The Institutions o

THE LAW OF SCOT

THE
INSTITUTIONS
OF
THE LAW
OF SCOTLAND

Deduced from its Originals, and *Collated* with the Civil,
Canon and Feudal Laws, and with the Customs of
Neighbouring Nations.

⟩ IN IV BOOKS ⟨

by *JAMES*, Viscount of *STAIR*,
Lord President of the Session
1693

EDITED BY
David M. Walker

THE UNIVERSITY PRESSES OF
EDINBURGH AND
GLASGOW
1981

© INTRODUCTION, TEXT, AND NOTES
DAVID M. WALKER
1981

EDINBURGH UNIVERSITY PRESS
22 GEORGE SQUARE
EDINBURGH
AND
UNIVERSITY OF GLASGOW PRESS
GLASGOW

ISBN 0 85224 397 9

PRINTED IN GREAT BRITAIN BY
WESTERN PRINTING SERVICES LTD
BRISTOL

∴

ADVERTISEMENT

In 1681 Sir James Dalrymple of Stair, Lord President of the Court of Session, published his Institutions of the Law of Scotland. *A second edition, revised and edited by the author himself, appeared in 1693. In 1695 Stair, by now raised to the peerage as Viscount Stair, the name by which he is universally known, died in office as Lord President, to which he had been restored in 1689 as a consequence of the 'Glorious Revolution' of 1688. Between 1681 and 1689 Stair had known loss of office, exile, accusation of treason, participation in plots of revolt, and ultimate return in the train of William of Orange. In commemoration of the tercentenary of publication of this classic work, the University Press of Edinburgh, with the generous assistance of Glasgow University Court and the Carnegie Trust for the Universities of Scotland, has undertaken the pious task of publishing anew an authoritative text of the* Institutions *of Stair. In this project the University Press has enjoyed the warm encouragement and support of Yale University Press. As the edition of 1693 is the latest which received revision and editing by Stair himself, it is the text of this edition which has been used, under the supervision of Professor D. M. Walker, Regius Professor of Law in the University of Glasgow, who has also provided an explanatory and expository Introduction. A decision to reprint a work designed, some 300 years ago, both for the practitioner and student of the Law of Scotland of the author's day, is itself a proof of the lasting value of the work to student, teacher and practitioner alike.*

It is to two great Scotsmen of the seventeenth century, co-evals and fellow lawyers, both of whom shared the vicissitudes of the times, that Scotland today owes her National Library on the one hand and in all probability the survival of her own system of law on the other. For the one she is indebted to Sir George Mackenzie—the 'Bloody Mackenzie' of Covenanting annals, who founded the Advocates Library, which (maintained and extended as a national heritage by the Faculty of Advocates) was finally given by the Faculty to the Nation in 1925 and became in name what it had long been in fact, the National Library of Scotland. For the other, Scotland owes a debt of permanent gratitude to Stair as philosopher, soldier, politician and judge.

It is difficult to exaggerate the impact of Stair's great work both on the development and indeed the continued survival of Scots Law. Stair is not only the first and greatest of our Institutional writers, the pillar on which the whole fabric of our Scots Law rests, but his Institutions are still the daily resort of the practising lawyer and their authority is still accorded the highest respect. While this of itself bears witness to the great and continuing value of the Institutions, it perhaps tends to conceal the greatest service which Stair rendered to the law of Scotland. Before he wrote, Scots law could scarcely be said to rest upon foundations of such breadth and strength to ensure its survival as an independent system of jurisprudence, in particular after 1707. From the publication of the first edition in 1681 until the Act of Union of the Parliaments of England and Scotland was less than 30 years. That Act gave statutory authority to the Articles of the painfully negotiated Articles of Union. That union was one which united Scotland with an England immeasurably superior in economic power and political influence and with a highly developed and long established legal system in the shape of the English common law—the product of centuries of growth under conditions of political and social stability far removed from the turbulent domestic history of Scotland, with a weak monarchy and feeble central government frequently at the mercy of a rebellious and lawless baronage. The Court of Session itself, the central organ of legal administration, was, when Stair wrote, not much more than 150 years old, with a bench that was all too often open to pressures both private and governmental.

It was true that in the 18th article of the Treaty of Union there occurred the provision 'that no alteration be made in Laws which concern Private Right except for Evident Utility of the subjects within Scotland'. Such a protective clause, however, could not serve as a sure defence against the influence, if not 'infiltration', of a more highly developed system of jurisprudence, while in any event it contained the seeds of its own destruction. Neither Articles nor Act contained any definition—if such indeed were possible or practicable—of 'evident utility'. The issue then was at the discretion and in the judgment of the Sovereign Parliament of the United Kingdom, in which the voice of Scotland was of necessity in a permanent minority. A further protective clause in the 19th Article made, it was assumed, provision for the continued independence of the Court of Session as a supreme Court and as interpreter of the Law of Scotland. It read 'that no causes in Scotland be cognoscible by the Courts of Chancery Queen's Bench Common Pleas or in any other Court in Westminster Hall and that the said courts or any other of the like nature after the Union shall have no power to cognosce review or alter the Acts or Sentences of the Judicature within Scotland or stop the Execution of the same'. This would appear at first blush to have been intended to secure the object of independence of the Scottish judicature. There was however no mention of the House of Lords, which in 1709 successfully asserted an appellate jurisdiction permitting it to review and alter decisions of the Supreme Court of Scotland. Then and for over a century and a half thereafter Scotland had, as of right, no judicial representation in the House of Lords. The letter of the Article was scrupulously observed: the House of Lords did not sit in Westminster Hall; whether the same could be said for the spirit is perhaps another matter. What can be said however is that in such a situation it would have been surprising had the influence of English Law and English legal concepts not been powerful enough to override and eventually eclipse a system so recently established and so lacking in historical social and political roots, unless the native vigour of Scots law had been strong enough to ensure its independent survival.

That the law of Scotland still survives today as a coherent and effective system of civil jurisprudence owes less to the withholding of Parliament's legislative hand than to the vigour and flexibility which it still possesses, which enables it to adapt itself to a social and economic structure far different from that of Scotland in the latter decades of the seventeenth century. For this, it can be argued with justification that the work of Stair is in large measure responsible and that his Institutions *fused the existing elements into a coherent and comprehensive whole, as a practical structure of law, based partly upon principles drawn from the jurisprudence of the Civilians and the Law of Rome and partly upon an ultimate ethical foundation. As it was put by a near contemporary, 'he hath therein so cleared up the springs and ground of our law that had been dammed up from ordinary observation by dust and rubbish, and reduced it into a sound and solid body (for which he deserves to be reckoned a founder and restorer of our laws) that if it were lost it might be retrieved and the tenor made, out of his excellent* Institutions'. *To put the matter conversely, without the support of Stair's* Institutions *and the lucidity and comprehension of the compendious statement of the law contained therein, what would have been the state of Scots Law after the Union and for the remainder of the eighteenth century? Craig's* Jus Feudale *in the field of feudal law and Mackenzie's* Institutes, *even supplemented by the suspect* Regiam Majestatem *and other works of doubtful or limited authority, were little enough, even supported by a few collections of reports of cases and books of* Practicks—*handbooks, in effect, of court procedure and forms—to provide the life blood of a system adapted to meet the needs of a growing commercial and industrial economy. It is not therefore difficult to see what the probable outcome would have been, especially in light of the great expansion of*

mercantile law in England, developed largely under the influence of
such great jurists as Lord Mansfield, during the latter part of the
eighteenth century.

To say this is not in any way to slight or decry the value or importance
of the works of Erskine and Bell, but the question may well be asked
whether, by the time they came to write, much more than the system of
feudal law and possibly the law of succession would have survived as a
living and recognisable legal system to expound or upon which to
comment. Erskine did not publish his Principles, until 1754 and his
Institutes did not appear until 1773, after his death. Bell's Principles, a work intended, in the words of its author, to achieve a comparatively modest purpose, 'to exhibit for the use of students and for
the sudden occasions of practice a concise and clear statement of the
principles and rules of the Law', only appeared in its first edition in
1829. Bell in effect was building on the foundations laid by his predecessors and, in the ultimate analysis, it may be argued, upon the
institutional writings of Stair.

Let Stair's own words express his purpose and design in his Dedication to King Charles II, prefixed to the first edition of 1681. He
called it a 'Summary of the Laws and Customs of your ancient
Kingdom of Scotland' : 'such just and convenient laws, which are here
offered to the view of the world, in a plain, rational, and natural
method ; in which material justice (the common law of the world) is
in the first place, orderly deduced from self-evident principles, through
all the several private rights thence arising, and, in the next place,
the expedients of the most polite nations, for ascertaining and expeding
the rights and interests of mankind, are applied in their proper places,
especially these which have been invented or followed by this nation.
So that a great part of what is here offered is common to most civil
nations, and is not like to be displeasing to the judicious and sober any
where who dote not so much upon their own customs as to think none
else worthy of their notice. There is not much here asserted upon mere
authority, or imposed for an other reason but quia majoribus placuerunt; but the rational motives, inductive of the several laws and customs are therewith held forth : And though the application of those
common rules to the variety of cases determined by our statutes, our
ancient customs, and the more recent decisions of our Supreme Courts,
be peculiar to us ; yet even the quadrancy of these to the common
dictates of reason and justice may make them the less displeasing, and
that no nation hath so few words of art, but that almost all our
terms are near the common and vulgar acceptation. Yea, the historical part, relating to the helps and expedients for clearing and
securing the rights of men out of the Word of God, the moral and judicial law contained therein, the civil, canon and feudal laws and many

customs of the neighbouring nations, digested as they fall in with the common rules of justice, may probably be acceptable to these who may and will allow time for their perusal.'

In this majestic and magisterial prose Stair sets out not only his purpose but the well-springs of his thought and the whole basis on which for him, as for many others in his own and succeeding generations in the pursuit and practice of the law, it was recognised that a durable and living system of civil jurisprudence must chiefly depend. The passing of more than three centuries has amply proved that perusal of the Institutions of Stair has proved acceptable and of profit to those who have, in his own phrase, allowed time for that perusal, not least perhaps because again in his own phrase 'we do always prefer the sense to the subtilty of law and do seldom trip by niceties or formalities.'

In presenting this in commendation of a tercentenary which neither Scotland nor the world of legal scholarship and study should neglect, the University Press pays its own tribute to a great lawyer, a great judge and a great Scotsman whose patriotism and love of his own country shines brightly from every page of that Dedication of the first edition to the King, and whose memory deserves the veneration of all who may seek or be called upon to study or to serve the law of Scotland or expound or follow its principles.

John Cameron

CONTENTS

PREFACE
AND ACKNOWLEDGMENTS

The initiative to publish a new edition of Stair's *Institutions* to mark the three hundredth anniversary of the first publication of the work came from the Hon. Lord Cameron, K.T., Senator of the College of Justice, who interested the Committee of Edinburgh University Press in the idea. Enquiries elicited warm support from Glasgow University Publications Board and it was decided that the edition should be undertaken as a joint venture by these two Universities.

The joint committee which has supervised the project wishes to make sincere acknowledgment of the financial assistance which alone has made publication possible. Edinburgh University Press has undertaken the whole work connected with production and borne the overhead expenses of publication and marketing. The committee gratefully acknowledges very generous financial assistance towards the costs of production from the Carnegie Trust for the Universities of Scotland and the University Court of the University of Glasgow, and assistance from the University Court of the University of Aberdeen, the Faculty of Advocates, the Society of Writers to Her Majesty's Signet, the Society of Solicitors in the Supreme Courts, and the Law Society of Scotland.

The editor is indebted to his colleague, Professor W. M. Gordon, for valuable assistance in identifying civil and canon law sources referred to by Stair, and to the staff of Edinburgh University Press for their careful attention to all matters of printing and production.

ABBREVIATIONS
USED IN THE TEXT AND NOTES

A.P.S.   *Acts of the Parliament of Scotland*, 1124–1707, Record ed., ed. Cosmo Innes and Thomas Thomson, 12 vols. (1814–75). Cited by volume, page and chapter number of Act.

B.S.   M.P. Brown, *Supplement to the Dictionary of Decisions*, 5 vols. (1826). Cited by volume, the letters B.S., and page.

B. Syn.   M.P. Brown, *General Synopsis of the Decisions of the Court of Session* omitted from Morison's *Dictionary of Decisions*, together with a selection from those in the MSS of the Advocates' Library and a collection of other decisions. 4 vols. (1829). Cited by volume, the letters B. Syn., and page.

Balfour   Sir James Balfour of Pittendreich, *Practicks or A System of the More Ancient Law of Scotland*, 1469–1579 (1754).

C.   The Code of the Emperor Justinian, edited by Krueger (Berlin, 1877), cited by book, title and section. Also in citations of Gratian's Decretum, Causa number, followed by quaestio and canon numbers.

Cl.   The Clementines, or Decretals of Pope Clement V, cited by 'Cl.' with book, title and chapter numbers.

Colvill   Alexander Colvill: *Practicks*, 1570–84 (MS in Advocates' Library).

Con.   The third part of Gratian's Decretum, *De Consecratione*, cited by Distinction and chapter.

Craig   Sir Thomes Craig of Riccarton, *Jus Feudale* (1655). There are also editions of 1716, 1732 and, translated by Lord President Clyde, 1934.

D.   The Digest of the Emperor Justinian, edited by Mommsen (Berlin, 1870), cited by book, title, section and, sometimes, paragraph number.

Dirleton   Sir John Nisbet, Lord Dirleton, *Decisions of the Lords of Council and Session*, 1665–77 (1698) (usually bound with his *Doubts and Questions in the Law, especially of Scotland*).

Dist.   The first part of Gratian's Decretum, cited by Distinction and chapter.

Durie   Sir Alexander Gibson, Lord Durie, *Decisions of the Lords of Council and Session*, 1621–42 (1690).

Extra or X   Decretals of Pope Gregory IX, cited by book, title, chapter and paragraph.

Extravagantes The Decretales Extravagantes of Pope John XXII and the Extravagantes Communes, cited by chapter, the abbreviation 'Xvag. Jo. XXII' or 'Xvag. Comm.', title and book, or as Extra, with title and chapter.

Fol. Dict. *Decisions of the Court of Session, abridged in form of a Dictionary* by H. Home, Lord Kames, and A. Fraser Tytler, Lord Woodhouselee, 2 vols. 1741; 4 vols. 1797; Supplement 1804.

Fountainhall Sir John Lauder, Lord Fountainhall, *Decisions of the Lords of Council and Session*, 1678–1712 (2 vols. 1759–61).

Gil. & Falc. Sir John Gilmour and Sir David Falconer, *Collection of Decisions of the Lords of Council and Session* (*Decisions*, 1661–6 by Gilmour, 1681–6 by Falconer) (1701).

Haddington Thomas Hamilton of Drumcairn, Earl of Haddington, *Practicks*, 1592–1628 (MS in Advocates' Library).

Harcarse Sir Roger Hog, Lord Harcarse, *Decisions of the Court of Session*, 1681–91 (1757).

Hope, Sir Thomas Hope, *Major Practicks*, 1608–33, edited by Lord
Maj. Pr. President Clyde, Stair Society, 2 vols. (1937–8). Cited by book, title and number of case.

Hope, Sir Thomas Hope, *Minor Practicks* (1726 and 1734).
Min. Pr. Cited by title and section.

Inst. *The Institutions of the Emperor Justinian*, edited by Krueger (Berlin, 1870), cited by book, title and section.

J. R. Juridical Review, 1889–

M. W. M. Morison: *Dictionary of Decisions of the Court of Session*, 1540–1808, 38 vols. (usually bound in 19) (1801–7). This work which reprints cases reported by older reporters, rearranged under alphabetical subject headings, is paginated consecutively throughout, a few numbers being printed twice. It is cited by the page. There is an Appendix, the titles of which are sometimes bound in at the end of each title in the Dictionary, but sometimes bound in a separate volume. Cases in the Appendix are cited by title and case number, e.g. M. Appx. voce Adjudication, no. 1. There is also a Synopsis in 4 volumes (usually bound in 2) and a Supplemental Volume of Tables and Indexes. The *Dictionary* is supplemented by Brown's *Supplement* and *Synopsis* (q.v.). George Tait published an *Index* to the *Decisions* in the original collections and in Morison's Dictionary, in 1823.

Maitland Sir Richard Maitland of Lethington, *Decisions, 1550–80.* (MS in Advocates' Library).

Nicolson Sir Thomas Nicolson, *Practicks* (MS in Advocates' Library). This is an unpublished manuscript in the Advocates' Library. The cases are collected under headings arranged alphabetically.

Nov. *The Novel Constitutions of the Emperor Justinian*, edited by Schöll and Kroll (Berlin 1877), cited by number.

Q. The second part of Gratian's Decretum, cited by Causa number, Quaestio number, and canon.

Regiam *Regiam Majestatem : the Auld Lawes and Constitutions of Scot-*
Majestatem *land.* By Sir John Skene, in Latin 1597, 1609 and 1613; in
English, 1609, 1774 and 1776. By Lord President Cooper
(Stair Society), 1947.

S.H.S. Scottish History Society.

Sext. Liber Sextus of the Decretals, published by Pope Boniface
VIII, cited by chapter, phrase Sext. or 'in vi to' or 'in 6', book
and number and rubric of title, or by 'VI,' or "Sext" with
book, title and chapter.

Sinclair John Sinclair: *Practicks*, 1540–9 (MS in Advocates' Library).

Spotiswoode Sir Robert Spotiswoode: *Practicks of the Law of Scotland*,
1541–1639 (1706). The cases are collected under headings
arranged alphabetically.

1 Stair Sir James Dalyrmple of Stair: *Decisions of the Lords of Council
and Session in the Most Important Cases Debate before Them*,
1661–71 (1683).

2 Stair Sir James Dalrymple of Stair: *Decisions of the Lords of Council
and Session in the Most Important Cases Debate before Them*,
1671–81 (1687).

X Decretals of Gregory IX, cited by chapter, the abbreviation
X, book and title, or X, (or Extra), book, title, chapter and
paragraph.

INTRODUCTION

1. *Stair's Career*

James Dalrymple,[1] author of the *Institutions*, was born in May 1619, son of James Dalrymple, the laird of Stair, a small estate in Kyle in Ayrshire, roughly midway between Ayr and Mauchline, and of his wife Janet Kennedy. He was educated at the Grammar School of Mauchline and, from 1633 to 1637, at Glasgow University, where he graduated in Arts with distinction. It was the time of Charles I's misguided attempt to maintain prelacy and impose a service-book on English Episcopal lines, known as Laud's Liturgy, on the Church of Scotland, and of the growing opposition in England to his personal government, of Hampden's refusal to pay ship-money (*R. v. Hampden* (1637) 3 St. Tr. 825), and other signs of resistance. In 1638 the National Covenant,[2] pledging signatories to defend the Presbyterian Church, secured the adherence of a large number of persons of all classes in Scotland, and later that year the General Assembly of the Church of Scotland meeting at Glasgow condemned the attempt to impose prelacy on the Church, condemned Laud's Liturgy, deposed the bishops and strengthened the position of the General Assembly.[3] The Covenanters raised an army to oppose the king, in which young Dalrymple obtained a commission and commanded a company of foot or a troop of horse in the regiment of the Earl of Glencairn, and he continued to serve until 1641, possibly participating in the First and Second Bishops Wars in which Scottish forces entered England in support of the English Parliament's stand against the King's personal government.

In March 1641, Dalrymple, on the solicitation, we are told, of some of his former teachers, became a candidate for an office of Regent in the University of Glasgow, and after competitive examination was elected. At that time the whole teaching of the liberal Arts in Glasgow University was in the hands of four Regents, who each took a year's intake of students (usually aged, on entry, about fifteen) through the whole four years' curriculum. In 1642 certain subjects were assigned to each Regent but the old system was reinstated in 1667. It was not till the following century that the system was permanently instituted whereby Professors were appointed who specialised in particular subjects. The subjects of Dalrymple's teaching are believed accordingly to have been mainly philosophy, and particularly logic.[4] He is reputed to have been a good teacher[5] and it is possible that this experience made him think much of justice and rights. There was at that time no Faculty of Law, nor teaching of law, save possibly in the context of ethics. His contemporaries on the staff at Glasgow included John Strang, Principal and professor of divinity, David Dickson and Robert Baillie, later (1660) Principal of the University, both teachers of theology, and talk with them and others such as George Gillespie, moderator of the General Assembly in 1648, must have confirmed a resolute Covenanting attitude to religion and theology, though as the Covenanters' views moved to extremes Dalrymple's did not move with them. In 1643 he married Margaret Ross, the daughter of a small landed proprietor of Balneil in Wigtownshire, and his second cousin.

He resigned his chair in 1647,[6] probably in September, and on 17 February 1648 was admitted an advocate of the Scottish bar. He had had no formal legal education—there was indeed none to be had in Scotland—and must have prepared himself by private study during his years as Regent. According to William Forbes[7] during his time in Glasgow he studied hard the Greek and Latin languages, with the History and Antiquities of Greece and Rome, in order to pursue the study of the Civil Law. At that time the literature of Scots law was very scanty.[8] Sir John Skene, Lord Clerk Register, had produced the *Lawes and Actes of Parliament* (1424–1597) based on earlier collections of statutes known as the Black Acts (being printed in blackletter) (1597 and 1611), editions of the two ancient treatises *Regiam Majestatem* and *Quoniam Attachiamenta* (1597, and, translated, 1609) and *De Verborum Significatione*, a valuable glossary of ancient legal terms (1597). Sir Thomas Craig's *Jus Feudale*, dealing with feudal land law, had been written by 1603 but was not published until 1655. Various collections of decisions and practical notes, known as *Practicks*, particularly those of Balfour, Hope, Nicolson, Haddington and Spotiswoode, existed in manuscript. There were various editions in print of the texts of the Roman law, Justinian's *Institutions*, *Digest*, *Code* and *Novels*, and of the canon law. But treatises on the law of Scotland there were none. Legal literature consisted largely of foreign books on Roman law.

In 1648 Puritanism finally triumphed in England. Charles I was tried and on 30 January 1649 was executed. Scotland was aghast.

In March 1649 Dalrymple, an advocate of one year's standing, was appointed by Parliament[9] one of a large commission, headed by the Lord Chancellor, for the revision and publication of the law of the country, to compile a formal model or frame of a book of 'just and equitable laws'. How he came to be chosen we do not know, but possibly because of his academic experience. But, like several previous commissions,[10] this one, if indeed it ever met, never reported, and nothing resulted. The experience may, however, have led him to think of a systematic statement of the laws of Scotland.

Later in 1649 and 1650 Dalrymple, appointed through Argyll's influence, went to Holland as secretary to the Commission of the Scottish Parliament sent to treat with the young Charles II at The Hague and Breda. On both occasions he was noted by the king for his abilities and good sense. Whether on these visits he looked at the local law, or its law books, we do not know.[11]

It would be surprising if he did not, but we have no certain evidence of this.

Charles II sailed to Scotland in 1650, landed at Garmouth at the mouth of the Spey, and was crowned at Scone on 1 January 1651, but in 1651 Cromwell and his generals defeated all forces supporting Charles II, who after his defeat at Worcester (1651) again escaped abroad; the Scottish Parliament ceased to meet and Scotland was an occupied country, nominally represented from 1654 by thirty members in the Commonwealth and Protectorate Parliaments.[12] Dalrymple was at this time probably engaged in legal practice. The Court of Session ceased, however, to sit after July 1651 and in May 1652 seven commissioners for the administration of justice in Scotland, four English and three Scottish, were appointed under the Great Seal of the Commonwealth.[13] The heritable jurisdictions of the feudal lords were abolished and new instructions issued for Justices of the Peace.[14] Two sheriffs principal were appointed for each county, one Scottish, one English, with authority to appoint deputies.[15] A Court of Admiralty was established.[16] In 1654 courts baron were erected in Scotland.[17] In 1654 Dalrymple and most of the other advocates refused the Tender, or Oath of Allegiance to the Commonwealth and Abjuration of Royalty, and for a time withdrew from the bar. The Tender had, it seems, to be abandoned. This withdrawal was traditionally regarded as the origin of written pleadings at the Scottish bar, a practice necessitated by the judges' ignorance of Scots law.[18]

In July 1657 Dalrymple, now aged 38 and of nine years' standing at the bar, on the recommendation of Monck to Cromwell,[19] was appointed by the Council of State for Scotland to fill a vacancy on the Bench and the appointment was confirmed by Cromwell. The courts, however, were closed between Cromwell's death in 1658 and the Restoration in 1660, so that he did not have much judicial experience at this time. At this time too he seemed to have been on intimate terms with Monck, the general commanding in Scotland, and to have recommended him, after Cromwell's death, to summon a Parliament and restore the king.

Charles II was restored in 1660 and shortly thereafter Stair was received with favour in London by Charles, knighted, and appointed one of the judges of the Court of Session in the fresh constitution of that Court in February 1661[20]. Sir John Gilmour was nominated President and, in the next year, Dalrymple was named Vice-President.

In 1662 Charles ordered the Lords of Session to make the Declaration which was incumbent[21] on all persons in public trust that to enter into Leagues or Covenants to take up arms against the king was unlawful, and that the National Covenant of 1638 and Solemn League and Covenant of 1643 were and are unlawful oaths. Dalrymple and some others declined to do so, and in 1664 his seat as a judge was declared vacant but Charles summoned him to London and, having allowed him to make a qualified declaration, reappointed him to the Court. He was also made a baronet of Nova Scotia (2 June 1664).

In 1669 he was a member of a Royal Commission to consider the Regulations of the three Supreme Courts of Scotland, Session, Justiciary and Exchequer, which finally, in 1672, produced a series of revised articles embodied in a statute concerning the Regulation of the Judicatories,[22] which, among other changes, established the High Court of Justiciary in the form it preserved until 1887.

In 1670 Dalrymple was appointed, on Lauderdale's nomination, to be one of the Scottish commissioners to treat with English commissioners for an incorporating union of the two kingdoms,[23] linked since 1603 by a personal union only. The proposals were for an incorporating union. Possibly at Dalrymple's prompting, the two legal systems were to remain separate.[24] The negotiations, however, came to nothing because of disputes on the ultimate appeal from the Scottish courts to Parliament, though there were other and deeper-rooted difficulties.[25] At the end of the same year Gilmour resigned the office of Lord President of the Court of Session and Dalrymple, by the influence of Lauderdale, was on 13 January 1671 appointed Lord President in his stead, to the consternation of Gilmour, who had relinquished the office, and of Nisbet, the Lord Advocate, who expected it, and was also made a member of the Scottish Privy Council. Stair 'by his wit and address, had insinuated himself so well with Lauderdale, whilst he was a Commissioner for the Union, that Lauderdale, who desired not to prefer Tweeddale's friends but to make new ones for himself, had contracted a firm friendship with him; which was much heightened by the Chancellor, who desired not the [Lord] Advocate's promotion, and by the Earl of Kincardine, who was Stair's great minion. And really Stair was a gentleman of excellent parts, of an equal wit and universal learning; but most considerable for being so free from passions, that most men thought this equality of spirit, a mere hypocrisy in him. This meekness fitted him extremely to be a President, for he thereby received calmly all men's informations, and by it he was capable to hear, without disorder or confusion, what the advocate represented. But that which I admired most in him was, that in ten years' intimacy, I never heard him speak unkindly of those who had injured him'.[26] In 1672–3 he sat also as M.P. for Wigtownshire and served as a member of the Committee of the Articles, which formulated the legislation for ratification by the full Parliament.

From 1670 to 1681 Dalrymple's life seems to have been less eventful. He sat for Wigtownshire in the Parliaments of 1672, 1673, 1678 and 1681 and was a member of the Lords of the Articles in 1672 and 1681. He was diligently occupied with the administration of justice in the Court, hampered by a shortage of capable men, and even of legally qualified men, on the Bench, and is believed to have drafted and secured the passing of the Act regulating the execution of deeds,[27] and other useful legislation. There is no indication that he approved of, still less participated in, the brutal persecutions of the Covenanters perpetrated at this time by Lauderdale's administration, or later by James, Duke of York, as Lord High Commissioner. He had to cope in 1674 with the dispute over the competence of appeal to Parliament which gave rise to a secession of the bar from Edinburgh and during the summer session of 1679 was absent, being in attendance on the King by the latter's command. This was the time of the debates on the Exclusion Bill to disable the Duke of York from inheriting the Crown.

In 1681, James, Duke of York, who had been Lord High Commissioner to the Scottish Parliament since 1679, obtained the passing of the Test Act[28] by which all office-bearers in church and state and many other classes of persons were obliged to take an oath acknowledging the Confession of Faith of 1560, accepting the royal supremacy as supreme governor of the realm, renouncing the Covenants (National Covenant and Solemn League and Covenant) and all leagues and meetings to treat of any matter of church or state, and forswearing all attempts to make any change in civil or ecclesiastical government. No conscientious person could take such an oath without qualification. It removed all security from the Protestant religion and Dalrymple suggested that reference to the first (John Knox's) Confession of Faith of 1560 (ratified by Act of Parliament in 1567) should be included in the test prescribed. This made the Test an inherently inconsistent document because it was antagonistic to prelacy and acknowledged the lawfulness of resistance to tyranny. Dalrymple declined to take this oath and was superseded as Lord President by Sir George Gordon of Haddo, and he then withdrew to his country house at Carscreoch in Galloway to oversee the printing of the first edition of his *Institutions*, which he had been compiling for a number of years. It was published at the end of that year.

There followed a considerable degree of persecution of those who would not take the Test and in September 1682 Dalrymple thought it prudent to take refuge in Holland and settled at Leiden where he matriculated at the University on 17 December 1682.[29] His wife and family, except his three eldest sons, joined him there in 1683. At that time civil law was being taught at Leiden by Noodt, Schulting and Johan Voet. There were numerous refugees from Britain in the Low Countries at that time and in 1686 John Locke wrote from Utrecht his *Letters on Toleration*. Whether Dalrymple ever met Locke is unknown; there is no evidence that he did. Whilst Dalrymple was at Leiden he published from Edinburgh the first volume of his *Decisions of the Court of Session*, 1661–71, dedicated to his former colleagues on the bench of that Court. The Preface is dated: Leiden, October 30 and November 9, 1683. This was the first volume of reports of decisions, as distinct from volumes of *Practicks*, to be published in Scotland. (Sir Alexander Gibson, Lord Durie's, *Decisions*, though collecting the decisions of an earlier period (1621–42) were not published until 1690). Stair's second volume, containing decisions of 1671–81, was published in 1687. Both are substantial volumes, and the cases are carefully presented. Also while at Leiden, he published his *Physiologia Nova Experimentalis* (published by Cornelius Boutestyn at Leiden, 1686) dealing with what we now call physics,[30] dedicated to the Royal

Society, of which a former President, Sir Robert Murray, had been Lord Justice-Clerk and a friend and colleague of Dalrymple's during Lauderdale's government of Scotland. This work was favourably commented on by Pierre Bayle and is said to have gained Dalrymple some reputation at the time as a philosopher.

In 1684 Dalrymple was charged with treason for alleged complicity in the Rye House Plot to assassinate Charles II and his brother James, Duke of York, and outlawed on 17 March 1685. Attempts were made to have him extradited to be tried in Scotland and he had to lie very low. In Scotland he was indicted for high treason[31] and the process was remitted to the Justiciary Court.[32] Some of his lands were forfeited.[33] In 1687 his eldest son John, now Lord Advocate, obtained a pardon for him, but he did not then risk returning to Scotland.

While in Holland, the hounding of him by James VII and II's agents drove him to turn away from his allegiance to the Crown; he supported Argyll's ill-fated expedition to Scotland in 1685; he became an active rebel against James VII and II; in 1687 he became a confidant and adviser of William of Orange, and in 1688 he was a party to the plan to bring William over to England to supplant James II; he sailed on the same ship as William to Torbay, and was closely involved in the settlement of the crowns of England and Scotland on William and Mary. From the beginning of the revolution he was ambitious to re-establish and expand his family's interest as much as possible. He became an active adviser of William and while the convention of 1688–9 was sitting was in London acting as an intermediary between William and Portland there and Melville in Edinburgh.[34] He and his son John were sworn of the Privy Council. In October 1689, after the assassination of Lord President Lockhart by a disgruntled litigant, he was re-appointed President of the Court of Session[35] and in 1690 was raised to the peerage, being created Viscount Stair and Lord Glenluce and Stranraer.[36] It was generally assumed that he had a large hand in nominating the judges of the new Court of Session. He also sat in the Parliament of 1689–90.[37] Thereafter until his death he continued to preside in the court but he was the target of various pamphlets charging him with various delinquencies during his political career, particularly with being a changeling or time-server, so that he felt obliged to publish his *Apology*,[38] seeking to vindicate his character and reputation. He was unpopular in 1688–9 and he and his eldest son John were subject to continuous violent attacks from the opposition in Parliament.[39] He was in bad odour, as responsible for the proposed nomination of the new Lords of Session.[40] An attempt was made to disqualify a peer from being Lord President.[40] The opposition sought to disrupt the working of the Court of Session, alleging that it was illegally constituted.[41] He was also assailed from many sides, by the High Church Party, the Jacobites, the Covenanters and many disappointed place-seekers. There was talk of impeaching him and his son John.[42] These years cannot have been happy. His wife died in 1692.

In 1692 his son, John, was implicated in the discreditable affair of the Massacre of Glencoe and in 1695 dismissed from the post of Secretary of State. In 1693 Stair, as we may now call him, was very unpopular; he was thought to have established too great an ascendancy over the court and was accused of altering the court's official judgments.[43] He dominated the court and allegations were persistently made that he used his power unfairly.[44]

In 1693 Stair published a second, extensively revised, edition of his *Institutions* and in 1695 *A Vindication of the Divine Perfections, illustrating the Glory of God in them by Reason and Revelation, methodically digested into several Meditations* (printed by B. Aylmer). He died on 25 November 1695 at his home in Edinburgh and was buried in St Giles Church there. After a period of political struggling he was succeeded as Lord President by his third son, Hew.

Stair accordingly was professionally involved in the working of the law of Scotland for 47 years and a judge for 38 years, with interruptions but including uninterrupted periods of 20 and 6 years on the Bench. By the time he published his *Institutions* he had had great experience of the law in action. He had also been involved in many of the most important governmental negotiations of the time.

His character has been variously assessed but contemporaries agreed in speaking of his outstanding ability and learning, mild temper and agreeable disposition. He certainly had a deep and thorough understanding of law and a strong desire to see it firmly established and maintained. That he changed his political views is undoubted but explicable. He supported Charles I until the king antagonised him by his attempt to supplant the Presbyterian form of worship and church government, and was later friendly with Monck, Cromwell's deputy in Scotland. Later he was well-regarded by Charles II and James VII and II but was driven by religious conviction to turn against James VII and to support William of Orange. In religion, though a strong Presbyterian he was not so hostile to Episcopacy as to oppose William's view that Episcopalians in Scotland who took the oath of allegiance should be given the same indulgences as dissenters were allowed in England.[45]

William Forbes,[46] writing within 20 years of Stair's death, gave the following 'short character' of him.

'During the long time he was a judge, none could ever stain him with the least malversation or indolence in his great trust, at a time when it would have been thought obliging and good service to men of power, who wanted nothing more than the least ground to call him in question. He could not endure to be solicited, or impertinently addressed to in matters of justice. The memory of the many good regulations in the form of process before the Session owing to his Lordship will never be obliterated. He had a stiff aversion from being concerned in criminal matters, either as a judge or a lawyer. In the matter of civil government he was always for sober measures. He thought it neither the interest nor the duty of kings to rule arbitrarily: both king and

people having their titles and rights by law; and an equal balance of prerogative and liberty being necessary to the happiness of a commonwealth. His
judgment never led him to use or approve severity against those, who being
sound in the fundamentals of religion, differed only in circumstantials. When
he sat in the Privy Council, he always interposed so far as he could with
safety, to rescue the suffering Presbyterians from feeling the sharp edge of
penal laws, to which they lay obnoxious in the reign of King Charles the 11
and suffered often public reproach for him so doing. Where he gave it as his
opinion, that the Privy Council, to whom the government and policy of the
nation was committed, ought to be equally prudent and just in applying the
severity of the laws: albeit judges in other courts are to walk by the letter of
the law, however rigorous and hard. He was a devout Christian, a sincere
Protestant, and a true son of the Presbyterian Church of Scotland, though
prudence allowed him not at all times to make a noise. He approved himself
to be of steady principles, in thrice forsaking his honourable and profitable
station, rather than comply with the corruption of the time. 1. He absolutely
refused to take the Usurper's Tender [the oath of allegiance to the Common-
wealth], and contentedly sat down with the loss of a beneficial employment
as an advocate, till he was dispensed with. 2. He risked his place of an ordinary Lord of Session in the year 1664, before he would sign, without a
commentary, the Declaration then imposed on all in public trust. And 3.
exposed himself to be shuffled out of his presidency (as he was) in the year
1681, by his boldly standing up in defence of the Protestant interest. In the
midst of the multiplicity of civil business, which his employment and character
brought upon him, he always found some time for the study of divinity,
wherein he arrived to a deep pitch of knowledge and directed everything else
to it. In short, he was indefatigable in business, even when he might have
used the privilege of his age to lie by and withdraw from it. He knew not what
it was to be idle, and took a strict account of his time: dividing himself between the duties of religion, and the studies of his profession, which he
minded more than the raising of a great fortune. He was sober, temperate
and mighty regular. He duly prayed always and read a chapter of the Bible to
his family before they sat down to dinner, and performed the like divine
service after supper: which he would not interrupt upon any consideration
of business, how important soever. He had a great spirit, and equal temper in
the harshest passages of his life: by the constant bent of his thoughts to what
was serious or profitable, he knew how to divert them from any uneasy
impression of sorrow. He was apt to forget, at least not to resent injuries done
to him, when it was in his power to requite them.

'His excellent writings will carry down his memory to the latest posterity.
His *Institutions of the Laws of Scotland* wherein that is compared with the
canon and civil laws, and the customs of neighbouring nations, are so useful,
that few considerable families in Scotland, not to mention professed lawyers,
do want them. He hath therein so cleared up the springs and grounds of our

law, that had been dammed up and reduced it into a sound and solid body (for which he deserves to be reckoned a founder and restorer of our law) that if it were lost, it might be retrieved and the tenor of it made up out of his excellent *Institutions*. He hath judiciously observed the Decisions of the Session from the restoration of the sovereignty, and re-establishment of the College of Justice to its ancient constitution and splendour, till August 1681: In which he hath not omitted any case of difficulty or importance determined when he was present on the bench; without expressing his own opinion when different from that of the plurality of the Lords, out of modesty and deference to their judgment. He wrote them *de die in diem*, commonly before dinner when fresh in his memory: And was the more fitted to do it, that he was not a day absent during that period of 20 years, except the time of the summer session 1679, when he attended the king by his majesty's special order. I have seen his *Physiologia Nova Experimentalis*. He wrote a treatise concerning the royal prerogative and the rights and privileges of the subject, and some sheets in vindication of the church government: but I don't remember to have seen either of these in print.[47] He wrote also a *Vindication of the Divine Perfections*, which was published in London in the year 1695, with a preface by Doctors W. Bates and J. Howe: wherein the learned divines gave this character of the book. "The clearness and vigour of the noble author's spirit are illustriously visible in managing a subject so deep and difficult. And in his unfolding the glorious and amiable excellencies of the blessed God, there is joined with the strength of argument, the beauty of expression, as may engage all readers to be happy in the entire choice of God for their everlasting portion. Which performance shews it to be a thing not impracticable, as it is more praise-worthy, amidst the greater secular employment, to find vacancy and a disposition of spirit to look with a very inquisitive eye into the deep things of God in which (if it were the author's pleasure to be known) would let it be seen, the statesman and the divine are not inconsistencies in a great and comprehensive mind".'

His family, immediate and remote, achieved considerable distinction, particularly in the law and the army. His family comprised (1) John (1648–1707), Master of Stair, and second Viscount. He became an advocate in 1672, was Lord Advocate 1687, a Lord of Session and Lord Justice-Clerk, 1688, Lord Advocate again in 1690 and, in 1691, joint Secretary of State for Scotland. He was implicated in the Massacre of Glencoe and, having been accused of exceeding his instructions, resigned, but later received a remission and was restored to favour. In 1703 he was made first Earl of Stair, Viscount Dalrymple, Lord Newliston, Glenluce and Stranraer. His second son, John, the second Earl, became a Field-Marshal and Commander-in-Chief of the forces in Great Britain, and his fifth son, George (1680–1745) became a Baron of the Court of Exchequer in Scotland in 1709.

(2) James (1650–1719), advocate 1675, and one of the Clerks of Session 1693, author and antiquary, created a baronet as Sir James Dalrymple of

Kelloch in 1697; he published *Collections concerning the Scottish History preceding the death of King David the First in 1153* (1705); his son John, and grandson William, were both advocates. His great-grandson, John, advocate 1748, was a baron of the Court of Exchequer in Scotland (1776–1806), and author of *An Essay towards a General History of Feudal Property in Great Britain* (1757), *Memoirs of Great Britain and Ireland* (1771) and other works. From him were descended the eighth and ninth Earls of Stair.

(3) Hew (1652–1737), advocate 1677, Dean of the Faculty of Advocates, 1695, commissary of Edinburgh, M.P., created a baronet as Sir Hew Dalrymple of North Berwick in 1698 and appointed Lord President of the Court of Session, 1698. His *Decisions of the Court of Session from 1698 to 1718* was published in 1758. His sixth son, Hew (1670–1755), was a Lord of Session, 1726–55, and of Justiciary, 1745–55, as Lord Drummore, and a more remote descendant, David (1719–84), became a judge as Lord Westhall in 1777. Another was General Sir Hew W. Dalrymple, Bart. (1750–1830).

(4) Thomas (1663–1725) studied medicine at Leiden and became First Physician to the King in Scotland.

(5) David (c. 1665–1721), advocate 1688, created a baronet as Sir David Dalrymple of Hailes, 1701, M.P., Lord Advocate, 1709–11 and 1714–20, Dean of the Faculty of Advocates, 1712–21; his grandson, Lord Hailes (1726–92), a Lord of Session, 1766–92, and of Justiciary 1776–92, was the distinguished scholar and antiquary, author of *A Catalogue of the Lords of Session from the Institution of the College of Justice* (1767), *An Examination of Some of the Arguments for the High Authority of Regiam Majestatem* (1769), *Tracts relative to the History and Antiquities of Scotland* (1800), and *Decisions of the Lords of Council and Session*, 1752–6 (1760), 1766–91 (1826), as well as lesser works. Stair had also five daughters and through their marriages other links were made between the Dalrymples and many other distinguished Scottish families.

2. *Scotland and Scots Law in 1681*

What was the state of Scotland and Scots law during the years between the Restoration in 1660 and 1681 when Stair's *Institutions* were published? After the turbulent years of the early and mid-seventeenth century, with revolt against monarchical misgovernment, the civil wars, the enforced union with, or rather subjugation to, England under the Commonwealth and Protectorate, the Restoration brought only comparative peace and calm. It was comparative only because the king's government was seeking to impose an ecclesiastical system unacceptable to the general body of the people, and it was being vigorously resisted. Hence there was the rigorous military repression of conventicles and Presbyterian dissent, the revolts suppressed at Rullion Green, Bothwell Brig and Aird's Moss, and the murder of Archbishop Sharp. There was, however, sufficient freedom from disturbance to allow an economic revival from the low point reached in the 1640s and 1650s. Industry and commerce both expanded, and agriculture developed. But the end of the Cromwellian Union brought an end of free trade with England and the colonies, and the English Navigation Act of 1660 hampered Scottish trade.

After the Restoration the Scottish Parliament was initially wholly subservient to the king. The Parliament of 1661 restored absolute monarchy, and the Committee of the Articles through which the king could control the legislation made by Parliament, and by the Act Rescissory of 1661 it annulled all the legislation of the Parliaments since 1633. Charles ruled Scotland through the Privy Council, and controlled Parliament through the Lords of the Articles, a recreated episcopacy and a tame Convention of Royal Burghs. As time passed, however, Parliament became less subservient and more independent; in 1673 the opposition Lords forced Lauderdale, the king's commissioner, to give way on finance and to dissolve Parliament, and thereafter royal policy was always liable to real opposition. Moreover, the acts of the administration were latterly repeatedly challenged as corrupt and unconstitutional. In 1674 the Convention of Royal Burghs was stigmatised as seditious for petitioning for the repeal of certain legislation. There were repeated appeals to the 'fundamental laws' of the Kingdom. In fact, the government of Scotland was becoming ministerial, for real authority lay with the king's ministers, and those opposed to the ministers appealed to the king, in whose name those ministers acted. Parliament became a platform for the opposition to the ministry.

Judicial independence was destroyed by the king's insistence in 1677 that commissions be *durante beneplacito*, while some of the judges, like Charles Maitland, Lord Haltoun, brother of Lauderdale, were totally unfit for their places. Haltoun abused his office to advance the interests of his clients and was ultimately convicted of embezzlement of the coinage and perjury. Lauderdale himself was an extraordinary Lord of Session and he and his nominees seem largely to have controlled the administration of justice, so that appeals for justice were in vain.

The Privy Council had jurisdiction in matters of state, the preservation of the public peace, punishment of riots and violent encroachments on lawful possession. Parliament had jurisdiction in cases brought by protestation for remeid of law from the Court of Session; this was not an appeal but an extraordinary remedy competent where the Session exceeded its authority or reduced or altered their own decrees *in foro*, or there was allegation of injustice or iniquity committed by the Lords.

The Courts Act, 1672, reorganised the Courts, establishing the High Court of Justiciary, consisting of the (lay) Justice-General, the Justice-Clerk and six of the judges of the Court of Session, a form it maintained until 1887, and made beneficial reforms in criminal procedures.

The Court of Session did not have a universal civil jurisdiction. It had jurisdiction in advocations from the Commissaries or in reductions of their decrees, but no original jurisdiction in divorce or confirmation of testaments, which belonged to the Commissary Court. The High Court of Admiralty similarly had exclusive jurisdiction at first instance in maritime causes though the Court of Session had jurisdiction to suspend or reduce its decrees. At the inferior court level sheriff courts, baron courts and regality courts exercised social control over most petty matters.

There was much legislation after 1660 of continuing significance and value, notably in the area of land law and conveyancing, such as the Subscription of Deeds Act 1681 (Stair's Act), the Entail Act 1685, the Prescription Acts of 1669 and 1695, the Blank Bonds and Trusts Act 1696, and the Registration Act of 1693 which perfected the system of land rights dependent on registration, completing the system inaugurated by the establishment of the Registers of Sasines in 1617. In the sphere of diligence the Adjudications Acts, 1661 and 1672, effected a major change while the Bankruptcy Act 1696 avoided certain preferences in favour of creditors. An Act of 1672 regulated tutors and curators of children. One of 1681 dealt with bills of exchange. An Act of 1669 made sheriffs and local justices local roads authorities, and bridges were built in many places. An Act of 1672 was the foundation of the Scottish poor law until 1845. In local government the office of commissioners of supply was created and in 1668 they were associated with the J.P.'s for administration of roads; they remained important officers of local government until 1889. Much of this legislation was in force for two centuries or longer.

Stair was a judge from 1657, reappointed to the restored Court of Session in 1661. Of his fellow-judges down to 1681 several have left a name and some claim to reputation. Sir John Gilmour, Lord President 1661–70, collected *Decisions*, 1661–6 (published, with Falconer's *Decisions*, in 1701); Sir John Nisbet, Lord Dirleton (1664–77) also collected *Decisions* and wrote Dirleton's *Doubts and Questions in the Law*, published together in 1690. Sir John Baird, Lord Newbyth (1664–81) compiled a manuscript *Practicks;* Sir Peter Wedderburn, Lord Gosford (1668–79) also collected *Decisions*; Sir Thomas Murray of Glendook (1674–81) printed folio and duodecimo editions of the Statutes from 1424; Sir David Falconer of Newton (1676–82), who was Lord President 1682–5 in succession to Stair, also collected *Decisions* (published, along with Gilmour's *Decisions*, in 1701); Sir Alexander Seton of Pitmedden (1677–89) published an edition of Mackenzie's *Law and Customs of Scotland in Matters Criminal*, to which he annexed a treatise on *Mutilation and Demembration*, in 1699; Sir Roger Hog, Lord Harcarse (1677–1700) collected the decisions of 1681 to 1692, published in 1757. This indicates that Stair was not alone on the post-Restoration bench in having capacity and interest in the law, and the fact that some other judges of the period have left no reputation does not necessarily mean that they were ignorant or inadequate. Haltoun, Lauderdale's brother, may be the worst of the period and was probably not alone, but by no means all the judges were scoundrels or legally incompetent.

During Stair's second tenure of the Presidency (1689–95) notable among his colleagues was Sir John Lauder of Fountainhall (1689–1722) whose collected *Decisions*, 1678–1712, were published in 1759–61 and are valuable and important as a source of knowledge of the period, not merely as reports of decided cases.

The literature of Scots law existing in 1681 immediately prior to the publication of Stair's *Institutions* was amazingly scanty. There were numerous individual statutes, and the collections of statutes known as the Black Acts (1555) and Skene's *Lawes and Actes of Parliament*, 1424–1597 (1597). Skene had also published his *De Verborum Significatione* (1597) and his editions of *Regiam Majestatem* (1597, 1609 and 1613). Apart from Stair's own *Decisions* (1683 and 1687) there were no printed reports. There were various manuscript collections of *Practicks*, or notes of statutes, cases and practical observations collected under alphabetical headings, the materials for treatises rather than texts in their own right. Of these, Stair certainly knew and used the collections of Haddington, Spotiswoode (published 1706), Nicolson, Sinclair, Maitland, Colvill and Hope. There were also manuscript collections of Decisions, a genus of literature developing from the *Practick* in the direction which led to the modern Session Cases. Stair knew in manuscript the collections of Gibson, Lord Durie (1621–42, published 1690) and of his colleagues Gilmour (1661–6) and Falconer (1681–9), published together in 1701, Dirleton (1665–77), published in 1698, Fountainhall (1678–1712), published in 1759–61, and Harcarse (1681–91), published in 1757. There were no textbooks or treatises. *Regiam Majestatem* stated the law of four centuries earlier. Craig's *Jus Feudale* was published in 1655, but dealt with land law only.

In view of this scanty literature, it is inevitable that reference should have been made to the texts of the Roman and canon law, and to continental literature founded thereon, just as in the twentieth century judges and practitioners so frequently, in default of indigenous literature, turn to English books.

Of these earlier writings on Scots law three, however, deserve mention, Craig's *Jus Feudale* and Hope's *Major Practicks* and *Minor Practicks*. The *Jus Feudale* is a detailed narrative account of a major area of the law, land law, based on principles and the earliest reasoned examination of a major area of Scots law. It was printed in Latin in 1655, 1716 and 1732 and again, translated by Lord President Clyde, in 1934. Hope's *Minor Practicks* is a small manual of Scots law, a concise and connected text in 16 titles, dealing with process, kirk-benefices, wills, bonds and assignations and property in land. It differs from other books entitled *Practicks* in not containing any references to decisions, books of authority, or practical observations and is not a true *Practicks*. It dates from about 1632. It has been printed twice, in 1726 by Alexander Bayne and in 1734 by John Spotiswood. The *Major*

Practicks is a true Practicks, a substantial work in eight parts, each divided into a number of titles, and these comprising a series of numbered notes, drawn from earlier sources, such as Balfour's *Practicks*, a summary of Acts of Parliament, Acts of Council and Session, and then practical observations, or case-notes. It covers the whole range of contemporary law in note form but it is not exhaustive, nor is it a connected or reasoned treatise. It covers 1608 to 1633. It remained unprinted until edited by Lord President Clyde and published by the Stair Society in 1937–8.

The paucity and poverty of this earlier literature brings out the more the incredible achievement of Stair. He first in Scotland wrote a connected narrative book covering the whole area of the private law, and in its size, scope, philosophic breadth and expository quality transcends by a huge margin all the existing literature.

The advances made by Stair on the previous literature can best be seen by looking at some representative topics. Take first the common contract of sale of goods. Craig does not treat of this. Hope's *Major Practicks* has three entries, extending in all to 20 lines, two quotations from *Regiam Majestatem* and on ea case of 1621. Take again liability for personal harm or injury. This too is outwith the scope of Craig. Hope's *Major Practicks* has a series of titles, Blood, Mutilation, Murder, Ravishing of Women, Slaughter and Assythment, comprising notes of points relative to the topic, but all dealing with it from the criminal standpoint; there is no discussion from the standpoint of civil liability, of delict or reparation of harm, still less is there discovery of principle or statement of general ideas. Take lastly succession to land on death. Craig of course deals with the topic at length but by reference to the civil law and the *Books of the Feus* only, with limited reference to Scottish practice. Hope's *Major Practicks* includes many pages on the topic with notes of many cases. His *Minor Practicks* treats at some length of Confirmation of Testaments and of Executors, and of Heirs. On all three topics Stair has a substantial amount to say: on sale, apart from his consideration of contracts generally (I, 10) he has a substantial discussion (I, 14). On liability for personal injury there is an extended examination in I, 9 distinguishing criminal and civil liability and treating of individual modes of causing harm, notably assythment, and moreover exploring the issues of concomitant accession and joint and several liability. On succession on death to land, there are two long titles (III, 4 and 5). On all three topics his examination is much longer, fuller, more thorough than any previous one and, above all, it is a systematic, reasoned exposition, supported by reference to authority, not just a collection of points.

3. *The Genesis of the* Institutions

It can only be speculation to try to determine what prompted Stair to essay writing a systematic textbook of Scots law. It was probably a combination of factors, the reading of Justinian's *Institutions* and *Digest* and acquaintance with some of the commentators thereon, and particularly Dutch works (even though he may not himself cite them), such as those of Joost van Damhouder (1507–81), Peter Peckius (1529–89), Paul van Merel (1558–1607) a teacher of Grotius, but particularly of Peter Goudelin (Gudelinus) (1550–1619), whose *De Jure Novissimo* (1620) is regarded as perhaps the first attempt at a systematic exposition of the law of the Netherlands,[48] and of Hugo de Groot (Grotius) (1583–1645), whose *Inleidinge tot de Hollandsche Rechtsgeleerdheid*, a systematic treatise on the law of the province of Holland, written in 1620, appeared in 1631 and is still the basic work on the Roman-Dutch law.[49] Stair in fact cites Grotius' *De Jure Belli ac Pacis* but not the *Inleidinge*;[50] he possibly could not at that time read the *Inleidinge*, which was not translated into Latin (by Van der Linden) or English (by Maasdorp, Lee and others) until long afterwards. When he was in Holland in 1682–8 he must, however, have acquired some familiarity with the language. He also cites Gudelinus several times. In his years in Holland he may also have seen Simon van Leeuwen's *Het Roomsch Hollandsch Recht* (translated by Sir John Kotzé as *Commentaries on the Roman Dutch Law* (1881)) which was widely used there as a student's textbook.[51] Apart from anything Stair may have seen on his own visits to Holland, Dutch books were not uncommon in Scotland. There are many of the seventeenth century in the Advocates' Library. Such books may have put into his mind the question: Why not an *Institutions* of the law of Scotland?

Whether he was to any extent prompted to write by the work of Sir Edward Coke in England is unknown. Coke attempted to give a reasonably complete exposition of English law, the first since Bracton, in his *Institutes of the Lawes of England* (First Part, or Commentary upon Littleton, 1628; Second Part, containing the exposition of many ancient and other Statutes, 1642; Third Part, concerning High Treason and other Pleas of the Crown, and Criminall Causes, 1644; Fourth Part, concerning the Jurisdiction of Courts, 1644). Coke, it has been said, rescued English law from declining into a stagnant marsh of detail; he effected the rescue with credit and ability, though not with perfection. Dalrymple must have heard of Coke; he certainly never refers to Coke and there is no evidence that Coke's work influenced him, though its existence may have encouraged him.

The *Institutions* may have started as no more than a diligent judge's notebook. In his *Apology* he wrote: 'for I did carefully and faithfully observe the debates and decisions of the Lords of Session during all the time I was in it, expressing mainly the reasons that the Lords laid hold on in all important cases, which were not come to be incontroverted as a beaten path, or were obvious to common capacities; and I did seldom eat or drink, and scarcely ever slept, before I perused the informations that passed every sederunt-day, and set down the decisions of the Lords (though sometimes not in the terms as they were marked by the clerks; for at that time the interlocutors were all upon their trust; without being revised and signed by the President, as they now are) while they were fresh in my memory, which were published in two volumes after my removal'. In the Advertisement to the second edition he says: 'The former edition was collected by me in many years, and designed chiefly for my particular use, that I might know the decisions and acts of Session, since the first institution of it, and that I might the more clear and determine my judgment in the matter of justice. And to that end, I made indexes of all the decisions, which had been observed by men of the greatest reputation, and did cite the same:'.

Another possible factor was his experience on the abortive Commission for the Restatement of the Law in 1649–50, which showed the need for a systematic treatise on the law. Another again may have been his experience as a Commissioner for Union in 1670, which seems to have brought home to him that in a Union with England the law of the smaller jurisdiction would be entirely at the mercy of the Parliament in which representation of the larger jurisdiction would necessarily predominate, who would from ignorance or bias always favour the legal approach more familiar to them. Stair was aware of the fundamental differences between Scots and English law and certainly wished to preserve Scots law inviolate. But preservation postulates knowledge of what the system is. Against the acceptance of this experience as alone motivating his writing is the known fact that manuscripts of at least parts or drafts of his book bear dates of 1666 and 1667. This cannot have been the prime or sole moving factor.

Not least it is quite possible that as a scholarly lawyer he was prompted to write simply by the appreciation that the sources of the law of Scotland were a disorderly jumble of materials, and that it was time somebody tried to put the materials into order and produce a systematic orderly account of what was growing up.

We do not know when he started to write. On the one hand the *Institutions* is not the book of an immature scholar or lawyer, and on the other hand, it must have been a number of years in the making. Probably the comparative calm and stability of the years after the Restoration on the one hand gave Stair the time and on the other prompted the view that reasonable peace and quiet called for an attempt at a systematic treatise on the whole private law. He began to collect the decisions of the Court of Session from 1661 and probably started to write his book then or, at least, shortly thereafter, and possibly even before. It could well have taken much of the spare time of a working judge for at least a dozen years. The extant manuscripts go back to the 1660s and 1670s. It seems possible that the negotiations for union with England in 1670 sharpened his resolve to preserve the independence of Scots law by stating it in systematic form. Latterly at least, in the 1670s, knowledge that he had been writing it is certain to have leaked out and manuscript copies would circulate, generating pressures for its publication.

His purpose was pretty certainly to reduce to order the growing volume of statute and case law and to provide Scottish judges and lawyers with a systematic statement of their country's private law. It was not primarily a study in general jurisprudence illustrated by Scottish examples, nor in how Roman law had been adopted and adapted in a country which had never been wholly within the Roman Empire. It was primarily a Scottish textbook. This is evidenced first by the heavy reliance on native, and what were then modern, authorities, namely Scottish statutes and Decisions.

The fact that Stair was writing a textbook for his country's governors and lawyers is seen also from another point; he wrote in English. Predecessors, such as Craig in Scotland, Gudelinus and Grotius in Holland and, much earlier, Bracton in England, had written in Latin. (Coke, too, wrote in English.) No doubt Latin was well known to lawyers in the seventeenth century, but to write in English largely excluded his work from continental jurists' ken. Furthermore, in the Dedication to King Charles II prefixed to the first edition, he speaks of presenting 'to your Majesty, a Summary of the Laws and Customs of your ancient Kingdom of Scotland'.

4. *Stair's Models*

It is plain that, certainly in his revised second edition of 1693, Stair's primary model in a very general sense was Justinian's *Institutions*.[52] But he did not slavishly follow or copy that model. The layout and order of treatment of topics in his *Institutions* diverges substantially from the Roman model.[53]

He was, however, clearly also familiar with the main works of the European jurists of the sixteenth and seventeenth centuries, several of whom were engaged in a similar task, seeking to write a systematic statement of the law of an emerging nation-state. The European jurist whom Stair cites most is Grotius, whose *De Jure Belli ac Pacis* sought to perform such a function for the major aspects of international relations, war and peace, on the basis of natural law, but whose *Inleidinge tot de Hollandsche Rechtsgeleedtheid* (Introduction to Dutch Jurisprudence) (1631), later translated into Latin by Van der Linden under the name *Hugonis Grotii Institutiones Juris Hollandici* (ed. Prof. H. F. W. D. Fischer, 1962), is a basic work on Roman-Dutch law, but he knew also Gudelinus' *De Jure Novissimo* (1620) which was perhaps the first attempt at a systematic exposition of the law of the Netherlands, and many of the treatises of the rather earlier European jurists. However, none of these appears to have been followed in detail; save in the most general way they were not models. There seems, in fact, to have been no single model nor any model followed closely.

5. *The Plan or Structure of the* Institutions

Stair was concerned not only to expound the law but to handle it as 'a rational discipline' (1,1,17). The plan or layout or pattern of his book is of importance and to this he clearly gave thought. More than one pattern can be discerned in the *Institutions*. In the first place there is what Professor Campbell[54] called the master-plan of the *Institutions*. It is based on Stair's recognition that the Roman classification in Justinian's *Institutions*, dealing with persons, things and actions, refers to 'the extrinsic object and matter, about which law and right are versant. But the proper object is the right itself, whether it concerns persons, things or actions, and according to the several rights and their natural order ought to be the order of jurisprudence which may be taken up in a threefold consideration; 1st, in the constitution and nature of rights; 2ndly, in their conveyance or translation from one person to another, whether it be among the living, or from the dead; 3rdly, in their cognition, which comprehends the trial, decision and execution of every right by the legal remedies',[55] or, in short, the nature of rights, conveyance of rights, cognition and enforcement of rights. As Professor Campbell observes:[56] 'Here already we have something different from Justinian, a universal plan for the exposition of rights, whatever their subject-matter, the excogitation of which indicates a high degree of abstract jurisprudential thinking. Whether it is of Stair's own devising I have not been able to discover.[57] This is the "master-plan" of Stair's *Institutions*. Books I and II deal with the constitution and nature of rights (but of the internal arrangement of these books more hereafter), Book III with their conveyance from one person to another . . . and Book IV with their cognition and enforcement'. But Stair does not apply his master-plan with ruthless logic and disregard of practical needs.

The second pattern or plan is that of Justinian's *Institutions*, treating successively of persons, things (including inheritance and the kind of incorporeal things called obligations, discussed in the order: contract, quasi-contract, delict and quasi-delict) and actions. In a very general sense Stair accepted this pattern but he turned it from a pattern of objects of law (law about persons, law about things, law about actions), into a pattern of substantive rights (rights against other persons, rights over things and rights of action). The Roman classification is based on the object and matter about which law and right are versant; but the proper subject of analysis is the right itself.

There is also a third pattern discernible in Books I and II. In I, I, I8 Stair says that 'the first principles of right are obedience, freedom and engagement' and at I, I, 23, following the passage already quoted, he says 'Whereby the whole method may be clearly thus: First, of the nature of those several rights; and because liberty standeth in the midst betwixt obligations of obedience, which are anterior, and of engagement, which are posterior (both which being of the same nature must be handled together), therefore liberty must have the first place; then next obligations obediential, and then conventional; and, after these, dominion in all its parts; and, in the second place, shall follow the conveyance of these several rights; and lastly, the cognition of all by judicial process and execution'. This explains why in Book I the titles deal with liberty and servitude, obligations in general (which are all restrictions on liberty), conjugal obligations, obligations between parents and children, obligations between tutors and curators and their pupils and minors, obligations of restitution, recompense and reparation and then obligations conventional or contracts, both contracts in general and the main particular species of contracts. This is why, unlike Justinian, Stair deals with obligations before things or property, and why he deals first with restitution and recompense, corresponding to the Roman quasi-contractual obligations, then with reparation, corresponding to Roman delictual obligations, and finally with conventional obligations, created by promises, pactions and contracts. In Book I accordingly his pattern does not wholly accord with his other plans. He does not there deal with the nature and constitution of rights, but with obligations as limitations on the right of liberty. But treating law as a collection of substantive rights, it is logical to treat of rights against persons, rights against persons arising from obligations, rights over things and rights of action.

The source of this third pattern, considering obligations both obediential and conventional, or legal and by agreement, as qualifications of liberty, is unknown but Professor Campbell observed that it accords closely with, and may well have been influenced by, the pattern of Books 2 and 3 of Pufendorf's *De Jure Naturae et Gentium*, published in 1672, which takes the primary idea of liberty, considers natural law as imposing duties which restrict man's liberty, and then general duties of reparation and duties created by agreement. In Pufendorf too obligations are examined before property. But Stair's work was substantially written before this work of Pufendorf was published. It may be, accordingly, that both Stair and Pufendorf were influenced by some earlier writer.

In his *Leviathan*, chapter 14, Hobbes adopts a generally similar approach, discussing obligation as contrasting with and as a restriction on liberty.

It is noteworthy also that at 1,9,4 Stair, when dealing with reparation, rejects the Roman classification into *furtum*, *rapina*, *damnum* and *injuria* and classifies harms by reference to the interest vested in the individual and infringed by the conduct in question, into injuries to life, members and health, to liberty, to fame, reputation and honour, to content, delight and satisfaction, and to goods and possessions. This again is remarkably modern and a great advance on classifications by modes of harm or means of wrongdoing. Stair may indeed have been on the verge of an analysis of law on the basis of the interests recognised and protected, an approach which did not reach development until the work of von Jhering, Roscoe Pound, and others in the twentieth century. But there are hints of this too in Pufendorf's *De Jure Naturae et Gentium* and Locke's *First Letter concerning Toleration* (1689) mentions the civil interests of life, liberty, health and indolency of body, and the possession of outward things, such as money, lands, houses, furniture and the like.

In practice Stair's layout provides a good practical working scheme of a book, by not insisting with complete strictness on his pattern of expounding the constitution and nature of rights, their conveyance and translation, and their cognition and execution. Thus he deals completely with contracts in Book I, save only their assignation and enforcement by action. In respect of real rights it is easier to apply the pattern and deal in separate books with ownership of land, its conveyance, and its vindication or enforcement.

6. *Stair's Sources*

The sources from which Stair drew the principles and rules which he stated were various. Some he cites and acknowledges, but there must be others which influenced him but which he does not mention.

In the first place there were principles of natural law, equity and reason, and the Bible (in the Authorised Version). He broadly equated the divine law, the law of reason, natural law and equity, as yielding principles discoverable by reason. The works of the natural lawyers, notably Grotius, aid in discovering these fundamental principles. These are non-legal, and moral or religious sources.[58]

Secondly he drew on the Roman law as finally settled by the Emperor Justinian in the sixth century A.D., to a lesser degree on the canon law of the Roman church, and on some of the commentators and humanists who wrote on the Roman law. There is repeated reference to the works of Balduinus, Clarus, Connanus, Cujas, Faber, Gail, Gothofredus, Gudelinus, Harprechtus, Hippolytus, Hotman, Matthaeus, Peresius, Rebuffus, Schotanus, Vinnius, Wesenbecius and Zoesius, and less common references to some three dozen more commentators on the civil law in the arguments addressed to, or the decisions of, the Court of Session in the years when Stair was a judge.[59] Some of these writers are expressly referred to in the *Institutions*, and others must have been more or less well known to him. We know from the references in the reported cases of the mid-seventeenth century that there were in use in the courts a great mass of continental treatises on the civil and canon law, and on various topics thereof. But Stair said himself (I,I,17): 'There is little to be found among the commentaries and treatises upon the civil law, arguing from any known principles of right; but all their debate is a congestion of the contexts of the law: which exceedingly nauseates delicate ingines [*ingenia*, brains], therein finding much more work for their memory than judgment in taking up and retaining the law-giver's will, rather than in searching into his reason'.

Thirdly, there were native sources, namely the Statutes of the Scottish Parliament, which he appears to have used as collected in Skene's *Lawes and Actes of Parliament* of 1597 (and later also in Murray of Glendook's editions, the folio of 1681 and the two duodecimo volumes of 1682), and the decisions of the Court of Session as collected by the collectors of *Practicks*, Hope, Haddington, Nicolson and Spotiswoode (none of which were then in print) and then by himself and later published in his two volumes of *Decisions*. There was also Craig's *Jus Feudale*, which had been printed in 1655. Though he says in his Dedication that 'the nauseating burden of citations are, as much as can be, left out', the citation of Scottish authority is very substantial, and it is the native sources which are the principal ones. English authorities had no weight; Glanvill, Bracton, Littleton and Coke are not mentioned, nor any English statute or case, though from casual comparative references he was clearly reasonably familiar with English law.

It is important not to overrate the importance of Roman or foreign sources; the *Institutions* is not just a Scottish translation of Justinian's *Institutions*, nor a statement of the Roman law with Scottish notes and comments, nor a Scottish version of a continental book, but an exposition of Scots law based predominantly on native sources, on his own observations of the operation of the Scots statutes and cases.

7. *Stair's Theory of Law*

Natural law thinking[60] goes back to the earliest speculation of the Greeks, the belief that in the physical sphere there was a body of principles explaining the behaviour of natural phenomena, animate and inanimate, and in the social sphere a body of principles discoverable intuitively and by pure reason setting standards of proper conduct. The theory has been used as a basis for speculation, a standard against which to measure existing institutions and rules, the justification for existing rules and for reforms, reactionary or radical. It has been an important idea in political and moral as well as legal thought, though with changing content and emphasis in different times and conditions.

The idea originated in Greek philosophy, particularly in Stoicism, and was carried over to Rome, not least by Cicero in his *De Republica* and *De Legibus*. In the works of the Roman jurists various versions of the idea are presented; the general view was to distinguish *ius naturale*, principles discoverable intuitively and accepted by reason as inherently right, *ius gentium*, principles generally accepted by and common to civilised peoples, and *ius civile*, the actual positive law of any particular community or state.

In the Christian fathers, notably St Augustine, the idea was developed that man had lived freely under natural law before his fall and had subsequently lived in bondage under sin and positive law. Gratian's *Decretum* identified the law of nature with the law of God; natural law was contained in and revealed by the Scriptures. The canonists made the canon law the principal vehicle in mediaeval times of the doctrine of the law of nature. Natural law was invested with a divine character; with it was contrasted mere human law, custom and man-made rules, mutable and with no higher authority than that of the sovereign person or body in the state.

The great mediaeval analysis of natural law was that of Aquinas (*Summa Theologica*, ia,iiae, Q.91) who distinguished the *eternal law*, or the government of the whole community of the universe by the divine reason, the *natural law*, the participation in the eternal law by which rational creatures

control their own actions and the actions of others, *human law*, being particular dispositions arrived at by an effort of reason from the precepts of
the natural law, and *a divine law*, necessary in addition to the natural law
and the humanly enacted law derived from it, to direct man to his destined
end of eternal blessedness. The Thomist system thus combines Greek
philosophy, Roman law, the teaching of the fathers of the church, and
principles of natural law. The supreme group of principles called for love of
God, love of one's neighbour according to the Golden Rule and generally the
performance of good and the avoidance of evil. The secondary principles,
derived from the first, were contained in the Ten Commandments, involving
obedience to parents and authority, protection of the person and life of another and of his property, truthfulness and fidelity to one's pledged word.
The third group consisted of concrete rules of justice formed by applying the
first two groups of principles to actual situations.

Among the later scholastics, particular interest attaches to the Spanish
theologian-jurists, notably Francisco Suarez (*De Legibus ac Deo Legislatore*,
1612), and Grotius, Pufendorf and Stair all drew on these thinkers. Suarez
emphasised the divine will instead of the divine reason as the source of
natural law.

Natural law was affected by the Reformation and the growth of distinct
Christian sects, the rise of the nation-states and the development of science.
The breakup of Christendom provoked a wide variety of statement, interpretation and application of the idea, and the rise of nation-states provoked
questions regarding relations between rulers and subjects and relations
between states, while scientific enquiry began to subject all natural phenomena
to free rational enquiry. In consequence there was a demand for a rational
basis for natural law.

Grotius was the founder of the modern theory of natural law. His views
are mainly set out in the *Prolegomena* to his *De Jure Belli ac Pacis* of 1625.
Echoing the Stoics, he saw the universe as dominated by a rational law of
nature. For man, natural law was the group of rules which followed inevitably from his nature; it was immutable but intelligible. If men were to live
with others, they must accept such principles as accepting human equality,
the principles of justice and equity, the keeping of promises, the compensation
for harm done, respect for property possessed by others, and so on. This
accordingly gave a set of moral standards, independent of both church
and state, rules not related to tradition but to the universal nature of
man to which rulers and subjects, states and private persons should be
subject.[61]

Stair defines law (1,1,1) as 'the dictate of reason, determining every
rational being to that which is congruous and convenient for the nature and
condition thereof; and this will extend to the determination of the indifferency of all rational beings'. 'Even God Almighty', he continues, 'though
he be accountable to, and controllable by none, and so hath the absolute

freedom of his choice, yet doth he unchangeably determine himself by his goodness, righteousness and truth; which therefore make the absolute sovereign divine law'. Divine law, that is, is supreme; God himself regulates his conduct in accordance with it and it determines the conduct of rational beings. 'The same is also the law of all rational creatures, by which they ought to determine and rule their free actions; but the congruity and conveniency of their nature affords them other dictates of their reason, which quadrate not with the divine nature, such as adoration, obedience, common to angels and men. And reason doth determine mankind yet further, from the conveniency of his nature and state, to be humble, penitent, careful and diligent for the preservation of himself and his kind; and therefore to be sociable and helpful, and to do only that which is convenient for mankind to be done by every one in the same condition . . . . This is that eternal law, which cannot be altered, being founded upon an unchangeable ground, the congruity to the nature of God, angels and men . . . . This is also called the law of nature, because it ariseth from the congruity or conveniency of nature, and thence is known by the light of nature'.

Accordingly divine law is sovereign; it is the eternal law and also called the law of nature. He continues (1,1,2): 'Correspondent to those dictates of reason (wherein law consists) which are in the understanding, there is an inclination in the will to observe and follow those dictates, which is justice . . . . There being nothing here proposed but the private rights of men, it is only requisite to consider the laws, by which private rights are constitute, conveyed, or destitute: and these are either divine or human'.

'Divine law is that mainly which is written in man's heart . . . . This is the law of nature, known naturally, either immediately, like unto those instincts which are in the other creatures, whereby they know what is necessary for their preservation. So the first principles of this natural law are known to men without reasoning or experience . . . . It is said to be written in the hearts of men' (1,1,3). Divine or natural law, that is, is mainly known instinctively or intuitively.

'With these common principles, with which God hath sent men into the world, he gave them also Reason, that thence they might by consequence deduce his law in more particular cases; and this part of the natural law is called the light or law of reason . . .' (1,1,4).

'This law is also called Conscience . . .' (1,1,5).

'This law of nature is also called Equity . . . . But equity is also taken for the law of rational nature, whereby nothing is to be done, which is not congruous to human nature . . . . And though equity be taken sometimes for the moderation of the extremity of human laws, yet it doth truly comprehend the whole law of the rational nature; otherwise it could not possibly give remeid to the rigour and extremity of positive law in all cases' (1,1,6).

Stair does not attempt to formulate a list of rights and duties which he attributes to natural law, but a substantial list could be compiled by attentive reading of the text. The principles so attributable can be classified as: 1. duties owed to God; 2. duties owed to oneself; 3. duties owed to the members of one's family; 4. duties owed to other persons generally; 5. principles relative to property; and 6. other miscellaneous principles.

'The law of nature is also termed the moral law . . .' (1,1,7). Accordingly, the first form of law is the divine law, law of nature, conscience, equity, the moral law, eternal, immutable, known in principle intuitively and in detail by the exercise of reason. He continues: 'Besides this natural, necessary, and perpetual law, God hath also given to men voluntary and positive laws, which though not at the pleasure of men, yet in themselves are mutable; . . .' (1,1,8). These include the ceremonial laws of worship; they are not written in the heart of man, nor deducible by reason from any principle (1,1,8). The prime positive law of God is the Judicial law prescribed to the people of Israel (1,1,9). This is accordingly the second form of law, divine positive law, stated in Scripture, but not eternal nor immutable.

He now treats of the third kind of law: 'Human law is that which, for utility's sake, is introduced by men: which is either by tacit consent, by consuetude or custom, or by express will or command of those in authority, having the legislative power'. It may be written or unwritten. 'The laws of men are either common to many nations, or proper to one nation, or peculiar to some places or incorporations in the same nation' (1,1,10). 'The law common to many nations is that which is commonly called *the law of nations*[62]. . . . But for the most part the law of nations is nothing else but equity, and the law of nature and reason . . . . This law is chiefly understood, when the common law is named among us; though the English so name the common current of their civil law, as opposite to statute and their late customs. Which is sometimes so taken with us. And oft-times by the common law, we understand the Roman law, which, in some sort is common to many nations' (1,1,11).

'The law of each society of people under the same sovereign authority, is called the civil law, or the law of the citizens of that commonwealth, though that now be appropriate to the civil law of the Roman commonwealth or empire, as the most excellent' (1,1,12). Then he gives a short account (1,1,12–14) of the three major systems of human laws, the civil law of Rome, the feudal law, and the canon law of the Roman church.

If the law of nature and reason were equally known to all men, he continues (1,1,15), it would be folly and fault to allow any other law. But because the main interest of men is to enjoy their rights in safety and security and also in confidence and quietness of mind, so that they may know what is their right and enjoy it, human laws are added, not to take away the law of nature and reason, but some of the effects thereof, which are in our power.[63] 'As by the law of nature man is a free creature, yet so as he may engage himself, and being engaged, by the same law of nature, he must perform: so men's laws are nothing else, but the public sponsions of princes and people; which therefore, even by the law of nature, they ought and must perform'. Human laws are accordingly introduced, he says: 1. to declare and clarify principles of natural law and equity in their application to particular cases; 2. to abridge equity in areas best left to natural feelings, honour and morality; 3. to supplement equity with formal safeguards, such as of sasine of land or intimation of assignations; 4. to modify equity, for example in succession to land; and 5. to adjust equity according to the requirements of time, place and public opinion.

Accordingly, he concludes, human laws are necessary. Happiest are the nations whose laws are nearest to equity, most declaratory of it, and least altering of its effects. Particularly so are those nations whose laws have developed by long custom based on discussion of particular cases. Statutes may easily leave gaps, which must be filled by recourse to equity. The best statutes are approbatory or corrected of customs. Though customary law has dangers, statutes tend to become so voluminous as to cease to be evidences of right and securities to people and 'become labyrinths, wherein they [people] are fain to lose their rights, if not themselves; at least, they must have implicit faith in those, who cannot comprehend them without making it the work of their whole life'. How prophetic! What Stair would have thought of twentieth-century statute law, sometimes beyond the comprehension of professional lawyers, can be imagined.

His theory may accordingly be summarised as follows: Law is the dictate of reason. It is distinguishable into 1. divine law (natural law, conscience, equity, the moral law), eternal and immutable; 2. positive divine law, found in Scripture, neither eternal nor immutable; 3. human law common to many nations (*ius gentium*); 4. human law proper to one nation (civil law); 5. human law peculiar to places or incorporations in the same nation. His view differs from that of Aquinas in equating divine, eternal and natural law, which Aquinas distinguished from each other. But his view is still fundamentally mediaeval in that natural law is a superior law, not merely a theoretical ideal standard, and it clearly owes much to the analysis of Aquinas[64] developed by later scholastic theologian-jurists such as Suarez in his *De Legibus ac Deo Legislatore* (1612). Even the judicious Hooker in his *Law of Ecclesiastical Polity*, Book 1 (1597) followed Aquinas closely, and this approach was not at all uncommon down to the early seventeenth century, prior indeed to the work of Bodin and Hobbes. Stair's law is accordingly not emancipated from religious superiority.

Stair's work indicates clearly that he was familiar with the Protestant version of revised natural law then current in Europe, as is evident from his references to Grotius. He was concerned not only to state the principles and rules established in Scots law in the late seventeenth century but to show that it was a rational discipline, a structure of basic principles from which conclusions could be deduced, and confirmed by the common dictates of reason. While there is no evidence that Stair and Locke ever met or were aware of each other's work, they shared some common assumptions, that there is a law of nature disclosed to men by reason, that men also need positive laws, that legislators and judges are instituted by agreement of men, and that the obligation to conform with laws and judgments derives from that agreement.[65]

His view, however, differs in certain respects from that of the contemporary continental natural lawyers. In the first place they held the view that a rational theory of law could be independent of theological presuppositions. The detailed content of the principle of natural law could be ascertained by deduction from man's nature as a rational being. Stair, on the other hand, was a convinced Protestant and Presbyterian and seems to have felt that he did not want to flout, or could not risk flouting, the accepted view of ecclesiastical opinion by giving primacy to reason and appearing to deny the influence of God in determining the principles which should govern human action, or by denying the freedom of the human will and stating that man is bound by a necessity in the nature and constitution of things in this world. The Westminster Confession of Faith (1644), ratified in 1690 as the main statement of faith accepted by the Presbyterian Church in Scotland, asserted both the freedom of the human will and the doctrine of effectual calling or divine predestination. Stair accordingly took a middle line. He asserted that law was founded primarily in the will of God, and that reason was subsidiary. Man was endowed with reason so that from its principles he might deduce God's law in particular cases. As Professor Campbell expressed it:[66] 'Stair was still prepared to rely on God at an indefinite number of points as the author of an indefinite number of principles of human action, which are directly known without reasoning or experience, which therefore do not require logical proof of their validity'.

In the second place the continental natural lawyers tended to accept a secular set of natural law principles, and held the view that a complete and self-sufficient system of law could be deduced by logic from these principles. Thus Grotius, in the *Prolegomena* to his *De Jure Belli*, contended that just as mathematicians treat their figures as abstracted from bodies, so in treating law he had withdrawn his mind from every particular fact. Stair did not, however, follow this line. He did not accept that reason by itself, applied to the principles implanted in man by God, could derive a satisfactory legal system. Some of his principles of law were asserted, he admitted, on the basis of mere authority, which no legal system could wholly dispense with. Only in the following century did the concept of law become wholly emancipated from religious overtones, and an imperative approach become fully established; as national law became prevalent and, in France, absolute government was established, the concept of law as enactment became the accepted one. This was foreshadowed by Hobbes and is exemplified by Burlamaqui, Rousseau and Blackstone.

Stair turns next to expound his view of what in modern terms we should call the sources of Scots law.

The customs of Scotland, he says (1,1,16) have arisen mainly from equity (i.e. natural law) and also from the civil, canon and feudal laws 'and therefore, these (especially the civil law) have great weight with us, namely, in cases where a custom is not yet formed. But none of these have with us the authority of law; and therefore are only received according to their equity and expediency, *secundum aequum et bonum*'. The law of Scotland, he continues, 'at first could be no other than *aequum et bonum*, equity and expediency . . . . Next unto equity [i.e. natural law] nations were ruled by consuetude, which declareth equity and constituteth expediency, and, in the third place, positive laws of sovereigns became accustomed, customs always continuing and proceeding . . . . In like manner, we are ruled in the first place by our ancient and immemorial customs, which may be called our common law; though sometimes by that name is understood equity [i.e. natural law] which is common to all nations, or the civil Roman law, which in some sort is common to very many . . . . In the next place are our statutes, or our acts of parliament . . . . Where our ancient law, statutes, and our recent customs and practiques are defective, recourse is had to equity, as the first and universal law, and to expediency, whereby the laws are drawn in consequence *ad similes casus*'. The hierarchy of sources is accordingly 1. Customs derived from natural law, civil (Roman), canon and feudal laws; 2. Ancient and immemorial customs – our common law; 3. Statutes or Acts of Parliament; and 4., failing other sources, Equity or natural law, expediency and analogy.

He then (1,1,18) states three first principles of equity (i.e. natural law), obedience to God, freedom of men, and man's power to limit his freedom by engagement, and three prime principles of positive law, society, property and commerce. 'The principles of equity are the efficient causes of rights and laws: the principles of positive law are the final causes or ends for which laws are made, and rights constitute and ordered [i.e. the objects of laws]. And all of them may aim at the maintenance, flourishing and peace of society, the security of property, and the freedom of commerce'. Obedience, freedom and engagement are then discussed (1,1,19–21).

Obedience[67] is the submission of man's will to God's will, intimated to him by the law of nature, light of reason and conscience, whereby men distinguish between right and wrong, duty and non-duty. From this arise what are called obediential obligations;[68] notably those between persons in a family and those called quasi-contractual. Obedience, that is, to the will of God imposes duties on human beings independently of their choice. Beyond the sphere of obedience is the sphere of freedom,[69] and beyond that the sphere of engagement,[70] wherein men voluntarily oblige or bind themselves in matters where they are free. Engagement is to Stair a fundamental concept, because Stair shared with Locke and the natural lawyers a contractarian view of government and political obligation. A man's freedom is in his own power and may be restrained by his voluntary engagements, which he is bound to fulfil (1,1,18).

He continues (1,1,22): 'The formal and proper object of law are the rights of men. A right is a power, given by the law, of disposing of things, or exacting from persons that which they are due. This will be evident, if we consider the several kinds of rights, which are three, our personal liberty, dominion and obligation . . . . Obligation is that which is correspondent to a personal right . . . . So dominion is called a real right', and then (1,1,23) he proceeds to the divisions of rights, public rights and private rights, the latter of which are to be considered in the order: 1. the constitution and nature of rights; 2. their conveyance or translation from one to another, and 3. their cognition, comprehending the trial, decision and execution of every right by the legal remedies. In relation to the constitution and nature of rights, liberty must be considered first, then obligations obediential and conventional, and finally dominion.

Not least interesting in relation to his own concept of law is Stair's own rhetorical question (1,1,17): Whether law may, or should, be handled as a rational discipline, having principles from whence its conclusions may be deduced? In other words, is law a body of principles which can be comprehended or grasped by the reason, or is it merely a collection of commands and prohibitions? Most lawyers, he said, think not, esteeming the law of a nation incapable of such a deduction, as being dependent upon the will and pleasure of lawgivers and introduced for utility's sake. This unfortunately has been the trend ever since Stair's day and more and more law, particularly statute law, can only be regarded as made from expediency and for reasons of utility, and can only with difficulty be fitted into any order or pattern. The Roman law, he points out, is largely the cause of this: 'There is little to be found among the commentaries and treatises upon the civil law, arguing from any known principles of right; but all their debate is a congestion of the contexts of the law; which exceedingly nauseates delicate engines,[71] therein finding much more work for the memory than judgement in taking up and retaining the lawgiver's will, rather than searching into his reason'.

But some recent learned lawyers, he says, have thought it both feasible and fit that law be formed into a rational discipline, as for example Duarenus and Grotius, and he gives his reasons. It is clear accordingly that this was part of Stair's purpose, to put the principles of law into order as a rational discipline, to state major principles, their subordinate principles and the qualifications thereof, in an understandable order and pattern, which will serve as the major premisses for deduction of conclusions in particular cases. This view is consistent with the standpoint of a natural lawyer, and opposed to the attitude of the mere positivist.

8. *Stair's Legal Concepts*

More than most writers of treatises on private law, particularly in the seventeenth century, Stair indicates his understanding of some of the general concepts of legal thinking which he uses in his work and which determined the structure of the book. These deserve consideration.

Rights. Stair appears to have distinguished natural rights (though he does not use the words) and civil rights, a distinction paralleled by his later distinction between obediential and conventional obligations. He seems to have accepted that a man has a natural right to those goods which are natural to rational beings, such as to life, liberty, the pursuit of happiness, and others. He does not, however, enumerate a list of natural rights. He seems moreover to hold the view (1,1,17) that 'in the matters of [natural] right, a man of reason, though without education, if not blinded or biassed with affection or interest, and marred with the statutes and customs of men (which are but as their contracts and matters of fact to him) would be able to discern right from wrong'.[72] Natural rights, that is, are known intuitively.

Just as natural rights are based on natural law, so civil rights are grounded in human positive law, which seeks to make natural rights effective in a community; the former are apprehended by intuition, the latter learned by the study of customs, statutes and other sources of positive law. 'The principles of equity [natural law][73] are the efficient cause of rights and laws; the principles of positive law[74] are the final causes or ends for which laws are made, and rights constituted and ordered.[75] And all of them may aim at the maintenance, flourishing and peace of society, the security of property, and the freedom of commerce' (1,1,18, *ad finem*). Natural law, that is, is the ultimate spring or force giving rise to natural rights and laws, the principles of positive law, the intended purposes or ends for which positive laws are made and civil rights constituted. Thus natural law ordains the protection of the person against assault and recognises a natural right to safety from assault; the principle of positive law seeking to secure the interests of individuals against infringement of safety of their persons is the end for which a rule of criminal law penalising assault is made, by custom, common law or statute.

'The formal and proper object[76] of law', he says (1,1,22), 'are the rights of men'. Rules of law, that is, are directed to defining and securing the rights of men. He continues: 'A right is a power, given by the law, of disposing of things, or exacting from persons that which they are due. This will be evident, if we consider the several kinds of rights, which are three, our personal liberty, dominion and obligation. Personal liberty is the power to dispose of our persons, and to live where, and as we please, except in so far as by obedience or engagement we are bound. Dominion is the power of disposal of the creatures in their substance, fruits, and use. Obligation is that which is correspondent to a personal right, which hath no proper name as it is in the creditor, but hath the name of obligation as it is in the debtor:

and it is nothing else but a legal tie, whereby the debtor may be compelled to pay or perform something, to which he is bound by obedience to God, or by his own consent and engagement. Unto which bond the correlate[77] in the creditor is the power of exaction, whereby he may exact, obtain, or compel the debtor to pay or perform what is due; and this is called a personal right, as looking directly to the person obliged, but to things indirectly, as they belong to that person. So dominion is called a real right, because it respecteth things directly, but persons, as they have meddled with those things. By which it is clear, that all rights consist in a power or faculty; the act whereof is possession, enjoyment or use; which is a matter of fact, and no point of right, and may be where no right is, as right may be where these are not'.

A right is accordingly, in his view, a legal power of disposal, or power of exaction; in Roman law *ius* was used sometimes in this sense, as in the phrase *ius testamenti faciendi*.[78] This is not complete, nor possibly of the essence of a legal right, which we now consider to consist in a legally assertable claim to do, or not to do, something, but it was an advance in conceptualising beyond anything earlier; most earlier writing had either not developed any clear conception of a right or had confused it with a rightful or just claim. But a legal right is not necessarily a rightful claim.[79] Stair seems to have been one of the first, if not the first, jurist to express in English this view of the right as a power, and the holder of it having freedom of choice in some matter or power in relation thereto.

Stair is most certainly right in observing that the act of a right, or exercise of it, in possession, enjoyment or use, is a matter of fact and independent of right, both legal and moral. Long before Hume made his famous observation of the distinction between 'is' and 'ought' Stair had observed it, and this distinction between matter of fact and point of right is important in his thinking: the legal order is an order of rights, as distinct from an order of conduct in fact: 'the proper objects of law are the rights of men' (1,1,22).

In the section quoted (1,1,22) Stair mentions the two categories of rights, personal right and real right. Personal right, he says, corresponds to obligation, that is duty, and looks directly to the person obliged and indirectly to things. Dominion, that is ownership, on the other hand, is called a real right because it concerns things directly and persons incidentally. This distinction hearks back to the Roman law. The Roman jurists distinguished broadly between *dominium*, or the relation between the holder of a right *in rem* and the right vested in him, and *obligatio*, or the relation between a creditor having a right *in personam* and the debtor on whom lay the correlative duty. These kinds of rights were themselves derived from the Roman distinction[80] between *actio in rem* and *actio in personam*, the former for the recovery of *dominium*, to assert entitlement to ownership of a thing, and the latter for the enforcement of an *obligatio*, claiming payment of money, performance of a contract or protection of some other personal claim. The right protected by an action *in rem* came to be called a *ius in rem*; that protected by an action *in personam* to be called a *ius in personam*, but both phrases came from the commentators rather than the Roman jurists themselves. In translation *ius in rem* became real right and *ius in personam* a personal right.[81]

Stair seems to be uncertain whether his distinction is not the same as that now called between personal rights and proprietary rights, the former dealing with elements of a man's personal condition, such as his liberty, freedom from harm, honour and reputation, the latter dealing with his rights in and over things of economic value, objects of property. Did Stair, that is, conceive of personal right as concerned with personal condition and real right as concerned with a man's property?[82] In modern analysis in these two antinomies personal and real do not correspond to personal and proprietary. In modern thinking the essential quality of a *ius in personam* is that it avails only against another determinate party, such as the other party to an obligation, whereas a *ius in rem* avails against persons generally, everyone. A right relative to a man's personal condition, such as his freedom from injury, is however *ius in rem* just as much as a right relative to his house or his books and some of the rights which are proprietary are *iura in personam*, such as against those indebted to him.

Stair further said that the several kinds of rights were three, personal liberty, dominion and obligation.[83] In 1,2,2 he affirms that there is a right of liberty, distinct from the dominion of the creatures and from obligation, and that this is evident from the fact that it can be referred to neither of these. This differs from both the Roman law and modern analysis, which regards the right to liberty, physical liberty, liberty from moral compulsion and other aspects of liberty, as a kind of *ius in rem*, valid against anyone and everyone. Is this because Stair conceived of dominion more narrowly than *ius in rem*, as a power over creatures and things rather than as an entitlement to assert one's claim against anyone and everyone?

Finally,[84] and briefly, Stair distinguishes public and private rights: public rights concern the state of the commonwealth, private rights are the rights of persons and particular incorporations. This is a transfer to the sphere of rights of the Roman law distinction between public law and private law.[85] It is an inaccurate distinction and might be better expressed as one between rights in public and in private law. Is, for example, dominion, a purely private law right? Is the right not to be assaulted a public or a private right? No modern analytical jurist seems to draw a distinction between public rights and private rights.

Duties. The concept of duty is hardly mentioned by Stair. It is subsumed in his concept of obligation and obligation (duty) is inadequately distinguished from obligation (link or bond).

Liberty. According to Stair (1,1,18) the first principles of equity [natural law] are '. . . 2. That man is a free creature, having power to dispose of himself and of all things, in so far as, by obedience to God, he is not restrained; 3. That this freedom of man is in his own power, and may be restrained by his voluntary engagements.' Later (1,1,20) he observes that where obedience to God ends, freedom begins, and man by nature is free in all things, where this obedience [to God] has not tied him, until he oblige himself, and at 1,1,21, he continues, that engagement begins where freedom ends, it being our voluntary obliging of ourselves, where, by nature, we are free. In 1,1,20, having discussed whether men truly are free, and concluded that they are, he adds that from freedom arises 'our personal freedom and liberty, whereby men are *sui juris*, but also their power of the disposal of other things within their reach, or that dominion which God hath given them over the creatures', that is personal liberty, and also liberty to have and exercise proprietary rights.

Stair's concept of liberty is that it is 'that natural power which man hath of his own person . . . a natural faculty to do that which every man pleaseth, unless he be hindered by law or force' (1,2,1). It is distinct from both the dominion of the creatures and from obligation, and its opposites are restraint and constraint. It is however not absolute but limited, 1. by the will of God and our obediential obligations to him, and to men by his ordinance (1,2,5); 2. by punishment for delinquency; 3. by engagement, as by imprisonment for debt; 4. by subjection to authority; and 5. by bondage, slavery or servitude. Injuries to liberty by constraint are punishable as delinquencies.

Later (IV,45,17) among general presumptions he mentions that liberty is presumed in opposition to slavery, freedom from all obligations by delinquence, freedom from conventional, though not from natural, obligations, and freedom against any servitude of land or other real bond.

Every engagement by voluntary obligation is a diminution of a man's freedom[86] because 'thereby we are either restrained from that power of disposal of the creatures,[87] or may be constrained to some performance contrary to our natural liberty'.[88] The principle of engagement gives rise to obligations by paction, promise or contract, and there is nothing more natural and consistent with principles of natural right than to stand to the faith of our pactions.

Obligation. Stair's conception of obligation[89] seems to be a confusion of two senses of that word, firstly, of obligation as meaning the duty or burden or liability incumbent on a person, corresponding to the personal right inhering in the creditor, what we now call duty, and secondly, of obligation as meaning a relationship, a legal bond or tie linking two or more distinct persons, and implying mutual rights and duties between the parties linked thereby. In the sentence in 1,1,22, already quoted, commencing 'Unto which bond . . .', it is obligation in the sense of duty, and not obligation in the sense of bond, to which the correlation in the creditor is the power of exaction. Similarly in 1,3,1, he says that what is a personal right in the creditor is in the debtor 'called an obligation, debt or duty'. He continues:

'Obligation is a legal tie, by which we may be necessitate or constrained to pay, or perform, something.[90] This tie lieth upon the debtor; and the power of making use of it in the creditor in the personal right itself, which is a power, given by the law, to exact from persons that which they are due'. In fact the tie of obligation lies on and between both parties, conferring on each rights to exact performance, and duties to perform. In fairness, however, this dualism of sense of the word *obligatio* is found in the Roman law, but in interpreting Stair one must frequently consider whether duty or bond is meant.

He then adverts to the quadruple categorisation of obligation in Roman law, into obligations *ex contractu, quasi ex contractu, ex maleficio,* and *quasi ex maleficio,*[91] but observes that obligations can be better distinguished 'according to the principle or original from whence they flow, in obligations obediential, and by engagement, or natural and conventional, or by the will of God and by the will of man'. This is a much better distinction, according to the source of the obligation in God or nature or in engagement or agreement. It is similar but not identical to that drawn by Pufendorf[92] between 'congenital' and 'adventitious', who also conceives of obligation as a bond or tie, but Pufendorf and Stair assign different particular obligations to their respective pairs of categories.

The term 'obediential' is interesting. It is not classical Latin, nor even the Latin of the Digest, but mediaeval;[93] first found in the phrase *potentia obedientiae,* used by Alexander of Hales, Albertus Magnus, Bonaventure and St Thomas Aquinas, *potentia obedientialis* occurs in Albertus Magnus[94] and in St Thomas Aquinas[95] in relation to miracles for the concept whereby a creature's being is subject or obedient to what God wills to do in it something beyond the activity of ordinary natural causes so long as no contradiction occurs. The latter phrase became the common one. This doctrine of obediential potency was taught by Augustine, formulated by mediaeval theologians and adopted as standard in theology.[96] The word is found in Cajetan, who particularly influenced the modern use of the concept of obediential potency for the relationship of intelligent creatures to the supernatural, and in Suarez, was common in theological contexts in the seventeenth century, and has continued into modern Catholic theology. Stair more probably got it from Suarez than direct from Aquinas. The word was quite common in seventeenth-century theology. Thus it is found in Samuel Rutherford's *Tryal and Triumph of Faith* (1645) xxv, 371—'power obediential to hear what God saith and do it'—and in Sir Matthew Hale's *Primitive Origination of Mankind* (1677) I, 138—'owes an obediential subjection to the Lord of Nature'.

Stair's meaning is, however, quite clear: 'Obediential obligations', he says,[97] 'which are put upon men by the will of God, not by their own will, and so are most part natural, as introduced by the law of nature, before any addition made thereto by engagement are such as we are bound to perform solely by our obedience to God: as conventional obligations are such, as we are bound by and through our own will, engagement or consent'.

'4. Obediential obligations are either by the will of God immediately, or by the mediation of some fact of ours;[98] such are obligations by delinquency, whereby we become bound to reparation and satisfaction of the party injured, and are liable in punishment to God, which may be exacted by those who have his warrant for that effect. Of these obediential obligations there be some which tie us to God alone; whereby there is no right constituted in man to exact the same as his own due, nor any warrant or command given him by God to exact them on his behalf; And some, though they constitute not a right in man, yet man is commanded and warranted to vindicate them; as the crimes of witchcraft, blasphemy, bestiality and the like; for which there is an express command to inflict punishment, though there be no injury done therein to man, of which there could be any reparation. . . . But these obligations, being among the public rights, belong to the magistrate, on whom is devolved the authority to vindicate for God as his viceregent, we shall not here insist on them, nor on those other obligations, whereby no right of execution is constituted in man for vindication, *et quae solum Deum habent ultorem* (such are the love and fear we owe to God, and dependence on, and confidence in, him) being now only to treat about the private rights of man. We shall therefore insist only on the obediential obligations that are betwixt husband and wife, parents and children, the obligations betwixt tutors and pupils, curators and minors, and the obligations of restitution and remuneration, and the obligations of reparation of delinquency and damage; and then we shall proceed to conventional obligations'.

Obediential obligations are accordingly those which men owe it to God to implement, performance of which is due solely by our obedience to God. The categories include (A.1) what later jurists called absolute duties, owed though no man has any right to exact performance, and also (A.2) those which man is commanded to vindicate though no man has right to performance. There are also (B) obligations owed by men to men, but springing from the will of God.[99] It may be objected that duties in categories A.1 and 2 are not legal duties at all, but religious or moral duties. The duty to love and fear God (in A.1) and to extirpate witchcraft, blasphemy and bestiality (in A.2) are not legal duties, though the latter category may be made legal duties by being incorporated in common law or enacted by statute. Duties in category B he conceives as binding by God's will or the law of nature, whether or not by positive law, but performance is exigible by man. Clearly accordingly the category of obediential obligations is different from and wider than merely obligations imposed by law, independently of human choice or volition. His basic distinction is not simply of obligations imposed by law and obligations undertaken voluntarily.

Contrasted with obediential obligations are conventional obligations, springing *ex conventione*, 'such as we are bound by and through our own will, engagement or consent' (1,3,3) to perform. Conventional obligations spring from man's natural capacity of engagement, to bind himself in favour of others. Later (1,10,pr.) he describes them as 'arising from the will of man, whereby our own will tieth us in that, wherein God hath left us free; for as obediential obligations descend from the principle of obedience to God, and have their rise and reason from his sovereign power to command, and our absolute obligement to obey; so, in his gracious goodness, in the greatest part, he hath left us free, and hath given power to none to exact, or compel us: yet, so he hath given that liberty in our power, that we may give it up to others, or restrain and engage it, whereby God obliges us to performance, by mediation of our own will; yet such obligations, as to their original, are conventional, and not obediential.

'Conventional obligations do arise from our will and consent; for, as in the beginning hath been shewn, the will is the only faculty constituting rights, whether real or personal; for it is the will of the owner, that naturally transferreth right from him to the acquirer; so in personal rights, that freedom we have of disposal of ourselves, our actions and things, which naturally is in us, is by our engagement placed in another, and an engagement is a diminution of freedom, constituting that power in another, whereby he may restrain or constrain us to the doing or performing, of that whereof we have given him power of exaction; and in the debtor it is the debtor's duty or necessity to perform'. Conventional obligations are constituted, he continues, by promise and by paction or contract.[100]

Stair's theory of reparation of delict. Stair's theory of delinquence or delict is plain; these obligations have their origin in the will of God, introduced by the law of nature (1,9,1) and have a two-fold nature, partly due to God, obliging to punishment, and partly to man, obliging to reparation, the 'obligation of repairing his damage by putting him in as good a condition as he was in before the injury' (1,9,2), a verbal formulation affirmed, albeit without reference to Stair, in judgments of the twentieth century. He goes on to develop a classification of harms by reference to the interests of the pursuer which are infringed, a theory not again developed until the late nineteenth and twentieth centuries. 'According to several rights and enjoyments, damages and delinquences may be esteemed. As, first, life, members and health . . . So the life of any being taken away, the damage of these who were entertained and maintained by his life, as his wife and children, may be repaired. So likewise the loss any man hath by the expenses of his cure, or the loss of his labour, and industry in his affairs, is also reparable. Next to life is liberty . . . The third is fame, reputation and honour . . . The fourth interest, that may be damnified, is our content, delight or satisfaction; and especially by the singular affection to, or our opinion of the value or worth of any thing that owners have . . . The last damage is in goods and possession' (1,9,4). The one element lacking in this analysis is an explicit distinction between intentional harms and unintentional or negligent harms, those done *dolo* and those done *culpa*. At least in the case of circumvention (1,9,9) this distinction is recognised, between *dolus malus* and *solertia* or error or mistake.

Stair's theory of contract. 'Conventional obligations do arise from our will and consent . . . but it is not every act of the will that raiseth an obligation, or power of exaction' (1,10,1). Stair accordingly accepted a will theory of contractual obligation, which did not become widely accepted until, and then under German influence, the nineteenth century. It is not, of course, he repeats (1,10,2) every act of the will that creates rights and duties, only engagement, 'that whereby the will conferreth or stateth a power of exaction in another, and thereby becomes engaged to that other to perform'. Neither desire nor resolution to contract will suffice to create obligation. He proceeds then (1,10,3) to distinguish (a) promises, not conditional on acceptance (1,10,4), (b) pactions or *duorum pluriumve in idem placitum consensus atque conventio*, a consent in their wills to oblige any of them (1,10,6), (c) offers, or promises conditional on acceptance (1,10,6) and (d) *nuda pacta*, but concludes (1,10,10) that pactions, contracts, covenants and agreements are synonymous terms; the only significant distinctions are therefore promises, conditional promises or offers, and contracts or agreements created by *consensus in idem*. 'It is the consent of two or more parties, to some things to be performed by either of them; for it is not a consent in their opinions, but a consent in their wills, to oblige any of them' (1,10,6).

This is all quite different from, and a much more subtle and penetrating analysis of obligations than, the classification of obligations according to the circumstances from which they arose, agreement, wrong, or otherwise, in Justinian's *Institutions*. Obediential obligations cover the area wherein man is obliged by God, conventional obligations the area wherein man is free, and may, by the exercise of his will, bind himself.

Stair's further distinctions of obligations (1,3,5) are more ordinary. They are (1) into natural and civil obligations, or those arising by the law of nature and not having remedies by civil law, and those having civil effect and execution, though possibly not binding by natural law; (2) principal and accessory obligations; and (3) obligations pure, conditional or uncertain, and to a day, or postponed.

Dominion. There arises from freedom, Stair says (1,1,20) not only men's personal freedom and liberty 'but also their power of the disposal of other things within their reach, or that dominion which God hath given them over the creatures'. Dominion, Stair says (1,1,22) is 'the power of disposal of the creatures in their substance, fruits and use . . . dominion is called a real right, because it respecteth things directly, but personal as they have meddled with those things'. Dominion, or real rights, is the subject-matter of Books II and III. 'Because that term [dominion] is more appropriated to the power of men over men, than over the creatures, it is therefore called a real right, or a right of things: for as obligation is a right personal, as being a power of exacting from persons that which is due; so a right real is a power of disposal of things, in their substance, fruits or use' (11, 1, pr.). Stair's concept of dominion seems to be based on the idea expressed in Genesis 1, 28–9, of the God-given dominion of man over all the creatures of the earth, air and sea. This gives inadequate place to rights in land, which occupy the major part of Books II and III, particularly when the word he uses must have come from *dominium*, of which the commonest phrase was *dominium ex iure Quiritium*, ownership of law by right of citizenship.

The Roman law, it will be remembered, dealt with things, *res*. Stair has taken a major step towards analytical abstraction in seeking to deal primarily, not with the kinds of things, but with the legal rights to and over kinds of things. To put it another way, he is primarily concerned with property as a right or bundle of rights, rather than with property, so-called, as a name for the objects of men's rights.

Conclusions on his use of concepts. Interesting and valuable as Stair's approach to the law from the standpoint of rights is, there are some other concepts which he does not discuss, notably personality, persons and the different status of persons. He does not take the point that rights attach only to those beings which have personality in law, that there are different kinds of legal persons, notably natural persons, societies and corporations, and that among natural persons there are different status-groups.[101] Nor does he devote space to examination of conduct, of acts and the mental state with which they are done.[102] In fairness to him, however, to expect such analysis is to expect too much, having regard to the state of knowledge in his time and the stage of maturity of legal analysis attained by text-writers. Judged by the standards of contemporaries, his jurisprudential powers are unusual and significant.

9. *The Standing of the* Institutions

Since its first publication in 1681 Stair's *Institutions* has held a unique place in Scottish legal history and in the literature of Scots law. It was the first book which sought to present in narrative form a systematic account of the whole private law of Scotland. It also very largely created Scots law as a rational system and its publication marks the beginning of modern Scots law. It is accordingly historically a text of the very first importance.

One of the achievements which can be attributed to Stair was to establish nascent Scots law as a system in which the lawyer questing for the solution to a problem would seek the appropriate principle within the ambit of whose application his case fell and to deduce syllogistically from that principle the solution to his problem, rather than to seek a previous decision of a court on facts which can fairly be regarded as similar to those raised by his problem and analogically to accept the judicial solution of the precedent problem as that applicable to the enquirer's problem. The validity of this claimed achievement can be established in two ways. In the first place, though Stair cites many decisions, there is no indication at any point that he regarded any of these decisions as a precedent in the modern sense, that is, as a prior decision which must subsequently be regarded as having persuasive force on the judges of a subsequent court, faced with an analogous problem, to decide in conformity with the *ratio* of the precedent, still less as a prior decision which, in some circumstances, was binding on the later judges, compelling them to decide conform to the precedent, unless they could find narrow reasons for regarding themselves as not bound. A decision was cited by him as an illustration, or an example, and no more. No doubt judges in the seventeenth century, as in the twentieth, liked to know how their predecessors had decided controversies of particular kinds, and to utilise their predecessors' wisdom, and doubtless they regarded consistency of decisions on similar points as conducive to justice but, particularly when the law was in a highly formative state, it is clear that they were free to differ from them. There was in Stair's time, that is, not even the beginnings of a doctrine of precedent, or of *stare decisis*. Decisions are evidence of our customs, not precedents. 'But there is much difference to be made betwixt a custom by frequent decisions and a single decision, which hath not the like force. Yet frequent agreeing decisions are more effectual than Acts of Sederunt themselves, who do easily go into desuetude' (1,1,16).

Indeed the distinction between basing decisions on principle or on authority, or between grounds of decision deduced from a general principle and rules binding merely because proceeding from a source recognised as stating rules with authority, is foreign to Stair. If any rules emanate from, and are stated with, authority, they are rules of the law of nature or God. The civil (Roman) law 'even though it be not acknowledged as a law binding for its authority' (1,1,12) is frequently followed for its equity, or consistency with natural law. Still less in Stair's strongly Protestant time did the canon law have authority but 'consideration must be had to these laws . . . as likewise containing many equitable and profitable laws' (1,1,14). Indeed 'these [the civil, canon and feudal laws] (especially the civil law) have great weight with us, namely in cases where a custom is not yet formed. But none of these have with us the authority of law, and therefore are only received according to their equity and expediency, *secundum bonum et aequum*' (1,1,16). To Stair the sources of law were equity, custom, and Acts of Parliament and even the last could fall into desuetude and cease to be authoritative (1,1,16).

In the second place, Stair regularly seeks to formulate and state propositions as principles capable of application to a great variety of particular cases. Take the common wrong of spuilzie (1,9,16–24) or roughly what a common lawyer would call conversion. He defines spuilzie (1,9,16), states the title requisite for pursuing for it, and how it must be done (1,9,17) and may be proved (1,9,18), and how it is elided, or the defences competent (1,9,19–24). Again in the common contract of sale, and in respect of the important problem of the passing of the risk of loss, Stair (1,14,7) poses the question, states the answer returned by the civil law, and continues: 'it is a general rule, that . . .'. 'Beside authority [i.e. the authority of the civil law, not of case-law] the main reason to the contrary is . . .'. As another example of his formulation of the law in statements of principle, take the subject of removing of tenants at the expiry of leases. Removing (11,9,38) is (A) summary without warning, or (B) solemn upon warning. Summary removing is (i) by paction, or (ii) by law. Solemn removing (11,9,39) had an old form (39 and 40) and the current form, which required title in the pursuer (41) but was subject to many exceptions or defences (42 and 43). On every point it would be possible to formulate a major premiss of law, or statement of a principle, which combined with a minor premiss of fact, or statement of the material facts of a problem, would inevitably lead to the conclusion or answer in point of law to the enquirer's quest. Let us take as an example the facts of probably the most famous case of the twentieth century, *Donoghue* v. *Stevenson*, 1932 S.C. (H.L.) 31; [1931] A.C. 562, which established the liability of a manufacturer to the ultimate consumer of his product for defect therein. Under the main head of liability arising *ex lege*, and the sub-head of the duty of reparation of injuries by delinquence, Stair says (1,9,4): 'according to several rights and enjoyments, damages and delinquences may be esteemed. As first, our life, members and health; which, though they be inestimable, and can have no price; yet there are therewith incident damages reparable; and that either *lucrum cessans*, or *damnum emergens* . . . the loss any man hath in the expense of his cure, or the loss of his labour, and industry in his affairs, is also reparable'. This principle is general enough to have sufficed for the decision of *Donoghue* in the way it was ultimately decided. Manufacturer's liability is but one species of the generic liability of persons for harm to one in life, members and health, wholly independent of contractual obligation. There is no warrant here for the heresy which, prior to *Donoghue* v. *Stevenson*, had inhibited the development of the principle of delictual liability to consumers, the view that if there was no contractual liability there could be no liability at all. The only factor not inherent in Stair's statement of principle but included in the *ratio* of *Donoghue* is the qualification that there should have been no reasonable probability of inspection of the goods between manufacture and consumption, which should have disclosed the defect. But by the early twentieth century regard for formulations of principle, as by Stair, had been largely forgotten, overwhelmed by citations of authorities, too frequently English, and, in this context, vitiated by the contract-tort dichotomy which obscured the true principle that a man might owe a duty to one *ex contractu* and also, quite separately, to him or to another or others *ex lege* and hence be liable to one for breach of contract and to another or others for reparation for delinquence or delict.

Can it be better expressed than in Stair's own words, in his *Apology* of

1690: 'but I may say without vanity, that no man did so much, to make the law of this Kingdom known and constant as I have done, that not only bred lawyers, but generally the nobility and gentry of the nation might know their rights; . . . And I did write the *Institutions of the Law of Scotland*, and did derive it from that common law that rules the world and compared it with the laws civil and canon, and with the custom of the neighbouring nations, which hath been so acceptable, that few considerable families of the nation wanted the same, and I have seen them avending, both in England and Holland'.

In the literature of Scots law the *Institutions* has always held a pre-eminent place, as the most authoritative and respected general treatise, and one of the few institutional works, statements in which, save where and when clearly overruled or rendered obsolete by later law, have an authority similar to that of decisions of the Court of Session and which settle the law. 'When on any point of law I find Stair's opinion uncontradicted I look upon that opinion as ascertaining the law of Scotland'.[103] 'Stair, Erskine and Bell are cited daily in the courts, and the court will pay as much respect to them as to a judgment of the House of Lords, though it is bound to follow a judgment of the House of Lords whatever the institutional writers may have said'.[104] Passages in the *Institutions* have been cited and founded on in countless arguments, judgments and later statements of the law and the examination of the ambit and applicability of any principle of Scottish common law is incomplete without consideration of what Stair wrote about the point. The *Institutions* is still in large measure a book of authority which can and should be examined and cited as providing an answer to modern practical issues, and still a living part of Scottish legal literature.

Stair's *Institutions* 'has long been accepted as the fountain-head of Scots law. Its outstanding feature is the emphasis consistently laid upon first principles, and the systematic development of these principles in harmony with the most enlarged and comprehensive views of comparative juris-prudence . . . . He ranged in a spirit of philosophic eclecticism over an immense field of enquiry, extending from the basic axioms of religion and ethics to the intricacies of early Scottish forms of process, and reduced the whole to an orderly and scientific system which has furnished the model and basis for all subsequent treatises of its kind'.[105]

Outside Scotland Stair's standing as a jurist of the first rank has hardly been adequately recognised. Joseph Story in the U.S.A. refers on many occasions to Stair and other leading Scottish jurists, but knowledge of Stair and his work is too often absent.

Inevitably as the law has developed, particularly in the twentieth century, with different social conditions and commercial practices, with increased statutory modification of common law, a great, indeed sometimes over-whelming, volume of case-law, the tendency, and the opportunity, to rely solely, or primarily, on a passage in Stair as providing the statement of principle which, applied to the facts, is decisive of the controversy, are less common than they were.

10. *The* Institutions *in its European Setting*

The writing and publication of Stair's *Institutions* is one example of a phenomenon widespread in Europe in the seventeenth and eighteenth centuries, the publication of a substantial and scholarly narrative work systematically setting out the law of a distinct state.[106] This phenomenon is on the one hand a natural result of the rise of the independent nation-states and on the other hand an early manifestation of the Enlightenment. The period is marked in legal history by the substantial emancipation of legal thought, analysis and exposition from Roman law on the one hand and from theology on the other, just as in other spheres it witnessed the beginning of modern science, the rise of deism, and the origins of modern philosophy in Descartes and Locke. It is noticeable that in all the European countries the word 'Institutions' or 'institutes' is frequently used to describe systematic expositions of the new discipline, the law of emerging states, and that everywhere the new discipline had similar characteristics; it challenged the standing of Roman and canon law as the learned law and largely replaced it. Roman law ceased to be the central topic of legal science and, though regard for it continued, and it frequently continued to be a preliminary topic of legal study, the new national systems of law, founded largely on native customs, legislation and decisions, replaced it. This national legal literature, moreover, was commonly in the vernacular, not in Latin.

In France the official compilation of the customs gave rise to a movement for the scientific study of the common customary law of France, and to such books as Guy Coquille's *Institution au droit français* (1607) and Antoine Loysel's *Institutes Coutumières* (1607) and later Gabriel Argou's *Institution au droit français* (1692) and Domat's *Les lois civiles dans leur ordre naturel* (1689–94).

In Germany the seventeenth century was notable as the era of the natural law jurists, above all Pufendorf, but also as the time of the establishment of German legal science. Hermann Conring gave a national basis for legal science in Germany by his *De Origine Juris Germanici Liber Unus* (1643), followed by Benedict Carpzov's *De Capitulatione Caesarea, sive de lege regia Germanorum* (1623) and David Mevius's *Commentarius in ius Lubecense* (1642–3). Christian Thomasius urged the teaching of Germanic law, and in the German language, and its establishment in practice, and one of his pupils Georg Beyer first gave lectures on German law, published posthumously as *Delineatio Juris Germanici ad Fundamenta sua Revocati* (1718). Slightly later Johann Gottlieb Heineccius expounded Roman law in his *Elementa iuris civilis secundum ordinem Institutionum* (1725) and Johann Stephen Putter wrote his *Elementa iuris Germanici privati* (1748) and other works on pure German law. Later in this stage of development in Germany

Johann Heinrich von Selchow wrote his *Institutiones jurisprudentiae Germanicae* (1757).

In the Netherlands, stimulated by international relations, trade and free philosophical and scientific research, there sprang up a vigorous school of legal learning. The first systematic treatise on the law of the Netherlands was Petrus Gudelinus' *De Jure Novissimo* (1620) but the greatest name is Hugo Grotius, who produced the masterly *Inleidinge tot de Hollandsche Rechtsgeleerdheid*, an introductory statement of a legal system based on Roman law and Germanic customary and local laws. Simon van Leeuwen's *Roomsch-Hollandsch Recht* (1664), though much influenced by Roman law, was practical and related to everyday life and Ulric Huber's *Heedendaegse Rechtsgeleertheyt* (1699) was and is of high standing. In addition there were many treatises on the Roman law and its relevance to contemporary Holland, the greatest being Johannes Voet's *Commentarius ad Pandectas* (1698–1704). In the southern Netherlands, now Belgium, Franciscus Zypaeus wrote a *Notitia Juris Belgici* (1655), the first dogmatic work on Belgian law; and Anselmo d'Anvers a *Codex Belgicus* (1649).

In Switzerland it was not until the eighteenth century that the idea of the unity of Swiss private law emerged, and the only work attempting an exposition of the entire private law valid in Switzerland was Hans Jacob Leu's *Eydgenössisches Stadt- und Land-recht* (1724–44), which sought to demonstrate the agreement between natural law and the law valid in Switzerland. Leu defined his work as Versuch eines Iuris Civilis Helvetici.

In Italy the local law was expounded along with Roman law in the major states from early in the eighteenth century, in such works as Francesco Rapolla's *Commentaria de iure regni Neapolitani* (1746) and Oronzio Fighera's *Institutiones iuris Regni Neapolitani* (1766).

In Spain legal science was intensely cultivated in the sixteenth and seventeenth centuries, particularly legal philosophy, public law, and international law, but there was a host of commentators on the private law such as Gregorio Lopez, commentator on the *Siete Partidas*, and Antonio Gomez, commentator on the *Leyes del Toro* and many textbooks of *derecho patrio* of which the earliest were Bermundez de Pedraza's *Arte legal* (1612) and Martinez Galindo's *Phoenix Jurisprudentiae Hispanicae sive Instituta Hispana* (1715) and the greatest, though not the first, was *Instituciones del derecho civil de Castilla* of Ignacio Jordan de Asso and Miguel de Manuel (1771). In 1713 the Consejo of Castille decreed that the study of Roman law be replaced by training in national law, and in 1741 that it be additional to Roman law.

In Scandinavia the seventeenth century saw much codification and the great jurists such as Rasmus Vinding were engaged in drafting codes rather than writing texts, but the effect was much the same, the rise of national law. Johannes Loccenius was the author of the first methodical work on the civil law of Sweden, *Synopsis juris privati ad leges Svecanas accommodata*

(1653), and was followed by Charles Ralamb (*Observationes juris practicae* (1679)) and David Nehrmann (*Inledning til den svenska jurisprudentiam civilem* (1729)).

England is something of a special case and stood outside this European trend. The English state began to be formed into a distinct nation-state earlier than these other countries, and accordingly there was from an early time a series of treatises on the law of that realm, particularly Glanvill's *De Legibus et Consuetudinibus Angliae* (c.1187), written from the standpoint of procedure, Bracton's *De Legibus et Consuetudinibus Angliae* (c.1256), based on the forms of action, with commentary and illustrations, Littleton's *Tenures* (c.1480), a study of land law from the standpoint of substantive law, rather than procedure, Cowell's *Institutiones Juris Anglicani ad Methodum et Seriem Institutionum Imperialium compositae et digestae* (1605), (translated as *Institutes of the Laws of England* in 1651), Coke's *Institutes of the Laws of England* (1628–44), the first to be written in English, and Wood's *Institute of the Laws of England* (1720). But none of these had the philosophic background, the breadth, or lucidity of statement of Stair. For a comparable work England had to wait for Blackstone in 1765. These apart, there are the books of authority on the criminal law of Hale, Hawkins and Foster.

Stair is accordingly one representative, and an early one, of the school of 'institutionalists' which emerged all over Europe in the seventeenth and eighteenth centuries, in succession to the glossators, commentators and humanists and those earlier jurists who had sought to marry indigenous customary and statutory law to the system and concepts of Roman law (a group represented in Scotland by Skene and Durie).

Apart from these general works on the private law of various countries, there were countless books on particular topics, notes of cases, collections of decisions, of opinions, and other writings. Grotius (*De Jure Belli ac Pacis* (1625)) built a body of rules for regulating international relations on the principles of natural law and, if not founded, certainly firmly established a body of doctrine which can be called international law.

11. *The Text*

The problem of what to present as the text of the *Institutions* is not without difficulty. There are in existence various manuscripts and five printed editions.

The first edition of the *Institutions* was published by the Heir of Andrew Anderson[107] at Edinburgh in 1681, after Stair had relinquished his first tenure of the office of Lord President of the Court of Session but before he withdrew to Holland. His contract with Anderson was dated 26th March 1681 and was preserved by Dallas of Saint Martin's[108] as a style for contracts to print a copyright work. It is reprinted in Aeneas Mackay's *Memoir of Stair* at pp. 173–6. The royal licence for printing the *Institutions* was obtained on 11 April 1681, but the book cannot have been published until much later in that year, unless indeed much of the work of type-setting had been done before the contract or the licence. Stair says in the Dedication: 'It is but little short of forty years, since I have followed the study and practice of law, constantly and diligently, so that those, who will not deny me reason and capacity, can hardly deny my knowledge and experience on the subject I write of. My modesty did not permit me to publish it, lest it should be judicially cited, where I sat: But now, becoming old, I have been prevailed with to print it, while I might oversee the press'. In his preface to the second edition Stair himself says that 'The former edition was printed when I was absent' but this must mean only absent from Edinburgh. In a letter of 1st July 1682 to the Marquis of Queensberry he wrote: 'I have ordered one of my books lately printed to be presented to your Lordship as a token of my most sincere affection'. He retired to Holland in September or October 1682.

It comprises a Dedication to the King, Charles II,[109] and an Index to (or rather a serial list of) the Titles of the whole book, with summaries or headings of the sections. The book is divided into two parts with separate title-pages, the first comprising Titles I–XXII (pages 1 to 444), the second Titles XXIII to XXXI (pages 1 to 192). Two distinct title-pages have been observed, so that there may have been two issues or impressions of this edition. Some copies have, bound in, with a separate title-page, *Modus Litigandi*, or Form of Process observed Before the Lords of Council and Session in Scotland (pages 1 to 44). There is no general index.

The second edition bearing to be 'Revised, Corrected and much Enlarged: With an alphabetical Index to the whole work' was printed by the Heir of Andrew Anderson in 1693. It comprises an Advertisement,[110] the text, now divided into four books (pages 1 to 763), an Appendix dealing with some recently enacted Statutes (pages 765 to 779), a list of printer's errors to be corrected, and the alphabetical index. The former first part had been divided into the first two Books, the second part is now the third Book and the fourth Book is a greatly expanded and rewritten version of the *Modus Litigandi*. The titles are now numbered serially within each book, and now number 91 in all, of which 52 are in the new Fourth book. Apart from the errors noted in the list of printer's errors there are also quite a number of other errors, as in some citations of the Roman law, and some statutory references.

In the Advertisement Stair points out that there were various omissions and mistakes in the first edition, that in this edition he had thought fit only to relate to the later and more authentic and useful collections of decisions, had divided this edition into four parts, divided the long titles in the first book and put them under more special titles, and divided the paragraphs: 'Though indeed this edition be in a great part new, by occasion of new Statutes of Parliament, Acts of Sederunt, and Decisions since the treatise was written, and by an entire addition to the fourth part, which was resolved and expressed to be added'. The author's changes were accordingly substantial.

The third edition 'was undertaken with a view to remove, by the help of several manuscripts, the obscurity which everywhere occurred in the former editions of this valuable system of law; and to add, in notes, the alterations which have been introduced since the 1693 (*sic*), by Statutes or Acts of Sederunt'. It was begun by John Gordon, advocate, who was responsible for the first 85 pages. Gordon (1715–75) passed advocate in 1737 and was joint professor of civil law at Edinburgh University 1753–4. After the press had stopped for some time the undertaking was completed by William Johnstone, advocate. Johnstone (1729–1805), second son of Sir James Johnstone of Westerhall, Bart,. passed advocate in 1751, sat as M.P. for Cromarty 1768–74, and Shrewsbury 1775–1805. He became extremely wealthy and when his wife succeeded to the estates of the Earl of Bath in 1767 he took the name of Pulteney. He was a director of the British Fisheries Society and gave his name to the Society's settlement at Pulteneytown, the southern part of the town of Wick, Caithness. He was a friend of Adam Smith. It was printed for G. Hamilton and J. Balfour, Edinburgh, in 1759.

It comprises the Advertisement to the 1693 edition, Index (more correctly a serial list) of Titles in the four Books, the Dedication of the 1681 edition, the text of the four Books (pages 1 to 786) and the Appendix (pages 787 to 801), alphabetical index, and a Table of the pages of the 1693 edition with the corresponding pages of this edition.

It is a useful edition. Alterations in the text are printed in italics, and those made without the authority of the manuscripts or decisions are bracketed and the former reading stated at the foot of the page. The decisions referred to are stated to have been examined and wherever the import of the decisions seemed to have been misapprehended, this is mentioned in notes.

The fourth edition was edited, with commentaries and a supplement, by George Brodie, advocate, and printed for Thomas Clark, Edinburgh, in 1826. Brodie (1786–1867) passed advocate in 1811 and became Historiographer-Royal for Scotland in 1836. There are separate title pages to the four Books bearing to be vol. I, vol. II, part III and part IV, the latter two dated 1827, but it is usually bound as one volume. The Appendix is reprinted and there is a Supplement by the editor and an Index. Brodie states in his Notice that he collated the three former editions with nine manuscripts in the Advocates' Library, and latterly with a tenth also, lent him by David Laing. 'But I must own that the chief advantage derived by me from the manuscripts has been that of greater confidence in the accuracy of the edition of 1693, which, as published by the author himself after a careful revision, ought, in my opinion, to be adhered to, unless when it is obvious, from the sense or the decision referred to, that a slight inaccuracy exists. In some instances of this description I have adopted the emendations of my predecessor, but rarely, never in any important instance, without stating the circumstances in a note. As for myself I have not presumed to alter or add one syllable. I cannot indeed approve of the liberties used with the text by the last editor, nor of the preference on many occasions given by him to manuscript copies—not one of which can, so far as I know, be traced to any authority—and to the first edition, which, as is stated by the author himself in his advertisement to the edition of 1693, was published in a very inaccurate form during his absence'. Unfortunately it must be said that collation reveals that Brodie took great liberties with Stair's text of 1693 and regularly changed words and sometimes transposed whole sentences or even paragraphs. His text is not an accurate version of the 1693 edition. Yet at one point in a note (p.75) he speaks of restoring the former arrangement 'not conceiving, like the last editor, that I am entitled to alter the text according to my own ideas of what it ought to be'. At various points Brodie introduced substantial footnotes stating the modern law on the topic. His Supplement runs to 165 pages, 100 devoted to sale and the remainder to shipping.

The fifth edition was edited by John Schank More, F.R.S.E., F.S.A. SCOT, Advocate, and appeared in two large volumes in 1832. More (1784–1861) passed advocate in 1806, published an edition of Erskine's *Principles* in 1827 and his edition of Stair in 1832. He succeeded George Joseph Bell as Professor of Scots Law in the University of Edinburgh in 1843 and held the chair till 1861. He was a great book collector, being said to have collected 15,000 volumes, and had an extensive knowledge of the literature of Scots law. In 1864 John McLaren, advocate (later editor of Bell's *Commentaries*, author of *Trusts*, which in its second and third editions became *Wills and Succession*, and a judge of the Court of Session) published, in two volumes, an edition of More's Lectures on the *Law of Scotland* 'to supply the want of a modern text-book'. The lectures show the influence of Stair and at many points resemble More's Notes to Stair.

In his Preface (p.xvi) More states that the 'third edition contains a number of additions and alterations, founded on certain manuscript copies; but it is doubtful whether, in many instances, these alterations can be regarded as amendments. The text of the second edition seems, on the whole, the best; but as the third edition has been said by a very competent judge [referring to Dodson's report of the judgment in *Dalrymple* v. *Dalrymple*, p. 1 (of Appendix)] to be "deemed far preferable to the rest"[111] and as it is undoubtedly that which is best known, and has been most esteemed by the profession, the text of the present edition has been reprinted from it . . . and most of the material alterations between the text of the third edition and of the first or second, have been pointed out in marginal notes, so that the text of this edition embraces all the advantages of any of these three editions'. More also reprinted most of the footnotes of Brodie's edition unchanged.

More's edition had appended to each volume very substantial notes, or rather essays, running in all to about the same length as the text, on the major topics of the text, bringing the statement of law down to his own time. The notes are of great interest and value in their own right[112] but are now very largely outdated. Since it was published this has been the edition in normal use.

It must, unfortunately but very plainly, be stated that all three previous editors have at many points taken liberties, frequently great liberties, with Stair's text, so that their editions are all, in different ways and to different extents, materially incorrect versions of what Stair published; they give neither the text of any manuscript, nor of the first nor of the second edition.

Among the liberties taken are adding, changing or deleting words or sentences, transferring sentences or sometimes whole paragraphs from one place to another in the text, altering the point at which a numbered section of a title commences, adding passages and citations from manuscripts or the first edition.

It follows from the transpositions, or alteration of the point at which a section commences, made by previous editors, that in some cases a reference in an older book to a passage in Stair, by Book, Title and section, will be inaccurate by reference both to Stair's second edition and to this edition, in that the words referred to may not be in this edition, or may be in the section before or after that referred to.

In particular, former editors seem to have ignored the fact that an author, when printing his work and particularly when issuing a revised second edition, may have changed his mind and may have wished to delete references given in his Ms. or first edition. Moreover, in the Advertisement to the second edition Stair himself said that he 'thought fit, in this edition, only to relate to the later and more authentic and useful collections'. Clearly he deliberately deleted some of the references which had been in the Ms. and the first edition. They are now interesting in a study of the development of his thinking, but no part of his final text.

Former editors, moreover, in many cases altered at their own hands the names of statutes or cases cited to accord with what they believed was the statute properly referred to, or the case under its true name. In the great majority of cases their references are probably correct and Stair's were wrong, but it seemed to the present editor wrong to alter the text in this way. He has accordingly in every case printed in the text what Stair printed, and has corrected the reference or the name in the square-bracketed notes. These editors also in many cases altered the text by incorporating matter from cases founded on, or to clarify Stair's meaning, or otherwise. In many cases their work was an improvement on Stair's text, but that is not the function of an editor, and the present editor has adhered scrupulously to the text of the second edition. If it is unclear or incorrect, the fault is that of the author, and it is not for an editor, without declaring precisely what he has done, to alter his author's text.

The problems of settling the text of an old book differ sharply according as it has, or has not, been printed in the author's lifetime and by his authority. In the case of a book never printed by the author in his lifetime, such as classical authors, or Biblical texts, or, among legal texts, Glanvill, Bracton and some others, the problems are of finding the manuscripts, collating them, discovering the stemma or pedigree of the manuscripts, and thereby determining which is the archetype or original manuscript, or at least that which is oldest and nearest to the author's time, and therefore presumably nearest to what he wrote, and if not his manuscript, a not too remote copy from it. In such a case the earliest manuscript is *prima facie* the basis of the text.

On the other hand, in the case, such as of Stair, of a book allowed by the author to be printed, and moreover later amended, revised and reprinted in his lifetime by his authority, it must be assumed that the last printed edition represents his concluded views. The manuscripts are accordingly superseded, and are interesting and valuable only as indicating the development of his views and thoughts, and changes in subject-matter as time passed. The manuscripts are not of equal authority with his revised printed text and it is quite wrong to produce a conflated version of manuscripts and printed text. He must be conceded the privilege of every text-writer, of changing his mind, or mode of expression, and of altering his text in a new edition. It must surely be taken that as authoritative statements the manuscripts and the first edition are superseded, save where the last printed edition is clearly defective. There is no evidence that Stair's copyist or printer have any responsibility for any changes .The second edition is not, however, perfect because there are in it quite a number of minor inaccuracies, the fault of author, copyist or printer, though of which does not greatly matter.

In settling the text of the *Institutions* here presented I have sought to follow the principles laid down by Sir Walter Greg[113] distinguishing between the two kinds of variants to be found in the different editions of a book, namely changes in substantives, such as words and phrases, and changes in accidentals, such as spelling, capitalisation and punctuation. Where a book has been published in an edition revised by the author, he points out, changes in substantives can usually, though not invariably, be attributed to the author, but changes in accidentals can often, though again not always, be attributed to the printer. Moreover, where an edition later than the first is known to have been carefully revised by the author that should be taken as the copy-text, rather than the first printed edition.

In the case of the text of Stair, there are three points of importance. His work was printed during his lifetime, though in his absence, presumably from a manuscript, which may or may not be a surviving one, and twelve years later, having been revised and materially altered by him, printed again, in part probably from a corrected copy of the first edition. This second edition was published less than three years before his death and, so far as is known, represents his final views on all the topics with which he deals. The existence of a half-page of Errata at the end shows that the second edition was carefully watched in proof. It must be taken that the manuscripts and the first edition were in his own view superseded. Secondly, Stair was a working lawyer and judge and his views must have changed and developed during the long period in which his work was being pondered, written and printed, and then reconsidered and revised, and it is not surprising if his later views differed materially from his earlier ones. Later views are not necessarily or always better than earlier ones but they must be taken as the author's concluded views. No doubt if he had lived another dozen years he might have changed his mind or altered his views on some points by reason of further consideration or changes in statute or common law determined by the court and given us a further revised edition. The development of the law in his time, and the evolution of his thought about it, is a study of immense interest, on which light may be cast by comparison of the manuscripts and the first and second printed editions, but the importance of his work today consists in his latest views; these are found in the second edition.

The second edition (1693) has accordingly been taken as the copy-text of this edition, as it was by Brodie. More, though he stated that he thought the text of the second edition the best, reprinted Johnstone's text, principally, it seems, because it was then the best known. The only modification here made of the text of the second edition as printed has been that the errors listed in the half-page of Errata at the end of that edition have been corrected in the text of this edition where they occur. The list of Errata has therefore not been reprinted in this edition. In particular I have not altered Stair's text merely because he has or may have misquoted a source, or possibly misinterpreted a decision. As in the case of any legal text-writer, whether the statement in the text is justified by the authority he cited for it must be judged by the reader and may be challenged; but it is not for the editor to substitute in the text what proposition he thinks an authority justifies for what Stair thought it justified. It would be utterly wrong for an editor to treat Stair as he might treat a modern textbook and substitute his view of what the law was, or now is, for Stair's statements. To do so would obscure Stair's own thought, in many places substitute the editor's words for those of Stair, and, in any event, radically alter the balance and substance of the text and probably inflate its size.

To present Stair's text for use in the latter twentieth century it has accordingly been accepted as impermissible to vary any word of the text of the second edition, save where a word appears plainly wrong, in which case what is thought to be the right word is added in square brackets, but permissible to bring spelling into line with accepted modern practice (including substituting modern s for the long s) and to limit the number of words italicised or endowed with a capital. I have, however, retained the ampersand where it is used by Stair, some of his use of italics, and, so far as possible, the punctuation of the second edition, lest in changing the punctuation there be any change of sense. But some of the punctuation seems quite bizarre, and this has been modified, but no more than seemed essential. The running headings of pages are unauthoritative and the editor's work.

The division of the work into Books, titles and sections, and the titles of these divisions, adopted in the second edition, has been uniformly followed since 1693 and is here followed, so that reference in other books to Stair, by Book, title and section, are generally equally valid for any edition after the first. The only exceptions are in those instances where an earlier editor had transferred a sentence or paragraph from one section to another, and where the sentence or paragraph is in this edition restored to where Stair printed it. In these cases a reference, based on Johnstone's, Brodie's or More's edition, will sometimes be found in this edition to be to the preceding or succeeding section, but it is never more remote than that.

It was thought better to make a fresh index for this edition rather than use that of the second or any later edition. The index of a book is unauthoritative.

12. *The Notes*

In preparing a modern edition of Stair there are many matters which could be dealt with in notes; in particular it would have been possible to prepare a full *apparatus criticus*, showing the readings of some or all of the manuscripts, and of the first and second, and possibly also of the later, editions, to seek to indicate the source of his thought on many points, to note all the subsequent cases in which particular passages in Stair have been cited, commented on or otherwise expounded, to compare his views with those of other writers, or to write what would necessarily be long and involved notes showing how the law stated by him on each point has developed and been modified since his time.

Considerations of the size and cost of production of this edition have, however, combined to dictate a minimal annotation of the text, confined to (1) giving also a reference to the Record edition of the Acts of the Parliament of Scotland for the statutes cited by Stair; (2) giving a reference to an original report and usually also to Morison's *Dictionary of Decisions* or other readily accessible series of printed reports for the cases referred to by Stair, usually merely by date and the names of parties; (3) giving a reference for passages from the Roman law, the Bible, or other sources cited by Stair; (4) giving some cross-references to other passages in the text dealing with the point; and (5) giving a brief biographical notice of the jurists whom he mentions. In addition, a few words now obsolete or unusual have been explained. More extensive annotation may ultimately be possible in a separate volume of notes and commentary.

In Stair's own printed editions there are no footnotes; all his references to sources and authorities are embodied in the text. Former editors transferred some of these references to footnotes, where they were mixed indiscriminately with the editor's own observations. In the present edition all references which are in Stair's 1693 text are restored to the text, and, to economise in cost, the editor's notes are run into the text rather than printed at the foot of the pages, but distinguished by being put in square brackets. Everything in square brackets is the editor's work. This distinguishes author's text and editor's work.

The identification of the statutes, cases and other sources referred to by Stair presents problems.

In respect of statutes Stair refers to them by year and chapter number, as printed in Skene's *Lawes and Actes of Parliament*. In most cases the statutes referred to are identifiable with certainty. In these cases the editor's note gives also a reference by volume, page and chapter number, to the Act as printed in the Acts of the Parliaments of Scotland (Record edition) in which the chapter numbers frequently, and the year sometimes, differ from those given by Skene. Thus Stair's reference to 'Act 1649, c. 29' is noted as [A.P.S. v, 504, c. 342]. In some cases, however, the year and/or chapter number of an Act cited by Stair does not appear to refer to a statute dealing with the subject-matter under discussion; it would seem that Stair, or his copyist or his printer, has made a mistake. In this case the bracketed note states what Act Stair probably properly had in mind, by reference to both Skene's and the A.P.S. citations, e.g. 'Parl. 1476, c. 67' [Act, 1475, c. 66; A.P.S. II, 112, c. 8]. Where modern legislation has conferred an authorised short title on an Act, that also is given in the note, e.g. Act 1621, 18, is noted as [Bankruptcy Act, 1621, c. 18; A.P.S. IV, 615, c. 18].

In respect of cases, Stair cited cases by the date and the names of the parties. Identification is frequently difficult because the older reporters were very uncertain or careless as to names of parties, spelling of names, attribution of names to pursuer and to defender, dates of decisions and other identifying characteristics. Nevertheless, the great majority of the cases referred to can be said with substantial confidence to have been identified.

I have wherever possible given a reference to the, or one of the, original reports and also to Morison's *Dictionary of Decisions*, as the place in which modern readers are most likely to read the report. Where a case is reported in more than one of the original reports and one of these is either volume of Stair's own *Decisions*, I have cited that report, on the assumption that, in writing his *Institutions*, he probably used his own collection of decisions rather than anyone else's. But the appearance in a note of a reference to an original report and to Morison's *Dictionary* does not imply that that is the only original report of the case. It seemed superfluous to list all the original reports of each case. This mode of annotation, incidentally, brings out the very substantial extent to which Stair relied on his own collections of *Decisions*, though he clearly also used the collections of Durie, Spotiswoode, Hope, Haddington and several others. Where the date, or the names of parties, in the printed reports differ materially from that quoted by Stair, mention is made in the note, e.g. where Stair cites "Dec. 11, 1622, Seton *contra* Elleis, the note is [*Sub nom. Seton and Eleis* v. *Acheson's Creditors*, Fol. Dict. 11, 256; M. 12599]; but the notes ignore mere variations of names, or spellings, or other discrepancies where there is little or no doubt as to the case cited.

In a small minority of cases the identification is not certain, but merely possible.

In a further small minority of instances, a case referred to by Stair has not been found in any printed volume. These cases are marked in the notes as "Not found". They may be from lost or unedited *Practicks* or from a note made by Stair himself and now lost.

Stair's references to the Roman law are in the older mode, with a reference to the lex, and sometimes section number, the abbreviation for *Institutions*, *Digest*, (the abbreviation ff. being used), *Code* or *Novels*, and the leading words of the Title. These have been translated in the notes into the more modern style of citation, giving the abbreviation for *Institutions*, *Digest*, *Code* or *Novels*, and the numbers for the book, title, lex and section as they appear in the Berlin Stereotype edition of the *Corpus Juris Civilis*. Some of Stair's citations are inaccurate, and in these cases the note gives what is believed to be the correct reference, which accordingly differs from the citation in the text.

To avoid interrupting the text, notes giving biographical information on the earlier jurists referred to by Stair have been collected in the List of Earlier Jurists referred to by Stair.

In respect of all sources cited it must be stated that the references given by the editor are by way of identification only, and imply no warrant by him that the statute or case is represented as good authority for the proposition for which Stair cites the source. As in any other treatise the reader must always consider for himself whether the authority cited vouches the proposition in the text.

In addition, I have, like the last two editors, drawn attention by cross-reference notes, either standing alone or combined with the note identifying a statute or case, to other passages in the *Institutions* bearing on the same point, e.g. [IV, 30, 3, *infra*].

In identifying the statutes and cases and the sources of the Roman, Biblical and other citations, it is proper to pay tribute to the previous editors, Brodie and More, who found references for many of them and whose work in this respect has generally been found very valuable and accurate.

NOTES

1. The general background of his time can be studied in the Edinburgh *History of Scotland*, vol. III by G. Donaldson and vol. IV by W. Ferguson. Fuller accounts of Stair's life can be found in Aeneas Mackay's *Memoir of Sir James Dalrymple, First Viscount Stair* (1873); his entry on Stair in the *Dictionary of National Biography;*

J. Murray Graham's *Annals and Correspondence of the Viscount and First and Second Earls of Stair* (1875); The Hon. Hew Dalrymple's article on the Stair family in *The Scots Peerage*, vol. VIII; and Dr G. M. Hutton's *Life* in *Stair Tercentenary Studies* (Stair Society, 1981). See also William Forbes's *Journal of the Session* (1714) Preface, xxix; Thomson, 'The First Viscount Stair' (1924) 36 J.R. 33; Duncan, 'Viscount Stair' (1934) 46 J.R. 103; Lord Cooper, 'The Scottish Legal Tradition' in *Selected Papers*, 177; Lord Cooper, 'Some Classics of Scottish Legal Literature' in *Selected Papers*, 39.

2. Text in W. C. Dickinson and G. Donaldson, *Source-Book of Scottish History* III, 95; G. Donaldson, *Scottish Historical Documents*, 194.

3. Documents in Dickinson and Donaldson, III, 105–13.

4. Glasgow University Library holds a book of 1646 entitled *Theses logicae, metaphysicae, physicae, mathematicae et ethicae, quas adolescentes hac vice ex Collegio Glasguensi cum Laurea emittendi publice propugnabunt, ad diem 27 Julii, Anno Domini 1646, Praeside Jacobo Darimplio*. This indicates the general scope of his teaching responsibility.

5. John Snell, later Seal Bearer to Sir Orlando Bridgman, Lord Keeper of the Great Seal of England, and to his successor the Earl of Shaftesbury, and founder of the Snell Exhibition to take a Glasgow student on to Balliol College, Oxford, pays him this tribute: *Munimenta Almae Universitatis Glasguensis*, III, 434.

6. Dalrymple seems to have retained an affection for Glasgow and the West. In Slezer's *Theatrum Scotiae* (1693) in which each section, with relative views, dealing with one of the cities and colleges of Scotland, is dedicated to a prominent noble, that on Glasgow, with views of the city and college, is dedicated to Dalrymple, by that time Viscount Stair and Lord President.

Glasgow University has not forgotten Stair.

In 1951 the General Council, the general body of graduates of the University, to mark the five hundredth anniversary of the foundation of the University, presented a handsome gateway and pair of wrought-iron gates to the University. The gates bear in five rows of panels the names of some of the most distinguished Glasgow men and women of each of the five centuries in the life of the University. One of the six names for the seventeenth century is Stair.

On 29 June 1953 Lord Cooper, Lord President of the Court of Session, a fine scholar and a great admirer of Stair, unveiled a large memorial tablet, erected by public subscription, and cut by Mr Hew Lorimer, RSA, in the University and spoke eloquently of Stair's great contribution to the making of Scots law. A brief report of the ceremony is in 1953 Scots Law Times (News) p.139. The inscription reads: JAMES DALRYMPLE/First Viscount Stair/Student in the College of Glasgow/1633–1637/Regent in the College/1641–1647/Senator of the College of Justice/1661–1671/President of the Court of Session/1671–1681 & 1689–1695/A supreme master of jurisprudence who in his *Institutions*/laid an imperishable foundation for the law of Scotland. It is situated on a wall facing the grand staircase leading up to the University Court Room, the Senate Room and the main University offices. The buildings are of course not those in which Stair studied or taught. He probably studied and possibly taught in the Pedagogy and the Arthurlie House on the east side of the High Street of Glasgow. The Old College was built in 1632–59 to the east of the original buildings, the High Street frontage being built last and covering the site of the old Pedagogy and the Arthurlie House. The Old College in turn was abandoned and later demolished when the University removed in 1870 to its present home on Gilmorehill, in the west end of the city.

In 1965 a Hall of Residence for students in Great Western Road, Glasgow, was named Dalrymple Hall. It was opened by the Earl of Stair and residents may wear a tie bearing the arms of Stair.

7. *Journal of the Session* (1714) Preface, xxx.

8. Lord Cooper, 'The Scottish Lawyer's Library in the Seventeenth Century' in *Selected Papers*, 276.

9. A.P.S. VI (2) 299, c.271.

10. There were earlier projects and commissions in 1425 (A.P.S. II, 10, c. 10); 1449 (A.P.S. II, 36, c. 10); 1469 (A.P.S. II, 97, c. 20); 1473 (A.P.S. II, 105, c. 14); 1566 (see A.P.S. I, 29); 1567 (A.P.S. III, 40, Appx. 42); 1574 (see A.P.S. I, 30; A.P.S. III, 89b); 1578 (A.P.S. III, 105, c. 18); 1592 (A.P.S. III, 564, c. 45); 1628 (see A.P.S. I, 34), renewed in 1630 (A.P.S. V, 209, c. 3; see also 225, 228; V, 39, c. 20), and 1633 (A.P.S. V,

46, c. 32); 1639 (A.P.S. v, 611); and later commissions in 1681 (A.P.S. VIII, 356, c. 94) and 1695 (A.P.S. IX, 362 and 455, c. 57). That of 1567 was directed to codify the laws dividing them into heads like the Roman law. (These dates are in the Old Style.) Lord Cooper in his Introduction to *Regiam Majestatem* (Stair Society, 1947), p. 4, erroneously dates the commission to which young Dalrymple was appointed as in 1631.

11. William Forbes (Preface to *Journal of the Session*, xxxi) says that when in Holland in 1649 and 1650 Dalrymple visited the universities and learned men there, particularly the great Salmasius. Salmasius (Claude de Saumaise, 1588–1653), French scholar, studied philosophy at Paris and law at Heidelberg. In 1631 he moved to Leiden to occupy Scaliger's chair. He was probably the most famous classical scholar of his day. At the request of Charles I he wrote a *Defensio Regio pro Carolo I* (1649), answered by John Milton in his *Pro Populo Anglicano Defensio* (1651). Dalrymple refers to Salmasius in his *Institutions*.

12. F. D. Dow, *Cromwellian Scotland*, *passim*.

13. *Scotland and the Protectorate* (ed. Firth, S.H.S.) 385. McMillan, 'Judicial System of the Commonwealth in Scotland' (1937) 49 J.R. 232; Cooper, 'Cromwell's Judges and their Influence on Scots Law' (1946) 58 J.R. 20, and in *Selected Papers*, 111; Mackay, *Memoir of Stair*, 56.

14. *Scotland and the Protectorate*, supra, 403.

15. *The Cromwellian Union* (ed. Terry, S.H.S.) 65.

16. *Ibid.*, 67.

17. *Scotland and the Protectorate*, supra, 99.

18. Mackay, *Memoir of Stair*, 61.

19. Thurloe, *State Papers*, VI, 367, 372; A.P.S. VI (2) 764 and 907. Monck's letter described him as 'a very honest man and a good lawyer'.

20. A.P.S. VII, 124.

21. A.P.S. VII, 377–8.

22. Courts Act, 1672; A.P.S. VIII, 80, c. 40.

23. A.P.S. VIII, 6; *The Cromwellian Union* (ed. Terry, S.H.S.), 188–207.

24. Ferguson, *Scotland's Relations with England*, 156.

25. See further, Defoe, *History of the Union of Great Britain*; Sir George Mackenzie, *Memoirs of the Affairs of Scotland*, 211; *Discourse concerning the Three Unions* in *Works*, 11, 664.

26. Mackenzie, *Memoirs*, 214.

27. Subscription of Deeds Act, 1681; A.P.S. VIII, 242, c. 5.

28. A.P.S. VIII, 243, c. 6; Dickinson & Donaldson, *Source Book of Scottish History*, III, 186–189; Donaldson, *Scottish Historical Documents*, 243–5. Additional Acts concerning the Test are A.P.S. VIII, 355, c. 91 and 471, c. 13.

29. *Volumen Inscriptionum sive Catalogus Studiosorum Academiae Leydensis*, 1677–97 p. 657.

30. See Lord Cooper, 'Stair the Scientist' (1955) 67 J.R. 23.

31. A.P.S. VIII, Appx. 32; see also pp. 40, 44, 49, 54, 62, 66, 70, 72.

32. A.P.S. VIII, 490, c. 52.

33. A.P.S. VIII, 646, c. 71.

34. P. W. J. Riley, *King William and the Scottish Politicians*, 16.

35. *Proceedings of the Estates in Scotland*, 1689–90 (ed. Balfour-Melville, S.H.S.) 11, 35, 48.

36. *ibid.*, 122, 153; A.P.S. IX, 112.

37. *ibid.*, 137, 161, 223, 227, 266.

38. 1690, republished by the Bannatyne Club, 1825, and in More's edition of Stair's *Institutions*, pp. xix–xxiv.

39. P. W. J. Riley, *King William and the Scottish Politicians*, 22.

40. *ibid.*, 23.

41. *ibid.*, 29.

42. *ibid.*, 30.

43. *ibid.*, 86.

44. *ibid.*, 120.

45. A.P.S. IX, 264 and 449.

46. *Journal of the Session* (1714) Preface xxxviii. At the end of the Preface Forbes mentions as among those who had given him information about Stair and other persons mentioned Sir Hugh (sic) Dalrymple of North Berwick, Lord President of the Session [Stair's third son] and Sir David Dalrymple of Hales (sic), late Queen's Advocate [Stair's fifth son]. There must have been many lawyers alive in 1714 who remembered Stair so that Forbes's account is probably substantially accurate.

47. Dr G. M. Hutton has identified at least five anonymous tracts, *A Discourse concerning the Nature, Power and proper Effects of the Present Conventions in both Kingdoms, called by the Prince of Orange* (1689); *A Political Conference between Aulicus, a Courtier; Damas, a countryman; and Civicus, a Citizen* (1689); *Plain Dealing :*

Being a Moderate General Review of the Scots Prelatical Clergies Proceedings in the latter Reigns. With a Vindication of the present Proceedings in Church Affairs There (1689); *A Vindication of the Proceedings of the Convention of the Estates in Scotland* (1689); and *A Farther Vindication of the Present Government of the Church of Scotland, established in a Presbyterian Polity* (1690) which can confidently, particularly on grounds of verbal similarities with Stair's other works, be said to be those referred to by Forbes. See also G. M. Hutton, *The Political Thought of Viscount Stair* (unpublished Ph.D. thesis, Birmingham University 1971).

48. Gudelinus' work, in six books, is constructed on a different plan and, certainly in layout, was not a model.

49. The standard edition is now, with Grotius' own corrections, edited by F. Dovring, H.F.W.D. Fischer and E. M. Meijers (Leiden 1952). There are English translations by Sir A. F. S. Maasdorp (*Introduction to Dutch Jurisprudence*, 1878) and R. W. Lee (*The Jurisprudence of Holland*, 1926 and supplemented by Lee's *Commentary* containing notes on Grotius by several distinguished jurists).

50. But there are possibly significant similarities between *Institutions* 1.9.4 and *Inleiding* 3.33.2 and 3.34.2, and with *De Jure Belli ac Pacis*, 2, 17, 13, 14.

51. This does not appear either to have been a direct model. It deals with persons, things, inheritance, obligations, crimes, courts and actions.

52. The plan of Stair's *Institutions*, so far as set out in the headings of the titles is, briefly, as follows:

Book I, Title 1, Common principles of law. 2, Liberty and servitude. 3, Obligations in general. 4-6, Family obligations, between husband and wife, parent and child, and guardian and ward. 7-8, Quasi-contractual obligations. 9, Delictual obligations. 10, Conventional obligations, by promise, paction, and contract. 11-17, Particular kinds of contracts. 18, Liberation from obligations.

Book II, Titles 1-12, Rights real or dominion, possession, property, servitudes, teinds, tacks, and prescription.

Book III, Titles 1-9, Assignations, dispositions, succession, executry and vitious intromission.

Book IV, Title 1, The Authority of the Lords of Council and Session. 2, The Order of discussing processes. 3, Ordinary actions generally. 4-41, Particular kinds of actions. 42-45, Proof. 46-52, Decrees and their execution.

53. The pattern of Justinian's *Institutions* is as follows:

Book I, Title 1, Of Justice and law. 2, Of the law of nature, the law of nations, and the civil law. 3-26, Persons, marriage and guardianship.

Book II, Titles 1-25, Things, wills, legacies and codicils.

Book III, Titles 1-12, Contractual obligations. 27, Quasi-contractual obligations. 28-29, Discharge of obligations.

Book IV, Titles 1-4, Delictual obligations. 5, Quasi-delictual obligations. 6-16, Actions and remedies. 17, Of the duties of a judge. 18, Of public prosecutions.

54. *The Structure of Stair's Institutions* (David Murray Lecture, Glasgow 1954), p. 11.

55. I, 1, 23.

56. *The Structure of Stair's Institutions*, p. 11.

57. It is of interest that while Stair did not in detail follow the arrangement of Grotius' *Inleiding*, Grotius in that work dealt with (Book 1) law in general, persons and domestic relations, (Book 11) real rights, and (Book 111) personal rights, arising from contract, unjust enrichment, delict. Grotius accordingly anticipated him in stressing kinds of rights rather than the subject-matter of rules.

58. It rather seems that Stair was interested in the sixteenth-century Spanish theologian-jurists such as Francisco Suarez and Luis de Molina. His concept of obediential obligations probably comes from St Thomas Aquinas through Suarez, who wrote a large *De Legibus ac Deo Legislatore* (Selections translated in Classics of International Law), and on *ius quaesitum tertio* (1, 10, 5) he refers to Molina, who wrote a *De Justitia et Jure*. On them see B. Hamilton, *Political Thought in 16th century Spain: a study of the political ideas of Vitoria, De Soto, Suarez and Molina* (1963); R. Wilenius, *The Social and Political theory of Francisco Suarez* (1963); H. Wright (ed.), *Francisco Suarez: Addresses in Commemoration of his Contribution to International Law and Politics* (1933).

59. See also Lord Cooper's discussion in 'The Scottish Lawyer's Library in the Seventeenth Century' in (1954) 66 J. R. 1, reprinted in his *Selected Papers*, 276,

of the extent of reference in the works of his contemporaries Mackenzie, Nisbet of Dirleton and Lauder of Fountainhall to the commentators and humanists.

60. On natural law thinking see Bryce, 'The Law of Nature' in *Studies in History and Jurisprudence, II;* Pollock, 'The History of the Law of Nature' in *Essays in the Law;* D'Entreves, *Natural Law;* Gierke, *Natural Law and the Theory of Society* (trs. Barker); Jones, *Historical Introduction to the Theory of Law;* Carlyle, *History of Mediaeval Political Theory in the West;* McIlwain, *The Growth of Political Thought in the West;* Cairns, *Legal Philosophy from Plato to Hegel;* Jolowicz and Nicholas, *Historical Introduction to the Study of Roman Law;* Schulz, *Principles of Roman Law* and *History of Roman Legal Science;* and works on jurisprudence and political thought generally.

61. Of other writers on natural law shortly before his own time there is no evidence that Stair knew of Richard Cumberland's *De Legibus Naturae Disquisitio* (1672) which also started from the work of Grotius, but attracted little interest at the time. Still less is Stair at all likely to have known of John Locke's *Essays on the Law of Nature* (first published, edited by W. von Leyden, in 1954) though Locke knew Suarez' book.

62. Stair means what the Roman jurists called the *ius gentium*. In later usage the law of nations or international law is not so much a law common to many nations as law applicable to and between nation-states.

63. This implies that human laws could not abrogate all the effects of the law of nature and reason.

64. Aquinas (Ia, IIae, Q. 90) defined law as 'an ordinance of reason for the common good, emanating from him who has the care of the community, and promulgated'.

65. D. N. MacCormick, 'Law, Obligation and Consent' (1979) *Archiv für Rechts- und Sozialphilosophie*, LXV, 387.

66. *Structure*, p. 28.

67. I, I, 19.

68. On these see further under Obligations, *infra*.

69. I, I, 20. On this see further under Liberty, *infra*.

70. I, I, 21.

71. *Ingenia*, brains.

72. cf. also I, I, 4.

73. Its first principles are obedience to God, the freedom of man, and voluntary engagements (I, I, 18 *ad initium*).

74. Its prime principles are society, property and commerce (I, I, 18, *ad medium*).

75. This distinction of efficient causes and final causes goes back to Aristotle, *Physics*, 198a, 20–5. An efficient cause is the agency which makes something, a primary source of change; a final cause is an end, that for the sake of which a thing is done.

76. The terminology of 'formal and proper object' is derived from Aristotelian metaphysics.

77. The use of the word 'correlate' is interesting, anticipating by more than two centuries the work of the analytical jurists, such as Windscheid, Thon, Bierling, and Salmond, and culminating in the work of Hohfeld (in his *Fundamental Legal Conceptions* (1913) 23 Yale L.J. 16, 30; (1916) 26 Yale L.J. 712), distinguishing between right, privilege, power and immunity and their correlatives, viz. duty, no-right, liability and disability. Stair's conception of 'power' seems to comprehend both Hohfeld's 'privilege' and his 'power'. His principle of freedom includes appreciation of what is inherent in Hohfeld's 'immunity'.

78. Dig. 28, 1, 6, pr.

79. Stair's concept of a right does not appear to owe anything to Pufendorf's *Elementorum Jurisprudentiae Universalis Libri Duo* (1660), Definition VII, which treats right as the moral quality by which we either command persons, or possess things, or by which things are owed to us. On 'rights' see further G. W. Paton, *Textbook of Jurisprudence* (4th ed. 1972), 284; H. L. A. Hart 'Bentham on Legal Rights' in *Oxford Essays in Jurisprudence, 2nd series* (1973); W. J. Kamba 'Legal Theory and Hohfeld's Analysis of a Legal Right', 1974 J.R. 249; R. H. S. Tur 'The Notion of a Legal Right', 1976 J.R. 177; D. N. MacCormick 'Rights in Legislation' in *Law, Morality and Society* (1977).

80. See Gaius, IV, 2; *Inst.* IV, 6, 1–15.

81. This is wholly unconnected with the distinction in English law between real and personal property.

82. In II, I, pr. he speaks of a real right as a power of disposal of things. This is rather what we would now call a proprietary right.

83. Compare also II, I, pr. where he repeats the triple distinction of rights, and says of dominion: 'But because that term is more appropriated to the power of men over men than over the creatures, it is

therefore called a real right, or a right of things: for as obligation is a right personal, as being a power of exacting from persons that which is due; so a real right is a power of disposal of things, in their substance, fruits or use.

84. I, I, 23.

85. Stair's words echo those of Ulpian in D. I, I, I, 2. On the distinction see J. W. Jones, *Historical Introduction to the Theory of Law* (1940), chap. 5.

86. I, I, 21.

87. i.e. restrained from exercising dominion, on which see I, I, 22.

88. i.e. liberty whereby men are *sui iuris*, on which see I, I, 20.

89. I, I, 22.

90. cf. Inst. III, 13, pr.; *Obligatio est iuris vinculum quo necessitate adstringimur alicuius solvendae rei secundum iura nostrae civitatis.*

91. Inst. III, 13, 2.

92. *Elementorum Jurisprudentiae Universalis Libri Duo* (1660) Definition XII. See also Pufendorf's *De Jure Naturae et Gentium*, Books IV–VII.

93. It is in Du Cange's *Glossarium Mediae et Infimae Latinitatis*, but not in relation to obligations or law.

94. *S.T.* 2. 8. 31. I. 4.

95. *De Virt. in com.* 10 *ad* 13.

96. See A. Darmet, *Les notions de raison séminale et de puissance obedientielle chez saint Augustin et Saint Thomas d'Aquin* (1934); L. B. Gillon, 'Aux origines de la puissance obedientielle' (1947) *Revue Thomiste* 47, 304.

97. I, 3, 3. See also I, I, 19, deriving them from the duty of obedience to God.

98. This seems to mean that the obligation is always potential but becomes actual only by the intervention of an act of the individual; thus the obediential obligations to a wife are incurred by marrying; the obediential obligation to make reparation to another for delinquency is not enforceable until or unless the person commits some delinquency against that other.

99. Examination of obediential obligations of class B occupies I, 4 to I, 9. Obligations of class A. 2 in Stair's view fall within public law, which he does not expound. It is hard to see how he could have brought those of class A. I within even public law.

100. Examination of conventional obligations occupies from I, 10 to I, 18 (the end of Book I).

101. But he mentions (IV, 47, 11) that a person denounced rebel or outlaw 'hath no person to stand in judgment', and at III,3,15 and IV, 52, 20, uses the phrase *persona standi in iudicio*. Incorporations are mentioned in several contexts.

102. *Culpa* and *dolus* are mentioned several times.

103. *Drew* v. *Drew* (1870) 9 M. 163, 167, per Lord Benholme.

104. Lord Normand, 'The Scottish Judicature and Legal Procedure' (Holdsworth Club, Birmingham University, Presidential address, 1941).

105. Lord Cooper, 'Some Classics of Scottish Legal Literature' (1929), *Scottish Bankers Magazine*, XXI, p. 259, reprinted in *Selected Papers* (1957) pp. 39, 43–4.

106. On this theme see further K. Luig, 'The Institutes of National Law in the Seventeenth and Eighteenth Centuries', 1972 J.R. 193.

107. Andrew Anderson was appointed printer to the Town and College of Edinburgh in 1663 and in 1671 received a royal patent which gave him a monopoly of printing in Scotland for 41 years. This was ratified by Act of Parliament in 1672. In 1687 the Town Council gave Anderson's widow the right to establish her presses in the College below the Library and there she remained till her death in 1716. Stair's book was accordingly published by the predecessors of the Edinburgh University Press.

108. George Dallas of Saint Martins, *A System of Stiles as Now Practicable within the Kingdom of Scotland*, 1697, Part II, p. 152; and in his second edition, 2 vols., 1774, vol. I, part II, p. 76.

109. Reprinted, *infra*, pp. 59–63.

110. Reprinted, *infra*, pp. 64–65.

111. This dictum is misattributed. In *Dalrymple* v. *Dalrymple* (1811) 2 Hagg. Consistorial Reports 54; 161 English Reports 665; a case, incidentally, dealing with the marriage of a descendant of Stair, the judge (Sir William Scott, later Lord Stowell), a very distinguished judge, but not a Scots lawyer, and sitting in the London Consistory Court, not a Scottish court, at p. 88 refers to Stair as 'a person whose learned labours have at all times engaged the reverence of Scottish jurisprudence'. The dictum referred to by More—'that published in 1759, chiefly by the care of the late Sir William Pulteney, is deemed far preferable to the rest'—is contained in 2 Hagg. C.R. (Appendix) 42; 161 Eng. R. 802, in

the answers of Robert Craigie, advocate, to interrogatories administered to him as to the law of Scotland relative to the case. It is a statement in evidence, not part of Sir William Scott's judgment. In any event, the observation was made before either Brodie's or More's editions were published and Craigie was accordingly only preferring the third edition to the first and second.

Also among the answers to interrogatories is that of David Hume, Professor of Scots Law in the University of Edinburgh, who answered (p. 77) that 'he considers Lord Stair as by far the ablest and most profound of the writers on the law of Scotland and his *Institute* (*sic*) as a work of higher authority than any of the other systems of the law, not excepting Sir Thomas Craig's work *De Feudis*'. Others who gave answers to interrogatories, including Henry Erskine (later Lord Advocate and Dean of the Faculty of Advocates) and Sir Ilay Campbell (late Lord President of the Court of Session) all speak of Stair as a very high authority.

In these circumstances it is submitted that this dictum is no authority for preferring Johnstone's text to any other. Of course in 1811, and when More wrote, Johnstone's edition was the best known—apart from those of 1681 and 1693 no other appeared between 1693 and 1826—and most esteemed because it was the latest and probably the commonest and best known.

112. In *Fortington* v. *Kinnaird*, 1942 S.C. 239, 265, Lord Justice-Clerk Cooper attached importance to the views expressed in More's Notes, as did Lord Jamieson at p. 289, and Lord Mackay at p. 276 said that the Notes 'carries almost the authority of a separate Institution'.

113. 'The Rationale of Copy-Text', *Studies in Bibliography* III (1950) (University of Virginia) reprinted in W. W. Greg, *Collected Papers*, ed. J. C. Maxwell (Oxford 1966).

DEDICATION TO THE KING
[PREFIXED TO THE FIRST EDITION, 1681]

MAY IT PLEASE YOUR MAJESTY
[CHARLES II]

I do humbly present to your Majesty, a Summary of the Laws and Customs of your ancient Kingdom of Scotland, which can be no where so fitly placed, as under the rays of your royal protection. I am confident it will tend to the honour and renown of your Majesty, and your princely progenitors, that you have governed this nation so long and so happily, by such just and convenient laws, which are here offered to the view of the world, in a plain, rational, and natural method: In which, material justice (the common law of the world) is, in the first place, orderly deduced from self-evident principles, through all the several private rights thence arising, and, in the next place, the expedients of the most polite nations, for ascertaining and expeding the rights and interests of mankind, are applied in their proper places, especially these which have been invented or followed by this nation. So that a great part of what is here offered is common to most civil nations, and is not like to be displeasing to the judicious and sober any where, who dote not so much upon their own customs as to think that none else are worthy of their notice. There is not much here asserted upon mere authority, or imposed for no other reason but *quia majoribus placuerunt*; but the rational motives, inductive of the several laws and customs, are therewith held forth: And though the application of those common rules to the variety of cases determined by our statutes, our ancient customs, and the more recent decisions of our Supreme Courts, be peculiar to us; yet even the quadrancy of these to the common dictates of reason and justice may make them the less displeasing, and that no nation hath so few words of art, but that almost all our terms are near the common and vulgar acceptation. Yea, the historical part, relating to the helps and expedients for clearing and securing the rights of men out of the Word of God, the moral and judicial law contained therein, the civil, canon, and feudal laws, and many customs of the neighbouring nations, digested as they fall in with the common rules of justice, may probably be acceptable to these who may and will allow time for their perusal. A quaint and gliding style, much less the flourishes of eloquence (the ordinary condiment and varnish, which qualify the pains of reading,) could not justly be expected in a treatise of law, which, of all subjects, doth require the most plain and accurate expression. To balance which, the nauseating burden of citations are, as much as can be, left out.

We do not pretend to be amongst the great and rich kingdoms of the earth; yet we know not who can claim preference in antiquity and integrity, being of one blood and lineage, without mixture of any other people, and have so continued above two thousand years; during all which, no foreign power was ever able to settle the dominion of a strange Lord over us, or to make us forsake our allegiance to your Majesty's royal ancestors, our native and kindly kings; whereas most of the other kingdoms are compounds of divers nations, and have been subjugated to princes of different and opposite families, and ofttimes foreigners. The great monarchies, which did design universality, are all broken in pieces, and there is no family that can claim a just title to redintegrate any of them. There is no Emperor or King except yourself, but knows to what other family their predecessors did succeed, and when, and by what means. It is evident, what a mixture hath been in Greece and Italy, in France and Spain, in England and elsewhere. This nation hath not been obscure and unknown to the world; but the most famous nations have made use of our arms, and have still, in grateful remembrance, retained trophies and monuments of our courage and constancy. There be few wars in Christendom, wherein we have not had considerable bodies of soldiers regimented and commanded by themselves, and ofttimes general officers commanding them and whole armies of strangers, with great reputation and gallantry, which did advance them above the natives of these countries where they served. Neither have we wanted the fame of learning, at home and abroad, in the most eminent professions, divine or human. And as every where the most pregnant and active spirits apply themselves to the study and practice of law, so these that applied themselves to that profession amongst us, have given great evidence of sharp and piercing spirits, with much readiness of conception and dexterity of expression; which are necessary qualifications both of the bench and bar, whereby the law of this kingdom hath attained to so great perfection, that it may, without arrogance, be compared with the laws of any of our neighbouring nations. For we are happy in having so few and so clear statutes. Our law is most part consuetudinary, whereby what is found inconvenient is obliterated and forgot. Our forms are plain and prompt, whereby the generality of the judicious have, with little pains, much insight in our law, and do, with the more security, enjoy their rights and possessions; which, by our public records, are better known than any where; by which we may, with the greatest assurance, trust or purchase, seeing no land-right is effectual against purchasers, by consent or by law, but where the ultimate perfection thereof, by seasin, or other evidents, is upon record, in registers set apart for the several rights, without mixture of any other, whereof there are authentic minute books kept, with the records, in each shire and jurisdiction, whereby, with the least pains or expense, all the rights, affecting any land within the course of prescription, can easily be found. We are not involved in the labyrinth of many and large statutes, whereof the posterior do ordinarily so abrogate or derogate from the prior, that it requires a great part of a life to be prompt in all these windings, without which no man, with sincerity and confidence, can consult or plead, much less can the subjects, by their own industry, know where to rest, but must give more implicit faith to their judges and lawyers than they need, or ought, to give to their divines. And we do always prefer the sense, to the subtilty, of law, and do seldom trip by niceties or formalities.

The greatest fixation and improvement of our law hath been by the establishment of the supreme civil judicature of the kingdom by King James the Fifth, in the institution of the College of Justice, consisting of fifteen ordinary Senators, in place of the King's Daily Council, which followed his residence and court, and of the Lords of Session who came in their place, and were nominated of the Estates of Parliament ambulatory; and the Senators of the College of Justice were invested with the powers of both, and their persons and the place of judicature became fixed, and hath so continued near the space of an hundred and fifty years. This Court was much improven by your Majesty's Royal Grandfather, who delighted exceedingly in it, and honoured it frequently with his presence, while he was in Scotland. So did your Royal Father when he came to Scotland to be crowned. And your Majesty hath owned and encouraged it more than any.

Your Majesty doth not demand or expect great revenues from this kingdom. That, which we can be useful in to your Majesty, is our personal service, and our firm adherence to your Crown and Monarchy, and to your Royal Family, in which we have peculiar interest, and which no time can communicate to any of your other dominions, which they neither can claim, nor should envy, that you are of our nation, and have governed us twenty centuries and more, and by us you are the most ancient King in the world, which is the most noble and resplendent jewel in your Crown. What family on earth can parallel that motto, which an hundred years ago was written about your royal ensigns upon your palace:

Nobis haec invicta miserunt
Centum sex proavi?

Therefore your Royal Family hath been betrothed to a virgin crown, which never knew another husband; and, though it hath been darkened with clouds and recesses, yet never was, and I hope never will be, in viduity. The mutual affection betwixt your Majesty's Royal Family and this nation is a prime interest to both, which should be much encouraged and improved. Your Majesty, without just ground of jealousy to your other kingdoms, may own a peculiar care of us, and we ought to avow a singular kindness to, and confidence in, your Majesty, and your royal successors. This might be so promoved, that your Majesty might, by treaties, have armies of this nation abroad, entertained without your charge, and ready at your call, (as you had

Douglas's regiment in France,) which might secure your peace at home, and make you stand in need of less aids from your people. You might also have thriving plantations abroad, if these, who every year go from this nation to seek their fortunes abroad, were directed and encouraged. And it is certainly a great interest to keep the nation at home in constant affection to your Majesty, and amongst themselves, that being so united and sensible of their true interest, they might be significant to your Majesty's service, which can be but of small effect, while they are dissatisfied or divided. Your Royal Grandfather did sopite and extinguish the feuds, which were frequent through this nation, while no place was free of an intestine and barbarous war betwixt most of the neighbouring families; whereof little remains but amongst some clans in the Highlands. There is little discord elsewhere, but the vying or envying for a greater share of your Majesty's favour and countenance. And there was never a King more fitted to prevent and cure these piques. Beside the benignity and gentleness, that hath been singular and constant in your Royal Family, no prince or person, by the general acknowledgment of the world, whether friends or unfriends, hath so little of suspicion or jealousy, resentment, revenge, austerity or severity, as your Sacred Majesty, or more of a noble enlargement and openness of heart and affection.

It is yet a greater glory to your Royal Family, that you have been Christian Kings, before any other family in Christendom were Kings; and that you and your subjects of Scotland have been least under the yoke of Rome in your sacred or civil interest. Their arms could never subdue you; but they turned on the defensive; and to exclude your valour, two of their most famous Emperors, Severus and Hadrian, were at an incredible cost to build two walls from sea to sea, the foundations of which are yet known, and a great part of Hadrian's wall from Carlisle to Newcastle is still standing. And, albeit the Roman art did prevail, more than their arms, in procuring a subordination and dependence of this church to the Bishops of Rome, and acceptance of the service and ceremonies, which they embraced not for many centuries after they were Christians, yet in their greatest devotion to the See of Rome, they kept always a considerable reserve, so that it was barratry (that is, proscription, banishment, and loss of lands and goods,) to purchase benefices from the Court of Rome; yea, it was not lawful to go to Rome without the King's licence. And the Roman yoke hath, by the good Providence of God, been fully rejected by three successive Kings during the space of an hundred and twenty-three years; and we have returned to the true, ancient and apostolic faith of Christ, warranted by the holy canon of Scripture. And your Majesty is the King in the world of the purest religion, and it is your greatest glory and interest, to be zealous and valiant for it, both at home and abroad, the steady pursuance whereof made a distaff not only peaceable and secure at home, but terrible to the popish kingdoms abroad.

I have, as distinctly and clearly as I could, by this Essay, given a view of law and of our customs, and the decisions of the Session, since the institution of the College of Justice, as they have been remarked and reported by the most eminent judges and pleaders from time to time: which I hope shall be more enlarged and improved by others. It hath been my aim and endeavour more than twenty years, in which I have served your Majesty as a Senator of your College of Justice; of which, by your Majesty's favour, I have been President near eleven years. It is but little short of forty years, since I have followed the study and practice of law, constantly and diligently, so that these, who will not deny me reason and capacity, can hardly deny my knowledge and experience in the subject I write of. My modesty did not permit me to publish it, lest it should be judicially cited, where I sat: But now, becoming old, I have been prevailed with to print it, while I might oversee the press. It was not vanity and ambition that set me on work; but, being so long a servant of God and your Majesty in the matter of justice, I thought it my duty not to smother my thoughts of the immaculate righteousness of God Almighty in his moral law, and of the justness and fitness of your Majesty's laws, that I might promote your honour and service, and the good of your subjects, which shall ever be the sincere endeavour of,

Your Majesty's
Most humble, most affectionate,
And obedient Servant and Subject,
JA. DALRYMPLE.

ADVERTISEMENT
[PREFIXED TO THE SECOND EDITION, 1693]

The former Edition of these Institutions being long ago wholly sold off, and many being desirous of a second, I did allow the printer to expede the same. And because there are several alterations and additions in this, that were not in the former edition, I thought fit to give the reader some account thereof.

First, The former edition was printed when I was absent, and the printer had not provided a skilful corrector, whereby several escapes in the impression occurred, and some parts of sentences in the copy were left out, and many of the citations being in figures in the copy were wrong printed, so that they could not easily be found; I did therefore revise them, and correct what I found wrong cited.

Secondly, The former edition was collected by me in many years, and designed chiefly for my particular use, that I might know the decisions and acts of Session, since the first institution of it, and that I might the more clear and determine my judgment in the matter of justice. And to that end, I made indexes of all the decisions, which had been observed by men of the greatest reputation, and did cite the same: But considering that the ancient decisions were before these trodden paths, which have since come to be fixed customs, and that there were not authentic copies of these old collections; I thought fit, in this edition, only to relate to the later and more authentic and useful collections.

Thirdly, In the former edition, I designed the treatise to be divided into three parts, as being most congruous to the subject-matter of jurisprudence. The *first* part, being concerning the *constitution* of original rights: The *second*, concerning the *transmission* of these original rights, amongst the living and from the dead: The *third*, concerning the *cognition* and *execution* of all these rights. Yet, finding it would be acceptable to divide the institutions of our law into four books, as the Institutions of the Civil Law are divided, and, especially, because there is a more eminent distinction in our law betwixt *heritable* rights of the ground, and *moveable* rights; I have divided this edition into four parts: The *first*, being of original *personal* rights: The *second*, of original *real* rights: The *third*, of the *conveyance* of both: And the *fourth*, of the *cognition* and *execution* of the whole.

Fourthly, In the former edition I made the titles as comprehensive as I could, that congenerous matters might be handled in the same titles; and therefore the whole treatise was contained in 31 titles: But now, I have divided the long titles in the first book, and put them under more special titles, and have divided the paragraphs, and joined them with the several titles accordingly.

Fifthly, In the former edition, I made no other Index than the titles, and summaries of the whole paragraphs thereof printed together, which might have gone far towards satisfaction, when the method was so natural: But now, the last part being added, the titles whereof are short, and needed no summaries of paragraphs; I have not reprinted the paragraphs of the former parts together, but at the several titles: And there is also an alphabetical index of the whole added.

In all which, there is no material change from what was in the first edition as things then stood; so that it will still be useful, and the titles may be cited, either by that or this edition: Though indeed this edition be in a great part new, by occasion of new Statutes of Parliament, Acts of Sederunt, and Decisions since the treatise was written, and by an entire addition of the fourth part, which was resolved and expressed to be added. And yet, it is still the same treatise, and therefore I thought it not proper to give it a new dedication.

I have been very sparing to express my own opinion in dubious cases of law, not determined by our customs or statutes, but have rather congested what the Lords have done, than what my opinion would have been in these cases when they were free. But I have used more freedom, in opening the fountains of law and justice, and the deductions thence arising, by the law and light of nature and of reason, which is the general rule of justice for the whole world. And the law and customs of nations, whether common or peculiar, should do no more, but clear and ascertain that general law of mankind, by describing the forms, orders and expedients, for making it effectual, and altering the course thereof of things which God Almighty hath left in the power of men, which, by their contracts or statutes, they may dispose of, as they see convenient.

I have omitted no material decision of the Lords that I found, especially where they were contrary, and seemed to be inconsistent, that judges might not be overruled by adducing some decisions, where others about the same time were opposite: But I have made use of few decisions in the last part, which doth more concern the form, than the matter, of justice. And I have truly related what were the forms, when I came to be a member of the College of Justice, and what improvement thereof hath been made by alterations and additions, as experience shewed to be requisite.

AN INDEX OF THE TITLES
CONTAINED IN THE FOLLOWING INSTITUTIONS

=====

BOOK I

BOOK II

BOOK I

Titles Contained in the First Book

BOOK I

Title 1. Common Principles of Law

MY design being to give a description of the law and customs of Scotland, such as might not only be profitable for judges and lawyers, but might be pleasant and useful to all persons of honour and discretion, I did resolve to raise my thoughts and theirs to a distinct consideration of the fountains and principles of the peculiar laws of all nations, which common reason makes intelligible to the judicious, when plainly and orderly proposed : and therefore have always in the first place set forth that common rule of material justice, by which mankind ought to govern themselves, though they had no positive statutes or customs ; and then, showing how these are thence introduced. I have therefore chosen the method I thought fittest for this purpose, and the terms most intelligible in common use, and have, as much as I could, forborn the terms of art. No man can be a knowing lawyer in any nation, who hath not well pondered and digested in his mind the common law of the world, from whence the interpretation, extensions, and limitations of all statutes and customs must be brought. I have therefore begun with the common principles of law, and thence have laid down the method I now follow, and have explained the general terms commonly made use of in law. And there is no term of which men have a more common but confused apprehension, than what law is : and yet there be few terms harder to be distinctly conceived or described. The clearest conception of it, I can find, is thus :

1. Law is the dictate of reason, determining every rational being to that which is congruous and convenient for the nature and condition thereof ; and this will extend to the determination of the indifferency of all rational beings.

Even God Almighty, though he be accountable to, and controllable by none, and so hath the absolute freedom of his choice, yet doth he unchangeably determine himself by his goodness, righteousness, and truth ; which therefore make the absolute sovereign divine law. The same is also the law of all rational creatures, by which they ought to determine and rule their free actions : but the congruity and conveniency of their nature affords them other dictates of their reason, which quadrate not with the divine nature, such as adoration, obedience, common to angels and men. And reason doth determine mankind yet further, from the conveniency of his nature and state, to be humble, penitent, careful and diligent for the preservation of himself and his kind ; and therefore, to be sociable and helpful, and to do only that which is convenient for mankind to be done by every one in the same condition. Whereof the rule in the gospel is excellent, *Do to all, as you would have them do to you* [Matt. vii, 12], which must be understood, if you were in their case, and they in yours. Heathen Philosophers came not the length of this positive law, but only to the negative, *Quod tibi fieri non vis, alteri ne feceris* [Lampridius in *Alex. Sev.* c. 51 ; Socrates earlier]. Thence also are the three common precepts in the Roman law, *Honeste vivere, alterum non laedere, suum cuique tribuere* [Inst. 1, 1, 3 ; D. 1, 1, 10]; all which are evidently the common interest and advantage of mankind. This is that eternal law, which cannot be altered, being founded upon an unchangeable ground, the congruity to the nature of God, angels and men ; and therefore God cannot deny himself, or act unsuitably to his divine perfections, (and therefore it is said, Shall not the judge of all the earth do right ? [Gen. xviii, 25] and that it is impossible for God to lie [Heb. vi, 18],) not by any fatal necessity, as if he had not power and freedom enough, but because his goodness, justice, and truth are as certain by his free choice, as are his omnipotency and sovereignty. This is also called the law of nature, because it ariseth from the congruity or conveniency of nature, and thence is known by the light of nature.

2. Correspondent to these dictates of reason (wherein law consists) which are in the understanding, there is an inclination in the will to observe and follow those dictates, which is justice ; and therefore it is described " constans et perpetua voluntas suum cuique tribuendi [Inst. 1, 1, 1, pr ; D. 1, 1, 10]; where, by the will, is not understood the faculty, but the inclination thereof, determined by the law, to give every one that which the law declareth to be due ; and it is divided into distributive and commutative justice [Aristotle, *Nic. Ethics*, Bk. v]. Distributive justice is the inclination to retribute rewards to the virtuous, and punishments to the vitious, proportioned to their actings : which is now almost wholly devolved upon public authority ; little remaining but encouragement and praise to the virtuous, and discouragement and discountenance to the vitious, as also the reserved powers of parents and masters. Commutative justice is the inclination to give every man his right; and though the name is taken from the interchange of private rights, yet it reacheth to all prestations, which are not by way of reward or punishment.

There being nothing here proposed but the private rights of men, it is only requisite to consider the laws, by which private rights are constitute, conveyed or destitute : and these are either divine or human.

3. Divine law is that mainly which is written in man's heart, according to that of the apostle, "For when the Gentiles, who have not the Law, (to wit, written in the Word) do by nature the things contained in the Law, these are a law unto themselves, which showeth the works of the Law written in their hearts; their conscience also bearing them witness, and their thoughts in the mean while accusing or else excusing one another."[1] This is the law of nature, known naturally, either immediately, like unto those instincts which are in the other creatures, whereby they know what is necessary for their preservation. So the first principles of this natural law are known to men without reasoning or experience, without art, industry, or education, and so are known to men every where through the world, though they keep no communion nor intercourse together : which is an unanswerable demonstration of the being of this law of nature. It is said to be written in the hearts of men, because, as law useth to be written on pillars [Exod. xxiv, xxxii, xxxiv] or tables [cf. The Twelve Tables of the Roman law] for certainty or conservation, so this law is written by the finger of God upon man's heart, there to remain for ever. Such are the common practical principles, that God is to be obeyed, parents honoured, ourselves defended, violence repulsed, children to be loved, educated and provided for.

4. With these common principles, with which God hath sent men into the world, he gave them also Reason, that thence they might by consequence deduce his law in more particular cases; and this part of the natural law is called the light or law of reason, and is called by Solomon "The candle of the Lord, searching the inward parts." Prov. xx. 27.[2]

5. This law is also called Conscience, which is said in the forecited place to bear witness, and thereby our thoughts do either accuse or excuse one another, according to the judgment or testimony we have of our own thoughts, as good or evil, consonant to, or dissonant from, the law of nature shining in the heart; and therefore conscience relates more to the principles of religion, than of morality. As when men's laws, to exclude evil customs, make exorbitant penalties, which in some cases judges modify, in others law or custom hath excluded their modification; yet the conscience of parties moves them not to take these exorbitant advantages, from which they can be excluded by the positive law of no nation. For instance, the law excludes discharges of debts, if a term be assigned to prove payment, and the term be circumduced; yet a conscientious creditor ought not to take twice payment : so a great estate may be carried away by apprising for a small sum, but just ones will not for conscience sake so extend it. This natural law, as it is derived from these principles, the nearer it is thereto, it is the clearer; and by the more immediate consequences it be derived, it is the surer : for as the body, in its progressive motion from one step to another, walketh surest by the

shortest steps; so doth the mind in deducing this divine law. Whence it is, that this part of the law of nature is not equally evident to all men; but the more of reason they have, the more clearness they have of it: which hath made men of reason, especially these who have exercised themselves in the inquiry of right, to be had in high esteem and admiration amongst men, who, though their invention was not so eminent, yet their judgment closed and went along with that, as having a native obligation in it. And so many times these "responsa prudentum" have been received with as much authority and more heartiness for laws, than the dictates of sovereigns. Cicero, in his Oration *pro Milone* [c.4], doth excellently set forth and distinguish this natural law from positive law; for, saith he, *Haec non scripta, sed nata lex, quam non didicimus, accepimus, legimus; verum ex natura ipsa arripuimus, hausimus, expressimus: ad quam non docti, sed facti; non instituti, sed imbuti sumus: ut, si vita nostra in aliquas insidias, si in vim, aut in tela aut inimicorum aut latronum incidisset, omnis honesta ratio esset expediendae salutis.*

6. This law of nature is also called Equity, from that equality it keeps amongst all persons, from that general moral principle, *Quod tibi fieri non vis, alteri ne feceris*, whereby just persons in their deliberations and resolutions state themselves in the case of their adversaries, and so change the scales of the balance; which holds most in commutative justice. So parents in the duties of children ought to consider, as if their children were their parents, and what in that case they would do to them: and children in their obedience ought to yield all to their parents that they would demand, if they were their children. But equity is also taken for the law of rational nature, whereby nothing is to be done, which is not congruous to human nature, and becoming the same; and whereby that is followed, which if it were generally observed in the same circumstances, mankind would be happy: whereby the common interest of mankind is preferred to the interest of any part of men; whereas vicious self-love preferreth the interest of a part to the interest of the whole. This law of the rational nature of man is not framed or fitted for the interest of any, as many laws of men's choice be: from the rigour whereof recourse ought to be had to this natural equity. For though men's laws be profitable and necessary for the most part, yet being the inventions of frail men, there occur many *casus incogitati*, wherein they serve not, but equity takes place [1,1,15,*infra*] and the limitations and fallancies, extensions and ampliations of human laws are brought from equity. And though equity be taken sometimes for the moderation of the extremity of human laws, yet it doth truly comprehend the whole law of the rational nature; otherwise it could not possibly give remeid to the rigour and extremity of positive law in all cases.

7. The law of nature is also termed the moral law, being the absolute and adequate rule of the manners of men for all times, places, and persons; and this denomination it hath commonly in opposition to the judicial and ceremonial law. The Roman law doth sometimes take the law of nature in a most strict sense, as it excludeth the law of reason, and as it is founded in the nature

of man, in so far as it is common with other animals, and therefore they define it to be *quod natura omnia animalia docuit*, as the conjunction of male and female, or marriage, the procreation and education of children, &c. But, even in that law, the law of nature is extended, and distinguished into the original and primitive law, and that which is derived thence, such as for the most part is the law of nations. And there is no doubt but there is more of the law of nature founded in the rational nature of man, as he is a rational and sociable creature, so that even that, which appeareth to be in the sensitive nature, is truly founded in the rational nature; and therefore is not properly communicable unto the beasts, who have no law but their natural instincts, having only some resemblance of the law of nature, therefore called τὰ μιμήματα τῆς ἀνθρωπίνης ζωῆς [Arist. *De Historia Animalium,* IX, 7].

The law of nature, as it is imprest upon our hearts, so in the goodness of God it is exprest in his word, wherein he hath not only holden forth these sacred mysteries, which could only be known by revelation, as having no principle in nature from whence they are deducible; but also, because through sin and evil custom the natural law in man's heart was much defaced, disordered, and erroneously deduced, he hath therefore re-printed the law of nature in a viver character in the Scripture, not only having the moral principles, but many conclusions thence flowing, particularly set forth. This analogy of the law of nature, even in the hearts of Heathens, and as it is set down in the law of God, evidenceth sufficiently, that both of them proceed from the same omniscient author.

8. Besides this natural, necessary, and perpetual law, God hath also given to men voluntary and positive laws, which though not at the pleasure of men, yet in themselves are mutable; and as they had a beginning, so some of them had, and others of them shall have, an end, when the occasion, exigence, and utility, for which they were constitute, shall cease. Such were the ceremonial laws, which containing a figurative and typical administration of the worship of God, shadowing forth Christ and his propitiatory sacrifice of himself, now when the sun of righteousness hath arisen, these shadows have flown away, and are in the Scripture repealed : in lieu whereof is the outward order of the worship and government of the Christian church. And the laws of God relating thereto, though we are to expect no change of them while time is, and are as binding to all to whom their lines are gone, as the natural law, yet are they no part of it, for they are not written in the heart of man, nor deducible by reason from any such principle. Such are the sabbath on the first day of the week, the particular offices in the church, their authority and maintenance. For though the law of nature doth teach, that God is to be acknowledged and adored, yet the empowering of some certain persons to be leaders in the public adoration, and the fixed time thereof, either as it was under the law, or as it is under the gospel, cannot be reached thence, but had its beginning, and hath been altered. Some also do account marriage in the degrees forbidden in

Leviticus [c.xviii,6 ; see Incest Act 1567, c. 14 (A.P.S. 111,26,c. 15) ; Marriage Act, 1567, c. 15 (A.P.S. 111, 26,c. 16)] to be by the positive law of God, though they acknowledge it not only to be given to the Jews, but to all men : yet the natural and universal aversion of marriage betwixt ascendants and descendants, and abhorrence of that brutish commixtion, which is observed in all nations, whom corrupt custom hath not so far depraved, as to forget not only this, but most of the uncontroverted laws of nature, do sufficiently evince the contrary. For if parents and posterity be all accounted as one degree, there is nothing prohibited by the law of God, but the very next degree of these who are in the place of parents, as uncles and aunts, or in the place of children, as nephews, nieces, or brethren and sisters. So that there can be no doubt, but the prohibition of commixtion of ascendants and descendants is purely natural.

9. The prime positive law of God is the Judicial Law, which God by the ministry of Moses prescribed to the people of Israel [Exod. xx] : wherein the Lord was pleased to be the particular law-giver and judge of that people, whom he had chosen from among all nations for a peculiar people to himself, and to whose inclinations it is befitted. There are not a few who esteem the judicial law obliging to all nations, mainly because it doth not appear in the gospel to be abolished, as the ceremonial laws are, and because of its excellency beyond the laws of Heathens or other men, who might not only err in expediency, rendering their laws unprofitable, but also might make them unjust and inconsistent with the immutable moral law of nature. Which reasons do sufficiently infer, that in the constitution of human laws chief respect ought to be had to the judicial laws of God ; and they assumed, where the inclination of the people, and their condition, do not render them inconvenient. But that these laws were accommodate unto the Jews' proper temper, is evident in the law concerning the bill of divorcement [Deut. xxiv, 1–4], which beareth to be permitted for the hardness of their hearts [Matt. xix, 8 ; Mark x, 5], which was natural and peculiar to them, of jealousy and bitterness against their wives ; therefore the Lord not only appointed trial, neither natural, necessary nor accustomed elsewhere, by those tokens of virginity for evidencing the wife's faithfulness, in not giving a polluted woman for a chaste, but also the extraordinary and miraculous trial by the water of jealousy : and therefore Christ did expressly abrogate that law, and show us, that Moses did not command to divorce, but for the hardness of their hearts only permitted it, and did command that, when the husband would put away his wife, he should give her a bill of divorce. But it doth not follow that the judicial law is in itself a law to all nations, or that the Lord purposed it so to be : but on the contrary it appeareth that his purpose was only to deliver it for a peculiar law to Israel, when he saith, "What nation is so great, that hath statutes and judgments so righteous, as is all this law, which I set before you this day ?" Deut. 4, verse 8.[3] And again the Psalmist saith, "He sheweth his word unto Jacob, his statutes and judgments to Israel. He hath not dealt so

with every nation, and as for his judgments, they have not known them." Psalm 147, verse 19.[4] And therefore the same law was not to Israelites and to strangers, even to proselytes, as appeareth in the matter of usury and bond-age, which were allowed as to strangers; but the former simply forbidden, and the latter limited as to Israelites. Neither is there any necessity of an ex-press abolition of this law in the gospel, seeing it was not given to all nations, and it doth yet bind the Jews, so far as it doth not build upon the ceremonial law. And therefore, that part of the judicial law, which is founded upon, or conducible to, the moral law, may be well received by other nations, to whose inclinations the same expediencies will agree, as most of the criminal laws are. And though they could suit with the frame and current of the laws already established, yet would they be far from making up a law to rule any nation now, after man's pravity hath so much increased vice and deceit; for that, which was sufficient in the simplicity of these times, would come far short in ours.

10. Human law is that which, for utility's sake, is introduced by men: which is either by tacit consent, by consuetude or custom, or by express will or command of these in authority, having the legislative power. And these were oft-times written; though sometimes also they were not written, as were Lycurgus's[5] laws, which not only were not written, but a law against it, that they should not be written. Hence is the distinction of laws, in written and unwritten, because of their original; for, *ex post facto*, customs or other un-written laws may be written by private persons, but they were not at first written by the law-giver. It is true the law is sometimes strictly taken in op-position to custom, as it comprehendeth equity or the natural law, and the edicts and statutes of nations and their law-givers. And sometimes more strictly, as in the vulgar distinction of law, statute, and custom; in which, law signifieth equity or the common law, as statutes and customs do the peculiar recent laws of several nations. And though that be only the law of man, which is voluntary and positive, constitute by man; yet equity and the natural law, in so far as it is allowed, declared and made effectual by man, is in so far ac-counted among the laws of men.

The laws of men are either common to many nations, or proper to one nation, or peculiar to some places or incorporations in the same nation, as were the municipal laws in the Roman republic. And such are still in most nations, not only in matters of lesser moment, but in the highest matters of private rights, as in succession, which is diversified in many provinces, in France, Germany, and the Netherlands, and England, as may be instanced in the Gavel-kind of Kent.[6]

11. The law common to many nations is that which is commonly called *the law of nations*, which stands in the customs owned and acknowledged by all, or at least the most civil nations. Which for the most part are nothing else but equity and the law of nature and reason; though in part also there be posi-tive laws, introduced by common consent of nations, and which do no less

oblige these nations, as importing their obligatory consent, than do the customs of particular nations and incorporations. Such are the laws of captivity and bondage, of these taken in war, the safety of ambassadors. Though more guilty of the common quarrel than the rest of the nations, from whom they are sent, yet for common utility's sake, while they act in and conform to that capacity, they are safe : otherwise there could be no commerce, orderly indiction of war, or pacification. And therefore the Romans, when they had to do with barbarous nations, who did not acknowledge this law, did send their ambassadors to their borders, and there did require reparation, and denounce war, because they could safely go no farther. And for the same reason, though slavery be against the natural law of liberty, yet it is received for conveniency by the nations, being more willing to lose liberty than life. Such also are the laws of hospitality, or the mutual trust betwixt the host and the guest, whom he hath willingly received in his house, whereby neither of them can act any thing prejudicial to the life or liberty of the other, while in that relation. Though otherwise they had just reason, and might do the same ; yet the doing of it then were a violating of the law of nations. But for the most part the law of nations is nothing else but equity, and the law of nature and reason, which standeth as the common rule among men, appointed of God, by which they may know, and crave each from other their rights ; and in case of refusal may vindicate the same by force. Wherein they are still regulate by the common law of reason, and the customs of nations, keeping a just proportion betwixt the wrong and reparation, though taken by force ; and not like Draco,[7] who made the punishment of all his laws death, (which therefore were said[8] to be written in blood,) so making the issue of every quarrel to be the conquest of the debelled,[9] and the swallowing up of all their rights, as if they had pactioned to put them all upon the issue of that war, whereas there is nothing in question by either part, but the striving for restitution of that right, or reparation of that injury, which the one owneth and the other denieth. This law is chiefly understood, when the common law is named among us ; though the English so name the common current of their civil law, as opposite to statute and their late customs. Which is sometimes so taken with us. And oft-times by the common law, we understand the Roman law, which in some sort is common to many nations.

12. The law of each society of people under the same sovereign authority, is called the civil law, or the law of the citizens of that commonwealth ; though that now be appropriate to the civil law of the Roman commonwealth or empire, as the most excellent. And because of that affinity that the law of Scotland hath with it, (as have also the laws and customs of the chief nations, to which the victorious arms of the Romans did propagate it, and its own worth, even after the ruin of the Roman empire which hath so commended it,) that though it be not acknowledged as a law binding for its authority, yet being, as a rule, followed for its equity, it shall not be amiss here to say something of it.

The Romans were first governed by kings, who gave them laws. Which, being collected by Papirius[10] in the time of Tarquinius Superbus,[11] were therefore called the Papirian law. *L. 2. sect. 1,2,3,ff. de origine juris* [D. 1,2,2]. Tarquinius and monarchy being thrown out, the Papirian law collected in his time and by name, was partaker of his hatred and contempt with the people: and there was no fixed nor written law among the Romans, till they sent the Triumviri, Postumus, Manlius and Sulpicius, to the Greek republics, to understand the laws of these commonwealths, and thence to frame a model of government and laws for the Roman state. Which they did, and made up the law of the Twelve Tables: which, being comprehended in few words and marrowy sentences, all written upon twelve tables, was fixed upon the most public market-place at Rome, that they might be easily known and kept in mind by all the citizens.[12]

These were so acceptable and satisfactory to the Romans, that they have been the foundation and principles of all that great body of law which afterwards they had; all which was ordered according to that ancient law, as extensions and limitations of it. Which was done at first by parts, by the *plebiscita*, laws enacted by the suffrage of the people; or by the *senatusconsulta ;* or by the edicts of the Prætors; or by the *responses* of the jurisprudents, who were authorized to give answer in dubious cases, as Cornelius, Nasica, Proculus, Sabinus, Gallus, Aufidius, Manlius, Scævola, Crassus, Juventius, Ulpianus, Paulus, Julianus, and others; and when the sovereign power was devolved upon the emperors, by their edicts, rescripts and decrees; until the Roman law increased unto so great a bulk, that there were thousands of books of law, in which the brevity and perspicuity of the twelve tables was then lost, as now the body of them through the injury of time has perished. But at last the emperor Justinian[13] did, by the pains of seventeen select Jurisconsults, pick out the marrow of all the ancient laws, and digest them in some method into the fifty books of the Digest or Pandects:[14] which therefore have the author of every law prefixed to it. He did also by Tribonian[15] and others collect the rescripts, decrees, and all the edicts of the emperors, which before were more imperfectly compiled in their Theodosian Codex,[16] and which thereafter he perfected, and named the Justinian Codex:[17] as posterior constitutions of the emperors were gathered together in nine collations, which were called the Novel Constitutions.[18] Justinian did also cause frame the four books of the Institutes,[19] as the sum and elements of the whole law. But as nothing human is stable, shortly after this greatest perfection of the Roman law, in the time of Phocas the emperor,[20] who reigned fourth after Justinian, and died in the year 565,[21] the Roman empire being opprest by the irruption of the Goths[22] and Longobards,[23] the Roman law did also lie under ashes above the space of five hundred years, until a new shape of the Roman empire being set up in Germany, Lotharius the emperor,[24] who flourished in the eleventh century, did again revive and restore the Roman law: which thence was every where taught in the schools, and enlarged with more vast heaps of commentaries and treatises than were these of the ancient lawyers, though not claiming the like authority.

13. In the interim did the feudal law or customs take rise among the Longobards and other nations, who, having expulsed out of Italy the Roman empire, were willing to change their barbarity, and to be successors to the Romans in their seats and civility ; and, that they might maintain their conquests, gave out all their lands to their soldiers and assecles,[25] as benefices to them for their service and assistance in their wars : the example of which, and the new interest it afforded to sovereigns, to have all their territories to hold of themselves, and most of their subjects by that new relation to become their feudataries and vassals, hath given the feudal law wings, whereby it hath spread itself over most of the world.

14. In the declining also of the Roman empire, the bishop of Rome, having mounted himself unto the imperial eminence of universal bishop, did, in imitation of the emperors, cause compile the canon law. And first, that part, which is called the Decretum,[26] was perfected by Gratian the monk[27] out of the fathers, doctors and councils, though much wrested and vitiate towards the interests and errors of the Roman church. And thereafter the Decretals[28] were compiled by pope Gregory IX out of the decretal epistles of the popes: which Boniface VIII augmented by addition of the sixth book of the Decretals ;[29] the first whereof is, in imitation of the Digest, made of the sentences of the ancient lawyers, and it out of the sentences of the fathers, doctors, and councils, of the church : and the latter, in resemblance of the Codex, is compacted of the rescripts of the popes. And that nothing may be improportional to the civil law, unto the Novel Constitutions do answer the Clementines[30] and Extravagants.[31]

This pontifical law extended unto all persons and things belonging to the Roman church, and separated from the laity all things that may relate to pious uses, or which may be claimed to be under the protection of his Holiness, as orphans, the wills of defuncts, the matter of marriage and divorce. All which he had obtained to be exempted from the civil authority of these sovereigns who were devoted to that See. These things being holy, were not to be temerate by the profane hands of princes or free people. And so deep hath this canon law been rooted, that, even where the Pope's authority is rejected, yet consideration must be had to these laws, not only as to these by which church benefices have been erected and ordered, but as likewise containing many equitable and profitable laws, which because of their weighty matter, and their being once received, may more fitly be retained than rejected.

15. Before we come to the customs of Scotland, there lies this block in the way of all human laws, that seeing, as hath been said, equity and the law of nature and reason is perfect and perpetual, then all laws of men's constitution seem not only to be dangerous, in that they may impinge upon the perfect law of God, but also to be useless and unprofitable, seeing men may live better and more safely by the divine dictates of God written in our hearts, than by

the devices of men; so that it may be thought, that those, who instead thereof embrace the laws of men, may meet with the reproof of the Israelites, who were said to reject God from reigning over them [1 Sam. viii,7]. This reason is so pressing, that if the law of nature and of reason were equally known to all men, or that the dispensers thereof could be found so knowing and so just, as men would and ought to have full confidence and quietness in their sentences, it would not only be a folly, but a fault, to admit of any other law. But the prime interests of men being to enjoy their rights, not only in safety and security, but in confidence and quietness of mind, that they may clearly know what is their right, and may securely enjoy the same; therefore human laws are added, not to take away the law of nature and of reason, but some of the effects thereof, which are in our power. And therefore, as by the law of nature man is a free creature, yet so as he may engage himself, and being engaged, by the same law of nature he must perform: so men's laws are nothing else, but the public sponsions of princes and people, which therefore even by the law of nature they ought and must perform. And therefore they are introduced:

First, For clearing and condescending on the law of nature and of reason. Such laws can none quarrel, because they do not alter, but declare, equity; and that very necessarily, because, though equity be very clear in its principles and *in thesi*, yet the deduction of reason further from the fountain, through the bias and corruption of interest, may make it much dubious *in hypothesi*, when it comes to the decision of particular cases in all their circumstances. And therefore it is necessary it be so fixed and cleared by statutes and customs suitable thereto, that the people may be secured.

Secondly, There be many points of right competent to men in equity, as it may be more profitable for the people to forbear the pursuance of them, than to be at the trouble and the expenses of the pursuit, as when human laws do cut off matters of less concernment, and in them rather take themselves to the honesty of their party, than to compulsion by remeid of law. Such are the remuneratory obligations of gratitude, and the inward obligations of the mind, as of affection, love, kindness, &c. according to the proverb, "We cannot poind for unkindness." It is not to be doubted but there be more such obligations, than are the obligations relating to outward performances of some palpable or sensible thing: and it may easily appear what vexation it might breed, if not only the latter, but also the former might all be pursued and extorted by compulsion of law. And none can think the law of nature injured, because of common consent men will spare themselves the labour to pursue those things which they may easily dispense with. And so likewise for the same reason, though by the moral law we are obliged to love our neighbour as ourselves, from whence arise the duties of charity and mercy, assistance and relief; yet for the most part men do not compel for the negative of these commands, but only for the contrary acts of injury by doing evil instead of doing good [cf. *Donoghue* v *Stevenson*, 1932 S.C. (H.L.) 31,44, per Lord Atkin].

Thirdly, For the security of the people, and anticipation of error and fraud, and that evident probation may be had, men do most profitably order deeds to be done in such a palpable and plain form, as it may easily appear, whether false or not. In which there can be no injury, seeing the manner of doing these deeds is free, and in our power. Thus, though the dispositive will of the proprietor be sufficient to alienate any thing that is his, and to constitute the right thereof in another, yet by the civil law and custom of most nations, delivery or apprehension of possession for conveying the right of goods is requisite, and seasin is necessary for conveying of the rights of lands by the feudal law: and so by our customs assignations are not effectual to transfer personal rights, till intimation follow. Our custom also appoints writ to be made, where it is easy and ordinary to be done: and therefore, as the penalty of the neglect or contempt thereof, doth exclude witnesses in matters of importance, and admitteth only writ, or oath of party, in cases where writ is accustomed. So the Romans ordained, that because in the agreements of the people, when they stood in mere conference, words were easy to be mistaken by themselves or witnesses, that therefore the parties should perfect such contracts by a solemn stipulation, wherein the one party did interrogate, if the other did agree to such terms as he exprest, and the other immediately repeated his answer, closing with him in terms: and therefore, if they did not so stipulate, they refused them action thereupon, as a naked paction.

Fourthly, Most nations for the flourishing of their families do otherwise dispose of their estates and possessions, and their laws do order them otherwise, than the law of nature doth. For the most part the heritage, and succession in the whole land-rights, belongs to the eldest son, as the stem and line of the family, and the parents are presumed to provide the rest of their children with competent portions ; though by the law of nature the right of succession doth belong to all. And, even this positive law, altering the course of the law of nature, hath its example from the judicial law of God, by which the males exclude the females, and the eldest hath a double portion.

Fifthly, According to the humours and inclinations of people, men do lay the heavier penalties upon the transgression of such laws, as stand in opposition thereunto, which may be altered when these inclinations alter: and when that humour becomes national, they forbear to make or exerce laws against them. So the Lord did frame the law of Moses for the humours of that people, in some things permitting without punishing the transgression of the most palpable and weighty laws of nature, as in *polygamy* and *divorce ;* and also extending the proportion of equality observed in the law of nature in *restitution* and *retribution*, as in theft. Hence it appears how necessary the laws of men are. Yet surely they are most happy, whose laws are nearest to equity, and most declaratory of it, and least altering of the effects thereof, except in cases eminently profitable, like unto these now pointed at. Yea, and the nations are more happy, whose laws have entered by long custom, wrung out from their debates upon particular cases, until it come to the consistence of a fixed and known custom. For thereby the conveniences and inconveniences thereof through a tract of time are experimentally seen; so that which is found in some cases convenient, if in other cases afterwards it be found inconvenient, it proves abortive in the womb of time, before it attain the maturity of a law. But in statutes the lawgiver must at once balance the conveniences and inconveniences; wherein he may and often doth fall short: and there do arise *casus incogitati*, wherein the statute is out, and then recourse must be had to equity. But these are the best laws, which are approbatory or correctory of experienced customs. And in a customary law, though the people run some hazard at first of their judges' arbitrement; yet when that law is come to a full consistence, they have by much the advantage in this, that what custom hath changed, that is thrown away and obliterate without memory or mention of it: but in statutory written law, the vestiges of all the alterations remain, and ordinarily increase to such a mass, that they cease to be evidences and securities to the people, and become labyrinths, wherein they are fair to lose their rights, if not themselves; at least they must have an implicit faith in these, who cannot comprehend them, without making it the work of their whole life.

16. Our customs, as they have arisen mainly from equity, so they are also from the civil, canon, and feudal laws, from which the terms, tenors, and forms of them are much borrowed; and therefore, these (especially the civil law,) have great weight with us, namely, in cases where a custom is not yet formed. But none of these have with us the authority of law; and therefore are only received according to their equity and expediency, *secundum bonum et æquum* [On the authority of the civil law see also Craig 1, 2, 14; Mack. 1, 1, 7; Bankt. 1, 1, 42; Ersk. 1, 1, 27 and 41. On that of the canon law see Craig 1, 3, 24; Mack. 1, 1, 8; Bankt. 1, 1, 42; Ersk. 1, 1, 28 and 42]. And though it may appear from some narratives of our statutes, that the parliament doth own the civil and canon laws to be our law, as in the revocation of King James IV Parl. 1493, c. 51 [A.P.S. 11, 236, c. 22], where it is said, "And since it is permitted by the constitutions of law, civil and canon, that minors may revoke," & Parl. 1540, c. 80 [A.P.S. 11, 372, c. 15]; (so likewise notars & forgers of false writs are ordained to be punished after the disposition of the common law, Parl. 1551, c. 22 [A.P.S. 11, 487, c. 17]; and in the act establishing religion, all acts contrary or constitutions canon, civil, or municipal, are abrogated, Parl. 1567, c. 31 [1567, c. 3; A.P.S. 11, 548, c. 4];) yet that amounts to no more, than that these laws are an example, after the similitude whereof the parliament proceeded. And though in the cases of falsehood the punishment be assumed, as in the civil law, which may make that a part of our law, yet it will not infer, that even in so far it was our law before, much less the whole. And there is reason for the abrogation of the canon law at the establishing of the protestant religion, because in the popish church it was held as an authoritative law: but since, it is only esteemed a law as to these cases that were acted by it, when it was in vigour; and in the rest, only as our customs

assume some particulars thereof, according to the weight of the matter. But for the full evidence of the contrary, there is an express and special statute, declaring this kingdom subject only to the king's laws, and to no other sovereign's laws, Parl. 1425, c. 48 [A.P.S. II, 9, c. 3], Parl. 1503, c. 79 [A.P.S. II, 252, c. 24]. Yea the law of Scotland regulates the succession and rights of Scotsmen in Scotland, though dying abroad, being resident there: as was found in the case of Colonel Henderson's children, who, having died in Holland, legated upon heritable bonds, according to the custom there, yet they were found not to be conveyed by testament, but to belong to his heirs, according to the law of Scotland, 9th December, 1623 [Haddington, *Fol. Dic.* 1, 320 ; M. 4481]. The like betwixt Melvil and Drummond, 3d July, 1634 [Durie, 723 ; M. 4483]. And in the case of the executors of William Schaw, factor at London, dying there, it was found that a nuncupative testament confirmed in England, being contrary to the law of Scotland, which admits of none such, was null, and the nearest of kin were preferred to the executor and universal legatar named there, January the 19th, 1665, Schaw *contra* Lewens [1 Stair, 252 ; M. 4494]. But as to the manner of probation, or subscription, the law of the place regulates it, 11th December, 1627, Falconar *contra* the heir of Beatty [Durie, 319 ; M. 4501]; and the 27th July, 1633, Gordon *contra* Morley [Durie, 691 ; M. 4461]; 15th February, 1630, Harper *contra* Jaffray [Durie, 493 ; M. 4431]. So a bond by an Englishman to a Scotsman, residing there, being after the style of England, payment thereof was found probable by witnesses, and by the oath of the cedent, against the assignee, 28th June, 1666, McMorlan *contra* Melvil [1 Stair, 382 ; M. 4447]. Yet a bond granted by Scotsmen to an Englishman in England, found regulate by the law of Scotland, and not to be taken away by witnesses, being after the style of Scotland, and registrable in Scotland, December 8, 1664, Scot *contra* Henderson and Wilson [1 Stair, 236 ; M. 4450]. But the law of England and other foreign nations being matter of fact to us, the same was found probable by the declaration of the judges there, January 18, 1676, Cunningham *contra* Brown [2 Stair, 401 ; M. 12323].

The law of Scotland (as of all other nations) at first could be no other than *æquum et bonum*, equity and expediency. For it is not to be supposed that any nation, at their first association and owning of government, did appoint positive laws; nor could they have customs anterior to their constitution: and yet it is necessarily implied that they must submit to, and be governed by a law, which could be understood no other than what their sovereign authority should find just and convenient. It may be, some cities at their first constitution might have enacted laws: but it cannot be found in all the records of antiquity, that ever any nation or country did so. Whatsoever be said of the Salic law of the French,[32] which they hold so ancient and fundamental, the same is either fictitious or long posterior to their constitution into a nation. And therefore, as in arbitriments parties are understood to submit themselves to arbiters *secundum arbitrium boni viri*, so nations of old submitted to their

princes, choosing rather to refer their interests and differences to the determination of their sovereigns, than that every one should be a judge to himself,
and should take and hold by force, what he conceived to be his right, without
any superior to himself to be judge to appeal to, and thereby live in perpetual
war. Whence government necessarily implies in the very being thereof a
yielding and submitting to the determination of the sovereign authority in
the differences of the people, though one or either party should conceive
themselves injured; that thereby private opinion may give place to public
authority, although they had natural power sufficient to withstand the same.
Otherwise they behoved to dissolve authority and society, and return to the
sovereignty of their private judgment and their natural force, from which
they did flee unto the sanctuary of government; which sovereignty, though it
may sometimes err, yet can be nothing like to these continual errors, when
every one owns himself as a sovereign judge in his own cause.

Next unto equity, nations were ruled by consuetude, which declareth
equity and constituteth expediency, and in the third place, positive laws of
sovereigns became accustomed, customs always continuing and proceeding,
so that every nation, under the name of law, understand their ancient and
uncontroverted customs time out of mind, as their first fundamental law. So
the Romans accounted their laws of the twelve tables: and when they did
express any thing to be *ipso jure*, they meant it to be such by that ancient law,
in opposition to their recent customs, introduced by their pretors and constitutions of their people, senate, and princes. The English also, by their common law, in opposition to statute and recent customs, mean their ancient and
unquestionable customs. In like manner we are ruled in the first place by our
ancient and immemorial customs, which may be called our common law;
though sometimes by that name is understood equity, which is common to all
nations, or the civil Roman law, which in some sort is common to very many.
By this law is our primogeniture, and all degrees of succession, our legitim
portion of children, communion of goods between man and wife, and the
division thereof at their death, the succession of the nearest agnates, the
terces of relicts, the liferent of husbands by the courtesy, which are anterior
to any statute, and not comprehended in any, as being more solemn and sure
than those are.

In the next place are our statutes, or our acts of parliament, which in this
are inferior to our ancient law, that they are liable to desuetude, which never
encroaches on the other. In this we differ from the English, whose statutes of
parliament, of whatsoever antiquity, remain ever in force till they be repealed;
which occasions to them many sad debates (public and private) upon old forgotten statutes. But with us the Lords of Session being by their institution
authorized with power to make rules and statutes to be observed in the manner and order of proceeding in, and administration of justice, Parl. 1537, c. 43
[College of Justice Act 1532; A.P.S. 11,335,c. 2], Parl. 1540, c. 93 [College of
Justice Act 1540; A.P.S. 11,371,c. 10]; therefore, as to the matter of justice,

their authority by their institution is utterly to decide and determine, but appellation to the king or parliament, Parl. 1457, c. 62 [A.P.S. 11,48,c. 3], renewed in the institution of the college of justice [See also IV, 1, 52–57]. Before the first institution appeals were in force, in place whereof reduction succeeded, so that the Lords' decreets upon debate, being formal, are irreducible upon alledgeance of iniquity, and extend not only to the interpretation of acts of parliament, but to the derogation thereof, especially so far as concerns the administration of justice, which is specially committed to them. Whereby all the old acts of parliament concerning the form of process are in desuetude : and so in several points more recent statutes. For instance, albeit by the act of parliament 1621, c. 18 [Bankruptcy Act, 1621 ; A.P.S. IV,615, c. 18], reductions of infeftments are appointed to be sustained by exception or reply, yet the Lords seeing that this is inconsistent with the necessary and ordinary form of process, whereby rights cannot be annulled or reduced, till the parties and their authors be called, that the same may be first produced, therefore they do not take away infeftments by exception or reply, notwithstanding of the said statute. But there is much difference to be made betwixt a custom by frequent decisions, and a simple decision, which hath not the like force. Yet frequent agreeing decisions are more effectual than acts of sederunt themselves, which do easily go into desuetude. Where our ancient law, statutes, and our recent customs and practiques are defective, recourse is had to equity, as the first and universal law, and to expediency, whereby laws are drawn in consequence *ad similes casus*. But if it appear that such cases have been of purpose omitted by the parliament, the Lords will not extend the same. As albeit by the act of parliament 1621, c. 6 [Diligence Act, 1621 ; A.P.S. IV,609,c. 6], composition to superiors for receiving apprisers be appointed, and the same in the next act [Adjudication Act, 1621 ; A.P.S. IV,611,c. 7] omitted, as to adjudgers ; therefore the Lords presuming thence, from the propinquity of these acts, that such compositions were omitted of purpose, they would not extend the benefit of the superior to a composition in adjudications, 21st of July 1636, Grierson *contra* Closburn [Durie, 819 ; M. 15042]. But now it is extended to adjudications : and in these the superior hath a composition by the act of parliament 23d December 1669 [1669,c. 18 ; A.P.S. VII,576,c. 39]. How far the civil, canon, or feudal law hath place with us, hath been already said. But it is not to be thought that the feudal law is our proper law, as Craig relates, lib. 1, dieg. 8, sect. pr. there being scarce any such thing as a common feudal law ; but it is local and customary to every place, and doth not extend to the half of our rights. Craig doth very well observe near that place [Craig, 1,8,11], that these books called *Regiam Majestatem* are no part of our law, but were compiled for the customs of England in 13 books by the Earl of Chester,[33] and by some unknown and inconsiderate hand stolen thence, and resarcinate into those four books which pass amongst us ; which though they be mentioned for to be revised and reformed with our former ancient laws, Parl. 1425, c. 54 [A.P.S. 11,10,c. 10], Parl. 1487, c. 115

[Not in A.P.S.], yet these do not acknowledge them, as already become our laws, but as much, as by alteration thereof, may become our law.[34]

The law of Scotland in its nearness to equity, plainness and facility in its customs, tenors, and forms, and in its celerity and dispatch in the administration and execution of justice, may be well paralleled with the best law in Christendom: which will more plainly appear, when the proportion and propinquity of it to equity shall be hereafter demonstrate.

17. Before we come to the common principles of law, this question would be resolved, Whether law may or should be handled as a rational discipline, having principles from whence its conclusions may be deduced? Most lawyers are for the negative part, commonly esteeming law, especially the positive and proper laws of any nation, incapable of such a deduction, as being dependent upon the will and pleasure of lawgivers, and introduced for utility's sake, and so frequently alterable, that they cannot be drawn from prior common principles, and keep the artificial method of rational disciplines: and therefore they rest satisfied with any order, whereby the particular heads and titles may be found. Whereunto the confused order of the civil law (which is the greatest blemish in it) hath been instrumental: for there is nothing more ordinary for learned men, than to maintain their authors, and, through their respect to them, not to be sensible of their tolerable errors. There is little to be found among the commentaries and treatises upon the civil law, arguing from any known principles of right; but all their debate is a congestion of the contexts of the law: which exceedingly nauseates delicate ingines,[35] therein finding much more work for their memory than judgment in taking up and retaining the law-giver's will, rather than searching into his reason. Yet there are not wanting of late of the learnedest lawyers, who have thought it both feasible and fit, that the law should be formed into a rational discipline, and have much regretted that it hath not been effectuated, yea scarce attempted by any; as Duarenus *de Ratione Discendi Docendique Juris*, and Grotius in his Prolegomena to his learned treatise *de Jure Belli ac Pacis*. For which there are many pregnant reasons.

First, As we have hinted before, equity or the law of nature standeth wholly in these practical principles, which are created in and with the soul of man, and arise in him without reasoning or debate, as naturally as the heat doth from the fire, or the light from the sun, and in these rules of righteousness, which are deduced thence by evident reason: so that law is reason itself, as to its principles about the rights of men, and therefore called the law of reason. And can there be any thing more congruous to a rational discipline than reason itself, and its principles?

Secondly, God in his goodness hath given man more radiant rays of reason, and preserved it more after his fall, about his rights of *meum* and *tuum*, than in any other science or knowledge: which for the most part are dubious and conjectural, and attainable only with great pains. But in the matters of right, a man of reason, though without education, if not blinded or biassed with affection or interest, and marred with the statutes and customs of men, which are but as their contracts and matters of fact to him, would be able to discern right from wrong : though he cannot be so distinct, as, by reflecting on his own knowledge, to take up, and hold forth the grounds upon which he doth proceed, or to reach matters of intricacy or difficulty, which require more eminent judgment and long experience.

Thirdly, God doth expostulate and argue with men, even for moral duties, from these common principles of righteousness, which their conscience cannot reject, as is evident everywhere in his Word. And therefore, seeing the law hath such principles, it may and ought to be held forth, as it is deduced from them.

As to the difficulties, which seem to arise from the variety and multiplication of positive laws, it will say nothing. For seeing positive law is only to declare equity, or make it effectual, and in some cases to lay aside the effects of it, for the profit of man now in his lapsed estate, it may be easily ordered, by bringing it to the parts of equity, whereunto it doth relate. And as a man's body may well be described, though it be not naked and in its pure naturals, and have its hair cut and ordered, and ornaments upon it ; all which will fall to be described as appendicles to the several parts of the body, which they adorn : so equity is the body of the law, and the statutes of men are but as the ornaments and vesture thereof ; and in the explanation of every part of it, will most fitly fall in accordingly. But the best demonstration of this will be ocular, by our delineation of equity and positive law together.

18. The principles of law are such as are known without arguing, and to which the judgment, upon apprehension thereof, will give it ready and full assent ; such as, God is to be adored and obeyed, parents to be obeyed and honoured, children to be loved and entertained. And such are these common precepts which are set forth in the civil law, to live honestly, to wrong no man, to give every man his right [Inst. 1, 1, 3 ; D. 1, 1, 10]. But here we shall speak of the most general principles, which have influence upon all the rights of men, leaving the more particular ones to the rights flowing therefrom in their proper places.

The first principles of equity are these : That God is to be obeyed by man. 2. That man is a free creature, having power to dispose of himself and of all things, in so far as by his obedience to God he is not restrained. 3. That this freedom of man is in his own power, and may be restrained by his voluntary engagements, which he is bound to fulfil. Or, to take them up more summarily, the first principles of right are obedience, freedom, and engagement.

There are also three prime principles of the positive law ; whose aim and interest is the profit and utility of man. As the natural law is *in æquo*, so the positive law is *in bono* or *utili :* and upon these two legs doth justice move, in giving every man his right. If man had not fallen, there had been no distinction betwixt *bonum* and *æquum :* nor had there been any thing more profitable, than the full following of the natural law. But man being now depraved, and wanting justice, or that willingness to give every man his right, and apt to fraud or force; therefore, in this estate it is profitable for him, to quit something of that which by equity is his due, for peace and quietness sake, rather than to use compulsion and quarrelling in all things; and to find out expedients and helps to make equity effectual: and therefore to make up societies of men, that they may mutually defend one another, and procure to one another their rights; and also to set clear limits to every man's property; and to maintain traffic and commerce among themselves and with others. So that the three principles of positive law may be society, property, and commerce. The principles of equity are the efficient cause of rights and laws: the principles of positive law are the final causes or ends for which laws are made, and rights constitute and ordered. And all of them may aim at the maintenance, flourishing, and peace of society, the security of property, and the freedom of commerce. And so the narratives of all statutes do commonly bear the motives introductory, towards some of these heads.

19. Obedience is that submission and sequacity of the mind and will of man to the authority and will of his Maker, immediately obliging without any tie upon him by himself, intimate to him by the law of nature, light of reason, and the conscience, whereby man distinguisheth betwixt right and wrong, betwixt what is duty and what is not duty. Hence do arise these obligations upon man, which are not by his own consent or engagement, nor by the will of man, but by the will of God. And therefore, these are fitly called obediential obligations. The first and most general whereof is, "To love the Lord our God with all our heart, and our neighbour as ourselves;" upon which, saith our Saviour, "hang all the law and the prophets." Matt. 22, vers. 40.[36] Which is a clear demonstration from his mouth of the dependence of the moral law upon this principle. Such are also the obligations betwixt husband and wife [1, 4, *infra*], parents and children [1, 5, *infra*], and the obligations of restitution [1, 7, *infra*], reparation [1, 9, *infra*], and remuneration [1, 8, *infra*]: in all which we are engaged, not by our will and consent. And such are the obligations which the civilians call *quasi ex contractu* [Inst. 3, 27], because they find them obligatory, and yet not by contract, and not adverting to this their rise from obedience, reduce them to contracts by a *quasi* [1, 7, 2, *infra*].

20. Where obedience ends, there freedom begins: and man by nature is free in all things, where this obedience has not tied him, until he oblige himself. It is a great mercy to man, that God hath obliged him only in a few necessary moral duties, and has left him free in much more, without any tie upon him as to the matter, but with a liberty *ad contradictoria*, that he may do or not do, and *ad contraria*, that he may do this or the contrary, providing that whatsoever he do, (even where he is free) be ordered and directed to the glory of God. It hath been the opinion of some, both learned and pious, that there is nothing indifferent *in actu exercito*, or as it is invested with circumstances, but that then every thing is a duty or a sin: and that, because all things must be done to the glory of God, and to mutual edification [I Cor.

x,31 ; xiv,26], from whence there is no exception, and so are not free; as that we must make account of every idle word [Matt. xii,36]; and that we are obliged to try all things, and to hold that which is best [I Thess. v,21]. Which reasons indeed conclude, that there is nothing free as to this contradiction, either to be done to the glory of God or not, and to edification and use or not ; but do not conclude that there is duty or necessity in the matter of the action itself: of which either part of the contradiction may be chosen, so that either part be useful and ordered to the glory of God. As saith the apostle [Rom. xiv,6], "He that observeth a day, observeth it to the Lord, and he that observeth it not, doth so to the Lord."

And likewise in that undeniable instance of marriage, wherein the apostle [I Cor. vii,38], debating of the conveniency to marry or not to marry, doth conclude, that he that marrieth doth well, but he that marrieth not doth better: whereby both parts of the contradiction are approven; and that, which is less profitable, is said to be well done. Therefore, there is a great difference betwixt duty which is necessary, and wherein we are obliged, though we mistake or be wilfully ignorant, by the very weight of the matter and absoluteness of the command : wherein the ordering of what is forbidden to God's glory will not justify, as we may not do evil, that good may come of it [Rom. iii,8]. As those who killed the apostles were far from being justified, though they thought they did God good service thereby [John xvi,2]. These things are *bona honesta, et mala inhonesta :* but matters of expediency are but *bona utilia,* and not *inhonesta.* And therefore, our duty in these is that which we conceive most to be for the glory of God, and good of ourselves and others; but if we do mistake, and choose that which is less expedient for these ends, we are certainly free.

God seemeth to do with men as princes do with their ambassadors, to whom they give some express instructions, wherein they have no latitude in their negotiations, with power for the rest to do as they shall judge most fit upon the place; wherein, if acting *bona fide* they mistake, and do not that which is most fit, they are not culpable. So man being sent into the world to behold the works of God, and to glorify him, for doing whereof he hath some rules written in his heart by the law of nature, and in the word of God, and for the rest is allowed to do as he conceiveth most conducible thereto, that whether he eat or drink, or whatsoever else he do, he do all to the glory of God, it were a sad rack to the consciences of men, if their errors and mistakes in the matters of expediency were to lie as a guilt upon their consciences : but that *bona fides* or *conscientia illæsa,* so much spoken of in the law, is that which cleareth and acquitteth men in such mistakas. From this freedom doth arise, not only our personal freedom and liberty, whereby men are *sui juris,* but also their power of the disposal of other things within their reach, or that dominion which God hath given them over the creatures.

21. As freedom began where obedience ended, so engagement begins where freedom ends ; it being our voluntary obliging of ourselves, where by

nature we are free. Every such obligation is a diminution of that freedom: for thereby we are either restrained from that power of disposal of the creatures, or may be constrained to some performances contrary to our natural liberty. Some hold it not lawful for us, "To give away our native freedom in whole or in part, or to bind ourselves where God has left us free, and that such engagements, except where they are profitable for us, or for an equivalent cause, are not obligatory." Which shall be more proper to debate, when we come to the obligations by paction, promise, or contract [1, 10, 10, *infra*], all which do arise from the principle of engagement: but it shall be sufficient here to conclude with the law, That there is nothing more natural, than to stand to the faith of our pactions [D. 2, 14, 1]; and this much for the common principles of law.

22. As to the object thereof, the formal and proper object of law are the rights of men. A right is a power, given by the law, of disposing of things, or exacting from persons that which they are due. This will be evident, if we consider the several kinds of rights: which are three, our personal liberty, dominion, and obligation. Personal liberty is the power to dispose of our persons, and to live where, and as we please, except in so far as by obedience or engagement we are bound. Dominion is the power of disposal of the creatures in their substance, fruits, and use. Obligation is that which is correspondent to a personal right, which hath no proper name as it is in the creditor, but hath the name of obligation as it is in the debtor: and it is nothing else but a legal tie, whereby the debtor may be compelled to pay or perform something, to which he is bound by obedience to God, or by his own consent and engagement. Unto which bond the correlate in the creditor is the power of exaction, whereby he may exact, obtain, or compel the debtor to pay or perform what is due: and this is called a personal right, as looking directly to the person obliged, but to things indirectly, as they belong to that person. So dominion is called a real right, because it respecteth things directly, but persons, as they have meddled with those things. By which it is clear, that all rights consist in a power or faculty: the act whereof is possession, enjoyment, or use; which is a matter of fact, and no point of right, and which may be where no right is, as right may be where these are not.

23. The Roman law taketh up for its object Persons, Things, and Actions, and according to these, orders itself [Inst. 1, 2, 12], but these are only the extrinsic object and matter, about which law and right are versant. But the proper object is the right itself, whether it concerns persons, things, or actions: and, according to the several rights and their natural order, the order of jurisprudence may be taken up in a threefold consideration, First, in the constitution and nature of rights; Secondly, in their conveyance, or translation from one person to another, whether it be among the living or from the dead; Thirdly, in their cognition, which comprehends the trial, decision, and execution of every man's right by the legal remeids. Whereby the whole method may be clearly thus. *First*, of the nature of those several rights; and

because liberty standeth in the midst betwixt obligations of obedience, which are anterior, and of engagements, which are posterior, yet both these, being of the same nature, must be handled together; and therefore liberty must have the first place; then next obligations obediential, and then conventional; and after these dominion in all its parts. And in the *second* place, shall follow the conveyance of these several rights. And, *lastly*, the cognition of all their judicial process and executions. Rights, in respect of the matter, are divided into public and private rights. Public rights are those which concern the state of the commonwealth; Private rights are the rights of persons and particular incorporations: of which in their proper places.

EDITOR'S NOTES

1. Rom. ii,14-15, where the reading is: 'For when the Gentiles, which have not the law unto themselves: Which show the work the law, these, having not the law, are a law unto themselves: which show the work of the law written in their hearts, their conscience also bearing witness, and their thoughts the mean while accusing or else excusing one another.'

2. The Authorised Version reads: "The spirit of man is the candle of the Lord, searching all the inward parts of the belly."

3. The Authorised Version reads: 'And what nation is there so great, that hath statutes and judgments so righteous as all this law, which I set before you this day.'

4. It is verses 19 and 20 and in the Authorised Version it reads "his statutes and his judgments . . .".

5. Lycurgus was the traditional founder of the Spartan constitution and military system. Opinions vary as to his date and there are doubts whether he was truly an historical character.

6. Gavelkind denoted the custom which applied from the Norman Conquest to 1925 to socage land in Kent, the most notable features of which were that land descended to all sons equally, it was devisable, and a husband who survived his wife was entitled to a life-estate in half of her land though issue of the marriage had not been born, all features different from the customs applicable elsewhere in England.

7. The Athenian lawgiver who in 621 B.C. drew up a code of laws with prescribed rules of procedure and fixed penalties, probably reducing to writing the customary law of his day. His laws were revised or repealed by Solon.

8. By the orator Demades.

9. *debellati*, subdued or conquered.

10. Sextus Papirius, who is said to have compiled a collection of *leges regiae*, or Publius Papirius, who made a collection of royal laws, or Gaius Papirius, who restored a collection of ordinances in the forum which had become illegible. Or there may have been a collection of pontifical law made when a Papirius was *rex sacrorum*.

11. Last king of Rome, traditionally 534-510 B.C.

12. The Twelve Tables, traditionally dated 451-450 B.C., possibly the work of a commission of ten, were regarded by the Romans as the basis of their entire legal system. Only fragments survive and modern reconstructions involve large elements of hypothesis; see Schöll, *Legis XII Tabularum Reliquiae* (1886); Bruns, *Fontes Iuris Romani Antiqui* (1919); Girard, *Textes de droit romain* (1923).

13. Byzantine emperor, 527-565 A.D.

14. The compilation of the Digest was ordered in 530 A.D. and it was brought into force on 30 December 533.

15. A learned jurist and official at Justinian's court who died c.543 A.D., director of the compilation of the *Digest* and the *Code*; see Honoré, *Tribonian* (1978).

16. An official collection made by order of Theodosius II and published in 438 A.D. containing in 16 books imperial constitutions from the time of Constantine to its own date.

17. The Code, containing imperial constitutions from the older collections and subsequent enactments, with the omission of obsolete matter, was published in twelve books in 534 A.D. It replaced an earlier edition of 529 A.D.

18. There was no official collection of the

Novels, and those known today are derived from three semi-official collections. The glossators divided the version known as the *Authenticum* into 12 *collationes*, nine containing laws glossed as of practical value, the rest being unglossed.

19. An official manual for law students having the force of an imperial statute, compiled by Tribonian, Theophilus and Dorotheus, published and having force from 30 December 533 A.D.

20. Byzantine emperor, 602–610 A.D.

21. *Sic.* Justinian died in 565, Phocas in 610 A.D.

22. The Ostrogoths entered Italy from 488 A.D. onwards.

23. The Lombards entered Italy from 568 A.D. onwards.

24. Lothar II, Holy Roman Emperor, 1133–1137 A.D. Stair's later editors consequently amended the word "eleventh" to "twelfth".

25. Attendants or followers.

26. Correctly called the *Concordia Discordantium Canonum*, a private collection in three books published about 1150, seeking to codify the scattered and conflicting canons of the Roman patriarchate. It never received papal sanction but at once became the basic text of canon law as studied in all the universities.

27. (c.1095–c.1159) a Camaldolese monk of Bologna.

28. The *Decretals* of Gregory IX, known as the *Liber Extra*, comprised decided cases in five books, and was officially promulgated in 1234.

29. The *Decretals* of Boniface VIII were promulgated in 1298 as a supplement to Gregory's five books and hence are called *Liber Sextus* or The Sext.

30. The *Decretals* of Clement V promulgated in 1313, but withdrawn and promulgated again in 1317 by John XXII.

31. *Decretales Extravagantes* of John XXII and *Extravagantes Communes* of Popes from Boniface VIII to Sixtus V, 1298 to 1484.

32. i.e. the laws of the Salian Franks, probably of the fifth century. See *Lex Salica*, ed. Hessels and Kern (1880); ed. Eckhardt (1953); *Pactus Legis Salicae*, ed. Eckhardt (1954). Stair probably knew the first printed edition, by Jean de Tillet, of about 1550, reprinted 1573, or that of Herold (1557) or one of several early 17th century editions, such as those of Lindenbrog (1602, 1609) or Bignon (1665).

33. The treatise *De Legibus et Consuetudinibus Regni Angliae*, in 14 books, which commences with the words *Regiam potestatem*, has traditionally been ascribed to Ranulf de Glanvill (c.1125–1190), Justiciar of England under Henry II, and been known as Glanvill, but may have been written by his kinsman and secretary Hubert Walter. The author of *Regiam Majestatem* clearly founded on it. Comparative texts are printed in A.P.S., I, 135.

34. On *Regiam Majestatem* see Craig I,8,II; Bankt. I,1,75; Ersk. I,1,32–36; Lord Hailes' *Examination of some of the Arguments for the High Antiquity of Regiam Majestatem* (1769) and in his *Tracts relative to the History and Antiquities of Scotland* (1800); Davidson's *Observations on the Regiam Majestatem* (1792); Chalmers' *Caledonia*, I,727; Pollock and Maitland, *History of English Law*, I, 223; Lord Cooper's Introduction to *Regiam Majestatem* (Stair Society, 1947).

35. *Ingenia*, intellects.

36. In the Authorised Version it reads: '37. Jesus said unto him, Thou shalt love the Lord thy God with all thy heart, and with all thy soul, and with all thy mind . . . 40. On these two commandments hang all the Law and the Prophets.'

Title 2. Of Liberty and Servitude

1. LIBERTY is that natural power which man hath of his own person, whence a free man is said to be *suæ potestatis*, in his own power; and it is defined in the law [Inst. 1, 3, 1] to be a natural faculty to do that which every man pleaseth, unless he be hindered by law or force.

2. That there is such a right, distinct from the dominion of the creatures, and from obligation, it is evident from this, that it can be referred to none of these, and yet is the most native and delightful right of man, without which he is capable of no other right; for bondage exeemeth man from the account of persons, and brings him rather in among things, *quæ sunt in patrimonio nostro ;* and the encroachments upon, and injuries against, the right of liberty, of all others are the most bitter and atrocious; for the non-performance of obligations or duties [due] to us, or the taking away, or detaining of the things of our property, are not to be compared with the laying violent hands on our persons.

3. This right ariseth from that principle of freedom, that man hath of himself and of other things beside man, to do in relation thereto as he pleaseth, except where he is tied by his obedience or engagement; and this part of it, which concerneth personal freedom, is maintained by that common received principle in the law of nature, of self-defence and preservation; for, as Cicero saith in his Oration *pro Milone* [c. 11], *Haec et ratio doctis, et necessitas barbaris, et mos gentibus, et feris natura ipsa præscripsit, ut omnem semper vim, quacumque ope possent, a corpore, a capite, a vita sua propulsarent.* And, as Gaius saith [D. 9, 2, 4, 1], *Adversus periculum naturalis ratio permittit se defendere,* which is only to be extended to private and unlawful violence.

4. Opposite unto liberty are restraint and constraint. Restraint hindereth man to be where, and go whither, he will : and constraint forceth him to do what he will not. Restraint is exercised by imprisonment and captivity, or in the hinderance of the use of things necessary for life, as meat, drink, sleep, &c. Constraint is exercised by beating, wounding, or the like force upon the body, or the fear of it, whereby any thing is extorted.

5. Though liberty be a most precious right, yet it is not absolute, but limited : *First,* by the will of God, and our obediential obligations to him, and to men by his ordinance. And though man hath power of his own person, yet hath he no power of his own life, or his members, to dispose of them at his

pleasure, either by taking away his life, or amputation, or disabling any member, either by himself, or by giving power to any other so to do, unless it be necessary for preserving the whole: but he is naturally obliged to God to maintain his life. So likewise men may be restrained or constrained by others, without encroachment upon the law of liberty, in the pursuance of other obediential obligations; as a husband hath power to restrain his wife from her liberty of going where she will, and may keep her within the bounds of conjugal society. So may parents restrain their children, and also constrain them to the performance of moral duties, and that without any engagement. We may also, without any injury, restrain a furious person, or one who is inferring violence to himself in his life or limbs, because this is not against any act of his lawful liberty, and is done as a duty in us of love and mercy. But in matters of utility and profit, where the natural liberty is not hemmed in with an obligation, there, unless by his own delinquence or consent, man cannot justly be restrained, much less constrained upon pretence of his utility or profit: for liberty is far preferable to profit, and in the matter of utility, every man is left to his own choice, and cannot, without injury to God and man, be hindered to do what he pleaseth, or be compelled to do what he pleaseth not, in things wherein he is free. As Grotius saith, *De jure belli*, *lib.2.Cap.22.parag.*12: "*Non enim si quid alicui utile est, id statim mihi licet ei per vim imponere. Nam his, qui rationis habent usum, libera esse debet utilium inutiliumve electio, nisi alteri jus quoddam in eos quæsitum sit.*"

6. Liberty may be diminished or taken away by our delinquence, in the way of punishment: for seeing it is a right in our own power, as goods and debts may be forfeited by our delinquence, so may our liberty in whole or in part.

7. *Thirdly*, our engagements do commonly import a diminution of our personal liberty, but much more, of that natural liberty of things without us. Whence it is, that the law alloweth personal execution or restraint, and incarceration of the debtor's person, until he do all the deeds that are in his power for the satisfaction of his creditor.

8. Liberty is diminished by subjection unto authority: for tho man by nature be a free creature and in his own power, he doth then become in the power of others, whether the authority be in the power of a society, where the suffrage of the plurality is preferred to the natural and free choice of particular persons, or whether the authority be stated in a few persons, or in one sovereign.

9. *Fifthly*, liberty is wholly taken away by bondage, slavery or servitude, which is diametrically opposite to liberty; for as liberty is that power, by which men are *sui juris*, so by servitude they became *alieni juris*, in the power of another, unto whom they became as the rest of their goods in their patrimony, and were possessed by them, and might been gifted, legated, sold and otherways disposed of at their pleasure, *l.4,ff. de statu hominum* [D.1,5,4,1], *l. qui in servitute 118,ff. de regulis juris* [D.50,17,118], so that masters had

among the Romans and almost everywhere, the power of the life and death of their slaves, §*1,l. de his qui sunt sui vel alieni juris* [Inst. 1,8,1; D.1,6,1], though the constitutions of the emperors did restrain that power to moderate chastisement, as appears by the former law, §*2. ibid* [D.1,6,2], and consequently servants being wholly their masters, they could have nothing of their own, *l. adquiruntur 10,ff. de adquirendo rerum dominio* [D.41,1,10], so that, that *peculium*, which their masters committed to them, to negotiate with, was wholly in their master's power, and might be taken away at his pleasure, l.4,*ff. de peculio* [D.15,1,4]; neither could they be liable to any obligation, *l. nec servus, 41.ff. de peculio* [D.15,1,41]; neither could there be any civil action for or against them, *l. in personam 22,ff. de regulis juris* [D.50,17,22]; *l.107,ff. ibid.* [D.50,17,107], neither could they be witness, procurators or arbiters; yea they were accounted as no body, or as dead men, *l.32 ibid.* [D.50,17,32]; *l.7,Cod. de testib.* [C.4,20,17]; *l.7.C. de judiciis* [C.3,1,7]; *l.7,ff. de recept. qui arbitr.* [D.4,8,7].

10. Bondage was introduced by the law of nations, and it is amongst the positive laws of nations settled by common consuetude. And it took first place in these who were taken in war, who being under the power of their enemies' sword, did lose their liberty in lieu of their life. Such also were these who sold their liberty, and gave it up, and were content to be perpetual slaves; as were the Jews bond-men, whose ears were pierced with an awl, as the symbol of their perpetual and willing servitude; the offspring of which servants remained in their servile condition; and by the custom of nations, and the Roman law, it followed the mother and not the father, *partus sequitur ventrem*. And in some cases, both by the judicial law and the Roman law, free parents might sell and give their children into bondage.

11. Bondage, though contrary to the nature of liberty, yet it is lawful, liberty being a right alienable, and in our disposal, so that the natural law constitutes us free, but puts no necessity on us so to continue. And therefore servitude is both approven in the Old Testament and in the New, where it is cleared against that obvious objection, that being made free by Christ we should not become the servants of men; to which the apostle answereth, "Art thou called being a servant (or slave) continue so, for nevertheless thou art Christ's free man." [1 Cor. vii,21–22] But yet Christian lenity and mercy hath almost taken away bondage, except amongst the Spaniards, Portugals, and other Christian nations bordering upon the Turks; where, because the Turks do extremely exercise slavery, especially upon Christians, their neighbours do the like, that they may have slaves to exchange with slaves. But little of slavery remains elsewhere among Christians, except the *adscriptitii*: who are not absolutely slaves, but they and their posterity are bound to several services to farms and villages, to which, by reason thereof only, they are in bondage; and their masters cannot apply them to other farms, or to other services; but they are fixed to, and follow those farms, and they are conveyed therewith. Such are the English villains; but in Scotland

there is no such thing.

12. There was formerly a kind of bondage in Scotland called Manrent, whereby free persons became the bondmen or followers of these who were their patrons and defenders; and these were rather *in clientela* than in bondage; but it is utterly now abolished, both by Act of Parl. 1457, c. 77 [A.P.S. 11, 50, c. 24], and Parl. 1555, c. 43 [A.P.S. 11, 487, c. 17], and by our custom.

13. From servitude among the Romans did arise Manumission and the right of patronage. Manumission is the demission of slaves, and the making of them libertines, whereby they became free, but with remaining thankfulness, reverence, and obsequiousness, and some other duties and offices to their former masters, then become their patrons : and if they failed therein, they forfeited their new-acquired liberty, and returned to their former condition of servitude.

14. In these therefore stood the right of patronage. And from this condition of libertines arose that distinction of men into these who were always free, who were called *ingenui*, and these who were bound, who were called *servi*, and these of a middle condition, who having been slaves, became free, and so were neither fully free, but had some duties lying upon them to their patrons, neither were fully bound as servants.

15. Servants with us, which now retain that name, are judged free persons, and have at most but hired their labour and work to their masters for a time, which is a kind of contract betwixt them, of which afterward.

16. The customs of this nation have little peculiar in relation to liberty directly ; but the injuries done against the same, especially of constraint, fall under the consideration of delinquences, and are so punished. The Romans had express laws *de libero homine exhibendo* [D. 43, 29], and *de privatis carceribus inhibendis* [C. 9, 5], and the English have their action of false imprisonment, determining with great exactness in what cases imprisonment is lawful, and in what not ; and how remeidable. It is also provided in the judicial law against stealers of men [Exod. xxi, 16]. But amongst us, as these crimes are very rare, so if unlawful restraint or unjust imprisonment should fall out, it remains to be punished amongst delinquences, according to the circumstances and atrocity thereof, and according to equity : and thence also a civil action for damage and interest ariseth.

Title 3. Obligations in General

RIGHTS called personal or obligations, being in nature and time for the most part anterior to, and inductive of, rights real of dominion and property, do therefore come under consideration next unto liberty.

1. The same right, as it is in the creditor, it is called a personal right, but as it is in the debtor, it is called an obligation, debt, or duty, which is retained as the more proper name, *Inst. de obligationibus in prin.* [Inst. 3, 13, pr.]. Obligation is a legal tie by which we may be necessitate or constrained to pay, or perform something [Inst. 3, 13, pr. ; see also D. 44, 7]. This tie lieth upon the debtor ; and the power of making use of it in the creditor is the personal right itself, which is a power given by the law, to exact from persons that which they are due.

2. Obligations by the Romans are distinguished in four kinds : in obligations ex contractu, vel quasi ex contractu, ex maleficio, vel quasi ex maleficio [Inst. 3, 13, 2]. Which distinction insinuates no reason of the cause or rise of these distinct obligations, as is requisite in a good distinct division ; and therefore, they may be more appositely divided, according to the principle or original from whence they flow, as in obligations obediential, and by engagement, or natural and conventional.

3. Obediential obligations are these, which are put upon men by the will of God, not by their own will, and so are most part natural, as introduced by the law of nature, before any addition made thereto by engagement, and are such as we are bound to perform solely by our obedience to God : as conventional obligations are such, as we are bound by and through our own will, engagement or consent.

4. Obediential obligations are either by the will of God immediately, or by the mediation of some fact of ours ; such are obligations by delinquence [1, 9, *infra*], whereby we become bound to reparation and satisfaction to the party injured, and are liable in punishment to God, which may be exacted by those who have his warrant for that effect. Of these obediential obligations there be some which tie us to God alone ; whereby there is no right constitute in man to exact the same as his own due, or any warrant or command given him by God to exact them on his behalf. And some, though they constitute not a right in man, yet man is commanded and warranted to vindicate them, as the crimes of witchcraft, blasphemy, bestiality, and the like ; for which there is an express command to inflict punishment, though there be no injury done therein to man, of which there could be any reparation [Exod. xxii, 18, 19, 28]. For the command, *Thou shalt not suffer a witch to live* [Exod. xxii, 18], takes place, though the witch have committed no malefice against the life or goods of man. But these obligations, being among public rights, belong to the magistrate, on whom that authority is devolved to vindicate it for God as his vicegereut. But we shall not here insist on them, nor on these other obligations, whereby no right of execution is constitute in man for vindication, *et quæ solum Deum habent ultorem*, such are the love and fear we owe to God, and deyendence on, and confidence in him. For being only to treat about the private rights of men, we shall therefore insist only on obediential obligations that are betwixt husband and wife [1, 4, *infra*], parents and children [1, 5, *in-*

fra], tutors and pupils [1,6,*infra*], curators and minors [1,6,*infra*], and the obligations of restitution [1,7,*infra*] and remuneration [1,8,*infra*], and the obligations of reparation of delinquence and damage [1,9,*infra*] : and then we shall proceed to conventional obligations [1,10,*infra*].

5. There is another distinction of obligations in the law, viz. natural and civil [cf. Inst.3,20,1]. Natural obligations are these, which have a tie by the law of nature, and do raise a right in the party to whom they relate : but the civil law or customs and constitutions of men do not second them with legal remedies or executions, but they remain only as bonds upon the good-will and honesty of these who are thereby bound, of which there are severals. As *first*, There be many natural obligations which have no civil effect, because they oblige to inward duties of the mind, which law doth not consider : as Cicero saith [Probably a reference to *De Officiis* III,c.17, though the text differs from that quoted by Stair], *Philosophum spectant quæ mente tenentur, Juridicum quæ manu tenentur.* Or *secondly*, Because though they oblige to outward performances, yet the manner and measure is left to the discretion and arbitriment of the obliged, as before hath been shown [1,1,20,*supra*]; though that in matters of expediency and utility, there be an obligation to do that, which is most conducible to these common ends to which we are obliged, yet in the particulars our acting *bona fide* makes us free. Or *thirdly*, Because, though absolute obligations lie upon the obliged, yet they relate to duties performable to God, whereof he hath given no power nor command to man. That there be some such obligations, that God hath authorised or commanded man to vindicate for him, and not all such, may be gathered from his own judicial law, in which many such are expressed, and many others omitted. Though these obligations be to duties relating to man, yet there is no correspondent right or power of compulsion in man : and so the creditor is God, and man is the third party, to whose behoof the obligation is imposed, but who hath neither power of exaction for himself, nor vindication for God. Such are the obligations of beneficence generally and particularly, of charity to the poor, assistance to these in hazard, and relief of the oppressed [1,1,15,*supra*]. For natural reason will teach us that, though these do naturally oblige us, yet they in whose favours they are, cannot compel us. For example, we are bound to give alms to the poor, yet none will affirm that the poor can extort it, or take it by force. It is true, that by the positive law of all nations, by their consociation, there is in the very nature of the association a duty of assistance for the common interest, into which they are associate : but that is not a natural, but a voluntary obligation flowing from their voluntary association or union. Likewise all people are bound to concur, and assist legal executions ; and in some places to contribute by such a proportion to the poor : but these are only positive laws, having the force and nature of contracts. Legal compulsion is also laid aside in matters of small moment, *nam prætor non curat minima*, and in some things of greater importance, wherein a way of procedure is prescribed, and as a penalty of non-observance of that

order, legal remedies are denied, when done any other way. So naked pactions among the Romans were ineffectual, when they did not interpose stipulation. And with us, agreements requiring writ are ineffectual, and may be resiled from, unless writ be interposed. Yea, in most matters of importance, obligations with us are ineffectual, unless proven by oath of party, or by writ. Civil obligations are these which have a civil effect and execution, though perhaps they be not naturally obliging; as with us an obligation in writ doth civilly oblige, and hath execution at the instance of the creditor's heir or assignee, though the debt was paid to the cedent or defunct, because the debtor hath not been so cautious as to keep a discharge in writ. But most part of obligations are both natural and civil : and there are many such particular obligations which will occur in their proper places.

6. There is a third distinction of obligations in principal and accessory : such are the cautionary obligations of surety and pledges, which are accessory to all other obligations ; of which in their proper places likewise.

7. The fourth distinction of obligations is in these, which are pure, conditional, and to a day. Conditional obligations are such as depend upon a condition ; and so are but obligations in hope, till the condition be existent. But obligations to a day are such as are presently binding, but the effect or execution thereof is suspended to a day. Betwixt which there is this main difference, that in conditional obligations the condition must necessarily be uncertain, either as being in the power of man's will, or as an accidental event. For if the condition be a thing certainly to come, though it may be conceived under the terms of a conditional obligation, yet it is indeed an obligation to a day. As if Titius be obliged to pay Mævius ten crowns, if an eclipse shall be such a day, upon which day, by the certain rules of astronomy, it is known that it is so to be, though perhaps it was uncertain to either, or both parties, yet it is not a conditional obligation, but the time of the eclipse is the term thereof. So likewise, if the condition be impossible *de facto*, or impossible *de jure*, that is, unlawful, *nam id tantum possumus quod de jure possumus*, then though the obligation be conceived in terms conditional, yet because the condition is not depending, and in itself uncertain, the obligation is not truly conditional, but is void and illusory, because of the legal impossibility of the condition. And if the obligement be founded on natural affection or charity, if the condition adjected may be an occasion to move the obtainer to do wrong, the obligation is valid and pure, and the condition is void, as not adjected, *nam conditio illicita est quasi non adjecta*. As when parents give bonds to children on condition that they marry not, or that they marry such a person, these bonds are valid : and the condition is void, as against the freedom of marriage, which the natural affection of parents obliges them not to violate. But if such a condition be imposed by any other, who hath no natural obligation, the condition is valid. Hence it appears, that such obligations, as are without conditions, are pure ; and such are simple which are not clogged with the running of a course of time, the adjection whereof is always in

favours of the debtor, as to the intervenient time, and in this also in favours of the creditors, that he needs use no interpellation or requisition of performance, *sed dies interpellat pro homine*, and the day being past, the debtor is *in mora*. But in simple obligations delay is only upon demand, and whensoever it is required, upon non-performance the debtor is *in mora*. Obligations *ad diem incertum* are in effect conditional, *nam dies incertus habetur pro conditione*, as a sum payable at such an age, which is frequently in provisions of children: if they die before that age, the sum is not due to their representatives, even after they might have attained that age; as was found January 17, 1665, Edgar *contra* Edgar [1 Stair 250; M.6325]; February 22, 1677, Belshes of Tofts *contra* Belshes [2 Stair 519; M.6327. See 1,5,6,*infra*].

8. A conditional obligation doth necessarily imply an uncertainty, and dependence of the effect of the obligation upon the existence of the condition; for, if the condition fail, the obligation is void. And oft-times obligations are conceived in conditional terms, though in effect there be no uncertainty of the condition, as to the being thereof, though it may be uncertain, as to the contractor's knowledge: as in obligations, where the condition is made of something past; or something that cannot but come, the coming whereof is the term of performance, and not a condition, and it is an obligation to a day, and not conditional. As on the contrary a conditional obligation may be, when it is not yet conceived in terms conditional: as when it is conceived to a day, if it be uncertain whether by the course of nature that day will ever come, it is no term but a condition. These uncertain conditions are of two kinds: voluntary, which depend upon the free choice of some persons; and casual, which depend upon the casual event of that which cannot naturally be foreknown. Amongst voluntary conditions, these are not to be numbered, which consist in the natural obligations of the creditor, which he is positively obliged to perform, and so are not looked on by the contractors, as an uncertain event in his choice: and therefore, though frequently such obligations in mutual contracts are conceived by way of provision or condition, and so may stop the effect or execution of such obligations, till the creditor's part be performed; yet that is rather, as the failzie or delay of the mutual cause of the obligation, than as the non-existence of a condition. And therefore, such contracts may, and ordinarily do receive execution, by poinding and apprising, before the performance of these provisions: which executions are not null, but will be preferred by their dates, to others proceeding upon pure obligations or to a day after the day is past. Yea, the other creditors cannot object the non-implement of the provisions, except they had interest, in so far as the fulfilling thereof would be to their behoof: which certainly they could do, if they were proper conditions; as they can do, when the condition is casual, or when it is voluntary, not being a part of the creditor's mutual obligement. In like manner the end and intent of an obligation, or the manner of performance thereof, is ordinarily exprest as a condition, though these be not real conditions, rendering the obligation uncertain.

A condition is oft-times implied in an obligation, though it be not exprest; as when a tocher is promised, this tacit condition is implied, if the marriage hold. And the condition may either be exprest or implied, as relating to the contracting, or to the performing of the obligation. As if the debtor said, on such conditions I shall become obliged, which differeth from this, that I oblige myself to pay or perform, when, or upon condition that such things shall exist. For in this case there is a present contract, though the effect be uncertain, and therefore arrestment and inhibition might be used thereupon. But in the former the very engagement is uncertain: as if one should promise to Titius, if he married Mævia, that he should contract with him for such a tocher; before such a marriage contracted or solemnized, neither arrestment nor inhibition would be granted thereupon [See I, 17, 15; IV, 20, 29, *infra*].

9. An offer hath the like implied condition of the other party's acceptance, and in that it differs from an absolute promise, so that if the acceptance be not adhibit presently, or within the time exprest in the offer, in which the other party hath liberty to accept, there ariseth no obligation, as was found June 25, 1664, Allan *contra* Collier [1 Stair 206; M. 9428]. And in mutual contracts the one party subscribing is not obliged, till the other subscribe, as being his acceptance. And a cautioner subscribing is not obliged, unless the principal party subscribe, that being implied as a tacit condition of his being cautioner [I, 10, 3 and 5, *infra*].

Title 4. Conjugal Obligations

THE first obligations God put upon man towards man, were the conjugal obligations, which arose from the constitution of marriage before the fall. From whence have arisen rights of the greatest consequence, as the husband's power over the wife and her goods; the mutual society of families, which is the only society immediately institute of God in the law of nature; and from whence is the power of parents over children; and the economical government of families, which of all others was the most absolute and full, extending not only to the determination of civil rights, but to the punishment of all crimes, till by the union of greater civil societies many of these powers have been devolved upon the common authority of the societies. And therefore these conjugal obligations deserve the first consideration.

1. Though marriage seem to be a voluntary contract by engagement, because the application of it is, and ought to be, of the most free consent, and because in matters circumstantial it is voluntary, as in the succession of the issue, and the provision of the wife and children; yet that marriage itself and the obligations thence arising are *jure divino*, appears thus. First, obligations arising from voluntary engagement take their rule and substance from the will of man, and may be framed and composed at his pleasure: but so cannot marriage, wherein it is not in the power of the parties, though of common consent, to alter any substantial, as to make the marriage for a time, or take the power over the wife from the husband, and place it in any other, or the right of provision or protection of the wife from the husband, and so of all the rest, which evidently demonstrateth, that it is not a human, but a divine, contract.

2. That marriage ariseth even from the primitive law of nature, and that it is the conjunction of two single persons, is evident not only from that natural affection, which all sorts of men in all places of the world (where no common example nor consent can reach) have unto a married estate; but as the lawyers say that it is founded in the common nature of man with other creatures, who have a resemblance of it in themselves, and it is given for the very example of the natural law, as contradistinct from the law of reason, and law of nations. For most part of the living creatures live and converse in pairs, and keep the common interest of their offspring, as is clear in all fowls whose wings have freed them from man's control, as many of the beasts of the field. And it is like, all of them would be so inclined, if their natural liberty were not restrained by man, by pursuing such as are wild, and making use of the tame, as they may be most profitable, preserving most of the female for increase, and destroying the male.

3. The affection of the property and chastity of women, and animosity and jealousy, that ariseth in men naturally upon the breach thereof, do evince, that by the law of nature every man ought to content himself with his own wife, and women not to be common. For as no man can endure the communication of his own, so it must necessarily follow, that he should not encroach upon another's property [Homer, Iliad, ix, 340–342]. And seeing nature holds not out a proportion betwixt the male and the female, whereby every man might appropriate more, it must, therefore, subsist in one: and so was the first institution by God; and all the posterior directions in his word are for a man and his wife, not his wives. And as the man hath not power over his body, but the wife [I Cor. vii, 4], so it were an absurd inconsistency, if that power were in many, and so behoved to resolve in a management by the common consent of the wives.

4. The degrees in which marriage is allowed or forbidden, are by divine institution: for the next degree collateral is only forbidden. For of ascendants

and descendants there is properly no degree, the great-grandmother being in that regard as near as the mother. And so the next collateral to all ascendants and descendants is in the same degree with brothers and sisters : and uncles and aunts, nephews and nieces, are alike in the propinquity of blood with these ; and the great-grandmother's sister with the mother's sister. Else if these were different degrees, there would many degrees intervene betwixt a person and his great-grand-aunt. But that there is a natural abhorrence of that promiscuous commixtion of blood, it is commonly acknowledged over all the world, as to all ascendants and descendants. And as to the next collaterals, the word of God cleareth it, not to have been a positive law given to the Jews, but to have been a common law to the Gentiles also. And therefore Lev. xviii. where the degrees of marriage are exprest, and unlawful commixtions forbidden, it is subjoined, ver. 24 and 25, *Defile not yourselves in any of these things : for in all these the nations are defiled, which I cast out before you. And the land is defiled : therefore I do visit the iniquity thereof upon it.* But unless these prohibite degrees of marriage were a part of the law of nature written in man's heart, or a common positive law known to all nations, the Lord, who hath declared that he will judge men by the law which is known, would not so have judged the Canaanites for the transgression of it.

5. The perpetuity of marriage is also evident by our Saviour's sentence against arbitrary divorce, which was permitted by the law of Moses for the hardness of that people's hearts. But the Lord cleareth up the ancient law of nature, "from the beginning it was not so," [Matt. xix, 8] which showeth the perpetuity of that law, and that it was before the judicial law. And therefore he concludeth, that whosoever putteth away his wife, except for fornication is an adulterer, if he marry another while she liveth.

6. For understanding of these conjugal rights, it will be necessary 1. to consider the constitution of marriage; 2. the dissolution of it; 3. the rights and interests thence arising. For the first, Marriage is defined by Modestinus to be the conjunction of man and woman to be comforts for all their life, with a communication of rights divine and human, *l. 1. ff. de ritu nuptiarum* [D. 23, 2, 1]. So the essence thereof consists in the conjugal society : the special nature of which society appeareth by the state, interest, and terms that the married persons have thereby.

It may be questioned whether the conjunction wherein marriage consists, be a conjunction of minds by mutual consent to the married state, and that whether privately or in the public solemnity ; or whether it requireth not a conjunction or commixtion of bodies. For clearing whereof consider, that it is not every consent to the married state that makes matrimony, but a consent *de præsenti*, and not a promise *de futuro matrimonio :* for this promise is only the espousals, which are premised to marriage, that so solemn an act might be with due deliberation. And therefore though, as other promises and pactions, espousals are naturally obligatory, and effectual also by the canon law, whereby the espoused persons may be compelled to perfect the marriage, unless there arise some eminent discovery of the corruption or pollution of either party, or defect or deformity, through sickness or some other accident : *Cap. ex literis Ext. de sponsalibus* [*Extra.*4,1,10] & *cap.2 eodem* [*Extra.*4,1,2] ; *c. Literis ult. de Conjug. leprosor* [*Extra.*2,4,25 and 4,8,3], yet by the civil law, there is place for either party to repent and renounce the espousals, *l.1.Cod. de sponsalibus* [C. 5,1,1]. Which is also the custom of this nation : for marriage uses not to be pursued before solemnization, *rebus integris.* So that the matter itself consists not in the promise, but in the present consent, whereby they accept each other as husband and wife : whether that be by words expressly ; or tacitly by marital cohabitation or acknowledgement ; or by natural commixtion, where there hath been a promise or espousals preceding, for therein is presumed a conjugal consent *de præsenti.*

The public solemnity is a matter of order, justly introduced by positive law, for the certainty of so important a contract, but not essential to marriage. Thence arises only the distinction of public or solemn, and private or clandestine marriages : and though the contraveners may be justly punished, (as in some nations by the exclusion of the issue of such marriages from succession,) yet the marriage cannot be declared void, and annulled ; and such exclusions seem very unequal against the innocent children. But by our custom, cohabitation, and being commonly repute man and wife, validates the marriage, and gives the wife right to her terce, who cannot be excluded therefrom, if she was reputed a lawful wife, and not questioned during the husband's life, till the contrary be clearly decerned, Parl. 1503, c.77 [A.P.S. 11,243, c.22]. So also a contract of marriage was found valid, against the husband's heir, though the marriage was never solemnized in kirk nor congregation, Hope, Husband and wife, Barclay *contra* Napier [Hope, *Maj.Pr.* 11,17,27 ; M.6115]. So likewise in the same case, a contract of marriage was found valid, and the man thereby obliged to solemnize the marriage, seeing he had procreate children with the woman, and by his missives had acknowledged he had married her, though by a contract, posterior to the contract of marriage, she had renounced the same [111,3,42,*infra*].

As to the other point, though the commixtion of bodies seem necessary for the constitution of affinity arising from marriage, yet the opinion of the canon law is true, *consensus, non coitus, facit matrimonium* [Decretum c.27, q.2,c.1 and 2]. But this consent must specially relate to that conjunction of bodies, as being then in the consenter's capacity : otherwise it is void. So the consent of persons naturally impotent or of a dubious kind, as hermaphrodites, where the one sex doth not eminently predomine, doth not make marriage. And the common essentials of consent must also here be observed : so that who cannot consent, cannot marry, as idiots and furious persons. Neither they, who have not the use of reason as, infants and those under age, who are not come to the use of discretion, unless *malitia suppleat ætatem*, that is, when the person is within the years of pupillarity, commonly established in law to be fourteen in males and twelve in females. Yet seeing marriage is a natural obligation, and not annullable by positive law, as to it regard must be had, whether the parties be truly come to discretion and capacity, whereof the commixtion of bodies is sufficient evidence. And this also is the sentence of the canon law [*Extra.* 4, 2, 14]. Errors also in the substantials make void the consent, unless future consent supervene; as it did in Jacob, who supposed that he had married and received Rachel, but by mistake got Leah, yet was content to retain her, and serve for the other also [Gen. xxix, 25–28. See I, 9, 9; IV, 40, 24, *infra*]. But errors in qualities or circumstances vitiate not, as if one, supposing he had married a maid or a chaste woman, had married a whore. So then it is not the consent to marriage, as it relateth to the procreation of children, that is requisite; for it may consist though the woman be far beyond that date: but it is the consent, whereby ariseth that conjugal society, which may have the conjunction of bodies as well as of minds; as the general end of the institution of marriage is the solace and satisfaction of man, for the Lord saw that it was not fit for him to be alone, and therefore made him an help meet for him. Yet though this capacity should never be actuate, as if persons, both capable, should after marriage live together, and it should be known or acknowledged that all their lives they did abstain, yet were the marriage valid as to the conjugal rights on either part. If it be asked, whether the consent of parents be essential to marriage; the common sentence will resolve it, *multa impediunt matrimonium contrahendum, quæ non dirimunt contractum*. So that consent is necessary *necessitate præcepti, sed non necessitate medii :* though by human constitution such marriages may be disallowed, and the issue repute as unlawful; but the marriage cannot be annulled. *L.* 11. *de stat. hom.* [D. 1, 5, 1] *l.* 13. §6. *ff. ad L. J. de adult.* [D. 48, 5, 14, 6]. By which laws, not only the issue of such marriages are excluded from succession, but the marriage itself is insinuate to be null : which human constitutions cannot reach; though the magistrate or minister, celebrator of the marriage, may refuse to proceed without consent of the parents. As by the law and custom of Holland, *Art.* 3, *Ord. pol.* it is statute, that before the celebration of marriage, there be three proclamations in the church or in the court; and that where the parties are minors, they be not married without consent of their parents, and where they are both majors, intimation must be made to their parents, who, if they appear not, their consent is presumed, and if they do appear and dissent, they must condescend upon the reasons, that it may be cognosced whether they be sufficient or not; and if the marriage do otherwise proceed, they account it null. Marriage is also void and inconsistent, when contracted within the degrees prescribed. Lev. xviii. Whereby the next degree collateral is only prohibite, both in consanguinity and affinity; which makes those joined in affinity in the same degree, as being by marriage one flesh. Neither can marriage consist where either party is married before. But the exclusion of further degrees by the canon law, as of cousin-germans, or of certain degrees in ecclesiastical affinity, or the prohibiting marriage to these *in sacris*, are these unlawful devices which cannot alter this divine contract, but become a cheat, putting parties in the Pope's power to approve or disapprove, as his avarice or interest leads. Neither do the civil constitutions of princes annul or dissolve marriage: whatever they may operate as to the interest of the married persons or their succession. As were the prohibitions of marriage between those of consular dignity and plebeian persons; between tutors and their children, and pupils; yea, between Jews and Christians; for even diversity of religion cannot annul it.

7. The dissolution of marriage is only by death. Adultery and desertion do not annul the marriage, but are just occasions upon which the persons injured may annul it, and be free: otherwise if they please to continue, the marriage remains valid. All do agree, that adultery hath some effect upon marriage. The canon law doth not thereupon dissolve it, that the party injured may be free to marry again, but only granteth separation. But our Saviour's precept cleareth the contrary: who in relation to the custom that then was of divorce for light causes, resolves, that putting away was not lawful, except in the cases of adultery, and so in that case approves the divorce, even as then used, Matt. 19 v. 9. It may be doubted whether the adulterer, after the dissolution of the marriage upon his default, may marry again? But though positive law, as a penalty upon adulterers, may hinder their marriage with the adulteress or otherwise declare such marriages, as to succession and civil effects, void; yet can it not simply annul it, and with any other person the adulterer may marry. With us marriage betwixt the two committers of adultery is declared null, and the issue inhabilitate to succeed to their parents, Parl. 1600, c. 20 [A.P.S. IV, 233, c. 29. See III, 3, 42, *infra*]. But otherwise even the person guilty may marry again.

8. The second ground of dissolution of the marriage is wilful desertion: which is grounded upon the answer of the apostle, I Cor. 7. 15, concerning the marriage of Christians with infidels, which he declares valid, unless the unbeliever depart, in which case he declares the Christian not to be under bondage: which cannot have any specialty, as to the party deserted as a Christian, and therefore must infer a general rule, that all married persons wilfully deserted are free. But this seems inconsistent with Christ's resolution, making adultery the only exception. Which is easily cleared, by adverting, that Christ's determination is not general of the dissolution of marriage, but of putting away by divorce, and so concludes no more, but that the putting away of the wife is unlawful, unless for adultery: but the wilful deserter is not put away, but goeth wilfully away. Yet from Matth. v. 32, and xix. 9, and Luke xvi. 18, it would appear, that by desertion the marriage is not dissolved, and that the person deserted may not marry again; because it is said, That whosoever marrieth her that is put away (or deserted) committeth adultery. But Christ speaks of these put away by the Jewish divorce, which, though permitted without punishment for the hardness of the Jews' hearts, was now under the gospel taken away: so that the person, so put away, remained in marriage, and the taking her in marriage by another became punishable as

adultery.

By the law of Scotland, dissolution of marriage for non-adherence, or wilful desertion, is expressly ordered, Parl. 1573, c. 55 [A.P.S. III,81,c. 1]. "That the deserter, after four years wilful desertion without a reasonable cause, must be first pursued and decerned to adhere, and being thereupon denounced, and also by the church excommunicate, the commissaries are warranted to proceed to divorce." But simple absence will not be accounted a man's wilful desertion, if he be following any lawful employment abroad, being content to accept and entertain his wife ; for she is obliged to follow him wherever he is.

9. The rights arising from marriage are the *jus mariti*, or conjugal power of the husband over the wife, her person and goods, and therewith by consequence the obligement for her debts. 2. His power, and the wife's security, whereby during the marriage she cannot oblige herself. 3. The husband's obligement to entertain the wife, and provide for her after his death. 4. Her interest in his goods and moveable estate at the dissolution of the marriage.

Jus mariti, as a term in our law, doth signify the right that the husband hath in the wife's goods. Yet it may well be extended to the power he hath over her person, which stands in that economical power and authority, whereby the husband is lord, head, and ruler over the wife, by the express ordinance of God, *Gen.* iii. 16, where the Lord says to Eve, *thy desire shall be towards thy husband, and he shall rule over thee.* Which though it may seem as a penalty imposed upon her, for being first in the transgression, and so not to be of the natural or moral law, which is perpetual, yet it is no more than a consequence of the moral law, whereby marriage being institute before the fall, the woman was made for the man, and not the man for the woman ; and therefore in that conjugal society, being but of two, the determination of things indifferent of their interest behoved to be in the man, and he had in so far the precedency and government of the wife ; but when through the fall the greatest measure of infirmity befel her, as being first in the transgression, whereby she became the weaker vessel, there was need, not only of a determination in things free, but an exaction of duties, whereinto she became less knowing and willing. Therefore, from that consequence, and not by any new imposition, the man became to have dominion over her, and power to make her to do these duties, which in her innocency she would have done of her own accord.

This power economical, as hath been said before, did naturally comprehend all authority, till most of it was devolved upon magistracy. Yet by this power, the husband may still contain the wife within the compass of the conjugal society ; and her abode and domicile followeth his ; and he hath right to recover her person from any, that would withdraw or withhold her from him, except in the case of an allowed separation for his injuries and atrocities, for which she might not be with him in security and safety.

From this power the husband hath over the wife's person, and conjugal society involved in the nature of marriage, arises according to the nature of society, a communion of goods betwixt the married persons; which society, having no determinate proportion in it, doth resolve into an equality : but so that, through the husband's economical power of government, the administration during the marriage of the whole is alone in the husband; whereby he having the sole and unaccountable administration, his power may rather seem to be a power of property, having indeed all the effects of property during the conjugal society, yet is no more than is above exprest.

This right of the husband in the goods of the wife is so great, that hardly can it be avoided by the pactions of parties, whereby if any thing be reserved to the wife during the marriage, to be peculiar and proper to her, excluding the *jus mariti*, the very right of the reservation becomes the husband's *jure mariti*, makes it elusory and ineffectual, as always running back upon the husband himself; as water thrown upon an higher ground doth ever return. And therefore a wife, before her contract of marriage, having disponed a part of her jointure, and taken a backbond for employing of it for the use of her future spouse and family jointly, though the husband by his contract of marriage renounced his right thereto yet he was found to have the power to manage it to the use of the family, February 9, 1667, Lord Collingtoun and L. Ratho *contra* tenants of Innertyle, and Lady Collingtoun [1 Stair, 438; M. 5828]. Nevertheless, by private paction the interest, and division, of the goods of married persons after the dissolution of the marriage, may be according to their pleasure, as they agree. And alimentary provisions, in case the husband cannot, or will not aliment the wife, are so personal to the wife, that *inhærent ossibus*, and recur not to the husband or his creditors, though constitute by the husband, without fraud of creditors, much more when constitute by any other.

10. Besides the obligations of the married persons, which are naturally in the minds and affections of each to other, there is outwardly the obligation of cohabitation or adherence, of which formerly; and the obligation of the husband to aliment and provide for the wife in all necessaries for her life, health, and ornament, according to their means and quality; to which he is naturally bound, though he had no means, but were to acquire the same; *for he that provides not for his own family, is worse than an infidel :* yet the civil effect thereof is only to give [to the wife] aliment and entertainment according to the man's means and quality; and so he is civilly bound *quoad potest*. Hence it is, that the aliment or furnishing of the wife is a debt of her husband's, not only for what is furnished by merchants and others *hoc nomine* in the husband's life, but even her mournings after his death, if it be proper for her quality to have mournings, burdens the executors of the husband, and not the wife, November 12, 1664, Lady Kirkassie *contra* Neilson [1 Stair 224; M. 5921]; July 7, 1675, Wilkie *contra* Morison [2 Stair 340; M. 5923].

Jus mariti is a legal assignation to the wife's moveable rights, needing no other intimation but the marriage; and is preferable to any voluntary right, prior to the marriage, if not intimate before the marriage, December 18, 1667,

Auchinleck *contra* Williamson and Gillespie [1 Stair 496 ; M. 6033].

11. The Roman law hath exceedingly varied in this matter from the natural law. For with them the wife was not *in potestate viri*, but either *in potestate patris*, or *sui juris :* and her goods remained fully her own, unless they had been constitute by her in a tocher, of which the husband had the administration and profit during the marriage *ad sustinenda onera matrimonii ;* and in which, after dissolution of the marriage, he had no interest, except by paction *de lucranda dote ;* and for security whereof the wife had *donationes propter nuptias* equivalent. Only *in dote æstimata*, the husband had power to dispose of the tocher for the value to which it was estimate of consent, to be paid at the dissolution of the marriage. All the other goods of the wife were *paraphernalia*, whereof she had the sole power and right.

12. The custom of most nations, even where the Roman law hath much weight, in this matter have returned to the natural course : as is observed by Chassanæus *ad Consuetudines Burgundiae, Tit. 4*, and Duarenus *tit. ff. de nupt.* [D. 23, 2] in relation to the custom of France ; Wesenbecius *in parat. ad tit. ff. de ritu nuptiarum*, and Covarruvias *Epit. 4. lib Decretal, part 2, cap. 7.* In reference to the customs of the Germans, Spaniards & most part of the nations of Europe, Gudelinus *de Jure Noviss.* [1, 7] showeth the same to be the custom of the Netherlands, in which they do almost in every thing agree with our customs. Yet if the marriage dissolve within year and day without a living child, all returns on either side, which was done in contemplation of the marriage, like to the general course of the civil law [1, 4, 19; 11, 6, 19, *infra*].

13. By the custom of Scotland the wife is in the power of the husband. And therefore, *First*, The husband is tutor and curator to his wife, and during her minority no other tutor or curator needs to be convened, or concur to authorize her : so it was decided, French *contra* French and Cranston, Hope *de minoribus* [Hope, *Maj. Pr.* IV, 9, 42 ; M. 2179]. But on the contrary, the wife is in no case convenable without calling the husband : and though she be married during the dependence, the husband must be cited upon supplication, and the process must be continued against him, for his interest : Spotiswood, Husband and wife, Baillie *contra* Robertson [Spotiswoode 154; M. 2192].

14. Yea, a wife's escheat or liferent falls not upon any horning execute against her during the marriage, because, being then under the power of her husband, she hath no power of herself to pursue, suspend, or relax, February 16, 1633, Stuart *contra* Bannerman [Spotiswoode, 153 ; M. 5734 and 6071]: and this was found, though the decreet was an ejection committed both by man and wife. Yet where the horning is upon a deed proper to the wife, as to divide her conjunct-fee-lands, horning is valid, or where the horning was upon a delinquence, as on lawborrows, Hope, Husband and wife, Lord Roxburgh *contra* Lady Orkney [Hope, *Maj. Pr.* 11, 17, 32 ; M. 6069].

15. In like manner a wife cannot pursue or charge without concourse of

her husband, and so letters not raised at his instance were reduced, though he concurred thereafter, July 27, 1631, Hay *contra* Rollock [*Sub nom. Napier* v *Rollock*, Durie, 602; M.6047]; the like Spotiswood, Husband and wife, Napier *contra* Kinloch [Spotiswoode, 159]. The like in a reduction of an heritable right, done by the wife's father on deathbed : which was not sustained, unless the husband had concurred, or had been called, in which case, if he refused to concur without just reason, the Lords would authorize the wife to insist, July 8, 1673, Hacket *contra* Gordon of Chapletoun [2 Stair, 206; M.6039]. But we must except from this rule, if the husband were inhabilitate or forfeited, March 26, 1622, Hamilton *contra* Stuart [1 Haddington, 313; M.4656]; or the wife being authorized by the Lords upon special consideration, the husband refusing to concur, January 9, 1623, Marshal *contra* Marshal [Durie 40; M.6036]: or that she were pursuing her husband himself, against whom ordinarily she hath no action except in singular cases, *ut si vergat ad inopiam*, or in case he had diverted from her, December 21, 1626, Lady Foulis *contra* her Husband [Durie 251 ; M.6158] : or if a wife with concourse of her friends, at whose instance execution was provided by her contract, were pursuing reduction of a deed, done by her husband in prejudice thereof, during her life, February 12, 1663, Lockie *contra* Paton [1 Stair 177; M.16090]: or that the obligation in its own nature require execution in the husband's life, as an obligement to infeft the wife in particular lands. But if it be a general obligement to employ money for her, or to infeft her in lands, &c. which the husband may at any time of his life perform, the wife will have no action against him : neither will she get inhibition upon supplication, unless the lords grant the same upon knowledge, that the husband is becoming in a worse condition, or that the wife hath quit a present infeftment for an obligation of another, in which case the lords granted inhibition, July 13, 1638, Lady Glenbervy *contra* her Husband [Durie 857 ; M.6053]. This delay of execution, where a term is not exprest, is upon consideration of merchants, who ordinarily having no other means than the stock with which they trade, it would ruin them, if they were necessitate to employ it on security, so soon as they are married ; and is not to be extended to others.

16. It was a privilege of women amongst the Romans *per senatusconsultum Velleianum*, that the obligations, by which they became surety, or interceded for others, were void. But our custom is, that a wife's obligation for debt, or personal obligement, contracted during the marriage, is null [1, 11, 3, *infra*], even though the bond were granted by her and her husband, containing an obligement to infeft the creditor in an annualrent out of their lands, and in this case the bond as to the wife, and an apprising thereon as to her liferent of these lands was found null : but here there was no special obligement of annualrent, or wadset of the wife's liferent lands, but generally out of both their lands, March 24, 1626, Greenlaw *contra* Galloway [Durie 198 ; M.5957]. The like Hope, Husband and wife, Douglas of Tofts *contra* Elphinstoun and Hamilton [Hope, *Maj.Pr.* 11, 17, 38 ; M.5975]. The like January 30,

1635, Mitchelson *contra* Mowbray [Durie 747 ; M. 5960] : in which case the bond being granted by the man and wife, and thereupon apprising deduced, though she did judicially ratify it upon oath, never to come in the contrary, yet the bond and infeftment, as to her liferent, was found null, seeing there was nothing to instruct her ratification, but the act of an inferior court, whereof the warrant was not produced. But a wife's obligation with her husband conjunctly and severally, obliging them to pay, and also to infeft in an annualrent out of either of their lands, was found null, as to the wife in the obligement to pay, but not as to the obligement to infeft, December 15, 1665, Elleis *contra* Keith [1 Stair 327 ; M. 5987]. Neither was a wife found liable for furnishing to the house in her husband's absence forth of the country, which did only affect her husband, Spotiswoode, Husband and wife, Howison *contra* Lady Louristoun [Spotiswoode 158 ; M. 5954]. The like January 29, 1631, Porter *contra* Law [Durie 561 ; M. 6071]. The like, though the cause of the bond was money advanced for the wife's necessary aliment, for which no process was granted against her till her husband was first discussed, December 21, 1629, Aiton *contra* Lady Hackertoun [Durie 477 ; M. 5952]. And also a wife's obligation without consent of her husband was found not to affect her, but him, though she was not *præposita negotiis*, but because she was *persona illustris*, and her husband out of the country, Hope, Husband and wife, Russel *contra* E. of Argyll [Hope, *Maj.Pr.* 11,17,30 ; M. 5878]: but a wife's bond for necessary habiliments for her body found to oblige herself, and not her husband's executors, for as to these she may contract, Haddington, July 6, 1610, Wise *contra* Lady Halyrudhouse [Haddington, *Fol.Dict.* 1,397 ; M. 5952]. This must be understood where the wife has an aliment constitute by her husband, or some other right exempt from his *jus mariti*. And it was so lately found in the case of Gairns, Merchant *contra* Arthur, December 19, 1667 [1 Stair 498; M. 5954]; and February 23, 1672, Neilson *contra* Arthur [2 Stair 77 ; M. 5984].

This privilege of wives was extended to obligations or dispositions made by a wife, though before completing the marriage, being after contract and proclamations, whereupon marriage followed, January 29, 1633, Scott *contra* Brown [Durie 665 ; M. 2710 and 6030]. The like specially where the proclamation was not only at the husband's parish church, but the wife's, July 8, 1623, Stuart *contra* Aitkin [*Sub nom. Macdougal* v *Aitken*, Durie 70; M. 6027]. The like of a disposition in favours of the wife's children after the contract and one proclamation, July 5, 1611, Fletcher in Dundee *contra* Brown [Haddington, *Fol.Dic.* 1,404 ; M. 6029].

Yet wives' obligations relating to their delinquence are not void, but only such as relate to their contract. So a wife was found obliged to fulfil an act of a kirk-session, under a penalty that she should forbear another man's company, which was found not to affect her husband's goods, but her own, Hope, Husband and wife, Bell *contra* Executors of Hog, and the kirk-session of St Cuthbert's [Hope, *Maj.Pr.* 11,17,25 ; M. 6068]. Here also are excepted obligements relating to dispositions of lands, annualrents or liferents: of which hereafter.

17. As to the husband's and wife's interests in their goods, by our custom, without any voluntary contract, there arises betwixt them a communion of all moveables, except the habiliments and ornaments of the wife's body, which, though they be superfluous, and the husband insolvent, are not arrestable for his debts contracted thereafter. The husband hath the full and sole administration of all moveable goods belonging or accrescing to the wife during the marriage, and the rents and profits of heritable rights, as being moveable. And therefore an heritable bond was found to belong to the husband *jure mariti*, because he was married before the term of Whitsunday, at which term the annualrents became payable, June 15, 1627, Nicolson *contra* Lyle [Durie 296; M.5798]; and a sum was found to belong to the executors of the first husband, though the term of payment was after his decease, and not to the wife or her second husband. Also a legacy, left to a wife, was found to belong to her husband, Hope, Legacies, Brown *contra* Bannatine [*Sub nom. Lawson* v *Ballantine.* Hope, *Maj.Pr.*IV,2,4; M.5798]. Likewise a husband was found to have right to a bond, blank in the creditor's name, which the wife during the marriage put in the hands of a third party, who filled up his own name therein, though the husband and wife were voluntarily separate, February 11, 1634, Drummond *contra* Captain Rollo [Durie 702; M.6152], except aliments duly and competently provided for the wife, which are not arrestable for the husband's debt. And a husband himself was found to have no access to a sum provided to a wife by her father for her aliment, July 4, 1637, Tennent *contra* Futhy [Durie 848; M.10372].

This communion of goods by our custom extended not to the wife's heritable rights, as lands, annualrents, heritable bonds, nor to liferents, but only to the rents and profits thereof during the marriage, which the wife cannot prejudge by any deed during the marriage. But as to the stock and profits, she may dispose thereof, to take effect after the dissolution of the marriage: as to which the wife may oblige herself personally in clauses relative to such rights, as clauses to infeft, clauses of warrandice, and clauses of requisition of sums for which her lands are wadset, such obligements being effectual against the wife. And this is the difference betwixt these and other personal obligements of the wife *stante matrimonio*, which, even though the husband consent to, are null, and oblige her not.

In the heritable rights of wives, bonds bearing annualrent, though without a clause of infeftment, are comprehended; for these remain heritable *quoad fiscum et relictam* by the act of Parl. 1661, c. 32 [A.P.S. VII,230,c.244]. And therefore a provision by a father to his daughter, bearing annualrent at five per cent. was found not to fall under the husband's *jus mariti*, June 28, 1665, Pitcairn *contra* Edgar [1 Stair 290; M.5775]; July 4, 1676, Rollo *contra.* Brownlie [2 Stair 436; M.2653].

The *jus mariti* is so effectual as to the moveable goods of the wife, that though a liferenter in her second contract of marriage reserved a part of her liferent lands to be solely at her own disposal, and that the husband in the same contract of marriage renounced his *jus mariti* thereanent, yet that renunciation was found to be his *jure mariti*, and so the profits of her liferent were affected by his creditors, it not being constitute as a formal and a proportional aliment, as was found in the case of the creditors of Mr. Andrew Hamilton *contra* Lady Carberry, his wife [Referred to in M. 5835], and lately July 13, 1678, Nicolson *contra* Inglis [2 Stair 631 ; M. 5834].

From this communion of goods it follows also that there is a communion of debts, whereby the husband is liable for the wife's debt, though it should both exceed her and his moveables and the profits of the wife's land, or of her other heritable rights. But this was not found to hold in matters of wrong or criminal things. And so the husband was found not liable for a spuilzie or wrongous intromission committed by his wife without his knowledge or approbation during the marriage, February 2, 1628, Scot *contra* Banks and Neil [Spotiswoode, 156; M. 6015]. These were done *stante matrimonio* without the husband's consent. And yet the husband, found liable for the damage of a mill demolished by his wife, as being *præposita negotiis*, and by his domestic servants, though he was out of the country himself, Spotiswoode, Husband and wife, Laird of Ludquhairn *contra* Earl Marischal [Spotiswoode, 154 ; M. 13982]. Neither was a husband found liable for the penalty of the contravening the act of a kirk-session, *ut supra*. Yet a husband was found liable for his interest for his wife's tutor-compts, not only for what she was liable for during her widowity, but during the time of a former husband, his successor being always first discussed as to what was done in his time, March 28, 1629, Matthison *contra* L. Wariston [Durie 443 ; M. 5875], yea, without the discussing of the successors of the former husband, *primo loco*, where the intromission was before both marriages, but prejudice to the defender to pursue the heirs of the first husband as accords, February 18, 1663, Dunbar of Hemprigs *contra* Lord Fraser [1 Stair 181 ; M. 2367]. But a husband was not found liable for furniture given by merchants to his wife without his consent, she having gone to London without his warrant, except in so far as her ordinary expenses would have amounted to if she had staid at home, though her husband had not inhibite her, July 6, 1677, Allan *contra* Earl and Countess of Southesk [2 Stair 534 ; M. 6005].

After inhibition against wives, the husband is not liable for any thing they contract, except what is furnished suitable to their quality, and where the husband cannot instruct that he sufficiently provided his wife otherways, July 25, 1676, Campbell *contra* Laird of Abden [2 Stair 458; M. 5879]. The like was found about the same time concerning furniture to the Lady Monteith [*Sub nom. Auchinleck* v *E. Monteith*, 1 *Fol. Dic.* 393; M. 5879].

But this obligement of the husband being only for his interest *jure mariti*, the debt itself doth not properly become his, but only it may take effect against his person and goods during the marriage. But if that interest were dissolved by his own or his wife's death, before the legal execution be complete, affecting his goods, there will be no further process against him or his heirs. Yea though there was litiscontestation before the wife's death, the husband was found free, albeit he was ordained by interlocutor to find caution to pay what should be decerned, July 11, 1664, Dunbar of Hemprigs *contra* Lord Fraser [1 Stair 212; M. 5862]. So likewise a husband was decerned with his wife for his interest, she dying before execution, he was free of the debt, December 23, 1665, Dame Rachel Burnet *contra* Lepers [1 Stair 329; M. 5863]. So likewise a husband decerned with his wife for his interest, having died before execution, his successors were found free of the debt, Hope, Transferring, Kinloch *contra* Dunbar [Hope, *Maj. Pr.* VI, 8, 14]. But the contrary was found where the husband was denounced upon the decreet, and had sold his wife's portion of land, *ibidem*, Earl of Murray *contra* Lord St Colmb [Hope, *Maj. Pr.* VI, 8, 16]. The like, where the decreet against the husband, after his wife's decease, was only found effectual, in so far as might extend to his wife's third part of his moveables, February 7, 1629, Brown *contra* Dalmahoy [Durie 422; M. 5932]. And a husband was found liable for his wife's debt after her death, in so far as might be extended to the benefit of her liferent duties resting at her death, February 1, 1662, Cunninghame *contra* Dalmahoy [1 Stair 90; M. 2816 and 5870]. So the husband is always liable for his wife's debt, even after her death, *in quantum est lucratus*, which cannot be understood to be by every benefit or tocher, marriage being an onerous contract where a tocher is given, *ad sustinenda onera matrimonii*, and, therefore, he can only be accounted *lucratus*, when the benefit he hath by his wife doth far exceed these *onera*, December 23, 1665, Burnet *contra* Lepers [1 Stair 329; M. 5863]. And even in case he be *lucratus*, the wife's heritage must be first discussed, January 23, 1678, Wilkie *contra* Stuart and Morison [2 Stair 601; M. 5868]. Yea, a husband being charged summarily for his interest upon a decreet obtained against his wife before the marriage, and being denounced thereupon, yet not being undertaken by him, or affecting his goods before his death, he was liberate, March 20, 1627, Knows *contra* Kneiland [Durie 292; M. 5862]. The like, though not only horning was used against the husband, but arrestment thereupon, January 23, 1678, Wilkie *contra* Stuart and Morison [2 Stair 601; M. 5868]. But a husband having given bond of borrowed money for his wife's furniture, was found liable therefor after her death, July 7, 1680, Slowan *contra* Lord Bargainie [2 Stair 782; M. Supp. 102]. But that the husband's lands or heritable rights will be liable for his wife's debt, there is neither decision nor ground for it, these not being *in communione bonorum*. It is more dubious, and, for any thing I know, undecided, whether the heritable debt of the wife will affect the husband *quoad mobilia*. But seeing it is a communion of goods only moveable, it should be also only of moveable debts, though *in cuommni forma*, as tutors or curators, so husbands will be decerned generally for their interest: yet with this difference, that tutors and curators will be liable in so far as they have the pupil's means; but I never heard that there was a distinction made, whether the wife's debt did exceed the third part of the man's moveables, which is her proportion of the same; but indefinitely it hath effect against the husband's person by caption, or his moveables by poinding. But a wife's heritable bonds become not her husband's, though uplifted by her, or made moveable by a charge, during the marriage, seeing she then re-employed the money for annualrent, February 21, 1679, Cockburn *contra* Burn [2 Stair 701; M.5793]: for the wife's charge is not to make her heritable sums moveable, but to recover them. And albeit there is no mention in our custom of affecting a wife's goods for a husband's debt, because all her moveable goods and sums become his by the marriage, except her *paraphernalia*; yet if a husband's heritable rights could be affected for his wife's debt, there were the same reason that her heritable rights should be affected for his debt. But a husband's heritable debt affects the moveable goods and sums in the communion, as being the husband's.

18. These are the interests of the man and wife during the marriage. But before we come to their interests after the dissolution thereof, it is to be considered, that by our customs donations between man and wife, *stante matrimonio*, are revocable by the giver during life. Which our customs have taken from the civil law, where this reason is rendered. *Ne mutuo amore invicem spoliarentur* [D.24,1,1]. Thus a donation betwixt a man and his wife was found annulled by the husband's revocation upon death-bed, subscribed by notars, because of his infirmity, Hope, Husband and wife, Earl of Angus *contra* Countess of Angus [Hope, *Maj.Pr.* 11,17,35]. And a husband was allowed to recall a bond granted to his wife, bearing, that he thought it convenient that they should live apart, and therefore obliged him to pay a sum yearly for her aliment; albeit it bore also, that he should never quarrel or recall the same, as importing a renunciation of that privilege, February 6, 1666, Livingston *contra* Beg [1 Stair 348; M.6153]. Yea, a donation by a husband to his wife was found revoked by a posterior right to his children, though it was not a pure donation, but in lieu of another right, and *quoad excessum* only, seeing it was *notabilis excessus*, November 20, 1662, Children of Wolmet *contra* Lady Wolmet [1 Stair 141; M.1730]. And an infeftment, bearing lands and a mill, was found revocable as to the mill, it not being expressed in the wife's contract, February 5, 1667, Countess of Hume *contra* Hog [1 Stair 436; M.8895]. This was extended to a wife's accepting of an infeftment in satisfaction of her contract, February 12, 1663, Relict of Morison *contra* his Heir [1 Stair 177; M.9148]. It is also revocable indirectly by the husband's posterior disposition of the lands formerly disponed to his wife in liferent, July 16, 1622, Murray of Lochmaben *contra* Scot of Haining [Durie 25; M.1300]. So a donation by infeftment, granted by a man to his wife beside her contract, was found revoked by an annualrent out of these lands granted to his daughter *pro tanto*, without mention of revocation, December 15, 1674,

Kinloch *contra* Raith [2 Stair 293 ; M.11345]. But donations by a man to his wife, who had no former provision nor contract of marriage, was found not revocable, being in satisfaction of the terce due by the marriage, March 25, 1635, Laird of Louriston *contra* Lady Dunipace [Durie 764; M.6132]. And where the husband granted infeftment of all that he then had, there being no contract of marriage, and thereafter a second infeftment, both *stante matrimonio*, the first was sustained, being in place of a contract of marriage, but the second was found revocable, November 23, 1664, Halyburton *contra* Porteous [1 Stair 229 ; M.6136]. And a provision to a wife, having no contract of marriage, was found revocable, in so far as it exceeded a provision suitable to the parties, June 27, 1677, Short and Burnet *contra* Murrays [2 Stair 531 ; M.6124]. Yet the want of a contract did not sustain a donation by a wife to her husband, to whom she assigned an heritable bond, the husband being naturally obliged to provide for his wife, and not the wife for her husband, December 15, 1676, Inglis of Eastshiels *contra* Lowry of Blackwood [2 Stair 480 ; M.6131]. Yea a donation by a wife, by assignation of her former jointure to her husband's behoof, was found revocable, though there was no contract, unless the husband had given a remuneratory provision, January 22, 1673, Watson *contra* Bruce [2 Stair 157 ; M.6129]. And a wife's consent to a contract of wadset of her liferent-lands with a back-tack to the husband, was only found valid as to the creditor, but revocable as to the husband, that she might enjoy the superplus of the benefit of a back-tack, more than the annualrent, June 28, 1673, Arnot *contra* Scot and Frier [2 Stair 196 ; M.6091]. But a donation by a husband to his wife's children of a former marriage was found not revocable, though done at his wife's desire, January 15, 1669, Hamilton *contra* Banes [1 Stair 581 ; M.6107], nor by a wife subscribing her husband's testament, by which her liferent-lands were provided to her daughter [1,9,8, *infra*], July 12, 1671, Murray *contra* Murray [1 Stair 755 ; M.5689]. As all donations are revocable for ingratitude, so are donations between husbands and wives for adultery, though the party injured sought not divorce, Hope, *Donation inter virum et uxorem*, Douglas *contra* Aiton [Hope, *Maj.Pr.* 11,8,6]. A bond conceived to a man and wife, and her heirs, found a donation by the man, whose means it was presumed to be, and revocable by him after her death, and a tack taken by him to himself and his wife in liferent, was found revoked by a posterior tack thereof to himself and his brother's son, December 21, 1638, Laird of Craigmillar *contra* relict of Nisbet [Durie, 869; M.6089]; yet thereafter it was found, in the same case, January 30, 1639, that in respect the tack was set by a third person, and that it did not appear to be by the man's means, that the back-tack to the wife was not revoked. But a donation betwixt man and wife altering their contract of marriage, being done before the marriage itself, was not found revocable, January 23, 1680, Hume *contra* Humes [2 Stair 746 ; M.6093]. Yet where the donation did bear date before the marriage, the husband's heir proving the writ antedated, and that it was truly after the marriage, the donation was therefore found revocable,

July 24, 1677, Earl of Dunfermling *contra* Earl of Callendar [2 Stair 547; M. Supp. 70].

19. To come to the interest of the husband and wife after the dissolution of the marriage, we must distinguish the dissolution thereof, which falls by death within year and day from the solemnizing thereof, and that which is dissolved thereafter. For by our custom, if the marriage dissolve within year and day after the solemnizing thereof, all things done in contemplation of the marriage become void, and return to the condition wherein they were before the same, and in this our custom agrees to the civil law. And so the tocher returns back to the wife, or these from whom it came: and she hath no benefit or any interest either in his moveables or heritables, by law or contract provided to her; nor hath he any interest in hers; unless there were a living child born, which was heard cry or weep: in which case marriage hath the same effect as to all intents and purposes, as if it had endured beyond the year. And this is extended to both the marriage of maids and widows, July 23, 1634, Maxwell *contra* Harestones [Durie 732; M. 6160]. And extended also to an infeftment by a husband to a wife, though it had no relation to the marriage, but was only presumed to be *hoc intuitu*, November 16, 1633, Grant *contra* Grant [Durie 692; M. 1743]. And is not only extended to the wife and husband and their heirs, but to any other person concerned, restitution being made *hinc inde* of all done *intuitu matrimonii*, Haddington, June 8, 1610, Laird of Caddel *contra* Ross [Nicolson, *Fol. Dic.* 1,413; M. 6167]. Yea a disposition by a father to a son of his estate, in contemplation of his marriage, which was dissolved within year and day by the wife's death, was found void, seeing the father persisted not therein, but infeft his second son, July 16th, 1678, Lord Burley *contra* Laird of Fairny [2 Stair 633; M. 6172]. And a tocher, paid within the year, was ordained to be repaid without any deduction for the wife's entertainment during the marriage, but only for her clothes which were before the marriage, and her funeral charges which were after the marriage was dissolved, February 23, 1681, Gordon *contra* Inglis [2 Stair 867; M. 5924 and 6180]. But gifts, given to the married persons by the friends of both sides, were divided equally, the marriage being dissolved within year and day, January 14, 1679, Waugh *contra* Jamison [2 Stair 670; M. 6179] If a living child was born, the marriage was found effectual, though both child and mother died within the year, Spotiswood, Husband and wife, Stuart *contra* Irving [Spotiswoode 159; M. 6182]. The reason why the child must be heard cry, is to make certain its lively ripeness, and not to leave it to the conjecture of the witnesses; and therefore it sufficeth not though they should declare that the child was living immediately before the birth, and appeared lively and full ripe when it was born, but that it was stifled in the birth [1, 4, 12, *supra*; 11, 6, 19, *infra*]. Yet a wife's infeftment was found valid till her tocher was repaid, though the marriage dissolved within the year, July 20, 1664, Petrie *contra* Paul [1 Stair 220; M. 9136]. But where a marriage continued a year, and a part of the next day after the year, the tocher was found

not to return, *nam in favorabilibus dies cœptus habetur pro completo*, February 25, 1680, Waddel *contra* Salmond [2 Stair 763; M. 3465].

20. Marriage dissolveth by divorce, either upon wilful non-adherence, or wilful desertion, or by adultery, the party injurer loseth all benefit accruing through the marriage, as is expressly provided by the foresaid act of Parl. concerning non-adherence, 1573, c. 55 [A.P.S. IV, 233, c. 29]. But the party injured hath the same benefit as by the other's natural death, March 21, 1637, Lady Manderstoun *contra* Laird of Rentoun [Durie 840; M. 1741]. But if divorce follow upon impotency, all things return *hinc inde*, because in effect there was no marriage, as was found in the process Earl of Eglintoun *contra* Lady Eglintoun [Haddington, *Fol. Dic.* 1, 415; M. 6185].

21. By the dissolution of marriage, there ariseth to married persons not only these rights, which by voluntary contract are constitute to either, and which are not proper here, but also these, which by law and custom are competent without any special convention or covenant. And these are either upon the part of the husband, or more frequently upon the part of the wife. To the husband is competent the liferent of the wife's heritage, which, because it is peculiar unto these nations, it is said to be the courtesy of Scotland or England. To the wife ariseth her share of the moveables, which is the half, where the man hath no children *in familia*, and the third, where there are such, and her terce, which is the liferent of the third part of his lands during her life. But of reversions, heritable bonds, dispositions, or rights of lands without infeftment, and of teinds, or tacks, or tenements within burgh, the relict hath no terce. These rights of terce and courtesy fall in to be considered among the feudal rights; and the relict's third or half of moveables in the succession of moveables, wherein it is a concomitant, and regulate according to that which is proper to the succession either of children or others, though as to the wife it be rather division of that communion of moveable goods that was competent to the married persons during the marriage; and therefore shall be insisted on no further here, but left to their proper places [11, 6 and III, 8, *infra*]. And so we shall proceed to the next kind of obediential obligations, and natural rights, which intervene betwixt parents and children.

22. Law and custom hath favoured and privileged wives in many cases *propter fragilitatem sexus*, whereby they are free from obligements for sums of money, and from personal execution by horning or caption, if it be not for criminal causes. Their contracts of marriage were commonly thought preferable to other personal creditors, February 8, 1662, Crawfurd *contra* the Earl of Murray [1 Stair 95; M. 2613]; November 8, 1677, Sinclair *contra* Richardson [2 Stair 555; M. 5648]; but there was a contrary decision upon full hearing *in præsentia*, Keith *contra* Leith, February 17, 1688 [1 Fountainhall 498; M. 11833]. Their share of their husband's moveables is not burdened with the husband's heritable debt, December 23, 1668, Mackenzie *contra* Robertson [1 Stair 576; M. 5784]; July 19, 1664, Scrimgeour *contra* Murray [1 Stair 219; M. 463]. Yea a gratuitous moveable bond granted by a

husband, payable at his death, whereby the whole executry would be exhausted, and the wife have no share, having no other provision, the same was not found to affect the wife's share; but otherwise such bonds, granted in *liege poustie* without fraud, were found to come off the whole head, and not off the dead's part only, December 8, 1675, Thomsons *contra* Executors of Eleis Thin [2 Stair 376; M.3593 and 5939]. And a wife was found not excluded from her share of her husband's moveables by a gratuitous disposition, by her husband to his brother, of all sums that he should have at his death, January 10, 1679, Grant *contra* Grant [2 Stair 668; M.3596 and 5943]. In like manner the infeftments and provisions of wives are effectual, although the tocher, which is the mutual cause thereof, be not paid, she not being obliged therefor herself, though the contract bore, that, the tocher being paid, it should be employed to the wife's use, July 5, 1665, Mackie *contra* Stuart [1 Stair 295; M.11205]. The like, though the contract bore that the husband should employ the tocher for the wife in liferent, albeit the tocher was lost through the father's insolvency, June 11, 1670, Hunter *contra* Creditors of Peter [1 Stair 678; M.1687]. The like, though the contract bore that the wife should have no benefit while the tocher should be fully paid, if the tocher could be recovered by the husband's diligence, November 21, 1671, Menzies *contra* Corbet [2 Stair 5; M.6066]. On the same ground a contract of marriage, bearing the one half of the tocher to the wife, failing children, albeit conceived *passive*, and not that the husband was to pay the same, or do diligence therefor; yet the husband was found liable to pay the half of the tocher, although it was not recovered, unless he had done the diligence of a provident man, which was found implied in his duty and trust as a husband, the wife being *in potestate viri*, July 14, 1676, Lockhart and L. Raploch her spouse *contra* Bonar [2 Stair 449; M.Supp.57]. And though husbands have no communion in the habiliments and ornaments of the wife, which cannot be affected for his debt; yet she hath her share of the habiliments of the husband, which falls in his executry; and he is obliged to pay all accounts for her habiliments, suitable to her quality. But where the wife had an alimentary provision for her habiliments, ornaments, and her other uses, the husband having furnished them, and received that sum, was not found liable to repay the same to her executors, February 2, 1667, Executors of Lady Piltoun *contra* Hay of Balhousie [1 Stair 434; M.5826]. Wives have not only a half or third of their husband's moveables when they survive, but have their aliment to the next term after the husband's death. Yea a wife was found to have right to the expenses of child-bed of a posthumous child, born after the father's death, against the eldest son, though he was not heir, but as having an universal disposition to his father's means, which was very considerable; and which disposition was granted after the posthumous child's conception, November 10, 1671, Hastie and Ker his Mother *contra* Hastie [2 Stair 1; M.416 and 5922]. And likewise, if the wife predecease, her executors have the half or third of her husband's moveables, the best of every kind being set aside as heirship moveables, though there could be no heir for the time, the husband being alive, December 8, 1668, Guidlat *contra* Nairn [1 Stair 568 ; M. 5404].

Title 5. Obligations between Parents and Children

THAT there are natural obligations betwixt parents and children, not proceeding from the consent of either party, or from the constitution of any human law, but from the obedience man oweth to his Maker, who hath written this law in the hearts of parents and children, as to their interests and duties, with capital letters, is evident by the common consent of all the nations of the world, how barbarous soever. And though evil custom hath put out the eyes of natural light in other things, yet in this the rays of the sun of righteousness are so direct, that their illumination cannot be extinguished. And these obligations are so firm, that in most things they cannot be taken off, nor discharged by men. Though children would discharge their parents of natural affection, education, provision, &c. or parents would free their children of reverence, obsequiousness, and of entertainment of parents not able to entertain themselves ; yet would these obligations still be binding upon either. These obligations are placed in the common nature that man hath with other animals, and so are given as evident instances of the law of nature, l. 2. *ff. de justitia et jure* [D. 1, 1, 2].

We shall then consider what these are : and first, what interests the parents have in the persons of their children ; secondly, in what they are naturally bound to their children ; thirdly, what interest the children have in the goods of their parents ; fourthly, what they naturally do owe to their parents ; fifthly, what they are bound in to each other.

2. For the first, ere we can distinctly know the power parents have over their children, we must distinguish the capacity and ages of the children : whereof there are three, infancy or pupillarity, minority or less age, and majority or full age. So doth Aristotle distinguish them *Polit. lib 1. cap. ult. Ethic. lib. 4. cap. 3 & lib. 5. cap. 10 ;* and after him Grotius *de jure belli & pacis, lib. 2. cap. 5.*

3. Infancy is, when the children are without discretion ; and then they are wholly in the power of their parents, who not only may, but must carry them whither, and keep them where they will ; and must also breed and order them according to their capacities, means and qualities. And this is rather an

act of dominion in the parents, than from any obligation of the children to submit to them.

4. It will not much be debated, but the direction of children in their minority is naturally stated in their parents, but the greatest question will remain, of their full age, when the children become able to govern themselves, and their own affairs: and as to that, it is the opinion of some, that it standeth alone, *in pietate et reverentia*, Steph. [Mathias Stephani] *Oeco. juris civilis, cap. 7* and *Vinnius, partitionum l. 1 cap. 7, in principio*, sheweth that the custom of Holland dissolveth the power of fathers by the children's age of 25 years.

5. Whatsoever may arise from the custom of nations, whereby the power of parents over their children in their full age is much diminished, yet by the original and pure law of nature, not only the tutory and protection of children's infancy with the care and direction of their minority, is in their parents; but there is also an economic authority in the father of the family over all his children and descendants, remaining in his family, whom he hath not elocat by marriage (which is also a natural bond) unto other families, whereby the females do naturally change their families, and become under the power of another family.

6. This is the only natural authority and government, which had in itself all authority, public, private, civil and criminal, till by human constitution and divine approbation, most of that power is now devolved upon magistrates. This power was not only before magistracy, but even remained thereafter with subordination thereto in most nations. As Cæsar, *de bello Gallico, lib. 2* writes, that among the Gauls and Belgæ parents had the power of life and death. The like power had the Romans anciently *l. in suis haeredibus, 11 ff. de liberis et posthumis* [D. 28, 2, 11], *l. libertati, 10. Cod. de patria potestate* [C. 8, 46, 10]. Aristotle testifieth the like of the Persians *lib. 8 Ethic. cap. 12.* And by the judicial law *Deut. 21 vers. 18*, the rebellious son, who obeyed not the voice of his father and mother, was to be brought forth before the elders of his city, and stoned to death, without other proof than the parents' testimony : so that the sentence was the parents', though the execution was to be public. Such authority was that of the patriarchs Abraham, Isaac, and Jacob, who with divine approbation made war, peace, and confederacies, which are now the public and proper rights of magistracy, and governed their own families, without any authority derived from others. And though Jacob's family arose to that greatness, that in it were many families, yet he remained the father and prince of them all : so that the several subordinate families had their subordinate authority over their wives and children ; and so their children were bound in obedience to them, but with the exception of their superior parents, to whom the first obedience is due ; as to the differences, arising between insubordinate posterity, they remained under the authority of the common fathers.

This natural authority reacheth all children, whether procreate of lawful marriage or not, so they be truly known to be children ; because the same foundation and common principles and duties are in both, though they have not the same interest in the father's goods, in respect of that community of goods betwixt man and wife in the conjugal society, even naturally, whence the goods are derived to the issue of the lawful marriage.

This paternal authority doth not necessarily carry the property and disposal of the goods of the children; but that they are capable of such by the gift of their parents, or others, or any otherways, even in infancy; and that they have the full dominion and administration thereof in their full age. And therefore bonds of provision by fathers to children, if delivered, are not revocable directly, nor indirectly, by contracting debts thereafter. And the delivery of such bonds of provision makes them irrevocable, whether the delivery be to the children, or to any other for their behoof; (which behoof will be presumed, unless the father express his mind at the delivery, that the writ is to be returned to himself, or depositate upon terms); and, therefore, a bond taken by a father in the name of his brother, the father obtaining an assignation from him to his daughter, the bond was not found revocable by the father, being registrate in the brother's name, November 20, 1667, Executors of Trotter *contra* Trotter [1 Stair 487; M.11499]. Children's provisions by bond, granted after testament, nominating them executors, was found not to import that they should have the executry, and that the heir is obliged to pay the bonds of provision, but the bond being moveable, should [first] affect the executry, Feb. 22, 1677, Belshes of Tofts *contra* Belshes [2 Stair 519; M.6327]. And a father, granting bond to a bairn in satisfaction of her portion natural, was not found thereby to apply that bairn's portion natural to the heir, executor or universal legatar, though they would be liable for payment of the bond; but to apply that bairn's share to the rest of the bairns, who thereby will have the whole bairns' part, February 17, 1671, Macgill *against* the Viscount of Oxford [1 Stair 723; M.8179]. For bonds of provision, delivered in *liege poustie*, do as other debts affect the whole executry; and where all the bairns had bonds of provision, none bearing "in satisfaction," they had also their bairns' part of the executry, July 16, 1678, Murrays *contra* Murrays [2 Stair 635; M.2372]. But bairns' provisions, payable at such an age, and not bearing the proportion of the deceasing to accresce to the surviving, the share of these bairns, who died before that age without issue, was not found due, February 22, 1677, Belshes of Tofts *contra* Belshes [2 Stair 519; M.6327. See 1,3,7,*supra*]. And whereas the delivery of writs in other cases is presumed from the date, if they be in the person's hands in whose favours they are granted: but in competition with other creditors, the delivery of bonds of provision is not presumed to have been from the date, but that must be instructed by some evidence, as taking seasin, registration, or witnesses, who saw the same in the hands of the children, or others to their behoof, and in that case they are valid, if there be no fraud or prejudice to creditors by insolvency. And, therefore, bonds of provision to children were reduced upon the eldest son's contract of marriage, though posterior, January 10, 1668,

Laird of Glencorse *contra* his brothers and sisters [1 Stair 501 ; M. 16995];
and a posterior tocher was preferred to a prior assignation to a bairn in
family unless the prior delivery were also proven, 14th November, 1676,
Major Inglis *contra* Boswells [2 Stair 462 ; M. 11568]; July 22, 1668, Johnston of Sheins *contra* Arnold [1 Stair 557 ; M. 958. See 1, 7, 14 ; 1, 8, 2 ; III, 8,
45–46, *infra*].

From this paternal power it follows, that the parents may contain and keep
their children in their families; and that they are obliged to employ their service and work for the common interest of the family; and what thence arises
is the parents', not their own; which doth always endure, till, by consent of
the parents they become *forisfamiliat*, whereby they may employ their work
and service for themselves alone.

Thus the interest of parents in the persons and good of their children, by
the law of nature, being cleared : as to the natural obligations of parents toward their children (beside their obligations that stand, and are acted in the
mind and affections, which the law respecteth not, but these only, *quæ non
mente, sed manu, tenentur*,) the main obligations are education and provision.
The education of children consisteth not only in the care and entertainment
of them during infancy, but especially in breeding of them for some calling
and employment according to their capacity and condition.

7. The duty of providing of children comprehends not only their aliment
and entertainment in meat, clothes, medicine and burial, which may be competent during the parent's life, but also competent provision after the parent's
death ; for the apostle saith, That he that careth not for his own family, is
worse than an infidel, *1 Tim. 5. vers. 8.* And in both, the ability of the parent
and the necessity of the children is to be considered. For if the children be
competently provided *aliunde*, the parents are not bound: and though the
children be necessitous, yet there must first be reserved for the parents that
which is necessary for subsistence; so that, when they are not able to entertain
their children, they may lawfully expose them to the mercy and charity of
others. But a father, though indigent, was decerned to receive his son (having
no means or calling) into his family, or to pay him a modification, January 13,
1666, Dick *contra* Dick [1 Stair 337 ; M. 409]. But a father was not found
liable to pay a merchant for furniture given to his son, where he gave his son
an allowance in money for his clothes, January 20, 1672, Wallace *contra*
Crawford of Camlarg [2 Stair 53 ; M. 13425]. Neither was a father found liable
for his daughter's bridel-furniture, to a merchant whom he prohibite to give
them off, but the daughter and her husband, July 10, 1672, Neilson *contra*
Guthrie and Gairn [2 Stair 98 ; M. 5878]. And a mother was found obliged to
receive her children into her family (but for no other modification) though
they were noble persons, there being none, representing the father, able to
entertain them, February 23, 1666, Children of the Earl of Buchan *contra* the
Countess of Buchan [1 Stair 365 ; M. 411].

As to the interest children have in the goods of their parents, it is to be considered, as either during the parents' life, or after their death. For the interest they have after their parents' death, it falleth in to be considered among the conveyances of rights by succession, of which in its proper place. But during the parents' life they have no real right of dominion or property in the parents' goods : for though the parents be obliged naturally to entertain and educate their children out of their goods, yet that is but a personal right, and entitleth not the children to meddle with their parents' goods upon that pretence ; as Solomon saith Prov. 28, vers. 24 : "Whoso robbeth his father and mother, and saith, it is no transgression ; the same is the companion of a destroyer."

8. The obligation of children toward their parents consists mainly in their obedience to them, and their duty to aliment and supply them in all their necessities according to the children's ability. Their obedience to their parents is much cleared from that power and authority their parents have over them, of which we have spoken already. For unto authority, or power of command, subjection or obedience answers, as the correlate : so that as the paternal power was most over the children when in their family, and least after their forisfamiliation, so are the duties of obedience proportional. But after emancipation, those duties are so far diminished, that little remaineth except that natural reverence, tenderness, and obsequiousness, that children do still owe to their parents in due order : which, though it hath no civil remeids, yet it remains a natural obligation to observe the parents' commands throughout their posterity ; as in that notour example of the Rechabites, Jer. xxxv. is clear, where they observe their father's commands in a free thing, though inconvenient, viz. To drink no wine, to build no houses, &c. and for their obedience the Lord promises there should not be wanting a man of them to stand before the Lord for ever. But while they are in the family, they are not only under the economic government of their parents, in so far as is not devolved upon the magistrate, but specially they are bound to abide with their parents, and to employ their service for their parents, and for the use of the family, whereunto their parents may compel them by their own proper authority. And parents have action against all others who shall hinder them to keep their children with them, or lead them whither, and employ them, as they please.

9. The obligation of aliment and relief to parents in necessity is due both by the law of nature, and hath in it also that remuneratory obligation, whereby children ought to retribute to, and recompense their parents for their education and entertainment. And though it be said 2 Cor. 12,14. That children ought not to lay up for the parents, but the parents for the children ; yet it is to be understood of that care, foresight, and providence, that parents ought to have, not only to provide things necessary for themselves, but for their children also after them ; which, being an ordinary duty, ought to be in their thoughts and consideration, and is not incumbent to the children; it being but rare and unexpected, that parents' necessities put them to expect

relief from their children; or else it is to be taken comparatively, that the
parents are rather to lay up for the children, than children for the parents.
Solon's law made the children infamous who did not aliment their parents.
And Cicero in his oration *De Responsis Haruspicum* saith, *Parentibus nos
primum natura constituit debitores, quos non alere nefarium est.*

In these natural obligations of aliment betwixt parents and children, the
order of nature must be observed, that the nearest are first to be preferred,
and the paternal line before the maternal, as being in another family : for even
the distinction of families, and union thereof in the paternal power, is
natural, as before is said. From the same ground, parents must first aliment
their children in the family : and amongst those that are emancipate, the
males are preferable to the females, who pass by marriage into other families.

10. As to the natural obligation of children amongst themselves, there is
no doubt but that there naturally lie greater obligations upon them, each to
other, than the common obligations betwixt man and man : Which are not
only greater in the measure and degrees, as to love them, assist them, support
them, and supply their necessities the more, by how nearer a degree of blood
they are bound to them than to others, which is commonly acknowledged by
all ; but the Romans and many other nations have acknowledged the natural
obligation of brothers and sisters to aliment each other ; though our custom
hath not authorized the same, unless the brother were heir to the father in a
competent estate, and the remanent children not at all provided : in which case
the lords have modified an aliment to them, January 24, 1663, the Children
of Wedderlie *contra* the Heir [*Sub nom. Netherlie*, 1 Stair 161; M.415]. Aliment was also found due by a brother to a sister of a second marriage (who
had a portion to be paid at her age of fourteen), and no annualrent or aliment
in the mean time, though they had a mother on life, February 11, 1663,
Frazer *contra* Frazer [1 Stair 176 ; M.415]. The like found due by an heir-male
to heirs of line till their marriage, seeing their portions bore no annualrent
January 8, 1663, Lady Otter *contra* Laird of Otter [1 Stair 152; M.414],
November 12, 1664, Daughters of Balmerino *contra* Heir-male thereof [1
Stair 225 ; M.Supp. 1]. It is also a natural obligation upon children, or kinsfolk descending from one common stock, to defend, and have the tuition of,
the pupillarity of that race which is incumbent ordinarily to the next degree
in that same family: and this is the natural rise of tutors, of which in the next
title.

11. The Romans did no more diminish the conjugal interests and obligations competent by nature, (as is before shown) than they have exceeded the
law of nature in the interests betwixt parents and children. For thereby the
parent's power was so great, that no nation hath the like, §2, *Institut. de patria
potestate* [Inst. 1,9,2] it being almost dominical, and the children as servants,
l. placet 79, ff. de acquirenda haered [D.29,2,79]. The father had also the power
of life and death *l. ult. Cod. de patria potestate* [c.8,46,10], *l. in suis 11, ff. de
liberis et posthumis* [D.28,2,11]. They had power also to sell their children

unto servitude. This was the ancient Roman law, whereof the austerity was by little and little corrected by their recent law; so that both in servants and children it was taken off, and this power retrenched to cases of extreme necessity *l.2, Cod. de patribus qui filios* [c. 4,43,2]. Children were permitted also to have goods of their own, which were called *peculium*, in which they were as free, and had all their rights and actions competent, as others; but with these restrictions, whereby the right of the father in the goods of the children was much abated; for in the *peculio*, which the sons acquired by arms, or liberal arts, the fathers had no power, which was called *peculium castrense vel quasi castrense l.2,ff. ad Senatus c. Maced.* [c.4,28,2]. Of other goods which befel the children, or were acquired, and came not from the father, which were therefore called *adventitious*, the father had the usufruct and administration only, but not the property or power of alienation *l.2, Cod. de bonis maternis* [c.6,60,2]. Only *in profectitio peculio*, which came from the father, he had full right and property, and all permitted to the son was to make use of, and manage it, until it was recalled by the father. In *peculiis castrensibus vel quasi*, children were as fathers of families, by recent law, *l. filius familias 39,ff. de oblig.* [D.44,7,39]. Yea even the usufruct ceased in goods given or left to the children, excluding the parents *Nov.117 in principio* [Nov.117, Cap.1]. 2. Next, where any thing was given or left to both jointly. 3. When the goods came by the father's fault, as when he did unjustly divorce with the mother *Nov.117 de haered.cap.10* [Nov.117,cap.10].

12. The custom of neighbouring nations does follow more closely the natural law, as the custom of France and the Netherlands is recorded by Gudelinus *De jure Noviss.cap.13*. And Matthias Stephanus testifieth the like of the custom of Germany *Oecon. juris civilis, lib.2.cap.67§4*. The custom of this nation also keepeth close to what is expressed before of the natural law, as to the interests and obligations of parents and children. And thereby aliments are frequently decerned to children, to be paid by their fathers, if they expel them from their families: and that not only by the act of parliament [Liferent Caution Act 1491, c.25; A.P.S. 11,224,c.6], providing aliment to heirs of lands, to be paid by the liferenters; but a father, though his son had no lands, was found convenable *super jure naturæ alendi liberos*, July 21, 1636, Laird of Ramorney *contra* Law [Durie 819; M.388]. So also by our custom a father is tutor of law to his sons being pupils. And, therefore, a father was found liable to the son for annualrent of his mother's third of moveables, remaining in the father's hands, February 4, 1665, Beg *contra* Beg [1 Stair 264; M.16273]. But a father was not found obliged for annualrent of a legacy belonging to his son, uplifted by him, seeing he alimented the son, December 15, 1668, Winram *contra* Elleis [1 Stair 570; M.11433]. A father is also curator to his children, especially when in his family, unless other curators be chosen by his consent. But a father, being poor, was not allowed to lift his son's money, without finding caution to make it forthcoming, February 12, 1633, Given *contra* Richardson [Durie 670; M.16263]. Neither might a

father, being *lapsus bonis*, assign a tack, acquired by him, to his son, though he might uplift the duties as administrator, January 29, 1629, Lands *contra* Douglas and Lands [Durie 419 ; M. 16250]. So deeds done by such minors, without their father's consent as lawful administrator, were found null, February 14, 1666, Fairholm *contra* McKenzie [Not found, unless same case as 1 Stair 409 ; M. 8959].

After pupillarity, a father is no more tutor to his children : and so might not discharge for his daughter, being past pupillarity, but only consent with her as curator, June 26, 1610, Forrest *contra* Forrest [Haddington MS]. A father is lawful administrator, both as tutor and curator, *honorarie*, of himself, without any cognition or solemnity ; and is not liable for omission ; neither is he exclusive of other curators. But deeds, done without a father's consent by a son, were found null, albeit the son resided not in his family, but followed the law, having no calling or patrimony to maintain himself, but living on his father's charges : neither was his father's subscribing with him found a sufficient authorizing of him, seeing he subscribed with his father as cautioner for him, December 7, 1666, Mackenzie *contra* Fairholm [1 Stair 409 ; M. 8959 ; 1,6,33, *infra*].

13. As to the father's power to keep his children within his family, and to apply their work for his use, though controversies in that point have seldom been moved, but the matter transacted by consent, it is not to be doubted but that children may be compelled to remain with their parents, and to employ their service for their use, even after their majority ; unless they be forisfamiliat by marriage, or by education in a distinct calling from their parents ; or unless their parents deal unnaturally with them, either by atrocity, or unwillingness to provide them with a competent marriage in due time, and with means suitable to their condition ; for that obligement to provide for them would be a ground of exception against them, if they would unjustly detain them in these cases ; or if the father countenance or allow the children to live by themselves, and to manage their own affairs apart ; from whence his tacit consent to their emancipation may be inferred. In which cases also Zasius *in l. utrum turpem 107, ff. De verb. oblig* [D. 45, 1, 107] and Matthias Stephanus *Oecon. juris civilis, lib. 2, cap. 1* doth declare that the conseutude of Germany is the same with our customs before expressed. The English account children to be emancipate so soon as they pass their minority, Cowell, *Institut. juris Anglicani*, Tit. 12 §4.

Title 6. Obligations between Tutors and Curators, and their Pupils and Minors; between Persons Interdicted and their Interdictors

TUTORS and curators, succeeded in the place of parents, and their obligations have a near resemblance; and therefore shall be here fitly subjoined. Though in the constitution and duties of tutors and curators the positive law predomineth, yet that without any positive law or contract there is a duty of tuition and protection of orphans, and specially upon these, who be relation of blood are their nearest kinsmen, and in place of their parents, it will appear by what ensueth; and what is superadded (either by the consent of parties, in curators, or by the law, in tutors, with the condition and interest of pupils and minors) cannot conveniently be separated. If there were no positive law, the natural infirmity of pupilage would not want its natural remedies, provided by Him, who is the father of the fatherless, and layeth his obediential obligations upon these whom, by the law written in their hearts, he hath bound to the performance of these duties, as is before [1, 1, 15, *supra*] shown. There is a common obediential, or natural obligation upon all men of love, mercy, and relief of the distressed, among whom infants and pupils who have no discretion, and cannot at all preserve or govern themselves, are the first. It hath been also shown [1, 5, 10, *supra*] that there is a more special obligation put upon those of one blood, one family, from one common parent, to help and support each other, of which in order.

2. The first and nearest degree is first and most obliged; hence ariseth that orderly and comely, natural, substitution of tutors for the preservation of pupils. First, The father's tutory and lawful administration whereof we have spoken already; and these failing by death or incapacity, the nearest degree

of agnates are in the place of parents, and are all jointly bound to this natural duty ; unless the parents, by their paternal power, have appointed and ordained others, whom they trust, to undertake that work. But because the privilege of primogeniture with us gives the succession to the eldest male and his representatives, therefore our law lays the burden of tuition, with the benefit of succession, to the male, to the next of line, if he be past twenty-five years of age ; if not, to the next agnate of that age ; but regardeth not the females or their succession, they not being so fit for the office of tutory, unless, upon particular confidence, they be named by the defunct.

And, lastly, the common obligation, that lieth upon people, hath devolved upon the magistrate, as representing them, the duty of being or appointing tutors for pupils. Hence doth arise the distinction of tutors in testamentar, constitute by the parent in his testament ; legitim, appointed by the law, which is of the nearest agnate ; and dative, which are ordained by the king.

3. The natural obligations of these tutors to their pupils are, first, to preserve their persons, and defend them against injuries and prejudices. And, therefore, they are named tutors, *quasi tuitores, l. 1. §ff. de tutelis* [D. 26, 1, 1]. 2. To aliment them out of the pupils' own means, according to the condition thereof ; and to educate them for a station in the commonwealth according to their quality and capacity. 3. To manage their affairs with such diligence as provident men use in their own affairs, that nothing may be lost, but every thing improven to the best advantage ; in all which they are not to exerce voluntary acts of dominion at their choice, as disposing of what is secure, but only necessary acts for the preservation and recovery of what will or may perish, and for improving the profits of it. 4. They are bound to give an account, and to restore to the pupil what is his own, so soon as he attains to the age of discretion.

4. On the other part, the pupil is obliged to the tutor, by the obediential bond of remuneration, or recompence of one good deed for another, to make up to the tutors whatsoever is wanting to them through their faithful administration. This is all the substance of the interests and obligations of tutors and pupils, which the positive law doth no more but declare, apply, and ascertain, by the form of entering that office, the security for performance of it, the fixed time of endurance thereof, which naturally is the age of discretion, in some sooner, in some later, in some never ; but, for certainty's cause, positive law determines a particular year in which, for the most part, discretion is attained.

That there are such interests and obligations even naturally, the light of nature will so easily go along, that it will rather need consideration than confirmation, the grounds thereof being commonly acknowledged and accustomed by all men, who are led by reason ; and it is so insinuate by the ordinary term of law, whereby these obligations are called *quasi ex contractu,* as arising from no contract betwixt the tutor and the infant or pupil, as not capable of contracting, and yet are not simply by the constitution of law ;

and therefore these obligations, not being by the will of man, must needs be obediential obligations by the will of God.

The Romans have in this matter kept clearly and closely by the law of nature; and therefore our customs have kept as near by them; and so have the customs of other nations. So says Gudelinus *de jure noviss. lib. 10. cap. 8 § fin.* that the custom of France and Netherlands hath very little altered in this from the Roman law. We shall therefore interweave the civil law and our customs, that it may appear how far they do agree and differ, and how they do quadrate to the law of nature; following this order: 1. What kinds of tutors there is, and what is the order of the same; 2. What the tutors' duties are in their entry, administration and accompts; 3. How tutories end; 4. The pupil's obligation to them therefore; and, lastly, The resemblance that curators and minors have with tutors and pupils.

5. As to the first, there be three kinds of tutors by the civil law and our custom (beside that of the father, who is called for distinction's sake, lawful administrator, of which formerly), and the tutors of idiots or furious persons. The first is the tutor testamentar or nominate; the second is, the tutor of law; and the third is the tutor dative; all which follow in course in the same order.

6. A tutor testamentar by the civil law behoved to be either named in the testament, or codicils confirmed by the testament *l. 3 ff. de testamentaria tutela* [c. 5, 28, 3] and could only be given to such as were *in patria potestate § 3 Inst. de tutelis* [Inst. 1, 13, 3]. But by our custom a father may nominate tutors to his children in any writ he pleases; but it is of a testamentary nature, always ambulatory and mutable during his life. A grandfather cannot name tutors to his oyes, because, his son being emancipate by marriage, they are not in his paternal power; neither can a mother or grandmother, who have also no such power. But any person that gives or dispones any thing to a pupil, may in that disposition name tutors; who are not properly such, but only have the trust and charge of the thing disponed, and as to it exclude all other tutors; which taketh place because that nomination is a quality and condition in the donation, January 31, 1665, Kirktouns *contra* L. of Hunthill [*Sub nom. Kirktons* v *Hunthill*, 1 Stair 261; M. 12531].

7. A tutor testamentar requires no preparatory solemnity to capacitate him to act, but the very nomination itself is sufficient: and, if it be in a testament, it is valid, though the testament be never confirmed, or be rejected by the executors. And so there needs no making of faith, or finding caution, because it is presumed, the father that did name him, did sufficiently know his faithfulness and fitness. And the confirmation of a testament, bearing that a tutor nominate accepted and made faith, was not found to instruct his acceptance, without the principal act subscribed by him were produced, or acts of administration proven, though it was thirty-seven years since the confirmation, January 31, 1665, Rutherfords *contra* L. of Hunthill [*Sub nom. Kirktons* v *Hunthill*, 1 Stair 261; M. 12531]. Neither was a tutory found instructed by a discharge as tutor testamentar, it being evident by the testament

that he was only overseer, June 10, 1665, Swinton *contra* Notman [1 Stair 279 ; M. 16273]. But a writ under the tutor's hand, designing him tutor, found to instruct, unless the contrary were proven by production of the tutory, December 2, 1668, Seatoun *contra* Seatoun [1 Stair 567 ; M. 2185 and 12767]. And a tutor nominate with other two, who accepted not, was only found liable from the time of his acceptance, by acting as tutor, and not for what was lost before ; although there was a considerable legacy left to him in the testament, and that shortly after the defunct's death he confirmed himself *qua* legatar, and had inspection of the defunct's writs, and subscribed an inventory thereof, whereof the testament was one, yet did not act as tutor for three years after : but he was not found to have right to the legacy, not having followed the defunct's will by accepting the tutory at first, February 2, 1675, Scrimzeor *contra* Wedderburn [2 Stair 314 ; M. 6357].

8. A tutor testamentar is ever preferred to a tutor of law or dative, even though the tutor nominate did forbear to act for seven years, and a tutor dative was constitute, and in possession of the custody of the pupil's person, December 17, 1631, Auchterlonie *contra* Oliphant [Durie 610 ; M. 16258], 6th July, 1627, Campbell *contra* Campbell [Durie 304; M. 16246] or though the tutor nominate had ceased six years, and was curator to a party, against whom the pupil had an action or process ; seeing in both cases no detriment could be shown by his forbearance. The like where the tutor nominate had abstained seven years, and yet was preferred to the custody of the pupil's person (here the pupil had no means to be administered) Spots. *de tutel.* Irving *contra* Irving [Spotiswoode, 348 ; M. 16260].

If there be no tutor nominate, there is place for tutors of law, who ordinarily are these who have the benefit of succession in the pupil's estate. And so by the Roman law, all the agnates of the nearest degree, as they were heirs, so were they also tutors by the law of the twelve tables *l. 5 & 6, ff. de legit. tut.* [D. 26, 4, 5 and 6] and so, after the succession was extended as well to the cognates as to the agnates, with the benefit thereof, the burden also of the tutory was extended *Nov. 118. cap. 5.* And with us upon the same ground, as the prerogative of primogeniture hath given the succession, not to the whole next degree of agnates, but to the eldest male and his issue, so the tutor of law is only one, viz. the nearest agnate or kinsman on the father's side, of twenty-five years of age, Parl. 1474, c. 51 [Tutors Act, 1474, c. 51 ; A.P.S. 11, 106, c. 6], where it is expressly declared, "That though the tutor of law be ordinarily heir, yet not always : for though the pupil have a younger brother, who is immediate agnate, yet the nearest agnate of twenty-five years old will be his tutor, passing by all others within that age."

9. The tutor of law is served, upon a brieve directed out of the chancery [IV, 3, 6, *infra*], by an inquest, as appears by the foresaid act of Parliament. But the brieve may be directed to, and served by, any judge-ordinary, though the pupil live not within the jurisdiction, March 8, 1636, Stewart *contra* Henderson [Durie 801 ; M. 9585]. Tutors of law, before they act, must find cau-

tion *rem pupilli salvam fore.* And by the act Ch. 2. Parl. 2. Sess. 3. Cap. 2 [i.e. Charles II, Parl. 2, Sess. 3, cap. 2; Tutors and Curators Act, 1672, c. 2; A.P.S. VIII, 59, c. 2], "All tutors and curators must make inventory of the pupil's estate, heritable or moveable, upon intimation to the friends on the father's side and mother's side, or if they appear not, by sight of the judge-ordinary; with three copies, one to the father's friends, one to the mother's friends, and one to remain with the clerk, without which, they can neither act nor authorise."

10. The tutor of law must serve himself within year and day from the time that he is in a capacity to be tutor, either counting from the defunct's death, or from the birth of the pupil if posthumous, or the ceasing of a just impediment. So that after the marriage of a tutrix testamentar, place was found for a year for the tutor of law to serve himself before a dative had access, July 15, 1631, Grant *contra* Grant [Durie, 596; M. 16257].

11. Where there is no tutor nominate, nor the tutor of law claimeth right within the year, there is place for a tutor dative; which, though by divers municipal customs may be constitute by the ordinary magistrate of the place, yet is most fitly constitute by the supreme magistrate; and so with us is given by the king in exchequer. And by the late Act of Parl. 1672 [Tutors and Curators Act, 1672 c. 2; A.P.S. VIII, 59, c. 2], it is appointed, "That before constituting of any tutor dative, the pupil's nearest friends on both sides shall be cited, that they may offer and inform concerning the fittest persons to be tutors." Tutors may be given to strangers' pupils in so far as concerns their lands in Scotland, December 17, 1627, Donaldson *contra* Brown [Durie 322; M. 4647]. In the giving tutors dative, though it be in the arbitrement of the king to choose whom he thinks fit, yet he will have regard to the interest of the pupil, to give a tutor either who was nominate by the father, but not legally, or who was nominate by the mother or grandmother, though having no legal power, or the nearest of kin, though they have neglected to serve within the year. But of all these he may take the best of such as offer or are willing, seeing with us all tutors are free to accept or refuse. But tutory being a public office it could not be refused among the Romans, unless the tutor had excuses allowed of the law *Tit. de excus. tut. ff. per totum.* [D. 27, 1].

Tutors dative must both make faith *de fideli administratione*, and find caution, the sufficiency whereof is in the magistrates' trust. And amongst the Romans an ordinary or inferior magistrate or his heirs were liable *pro dolo aut lata culpa*, if the caution taken by them were not found sufficient, *Tit. ff. de Magistratu conveniendo* [D. 27, 8]; but not the greater magistrates, as the Pretor, or President, who, through the eminency of their office, could not so particularly know, but were necessitate to trust to the relation of others, *l. 1. ff. tit. eodem.*

12. These that act as tutors, not knowing but that they are such, or otherways fraudulently knowing they are not such, are therefore called pro-tutors; and are liable for all the duties of real tutors during the time of their acting.

And by the civil law they were liable to make up his interest, whom by fraud they had deceived by acting as tutors *Tit. ff. quod falso tut.* Whence it follows, that such actings were not void. But if the person had been long holden and repute tutor, the deed would likely be sustained, unless annulled because of the pupil's lesion. There had no decision occurred with us, to show whether pro-tutors are obliged for their intromission only, or also for their omission : But a case occurring June 10, 1665, Swinton *contra* Notman [1 Stair 279; M. 16273], who, being nominate an overseer, intromitted, after long debate the lords found that an overseer acting under the name of tutor (but by a false designation, contrary to the testament), should be liable only for such kinds of things, and for the annualrents thereof, as he intromitted with; for seeing he had no law or custom regulating the case, the defender could be only condemned according to equity; but they declared by an act of sederunt, that whosoever in time coming meddled with pupils' or minors' means as pro-tutors or pro-curators, should be liable from henceforth as tutors or curators for intromission and omission, June 10, 1665, Swinton *contra* Notman [1 Stair 279, M. 16273].

13. Tutors do use ordinarily to name factors, who do not exoner the tutors of any of their obligations; but both the tutors, and they, in the same terms as the tutors, are liable to the pupils, if they be factors generally constitute. March 28, 1632, L. of Ludquhairn *contra* L. of Haddo [Durie 633; M. 9503]; July 18, 1635, Edmonston *contra* Edmonston [Durie 772; M. 16264].

14. If there be more tutors nominate or dative, and no quorum exprest; if some of them die, the office is not void, but the rest of them may act. And so it was found in tutors nominate, Hope, Executors, Stuart *contra* Kirkwood and Moor [Hope, *Maj. Pr.* IV, 4, 49; M. 14693]. The like though some of the tutors accepted not, Hope, Tutors, Ruthven *contra*   [Hope, *Maj. Pr.* IV, 10, 50]; *ibid.* Faside *contra* Edmonston [Hope, *Maj. Pr.* IV, 10, 50; M. 16240]; February 14, 1672, Eleis *contra* Scot [2 Stair 69; M. 14695]. But a tutory to two, bearing to them jointly, was found void by the death of either, January 17, 1671, Drummond of Riccartoun *contra* Feuars of Bothkennet [1 Stair 704; M. 14694]. And where there are many tutors nominate, they may be either with or without a quorum; and either definitely, or by a distinct division, in which case each are but liable for their own division, *l. 2. C. de dividen. tut.* [c. 5, 52, 2].

15. As to the duties of tutors, they are alike in them all. And the first is the custody of the pupil's person; wherein a tutor was preferred to the pupil's mother, offering to entertain him gratis, though the person nearest to succeed was married upon the tutor's sister; here the tutor was nominate, and the mother married, July 4, 1629, L. of Langshaw *contra* Moor [Durie 455; M. 16252]. The like, where both the tutor and the mother offered to aliment the pupil gratis; but the mother's second husband had apprised the pupil's lands, and the pupil was a lass only of five years old, February ult. 1632,

Gordon *contra* Corsan [Durie 625 ; M. 16259]. A tutor was found to have the
custody of his pupil, (who was an heretrix) and not her mother, though she
offered to entertain her gratis, being married to a second husband, February
5, 1675, Fullartoun *contra* Lady Boyn [2 Stair 317; M. 16291]. Yea, a tutor
obtained his pupil's person to be removed from her mother, though unmarried, at the pupil's age of eleven years, albeit the pupil was valetudinary,
and she was appointed to remain with one of her father's friends, to the effect
that she might not be influenced as to her marriage by her mother or her
friends, February 6, 1666, L. of Dury *contra* Lady Dury [1 Stair 348;
M. 16277]. But, if the tutor be immediately to succeed to the pupil, he hath
not the custody of his person, which is to be with his mother or some other
person at the arbitrement of the lords, and a modification to be for the pupil's
aliment according to his means. But if there be any other immediate successor, though the tutor was next, he had the custody of the pupil's person,
Nicolson, *ubi pupilli*, Forrester *contra* Smith [Not found].

Of old, tutors were excluded by the donatars of ward from custody of the
ward-pupil's person. January 15, 1549, Laird of Achnames *contra* Lord of
Elphingstoun and L. Lethingtoun [Probably *Laird of Achans* v *Livingston*,
Sinclair *Prac.*; M. 16220], March 16, 1565, Weir *contra* Lockhart [Not
found] and July 14, 1566, Weir *contra* L. of Lee [Maitland, *Fol. Dic.* 1, 48 ;
M. 605]. *Spots. hic.* Hamilton *contra* L. of Ganstoun [(1546) Spotiswoode
211 ; M. 9055]. Since that time tutors are preferred in the custody of their
pupil's person to the donatar of his ward.

16. The next duty of tutors is to authorize the pupil in actions of law ;
which, though it be done ordinarily by all the tutors, when they are more, yet
one of three was admitted to authorize a pupil in a pursuit against the other
two to accept or renounce, though they were all named jointly, March 8,
1628, Muir and Thomson *contra* Kincaid [Durie 356 ; M. 1349].

17. Tutors or their factors are presumed to do that to the behoof of the
pupil, which they ought to do ; and though it be done *proprio nomine*, it accresceth to the pupil, July 18, 1635, Edmonston *contra* Edmonston [Durie
772 ; M. 16264]. And so a tack of the pupil's rents, taken by the tutor's factor
to himself and his wife in liferent, was found to accresce to the pupil, except
as to the wife's liferent-lands, March 28, 1632, L. of Ludquhairn *contra* L.
of Haddo [Durie 633 ; M. 9503 and 16260]. This is presumed *præsumptione
juris ;* so that the narrative, bearing another cause, is not respected. And
therefore a tutor acquiring a discharge or assignation of an annualrent due by
the pupil to his mother, the same was found to accresce to the pupil, though
it bore Love and favour, and for the tutor's pains and discharging the office,
March 5, 1629, White *contra* Douglas [Durie 433 ; M. 16251]; Hope, Tutors,
Dewar *contra* Dewar [Hope, *Maj. Pr.* IV, 10, 54 ; M. 16241]. Neither hath the
tutor ordinarily action against the pupil, till his office end ; and then he may
pursue as a stranger. Hope, *de Minoribus*, Naismith *contra* Naismith [Hope,
Maj. Pr. IV, 10, 58 ; M. 16247]. Likewise he may apprise the pupil's lands for

his own debt, the pupil having other tutors. Hope *de heredibus*, &c. White *contra* Calderwood [Hope, *Maj. Pr.* IV, 5, 68; M. 386]. So a tutrix, nominate *sine qua non*, was admitted to pursue a registration of her contract of marriage against her pupil, there being more tutors nominate, and she having renounced her office, though she had acted by subscribing deeds, not hurtful to the pupil, July 30, 1625, Lady Stoniehill *contra* her Son [Durie 185; M. 16245].

18. Tutors may only do necessary deeds for their pupils: either such as the pupil is obliged to do, as payment of his debts, which the tutor may do willingly without compulsion of law ; or otherwise deeds necessary for management of his estate, and setting of his lands, or labouring the same, uplifting his rents and annualrents, uplifting the sums that are not secured, carrying on any work which was left to the pupil, which cannot otherwise be disposed of.

But tutors cannot sell the lands or heritable rights of their minors, without an intervening decreet of a judge, *tit. ff. de rebus eorum qui sub tutela* [D. 27, 9] and any such alienation is null, without the cognition aforesaid. And albeit this restriction of the tutors' power hath been introduced from the example of the Roman law, which at first did only extend *ad prædia rustica et suburbana*, the same was afterwards extended *ad prædia urbana* ; and is so extended by our custom. And therefore a house in Edinburgh being sold by a tutor without antecedent authority of the lords, the same was declared to belong to the pupil, albeit the house was raised several stories high, and the acquirers were only found to have right to the meliorations, in so far as profitable to the pupil, who was put not to prove lesion by the sale, February 5, 1692, Sandilands *contra* L. of Nidderie [Not found]. And the authority of the lords is interponed upon a process, which must be by calling the creditors of the pupil and his nearest friends to hear and see it found that there is a necessity to sell the whole, or a part of his heritable rights, and that the rate thereof may be determined: in which it must appear, that the pupil's debt cannot otherwise be satisfied.

The law allows the like in the case of the pupil's aliment, if it cannot be afforded otherwise ; and alienations so made are not easily reducible, or the pupil or minor restored against the same, if the true cause hath been known to the judge ; but not so, if that hath been latent, either *dolo* or *lata culpa*, *l. 11. C. de præd : minor non alien* [C. 5, 71, 11]. And therefore a tutor's assignation of his son's and pupil's mails and duties for the tutor's own debts was found null by exception, even at the pupil's tenant's instance, Spots, Assignation, Lands *contra* Lands [(1629) Spotiswoode, 200; M. 16250; I, 5, 12, *supra*]. Yet a tutor's ratification of a reducible decreet, given against his minor, was found valid, though voluntary, being *in re antiqua*, Spots, Tutors, Earl of Kinghorn *contra* Strang [(1631) Spotiswoode 347 ; M. 16256].

19. Tutors and pro-tutors are liable for annualrents of their pupil's monies, which they are obliged to make profitable, in so far as they are either liquid sums, that they had in specie, or which the tutors took up, which was made up of their pupil's moveables, or rents of lands after a term in money-

rent, and a year in victual, from the term of payment, in so far as it is not employed for their own use, or profitably for paying of their debts or annualrents, alimenting them, or other uses necessary; according to the ancient law of the Romans, which obliged the tutor after he had the money two months in his hands. But by the novel constitutions, *Nov.72, cap.6 de administrat. pecun. pupilli*, it is left to the arbitrement of the tutor, either to keep the pupil's money by him, or to employ it for profit; but it is not so by our custom; for it was lately found that a tutor by his office and diligence was obliged to lift and employ the pupil's annualrents of sums in secure hands once in his tutory, and so pay annual for the annualrents of his pupil's sums, omitted to be uplifted by him, yet only from the expiring of the tutory, January 27, 1665, Kintor *contra* Boyd [1 Stair 258; M.503]. So a tutor was found liable for the annualrent of his pupil's annualrent, within a year after his acceptance, but not for the current annualrent during the tutory, he leaving the same employed for annualrent at the ish thereof, February 27, 1673, Douglas *contra* Gray [2 Stair 181; M.501]. A tutor's heir, being minor, was found liable only for annual of his pupil's sums, after the intenting of the cause, the pursuer being silent twenty-five years, February 22, 1634, Davidson *contra* Jack [Durie 705; M.506]. Neither was the heir found liable for annualrent where the father died during his tutory: Hope, *de hered.* Graham *contra* Crichton [Hope, *Maj.Pr.* IV,4,50], January 21, 1665. Kintor *contra* Boyd [1 Stair 258; M.503]. But pupils' annualrents bear not annualrent from a year after they are due, as their silver-rent of lands do bear, but only from the end of the tutory: July 18, 1629, Nasmith *contra* Nasmith [Durie 465; M.6522].

20. Tutors are liable for their minors, and must be convened with them by their creditors, for their interest; and are also decerned with them for their interest. Upon which decreets personal execution is competent against tutors for any deed, prestable by them by their office. For example, they may be compelled to receive vassals, whom the pupil's predecessor was obliged to receive; or grant tacks of lands, or charters, or seasins, where there hath been a disposition before. But in decreets for payment of liquid sums, execution cannot be made against the means of tutors, unless they be specially decerned to make forthcoming so much of the pupil's means as they have in their hands, for satisfying of the debt, in whole or in part: which, though it be oft done by a second process, yet may be a distinct member of the first, or by way of special charge in the discussion of a suspension, raised by the tutor against creditors on that or other grounds. But the tutor's oath was not sustained to prove against the pupil an agreement made by the defunct, though there were concurrent probabilities and testificates, December 7, 1664, Eccles *contra* Eccles [1 Stair 236; M.16270]. Yet the tutor's oath was sustained against the pupil, as to the tutor's intromission in name of the pupil, that being *factum proprium*, obliging also himself; and yet he was not holden as confest, as being a party; but was compelled to depone by caption, June 27, 1665, Cant *contra* Loch [1 Stair 288; M.12029].

21. The last duty of tutors is to make an accompt, and to restore and re-fund; wherein they will be liable to account and satisfy for the pupil's whole means and estate, not only for their intromission, but for their omission; and for such diligence as they use in their own affairs, which seems sufficient in tutors testamentar, seeing the office is gratuitous and free, and not sought by them. But in tutors of law and dative, who ordinarily seek the office, and offer themselves, both the diligence accustomed by provident men, and such as they use in their own affairs, may be justly required; and by the civil law all tutors were liable *pro dolo, culpa et negligentia, l. 33 de administratione et periculo tutorum, &c.* [D. 26, 7, 33].

22. That tutors are liable, not only for what they did intromit but what they might have intromitted with by diligence, and particularly, with the rents of the pupil's lands, wherein his predecessors died infeft, and in possession, though the pupil himself was not infeft, was found, January 26, 1628, Commissary of Dunkel *contra* Abercromby [Durie 333; M. 3502]. Yet a tutrix was found only liable for her intromission, in respect she continued but some months, and the place where the minor's goods were, was infected with the plague, Hope, *de Tutoribus   contra* Cathcart [*Sub nom. Ryside* v *Cathcart* (1610) Hope, *Maj. Pr.* IV, 10, 4; M. 16239]. Neither was a tutor found liable for a sum due to the pupil, as not doing diligence by horning and caption for uplifting thereof, unless it were alleged that by diligence he might have recovered it; and that the debtor was become worse, July 2, 1628, Hamilton *contra* Hamilton [Durie 379; M. 3502]. The like, where the tutor offered to prove by the neighbourhood that the debtor during his tutory was repute and holden insolvent, February 6, 1623, Watson *contra* Watson [Durie 45; M. 3501 and 16242].

23. Co-tutors, both by the civil law and our custom, are liable *in solidum*; and so some of them were decerned for the whole, though the rest were not convened, February 22, 1634, Davidson *contra* Jack [Durie 705; M. 506]. They were also found liable *in solidum* though they had divided the tutory among themselves; but if the same were divided by the testator or a judge, the tutors were only liable for their share, and not for the rest, unless they have by fraud and supine negligence omitted to pursue the other suspect tutors to be removed, *l. 2. C. de dividenda tutela* [C. 5, 52, 2]. The benefit of the order of discussing, competent of the law, was that tutors who did administrate were only liable for their parts *primo loco*, if the rest were *solvendo*, *l. 3. C. de dividenda tutela* [C. 5, 52, 3]; and that they should be first discust, who had administrate and intromitted, before them who had neglected or forborn, *ibid*. These our custom followeth not. Yet a tutor was not found to have interest to cause the co-tutors find caution to warrant him for their acting without him, or against his mind, where they did out-vote him, or else to quit the tutory; but was left to his ordinary course, to remove them if they malversed, June 27, 1672, Stirling *contra* his Co-tutors [2 Stair 91; M. 16286].

24. Tutory is finished, first, by the death either of tutor or pupil: se-

condly, by the marriage of a tutrix testamentar, which no provision, even of the testator can dispense with : thirdly, by the tutor's renouncing the office; after which, though he were tutor testamentar, he cannot resume the office, July 6, 1627, Campbell *contra* Campbell [Durie 304; M. 16246]; but forbearance for six or seven years doth not extinguish the office of a tutor testamentar by the former decisions; the like, December 17, 1631, Auchterlonie *contra* Oliphant [Spotiswoode 348; M. 16258]: fourthly, by fury, lethargy, or any natural defect of the tutor, rendering him unable to exercise his office : fifthly, and most ordinarily, by the pupil's running the years of his pupillarity, which in men is fourteen years, in women twelve. But if the tutors continue to act till majority, they are liable as curators. Yet the express appointment of the defunct, that the tutors continue curators, cannot extend the tutory after pupillarity, or hinder election of curators, if the minors think fit to choose others, February 6, 1633, Harper *contra* Hamilton [Durie 668; M. 16262].

25. The tutory, appointed to idiots and furious persons, is prescribed by act of Parl. 1585, c. 18 [Curators Act, 1585; A.P.S. III, 396, c. 25], whereby the nearest agnates or kinsmen of natural fools, idiots, or furious persons, should be served, received and preferred to their tutory and curatory, according to the common law; where, by the common law, the civil law is understood. And though the Act seems only to hold out tutors of law where any are served; yet, seeing it is according to the disposition of the civil law, it excludes not tutors testamentar during such persons' pupillarity, nor tutors dative, if the nearest agnate serve not : but ordinarily the tutors of idiots are the tutors of law. This act, by custom, is extended to deaf and dumb persons, though they be not expressed, who have tutors in the same manner, albeit they have sufficient judgment, since they cannot act by it. These tutors have greater privilege than other tutors, because they are ordinarily the heirs of such persons; and, therefore, their not serving within the year and day from the idiotry or furiosity, after pupillarity, albeit datives be constitute, the tutors of law recall them, and call them to accompt; which was so found, though the tutor was not served till five years after the idiot's majority, February 22, 1628, Colquhoun *contra* Wardrope [Durie 349; M. 6276], January 21, 1663, Stewart *contra* Spreul [1 Stair 159; M. 6280]. These tutors must be served by a brief of idiotry, and by inquest, Parl. 1476, c. 67 [Act 1475, c. 66; A.P.S. II, 112, c. 8], by which the time of the idiotry or furiosity must be determined : and all acts during that time are declared null. They are liable in all other things as other tutors, for finding caution, inventory, and being countable for intromission and omission. Their tutory ends not by lucid intervals, but by full recovery of the furious persons their judgment.

26. When tutory is ended, whatsoever the tutor acted in name of the pupil, the pupil hath thereupon action, as if it had been done by himself, *l. 2. ff. quando ex facto tutoris* [D. 26, 9, 2]. So whatever was decerned against the tutor *hoc nomine*, ceaseth when the tutory is ended *l. fin. C. de per tut* [c. 5, 38, 6] and the action is competent against the pupil; as likewise, if the

pupil be advantaged by the fraud of the tutor, he may be therefore convened, *l.3.ff. quando ex facto tutoris vel curatoris* [D.26,9,3].

27. Lastly, tutory ceaseth by the action of removing suspect tutors, which was a popular action competent to any, *l.1.§6.ff et §3. Inst. de susp. tut.* [D.26,10,1,3 and 6]; but ordinarily it is done by the overseers, mother or friends of the pupil, or by the other tutors; The grounds whereof are not only his malversation, as it was found a malversation, that the tutor had not made inventory conform to the late act of parliament, July 7, 1680, Gibson *contra* Lord Dunkel and Thomson [2 Stair 781; M.16299], but any thing incident, or appearing to weaken his trust, as if he become insolvent, or his cautioner become such.

After tutory is ended, the tutor hath no action against his pupil *ante redditas rationes*, till he make his accounts, January 24, 1662, Cranston *contra* Earl of Wintoun [Not found]. Neither hath the tutor's assignee action against the pupil before the tutor's accounts be made, albeit assigned to a liquid sum, unless the assignee find caution for the tutor, January 24, 1662, Ramsay *contra* Earl of Winton [1 Stair 87; M.9977]. Neither, for the same reason, had the tutor's assignee action against the pupil as heir to his father, though it was ten years since the pupillarity was past, July 7, 1676, Spence *contra* Scot [2 Stair 442; M.9982]. But a tutor was not found liable for the services he got of the pupil's tenants in kind, January 11, 1668, Grant *contra* Grant [1 Stair 502; M.12172]. Yea a tutor having counted, and given bond for the balance, being charged with other articles, though these were not instantly liquidate, yet the extract of a decreet upon the bond was stopped for a time, till the additional articles should be closed; but the bond was not reduced, as being *in confinio minoris ætatis, et ante redditas rationes*, December 5, 1671, Scot *contra* Eleis [1 B.S.644]. In a tutor's accompts, it was a sufficient instruction of an article of the charge, a bond due to the defunct, produced by the pupil. Nor was the tutor liberate, upon alleging he knew not of it, but it was presumed to have been in the charter chest, unless the tutor could instruct, that he had made search in the charter chest, and neither found this bond, nor any inventory relating thereto; so the tutor was found liable, though the sum was lost by the debtor's becoming insolvent during the tutory, June 24, 1680, Cleiland *contra* L. of Lamingtoun [2 Stair 777; M.12451]. Neither did a tutor get any further allowance for his pupil's maintenance, than the annualrent of his stock, though he expended more, November 17, 1680, Sandilands *contra* Tailzefer [2 Stair 799; M.16300].

28. The reciprocal duty of pupils to tutors after the tutory is ended, is to restore and make up to them whatsoever they wared out profitably, or is so wanting to them by that office, wherein the expense of obtaining the tutory itself will be a part. But tutory being a free gratuitous office, the pupils are not liable to their tutors for any allowance, salary, or satisfaction for their pains, but only for their expenses. And if a tutor hath not made inventory conform to the late act of parliament, he loseth his expenses, as a penalty for

not making inventory, even though the pupil was *lucratus* thereby [Act1672, c.2; A.P.S. VIII, 59, c.2; and A. S.25 Feb. 1693].

29. Curatory hath such a resemblance with tutory, that, though the constitution of curators be not of the law of nature, which leaveth all persons of discretion free, but of positive law, whereby a way is provided for the levity and facility of minors, yet to shun repetition it will be most proper here to annex that office, and the obligations therefrom arising betwixt curators and minors. And in these we shall only touch the difference betwixt tutors and curators (supposing the rest as common to both) which is chiefly in these points.

30. *First*, In the election and constitution of curators, which is done by way of process at the instance of the minor before any judge-ordinary whatsomever, whereby he citeth two or three of his nearest kinsmen on both sides, upon nine days warning, and all others having interest, generally at the market-cross, to hear and see curators decerned to him [Act 1555, c. 35; A.P.S. 11, 493, c. 8]; and it is in his option whom to choose, as it is in their option also to accept or refuse. He may also make any number a quorum, or adject any condition he thinks fit in their election. And the parties compearing must accept and make faith *de fideli administratione*, and find caution. Their acceptation must be by subscribing the act of curatory, especially if the election be in an inferior court, for want whereof an act of curatory before the baillies was found null, Hope, Curators, Sibbald *contra* Hay and Lindsay [Hope, *Maj. Pr.* IV, 10, 55; M. 16246]. Curators also may be chosen by procuratory without the minor's presence, so that the procuratory express the curator's names: Hope, Curators, Marquis of Hamilton *contra* his Curators [Hope, *Maj. Pr.* IV, 10, 57; M. 16245]; yea being done in England, according to the custom there, it is sufficient to authorize the minors here. Hope, *de tut.* L. Posso *contra* Nasmith [Hope, *Maj. Pr.* IV, 10, 56; M. 4455]. Though the minor may choose curators whom he pleaseth, yet he may not choose rebels unrelaxed, if it be objected and verified at the election by his friends. July 4, 1629, Corbet of Ardill *contra*   [*Sub nom. Corbet of Ardill* v *His nearest of kin*, Durie, 456; M. 10155].

31. Curators are of two kinds, *ad lites* and *ad negotia*. The former are appointed for authorizing judicially in process; the other are mainly for extra-judicial affairs. Curators *ad lites* are so far necessary, that they must be given by the judge ordinary, before whom any action is pursued, for authorizing of the minors either *passive* or *active*, §2. *Inst. de curat* [Inst. 1, 23, 2] and they will be given upon the desire of either party. Their office seems to reach no further than to faithfulness and diligence in the processes whereunto they are elected. There are sometimes curators named to pupils to supply the defect of their tutors, as if their tutor be concerned, or be absent, or incapable to act for a time. These, though for a distinction from tutors they be called curators, yet their office *pro tempore* is of the same nature with tutors.

32. Curators *ad negotia* are in the minor's option, and must be freely

chosen : so that, though a minor's father named his tutor expressly to continue their office till the pupil's majority, yet it was found not to hinder the
minor to choose curators, or to disown his tutors after his pupillarity, February 6, 1633, Harpers *contra* Hamilton [Durie 668 ; M. 16262]. Minors having
chosen no curators are in the same condition for extrajudicial acts alone, as if
they had curators ; in either case the deeds are revocable, and reducible upon
enorm lesion.

33. But if once they choose curators, all deeds, done by them without consent of their curators, are *eo ipso* null by exception, without necessity to
allege lesion, December 19, 1632, Maxwell *contra* the E. of Nithisdale [Durie
660 ; M. 2115] ; and that so exactly, that the minority was counted *de momento
in momentum*, though the minor wanted only twelve hours of twenty-one
years, June 26, 1624, Drummond *contra* L. of Cuninghamhead [Durie 130 ;
M. 3465]. This was extended to a judicial act, whereby the minor enacted
himself cautioner, Hope, *de Minoribus*, Paterson *contra* Wishart [Hope,
Maj. Pr. IV, 10, 52 ; M. 16241] ; and extended also to a minor's service, without consent of his curators, and that by exception, without instructing lesion,
Spots. *de Minor.* Simpson *contra* Laird of Balgony [Spotiswoode, 137 ;
M. 2729] ; and to a tack taken by the minor without consent of his curators
Hope *de minoribus*, Seton *contra* L. of Caskiben [Hope, *Maj. Pr.* IV, 9, 39 ;
M. 8939] : and extended to deeds done by minors in their father's family, without their father's consent, and so it was found, that a minor's bond, subscribing
cautioner with and for his father, was null ; and that his father, as lawful
administrator, could not authorize him to be cautioner for himself : here the
minor was a student at law, but entertained by his father, and not *forisfamiliat*, December 7, 1666, Mackenzie *contra* Fairholm [1 Stair 409 ; M. 8959] ;
July 25, 1667, *inter eosdem* [1 Stair 480 ; M. 8960 ; 1, 5, 12, *supra*]. Yet the deed
was sustained, being a bond of borrowed money, the creditor proving by
witnesses that the sum was converted for the minor's use profitably, December
11, 1629, Gordon *contra* Earl of Galloway [Durie 473 ; M. 8941]. This is according to that common ground of equity, *nemo debet ex alieno damno lucrari :*
hence flows *minor tenetur in quantum locupletior factus.* But though there was
some onerous cause of minors' deeds, yet unless it were liquid as delivery of
money, it is not receivable by way of exception or reply, but only is reserved
to the creditor to pursue as accords, and the minor's deed was found void
notwithstanding, December 19, 1632, Maxwell *contra* Earl of Nithisdale
[Durie 660 ; M. 2115]. But this was not extended to necessary furnishing of
clothes, taken on without consent of curators, which was sustained by way of
reply, February 5, 1631, Inglis *contra* Executors of Sharp [Durie 565 ;
M. 8941].

34. The civil law seems not to require the consent of curators, as necessary to concur with the minor in the making his latter will, but only to deeds
among the living ; because law hath rejected all ties and hinderances of full
liberty in testaments of defuncts in the disposal of their goods ; and therefore

if a minor having curators do in his testament say, *quæstionem curatoribus meis nemo faciat, eam nam ipse tractavi*, in that case curators are liable for restitution of what they have of the minor's goods by fraud, but not for a complete diligence *l. 20 § 1.ff. deliberatione legata* [D. 34, 3, 20, 1 (properly *de liberatione legata*)]. I have not observed it directly controverted and determined, whether by our custom minors, having curators, may test without their consent; but indirectly, a minor making his curator his executor and universal legatar, though the minor was with the curator when he tested and died shortly after, and his nearest relations were not acquainted whom he had named in a former testament, it was sustained, no threats nor importunity being alleged, November 30, 1680, Stevenson *contra* Allans [2 Stair 807; M. 8949].

35. Curators differ in their office from tutors mainly in this, that tutors are given chiefly for the pupil's person, but curators are given for the right managing of their goods and affairs: secondly, tutors act for, and in the name of, their pupils, who in their pupillarity have no discretion, but curators cannot, and are only obliged by their office, to authorize their minors, and act with them by consenting to their deeds; for instance, curators cannot discharge for their minors, but only consent to their minors' discharge. And so fathers, after their children's pupillarity, can only consent with their children, as their lawful administrators, whereby they are tutors in the children's pupillarity, and curators in their minority without election or formality, June 20, 1610, Forrester *contra* Forrester [Haddington MS; M. 16238]; January 9, 1675, Mactintosh *contra* Frazer of Strichen [2 Stair 303; M. 11239].

36. Their duty is to see to the minor's affairs, that they get no detriment; and they must answer, not only for the deeds whereunto they consent, but for their omission, and for any detriment the minor suffereth by their negligence; and, therefore, a curator was found liable for intromission and omission, albeit the act of curatory did not bear that he compeared and did find caution, seeing he accepted thereafter, by subscribing a writ with the minor as his curator, which was found to oblige him from the time of the acceptance, November 18, 1671, Cass *contra* Elleis [2 Stair 3; M. 3504]: but curators, continuing to uplift their minor's rent after majority, were found not liable for omissions these years, unless they had a distinct factory continued *per tacitam reconventionem, ibidem*. And, therefore, they must not only be counsellors to the minors, showing them what they ought to do, and requiring them to do the same; but specially they must cause them constitute factors, and grant procuratories to persons for uplifting their money, whether it be the stock, of that which may be in hazard, or annualrent, or rents and to grant procuratories for pursuing their actions, and putting them to execution. For, seeing they must be accountable, they must not suffer the minor to have his own goods and his own money in his own hand, lest he lose and mispend them; and these procuratories may be given to some of themselves: and in many things their very office includes a procuratory, being less than curatory.

But though they may intromit with the pupil's means themselves, yet they are not obliged to be servants or factors; but may authorize such, being liable always that they acted therein profitably. But if the minor will not authorize such, nor do these deeds needful and profitable for his affairs, the curators may crave to be exonered. So they may also do, if he meddle with his own means, and will not be restrained. Or if any of the other curators act unprofitably, or without consent of the rest, the curators must do diligence to remove them, as suspect and malversant. Curators are to recover that which was unwarrantably meddled with; otherwise they are liable, not only for their own omissions or intromissions, but for the other curators, and so are all liable *in solidum*, as hath been said of tutors, February 11, 1630, Guthry *contra* Guthry [Durie 491; M. 14640]. And they are liable for annualrent of minor's means, as tutors are, February 24, 1627, Guthry *contra* Guthry [Durie 281; M. 507]; yea, their heirs, though minors for the time after expiring of the curatory, ibid. Where the curator's heirs are found liable for the annualrent of a sum consigned to the minor; yet if curators die before their minor become major, they are not liable for annualrent. But curators, expressly chosen with a quorum, and with this condition, that they should be only obliged for deeds, whereunto they consented, and be free of omissions, were so approven by the lords during their office. But where the act of curatory bore that the curators were named jointly, and three of them to be a quorum, two only accepting, the curatory was found null, January 25, 1672, Ramsay *contra* Maxwell [2 Stair 55; M. 9042]. But where they were not named jointly, the death of one did not annul the curatory, January 4, 1666, Fairfoul *contra* Binning [1 Stair 332; M. 16277]; or the not acceptance, February 11, 1676, Turnbull *contra* Rutherford [2 Stair 414; M. 9162]. And though there be a quorum constitute, all the curators are liable for diligence; and if any quorum act hurtfully, they must crave them to be removed, and what they have so done, to be restored.

Curators are not simply liable for all their pupil's means, which may be lost without their fault: neither to do diligence in all cases, but where diligence might be profitable, as hath been said of tutors [1, 6, 22, *supra*]. Curators, being elected by authority of a judge, cannot be liberate by the minor's consent. Neither did a decreet against a minor, on his consent, liberate curators from their office, July 21, 1664, Scot of Braidmeadow *contra* Scot of Thirlstane [1 Stair 220; M. 16269]. Curators may not authorize their minors, where hazard predomines; nor may they buy lands with their minor's money; but they may give it out on land security, and may relieve the minor's estate of burden, though there might be latent hazard of security. So the curators of Fletcher of Aberlady, having liberate his estate of a liferent, and caused the minor to swear not to quarrel the bargain, and gave their own warrandice to the liferenter, were not found liable to their minor's heir; albeit the liferenter had a cancer in her breast, and died shortly after the bargain, seeing they knew it not, and acted prudently; and the minor's heir was excluded by his predecessor's oath, given before the late act of Parliament [Oaths of Minors

Act, 1681, c. 19; A.P.S. VIII,352,c.85] because he pursued on his predecessor's lesion, who was minor and swore; January 1691, Fletcher of Aberlady *contra* Murray of Blackbarony and others [Not found].

37. Curators are appointed in the law, not only for that ordinary levity and weakness incident to minority, which therefore runs only to twenty-one years complete, at which time, by our custom, minority endeth ; but also in case of known or conspicuous levity, though after majority. Such were the curators of prodigals, to whom, as to furious persons, curators were constitute their nearest agnates. Instead of this our custom hath interdictions, whereby persons acknowledging their own weakness and levity, and readiness to hurt themselves, do therefore bind themselves, that they shall not act without the consent of these persons interdictors therein mentioned; who thereby become as curators, though they be not obliged for intromission or omission, but only to consent with the persons interdicted, and for their fraud and fault in consenting.

38. Interdictions [IV, 20, 30 *et seq.*, *infra*] are most fitly made judicially, upon cognition of the cause; by which after trial the person craving to be interdicted, acknowledging his own lavishness and prodigality, interdictors are appointed by the judge competent, and that either at the instance of the party himself, or of his friends. Yea the lords *ex proprio motu* did interdict a person who was evidently lavish, and had thrice made opposite rights of the same subject ; and that *incidenter* in another process where his levity did so appear, February 17, 1681, Robertson *contra* Gray [*Sub nom. Gray* v *Robertson*, 2 Stair 861 ; M. 7134]. That this is the genuine way of interdictions, is clear by the narrative of the act of parliament 1581, c. 119 [A.P.S. III, 223, c. 24] ; and therefore an interdiction was reduced, only because it was done *sine causa cognita*, Hope, Interdictions, Robertson *contra*   [Hope, *Maj. Pr.* II, 16, 11 ; M. 7158] : but there has not been a just ground for the interdiction alleged and instructed.

39. The more ordinary way of interdictions is of consent ; whereby the person interdicted, acknowledging his own lavishness, doth, by a writ under his hand, interdict himself. And this is reducible, if the narrative was not true, but the person interdicted was prudent and provident, December 20, 1622, Campbel *contra* L. of Glenurchy [Durie 40 ; M. 7158] ; and December 4, 1623, Geichan *contra* Hay and Davidson [Durie 86 ; M. 7160]. Interdictions use also to be in the way of obligation not to contract debts or dispone lands without consent of such persons, and inhibition registrate thereupon; which was sustained, though not in the ordinary style of interdiction, the person obliged being known insufficient to manage his own affairs through levity or prodigality, November 10, 1676, Stewart *contra* Hay of Gourdie [Direlton 186; M. 3092 and 7133]. But a bond bearing that a man should not sell or dispone without consent of his wife, on the narrative of his facility, whereon inhibition was used, was found not to be valid as an interdiction, as inconsistent, binding a man to the direction of his wife; but that it was only valid to secure

the wife's own interest by an aliment according to her quality, as an inhibition, February 27, 1663, Lady Milton *contra* L. Milton [Stair 189; M. 9452].

40. Interdictions must be published at the market-cross of the head-burgh of the shire where the party dwells, and within forty days after publication of the same, with the executions thereof, must be registrate by the sheriff-clerk of that shire, in the register of interdictions and inhibitions within the shire. The interdiction must be also registrate in the register of inhibitions of any other shire where the lands of the interdicted person lie; otherwise, if it be not published, [and registrate in the shire where it is published], it is absolutely null, and hath no effect as to lands or heritable rights in any other shire, unless it be also registrate there, Parl. 1581, c. 118 [1581, c. 119; A.P.S. III, 223, c. 24]; February 11, 1662, Ramsay *contra* Maclellan [1 Stair 96; M. 7131]. Yet it needs not be intimate to the party interdicted, December 11, 1622, Seton *contra* Elleis [*Sub nom. Seton and Eleis* v *Acheson's Creditors, Fol. Dict.* 11, 256; M. 12599].

41. The effect of interdictions, by custom, is retrenched only to the preservation of heritable rights, and doth not extend to moveables, or personal execution against the person interdicted; so that he may dispone his moveables, or upon any personal bond granted by him, his moveables may be poinded, arrested, and made forthcoming, and his person incarcerate, though the style of interdiction doth expressly prohibit alienation of moveables, July 11, 1634, Bruce *contra* Forbes [Durie, 725; M. 7130]; June 20, 1671, Crawford *contra* Haliburton [1 Stair 736; M. 2741]. Also he may thereupon be denounced, though thereby his liferent fall in prejudice of the heritage. Haddington, February 8, 1610; Hay of Brunthills *contra* his Father and Sister [Not found]; and December 21, 1610, L. Broxmouth younger *contra* Relict of Wauchop [*Fol. Dict.* 1, 481; M. 7164]. But interdiction hath effect in favours of the heir of the interdicted person, that neither his heritage can be affected upon any obligation granted by his predecessor after interdiction, neither can any personal execution by caption and horning be against him, as would have been against his predecessor. But such bonds will take effect against the heir, as meddling with the heirship moveables, or other moveables of the defunct. The reason wherefore moveables are excepted both from inhibitions and interdictions is, because they are of less moment, and the traffic of them must be current and free. And therefore these remeids being but by positive law, and not by natural equity (by which the engagement or disposition of any person, having the use of reason, is effectual, though lavish), positive law prohibiteth and voideth such only as to lands, heritage, or as being of the greatest importance; in which even a tack to a kindly tenant, set without consent of the interdictors, was found null, Hope, Interdict. Douglas *contra* Cranston [Hope, *Maj. Pr.* II, 16, 9; M. 7148]. Interdictions do not make void all posterior obligations, but only such where there is lesion: and therefore, where there is a just and onerous cause, the obligation or deed is good, though without consent of the interdictors, July 29, 1624, L. of Collingtoun *contra*

Hall [*Sub nom. Collington* v *Faw*, Durie 142; M.7148]; November 10, 1676, Stuart *contra* Hay of Gourdy [2 Stair 461; M.3092 and 7132].

42. The remeid by interdictions is only by reduction, and not by exception or suspension, March 17, 1630, Sempil *contra* Dobie [Spotiswoode 121; M.2740]; January 22, 1631, Hardie *contra* McCalla [*Sub nom. Hardie* v *McCaula*, Durie 558; M.2740]. Yet interdiction is sustained by way of reply, seeing the pursuer thereby doth only delay himself, February 13, 1662, Lockhart *contra* Kennedy [1 Stair 98; M.2741]. It is a competent ground of reduction at the instance of the interdicted person, his assignees or heirs, and it is also competent, at the instance of the interdictors, without consent of the person interdicted, Haddington, December 21, 1610, L. Broxmouth younger *contra* Relict of Wauchop [*Fol.Dict.* 1,481; M.7164].

43. Interdictions cannot be taken off by consent of the interdictors or interdicted persons, though they should renounce or discharge them, but only by the act of a judge competent, finding the grounds thereof either not true, or otherwise that the person interdicted is come to a more stable deportment, Hope, Interdict. Anderson *contra* Interdictors of Craig [*Sub nom. Sanderson* v *Interdictors of Craig*, Hope, *Maj.Pr.* 11,16,10; M.7165], December 4, 1623, Gichan *contra* Hay and Davidson [Durie 86; M.7160], which is to be understood of interdictions laid on by authority of a judge *causa cognita*.

44. There are other two privileges of minors, which can nowhere be so conveniently spoken to as in this place. The one is, that minors are restored against deeds done by them in their minority to their enorm lesion. The other is, *Minor non tenetur placitare super hereditate paterna* [R.M. III,32,15; *Statuta Willelmi regis*, c.39].

As to the first, minority and lesion are the ordinary ground of reduction. But because they are *facti*, and abide probation, they are not receivable by exception, unless he who pursues the minor can instruct his pursuit; but if he take a term to prove, the minor may take the same term to prove his minority, which doth not acknowledge the libel, or free the pursuer from probation thereof.

There is no difference as to the restitution of minors, though the deed be done with consent of curators. Nor did it exclude a minor reducing, because his curators had received the money in question, and so were liable to the minor for misemploying it, upon pretence that his lesion could not be known till they were discussed, July 2, 1667, Lord Blantyre *contra* Walkinshaw [1 Stair 468; M.2215 and 8991]. The reason is, because the minor lesed may pursue both. But this remeid is not competent for every small lesion, but it must be enorm, which is in *arbitrio judicis*. Neither is a minor restored against lesion, which falls not by levity but by accident, as by shipwreck, as if the minor be a trading merchant, Hope, *de minoribus*, Edgar *contra* Executors of Edgar [Hope, *Maj.Pr.* IV,9,36; M.8986]. Neither because he was bound conjunctly and severally for ware with another merchant, who was in society with him in trading, June 20, 1676, Galbraith *contra* Lesly [2 Stair 428 ; M.9027]. Because trading merchants and others exercising trade, requiring peculiar skill, capacity, and understanding, are held rather to design to deceive, than to be deceived ; as was found in the case of a notar-public, July 19, 1636, Gardner *contra* Chalmers [Durie 818 ; M.9025].

Neither was a minor restored against his judicial confession upon oath, upon point of fact, and swearing never to come in the contrary, November 28, 1626, Hope and Nicolson *contra* Nicolson [Durie 238 ; M.Supp.33]. Neither was a minor restored against his promise upon oath, to quit twenty chalders of victual, provided to him by his contract of marriage, as not lesed by keeping his oath, which is conform to the Authentic *Sacramenta puberum* [Auth. *Sacramenta puberum* ad C.2.27(28)1. See also *Libri Feudorum* 2,53, 10], January 15, 1634, Hepburn *contra* Hepburn and Seton [Durie 697 ; M.8921]. And it was found relevant against restitution of a minor of ba ond granted for a debt of his father's, whom he represented not, that he swore to perform the same, February 10, 1672, Wauch *contra* Baillie [2 Stair 69 ; M.8922] But the oaths of minors being elicit with the same facility as their bonds and obligations are, therefore they are lately altogether discharged by act of parliament with great severity, and declared void and null, Act.19. Par.3 Ch.2 [i.e. Parliament 3, Charles II, Act 19, i.e. Oaths of Minors Act, 1681, c.19 ; A.P.S. VIII,352,c.85 ; see I,17,14,*infra*].

A minor hath not the privilege to reduce a disposition of land without the authority of a judge, as in the case of pupils, unless he also allege lesion, February 2, 1630, Hamilton *contra* Sharp [Durie 488 ; M.8981]. The like, though the minor had no curators, December 13, 1666, Thomson *contra* Stevenson [1 Stair 411 ; M.8982]. Neither is restitution competent, unless reduction be intented within the age of twenty-five years complete. For with us majority is at the age of twenty-one years complete ; and there are four years allowed to minors to intent reductions, which therefore are called *anni utiles*.

A minor was restored against his contract of marriage, wherein he was obliged to infeft his first-born son in fee of his whole estate, which was very considerable, having gotten but ten thousand merks of tocher, March 7, 1623, Lord Bargeny *contra* his Son [Durie 56 ; M.10418]. The like, where a minor getting but a thousand merks of tocher, provided five thousand merks to his wife's father in case of no succession ; but a minor not restored against that part of his contract, providing all his means acquired and to be acquired in liferent to his wife, July 4, 1632, Davidson *contra* Hamilton [Durie 639 ; M.8988]. A woman minor was restored against the exorbitancies of her contract of marriage, November 22, 1664, Macgill *contra* Ruthven of Gairn [1 Stair 227 ; M.5696] ; but here she was only restored to a suitable liferent, but not against that provision in her contract, providing her lands and sums to the heirs of the marriage ; which failing, to the man's heirs. The like, where the wife disponed her lands to her husband, whose means were altogether unanswerable, Spotiswoode, Husband and Wife, Fleming *contra* Hog [Not found].

Minors are also restored against judicial acts to their lesion; as against a decreet of exoneration of a tutor, with concourse of curators, before the lords *in foro contradictorio*, December 1, 1638, Stuart *contra* Stuart [Durie 863; M.9008]; Hope, Universal and lucrative Successor, Knows *contra* Knows and Watson [Hope, *Maj.Pr.* IV,9,32; M.8968]; and against a defence proponed by an advocate without special mandate, which did homologate a deed in minority, February 14, 1677, Duke and Duchess of Buccleugh *contra* Earl of Tweeddale [2 Stair 504; M.2369]; in which case it was found, that accepting an illiquid right for a liquid was no enorm lesion, inferring restitution.

But restitution is excluded *si minor se majorem dixerit ; nam deceptis, non decepientibus, jura subveniunt* [C.2,42,2], as where the minor's bond bore expressly that he was major, and the creditor knew not he was minor by his aspect or otherwise, nor did fraudfully induce him to insert his majority, February 23, 1665, Kennedy *contra* Weir [1 Stair 274; M. 11658]. It is also elided, if it be proven that the deed in question was profitable, as that the sum in question was wared upon the minor for meat and clothes, though his father gave him a sufficient allowance, seeing he was then abroad from his father, Hope, Minority, Creich *contra* Walker [Possibly *Creich* v *Dalhousie*, Hope, *Maj.Pr.* VI,37,25]. It is also elided by deeds of homologation after majority, July 19, 1636, Gardner *contra* Chalmers [Durie 818; M.9025]. But where majority was alleged against a minor's restitution, neither party was preferred in the probation, but witnesses allowed *hinc inde*, February 20, 1668, Farquhar of Tonley *contra* Gordon [1 Stair 528; M. 5685]. And lesion needs not be proven by the minor granting bonds of borrowed money; for the misapplication is presumed unless the contrary be proven.

This privilege is not only competent to the minor himself, but to his heir, who if he were minor may reduce the deed done in his precedessor's minority; the rule whereof in the several cases, which may occur, is well deduced from the redemptions of apprisings led against minors. For the act Parl. 1621 [Diligence Act 1621, c.6; A.P.S. III,609,c.6], anent apprisings, orders the interest of minors in redeeming apprisings thus: that if a minor, having right to redeem comprised lands, decease before his age of twenty-five years complete, and another minor be heir, or succeed to him in his right of reversion, that minor shall have the same time to redeem, as if the apprising had been led against himself; but a major succeeding to a minor in the right of reversion, if that minor died within seven years after the apprising, the major hath as much time to redeem as rested of the seven years, but no *anni utiles* after; and if the minor, who had right of reversion, outlive the seven years, but die *intra annos utiles*, the major succeeding hath a year to redeem, though there be not so much resting of his predecessor's *anni utiles*; but though more be resting, he hath only a year. There being no speciality as to minority in apprisings and other rights, and this rule is to be followed in all cases of minority.

Minority and lesion is also relevant at the instance of a minor's creditors, seeing the minor *intra annos utiles* had intented reduction. But the privilege of restitution is not competent to minors upon revocation, unless they intent reduction and declarator *intra annos utiles ;* which was found to hold in the king's revocation as to lands not annexed, Spots. Revocation, Pringle *contra* Ker [*Sub nom. Hoppringle* v *Ker*, Spotiswoode, 306].

45. The other privilege of a minor is, *quod non tenetur placitare super hereditate paterna ;* which though it be not *peremptorium causæ*, delaying only pursuit till majority, yet there is no necessity to verify it instantly, but a term will be granted to prove the same, February 24, 1676, Kello *contra* Kinnier [2 Stair 421 ; M. 12068]. And this privilege is introduced in favours of minors, that they be not put out of their father's heritage, whereof he died in peaceable possession. For though their privilege of restitution might recover such rights by reduction, yet the minor would lose the fruits and profits *medio tempore*, and until their rights were produced and made clear in reduction ; which might be of great importance to them : for if a minor of a year old were dispossessed of his father's inheritance, he would lose at least twenty years fruits of it ; and therefore the law hath introduced this privilege in favours of minors, beside the privilege of restitution, wherein minors are not in contradistinction to pupils, but the privilege is chiefly competent to pupils. And though it bear only *de hereditate paterna*, yet thereby minors succeeding immediately to their grandfather or other predecessor, who died in possession, it is not like the privilege would be denied to them, though I have not found it controverted or determined, seeing the law under the name of father doth ordinarily comprehend grandfather, great-grandfather and all predecessors in a direct line, who come all under the designation of forefathers, as all successors in the right line come under the name of children ; and it holds alike in the heirs of mothers, grandmothers, &c.

But the law indulgeth this favour only as to the heritage of fathers; and therefore neither the style nor custom hath extended it to collateral succession, as to brothers or uncles, wherein minors, if they be excluded, can only be restored by minority and lesion, so soon as their predecessor's or author's rights can be found.

Neither was ever this privilege extended further than to minors in possession of the heritage of their forefathers, who died in peaceable and lawful possession, and to whom the minor immediately succeeded. For there is no privilege to possession, *vi, clam, aut precario*, though law or custom hath not determined how long possession of the defunct is required to exclude clandestine or momentary possession. But the continued possession of the defunct, with his author, may be accounted sufficient ; or the defunct's possession by his father's liferenter, whose right is granted by him or reserved in his right, but not to the possession of singular successors by redeemable rights, as wadsetters or apprisers, nor any other liferenter than the father's relict.

Neither hath there been any exception made of the pursuits at the instance of minors against minors, as being both privileged, there being no parity in recovering and retaining possession; but where a minor was put from possession by a decreet of removing, obtained by a minor, from lands wherein her father and herself were infeft, and in possession, she was not excluded to reduce that decreet of removing upon the minority of the other minor, whose father died not in possession, June 18, 1680, Lyle *contra* Dons [2 Stair 771; M.9106].

This privilege will not only exclude possessory judgments, such as removings or mails and duties, but also declarators or reductions; as to which it hath been variously decided, whether it should stop certification *contra non producta*, especially in the case of improbation. And though it cannot exclude improbation where the writs are produced, or where they are in the hands of the minor and his tutors or curators, if that shall appear by their writ or oath; yet where the minor produced his father's infeftment, and proved his father's possession, he was found obliged to produce no further, January 31, 1665, Kello *contra* Pringle and the L. of Wedderburn [1 Stair 269; M.9063], so that it cannot defend simply against production. But if it could not defend against production of any further but the father's infeftment, and that certification in improbations would be granted in all other rights; if these certifications could take effect, the privilege might be wholly evacuate; and if they should take no effect till majority, certifications in improbations should not be granted, being hardly reducible, even though in absence. And though it was not sustained against production in a reduction, November 27, 1678, Guthry *contra* L. of Guthry [2 Stair 647; M.9069], yet in that case the minor's right was only an apprising at his father's instance, upon which his father was never infeft.

This being a feudal privilege, whereof there is no mention or foundation in the civil law, it is only competent to minors, whose fathers were in possession by virtue of infeftment, as in the former case of apprising or where the father had a disposition without infeftment. January 31, 1665, Kello *contra* Pringle [1 Stair 269; M.9063]. Where the reasons of reduction being probable by witnesses, their oaths were taken to lie *in retentis*, lest the probation might perish in the mean time, and so followed, February 15, 1678, Gordon *contra* Maxwell [2 Stair 614; M.6144]. But the want of infeftment of the father's author was not found relevant, January 18, 1667, Chapman *contra* White [1 Stair 427; M.9066].

Neither will this privilege exclude the father's obligement to denude himself of the infeftment in question, Spots, Minor, Hamilton *contra* [Probably *Hamilton v Cambuskeith* (1634) Spotiswoode 211; M.9094]. For there is no competition of rights, but implement of an obligement. And so it was not sustained in a reduction upon a clause irritant in a feu, Hope, *de Minoribus,* *contra* Mitchel [Sub nom. *Inchaffray v Mitchell*, Hope, *Maj.Pr.* IV, 9, 37; M.9096]: neither to exclude reductions *ob non solutum canonem* by the father, though the feu contained no conventional clause irritant, February 20, 1633, Lennox *contra* McMurren [Durie 675 ; M.6435]. Neither did it exclude the probation of the tenor of a charter, which might exclude the minor's right, February 15, 1628, the Master of Jedburgh *contra* the Earl of Home [Durie 345 ; M.9083] ; albeit it would exclude process upon that charter.

Neither doth it exclude processes in relation to marches, perambulation, or division of lands, July 27, 1675, Robertson *contra* Stuart [2 Stair 362 ; R.9097]. Neither did it exclude the nullity of a disposition by a wife to her husband dying within the year, February 15, 1678, Gordon and her spouse *contra* Maxwell [2 Stair 614 ; M.6144].

But this privilege was found not only competent to defend minors in their property, but in their commonty, Hope, *de minoribus*   *contra* Mitchel [Probably Hope, *Maj. Pr.* IV, 9, 37, *sub nom. Inchaffray* v *Mitchell*]. Yet where the interest of a minor is not the chief right, but a major's right, whereby the minor's would fall in consequence, the process doth not proceed but against the major having a partial interest by the same evidents, November 25, 1624, Hamilton *contra* Matthison [Spotiswoode 210 ; M.9058], Spots, Minors, &c. Hamilton *contra* Christie [Spotiswoode 210 ; M.9058]. Or where a major lifrenter is called with a minor fiar, the process proceeds against the liferenter, but the minor is as not called, March 21, 1628, Bamanno *contra* Zule [*Sub nom. Bamanno* v *Yule*, Durie 366 ; M.9062] ; July 15, 1665, Borthwick *contra* Skein [1 Stair 298 ; M.9065]. This privilege is not relevant against the faults of the father, or his authors, as to his possession or right. And, therefore, it will not defend against forfeiture of the father's author, whereby the father's right fell in consequence, Spots, Minor, Hamilton *contra* Gaston [(1546) Spotiswoode, 211 ; M.9055]. Neither against recognition, February 19, 1662, Lady Carnegie *contra* Lord Cranburn [1 Stair 103 ; M.10339]. Neither will it defend against the superior, or his donatar, pursuing for any casualty of his superiority.

Title 7. Restitution

1. *Restitution of other men's Goods a Natural Obligation.*
2. *Restitution is not solely an effect of Property.*
3. *Restitution of things straying or waith, and lost.*
4. *Restitution of things* bona fide *acquired, not from the right Owner.*
5. *Restitution of things recovered from Thieves, Pirates, and Robbers.*
6. *Restitution not competent of things recovered from Public Enemies.*
7. *Restitution of things,* quæ cadunt in non causam, et causa data causa non secuta.
8. *No Restitution of things given* ob turpem causam.
9. *Restitution of* indebite solutum, *except by Transaction or Litiscontestation.*
10. *Restitution reacheth also the Fruits not consumed.*
11. *Restitution is grounded on the having anything which ceasing without fault, the Obligation of Restitution ceaseth.*
12. Bonæ fidei possessor facit fructus consumptos suos.
13. *Restitution by Heirs.*
14. *From Restitution arises the Action of Exhibition and Delivery :*
15. *And the Division of Things common without Society.*

THE obligations, whereby men are holden to restore the proper goods of others, are placed here among natural or obediential obligations, because they are not by contract or consent, neither have they their original from positive law. For though there were no positive law, these obligations would be binding; and they are obligatory among persons, who are not subject to one positive law. And, therefore, seeing they are not obligatory by the will or law of man, of necessity they must have their original from the authority and command of God, and that obedience we owe thereto by the law written in our hearts.

We are not here to speak of the obligations of restitution, which are by any voluntary engagement, or which are by delinquence, but of these only, whereby that which is another's coming in our power, without his purpose to gift it to us, and yet without our fault, ought to be restored, as things straying, or found, or recovered from pirates, thieves, &c. or bought *bona fide*, or the like.

2. Restitution of things belonging to others, may seem to be an effect of property, whence cometh the right of vindication or repetition of any thing; but, beside the real action, the proprietor hath to take or recover what is his own, (which doth not directly concern any other person, and so, being no personal right, hath no correspondent obligation upon the haver of that, which is another's, to restore it,) there is a personal right, which is a power in the owner to demand it, not only when it is in the possession of the haver, but if he hath fraudfully put it away; and yet it is his once having it that obliges him, and his fraudulent away-putting, though it be a delinquency, yet it gave not the rise to the obligation, but only continues it in the same condition as if he yet had it; so in that case his obligation is more palpable; for vindication of the thing, where it is not, cannot take place, though *pro possessore habetur qui dolo desiit possidere*, that is only *fictione juris ;* but the obligation to restore is direct and proper. The learned Grotius *de jure belli*, *l.* 2 *c.* 10, maketh such obligations, as arise from dominion and property, to be by tacit consent or contract, whereby the nations, who have agreed to appropriate things common to men, have also tacitly agreed that each man should restore what is the property of another. Yet this will not hold, if we consider that, though for the most part property be by consent, yet in many things it is without consent, as things which have their specification from their owner [by] his skill or industry, and others, as will appear in its own place; and, therefore, it is most just and sure to attribute such obligations to the law of God written in our hearts rather than unto any other conjecture of supposed consent. To this agreeth the Roman law, which holdeth these obligations not to be *ex contractu, sed quasi ex contractu*, neither doth account them obligations *ex lege ;* and if they were of tacit consent, these obligations were *ex contractu, l.* 2.*ff. d. Pact.* § *sed etiam* [D. 2, 14, 2]; for that tacit consents produce true, and not *quasi* contracts. See *l. 4. pro socio* [D. 17, 2, 4] *l. 18. Funct.* [D. 17, 1, 18] *l.* 6 § 2.*ff. Mandati* [D. 17, 1, 6, 2] *l. 13 ult. ff. Locati.* [D. 19, 2, 13].

3. There is many ways, by which the things of others may come to our hands, without our fault or delinquence. As first, Things straying, concerning which, the Lord hath ordained, Deut. 22. vers. 1,2,3: "To bring again unto their brother that which went astray, and if he were not near, to keep it till he sought after it, and then restore it ; and to do so with all things lost by him ;" wherein there seemeth something to be mixed of positive law, as the taking of it home to him, or keeping of it for his brother : whereas the simple natural obligation of restitution obliges to no duty of custody or pains, but only not to conceal that which is another's, and to restore it when demanded. And such is the custom of Scotland, that waith or straying goods must be proclaimed, and intimate to be waith ; and if the owner make them appear to be his, he may have them, satisfying for what was wared upon them for their preservation, as grass, &c. and if none appear within such a time, custom hath added that waith or strayed goods become public, and escheat to the king or others, to whom he hath disponed or committed that power, And this intimation is so far requisite, that if the goods be meddled with, or disposed of otherwise, it is theft. But though the publication maketh the goods public, and the meddling therewith to be without fault ; yet so that, if there do never any owner appear, the things do become really and absolutely public. And they do not become the possessor's by that ancient law, *quod nullius est, fit occupantis ;* which takes place amongst us only in things which were never known to have an owner, as pearls or stones found on the shore, and many others : but therefrom are excepted waith goods, and goods by shipwreck, which become escheat, as public. *Secondly*, Things lost, of which we see the rule for Israel, Deut. 22, how far they may be possessed without delinquence. In these our custom agrees with the Roman law, and other nations, except in the matter of waith and wrack goods, of which before, that such things, not being concealed, may remain with the possessors ; and if none claim them, they become their own ; and they may dispose of them, if they cannot be conveniently preserved without hazard [11,1,5 ; 111,3,27,*infra*].

4. *Thirdly*, Things belonging to others coming to our hands without delinquence, which we acquire *bona fide* either the property, use, or security thereof by pledge or deposition. In such cases we are bound to restore them to the owner, though thereby we lose what we gave, except in some cases, wherein positive law secures the buyer, and leaves the owner to seek the seller. And this restitution takes place, notwithstanding any obligement in the contrary : whereof we have an excellent species in the law *l. bona fide 31 §1.ff. Depositi* [D. 16,3,31,1]. A robber depositate with Seius that which he spoiled or robbed from Mævius ;—to which is Seius obliged to restore ? If he look only upon his engagement, truly to the robber ; but if upon the whole matter, certainly to Mævius. For the precept of law is to render every thing to the owner ; and therefore no promise or engagement can here prevail against the natural obligation of restitution, because, that being natural and indispensable, the engagement, whether ignorantly or wittingly made, to restore that

which the engager knows to be another's, is a delinquence inferring punishment for engaging, but no obligement to perform. So also he, who ignorantly takes in custody or pledge that which is his own, though thereby he promise to restore it ; yet his obligation, being by error in the substance of the contract, makes it void, and he may retain or recover it as his own.

5. *Fourthly*, Things recovered from thieves, robbers or pirates, are liable to this obligation of restitution ; wherein these things may be lawfully detained for the expenses and labour in recovery, especially if the labour was undertaken of purpose to recover such things : and if it was but by accident, the recoverer projecting some other thing, the satisfaction is due, as a remuneration of the trouble and pains, which it might have cost the owner in the recovery ; which with the expenses following thereon, being saved to him, he ought to recompense to the author thereof the profit accressing to him.

6. The greater doubt remaineth, Whether what enemies has possest, being recovered by a nation or party, ought not to be restored to the proper owners of that nation, who bore the equal expense of the war, and who being any way engaged in that quarrel, cannot but acknowledge the war of their enemies to be unjust. And, therefore, as to these things, I think that equity would require restitution upon satisfaction and gratification of the favour received : which ought to take place, unless by the peculiar customs of nations it hath been otherwise agreed, which may alter or derogate from this common law ; and therefore David, recovering back his wife and his spoil from his enemies, delivered every man his own, *vide infra, Tit. 12. Rights real.* §*43*.

7. *Fifthly*, The duty of restitution extendeth to those things, *quæ cadunt in non causam*, which coming warrantably to our hands, and without any paction of restitution, yet if the cause cease by which they become ours, there superveneth the obligation of restitution of them ; whence are the condictions in law, *ob non causam* and *causa data, causa non secuta*, which have this natural ground, and of which there are innumerable instances, as all things that become in the possession of either party in contemplation of marriage, the marriage, which is the cause, failing to be accomplished, the interest of either party ceaseth, and either must restore, or if it be dissolved within year and day, without a living child born, our custom makes all to return, as if there had been no marriage ; of which formerly, *Tit. Conjug. Obligat.* [1, 4, 19, *supra*].

8. But there is not the same ground for things given for an unjust cause, as *ob turpem causam ;* in which the will of the owner, and his purpose to transfer the property is effectual, though his motive was not good. But positive law doth sometimes obviate the inconveniency by such donations, and makes them void, and either to return, or become caduciary and escheat. But in things received *ex turpi causa*, if both parties be *in culpa, potior est conditio possidentis ;* so there is no restitution. As for these things which are attained by force or fear, they have their original from delinquence, and come not under this consideration.

9. *Sixthly*, Restitution extendeth to *indebite solutum*, when any party through error delivereth or payeth that which he supposeth due, or belongeth to another; if thereafter it appear that it was not due to that other, he who receiveth it is obliged to restore, and yet not by paction or contract. Therefore the law calleth this *promutuum vel quasi mutuum* [Cujas, *paratit. ad C. de condictione indebiti*], having in it the same natural obligation which *mutuum* or loan hath by voluntary engagement. There is this exception against *indebite solutum*, that it cannot be repeated, when the creditor gets that which is due to him, though not due by that party who paid the same, *l.2. C. de condict. indeb.* [C. 4, 5, 2] *l. 44. ff. eod.* [D. 12, 6, 44], which was not found, when the payment was made to an executor-creditor, pursuing upon his confirmation, and before sentence obtaining payment from the debtor's heir, who was decerned to refund, upon a discharge of the debt, granted to the defunct debtor, whereby it appeared the debt was not truly due, but twice paid, January 10, 1673, Ramsay *contra* Robertson [2 Stair, 146; M. 2924] *nam jus non patitur idem bis solvi*.

Positive law, for utility and quietness sake, excepteth transactions, which are properly such, and which are of two sorts, the one extrajudicial, when in any matter doubtful and debateable, either party to shun the hazard and trouble of legal diligence, is willing to transact and agree, so as thereby they quit or abate part of what they claim as their right, and so they tacitly renounce all future question upon any appearing of right, either judicially or extrajudicially; and, therefore, what either quitteth to other of their rights is due for the same cause; and hath in it, either expressly or implicitly, that the transaction shall not be ransacted upon any thing that shall accidentally appear thereafter, fraud and force only, as the common exception in all human actions, being excepted: and therefore such things, though they appear not to be the havers, are not to be restored. The other transaction is judicial by litiscontestation, when any cause in difference is referred to the oath of the party, or other probation, and particular diets for that effect assigned, wherein, if either party fail, he loseth what is referred thereto by his implicit consent; and when the right of any thing is referred to the haver's oath, and he sweareth it to be his own, though thereafter it may be made palpably appear not to be so, yet it will not be restored because of the owner's reference, implying that condition, that he shall stand to his oath, without questioning right or wrong, because an oath is an end of all controversy, though the swearer may be punished as a wilful perjurer. And thus most of things that become ours by sentences and decreets of judges, are not liable to restitution upon any subsequent question; of which afterwards in their proper places [1, 17, 2; IV, 39, 1, *infra*].

10. Under restitution doth fall not only the things of others, but their natural birth and fruits extant, not *bona fide* consumed; which are accounted as parts of the things, being accessory thereto, and belonging to the same owner: but industrial and artificial profits, in so far as they arise from the

haver's industry and not from the thing, fall not under restitution, if once separate therefrom.

11. In all these, the obligation of restitution is formally founded upon the having of things of others in our power, and therefore, that ceasing, the obligation also ceaseth. As he who *bona fide* did buy that which did belong to another, if while he hath it, it appeareth to be that other's, he must restore it without expectation of the price he gave for it, but as to that he must take himself to his warrandice, (express or implied) against the seller: but if *bona fide* he has sold it before he be questioned, he is free, and not obliged to restore it; though in so far as he is profited in receiving more for it than he gave, he be liable by the obligation of remuneration or recompense, of which in the next title. And as to the fruits of that which is another's, the obligation of restitution takes only place against the haver, where they are extant; and therefore, where they are neglected, or being reaped have perished, yea where they are consumed by the haver's making use of them, the obligation of restitution takes no place, though the obligation of recompense hath place in so far only as, by such fruits the haver conceiving them to be his own, is gainer, and in better condition than if he had not had them; but if he have increased his spending *bona fide* because of his having, he is free, *l. 25. § dum re sua 11 de Pet. haered.* [D. 5, 3, 25, 11]. Under his profiting comes his paying of his debt, or even his beneficence, where it appears he would have gifted, whether such a thing had come to his hand or not, for in either case he is *locupletior*, and must recompense. So that if he had sold or delivered that which was another's and which came to him without price, he is not obliged to restore the thing, but to recompense what he hath enriched himself by the price; and that without any question of the proportionable value of it to the thing.

12. In the enjoyment of fruits, the positive law of the Romans, and of this and most other nations, hath not only owned what is before said of restoring no more than that, by which the haver hath profited; but hath extended it this much farther, for utility and common quietness sake, that *bonæ fidei possessor facit fructus perceptos et consumptos suos;* whereby what fruits he, who hath possessed *bona fide*, hath consumed, though he have profited, and been enriched thereby, he is not obliged to restore the same: Which doth much secure and quiet men's enjoyments, that they may freely use and enjoy that which *bona fide* they have, and to shun the hazard of their ruin by answering for the bygone fruits, or their great vexation in clearing, whether they be enriched thereby or not, *vide infra Title 12, § 23* [11, 1, 23, *infra*].

13. Amongst these obligations neither by contract nor delinquence are commonly accounted the obligations, which are incident to these who enter heirs or are successors to others; whereby they are obliged to perform all their predecessors' obligations, and satisfy their debts in such manner as in law is prescribed; and yet it is not by their own engagement, nor by their fault but by their fact of entering heirs. Such also are the obligations upon executors

to satisfy the children and relict, legatars and creditors of defuncts, by or for whom they are intrusted. And indeed the restitution of the relict's part is properly such ; as also the legatar's, to whom the right by the legacy is transmitted oft-times of peculiar things: the giving also to children, or nearest of kin, is a restitution, because the property of the defunct's goods by his will, expressed or presumed, is transmitted to them after his death. But for payment of the defunct's debts, they are not properly by restitution, because the creditor hath no property in the goods, but an obligation upon the person, representing the defunct, and they arise either from that natural obligation that lies upon children from their parent's engagement, of which before [1,5,9,*supra*]; or by the natural obligation of remuneration or recompence, by which these successors, in so far as they are profited by the succession of the defunct, they must satisfy or recompense. And the positive law in some cases makes them liable simply, yet in equity they are liable in so far as they are gainers, *secundum vires hereditatis et inventarii.*

In the restitution of the goods of others, though the ground thereof be the having of that which is to be restored, yet if the haver cease to have through his own fraud, his delinquence therein obliges him to reparation, as if he still had it, according to the maxim of law, *pro possessore habetur, qui dolo desiit possidere, l. 11 de R.J.* [D. 50, 17, 131] and this extendeth not only to the thing itself, which he must restore, though he hath fraudulently put it away, or at least the value of it ; but also it extends to the fruits which he hath enjoyed *mala fide*, and after he knew, and had intimate to him, the right of another. So that such fruit must be restored, though the enjoyer become not the richer thereby.

14. From the right of restitution ariseth the action of exhibition and delivery. The exhibition is but preparatory to the delivery, that thereby the thing in question may be known to the parties, judge and witnesses ; and therefore *majori inest minus*, he that hath right to crave delivery hath much more right to crave the production, or the inspection. This action may be raised or intented concerning any moveable things that can be conveyed before the judge or his delegates ; as if the question were of an horse, if he be extant, he may be fitly craved to be exhibite, that the witnesses may be in a clearer capacity to depone to whom he doth belong ; but the ordinary subject of this action is exhibition and delivery of writs ; wherein the tenor and style of the action is, that the defender hath, or had, and fraudfully put away the writs in question. Whose having is probable by witnesses ; and relates not unto the time of probation, but unto the time of the citation. For if after citation the defender had the thing in question, he ought to have acknowledged it ; and if he have justly or necessarily put it away, or wanted it, he ought to have pleaded that as a defence, which therefore would exeem the pursuer from probation of the libel, as being acknowledged by the defence, and so being omitted, and the pursuer proving his libel, the exception is not competent ; but the defender is accounted as a fraudful away-putter after citation :

so that this defence, that the writs in question were given to be registrate, and were burnt in the tolbooth, was found relevant, and probable by the members of court, Haddington, January 12, 1610, Home *contra* Wilson [Not found].

There is a second member in this action, to wit, that the defender at any time before the citation had the writs in question, and fraudulently put them away, and is therefore repute as haver of them. Both these members must be proven : for it will not be sufficient to prove that the defender had the writs before the citation ; but it also must be proven that he fraudfully put them away ; which, therefore, being a matter of fraud, concerning the mind and purpose, is not probable by witnesses, but by writ or oath of party, November 17, 1627, Inglis *contra* Kirkwood [Durie 313 ; M. 3976]; January 30, 1629, Captain Crafurd *contra* L. Lamingtoun [Durie 420; M. 12374]. Yet if fraud otherwise appear, witnesses will be admitted to prove the having before citation, that the haver may instruct that he warrantably put the same away, July 14, 1666, Fountain and Brown *contra* Maxwell of Netheryet [1 Stair 397 ; M. 3978]. But witnesses will not be admitted to prove the delivery of any writ by the granter thereof, whether it be bond or assignation, as being *chirographum apud debitorem repertum, quod præsumitur solutum, l. 2§1.ff. de Pact.* [D. 2, 14, 2, 1] which was sustained as to an assignation in the hands of the granter's son, who did his affairs ; and witnesses were not admitted to prove that the same was delivered to the son, as agent for the pursuer ; December 14, 1666, Fairly *contra* the executors of Sir William Dick [*Sub nom. Fairlie* v *Dick's Creditors*, 1 Stair 412 ; M. 12278]. This presumption is stronger in relation to bonds, which are most ordinarly taken away by retiring the same, without taking discharge ; and therefore, being found in the hands of the debtor or his heir, they are presumed to be satisfied and retired ; or being in the hands of a cautioner, if it appear by his oath, or other evidence, that he got the bond from the principal debtor to take his name from it ; June 26, 1623, Carmichael *contra* Hay of Munktoun [*Sub nom. Monkton* v *Carmichael*, Durie 66 ; M. 11404] : otherwise the presumption would not hold by by the bond's being found in the hands of a cautioner, or of an executor, for whom simple retiring of the bond will not be sufficient without discharge or assignation.

Exhibition and delivery is competent to any party, in whose favours a writ is conceived, without necessity to prove that it was delivered. For that is presumed, if the writ be out of the granter's hand ; so that the granter is necessitate to prove that the writ was depositate upon terms not performed, or that it was lent, lost, stolen, or passed otherwise from him than by delivery ; for prevention of which, the English custom is good, that the writ bears, not only signed and sealed, but delivered before the witnesses. But, seeing with us delivery is presumed, it is ordinarily required that the granter of the writ be called in the exhibition, that he may be heard to propone any thing that may take off the presumption. Yet this will not be necessary in recovering securities of land or other real rights, especially if the pursuer be in possession. But in several cases writs are effectual without delivery:—As, first, writs granted by parents in favours of their children; November 11, 1624, bairns of Eldersly *contra* his heir [Durie 145; M.6344]: Secondly, mutual contracts or minutes; June penult. 1625, Valence *contra* Crawford [Durie 167; M.12304]: Thirdly, writs bearing a clause dispensing with delivery: Fourthly, by reservation of the granter's liferent, and power to dispone; June 19, 1668, Hadden and Lawder *contra* Shoarswood [1 Stair 541; M.16997]: Fifthly, an assignation taken by a debtor in name of his creditor, for his creditor's relief as cautioner for him, intimate by the debtor was found effectual without delivery; January 18, 1677, Dich of Grange *contra* Oliphant of Gask [2 Stair 496; M.6548]; February 24, 1680, McLurg *contra* Blackwood [2 Stair 762; M.845]. The like was found where the debtor took a bond in name of his creditor, which was presumed to be for that creditor's satisfaction or security, and not in trust, and not affectable by arrestment for the procurer's debt, before it was delivered; July 12, 1677, Bain *contra* Mcmillan [2 Stair 537; M.11495; 1,8,2, *infra*]. But where the bond was taken blank, and arrestment laid on before it was filled up with the creditor's name, or delivered to him, the arrester was preferred; February 27, 1678, Campbell and Cunninghame *contra* Bain and Mcmillan [2 Stair 618; M.9128].

Delivery of bonds of provision to children in the family is not presumed in competition with creditors, though their debts be posterior to the dates of the bonds of provision, unless the delivery thereof be proven anterior to the debts: otherwise creditors would be most insecure by parents making large bonds of provision, which they ordinarily keep by them; which will not be extended to bonds taken from debtors in the names of children, or wherein they are substitute, these not being latent, but known to the debtor [1,5,6, *supra*]. But the simple proving the having of writs, after citation is sufficient to infer the conclusion, unless the lawful cause be alleged in the defence and proven, and the having of writs, though of great importance, is probable by witnesses.

For the better discovery of the havers of writs, the Lords, by a late act of sederunt, February 22, 1688, ordained defenders in exhibitions to depone if ever they had the writs in question, and when and how they ceased to have them, and whether or not they know who had had them afterward, or who now hath them. Whereas before they did only depone they had them not since the citation in the exhibition, or did not at any time fraudfully put them away; whereby they were judges of what did import fraudful away-putting: whereas this special way of their examination gives the Lords opportunity to judge whether the way they ceased to have them was fraudulent or not.

15. Under the obligation of restitution is comprehended the obligation of division, whereby what we possess in common with others, or indistinct from that which they possess, we are naturally obliged to divide it with them, whensoever they desire to quit that communion; for thereby we restore what is their own, and we are not obliged thereto by any contract or delinquence. It

is true the contract of society includeth the obligement to divide after the society is ended. But communion falleth many times, where there is no society or contract, as by succession, legacy, gift, &c. Hence arise these three actions frequent in the Roman law, *actio familiæ erciscundæ*, [D. 10,2] *actio de communi dividundo* [D. 10,3], and *actio de finibus regundis* [*Sub nom. finium regundorum*, D. 10,1]. The first is the division of that which falls by succession. The second for division of that which is otherwise common. The third for distinction and clearing of the marches of contiguous grounds. In these either party may be pursuer; and he is held to be pursuer who did first provoke to judgement. But because they do chiefly concern immoveable or ground-rights, we shall say no more here of them, but leave them to their proper places, to be treated of hereafter [IV, 3, 12; IV, 27, *infra*].

Title 8. Recompense or Remuneration

THE obligation of remuneration or recompense is that bond of the law of nature, obliging to do one good deed for another, and it comprehends, *first*, all obligations of gratitude, which are generally acknowledged by all nations, the breach whereof is abhorred; *si ingratum dixeris, omnia dixeris.* Yet because the complaints of ingratitude are so frequent and unclear, every one esteeming highly of the demerit of his own actions, therefore most of them are laid aside without any legal remedy.

2. That which is done *animo donandi*, though it doth induce an obligation upon the mind and affection of the receiver to be thankful, yet doth not bind to the like liberality in case of necessity, *l.25.§11.ff. de Pet. haered.* [D. 5,3, 25,11] but in few cases; as a master gifting liberty upon this ground did put an obligation upon the servant, who thereby became free, *l.1 C. de revoc. don.* [C.8,55,1]; whence also arose that right of patronage, of which before [1,2,13–14, *supra*]. But that is rather by a positive law and tacit consent, as a condition implied in the gift. So also in every gift there is a correspondent duty of gratitude; and therefore, by ingratitude the donation becomes void and returns. Which the Romans extended only to the donor, not to his heirs, *l.1 et l. ult. C. de revoc. don.*[C.8,55,1 and 10], nor against the donatar's heirs, *l.7. C. eod.* [C.8,55,7] and betwixt these in a few cases exprest *in d. l. ult.* so that it is penal. But the matter is more clear when the good deed is done, not *animo donandi*, but of purpose to oblige the receiver of the benefit to recompense. Such are the obligations *negotiorum gestorum;* and generally the obligations of recompense of what we are profited by the damage of

others without their purpose to gift, or as the law expresseth it *in quantum locupletiores facti sumus ex damno alterius, l.13. in fin. & l.14ff. de Cond. indebit* [D. 12,6,13 and 14]. It is a rule in law, *donatio non præsumitur ;* and therefore, whatsoever is done, if it can receive any other construction than donation, it is constructed accordingly. Whence ariseth that other rule of law, *debitor non præsumitur donare, l.25.ff. de Probat.* [D.22,3,25] so that any deed done by the debtor is either presumed to be in security, or in satisfaction of his debt. As if he assign his creditor to any thing due to him, or dispone any thing to him, it is understood to be in security or payment; unless the deed express it to be a donation, or done for love and favour. Yea, trust is rather presumed than donation ; as if a man take a bond, assignation, disposition, or other right in another man's name, it is held to be a trust ; and he may force that other to denude himself, if he was not creditor to the acquirer [1,7,14,*supra*]. Yet these rules have their limitations. As, *first*, bonds, assignations or other rights in the names of children unforisfamiliat and unprovided, are presumed to be donations, because of the parent's natural affection and natural obligation to provide children *vid. l.26.ff. de Prob.* [D.22,3,26], which was extended to some goods and money of a small value, delivered by a rich brother who wanted children, to his brother who was no merchant ; which was presumed to be *animo donandi*, and was not imputed in part of an annual legacy, left thereafter by that rich brother to the other, November 13, 1679, Anderson *contra* Anderson [2 Stair 705 ; M.11509]. Yea an assignation to one's nearest of kin *mortis causa* was found a donation, and not in satisfaction of a debt due to that party, June 16, 1665, Crookshank *contra* Crookshank [1 Stair 282 ; M.11489]. And bonds of provision to children are not interpreted in satisfaction of prior bonds, but to be a further addition ; and so are any other rights taken in the name of children, especially if unforisfamiliat. Yet a tocher in a contract of marriage was found to be in satisfaction of all former provision, though it did not so express, June 29, 1680, Young *contra* Pape and Vauns [2 Stair 778; M.11476; 1,5,6,*supra*]. And aliment to children is ordinarily interpreted to be *ex pietate*, and not to oblige them ; as was found in the case of a mother, where the children had no considerable estate, February 2, 1672, Captain Guthry *contra* L. Mackerston and his brother [2 Stair 57; M.10137]; the like, though the mother was married, alimenting her daughter, who was apparent heir to her father, though she renounced to be heir, July 16, 1667, Hamilton *contra* Symonton [1 Stair 474 ; M.382]; the like was found in the mother's father alimenting his oye, July 21, 1665, L. of Ludquhairn *contra* L. Gight [1 Stair 301 ; M.11425]; and in the case of a grandmother alimenting her oye in the father's life, till she require the father to take her home, June 11, 1680, Gordon *contra* Lesly [2 Stair 770 ; M.11427]. Yet aliment by a sister's husband, who was also debtor, was not found to be a donation, seeing it began in minority, and was continued after though without paction, February 16, 1681, Spence *contra* Foulis [2 Stair 860; M.11437].

In all cases aliment or entertainment, given to any person without paction, is presumed a donation, if the person was major, and capable to make agreement. But entertainment to minors or weak persons doth ever infer recompense according to the true value of the benefit received. And in the case of these, who are in use to furnish provisions for money, the presumption ceaseth, and recompense is due.

In like manner where more persons are bound for the same debt, when any one payeth the whole debt, or more than his share, recompense by way of relief is due, although there be no clause of relief. And generally the delivery of any thing is not presumed to be a donation, but for recompense or loan. And so the delivery of victual to an ordinary buyer or seller of victual was found to infer the ordinary price, though no agreement or price was proven, unless the receiver instruct another cause of the delivery, June 15, 1667, Home *contra* Jameson [2 Stair 523; M.11508; IV,45,17,*infra*].

3. Likewise the obligation betwixt negotiators and these, to whose behoof they negotiate, ties to recompense what others (without our command, knowledge, or presence), have necessarily or profitably done for carrying on of our affairs, *l.2.ff. de neg. gest.* [D.3,5,2] and these deeds must be done without command or commission, otherwise they come in the nature of the contract of mandate or commission; yea what is done in our presence, with our knowledge, in our affairs, is repute as with our tacit consent and commission, *nam qui tacet, consentire videtur.* They must also be done for the carrying on of our affairs, for a negotiator cannot begin any new business, but only carry on that which is begun, *l.11.ff. eod.* [D.3,5,11] and they must be necessarily or profitably done, otherwise he hath his labour for his pains, and he that set him on work must pay him his expenses. And, lastly, though these deeds may be done without knowledge or consent, yet they may not be contrary to our will and command; for such obtruders can expect no recompence, *l. final. C. de neg. gest.* [C.2,18,24]; though, if no positive law hinder, we may be liable even to such *in quantum facti sumus locupletiores.* But the obligement to the negotiators is greater; for if they do that which is necessary or profitable for carrying on our affairs, though by some accident that affair may perish or miscarry, and we no richer, but, it may be, poorer, yet are we obliged, *l.10.ff.§.1 eod.* [D.3,5,10,1].

The ground of these obligations is, because it is frequent for men to go abroad upon their affairs, supposing quickly to return, and leave no mandate for managing of them, *Inst.* §*1 vers. idque utilitatis, de oblig. quæ quasi ex contr. nasc.* [Inst. 3,27,1] and yet being detained from them beyond expectaction, they may be easily lost; for instance, some redemptions must be peremptor, and the failure therein hath a great inconvenience; or the perfecting of some great bargain, a great part whereof is already done, and the not perfecting the rest loseth the whole; or the management of any work of great profit, that for want of some pains or expenses might be lost. These who interpose themselves in such cases, do necessarily and profitably for the good of the absent, and so are under no delinquence ; neither are they presumed to gift their pains and expenses ; nor have they any conventional obligation upon their part : and yet, though there were no positive law for it, the very light of nature would teach us it ought to be recompensed. And therefore can be no other than an obediential or natural obligation, by the authority of God, and our obedience to him. Grotius *l.2. cap. 10. de Jure Belli*, §8, doth not own this obligation as natural, but as arising *ex lege civili : nullum enim* (saith he) *habet eorum fundamentorum, ex quibus natura obligationem inducit ;* but the contrary appeareth not only from what is said, but by the testimony of the law itself, which reckons the obligations *negotiorum gestorum*, not among contracts, or obligations, or actions *ex lege*, but amongst these which are *quasi ex contractu*.

That this obligation is effectual, if it be diligently carried on, though the success answer not, is acknowledged in law, and set forth by an excellent species by Ulipan *l.10§1.ff. de negotiis gestis* [D.3,5,10,1]. "It sufficeth (saith he) if the negotiator did act profitably, although the affair had not the effect : as if he had cured a sick servant, if, notwithstanding the cure, the servant died, he hath this action competent to him."

4. From this obligation there arise mutual actions : the one direct, whereby he whose affair is managed, craveth accompt and restitution of the negotiator, and reparation of what he hath done amiss ; and the contrary action to the negotiator, whereby he craveth recompence and satisfaction of what he hath profitably expended, and for his labour and pains ; but the action is valid on either part, whether intented *directe* or *utiliter, l. Actio 47.ff. de negotiis gestis* [D.3,5,47].

5. The negotiator is holden not only to answer for fraud, but *pro culpa levi*, for his fault, though light ; yea, if any other negotiator offered, whom he excluded, for the lightest fault. He may be made also to follow forth his negotiation, according to the precept, *susceptum perfice manus, l.6 § ult. de neg. gestis* [D.3,5,6,12], *l.21.§2.ff. eod* [D.3,5,21,2]. But this, and the exactness of diligence, is introduced by positive law, equity leaving the negotiator free, if he hath acted profitably, though he might have acted more profitably, in making his party liable to him according to his acting.

6. The other obligation of recompense is for that whereby we are enriched by another's means, without purpose of donation, which is only presumed in few cases, as he who even *mala fide* buildeth upon another man's ground, or repaireth unnecessarily his house, is not presumed to do it *animo donandi*, but hath recompence by the owner *in quantum lucratus, l.38.ff. de hereditatis petitione* [D.5,3,38]. This remuneration is a most natural obligation ; as Cicero *l.3, de officiis* [s.5], saith, "That it is against nature for a man upon another's damage to increase his profit;" and again, "Justice suffers not, that with the spoil of others we should augment our own riches;" and, therefore, this is a common exception in all positive laws, that every one should be liable *in quantum locupletior factus est*. So pupils, though they cannot

oblige themselves by contract, yet if they receive that which is another's, they are liable to recompence *in quantum locupletiores facti, l. sed mihi 3.ff commodati* [D. 13, 6, 3], *l. 5. ff. de auct. tut.* [D. 26, 8, 5]. Minors also, though by positive law they are not liable for what they borrow, and receive, and mispend, yet they are liable *in quantum locupletiores facti sint*.

7. Hence arises the action in law *de in rem verso* [D. 15, 3]; whereby whatsoever turneth to the behoof of any makes him thereby liable, though without any engagement of his own.

8. We are enriched either by accession of gain or prevention of loss. Whence is the obligation of contribution for making up of goods thrown overboard to lighten ships in danger of shipwreck, whereby the loss of all is prevented, *l. 2. ff. ad legem Rhodiam de jactu* [D. 14, 2, 2], by which, whatsoever is thrown out to lighten a ship, for preventing of shipwreck, is to be satisfied by the contribution of all who enjoy that common benefit of safety from shipwreck, proportionally, according to the value of what is thereby saved: wherein the owners of the ship bear their share *l. 2. §2. eodem* [D. 14, 2, 2, 2], and wherein not only jewels, though of small weight, but even the clothes and rings of passengers bear a share; and the master of the ship may detain their goods till their share be paid *l. 2. §1. eodem* [D. 14, 2, 2, 1]. Which holds also when there is hazard of naufrage by entering a shallow river or port; if a part of the goods be put in a boat, and it perish, the value thereof is to be satisfied by contribution *l. 4. in pr. eod.* [D. 14, 2, 4, pr.]. Contribution is also made for what is paid for redemption of ships from pirates: which is not extended to things taken away by pirates or robbers out of ships, *l. 2. §3. eod.* [D. 14, 2, 2, 3]. This *lex Rhodia* is now become the law of nations, as commonly received by all for its expediency to prevent shipwreck, and to encourage merchants to throw out their goods, when thereby they will but bear their share of the loss. But this law is not declaratory of pure equity, but doth hold by custom; otherwise what any party doth for his own profit, though it have a consequential advantage to others, it will not oblige them to bear a share of the expenses; nor will it be interpret as *negotium gestum ;* for he who improves any right, though it becomes simply void, and another right beside his be preferred, yet he was doing his own business, not theirs, and can claim no share from them of his expenses *l. 6. §3 & 4. ff. de neg. gest.* [D. 3, 5, 6, 3 and 4]. So it was found, that, to evite capture by a privateer, a skipper having, by consent of some merchants aboard, and of the company, made a hole in the bottom of the ship, that he might run near the shore at a creek, and opening the hole, make the ship so far sink that she could not be carried off by the privateer, yet that privateer having reached her near the shore, but before the hole was opened, and having agreed for a ransom, for which the merchants contributed, the ship having been wrecked five days after by a storm, which she might have prevented by going off before the storm arose, the merchants and passengers were not found liable to contribution of their shares for the loss of the ship; June 15, 1680; Lesly and Millers *contra*

Logan, Weir, and others [*Sub die* 15 January, 1680, 2 Stair 737; M.13417]: *vide l.2.§.1. in fine, ff. ad L. Rhod. de jactu* [D.14,2,2,1], and *l.4.§.1. eod.* [D.14,2,4,1].

9. From the natural obligation of recompence doth arise the obligation of relief, whereby, when many persons are obliged *in solidum*, and thereby liable conjunctly and severally, payment or satisfaction made by one for more than his own share, doth oblige all the rest *pro rata*, although there be no conventional clause of relief, nor any law or statute but the natural obligation of recompence; for he who paid, not only for himself, but for others, is not presumed to do it *animo donandi*, as was found in the case of co-principals, June 19, 1662, Wallace *contra* Forks [1 Stair 111; M.3346]; June 28, 1665, Monteith *contra* Anderson [1 Stair 288; M.1044]. And, upon the same ground, relief is competent amongst cautioners, without any clause of relief, because the payment of one liberates all; June 27, 1675, Monteith *contra* Roger [*Sub die* January 27, 1675, 2 Stair 312; M.3351]. Yea, relief was found competent to a cautioner, who, in a new bond of corroboration, had engaged for the debt with the principal, and that against the cautioners in the first bond, though he had no assignation to the clause of relief granted to the first cautioners, Spotiswoode, Cautioners, Lybrak *contra* Vauns [(1636) Spotiswoode 34; M.2118]. The same must hold in co-tutors, co-curators, and wherever more debtors are liable *in solidum* for the same debt or deed [1,17,13,*infra*].

Title 9. Reparation, Where, of Delinquences and Damages Thence Arising

AMONGST obligations obediential we have placed these which are by delinquence; because they arise without any convention, consent, or contract, either particularly, or only by virtue of any positive law; and, therefore, they must needs have their original from the authority and will of God, and of our obedience due thereto. For though they do proceed from our fact, and from our will, whence that fact is voluntarily committed, yet it is not from our contracting will: and, therefore, these obligations do not receive their effect, and measure, or extent, by our will.

1. That obligations of delinquence are introduced by the law of nature, the suffrage of all men and all nations will evince, who do everywhere acknowledge the reparation of damages, and punishment of crimes and injuries, as having by nature a clear evidence and sharp sense thereof; and thereupon can, without reluctancy, concur with the magistrate in the punishment of citizens, and of enemies by the sword.

But it may be doubted how the law of nature, which is perpetual, and had place chiefly in innocency, can prescribe any thing in relation to delinquency or malefice, which was not to be found in that condition. This will be easily cleared, if it be considered that, though man was made in the state of innocency, yet he had a natural instability, for which God did warn and arm him; and though the principal and direct law of nature did teach man to love his neighbour as himself, yet he could not but by consequence know, (though he had stood in innocency, as the angels do,) that any who acted against that royal law of love by doing evil to his neighbour, and taking away from him that which is his, ought to repair him, and to be liable to divine justice, which is that certification which God put upon his natural law, as he did more expressly upon the forbidden fruit, *morte morieris.*

2. The obligation of delinquence then, is that whereunto injury or malefice doth oblige, as the meritorious cause thereof. And it is twofold: either that which relateth to God, or that which relateth to man. The former is the obligation of punishment, pain, or penalty: for unto God there can properly no reparation be made by the creature, whose duty and service is due to him; so that to him the creature is obliged to underly the punishment. In reference to man is the obligation of repairing his damage, putting him in as good condition as he was in before the injury; and this only is man's part for himself. For the inflicting of punishment is for God, in so far as it is authorized or allowed by him; but it is not for, or from man of himself: "Revenge is mine; and I will repay it, saith the Lord." [Rom. xii, 19.] For, as hath been said before [1, 1, 22, *supra*], an obligation in the debtor, hath a correspondent power of exaction in the creditor, which is the personal right. So in delinquence the power of exaction of reparation of his damage is man's for himself, but the power of exacting punishment is in God; and as for him or from him it is committed to man, it is but a ministerial power, and not dispensable at man's pleasure, and hath an obligation whereby man stands bound to God for doing his duty therein. Though positive law and pactions of men, and in some things the positive law of God itself, may constitute a penalty, and employ it for the proper use of the injured; yet it is not a proper punishment,

that hath its force by paction or positive law, and not by the law of nature. The obligation to punishment, arising from delinquence, and man's power and duty to inflict the same, is a public right, which, though naturally it did concern every man, yet is now with divine approbation for most part devolved upon public authority, which is said, Rom. 13, vers. 3, 4 "to be a terror to evil doers ; and not to bear the sword in vain, for he is the minister of God, a revenger, to execute wrath upon him that doth evil : " By which it is clear, that the magistrate, as he executeth revenge, doth it not of or for himself, nor for, or from the people, as their proper right or power of exaction, but, therein as he is the minister of God, he doth it for, and from God. Even though his authority and commission were not immediately from God, but from man, yet he stands in the place of these men to God, to execute that revenge, which they themselves were naturally obliged unto. But how far man's natural duties, or the magistrate's, in the punishment of crimes reacheth, the lines of the law of nature are become dark in many points. It is manifest and agreed by all, that, though in all damages done to man there are also punishments which may be inflicted by God, yet where the matter is chiefly man's interest, and so reparable to him, none will think that it is a duty, in all of these cases, to inflict vengeance on such. Neither doth any own a power and necessity to inflict punishment for man's spiritual delinquences, standing in his mind and affection, as for want of love, confidence, hope, &c. *Cogitationis pœnam nemo patitur, l.18.ff. de Poenis* [D.48,19,18]. In some things also the power of punishment is no less evident, even when there can be no reparation to man, as in that general precept of equal crimes and punishments, life for life, eye for eye, tooth for tooth, &c. [Deut. xix,21]. But there are many middle crimes that are much more unclear, wherein the word of God, even in the judicial law, is an excellent light ; for we may safely conclude, that it would be no injustice or intrusion for man to vindicate these crimes for God, which himself gave order to revenge. But our purpose being here only to insist in private rights, we shall not follow these, nor the many sublime questions that arise on that matter, but shall return to the private rights of men, arising to them by delinquence, of exacting reparation of their damages inferred thereby.

3. Damage is called *damnum, à demendo*, because it diminisheth or taketh away something from another, which of right he had *l.3.ff. de damn. inf.* [D.39,2,3]. The Greeks, for the like reason, call it ἐλαττον, by which man hath less than he had. It is not every damage that raiseth this obligation ; for some damages may be just, as these which are inflicted by way of punishment, and others may have their reparation arising from contracts, whereby, though a delinquence may arise in non-performance of the contract, yet the original cause of the obligation is the contract. Some also arise from deeds or things, the non-performance whereof is a delinquence ; as in the obligations of restitution and recompence. But here are only understood obligations which originally arise from delinquences as the first cause thereof.

4. Delinquence in the Roman law [Inst. IV, I, pr.] is reduced into these four, *furtum, rapina, damnum, injuria ;* wherein we shall not insist, but follow private delinquences, and obligations and actions thence arising, as they are known by the terms in our law, in so far as they use to be civilly prosecute. For though in public crimes, which are criminally pursued, there is competent reparation, either from the nature of the crime, or from law or custom; yet that is incident unto a public right, and not ordinary; therefore, it shall in general suffice here to consider, that, according to several rights and enjoyments, damages and delinquences may be esteemed.

As *first*, Life, members, and health; which, though they be inestimable, and can have no price, *l. 3. ff. si quad. paup.* [D. 9, I, 3], yet, there are therewith incident damages, and that either *lucrum cessans* or *damnum emergens*. So the life of any being taken away, the damage of these who were entertained and maintained by his life, as his wife and children may be repaired, see *Cuja.* [Jacques Cujas] *Obs. 14. c. 4*. So likewise the loss any man hath by the expenses of his cure or the loss of his labour, and industry in his affairs, is also reparable *d. l. 3. si quad. paup.* [D. 9, I, 3].

Next to life is liberty; and the delinquences against it are restraint and constraint: And though liberty itself be inestimable, yet the damage sustained through these delinquences are reparable.

The third is fame, reputation, and honour, which is also in some way reparable *l. 5. §1 in fin. ff. qui satisdare coguntur* [D. 2, 8, 5]. *l. 31. §5. de rebus Auth. Jud. Poss.* [D. 42, 5, 31, 5]. *l. 15. §31, 33 & l. 19. l. 20. ff. de Injur.* [D. 47 10, 15, 31 and 33; D. 47, 10, 19 and 20]. *First*, by making up the damage that is inferred in men's goods by the hurt of their fame, whereby their gain ceaseth, in that being repute such persons they are disenabled for their affairs. As if a merchant be called a bankrupt, it may not only hinder his traffick, but make all his creditors fall upon him suddenly to his ruin. So if a man be called a cheater, deceiver or the like, it disables him to manage his affairs, men being unwilling to meddle with such. And if a man, being about to marry, be called impotent, or infected with any noisome disease, he may be damnified in his match and tocher. Such actions upon injurious words, as they may relate to damage in means, are frequent and curious among the English; but with us there is little of it accustomed to be pursued, though we own the same grounds, and would proceed to the same effects with them, if questioned. *Secondly*, damage in fame or honour is repaired by homage, acknowledgment or ignominy put upon the delinquent. *Thirdly*, by equivalent honour and vindication of the injured. Slander is competent to be judged by commissaries; and therefore a decreet of the commissaries of Edinburgh, upon a pursuit for slander and defamation, decerning the slanderer to make acknowledgment of the injury before the congregation, and to pay an hundred pounds Scots to the party, and as much to the poor, was sustained by the lords, February 5, 1669, Deans *contra* Bothwell [1 Stair 598; M. 7577].

The fourth interest that may be damnified, is our content, delight, or satisfaction; and especially by the singular affection to, or our opinion of, the value or worth of any thing that owners have, in which consideration it is said, that every thing is to every man as he esteemeth it. And though this be not the intrinsic value of the thing, nor the common rate of it in the account of men, but *pretium affectionis*, the rate that the affection of the owner puts upon it; yet that being free to him, and his right, his damage therein ought to be repaired according to the value himself esteemed the thing taken from him worth. On this ground, in most actions in the civil law, wherein there is force or atrocious injury, reparation is to be made according to the reasonable estimation of the injured: And, therefore, he hath *juramentum in litem*, his oath to declare how much he accounted himself damnified; the exorbitancy whereof might have been taxed by the judge; but otherwise, though his estimation be much above the common value, it were receivable. This hath also place with us, as in actions of spuilzie, and other delinquencies by violence.

The last damage is in goods and possession; the redress whereof is more clear, because the things themselves are more valuable and estimable. In all reparations the natural fruits and profits of the things taken away come in as part thereof; and in many cases, the industrial fruits and profits which the owner might have had, at least used to make thereof.

Reparation is either by restitution of the same thing, in the same case, that it would have been in if it had remained with the owner, and this is most exact; or, where that cannot be, by giving the like value, or that which is nearest to make up the damage, according to the desire of the damnified. And if none be found fitter, reparation must be made in money, which is the common token of exchange and hath in it the value of every thing estimable.

5. In the reparation of delinquences it would be considered, when many have a hand in it, who are to be liable, and how far; for in some cases the delinquence is committed by one principally, and others are but accessory; in other cases the delinquence is equally and principally committed by more, though unto these also there may be accessories.

Accession to delinquence is either anterior, concomitant, or posterior to the delinquence itself. Anterior is, either by counsel, instigation or provocation; or by connivance in foreknowing, and not hindering these, whom they might and ought to have stopped, and that either specially in relation to one singular delinquence, or generally in knowing and not restraining the common and known inclination of the actors towards delinquences of that kind, as when a master keeps outrageous and pernicious servants or beasts. And, therefore, in many cases, even by natural equity, the master is liable for the damage done by his beast; as is clearly resolved in the judicial law, in the case of the pushing ox, which if it was accustomed that he pushed before time, the owner is liable for the damage thereof, as being obliged to restrain it, but if not he is free. So the like may be said of mastives and other dogs, if they be accustomed to assault men, their goods or cattle, and be not destroyed or restrained, their owner is liable. The remeids adhibite by the Romans, see *l. 40. et seqq. de œdil. ed. tot. tit. ff.* [D. 21, 1, 40] *et Inst. si quadr. paup. fecisse dicatur* [Inst. 4, 9].

Hence also is that famous edict of the prætor in the Roman law, *Nautæ, caupones, stabularii, quod salvum fore receperunt, nisi restituant, in eos judicium dabo* [D. 4, 9, 1, pr.]; by which the masters of taverns, stables, or ships, are liable for restitution of the damages that may be sustained by their servants, or any other that shall happen to be there for the time, in what is brought aboard upon the account of their employments. *l. 1. § ult. in fin. l. 2 & 3 in pr. ff. Nautae caup. stab.* [D. 4, 9, 1, 8; D. 4, 9, 2 and 3] but these obligations are rather introduced by statutory law for common utility, than by natural obligation.

Concomitant accession is, when the accessories are not equally concurrent in the act, but countenance, or otherwise assist, abett, cherish, praise, or connive at the delinquence. Posterior accession is by ratihabition, approbation, praise, gratification, defence, or support of the delinquents in order to the delinquence; all which accessions in our law are called *art and part*.

As to the question then, Who of these co-operants are obliged, and how far? *First*, It is clear that, where the delinquence is committed by many alike, there all of them are liable alike. But whether in equity they be all liable *in solidum*, or for the whole reparation, it is not so clear. Positive law hath made them all liable *in solidum*, for the repressing such concurrences, and that the injured be not put to the trouble of seeking in by parts from the several delinquents. Yet equity would rather lay the reparation of every man's part first upon himself; and, in case of his not being found solvent or sufficient, upon the rest, making up with all the trouble of obtaining reparation from many, by refunding the expenses in obtaining thereof, and the labour, and pains, and content of the injured. As to the obligation of punishment of many concurring delinquents: if an army, or part of it, in a mutiny all shoot at one person, if he be killed, it would not be thought just, for that one's life, to take the lives of all; and, therefore, because it cannot be known whose ball killed the man, it is accustomed, and not without good ground, by lot to single out who are to suffer, and the rest are free. From whence it may be gathered, as in the punishment, so in reparation, fellow delinquents, *socii criminis*, are to concur in the reparation, as they concurred in the action; though, as hath been said, positive law doth well to make all liable *in solidum*; yet so, that the satisfaction of one or more liberates the rest. But when it is not the private interest, but the public punishment of a crime, it should be extended so far as may restrain the crime. *Secondly*, As to the accessory delinquents. Though delinquents by command be numbered among them, yet (as we say) He doeth that causeth do; therefore, such are proper efficients, though mediate, and, therefore, no less liable than concurrents, *l. 15. ff. ad leg. Cor. de sicar.* [D. 48, 8, 15].

Thirdly, Other accessories, albeit by positive law they are oft-times all or many of them made liable *in solidum*, yet, as was said of concurrents, in equity they are liable but according to the influence they had in the delinquence. But in these the obligation may be much more to the punishment, where the will comes in to be considered with the act, than in the reparation, where the damage (which is the outward and more conspicuous thing) is mainly considered. Hence we shall insist no further, but come to the obligations by delinquence, which are civilly cognoscible by our custom, according to their known names and titles in our law ; which though they do rather signify the acts or actions, whereby such obligations are incurred or prosecute, than the obligations themselves, yet will they be sufficient to hold out both.

6. These are either general, having no particular name or designation: and such are pursued under the general names of damage and interest. Which hath as many branches and specialties, as there can be valuable and reparable damages : besides those of a special name and nature, which are chiefly these, assythment, extortion, circumvention, spuilzie, intrusion, ejection, molestation, breach of arrestment, deforcement, contravention, forgery, which comes in more properly in the process of improbation [IV, 20, 5, *infra*].

7. Assythment, as it signifies the reparation made, so it insinuates the obligation to repair damage, sustained by slaughter, mutilation, or other injuries in the members or health of the body; but it is chiefly pursued by the wife, children, or nearest of kin of parties slain. In other cases it is competent to the party mutilate or hurt, or otherwise prejudged by the mutilation or hurt. And though the private interest be only for reparation of damage and loss; yet our custom applyeth much of that, which is penal therein to the injured. And, therefore, consideration is had of the ability and estate of the offender, and the assythment is accordingly modified, all circumstances being considered ; and that either against the principal offender or the accessories. So it was found in the pursuit at the instance of Patrick and Isabel Greers, for the assythment and slaughter of their brother, against Thomas Horn, baxter, Nicolson, *de sicariis* [*Sub nom. Drews* v *Horn*, Haddington, *Fol. Dic.* 11,341 ; M. 13904]. This action was so favourable, that it was sustained, though there was no particular quantity of damage libelled, but the same referred to to the lords, Spotiswoode, Summons and Libel [Spotiswoode, 320]. Yea it was sustained at the instance of some of the kin, though not of the nearest degree, and though there were no concurrence of the four branches of the slain. It is a sufficient proof in this action, if the defender have taken remission, as was found in the case of Greers foresaid, and the like is observed, Haddington, January 25, 1611, Drew *contra* Hume in Montrose [Haddington, *Fol. Dic.* 11,341 ; M. 13904], where the defender was not freed, though he had an acknowledgment under the defunct's hand, that he was the cause of the wound, and therefore quit the wrong. So Assythment is a privileged action, as recent spuilzie is, Parl. 1528. c. 7 [A.P.S. 11,332,c. 3].

8. Extortion signifies the act of force, or other mean of fear, whereby a person is compelled to do that which of their proper inclination they would not have done. It doth also imply the obligation of the injurer to the injured,

to repair his loss and damage by such acts; and things so done are said to be done *vi majori* or *metus causa*, by force or fear. Deeds or obligations extorted are in their own nature, and in equity, efficacious because they have truly the consent or act of the will, by which such rights are constitute. *l.21.§5.ff. Quod metus causa* [D.4,2,21,5], and therefore the Romans had no civil remeid in their ancient law for such, till the edict of the prætor *Quod metus causa gestum erat, ratum non habebo, l.1.ff. quod metus causa* [D.4,2,1]. But by that edict, and the custom of this and other nations, such deeds and obligations as are by force and fear, are made utterly void; though in equity the effect almost would be the same: for seeing the delinquence done by extortion obliges to reparation, if any should be pursued upon an extorted obligation, he would have the exception of compensation upon the obligement of reparation, and so might also by action obtain such an obligation or other right to be annulled.

This edict was not competent upon every force or fear. But first, it behoved to be unlawful, *l.3.§1.ff. quod metus causa* [D.4,2,3,1], secondly, such as might befall a constant man, as of life, *l.6,7,8,9.ff.l.9 c.eodem* [D.4,2,6-9], or torment of the body, *l.4.c.eodem* [D.4,2,4], or of bondage, *l.8.§1.ff eodem* [D.4,2,8,1], or the loss of estate, *l.9.ff. quod metus causa* [D.4,2,9], or infamy, or disgrace, *l.8.§2.ff. eodem* [D.4,2,8,2], or of bonds and prison, *l.22.ff. eodem* [D.4,2,22], but only unlawful and private, and not public imprisonment, *l.3.§1.ff. eodem* [D.4,2,3,1], it was not competent upon reverential fear, *l.6. C. de his quæ vi* [c.2,19,6]; nor upon fear contracted upon power and dignity, nor of threats, *l.9. C. eodem* [c.2,19,9], except they were from powerful persons, *l.23.§1, quod metus causa* [D.4,2,23,1], and the effect of the edict was, being pursued within a year, (which afterwards was made four years, *l.7. C. de temp. in integrum rest.* [c.2,52,7], in place of *annus utilis*, unless reparation was made before sentence), the party was condemed in the quadruple, and the penalty was triple, and applied to the injured; and after a year, simple reparation, *l.14.§1.ff. eodem* [D.4,2,14,1]. Our customs go much along with the course of the civil law in this, but so as not bound thereby, respecting most when the true reciprocal cause of the obligation or deed is force or fear, not being vain or foolish fear. And it is competent ordinarily by way of action, or sometimes by exception, Spots, Exceptions, Tenants of Cockburnspath *contra* E. Home [(1546) Spotiswoode, 109]. But it was elided by a judicial ratification of the deed upon oath [1, 17, 14, *infra*], July 8, 1642, Grant *contra* Balvaird [Durie 898; M. 16483]. Extortion is more easily sustained in the deeds of weaker persons; and therefore extortion was found relevant to reduce a disposition by a facile weak person, who was apprehended by the purchaser upon a caption of a third party, and detained by his servants and officers, and not by messengers, and kept latent in obscure houses, and carried from place to place in the night, till he subscribed a disposition of his whole estate for a cause not near the third of its value; albeit there was produced a cancelled minute to the same effect with the disposition in question, wherein the two actors of the force were witnesses insert, but the disponer's name, nor no part of it, was to be seen, but a lacerate place, as if it had been cancelled, without any anterior adminicle to astruct the truth of it: January 10, 1667, Stewart of Castlemilk *contra* Whiteford and the Duke of Hamilton [2 Stair 489 ; M. 16489]. Extortion falls most to be controverted in deeds done by wives; and therefore, when the deed is extremely to their prejudice, and to the behoof of their husbands, it is presumed as done *ex reverentia maritali*. Thus, a wife's discharge of her whole contract was found null, without alleging any compulsion, January 9, 1623, Marshall *contra* Marshall [Durie 40 ; M. 6036]. But ordinarily marital reverence is not sufficient, though the husband were *vir ferox*, and was thereafter divorced: Hope, Husband and Wife, Hepburn *contra* Nasmith [Hope, *Maj. Pr.* 11, 17, 31 ; M. 6069 and 16482].

It was also found relevant to reduce a wife's consent to her husband's disposition, that before, he had beaten, menaced, and extruded her for not consenting; but in this case it being alleged, that the wife appeared well content at the subscription, witnesses were examined *hinc inde ex officio*, for trial of the truth, July 18, 1632, Cassie *contra* Fleming [Durie 634 ; M. 10279], where this case of *vis et metus* is accurately debated and determined. But a wife subscribing her husband's testament, containing provisions prejudicial to her contract of marriage was not reponed, as having done it *ex reverentia maritali*, at her husband's desire, who was *moribundus*, he having lien long sick, and she having married within a year thereafter, and the deed done to her only daughter, January 24, 1674, Murray and Jaffrey *contra* Murray [2 Stair 256 ; M. 6525 ; 1, 4, 18, *supra*]. Upon the like ground extortion will be the more easily presumed and sustained in the deeds of the persons, who are weak and infirm of judgment or courage, as said is, than of these who are knowing and confident; and more easily in deeds and obligations gratuitous and free, than in such as are for an onerous cause, which will not easily be annulled, unless manifest lesion do appear, or that the compulsion be very evident. Yet the resignation of the earldom of Morton, in the hands of king James V was reduced, because the resigner was then imprisoned by the king, without any visible cause, and was discharged the same day he made the resignation, Sinclair, April 12, 1543, Earl of Morton *contra* the Queen [Sinclair's *Prac.*; M. 16479]. And a disposition granted by the Lord Gray and his Lady to a great man for the time, after menaces, and without an adequate onerous cause, was reduced *ex capite metus*, and upon concussion, February 22, 1688, Lord and Lady Gray *contra* Earl of Lauderdale [1 Fountainhall, 499 ; M. 16501]. And the like sustained against a decreet at the king's instance against the master of the mint, and assigned to the lord chancellor, together with the bond and transaction thereupon, Earl Lauderdale and Lord Haltoun *contra* Earl Aberdeen, January 13, 1692 [Harcarse 154 ; M. Supp. 88 ; 1, 17, 11, *infra*]. So *metus* was sustained to reduce a bond granted by a party, because he was taken by caption, being sick, January 22, 1667, Mair *contra* Stuart of Shambelly [1 Stair 429; M. 16484]. It was also sustained to reduce a bond granted by two sons for freeing their father, who was taken by a caption, though the charge was suspended, (he being carried to the hills and menaced for his life); though the sons got abatement, and so there appeared a transaction, December 8, 1671, McNish *contra* Spalding and Farquharson [*Sub nom. McIntoshes v Spalding and Farquharson*, 2 Stair 20; M. 16486].

9. Circumvention signifieth the act of fraud, whereby a person is induced to a deed or obligation by deceit, and is called *dolus malus*, in opposition to *dolus bonus*, or *solertia*, *l.1.§3.ff. de dolo* [D. 4, 3, 1, 3] *& l.16.§4. de minoribus* [D. 4, 4, 16, 4]; and it must needs be the cause of the obligation or deed, and so not be known to the party induced, before it can have any legal effect, *l.34. C. de Transact.* [c. 2, 4, 34]. For he who knoweth the snare, cannot be said to be ensnared, but to ensnare himself; and though deceit were used, yet where it was not deceit, that was the cause of the obligation or deed, but the party's proper motion, inclination, or an equivalent cause onerous, it infers not circumvention. So neither doth error nor mistake, though it be the cause of the obligation or deed, and be very prejudicial to the erring party. And though, if it had been fraudulently induced by the other party, it would have been sufficient; yet not being so, there is no circumvention: and the deed is valid, unless the error be in the substantials of the deed, and then there is no true consent, and the deed is null; as if one married Sempronia, supposing she were Mævia, the marriage hath no further progress (but by subsequent consent) and it is void. But if he married Sempronia, supposing her to be a virgin, rich or well-natured, which were the inductives to his consent, though he be mistaken therein, seeing it is not in the substantials, the contract is valid [1, 4, 6, *supra*; IV, 40, 24, *infra*]. But if the error or mistake, which gave the cause to the contract, were by machination, project or endeavour, of any other than the party errant, it would be circumvention, *l.2.§1.ff. de doli mali et met. exceptione* [D. 44, 4, 2, 1]. So that there is nothing more frequently to be adverted, than whether the error be through the party's own fault, or through the deceit of another; and therefore *errore lapsus* and *dolo circumventus* are distinct defects in deeds.

10. The Roman praetor, among other perpetual edicts, did give this of fraud; *Quae dolo facta esse dicuntur, si de his rebus alia actio non erit, et justa causa esse videbitur, judicium dabo*, *l.1.§1.ff. de dolo malo* [D. 4, 3, 1, 1]. This edict was competent either by way of action or exception, *l. finali.ff. eodem* [D. 4, 3, 40], and, in hatred of fraud, these who were condemned in this action became infamous, *l.1.ff. de his qui notantur infamia* [D. 3, 2, 1]. And therefore, as the edict expresses it, it was not competent, if there was any other more favourable remeid: neither was it competent for a very small sum, not exceeding two crowns, *l.9.§finali.ff. de dolo malo* [D. 4, 3, 9, 5], neither was it competent to children against their parents, nor to the vulgar against these of consular dignity, nor to vile persons against those of an orderly life, *l.11.ff. eodem* [D. 4, 3, 11]. It was also personal, and reached no further than the per-

son committing the fraud, and not *in rem*, reaching the thing, if lawfully it came to any other not partaking of the fraud : *dolus auctoris non nocet successori*, *l. 4. §27. ff. de doli & mali & metus exceptione* [D. 44, 4, 4, 27], *nisi in causa lucrativa, ibidem* [This should read *l. 4. §30 eodem*, i.e. D. 44, 4, 4, 30]. So that the deed, done thereby, was not rendered null, as in extortion ; but reparation given to the injured to the single value only, infamy being a sufficient penalty, but according to the estimation of the party injured by his oath *in litem*, *l. 18. ff. eodem* [D. 44, 4, 18], *l. 68 ff. de rei vind.* [D. 6, 1, 68], *l. 5. §3. ff. de in lit. Jur.* [D. 12, 3, 5, 3], *l. 2. C. eod.* [C. 5, 53, 2].

The Romans had also their *actio redhibitoria et quanti minoris*, whereby the deceived might obtain what damage they had sustained by the fraud, or might thereby annul the bargain. And where the lesion was very great, fraud was presumed, *l. 36. ff. de V.O.* [D. 45, 1, 36], as when the price exceeded the double value of the ware, *l. 2. C. de rescind. vend.* [C. 4, 44, 2]. But they did not consider small differences betwixt the ware and price, which would have raised multitudes of debates hurtful to trade, the design whereof is to gain, and therefore nothing to induce a moderate gain was questionable. As when merchants set out their ware, or though they should falsely assert it cost them so much, and others had given them so much, or that the ware was fashionable or good, *l. 19. in pr. ff. de Aedil. edicto* [D. 21, 1, 19, *in pr.*], *l. 18 in pr. eod.* [D. 21, 1, 18, *in pr.*], there was no civil remeid, unless the damage were considerable. In which sense only it is true, *in commercio licet decipere ; l. 16. §5. ff. de Minorib.* [D. 4, 4, 16, 5. This should be §4] because, though it be not simply lawful, yet it is against no civil law. But the sophistication of ware, or concealing of the insufficiency thereof, was held fraudulent, and reparable *actione redhibitoria, aut quanti minoris*.

We have the more fully summed up the sentiments of the civil law in the matter of fraud, because it is most equitable and expedient, and therefore is generally followed by our custom ; which regardeth not inconsiderable damages in traffic, that it may be current and secure. For nothing is more prejudicial to trade, than to be easily involved in pleas ; which diverts merchants from their trade, and frequently marrs their gain, and sometimes their credit. Therefore we allow not the quarrelling of bargains upon presumed fraud *ex re ipsa*, although that which is bought be within the half of the just price ; if there be not sophistication, or latent insufficiency, which we exactly consider, because it is destructive to trade. Vide Tit. 10, §14 & 15 [1, 10, 14 and 15, *infra*].

11. Fraud is not to be presumed, but must be proven, *l. 18. §1. ff. de Prob.* [D. 22, 3, 18], *l. 6. C. de dolo* [C. 2, 20, 6], and is always competent to be proven by the oath or writ of the party committing the fraud, when the question is betwixt himself and the party prejudged ; whereby it may be proven that he designed to deceive, or that he did such acts from whence fraud is presumed ; which by his oath he may qualify what he did, and why he did it ; and if there be a probable construction that the deeds done were

not to deceive, fraud will not be thence presumed : and will be hardly presumed in a person of entire fame and honest life ; but much more easily in these who have been found to defraud, or are so reputed. And it being ordinary for parties to allege contrary, or different circumstances to infer or exclude fraud, therefore the lords do neither give the benefit or burden of probation to one party ; but do state the points of moment alleged, or what others they think fit for clearing the truth, and allow either party to prove where their allegeances are not contrary ; and where they are contrary, there are abstract queries stated, as to which either party may adduce such an equal number of witnesses as is prescribed, as whether a writ was read at the signing, and what the condition of parties then were, (for the not reading of a writ at subscribing will not alone infer fraud, because it might have been read before). Yea it was not sustained to be proven by witnesses, that a writ was not read at subscribing, though there was great lesion to the subscriber in favour of his curator *sine quo non*, within six months after his majority, *ante redditas rationes*. And that a wadset was communed, yet the writ bore an irredeemable disposition, July 4, 1635, L. Monimusk *contra* L. Lesly [Durie, 770 ; M. 4956] : but these circumstances would have been certainly relevant by the oath of the party, or writ. Neither were witnesses admitted to prove circumvention in causing a testator give warrant to a notar to subscribe a testament unread, of a tenor contrary to what the testator expressed, Hope, Testament, nearest of kin of the Lady Innerlieth *contra* her Executors [Hope, *Maj. Pr.* IV, 1, 14 ; M. 6846]. Neither were witnesses admitted to prove the fraud of a debtor, retiring a bond from a person, whose name was only in trust for another to whom the debtor had paid annualrent. July 4, 1622, Barclay *contra* Cuningham [Not found]. But where the deeds alleged can have no fair construction, but do infer fraud, witnesses are receivable and thereupon bond and ratification for a considerable estate were reduced, March 1682, Bannatine *contra* Bonnar and Neilson [Harcarse 123 ; M. 5581] ; March 1682, Ogilvy *contra* Gourlay [Probably 1 Fountainhall 175]. So a collusion betwixt a creditor and debtor, whom the creditor brought home from abroad, that he might prevent the diligence of another creditor, who had denounced that debtor's lands to be apprised upon sixty days, but upon return of the debtor, this creditor denounced upon fifteen days, and so did first apprise, yet the first denunciation and last apprising was preferred, Hope, *de dolo*, Wardlaw *contra* Dalziel [(1620) Hope, *Maj. Pr.* VI, 28, 58 ; M. 2427]. And the liferent escheat of a vassal was excluded, because the superior, upon whose horning it fell, had taken payment of the debt, and had not acquainted the vassal that he was denounced, that he might have relaxed within the year, as was found in the same case, *ibidem*. Though this case, and that of latent insufficiency, be rather *lata culpa, quae dolo aequiparatur ;* for the difference betwixt *dolus* and *lata culpa* is, that *dolus est magis animi*, and oftentimes by positive acts, and *lata culpa* is rather *facti*, and by omission of that which the party is obliged to show. A discharge as to an assigny was reduced to a bond granted by one brother to another, the discharge being of the same date with the bond, which could have no construction, but that the brother by assigning the bond might deceive, unless there were instructed a just cause of that date, December 4, 1665, Thomson *contra* Henderson [1 Stair 320 ; M.4906]. And a discharge by a son to his father, of a sum provided to him by his contract of marriage, without satisfaction, but upon agreement betwixt the father and the son the time of the contract, that the sum in the contract should be discharged gratis, was found fraudulent and null, as to the son's creditors, who traded with him even after the discharge, January 21, 1680, Caddel *contra* Raith [2 Stair 473 ; M.4275]. And a liferent by a husband to his wife of his whole estate, providing she disponed the half to the children of the marriage, was found fraudulent as to that half, and the creditors of the husband preferred to the children therein, December 23, 1679, Erskine *contra* Carnegies and Smith [2 Stair 726 ; M.968]. But where the liferent was but suitable to the parties, a clause therein, that so much of it should be applied for the aliment of the children, that clause was not found fraudulent in prejudice of the husband's creditors, but was sustained to the children, it flowing only from the mother, November 16, 1665, Wat *contra* Russell [1 Stair 308 ; M.10378].

12. Under fraud simulation and collusion are comprehended. Simulation occurs mainly in two cases ; in gifts of escheat and liferent, and in dispositions, *retenta possessione*. For, although the disposition be delivered, and that there be instruments of delivery of the goods disponed, yet if the natural possession be retained, the disposition is presumed similate, and others affecting the things disponed by legal diligence, or by natural possession, are preferred [11,3,27; 111,2,12,*infra*]. So simulation in gifts of escheat and liferent is very frequent ; and easily presumed, *retenta possessione*, Vid.Tit.25.§12[111,3,21, *infra*].

13. Collusion occurs chiefly when the debtor or common author opposes some creditors, and concurs with others, that these may attain the first complete diligence ; which imports direct fraud : or if he oppose one, though he do not concur with another, but only not oppose that other, his opposition is holden as fraudulent, as supra in the case, Wardlaw *contra* Dalziell [(1620) Hope, *Maj.Pr.* VI,28,58 ; M.2427]

14. Fraud gives remeid by reparation to all that are damnified thereby, against the actor of the fraud, either by annulling of the contract or other deed elicit or induced by fraud, or by making up the damage sustained by the fraud, at the option of the injured ; and so fraud was sustained at the instance of a seller, to annul a bargain of wines, delivered to a skipper upon the buyer's order, because the time of that order the buyer knew himself to be insolvent, which might appear by his books ; and though the wines were arrested by a creditor of the buyer's in the ship, and a decreet for making forthcoming recovered ; yet the wines were ordained to be restored to the seller, December 22, 1680, Prince *contra* Pallat [2 Stair 823 ; M.4933].

15. Reparation of fraud is not only competent to the party defrauded, but also to his creditors or assignees; for which the Romans had a peculiar remeid *per actionem Paulianam* for annulling all deeds *in fraudem creditorum* [D. 42, 8]. In imitation whereof the lords of session made an act of sederunt in July 1620, against unlawful dispositions and alienations made by dyvours and bankrupts, which was ratified by act of Parliament, 1621. c. 18 [Bankruptcy Act, 1621, c. 18; A.P.S. IV, 615, c. 18]; by which act of sederunt the Lords declare, "That, according to the power given to them to set down orders for administration of justice, meaning to follow and practise the good and commendable laws, civil and canon, made against fraudful alienations in prejudice of creditors, against the authors and partakers of such fraud, that they will decern all alienations, dispositions, assignations and translations, made by the debtor of any of his lands, teinds, reversions, actions, debts, or goods whatsoever, to any conjunct or confident person, without true, just and necessary causes, and without a just price really paid, the same being done after contracting of lawful debts, to have been from the beginning null, by way of action or exception, without further declarator: but prejudice to purchasers of the bankrupt's lands and goods for just and competent prices, or in satisfaction of their lawful debts, from the interposed persons: But the receiver of the price from the buyer, shall be holden to make it forthcoming to the creditors. And it shall be sufficient to prove by writ or oath of the receiver of the disposition from the bankrupt, that the same was made without a true and just cause, or that, the lands and goods being sold by him that bought them from the dyvour, the most part of the price was converted or to be converted to the bankrupt's profit and use. And in case the bankrupt or interposed person shall make any voluntary payment or right to any person he shall be holden to make the same forthcoming to the creditor having used the first lawful diligence; and he shall be preferred to the con-creditor, who, being posterior to him in diligence, hath obtained payment by the partial favour of the debitor, or his interposed confident, and shall recover from the said creditor what he hath so obtained: but what the interposed person hath paid or assigned to the bankrupt's lawful creditor, before preferable diligence done by others, shall be allowed to him; and he shall be liable to make forthcoming the rest of the price. Yea the said bankrupts and interposed persons, and all others who shall give counsel and assistance in devising and practising the fraud, shall be holden infamous, incapable of honour, dignity, or office, or to be witnesses or assizers."

This excellent statute hath been cleared by many limitations and extensions, in multitudes of decisions occurring since, relating to defrauding of creditors: which, being of the greatest importance for public good and security, we shall distinctly and in order hold forth the several cases wherein there have been decisions in this matter.

First, then, though the statute be only in favours of anterior creditors, for annulling posterior deeds; yet it is not exclusive of other remeids for annulling deeds done in defraud of creditors, though contracting after these deeds, where fraud in the design doth evidently appear: whereof we shall now instance several decisions. So a bond granted by a father to a son *forisfamiliat*, payable after the father's death, was reduced at the instance of the father's posterior creditors, continuing traffic with him, February 12, 1669, Pott *contra* Pollock [*Sub nom. Pollock* v *Pollock*, 1 Stair 602 ; M. 4910]. And a bond payable only by the granter's heir, if he had no heir of his own body, was reduced as fraudulent, January 24, 1677, Blair of Ardblair *contra* Wilson [2 Stair 498 ; M. 4927]. And a disposition of lands, purchased by a merchant to his son, was found affectable for the debts of merchants strangers, who began to trade with the father before the disposition, and continued after, even as to the posterior debts, seeing the father continued still to act as proprietor, though by his compt-book it appeared he knew himself to be insolvent: and though the son's infeftment was public and registrate, which stranger merchants were not obliged to know, July 2, 1673, Street and Jackson *contra* Mason [2 Stair 197 ; M. 4914]. Yea an infeftment by a father to his eldest son, an infant, was reduced at the instance of posterior creditors, his neighbours, where the seasin was registrate, seeing the register was carried out of the country, and the father continued to act, not as liferenter, but as proprietor, December 4, 1673, Reid of Ballochmiln *contra* Reid of Daldilling [2 Stair 234 ; M. 4925]. And generally latent rights amongst confident persons are reducible by posterior creditors. But the liferent of the whole conquest of a merchant, provided in a contract of marriage to his wife, being an ordinary clause, was not found fraudulent, February 10, 1674, Marion Gray *contra* the son and creditors of her husband [2 Stair 263 ; M. 977].

Secondly, Though this statute bears all alienations, without a cause onerous, in prejudice of prior creditors to be null *ab initio*, and without declarator by exception or reply ; yet custom hath found this inconsistent with the nature of infeftments, which cannot be reduced till they be first produced, and all the authors called ; which cannot be by way of exception, but by action [1, 1, 16, *supra*]. Yet a disposition of moveables was found annullable by reply, June 16, 1671, Bowers *contra* Lady Couper [1 Stair 734 ; M. 2734] ; and likewise a profitable tack, February 6, 1662, Doctor Hay *contra* Marjory Jamieson [2 Stair 63 ; M. 1009]. Neither are the receivers of such alienations countable for the profits *ab initio*, till they be put *in mala fide* by the pursuits of anterior creditors ; whose rights they are not presumed to know till they be produced and found preferable, either evidently, when the case is clear to common apprehension, or *in dubio*, when it is so found by the judge.

Thirdly, Though the title of this statute, and much of the body of it, be against the alienations of bankrupts in prejudice of their creditors ; yet the statutory part declares all alienations to any conjunct or confident person without a just price, being in prejudice of anterior creditors, to be annulled, which hath always been extended, not only to dispositions of bankrupts made to confident persons, but to any person, without a competent price, or equivalent cause onerous; and therefore such gratuitous deeds are reducible by anterior creditors, though the granter was not then bankrupt, as a broken merchant flying. But if he were before, or did by these fraudulent deeds become, insolvent, §*3 Inst. quibus ex caus. manumit.* [Inst. 1,6,3], Hope, Usury, Pringle *contra* Ker [Hope, *Maj. Pr.* 11,13,32 and 41; M.931]; February 16, 1628, Kilgour *contra* Thomson [Durie 347; M.910], January 17, 1632; Skene *contra* Belston [*Sub nom. Skene* v *Betson*, Durie 611; M.896]; yea, if thereby his estate cannot afford ready satisfaction or security, as being incumbered with many apprisings or adjudications, though the reversions may be equivalent to all his debt, yet anterior creditors may reduce gratuitous deeds done by such persons, it being more fit that anterior creditors should be preferred, and the obtainers of these gratuitous rights should be put to recur upon the reversions by their warrandice, February 10, 1665, Lady Craig *contra* Lord Loure [*Sub nom. Lady Greenhead* v *L. Lourie*, 1 Stair 266; M.931].

But there is nothing in this statute, or by custom, to annul any gratuitous deed in favours of wives, children or strangers, if at the time of the granting and delivery thereof the granter had an estate sufficient for these and all his debts, unaffected by apprising, adjudication or arrestment. Neither will inhibition suffice, nor apprising or arrestment for small sums, be a ground for this reduction. For competent provisions to wives or husbands are not accounted gratuitous, but onerous *ad sustinenda onera matrimonii, arg. l. ult. §1. in fine & §2. junct. cum.* [D.42,8,25,1 and 2], *l.6.§11.ff. Quae in frand. cred.* [D.42,8,6,11] and for other mutual provisions. But if exorbitant, they will be liable *in quantum locupletiores facti*, December 23, 1665, Burnet *contra* Lepers [1 Stair 329; M.5863]. Neither are provisions or gifts to children annullable by anterior creditors, if the granter had then a visible estate, sufficient for these and all his debts, as was found in a provision by a father to his son by his contract of marriage, though the son received the tocher, June 22, 1680, Grant of Cairnhaugh *contra* Grant of Elchies [2 Stair 773; M.100]; November 10, 1680, McKell *contra* Jamieson and Wilson [2 Stair 795; M.920]. Yea the portions of children were not excluded by prior creditors, their father having then a sufficient visible estate, though *ex eventu* it proved insufficient, by running on of annuals, and accumulations of apprisings, December 11, 1679, Creditors of Muswal *contra* Children of Muswal [2 Stair 720; M.934]; June 30, 1675, Clark *contra* Stuart and Williamson [2 Stair 336; M.919]. And so a disposition by a grandfather to his oye was not annulled by anterior creditors, March 6, 1632, L. Grantoun *contra* Ker [*Sub nom. L. Garthland* v *Ker*, Durie 626; M.915].

Fourthly, Though this statute requires a just price, it did not annul a disposition, albeit a prior creditor offered a greater price, if the price received was the ordinary rate of the country, *d.l.6. in pr. eod.* [D.42,8,6,pr.] and though there was a personal reversion to the disponer's eldest son only, January 16, 1677, E. Glencairn *contra* Brisbane [2 Stair 494; M.1011]. The like, where the pursuer had obtained a prior minute of sale for a greater price:

yet it did not reduce a posterior infeftment purchased *bona fide*, though for a lesser price, being competent, July 18, 1677, Murray of Kilor *contra* Drummond of Machanie [2 Stair 543 ; M. 1048].

Fifthly, Though the statute mentions only the annulling of dispositions, &c. yet it is ordinarily extended to bonds or obligements, whereupon apprising, adjudication or arrestment follows, and likewise to renunciations and discharges of personal faculties and reversions.

Sixthly, Though dispositions or other rights be for equivalent causes onerous; yet by the posterior part of the statute they are accounted fraudulent and reducible, if the bankrupt, or the interposed person in trust, do, by voluntary gratification prefer one creditor to another, who hath done more timeous and lawful diligence ; December 11, 1691, the creditors of Lantoun and Cockburn competing [Possibly Harcarse 172 ; M. 1293 or 2841], where the Lords found that the execution or the charge given upon letters of horning against a debtor, who is *obæratus*, and burdened with great debts, and against whom several legal diligences are beginning to be raised and execute, albeit the debtor do not appear at the time to be altogether insolvent, and not prove to be so by the event, and likewise the executions upon letters of inhibition against the debtor himself so burdened, do render the debtor incapable to grant voluntary rights and infeftments in prejudice of the other creditors their said prior diligence. But where a debtor of an entire estate pays his lawful creditor, or satisfies him by dispositions or assignations, neither the tenor nor extension of the statute reacheth these cases, albeit there be inchoate and incomplete diligence at the instance of other creditors against him.

Seventhly, Where that clause of the statute bears the annulling of deeds done in gratification, or preference of one creditor to another, who hath done more timeous diligence by inhibition, horning, arrestment, comprising or other lawful mean, duly to affect the dyvour's lands or goods, or price thereof ; the meaning is, that when these diligences are not complete, but inchoate, and the creditor is *in cursu diligentiæ*, the debtor or his trustee cannot prevent the course of that diligence by preferring another creditor doing less diligence. For, if the meaning were of an apprising perfected by infeftment, or arrestment by a decreet to make forthcoming, there needed not this remeid ; for these diligences, being complete, would exclude any other posterior disposition or diligence : yea inhibition, if the executions were complete and registrate, would of itself be effectual to reduce posterior deeds *ex capite inhibitionis*. But if these diligences be only inchoate as if the inhibitor had begun his execution, but had not completed it at all at the market-crosses requisite [IV, 50, 10, *infra*], yet any disposition, infeftment, or other real right made to another creditor *medio tempore*, less vigilant, is annullable thereby, December 15, 1665, and February 27, 1667, Eleis *contra* Keith and Wishart [Dirleton 4 and 1 Stair 457 ; M. 5988 and 7020] ; or if lands be denounced to be apprised, or summons of adjudication be execute, rights thereafter made to other creditors doing less diligence, though *in cursu diligentiæ* with the first, are thereby reducible, although done before the decreet of apprising or infeftment. But inhibition, apprising or adjudication, inchoate, have no effect as to moveable rights, not being, as the statute requires, diligences which duly can affect that subject. Neither doth the laying on of arrestment affect heritable rights, and so cannot hinder the debtor to dispone these to lawful creditors doing less diligence. But horning is a diligence, relating both to the moveable estate, by single escheat, and to the heritable estate, by liferent escheat; and therefore after the charge of horning it is effectual, February 12, 1675, Veitch *contra* the Executors of Ker and Pallat [2 Stair 321; M. 1073]; July 18, 1677, Murray of Kilor *contra* Drummond of Machany [2 Stair 543; M. 1048]; January 25, 1681, Bathgate *contra* Bogil [*Sub nom. Bathgate* v *Bowdoun*, 2 Stair 841; M. 1049]; and lately in the forecited case of the Creditors of Cockburn and Lantoun [Possibly Harcarse 172; M. 1293 or 2841], which occasioned a difficulty in the ranking of the voluntary rights and adjudications, which the Lords have determined, which see in Title Infeftments of Property, §ult. [11,3,81,*infra*; see also IV,35,17–18,*infra*].

But this statute will not annul dispositions or other rights made in favours of these persons, who have used the most effectual diligence duly to affect the subject, because this prevents expenses, and is prejudicial both to the debtor and co-creditors, and is not contrary to this statute.

Neither will dispositions or other rights, for equivalent causes onerous, made to creditors, be annulled if not done *in cursu diligentiæ*; but if the co-creditor insist not in his inchoate diligence till it be complete, he hath not the benefit of the statute *nam vigilantibus et non dormientibus jura subveniunt, l.24.ff. Qua. in fraud. cred.* [D. 42,8,24], and therefore a disposition was not reduced at the instance of a creditor who had apprised before a disposition but for several years had neither obtained infeftment nor charged the superior, February 8, 1681, Neilson *contra* Ross of Pittendreich [2 Stair 856; M. 1045]. But how long this negligence must be to exclude it, must necessarily be *in arbitrio judicis*. Neither will this clause of the statute annul dispositions made to buyers for a just price paid, where the price was not an anterior debt due to the buyer; for there, there is no preference of one creditor to another, but a lawful bargain in commerce, where the buyer neither doth, nor can, know inchoate diligences, but only such as are complete and registrate, except in the case where the subject becomes litigious, which is not to be extended to every diligence in prejudice of purchasers of lands, whereby rights would become very uncertain, especially when irredeemable rights are purchased; but against the purchasing of bonds, annualrents, or wadsets, it may be more extended as in the former case, February 8, 1681, Neilson *contra* Ross of Pittendreich [2 Stair 856; M. 1045], where this defence was also sustained, that the disposition was for a price paid and for no anterior debt. And in the former case Bathgate *contra* Bogil [*Sub nom. Bathgate* v *Bowdoun*, 2 Stair 841; M. 1049], the disposition after horning, though it was in the terms of sale, was only annulled because it was granted for anterior debts due to the buyer, in prejudice of another creditor's prior diligence, and so fell under the act of Parliament.

Fraud is no *vitium reale* affecting the subject, but only the committer of the fraud and these who are partakers of the fraud, as is clear by this statute bearing an exception of lawful purchasers not partakers of the fraud. But where the right purchased hath evidence of fraud in itself, the purchaser, though for a just price paid, is thereby partaker of the fraud, and so may be excluded ; as if the right acquired bore "for love and favour :" or if it be betwixt conjunct persons, the purchaser must instruct the cause onerous; as when the right purchased was from one brother to another, December 23, 1679, Gordon of Troquhen *contra* Ferguson of Keiroch [2 Stair 726 ; M. 1012]; January 24, 1680, Crawfurd *contra* Ker [2 Stair 747 ; M. 1012].

Eighthly, Though the manner of probation by this statute, be by the oath of the purchaser or writ, yet the narrative of such rights being betwixt conjunct persons, albeit it bear causes onerous, must be otherwise astructed, wherein witnesses and other evidences will be received [111, 7, 2, *infra*], which is not only sustained as to dispositions by parents to children, but by brothers and sisters to brothers or to good-brothers and good-sisters, yet not to two persons marrying two sisters, where there is but *affinitas affinitatis :* it hath also been extended to uncle and nephew, where other circumstances concurred, January 18, 1678, Kinloch of Gourdie *contra* Blair [2 Stair 595 ; M. 889], December 18, 1673, Creditors of Tarsapy *contra* L. Kinfanes [2 Stair 243 ; M. 900]. The like effect is in rights acquired in name of children in the family who have no visible estates, for these are held fraudulent, and may be affected for the father's debt, as hath been frequently decided and observed *supra*, §15. *in pr.*

16. Spuilzie [IV, 30, 1, *et seq.*] is the taking away of moveables without consent of the owner or order of law, obliging to restitution of the things taken away, with all possible profits, or reparation thereof, according to the estimation of the injured, made by his *juramentum in litem*. Thus things stolen or robbed, though they might be criminally pursued, as theft or robbery, yet they may be civilly pursued for as a spuilzie.

Spuilzie *inurit laben realem*, whereby the goods may be recovered from purchasers *bona fide*, November 21, 1677, Hay *contra* Leonard and others [2 Stair 561 ; M. 10286]. The profits of things spuilzied are called violent profits, because they are not such ordinary profits as the person spuilzied used to make of the goods, but such as he might have made thereof, as where the things spuilzied have profits, as horse, oxen, or other cattle, and instruments, or other tools. But corns and the like have no profits. The violent profits of a horse spuilzied in labouring time, was modified to five shillings Scots *per diem*, February 28, 1668, Lord Justice Clerk *contra* Hume of Lenthill [1 Stair 538 ; M. 13985]. But the modification depends much upon the violence and atrocity of the spuilzie, and the arbitriment of the Judge.

17. In spuilzies the pursuer needs no other title but possession, from

whence in moveables a right is presumed; and therefore, [process for] a spuilzie of goods in coffers was sustained upon the pursuer's having the keys, and the defender's breaking up the coffers, not being done by parents or masters, July 25, 1676, Maxwell *contra* Maxwell [2 Stair 458; M. 14729]. A relict in possession was admitted to pursue a spuilzie of corns, sown and reaped by her husband, though not confirmed by her, July 26, 1626, Russel *contra* [*Sub nom. Russel* v *Kerse*, Durie 228; M. 14733]. Spuilzies must be by unlawful meddling or accession thereto; and therefore it was found relevantly libelled, that the goods spuilzied were immediately received into the defender's house, January 26, 1628, E. Roxburgh *contra* L. Lugtoun [Durie 334; M. 379]; yet a spuilzie was not sustained against a person as accessory, who being charged by the messenger, did apprise the goods upon the ground, though in other solemnities the poinding was illegal, for which he was not answerable, Hope, Spuilzie, Butter *contra* Gordon [Hope, *Maj. Pr.* VI, 18, 61].

18. In a spuilzie, the fact being proved or acknowledged, as to some particulars libelled, the pursuer's oath will be admitted to prove the rest of the libel, though consisting of divers kinds of things, March 8, 1628, Broun *contra* Murray [Durie 356; M. 9361].

19. Spuilzie is elided, *First*, if the deed was warrantably done, at least *bona fide* by a colourable title, as by custom; and so the spuilzie of a horse was elided, because he was meddled with, as being carrying corn out of the thirle to another mill, according to the custom of the country, whereby the horse is forfeited to the master of the mills, and the corn to the miller, January 22, 1635, Menzies *contra* [*Sub nom. Menzies* v *McKay*, Durie 743; M. 1815; see Craig, *J.F.* 11, 8, 9] but was not elided by a disposition of the goods libelled for relief, being meddled with *brevi manu*, seeing distress was not instructed, July 19, 1633, Kirkwood *contra* Ferguson [Durie 686; M. 2117]; so where there was a disposition, and instrument of possession, albeit the disposition was *omnium bonorum*, and possession retained for two years, yet it was found sufficient *contra spolium*, especially seeing there was no violence used in attaining real possession of the goods, January 30, 1662, Irvine *contra* M'Cartney [1 Stair 89; M. 14750]. And the spuilzie of a horse was elided, because the pursuer having committed hamesucken and slaughter, was taken by the defender with a horse, as being Baillie of the barony where he did it; Had. January 8, 1611, Baillie *contra* Lord Torphichen [Haddington; M. 4797]. And a spuilzie of corns was elided by the defender's entering in possession of the corns upon the ground, whereupon the corns were growing; Hope, Spuilzie, Eliot *contra* Lord Buccleugh [Hope, *Maj. Pr.* VI, 18, 72; M. 14761]. It was also elided as to a messenger, because he poinded the goods libelled by virtue of letters of poinding directed against the pursuer, unwarrantably raised, seeing there was no conclusion in the decreet against him; March 4, 1628, Scot *contra* Banks [Durie 353; M. 6016]. Or if the defender meddle with goods by a title or warrand from any other party to whom they

belonged; and though this be contrary to the libel it will be sufficient; and if either party allege right, the most pregnant will be preferred [IV, 39, 4, *infra*].

20. The second exception in spuilzies is voluntary delivery, which was sustained, though it seemed contrary to the libel; Spotiswoode, Spuilzie, Cunninghame *contra* M'Culloch [Spotiswoode 90].

21. The third exception against spuilzie is, that the goods libelled were lawfully poinded; for, though the decreet whereupon the poinding was raised should be reduced for want of formality, yet it will not be a spuilzie, unless it proceeded *mala fide* or *spreta authoritate judicis*, as when a decreet pronounced was used after advocation intimated to the party, though the inferior judge refused to receive, or record it judicially; or when the debt contained in the decreet was fully satisfied before the poinding; Spots, Spuilzie *contra* Broun [*Sub nom. Vans* v *Brown*, Spotiswoode, 88]. But the exception of poinding will be elided by this reply, That the pursuer offered the sum poinded for, at the time of the poinding, when the poinded goods were offered.

22. The third and most ordinary reply against poinding is, that the goods were not poindable, as being plough-goods, which are not poindable the time of ploughing the ground, if there be any other goods upon the ground sufficient for paying the debt, according to the act of parliament, 1503, c. 98 [Diligence Act, 1503, c. 98; A.P.S. 11, 254, c. 45; IV, 47, 34 *infra*]. And it was found sufficient, that there were other goods upon the ground, without necessity to allege, that they were the debtor's proper goods; or that the goods poinded were then in labour, being two or three days before in the plough, December 10, 1631, Gibson *contra* Corsby [*Sub die* Dec. 1, 1630, Durie 544; M. 10512]. Yea poinding of plough-goods was found a spuilzie, being done in the ordinary time of plowing, though the goods were not yoked that year, because of frost; June 7, 1678, Wood *contra* Stuart [2 Stair 621; M. 10516]. There is another reply against poinding, that the goods poinded were not the debtor's, but another offered to depone they were his, or that this offer was made by his warrand, or by his servant; but it is not enough that this offer was made by these who had no direct, or presumed commission; July 6, 1666, Corbet *contra* Stirling [1 Stair 391; M. 10602]. This offer must be made before the solemnity of poinding be ended, but an offer was not sustained, being offered about an hour after, to give summary restitution; July 9, 1675, Cotts *contra* Harper [2 Stair 342; M. 10513]. But this oath will not exclude probation, that the goods were the debtor's, or another's by way of declarator, that thereafter they might be affected by poinding, but is only like an oath of calumny, that *in possessorio* hinders poinding.

23. The [fourth] exception against spuilzie, is restitution of the goods spuilzied within twenty-four hours, *re integra*, and is also elided by restitution of the goods, if they be accepted and kept by the pursuer.

24. There is also a common exception against spuilzies upon prescrip-

tion of three years they not being pursued within that space, after the committing thereof, and that by express statute, Parl. 1579, c. 51 [Prescription
(Ejections) Act, 1579, c. 81; A.P.S. III, 145, c. 19]. But this prescription is
only against the spuilzie as such, so that it taketh away the privilege thereof,
as to the violent profits, *et juramentum in litem ;* yet it may thereafter be pursued, as wrongous intromission for restitution only; and if many be pursued
they are not liable *in solidum,* but equally, unless a greater intromission of
some of them be proven, January 17, 1668, Captain Strachan *contra* Morison
[1 Stair 508; M. 14708], which also is competent in many cases, where spuilzie
is either not sustainable, or elidable in its atrocity as a spuilzie, *nam levis exceptio excusat a spolio,* and yet action for restitution remains; and sometimes
the spuilzie may be restricted thereto, if the pursuer please so to do, before
litiscontestation; or otherwise he hath therefore a several action, as if spuilzie
be pursued, and an exception of lawful poinding admitted to be proven, the
defender will be assoilzied from the spuilzie, even though the decreet, whereupon the poinding proceeded, be reduced for informality; and yet he will
have a several action for restitution, which may also be decerned in the action
of spuilzie. But spuilzie is not elided by masters of the ground their bringing
back the goods of their tenants, by virtue of their hypothec, *ex intervallo ;*
February 9, 1676, Park *contra* Cockburn of Rysely [2 Stair 412 ; M. 6204].
Neither was the spuilzie of a horse elided, because he was found in the skaith,
and was offered back within forty-eight hours, upon payment of the skaith,
unless he had been put in a poind-fold, or safe place, having water, grass, or
fodder, and that by the sentence of a judge the skaith hath been estimated,
and the horse poinded therefor; February 10, 1676, Duncan *contra* Kids
[2 Stair 414; M. 10514]; December 2, 1679, Beaton *contra* Hume [2 Stair
712; M. 14751]. So spuilzie was not elided upon alleging the pursuer had
spuilzied or reset as much of the defender's goods, by the act 112. Parl. 7
[1581, c. 112; A.P.S. III, 218, c. 16], and act 16. Parl. 10. K. James VI.
[1585, c. 16; A.P.S. III, 379, c. 13] unless the pursuer had been a broken man
and notorious thief of a clan, who could not be reached by the ordinary
course of law, November 29, 1678. More *contra* M'Federick [2 Stair 649;
M. 14729].

25. Intrusion and ejection [11, 1, 19–20; IV, 28, 1, *infra*] are delinquences
in lands and immoveables, as spuilzie is in moveables, and they differ in this ;
that intrusion is the entering in possession, being for the time void, without
consent of the parties interested, or order of law ; *l. ult. C. unde vi* [C. 8, 4, 11],
but ejection, as its *etymon* intimates, is not only the unwarrantable entering
in lands, but the casting out violently of the then possessor *toto Tit. ff. de vi &
vi arm.* [D. 43, 16]. In this there is violence, in the other wrong, but no violence
in the entry, though it be a violent detention ; and, in either case, the injured
must be at least repute in possession : but as the possession must begin by
some bodily act, *l. 8. ff. de A. vel A. P.* [D. 41, 2, 8], it may be continued alone
by the act of the mind, *l. 25 § 2 eod.* [D. 41, 2, 25, 2], willing or affecting the

possession, which is conjectured or presumed from circumstances: *l.6§1 &*
l.7.ff. eod. [D. 41, 2, 6, 1 and 7; 11, 1, 20, *infra*] for if it be but a short time since
the possessor did corporally possess, and nothing appear that he hath relinquished his possession, or his affection thereto ceased, then he is still possessor, and is so presumed, because of his interest; but if his abstinence be
total, or long, that he hath retained nothing, as the keys, or keeping of doors
close, then the possession is holden as relinquished; and he who enters by a
real or colourable title, is no intruder, and cannot be extruded, but by warning, and process of removing; and therefore, though intrusion be said to be in
the void possession, it is only meant as to corporal possession, there being still
a presumed possession *animo* on the part of the injured. In other things intrusion and ejection do in all things agree; so ejection must be pursued within
three years, parl. 1579, cap. 81 (Prescription (Ejections) Act, 1579, c. 81;
A.P.S. 111, 145, c. 19], which is extended to intrusion by these words of the
statute, *That ejection, and others of that nature, be pursued within three years*
after committing thereof, Had. February 2, 1610, L. Craighall *contra*
[*Sub nom. Craighall* v *Kinninmouth*, Haddington, *Fol. Dict.* 11, 119; M. 11068].

26. Ejection is only competent to the natural possessors, possessing by
themselves, their hinds and cottars; but not to an heritor for ejection of his
tenants, unless the tenants concur, Hope, Ejection, Cunningham *contra*
M'Culloch [Hope, *Maj. Pr.* VI, 15, 34; M. 13879]. This must be understood as
to the oath *in litem,* for none can have the price of affection, but the natural
possessor, nor the violent profits, unless the tenants insist not; in which case
the heritor may claim them, and in all cases may pursue the ejector or intruder to pay the rent, or remove without warning. So intrusion or ejection is not
committed, but by entering into the natural possession, or at least by out-
putting, or inputting of tenants: for though possessors invert their master's
possession, and pay their rents to another, this will not infer intrusion or ejection: but in both these cases, there are other remeids in law, by removing, or
action for maills and duties, which is competent against intromitters. Though
ejection and intrusion prescribe by this statute, yet it is only as such, for
taking away of it singular privileges, viz. the violent profits; but though they
be not pursued within three years, yet they are competent, being libelled and
restricted to restitution of possession, and the ordinary profits; and in this
they differ from removing, which cannot be pursued but upon warning forty
days preceding Whitsunday; but these may be pursued at any time without
warning, March 16, 1627, Hay *contra* Ker [Durie 292; M. 11069]; Spotiswoode, Ejection, Mowat *contra* Davidson [(1627) Spotiswoode, 92]; July 15,
1626, M'Fedrick *contra* McLachlan [Durie 219; M. Supp. 32]. Ejection and
intrusion are founded especially upon possession, and the pursuer needs not
dispute his right, neither his entering in possession, which, though it were
vitious, yet if it be continued by a considerable space, and the possessor be
then ejected, he will not be excluded, by alleging his entry was vitious, as if he
had entered in the vice of a tenant, removed by the defender. Yea ejection was

sustained at the instance of infants, whose father died in possession, and had an old infeftment, albeit a decreet of removing was obtained against the mother, they not being called, nor was the ejector allowed *in hoc processu* to dispute the infant's right. But *spoliatus* was found instantly to be restored to possession, February 19, 1663, Scot *contra* E. Hume [1 Stair 183; M. 10602]. Here the heir, though in the mother's family, was not held as removed as her bairn; yet the spuilzie was restricted to re-possession.

27. Ejection or intrusion are excluded, by alleging the pursuer relinquished the possession, or did voluntarily remove, which must be proven by writ, or oath of party, if there be no matters of fact, from whence the dereliction doth evidently appear, as transporting of the parties goods, June 19, 1634, Colonel Ruthven *contra* Gairn [Possibly 1 Stair 115; M. 393]. This was also found proven by instrument, and the witnesses insert, though the pursuer libelled violence, contrary to the instrument, Hope, Ejection, Cunningham *contra* M'Culloch [Hope, *Maj. Pr.* VI, 15, 34; M. 13879]. And also found proven by a renunciation, attested by an act of the defender's court, and other circumstances, Hope, Ejection, L. Monymusk *contra* His tenants [Hope, *Maj. Pr.* VI, 15, 32; M. 13879]; the like upon voluntary removing, and renouncing in the pursuer's master's court, Had. June 15, 1610, Brown *contra* [Not found]. Ejection was also elided by voluntary removing or renouncing, after the defender's entry. But ejection was not elided by a personal obligement, to possess the ejector, or by a decreet-arbitral, seeing the entry thereto was not by order of law, or consent to possess, Spots, Arbiter, Wood *contra* Scot [Spotiswoode, 14; M. 624].

Violent profits in ejection and intrusion within burgh, are ordinarily sustained for the double maill; but in landward, the violent profits are accompted by the quantity of the seed the land can sow, and the increase such lands can yield deducing the expences of seed and labourage, and the profits the sums can yield which the land can hold, wherein are comprehended the calves and milk of cows; and the wool, lambs, and milk of sheep, deducing the expences of herding [11, 9, 44; IV, 29, 3, *infra*]. In ejection and intrusion, the defender must find caution for the violent profits at the first term of litiscontestation, or otherwise, decreet is to be given against him, Parl. 1594, cap. 217 [Ejection Caution Act, 1594, c. 217; A.P.S. IV, 68, c. 27].

Succeeding in the vice is a kind of intrusion; but because it is ordinarily consequent upon removing, it is spoken to, Title, Tacks 19, §45 [11, 9, 45, *infra*].

28. Molestation is the troubling of possession chiefly in and about marches of lands [IV, 27, 1, *infra*] whereby the party injurer is obliged to refund the damage to the party injured, and the marches being cognosced, he will be decerned to desist, and cease from troubling in time coming; whereupon all personal execution is competent. It is also competent when possession is troubled otherwise. This is ordinarily a mutual action, and probation allowed *hinc inde;* for it is the same with the Roman action *finium regundorum l. 13. ff. de judiciis*

[D. 5,1,13] and in case of further trouble, *lawborrows* and *contraventions* will be sustained, after the marches are cognosced, which otherwise can have no effect, while the marches and possession are dubious. The process whereby molestation is determined, is called a *cognition*, the whole course whereof is clearly ordered and set down by the statute of Session, ratified in Parliament 1587, cap. 42 [A.P.S. III,445,c.23] whereby it is clear that molestations were of old decided by sheriffs, bailies of regalities, and other judges ordinary where the lands lay, by the determination of an assize, or inquest of the best and worthiest of the country, and they may be still so pursued : but, if before the Session, the Lords are not to hear and determine the causes themselves, but to remit the same to the judges ordinary ; or in case they be suspect, to name others as judges delegate for that act, except only in those molestations which do concern any of the Lords of Session, which are to be heard and determined before themselves. The said Judges Ordinary, or delegates, are first to hear parties debate, and to determine the relevancy of the points to be proven ; the probation must be before the inquest, and must be decided by their verdict ; the most part of the inquest is to be landed men, worth three hundred merks of rent and above, in the parish where the lands lie, or failing them in the next adjacent parishes, as is fully set forth in the said statute. In these cognitions, the superior must be called in all the diets of process, Hope, Cognition, Calder *contra* Purves of Confirdie [*Sub nom. Calder* v *Forbes*, *Hope, Maj.Pr.* VI,21,42]. And if the cognition be pursued by a liferenter or others, the heritor must be called, or otherwise the cognition is null.

29. Breach of arrestment and deforcement [IV,49,3–4 and 7,*infra*], are by our law and custom in all things equiparate, both being violations of legal acts ; and concerning both, it is statute, Par. 1581, cap.117 [Lawburrows Act, 1581, c.117; A.P.S. III,222,c.22], that breakers of arrestment, or the deforcers of poinding, or any other legal execution, shall escheat their whole moveables, and the party injured shall be first paid of his debt and damages, for which he shall have ready execution against the injurer ; which is further extended, Par. 1592, cap.150 [Deforcement Act, 1592, c.152; A.P.S. III, 577,c.72], that the one half of the escheat of the moveables shall belong to the party injured, if the executor of the process or letters be deforced or molested in the execution, which yet shall stand as a valid execution, which must be understood in executions of summons, or charges of horning ; though the latter Act be more favourable to the injured, yet being in his favours, he may make use of the first, which will infer a personal obligement upon the deforcer, or breaker of arrestment, to pay the sums due to the injured, whereupon the arrestment or execution did proceed, with the damage and interest, July 25, 1633, Mitchell *contra* Laws and Stuart [Durie 691 ; M.2916]: the like was found in the deforcement of a caption, and that the pursuer's having insisted criminally, *ad vindictam publicam*, did not hinder him to insist civilly for private interest, December 13, 1672, Murray *contra* French of Frenchland [2 Stair 133 ; M.2917]: which takes no place where the arrestment is not

for debt, but upon controverted rights and possession, which hinders not continuation of possession, but only innovation, as when tenants continue to pay controverted farms to the former possessor [1, 18, 3, *infra*].

Deforcement of a poinding was elided, because the same was not done in lawful time of day, but before the sun, but was not elided, because the goods were attested to belong to another party, whose oath had been made thereon the time of the poinding; neither when kept on the ground for the master's rent by his servants, seeing they expressed not that cause, nor craved not security therefore from the poinder, February 1, 1628, Lord Halkertoun *contra* Kadie and Grieves [Durie 338; M. 3426]: but if it had been expressly for the rents resting, it would not infer deforcement, if such were truly resting. Neither doth resistance of poinding of plough-goods in labouring time, where there were other goods sufficient, infer deforcement: so stopping of poinding by the master of the ground, or landlord of an house for that year's rent, infers not deforcement, December 7, 1630, Dick *contra* Lands [Durie 545; M. 6243] or that he hindered entry, unless there were special warrant in the letters to make open doors.

30. Contravention, as it signifies any act done against lawborrows, so it implies the obligation of the contravener, and the personal right, which the user of the lawborrows hath thereby, and likewise the action, by which it is pursued [IV, 48, 1, *infra*]. For the uptaking of all, it must be considered what lawborrows are, which the word itself insinuates to be caution found to do nothing but by order of law; for a burrow or burgh, in our ancient language, is a cautioner, and lawborrows is caution to keep the law, the reason hereof is the safety and security of the people, who in equity have no more than the reparation of the damage they sustain through delinquences or illegal acts; but, to prevent such, and terrify evil doers, a greater penalty than reparation is appointed, according to the quality and estate of the injurer, Par. 1593, cap. 166 [A.P.S. IV, 17, c. 9], where the half of the penalty is applied to the injured, and the other half to the public, Par. 1581, cap. 117 [Lawburrows Act, 1581, c. 117; A.P.S. III, 222, c. 22]. By the narrative of which statute it is clear, that before lawborrows were granted only for safety against bodily harm, in the persons of the complainers, yet, for the reason therein expressed, the same was extended, *That the complainers, their wives, bairns, tenants, and servants, shall be harmless and skaithless in their bodies, lands, tacks, possessions, goods and gear, and no ways molested or troubled therein, by the persons complained on, nor no others of their causing, sending, hunding out, resetting, command, assistance, and ratihabition, whom they may stop, or let, directly or indirectly, otherwise than by order of law or justice.* By the same statute it is also evident, that lawborrows are granted upon the supplication of parties fearing harm, who without citing the other party, but making faith upon their complaint, have letters of horning, summarily to charge the party complained on, to find caution *ut supra*; and if caution be found, the action of contravention doth proceed upon, and conform to the act of caution; but if obedience be not

given, the complainer may proceed to denunciation or caption; but the contravention will proceed, though there be no caution found, but only a charge upon the letters without denunciation, unless the charge be suspended, as uses to be done when the penalty charged for is exorbitant, and not conform to the act of parliament, January 8, 1628. Semple *contra* Cunninghame [*Sub die* July 8, Durie 385; M. 8032].

Contravention may proceed upon any delinquence, according to the tenor of the act of caution or letters of lawborrows, which, though very comprehensive, yet is not sustained upon any illegal deed, when the matter of right is dubious, as in matters of molestation, before the cognition, or before the marches be clear, Spots, Contravention, Lord Balcaskie *contra* Strang [(1591) Spotiswoode 74; M. 8026]. Neither upon a deed done by a colourable title, though afterward reduced, as entering in possession by a null decreet, Hope, Contravention, Moorhead *contra* Lord Barskub [*Sub nom. Muirhead* v *Barsinok*, Hope, *Maj.Pr.* VI, 35, 33; M. 8031]. Neither upon pasturing upon bounds controverted, or where there was no violence or unlawfulness in pasturage, upon clear marches, July 14, 1626, L. Grange *contra* Lesley [*Sub nom. Grange* v *Betson*, Durie 217]. Neither upon a deed of spuilzie against the pursuer's tenant not complaining, though the lawborrows bears, men, tenants, and servants to be harmless, which was esteemed *stilus curiæ*, January 28, 1632, Grant *contra* Grant [Durie 615; M. 8036]; and February 9, 1633, Lindsay *contra* Dennistoun [Durie 670; M. 8040]. Neither was it sustained upon deeds done by the defender's tenants, without alleging command or ratihabition, unless the deeds be manifest, or known to their masters, as in conveening daily, and cutting another's woods, Had. July 9, 1611, Vauns *contra* Balnagown [Haddington, *Fol.Dict.* II, 343; M. 13984]. Neither upon deeds done by servants without warrand, unless they be menial servants, Hope, Contravention, Galbraith *contra* Anderson [Hope, *Maj.Pr.* VI, 35, 34; M. 13984]: yet contravention was sustained upon hurt done to the pursuer's servant, though he was then rebel, being afterwards relaxed, Hope, Horning, Bruce of Clackmannan *contra* Bruce [Hope, *Maj.Pr.* VI, 27, 72]. It was also sustained upon attempts of injury, though there was no hurt, as a stroke on the cloathes, and upon offer to strike with a whinger, Had. December 21, 1609, L. Greenyards *contra* L. Clackmannan [Haddington, *Fol.Dict.* I, 534; M. 8030]. And also upon a violent troubling the pursuer, without order of law, though without damage, Spots, Contravention, L. Balcaskie *contra* Strang [(1591) Spotiswoode 74; M. 8026]. It is also sustained upon a delinquence, though there be another action competent therefor, as for molestation, Had. November 29, 1609, Dundas *contra* Cumming of Ironside [Not found]. Or for violent possession after warning, Hope, *de actionibus*, Cunningham *contra*   [Hope, *Maj.Pr.* VI, 1, 8]. But, if the other ordinary action was insisted in, and decreet obtained, contravention was not sustained, though the other were offered to be renounced, Hope, Contravention, Johnstoun *contra* Charters [Hope, *Maj.Pr.* VI, 35, 28].

Contravention was elided by the pursuer's granting a factory after the deeds libelled to do the like, reserving only damage and interest, January 11, 1633, Dennistoun *contra* Lindsay [(1633) Spotiswoode 75 ; M. 8038]. Contravention on several deeds may be sustained, *separatim toties quoties :* and against many contraveeners, contraveening in one act ; but in such cases the Lords will modify and lessen the penalty, within the rates of the act of parliament, Had. November 29, 1609, Dundas *contra* Cumming of Ironside [Not found]. Contravention is not found pursuable before any inferior judge, otherwise the decreet thereon will be null by exception, Had. July 6, 1611, Kennedy *contra* Kennedy of Garriehorn [Haddington, *Fol. Dict.* 1,493; M. 7307]. In contraventions, the King's Advocate must concur for the King's interest, but he cannot insist alone, as when the private party hath discharged the deeds, even after the intenting of the cause, Hope, Contravention, Forrest *contra* Turnbul [Hope, *Maj. Pr.* VI, 35, 31 ; M. 7898].

Title 10. Obligations Conventional, by Promise, Paction, and Contract

FROM obediential obligations, flowing from the will of God, order leads us next to conventional obligations, arising from the will of man, whereby our own will tieth us in that, wherein God hath left us free : for as obediential obligations descend from the principle of obedience to God, and have their rise and reason from his sovereign power to command, and our absolute obligement to obey ; so in his gracious goodness, in the greatest part he hath left us free, and hath given power to none to exact or compel us : yet so as he hath given that liberty in our power, that we may give it up to others, or restrain and engage it, whereby God obliges us to performance, by mediation of our own will: yet such obligations, as to their original, are conventional, and not obediential.

Conventional obligations do arise from our will and consent ; for, as in the beginning hath been shown, the will is the only faculty constituting rights, whether real or personal ; for it is the will of the owner, that naturally transferreth right from him to the acquirer : so in personal rights, that freedom we have of disposal of ourselves, our actions and things, which naturally is in us, is by our engagement placed in another, and so engagement is a diminution of freedom, constituting that power in another, whereby he may restrain, or constrain us to the doing or performing of that whereof we have given him power of exaction ; as in the debtor, it is the debtor's duty or necessity to perform. But it is not every act of the will that raiseth an obligation, or power of exaction : and therefore that it may appear what act of it is obligatory.

2. We must distinguish three acts in the will, desire, resolution, and engagement. Desire is a tendency or inclination of the will towards its object, and it is the first motion thereof, which is not sufficient to constitute a right ; neither is resolution (which is a determinate purpose to do that which is desired) efficacious, because, whatsoever is resolved or purposed, may be without fault altered, unless by accident the matter be necessary, or that the resolution be holden forth to assure others ; the alteration whereof, without evident ground, importeth levity and inconstancy, and sometimes deceit and unfaithfulness : but still resolution is but an act of the will with itself, as deliberation is of the understanding, acting with itself, and it is unquestionable, nothing can be obliged to itself, though it be obliged to God, or to another in relation to itself : and therefore, if a party should express a resolution, to give unto, or to bestow upon another, any thing, though that resolution related to the good of another ; yet it is not obligatory, nor can that other compel the resolver to perform, though it were never so fully cleared, or confirmed by word or writ. So it was found, that a resolution expressed both by word and writ, in favour of near relations, did infer no obligation, February 27, 1673, Kincaid *contra* Dickson [2 Stair 181 ; M. 12143]. It remaineth then, that the only act of the will, which is efficacious, is that whereby the will conferreth or stateth a power of exaction in another, and thereby becomes engaged to that other to perform.

3. Again, we must distinguish betwixt promise, pollicitation or offer, paction and contract, the difference amongst which is this, that the obligatory act of the will is sometimes absolute and pure, and sometimes conditional, wherein the condition relates either unto the obligation itself, or to the performance ; such are the ordinary conditional obligations, which, though they be presently (upon the granting thereof) binding, and cannot be recalled, yet they are only to be performed, and have effect, when the condition shall be existent : but when the condition relateth to the constitution of the obligation, then the very obligation itself is pendent, till the condition be purified, and till then it is no obligation [1, 3, 8, *supra*]; as when any offer or tender is made, there is implied a condition, that before it become obligatory, the party to whom it is offered must accept ; and therefore an offer by a son, to pay a debt due by his mother, made known to be accepted at such a time, and in such a place, was found not obligatory after the mother's death, unless it had been so accepted, June 24, 1664, Allan *contra* Collier [1 Stair 206 ; M. 9428 ; 1, 3, 9, *supra*; 1, 10, 5–6, *infra*]. So then, an offer accepted is a contract, because it is the deed of two, the offerer and accepter.

4. But a promise is that which is simple and pure, and hath not implied as a condition, the acceptance of another. In this Grotius differeth *de jure belli, lib.2.cap.11.§14* holding, "that acceptance is necessary to every conventional obligation in equity, without consideration of positive law ;" and to prevent that obvious objection, that promises are made to absents, infants, idiots, or persons not yet born, who cannot accept, and therefore such obligations should ever be revocable, till their acceptation, which in some of them can never be; he answereth, that the civil law only withholdeth, that such offers cannot be revoked, until these be in such capacity as to accept or refuse. Promises now are commonly held obligatory, the canon law having taken off the exception of the civil law, *de nudo pacto.* It is true, if he in whose favour they are made, accept not, they become void, not by the negative non-acceptance, but by the contrary rejection. For as the will of the promiser constitutes a right in the other, so the other's will, by renouncing and rejecting that right, voids it, and makes it return. This also quadrates with the nature of a right, which consisteth in a faculty or power which may be in these, who exerce no act of the will about it, nor know not of it; so infants truly have right as well as men, though they do not know, nor cannot exerce it. Promises with us are not probable by witnesses, though within an hundred pounds, July 3, 1668, Donaldson *contra* Harrower [1 Stair 548; M. 12385]; February 9, 1672, Wood *contra* Robertson [2 Stair 68; M. 12225]. The like was found of a promise engaging for a party, who bought goods, not being a partner in the bargain; for promises, when they are parts of bargains about moveables, are probable by witnesses, January 19, 1672, Dewar *contra* Brown [*Sub nom. Deuchar* v *Brown*, 2 Stair 50; M. 12386]. And the reason that our custom gives no legal remedy for performance of promises of things of importance by witnesses, is the same that the Roman law gave no action upon naked pactions, to prevent the mistakes of parties and witnesses in communings, that they should use a set form of words in stipulations so now, when writ is so ordinary, we allow no processes for promises, as a penalty against these who observe not so easy a method; yet the promise obliges the conscience and the honesty of the promiser.

5. It is likewise the opinion of Molina, cap.263 [On the whole section see *Carmichael* v *Carmichael's Executor*, 1920 S.C. (H.L.) 195 ; *Allan's Trs.* v *I.R.C.*, 1971 S.C(H.L.) 45. See also Smith, *Studies Critical and Comparative*, 183 ; Cameron, 1961 J.R. 103 ; Rodger, 1969 J.R. 34, 128 ; McCormick, 1970 J.R. 228] and it quadrates to our customs, that when parties contract, if there be any article in favours of a third party, at any time, *est jus quæsitum tertio*, which cannot be recalled by both the contractors, but he may compel either of them to exhibit the contract, and thereupon the obliged may be compelled to perform. So a promise, though gratuitous, made in favour of a third party, that party, albeit not present, nor accepting, was found to have right thereby, Had. November 25, 1609, Achinmoutie *contra* Hay [*Sub nom. Auchmouty* v *Mayne*, Haddington, *Fol.Dict.* 11, 200 ; M. 12126]. Promises de-

pendent upon acceptance may either be made by way of offer, or when the promise requires some things to be done on the part of him to whom it is made, not as a condition annexed only to the performance, for then the promise is presently obligatory, though the effect be suspended till the condition exist, but if the condition be so meant or expressed, that it must precede the obligation itself, as in mutual contracts, the one party subscribing is not obliged until the other also subscribe, or that the other party accept or consent: and so a contract being registrate, was found orderly proceeded, though he who registrate it had not subscribed, seeing at the discussing he did summarily consent to the registration thereof against himself, February 9, 1627, M'Duff *contra* M'Culloch [Durie 270 ; M. 8406 ; 1,3,9,*supra ;* I, 10, 3 and 6,*infra*]. Hence is our vulgar distinction betwixt obligations and contracts, the former being only where the obligation is μονοπλευρος, on the one part: the other where the obligation is δευπλευρος, obligatory on both parts, whereby both parties are obliged to mutual prestations.

6. *Pactum* or a paction, in the law is defined, *duorum pluriumve in idem placitum consensus atque conventio, l. 1. §2.ff. de pactis* [D. 2, 14, 1, 2], *et l. 3. ff. de pollicit.* [D. 50, 12, 3]. It is the consent of two or more parties, to some things to be performed by either of them; for it is not a consent in their opinions, but a consent in their wills, to oblige any of them: and it is much to be considered, whether the consent be given *animo obligandi*, to oblige or not; for the same words will sometimes be interpreted as obligatory and sometimes not, according to the circumstances; as if it be jestingly or merrily expressed, whatsoever the words be, there is no obligation ; because thereby it appears there is no mind to oblige ; or if the words be in affairs or negotiations, they are interpreted obligatory, though they express no obligation but a futurition, which otherwise would import no more than a resolution; as Titius is to give Mevius an hundred crowns, in any matter of negotiation, this would be obligatory, but otherwise it would be no more but an expression of Titius's purpose so to do ; yet because it is inward and unknown, it must be taken by the words or other signs, so if the words be clearly obligatory and serious, no pretence that there was no purpose to oblige will take place. If the promise be pendent upon acceptation, and no more than an offer, it is imperfect and ambulatory, and in the power of the offerer, till acceptance; and if he die before acceptance, it is revoked as a commission or mandate, which necessarily imports acceptance, and expires by the mandator's death, *morte mandatoris perit mandatum ;* so acceptance cannot be by any third party, unless he have warrant for the effect ; and so if a promise be made by one to another in favours of a third, importing the acceptance of that third, it is pendent and revocable by these contractors, till the third accept [1,3,9,*supra ;* I, 10,3 and 5,*infra*].

7. The Romans, that they might have clear proof of pactions and agreements, would second none with their civil authority, but such as had a solemnity of words, by way of stipulation, whereby the one party going be-

fore, by an interrogation, the other party closed by an answer conform, which was both clear to the parties and witnesses; or otherwise, unless there were the intervention of some deed, or thing beside the consent, or that it were a contract allowed of the law, or such other paction as it specially confirmeth, without all which, it was called *nudum pactum inefficax ad agendum.* We shall not insist in these, because the common custom of nations hath resiled therefrom, following rather the canon law, by which every paction produceth action, *et omne verbum de ore fideli cadit in debitum, C. 1 & 3 de pactis* [C. 2, 3, 1 and 3]. And so observeth *Guidelinus, de jure Nov. l. 3. cap. 5. §ult.* and *Corvinus, de pactis.* We have a special statute of session, November 27, 1592, acknowledging all pactions and promises as effectual [A.S. 27 Nov., 1592]: and so it hath been ever since decided, January 14, 1631, Sharp *contra* Sharp [Durie 553; M. 4299 and 15562; I. 13, 14, *infra*].

8. Even *pactum corvinum de hæreditate viventis*, is found binding with us, though among the most odious, July 6, 1630, Aikenhead *contra* Bothwell [Durie, 525; M. 9492]. But *pactum de quota litis*, whether it be a naked paction or promise, or a mutual contract, is rejected both by the civil law and our custom; whereby advocates, in place of their honorary, take a share of the profit of the plea; which is to prevent the stirring up, and too much eagerness in pleas, and was extended to an agent or writer, if he had made such a paction before, or during the plea; but not after all plea was ended, having given bond to an apparent heir to denude himself of a right he had acquired for sums of money, getting his expenses, and a fourth part for his pains and hazard, February 24, 1675, Hume *contra* Nisbet, writer [2 Stair 326; M. 9496; I, 14, 2, *infra*]. Yea, an advocate taking assignation to a part of a plea, it was found, *pactum de quota litis* and process was thereby excluded, though proponed by the debtor, and not by the party with whom the paction was made, but it was not found probable by that parties' oath alone, as being but one witness, June 23, 1680, Ruthven *contra* Weir [*Sub nom. Weir* v *Callender and Ruthven*, 2 Stair 774; M. 9499].

9. If the matter be of great moment, or which requireth to its perfection, solemnity in writ, all such agreements, promises, and pactions, are accounted imperfect, and not obligatory until writ be subscribed, such as dispositions of lands and heritable rights, tacks, rentals, and assignations to writs, &c.; in all which, there is *locus pœnitentiæ* even after the agreement, and either party may resile, till the writ be subscribed and delivered. And it was so found, though the buyer, by a missive letter, wrote, that he thought he would not be able to furnish the money, but that he would not pass from the communing, seeing there was no minute nor obligation otherwise, January 28, 1663, Montgomery of Skelmorly *contra* Brown [1 Stair 163; M. 8411]. So it was also found, that a cautioner subscribing a bond, might resile before it was delivered by him, though it was subscribed, and delivered by the principal and other cautioners before, March 5, 1628, M'Gil *contra* Edmonstoun [Durie 355; M. 16991]. The like of a bargain of land, agreed upon by word, some

things being done by the buyer in contemplation thereof, being restored, December 5, 1628, Oliphant *contra* Monorgan [Durie 406; M. 8400]. The like in a tack for several years, which was found to endure but for one year, though the tacksman was thereby in possession, January 24, 1630, Lowry *contra* Ker [*Sub die* January 29, Durie 487; M. 12736]; July 16, 1636, Keith *contra* his tenants [*Sub nom. Keith v Johnston's Tenants*, Durie 816; M. 8400]. Neither is there *locus pœnitentiæ in pactis liberatoriis*, where any right is passed from or restricted, and no new right to be made, December 12, 1661, Hepburn *contra* Hamilton of Orbistoun [1 Stair 67; M. 8465]. The like in restricting an annualrent to a part of lands affected therewith, February 8, 1666, Ker *contra* Hunter [1 Stair 352; M. 8465]. *Locus pœnitentiæ* was found competent to a defender, who produced a right granted by the charger, with a blank assignation to instruct compensation, which he got up before it was delivered to the charger, or any decreet thereon; and no minute of the decreet being extant, the suspender was found *in tuto*, to make use of the right compensed on, December 9, 1674, Lo. Balmerino *contra* the Tenants of North Berwick and Creditors of Sir William Dick [2 Stair 289; M. 8416]. Yea, *locus pœnitentiæ* was found competent to resile from a bargain, which might have been valid without writ; because it was expressly agreed to be redacted in writ, January 12, 1676, Campbell *contra* Douglas [2 Stair 396; M. 8470].

The other remedy we have instead of stipulation, is, that by a statute of Parl. 1579, cap. 80 [Subscription of Deeds Act, 1579, c. 80; A.P.S. III, 145, c. 18], all writs of great importance are to be subscribed by the party, or by two notaries, and four witnesses, wherein custom hath interpreted matters of importance to be that which exceeds an hundred pounds Scots; and it is so far extended, that, in matters where writ may, and uses to be adhibited, probation is not admitted by witnesses, but only by oath of party, or writ: and by these remedies, very necessarily introduced, the inconveniences foresaid are sufficiently caveated.

10. But let us inquire whether promises, or naked pactions, are morally obligatory by the law of Nature. Few do contravert it, yet Connanus, *lib. 1. cap. 6, lib. 5. cap. 9* holdeth, that promises, or naked pactions, where there is no equivalent cause onerous intervening, do morally produce no obligation or action, though in congruity and decency it be fit to perform, lest it be an argument of levity; against which, there is not only the testimony of the canon law, which insinuates an anterior reason to its own position; but also the civil law, *l. 1. ff. de pactis* [D. 2, 14, 1] "There is nothing (says it) so congruous to human trust, as to perform what is agreed among them;" and the edict *de constituta pecunia*, saith, "It is suitable to natural equity;" and saith further, "That he is debtor by the law of nature, who must pay by the law of nations, whose faith we have followed", *l. Cum amplius, ff. de regulis juris* [D. 50, 17, 84]; but especially this is confirmed by the law of God, Prov. 6. 1 "If thou be surety for a friend, if thou hast striken thy hand with a stranger, thou art taken with the words of thy mouth;" and the performance

of words is acknowledged "a part of God's righteousness," Nehemiah 9, vers. 8; Hebrews 10, vers. 23, where it is acknowleged "a part of God's faithfulness." And if promises were not morally obliging, they could have no effect, but by positive law (which is no more itself than a public paction, *communis reipublicæ sponsio, l. 1. ff. de L. L.* [D. 1, 3, 1] *et communis sponsio civitatis, l. 2 eod.* [D. 1, 3, 2] and so *laborans eodem morbo*) and then all pactions and agreements among nations would be ineffectual, and all commerce and society among men should be destroyed : Pactions, contracts, covenants, and agreements, are synonymous terms both in themselves, and according to the recent customs of this and other nations ; so that it will be unnecessary to trace the many subtilties and differences amongst pactions and contracts in the Roman law.

11. This much only in a word for clearing this matter : Their contracts were of four kinds, either perfected by things, words, writ, or sole consent *§2. 1. de obl.* [Inst. 3, 13, 2] *l. 1. ff. de O. & A.* [D. 44, 7, 1]. Contracts by intervention of things, remain naked pactions, ineffectual, until something be given or done by either party to other ; such are all these contracts, which are called *innominati*, which have not a special name and nature acknowledged in the law, *l. 2 & seqq. de præsc. verb.* [D. 19, 5, 2 *et seqq.*] *l. 72 ff de Pact.* [D. 2, 14, 72] *l. 10. C. eodem* [C. 2, 3, 10] ; and therefore oblige not by sole consent, but the giving or doing of the one party obligeth the other, as permutation, excambion, or exchange, when either a thing is given for another, or a thing is given for a deed, work, or use, or one deed or work is done for another, for the which the law hath no special name ; and therefore names them, *do ut des, do ut facias, facio ut facias.*

Amongst real contracts, the law numbereth *mutuum* and *commodatum*, for which we have but the sole name of loan, deposition or custody, *pignus* or pledge, of which hereafter.

Contracts perfected by words are stipulations, which being wholly out of use, we shall say no more of them, than what before is hinted. The third kind of contracts are these, which have their force by writ; and therefore are called *chyrographa*, or the hand-writ and subscription of the debtor, by which he acknowledgeth the receipt of so much money, either in borrowing, or tocher, and accordingly is obliged to pay at his day, or at the dissolution of the marriage. These writs, for the space of two years after their date and delivery, did not prove the receipt of the money as they expressed, but during that time, if the creditor pursue thereupon, he must prove the delivery of the money ; and that law presumed, that the writ was given *spe numerandæ pecuniæ*, upon hope of delivery of the money : but, after the two years, it presumed the money to be delivered, after which the writ is probative, and is the cause of the obligation, whether the money was delivered or not ; and after which the debtor could not prove the not delivery of the money, even by the oath of the creditor *l. in contractibus, C. 14. de non numerata pecunia* [C. 4, 30, 14] but this is also changed with us, and with our neighbour nations, as Balduinus testifieth, *ad titulum Inst. de lit. oblig.* [Inst. 3,21] and Boetius *de consuetudine, tit. de jurisdict. ;* and Rebuffus *Tom.1 Const. in Proæm. num.59.* So now the custom is, that the writ is not the substance of the obligation, but is only a probation of the promise, though in some cases it be a necessary solemnity till which the parties may resile, as hath been formerly shown : but the writ being subscribed and delivered, proves from its date, and is valid, unless it be improven ; yet so, as it admitteth contrary probation by the creditor's oath or writ, even though the writ bear the numeration of money, and do expressly renounce the exception of not numerate money.

The last kind of contracts are these, which are by sole consent, as are the contracts of sale, location or hyring, society, and mandate or commission ; but not only these, but all other promises and pactions are now valid contracts by sole consent, except where writ is requisite, as is before expressed ; and this consent may be either expressed by word, writ, or fact, by doing deeds importing consent, which therefore is called homologation [1,10,15 ; II,11,24 ; IV,40,29,*infra*] whereof acceptance of any right is a special kind and it takes place in many cases, but it cannot take place unless it be proven, or presumed that the homologator knew the right ; and therefore a bond drawn in name of several apprisers, to communicate their rights, and subscribed by some, was found not homologated by one who subscribed not, seeing it appeared not that he knew thereof, though *de facto*, he concurred in pursuits with these apprisers to exclude other rights, July 6, 1661, Telzifer *contra* Maxtoun and Cunningham [1 Stair 51 ; M. 5633]. Neither doth homologation take place, where the deed done may be attributed to another cause ; and so possessing lands, whereof there was an infeftment granted, in satisfaction of a wife's contract was not inferred, where she was apparent heir to another person infeft, December 12th, 1665, Barns *contra* Young [1 Stair 325 ; M. 5685]. Neither doth payment of one article of a decreet-arbital, homologate articles of a different nature, November 22, 1662, Primrose *contra* Dune [1 Stair 144 ; M. 5702]. Homologation of a father's legacy, as to his children, was inferred by his relict's confirming the testament without protestation not to approve that legacy, February 19, 1663, Muir *contra* Stirling [1 Stair 183 ; M. 6107]. But where a relict in the confirmation, protested not to prejudge her own right, by a provision contained in the testament, in favours of her daughter, it was not found to homologate the same, July 12, 1671, Murray *contra* Murray [1 Stair 755 ; M. 5689 ; 1,9,8,*supra*]. Homologation of a feuar's right was not inferred by acceptance of two years' duty, after declarator of the nullity, further than that no more could be demanded for these two years, June 6, 1666, E. Cassils *contra* Sir Andrew Agnew [1 Stair 373 ; M. 6408]. Neither did the payment of some years' annualrent homologate a decreet of poinding the ground, as being an act necessary to shun poinding of the tenants, February 9, 1672, Cockburn of Piltoun *contra* Halyburton and Burnet [2 Stair 67 ; M. 9009]. Neither did a minister's receiving a tack-duty of teinds, hinder him to reduce the tack thereafter, as being without consent of the patron, February 27, 1668, Chalmers *contra* Wood of Balbegno [1 Stair 538; M.5698]. Neither did the payment of annualrent after majority, by a minor cautioner, paying it with the principal's money, and taking discharge to him only, hinder the minor to reduce, February 14, 1668, Mackenzie *contra* Fairholm [1 Stair 524; M.5639]. Neither did the payment of annualrent to an indigent sister after majority, exclude reduction upon minority; but registrating the contract after majority without charge or execution, was found to infer homologation, June 28, 1671, Hume *contra* L. Rentoun, Justice Clerk [1 Stair 741; M.5688]. Neither did the confirming of a sum as moveable, hinder the confirmer to recover it as heritable, June 28, 1672, Kilgour *contra* Menzies [2 Stair 93; M.11516]; December 23, 1673, Mitchel *contra* Mitchel [2 Stair 246; M.5646]. Neither doth the granting of a precept of seasin on obedience, import acknowlegment of right, or exclude reduction and improbation, December 20, 1662, L. Mochrum *contra* L. Myretoun and Airiolland [*Sub nom. Mochrum* v *Airiolland*, 1 Stair 151; M.6715]. Neither was a decreet found homologated by taking discharge and giving a bond without abatement, which might import transaction, the grantor being in the messenger's hands, under caption, July 3, 1668, Rew *contra* Houstoun [1 Stair 547; M.16484]. Neither was homologation of the truth of a debt, inferred by granting bond by a party in prison, for not finding caution *judicatum solvi*, February 18, 1680, Burnet *contra* Ewing [*Sub nom. Ewing* v *Burnet*, 2 Stair 758; M.16494; 1,9,8, *supra*]. Neither did allowance to a tenant in his rent of annualrent paid by him, exclude reduction of the bond of minority, though the allowance was after majority, December 14, 1675, Moodie *contra* M'Intosh [2 Stair 380; M.5693]. Neither accepting a bond jointly with another, did it homologate the right of that other, February 1, 1766, Veitch *contra* Ker and Pallat [2 Stair 408; M.5646].

Consent may be adhibited by signs, as the borrowing of a watch by a sign made by the borrower's hand, was found to oblige him to restore, though another instantly borrowed it that same way from him; nor was the first lender's silence in an act so subite, interpreted a consent to the second loan, July 3, 1662, Lord Cowper *contra* Lord Pitsligo [1 Stair 119; M.5626]. But a dumb man subscribing a discharge, was not found to infer his consent, in favour of his sister, seeing he knew not what it imported, July 9, 1663, Hamilton *contra* Esdell [1 Stair 197; M.6300]. Neither was consent to a march inferred by the one heritor's building a dyke, and another's silence for a time, January 8, 1663, Nicol *contra* Sir Alexander Hope [1 Stair 153; M.2201]. Neither was the knowledge and silence of a husband found to infer his consent to his future spouse renouncing a part of her jointure after proclamation, and yet going on in the marriage, January 5, 1666, Lady Bute and her husband *contra* Sheriff of Bute [1 Stair 333; M.6031]. And albeit consent to the contents of a writ, is not always inferred from subscribing as a witness; yet in some cases it is, when the consent relates not to the tenor, but to the time of subscribing, as an heir's subscribing as a witness to a writ on deathbed, June 25, 1663, Stuart of Ascock *contra* Stuart of Arnholm [*Sub die* Jan. 25, 1 Stair 195; M. 5674]. But the consent of a party to a decreet, was not found probable by the decreet, without a warrant under the consenter's hand; seeing it appeared that the minute of the decreet on the judicial consent, was not instantly written, but long after, and it was no ordinary point in process consented to, but a transaction of a special nature, July 24, 1661, L. of Buchanan *contra* L. Coll. Osburn [1 Stair 53; M. 12528]: but one of the parties having offered implement by instrument, instructed by the witnesses insert, was not suffered to quarrel his consent, as not under his hand, February 4, 1671, Lowrie *contra* Gibson [1 Stair 715; M. 5622]. But consent was not found to be inferred by the subscribing witnesses as to the contents of the writ, February 1, 1676, Veitch *contra* Ker and Pallat [2 Stair 408; M. 5646]. Yea though the writ did bear the witness to be cautioner, unless it were proven by the witnesses insert, that the writ was fully read to that witness before he subscribed, July 26, 1672, Gordon *contra* Menzies [2 Stair 111; M. 5646].

12. All pactions and contracts being now equally efficacious, may, according to their subject matter, be taken up thus: They are either merely gratuitous, as he who obliges himself to bestow a horse is thereby bound, but there is no obligation on the other; but if the donation be perfected by a present tradition of the thing gifted, there is no obligation contracted on either hand; or next, the obligation is gratuitous on the one part as loan, which is either by the free lending of things consisting in number, measure, and weight, which the law regardeth as a quantity, without regard to the individual body or thing, such being commonly of equal value, according to their quantities, and are called fungibles, as money, corn, wine, either where the loan is expressly, or implicitly, for the re-delivery of the like quantities, though not the same very thing; *pr. Inst. Quib. mod. re cont. oblig.* [Inst. 3, 14, pr.]. Or otherwise, it is the lending the use of a particular thing, to be delivered again, the same in substance. The former is called *mutuum*, the latter *commodatum :* in both if the thing lent be not delivered, this will be effectual to cause it be delivered, though it be gratuitous, if it be in the lender's power, §2 *d. tit. in fin.* [Inst. 3, 14, 2] but on the part of the borrower it is onerous, for he is obliged either to restore the same body or the same quantity. Such also is commission or mandate, whereby the mandator doth freely undertake, and is obliged *susceptum perficere manus,* §*antep. Inst. de mand.* [Inst. 3, 26, 11] *l. 17* §3 *ff. commodat.* [D. 13, 6, 17, 3] and that freely; §*ult. d. tit.* [D. 13, 6, 17, 5] but he is onerously obliged to restore what by the mandate he hath from the mandator, as the mandator is obliged to refund him his interest and expenses. Such also is the contract of custody or *depositum,* which is a kind of commission, whereby the depositar undertakes the custody of the thing deposited. Pledge is also a kind of commission, whereby the thing impledged is given to a creditor for his security, that he may detain, and in case of not payment, he may sell it, and pay himself by the Roman law. but he can only detain it for security, till he poind it, by our custom. The other contracts

are such as are onerous on both parts and obligatory on both parts, and in them there is also always *quid pro quo*, according to the nature and intent of these contracts, observing in them an equality of the deeds or things to be done or given on either part, as not being of their nature or of the direct purpose of the parties, gratuitous or donative.

For uptaking of these we must consider, that all that can come in these obligations, is either something to be given, or the use or fruit of something, or the labour, work, or deeds of persons; and among things, special considerations is had of money, which is the common token of exchange; and therefore there are special contracts in relation to it, different from the exchange of other things. So then all these permutative contracts are either of things for things, as are permutation, excambion, barter, &c. Or of things for numbered money, and that is sale; or money for money, as by bills of exchange.

Secondly, profit, use, fruit, or work, may be either exchanged with things, and this hath no proper name, but is called in law, *facio ut des ;* or otherwise may be exchanged for the like use, profit, or work, neither hath this a proper name, but is called *facio ut facias :* but if the use and profit of things, deeds, or industry of persons be exchanged for money or other fungibles, it is called location and conduction, *Vide l.5 §1 & 2. de Praescr. Verb.* [D. 19, 5, 5, 1 and 2].

And, *lastly*, if the contract be not to exchange totally things, use, or work, for the like, but to communicate them together, where there is an exchange in part, there arises the contract of society, in which sometimes money or things are communicated, and the property constituted in the society without division; or sometimes the use of things, or money, are by the society communicated on the one part, and the substance of money on the other, so that the property of the one's money remains his own, and the profit becomes common; or there may be communication of work with money, or work with work : and though these be the most ordinary contracts among men, yet there be as many varieties as the conjunction of variety of these things, in the various use or humours of men, can make up; as the contract of assurance, where money or things are given, for the hazard of any thing that is in danger, whether it be goods or persons.

We shall only then touch the common requisites, first, of all contracts, and next, the specialities of such prime ones, unto which law or custom hath given a special nature, that by the very naming of the contract and agreement, all the obligations, interests, and consequences thence arising, are commonly known and presumed, and are as effectual as if they were all expressed, without necessity to dispute precisely what reason and equity will conclude, from the nature of what is done or said. This seems to be the only profitable distinction betwixt contracts nominate and innominate; for in all contracts, not only that which is expressed must be performed, but that which is necessarily consequent and implied; but in nominate contracts, law hath determined these implications. We shall therefore speak specially of the contracts of loan, commission, custody, pledge, excambion, sale, location, and contracts usurary and society, and transaction may well be numbered amongst mutual onerous contracts, for thereby either party quitteth a part of what he claims, for shunning the hazard and expences of law, of which hereafter [1,17,2, *infra*].

13. For the common requisites and properties of contracts, *First*, They must be deeds of the rational appetite or will, which, as we have said, can only constitute rights : therefore the consent of infants can work nothing, because they have not the use of reason, and though equity keepeth not one time for the attainment of reason, but takes it as soon as truly it is, which in some is much sooner and in some much later ; yet positive law, following that which is most ordinary for stability's sake, fixes it at the end of pupillarity, which in men is fourteen and in women twelve years of age ; so neither infants, idiots, nor furious persons, except in their lucid intervals, can contract; and this is to be cognosced by an inquest upon a brieve out of the Chancellary, called the brieve of idiotry, which is mainly for appointing the nearest agnat to be tutor to such : and the deeds of idiots are not only void after this inquest, but after their idiotry or furiosity, whenever it began, which therefore must be cognosced ; yet it may be sustained by reduction without a brieve at the furious person's instance convalescing, and at the instance of the furious person's heir, July 26, 1638, Loch *contra* Dyke [Durie 861 ; M. 6278 ; 1,3,42,*supra*]. But it was not found competent by exception, Spots. Idiots, Crawfurd *contra* Kinneir [Spotiswoode, 162 ; M. 6275]. Furiosity taketh away the escheat of those who are self-murderers, being then furious, not knowing what they did, Hope, Horning, Reidpeth *contra* Wauchop [Hope, *Maj. Pr.* VI, 27, 80 ; M. 3440].

Secondly, These also who through fear, *l. 8 & 9. C. de Jur & fact. ign.* [C. 1,8,8 and 9] or drunkenness, or disease, have not for the time the use of reason, do not legally contract.

Thirdly, These who err in the substantials of what is done, contract not, *l. 9. ff. de cont. empt.* [D. 18,1,9]. We shall not here debate of the effect of extortion, error, or circumvention, what influence they have upon contracts, of which in the former title. These who are deaf or dumb may contract, if they have the use of reason, and if it appear they understood what was done, and expressed their consent, by their ordinary known signs. And, lastly, Positive law for utility's sake hath disabled minors having curators, to contract without their consent ; Like unto these are persons interdicted, *l. 3. C. de in integ. restit.* [C. 2,21,3] *l. 40 de R. I* [D. 4,1,40] of which before, *Tit. Tutors and Curators, §37* [1,6,37,*supra*].

This much, in the first place, as the requisites in the persons contracting. *Secondly*, In the act of contracting, it must be of purpose to oblige, either really or presumptively, and so much be serious, so that what is expressed in jest or scorn makes no contract.

Thirdly, In the matter of contracts it is requisite, that it be of things in our power in their kind ; and so contracts of impossibilities are void, § *10. Inst. de inut. stip.* [Inst. 3, 19, 11]. And contracts in things unlawful are also void, *Arg. l. 15. ff. de cond. inst.* [D. 28, 7, 15]. But though the particular thing be not in our power, and yet be not manifestly impossible, the contract is obligatory ; and albeit it cannot obtain its effect, upon that thing, it is effectual for the equivalent, as damage and interest. Contracts may intervene where there intercedes a natural and obediential obligation, where it hath this use, to declare and express the natural obligation to avoid debate thereupon : But the proper matter of contracts, are things free, and the declaration or acknowledgement of necessary duties may be free, though the duty itself be necessary ; yet where obediential and conventional obligations are concurring, they are both obligatory.

14. It is the property of permutative contracts, that the purpose of the contractors is to keep an equality in the worth and value of the things, fruit, or works interchanged, the value whereof is regulated according to the common esteem and custom of men in every place, and it is liquidated or known by money or some fungible like unto money, as sugar and tobacco in the American islands : for money being the common token of exchange, and therefore having virtually in it all things, they are accounted better or worse, or equal, according to the common rate of the place, as they are worth in money for the time : the prime grounds of this common estimate are Necessity, Utility, and Delectation, whether it be real or imaginary, as Pliny, lib. 9. cap. 55 *margaritis pretium luxuria fecit,* such is the value of portraits, tulips or other flowers, upon which, in some places, a far greater rate hath been put, than any usefulness thereof would allow; hence it is that the rate of things does frequently change, as the necessity or esteem of them changeth, and the more they abound, the easier is their rate.

But the question is here, Whether in these contracts there be a moral necessity to keep an exact equality, that whosoever *ex post facto*, shall be found to have made an unequal bargain, the gainer ought to repair the loser. In this the Romans did not notice every inequality, but that which was enorm, above the half of the just value; which our custom alloweth not, June 23, 1669, Farie *contra* Inglis [1 Stair 623 ; M. 14231 ; 1, 9, 11, *supra*]. And the opinion of Grotius *de jure belli*, lib. 2. cap. 12. § 11, is for the affirmative upon this ground chiefly, that the purpose of the contracters is to give one thing for another of equal value, without purpose to gift on either hand. Yet the contrary opinion is more probable in some cases, wherein, though it be the purpose of the parties to interchange things of equal value without donation, yet that equality hath no determinate or certain rule, but their own opinions : for, as is said before, the special affection and opinion of the owner, is a piece of his interest and enjoyment ; and if the thing be taken from him unwarrantably, and cannot be restored, the reparation is not according to the common rate, but *secundum pretium affectionis*, according to the value the owner had of it ; and if that owner sell it for the rate he thought it worth, it would be thought no less than cozenage, for the buyer to offer but what others thought it worth : If then the particular value or esteem be the first rule in such contracts, when both parties being free, do agree upon such a rate, there is here no donation, but a particular estimation, wherewith either party ought to rest satisfied. It is true, where there is no rate agreed upon, the common rate must be the rule, but it cannot always be a rule, seeing the public rate doth but arise from the private rate, otherwise rates should never change, except where by public authority they are determined, which is but seldom. But ordinarily the change of rates begins at particular persons, and the second contractors use for a pattern the first; and the fuller the example be, the stronger it is until it become common ; and therefore it is safest to conclude with the law, *l. si voluntate, C. de rescin. vend.* [C. 4, 44, 8] which saith, This is the substance of buying and selling, that the buyer having a purpose to buy cheap, and the seller to sell dear, they come to this contract, and after many debates, the seller by little and little diminishing what he sought, and the buyer adding to what he offered, at last they agree to a certain price, or as Seneca says, *lib. 6, de beneficiis, cap. 15.* "It is no matter what the rate be, seeing it is agreed between the buyer and the seller; for he that buys well, owes nothing to the seller". Therefore, the equality required in these contracts, cannot be in any other rate than the parties agree on; but in other things this equality ought to be observed, as in any Penalty adjected, or Clauses irritant, which therefore ought to be and are reduced to the just interest, whatever the parties' agreement be. So then, seeing promises and contracts are morally binding, permutative contracts must also be such, else they should not bind by virtue of the consent, but by reason of the matter; but in them, as in all others, if any party hath disadvantage by fraud or guile, it ought to be repaired; but not by virtue of the contract, but from the obligation arising from that delinquence: and so "unjust balances are an abomination to the Lord," because of the deceit thence arising: as also false money, and insufficient ware by any latent insufficiency or defect which was not obvious and easily perceivable by the acquirer, in which case there can be no presumption of fraud, "his eye is his merchant", *l. 1 §6. ff. de aedil. edict.* [D. 21, 1, 1, 6]. But in others, according to the sentence of Ambrose; "In contracts," saith he, "even the defects of the things which are sold ought to be laid open, and unless the seller intimate the same, there is competent to the buyer an action of fraud." So also, if the buyer take advantage of the ignorance and simplicity of the seller, and where there is no alteration of the common rate, nor ground thereof, asketh or craveth more if it be not deceit, at least it is against charity and honesty: so it is when ware is kept up till pinching necessity, which raiseth extreme dearth, or when some special necessity of an acquirer puts him so upon the mercy of the disponer, that he may take a price, even above that which himself accounts the thing worth; in such cases, there is the violation of the natural obligation of charity, whereby men are bound in some cases, to gift freely to the necessity of others, but frequently we are obliged to exchange what our necessity may spare, to supply others' necessity for the like, which they may spare, and so without injury, in case of necessity, men may be compelled to sell that which is their own.

15. This agreeth with our custom, by which only a latent insufficiency of the goods and ware, at the time of the sale and delivery, is sufficient to abate or take down the price [1, 9, 11, *supra*], but not, unless when the insufficiency appeared, the thing bought be offered to be restored (if it be not carried abroad before the insufficiency appear) after which, retention is accounted an acquiescence in, and homologation of the contract [1. 10, 11, *supra*]. So no other than the latent insufficiency of wines, as being mixed with peary, &c. is relevant to liberate from a bond granted for the price thereof. But the insufficiency of a horse was not sustained to liberate from the price, he not being offered back when that appeared, January 9, 1629, Brown *contra* Nicolson [Durie 412; M. 8940]. And the insufficiency of skins received upon trust, was found only probable by the oath of the seller, after the buyer had sold them again, July 7, 1675, Paton *contra* Lockhart [2 Stair 340; M. 14232].

16. Before we come to the special contracts, this question, which is of much importance in practice, would be resolved, whether in mutual or reciprocal contracts, a party contractor, or his assignee can obtain implement of the articles of the contract in his favour, till he fulfill or cause to be fulfilled the other part. Our decisions have been exceeding various in this matter, for clearing whereof, several cases must be distinguished: *First*, In the case of the contractors themselves: and in that case, either the mutual obligements are conceived conditionally, that the one part being performed or upon the performance thereof, the other part shall be performed; or where the obligements are not conceived conditionally, yet they are properly mutual causes each of other; as in Sale, the obligement to deliver the ware and to pay the price; in Permutation, the things exchanged and mutual obligements for delivery thereof, are the mutual causes each of other; in Location, the use of that which is set for hire and the hire, are mutual causes, and so are the obligations *hinc inde*. Otherwise the obligements are not the proper causes each of other, but either wholly different matters, which are frequently accumulated in the same contracts; or the one is but the occasion and motive, and not the proper cause of the other. So the case of assignees must be considered in all these.

For the *first*, the civil law is for the negative, that in reciprocal contracts, neither party can have effectual action, except he perform the whole contract on his part [D. 19, 1, 13, 8]. As to the first member of the first case, there is no question; but when the mutual obligements are conceived conditionally, he that demands the one part, must perform the other. As to the other member, when the obligements are mutual causes each of other expressly, as when the contract bears, "for the which causes," or when by the nature of the thing it appeareth so to be; it is most consonant to reason, to the civil law, and our practice, that neither party should obtain implement of the obligements to him, till he fulfil the obligements by him.

As to the *second* case ; Whether an assignee charging or pursuing upon a mutual contract, be in any better case than the cedent, or can crave implement, till the cedent's part be performed, the difficulty is here, that if assignees be clogged with the obligements of the cedent, it will mar commerce, and render such contracts ineffectual, as to summary execution, and so obligements therein for liquid sums of money, might not be poinded or apprised for, nor any execution valid thereupon ; but this will not follow, for though these executions be summarily used, they will stand valid, only the effect will be suspended, till the other part be performed. But the assignee having no title whereby to compel his cedent to perform his part ; therefore the other contractor must either be decerned to assign his part of the contract to the assignee, that thereupon he may insist for performance, and that before the extract of his decreet or rather execution may be sisted, except as to adjudication for his security, till he procure implement of his cedent's part ; or otherwise that he find caution, that the other contractor using diligence against his cedent for performance, that the assignee shall make up what shall be wanting to him as was done in the case betwixt Cunninghame *contra* Ross, [February 15, 1627, Durie 274; M. 12453], wherein an assignee upon a contract for the price of lands, by which contract his cedent was obliged to cause the tenants pay certain bygone farms, therefore the assignee was ordained to find caution for satisfying of these farms against the cedent, Feb. 15, 1627 Cunninghame *contra* Ross [Durie 274; M. 12453]; Hope, Contracts, L. Renton *contra* Douglas [Hope, *Maj. Pr.* II, 1, 27]. And though a donatar was found to have right to the price of lands due by a contract, though the rebel had not performed his part of the contract, Hope, Cessio bonorum, Balfour *con.* Futhie [Hope, *Maj. Pr.* VI, 30, 20; M. 2207], where there was nothing alleged of the insolvency of the cedent. Yet a donatar pursuing for the price of feus, the feuars were assoilizied from the declarator, till the donatar obtained the feus to be perfected ; but here it was known, the donatar was in trust for the rebel, who was in power to perform, January 28, 1673, Lord Lyon *contra* Forbes [2 Stair 160 ; M. 5078]. But there can be no reason that the one part of the mutual cause should be effectual without the other, for if the cedent's backbond apart would affect the assignee, much more when it is in the same contract ; yea, though the matter proceed not by way of contract but by bonds apart ; if thereby it appear, that these bonds are mutual causes one of another, the effect should be the same, and though there be no more to prove that they are mutual causes, but that they are of the same date, and before the same witnesses, the Lords will readily examine the witnesses insert, *ex officio*, whether they be mutual causes each of the other ; and therefore, where a bond apart did bear that the creditor should ratify a disposition of the same date, at his majority, under a great penalty ; a bond granted apart to that party of that same date, being assigned, the assignee was found to have no power to uplift the principal sum, till the cedent either ratified it at his majority, or were past his *anni utiles*, without reduction, November 14, 1628, Cumming *contra* Cumming [Durie 396; M.9147]. In this case the bond assigned did expressly bear the price of the land, to which the other bond of the same date was relative. The like was found, as to writs of the same date, with a contract anent the same matter, though not mentioned in the contract, Hope, Contract, Duncrub *contra* Chapman [*Sub nom. Duner* v *Chapman*, Hope, *Maj.Pr.*11,1,17]. But if in contracts or mutual bonds, the mutual obligements have different terms of performance, a pursuit upon the one part will not be stopped by not perform- ance of the other part, while the term agreed for the performance is not come, November 28, 1676, Carmichael of Balmedy *contra* Dempster of Pitliver [2 Stair 469; M.9163], this was between the parties contractors; but when a prior bond of borrowed money is given with mention of the cause, the meaning of contractors must be, that there should be no effect thereupon as to singular successors, yea even as to contractors, when there is no backbond or condition, but a simple bond of borrowed money, which imports accept- ilation or innovation of the former mutual obligement, for in both the former cases, the cause was expressed not to be borrowed money.

Title 11. Loan or *Mutuum* and *Commodatum*, Where, of Bills of Exchange

HAVING thus treated of contracts in general in the preceding title, we come now to particular contracts, according to the order proposed. Loan compre- hendeth both the contracts in the law called *mutuum* and *commodatum;* by the former, a thing fungible is freely given, for the like to be restored in the same kind and quantity, though not the same individual. A fungible is that which is estimated according to the quantity, and is not easily discernible nor noticed in the individual or particular body, but only in the like quantity of the same kind, the chief of which is money, where ordinarily the extrinsic value and common rate is regarded, without respect to the matter, and so what is borrowed in gold may be paid in silver, according to the common rate of the place, unless it be otherwise contracted: such also are wine, oil, and grain, wherein the quantity is ever respected in the same kind, as in the loan of wines, payment must be had not only by the wine of the same country, but if there be any difference, by the wine of the same place of the country, and so of all the rest; for it is never accounted a quantity, where there can be other differences remarked. These fungibles have no fruit or use, if they be retained, and therefore the end of the contract, and purpose of the contractor is, that the property thereof shall pass to the borrower from the lender, and may be by him alienated; and thence is its name for *mutuum est quasi de meo tuum, l.2.ff. de rebus creditis* [D. 12, 1, 2, 2]. Salmasius alone denies this, holding that the intent of this contract, *non est transferre dominium*, but to give the use, and that the alienation falls of accident, because law makes no difference of quantities of the same kind; so that if money be found, restitution may be made without any contract, though not in the same money but in the like, wherein there is no consent, and so can be no alienation.

2. Yet the common opinion holds, that the purpose of the contractors is to alienate, because they know without it there can be no use: and if a fungible be not lent to that purpose, but only to be detained, as in some cases it may, as money to make a show with, to appear rich, or to make a simulate consignation, there the borrower without injury, could not alienate, neither is there *mutuum* in that case, but *commodatum;* and he who findeth, unwarrantably alienateth his neighbour's money, and may be compelled, not only to render the like in current money, but to render the same species and piece of money. So he who hath the custody of money, if he meddle with it, commits theft by the law. Hence it follows that *in mutuo* the whole peril of the thing lent, after delivery, is the borrower's, *ejus est periculum cujus est dominium ;* so that money, or any other fungible thing lent, though it were immediately taken away by force, or destroyed by accident, the borrower is obliged to pay it; so that the transmission of the property of things lent *mutuo*, is so necessary, that without it, it cannot consist; and if a paction or condition be adjected, though with interposition of a stipulation, that the thing lent shall not be alienable, it destroys the contract, and changes it into *commodatum*.

It is not here necessary to repeat the general requisites of *mutuum* common to other contracts, as that it must be done by an act of the will, with under-standing, and so is impeded by error in the substance of the contract, and cannot be effectuated by infants, furious persons; nor by the civil law could it be done by prodigals, which we notice not, unless they be interdicted : neither by minors having curators without their consent. Nor can they who have not the right of property lend, except by commission, because they can-not transmit more than they have ; but *mutuum* may be constitute by such as can contract effectually, having all the former requisites of the lender.

3. The civil law had this exception further, *per senatus consultum Macedonianum* [D. 14, 6 ; C. 4, 28], prohibiting and annulling all lending to sons in the family, which our custom owneth [not], and looketh upon sons at most, as under the privilege of minors, if within age; and if they contract without their father's consent, who is their lawful administrator, their deed is annullable, unless it be of small importance, or be in such matters wherein

they use to negotiate. Our custom instead of the *senatus consultum Velleianum* [D. 16, 1 ; C. 4, 29], in favours of women, whereby they could not interpose as cautioners, or any ways of surety for others, hath indulged the favour to wives, that while they are married, they cannot effectually oblige themselves, otherwise than in reference to their lands, of which formerly, Title. Conjugal Obligations § 16 [1, 4, 16, *supra*].

4. Because of the matter, things cannot fall under *mutuum*, which cannot be alienated, and which are not properly fungible (as money, corn, wine, oil); and I doubt not but oxen, kine, and sheep, are mutuable, as is ordinary in steel-bow goods, which are delivered to the tenant with the land, for the like number and kind at his removal.

5. As to the specialities of *mutuum*. First, It is not contracted without delivery of the thing lent, and it hath very little, either by the civil law, or our customs, as a nominate contract, but what is competent by the obligation of restitution or recompence; and, therefore, *promutuum, per indebite solutum*, where there is no contract, is equiparate to *mutuum ;* for the like, not only in kind but in value, must be repaid, though nothing be expressed thereof; as he who lent so much wine, is not obliged to accept the same kind of wine, but also the same value; as if he lent old wine, he is not obliged to take new, which is accounted worse, *l. 3. ff. de rebus creditis* [D. 12, 1, 3], and this is rather by that equivalence, due in recompence, than by any tacit paction, understood to be implied in this contract. And it were more convenient for commerce that there should be understood a contrary paction, that being repaid in the same kind, there should be no debate of the equivalent value, which leaves a perpetual incertitude in all such contracts, raising ever a quarrel, that the re-payment is not as good as the thing lent, according as there is difference of the goodness of wines, in the same country, yea, in the same field. Likewise there is difference in kinds of money, silver, or gold, and in the intrinsic and extrinsic value; wherein the common opinion is, that not only the extrinsic, but intrinsic, value is to be respected, that the same weight and species of money may be repaid. But none make difference of gold or silver, not allayed; and all reject copper or layed money. Our custom was to have re-payment of the same intrinsic value, as appears Parl. 1451, cap. 36 [A.P.S. 11, 39, cc. 1–18], Parl., 1457, cap. 19 [1456, c. 58; A.P.S. 11, 46, c. 7], Parl. 1555, cap. 37 [A.P.S. 11, 494, c. 10]; but that was well altered by a posterior custom, allowing the current coin for the time, by the extrinsic value to be sufficient, in all redemptions, much more in personal contracts, which is most convenient, seeing money is regarded as the token of exchange, and as a fungible, not as a body, *l. 1 in pr. ff. de Act. empti* [D. 19, 1, 1]; and it is not to be supposed that if the lender had kept his money from the present borrower, that he would have lost the profit of it, or keep it up till the extrinsic value might change to his advantage, or that the borrower was to keep it by him, but to make present use of it; for which cause we notice not the intrinsic value, even as it was at the term of payment.

6. The civil law gives so little to *mutuum*, by the nature of the contract, that it is amongst the contracts *stricti juris*, where nothing is understood but what is expressed, or necessarily consequent therefrom : and therefore there is no annual or profit due *in mutuo* ; yea, though it be expressed by paction, it will not suffice by the civil law, unless it be by stipulation. So we allow no profit *in mutuo*, unless it be so agreed upon, which may be by paction, even *ex intervallo* ; in which case it retains the name of *mutuum*, though it be rather location of the use of the fungible, for the annual, as a competent hire, and so we shall speak to annualrents not here, but in location. Yet the law did allow to *mutuum*, that any thing might be transchanged into a fungible, as the price thereof, and that fungible constitute *in mutuum*, which is equivalent, as if the fungible had been really delivered, *l.11.ff. de rebus creditis* [D. 12, 1, 11]. And any contract is easily changed *in mutuum*, *per fictionem brevis manus*, as if all these alterations had been actually made *l.9 §9 de reb. cred.* [D. 12, 1, 9, 9]. But if it were but acknowledged, *per chyrographum*, that money was delivered, the exception *de non numerata pecunia* was competent. With us the transmission from any other cause is sufficient, and the acknowledgement of the receipt of money proves, unless the contrary be proven by writ or oath of party.

7. The ordinary way of *mutuum* amongst merchants is by bills of exchange, or letters of credit, which have several specialities, which arise from the nature of these acts, and from custom, especially these common customs of merchants, observed in cities of greatest trade in the neighbouring nations. The nature and ordinary tenor of these bills of exchange is, that the drawer of the bill orders such a merchant, his correspondent, to pay the sum contained in the bill upon sight, or at such a certain time, or at such usance, and that for value received ; wherein there is implied a mandate to the correspondent, and an obligement upon the drawer of the bill, to make that mandate effectual, wherein *mutuum* is implied, if the value received by him be numerate money, or if any other causes, such as delivery of ware, and there is in it *fictio brevis manus*, as if the ware were sold to the drawer of the bill, and the sum in the bill were the price received, and delivered again in loan. There useth two or three bills to be drawn for the same sum, which do bear to be the *first*, *second* and *third bill*, and the payment of any one satisfies all. The fixed form by custom of making use of these bills, is by presenting them to him upon whom they are drawn, and if he accept the bill, he writes thereupon, *Accepts*, which if it be simply, he becomes liable in the terms, and at the time mentioned in the bill : but sometimes the accepter doth qualify his acceptance, which the creditor by the bill may refuse, and require either simple acceptance, or may protest for non-acceptance ; but if he suffer the acceptance to be qualified, it imports his consent, and he cannot protest for non-acceptance, as if the acceptance be to a longer day than that which is contained in the bill, or if it bear acceptance, "if provisions come betwixt and the day ;" or, "if ware or bills in hand do raise the sum." At or after the day,

the bill is again presented, and if payment be not then made, the creditor in the bill protests for not-payment, and both these protestations must be by instrument of a notary, either for non-acceptance or not-payment: which instruments with the bill, make sufficient probation, both against the drawer of the bill, and against him upon whom it was drawn; and neither witnesses, nor the oath of party will be sufficient to supply the protest: so that the instrument or protest is not only a proof, but a solemnity requisite. These protests may be taken against him upon whom they were drawn, either personally, or at his dwelling-house, which was sustained, though before presenting of the bill, the party upon whom it was drawn was dead, July 8, 1664, Kennedy *contra* Hutchison [1 Stair 211; M. 1496].

Upon bills so protested, the creditor in the bill hath action, both against him upon whom the bill was drawn, if through his fault, he hath either refused to accept or to pay; and so if he had provisions in his hand, he will be decerned to pay; and if without provisions he accept and pay, the drawer of the bill becomes his debtor, *ex mutuo*, or *ex mandato*. The creditor in the bill may also return upon the drawer of the bill, who will be decerned to pay the sum, with the damage the creditor hath sustained through its being protested; wherein will be comprehended the expenses of the pursuit against the correspondent, and the profit the creditor in the bill might have made, if according to it he had received his money, which will differ in several persons and cases; as if the creditor in the bill be not a merchant, the ordinary damage will be the exchange, that is, the rate ordinarily given at that time, for answering money from the place at which the bill was drawn, to the place to which it was directed; but if the creditor in the bill was a merchant, and was to trade with the sum in the place to which the bill was direct, he hath also no more but exchange; but if he was to trade in any other place, before he returned to the place where the bill was drawn, he will not only get exchange, but re-exchange, as being damnified in the profit of his ware that he was to buy at the place to which he was bound, from that place to which the bill was direct, for the ware he was to buy there, and for the loss of his profit of the ware he was to buy at the second port: but though there might be farther progress in his traffic, his damage is no farther extended than to exchange and re-exchange; he hath also re-exchange, if wanting credit at that place, he be necessitated to return empty, or buy on trust: and in all the oath of the creditor in the bill, concerning his design with the bill, must be sufficient probation, and is taxable, as all oaths *in litem* are when they appear exhorbitant. If the bill of exchange be unsatisfied by an interveening accident, which the drawer could not prevent, the damage will be modified or taken off; as in the former case [1 Stair 211; M. 1496], the correspondent upon whom the bill was drawn, dying before the day of payment, the creditor in the bill having protested at his dwelling-house, and not insisting against his successors, but returning against the drawer, he got no exchange, or re-exchange; yet certainly the drawer of the bill being thereby obliged to deliver the money at the place to which the bill was directed, it had been no stretch to give him exchange.

But if the correspondent, upon whom the bill is drawn, break, or become insolvent, full damage will be due by the drawer, whose part it was to have his money in secure hands; unless the correspondent's insolvency be by the delay, or fault of the creditor in the bill : for though there be no determinate time, at which he is obliged to present it, yet conveniency and ordinary diligence is implied ; but if the delay fall by an accident, though the correspondent break before the bill be presented or paid, the drawer of the bill will be liable for the value received, but for no damage, July 1, 1676, Doctor Wallace *contra* Simson [2 Stair 435 ; M. 1545].

These bills of exchange are probative, though they neither have witnesses nor be holograph, by the custom of merchants, because of the exuberant trust among them, and because they do not lie over as other securities, but come quickly to be questioned, if they be not satisfied. Yea, a bill of exchange by a drover, neither having subscription of his name, nor initial letters thereof, but a mark, at which the writer of the bill wrote, "This is the mark of the drawer of the bill," the writer and several witnesses being examined, *ex officio*, and deponing, that it was the drover's custom to mark bills thus, which he readily paid, though of greater sums than this, which was an hundred pounds sterling, and one witness deponing, that he saw him set to his mark to this bill, the bill was sustained, Feb. 26, 1662, Brown *contra* Johnstoun [1 Stair 105 ; M. 16802].

Bills of exchange are also transmitted, without any formal assignation or intimation, by a note upon the bill itself, ordering it to be paid to such another : and bills of exchange have now summary execution, by horning, as if they did contain a clause of registration, by the act 20, Par. 3, chap. 2. l. 2, [Bills of Exchange Act, 1681, c. 20 ; A.P.S. VIII, 352, c. 86], which was very fit for the expediting of commerce. The first order carries the right of the sum in the bill, without necessity of intimation, yet payment made *bona fide* by a posterior order, secures the payer [III, 1, 12, *infra*].

Bills or precepts, not being amongst merchants or *in re mercatoria*, import only warrandice upon the drawer, and give action against the person upon whom they are drawn, but neither require the solemnities, nor have the privilege or effects of bills of exchange, but have only the effect of assignations from the drawer upon him upon whom they are drawn. Yea, a bill of exchange amongst merchants, not bearing value received, was found only as an assignation, without a cause onerous, but not as a mere factory, which the drawer might recall, and by a posterior bill exclude the former, July 24, 1691, Hume *contra* Hamilton [Not found].

Letters of credit among merchants, are equiparate to bills of exchange in some cases, but in others they are but cautionary for these in whose favours they are granted ; and therefore a merchant's letters of credit, to honour another merchant's bills, was only found effectual as to such bills as were accepted and paid, and whereof re-payment was not made, and advertisement given to the writer of the letters, of the particular bills not paid in due time, before the other merchant became insolvent, January 7, 1681, Ewing Merchant in London *contra* Burnet [2 Stair 828; M. 8219]. Vid. *Marius upon Bills of Exchange, lex Mercatoria &c.*

8. The other kind of loan is called *commodatum, quasi commodo datum,* and it is a contract whereby the use of any thing is freely given to be restored, the same without deterioration; if it be not freely lent, but for a hire, it is location; if the like be restored, it is *mutuum ;* but if it be lost through the commodatar's fault, or otherwise deteriorate, the value must be restored, either as it was estimate by the parties before hand, which changeth not its nature §2 *Inst. Quib. mod. re cont. obl.* [Inst, 3, 14, 2], *l. 1.§3 & 4ff. de O. & A.* [D. 44, 7, 1, 3 and 4]. Or if there be no estimation, then the estimation is to be according to the rate of the thing lent, at the time and place appointed in the contract, *l. 5 in pr. ff. Commod.* [D. 13, 6, 5 *in pr.*]; or as it was worth the time of the sentence. But restitution must be made without deterioration, except such as necessarily follows the use for which it was lent; as clothes lent may be worn, and cattle lent become older, *d. 1. 5.§4.* [D. 13, 6, 5, 4]; Or if a horse be lent for a long journey, and therefore become leaner, without the borrower's fault, he is not obliged to make up the same, *l. fin. ff. Commodati* [D. 13, 6, 23]; but all other deteriorations must be made up; and it must be lent for use, that it may differ from depositation, which admits of no use, but custody, and so is not for the benefit of the depositar, but of the deponent, or him who depositeth.

This contract may be celebrated amongst all that have the common requisites of contracting; yea, if the lender have the possession, he may lend, though he have no property; and servitudes and habitation may be lent *l. 1.§1 in fin. ff. h. tit* [D. 13, 6, 1, 1]. And though the lender have neither right nor lawful possession, the law saith, *l. si servus ff. Commodati* [D. 13, 6, 22], that this contract hath effect, which is only to be understood, that the action *commodati* is competent, but not as to all effects; for the borrower cannot effectually detain the thing lent to his day, or any fruit thereof, seeing the lender had no title; but his having or detaining is not theft nor robbery; as when a depositar lendeth the thing depositate.

All things may be lent that can have any use without consumption of their substance, and so fungibles cannot be lent, unless they be given *ad pompam,* as money lent to seem rich, or to make a simulate offer or consignation, *l. 3.§fin. l. 4. ff. h. t* [D. 13, 6, 3, 6 and 4].

9. As to the diligence due by the borrower, the case must be distinguished; for some things may be lent only for the behoof of the lender, as he who lends clothes or instruments, to his servants for his own use and honour: sometimes to both the lender and borrower's use, and oftest to the borrower's use alone: in all cases, the borrower is obliged *de dolo ;* yea, no paction can be valid in the contrary, as being against good manners; *l. 17. in pr. ff. hoc.*

tit. [D. 13,6,17,*in pr.*]; *l.23ff. de R. Juris* [D. 50,17,23]. In no case is the borrower obliged for any accident, as death, naufrage, burning, unless he hath undertaken that hazard, either expressly or tacitly, as *in commodato æstimato*, which imports, that if the thing perish, it is lost to the borrower, and he must pay the price ; *l.5 §3ff. commodati* [D. 13,6,5,3]. For, as *in dote æstimata*, so in *commodato æstimato*, it is in the debtor's option, whether to restore the thing itself entire, or the price to which it is estimated ; but if the estimation be only in the case of the deterioration, or loss, it doth no more but save questions as to the value, and is not *commodatum æstimatum*, as was found, Nov. 17, 1668, betwixt the towns of Arbroath and Montrose [Possibly *Duncan* v *Arbroath*, Nov. 17, 1668 ; 1 Stair 563 ; M. 10075]: Or that the borrower hath applied the loan to another use than it was lent for ; in which case it perisheth to him, yea, he committeth theft in that misapplication *l.5.§8ff. commodati* [D. 13,6,5,8]: so if a fault precede occasioning the accident, as if money lent for show, being carried abroad, be taken by robbers, *l.5 §4ff.h.t* [D. 13,6,5,4]; *l.1 §4ff. de O. & A.* [D. 44,7,1,4]. But in the first case, the borrower is only holden for the grossest faults and negligence ; in the second, for ordinary faults, *culpa levi ;* in the last, for the lightest fault, and is obliged for such diligence, as the most prudent use in their affairs *d.l.5 §2.ff.Commodati* [D. 13,6,5,2 ; 1,15,5,*infra*].

10. *Precarium* is a kind of *commodatum*, differing in this, that *commodatum* hath a determinate time, either expressly, when the use of a thing is given to such a day, or such an use, which importeth a time, as lending a book to copy, must infer so much time as may do it ; and lending a horse to ride a journey, must import a competent time. But *precarium* is expressly lent, to be recalled at the lender's pleasure; *l.1ff. de Precario* [D. 43,26,1]; *l.2 §2 eod.* [D. 43,26,2,2], and if nothing be expressed, it is presumed in law, *commodatum* during the use granted, unless there be no special use expressed, and then it is esteemed *precarium*, because there can be no time consequent upon general use, *d.l.2 §3* [D. 43,26,2,3].

11. *Commodatum* is ended by the ending of the special use, for which it is granted, or the time prefixed, *l.17.§3ff.Commodati* [D. 13,6,17,3]; or by revocation, if it be precarious, or by perishing of the matter lent; but *precarium* is not finished by the death of the lender, till his heir recall it : but it is finished by the death of the borrower, unless it be otherwise agreed.

12. From *commodatum* arise two actions, the direct, whereby the lender may call for the thing lent : *l.5 §9.h.t.* [D. 13,6,5,9], and the contrary, whereby the borrower may call for his expenses, wared out necessarily, or profitably on the thing lent, more than is necessary to preserve it in the case it was lent, which he may use by way of exception, to have retention till the same be satisfied, *d.l.17 §3.* [D. 13,6,17,3].

Title 12. Mandate or Commission, Where, of Trust, &c.

COMMISSION is called in law *mandatum*, either because it useth to be expressed by way of command or precept, though this be special in a precept, that most mandates are free, and may be refused, but precepts may not, when the party upon whom they are drawn, hath provision from the drawer : or otherwise it is called *mandatum, quasi de manu datum*, because it is given out of the hand, or the management of the mandant given to the trust of the mandatar. The requisites of this contract, must be first, a desire, warrant, or order, upon the part of the mandant to the mandatar, to do some affair, to the behoof of the mandant only ; or of the mandant and mandatar, as to manage that which they have in common ; or to the behoof of a third party only; or of a third party and the mandatar, or of the three jointly; for if to the behoof of the mandatar only, it inferreth no obligation, but rather is a mere counsel, in whatsoever terms it be expressed; as if Maevius desire or command Titius, not to employ his money upon annualrent, but to buy land therewith, or particularly to buy such land, there ariseth thence no obligation: it is true in crimes, such desires may infer punishment, *l. 11 § 3 ff. de injur.* [D. 47, 10, 11, 3] *l. 5 C. de accusat.* [c. 9, 2, 5]. But no obligation in favour of the party desired. Or when a commission is granted only to the behoof of the receiver, it transmitteth a right to him, and no obligation upon him. So personal rights are transmitted by assignations, which are procuratories, but to the procurator's own behoof; such are also precepts for taking seasin or possession, *vid. tit. Inst. de mand. usque ad § 8* [Inst. 3, 26, 1–8].

2. As to the terms in which mandates or commissions are expressed, if it be any way to the behoof of the mandant, there is no difference what the expression be, unless the words be *mendicatorie*, importing the desire of a donation ; but if it be only to the behoof of the mandatar, or of a third party, or both, without any behoof of the mandant, then it must be considered, whether the words import only a counsel, that the mandatar do such a thing upon his own accompt ; in which case there is no contract, nor obligation, unless it appear that it was upon the mandant's accompt, or a third party's, or by fraud, *l. 47. de R.I.* [D. 50, 17, 47].

3. The second requisite is the consent or acceptance of the mandatar,

which completeth this contract, which is perfected by sole consent, and may
be either by word or deed, from whence the warrant of the mandant, and
acceptance of the mandatar may be inferred, or by any other sign, as by
pointing with the hand, or beckoning with the head : and albeit it was free
to accept or consent, yet it is obligatory and necessary to perform, *d.l.17§3
in med.ff.commod.* [D.13,6,17,3] unless *re integra* the mandatar renounce,
so that the mandator be not hindered in obtaining thereafter another
mandatar. *§9 & §11 Inst.h.tit.* [Inst. 3,26,9 and 11].

4. The third requisite in a mandate is, that it be in relation to a thing
lawfully to be done ; for it cannot reach to what is already done, and being
in a matter unlawful, albeit it be accepted, it obliges not the accepter to perform, and if it be performed, it obliges not the mandant to make up the
mandatar's damage : but in this, as in other things unlawful, albeit both
parties be in the fault, *potior est conditio possidentis,* and he who is actually
free of the loss, hath the advantage, *l.12 §11,ff.h.tit.* [D.17,1,12,11] *vid.
supra §1. in fin.* [1,12,1 *in fin., supra*].

5. The last requisite in mandates is, that the acceptance must be free,
not only in so far as the mandatar may freely accept or refuse, whereby a
proper and voluntary mandate, differs from a necessary command or precept,
which is no proper mandate, because it is not inferred by consent, but also
in so far as acceptance must be gratuitous ; otherwise the contract thence
arising is not mandate, but location, *l.1 §4ff.h.t* [D.17,1,1,4]. Yet honoraries
or salaries, for performing of things, having no proper price or estimation,
alter not the nature of this contract, as the salaries or honoraries of physicians
for procuring of health, which hath no price ; or of judges or advocates for
giving or procuring of justice.

6. It is implied in the nature of a mandate, that it is personal, depending
upon the singular choice of the mandant, which he hath made of the mandatar's person ; and therefore it is neither continued in the heir of the
mandant, or of the mandatar ; but *morte mandatoris perimitur mandatum,*
which holdeth also upon the death of the mandatar ; for this contract arising
from a singular affection or friendship betwixt both, the removal of either
resolves that tie ; so that in delegation, which is a mandate by a creditor to
his debtor, to pay the debt to the creditor of his creditor, it was found to
cease by the death of the creditor mandant ; and that a letter written by him
to his debtor to pay his creditor, was no warrant to pay, after the debtor
knew that his creditor the mandator was dead, Feb. 2. 1628, executors of the
Laird of Duffus *contra* Forrester [Spotiswoode, 123 ; M.3166]. But here
there is an exception, *si res non sit integra,* if the matter of the mandate be
not entire, but that the mandatar hath entered upon, and performed a part
of his commission ; for in that case it continueth after the death of either
party : it hath also the exception *bonæ fidei,* if the mandatar perform the
mandate, though after the mandant's death, if he knew not that he was dead,
albeit the matter was entire at the time of his death, *§10.Inst.h.tit.* [Inst. 3,

26,10]. In general or complex mandates, the performance of a part doth not continue all the several members or different natures of the mandate, but only that particular whereof a part is done.

7. Here there ariseth a question, whether a mandatar may intrust another person, or sub-commit his mandate, wherein the civil law, and most of the doctors are in the affirmative. But the nature of the contract inferreth the contrary, which ought to take place, unless law or custom were opposite, which is not with us. The reasons for the negative are pregnant; first, because the singular and personal fitness of the mandatar is chosen by the mandator, and so cannot without his consent be altered. Secondly, It is a common ground, that which belongeth not to heirs, belongeth much less to assignees or substitutes. Thirdly, It is a common brocard, *delegatus non potest delegare*, especially in the matters of jurisdiction, which the doctors acknowledge, but say that it is introduced by the law, against the nature of this contract; but they should rather say, that the power of sub-committing in extrajudicials is so introduced. It is true, the reasons foresaid fail in some cases, as if the mandate be of a nature so common, that there is no distinction of the fitness of persons; as precepts of seasin, which are therefore directed blank, that any person's name indifferently may be filled up; or if the mandate be so general, that it cannot all be performed by one.

8. It is also consequent from the nature of this contract, that it is ambulatory and revocable at the pleasure of the mandator, even though it bear a definite term; because that being introduced in favours of the mandator, it cannot hinder him, *nam cuique licet juri pro se introducto renunciare*, which holdeth not when the mandate is partly to be the mandator's own behoof; for then the interest not being wholly the mandator's, he cannot alter the time agreed upon without consent of the mandatar: yea, if the mandate be wholly to the behoof of the mandatar, it may be, and frequently is irrevocable, and containeth a clause *de rato*, as is ordinary in assignations, and procuratories of resignation, and precepts of seasin, bearing to be "an irrevocable power and warrant."

9. The obligation arising from mandate is chiefly upon the part of the mandatar, to perform his undertaking, wherein he is obliged to follow the tenor of his commission, *in forma specifica*, in so far as it is special and express, wherein if he transgress, some of the ancient lawyers denied him repetition of his expenses, not only as to the excrescence above his commission, but for all: as having received commission to buy such a field, for one thousand crowns, he had bought it for one thousand two hundred, he should have repetition of nothing: but Proculus, *l.3 §ult.l.4ff. Mandati* [D. 17,1,3 and 4], thought that he should have action for that part contained in the commission, which, as the more benign opinion, Justinian followeth §8 *Inst.h.tit.* [Inst. 3,26,8] and where the mandate is not special, it must be performed *secundum arbitrium boni viri*.

10. As to the diligence whereunto mandatars are obliged, the Doctors

are of diverse opinions; the law inclineth most, that mandatars are obliged for the exactest diligence, and for the lightest fault, *l.13 & l.23 C.h.tit.* [c.4, 35,13 and 21]. But by the nature of the contract, mandatars, seeing their undertakings are gratuitous, they ought to be but liable for such diligence as they use in their own affairs; and the mandator ought to impute it to himself, that he made not choice of a more diligent person, which our custom followeth, but still there must be *bona fides, l.10.ff.h.tit.* [D.17,1,10]. A commission to receive money abroad, was found to infer no diligence, July 17, 1672, E. Weems *contra* Sir William Thomson [2 Stair 105 ; M.3515]. The like of a commission to a buyer, to infeft the seller and himself, and to do all other things necessary for his security, Dec. 16, 1668, Fraser *contra* Keith [1 Stair 571; M.6953]. So the obligation upon the part of the mandator, is to refund to the mandatar his damage and expense, and to keep him harmless; but this extends not unto casual damages, as if the mandatar were spoiled in the way, or suffered shipwreck in going about the execution of the mandate, *l.26.inter causas, §6 non omnis ff. Mandati* [D.17,1,26,6], but this is to be limited, unless the mandate do specially require concomitant hazard, as if a mandatar be sent through a place where there are forces of enemies, robbers, or pirates, commonly known to haunt the place, by which he must pass.

11. As to the special kinds of mandates, they are either express, or tacit, to one mandatar, or more, general or special, to be performed in the mandatar, for the mandator's behoof, or in the name of the mandator. As also, amongst mandates are comprehended the commissions of institors, and exercitors, and all precepts, procuratories, assignations and delegations.

12. A tacit mandate, is that which is inferred by signs, and is not expressed by words; as he who is present and suffereth another to manage his affairs without contradiction gives thereby a tacit mandate, *l.qui patitur, 18.* [D.17,1,18] *l.qui fide alterius 53,ff.mandati* [D.17,1,53], for in this, *qui tacet consentire videtur.* So he who whispereth his servant in the ear, if he immediately kill or wound any person present, is presumed to give command to the servant so to do, if there was capital enmity betwixt him and that person before. In like manner, the giving of evidents or writs, yea, which is more, the having of these, though the giving appear not, is presumed to constitute procurators; as is evident in the having a precept of seasin, which is sufficient, without any other power given to the bailie or attorney. And advocates are presumed to have warrant from parties for whom they compear, without producing any mandate, not only upon production of the parties' evidents, or special alledgeances in point of fact, which if wanting, the compearance of procurators in inferior courts, is held as without warrant, and the decreet as in absence; but even without these, if advocates do no more but appear, and take a day to produce parties to give their oaths, the decreet is not in absence. Hence a wife having her husband's bond in her hand, impignorating it for an hundred pounds, the impignoration was found valid

against the husband, the wife's warrant being presumed by her having the bond, Feb. 4, 1665, Paterson *contra* Pringle [1 Stair 264; M.11604]. And the warrant of a servant's taking off furniture for his master, and giving receipt in name of his master, and for his use, found not to oblige the servant to pay, or instruct his warrant, which was presumed to be known to the merchant, unless the servant had otherwise employed the furnishing, Nov. 17, 1665, Howison *contra* Cockburn [1 Stair 309; M.11604]. And a warrant was inferred, by the presence of him who had commission to do, and hindered not, Feb. 23, 1667, L. Rentoun *contra* L. Lambertoun [1 Stair 450; M.9395]. And a warrant of a factor or agent, for charging and denouncing a daughter and her husband upon a bond granted to her mother, was presumed from having the bond, Dec. 23, 1673, Dalmahoy *contra* Lo. Almond [*Sub nom. Almond* v *Dalmahoy*, 2 Stair 244; M.5865].

13. Mandates given to more persons, may be either to each, or some of them severally, by divers warrants, or to more by the same warrant, whereupon these questions arise; *First*, When there are many mandatars jointly, whether they must all necessarily join before they can act, so that if one die, the commission is void? Or whether it be understood to the survivors, or to the plurality of them? *Secondly*, Whether mandatars be all liable *in solidum*, or but *pro rata*.

As to the *first* question, If many mandatars be constitute severally, or with a quorum or plurality expressed, there is no debate, but if otherwise, the case is very doubtful, and there be pregnant reasons and testimonies upon both parts: but this seemeth to prevail as the general rule, that mandates jointly given, can only be jointly executed; *First*, Because by the nature of this contract the personal and singular fitness and industry of mandatars is chosen; and therefore this being a special trust, when it is given to many, it is presumed, that the constituent trusts them all jointly, and not a part of them. *Secondly*, A mandate given to ten, cannot be regularly understood, given to any lesser number; or it being given to Titius, Seius, and Mævius, that it is given to any two of them. It may be objected, that where there are many executors or tutors, without mentioning a quorum, the death of one makes it not to cease, Hope, Executors, Stuart *contra* Kirkwood and Moor [Hope, *Maj. Pr.* IV, 4, 69; M.14693]: or the death or non-acceptance of some of them, [1, 6, 14, *supra*] ibid. Ruthven *contra*   [Hope, *Maj. Pr.* IV, 10, 50; M.16240] ibid. Fauside *contra* Edmonston [*Sub nom. Fawside* v *Adamson*, Hope, *Maj. Pr.* IV, 10, 50; M.16240]; and therefore, this being the most important trust, the like must hold in all other cases. It is answered, that the parity holds not; for the deeds of defuncts in their latter will are always extended, that the act may stand: but in contracts it is contrary, where words are interpreted more strictly; and in this case, the difference is clear, that a mandator, *inter vivos*, giving power, it is strictly to be interpreted; because the power failing, returns from the mandatars to the mandator himself: But a power given by a defunct in contemplation of death, cannot return; and therefore the defunct is presumed to prefer all the persons nominate, to any other that may fall by course of law. *Vid.Tit.6 §36 in fin. supra. Obligations between Tutors and Pupils, &c.* [1,6,36,*supra*].

But this rule, as it is founded upon the singularity of the choice, it faileth and must be limited, where that ground ceaseth, and is preponderate: as *First*, if the deed to be done, be common and ordinary; there, not only the plurality, but any of the mandatars will suffice; so any of more curators may authorise a minor. *Secondly*, If the thing to be done be to the advantage of the constituent, and hath not a considerable hazard or power to infer his disadvantage; as if a commission being begun to many, of things which admit no delay, it may be done by any part of the mandatars, and they will have *actionem mandati*, and not *negotiorum gestorum* only. So ambassadors sent to solemnise a marriage, or receive a crown, though some of them should die, or dis-assent, unquestionably the plurality might proceed. But it would not be so in a treaty for marriage or peace, much less for surrendering a kingdom, city, or fort; and therefore it cannot always be thought, that a plurality is understood, though not expressed. *Thirdly*, In cases necessary, where matters may not be delayed, plurality is always understood, as in commissions for ordinary jurisdictions. *Fourthly*, Where the consuetude of the place, or of the mandator himself, useth to allow a plurality, there it is understood, though not expressed.

14. As to the other question [1,16,6,*infra*], where more mandatars are constitute severally, they are no doubt liable *in solidum*, because they are constitute *in solidum ;* but when they are constitute jointly, or added, the doubt remaineth. For the affirmative is, *First*, The authority of the civil law, *l.Creditor mandatorem, 60 § duobus, 3 ff.Mandati* [D.17,1,60,2]. *Secondly*, albeit the obligation of many, for payment of a quantity, make them liable but *pro rata*, yet where it is a fact, they are liable *in solidum*. And so tutors and curators are liable severally *in solidum ;* but executors are not, because their duty is to pay *secundum vires inventarii ;* and therefore *in rigore juris*, mandatars being malversant, or grossly negligent, are liable *in solidum*, if they may act severally, especially in acts indivisible [1,17,20,*infra*].

15. General mandates do occasion the most debates in this contract; for there is much more clearness where the mandate is special; which useth to be distinguished in *determinate*, when both matter and manner are special, and *indeterminate*, when the matter is special, but the manner is not specified; in the former the precise tenor of the commission must be followed; and yet if any part thereof be, or become unprofitable, and evidently and consider-ably hurtful, the mandatar in the latter case may safely, and in the former case, must necessarily do what is best *secundum arbitrium boni viri*, and must do the like in all indeterminate mandates. But the great question is, How far general mandates may be extended; and in what cases they are not effectual; but there is necessarily required special mandates, which refer to the pleasure, choice, or opinion of the mandatar, as if it have a clause *cum libera aut plena*

administratione or the like; or where that is wanting, the doctors enumerate multitudes of cases, whereunto general mandates are not to be extended.

First, In the contracting of marriage no general mandate, albeit *cum libera, &c.* is sufficient, because the affection and choice of the person is singular, and incommunicable. And albeit Abraham's commission to Eleazar, to take a wife for his son of his kindred [Gen. xxiv, 4], was valid, though not special as to the person; yet the case was singular, there being so few families that worshipped the true God to choose upon. But recenter customs require it to be special, even as to the person, as well as to the family. *Secondly*, No general mandate, though *cum libera*, can be extended to any thing that may import a fault or crime. *Thirdly*, No general mandate can reach to donations, or mere liberality, and yet doth not hinder gratifications for services done, or upon the expectation that the receiver may probably be induced thereby to do matters of importance; as the gifts of ambassadors, or generals, are not only valid as to the receivers, but as to the mandators, if there was probable reason. *Fourthly*, General mandates extend not to alienation of immoveables; but that must be specially expressed. *Fifthly*, General mandates extend not to submissions or transactions, nor to insist in any action criminal or famous, or to annul that which is specially done by the constituent, or to dispose of that which was specially reserved before, either by law or deed, as *regalia*, or things peculiarly reserved to princes. *Sixthly*, A special mandate is required, to enter any party heir to his predecessor. The civil law numbered *additionem hæreditatis inter actus legitimos* and so excluded even a special mandate therein: but our customs allow the same; and because heirs are liable *in solidum* to all their predecessor's debts, therefore a special mandate is necessary. *Seventhly*, Where, in general mandates, some things are specially expressed, the generality is not extended to cases of greater importance than these expressed.

16. Amongst mandates are all offices, which do ever imply a condition resolutive upon committing faults; but not such as are light faults, or of negligence, but they must be atrocious, at least of knowledge and importance: upon this ground it was, that the town of Edinburgh having deposed their town-clerk from his office which he had *ad vitam*, the sentence was sustained, if the fault were found of the clerk's knowledge, and of importance, and it was not enough that no hurt followed, and that he was willing to make it up, February 14, 1665, Town of Edinburgh *contra* Sir William Thomson [*Sub nom. Thomson v Edinburgh*, 1 Stair 269; M. 13090]. But the office of a commissary-clerk was not found extinct by his being at the horn for a debt, or being sometimes out of the country, having power of deputation, February 6, 1666, Archbishop of Glasgow *contra* Commissar Clerk of Dumfries [*Sub nom. Archbishop of Glasgow v Logan*, 1 Stair 347; M. 13093]. The office of a commissary doth also import, as a necessary condition, that the commissary be qualified to discharge the office in his own person, though he have deputes, seeing he must answer for, and over-rule his deputes, February 14, 1666,

Archbishop of Glasgow *contra* Commissar of Glasgow [1 Stair 355; M. 13094].
Where it was also found, that by the commissary's instructions they must reside in the place of the commissariot under the pain of deprivation, notwithstanding the common custom in the contrary, which only excused from bygone faults.

17. Trust is also amongst mandates or commissions, though it may be
referred to deposition, seeing the right is in custody of the person intrusted [1,13,7; IV,45,22,*infra*].

Mandatars in the law could not oblige the mandator, or directly acquire to
him; but they could only oblige themselves, and acquire to themselves, and
thereafter transmit to the mandators; and that because in most contracts,
thereby the person contractor behoved immediately to act, and no person
interposed, which our custom regardeth not; and therefore mandatars may
act in their own names; in which case the right, whether real or personal,
standeth in their person; as he who by commission acquired lands or goods
in his own name; the real right thereof is in his person, and there lies an
obligation upon him, if he was commissionate, to transmit them to his constituent. But he may also acquire, transact, or contract in name of the constituent; in which case the real right stands immediately in the person of the
mandator, and the obligation constitutes him creditor, and there is no obligation betwixt the mandatar and the third party; nor is the mandatar obliged to
instruct that he had commission, but that is upon his hazard who acted with
him, unless the contrary be proven by his oath or writ; and therefore a servant, though by a ticket he acknowledged he had taken off such furniture for
his master's use, was not found obliged to pay, or to instruct his warrant,
especially after his master's death: but the warrant was presumed as known to
the merchant, November 17, 1665, Howison *contra* Cockburn [1 Stair 309;
M. 11604]. Trust in the right of lands, sums or goods, to the behoof of another,
doth frequently occur; and because fraud is ordinarily in it, it is not only
probable by writ or oath of the trustee, but sometimes witnesses are examined
ex officio, to find out the truth, February 22, 1665, Viscount Kingstoun *contra*
Colonel Fullertoun [1 Stair 273; M. 12749]; February 6, 1669, Rule *contra*
Rule [1 Stair 598; M. 16167]; February 24, 1669, Earl of Annandale *contra*
Young [1 Stair 612; M. 16168], June 19, 1669, Scot *contra* Langtoun [1 Stair
620; M. 12316]. Yea trust has been found probable by presumptions only,
January 12, 1666, Executors of Stevenson *contra* Crawford [1 Stair 337;
M. 12750], January 22, 1673, Watson *contra* Bruce [2 Stair 157; M. 6129]. But
it was not found proven by a declaration upon death-bed, in prejudice of the
heir, November 26, 1674, Paton *contra* Stirling of Airdoch [2 Stair 284; M.
12588].

A person intrusted in a disposition of lands, having compounded for the
intruster's debts, was found to have no interest to burden the intruster with
more than what he truly paid out, Nov. 15, 1667, Maxwel *contra* Maxwell
[1 Stair 485; M. 16166]. Neither was a person intrusted for payment of the

intruster's creditors, found to have power to prefer them to the more timeous diligence of others, by inhibition or apprising, though only done against the intruster, July 24, 1669, Crawfurd *contra* Anderson [1 Stair 645; M.1196]. And a person receiving money to buy goods for another, but having bought and received them in his own name, without mention of the truster, the property thereof was found to be in the person intrusted, and his creditors arresting were preferred, January 24, 1672, Roiston *contra* Robertson and Fleming [*Sub nom. Boylstoun* v *Robertson and Fleming*, 2 Stair 54; M.15125]. Yet trust in sums, or personal rights, after the death of the person intrusted, was found not necessary to be confirmed, as *in bonis defuncti* of the intrusted person, but that the trust might be proven against the debtor, and the nearest of kin of the person intrusted, June 9, 1669, Street *contra* Home of Bruntfield [1 Stair 616; M.15122]. But trust in an infeftment of annualrent, found not to make the person intrusted liable for omission, but only for intromission, December 18, 1666, Cass *contra* Wat [1 Stair 415; M.3536]. The like in an assignation in trust, which was not found to infer an obligement to do diligence, if the assignee was not required either to do diligence, or denude; but he having transferred without warrant, was found liable for the sum, albeit he offered to procure a reposition, July 18, 1672, Watson *contra* Bruce [2 Stair 157; M.6129]. And an assignee in trust, that the sum might be included in his apprising, giving backbond to be comptable in case of payment, having disponed the apprising without reservation, was found liable for so much of the sum intrusted as might have been recovered, January 5, 1675, E. of Northesk *contra* L.Pittarro [2 Stair 300; M.16172].

Trust was inferred by a grandfather's delivering of a disposition, conceived in favours of his grandchild, the disponer at the delivery not having expressed the terms of the trust, or his design, and having recalled and received back the disposition, and disponed the half of the lands therein to another; it was thence found, that the disposition was not absolute and irrevocable, but was intrusted in that third party, to be recalled if the disponer pleased; or otherwise to be delivered to the oye, January 25, 1677, Ker *contra* Ker [2 Stair 499; M.3249; I, 13, 4,*infra*]. When trust is referred to a party's oath, whether such a right standing in their person be in trust to the behoof of another, they use commonly to depone, that it is to their own behoof; which being found dubious and fallacious, what the meaning of such words were, special interrogators are allowed to expiscate the truth; and parties use to be reexamined thereupon, as whether the deponent's meaning by these words, that the right was to his own behoof, and not to another's, was only, that he gave no promise or backbond, to apply the right or benefit thereof, in whole or in part, to another: Or whether the true meaning of the design was, that the other put him upon acquiring that right, as being a gift of non-entry of lands, bought by that other, so that the whole benefit should not be applied to the acquirer himself; for it was not presumable that he would put another upon taking the gift of non-entry of the lands he himself had bought, to be made use of to the full extent; which being so acknowledged, the gift was found so far to the behoof of the buyer, that the seller by the warrandice should pay no more for the non-entry, than the acquirer of the non-entry gave truly for it, seeing the buyer had communed with the superior, and brought the non-entry to the same rate, and then put his cousin-german to acquire it, February 2, 1681, Mr. Balmerino *contra* L.Powrie [2 Stair 850; M.Supp.113]. Upon the same ground a donatar of a liferent escheat being examined, whether it was to the behoof of his good-brother, who having deponed, that it was to his own behoof, and dying before he was re-examined, his oath was interpreted only, that he had given no backbond, or promise in favour of his good-brother; and therefore by pregnant presumptions the trust was inferred, as that the brother only was concerned in that liferent; that he managed it, and was at all the expenses of the process; that the donatar's successors never owned it, nor confirmed the benefit of the gift, February 11, 1679, Forbes of Balvenie *contra* L.Boyn [2 Stair 690; M.16178].

18. The law for utility of commerce did, against the common rules foresaid, constitute an obligation upon exercitors, by the deed or contract of masters of ships. An exercitor is he to whom the profit of vessels or ships, whether upon the sea, rivers, or lakes, belongeth; whether he be owner of the ship, or have only hired the same. The master of the ship is he that hath the command thereof, who therefore may contract and borrow money for reparation of the ship, or out-rigging thereof, or for the entertainment of the mariners, or any other thing for the use of the voyage. And thereby not only the master contractor, but the exercitor who constitutes him is liable. Yea, if the master substitute another master, his engagement also obligeth the exercitor; so that whosoever he be that contracts with him who for the time officiates as master, obligeth the exercitor in what was borrowed for the use of the ship, company or voyage. And there seems no necessity of showing a commission, but the exercising of the office is sufficient; and thereby the ship and out-rigging is hypothecated and affected. Yea, if there be many exercitors, they are all liable *in solidum ;* and if there be many masters the contract of one of them obligeth the exercitors jointly. Neither needs he who contracts with the master, instruct that the money borrowed was actually employed for the use of the ship, company or voyage; but this much he must make appear, that when he lent the money, there was such need of it; albeit he be not obliged to take notice whether the master misemployed it or not, because the exercitor should have looked whom he trusted. If the master be constitute with power to buy ware, and load the ship, the exercitor is liable to these who contract with him upon that account: but this is not presumed upon acting as master, unless his commission appear; and so the master's extraneous contracts oblige not the exercitors, albeit their faults do, by the edict *nautæ, caupones, stabularii* [D.4,9], all which is clear from the title,*ff. de exercitoria actione per totum* [D.14,1], and is generally in vigour with us, and all Admiralties, who are proper judges of these matters, in the

first instance [1, 13, 3, *infra*].

19. After the similitude of the Exercitory action, the prætor by the perpetual edict, did introduce the Institory action, in which the contracts of institors in relation to that wherein they were intrusted, their prepositors are obliged; and as exercitors are as to maritime matters, so prepositors are correspondent in traffic at land; and institors are these who are intrusted in such affairs, corresponding to the masters of ships; which institors are these who are intrusted with keeping of shops, buying or selling of ware, keeping of cash for exchange, and such as are sent abroad to buy ware. And these who are intrusted with the labouring of any field, or any other like business. And it is alike of whatsoever sex or age they be, though even they be pupils who cannot oblige themselves, or minors, who have the benefit of restitution, yet both do effectually oblige their prepositors: and if there be more prepositors, they are liable *in solidum*. But such obligations reach no further than what is contracted for the use of the affair wherein they are intrusted. Neither are the prepositors obliged, if they have intimated to the party contractor not to contract with their institors. But if they contract *bona fide*, albeit the institor be limited and prohibited to contract, in such cases the creditors contracting *bona fide* with them are secure. All which appears, *tit. de instit. actione,ff. per totum* [D. 14, 3]. But our custom hath not so fully owned the Roman law as to institors, as it has to exercitors.

Title 13. Custody or Depositum

CUSTODY is called in the law *depositum* or *commendatum*, to which we have no suitable term in our law, but this contract is most fitly expressed by the duty and obligation thereof, which is to keep or preserve that which is given in custody, and it is here subjoined to mandate, because indeed it is a kind of it. For the lawyers do not so much notice the accuracy of logical divisions, whereby no member can comprehend another, as the usual terms known in law; and therefore do handle *mandatum, depositum et pignus*, severally, though all of them be truly mandates, and therefore *depositum* also may be fitly defined, to be a mandate or commission, given and undertaken, to keep and preserve someting belonging to the mandator or some third party; and therefore, whatever hath been before said of mandates, must be here understood of custody, and needs not be repeated, except what is special in custody.

2. The civil law maketh a difference in the diligence of mandatars, and depositars, that these are liable only for fraud, whereof alone the prætor's edict makes mention *l.1* §*1.l.20.ff.depositi* [D. 16,3,1,1], *l.23.ff. de regulis juris* [D. 50,17,23], whereby the depositar, though he lose the thing depositate, without fraud, is free, but it is extended to *lata culpa*, or the grossest fault, *quæ dolo æquiparatur in jure, l.quod Nerva,32,ff.depositi* [D,. 16 3,32], where the diligence opposite to grossest faults is excellently described, by such diligence as men ordinarily do, or the depositar doth, in his own affairs. But mandatars are liable for the lightest fault, yet, as is shown before [1,12,10, *supra*], that is by the constitution of the civil law, and not by the nature of the mandate : for surely the reason and ground of the diligence of both is alike, as being gratuitous, and at the free choice of the constituent, who therefore should demand no more in either case, but such diligence as the person intrusted uses, or men ordinarily do in their own affairs ; unless it be otherwise agreed, or that the depositar hath procured the custody when others offered, *l.1.* §*35.ff.depositi* [D. 16,3,1,35]; or that he have any honorary or salary therefore ; which may be consistent here, or in any other mandates, when in the meaning of the parties, it is not an equivalent satisfaction to the benefit received, which ordinarily is not esteemable, as the salaries of physicians for the preservation of health, or life, and curing any member, or of judges or lawyers for the doing or procuring of justice ; and therefore is called an honorary, and the contract is esteemed notwithstanding free : Or, as in depositations made in case of naufrage, fire, tumult, or falling of houses, where the positive law giveth the double in case of denial of the thing depositate, in commiseration of these cases for the public good *l.1.ff. depositi* [D. 16,3,1]; but these cases must be evident, and the only causes of the contract, *l.1.* §*3.ff.depositi* [D. 16,3,1,3].

Hence it followeth, that depositars are not liable for light faults, or the perishing or deterioration of the thing depositate by casualty or accident ; yet it may be questioned, if the depositar delay, and do not re-deliver, whether in that case he is liable to make good the thing perished. The same question is also in mandates, and the law is for the affirmative, in this and all other cases, unless the thing after the delay would have the same way perished, if it had been restored, *l.5.ff. de rebus creditis* [D. 12,1,5], *l.12.* §*3.ff. depositi* [D. 16,3,12,3]; where the depositar's peril is that if the thing perish, after sentence or judgment *in actione depositi*, if the depositor do not then deliver, the loss is his, not the deponent's ; the reason hereof is rendered by the doctors, because if the thing had been restored, the owner might have sold it, and so though it had perished, he had been no loser. Yet this is partly penal, and the adequate ground of it must be by the obligation of reparation of the damage sustained by that delinquence, in not restoring the thing depositate to its owner when required ; and therefore it is to be measured according to the true interest ; and though possibly the owner might have sold it before it had perished, yet unless there had been a known occasion, or offer to have bought or purchased it at the time of the remaining of it after delay, equity would not conclude the making up of what had so perished. In this we are not bounded with any positive law or custom, and therefore equity in it with us may take place; and we are not severe in the diligence of mandatars, as appears from the former paragraph, neither yet in custody; and therefore a person having received money in keeping, and it being demanded, he did declare, that it was sent with his own to Dundee for safety, and that the owner might have it there, for the sending for; and thereafter, Dundee being taken and plundered, he was liberate, giving his oath that the money he got in keeping was lost there, July 19, 1662, Fiddes *contra* Jack [1 Stair 130; M. 12310]. And a horse being put in the park of Holyroodhouse for grazing, though he was lost, the keeper was found free; because there was a placard on the entry of the park, that the horse to be put there was upon their master's peril, though this horse was delivered to a servant, who said nothing to him of the placard, Nov. 16, 1667, Whitehead *contra* Straiton [1 Stair 486; M. 10074].

3. In the civil law there is a deposition of a special nature, introduced by the edict, *nautæ, caupones, stabularii, quod cujusque salvum fore receperint, nisi restituant, in eos judicium dabo, l.1.ff.eodem* [D. 4,9,1]. By this edict, positive law for utility's sake, hath appointed, that the custody of the goods of passengers in ships, or voyagers in inns, or in stables, shall be far extended beyond the nature of depositation, which obligeth only for fraud, or supine negligence, them (who have expressly contracted) for their own fact. But this edict, for public utility's sake, extendeth it: First, To the restitution of the goods of passengers and voyagers, and reparation of any loss or injury done by the mariners, or servants of the inn or stable, *l.1 §8. eodem* [D. 4,9, 1,8]. Whereas by the common law, before that edict, in this and other such cases, there is no such obligement; much less are persons now obliged for their hired servant's fact or fault, except facts wherein they are specially intrusted by them; but because the theft and loss of such goods is very ordinary in ships, inns, and stables, therefore this edict was introduced for the security of travellers, *l.1.§2.eodem* [D. 4,9,2]. Secondly, The edict extends this obligement, even to the damage sustained by the act of other passengers or voyagers in the ship, inn, or stable, for the which, the master of the ship, inn-keeper, or keeper of the stable, could be no ways obliged, but by virtue of this edict, *d.l.in fin.l.2 & l.3. in pr. eodem* [D. 4,9,1,2 and 3]. Thirdly, they were made liable for the loss or theft of such things absolutely, from which they were free by no diligence, but were not liable for accident or force, *d.l.3 §1. in fin.* [D. 4,9,3,1 *in fin.*] that is, sea-hazard must always be excepted.

By *nautæ* in this edict are understood, not the mariners, but the exercitors or owners of the ship, to whom the profit belongs, and so the master of the inn or stable, and by the Edict they are only liable for that, *quod salvum fore receperint*, which they received in custody, either by themselves, or such others as they intrusted, to admit passengers or voyagers, their goods and horses, *l.1.* §*2, eodem* [D.4,9,1,2], whether the same be ware,, clothes clog-bags, or other furnishing for passengers or voyagers, or the furniture of horses in stables, *l.1.* §*6. eodem* [D.4,9,1,6], or what other things are brought in : and by the common law, albeit the things brought in were neither known or shown to the master of the ship, inn, or stable, they are liable for restitution, *l.1.* §*8. eodem* [D.4,9,1,8]. And if any thing be wanting, the party loser hath *juramentum in litem*, and is not obliged to show what is in his clog-bag, pockets, &c. *Gloss, ibid.* The reason of all which is rendered, *l.1. eodem.* [D.4,9,1], because it is in the master of the ship's option, to receive such persons or not; and consequently, if he doubt of their trust, in case they allege any thing wanting, he may refuse them access, unless they show what they have, otherwise he is presumed to trust their oath, without which this benefit would be useless: but *L.L.Navales Rhod.* [Not found] §*14*, ordains the money to be depositate with the skipper, otherwise he is not liable; and §15, the owner has no more but the skipper, seamen, and passenger's oaths for his money. They are also by this Edict, not only liable for what is received and entered into the ship or inn; but also, if it be expressly received for that end elsewhere, as on the shore, by these having power, and if it be lost before it be entered in the ship, *l.3 ibid.* [D.4,9,3]. Neither are these persons liberate, by bidding each man look to his own goods, unless the passengers consent, *l.7 eodem* [D.4,9,7], but their silence will not import their consent, when they are entered and in their passage; yet if it should be so expressed before, or at their entry, when it is free to them to enter or not, such silence would sufficiently infer consent. Neither are they free, though the passenger take the key of the chamber or chest himself, which is but *propter majorem securitatem*, and not to liberate their obligement, especially seeing they may have other keys, which the passengers cannot know.

   This excellent Edict being but positive law, it will be effectual with us only in so far as the common customs of nations have owned it, especially in maritime matters, betwixt us and other nations, or in so far as our own custom hath received it at home; but the evident expediency thereof cannot but make it acceptable any where, where the least respect is had to the civil law; so a chapman depositating his pack with a creditor, had his oath *in litem*, as to the particulars therein contained, reserving the Lords' modification, Jan. 3. 1667,   *contra* Brand [1 Stair 423; M.1817]. And lately an inn-keeper in Edinburgh was found liable for a cloak brought into his tavern, without necessity of proving either that it was delivered to the master or his servants, or that they stole the cloak, January 17, 1687, Master of Forbes *contra* Steill [*Sub die.* February 17, 1 Fountainhall 448; M.9233]. So a skipper was found liable for the damage of ware, by the spouting of the pump, although the ship was tight at the loosing, and that the owner of the ware was on board, and had put the ware near the pump, that it might not be easily found out by capers, seeing there was no extraordinary accident by stress of weather, Nov. 7, 1677, Lourie *contra* Angus [2 Stair 553; M.10107].

The like was found in the damage of ware by the sea-water, though the ship was repaired in the port, and the damage was befallen by a leak, struck up in that same road, after the reparation, seeing there was no extraordinary stress of weather, or other accident that could not be prevented, July 24, 1680, Lawmont *contra* Boswell [2 Stair 791; M. 10110].

4. Depositation of writs falls most frequently in question with us, by which the depositar is trusted with the keeping of the writs and the delivery thereof, according to the terms of depositation, express, or presumed. The terms presumed are, that the depositar should give back the writ to the depositor, if he require it, and if not, to the person in whose favours it bears to be granted, as was found in the case of Ker *contra* Kerrs [2 Stair 499; M. 3249; I. 12, 17, *supra*], Jan. 25, 1677, where the case was a disposition of a tenement, by a grandfather to his oye, merely gratuitous, given to a third party, without expressing any terms of depositation. But if the terms be expressed, they are to be faithfully observed by the depositar, who is trusted, and which are always probable by his oath, if they be not in writ, signed by the depositor; in which case, the oath of the depositar cannot be received against the depositor's writ, or even besides the same; and therefore a depositor's oath was not found receivable, to prove that the deopsitar passed from the writ depositate, and ordained it to be cancelled, Feb. 24, 1675, Cowan *contra* Ramsay [2 Stair 327; M. 12379]. But the depositar's oath will not prove that the writ was depositate, but the oath or writ of the granter; because delivery is presumed, unless the contrair be proven by the oath or writ of him in whose favours the writ is conceived, unless it be in the hand of him who granted it; yea if the haver allege, that though the writ be in the name of a third party, yet he made use of his name to his own behoof, he must instruct it by the oath of that third party, or other evidences.

5. Under custody is contained sequestration, whether of consent, where any thing litigious or controverted is intrusted in the hand of a third party, till the rights and possessions of the pretenders be cleared, or by authority of a judge, which is a part of judicial process, of which hereafter [IV, 41, 7 and 50, 27, *infra*].

6. Consignation is also a kind of custody, whereby the consigner depositates in the consignatar's hands, the sum or thing which is refused by the creditor, to the creditor's behoof, wherein the consignatar is but the interposed person, either by consent, as it is frequently provided by clauses of consignation, or by law; and the contract of custody standeth betwixt the creditor and the consignatar, by which he is obliged to keep, and restore to the creditor; and thereby the debtor orderly consigning is liberated, and is not obliged to uplift sums consigned from the consignatar, and make them forthcoming to the creditor, July 28, 1665, Scot *contra* Somervail [1 Stair 304; M. 10118], unless the consignation be simulate, or taken up again by the consigner. And where the law condescends on consignatars, the consigner is liberate, and not liable for the consignatar's sufficiency, or faithful-

ness ; as where consignations are to be legally in the hands of the Clerk of the Bills, Feb. 15, 1673, Mowat *contra* Lockhart [2 Stair 173 ; M. 10118] ; yet if the consignation hath not been orderly, but by the fault of the consigner, if the public consignatar prove insolvent, the peril is the consigner's. In conventional obligations, where the choice of the consignatar is in the consigner, the consignation is upon the peril of the consigner, if the consignatar was insolvent, which uses ordinarily to be expressed, but though it were not, it is implied [1, 18, 4, *infra*].

7. Trust is also a kind of deposition, whereby the thing intrusted is in the custody of the person intrusted, to the behoof of the intruster, and the property of the thing intrusted, be it land or moveables, is in the person of the intrusted, else it is not proper trust : so if it be transmitted to singular successors, acquiring *bona fide*, they are secure, and the trustee is only liable personally upon the trust ; but such trusts being of importance, albeit writ useth not to be adhibited in them, they are not ordinarily proven but by writ, or oath of party, yet witnesses are used *ex officio*, and the trust of an assignation found proven thereby, Feb. 22, 1665, Viscount Kingstoun *contra* Col. Fullertoun [1 Stair 273 ; M. 12749]. And a bond being in trust to another party's behoof, was found proven by presumptions, Jan. 12, 1666, Executors of Stevenson *contra* Crawfurd [1 Stair 337 ; M. 12750 ; 1, 12, 17, *supra*]. The reason of using witnesses in trust, is, because writ is seldom used therein ; for if writ be granted by backbond or declaration, it is not properly trust ; but where the thing entrusted is alienated, yet so as the trustee believes that the disponer designs not donation, or alienation, but trusts, that, on demand, the person trusted will denude himself.

8. This is singular in the law of deposition, that there is no exception of compensation competent against it, *l. pen. C. depositi* [C. 4, 34, 11 ; 1, 18, 6, *infra*], which Donellus and most interpreters account to be introduced only by Justinian, and was not so before, nor by the nature of this contract, nor by equity. But the contrary appeareth, because the very intent and nature of this contract is, that the thing depositate must be kept and restored whensoever demanded, yea, though it had a term, yet unless there were a salary, or some interest in the keeper, it may be demanded whensoever ; because the term is in favours of the depositor, not of the depositar, whom it bindeth during that time, and so it may be renounced by the depositor at any time, *nam cuique licet juri pro se introducto renunciare ;* and therefore it is the nature of this contract, that the thing depositate should be restored upon demand, and his accepting thereof so, is a tacit quitting of any objection in the contrary. But the convincing reason is, that compensation is only in things of the same nature and liquid ; but in deposition, the dominion and possession of the thing remaineth in the depositor, though it be numerate money consigned, and to meddle with it is unwarrantable, and accounted in law theft, as being *contrectatio rei alienæ ;* and therefore, that being a thing it cannot be compensed with *mutuum*, where the property and dominion is

in the borrower, and but a personal obligation to repay, which cannot be compensed with a body, the property whereof is not alienated. The like therefore holdeth in money found, or any other way in the detainer's hands, without right to the property of it.

9. The question is also moved here, Whether the thing depositate may be detained for the necessary and profitable expenses wared upon it. Though law and most interpreters favour the negative, upon the same ground that compensation is excluded; yet the affirmative is to be preferred, because as the contrary action is competent for the melioration, so much more the exception, it being a part of the same contract [1,18,6,*infra*]; and therefore the Lord Balmerinoch, having by his own missive and backbond, acknowledged that the estate of Jedburgh was disponed to him in trust, to the behoof of Earl Somerset, all the expense on the land, or for Somerset, in contemplation of the trust, was found competent against Earl Bedford, who had adjudged Somerset's right, Feb. 18, 1662, *inter eosdem* [*Sub nom. E of Bedford* v *L. Balmerino*, 1 Stair 101; M.9135], where retention was only sustained, if Balmerinoch found caution for the superplus. And in all cases in the law where action is competent, exception is also competent, and so with us, if instantly verified. Amongst the Romans there was an edict of the Prætor, *in deposito*, to this effect, that depositars should be obliged to restore or make up the single value; but in things depositate through the present occasion of tumult, fire, falling of houses, or shipwreck (in the case of not due restitution) these persons were liable for the double, *l.1.ff.depositi* [D.16,3,1] wherein there is much utility to secure persons depositating of necessity in these deplorable cases; but as yet it hath not been allowed by our custom.

10. It may be questioned, if any thing be depositate to more depositars, whether they are liable *in solidum*; so that the deponent may crave restitution, or reparation from every one, for the whole value, or for his share only? The civil law is clear for the affirmative, that all are liable *in solidum*, *l.1* §*43*, *eodem* [D.16,3,1,43], and upon good reason; because it is fidelity in preserving one individual that is undertaken, which therefore *de natura rei*, must oblige every person to the whole, seeing he is not obliged to restore a part of the thing depositate, but the thing itself; and this being consequent to the nature of deposition, will no doubt be followed by us. *In deposito*, by the civil law, the deponent hath *beneficium juramenti in litem*, or to prove the particulars or quantities wanting, and their value *secundum pretium affectionis*, because of the exuberance of trust in this contract, *l.1* §*26ff. depositi* [D.16,3,1,26] but not the depositar in the contrary action, *l.5 eodem* [D.16, 3,5], where the reason is added, because there is no breach of faith nor trust there, but damage and reparation in question: the depositar also detaining, being condemned, becomes infamous, *l.1.ff.de his qui infamia notantur* [D.3,2,1]. Hence it is from this trust, that if a chest or other continent sealed, be depositate, action is competent for all that was therein shown or not *l.1.* §*41.eodem* [D.3,2,1,41]; and therefore in such cases, the deponent's

oath *in litem* must be taken, or else his interest perisheth, which is suitable to our custom, as before mentioned in the case of innkeepers, *supra*, §*3* [1, 13, 3, *supra*]. And there is good reason and equity *pro pretio affectionis* also, but I have not observed it questioned or decided. So this being a contract of greatest trust, restitution is to be made *cum omni causa*, as fruits and birth, and annualrent *post moram*, *l.2.C. depositi* [C. 4, 34, 2]; but annualrent with us is not due *sine pacto*, but may be made up by the Lords their modification of damage and expenses.

11. Pledge either signifies the thing impignorated or the contract of impignoration, in the same way as *pignus* in the law is taken; and it is a kind of mandate whereby the debtor for his creditor's security gives him the pawn, or thing impignorated, to detain or keep it for his own security, or in case of not-payment of the debt, to sell the pledge, and pay himself out of the price, and restore the rest, or restore the pledge itself upon payment of the debt; all which is of the nature of a mandate, and it hath not only custody in it, but the power to dispone in the case of not-payment: but if the profit of the pledge be allotted for the profit of the debt, which is called ἀντιχρησις, it is a mixt contract, having in it a mandate, and the exchange of the usufruct, or use of the pledge for the use of the debt. Our custom allows not the creditor to sell the pledge, but he may poind it, or assign his debt, and cause arrest it in his hand, and pursue to make forthcoming; but there being a real right of the pledge, no other diligence will affect it further, than as to the reversion of it, on payment of the creditor's debt.

12. This contract hath this special in it, that it is not merely to the behoof of the constituent, as ordinarily mandates are, but it is to the behoof of the hypothecat for his security; and so ends not with the death of either party, nor is revocable as other mandates, but passes to heirs and assignees; and therefore requireth greater diligence than mandates, viz. such diligence as prudent men use in their affairs, but obligeth not for the lightest fault, *l. 23. ff. de reg. juris* [D. 50, 17, 23]. This is also singular in wadsets, or impignorations, that thereby there is constitute a real right in the pledge, which no deed or alienation of the constituent can alter or infringe, which is not so in mandates, or things depositate, nor in location, whereby there is only a personal right; and if the property of the thing be alienated from the constituent, the personal right hath no effect, as to the thing about which it is constitute; but there is here a real right, of which hereafter amongst other real rights, Tit. Wadsets [11, 10, *infra*].

13. We shall not insist in the manner of the sale of pledges prescribed by the Roman law, and the intimations or denunciations requisite to be made to the debtor, that being wholly changed by our customs. For in wadsets of lands the wadsetter hath a disposition of the property, but with a reservation or paction, to sell back again to the debtor, upon payment of the debt; and so the wadsetter cannot by virtue of the impignoration, sell the lands and pay himself, but all he can do is to affect the wadset lands by legal diligence,

as an other creditor ; and if any other prevent him in diligence, they acquire
the right of reversion, and no posterior diligence of his can take it away, or
capacitate him to acquire the full property of the pledge, or to alienate it
simply to another. The like is in the impignoration of moveables, which
cannot be thereby sold, but the creditor may affect them by his legal diligence,
by poinding thereof, as said is.

14. In impignoration either of heritable or moveable rights, the civil
law rejected *pactum legis commissoriae, l.3.Cod.de Pact.* [c.2,3,3] which we
call a clause irritant, whereby it is provided, that if the debt be not paid at
such a time, the reversion shall be void. Our custom doth not reject such
clauses, but in the contrary, by act of sederunt, Nov. 27, 1592, [See I,10,7,
supra ; II,10,6; IV,18,3,*infra.*] it is declared, "That the Lords would
decide in all clauses irritant, whether in infeftments, bonds, or tacks,
according to the express words and meaning thereof precisely;" yet the
Lords allow such clauses to be purged by performance, before sentence
declaring the clause irritant committed, or will supersede the extracting of
the decreet for a time for that effect, as they see cause ; so in such a process,
though the irritancy was committed long before, yet by payment at the bar
it was allowed to be purged, even though the party after the irritancy got
possession, Hope, Clause irritant, Edgar *contra* Gordon of Earlstoun [Hope,
Maj.Pr. III,23,16 ; M.11068]. And albeit the money was not ready to purge
at the bar, so that the failzie was declared, yet it was superseding extract for
a time, that it might be purged in the mean time, February 7, 1628, Pringle
contra Ker [Durie 341 ; M.7203]. But where the requisition was on ninescore
days, there was no time granted after the decreet to purge, July 19, 1625,
Nairn *contra* Napier [Durie 178 ; M.7202]. Yet this clause is so odious, that
it was elided by the wadsetter's possession of a part of the lands, and thereby
getting a part of his annualrent, March 18, 1629, Barclay *contra* Stevenson
[Durie 438 ; M.7183]. The like by accepting of payment of annualrent after
failzie, Hope, Clause irritant, Naismith *contra* Kinloch [Hope, *Maj.Pr.* III,
23,13 ; M.7254]. The like by payment of annualrent, or by compensation
therewith, Barns *contra* Barclay, ibid [Not found]. And the reason of the law
and our custom is, because impignoration is a permutative contract, wherein
equality is meant and required ; so clauses irritant are redacted to equality,
and respect is not had to the terms and expressions of the contract, but to
the thing truly done : and therefore, though sale of lands with a reversion be
expressed, yet if there be not a competent equivalent price, and that it be
not a real and proper sale, but only a wadset under that conception, the
clause irritant hath no further effect than is before expressed ; but if it be a
true sale and competent price, the clause irritant is not penal, but hath its
full effect ; whereas otherwise it is still purgeable till declarator, which
therefore is necessary, even though the clause irritant bear, that the reversion
shall be null without declarator, for the remedying of the exorbitancy of
such clauses irritant, which must be a process to declare the same, that the

reverser may purge at the bar, or lose the reversion [II, 10, 6; IV, 18, 3, *infra*].

Impignoration is either express by the explicit consent of parties, or implicit, which is introduced by law, without consent of parties; of which tacit hypothecations, there have been many in the civil law; as in the ware, for the price; in houses for expenses in preservation or melioration, or for money lent for that use; to a wife in the goods of her husband for her tocher; to pupils and minors in the goods of their tutors and curators for their duty and administration; to pupils in the goods of their mother, being their tutrix, or in the goods of her second husband if she did not make an accompt and procure a new tutor before her marriage; to legators in the goods of executors; to the fisk for their tribute, or their contracts; to cities in the goods of their administrators. But our custom hath taken away express hypothecations, of all or a part of the debtor's goods, without delivery, and of the tacit legal hypothecations hath only allowed a few, allowing ordinarily parties to be preferred according to the priority of their legal diligence, that commerce may be the more sure, and every one may more easily know his condition with whom he contracts : and therefore goods sold were not found under any hypothecation for the price, June 14, 1676, Cushney *contra* Christy [2 Stair 425 ; M. 6237].

15. Yet with us there remains the tacit hypothecation of the fruits on the ground in the first place, and they not satisfying, of the other goods on the ground belonging to the possessor, for the terms of the year's rent when the crop was on the ground, but not for prior or past years [IV, 25, *infra*]; and therefore all masters of the ground or their assignees, having right to the mails and duties, have interest to recover the rents thereof from all intromitters with the fruits, rents, or profits thereof, though upon a title, unless their title be preferable, or at least have the benefit of a possessory judgment. This was extended to intromitters, though they bought the corns which grew on the ground in public market at Yule, albeit the heritor had poinded a part of the crop, for the rent of a prior year, unless at the term of payment, Candlemas, there were sufficient fruits on the ground to satisfy the rent, March 29, 1639, Hay *contra* Eliot [Durie 886; M. 6219]. Secondly, It is extended to intromitters with the crop and goods of the ground, though lawfully poinded from the tenants for their just debts, unless they left as much upon the ground as might satisfy the rent, besides the household stuff, July 25, 1623, and Feb. 3, 1624, Hays *contra* Keith [Hope, *Maj. Pr.* VI, 19, 10 and 11; M. 6190]. The like, wherein the present crop was not accompted, but left for the subsequent rent, of which the terms were not come, June 29, 1642, Lord Polwart *contra*   [Durie 897; M. 6221]. Thirdly, It is extended, that thereby the master of the ground may summarily stop poinding, unless sufficient goods be left to pay the rent, beside the plenishing of the house, Feb. 3, 1624, Hays *contra* Keith [Hope, *Maj. Pr.* VI, 19, 10 and 11; M. 6190]. Fourthly, This is extended against the donatar of the

tenant's escheat, intromitting thereby, who was found liable, though no action was moved by the master of the ground for seven years in the foresaid case, Hays *contra* Keith [Hope, *supra;* M.6190]. The like is sustained as to the goods of the possessors of houses, though *invecta et illata* only, all intromitters therewith being liable for house-mails; and the goods may be stopped from poinding for the possessor's debt, without deforcement, as being *invecta et illata ;* but this extends only to one year, or two terms' mail, December 7, 1630, Dick *contra* Lands [Durie 545 ; M.6243]. But the hypothecation of the fruits of the ground is greater than of the tenant's other goods; for the fruits are liable according to the value thereof for the rents, though there remain other goods sufficient to pay the rents on the ground, seeing there remained not sufficient fruits to pay the same; March ult. 1624 La.Dun and her Spouse *contra* L. of Dun [Haddington MS; M.6218]. This hypothecation of the fruits for the rent was extended to a town setting their customs, even against the sub-tacksman not bound to the town, who were preferred to the tacksman's creditors in a double poinding, January 31, 1665, Anderson and Proven *contra* the Town of Edinburgh [*Sub nom. Edinburgh* v *Provan's Creditors*, 1 Stair 260 ; M.6236]. It was also extended to the setter of a fishing against the donatar of the tacksman's escheat, who was found liable to restore, July 4, 1667, Cumming of Alter *contra* Lumsdean [1 Stair 469 ; M.6237]. This hypothecation was found to give the master of the ground right, not only to detain but to bring back the tenant's goods to the ground *de recenti*, December 11, 1672, Crichton *contra* E. of Queensberry [2 Stair 132 ; M.6203]; but not *ex intervallo*, February 9, 1676, Park *contra* Cockburn of Riselaw [2 Stair 412 ; M.6204]. But this hypothecation was not extended to an appriser without diligence or possession, July 29, 1675, Lord Panmuir *contra* L.Collistoun [2 Stair 362 ; M. 14088].

16. The like hypothecation is competent to teind-masters for their teinds, even though the heritor get the rent for the whole profit of the land, stock and teind jointly, he is thereby liable as intromitter; which was extended to ministers for their benefices or stipends, whereby they may have access to any intromitter with the teinds, out of which the stipend is modified, not only for the intromitter's proportion of his lands, but *in solidum* for his whole teind, according to the value of his intromission, July 6, 1625, Morton *contra* Scot [Durie 174 ; M.14784]; which held, though the intromitter had a wadset of stock and teind, whereby he had but his annualrent, March 21, 1633, Key *contra* Gray and Carmichael [Durie 682; M.14786]; and this was found not only in beneficed ministers, but in stipendaries, who may either take them to the tenants, or the masters intromitting, Spots. Kirkmen, Ker *contra* Gilchrist [*Sub nom. Kirk* v *Gilchrist*, Spotiswoode 191 ; M.14786]. The preference of relicts for implement of their contracts of marriage, out of their husband's moveables, in their hands, to other creditors, is not an hypothecation, but a personal privilege, which, by a late decision [Possibly

Keith v Keith, 1 Fountainhall 498; M.11833], hath not been sustained, but according to their diligence, *Vid.supra.Tit.4. §22* [1,4,22,*supra*].

Title 14. Permutation and Sale, or Emption and Vendition

PERMUTATION or excambion and sale, are so congeneous contracts, especially in our customs, that the same work will explain both, by holding out in what they do agree, and in what they differ. Permutation or exchange, is a contract whereby one thing is agreed to be given for another, which, if it be money, as it is current for goods or ware, (under which all things which can be bought are comprehended) then it is sale, or emption and vendition. Sale hath been very antiently and generally distinguished from all other permutations of one thing for another, which is called barter, or excambion; the reason whereof is, that by that mutual obligation of mankind to exchange, what they may spare from their own necessary use, with what others are willing to give in exchange thereof equivalent thereto, and useful to the receiver, which is comprehended under the general term of commerce, of which in the first title; therefore exchange may warrantably be urged and compelled, not only by civil authority between subjects of the same common-wealth, but also between insubordinate commonwealths. Commerce and free trade is by the law of nations, and cannot be effectual or useful by barter only; therefore common tokens of exchange have been invented and allowed over all the civil nations of the world, as comprehending the value of every thing venal, and which were chosen of the most durable metals, and nearest to the intrinsic value of things, such as gold and silver: and lest the currency of commerce might be retarded upon debates of the intrinsic value of these metals, they have always been stamped by public authority, that they might be current amongst the subjects of that commonwealth; and in comparison with the coined money of different commonwealths, regard is had so far to the intrinsic value, that the weight and fineness of the several coins is known, and thereby the proportion of current money in the several commonwealths, and so is current in all places that admit other coins than their own: yea, in some civil commonwealths, other tokens of exchange have been current as well as money, as for a long time tobacco in the American islands, and copper or tin in smaller payments in several countries amongst themselves.

The first impressions that were upon money were the shapes of cattle, and therefore money was thence called *pecunia*, and the first and most ordinary exchange or barter being of cattle, by this means a great advantage has accrued to mankind; for if men were obliged to exchange what exceeded their use, but for other things whereof they had use, it might be long ere that case occurred: but as the wise man saith, money answereth all things. And because gold and silver are durable metals, and continually raised out of the ground, by the abundance thereof, the extrinsic value is so lowed, that now the ounce of gold or silver is not the tenth part of the value that sometimes it was of; and so money becomes bulkish and heavy, uneasy to be transported, therefore bills of exchange do supply that inconvenience, of which *supra, Tit. Loan or Mutuum.* §*7* [1,11,7,*supra*].

These contracts of permutation or barter and sale, agree in this, that both are perfected according to law and our custom, by sole consent, naked pactions being now efficacious; and though neither of the things exchanged be delivered, the agreement is valid. But if there be any latent vitiosity, if it impede the use of the thing bought, the Romans gave *actionem redhibitoriam*, to restore and annul the bargain, or *quanti minoris*, for making up the buyer's interest: but if the seller was ignorant of the vitiosity, or insufficiency, he is not liable to make it good, unless he affirm it to be free of that, or in general, of any other faults: but if he knew the vitiosity, he is liable, if it were not shown to the buyer, or of itself evident or unknown, in which case the seller is not obliged, if he do not expressly paction; as if the seller commending his ware, say that a servant is beautiful, or a house well contrived, he is not liable to make it good; but if he say the servant is learned, or skilful in any art, he must make it good, *l. 43. ff. de cont. empt* [D. 18, 1, 43]. Our custom alloweth the making up of latent insufficiency, of which before, *Tit. 10.* §*15 and Tit. 9* §*10* [1,10,15; 1,9,10,*supra*].

But these contracts differ, First, In the materials, which in sale must be money as such, and as a liquid price, else if it be respected as a body, or indefinite quantity, as uncoined or uncurrent money, or if it be bought by the weight, or intrinsic value; or if money of one country be exchanged with money of another country, having no common standard, here is no sale but exchange; neither is exchange of money sale, because it is not as a liquid quantity, as when so much English money is given for the Florence crown, or gilder, and the remitting thereof. The price must be also certain, or which may be ascertained, *as such a person gave*, or *as shall be had from others by the seller for the like goods*, or *as such a person shall appoint*, which, if exorbitant, may be redacted *ad arbitrium boni viri*, which seems to consist, even though the arbitriment be made the buyer's, or the seller's, to determine the price.

Secondly, Excambion and sale differ mainly in this, that in sale, delivery of the goods or things bought, with the obligation of warrandice in case of eviction, which is implied in sale, though not expressed, is the implement of it on the seller's part, and even though the buyer know, and make it appear, that it were not the seller's, yet he could demand no more but delivery and warrandice; but contrariwise, the price must be made the seller's, and he may refuse it if he can show another's right, which can rarely occur, seeing money is a fungible, and cannot be distinguished from other money.

But in excambion, delivery must be made on either part, and the thing delivered must become thereby the receiver's, else, if it appear to be another's, it may be refused before delivery, and if it be evicted after, the contract becomes void, and the other party hath regress to what he gave in excambion, which followeth even singular successors, though it be not so expressed, and though the singular succession was by apprising and other legal diligence, prior to the eviction, November 25, 1623, E. Montrose *contra* Ker [*Sub nom. E. of Melross* v *Ker*, Durie 83; M. 3677]. And that without necessity to instruct, that he who craves regress had right when he changed, any further than by the narrative of the excambion, which was of an old date, in a charter from the king, bearing, these lands to have been disponed in excambion for the defender's lands, and that the excamber and his heirs should have regress, without mention of assignees, albeit the pursuer was assignee, July 14, 1629, L. Wardness *contra* L. Balcomy [Durie 461; M. 3678]; where it was also found, that no person needed to be cited, to obtain regress, but the present proprietor of the lands excambed, and the successor of the contractor, and no intervenient authors, July 2, 1629, *inter eosdem* [II, 3, 50, *infra*].

2. Sale may consist in all things which are not prohibited, such as buying of pleas by members of the College of Justice, which is prohibited by act of Parliament [Land Purchase Act, 1594, c. 220; A.P.S. IV, 68, c. 26], and which is understood of all persons having employment about the Session, as advocates, clerks, writers, &c. agents and their servants; wherein by pleas are not understood things wherein there may be controversy, but wherein there is process actually depending, called and not decerned, July 6, 1625, Mowat *contra* McClane [*Sub nom. Mowat* v *McLellan*, Durie 174; M. 9496]; July 30, 1635, Richardson *contra* Cranston-Riddel [*Sub nom. Richardson and Riddel* v *Sinclair*, Durie 776; M. 3210]. But the prohibition doth not annul the right or hinder process, but is a ground whereupon deprivation may follow by the Act, as in the former case, Had. June 5, 1611, Cunninghame *contra* Maxwell of Drumcoltrane [Haddington, *Fol. Dict.* II, 24; M. 9495; I, 10, 8, *supra*].

Sale being perfected, and the thing delivered, the property thereof becomes the buyer's, if it was the seller's, and there is no dependence of it, till the price be paid or secured, as was in the civil law, neither hypothecation of it for the price, Hope, *de empto*, Parker *contra* Law [*Sub nom. Park* v *Findlay*, Hope, *Maj. Pr.* II, 4, 3]. In sale there may be earnest interposed, or reversion granted, or the commissory paction or clause irritant adjected, that if the price be not paid, the sale shall be void; or the same may be conditionally, if the price be paid by such a day; or if any other offer not a better price in such a time; or with condition not to sell without consent, of which in order.

3. As to the first, Though giving of earnest be very ordinary in bargains

of sale and others, yet it is no less dubious, what the nature and effect thereof is, some holding it to be, to the effect the bargain may be evident and certain : for though sale be perfected by sole consent, yet it is not always evident to the parties and witnesses, whether it be a communing or a contract; and therefore, to make it sure to both, merchants, who may not hazard upon dubious interpretations, do give earnest as an evidence of the bargain closed and perfected : but others think, that the effect and intent of earnest is, that the giver of the earnest may resile from the bargain if he please to lose his earnest, and the taker may resile if he return the earnest with as much more. The civil law, *l.17.C.de fide instrumentorum* [c.4,21,17] & *Inst.de empt. vend. in pr.* [Inst.3,23,*pr.*], and many interpreters seems to favour this construction : yet many texts in law adduced by Wesenbecius, Faber and others, are for the former opinion, and they do interprete the contrary places, not to be of sale perfected, but of an antecedent promise or paction, to buy or sell. It hath not oft occurred (so far as I have observed) to be decided with us, which of these opinions is to be followed, but the former seems to be preferable, because ordinarily with us earnest is so inconsiderable, that it cannot be thought to be the meaning of the parties to leave the bargain arbitrary, upon the losing or doubling thereof. To this also suits the sense that earnest is taken in the Scripture for evidence and assurance, making the matter fixed and not arbitrary, which at least evinceth, that the word hath been anciently so taken, whatever hath been the custom and constitution of the Romans. Earnest also is reckoned as a part of the price with us, and thereby it stands not *in nudis finibus contractus, nec est res integra ;* so that neither party can resile therefrom.

4. Reversion, or the paction of redemption, though ordinarily it is used in wadsets (which, albeit they be under the form of sale, yet in reality they are not such, there being no equivalent price) yet reversion may be where there is a true sale, and this paction is no real quality or condition of the sale, however it be conceived, but only a personal obligement on the buyer, which therefore doth not affect the thing bought, nor a singular successor. And though reversion of lands and heritable rights be made as real and effectual against singular successors, when it is engrossed in the bargain or duly registrate, yet that is not by the nature of the thing, but by statute [Reversion Act, 1469, c.27; A.P.S. II,94,c.3; II,1,42; II,10,3,*infra*] and takes no place in other cases, as in reversion of moveables, which are sold under reversion; but if moveables be impignorate, the reversion is a part of the contract, and is effectual against singular successors.

As to the other pactions adjected to sale, sometimes they are so conceived and meant, that thereby the bargain is truly conditional and pendent, and so is not a perfect bargain, till the condition be existent; neither doth the property of the thing sold pass thereby, though possession follow, till it be performed ; as if the bargain be conditional, only upon payment of the price at such a time, till payment, the property passeth not unto the buyer. But there are many other adjections, which are expressed under the name of conditions and provisions, which are not inherent as essential in the bargain, but extrinsic personal obligements, the existence whereof doth not annul the sale, or suspend or annul the property in the buyer, at least in his singular successors; as hath now been said in reversions, and is frequent in many other cases.

5. In sale there uses to be adhibite a clause irritant, or resolutive clause, that if such a thing or case were, or were not, in that case the bargain should be null and void, as if it had never been made and granted : whence ariseth a very subtile debate, whether such clauses, whatsoever their tenor be, are effectual, and follow the thing to singular successors, and do render the bargain and property acquired null in itself ? Or whether such be but personal obligations only ? Which, though they may annul the property or bargain, if it remain in the hands of the contractor, cannot reach it, if it be in the hands of a third party; this being the question, for clearing thereof, it appeareth,

First, That if such conditions or resolutive clauses do stop the transmission of property, and be so meant and expressed, then, as is said before, the bargain is pendent, and the property not transmitted, and the seller remains the proprietor; but if by the contract and clause, the buyer become once the proprietor, and the condition is adjected, that he shall cease to be proprietor, in such a case, this is but personal; for property or dominion passes not by conditions or provisions, but by tradition, and other ways prescribed in law; so that these conditions, however expressed, are only the foundation, upon which the property might pass from the buyer, if the thing bought remain his, unless by law or statute it be otherwise ordered, as in reversions of lands, alienation of feudal rights, which become void and return if alienate, and not payment of the feu-duty, whereby the feu-right becomes void; but all these are by law and custom, and not by private paction.

Secondly, The doubt remains if such personal conditions with such clauses resolutive be in the body of the bargain, whether it be effectual against singular successors, who cannot but know their author's rights ? And, therefore, are *in dolo et mala fide*, if they acquire such rights in prejudice of the conditions thereof; and so *ex dolo*, at least such clauses will be effectual against singular successors; but first, This hath no force where the acquisition is not voluntary but necessary for satisfaction of debt, by apprising and other legal diligence; in which ordinarily the acquirer doth not, neither is supposed to know his author's right. Secondly, If the bargain be so necessary that the purchaser be a creditor, and hath no other probable way of payment; in which, though he see his author's right bearing such clauses, yet he acteth upon necessity, for his own satisfaction. Thirdly, These who acquire such rights without necessity, and see therein such conditions in themselves personal, though having resolutive clauses, do not thereby know that the third party hath the right, *jus in re*, but only *jus ad rem ;* and, therefore, if they acquire such rights, the property is thereby transmitted. And though there may be fraud in the acquirer, which raiseth an obligation of reparation to the party damnified by that delinquence, yet that is but personal; and another party acquiring *bona fide* or necessarily, and not partaking of that fraud, is *in tuto*. But certain knowledge, by intimation, citation, or the like, inducing *malam fidem*, whereby any prior disposition or assignation made to another party is certainly known, or at least interruption made in acquiring by arrestment or citation of the acquirer, such rights acquired, not being of necessity to satisfy prior engagements, are reducible *ex capite fraudis*, and the acquirer is partaker of the fraud of his author, who thereby becomes a granter of double rights; but this will not hinder legal diligence to proceed and be completed and become effectual, though the user thereof did certainly know any inchoate or incomplete right of another.

6. But it is more doubtful, and not yet clear by custom, whether a voluntary right taken for satisfaction of a prior debt, by him who certainly knew of a prior disposition or assignation, though not perfected, would be reduced as fraudulent. So the relating of one right unto another right, without any invalidity thereof expressed, was found to infer an acknowledgment of it, February 15, 1637, Lawder *contra* Goodwife of Whitekirk [Durie 826; M. 1692]. Of late the like conditions have become very ordinary, that thereby property may become inalienable and as a perpetual usufruct. Yet it seems such are neither expedient for commerce nor consistent with the nature of property, whose main effect is alienation or disposal of the substance of the thing, as usufruct is of the fruits; and, therefore, it were safest upon such clauses to use inhibition; yet they may be effectual against lucrative alienations or donations in respect that by these clauses, at least the parties are personal creditors, and so alienations gratuitous, to their prejudice, may be annulled by the statute 1621, cap. 18 [Bankruptcy Act, 1621, c.18; A.P.S. IV, 615, c.18]. But of late it hath been found, that a clause irritant being in a tailzie, and in the seasin, both of the first heir, and of the last, that it did annul the creditor's rights and apprisings, and the next, who might have been heir of tailzie, had access to the land without being heir to him, who incurred the clause irritant by his debt, Feb. 26, 1662, Lord Stormont *contra* Creditors of the E. Annandale [1 Stair 106; M. 13966]. And now there is a special statute regulating tailzies and clauses irritant therein; of which hereafter, Title Infeftments [11, 3, 58, *infra*].

7. Sale being complete, the question is, if the thing should perish by accident before delivery, and not after delay, and without the fault of the seller, whether the hazard be the seller's or the buyer's? By the civil law the buyer hath the peril, *l. 34. §6. ff. de contrahenda emptione* [D. 18, 1, 34, 6]. *l. 14 de furtis* [D. 47, 2, 14]. *l. 1. Cod. de periculo & com. rei vend.* [C. 4, 48, 1] and the peril is not the seller's, unless expressly he take the hazard, or that the buyer buy *per aversionem; l. 62. §2. ff. de contrahenda emptione* [D. 18, 1, 62, 2]; all which putteth both the peril and profits of the thing upon the

buyer, *ejus est periculum cujus est commodum ;* and it is far more clear, that the accessions, fruits, and profits of things bought are, the buyer's, even before delivery; and by the same ground, the peril must be his also. But on the other part, that the loss is the seller's is the opinion of others, because the seller, after the sale, is debtor for the delivery; and it is a general rule, that the debtor is never obliged for the hazard of accidents, when he is debtor for a certain body ; but all agree, that if the sale were of a fungible, as wine, oil, or grain, not considered as a particular body, as the wine in such a cellar, or the grain in such a house, but generally so much grain or wine, as a mere fungible, in that case the peril would be the seller's ; because the perishing of any one particular could not be the buyer's. But beside authority, the main reason on the contrary is, that every thing perisheth to its owner, and before tradition, the seller is proprietar of the thing sold. I have not observed it debated or decided with us, if the thing sold should thereafter perish, that yet the price is due ; and if by common custom, the seller had not forborn, in that case doubtless the buyer would not have paid willingly ; which therefore seems to be our custom, seeing none have obtained the price, who did not deliver, or offer the thing sold, which is also the opinion of Cujac, *ad l.33.ff.Locati ;* yet the peril of a house sold, and thereafter burnt, was found to be the buyer's, though the disposition bore an obligement to put the buyer in possession, because the buyer did voluntarily take possession and re-builded the house and was infeft before the burning, Dec. 13, 1667, Hunter *contra* Wilsons [1 Stair 493 ; M. 10067]. In sale, absolute warrandice is implied, which is not to be extended to moderate servitudes, as aquæducts and city-servitudes *l.66.ff.de contrahenda emptione* [D. 18,1,66], of which afterwards, *Title Infeftments,* §*Warrandice* [11,3,46,*infra*].

Title 15. Location and Conduction, Where, of Annualrent and Usury

LOCATION and conduction is a contract, whereby hire is given for the fruits, use or work of persons or things. This contract keepeth a great proportion with sale; for as no sale can be without a price, so no location without an hire, and as the price must be certain, either being expressly named, or indirectly, being the price that such another gave for the like, or that such a person should think reasonable, both which become certain, if the price given by that other party appear, or if that third person modify the price, otherwise the sale is void and pendent, and imperfect, till that be performed : So in location the hire must be the same way ascertained ; for if the price be but made *ex post facto*, it is no proper location; as he who gives his cloth to be dyed, and promiseth to agree for the cloth, as the dye shall be in fineness, this is no location but an innominate contract, *Pr. & §1.Inst. de Locat.cond.* [Inst. 3,24,Pr. and 1] *& l.25. in prin.ff.eod.* [D. 19,2,25].

But it is controverted, whether sale and location do also agree in this, that as the price must be in current money, so also the hire. This question was of much moment in the Roman law, because location was a nominate contract, perfected by sole consent; but other contracts innominate were but naked pactions, till the thing agreed upon was interposed; and therefore it is there accurately debated, some holding, that money only can make the hire in a proper location, and some that any other liquid quantity or fungible is sufficient, as oil, grain, &c. But with us, all agreements being effectual by sole consent, we need not much debate; and therefore, seeing all the effects and conditions competent, where the hire is money, are also competent where it is any other fungible, we agree with that opinion, that such are proper locations.

Sale and location differ mainly in this, that the intent and effect of sale is to alienate the substance of the thing bought, and state the property thereof in the buyer; but in location, the ordinary intent thereof is, that the substance and property of the thing is not alienate, but remains in the setter, and the taker hath only the fruits and works thereof, which must not be already done and extant, but that which is to be done, *et in spe ;* as for instance, a bargain for the fruits of a field, which are already growing, is no location, but sale, and so of use or work already performed; and therefore, in the nature of this contract, there is an hazard and uncertainty in the conductor, of the quantity or value of the fruits, use or work, the peril and profits whereof is the conductor's.

2. But here ariseth the question, that in the case of the sterility of the ground set, or the absolute ceasing of the use, fruits or work, whether the hire be due or not? The determination whereof will clear the exception of the former rule, concerning the peril and quantity of the use, fruits and work locate; and therefore, *first*, where the use, fruits and work, doth altogether cease, without the fault of the conductor, there the hire must also cease, because the one is given as the cause of the other, and the peril undertaken is not of the being, but of the quantity and value thereof: for instance, if land taken be inundate or sanded, and so have no fruit, it is the common opinion of all, that the hire or cane ceaseth to be due for that time: or if a horse, or a servant hired die, the hire or fee is but due according to the time of their life; but if they be sick or unprofitable for a time, yet with hope of recovery and profit, in that case there is no abatement.

Secondly, Though the opinion of the learned be very diverse, in the matter of the barrenness of the ground, some accounting it if the half of the ordinary increase fail, some if the third, and some leaving it to the common estimation of the place what is called barrenness, or to the arbitriment of the judge; yet

I think it more rational to determine that case with the rest, upon the former ground, that if there be any profit of the fruit above the expenses, or work, the rent or hire should be due, *vid. l. 15. ff. h. t.* [D. 19, 2, 15].

3. The like is in vastation by public calamity, which hath been frequently decided upon occasion of the late vastations, but this will not extend to private accidents befalling the crop after the growing or reaping, even though by accident it should be destroyed or burnt without the taker's fault, the hazard being his own, because it is not then respected as the fruit, but as a body in being, whereof he hath the property and peril : but in public calamities by war, not only the crop is taken away, but the tenants are disabled, and hindered to labour, and therefore must have abatement, *d. l. 15. §4. ff. h. t.* [D. 19, 2, 15, 4]. But the plenty of a former year doth not compense the sterility of a latter, *l. 8. C. de locato* [C. 4, 65, 8]. Neither is there any abatement, where the hire is a proportion of the fruits, *l. 25. §9. ff. h. t.* [D. 19, 2, 25, 9]. Yea, it is more agreeable to the nature of this contract, that no respect should be had to any prior or posterior year, because there are as many locations as there are years.

4. Seeing the intent and effect of location is not to alienate the property of the thing locate, it followeth, that this contract is merely personal, and thereby there is no real right in the thing whose use fruits or work are locate ; so that if the property of these things be alienated from the locator, the interest of the conductor ceaseth, and a singular successor may recover it from the conductor notwithstanding the location, which reacheth it only by the personal contract, as it did belong to the setter, *l. 9. C. h. t.* [C. 4, 65, 9]; and so it would be in our tacks or rentals by their own nature : but it is otherwise provided by a special statute, of which hereafter, *Title Tacks.* §2 [11, 9, 2, *infra*]. Likewise we shall speak nothing here of feu-farms, which, though they are locations, yet by the law they become real rights, leaving these to their own place, *Tit. Infeftments* [11, 3, 34, *infra*].

5. From this contract the conductor's obligation is to pay the hire, and after the end of location to restore the thing locate, making up all damages ; in which the conductor is liable even for light faults, and must use such diligence as prudent men use in their affairs, but is not liable for casual or accidental perishing of the thing locate. Some hold him liable for the most exact diligence and lightest fault ; but others with better reason are for the contrary, it being the common rule in diligence, that in that which is only to the behoof of the keeper he should use most exact diligence, and is liable for the lightest fault, as it is in loan; and these who have the custody only for another, are liable for the grossest fault which is equivalent to fraud ; and for such diligence as is commonly accustomed by every man; but these who have the custody partly for themselves and partly for others, are in the middle way obliged for such diligence as themselves, or prudent men use in their affairs [1, 11, 9, *supra*].

6. The obligation on the part of the locator, is to deliver the thing locate,

and to continue it during the time of the location, and to refund to the conductor his necessary expenses employed upon the thing hired, unless the
custom of the place be otherwise; and so the reparation and upholding of
houses set in *prædiis urbanis* lieth upon the setter, if it be not otherwise
agreed: but in lands or *prædiis rusticis*, the tenant is obliged to keep the land
and houses in as good condition as he got them, and may not destroy mosses
nor rive out meadows, and is liable for the damage though there be no such
provision in his tack, February 6, 1633. L. Haddo *contra* Johnstoun [Durie
669; M. 7540; 11,9,31,*infra*]; neither hath he reparation for any building or
policy which he maketh, which is accounted as being freely done without
expectation of recompence, if it be not otherwise agreed, or that the rent be
raised thereby.

7. Next, as to such contracts, whereby money, or any fungible is lent
for the like in kind again, with such a hire for the use thereof. These are
called usurary contracts, and they cannot be comprehended under loan,
because they are not gratuitous, or under location, because the property and
substance is alienate. Usurary contracts come nearest to location; but to
repress the exorbitance of usurers, the civil law rejected usurary contracts,
and admitted only of the profit of fungibles. In some cases the judicial law
also rejecteth them, and prohibiteth usury to be used among the Jews,
though they might use it with other nations. So doth the canon law disapprove it, and most nations, where that law is in vigour; yet we, and
generally other Protestant nations, do allow of the profit of money, or other
fungibles, it being within the proportion allowed in law, which sometimes
was ten for each hundred, till the year 1633, thereafter eight [Act 1633,
c. 21; A.P.S. v, 39, c. 21], and now six since the year 1649 [Act 1649, c. 29;
A.P.S. v. 504, c. 342] And therefore usurary contracts with us, are only such,
wherein there is unlawful, or exorbitant profits beyond the law. The civil
law allowed *usuras centesimas*, viz. one of a hundred monthly; and their
usuras besses, *semisses*, and *dodrantes*, in their several cases. We have only one
measure for all. *Fœnus Nauticum* is where so much is given, not only for the
profit of the money, but for the hazard and peril of the ware bought thereby,
or of other fungibles, by sea; and so it is a mixed contract; and in both cases
profit or annualrent is lawful, as having no moral countermand, and so being
free, is not only subject to our pactions and promises, which we are morally
obliged to observe, but hath also in it permutative justice, in that money,
wine, oil, grain, or the like, have a real use profitable to men, by the exchange
thereof and increase that may accrue thereby, and for which proportionable
hire may be lawfully and profitably constitute. These usurary contracts
therefore are to be reduced, not to loan but to location, though by accident
they have that difference from the rest, that the property is alienate; because
there can be no use of money or fungibles otherwise. There are three kinds
of usurary contracts, legal, pactional and penal: legal are these wherein
annualrent is due by law without consent or fault; pactional are these

wherein annualrent is promised; penal are these which are by the modification of judges, as the damage of parties: but in foreign bills of exchange
annualrent is now allowed without paction, by the act 20 Parl. 3 Ch. 2 [Bills
of Exchange Act, 1681, c. 20; A.P.S. VIII, 352, c. 86].

The penalty of exorbitant usury with us was, that the debtor for such
usury, revealing the same, should be freed of the contract, and if he did not,
any other revealing it should have right to the sum given out upon usury,
and profit thereof, Parl. 1594, c. 22 [Act 1594, c. 222; A.P.S. IV, 70, c. 32],
but afterwards all taking of more annualrent than ten *per cent.* directly or
indirectly, as by taking of victual within the ordinary prices, or buying
victual for the annualrent with exorbitant prices, in case of not delivery, or
by improper wadsets, having greater backtack duties than effeiring to ten
per cent. or otherwise, do confiscate their moveables, and the sums so given
out, which the party cannot renounce, but the King's Advocate hath interest
to pursue therefor, without the party's concurrence; and if he concur, he
shall have restitution of what more annual he paid nor ten *per cent.* Parl.
1597. cap. 247 [Act 1597, c. 251; A.P.S. IV, 133, c. 118; also Act 1597, c. 263;
A.P.S. IV, 138, c. 30]. But the annual was retrenched to eight *per cent.* Parl.
1633, c. 21 [Act 1633, c. 21; A.P.S. V, 39, c. 21] and to six *per cent.* Parl.
1649, c. 29 [Act 1649, c. 29; A.P.S. V, 504, c. 342], revived Parl. 1661, c. 49
[Act 1661, c. 49; A.P.S. VII, 320, c. 345]. But whether proper wadsets without back-tack, though the rent be much more than the ordinary annualrent,
be an usurary contract, and falls under the general clause of the said act,
though it hath sometimes been essayed, yet it hath not been decided. The
main reason that the parties found on is, on the one part, that there is indirectly more than the ordinary annualrent, and so falls under the act 1597:
And, on the other part, that improper wadsets are there expressed, and
proper wadsets seem *ex proposito* omitted; likeas in proper wadsets all
hazard lies upon the wadsetter, of setting the land, of dead, poor, and waste.
But we shall leave this to every man's private judgment, till public judgment
cast the balance; only all proper wadsets before 1661, are restricted to the
annualrent by the act of Parliament 1661, c. 62 [Diligence Act, 1661, c. 62;
A.P.S. VII, 319, c. 344]. And if upon offer of security, the wadsetter will not
quit possession, he is countable from the offer, as hath been often decided
since that Act.

There uses also in wadsets and reversions, to be included a condition to
set the wadset lands for such a time, to begin after redemption, which, if it
be far within the true worth, is usury, and is declared so, Parl. 1449, c. 19
[Lease Act 1449, c. 19; A.P.S. II, 35, c. 6; II, 10, 10, *infra*]. "That lands
provided to be set for tacks, not near the true worth, the same shall not be
kept." Yet such a tack was sustained, seeing the wadsetter had not his full
annualrent, by reason of a liferent reserved in the wadset, and the wadsetter
was the constituent's brother, and so it was like to be his portion natural
whereof the tack was a part, Jan. 21, 1662, L. Polwart *contra* Hume [1 Stair

84; M.16408]; but in other cases, such a tack was found null by the said act, but not by the act betwixt debtor and creditor, February 15, 1666, Lo. Ley *contra* Porteous[1 Stair 356; M.16523].

8. This much for usury or annualrent by contract or paction. It is also due by the law, and by the obligation of recompense and reparation; and in the civil law, in all contracts *bonæ fidei*, it is due *ex mora*, by the delay of the debtor, which is understood after he shall be required for the same, or that the term is past, *nam dies interpellat pro homine* [1,3,7,*supra*; 1,17,15,*infra*], and in other contracts by litiscontestation, *l.2 & l.35.ff.de Usuris* [D.22,1,2 and 35]: But our custom hath little use of that distinction, neither followeth that rule, but, 1mo, Where annualrent is not agreed upon, ordinarily it is not due till horning be used against the debtor, and that by a special statute of Parliament, 1621,cap.20 [A.P.S. IV,623,c.20]. Yea, though the horning was not registrate, and so null, as to escheat, it was found valid as to the annualrent, February 11, 1673, Smith *contra* Wauch [2 Stair 171; M.491]. But it was found not competent by way of special charge in the suspension of the principal debt, but by ordinary action, July 2, 1629, Purveyance *contra* L.Craigie[Durie 455; M.14990], where Dury's opinion is, that if the charger had raised horning upon the act of Parliament, it would have been sustained summarily, and is now ordinarily sustained summarily by a special charge, when the sum is charged for or suspended; but it being once due, it not only continueth during the life of the person denounced, but still thereafter till payment, July 8, 1642, Huntly *contra* Heirs of Mr John Manson[Durie 898; M.497]. 2do, Annualrent provided by a bond for one year, though it express not for all years thereafter, yet continueth due till payment, December 2, 1628, Zair *contra* Ramsay [Durie 403; M.484]. The like where one term was only in the bond, Spots. Usury, Keith *contra* Bruce [Spotiswoode 353; M.486]; and where annualrent was promised for time bygone, by a letter, it was found still due till payment, January 13, 1669, Home *contra* Seaton of Menzies[1 Stair 580; M.486]. 3tio, It is due by use of payment only, without express paction, March 4, 1628, Forrester *contra* Clerk [Spotiswoode 353; M.482]. 4to, Annualrent is ordained to be due to cautioners by their principals, for sums paid by them as cautioners, by the clause of relief, as being damage and interest, though the bond bear no annualrent, by statute of session, December 21, 1590; Hope, Usury, Torry *contra* Dowhill [Possibly *Dury* v *Coldwell*, Hope *Maj.Pr.* 11,13,40]; December 4, 1629, Cockpool *contra* Johnstoun [Durie 473; M.2115], where the clause of relief bore only to relieve the cautioner of his cautionry, and not of all damage. The like, though there was no further distress against the cautioner but registration, January 24, 1627, L.Waughton *contra* L.Innerweek [Durie 262; M.519]; and this was extended to co-principals, having a clause of mutual relief of cost, skaith, &c. November 15, 1627, Black of Largo *contra* Dick [Durie 312; M.520]. 5to, Annualrent is due without paction, by tutors and curators to their pupils, of which formerly in the Tit.Obligations betwixt them [1,6,

19, *supra*]. 6to, Annualrent was found due without paction, by an heir male for the portion of the heir female, though not required for many years, and that still from the term of payment, Haddington, July 5, 1610, Colquhoun *contra* L. of Luss [Colvill, *Fol. Dict.* 1, 44; M. 560]. The like by a husband, who was found obliged to his wife for the annualrent of the tocher payable by the father, though the tocher was never paid, Hope, Husband and wife, Baird *contra* Gordon [*Sub nom. Hervey and Baird* v *Gordon*, Hope, *Maj. Pr.* 11, 17, 44], Spots. Usury, Skeen *contra* Hart [Not found]. 7mo, Annualrent was found due for the price of lands possessed by the buyer, without paction, Hope, Usury, Stirling *contra* Ogilvy [Hope, *Maj. Pr.* 11, 13, 24]; Feb. 17, 1624, Dury of that Ilk *contra* Lo. Ramsay [Durie 110; M. 542], and *L. 2. ff. de Usur.* [D. 22, 1, 2]. The like though the delay of payment was not the debtor's fault, November 14, 1628, Cuming *contra* Cumming [Durie 396; M. 9147]; Spots. Usury, Home *contra* L. Renton [Spotiswoode 352; M. 545]. Annualrent not sustained without paction, for a sum lent to an old man, on condition, that if he died without heirs, the creditor should become the debtor's heir, and yet he having heirs, annualrent was not found due, December 11, 1662, Logie *contra* Logie [1 Stair 149; M. 489]. But the Lords do sometimes allow annualrent, or an equivalent expense among merchants; and they did so determine in a provision by a father to his natural daughter, payable at her marriage, which was found so favourable not to hinder her to marry, that annualrent was allowed her, seeing the condition was in her power, June 25, 1664, Inglis *contra* Inglis [1 Stair 208; M. 561]. The Romans allowed annual till it equalled the principal, but no further, *l. 10 & l. 27. §1 & l. 29. C. de usuris* [c. 4, 32, 10 and 27, 1, and 29]: but our custom hath no such restriction. Yet we restrict the English double bonds to the single sums and annualrent thereof, but no further than till it be equivalent to the principal; seeing by the tenor of such bonds, it appears to be the meaning of the parties, that no more should be demanded in any case, January 2, 1679, Frazer and Burnet *contra* Hamilton [2 Stair 678; M. 564].

Annual upon annual is condemned by all when it is comprehended in the first paction, but it is ordinary with us, by posterior contracts to accumulate annualrents and make it a principal, and so both that which was first principal, and that which was once annual, bears annual, which the Romans did not allow, *l. 28. C. eod.* [c. 4, 32, 28] so also annual, by virtue of the act of Parliament, if decreet follow thereupon and horning, it will bear annual, seeing there is no limitation; but this will not be extended to annuals in time coming, after the horning. And lastly, Annualrent paid by a cautioner, by the said statute of session, will bear annualrent, because to him it is a principal. Annualrent was also found due without paction for money expended, according to the custom of Bourdeaux, Dec. 8. 1677, Peron *contra* Morison [*Sub nom. Aperon*, 2 Stair 573; M. 4529].

All things may fall under location that can have any use, fruit, or work, but real servitudes cannot be set severally, but only as accessories to the thing which they serve. Works which can be locate, 1mo, Must be lawful. 2do, They must be performable in that which belongeth to the conductor, or in reference to his person; for work employed upon the worker's own matter is no location; as if a goldsmith be employed to work such a piece of work in his own metal, and the same to be bought as it is so wrought, it is sale and not location, unless there be two distinct bargains, one for the metal, which is sale, and the other for the workmanship, which is location; and if the work is to be employed on that which concerns a third party, it is not location, but mandate.

Title 16. Society, Where, of Copartnery

SOCIETY is not so much a permutative, as a commutative contract, whereby the contractors communicate each to other some stock, work or profit. The effect of society is, that thereby something which before was proper, becometh, or is continued to be common to the copartners, and it is either a stock, or the profit of a stock, or work, labour or industry: yet this communication is not effectual to transfer the property in part, or to communicate it, without delivery or possession, by which property by positive law is conveyed. There is oft-times a communion without society, because it is of accident, as legators, heirs or acquirers of the same thing *pro indiviso ;* but if there be interposed a contract thereupon, to continue that communion for the common profit of the contractors, it becometh a proper society.

2. The matter of society are things, fruits, work or industry, and that variously: for sometimes the thing or stock is only put in by one, and the work and industry about it by another; as where a stock is given in partnership to a merchant to trade with, here it may be that the merchant's skill and pains is balanced with the profit of the stock of the other, who doth not, nor cannot make that use of it: or land is set to husbandmen to be laboured, and the increase to be common: sometimes each partner bringeth a stock to the society, and their work or pains withal, and sometimes only work, and the profit thereby is made common: and sometimes the one communicateth the stock itself, whereby the property thereof becometh common to himself and other partners, and the profit accruing thereby; and the other bringeth in a stock, but doth not communicate itself, but the profit thereof, in all which the interest and shares may either be equal or unequal; but without work and industry by the partners, or others, there can be no society, because there can be no profit, or hazard of profit or loss.

3. The nature of this contract is, to have in it equality of profit and loss

proportionable to the value and worth of the stock and work, which is un-alterable and indispensible by the nature of this contract; and scarcely can any paction or indirect course be effectual in the contrary, because thereby the contract would become usurary and void; which equality, as to the work and industry, is illiquid, and the value thereof is esteemed according to the common estimate; but where there is a special value set upon it, by the private consent of parties, which (as was said before of the private rate of parties, *Tit. 10. §14* [1, 10, 14, *supra*]) without fraud is sufficient: so some-times the value of the work is estimated equal to the stock or industry of the other partners, and sometimes the half, third, or other proportion of it: but where the matter is clear, or where the society consists of a stock in money, the profit must necessarily be proportionable thereto, and the hazard or loss accordingly; but if it be agreed, that where the stocks are equal, the one should have one third, and the other two thirds of the profit or loss, or that one should bear the hazard of the stock of both, and the profit should be equal, or any other inequality, it is clearly usurary, unequal and unjust, *l. 29. pr. & §1. ff. h. t.* [D. 17, 2, 29, *pr.* and 1]. But if the one has only loss, and the other all the gain, it is called *societas Leonina, d. l. 29. §ult.* [D. 17, 2, 29, 2]. Neither doth it subsist as a donation, unless so specially expressed and really meant; for oft-times, to make inconsistent contracts subsist, it is agreed, that the inequality, if any be, shall be a donation; but that is a mere colour, and doth work no effect, seeing the intent of the contract is truly to communicate like for like, and not to gift, and that addition is but simulate or fraudulent. Hence society may be described "a contract, for communicat-ing the profit or loss of that which is brought into the society, proportionably according to the share and interest of each partner." It is true, that if there appear no inequality in the stock and industry of the partners, when no proportion is expressed, equal share of profit and loss is understood, *l. 5. §fin. ff. h. t.* [D. 17, 2, 5] & *§3 Inst. h. t.* [Inst. 3, 25, 3], or if the skill or in-dustry of some of the partners be of great importance, the society may con-sist in these terms, that those persons shall have no share of the loss, and shall have such a share of the profit according to the sentence of Sulpitius; but if such inequality appear not, the sentence of Mucius rejecting such inequality of shares is just, and there is no contrariety between the opinions of both, *§2. Instit. h. t.* [Inst. 3, 25, 2].

4. It remains to consider, what are the effects of society while it is, and how it ceaseth. As to the First, the disposal and management of all the affairs of societies is in the whole partners; and each of them (though having an unequal share) hath an equal vote, unless it be otherwise agreed, and the common rule is, *potior est conditio prohibentis, l. 28. ff. Comm. divid.* [D. 10, 3, 28]. So that every one hath a negative vote, in acts that are not necessary for the design of the society, unless by the custom or paction or deed of the parties it be otherwise ordered; as where it is the custom of the place, that in such societies there should be a plurality; or when it is agreed, that the

minor part should give place to, and is comprehended in, the acts of the major part; or when the society hath been accustomed to act in such a way, not only the greater part, but even one or more of the partners may continue that way; which is still held to be the mind of the whole, unless the contrary be expressed; and therefore it was found, where one of more partners in a ship, had fraughted her to a dangerous voyage, without the others' consent, yet he was not found liable for her value, being lost by accident, where no just objection could be made against the skipper's skill, July 22, 1673, Sim *contra* Abernethy [*Sub nom. Swyne* v *Abernethy*, 2 Stair 218; M. 14565]. Yea the protesting of any of the owners against the skipper and major part, will not make them liable for the protester's part of the ship, if she be cast away, though it be the law in maritime cases in some places; because of the ordinary or usual remeid here, of a roup at the half or major part of the owners against the rest, or a set at any of the owners' instance against the whole, either to take his part at such a rate, or quit their parts at the same price, or roup his own part when he pleases. So letting out of lands, or setting out of houses, employing of monies in a society, may be continued by one or more of the partners, and their actings with extraneous persons, in name of the society, do constitute the whole society debtor or creditor, or doth acquire to them, or dispone from them. It is also consistent with the nature of this contract, to give a negative vote to one or more of the society, whose interest in the stock, or whose skill and industry is esteemed the greatest; but the simple nature of the society itself is the most tender engagement; and so if it be not otherwise provided, it is always dissolvable at the option and the choice of any of the society, and it implies that the management is in the whole partners equally, and that every one hath a negative vote; and therefore, when it is contracted to a time that it may not be parted from, in that case the interest and end of the society is changed, and if the minor part will not cede to the major part, or to arbitriment, it must be decided by the Judge Ordinary which of the parts is most conduceable to the society; as in ships, as said is; so in heritage *actione familiæ erciscundæ*, *ff. 10. tit. 2* [D. 10.2,]. *C. 3. tit. 36* [C. 3, 36]. And in other things, as legacies, &c. *actione de communi dividundo*, *ff. 10. tit. 3* [D. 10, 3]. *C. 3. tit. 37* [C. 3, 37]. And with us, when many creditors are concerned in a bankrupt's estate, it is divided by roup and sale, conform to the 17th act, Parl. 3. Ch. 2d. [Judicial Sale Act, 1681, c. 17; A.P.S. VIII, 351, c. 83], and which is enlarged by act 20, Parl. 1 K.W. & Q.M. [Judicial Sale Act, 1690, c. 20; A.P.S. IX, 195, c. 49], wherein the English are very frequent and exact upon commissions of bankrupt. So a wife is kend to the terce of her husband's lands by a brief out of the chancery, of which *infra*, Title Liferents, §12 [11,6,12, *infra*]. But this being so great a retardment upon the management of the affairs of society by consent, it looseth the fraternity among the partners, and is sure to lose the pleasure and readily the profit of all; and therefore the Romans did upon good grounds annul and disown all pactions, whereby society did continue beyond the life and pleasure of any of the partners, except in some few cases, *l.63 in fin.ff. h.t.* [D.17,2,63 *in fin.*] *l.77 §20 de Legat.2* [D.50,7,20] *l.14 & l.70.eod.* [D.17,2,14 and 70].

5. Society by consent then is finished : *First*, When the matter whereupon it is contracted is extinct, *§6.Inst.h.t.* [Inst.3,25,6]. *Secondly*, By the death or incapacity of any of the partners to act in the society ; for it being one individual contract of the whole, and not as many contracts as partners, it is like a sheaf of arrows bound together with one tie, out of which, if one be pulled, the rest will fall out, and the personal humour of the partners is so chosen, that it is not supposed to be communicated to their heirs or assignees, unless by custom or paction the contrary be provided, which no doubt is consistent with, though not consequent from, the nature of society, *§4 & seq.Inst.hoc.tit.* [Inst.3,25,4 *et seq.*] *l.4 §1.l.59.l.63 §ult.l.65 §9 ff. eod.* [D.17,2,4,1 ; 59 ; 63,10 ; 65,9]. *Thirdly*, It is most consonant to the nature of society to be dissolved at the option and pleasure of any of the partners, it being very contrary thereto, and much impeding of the ends of it, that any should be continued a partner against his own will ; and therefore ordinarily, not only the express renunciation of the society, but any contracting or acting separately in the matter of the society dissolveth it ; yet *propter bonam fidem*, whatsoever is done with, or by the society, before the dissolution thereof be known, is valid ; but this dissolution at pleasure may be altered by custom, or consent of parties, *d. §4,Instit.h.t.* [Inst.3,25,4]. And to sum up all, in society proportionable equality is essential and inseparable, and all the other specialities are congruous and convenient, and therefore understood, if by custom or consent it be not otherwise ordered, *§1 Instit.h.t.* [Inst.3,25,1].

6. The same question is incident here, that before hath been touched concerning mandates [1.12,13–14,*supra*], when one or more of the parties act in the matter of the society, whether thereby the whole society be obliged by the obligations of these ? Whether obligations made to these, constitute the society creditor ? Or whether real rights acquired by these are *ipso facto* common to the society ? Or if there be but an obligation upon the actors to communicate the property always remaining in the actors, till they effectually communicate ? The resolution of this being the same with that in mandates, we refer you thither, and say only this in general, that when these parties only act in name of the society, and by its express warrant, or by what they have been accustomed to do, in so far they are not only partners but mandatars, and it hath the same effect, as if the society had acted itself ; but when they act not so, there doth only arise an obligement upon the partners-actors to communicate, in the mean time the property remaineth in the actors ; and if transmitted to others before this communication, the society will be thereby excluded, but the actors will remain obliged for reparation of the damage and interest of the society ; and this will hold, though things be bought or acquired by the common money of the society ; but all the natural

interest, birth, fruits, and profit of the society, is of itself, and instantly common to the society.

7. Partners are liable each to other, for such diligence as men do ordinarily use, or the partners themselves use, in their own affairs; for this contract being undergone for the mutual good of the parties, the diligence keepeth the middle way betwixt exact diligence and supine negligence: but none of them are liable for what is lost by force or accident, without their fault, §*ult. Inst. h. t.* [Inst. 3, 25, 9].

8. Society hath as many divisions, as it hath various and multiform matter in which it may be contracted; but that which is most noticed in law is, that some societies are common and general, whereby parties communicate all their goods, rights and interests communicable, which the Greeks call κοινωνιαν; *Inst. pr. h. t.* [Inst. 3, 25, *pr.*] others are particular of one or more of these, *l. 52. §5. ff. eod.* [D. 17, 2, 52, 5]. Upon the first there are many questions arising, as how far the partners may gift, or educate and provide their children, so as that the rest are obliged or understood to concur: but such societies being altogether unaccustomed here, it shall be vain to debate the properties of them, but proceed to accessory obligations.

Title 17. Accessory Obligations, Where, of Transaction, Caution, Oaths, and Other Accessories

1. THESE being the several kinds of pactions and contracts arising from the matter, there are other distinctions of them from their adjuncts or circumstances, of which this is the chief, that contracts may be celebrated, either immediately, or mediately by the interposition of other persons, as mandatars or commissioners; concerning which it hath been shown before, that as there is a contract betwixt the mandant and mandatar, so oft-times there is a contract engaged betwixt the mandant and a third party, who hath acted with the mandatar according to his warrant: in which case ordinarily there is no contract or obligement, betwixt the mandatar and the third party: as he who buys land in name, and to the use of another, by his warrant, the lands are acquired to him who gave the warrant, and he is obliged to pay the price to the seller, but not to his mandatar, so the seller is obliged to

deliver and warrant him, and not the mandatar. But to all manner of promises and contracts, transactions, caution, and oaths may be interposed.

2. Transaction may be interposed in the matter of all contracts, and it is a most important contract, whereby all pleas and controversies may be prevented or terminated; for thereby all parties transacting, quit some part of what they claim, to redeem the vexation and uncertain event of pleas. It is therefore the common interest, that transactions should be firmly and inviolably observed, which, both by the Roman law and our customs, hath been held as sacred, and necessary for men's quiet and peace.

It must therefore be accurately considered what a transaction is, and what are the necessary requisites thereto. The word transaction is variously taken; so the administration of any affair is commonly called a transaction, and particularly the public transactions; and in other cases even where the name of transaction is used, there is no transaction in the sense here proposed; for it is very ordinary in any contract to say, It is transacted, agreed, and finally contracted; but a proper transaction must imply the doubtful event of a plea : and therefore, when parties commune, and come to an agreement, by clearing the point of right in their claims on either side, though either party pass from much they claimed, there is no transaction, albeit thereby the vexation of a plea be shunned : for it is more the uncertain event than the trouble of legal process that makes a transaction; and therefore when a real transaction is meant, it is fittest to express it in clear terms, that in the differences among parties in such points that are, or may be controverted, both parties acknowledge that the matter is dubious, and the event is uncertain; and therefore either party remits their claims, and come to a middle agreement, wherein it is not necessary that either party remit equally, nor will an inconsiderable abatement infer transaction, or the quitting of penalties though considerable : yet though the express terms of transaction be not used, or the descending from mutual claims, there may be a true transaction; as when parties during the dependence of processes come to agree, giving and taking less than they pleaded, otherwise such an agreement is no transaction, January 10, 1673, Ramsay *contra* Robertson [2 Stair 146; M. 2924].

And if the matter be the evident ground of a dubious plea, whether it be by the uncertainty how the judges will determine, or the uncertainty what effect the execution may have, and even after decreets *in foro contradictorio*, if there remain doubtfulness and uncertain event, there may be place for transaction; as where there is doubtfulness of informality or nullity, whereby decreets may be laid open, and all the interlocutors and probations may be altered; or where these things that were not competent during that decreet, may come to be competent after, or new matter may occur, without fraud or concealment to make delay, *l. 32. Cod. de transactionibus* [C. 2, 4, 32].

A bond granted for a sum in a decreet, and caption thereon was found no transaction without abatement, and so the decreet and bond were found reduceable, July 3, 1668, Row *contra* Houstoun [1 Stair 547; M. 16484]. Nor was giving a bond for accounts without abatement found a transaction, February 18, 1680, Burnet *contra* Ewing [*Sub nom. Ewing* v *Burnet*, 2 Stair 758; M. 16494; 1,7,9; 1,9,8,*supra*]. And albeit it be much controverted, whether solemn and formal decreets can be altered *ex instrumentis de novo repertis*, yet it is generally held that transactions are not ransacted thereby, *l. 19. Cod. de transactionibus* [C.2,4,19]. Neither is transaction convelled upon such grounds of force or fear, as would convel other contracts, but such fear as imports imminent hazard of death or torture, *l. 13 eodem* [C.2,4,13], whereunto the doctors add some other cases, as the imminent fear of the ruin of men's fortunes and estates, yea it must be a fear imminent at the time of the agreement, for no preceding fear will be relevant if the occasion of it be past. Neither doth fraud or circumvention dissolve transactions, if it be but in the motives inducing the agreement, unless it be a deception in the very substance of the act, *l. 22 C. eodem* [c. 2,4,22]. Neither will error or mistake in the matter ransact transactions, if the error be about any circumstantiate quality, or quantity, and not in the substance of the matter.

3. Caution or surety is the promise or contract of any, not for himself, but for another; and therefore this being a gratuitous engagement, having no equivalent cause onerous as to the cautioner, it required a stipulation among the Romans to make it effectual, though it was sometimes by mandate or commission, but now every promise and paction, according to the law of nature, being effectual, it is valid without stipulation.

Caution is interposed any way, by which the consent is truly given, and it may be either by mandate or commission, when the mandator giveth order or warrant to contract with any other party, to that party's behoof; for then that party is the principal debtor, and the mandant is cautioner, or it may be by taking on the debt of another freely. This cautioner in the law is called *ex-promissor*, but is more improperly a cautioner, seeing himself is principal, having but an obligation of relief as mandatar, or negotiator. But the most proper and ordinary cautioner is he who is obliged with, and for, the principal debtor, and is called *ad-promissor* or *fidejussor*, because upon his faith or trust the creditor contracteth. These cautionary promises or contracts are of the same kind or nature with these of which we have now spoken; yet have they something peculiar, which we shall shortly touch, and which resolve in these questions, *First*, Whether cautioners are liable and convenable simply, or in so far as the principal debtor is not *solvendo*, or after discussing of him? *Secondly*, Whether cautioners are liable *in solidum*, or *pro rata*.

4. As to the first, the nature and intent of surety is, that the creditor may be secure of his debt; and therefore cautioners are not ordinarily decerned to pay till the creditor assign the debt, and all security they have for it from the principal, if they have not a distinct interest to retain the security, January 10, 1665, Lesly *contra* Hay [*Sub nom. Lesly* v *Gray*, 1 Stair 247; M. 2111]; and July 10, 1666, Dame Margaret Hay *contra* Crafurd of Kerse

[*Sub nom. Hume* v *Crawford*, 1 Stair 393 ; M.2112 and 3347], where the Lords refused to cause the creditor assign against the co-cautioners, where there was no clause of mutual relief, but that was implied though not expressed.

5. Cautioners cannot be pursued till the principal debtor be discust, unless it be otherwise contracted, or provided by the custom or law of the place. It was contrary by the ancient Roman law, *l.jure nost.5.C de fide.juss.* [c.8,40,5] which was corrected by the Authentic constitution, *Coll.1.Tit.4.* [Nov.4,tit.1]. With us cautioners are frequently bound for, and with, the principal, as full debtors, conjunctly and severally, and thereby *ex pacto* the question ceaseth ; but otherwise the cautioner is understood to be obliged for the principal debtor's performance, and so is liable only *subsidiarie* after the principal is discust, and especially where the performance is a trust or deed proper to the principal debtor. Thus cautioners for executors are only liable after the executors are discust, at least by horning executed, Had. June 27, 1610, Scrogie *contra* Constable of Dundee [Haddington, *Fol. Dict.*1,249 ; M.3587]. The like, though the executor was alleged to be bankrupt, July 24, 1662, Brisbane *contra* Monteith [1 Stair 134 ; M.3588]. But a cautioner for an executor was decerned with him, superseding execution against the cautioner, till the executor were first discust, Dec. 2, 1662, Douglas *contra* La. Ormistoun [*Sub nom. Douglas* v *Lindsay*, 1 Stair 147 ; M.8125]. And executors were not holden discust by horning, till poinding were essayed, and search made for his moveables, though none was condescended on, February 12, 1623, Arnot *contra* Abernethy [Durie 45 ; M.3587]. The like, that search behoved to be made, both for moveables and lands, and they apprised, if any were ; and that horning and caption sufficed not, Hope, Executors, Stuart *contra* Fisher [Hope, *Maj.Pr.* IV,4,40 ; M.3588]. But there is no necessity in discussing the cautioner to call the executor who was discust, December 5, 1623, Rochead *contra* L.Manderston [Durie 87 ; M.2190]. So the diligence for discussing must be according to the estate of the principal debtor : if he have moveables they must be poinded ; if lands, they must be apprised ; if debts, they must be arrested and made forthcoming ; and if there is none of these to be found, discussion by horning and caption is sufficient, though he be not taken by the caption.

6. Cautioners for curators are not liable till they be discust ; yet they were decerned for constituting the debt, with this quality, that before execution against the cautioners, the curators should be discust in their persons, goods and lands, Nov. 20, 1627, Rollock *contra* Corsbie [Durie 314 ; M.2074].

7. Cautioners for factors, as for the factors in Camphire [Campveere or Veere in the Netherlands, the Scottish Staple town in the sixteenth and seventeenth centuries. See Davidson and Gray, *The Scottish Staple at Veere* (1909) ; *Journal of Thomas Cunningham* (ed. Courthope, S.H.S., 1928)] to the burrows, found not convenable till the factors were discust, July 8, 1626, Smith *contra*   [Durie 211 ; M.Supp.30]. And cautioners for these

factors were not found liable for the goods sent to a factor, after he was known to the pursuer to be bankrupt, March 4, 1630, Ritchie *contra* Paterson [Durie 499; M.12427]. Cautioners in suspensions are only liable after discussing the suspenders, and because by the tenor of their act or bond they are bound to pay what shall be decerned against the suspender; if the decreet suspended be turned into a libel, or if the reason of suspension was relevant and instructed, though it were elided by an answer emergent after the suspension, they are free; Spots. Suspension, Weir *contra* Baillie [Spotiswoode, 325; M.2142]. And because of the tenor of the bond, if the suspender die before he was discust, the cautioner was free, seeing the bond of caution bore, that the cautioner shall pay what shall be decerned against the suspender. Yet by the act of sederunt anno 1649 [A.S. 29 Jan. 1650], all cautioners were declared liable, though the suspender died, if the charge being transferred against his heir or executors, the letters were found orderly proceeded, which is in use whensoever the creditor insists on the suspended decreet, and obtains sentence by transference. A cautioner in a suspension of a real action of poinding the ground, was not found liable to pay the annualrent suspended, but to warrant it, Feb. 18, 1623, Blackburn *contra* Drysdale [Durie 47; M.2141]. And a cautioner in a suspension was found liable, though his bond of cautionry contained a clause of relief, which was not signed by the suspender, seeing the bond did not oblige the principal and the cautioner to perform what should be decerned, but only the cautioner to perform, and the principal to relieve him, Jan. 6, 1681, Home *contra* Home [2 Stair 827; M.2142]. In which case, it was only found necessary to discuss the suspender and not the cautioner, in the first suspension, *Ibidem*.

8. Cautioners for loosing of arrestments, are not cautioners for those in whose hands arrestments are made, but for the debtor, whose goods or money are arrested in lieu of the arrestment; and yet they are no farther liable than in so far as was in the hands of the person against whom the arrestment was used, who therefore must be pursued before, or with, the cautioner, that the debt may be constitute, June 21, 1626, L. Balmerinoch *contra* L. Lochinvar [Durie 204; M.788]. And it may be constitute against the cautioners by the oath of these in whose hands arrestment was made, Feb. 2, 1627, *inter eosdem* [Durie 267; M. 789].

9. Cautioners are liable according to the oath of the principal debtor, which is a sufficient probation against them, because their obligation being accessory, it is liable to the same probation with the principal, as is clear from the case last instanced. But it is more dubious, whether the cautioners run all other hazard with the principal debtor; wherein, though the cautioner of an executor was not admitted to propone exhausting, being proponed by the executor himself, and he failing therein, March 4, 1623, Wood *contra* Executors of Ker [*Sub nom. Wood* v *Wood*, Durie 54; M.14049]; yet it was found, that where exhausting was omitted by the executor, it was admitted for the cautioner, being instantly verified, July 9, 1623, Arnot *contra* Execu-

tors of Hume and Mastertoun [Durie 71 ; M. 14051]. And likewise, though the principal intented reduction, but was holden as confessed by his oath *de calumnia*, yet that was found not to prejudge the cautioner, or to exclude him from insisting, in proving that same point, Jan. 22, 1629, Lord Carberry *contra* Kello [*Sub nom. Fairbairn* v *Kello*, Durie 416 ; M. 14053]. Whence we may conclude, that collusion or wilful omission, or negligence of the principal, hindereth not the cautioner ; but if the principal, proponing any reason of defence, used probation by witnesses which was not found to prove the same, it would not be again admitted to be proven by the cautioner, with other witnesses ; yet a cautioner was not secluded to prove a defence, wherein the principal succumbed, it not being intimate to the cautioner, Dec. 11, 1673, Earl of Kinghorn *contra* E. Wintoun [2 Stair 238 ; M. 14062]. But this was a defence upon a writ, not by witnesses, against the principal finding caution to be answerable to what should be decerned.

10. Cautioners use to be given before the Admiral, or other Courts, where the defender is attached to be put in prison till the process be discussed and the decreet satisfied ; which is sometimes only *judicio sisti*, that the party shall appear at all the diets of process, or *judicatum solvi*, or both ; to which, caution as law will, is equivalent, importing that the defender shall do all that law requires in the present case, Jan. 31, 1633, Stevenson *contra* Law [Durie 666 ; M. 4832] ; and Nov. 16, 1636, Stuart *contra* Gedd [Durie 821 ; M. 2033]. So though advocation be obtained, the cautioner, as law will, must sist the principal when he produces the advocation, who must then remain in ward, as he was before caution was found, till the cause be discussed, as was found, Feb. 20, 1666,   *contra* M'Culloch [1 Stair 360 ; M. 369]. The like found that a cautioner, *judicio sisti aut judicatum solvi*, was liberate by putting the party in prison, though not at the calling of the cause, July 10, 1666, Thomson *contra* Binnie [1 Stair 392 ; M. 2034].

11. Cautioners may be accessory to obligations, though the principal debtor be not liable by any statute or custom, it giving him a special privilege ; as minors, or wives clad with husbands, Nov. 28, 1623, Shaw *contra* Maxwell [Durie 83 ; M. 2074]. But where the obligation is in itself null, and hath not so much as a natural obligation ; if the principal be free, the cautioner is also free ; as if the principal did not at all, or did not validly subscribe, Hope, *fidejussor* [Hope, *Maj. Pr.* 11, 11]. The like may be said of obligations by pupils, fools, or furious persons, whose cautioners are free with themselves. But a cautioner was found liable for the whole sum, though the principal party subscribed but by one notary, whereby he would be only liable for a hundred pounds, July 8, 1680, Johnston *contra* L. Romano [2 Stair 784 ; M. 2076]. And a cautioner was found liable, though the creditor, having received a disposition of moveables from the principal debtor in security of his sum, promised not to trouble his person or goods, reserving power to distress the cautioner, July 10, 1680, Leitch of Mousie *contra* Hadderwick [2 Stair 784 ; M. 2077], but cautioners are free with the principal, if the

obligation were obtained *vi aut fraude*, though the cautioner were bound as full debtor, Jan. 13, 1691, Lord Hatton *contra* E. Aberdeen [Not found]; for in such cases there is *labes realis, quæ rei inhæret* [1,9,8,*supra*].

12. As to the other question, Whether cautioners be liable *in solidum*, unless they be expressly bound conjunctly and severally: If they become cautioners at divers times, without relation one to the other, there is no doubt but, as they obliged themselves, so are they all liable *in solidum ;* but when they oblige together, or with relation to one another, the nature of the deed importeth no more than surety; so that each is liable for what is wanting by the principal, and what is wanting by the other cautioners: but this holds even when parties are bound, not only as cautioners for, but as principals with, the debtor, for then they are liable only *pro rata*, unless they be bound conjunctly and severally, or when the matter of the obligation is an indivisible fact [1,17,20,*infra*].

13. Cautioners ordinarily have no action against the principal debtor, till they be distressed, unless the clause or bond of relief bear, "to free, relieve and skaithless keep them ;" yet where an executor was becoming poor, the cautioner pursuing him to relieve him, or find caution, was thought by the Lords to have interest so to do, Jan. 19, 1627, Thomson *contra* Heriot [Durie 259 ; M. 2113]. If a cautioner pay, without intimation to the principal debtor in due time before litiscontestation, it is on his peril, and the principal is not obliged to relieve him, if he had a competent defence, that would have excluded the creditor, Dec. 19, 1632, Maxwel of Gribtoun *contra* E. Nithsdale [Durie 660 ; M. 2115].

Cautioners getting assignation from the creditor, whether they insist in the creditor's name, or their own as his assignee, are obliged to allow their own part; July 8, 1664, Nisbet *contra* Leslie [1 Stair 211 ; M. 3392]; in this cause there was a clause of mutual relief amongst the cautioners. Co-principals bound conjunctly and severally, are mutually as cautioners for their shares, liable to relieve each other though there were no express clause of relief, which holds also in co-cautioners, though there were no clause of mutual relief amongst them, June 19, 1662, Wallace *contra* Forbes [1 Stair 111 ; M. 3346; 1,8,9,*supra*]. Co-cautioners were found liable for relief *ex natura rei*, without an express clause of relief, Jan. 27, 1675, Monteith *contra* Rodger [2 Stair 312 ; M. 3351]. Cautioners having paid, if they seek their relief from the other cautioners, any ease they get on special favour to themselves, hinders them to obtain of the rest their full proportion ; as if they got ease by transaction, or upon account of questioning the debt, they can ask no more than what they truly gave out, allowing their own share, as was found in a charge to the cautioner's behoof against the co-cautioner, July 27, 1672, Brodie *contra* Keith [2 Stair 111 ; M. 3393]; June 28, 1665, Monteith *contra* Anderson [1 Stair 288 ; M. 1044]. A cautioner in a suspension of a bond, wherein there were four cautioners, being distressed, and having paid and obtained assignation from the creditor, was found to have access against the first four cautioners, allowing only his own fifth part, Feb. 23, 1671, Arnold of Barncaple against Gordoun of Holm [1 Stair 728 ; M. 14641].

14. As caution, so oaths are accessory to all promises, pactions, and contracts : not only these declaratory oaths, which are ordinary in the discussing of rights, whereby all persons are bound to declare the truth upon oath as witnesses, or as parties against themselves in civil causes, but promissory oaths, whereby they promise to observe or fulfil any thing *activè*, or *passivè* never to quarrel it ; concerning which oaths there is no small matter of debate among lawyers, what effect they have. All do agree, that, in so far as any promise can be effectual, a promissory oath is valid, and hath this much of advantage, that the creditor is the more secure, because he may justly expect the debtor will be more observant of his oath than of his ordinary paction, seeing the penalty of the violation of an oath deserves a more atrocious judgment than any other, God being called as a witness and a judge ; which effect it hath, though adhibited to that which by the matter hath an anterior obligation ; as obligations betwixt husband and wife, parents and children, in these things in which they are mutually obliged, or where there hath preceded or is conjoined an obligatory contract, which of itself is binding without an oath. *2do*, All do also agree, that oaths interposed in things unlawful, not only as to the matter, but as to the manner, are not obligatory ; so no man justifieth Herod, for taking John Baptist's head without a cause, upon pretence of his oath. *3tio*, All do agree, that in matters free and in our own power, as contracts are obligatory, so oaths are much more.

The question then remains, Whether, in acts *civiliter* inefficacious, the interposition of an oath can give efficacy ? or whether that which is done *indebito modo*, becomes valid by an oath to perform it, or not to impugn it, and if that efficacy will not only extend to the swearer, but to his heirs or successors ? Of this, there are multitudes of cases and examples debated among civilians. As by the civil law naked pactions are not efficacious to ground any action upon ; *Quæritur*, Whether, if the paction be with an oath, the creditor may not effectually pursue thereupon ? By law likewise the deeds of minors, having curators not consenting, are null ; but if the minor swear not to quarrel them, *quid juris* ? Minors lesed have by law the benefit of restitution, but if they do the deed upon oath to perform it, or not to quarrel it, whether, if they pursue to reduce it, will they be excluded by their oath ? or if a wife be obliged personally for debt, and swear to perform it, or never to come in the contrary, whether yet she may defend herself with her privilege ? or if a woman's land, given her for security of her tocher *donatione propter nuptias*, being sold by her husband with her consent, which the law declareth null, whether her oath interposed will validate it ? or if *pactum legis commissoriæ in pignoribus* confirmed with an oath will be valid ? or if an oath for performance will exclude the common exceptions of fear, force, or fraud ? And innumerable such cases, whereby positive law prohibiteth any act to be done, or declareth it void simply, or void if it be not done in such a manner, and with such solemnities.

For clearing these and the like cases, we are chiefly to consider, *quæ sunt partes judicis*, or what is the judge's duty in deciding cases wherein oaths are interposed, rather than what concerns the parties, and the obligations upon their consciences by these oaths *in foro poli ;* and therefore we shall take up the matter distinctly in these ensuing points.

First, If an action be pursued upon a ground ineffectual in law, albeit the defender hath interposed an oath never to come in the contrary, yet that would not be sustained by the judge, though the defender should not appear or object, which is ineffectual of itself; in that case the interposition of an oath hath no effect: As if by the civil law an action were intented upon a promise or a naked paction, with an oath interposed, the action would not be sustained, albeit the defender should not appear, or appearing should not object, that it were a naked paction: Or, if a declarator should be intented, to declare *pactum legis commissoriæ in pignoribus* to be valid and effectual, though it were libelled that the other party did swear never to come in the contrary, yet the judge could not sustain such an action; nor generally can sustain any action which is unjust or irrelevant, albeit it should not be opposed, but consented to simply, or with an oath never to quarrel it; because in such cases *pactis privatorum non derogatur juri communi.* For the consent or oath of no party can make that just which is unjust, nor can make that sufficient or effectual, that is deficient in its essentials. As if any party should grant a disposition of lands or annualrents, and declare, that it should be effectual for poinding the ground without infeftment, and should swear never to come in the contrary thereof, if thereupon the obtainer should pursue a poinding of the ground, the same could not be sustained, because these rights are defective in their essentials, wanting infeftment: and yet in these cases, if the party should object, or any way hinder the effect of his oath, he contravenes the same; but the judge not sustaining the same doth no wrong, because his not sustaining proceeds upon a defect of an essential requisite, and not because of any exception or objection of the party. From this ground it is, that if a wife be pursued or charged upon a bond for debt subscribed by her, bearing expressly her to be designed a wife, though it were condescended on, that she made faith never to come in the contrary, the Lords would not sustain the pursuit or charge; because by the very action itself it appeareth, that the summons or charges are irrelevant and contrary to law, which declareth a wife's bond for debt *ipso jure* null; and therefore, though she may be faulty in suspending, or hindering the performance of the engagement of her oath, the Lords do justly reject such an irrelevant libel or charge, as they did betwixt Birsh *contra* Douglas [1 Stair 181; M. 5963] Feb. 18, 1663, where her bond was suspended *simpliciter*, as being expressly granted by a wife, though she judicially made faith never to come in the contrary: Or if the husband should suspend, and allege, that such an obligation or oath could not be effectual against his goods, or the person of his wife in his prejudice, there could be neither wrong on his part, nor on the judge's part, as said is.

Secondly, If either action or exception be founded upon that which is not defective in essentials, but in circumstantials, ordained and commanded by law, the defect thereof may be supplied by the other party's consent, much more by their oaths ; and in these cases *quæ fieri non debent, facta valent :* for every prohibition of law doth not annul the deed done contrary thereto, but infers the penalty of law upon the doers ; as tacks of teinds are prohibited to be set by prelates for longer than nineteen years, and by inferior beneficed persons, for longer than their life, and five years thereafter, under the pain of infamy and deprivation, Parl. 1617, cap. 4 [Act 1617, c. 4 ; A.P.S. IV, 534, c. 4]. Yet it was found, that a tack granted for a longer time was not thereby null, Nov. 9, 1624, Hope *contra* the Minister of Craighall [Durie 144 ; M. 7943]. So likewise members of the College of Justice are prohibited to buy pleas [Land Purchase Act, 1594, c. 220 ; A.P.S. IV, 68, c. 26], yet the right acquired contrary thereto was not found null or process refused thereupon, but that it might be a ground of deprivation, Had. June 5, 1611, Cunningham, Advocate *contra* Maxwell of Drumcoultron [Haddington, *Fol. Dict.* II, 24 ; M. 9495]. In like manner the solemnities of marriages are prescribed in the law, and all persons are prohibited to proceed any other way ; so they are appointed to be publicly solemnized by a minister, and the consent of parents are required ; yet the want of these will not annul the marriage, because it is a divine contract which cannot receive its essentials from positive law or statute ; whence it is justly said, *Multa impediunt matrimonium contrahendum, quæ non dirimunt contractum* [1, 4, 6, *supra*].

Some deeds are declared null *ipso jure,* and others are only annullable *ope exceptionis,* or by way of restitution, or at least, where something in fact must be alleged and proven, which doth not appear by the right or deed itself ; and so belongeth not to the judge to advert to, but must be proponed by the party. In these an oath interposed doth debar the swearer from proposing or making use of such exceptions and alledgances ; and therefore, neither may the party justly propone the same, nor the judge justly sustain the same ; for there be many things of themselves relevant and competent in law, which yet may be excluded by a personal objection, against the proponer ; for in many cases, allegances competent to parties may be renounced, so that though they be relevant, that personal objection will exclude the proponer, but his oath is much stronger than his renunciation, and therefore, seeing such points are not *partes judicis,* nor consisting in any intrinsic nullity or defect, though the law allow or prescribe them, yet it doth not mention or express, that though the party in whose favours they are introduced renounce them simply, or with an oath, that these shall be admitted ; and therefore they are justly to be repelled, being *in detrimentum animi* of the proponer. This ground solveth most of the cases before proponed ; for if a minor pursue restitution upon minority and lesion, his oath to perform, or not to quarrel the deed in question, excludes him, both by the civil law and our custom ; for by the Authentic *sacramenta puberum sponte facta, super contractibus rerum suarum non retractandis, inviolabiliter custodiantur, C. si adversus vend.*, and it was so decided in an obligement by a minor, to quit twenty chalders of victual, provided in his contract of marriage, Jan. 15, 1634, Hepburn *contra* Seaton [Spotiswoode 205 ; M. 8959], where it was found, that the oath was valid, though not judicial. The like was found, that a minor having given a bond for his father's debt, whom he represented not, and being sworn not to come in the contrary, the same was not reduced upon minority and lesion, Feb. 10, 1672, Waugh *contra* Bailzie of Dunraget [2 Stair 69 ; M. 8922]. Upon this same ground, a minor having curators not consenting, swearing to perform his obligation, or never to come in the contrary, his exception of its being thus null, because it consists in fact, and most be proven that he was minor, and that he had curators, may justly be repelled, and he excluded from proponing thereof, in respect of his oath, seeing it is not the part of the judge to know or advert thereto ; but his curators who have not sworn, may, yea must propone that nullity, because they have not sworn. But to prevent the inconveniency of inducing minors so to swear, it is declared by the 19th act, Parl. 1681 [Oaths of Minors Act, 1681, c. 19 ; A.P.S. VIII, 352, c. 86], that the elicitor shall be infamous and the contract null, and the nullity may be declared at the instance of any relation to the minor ; but it is the judge's part to advert to the nullity, and therefore, though the swearer is not allowed to object against his oath, yet any friend might, if the judge reserves it. *Vid. supra Tit. 6 §44* [1,6,44, *supra*].

On this ground likewise, the exception or reason of reduction upon force or fear is excluded, if the party have sworn to perform or not quarrel the deed, which is the sentence of the canon law, not only as to wives' consent to the alienation of lands given to them *donatione propter nuptias*, which is both null, and presumed to be granted upon her fear or reverence of her husband, *C. licet mulieris, l. 6 de jure jurando* [Sext. 2, 11, 2] *C. cum continget, de jurejurando* [*Extra.* 2, 24, 28], whereby such consents and oaths being interposed, are declared to be valid ; but generally, no deed having an oath interposed can be recalled upon an alledgeance of force or fear, *C. 3 & 4, de iis quæ vim metumve* [*Extra.* 1, 40, 3 and 4]; and albeit the Pope assumes to himself liberty "to absolve from such oaths as are done upon fear," yet they are declared of themselves to be valid, which our custom followeth, and was so determined, Parl. 1481, cap. 83 [A.P.S. II, 140, c. 14], and was so decided by the Lords, July 8, 1642, Grant *contra* Balvaird [Durie 898 ; M. 16483 ; 1, 9, 8, *supra*], where a wife was excluded from the reduction of the alienation of her liferent lands *super vi et metu*, because she had judicially ratified the same, and sworn never to come in the contrary ; neither was it respected, that the oath as well as the disposition was by force and fear ; for this is the great foundation of all public transactions betwixt different nations, where oft-times the one party is induced through fear, to that which otherwise they would not yield to, and yet both parties acquiesce in the religion of an oath interposed; so the oath of Israel to the King of Babylon was binding upon them, though thereby the people of God subjected themselves to a Heathen King; and therefore they are accused by Jeremiah for the breach thereof, and likewise for breaking the oath to their servants, whom they manumitted upon mere necessity for their defence.

From this reason also it is, that the exception or reason of reduction upon deception, fraud or circumvention is excluded, if an oath be interposed, whereof we have the most eminent example of the oath of the people of Israel to the Gibeonites who purposely deceived and circumvened them, feigning themselves to be a people far off, though they were of the Hivites whom Israel was commanded utterly to destroy; against which judicial precept, they being induced through error and deceit to swear, the oath was binding on them and their posterity, and was punished upon Saul for breach thereof. From this instance we have occasion to return to the last case; whether oaths be only personal, obliging the swearer, and so inherent to their persons that they bind not their heirs? Wherein some are for the affirmative, that even heirs are obliged as being *fictione juris eadem persona cum defuncto ;* which is also fortified by the punishment in the successors of Israel in the days of Saul; but I rather incline to the negative, that heirs are not obliged, but only the persons who swear, which is the more common opinion of lawyers, civilians, and canonists; nor doth the instance infer the contrary, because oaths by societies and incorporations, continue not as they are heirs, but because the society dieth not, and is ever the same, especially in contracts betwixt nations, where the parties intend not to oblige particular persons then living, but the nation; neither doth the fiction of law operate in this case; for no position or fiction of law can either extend or abridge the obligation of an oath, which is *alterius et superioris juris.* Yet in the process between the tutor and curators of Aberlady, the oath of the [minor] predecessor was found valid against his heir, excepting upon his predecessor's interest, being an oath before the act Parl. 1681 [Oaths of Minors Act, 1681, c. 19; A.P.S. VIII, 352, c. 85], Jan.   1691, [Not found]. *Vid. supra. Tit. 6 § 36 in fin.* [1, 6, 36, *supra*].

There remains yet this objection, that if oaths be so effectual, great inconveniencies will follow, a door being opened to force and fraud; for by the same facility that parties are induced to act, they will be induced to confirm it by an oath. It is answered, *Incommodum non servit argumentum ;* which therefore was not regarded in the case of Grant *contra* Balvaird [Durie 898 ; M. 16483], but there may be a remedy by severe punishment upon parties, who shall induce others to swear to their own hurt, which the Prince may inflict, and repair the damage of the læsed, and is partly remedied by the said act, Parl. 1681 [Oaths of Minors Act, 1681, c. 19; A.P.S. VIII, 352, c. 85]. It is true, if the fear be such as stupifieth, and takes away the act of reason, there is nothing done, because there can no contract in its substantials consist without the knowledge and reason of the party; or if the deceit be *in substantialibus*, as if a man should by mistake marry one woman for another, there is nothing done, except when an act of reason is exercised: but upon motives by fear, error, or mistake, the deed is in itself valid, though annullable by fear or fraud, which are excluded by the oath, against which they cannot be alleged by the party who hath sworn, but may be proponed by his heirs, executors, or cautioners, or any other having interest.

Having now spoken of the several kinds of obligations, before we go over to real rights, it is fit to touch the common considerations that fall into all or most obligations, as to the implement or performance thereof, viz. delay, interest, profit, time, place, and manner of performance.

15. Delay or *mora*, is not that time, which by the adjection of a day or condition, or which by law is allowed, to perform, but that time which runs after lawful delay is past, and is the debtor's fault in not performing his obligation; so that it seldom makes any part of the contract whereupon the obligation ariseth, except penalties be adjected in case of delay, or an estimation made of the interest. Delay is incurred in pure obligations by interpellation or requisition; for when no term is prefixed, the option of the creditor is the time of performance; and though requisition be most clear and secure by the instrument of a notary, and therefore verbal requisition by a merchant to a skipper, to loose after the ship was loaded, was not found sufficient without an instrument, where the charter-party had no definite term, but to do diligence to transport the goods, Feb. 14, 1678, Calderwood *contra* Angus [2 Stair 613; M. Supp. 78]; yet in some cases, that is not necessary, but being naked emission of words, it will only be probable by the debtor's oath or writ. In obligations to a day, delay is incurred by the passing of the term; *nam dies interpellat pro homine* [1, 15, 8, *supra*]. In obligations conditional, delay cannot be till the condition be purified, and even then either requisition or a term is requisite; for it is frequent in obligations conditional to add a term also; so that the existence of the condition makes the conditional obligation to become pure, and so requisition is to be used before delay if no term be expressed. But if there be no party who can require or be required, delay is incurred if performance be not made so soon as it can be; as is in the case of restitution of things found, or come in the hands of others without contract, which is seldom known to the owner. So also in obligations due to pupils delay is incurred without requisition, *l. 1* §*ult. de usuris* [D. 22, 1, 1 or C. 4, 32, 1]. And in obligations by delinquence, delay is without requisition, and runneth from the first time performance can be made.

Legal execution is not competent ordinarily till delay, because none should be pursued till he have failed; yet in some cases the debtor may be pursued before the term, to pay at the term, as *si vergat ad inopiam*. Yea in removing it seems very expedient to pursue the party warned even before the term, to remove at the term, otherwise the lands cannot be safely set, the tenant not knowing if others will remove willingly, and may not be uncertain in that point, which is a public interest, for setting land and preventing waste; but upon all obligations which are truly contracted, the legal diligences of arrestment or inhibition may be used even before requisition or the term of performance [I, 3, 8, *supra* ; IV, 20, 29, *infra*]. The ordinary effect of delay is, that when the obligation is to give or deliver any thing, if it perish even without the debtor's fault, it perisheth to the debtor, and must be made good to the creditor, unless it appear that it would have so perished with the creditor, which seldom can be made appear; because it is ordinarily presumed, that if the thing had been delivered, the creditor would have disposed of it, and so been free of the hazard, especially if it be a thing for sale, not for keeping, and if any occasion was offered to have disposed thereof [I, 13, 2, *supra*].

16. The next effect of delay is the interest or damage of the creditor; for if the obligation be performed within the due time and in due manner, there is no interest; if not, after the delay incurred by requisition or term, it is in the creditor's option to pursue for performance, or for damage and interest. But in some cases, delay may be purged, which is much *in arbitrio judicis*, and is always granted in things penal, where the penalty is great, and exceeds the true interest, as in non-payment of feu-duties, which infers the loss of the feu; and in clauses irritant, in wadsets, when delay is purged, the hazard returns upon the creditor, and the debtor is free, if the thing to be delivered perish; but if the creditor do again require after the former delay is purged, delay is again incurred by that new requisition.

This is a general rule *locum facti imprestabilis subit damnum et interesse*, yet in some cases if the delay be wilful or fraudulent, that the thing might become imprestable, all personal execution by escheat and caption will proceed. Interest may either be competent for the whole obligation as when it is imprestable, or when any part or qualification is unperformed for the value thereof. Interest doth both comprehend *damnum emergens et lucrum cessans*; the first is commonly competent, the last but in some cases, and that ordinarily for such gain as the creditors used to make; and so the delay of bills of exchange, gives exchange and re-exchange, as the creditor's condition requires [I, II, 7, *supra*], but would give neither, when not drawn for the use of a merchant, or him that behoved to obtain the sum for a merchant, for present use. In ejections, spuilzies, and other atrocious delinquencies, the greatest profits that might have been made, are allowed as the creditor's interest. In obligations which are not *in dando* but *in faciendo*, the common opinion of the doctors is, that there can be no pursuit for performance, but only for interest; for before the delay there is no pursuit, and after, the creditor cannot pursue for performance, but for interest, *l. 13. in fine ff. de re judicata* [D. 42, 1, 13]; but it seems more suitable to equity, that it should be in the creditor's option even after the delay, either to suit for performance or interest, as he pleaseth, if both be prestable.

In obligations *in dando*, where there is delay incurred, it will not be purged by offering performance, especially if the thing have a certain definite season of its use, as grain of such a year, if it be not delivered *debito tempore*, the delay will not be purged by offering it after, but the price comes in place of it.

There is a constitution of Justinian, restricting interest where things certain are in the principal obligation, to the double, and in others, allowing judges to inquire what damage truly is sustained, and to determine accordingly, *l. unic. C. de sent. quæ pro eo, quod interest* [C. 7, 47]; wherefore we extend not annuals in the English double bonds beyond the stock, because they are penal, and should do the like in any penal annuals, but not in conventional annuals. These who remove not after warning within burgh are only liable for double mail that they paid, if it were not considerably within the just rent.

In interests, the value thereof may either be that which is agreed by parties which, if high and penal, may be modified, or ordinarily the common rate, and sometimes *pretium affectionis*, in these cases, where the creditor hath *juramentum in litem*, the value was estimated by the Romans, in *bonæ fidei judiciis*, as at the time of sentence, in *stricti juris*, as it was worth the time of litiscontestation; this distinction is not now of much use with us, and therefore it is rather in the arbitriment of the judge to ponder all circumstances, and accordingly modify the value either as at the time of delay or citation, litiscontestation or sentence.

17. Profit which comprehends fruits is a part of the creditor's interest in sale; for by the special nature of that contract all accessions and fruits belong to the buyer from the time of the sale, and so it is a part of that contract; but in other contracts it is only due *post moram*, and is no part of the contract. The sentence of the Roman law is in this, as in the estimation *in actionibus bonæ fidei*, and *in arbitrariis* fruits and profits become due from delay, which also takes place in legacies; but in these which are *stricti juris*, if the obligation be to deliver that which was the creditor's before, the fruits and profit follow the property, and are due from delay; but where the property was not the creditor's, the fruits are not due till litiscontestation, *l. 3 & l. 34 & l. 38 ff. de usuris* [D. 22, 1, 3; 34; 38].

18. The time of performing obligations is at, or before, the term; in obligations not to a day, so soon as requisition is made; which cannot be understood in that instant, if the thing require more time to perform it, but such time is allowed, that by ordinary diligence it may be performed; *Vid.* §5 *Inst. de V. O.* [Inst. 3, 15, 5] so that delay is not understood till that be past; as when a party is obliged to do a work, he must have so much time as the work requires; or if money be required, if the debtor offer within twenty-four hours, it would not infer delay; for it is not his part to carry a sum of money about him, nor to have it ready at each instant, *et nec cum sacco adire debet, l. 105 de solut.* [D. 46, 3, 105]. And passing an instant, the strictest time law respecteth is an artificial day or twenty-four hours; if the debtor offer

before the day the creditor cannot refuse it, seeing the day is in favours of the debtor, and so may be renounced by him; if a term be expressed, there needs no requisition; *nam dies interpellat pro homine*, as said is.

19. The place for performing obligations, if it be expressed, is to be observed, and another place cannot be obtruded, though it may seem as convenient for the creditor, unless there be not safe access to that place, in which case the debtor may offer, and the creditor may pursue, as if no place were named; in which case he hath the choice to pursue, either in the place of the contract, if he find the debtor there, or wherever the debtor is convenable; and even where the place is expressed, the creditor may elsewhere pursue for performance, if he allow the debtor's damage, in not paying at the place appointed; but if the thing to be performed, be delivery of a certain species or body, which cannot follow a man, as a horse or a dog, but an inanimate body, as a coach, coffer, cabinet, or the like, if no place be expressed, the place where it is must be understood; but if it be a quantity simply, the place of contract, or where the debtor resides, is understood; for the debtor is not presumed to follow the creditor's residence, if custom or paction be not otherwise.

20. As to the manner of performing obligations, the main question is when there are *correi debendi*, whether performance must be by all *in solidum*, or but *pro rata* ? [1,13,10; 1,17,12,*supra*.] For eviting the question, 1°, Debtors use to be bound conjunctly and severally, but when that is omitted, the debtors are understood to be but bound conjunctly *et pro rata ;* for *in dubiis potior est conditio debitoris :* if the debtors were bound by several obligations, not relating to others as becoming parts of the same obligation, all are bound severally and *in solidum ;* but when they are bound together in one bond, and so *correi debendi*, by the ancient Roman law they were all liable *in solidum*, which was altered by Justinian's Novel Constitution [Nov. 99,c.1], giving the benefit of division *pro rata*, as to these who are solvent and not far absent, unless the matter of the obligation be indivisible, as the delivery of a man, an horse, or any thing which law considers not as quantity or *genus*, but as *corpus ;* for oft-times that cannot be divided without destruction of the thing, and always it is the creditor's interest that it should not be divided. 2°, Obligations *in faciendo*, are ordinarily indivisible, *l. stipul. 2 ff. de verborum oblig.* [D.45,1,2] as was lately found in an obligation by two owners of a ship, to carry corns from one port to another, both were found liable *in solidum ;* or if the obligation be *in non faciendo*, that such a thing shall not be done, but that they shall hinder, each is obliged *in solidum*, June 14, 1672, Sutherland and Grant *contra* Flat [*Sub nom. Groat & Flatt* v *Sutherland*, 2 Stair 84; M.14632; 1,12,14,*supra*]. This also concerns the manner of performance, that in alternatives *electio est debitoris*, whose part is more favourable, but the adjection of a penalty or estimation, makes not the obligation alternative: but if any of the members of the alternative become not entire, the debtor cannot offer that member, January 18, 1675,

Collector of the King and Lords' taxation *contra* Inglis of Straitoun [2 Stair 305; M. Supp. 33].

The manner also of performance admits not that the debtor may perform by parts that which he is obliged to by one obligation, if it be not that, which cannot be performed all at once, as the performance of some acts, requiring divers seasons; but otherwise it must be done without intermission, for neither can money or grain be all delivered at one instant; but that is understood to be performed together, which is without intermission; yet the civil law favours the debtor so far, that the creditor cannot refuse to accept a part of the money due, which our custom allows not.

Title 18. Liberation from Obligations.

HAVING thus gone through the constitution and effects of Conventional Obligations, it is requisite, in the next place, to consider their destitution, and how they cease, which we have expressed in the general term of Liberation, comprehending not only payment, but all the ways by which obligations or bonds are dissolved or loosed, and debtors liberated. We are not here to speak of the objections competent against obligations from their nullities, for such were never truly obligations; neither of the common exceptions against them, and other rights, as prescription, litiscontestation, *res judicata*, circumvention, extortion, &c. of which in their proper places; but only of the proper ways of taking away obligations; and these are either by contrary consent, or by performance, or the equivalent thereof.

1. *First,* As consent constituteth, so contrary consent destituteth or extinguisheth any obligation, whether it be by declaration, renunciation, discharge, or *per pactum de non petendo*, which may be extended, not only to conventional, but to natural obligations, as to any duty omitted or transgressed which is past, though not to the discharge of the obligation itself as to the future; for love to God or our neighbour, and most of the duties betwixt husbands and wives, parents and children, cannot be discharged as to the future; neither can future fraud or force be effectually discharged, for such *cadunt in turpem causam*.

A discharge of a sum payable to a man and his wife, and the bairns of the marriage, subscribed only by the husband, excludes the wife from her liferent-right to that sum, January 21, 1680, Caddel *contra* Raith [2 Stair 743; M. 4275]. Neither was a discharge to a cautioner upon payment found competent to the principal debtor, unless the cautioner concur; for the principal may be distressed by the cautioner, using the name of the creditor as his cedent, July 13, 1675, Scrimzeour *contra* E.Northesk [2 Stair 343; M.3550]. A discharge to one of more debtors, viz. co-tutors, found not to liberate the rest, except in so far as satisfaction was made, or as the other co-tutors would be excluded from relief by the party discharged, December 19, 1669, Seatoun *contra* Seatoun [1 Stair 575; M.3547]. But payment made by one party whose lands were affected by inhibition, did liberate the rest *pro tanto*, though it bore not in satisfaction, but to restrict the inhibition, January 5, 1675, Ballantine *contra* Edgar [2 Stair 299; M.7807]. Discharges by masters to tenants for rent, by their subscription, without witnesses, though not being holograph, are sustained even against singular successors, in regard of the custom so to discharge, November 7, 1674, Boyd *contra* Story [Dirleton 76; M.12457]. And by the same custom, receipts and discharges of merchants and factors, *in re mercatoria*, are sufficient by the party's subscription, albeit neither holograph, nor with witnesses [IV,42,6, *infra*].

The main question remains, how far general discharges are to be extended, which are of two sorts: one where there are particulars discharged with a general clause, and then the general is not extended to matters of greater importance than the greatest of these particulars, unless both be of one kind, as a greater sum with lesser sums expressed, February 24, 1636, Lawson *contra* L.Arkinglas [Durie 797; M.5023]. The other is, where the discharge is only general without particulars, which useth not to be extended to clauses of warrandice, clauses of relief, or obligements to infeft, or to purchase real rights; and therefore a discharge of all debts, sums of money, bonds, obligations, clags, claims, for whatsoever cause, was found not to discharge a contract for purchasing an apprising of lands, and disponing the same, November 19, 1680, Dalgarno *contra* L.Tolquhon [2 Stair 802; M.5030]. Neither was a discharge wholly general, extended to an obligation by the party discharged as cautioner, unless it were proven that the discharge was granted upon satisfaction of that debt, Hope, Bonds, Ogilvie *contra* Napier [Hope, *Maj.Pr.* II,14,13]. But it was extended to contravention, though there was a decreet suspended after the discharge, Hope, Contravention, L.Aitoun *contra* his Brother [Hope, *Maj.Pr.* VI,35,30]. Yea a general discharge in a decreet-arbitral, was found to liberate the submitter-cautioner, Hope, Bonds, Lady Balmastiner and her Son *contra* Weddel [Hope, *Maj.Pr.* II,14,14; M.5023]. Neither was a general discharge found to extend to a sum assigned by the discharger before the discharge, albeit the assignation was not intimated, seeing the discharger was not presumed to know the want of the intimation, unless it were proven that the sum was particularly communed upon, or satisfied at obtaining the general discharge, February 3, 1671, Blair of Bagillo *contra* Blair of Denhead [1 Stair 714; M.940]. Neither was a general discharge extended to sums, whereunto the discharger succeeded after the discharge, February 14, 1633, Halyburtoun *contra* Hunter [Durie 673 ; M. 5042].

2. Three subsequent discharges do presume that all precedings are past from; as, first, the discharges of three immediate subsequent years' rent, Had. June 21, 1610, Howison *contra* Hamilton [Not found]. This was sustained, though the discharges were only granted by a chamberlain, Hope, Clause irritant, Lord Wedderburn *contra* Nisbet [Hope, *Maj.Pr.* 111,23, 14 ; M. 7181]. This was sustained to purge a clause irritant, yea, though some of the discharges were granted to the father, and the rest to the son as heir, February 17, 1631, Williamson *contra* L. Bagillo [Durie 570 ; M. 11393], which was extended to bygones, though a bond was granted for them, the bond bearing expressly for a term, and having lain over very long, and all subsequent terms paid, March 18, 1634, Douglas *contra* Bothwel [Durie 713 ; M. 11395]. But discharges of three subsequent years, granted by merchants who had bought farms, did not liberate from former years, Had. March 26, 1626, Master of Corstorphin *contra*   [*Sub anno* 1636, Durie 807; M. 11396]. Neither where the discharges were not in writ, February 19, 1631, Moristoun *contra* Tennents of Eastnisbet [Durie 572 ; M. 11394]. Neither where the payment of three terms was acknowledged by the party's oath, which bore not three terms immediately subsequent, Had. March 26, 1622, Kennedy *contra* Dalrymple of Stair [Haddington, *Fol. Dict.* 11,136 ; M. 11393]. Nor where there were two years' discharges, and receipts making up the third, March 23, 1631, L. Rosyth *contra* Wood [Durie 585 ; M. 11395]; and therefore receipts, though being joined they would make up more than three years, yet infer not this presumption, that all preceding years are paid; yea, one discharge for three consequent terms or years, would not infer the same; for the presumption is mainly inferred from the reiteration of the discharges without reservation, which no prudent man is presumed to do. The presumption is also introduced in favour of debtors, that they be not obliged to preserve forty years' discharges; and therefore, if the payment be annual, there must be three discharges of three years immediately following one another, as in the payment of farms; but if the payment be termly, as in annualrents, or silver rents, the ground of the presumption holds by three several discharges, of three immediate subsequent terms, Hope, Bonds, Weyms *contra* La. St. Columb [Hope, *Maj.Pr.* 11,14,15 ; M. 11391]. But as to the discharges of factors or chamberlains, three subsequent discharges are only sufficient against the chamberlain, during his commission, and against his constituent, who gave him power to discharge, during that commission. But the strongest of these presumptions admits of contrary probation by the debtor, that he knows there are preceding rests, which his writ will not prove, though he should acknowledge in writ, so much resting at such a time; for three subsequent discharges thereafter, will presume these rests paid, though still his oath may prove it is not paid ; so that the strongest of these presumptions, though they be *præsump-*

tiones juris, yet they are not *præsumptiones juris et de jure*, which admit of no contrary probation.

The more proper way of dissolving obligations is by performance, by which they attain their effect, and that is either by payment or consignation; the more improper ways are acceptilation, compensation, innovation, confusion; of which in order.

3. Payment is the most proper loosing of obligations, and therefore retaineth the common name of solution, *l. 49 and l. 80 ff. de solut.* [D. 46, 3, 49 and 80]. In many cases payment made *bona fide* dissolveth the obligation, though he to whom it was made had no right for the time. So payment made to a procurator was thought sufficient, albeit the procuratory were thereafter improven, seeing there was no visible ground of suspicion of the falsehood of it, February 1, 1665, Elphingstoun of Selms *contra* Lo. Rollo and Laird of Niddery [1 Stair 262; M. 17018]. And payment made to a minister, though he was deposed, having continued to preach after the term, before intimation of the deposition, was sustained, but not for terms after the intimation, January 10, 1679, College of Aberdeen *contra* E. Aboyn [2 Stair 668; M. 14791]. So also payment made by a debtor to his creditor *bona fide*, was found sufficient to liberate against an appriser, who had apprised the right of that sum before payment made, albeit the apprising as a judicial assignation needs no intimation [III, 1, 13, *infra*], as was found in the case of Thomson *contra* Douglas Lady Longformacus [Not found]. And payment made *bona fide* to a donatar, was found relevant against a prior donatar, Hope, Horning, Wright *contra* Wright [Hope, *Maj. Pr.* VI, 27, 99]. And most ordinarily, payment made *bona fide* by tenants to their old master, is found relevant against singular successors, though publicly infeft, using no diligence to put the tenants *in mala fide*, Spots. Apprising, Lord Lowdoun *contra* Tennants of Jedburgh [*Sub nom. E of Lothian*, Spotiswoode, 54; M. 14087]. And payment by tenants to their master, was sustained against the donatar of his escheat, not having obtained special declarator, Had. February 10, 1610, Blackburn *contra* Wilson [Haddington, *Fol. Dict.* I, 113; M. 1786]. Neither will citations against tenants, or arrestments upon the titles of singular successors, put them *in mala fide* to pay to their master, till the titles of singular successors be judicially produced against the tenants compearing, because tenants are not obliged, as purchasers, to search registers to find their master's rights, or the rights of singular successors; yea, the arrestments of their master's rents, not insisted upon and their masters' debts instructed, before the term, seem not to infer double payment against the tenants, paying after their terms are past [1, 9, 29, *supra*; IV, 4, 33, *infra*]: but payment made before the hand doth not liberate, even against a donatar arresting and doing diligence after payment, before the term, February ult. 1628, La. Lauchop *contra* Tennents of Cleghorn [Durie 352; M. 10022]; February 5, 1667, Lady Traquair *contra* Houatson [1 Stair 435; M. 10024]. But it will not be accounted payment before hand, if by the condition of the tack, the first term's payment be made

at the entry, and the tenants to be free at the ish, January 7, 1662, Earl of Lauderdale *contra* Tennents of Swintoun [1 Stair 75; M. 10023]. Neither will a discharge freely granted, without true and real payment be sufficient, though it bear payment, to obtain the privilege of payment *bona fide*, as was found in the foresaid case, Thomson *contra* Douglas [Not found; 1,18,5, *infra*]. Payment made by tenants *bona fide*, to their master of stock and teind *promiscuè*, as they had been accustomed, found to liberate from their teind-master, who had inhibite and intimate the same to the tenants, seeing the proportion of the duty they paid for teind was not known, December 13, 1627, Hepburn *contra* Tennents [Durie 320; M.1779]; March 21, 1628, Murray *contra* Tennents of Inchaffray Abbey [Durie 366; M.1780; 11,8,23,*infra*]. Yea payment made of a part of the price of lands to the disponer's bairns, to whom it was destinate, was found relevant, albeit after a reduction depending of that disposition; seeing there was no reason filled up against the bairns' interest, nor they cited, July 19, 1662, Montgomery *contra* Wallace [1 Stair 131; M.1789]. Payment of a tocher contracted by a wife was inferred by presumption that the wife lived twenty-two years, and that the husband acknowledged in his testament that she had paid the tocher, February 16, 1671, Dods *contra* Scot [1 Stair 722; M.12584]. Payment is always presumed by retiring of the principal bonds, *nam chyrographum apud debitorem repertum præsumitur solutum.*

Missives or narratives in other writs, will not instruct where the principal writ itself is not produced, and therefore is held as retired, albeit these are adminicles to prove the tenor, if the *casus amissionis* be so far instructed, as to take off the presumption that the writ was retired. Payment made indefinitely by a debtor for several sums is generally ascribed to any of these sums that the debtor pleaseth to apply it to; because the case of the debtor is favourable and the creditor granting a receipt indefinitely, it is interprete against him, the matter remaining entire as it was the time of the receipt: but where the debtor became bankrupt after the indefinite receipt, the same was not found applicable to a sum having caution, there being another sum which had no caution, which would have been lost by that application, Feb. 13, 1680, Moncrief *contra* Cameron [*Sub nom. McReith v Cameron*, 2 Stair 757; M.6801]. But where the debtor makes no application, but his creditor or singular successor does count the application, *præsumitur in duriorem sortem*, as if for one debt there be a bond bearing annualrent, and another debt bearing no annualrent, the indefinite receipt is to be imputed to the bond bearing annualrent; or where the one security hath a greater penalty, legal or conventional, in case of not payment, as apprising or adjudication, whereof the legal is near to expire.

4. Consignation [1,13,6,*supra*] in case of the absence, lurking, or refusal of the creditor, is equivalent to payment, and where it is not otherwise agreed (with us) it is ordinarily done in the hands of the Clerk of the Bills, by way of suspension, and it stops the running of annuals, and all other

inconveniencies upon the debtor, and the consigner is free, though that which is consigned be lost by the keeper's being bankrupt, *l.19.C.de Usur.* [c.4,32,19] or otherwise, if it was the creditor's fault who charged for more than was due, as if he charged for the whole penalty, which ought to be modified : and there is no necessity in that case to consign the penalty, but to offer what shall be found due ; so if the fault be the consigner's, if the money be lost, it is lost to him. It was so found, that a sum consigned in the hands of the Clerk of the Bills upon obtaining suspension, the consigner having first offered by instrument the principal sum and annualrent, and so much of the penalty as the charger would depone he had truly debursed upon oath, the instrument being also instructed by the oath of the witnesses insert, the consigner was declared free, though the then Clerk of the Bills was become insolvent, July 28, 1665, Scot *contra* Somervail [1 Stair 304; M.10118]. So that in consignation of sums, for which there is a charge of horning, if the charge be for more than what is due, consignation may be warrantably made, without offer of what is due ; but otherwise, the offer of what is due should precede, else the peril is the consigner's, if the sum consigned be lost [11,10,18,*infra*]. But if when the consignation is *authore prætoris* either by deliverance of the Lords, or by the Ordinary passing bills of suspension upon consignation, it stops the course of annuals *l.6.C.eod.* [c.4, 32,6], because there is always a several reason of suspension, which ought to be relevant, though consignation would make it pass without instruction ; for then consignation is only for the creditor's security in place of caution ; and seeing the creditor may quickly discuss the suspension, and will be heard to answer summarily upon the bill, albeit at discussing, the reason be not found relevant, or not instructed, annual is not decerned after consignation, being *modica mora ;* yet if the sum were lost, the peril would be the consigner's, not having first offered all that was due by instrument ; and though the creditor be uncertain, lurking or out of the country, the Lords upon supplication will grant letters of requisition and offer, to be execute at the market-cross of Edinburgh and pier of Leith, where all men are presumed to have procurators to answer for them *tanquam in communi patria :* but if an offer be made of all that is due, and not accepted, it is a relevant reason of suspension, upon production of the instrument, and consigning the principal and annual, though no part of the expenses be consigned, till they be modified. If the consigner's reason be found relevant and instructed, the charge will be suspended *simpliciter*, and the decreet will contain a warrant to the Clerk of the Bills, to deliver up the consigned sums to the charger, who must bear the expenses of consignation ; but if the suspender be *in mora aut culpa*, as if he do not consign the expenses modified by the Lords, whereby the charger will be put to a new charge, he must bear the expenses of consignation. But if an assignee or singular successor charge for more than is due, the hazard will not be his, who may be ignorant of his cedent's discharges, and therefore the suspender ought to produce to him the discharges, and offer to him what is due, which if he omit, the hazard will be his. As to the obligements upon the consignatar, these shall more properly come in, with redemption of wadsets, where consignations are most frequent. *Infra, Title Wadsets* [11, 10, *infra*].

5. Acceptilation is the solution of an obligation, by acceptance of that which is not the direct performance of the obligation, in satisfaction thereof, either really, or imaginarily by acknowledgement thereof, as if it were truly performed. The Romans did only allow acceptilation as a liberation from stipulations, and therefore, before any other obligation could be dissolved by acceptilation, it behoved to be innovated, by a stipulation, engaging for the same matter, and the acceptilation itself could only be by stipulation, by the interrogation of the debtor, *quod ex tali stipulatione debeo, acceptum fers*, to which the creditor answered, *acceptum fero ;* whence it had the name of *acceptilatio*, expressing an acknowledgement of the receiving and accepting of the performance of the obligation, and of present bearing and having the same, which was valid and effectual though the creditor, neither then nor before, had received any performance of the obligation, and needed no other probation : nor doth it admit of a contrary probation, that nothing was truly received, in respect that the sole will of the creditor may evacuate the obligation, by discharge or renunciation ; and therefore acceptilation without any performance is sufficient, and is the more solemn and secure way of exoneration.

Where there are many co-debtors, the discharging one liberates not the rest if they be co-principals, unless the discharge be impersonally conceived, that the thing obliged shall not be demanded ; or that the renunciation or discharge be granted to the principal debtor ; for thereby the obligations of the cautioners being accessory, are understood also to be renounced : But acceptilation extinguisheth the obligation as to all the debtors ; because it importeth an acknowledgement of performance.

Acceptilation with us may be of any obligation, and requireth no stipulation ; but, as the acknowledgement of payment liberates all the debtors, so the acknowledgement of any satisfaction which importeth payment, or any thing accepted as equivalent, hath the same effect ; and therefore we use more the term of satisfaction than acceptilation ; which satisfaction, if it be upon grounds equivalent to payment or direct performance, it is equiparate thereto in all points, and hath the privilege of payment made *bona fide*, to liberate, though the obligation be not performed to the party having the present, and better right ; but otherwise, neither the acknowledgement of payment or of satisfaction, or any discharge, hath the privilege of payment made *bona fide*, which is mainly founded upon this ground, that *bona fides non patitur ut idem bis exigatur, l. 57. ff. de R.I.* [D. 50, 17, 57].

6. Compensation is a kind of liberation, as being equivalent to payment ; for thereby two liquid obligations do extinguish each other *ipso jure* [But see Ersk. III, 5, 12 ; Bell, *Comm.* II, 124], and not only *ope exceptionis* ; for

albeit compensation cannot operate if it be not proponed, as neither can payment, yet both *perimunt obligationem ipso jure*, and therefore are not arbitrary to either party, to propone or not propone, as they please; but any third party having interest may propone the same, which they cannot hinder; for instance, if a cautioner be distressed, he can propone payment, or compensation, upon the like liquid debt due to the principal debtor, which he cannot hinder; and therefore a liquid clear debt, though bearing no annualrent, compenseth another debt bearing annualrent, not only from the time compensation is proponed, but from the time that both debts came to be payable, from which time it stops the course of annualrent, as is clear by many laws, *Digest. et Cod. de compensationibus* [D. 16,2 ; C. 4,31], which is constantly followed by our custom, wherein positive law for utility's sake hath influence, to shun the multiplication of pleas; for otherwise, if compensation were rejected, the creditor would proceed to execution, and the debtor would be put to a new action, which is very inconvenient; and therefore when a debtor forbeareth to insist for a liquid debt, after the term is past, it is presumed to be on that account, that the creditor oweth him the like, or a greater sum, *et frustra petit quod mox est restiturus*. But otherwise compensation is neither payment formally nor materially; for when a creditor borroweth from his debtor a sum, and expressly obligeth him to pay the same, it is so far from being done for payment of a sum, formerly due to the debtor, that there is an express obligement to pay the same in numerate money, at a day, and yet if that posterior debt be insisted on, it may be compensed with the prior.

If compensation be renounced it will be excluded by that personal objection, which will take no place against other parties' interest; for thereupon compensation would be admitted for a cautioner, for a debt due to the principal, though the principal should renounce compensation; or if the compensation be indirectly renounced, by giving a bond blank in the creditor's name, which is understood as done of intention, that the bond may pass to singular successors without a formal assignation or intimation, but by filling up the party's name who gets the bond, who charging thereupon will not be compensed by any debt of the party, to whom it was first granted, Feb. 27, 1668, Henderson *contra* Birny [1 Stair 538 ; M. 1653 ; III,1,5,*infra*]. And on the same ground, a bond of corroboration, bearing a general exclusion of suspension, was found to exclude compensation, though the bond was granted under caption, without any transaction or abatement, June 28, 1672, Murray *contra* Spadin of Assintully [*Sub nom. Murray* v *Spalding*, 2 Stair 92 : M. 16487].

Compensation is described by Modestinus, *debiti et crediti contributio, l. 1. ff. de compensationibus* [D. 16,2,1] which description is neither clear nor full: it is not clear whether the contribution be by concourse of two debts, or by proponing of the compensation: neither is it full by expressing what kind of debts are compensable, for they must be commensurable and liquid, being considered as fungibles, indecernable in the value, or in the individuals, as money, wine, oil, grain, &c. Or if both obligations be in general, as if either party be obliged to deliver a house, a sword, &c. for then no speciality being expressed, the obligations are commensurate, and so compensable. But obligations of a particular body are not compensable by money ; and therefore money depositate being demanded, cannot be compensed by a debt due to the depositar, because the money depositate was not delivered as a fungible to be restored in the same kind, but in the same individual ; and likewise, acceptance of depositation imports so much trust for ready delivery, that compensation is understood thereby to be renounced, *l. penult. C. depositi* [C. 4, 34, 12], *vid. supra h. t.* [1, 13, 8, *supra*].

Upon the same ground, compensation is not relevant upon sums secured by an heritable infeftment, whereby lands or annualrents are disponed for these sums ; for though impignoration be intended, yet the contract being in the form of vendition with a reversion, the sum lent becomes the debtor's, as the price of the land or annualrent, and is no more the creditor's, unless there be a clause of requisition, that he may return to his money, or pass from his infeftment, or a clause to repay upon a simple charge ; and therefore, till the requisition or charge, there can be no compensation, except upon the bygone annualrents, due by the infeftment, which remain still moveable and compensable, January 2, 1667, Oliphant *contra* Hamilton [1 Stair 422 ; M. 2171]. But compensation was sustained upon liquid sums, though apprising was led thereupon, unless it were clad with possession and expired, June 18, 1675, Lyes Burnet *contra* Forbes of Blacktoun [2 Stair 330 ; M. 286]. The like was found as to a sum apprised for : but not upon a wadset, requiring requisition, unless requisition were made, November 12, 1675, Home of Plandergast *contra* Home of Linthil [2 Stair 368 ; M. 2633]. The reason of the difference is, because apprisings or adjudications during the legal are extinct, in any way that the sums whereon they were led become extinct, and need no re-investiture of the debtor as wadsets do. But by a liquid debt, is not understood a debt, for which there is a decreet, or *quæ habet paratam executionem*, but it is sufficient that the debt itself is liquid of the same kind with the charge ; and therefore, compensation is competent against sums due by registrate bonds, upon sums due by bonds, though not registrate, yea, though not registrable.

Compensation is also competent upon debts which are not liquid, so soon as they become liquid, either by a liquidation of consent, or by a decreet, which was sustained, though the decreet was after the charge, Dec. 23, 1635, Keith *contra* L. Glenkindie [*Sub nom. L. Keith and Glenkindie* v *Irvine*, Durie 787 ; M. 10185]. Yea, a decreet of liquidation against a principal, was found sufficient to infer compensation against the cautioner, or his assignee, though not called to the decreet, it being without collusion, June 24, 1665, Irving *contra* Strachan [1 Stair 287 ; M. 14060 ; 1, 17, 9, *supra*]. And compensation was sustained against an assignee, upon a debt due by the cedent, though liquidate after the assignation, in respect the assignation was gratuitous, Jan. 18, 1676, Crokat *contra* Ramsay [2 Stair 400 ; M. 2652] : but compensation ought no further to be drawn back than to the liquidation ; and so farms being liquidate will stop the course of annualrent, from the time of the liquidation, but not from the time the farms were due, unless it were money-rent ; but farms or services only from the liquidation, December 4, 1675, Watson *contra* Cunninghame [2 Stair 375 ; M. 2684]. So compensation is relevant, not only upon a debt of the creditor's own, but if he be creditor by assignation, the debt is compensable by a liquid debt, due by the cedent, before he was denuded by assignation and intimation, because the compensation was effectual *ipso jure*, from the concourse of the two liquid debts *inter eosdem*, Feb. 14, 1633, Keith *contra* Heriot [Durie 672 ; M. 2601] ; March 16, 1639, Forsyth *contra* Coupland [Durie 885 ; M. 2650 ; III, 1, 20, *infra*].

Compensation by our common consuetude, is also relevant upon a debt assigned to the compenser, albeit the debtor pursued or charged do seek out and acquire a debt of the charger's even after the charge, which is a further benefit introduced by custom, though it hath this inconveniency, that a creditor can hardly recover any debt, if he be due debt to others himself ; but if an assignee charge for a debt, the debtor will not have compensation upon a debt of the cedent's, assigned to him after the intimation of the charger's assignation, for these two debts never concurred *inter easdem partes ;* for though the debtor may always compense the assignee upon the cedent's debt before the assignation, if it was originally due to the debtor himself, but after the cedent is denuded by intimation, the debtor cannot acquire a debt due by the cedent to another, therewith to exclude the assignee ; otherwise the debts do never concur betwixt the same debtor and creditor, Jan. 22, 1663, Wallace *contra* Edgar [1 Stair 161 ; M. 837] ; July 4, 1676, Rollo *contra* Brownlie [2 Stair 436 ; M. 2653]. The reason is, because, after a charger's cedent is denuded by his assignation to the charger, he is no more creditor to the person charged ; and therefore that person taking assignation to the debt due by the charger's cedent, could not compense the charger, much less his assignee. But heirs and executors are accounted *eadem persona cum defuncto ;* and therefore compensation may be both upon and against their debts : so compensation was admitted against an heir or executor, upon debt due by the defunct to the defender's father, whom he represented, Spots. hic. Cassmire Pyet *contra* Russetter [Not found]. And compensation was admitted against an executor upon a legacy left to the defender, though there was no sentence thereupon, Spots. Executors, Williamson *contra* Tweedies [Spotiswoode 118; M. 2613]. It was also admitted for an executor, upon a debt due by the pursuer to the defunct, though the executor had not confirmed that debt, but he behoved to eik the same, Had. Dec. 7, 1609, Aikman *contra* La. Brughtoun [Not found].

But compensation is not competent to a debtor of a defunct, taking assignation to one of the defunct's debts after his death, which is upon account of the privilege of the creditors, who have access to the defunct's estate according to their diligence; and therefore the executor cannot prefer one to another, much less can a debtor of the defunct, by taking assignation to the defunct's debts, prefer that creditor to the rest of the creditors of the defunct, Feb. 8, 1662, Crawfurd *contra* E. Murray [1 Stair 95; M. 2613]; Feb. 14, 1662, Children of Mouswall *contra* Lowrie of Maxweltoun [1 Stair 100; M. 2614].

Compensation was found competent against a donatar upon a debt of the rebels before the rebellion, for which the compenser was cautioner, though he paid thereafter, Feb. 3, 1635, Innes *contra* Lesly [Durie 749; M. 2620]; Jan. 23, 1669, Drummond *contra* Stirling of Airdoch [1 Stair 590; M. 2621]. So compensation is competent against factors, procurators or commissioners, upon their constituent's liquid debt, but none upon their own debt; for they are not creditors as to their constituent's sums. Yea, a factor being charged by his constituent for his intromission with his rents, was not admitted to compense the same with a debt due by his constituent, whereunto the factor took assignation; neither was a chamberlain accounted a debtor to his constituent, as by a liquid debt, but that his constituent's rents were in the property of his master, and only in the factor's custody as a servant, Nov. 9, 1672, Pearson *contra* Murray, alias Crichton [2 Stair 115; M. 2625].

Compensation takes no place in the provinces of France, which acknowledge not the Roman law, but a consuetudinary law, without a privilege from the King, as is observed by Gregorius Tholosanus upon compensation. And it seems not to have been competent by the law of Scotland, before the act of Parl. 1592, cap. 143 [Compensation Act 1592, c. 143; A.P.S. III, 573, c. 61], whereby it is statute, "That any debt *de liquido in liquidum*, instantly verified by writ, or oath of party, before giving of decreet, be admitted by all judges within the realm, by way of exception; but not after the giving thereof, in the suspension, or in the reduction of the same decreet:" So that if the charge or pursuit be instantly verified by writ, the defender will not get a term to prove compensation; but if a term be assigned to the pursuer, the same would be assigned to the defender to instruct any debt wherewith he would compense by writ or oath, yea by witnesses if the probation can be closed as soon as the pursuer's probation; for the statute bears, "compensation to be in liquid debts instantly verified before the decreet," although it mention not probation by witnesses, it doth not exclude the same; but it excludes compensation after the decreet, either by suspension or reduction, which seems to import more than the rejection of compensation, because it was competent and omitted, which hath been always a common objection against any reason of suspension or reduction; but that compensation should not be admitted after decreet, though the decreet were in absence, unless it were reduced upon improbation of the executions, or other nullity, or by purging the contumacy in not compearing; so compensation was not sustained against a sheriff's decreet, though in absence, July 25, 1676, Wright *contra* Sheill [2 Stair 456; M. 2640]. And the taking assignation to the debts of the cedents after decreet, should not found a compensation, as being against the letter of the statute; for though it seem an emergent reason, which would be sufficient against competent and omitted, yet not against the speciality of this statute, excluding all compensation after decreet. But this statute is to be understood only of decreets proceeding upon citation, and not decreets of registration, which are summary and of consent, by the clause of registration.

Compensation is sometimes elided by recompensation, which doth but seldom occur, and hath not been distinctly determined as to the several cases in which it may occur. There may be several debts due by, and to, the same persons, and they may insist by pursuit or charge for some of them, and not for others; if there be more debts on either hand, they must be determined by an accompt of debit and credit; but if the pursuer be creditor in two liquid debts due by the defender, and the defender be creditor to him in one liquid debt, three cases may occur; for either the defender's debt is anterior to both the pursuer's debts, or posterior to both, or is betwixt the two debts of the pursuer or charger. The ground for resolution of these cases, is that which hath been said, that liquid debts due by, and to, the same persons, concurring at the same time, extinguish each other so far as they are equal: so then if a creditor, having two debts due to him by the same debtor, and if the debtor be creditor to him in a debt prior to both, the first debt of the two being pursued for, the defender hath compensation on his debt prior to both, because these two debts, so soon as they concurred, did extinguish each other, but the pursuer cannot recompense with his second debt, because there was no extinction betwixt it and the defender's debt, but only between the pursuer's first debt, and the defender's anterior debt; but if the pursuer insist for his second debt, the defender proponing compensation upon that debt, the pursuer hath recompensation upon his first debt.

If the defender's debt be posterior to both the pursuer's debts, the concourse and extinction is only between the pursuer's second debt and the defender's debt, yet compensation being equivalent to indefinite payment, wherein the favour of defenders gives the option to ascribe the indefinite payment to either of the debts he pleaseth; therefore, whether the pursuer insist on his second or first debt, he cannot recompense with the other: this doth also agree with that ordinary presumption, that a creditor would not give bond to his debtor, but would only give him discharge and allowance in what he was before owing to him, and so in that case there is no recompensation.

The third case is, if the defender's or suspender's debt be in the middle, between a prior debt of the pursuer's, and a posterior, then a middle debt concurring with the prior debt, there is mutual extinction; and therefore, if the pursuer insist on his prior debt, and the defender crave compensation on his middle debt, the pursuer cannot have recompensation on his posterior debt; but if the pursuer insist on his posterior debt, if the defender compense not his middle debt, the pursuer may recompense with his prior debt.

7. Retention is not an absolute extinction of the obligation of repayment or restitution, but rather a suspension thereof, till satisfaction be made to the retainer; and therefore it is rather a dilatory than a peremptory exception, though sometimes, when that which is due to the retainer, is equivalent to the value of what is demanded, if either become liquid, it may turn into a compensation. Such is the right of mandatars, impledgers, and the like, who have interest to retain the things possessed by them, until the necessary and profitable expenses wared out by them thereupon be satisfied.

8. Innovation is the turning of one obligation into another; and if it be a third person becoming debtor for relief of the former debtor, it is called Delegation. Innovation is not presumed by granting of a new obligation, either by the debtor or another; but it is rather held to be as caution or corroboration of the former obligation, consistent therewith; and in the civil law it is never esteemed innovation, unless it be so expressed, *l.ult.C. de novationibus* [c.8,41,8]; but with us, though it be not named, yet, if it appear to have been the meaning of the parties, not to corroborate, but to take away the former obligation, it is a valid innovation: so it is ordinarily inferred, when a posterior security bears, "in satisfaction of the former obligation," though it did not renounce or discharge it, nor expressly innovate it, Dec. 6, 1632, Chisholm *contra* Gordon [Durie 656; M. 16472]. The like where the posterior bond bears, "in full satisfaction of the sum, for which the former was granted," though it made no mention of the former security, July 23, 1633, Lawson *contra* Scot of Whiteslade [Durie 689; M. 11519].

9. Confusion of obligations is, when the creditor and debtor become one person, as when the one succeedeth as heir to the other, or becomes singular successor in the debt; for thereby the obligation is ineffectual, seeing none can be creditor or debtor to himself, which was extended so far, that an heir-portioner being debtor, by meddling with the defunct's means, and thereafter her husband taking assignation to a debt, and pursuing another representing the defunct thereupon, the exception of confusion was found relevant, because he was creditor as assignee, and debtor as the intromitter's husband, Spots. Assignation, Muir *contra* Calder [Spotiswoode 22; M. 831]. But where an apparent heir gave a bond and whereupon adjudication was used of his predecessors' estate, his taking assignation to that adjudication was not found to extinguish the debt by confusion, though rights so taken will not free the assignee of behaving as heir, if his assignee intromit [III,6, 14,*infra*]; whereupon there was an act of sederunt made as to all cases thereafter in the case of the Creditors of the Earl of Nithsdale, Jan. 22, 1662 [*Sub nom. Glendinning* v *E.Nithsdale*, 1 Stair 86; M. 9739]. But if by different successions, the debtor and creditor should become distinct, the obligations would revive, as in many cases may occur; and so confusion is not an absolute extinction, but rather a suspension of obligations.

Confusion doth not always take place, where the same person who is debtor succeeds to, or takes assignation, as is evident in cautioners taking assignation to bonds, wherein they are debtors as cautioners, yet may pursue the principal, or co-cautioners as assignees, and will not be excluded upon alledgance of confusion, which is only relevant when that debtor who hath no relief, becomes also creditor by succession or assignation. And so an executor taking assignation to an heritable debt, may thereupon pursue the heir for relief : or any heir-male of tailzie or provision, taking assignation to his predecessor's debt, may, as assignee, have recourse against the heir of line, of conquest, or executor. Yea, if any person take assignation to a debt, due by his predecessor, to whom he is heir-male, if there be no heir of line or executor, though during his life the assignation can have no effect, yet after his death, his heir-male will succeed to him in that assignation, and may thereupon pursue his heir of line, or executor for payment; for the taking of an assignation, and not a discharge, did clear the mind of the defunct, that the debt and credit would divide after his death, and that his heir-male would succeed to him *in credito*, and his heir of line *in debito*.

THE END OF THE FIRST BOOK.

BOOK II

Titles Contained in the Second Book

BOOK II

Title 1. Rights Real or Dominion; Where, of Community, Possession, and Property

HAVING gone through the first two branches of private rights, personal freedom and obligation, how they are constitute and how extinguished, we come now to the third, which is dominion: but because that term is more appropriated to men over men, than over other creatures, it is therefore called a right real, or a right of things: for as obligation is a right personal, as being a power of exacting from persons that which is due; so a right real is a power of disposal of things in their substance, fruits, or use.

1. For unfolding this right, and the progress thereof, both according to the order of time and nature, advert, First, that when God created man, he gave him dominion or lordship over all the creatures of the earth, in the air,

and in the sea, Gen. i. verses 28 and 29, with power to man to dispose of the creatures, even to the consumption thereof; and it is like, that during man's innocency, there was upon the part of the creatures a great subjection and subserviency to man, till afterwards, when he revolted from God, the creatures revolted also from him. This dominion of the creatures was given by God, when there was yet no man but Adam and Eve only; whence some do infer, that Adam was not only governor of this whole inferior world, but that he was proprietor of it, and that all rights of government or property, behoved to be derived from his disposal, or by succession to him, and that his monarchy did descend by primogeniture of his male race; so that if the person could be known, that doth by progress represent Adam, he would be the only righteous Monarch of the world; but the text cleareth the contrary, for in the 28th verse, God saith to Adam and Eve, "increase and multiply, and replenish the earth, and subdue or subject the same, and have dominion over the fishes of the sea, the fowls of the heaven, and all living things which move upon the earth." This gift, therefore, could not be to Adam and Eve, who could neither replenish the earth nor subjugate nor subdue it; but it was to mankind, which then was in their persons only; and it did not import a present right of property, but only a right or power to appropriate by possession, or *jus ad rem*, not *jus in re ;* so that what was not subdued and possessed, was no man's, and every man had right to subdue and possess, and thereby had right to that, which before belonged to none as well as Adam. And in these first ages, there was no property distinct from lawful possession, not only of moveables, but even of parts of the earth; for when possessors removed from these parts, they ceased to be theirs, and became the next possessor's; and therefore the Scripture calleth them possessions, without mention of any other property. Adam's dominion was of his posterity, as he was their father, and so indirectly he might overrule their possessions; but they derived no right from him thereto, but to what he gifted, being then in his possession, which was common to all other fathers.

It is a false and groundless opinion which some hold, that man by his fall hath lost his right to the creatures, until by grace he be restored, and that the sole dominion of them belongs to the saints, who may take them by force from all others. For by the whole strain of the law of God, he still owneth dominion and property of the creatures in man, without distinction, and prohibiteth all force or fraud in the contrary, which sufficiently cleareth that subtilty of man's forfeiture; for though sin maketh man obnoxious by way of obligation to punishment, by God's exterminating him from the use and comfort of the creatures; yet that obligation doth not infer the actual ceasing of man's right, much less the stating of the rights of mankind in a small part of them.

This dominion of the creatures being given to man without distinct proportions or bounds, it necessarily followeth, that by the law of nature, the birth and fruit of both sea and land were acquirable by all mankind, who had equal interest therein, and every one might take and make use thereof, for his necessity, utility, and delight; yet the use and fruit thereof must in some cases, and might in all cases, become proper, as what any had taken and possessed for his use, became thereby proper, and could not without injury be taken from him, much more the things which had received specification from his art or industry became proper, and all others might be debarred from any profit or use thereof; but so, that some part or use thereof might be communicate to others, which being the lesser, and not reaching the power of the substance of the thing, is therefore called a servitude, whereby that which is proper to one, serveth another in part. And when the proprietor giveth not the fruit, or use, but only the holding, or the detention of the thing to another, for his security of some debt, or obligation of the proprietor's to him, that right is called a pawn or pledge; so that in whole, all real rights are either that original community of all men which could not be affected, or the interest which possession giveth, or property, servitude, or pledge; of which in order: And first, generally as they were of old, common to both things moveable and immoveable; and then specially in relation to things immoveable, and to heritable ground-rights of the earth, and things fixed thereto, which now by the feudal customs is much changed from what it was, and yet is in moveables.

2. The distinction of moveable and heritable, is very necessary to be here known, as being the common materials of real rights, and having a general use, in the constitution and transmission of rights, amongst the living, and from the dead; succession being now totally divided, in moveable, and heritable or immoveable rights. Any thing is called moveable, which by its nature and use is capable of motion, as things immoveable are the earth, sea, and things fixed to the earth, not to be removed therefrom, as trees, houses, &c. which though they may be possibly moved, yet it is not their use so to be; the superfice of the earth is immoveable, though it may be moved from one place to another place of the earth: the sea also is immoveable, though it hath its agitation by ebbing and flowing, which is not the use man maketh of it. These things with us are called heritable, because they descend not to executors, to whom only moveables befal, but to heirs: and so the distinction cometh ordinarily of moveables and heritables; as that which is fixed to, or is a part of the ground, is counted immoveable, as trees and grass, and all the natural fruits of the earth; yet industrial fruits, as corns, are accounted moveable, and belong not to the heirs of defuncts, but to their executors, when they are sown or growing upon the ground at their death, as well as when they are reaped, and so fall under single escheat, Feb. 2, 1627, Somervel *contra* Stirling [Durie 267; M. 5074].

3. The distinction of heritable and moveable is derived to obligations, as the matter thereof is heritable or moveable, and so all dispositions or obligations for constituting any right of the ground, in property, community, or servitude, are heritable, although they have not yet attained their effect, and become real rights complete; as dispositions of lands, annualrents, pasturages,

thirlage, &c. which is so far extended, that all which is by destination to have its accomplishment by a real right of the ground, is heritable; as bonds bearing a clause of annualrent, which, because annualrents were usually by infeftment, therefore the very provision of annualrent, though but a personal obligement to pay it yearly or termly, without mention of infeftment, made the provision or bond heritable, and not to descend to executors, children, or wives, but to heirs only, till the act of Parliament 1641, revived Parl. 1661, cap. 32 [Bonds Act, 1661, c. 32; A.P.S. VII, 230, c. 244], whereby such bonds as were or should be made after that act 1641, bearing only a clause of annualrent, and no obligement to infeft the creditor in an annualrent, were declared to be moveable as to the defunct's children or nearest of kin, but not as to the wife or fisk, to fall under single escheat; and that because many have their estates and stocks in money, and take obligement for annualrents, for the profit thereof, without purpose to exclude their younger children therefrom. But wives are excluded [1, 4, 17, *supra*], because they are ordinarily provided by their contracts of marriage. But before this Act, all such bonds were to all effects heritable; yet so, as sums destinate for annualrent, though *de facto* they bore none, are heritable *quoad* the party who destinate; as when a tocher is conditioned by a wife's father or brother to be paid to her husband, who is obliged to employ it upon annualrent, this sum as to the husband is heritable, and excludes his executors; but as to the debtor who was neither obliged to pay annualrent or employ it, it is moveable, and so would affect the debtor's executors and exhaust his moveables, but would only belong to the creditor's heirs, Jan. 19, 1637, Robison *contra* Seton [Durie 824; M. 5489]; July 25, 1662, Naismith *contra* Jaffray [1 Stair 135; M. 5483]; and lately Nov. 19, 1691, Fleming *contra* Bell [Not found]. And this was so far extended, that when the destination was by a distinct article or bond, yet the executor might be compelled to assign, or repay the sum to the heir, Spots. *Juramentum de calumnia,*   *contra* Watson [Not found in Spotiswoode]. *Idem, de hæredibus,* Executors of Seton *contra* Robison [Not found in Spotiswoode]. And bonds also become heritable by distinct supervening rights, as by a several disposition of the debtor's whole goods and lands, with an obligement to infeft, and also by supervening apprisings or adjudications.

4. But even complete heritable rights themselves, containing personal clauses of requisition, become moveable by the requisition or charge; which is *pro tempore* a passing from the infeftment, and taking the creditor to the personal obligement: yet so, as whenever he pleaseth to pass from the requisition or charge, it convalesceth, and is not excluded by intervening rights; and so was found moveable by a charge, though but against one of the cautioners, not only as to him, but as to all the debtors, seeing thereby the creditor had taken his option, Jan. 24, 1666, Colonel Montgomery *contra* Stuart [1 Stair 343; M. 5584]. But the showing the defunct's mind to require, is not sufficient to make the sum moveable, unless it be done *habili modo ;* so a requisition being disconform to the clause of requisition, was found not to make the sum

moveable, Jan. 18, 1665, Stuart *contra* Stuart [1 Stair 251; M. 5587]. Yea, a charge upon a bond of corroboration, accumulating the principal and annual in a former security by infeftment, and bearing, "but derogation of the former security," was found to make the whole sum moveable, and to belong to the executor, without necessity to instruct a warrant to give the charge, which was presumed, albeit the defunct upon death-bed expressed that the sum belonged to his heir, June 25, 1672, Executors *contra* Heir of Sir Robert Seton [2 Stair 89; M. 5572]. But sums were not found heritable, because a disposition of land did bear, as the condition of the reversion, that the land should not be redeemed, or the acquirer denuded, till he were satisfied of all sums due to him, or which should be due to him by the disponer; neither yet when the sums are in the dispositive clause, to be contracted thereafter; but only sums which are the anterior causes of the disposition, for thereby the creditor doth not make such sums *jura fixa*, nor are they the causes of the disposition, Feb. 18, 1676, Wauch *contra* Jamison [2 Stair 417; M. 5526]. Sums are also heritable, when executors are expressly excluded; and a charge or decreet for such sums will not make them moveable, July 13, 1676, Christy *contra* Christy [2 Stair 447; M. 5580], and finally so determined, Dec. 30, 1690, Heirs and executors, Bonar *contra* Gray of Innerichty [Not found], the reason whereof is, because the mind of the creditor, by calling for his money, is not to retain it in his hands as moveables: but to make it a fixed right for his heir, seeing he excludes his executors. And for the like reason, wives charging for their heritable sums, the stock whereof is not in their husbands' power, are not presumed thereby to make them moveable, and to fall in the power of their husbands [1,4,17,*supra*]. And if any party in his process or charge should so declare his intent, it would not make the sum moveable: but requisition or a charge will make sums, which were heritable by infeftment or destination, moveable; and so likewise will a decreet for payment, Dec. 13, 1676, Fairholm *contra* Montgomery [2 Stair 477; M. 9844]. Sums consigned by an order of redemption do not thereby become moveable till declarator of redemption, or till the creditor accept of consignation, and insist for the consigned sums, which if he do not, his executor cannot recover the same, but his heir, to whom the wadset right belongs [11, 10, 22, *infra*]. For it is not in the power of the debtor to alter the condition of his creditor's sum, and to make it either heritable or moveable, without consent of the creditor, or the authority of a judge: but the consigner may take up his sum consigned, and pass from his order *re integra*, Jan. 21, 1673, Nicol *contra* Lowrie [2 Stair 152; M. 14095]; June 18, 1675, Lo. Lie *contra* Foulis of Blacktoun [*Sub nom. Leys* v *Forbes*, 2 Stair 330; M. 286].

The requisition or charge may not only be past from expressly, but tacitly, by taking annualrent thereafter, if it be for terms thereafter, as in the last case, and Spots. Assignation, Donaldson *contra* Donaldson [Spotiswoode 18]. Requisition or a charge makes bonds heritable (even after the act 1641) moveable as to the relict. The like is when they become otherwise simply moveable: but sums only heritable by destination for annualrent, are moveable till the first term of payment of the annualrent be past, and though the term of payment of the principal be not come, yet if the first term of payment of annualrent be past, the sum is heritable, July 31, 1666, Gordon *contra* Keith [1 Stair 403; M. 5505]. And if the debtor die before that time, such sums affect his executors, June 29, 1624, Smith *contra* Relict of Sanderson [Sub nom. *Smith v Anderson's Relict*, Durie 132; M. 5503]; or by the creditor's death before the first term of the annualrent, they fall to his executors and wife, Feb. 12, 1623, Wallace *contra* McDowal [Durie 45; M. 6123]. And generally all rights and obligements, having a tract of future time, are heritable as to the executors, who are thereby excluded, though they no way relate to infeftments, or lands, as pensions, tacks, &c. [III, 5, 6, *infra*]. But as to the fisk, where the distinction is betwixt moveables, liferent rights and heritable rights, the first is carried by single escheat, the next by liferent escheat, and the whole by forfeiture. All rights relating to infeftment by destination, are heritable or moveable in the same manner as betwixt heirs and executors: but rights having a tract of time, but not for a liferent, are moveable, and fall under single escheat [III, 3, 15, *infra*], yet the bygones of annualrent by infeftment, are still moveable [II, 4, 10; II, 5, 14; III, 1, 28, *infra*] but as to both effects, assignations to liferent tacks, make them moveable, and to fall under single escheat, Hope, Horning, Ker *contra* Ker [Hope, *Maj. Pr.* VI, 27, 111 and 120; M. 5071]. Clauses also of relief in heritable bonds are moveable; and the *jus mariti* of husbands, though they carry the profit of the wives' heritable rights, or rights of liferent, fall under the husband's single escheat.

5. To return to the several kinds of real rights, the first is that of commonty, which all men have of things, which cannot be appropriated. As first, The air is common to all men, because it can have no limits or bounds, and because all men every where must necessarily breathe it. Secondly, Running waters are common to all men, because they can have no bounds; but water standing, and capable of bounds, is appropriated. Thirdly, The vast ocean is common to all mankind as to navigation and fishing, which are the only uses thereof, because it is not capable of bounds, but where the sea is enclosed, in bays, creeks, or otherwise is capable of any bounds or meeths, as within the points of such lands, or within the view of such shores, there it may become proper, but with the reservation of passage for commerce, as in the land; so fishing without these bounds is common to all, and within them also, except as to certain kinds of fishes, such as herrings, &c. Fourthly, All the wild and free creatures, which are in the property of none, are in some sort common to all, as fishes, fowls, bees, &c. so as to that common right of appropriation by subduing and possession; which yet is restricted as to some kinds, as hawks and swans in some countries, and whales, extraordinary great fishes, salmon and herring-fishings, &c. which are *inter regalia*, or are excluded from the property of the commons. Such also is the right of appropriation by possession of gems and precious stones on the shore, or things relinquished by the proper

owners, except where there is a national community, that people or their authority do possess in common, not only some reserved rights of the earth, but also the rights of precious things, or things relinquished, or lost by ship-wreck; or otherwise, whereby the imaginary possession of having such within their territories, is sufficient by the custom of nations to appropriate them, and to exclude other nations, or single persons of that same nation from them [III, 3, 27, *infra*]. So with us, treasures hid in the earth, whose proper owners cannot be known, are not his in whose ground they are found, nor the finder's, but belong to the King; and things strayed, or waith, whose owners cannot appear, are public [1, 7, 3, *supra*]. But shipwreck is not to be made use of by the King in Scotland, in prejudice of the owners of such countries as use not that law themselves, but they shall have the same favour here, as they keep to ships of this country broken and shipwreckt with them, Par. 1429, cap. 124 [A.P.S. II, 19, c. 15]. Fifthly, Of things appropriated there remains still the common use of ways and passages, which is like a servitude on property; for this is necessarily required for the use of man; and therefore understood as an use reserved, both in their tacit consent to appropriation, and in their custom, *l. 1 & l. 2, ff. de locis et itineribus publicis* [D. 43, 7, 1 and 2], *arg l. 2, ff. de via public. &c.* [D. 43, 11, 2]. So all nations have free passage by navigation through the ocean, in bays and navigable rivers; and have also the benefit of stations, or roads and harbours in the sea or rivers; and have the common use of the shores for casting anchors, disloading of goods, taking in of ballast, or water rising in fountains there, drying of nets, erecting of tents, and the like, *§5. Inst. de rer. divis.* [Inst. 2, 1, 5]. Yet doth the shore remain proper, not only as to jurisdiction, but as to houses, or works built thereupon; and as to minerals, coals, or the like found therein, and so is not in whole common, but some uses thereof only. Nor doth it follow, that these uses are not common to all men, because they are denied to enemies; for, as for these, as we may take away that which is in their power in some cases, so much more may we detain from them that which is our own; and as we pursue their persons and goods in their own bounds, much more in ours. The shore in the civil law is defined to be so far as the greatest winter tides do run *§3 Inst. de rerum divisione &c.* [Inst. 2, 1, 3], which must be understood of ordinary tides, and not of extraordinary spring tides. But the use of the banks of the sea, or rivers, to cast anchors or lay goods thereon, or to tie cables to trees growing thereon, or the use of ports, which are industrial, or stations made by art, or fortified for security, are not common to all men, but public to their own people, or allowed to others freely for commerce, or in some cases are granted for a reasonable satisfaction of anchorage, portage, or other shore-dues, which oft-times belong to private persons, by their proper right, or by custom, or by public grant; but stations in these rivers, by casting of anchor remain common, and ought not to be burdened. So also ways or pass-ages in the land are common to all, and may not be justly refused by one nation to another; and being refused, have always been accounted lawfully forced:

as Plutarch relates of Cimon, who going to Lacedæmon, forced his passage through Corinth; and Agesilaus returning from Asia, craved passage through Macedon, and while they craved time to consult of an answer, he conceiving delay to be a denial, said, Consult you, but I will pass. But to take away all questions, whether these were by might or right, we have a divine example of Moses, Numb. xx. verses 17 and 19, where Israel in their way to Canaan, craved passage of Edom, by the highways, and offered payment even for their water, which was to be understood of their standing water, as wells, which were rare and precious there, and did the like with the Ammonites; and upon their refusal, forced it by war.

6. There is also in property implied an obligation of commerce, or exchange, in case of necessity; for without this, property could not consist, seeing by the division inferred therethrough, every man cannot have actually all necessaries without exchange, which being denied in cases of necessity, or where there is no common authority, it may be taken by force; as these who pass through the territories of others, if by their opposition, or otherwise, they be short of provision, they may lawfully take the same for money, as is implied in Moses' offer to Edom; yea, there is implied in property, an obligation to give, in cases of necessity, to these who have not wherewith to exchange, and cannot otherwise preserve their life, but with the obligation of recompence when they are able; for human necessity doth also infer this: but it must be a real, and not a pretended and feigned necessity: so David being hungry, ate the shew-bread, though appropriated to God; and the disciples being hungry, ate the ears of corn; and this is the ground of the obligation, to aliment the poor, which though it also floweth from the obligation of charity, yet, (as hath been spoken before) that obligation hath no determinate bounds, but is left to the discretion of the giver, not of the demander, and so can be no warrant for taking by force, and without the proprietor's consent.

7. The commonty that is of grass and fruits growing upon the highways, followeth the commonty of the ways themselves: but the common use of natural fruits brought forth without industry, even in proper fields, as of nuts, berries, or the like, or the promiscuous use of pasturage in the winter time, accustomed in many places of Scotland, are no part of this commonty, but are for the most part permitted as of little moment, or disadvantage; and therefore may be denied without injury. And so by act 11, Parl. 1686 [Winter Herding Act, 1686, c. 11; A.P.S. VIII, 595, c. 21], all persons are ordained to herd their horse or nolt all winter in the day, and house them in the night, and half a merk is appointed for every beast taken by any person on their own grass, before the beast be re-delivered.

8. The second step of real right is Possession, which, as it is the way to property, and in some cases doth fully accomplish it, so it hath in it a distinct lesser right than property, which hath no other name than possession, though it be more *facti* than *juris:* and seeing possession is a common precognite to the most of real rights, it fitly falleth in here to be considered, both as it is a

fact, and as it is a right; for as it is a fact, it is not only requisite to constitute real rights, but is also an effect thereof, when constitute.

9. Possession hath its name from its special kind, for it is as much as *positio sedium*, expressing the way of possession of the earth, (at first common) by families, nations, or persons, in fixing or settling their seats or habitations there, evidencing their affection and purpose to appropriate these seats, which therefore was not understood by their passing through it, but by fixing in it; and therefore territories of old were called possessions. That we may then take up aright the nature of possession, wherein it doth consist, and how it is begun, continued, interrupted, and lost, we must, first, distinguish the several kinds of possession: and, secondly, collect the common nature wherein they agree: and thirdly, the point of right thence arising. As to the first, The reason why the kinds and distinctions of possession are so much multiplied, is, because by positive law and the custom of nations, property and servitude cannot be constitute without possession, though it be not natural, or necessary to these rights, but by the will and constitution of men; therefore it receives diversification at their pleasure. So what men think fit to call or esteem possession, is enough to constitute property, seeing without any such thing it may be constitute, as afterward it will appear.

10. Hence ariseth the distinction of possession, in natural and civil; the former being that which is, and the latter that which is holden or repute such; under which there are degrees, as it cometh nearer to the natural possession. We shall proceed in order from the more plenary and plain possession, to these which are less clear.

11. First then, The clearest possession is of moveables, and it is the first possession that was amongst men, for so did the fruits of things become proper; and thereafter ornaments, clothes, instruments, and cattle became proper, the possession whereof is simple and plain; holding and detaining them for our proper use, and debarring others from them, either by detaining them in our hands, or upon our bodies, or keeping them under our view or power, and making use of them, or having them in fast places, to which others had no easy access. This possession of moveables was so begun and continued, and by contrary acts interrupted and lost, when others exercised the same acts, either without the possessors' consent, or by their tolerance, or tradition and delivery, or by forsaking or relinquishing them, so that in the matter of possession of moveables there can be little controversy.

12. Secondly, Possession of the ground is also clear in many cases; as First, In habitations, whether in caves, tents, or proper houses; Next in gardens, inclosures and plantations; Thirdly, In fields by pasturage or tillage; in so far as these acts extend, so far these are all most natural possessions. But after that most ancient simplicity, rights, and the ways of acquiring thereof were multiplied; and therefore possession could not be entire, but behoved to be divided amongst the several interests; and then did the difficulties arise, as when one had the property, a second the fruits, a third the use, a fourth the

servitudes in some part, a fifth the detention for security, a sixth the custody or location; and all these exercised, either by the parties themselves, their servants or children in their power, and their procurators in their name: yea, and by opposite and interrupting acts, many at once pretending to the same kinds and parts of possession, all which occasion much difficulty in the matter of possession.

13. So then the third kind of possession was, when the earth began to be divided by limits and bounds, and to have common denominations, then the possession of the whole was attained by exercising possessory acts upon a part; as he who possesseth a field, needs not go about it all, or touch every turf of it, by himself or his cattle, but by possessing a part, possesseth the whole, unless there were contrary possessory acts. So possession of the greater part of lands, contained in one tenement, was found sufficient to validate a base infeftment as to the whole, and to exclude a posterior public infeftment, for removing the tenants from a part of the tenement, though the base infeftment had possession several years, and had attained or pursued for no possession of these tenements, Spots. Removing, Hunter *contra* Hardie [Spotiswoode 287; M. 13793], observed by Dury, Jan. 14. 1630 [11, 3, 27, *infra*]. The like of possession of a part of teinds in a tack, found sufficient to validate the tack as to the whole, Spots. *De possessione*, La Merchistoun *contra* L. Wrightshouses [Spotiswoode 230; M. 15625].

14. Fourthly, Possession civil is extended to uplifting of mails and duties, which is sufficient to introduce and preserve property, though the pasturage and tillage, and all other natural deeds of possession be in others, who are properly called possessors; who hold and possess for themselves in so far as concerns the excrece of the profits above the rent, as to which they possess in the name of their masters; and therefore this possession is partly natural to the masters of the ground and partly civil by their tenants.

15. Fifthly, Possession is attained symbolically, where there is not use of the whole or a part, but only of a symbol or token, and this is when the thing to be possest is present; as the civil possession by infeftment, by delivery of earth and stone upon the ground of the lands, or a penny for an annualrent, or by delivery of a parcel of corns for a stack or field of corn, or some of a herd or flock for the whole flock, being present; in which the symbols being also parts of the thing to be possest, have some affinity to natural possession.

Sixthly, Civil possession is by a token or symbol, which is no part of the thing to be possest, but is a token only to represent it, as either having some resemblance with it, as the delivery of a copy or scroll for an office, or otherwise hath no resemblance, but is a token merely supposititious to represent it; as delivery of a baton in resignation, or delivery of a thing bought or sold, by a wisp of straw, which ordinarily is in absence of the thing to be possessed.

16. Seventhly, Possession is attained or retained without symbol, and without interposition of any person in our power, or procurator, but only by

conjunction of interest: so when the property of land is granted to one, and the usufruct or liferent to another, or when the liferent is reserved, the possession of the liferenter is held to be the possession of the fiar, as to all other third parties and rights. And a husband's possession of lands by himself, or any deriving right from him, is held to be the wife's possession, either by her liferent, or conjunct fee infeftment [11, 3, 27, *infra*].

17. The several kinds and degrees of possession being thus laid open, it will be more easy to take up the common notion and nature of it, and it may be thus described. Possession is the holding or detaining of any thing by ourselves, or others for our use. It is not every holding or detaining which makes possession; for depositars do detain, but because it is not for their use, they do not possess. To possession there must be an act of the body, which is detention and holding: and an act of the mind, which is the inclination or affection to make use of the thing detained; which being of the mind, is not so easily perceivable as that of the body; but it is presumed whensoever the profit of the detainer may be to make use of the thing; but where it may be wrong, or hurtful, it is not presumed: As he who taketh another man's horse by the head, or keepeth that which is waith, or taketh in his hands the money or goods of another, which, if it were to make use of, it would infer theft, and therefore such detention is not presumed to be possession. He also, who detaineth or holdeth a thing not at all for his own use, but for another's who doth detain by him, as by his servant or procurator, doth not possess: But otherwise, if he have no warrant from another, but only intended or is obliged that it shall be to the behoof of another, in that case he is possessor; because the real right is in him, and there is upon him only an obligation to make it forthcoming to another: and they who possess partly for themselves and partly for others, as tenants, have possession only in part.

18. To come now to the requisites for entering and beginning possession, there must be both detention of the body, and the detention of the mind, for use; for neither of the two alone can begin possession. Corporal possession alone, can neither begin it nor continue it; and if any act of the mind were enough, possession would be very large and but imaginary; but the manner of this seisure of possession to begin it, is very diverse, even by all the several ways which are before set forth, *l. 3. § 1, l. 8. ff. h. t.* [D. 41, 2, 3, 1 and 8] *l. 153 de R.I.* [D. 50, 17, 153].

19. Possession being once begun, it is continued, not only by reiteration of possessory acts, but even by the mind only, though there be no outward acts exerced, and the mind and affection to continue possession is always presumed unless the contrary appear; so that if the thing once possessed be void as to outward acts, yet it is held possessed by the mind; and any contrary act of others entering to that possession, is unwarrantable and intrusion. For as hath been before shown, intrusion is where the entry is made in possession without violence, but without warrant or consent, as ejection is by violence: but these contrary acts, though unwarrantable, yet they take away the posses-

sion that is detained by the mind, *vid. l. 6. pr. & §1 h. tit.* [D. 41,2,6,pr. and 1; 1,9,25,*supra*].

20. Possession then is lost by a contrary possession, and it is interrupted by contrary acts, and attempts of possession, which if they do not attain the effect to expulse it, it is called a troubled or disquieted possession; for nothing can be possessed *in solidum* by more than one, either simply or in relation to the same right; as there cannot be more proprietors than one of the same kind, though one be superior and another vassal; so more liferenters cannot possess *in solidum;* and therefore the entry to possess that which is already possessed, must expulse the prior, or else introduce a partial and common possession. Yet it is not the contrary attempts, or every act that expelleth a prior possession; but if the same be violent, the prior possessor hath the benefit of a possessory judgment, *l. 1. § 27. ff. de vi et vi armata* [D. 43, 16, 1, 27], and may lawfully use violence to continue possession, which afterwards he may not, for recovery thereof, when it is lost, though unwarrantably or violently, unless it be *ex incontinenti, l. 3. § 9. d. t.* [D. 43, 16, 3, 9]. Thus possession is transferred from one to another: but possession is simply lost, when it is forsaken and relinquished. It is not easy to be known when possession is detained by the mind and when relinquished: wherein there is a general rule, that dereliction is not presumed except it appear by evident declaratory acts or circumstances, as when it is thrown away in any public place where it cannot but be taken up, or when another is suffered to possess without contradiction, or when possessory acts have been long abstained from; all which conjectures are *in arbitrio judicis.*

21. From what hath been said, the ordinary distinctions of possession may be easily understood, as being either natural or civil, continued quiet and peaceable, or interrupted and disturbed, lawful or unlawful. Under which distinction are comprehended *possessio bonæ fidei*, which may be called innocent possession, and *malæ fidei* or fraudulent; and possession public, or clandestine, and long possession, momentary, or precarious.

22. To come to the right implied in possession, it is mainly in two points; First, In the right to continue it against all illegal contrary acts. Secondly, In the right of appropriation of the fruits consumed *bona fide*. Both these are introduced by positive law, for utility's sake: for, by equity any man might at any time recover the possession of that which is his own, by force, and all the fruits thereof, whether extant or consumed; but civil society and magistracy being erected, it is the main foundation of the peace, and preservation thereof, that possession may not be recovered by violence, but by order of law; and therefore there is no more allowed to private force, than to continue possession against contrary violent and clandestine acts, immediately after acting of the former, or notice of the latter: but a violent, clandestine, and unlawful possession may not be troubled though there be an evident right; much less may possession be entered where there was a right in a person, to whom another is or may be heir in that thing; for as they are accounted as one person

in law, so their possession is accounted as one possession. Like unto this is the right of apparent heirs to possess their predecessors' rents though they be not infeft, which will not only exoner the possessors, but if the apparent heir die un-infeft, his nearest of kin will have right to the rents resting from his predecessor's death to his own death; and these will be subject to his own proper debts, albeit they will not affect the land itself; but the next apparent heir must enter to the defunct last infeft, and his person and estate will only be liable for the debts of the defunct to whom he entered. And the rents resting for the years of the apparent heir's time, when he might have entered, belong to his executors, *vid. infra, Title Heirs* [11, 6, 17; 11, 3, 16; 111, 5, 2, *infra*].

23. The other possessory right is that which was allowed in the civil law, *bonæ fidei possessor facit fructus consumptos suos; l. certum 22, Cod. de rei vindicatione* [C. 3, 32, 22]; the reason whereof is, because they who enjoy that which they think their own, do consume the fruits thereof without expectation of repetition or accompt, else they are presumed to reserve them, or employ them profitably for restitution; and if it were otherwise, there could be no quiet or security to men's minds, who could call nothing securely their own, if the event of a dubious right might make them restore what they had consumed *bona fide;* and as this is in favours of the innocent possessor, *add. l. 136 de R.I.* [D. 50, 17, 136], *l. 25. § 11 de Pet. hæred* [D. 5, 3, 25, 11], so it is in hatred of the negligence of the other party not pursuing his right.

24. This right is only competent to possessors *bona fide*, who do truly think that which they possess to be their own, and know not the right of any other, *l. 109. ff. de V.S.* [D. 50, 16, 109]. But private knowledge upon information, without legal diligence, or other solemnity allowed in law, at least unless the private knowledge be certain, it is not regarded, nor doth constitute the knower in *mala fide*, March 14, 1626, Nisbet and L. Westraw *contra* Williamson [*Sub nom. Westraw* v *Williamson and Carmichael*, Durie 192; M. 859]. But a mother was not found to enjoy this benefit in prejudice of her children, there being several presumptions of her knowledge of their right, Nov. 20, 1662, Children of Wolmet *contra* Lady Wolmet and Dankeith her husband [1 Stair 141; M. 1730]. In some cases a citation and production of any other evidently preferable right is sufficient, when the possessor hath no probable title; but where he hath a double title, *mala fides* is only induced by litiscontestation, or sentence. In reductions, whether the defender is liable for the bygone profits, from citation, litiscontestation, or decreet, is in the arbitriment of the judge, July 12, 1627, L. Pitmedden and Lo. Elphingstoun *contra* Smith [Durie 306; M. 13824]. The like in a tack reduced upon a failzie, Hope, Reduction, Seton *contra* Seton [Hope, *Maj. Pr.* VI, 38, 19; M. 7201]. The like, Had. June 28, 1610, Hunter *contra* Lord Sanquhar [Haddington, *Fol. Dict.* I, 111; M. 1753]. The like, as to a decreet of removing reduced, and the violent profits found due only after litiscontestation in the reduction, Had. Jan. 24, 1611, Jousie *contra* Mortimer [Not found]. And found only to take effect after sentence, in a reduction of an apprising, because the half of the sum was

paid, Hope, Poinding, Lamb *contra* Smeaton Hepburn [Hope, *Maj. Pr.* VI, 28, 49; M. 95]. And though the possessor's right was but a tack, which fell in consequence with the setter's infeftment, reduced in parliament, yet the tacksman's possession *bona fide* was sustained, though he needed not to be called to the decreet of parliament, seeing on that decreet there was nothing done to make him know it, or put him *in mala fide*, July 19, 1664, Douglas and Sinclair of Longformacus her spouse *contra* L. Wedderburn [1 Stair 217; M. 7748]. Upon this ground an adjudger was preferred to the bygone duties uplifted by him, to a prior appriser, who charged the superior to infeft him before the adjudication, December 1, 1632, L. Kilkerran *contra* Ferguson [Durie 654; M. Supp. 67]. This was extended to the profits uplifted by infeftment upon a disposition, though granted after the liferent-escheat fell, in prejudice of the superior and donatar, July 3, 1624, Muir *contra* Hannay and the E. Galloway [Durie 137; M. 3638]; and was extended to a tack or feu of ward-lands not confirmed by the superior, in prejudice of his donatar of the ward, March 13, 1627, L. Ley *contra* Bar [Durie 290; M. 15316]. And was extended to the profits of a procurator-fiscal's place, wherein the incumbent served three years without interruption, though his right was reduced thereafter, and declared null *ab initio*, Feb. 17, 1624, Thomson *contra* Law [Durie 111; M. 1737]. It was also extended to one, who, having a posterior right of reversion, first redeemed and possessed thereby, as to bygones before the citation, though he had not possest so long as to give him the benefit of a possessory judgment, Nov. 18, 1664, Guthrie *contra* L. Sornbeg [1 Stair 226; M. 861]. It was also sustained against a minor, reducing upon minority and lesion, yet the possessor by virtue of his contract, was secure as to bygones, before citation; here there was a probable cause of contracting for an onerous consideration, though not fully equivalent, Feb. 16, 1666, Earl Wintoun *contra* Countess of Wintoun [1 Stair 357; M. 9047]. Upon this title, a tenant was liberate from removing upon a warning by a fiar after the death of his father the liferenter, in respect he set the tack without mention of his liferent, and was reputed fiar; and therefore the son was put to a new warning, Feb. 16, 1669, Hamilton *contra* Harper [1 Stair 606; M. 13827].

Possession *bona fide*, was found to liberate an appriser from being comptable to the other apprisers within year and day, July 17, 1675, Baird *contra* Johnstoun [*Sub nom. Boyd* v. *Justice*, 2 Stair 351; M. 10651]. It was also sustained against the donatar of forfeiture, Jan. 28, 1679, L. Blair *contra* La. Haslehead [2 Stair 682; M. 7871]. It was also sustained upon an infeftment for relief, whereby the rents were to be imputed in satisfaction, both of the principal and annual, Feb. 8, 1676, Scrimzour *contra* E. Northesk [2 Stair 411; M. 1751]. Yea, it was sustained, though the possessor's author's title was forged, he being a singular successor, not accessory to, or conscious of the forgery, even after improbation of his title was proponed by exception, but not sustained, but reserved by way of action, in which the title was found false, yet the *bona fides* was extended to the rents spent, till he was put *in mala fide*, by probation of the forgery; but he was found liable *in quantum lucratus*, for getting more price for the land in question, than he paid to his author therefor, Jan. 18, 1677, Dick of Grange *contra* Oliphant [2 Stair 496; M. 6548]. But no unlawful possession is valid in this case, if it be vitious, violent, clandestine, or momentary: but it is not so evident when a possession is accounted momentary; sure little time will suffice in moveables, but in lands more time is required, as a year or term, or thereby.

This right is different from the possessory judgment competent upon infeftments, which require longer time; and because it is an effect of infeftments, tacks, or the like, we shall speak thereof in these titles [11,7,22; IV,3,47; IV,17,2–3; IV,22,5 and 8; IV,26,3; IV,45,17,*infra*]. If the possession *bona fide* be by virtue of a colourable title, though perhaps null in itself upon informalities requisite in law, or upon inhibition, interdiction, or want of power in the granter, it is effectual; yet when by a common or known law, the title is void materially, in this case the possessor is not esteemed to possess *bona fide*, it being so evident, *nam ignorantia juris non excusat:* as if a relict should possess lands or others, the marriage being dissolved by her husband's death within year and day, November 16, 1633, Grant *contra* Grant [Durie 692; M. 1743]. Hereby it is evident, that possession hath much in it distinct and several from fact [11,1,8,*supra*], and therefore it stands in place of a title in all Ejections and Spuilzies.

25. By the canon law, which is so far allowed by our custom, *possessor decennalis et triennalis non tenetur docere de titulo etiam in causa falsi*, whereupon prebendars were assoilzied from production of their provisions, in an improbation, Hope, Improbation, B. of Galloway *contra* the Prebendars of the Chapel-Royal [Hope, *Maj. Pr.* VI,24,80; M. 15627]. But this hinders not reduction, where the title is supposed, but craved to be reduced upon a better right, as when the debate is, who hath the right of patronage, E. Wigtoun *contra* L. Drummellier [Not found], Had. July 24, 1622, E. Wigtoun *contra* Bishop of Glasgow [Not found]; for in these cases an ecclesiastical person's title was to be reduced *in consequentiam* with the patron's title, which hath not this privilege. This possession must be as being holden and repute a part of the benefice, and must be proven by witnesses; and therefore the possession of lands by tolerance, was found probable by witnesses, to elide thirteen years' possession thereof by a minister, who pretended to it as a part of his glebe,   Ministers of   *contra* D. of Buccleugh [June 22, 1671, *D. Buccleugh* v *Parishioners of Hassendein*, 1 Stair 739; M. 12401]. But if the church-men's title can be found, their possession will be ascribed thereto, and regulated thereby: and therefore the bishop of Dumblain, as Dean of the Chapel-royal, having long possessed ten chalders of victual, as a part of his benefice, there being found a mortification of that victual by the King, bearing the King to have had right by disposition from another, and that other's right being produced, it did bear a reversion in the body thereof for seven thousand merks, which being paid to the king when the bishops were

suppressed, and his grant of redemption thereupon voluntarily, without an order or sentence, the church-men's possession more than thirteen years before the redemption, and thirteen years after the redemption, was elided by the reverser's right and redemption. Neither did the act of sederunt, after the reformation, declaring ten years' possession of kirklands, before the Reformation, and thirty years after, to import a right to sustain this churchman's possession; that act being only for feus, granted by churchmen, not for rights granted to churchmen, July 11, 1676, Bishop of Dumblain *contra* Kinloch [2 Stair 444; M.7950]. And it was found that thirteen years' possession of vicarage by a minister, did not prefer him to a tacksman, where the minister's title was a decreet of locality produced. and not containing the teinds in question, February 24, 1681, Doctor Lesley *contra* the Minister of Glenmuck [2 Stair 868; M.11001]. This right in favour of churchmen, is by a rule of chancellary of Rome, which hath been continued after the Reformation, as being convenient, that less time and title should give right to the church benefices, whose mortifications may be more easily lost, or suppressed, than other rights. There is also another rule in that chancellary, that *triennalis pacificus possessor beneficii est inde securus;* this rule gives not right to the church, but prefers one churchman to another, if he continue to possess three years, without interruption, though he could not defend himself by his right [11,8,29,*infra*].

There is a third benefit by possession of benefices and stipends, which is by seven years' peaceable possession, whereby they have the benefit of a possessory judgment, and cannot be called in question but by reduction, or declarator; and therefore a minister's possession of his stipend for seven years, was continued, though it partly affected the stock, and no title produced but a horning upon a decreet of locality, which was lost and never booked, December 6, 1672, Veitch *contra* L. Wedderly [2 Stair 129; M.10640]. And a minister having possessed his stipend seven years after the restitution of bishops, was preferred to a dean, who had a right before the year 1637, and though all bishops and deans are restored by act of Parliament, to their rights and possessions as before 1637, until the dean's right were declared *in petitorio*, February 9, 1675, Dunlap *contra* the Parochioners of Skeen [2 Stair 320; M.Supp. 36]. And by an act of sederunt, possession of benefices, or ecclesiastical rights, thirty years after the Reformation, or ten years before, is appointed to stand as a valid title, Hope, Possession, E. Hume *contra* E. Buccleugh [Hope, *Maj. Pr.* III,21,27; M.7972].

26. So also possession of a forfeited person five years, he being reputed as heritable possessor, is appointed to stand as a valid right to the king, and his donatar of the forfeiture, Parl. 1584, cap. 2 [A.P.S. III,349,c.6]. And so it was found, though the donatar was nearest of kin to the forfeited person, and might have been presumed to have had his right, July 19, 1623, L. Maxwel *contra* L. Westraw [Durie 72; M.10599], where Hope observes, "That the donatar made faith, that he had just reason to affirm the that rights were

wanting," Hope, Possession. This was sustained, though it was offered to be proven, that the rights were reduced *in foro contradictorio*, upon recognition, Had. Feb. 20, 1611, Hairstones *contra* Campbel [Not found]. The like, though the forfeited person's predecessor was denuded, by a public infeftment of wadset, and possessed also by a back tack, seeing the wadset might have been renounced; therefore it was left to the inquest, appointed to cognosce by the act of Parliament, whether the possessor was reputed as heritor, or as a back-tacksman, as was found in the case of Scot of Scotstarbet *contra* Tenants of Garvock [Not found]. So effectual is possession *active*, besides that it is the ground of prescription, whereby property and all other rights are introduced; and *passive*, it is sufficient to hold out all others, who have not a good right, and it is always favourable in dubious cases; from the experience whereof is the vulgar saying, "that possession is eleven points of the law:" but the said case is altered by a clause in the Parliament 1690, cap. 33 [A.P.S. IX, 224, c. 104];—That all estates forfeited shall be subject to all real actions and claims against the same, though they be not raised nor insisted on within the five years preceding the forfeiture, excepting bygone feu-duties, annualrents, and other annual prestations.

27. Possession, as distinct from right, is ascribable only to that title by which it did begin, in prejudice of him from whom the possession was acquired, and to whom it must be restored, notwithstanding any other right in the possessor, to which he might ascribe it, and which, after he had quit the possession, might recover it, Spots. Possession, Herreis *contra* Anderson [Spotiswoode 229; M. 9217]; *Idem*, Elphingston of Selms *contra* Guthrie [Spotiswoode 276; M. 13270]. Possession attained without process, by one who had in his person both a wadset and an apprising of the lands, was found only ascribable to the apprising, that the same might be satisfied by intromission, as being *jus nobilius et durior sors*, as was found in the case of the Earl of Nithsdale *contra* Countess of Buccleugh [Possibly 1 Fountainhall 387; M. 546]. But as to all others from whom the possession flowed not, the same may be defended upon all rights in the possessor, or him from whom he hath tolerance or right.

28. The main real right is property, standing in the middle betwixt community and possession, which precede it, and servitude and pledge which follow it, of which *infra*, Title Servitudes [11, 7, *infra*]. But the nature of Property is best understood, when it is compared with community; for in this they both agree, that either hath a power to dispose of things; and in this they differ, that community is a promiscuous and a conjunct power, but property is a disjunct and separate power of disposal, which, if it be with diminution of any part of the fruits or use, it is a diminished property, and that diminution is called a Servitude or Pledge; but though the proprietor, and these who have servitudes, have both the power of disposal of the same thing, yet in this they differ from community, that it is not promiscuous, but a distinct power, relating to distinct effects and interests. The way to distinguish betwixt pro-

perty and servitude is, that the greatest interest retaineth the name of property, which hath in it a power of disposal of the substance of the thing, or
alienation thereof; whereas servitude is the lesser right, and reacheth but the
fruits or use in part, or for a time. It will be here proper to inquire into
the manner of the constitution of property, where it was not; as for the
transmission of property, (being constitute) from one to another, it
comes in afterwards amongst conveyances, or transmission of rights, *infra*,
lib. 3.

29. The first and most simple way of constitution of property, is by
possession of things belonging to man; for, as before is shown, the original
condition of the creatures did necessarily carry this with it, that every one
might possess that which was possessed by no other, in so far as his use
required, and might not be lawfully dispossessed thereof without his own
consent, which made it to become proper to him, and that he might defend
violence against his possession of it. This property began first in moveables,
clothes, and ornaments of the body, instruments for subduing the creatures,
as darts, which are the most ancient instruments of force, while man was
satisfied with the natural fruits of the earth, and such other creatures as for
his use and delectation, he seized on for the time.

30. *Secondly*, Appropriation was by man's industry and possession by
subduing and taming the creatures, and his affection to make use of them, not
for a time, but constantly; for thereby not only his common right and possession, but his industry and labour did properly intitle him to these things he
possessed: thus when man made use of the other creatures, not by his own
strength alone, nor by darts, stones, or the like; but made use of one creature
to master others, as hounds, hawks, &c. these instruments of pleasure managed by him, became unquestionably proper to him; then man proceeded also
to subdue and make proper cattle, as cows, oxen, sheep, horse, mules, camels,
&c. by constant use-making of their birth, fruits and work.

31. *Thirdly*, Property having extended itself to the ground, appropriated
seats for habitation, and fields for pasturage and tillage, and that for a constant
abode; whereas at first, though man's use-making of the earth did introduce
some kind of property in it for the time, yet was it without a purpose or evidence of a constant or perpetual appropriation; but men moved with their
cattle from place to place, without fixing in any one place. This fixation of the
ground began first in houses and wells, which in the places of the world first
inhabited by man were rare, and of great necessity and use, and therefore
digged with industry, and preserved with great earnestness.

32. *Fourthly*, When man increased upon the earth, and societies began to
be erected, they possessed whole countries, and divided them amongst them
by meiths and marches; and when any one of them swelled to that greatness,
that their territories could not contain them, either the whole or the excreass
of them removed to places of the earth not then inhabited, and fixed seats for
themselves: though the unjust ambition of some of them made them expel

others; yet that, as contrary to the law of nature, was abhorred, and gave occasion to the rest, from the same law, to concur with and maintain the oppressed.

33. And therefore, *Fifthly*, Property is introduced by possession of things, which are yet simply void and belong to none, and that without limitation. This is acknowledged by the law of nations, and their common consent, whence is that principle, *Quod nullius est, fit primi occupantis:* And all these ways of appropriation are by possession or occupation, and thus are all free creatures appropriated, as fowls of the air, wild beasts of the earth, fish of the sea, without distinction, upon whose ground they are taken; and though men may be hindered to come within the grounds of others, *l. 16 de serv. pr. rust.* [D. 8, 3, 16] § *12 Inst. de rer. div et acq. &c.* [Inst. 2, 1, 12], there being now no ground for passage upon account of hunting, hawking, or fishing: Yea though in some nations, the use of some of these free creatures be prohibited to any but to the sovereign power, yet the personal restraint hindereth not, but he who seizeth upon any wild creature in another man's bounds, it becometh his own *arg. d.* § *12* [Inst. 2, 1, 12], though he be punishable for that trespass; *Vid. l. 13* § *ult. in fin. ff. de injuriis* [D. 47, 10, 13, 7]; and positive law may make a part of the punishment to be the loss of what he hath taken. So likewise, it is the first seizure that introduceth property, and not the first attempt and prosecution; as he who pursueth or woundeth a wild beast, a fowl or fish, is not thereby proprietor, unless he had brought it within his power, as if he had killed it or wounded it to death, or otherwise given the effectual cause whereby it cannot use its native freedom; as at the whale-fishing at Greenland, he that woundeth a whale so that she cannot keep the sea for the smart of her wound, and so must needs come to land, is proprietor, and not he that lays first hand on her at land. Though the falling in upon another's game when he alone is in prosecution, may be uncivility or injury, yet it hindereth not the constitution of property; though it be a just ground to annul the right of the first possessor, and make him restore to the first prosecutor, if he continue his pursuit with a probability to reach his prey. And therefore, in the last Dutch war, a frigate of the King's called the Nightingale, and a French frigate being then auxiliary to the King in that war, having rencountered a Dutch privateer who had possessed and manned three prizes, and having debelled him, in the mean time the prizes made sail to escape; but while the two frigates were taking two of these prizes, a Scottish privateer attacked the third, called the Tortoice, and made her strike sail; but not knowing whether the other frigates were friends or foes at such a distance, did not board her till they came near; and the French frigate being nearer than the English frigate, both the French frigate and the Scottish privateer claimed the Tortoice as their prize. The English Captain sent the prize to Leith, and declared the case under his hand; whereupon the Admiral adjudged the Tortoice prize to Rankine the Scottish privateer; but the matter being brought before the Lords by reduction, the French privateer pursued not, but the King's Advocate; yet the Lords, found

that the frigate under the King's pay having defeat the Dutch privateer, who was possessed of the Tortoice, and being in view and prosecution of her, that Rankine's capture and possession was injurious, otherwise than to assist the first attacker; unless it were proven, that the prize would have escaped if it had not been stopped, and forced to strike sail to Captain Rankine, February 15, 1677, King's Advocate *contra* Capt. Rankine [2 Stair 507; M. 11930].

The creatures are understood to be free while they are not within the power of any; but fishes within ponds are proper, and fowls, though never so wild, while they are in custody. Amongst these free creatures, these which are tame are not comprehended, but only these which are wild; which, if they be tamed, contrary to their nature, are so long proper as their tameness remains; but if they return to their ancient wildness, their property thereof is lost so soon as the owner ceaseth to pursue for possession; and it is so long continued, or understood to be continued by the mind, having once begun to be possest by bodily acts; and therefore the prosecution of wild creatures will not begin, though it may continue the property of them. Bees are numbered amongst these wild creatures, which therefore are not proper though they hive in trees, more than fowls who set their nests thereupon, but if they be within a skep, or work in the hollow of a tree, wall, or in a house, they are proper; or while they hive, or flying away are pursued by the proprietor; but thereafter they belong to him who next getteth them in his power: as also these which were tamed and become wild, become theirs who regain and tame them again, and return not to their first owner. Thus also gems, pearls, and precious stones, are appropriated by the finders: And likewise lands not possest; or which do arise of new, as do some islands in the sea, or more frequently in public rivers, which by the civil law are accounted to accresce to these, whose ground lies nearest, proportionably according to that part of the ground that fronts them; but where such civil constitution is not, such islands are public as the rivers are in which they are bred. *Vid. Inst.* § *12, 13, 14, 15, 16, 17, 18, 22, h. Tit.* [Inst. 2, 1, 12–18 and 22]. *Adde l. 3.* § *14. ff. de acquir. poss.* [D. 41, 2, 3, 14] *l. 8.* § *1 & 2 ff. famil. arscis.* [D. 10, 2, 8, 1 and 2].

34. The next way of appropriation is by accession, whereby the accessories of things proper are also proper, as the birth of all cattle and their fruits. It is likewise a natural acquisition of property, which ariseth by accretion of parts, accretion of birth and of fruits, and even the dung or any other profit, followeth the property of that whereunto it is accessory; because by common utility that is understood to be comprehended in the common consent of mankind. So trees and all plants, as the birth of the earth, are carried therewith, while they are growing thereupon, even to singular successors; but if separated or contained in moveable boxes, they are not so carried with the ground as accessories, but are separate moveables. So likewise the natural fruits of the ground, as grass and herbs, are carried as the fruit thereof and accessory thereto. But by our custom, corns and industrial fruits are esteemed as

distinct moveables, even before they be separated or ripe, and belong not to purchasers of land or heirs.

These are the ways of constituting property by natural equity, without consideration of the positive law of any particular nation: but no doubt, as the sole dispositive will of the owner may state the property of what is his and fully at his disposal, in another, so may the public consent of any people introduce ways of appropriation, as they find most convenient for public good, and that either expressly by statute, or declaration of the legislative authority, or tacitly by consuetude; and albeit it be a good and solid rule, *Quod meum est, sine me alienum fieri nequit*, yet it hath the exception of public sanction or common custom; and so though it be not by the sole and proper consent of the owner, yet it is by the consent of that society of people or their authority, wherein the submission or consent of every one in the society is implied, in so far as the design of association extends: and therefore first, in fungibles and all such things as are not discernible from others of that kind, possession is generally esteemed to constitute property, which is most evident in current money, which if it be not sealed, and during its remaining so, is otherwise undiscernible, it doth so far become the property of the possessor, that it passeth to all singular successors without any question of the knowledge, fraud, or other fault of the author; without which, commerce could not be secured, if money, which is the common mean of it, did not pass currently without all question, whose it had been, or how it ceased to be his; *l. si alien. 78 ff. de solutionibus* [D. 46, 3, 78]; and though that law is in the case of commixtion of money with another's money, who was not owner of it, whereby it is esteemed as consumption of the money commixed, yet that ground doth necessarily reach all money, so soon as it passeth to any singular successor by commerce, for thereby it is consumed in the same way.

35. Secondly, Upon the like ground it is, that appropriation by alluvion, is admitted in all nations, for thereby the adjection of another's ground insensibly, and unperceivably, by the running of a river, becomes a part of the ground to which it is adjected; because it is uncertain from whose ground such small and unperceivable particles are carried by the water, and thereby also the frequent questions that would arise betwixt the proprietors upon the opposite banks of rivers, are prevented; and though the adjection may be perceivable and considerable in a tract of time, it maketh no difference, if at no particular instant the adjection be considerable; as the motion of the palm of a horologe is insensible at any instant, though it be very perceivable when put together, in less than the quarter of an hour.

36. Thirdly, Upon the same ground, confusion of liquids, which are not afterwards separable, altereth the property, in so far, that what before belonged to several owners severally, becometh now to belong to the same owners *pro indiviso*, according to the proportion of the value of their shares; neither is there any difference, whether the confusion be made by the consent of parties, by accident, or by mistake, or fault, the effect being the same in all:

for, because the parts are undiscernible and inseparable so as to give every owner the individual body he had before; therefore he can only receive by equivalence, the like value by division.

37. Fourthly, Upon the same ground, commixture of grain or other arid bodies, belonging to diverse owners, which cannot be easily separated, or of any materials in one mass, work or artifice, if they be not separable, they induce a communion proportionable to the value of the several ingredients: and though all the ingredients remain without alteration of their substance, so that in subtility, the property of each part might be considered as remaining with the former owner, not only in commixture, but in confusion, alluvion and money, yet public authority for utility's sake, constituteth or declareth the property in manner foresaid, which is also consequent from necessity, and the nature of the thing, though there were no positive law: and such commixtures are not like the commixtures of a flock, where every individual is discernible and separable, as having the several marks of their distinct owners; and if a commixture in that case should become undiscernible, it would of necessity introduce a community; as if different flocks of unmarked lambs should in any way fall to come together, so that the owners, or the servants, could not distinguish their own, there were no remedy but to divide according to the number belonging to the several owners, and till that division were made, every owner had a proportionable interest in every individual, seeing none of them could say or instruct this or that to be properly his own.

38. Fifthly, Positive law for the common benefit, constituteth property by necessary conjunction in constructure; such is the Roman law *de tigno juncto*, whereby a beam, or any other material built in a house, becomes proper to the owner of the house or building, that policy be not prejudged by demolishing of buildings; which therefore taketh effect whether the materials be made use of *bonâ* or *malâ fide ;* yea, though the materials were affected with theft, which in other cases is *labes realis*, the public interest would not suffer demolition, but give the prior owner the value, *secundum pretium affectionis*, and further punish the transgressor; as the Roman law gave the double value; but if before receiving of that satisfaction, the building come to be demolished, there is no doubt but the owner of such materials will recover the same, *rei vindicatione.*

39. Upon the like ground of common utility, the Roman law did constitute property by contexture, whereby the materials wrought into cloth, garments, or other artifact, did become the property of the owner of that artifact, if without destruction thereof, or considerable detriment thereto, such materials could not be separated therefrom; in which they made no difference, whether these materials were made use of *bona* or *mala fide ;* nor did the inherent *labes* of materials stolen, hinder the accession and appropriation thereof by contexture, §26. *Inst. de rerum divisione* [Inst. 2, 1, 26]; but both in constructure and in contexture, he who thereby acquireth the property of materials belonging to other owners, seeing the restitution thereof ceaseth, he is

liable, not only for recompense, *in quantum locupletior factus est*, but also for reparation of the damage of the former owner, in which the manner of acquisition is considered; for, if the materials of others be made use of, in constructure or contexture *bona fide*, the ordinary value thereof is only due, but otherwise the greatest value, according to the estimation of the former owner *per pretium affectionis*.

In contexture it is considered, what is the design of the artifact, that it may appear what is principal, and what is accessory; as in cloths, the materials, though much more precious than the cloth, are accessory thereto, and the property of the whole befalleth not to the owner of the materials, but to the owner of the cloth. And precious stones set in rings are accessory thereto, though more precious than the gold, or any other material of the ring. But otherwise, if a gem be set in gold, the gold becomes accessory thereto, and wherever the case is dubious, that which is of greatest value carrieth the property of the whole. Albeit that controversies of this nature have been seldom moved with us, as to constructure, or contexture; yet it is not to be doubted, but we would proceed upon the like grounds of equity and utility.

Upon the like ground of accession, questions in relation to pictures are to be resolved; for if the ground, board, or table of a picture belong to one, and the same be painted by another, either for his own use, or for the use of a third party, there doth not continue two distinct properties, one of the board, and another of the picture, nor a communion by proportion of interest, but the property of the whole befalleth to one, as to which, there was a contrariety betwixt the two Roman jurisconsults, Paulus and Gaius, for Paulus allowed the picture to follow the board, as accessory thereto, and carried therewith; *l. in rem 23, §3 ff. de rei vindicatione* [D. 6, 1, 23, 3] but Gaius on the contrary attributed the board as accessory to the picture *l. 9, §2. ff. de acquirendo rerum dominio*, [D. 41, 1, 9, 2]; and though both sentences be confirmed by Justinian in the Digests; yet in the Institutes he prefers the opinion of Gaius, *§34 Inst. de rerum divisione*, [Inst. 2, 1, 34] upon that reason, that it were ridiculous, that a precious picture of Apelles should follow a board, though of the lowest value, albeit before, precious stones, though of greater value than cloth, were declared by him to be carried therewith. Positive law may determine this point either way, without injustice, according to equity and expediency; but there are diverse cases in the matter, which should be diversely resolved; as, if any picture be painted upon a wall, or other immoveable, it doth necessarily cede to the ground thereof, and quality, wherever the picture is, for ornament of its ground, as when a shrine, or cabinet, or the like moveables, are painted, because the adorning of the ground is in that case designed; but a face, or any other picture where the board is only designed for it, the board is most conveniently esteemed as accessory thereto; and in all cases, the owner of the whole is liable *in quantum lucratus est*, even though the painting be done by him who knew that the ground was not his own; for in that case, the presumption is not strong enough, that he did it *animo donandi*; for it cannot be imagined, that the making use of an inconsiderable board of another, should infer the purpose of gifting a fine picture thereupon, neither that they who paint a wall, shrine, or box of others, being artisans, who work for profit, did the same to gift, but to oblige the other party. So writing upon parchment, paper or other tables, was by the Roman law accounted as accessory thereto §*33 Inst. de rerum divisione*, [Inst. 2, 1, 33] *l. 3, §pen. ff. ad exhibendum*. [D. 10, 4, 3, 14], which is very dissonant from that which is there determined of pictures: and therefore, is every where in desuetude, as is observed by Grotius, Minsynger and others, both as to writing and printing, in the same way as painting; for if the writing be upon the wall or other moveables of another, or if it be upon the books of others, it cedeth thereto; but if it be upon paper or parchment, the design and use whereof is for writing, and the use whereof is consumed and lost by writing, it doth follow the writing; and it were very unreasonable to think, that the evidents and securities of lands, or any manuscript, should be accessory to the paper or parchment whereon they were written, and which were only designed to bear and preserve the writ, and not to be carried therewith.

40. It is a rule in the Roman law, which we follow, *inædificatum solo cedit solo ;* for thereby all buildings of houses, walls, wells, dykes, &c. and generally, all things fixed to the ground, or walls, are accounted as parts of the ground, and pass therewith, (though not expressed) to all singular successors; and not to executors, but to heirs; and thence, not only the materials of others become the owners of the ground, on which they are builded, and for preserving of policy, cannot be demolished, as hath been said of constructure: but likewise, he that builds with his own materials upon another man's ground, the same accresce to the ground, and if the owner of these materials knew the ground to be another's, the Roman law gave him no recompence therefor, but presumed it to be done *animo donandi*, which is rather penal, in hatred of these who encroach upon the ground of others, than from any sufficient ground of presumption; and therefore our custom doth allow a recompence to the builder, in so far as the heritor was profited thereby, in that he might get a greater rent for that building, Feb. 5, 1692, Sandilands *contra* L. Niddrie. [Not found]. But building of houses by tenants for their own use, though at their removing they leave the land in better condition than at their entry, they get no satisfaction therefor without paction. And a liferenter having rebuilded a jointure-house which was burnt by accident in her widowity, and rebuilt by her second husband, was found to have no satisfaction therefor, except the house had been accustomed to be set for rent, and that the liferenter or her husband had no power to demolish any thing that was fixed to the ground, Feb. 2, 1672, Captain Guthrie *contra* L. McKerstoun [2 Stair 57; M. 10137]. And an appriser having re-built a burnt house, was not presumed to gift the same to a liferenter, albeit her seasin was registrate, but she had her option, either to get so much out of the rent of the tenement, as it was worth before the reparation; or to have the possession of the tenement, paying the annualrent of the sums

necessarily and profitably wared upon the reparation thereof, during her life, Jan. 24, 1672, Hacket *contra* Wat [2 Stair 54; M. 13412]

41. There remains to be cleared, that appropriation which is by specification, whereby, of materials belonging to other owners, a new species is produced, whether the product belongs to the owners of the materials, or to him for whom the work is made; as to which the two great sects of the ancient lawyers were divided, Proculus and his followers attributing the property of all the materials to him that made the work, and Sabinus and his, attributing the whole to the owner of the materials: but Tribonian midseth the matter thus, that if the product can easily be reduced to the first matter, the owners of the matter remain proprietors of the whole, as when a cup or other artefact is made of metal; but otherwise the materials cedes to the workmanship, not only when the materials are consumed, but even when they remain, and cannot be reduced to their first nature; as wine of other men's grapes, malt of other men's bear, cloth of other men's wool, and even a ship of other men's timber; but not by malting of barley, or dying of cloth, or the like, which change not the species. Conanus, is of opinion, that whether the workmanship or the materials be more precious, the property is carried by the value. And Grotius is of opinion, that there ariseth a communion, as in confusion of liquors, proportioned according to the value of the materials and workmanship. Positive law, or custom, may, without injustice, follow any of these ways, reparation being always made to the party who loses his interest, unless the presumption be strong enough to infer, that the workmanship was performed *animo donandi*, by him who knew the materials belonged to another.

42. In immoveables the constitution or transmission of property, is expressed in writ, and is parted in many interests; but in moveables, property is simple and full without servitude, and there is no other interest in them, unless they be impledged [1, 14, 4, *supra*]; neither needs the title, constitution, or transmission, of property in moveables, be instructed by writ, but is presumed from possession; and therefore, for the restitution or recovery of moveables from the possessor thereof, it is not sufficient to instruct that the pursuer had a right thereto, as by the birth or fruit of his ground or cattle; or as being bought by him, and in his possession; but he must instruct the manner how his possession ceased, as being either taken from him by violence, or by stealth, or having strayed, and being lost or the like; and the reason thereof is, because moveables pass without writ, and oft-times without witness; and therefore, whatever right parties once had to moveables, it is presumed to be transmitted by donation, sale, or otherwise, unless it be proven that he lost possession, as aforesaid; or otherwise, that it be proven by the defender's oath, that when he acquired right, he knew the thing in question to be the pursuer's proper goods; for in that case, even his private knowledge will prejudge him, though he had bought it at a competent rate; though it be not so in heritable rights, to whose constitution and transmission, writ and solemnities are necessary; neither will it avail, though it were a horse bought in public market

and booked there; for we have not the privilege of fairs which the English have, that horse bought in public market should be secured to the buyer, without further question, but he buys the same with the peril of the seller's right, March 19, 1639, Ferguson *contra* Forrest [Durie 885; M. 4145]. Hence it is, that in all actions for recovery of moveables, there is no more libelled, than that the moveables were the proper goods of the pursuer, and in his possession, for such a time, by using the same as his own proper goods, and condescending how he ceased to possess, as being lent by him, which was found relevant to be proven by witnesses, though the question was of a book of considerable value, Jan. 27, 1665, Scot *contra* Fletcher [1 Stair 258; M. 11616]; or that the goods did stray, Feb. 3, 1672, Scot of Gorrenberry *contra* Eliot [2 Stair 59; M. 12727]; or if the goods were in the possession of a defunct at his death, the presumption of sale ceaseth; or if there be a stronger contrary presumption; as was found in the case of jewels, which the defender neither could use as proper to his quality, nor was he a merchant or jeweller, these jewels being once impignorated by writ; in that case possession was not found sufficient to infer property, Dec. 12, 1665, Ramsay *contra* Wilson [1 Stair 326; M. 9114]. And even in the case of ships of war which are the most considerable moveables, property was presumed by possession without writ, July 26, 1673, Captain Hamilton *contra* the Owners of the Statine [2 Stair 221; M. 11925, 12774]; and the property of money was inferred, by having the key of the chest in which the money was unsealed, unless a contrary positive probation were adduced, June 18, 1675, Taylour *contra* Rankin [2 Stair 333; M. 9118]. Yea, moveables acquired *bona fide*, for onerous causes, were found not liable to hypothecation or to the conditions of a written disposition of them, unless they had been affected with diligence, when they were in the hands of him to whom they were disponed with these conditions, Dec. 17, 1675, Creditors of Mastertoun *contra* Creditors of Thin [2 Stair 387; M. 11830; I,14,4, *supra ;* III,2,7; IV,30,9–10,*infra*].

Title 2. Reprisals, Where, of Prizes, &c.

THESE being the ways of appropriation by private right, appropriation by public right is by war and force, where there is no common judge or authority; for in that case equity, and that common justice which is acknowledged by all nations as the rule of right and wrong, especially in so far as it is owned by the law of nations, is a sufficient warrant for obtaining satisfaction by force, where it is denied by justice: But our design here being only to consider private rights, we shall but notice that which by public authority is allowed in these cases to be the peculiar right of private persons, which doth only reach moveables seized upon by reprisals, or the goods of enemies or their partakers taken in public war.

1. *Reprisals*, or letters of marque, are granted by princes or states, by their warrant or commission, to seize upon the goods of all persons under the dominion of such princes or people, who have refused to make just reparation, for the wrongs and damages done by any of their subjects, which the law of nations doth justly and necessarily allow for the common good of mankind: for if private persons be injured, by these who are not under one common authority with them, by piracy, pillage or otherwise, oft-times they cannot know the injurer, and all force being stated in public authority, they cannot make use thereof to redress or revenge themselves; and therefore they can only make application to the sovereign authority of that society of people, whereof they are members, and represent and instruct the injury and damage sustained by them, by the subjects of these princes or states, and thereupon desire that a redress may be demanded, which is ordinarily done by ambassadors or other ministers of state: and if redress be not so obtained, the sovereign authority of the persons injured may, and ought to give commissions for seizing upon the goods of any of the people of that society, whereof the injurers are members, till just satisfaction and reparation be obtained; and though there be that singularity in it, that the goods of these who did not the injury, are taken to satisfy the same; yet therein there is not only necessity, but moral justice, allowed and approven by the custom of all nations, by their common consent; for without this societies could not be preserved; and therefore, the public association of people implieth this in it, that the society is liable for reparation of the injuries and damages of any of their society, when reparation is refused.

2. Reprisals ought to be limited to a just satisfaction, and therefore what is thereby seized ought to be adjudged in the Courts of Admiralty, wherein it ought to be proven, that the goods seized belonged to persons of that society, of which the injurer is a member, and to be valued according to the rate they are worth, where they are brought in, and to be adjudged, in satisfaction to the injured of their damage and interest, in whole or in part; so that the excress should be forthcoming to the owner thereof; the expences of recovery being also satisfied; and, so soon as satisfaction is obtained, the reprisals ought to cease: neither doth the use-making of reprisals in this just order and measure, import the breach of treaties, or

common peace, or infer public war, though they may become the occasion thereof.

3. But when the injury is public and atrocious, the law of nations hath necessarily and justly allowed public war, not only to reach the moveables of public enemies, but their territories, jurisdictions and estates, wherein the proportion of satisfaction cannot be so measured, nor is it so considered as in reprisals. That which accrueth to private persons in war, is only the giving of quarter, or getting of spoil, in so far as the same is allowed, or permitted by the commanders-in-chief, or warranted by public authority; as is ordinary to the soldiers upon defeats of their enemies to seize upon, and appropriate to themselves such moveables as are upon their enemies persons, or in their baggage: and sometimes for the encouraging of soldiers besieging, and for the obstinacy of the besieged, the plunder of places gained by force, is for some time permitted, and ceaseth so soon as countermanded. In other cases, what belongs to enemies is confiscated for public use, and then soldiers ought to be contented with their wages.

4. The main private interest in public war, is that which accrueth by commissions granted by the Admiral, for seizing and appropriating of the ships and goods of public enemies, and of these who become partakers of the war, and who carry not themselves as friends, or neuters, to the princes or states engaged in the war: for by our custom, albeit such ships and goods be confiscated as public, belonging to the King or States; yet private persons who undertake these commissions, have for their expenses the profit of these seizures, paying a fifteenth part thereof to the King, and a tenth part to the Admiral.

There have been many questions as to the rights and interests of allies and neuters, very fully and accurately debated, and decided in the Session, upon occasion of the late wars betwixt the King and the States of the United Provinces [First Dutch War, 1652–54; Second Dutch War, 1665–67; Third Dutch War, 1672–74] which, because they are of great use, for clearing the important points that occur in these controversies, and for vindicating of the public justice of this kingdom, we shall in the clearest and shortest method we can, give account of what hath been determined in all the prizes which came before the Lords of Session in these wars.

5. The Lord Admiral of Scotland is the Judge Ordinary and the sole Judge in the first instance of all prizes taken at sea; but in the second instance the Lords of Session, who are the Supreme Judges in all civil causes in Scotland, which are not determined by, or depending before the Parliament or their commissioners, so upon complaint of iniquity committed by the Admiral, before final sentence, the Lords did advocate such causes, wherein they found the iniquity alleged and instructed; and in the second instance, after sentence, the Lords do grant letters of suspension, or reduction of the Admiral's decreets, whereupon all intricate and difficile questions in matters of prizes come to be debated and determined by the Lords. Where there is no question, when

the goods and ships seized belong to enemies, but only when they do belong, or are pretended to belong to allies or neuters, the ships being furnished with many false and double documents for that effect. So the Lords, upon complaint of iniquity committed by the Admiral, (it being alleged that the Lords were not judges in the matters of prizes in the first instance) yet they found, both by the amplitude of the power of their jurisdiction, and by the custom in former times, that it was competent to the Lords to advocate causes from the Admiral upon iniquity, albeit the process cannot begin before them in the first instance; for as they are the King's ordinary council, all matters, not belonging to the jurisdiction of another court, belongeth to them; and therefore they may, and oft have advocate causes from the Justice-General, and other Judges in criminal causes: albeit the Lords cannot decide these causes, as being only judges in causes civil, yet they may advocate the same, that in case the reasons of advocation be relevant and proven, they may remit the cause to the proper and competent Judge, if the reason of advocation be upon incompetency, or to other unsuspect Judges, if the reason be upon the suspicion of the Judge, as being concerned in the cause, or nearly related to the parties, or having enmity against any of them: and therefore, the Lords in the advocation raised by the owners of the ship called the Bounder against Captain Gillies [2 Stair 185; M. 11907], it being alleged that the Admiral had committed iniquity, in granting a conjunct probation for proving the property of the ship and loading; the Lords found this no relevant ground of advocation of the cause, it being *in arbitrio judicis* whether to grant a conjunct probation before answer to the relevancy of the reasons of adjudication, or to discuss the relevancy first, and then to admit the points found relevant to probation; but in the other way, witnesses are adduced for either party: yet this being only *ex nobili officio*, the Lords remitted the cause to the Admiral, and ordained him to proceed to discuss the relevancy, there being pregnant grounds of adjudication instantly verified, June 12, 1673, and upon his refusal, they did advocate the cause to themselves; they did also ordain the Admiral to proceed upon the evidences adduced to adjudge or assoilzie, without allowing a conjunct probation before answer, and declared, that if he proceeded not accordingly, they would advocate the cause, albeit the Danish treaty bear, "that their ships shall not be meddled with, or their goods disloaded, till they be adjudged in a Court of Admiralty;" for the Lords are the King's great Court of Admiralty, in the same way as his commissioners in England are judges in the second instances, of prizes brought before the Admiral of England, December 17, 1673, Captain Stuart *contra* the Owners of the Danish ship Seal Fish. [2 Stair 241; M. 11926]. But advocations, as they are now discharged from the Admiral in maritime causes, by Act 16. Parl. 2, Sess. 3, Charl. 2, 1672 [Courts Act, 1672, c. 16; A.P.S. VIII, 80, c. 40], so they may seem discharged from the Lords of Justiciary by their late constitution, *Ibid*.

6. When questions concerning prizes come before the Lords, they do not exclude the defences of strangers, as being competent and omitted in the first

instance, though that be a rule by our custom, but do proceed according to the common law of nations, and so they decided, July 23, 1667, Hans Jurgan *contra* Capt. Logan [1 Stair 477; M. 12222], which was the first case occurring in that question, and was always followed thereafter: for the rule by which the Lords have always proceeded in the matter of prizes hath been the law and custom of nations; and therefore the tenor of the Admiral's commission was not found to be the rule, Feb. 21, 1668, Bartholomew Parkman *contra* Capt. Allan [1 Stair 529; M. 11867]. And the treaties betwixt the King and his allies, in so far as they differ from the common law of nations, have always been allowed by the Lords, as exceptions from that general rule, and good defences to the people comprehended in these treaties. In dubious cases the Lords have proceeded by the King's instructions, ordinarily adhibited to the admiralties of all his kingdoms, that they might keep one uniform rule with strangers, in which, not only respect hath been had unto justice, but even favour towards allies, and policy and prudence towards all neuters, that none of them might receive offence, by the extension of justice in favourable cases.

7. The ground of justice for confiscating the ships of those who are not enemies, is, that they have assisted the enemy in carrying on the war, and thereby became accessories to the war, and by that delinquence, do confiscate the ships and the loading, by which they have had accession: for the law and custom of nations hath very fitly restricted the reparation of this delinquence, so as not to state the parties offenders as enemies, and thereby to make all their goods confiscable as enemies goods, but doth limit the same to these ships, in which the concourse is acted, if they be seized in that voyage, in which they give assistance or in their immediate return with counterband, and the like.

Engagement in war by princes and states, cannot justly hinder the free trade of other people, upon whom neither party hath either obligation or jurisdiction; but the common consent and custom of nations requireth an equality and neutrality in all other parties, that they concur not in the war with either party, forbearing assistance in the war, which is by furnishing them with men, instruments of war, materials, specially such as are requisite for the present war, money furnished for public use, and in some cases victual, as when it is carried to places besieged; and other things which have promiscuous use in peace and war, when there is a special application thereof to the necessary use of the war, as iron, brass, lead, pitch, tar, and the like, which are therefore called counterband goods, or prohibited goods: and by the denunciations of war, intimation is ordinarily made to neuters, from what things to abstain, as from carrying of counterband goods towards enemies' ports, or carrying the goods and ware of enemies, whereby their trade is promoted, and they enabled to maintain the war; or by carrying on their trade under the colour of the trade of neuters; and therefore, in time of war, neuters do instruct their vessels with passes and other documents, for proving that the bottom and goods belong to their subjects, who are free-men, and that the parties engaged in the war, or any of their subjects, have no interest therein; which passes are upon the oaths of the owners of the ship, or masters thereof, and those who embark the loading; and where there is any treaty, the formula of such passes useth to be expressed, always including an oath, and to be given by such magistrates as are agreed upon in the said treaties.

8. Seeing then the accession of neuters is a delinquence, it can have no place where there is not a public denounced war, which is presumed to be known to the delinquent; and therefore the ship and goods belonging to neuters, were not found prize, because carrying counterband goods towards the enemy's ports, unless the war had been notourly known at the place where they loosed, and acts of hostility, and declaring of prizes, in neighbouring places was not found sufficient, July 23, 1667, Hans Jurgan *contra* Capt. Logan [1 Stair 477; M. 12222]. The like was found of a ship of Hamburgh, carrying counterband goods to Danish ports, after acts of hostility betwixt the King and the Danes, because the ship was taken before the proclamation of the war against the Danes, Feb. 25, 1668, Merchants of Hamburgh *contra* Capt. Dishington [1 Stair 533; M. 11876].

9. If ships have in them counterband goods, they may be brought up, if the port be not expressed upon oath, and be a free port, or be contradicted by the oaths of the skipper and company, which infers a full probation, in case they acknowledge an unfree port; and a presumptive probation, in case the pass bear not a free port, is a ground of seizure; yet it admits a contrary probation, for proving of the true port, Jan. 21, 1673, Hendrick Anderson, Master of the Sun of Dantzick *contra* Capt. Douglas [2 Stair 154; M. 11889]. The like was found, where the pass made the port uncertain and ambiguous, bearing London to be the port, but a greater fraught promised, if the ship was brought up into Holland, which was found to be elided by a positive contrary probation, Feb. 19, 1673, the owners of the Palm-tree and Patience *contra* Capt. Achison [2 Stair 173; M. 11894].

10. Amongst counterband, pitch and tar were found comprehended, January 14, 1668, Capt. Allan *contra* Parkman [1 Stair 502; M. 11865]; timber proper for shipping, as masts, &c. is unquestionably counterband, but timber of promiscuous use, is not counterband, except in special cases, for the peculiar use of the war. There is a particular article in the first treaty betwixt the King and the Swedes, by which it is declared, that in regard the most of the materials of the Swedish trade are pitch, tar, masts, &c. which are counterband, yet the King declares, these shall not be seized upon that account, which was not found sufficient to defend a Swedish ship carrying such counterband goods, they not being the product of their own country, January 14, 1668, Capt. Allan *contra* Parkman [1 Stair 502; M. 11865]. In the last treaty betwixt the King and the Swedes, there is an article, bearing, "That counterband shall be prize, *si deprehendatur;*" and therefore, it was thereby inferred, that the ship and remanent loading was not prize, July 18, 1673, Capt.

Winchester *contra* the Owners of the St Andrew [2 Stair 216; M. 11913]. The like July 24, 1673, Capt. Donaldson *contra* the master of the King David [2 Stair 220; M. 11902].

There was the like article, both as to counterband, and enemies goods, in the treaty at Breda [1667], betwixt the King, the Dutch, the French, and the Danish, at the pacification of the first Dutch war; but that pacification being broken by the second Dutch war, it was not found effectual in the subsequent war, upon a letter from the King, But a ship was not found prize for carrying of victual or money to an enemy's country, July 16, 1673, Capt. Lyel *contra* the master of the Leopard [2 Stair 213; M. 11920].

11. There is no doubt but carrying of soldiers to the enemy's country, of what nation soever they be, is counterband, and useth to be expressed in the treaties of allies generally, under the name of men, which can only be understood of strangers when they are actual soldiers in the enemy's service, for thereby there is a greater participation of the war, than either by carrying of enemies goods, or by carrying the instruments of war towards the enemy's ports; but otherwise passengers who are neuters, may freely go to the ports of enemies for trading, travelling, or any other end, not being found or presumed to become citizens or soldiers there, but residing only as factors for strangers; and so not contributing with the enemy to the war, they do not exceed the bounds of neutrality.

12. The difficulty is greater in case persons belonging to the enemy's country, be carried in the ships of allies or neuters, and there is little doubt but the persons of enemies, residing in the enemy's country, and contributing to the war, hath the same or more effect, than the carrying of their goods, though that hath not occurred to be determined with us, and there is less doubt, that being born in the enemy's country, or having resided there as citizens, but having left the same before the war, doth no further state them as enemies, than that by their language, or other evidence, they are presumed to be enemies, unless they make it appear, that they had left the enemy's country, and fixed their residence elsewhere: neither will any burdens imposed upon their lands or houses, import their concourse in the war as enemies. There was a special concession by the King in favours of the King of Spain, that because the language of his subjects in the Netherlands, is the same with these of the United Provinces, that there should be no seizure of the ships belonging to his subjects, upon account of being served, or navigated by Hollanders. There is also an article in the Swedish treaty, that it should be free for them to make use of Dutch masters for navigating their ships, provided that these masters fix their domiciles in Sweden, and become citizens and inhabitants there.

These concessions gave great occasion of doubt, whether these or other allies or neuters, might make use of Hollanders as mariners, or servants in their ships, because, if without that concession they were free to hire Hollanders for servants, they might hire them for masters of ships, as well as other mariners, and so needed no such privilege, and therefore run no hazard by being navigated by Hollanders; but if they might not lawfully make use of a Hollands master, till they had it by special privilege, *a pari* they could not make use of Hollands mariners. It is clear, that the being by nation Hollanders inferreth no hazard, either as to the masters or seamen; for the war is only with the citizens and inhabitants of the enemy's country, so that the true domicile or residence is the main point in question. There is also great difference betwixt the master or stearsman, and the common mariners; for the master is in possession of, and entrusted with the ship, which is affected both with his delinquence, and by his contracts of bottomry; and therefore his oath alone is always accounted sufficient probation, as to the property of the ship, and frequently the stearsman is entrusted with the loading; in which case also his oath will be sufficient probation as to the property thereof; but the oaths of the mariners have only been made use of as ordinary witnesses, proving by the concourse of two or more; and the confessions of the master, stears-man, or company at sea when they were taken, have not been allowed as sufficient probation, to confiscate the ship or loading; yea, though renewed after they came to land, but only when taken judicially; and very little use hath been made of the oaths of the privateer, or his company, for proving against strangers, but only their own oaths, and other evidences; but the oath of the skipper alone was found to prove against his owners, July 13, 1669, Capt. Wood *contra* Neilson [*Sub nom. Wood* v *Boyneilson*, 1 Stair 636; M. 11884].

The taking the privilege for a Hollands master, upon the considerations aforesaid doth not import, that mariners may not be made use of who are by nation Hollanders, if they reside not in the jurisdiction of the enemy; neither will the being of some of them aboard, infer such evidence, that the whole ship and loading belong not to neuters and free-men; but if the most part of the company be Hollanders, or if the master be a Hollander, the presumption is strong, and gives sufficient ground for seizure; and therefore it is fitly declared by treaties, that if the master by nation be a Hollander, the pass shall bear expressly, "That it is sworn upon oath, that he is citizen and inhabitant in Sweden."

13. The King by his proclamation of the first war against the Dutch [1665], did command to seize and make prizes of all ships, where there were found any number of men belonging to the enemy; and therefore a Swedish ship was found prize, because navigated with Hollanders, all or the most part of her company being such, albeit she had a pass from Sweden in the terms of the formula contained in the Swedish treaty; and albeit the treaty bear, that where such a pass is, *in bona aut homines nullo modo inquiratur;* because in that same article it is subjoined *nisi gravis suspicio subsit,* and it was a most weighty ground of suspicion, that the ship or goods belonged to Hollanders, that the company acknowledged that they resided in Holland, and were taken on there, immediately before this voyage in this process: Where it being alleged,

that the confession of the company, taken by an Admiral Depute at Cromarty, was extorted by holding swords and pistols to their breasts, or that the same was so extorted at sea, when they were taken, it was found sufficient to enervate their testimonies, if they were made to swear at sea, the privateer and company having swords and pistols in their hands; because to evite the infamy of perjury, they might adhere in their judicial re-examination to their testimonies taken at sea upon oath, albeit not true; or if by force or just fear they did so depone before the Admiral-Depute, February 25, 1668, The Owners of the ship called the Castle of Riga *contra* Cap. Seton [1 Stair 534; M. 11862]. The like was found, where a great part of the company were Hollanders, June 30, 1668, Paterson *contra* Cap. Anderson [1 Stair 544; M. 11877]. And in the case betwixt Captain Allan and Parkman, decided July 9, 1668 [1 Stair 550; M. 11869], the ship was found prize, for having a number of Hollanders sailors, viz. three, the company being nine, and for having a small parcel of tar, as counterband aboard, and having aboard the product counterband, taken in the immediate return of that voyage; upon all which grounds jointly, the said ship was declared prize.

But in the second war [1672–74] there hath no ship been declared prize upon account of the company's being Hollanders, neither because the master was a Hollander, if he were not also a part-owner, albeit two of the company were Hollanders, July 24, 1673, Captain Bennet *contra* the Owners of the Pearl [2 Stair 220; M. Supp. 23]. But the master being a Hollander, was found a sufficient ground of suspicion and seizure, but not of confiscation, the property being proven to pertain to free men; and therefore probation was allowed to either party, July 16, 1673, Captain Lyle *contra* the master of the ship called The Leopard [2 Stair 213; M. 11920]. For the hiring of the enemy's people is no assistance to them in the war, but rather a weakening of them, so that if these of the enemy's country be only aboard as servants to neuters, and not upon their own account, either as traders or passengers, there hath been no inquiry in the last war as to their residence, neither hath any thing as to that point been mentioned in the last proclamation of war, or in his Majesty's instructions to the admiralties of his kingdoms: and though the law might have reached ships navigated by Hollanders, residing in Holland, and not changing their domicile, yet in favour and prudence, that ground hath not been sustained, it being more the King's interest to allow his enemies to withdraw from their country, than to force them to serve only there.

14. Counterband is not only a cause of confiscation, when taken going towards enemies' ports, but also when the ship is taken in her return from the enemy's port in the same voyage, for then the delinquence is complete, whereas it had not taken effect before the ship attained the port; and yet might be justly seized before the full effect, because the seizure of the ship in her voyage is the impediment that the effect is not attained; and therefore, the common custom of nations hath allowed such seizures; for otherwise it were impossible to hinder neuters to carry counterband goods to enemies, for carrying

on the war; neither will the pretence of altering their resolution, to sail to or disload in a free port, be a sufficient defence, unless the ship were actually stearing another course: but if a ship should be pursued to be searched for counterband in her passage to an enemy's port, and should be waited for till her return, and taken as she came from that port, there could be far less pretence to excuse that delinquence; and therefore, it was one of the grounds of confiscation of Parkman's ship, taken by Captain Allan, that she was taken in the return of the same voyage, in which she carried counterband to the enemy's ports, July 9, 1668 [1 Stair 550; M. 11869]. And though in that case the reason was libelled that the ship was taken, having in her the product of counterband, as having the same effect with counterband itself, *quia surrogatum sapit naturam surrogati*, yet without that, in the foresaid case of Captain Lyle [2 Stair 213; M. 11920], it was found sufficient that the ship was taken in the return of that same voyage, in which she carried counterband without mention of the product thereof, July 16, 1673, in which case it was found necessary, that the ship belonged to the same owners, that had carried in the counterband; so that though the ship had been light without any loading, she would have been prize, unless she had been a Swedish ship, and so secured by the Swedish treaty, confiscating only counterband when it was actually taken. But it is a most convenient moderation of the law of nations, that the delinquence of carrying counterband, is followed no farther than the immediate return of that voyage, otherwise it would be the foundation of marring trade, by perpetual quarrels, upon pretence of counterband carried in to enemies in former voyages, and in these wars there has been no occasion to determine, whether it be a cause of confiscation, if a ship be taken in her return of that voyage, wherein she was loaded with enemies' goods.

15. The Dutch by their declaration did prohibit all friends and allies, not only to carry counterband-goods to any port in the King's dominions, but to be found therewith upon his coasts, or diverting from their voyage, which they might make with counterband towards the King's ports; holding that for a sufficient probation of their intending these ports, which is like they would not take off by documents aboard, expressing their own ports, or the ports of neuters, it being so easy to procure false and colourable documents; yet that was never sustained as a relevant ground of adjudication with us. So that by what hath been said, the confiscation of the ships and goods of allies and neuters, upon account of counterband, and the assistance given to enemies thereby, hath been fully cleared.

16. The other chief ground of confiscation of ships and goods of neuters, is by their concourse with enemies, in carrying on their trade; and therefore, in all the treaties, the *formula* of passes doth require, that it be attested upon oath, that the ship and loading belongs to the subjects of that ally, and no part thereof to the King's enemies; and likewise the particular kinds and quantities of the cargo, and the owners thereof, and of the ship, must be expressed. Some are of opinion, that an unfree ship confiscates the loading as accessory

thereto, but with us an unfree loading, or a part thereof, doth not confiscate the ship, which is but a groundless subtility; the reason of this confiscation being the partaking with enemies in carrying on of their trade, it taketh place alike in the ship and loading, or any part thereof; but it being a delinquence, it hath still the exception of the *bona fides*, and ignorance of these who partake in that conjunction of trade. But though the society or partnership was entered into before the war, it was not found to liberate, seeing there was time and opportunity to dissolve it thereafter, July 17, 1673, Master of the Golden Falcon *contra* Capt. Buchanan [2 Stair 215; M. 11922].

17. That a part of the ship belonging to an enemy, doth confiscate the whole ship, and loading, hath been oft-times decided, even in the case where the master being a part-owner, was hired by the Swedes, or other allies, and was a sworn citizen in Sweden; unless it were sufficiently instructed that he were an inhabitant and residenter there, and had changed his domicile from Holland, and carried his wife and family, if he had any, to a neutral place. Neither was the production of a burgess-brief in Sweden found sufficient, seeing the skipper by his oath acknowledged, that he left his wife lying-in at Amsterdam, February 28, 1673; and July 18, 1673, Master of the Elsingburg *contra* Capt. Douglas [2 Stair 182 and 216; M. 11905]. The like was found, because the master by his oath acknowledged, that he was a Hollander, and a part-owner, and that the evidence that his domicile was still in Holland, was more pregnant than that he had changed the same to Copenhagen, June 25, 1673, Captain   *contra* Master of the Saint Mary [2 Stair 191; M. 11915]. The like was found, where the skipper's oath bore him to be a part-owner and a Hollander, and that he intended to change his domicile, but had not done it, though he produced a Swedish burgess-brief, July 10, 1673, Captain Fraser *contra* master of the Young Tobias [2 Stair 208; M. 11920].

18. The loading belonging to enemies, was also found to make the ship prize, seeing it appeared that they knew the same to belong to enemies, when unloaded, and had no privilege by treaty, July 15, 1573, Captain Wilson *contra* the master of the ship called the Venus [2 Stair 212; M. 11918]. In like manner, the most part of the loading being proven to belong to a Jew, residing and trafficking in Amsterdam, the loading was found prize, but the ship belonging to Lubeck was found free, because she loosed from Lisbon before the certainty of the war, and so was in *bona fide* to engage for a freight with a Hollander; neither was it respected that this Jew was an agent for the King of Portugal, seeing he was a residing trafficking merchant in Holland, February 11, 1673, Earl of Kincardine *contra* the master of the St Andrew [2 Stair 171; M. 11893]; but thereafter this ship was also found prize upon other grounds.

19. The greatest difficulty in the matter of prizes is, the discovery and probation of the interest of enemies. If probation be not had from the oath of the skipper and company, or from the documents found aboard, there remains no more but presumptive probation, which sometimes is so pregnant as it admits no contrary positive probation, and oft-times it doth admit the same,

and then there is probation allowed to either party, for clearing the matter of fact, either as to the property of the ship or goods, the true residence of the master, or the port truly intended, or any other matter of fact, whereupon confiscation or liberation may be inferred.

In the second Dutch war [1672–74], they had found out so cunning contrivances to cover their trade, that the same could hardly be so far discovered as to make a lawful probation; for they did not only procure passes from the Swedes and Danes, and other allies and neuters, and upon the privilege granted to them of Hollands masters, did send persons intrusted by them, as masters or steersmen to manage their trade, under pretence of fixing their domiciles in Sweden, or in Denmark, conform to these treaties: but also, they intrusted their money to merchants, or factors belonging to the countries of allies and neuters, who bought ships and goods in their own names, but to the use and behoof of the Hollanders, and upon their risk and advantage and profit, so that they had a pretence to depone, that the property of ship and goods did belong to these free men, who bought them, because there lay only an obligation of trust upon them, to communicate the same to Hollanders; as did appear by a report returned from the Magistrates of Stockholm, upon a commission from the Lords for clearing the property of the ship called The Wine-Grape, and her loading; for the persons, who by the pass made faith as owners, being interrogate, "Whether they had lent their names for the behoof of the Dutch, or had bought the ship and goods for their use, so that the benefit or loss was to redound to the Dutch;" they declined to give a direct answer upon oath denying the same, and only asserted, that they ought not to be interrogate upon such indirect dealing, or the like, or to that purpose: yea, use was made of the names and trust of his Majesty's subjects, to colour the Dutch trade, and many passes were procured from the Admiralty of England for the same effect: all which were the more easily obtained, because the sufferings of innocent merchants, upon account of their governors, was generally pitied, and the profit of privateers was as generally hated and envied.

20. The ordinary ground of a presumptive probation of the interest of enemies, by the custom of nations are these: First, if in the time of war ships were not instructed with passes upon oath, expressing the owner of ships and loading; and therefore the want of passes, or the want of documents for instructing the property of the ship and loading, or any part thereof, the same is presumed to belong to enemies. Secondly, False or forged documents. Thirdly, Double documents. Fourthly, Destroying of documents, as throwing the same overboard, or throwing them away at the time of the capture, infer that the ship or loading, or some part thereof, belonged to enemies, and likewise the having aboard double flags, to be made use of at divers occasions.

21. As to the first ground of confiscation upon want of documents: First, There is no necessity to have aboard a vendition of the ship in writ; because in ships, as other moveables, property is presumed from possession, July 26, 1673, Captain Hamilton *contra* the master of the ship called the   of

Stattin [2 Stair 221; M. 11925 and 12774]. Neither doth the want of a pass, conform to the *formula* in the treaties, as being defective and not expressing the port to which the ship was direct, infer confiscation: in this case there was no counterband goods aboard, so that though the true port had been the enemy's port, it would not have inferred confiscation, January 21, 1673, Anderson, master of the Sun of Dantzick *contra* Capt. Douglas [2 Stair 154; M. 11889]. The like was found, February 19, 1673, the owners of the Palm-Tree and Patience *contra* Capt. Achison [2 Stair 173; M. 11894], and upon February 27, 1673, the owners of the King David *contra* Capt. Donaldson [2 Stair 220; M. 11903]; where a Swedish ship wanting a pass, conform to the Swedish *formula*, and not being upon oath, though these were found presumptive probations of the interest of enemies; yet not so pregnant as to exclude a contrary positive probation, that the property of the ship and goods belonged to free-men; and the not expressing the port in the pass of a Swedish ship, was not found so to infer the goods to belong to enemies; but that it admitted a contrary probation, that the ship and loading belonged to free men; and because the loading was pitch and tar, which is counterband, the not expressing the port being essential as to counterband, would have confiscated the ship and loading, unless it had been secured by the Swedish treaty, declaring pitch and tar, and others, being the growth of Sweden, not to be counterband, February 28, 1673, the master of the St. Peter of Stoad *contra* Capt. Stuart [2 Stair 182; M. 11904].

Passes for ships in time of war, must be renewed for every voyage, and cannot otherwise express the kinds and quantities of the cargo, which was sustained as one of the reasons of the adjudication of the ship called The Elsingburg, at the instance of Captain Dowglas, decided July 18, 1673 [2 Stair 216; M. 11905]; yet a ship was not found prize as wanting a pass for the present voyage, in respect she having loosed at Nantz, and having there a particular pass, she was forced into England by stress of weather, and there sold her loading, and went back to Nantz, and took in the like loading for the same owners and port, and therefore altered not the first pass, June 17, 1673, Captain Donaldson *contra* Master of the Deborah [2 Stair 188; M. 11913]. It is likewise most necessary, that passes be truly granted upon oath made, which is the greatest security against colourable documents, and therefore it was sustained as one of the grounds of the adjudication, of the ship called the St. Mary, that the master by his oath acknowledged, that he had not made faith, as the pass bears, as was found June 25, 1673 [2 Stair 191; M. 11915], and upon that reason the ship was found prize; in which case also one witness deponed, that papers were thrown overboard, July 9, 1673, Captain Gillies *contra* the Owners of the Bounder [2 Stair 207; M. 11909].

22. Double documents infer confiscation, but that is chiefly understood, when the documents are contrary in material points; but where there was one pass from the college of commerce, and another from the King of Sweden, having some contrariety, but not in material points, the same was not found

to make the ship prize, June 13, 1673, Capt. Winchester *contra* the Owners of the St Andrew [2 Stair 187; M. 11912].

23. The throwing of papers overboard, or destroying the same at the time of the capture, is a most pregnant ground of confiscation; for thence it is presumed, that these papers would have instructed the property to belong to enemies; and therefore being proven but by one witness, it put the burden of probation upon the strangers, that the ship and loading belonged to free men, February 28, 1673, the master of the White Dove *contra* Capt. Alexander [2 Stair 183; M. 11906]; regard was also had to the same, though but proven by one witness, in the confiscation of the Bounder, July 9, 1673 [2 Stair 207; M. 11909]; and if there were concurring witnesses in this point, it would infer *præsumptionem juris, et de jure*, not admitting a contrary probation.

24. Ships have oft-times been found prize by the concourse of several evidences of a contrivance, under colourable documents; and therefore a ship was found prize, because the pass did not mention the port, which a toll-brieve bore to be Breme, and the master by his oath acknowledged the port to be Amsterdam, and that the owners were other persons than were expressed in the pass, and that the master resided in Holland, though the pass bore him to be a burgess in Dantzick, against which a contrary probation was not admitted, January 23, 1673, the owners of the Crown of Dantzick *contra* Capt. Lyon [2 Stair 160; M. 11892]; a ship was also confiscated because the master and steersman deponed that they knew not to whom the goods belonged, but that they had order from a merchant in Amsterdam, to consign them in the packhouse of Stockholm, to be delivered to such persons as should show such marks, July 10, 1673, Captain Fraser *contra* Master of the Flying Hart [2 Stair 207; M. 11919]; and in like manner the Fortune of Trailsound was found prize, July 22, 1673 [2 Stair 218; M. 11923], because it was acknowledged upon oath, that if the ship were taken by Hollanders, the company should depone the goods belonged to the tar-company in Stockholm, as the pass bears; and if it came safe to Scotland or England, they should declare the same belonged to Samuel Souton an Englishman residing in Sweden.

25. Albeit a part of the ship or loading be found to belong to enemies, and that thereby the whole becomes prize, as being partners with the enemy in carrying on their trade, yet these who can show that they were in an invincible ignorance of the interest of an enemy, and did all they could do to secure against the same, by taking the oaths of the owners of the whole ship and loading, that the property belonged to themselves, and no part thereof to an enemy, it would take off the delinquence of that party, and preserve their interest, which was never pleaded during these wars, but by some of the King's subjects; as in the first war, the King having by his proclamation, warranted all ships even from enemies, to be employed for bringing timber for the rebuilding of London, a great part whereof was then lately burnt, certificates and passes being always had from the Duke of York, then Lord High Admiral of England; whereupon John Dyson, merchant at London,

fraughts a ship of Norway, whereof Boaz Neilson was master, called the Raphael, to import to London six thousand deal-boards; the ship in her voyage to London was taken by Captain Wood, and the whole ship and loading adjudged as prize, which being brought before the Lords by reduction, they found that the ship and loading became prize, because there were found aboard fifteen hundred deals belonging to the owners or company, who then were in enmity in the Danish war; and yet the six thousand deals belonging to the London merchant, who had contracted *bona fide* by the King's proclamation, did not become prize with the ship, as was decided July 13, 1669 [*Sub nom. Wood* v *Boyneilson*, 1 Stair 636; M. 11884]; for the London merchant not being on the place of embarking, could not know whether there was more entered than the deals he fraughted, or whether the owners gave truly an oath upon the property and quantity of the loading. And in like manner, Sir Francis Clark, merchant at London, having ordered a parcel of brass-wire to be brought home to him from Sweden, the same was embarked in the ship called the Calmer, which was taken in her voyage to London by Captain Smeatoun, and was adjudged prize by the Admiral, because the pass was convelled by the master's oath, yet the parcel of brass-wire belonging to Sir Francis Clark was found not to be prize, December 13, 1673, Sir Francis Clark *contra* Capt. Smeatoun [2 Stair 240; M. Supp. 28]; and that because Sir Francis, residing in England, and not being upon the place of embarking, could not know the falsehood or simulation of the pass, or other grounds of confiscation; and albeit there was no document aboard for this parcel of brass-wire, which would have inferred a presumptive probation against allies or neuters, that the same belonged to enemies, yet the same or any other presumptive probation, though so strong against neuters, that it would admit no contrary probation, yet as to the King's subjects residing in his dominions, who could not trade but under colourable documents, it was not found *dolus malus*, unless they had, or could have known the interest of any of the King's enemies. Likewise, some merchants in Hull, having embarked a loading in a ship of Hamburg, called the Lyveday, the Admiral found the loading prize, because there were double and forged documents made use of, against which no contrary probation could have been admitted; for neuters who being free with all parties engaged in the war, had no reason to make use of false or double documents, so that it necessarily inferred that the ship or loading belonged not to neuters but to enemies; yet the matter being brought in question by reduction, the Lords found that there being no ground of confiscation of the ship, but it was a free Hamburg ship, except upon account of the colourable documents for the loading, they admitted a contrary probation that the property of the loading belonged to the merchants of Hull, November 14, 1673, master of the Lyveday *contra* Capt. Middletoun [2 Stair 229; M. 11925].

26. We have now gone through the ordinary grounds of adjudication of prizes; there are some other grounds that have been alleged for confiscation, but have not been sustained; as 1°, it was not found a ground of confiscation

of a ship or loading, that the same belonged to the subjects of the Duke of Holstein, who held some of his estate of the King of Denmark, then a declared enemy to the King, unless the Duke of Holstein had contributed to the war, as was found January 4, 1667, Herrison *contra* L. Ludquharn [1 Stair 418, 425; M.11858]; neither that the ship wanted a vendition in writ, July 26, 1673, Captain Hamilton *contra* master of the ship called ———— of Stattin [2 Stair 221; M.11925 and 12774]; neither was it found a relevant ground of confiscation, because the ship was bought in Holland, and taken at sea ere she touched any other ground, February 21, 1673, the owners of the ship called the Prince of East-Freezland *contra* Capt. Binnie [2 Stair 177; M. 11897]; the like was found in the foresaid case of Captain Hamilton [2 Stair 221; M.11925 and 12774]; neither did the insurance of ship or loading in Holland infer a sufficient ground of confiscation alone, though it might concur with others as an adminicle, albeit the insurance was alleged to put the risk and hazard of the capture upon the King's friends, without detriment to his enemies; yet the Lords found, that seeing the property of the goods insured did remain in the King's allies, the same ought not to be confiscated, neither was it alleged, that the insurance was expressly against capture, but only against hazard at sea in general, July 22, 1673, Captain   *contra* the Owners of the Fortune of Trailsound [Stralsund] [2 Stair 218; M.11923].

This further is to be observed, that when the ships of neuters have aboard counterband, the defect of documents for the counterband, or double, or colourable documents to cover the same, will not infer confiscation, if the property be proven to belong to free men, and that the true port intended was not an enemy's port; because in such cases neuters have necessity of colourable documents; but as to the property of ships and goods, they have no such necessity; and therefore, contrary probation is not admitted against the ordinary presumptive probation, by wanting of documents, concealing or destroying of documents, or making use of double or false documents.

When prizes adjudged by the Admiral are rouped and sold, if by reduction, they be liberated by the Lords, the owners are decerned *in solidum,* to restore the price, the ship and loading being indivisible, though oft-times some are assumed as owners who are not solvent, June 10, 1680, the Ann of Christiana *contra* Captain Martin [2 Stair 769; M.14672]. And if the ship and loading be orderly rouped, upon the Admiral's warrant, or sold upon his decreet, before the same be called in question by citation upon reduction, albeit the Lords thereafter liberated the ship, they will decern no more but the price obtained by the roup before the Admiral's adjudication, or the price obtained by sale, *bona fide,* after the Admiral's decreet: and if the King's fifteenth part, and the Admiral's tenth part, be *bona fide* paid, they are liberated *pro tanto,* and the strangers must have recourse to the Treasury, and against the Admiral for repetition.

Title 3. Infeftments of Property, Where, of Charters, Seasins, Resignations, Confirmations, &c.

THE Roman empire in Italy, being long oppressed, was at length suppressed by the inundation of the Longobards, and other barbarous nations, who seated themselves there, and divided these beautiful countries amongst their captains, and they subdivided the same to their soldiers, for their military service; and as they were the authors of this new right; so did they term it by a new and barbarous name, *Feudum*, which the Germans call *Fiff*, and we with the English call a *Fee*. Concerning which there was no common written law; but the several provinces had their diverse customs, as they thought most suitable to the nature of this right, and their own utility. As to these books annexed to the civil law [The *Libri Feudorum* were in the sixteenth and seventeenth centuries frequently printed at the end of volumes containing the *Corpus Juris Civilis*], called *Libri feudorum*, though they have great respect amongst lawyers, yet they are but the observations of private persons, and so not a written public law.

By this irruption, which happened in the sixth century, the Roman civil law was sopite for five hundred years, and was revived in the eleventh [This should be "twelfth"; cf. 1,1,12,*supra*] century, and did take in with it the feudal customs, which have been propagated through the most civil nations in the world; not only for strengthening them towards war, but because sovereigns had thereby a new interest over their subjects, thereby becoming their feudatars and vassals, owning always to them fidelity, and oftest following them as their clients and assecles, acknowledging them as their lords, superiors, and paramounts in their lands and heritages, which are all derived, mediately or immediately from the sovereign authority, as the common and supreme superior of all the subjects, who have no more than the right of unfixed moveables.

2. And thence also ariseth the feudal jurisdiction, whereby not only the sovereign power, but all superiors do by the advice and assistance of their vassals, who are called peers of their court, order and determine all things, not only relating to themselves and their vassals, but to all others, who are locally within their territories, both in civils and criminals, in so far as they derive jurisdiction, civil or criminal, from the sovereign power, immediately or mediately. No nation is more exact in this than Scotland, wherein the King as supreme superior, ruleth by his vassals assembled in parliament; in which at first all were personally present who held lands immediately of him, as barons great and small, free-holders of any moment, holding a forty shilling land of old extent of the King, and prelates for church lands; the free-burghs were also represented in parliament by their commissioners, as holding their burgage lands, and their freedoms and privileges of burghs, as feudatars of the King; so that there was not one foot of ground in Scotland whose lord was not present in Parliament, by himself or his delegate. But when fees holden of the King became sub-divided, and multiplied, two or more commissioners were admitted in Parliament, in name of the meaner barons and freeholders; and all were accounted great barons, who held an hundred merk

land or above of the King, and the rest meaner barons, Parl. 1503, cap. 78 [A.P.S. 11,252,c.23]. So also other superiors have their courts, consisting of their vassals, who are obliged to answer suit thereto, who as a jury, gave doom and judgment of old, when all matters proceeded by jury or inquest, as it was also in the King's court by sheriffs, bailies, &c. of which the shadow or formality yet remaineth, of having a doomster as a member of court to pronounce sentence, though inquests be in most things laid aside through recent use and custom.

3. The very right of superiority carries this right of jurisdiction over the vassals, unless by their infeftments, or prescription, they be exempted, by having courts and their issues in their infeftments. Our learned countryman, Craig of Riccarton, hath largely and learnedly handled the feudal rights of this and other nations, in his book *De Feudis;* and therefore we shall only follow closely what since his time by statute or custom hath been cleared or altered in our feudal rights, which is very much; for he having written in the year 1600, there are since many statutes and variety of cases, which did occur, and were determined by the Lords, and have been *de recenti* observed, as they were done by the most eminent of the Lords and lawyers, as by Haddingtoun, who was president of the Session [1609–13, 1622–23], and by president Spotiswoode [1633–41], and by Dury, who continued in the Session from the year 1621 until his death in the year 1642. And though these decisions have been intermitted since that time, till King Charles II's return, the loss is not great, these times being troublesome, and great alterations of the Lords; but the decisions of the Lords have been constantly observed since that King's return, by which most of the feudal questions are determined; and these things which Craig could but conjecture from the nature of the feudal rights, the customs of neighbouring nations, and the opinion of feudists, are now commonly known, and come to a fixed custom; neither doth he observe any decisions particularly further than his own time, in which our feudal customs could be but little determined, seeing the Lords of Session were mutable and ambulatory, till the year 1540, in which King James V did perfect the establishment of the Session in a College of Justice [College of Justice Act, 1540, c.93; A.P.S. 11,359,c.10], who at first, could not be so knowing and fixed in their forms and customs; and therefore, it cannot be thought strange, if the feudal customs, as they are now settled, do much differ from what Craig did observe: he hath indeed very well observed the origin and nature of feudal rights, and the customs of Italy where they began, and of France and England, whence they were derived to us; and therefore, we shall say little as to these; and so much only of the rights themselves as must necessarily be introductory to our fixed customs, in which we shall follow that same method (as most accommodated to the matter) which we observed in the former title of Real Rights. But there being in feudal rights nothing of that original community there spoken of, but only promiscuous properties of incorporations or persons, or otherwise a servitude of common pasturage, &c. therefore, we

shall first speak of the right of property of lands, both in relation to the superior and to the vassal: next, of the servitudes competent in fees; which comprehending all rights, not reaching the alienation of the substance, but only the lesser interests extending to the profits or use of hereditaments, it must comprehend both the interest introduced by law, as teinds, and these that are by consent, by infeftments or other grants, or long possession; as life-rents, conjunct-fees, terces, and the right of courtesy, annualrents, pensions, rentals, tacks, &c. or real servitudes, as thirlage, pasturage, &c.: and lastly, feudal pledges, which are called wadsets. But in all, we are here only to speak of the constitution of feudal rights, leaving the transmission thereof to heirs, or singular successors, to the third book of the Institutions.

4. The property of all lands and immoveables, or hereditaments, is either allodial or feudal. Allodial is that, whereby the right is without recognisance, or acknowledgment of a superior, having a real right in the thing; thus are moveables enjoyed; and lands and immoveables were so till these feudal customs. Now there remains little allodial; for lands holden feu, or burgage, or lands mortified, are not allodial, seeing they acknowledge a superior having the direct right, and to whom there must be some rent or return, though they be not so proper fees, as land holden ward. Yet the superior's right in the sovereign power, is not feudal, but allodial with us, though some kingdoms be holden of superiors as feudal. The gleibs of ministers seem to come nearest to allodials, having no infeftment, holding, rent or acknowledgment, though they be more properly mortified fees, whereof the liferent-escheat befals to the king only [11,3,40; 11,4,63,*infra*].

Kirks and kirk-yards are only allodial, without any acknowledgment of a superior, but they are destinate for pious uses, and are ordained to be upheld and repaired, Parl. 1563, cap. 76 [A.P.S. 11,539,c. 12]. And the parishioners of every parish are ordained to build and repair kirk-yard dykes, with stone and mortar, two ells high, and to make kirk-styles therein, Parl. 1597, cap. 232 [Kirk Dykes Act, 1597, c.232; A.P.S. iv,131,c.3]. The manner of repairing kirks was remitted to the Council by the said first act of Parliament, and thereupon an act of Council was made, which is ratified, Parl. 1572, cap. 54 [A.P.S. iii,76*,c.15], but it is not repeated in the ratification, but only in general, that the parishioners were warranted to name persons to stent their neighbours.

5. A fee signifieth either the right itself, or the thing affected with the right, whether it be corporeal, as lands, lochs, woods, fortalices, mills; or incorporeal, as annualrents, fishing, jurisdiction, pasturage, or the like.

Fees at first were only granted for fidelity and military service; and therefore they implied. 1. A free and gratuitous donation, as to money, or other anterior cause. 2. None could succeed therein, but such as could perform that service, whereby women were excluded. 3. They could descend to none but to the male issue of the first vassal's body, which ceasing, they became void, and could not be transmitted to the collaterals, or to the ascendents of the first vassal. 4. Whensoever they were open, or void by the death of the vassal infeft, they returned to the superior, until the vassal's heir were capable of military service, which was esteemed to be so soon as he attained majority, and while they were in non-entry by the negligence of the vassal, not demanding infeftment; but in his minority, when he was unable to serve, both the lands and the vassal were in the hands of the superior in ward and custody, or of his donatar beside which he had then no other profit of his fee.

In all fees, fidelity by the vassal to his superior is necessarily implied, and if any thing were acted contrary to fidelity and gratitude, against the life and fame of the superior, to the great prejudice of his estate or nearest relations, the fee became void; wherein is also comprehended the vassal's disclaiming of his superior, or owning another in his place; or infefting another vassal without his superior's consent.

Fees are not only unalienable without consent of the superior, for the reasons now adduced; but they are *stricti juris*, and there is no obligement upon the superior to receive any stranger, or singular successor to be his vassal, except what the law hath introduced by statute or custom, in favour of creditors, for obtaining satisfaction of their debts, by apprising or adjudication, whereby the superior may be compelled to receive singular successors: yet the disposition, procuratory, or precept of seasin before infeftment are assignable, and the superior may be compelled to receive assignees, if the disposition be in favour of assignees: but infeftment being once taken, he is not obliged to receive any assignee or singular successors, otherwise than in obedience of horning upon apprising or adjudication, getting a year's rent for accepting a new vassal [11, 4, 32, *infra*].

6. These being the ancient requisites of fees, that is a proper fee which hath them, and the want of any of them makes it improper in so far; but most of them are now changed by the tenor of the infeftment; as when the fee is granted to the vassal, and the heirs of his body, it is so far improper, that women may succeed; if it be granted to him and his heirs simply, then his collateral heirs or ascendents may succeed: or if to his heirs-male whatsoever; much more if to the heirs or descendents of other persons in tailzies. Fees are also granted, not for military service, or service indefinitely, but for some definite particular service, as for carrying of a sword, or other ensign of honour, before the superior on solemn days; or not for service at all, but for some rent, which is either inconsiderable, as a mere acknowledgment of the superior, as a penny money, or a grain of pepper, a rose, &c. or for a feu-farm duty in money, or any fungible, or other performance: or, when the avail of the marriage, and profit of the ward is taxed to such a sum.

Hence we may consider, what remains as to the essentials of fees, and common interests thereof, which are these.

7. First, There must remain a right in the superior, which is called *dominium directum;* and withal, a right in the vassal, called *dominium utile:*

the reason of the distinction and terms thereof is, because it can hardly be determined, whether the right of property is in the superior or vassal alone, so that the other should only have a servitude upon it; though some have thought superiority but a servitude, the property being in the vassal, and others have thought the fee itself to be but a servitude, to wit, the perpetual use and fruit; yet the reconciliation and satisfaction of both, have been well found out in this distinction, whereby neither's interest is called a servitude; but by the resemblance of the distinction in law, betwixt *jura et actiones directæ*, and those which for resemblance were reductive thereto, and therefore called *utiles*, the superior's right is called *dominium directum*, and the vassal's *dominium utile*, and without these the right cannot consist.

Secondly, as there must be a right in the superior, and another in the vassal, so the vassal in his right must necessarily hold of, and acknowledge the superior, as having the direct right in the fee, otherwise the two distinct rights without this subordination, will make but two partial allodial rights.

8. Thirdly, There is necessarily implied in fees, some rent or return to the superior for the fee, which may be either service, money, or other fungible, or prayers and supplications, as in fees mortified to the kirk, or other performance, or at least the vassal's fidelity to the superior, implying, not only negative, that he may not wrong the superior, but positive, that he must reveal to his superior any design against his life or fame.

9. Which fidelity, though it be not expressed, yet it is necessarily implied in all kinds of fees, and cannot be taken away by any paction to the contrary, without destroying the very nature of this right.

10. To come now to the constitution of the property of lands, in fee and heritage, the feudal contract is of itself alienative, as loan, sale, exchange, and the contracts in law, called, *do ut des*, and *do ut facias*: of which two last, the feudal contract is a kind, seeing thereby land or other immoveable is given, for giving or doing something; therefore, as in others, so in it, the will of the owner must constitute the right in the vassal; and seeing by the custom of nations, some kind of possession is necessary to constitute or transfer property, the superior's delivery of possession to the vassal, or acknowledgment and approbation thereof in the vassal, to be holden by him in fee, were sufficient to constitute and perfect the fee.

11. And therefore, in the udal right of lands in Orkney and Zetland, whereby, without any infeftment, investiture or other right or writ, they enjoy lands and hereditaments, it sufficeth them to instruct by witnesses, that they have possessed, as being holden and repute heritable possessors of such lands; but the law and custom of Scotland hath, as in all other places, necessarily required writ, not only for evidence of the constitution of this right, but as solemnities for the perfecting and solemnizing thereof, without which it becomes not a complete real right of the ground, except where such writs have been destroyed, or lost in times of trouble, and then a proving the tenor of them must be used: or in some cases the heritor may be cognosced

by an inquest, as heritable possessor. But ordinarily writ is requisite, which writs are called an infeftment, or an investiture.

12. Infeftment or *infeudatio*, signifieth the right constitutive of a fee, as its etymon indicateth: so also investiture is the same, more metaphorically, as we are said to be invested or indued with any right, as men are covered with a garment or cloak, and denuded and divested thereof, when it is extinct or transmitted: so both infeftment and investiture signify the writs, which are evidents, signifying the acts constituting the fee; and these are two, the dispositive will of the superior, and his delivery of possession by himself, or his bailie in his name, to the vassal, or his procurator or attorney.

13. Of a long time, infeftment hath required writ as a necessary solemnity, and not only as a mean of probation that the superior did truly dispone to the vassal, any immoveable in fee and heritage, and that accordingly the vassal attained possession, natural, civil, or symbolical; for if writ were adhibited only for probation, other probation might also be admitted, not only against the superior, or his heirs by their writ or oath, but even against their singular successors, or other competitors, by whose oath of knowledge or writ, the truth of the infeftment, and of these two necessary acts to constitute a fee, might be proven; and albeit the superior's oath would not prove against a singular successor, yet his writ anterior to that singular successor's right, acknowledging, that he had at such a time invested such a person as his vassal, and entered him in possession, would prove against his assignee; but neither of these ways would constitute a fee, and supply a written infeftment, except where the peculiar custom of fees without writ hath been immemorial, and therefore sustained as sufficient: and albeit it be provided by ancient statutes [Rob.III,c.36 (not in A.P.S.); IV,45,17,*infra*], that the heritable possessors of lands may be cognosced by inquest, yet that was only upon consideration of calamity and war, whereby writs were destroyed, and where no competition was by any pretending a written infeftment, and possession conform, the question being only betwixt the superior and his vassal, who with his predecessors had been in immemorial possession, as being holden and repute heritable possessors, by performing the deeds proper to vassals of such lands, and so holden and repute as heritable possessors by the neighbourhood: which I have not heard to take effect for others, but the King's immediate vassals, who claims property in no lands as supreme superior, but what is annexed to the crown, or whereof the property is acquired to the King, by the casualities of his superiority, or by acquisition from other proprietors: and therefore he doth never exclude the ancient heritable possessors, though they have lost their rights by public calamity, wherein not only adminicles in writ, but the testimonies of witnesses above exception are received: whereby if the right be not proved to be blench, or feu by the Exchequer Rolls, which bear all the King's property and the reddendos thereof, or by Eques made in Exchequer, the fee will be held ward, and according to the probation and verdict of the inquest, charters will be granted by the King in Exchequer, and so

there scarce can be pretended any fee, which hath not been already established by writ, except in Orkney and Zetland.

14. The writ requisite to constitute a fee, must contain the present dispositive act of the superior, by which he dispones to the vassal and his heirs the fee, in whatsoever terms he expresseth it, whether he gift, grant, alienate, sell, or dispone, though these several terms expressed, may import a different title and warrandice, yea, albeit no cause or title be expressed or implied, but only that the superior dispones: or though the cause or title insinuated be not true, yet it was sufficient with possession, until the solemnity of instruments of seasin was introduced, and is still sufficient when seasin is rightly adhibited; for we follow not that subtility of annulling deeds, because they are *sine causa*, but do esteem them as gratuitous donations; and therefore narratives expressing the cause of the disposition, are never inquired into, because, though there were no cause, the disposition is good, and albeit neither the *tenendas*, *reddendo*, or the *modus acquirendi*, be expressed, yet if the property was the disponer's, and he do but express the disposition to be in fee and heritage, it is valid; for the *reddendo* is understood to be services, accustomed in ward-holdings; and thereby will be carried (though not expressed) all the parts and pertinents of the fee.

And therefore any disposition *per verba de præsenti* in fee, is valid as to that part of the infeftment, and although the disposition contained an obligement to grant charters, yet the not granting thereof doth not prejudge. And though charters be granted relative to prior obligements, yet they are good, without necessity to prove these. Nor will it be sustained, for the superior or any competitor to say, that if the prior obligation, disposition, or contract, were produced, it would be found conditional, or have clauses in favours of the superior, or that competitor, whether generally or particularly alleged: but if these were lost, the charter is sufficient, and no more is understood to be in the real right, than what is contained in the charter; yea, though the charter bear, that it is granted "according to the provisions and conditions contained in such a contract, disposition, or bond," which may import, that the superior by granting the charter without these, hath not past from them; and therefore, he may insist upon them as personal obligements, and the vassal will be obliged to produce the same *ad modum probationis*, by exhibition or incident diligence, whereupon he must depone, whether he has them, or had them since the citation, or did at any time fraudulently put them away: but if without fraud they be lost, the charter is sufficient; yet if any other should found relevant alledgeances upon the original disposition, if they be sustained, he will get diligences to cause the same be produced *ad modum probationis*.

Precepts of *clare constat* [III, 5, 26, *infra*] are also sufficient, seeing they contain a precept to infeft such a person as vassal, which implies the dispositive will of the superior; and therefore is valid in place of a charter from its date, albeit it hath no effect against singular successors, as to that vassal's predecessor's rights, which must be instructed by the rights themselves, and not by the superior's acknowledgment.

And for the same reason, other precepts of seasin, not relating to particular charters or seasins, but either simple, or bearing *secundum chartam conficiendam*, are sufficient, although these charters be never granted: but there will be understood a proper ward-holding gratuitous, without warrandice, extending only to the heirs of the vassal's body, but not reaching to collaterals or ascendents, unless the precept express or insinuate an onerous title, as vendition, excambion, &c.

But since writ became to be an essential solemnity of fees, the superior's present dispositive act must be in writ, but his preterit declaratory act, acknowledging such a person and his predecessors to be vassals, and have the fee, or his obligement to grant the fee, though never so express, which relates not to a disposition *de futuro*, will not supply a charter, though clad with real possession, or having seasin by instrument, bearing to be *propriis manibus:* Yet in some cases, adminiculation of a seasin will suffice, as in the liferents of wives being proportional, or in very ancient rights, or where in competition no better right is shown; and in rights of property that are old, though the mediate warrant of the seasin be lost, the obligement to grant such infeftment will be valid, not only against the superior, or his heirs and successors, but against others having singular titles.

Much less is it necessary to have formal and ample charters in the best style upon parchment, in Latin, sealed; albeit vassals are obliged to accept no other, and the notaries, drawers of informal charters, may be deposed and censured, yet the right will not be annulled, or postponed to posterior, more formal, and solemn rights, for want of these formalities.

15. The formal tenor of charters is different, according to the several kinds of infeftments; whereof some are original infeftments, by which the fee was first constituted, and therefore are most plain and simple, containing the dispositive clause, relating or insinuating the title or original of the right. If it be an original charter from the King, it begins with his royal title, etc., and bears the consent of the treasurer, or commissioners of the treasury, and bears a narrative of the motives, inducing the King to grant the same; and if it be ward or blench, in burgage, or mortification, it bears, *Damus, concedimus et in perpetuum confirmamus*. But if it be a feu-charter, it bears, *Arendamus, locamus, in emphyteusin dimittimus, et in perpetuum confirmamus;* and then follows the clause *tenendas*, and the clause *reddendo*, which if it be ward, bears, *Servitia debita et consueta:* if blench, the particular blench duty, *nomine albæ firmæ:* if feu, the particular feu-duty, and sometimes the duplication thereof, and the marriage of the heir: if burgage, it bears, *Servitia burgalia:* if in mortification, it bears, *Preces et supplicationes*. And ordinarily warrandice, which, though very ample, hath no effect; for if the right prove invalid, there is no action against the King, who doth always dispone *plenissimo jure*, but *periculo petentis;* especially when he dispones as supreme superior, by the right of his

crown: but if he dispone for a price or cause onerous, as for sums of money, or by excambion, lands acquired by him, being no part of the revenue of the crown, or annexed property in these *utitur jure privato*, and his warrandice may have effect, as to his private patrimony, but not as to the patrimony of the crown.

Charters granted by the King of fees by progress, are either upon resignation or by confirmation, or upon apprising or adjudication, which differ from original charters, in their several specialities; as, charters upon resignation, after the dispositive clause, bear the conveyance, "That the lands or others were resigned in the hands of his Majesty, or his commissioners, by a procuratory of resignation apart, or in a disposition or contract, expressing its date, in favours of the acquirer, his heirs or assignees;" whereupon resignation being made in the resigner's life, the charter will be granted to him, or to his heirs served generally, or to his assignees, having right by assignation to the procuratory of resignation.

Charters of confirmation do deduce the right to be confirmed, which, if it be a charter *à se*, bearing, "to be holden from the disponer of the King," and expressing the *tenendas* and *reddendo*, the King's charter doth in the like style, generally relate the charter to be confirmed, and then ratifies, confirms, and approves the same in all the heads and articles therein, and then subjoins the tenor and words of the charter.

There is another kind of charter of confirmation by the King, of charters granted by his vassals to their sub-vassals, not to be holden *à se* of the King, but *de se* of the disponer. The effect of which confirmation is to secure the acquirer against the forfeiture, or recognition of his superior.

Charters by the King upon apprising or adjudication, do either narrate the apprising or adjudication before the dispositive clause; or otherwise after the dispositive clause, by the clause beginning, *Quæ quidem terræ per prius hæreditarie pertinuerunt ad A. B. &c.* "That the lands and others in the charter, were apprised or adjudged from the former vassal, or his apparent heir, lawfully charged to enter heir in special;" and expresses the date of the apprising or adjudication, and the sums therein contained, and bears, in the *reddendo*, the duties and services, due and accustomed before the said apprising or adjudication; likewise the King's charters bear as witnesses, "several officers of state, and the director of the chancellary, &c."

The King's charters must pass in exchequer upon a signature signed by the King, or by his treasurer, or commissioners of the treasury, and a *quorum* of the exchequer; which signature is recorded in the books of exchequer, and then passeth under the signet, and then under the privy seal, whose warrant is the signature, and then under the quarter seal, which is called the testimony of the Great-seal, and lastly under the Great-Seal itself.

Charters by subjects in most things agree with the King's charters, but differ in these points, that they begin not with their titles, but thus, *Omnibus hanc cartam visuris vel audituris;* and then follows the superior's title or designation. And in original charters, the special cause is narrated, as for implement of a certain contract, disposition, or obligation; in them also the warrandice is more particularly expressed, because it is effectual according to its tenor.

In the charters granted by subjects, the precepts of seasin were ordinarily engrossed, and now by the late act of Parliament 1672, cap. 7 [Writs Act, 1672, c. 7; A.P.S. VIII, 69, c. 16], precepts of seasin are appointed to be insert in the King's charters, which before could only pass by a writ, under the quarter-seal, or testimony of the Great-seal.

In all charters, both by King and subjects, the clause *tenendas* useth to be insert, expressing the lands, or others by their ordinary designations, and then adding, *Per omnes suas metas antiquas et divisas, prout jacent in longitudine et latitudine, cum domibus, ædificiis, boscis, planis, moris, maresiis, viis, semitis, aquis, rivolis, stagnis, pratis, pascuis et pasturis, molendinis et multuris, et eorum sequelis, aucupationibus, venationibus, piscationibus, petariis, turbariis, cuniculis, cuniculariis, columbis, columbariis, hortis, pomariis, fabrilibus, brasinis et brueriis, genistis, sylvis, nemoribus et virgultis, lignis, lapicidinis, lapide et calce, cum curiis et earum exitibus, herezeldis, blooduitis, et mulierum merchetis, libero introitu et exitu, ac cum omnibus aliis libertatibus, commoditatibus, proficuis, asiamentis, ac justis suis pertinentiis quibuscunque, tam non nominatis quam nominatis, tam subtus quam supra terram, procul et prope ad prædictas terras spectantibus, seu spectare valentibus, quomodolibet in futurum, libere, plenarie, quiete, integre, honorifice, sine aliquo impedimento, revocatione, contradictione, aut obstaculo qualicunque.*

In the charters by the King or subjects, there may, and useth to be insert a clause *de novo-damus*, which doth dispone the fee, as by an original right, in case the disponer's right should be found defective, and to secure against any title proper to the superior, either as to the property, or any servitude or casuality; which clauses use to be very full, and to express "all nullities, title, or interest in the superior, with supply of all defects;" and bearing all the particular casualities, with which the fee might be burdened, which are effectual, and extended to the full against subjects. But as to such clauses in the King's charters, they are fully extended as to all interest in the King, relating to the property, such as "nullities, forfeiture, recognition, purpresture, disclamation;" but the general words *Pro omni jure, titulo et interesse*, are not extended against the King, to any casuality of superiority, (not reaching, but burdening the property,) except such only as are particularly expressed: and therefore a *novo-damus*, in a bishop's charter from the King, disponing a patronage *pro omni jure*, was found to give the bishop's successor right to that patronage, though it was a laick patronage, without necessity to instruct that the bishop had any pretence of a title thereto before, but that the *novo-damus* was as effectual as an original right, Feb. 29, 1680, Sir John Scot of Ancrum *contra* Archbishop of Glasgow [2 Stair 765; M. 9339]. But a *novo-damus* by the King, bearing *pro omni jure, titulo et interesse*, and expressing ward, was found not to exclude the King's donatar from the marriage, as being a casuality differing from the ward, which useth to pass by a several gift, July 17, 1672, Lord Hatton *contra* the Earl of Northesk [2 Stair 98; M. 6508].

The reason of the different extension of the clause *de novo-damus*, as to the King and subjects, is, because subjects are presumed to take special notice of all clauses that they insert in their charters, which *in dubio* are interpreted *contra proferentem*. But these clauses do more easily pass by inadvertence in Exchequer; and therefore their gifts are more regulated by their acts, than by the common style thereof. For though gifts of ward comprehend non-entry, ay and while the entry of the righteous heir; yet by act of Exchequer, it is only extended to three terms after the ward, though the old style be still continued.

Charters do also comprehend several conditions and provisions, of which hereafter. And some charters do express a bounding, which is ordinary in these within burgh. And some do express a particular enumeration. And some have only the general name of barony, or tenendry, or some other common designation, under which there may be particular designations comprehended. And some charters bear "courts and their issues," or particularly "infangtheif, outfang-thief, pit and gallows."

16. These charters, or other writs in place of charters, though they do never so fully comprehend the dispositive will of the superior, yet they never become a real right till they be completed by seasin, which imports the taking of possession; for seasin and seizure are from the same original, signifying laying hold of, or taking possession: and disseasing is dispossession; and therefore, it is a needless question, whether seasin or possession are distinct, and which are most effectual; for till the solemnity of instruments of seasin was introduced to accomplish the real right of fees, possession was necessary to be joined to the disposition, which possession might either be natural by actual inhabitation, manuring or stocking of the ground, *positione sedium;* or might be civil, by uplifting the fruits and duties: or it might be symbolical, *positione pedum*, by entering upon the land as vassal upon the superior's warrant. But if this symbolical possession were *retenta possessione naturali*, the superior disponing to another, who first attained the natural possession, he would have been preferred to the symbolical possession, as being suspect and simulate, *retenta possessione;* therefore till the time of King James the first, any charter, disposition, or precept from a superior to a vassal, mentioning his heirs, or an heritable right, with true and real possession, without simulation, was sufficient to complete the fee. So a charter with natural possession was sustained, being in the reign of Robert II, June 24, 1625, Town of Stirling *contra* L. of Urkle [*Sub nom. L. Urthill*, Durie 166; M. 6621]. And also before the reign of King James I, Hope, Seasin, Earl of Marr *contra* Bishop of Aberdeen [Hope, *Maj. Pr.* III, 6, 41].

But King James I. having been long detained in England, being taken in his voyage coming home from France [James I was captured at sea in 1406, on his way to France, and detained in England until 1424], did thence bring in the solemnity of seasins by the instrument of a notary, about the year 1430, as Craig relateth *l.2,dieges.7*, near the beginning, [11,7,2; see also IV,3,4, *infra*], and yet saith, that long thereafter, even near to his time, the bailie's seal upon the superior's disposition, charter, or precept, was sufficient to instruct delivery of possession.

Neither was there necessity then in any case to prove the delivery, or the superior's entering the vassal in possession, but that was presumed from the possession itself: and therefore, it needs not be debated how the vassal entered in possession, or what warrant the bailie had to give him possession, or what warrant the person who received the possession for the vassal had, as his procurator or attorney; for all these powers were presumed. Neither were precepts of seasin, or attornies then in use; for as this solemnity of an instrument of seasin was introduced from England, so was the name of attorney, which is frequent there, but seldom used here, except in cases of seasin.

After instruments of seasin became in use, they were not only sustained as the mean of probation, that possession or seasin was given or taken, but they were the necessary solemnities to accomplish the right, which could not be supplied by any other mean of probation; though the superior with a thousand witnesses, should subscribe all the contents of a seasin, it would be of no effect to make a real right without the attest of a notary, in which sense the vulgar maxim is to be understood, *Nulla sasina nulla terra*, which is not only necessary to the first vassal, but must be renewed to all his heirs and successors; although by the custom of France, the vassal being once infeft, his heirs need not be infeft, but do continue to possess by his right, as the heirs of tacksmen do with us: but every heir must be infeft in fees, otherwise, if they die uninfeft, they never attain the real right, but only a possessory title to the fruits and rents, from the predecessor's death till their own death, which will belong to their executors, in so far as unuplifted from their predecessor's death, till their own death, or renunciation to be heir, and will be affected for their proper debts, which will not affect the heritage, or the next heir entering, who must enter to the defunct, who died last infeft, and will be liable for his debts, but not for the debts of his apparent heir, who was never infeft, except there be a competition upon the defunct fiar's debts, which will be preferred to the apparent heir's executors-creditors, but if there be no debts of the last infeft or apparent heir, the rents will remain *in hæreditate jacente*, and will belong to the next heir without confirmation. [See also 11,1,22; 11,6,17; 111,5,2,*infra*.]

17. Let us then consider the formal tenor of an instrument of seasin, and the meaning thereof, and then consider the essentials and necessary requisites thereto, and how far unformal seasins have been sustained. A formal seasin is the instrument of a notary-public, bearing the delivery of symbolical possession, by the superior or his bailie, to the vassal or his attorney, by delivery of earth and stone, and other symbols accustomed upon the ground of the fee; which instrument should contain the name of God, as its initial words, *In Dei*

nomine, Amen, that it may keep the notary in remembrance of his faith and trust, deterring him to take the name of God to a falsehood or lie. 2. It should bear the date by the day, month, and year of God, and was accustomed to have the indiction and name of the Pope, which since the Reformation hath not been in use: but it should contain the name of the King, and the year of his reign. 3. It bears the appearance of the vassal or his certain attorney, which is sufficiently instructed by having of the precept of seasin in his hands, which is but *præsumptio juris,* and doth not exclude a contrary probation, especially as to the heir of the first vassal, who, by taking infeftment, becomes liable for all his predecessor's debts, and therefore if the superior should grant a precept of *clare constat,* the bearer thereof, as attorney for the apparent heir, taking seasin, would involve the apparent heir in all his father's debts; and therefore it may be proven by the superior and attorney's oaths, that the precept of seasin was without warrant from the apparent heir, and so was fraudulent and collusive, to involve him in his predecessor's debts, and in an overburdened and hurtful succession. 4. It must bear the delivery of the precept of seasin to the superior, if he be present, or in his absence, to his bailie, whose warrant is secured, because there is a blank left in the precept for his name, in which blank any person's name being filled up, he is sufficiently authorised as bailie in that part, specially constitute. 5. It bears the bailie's accepting of the precept, and delivering of it to the notary in presence of the witnesses. 6. It must bear the notary's reading of the precept, and exponing it, if it be in Latin, and then the words of the precept should be engrossed. 7. It bears the superior or the bailie's delivering of earth and stone of the land to the vassal, or to his attorney, bearer of the precept; or delivery of any other accustomed symbol, as a penny for an annualrent, a net for fishing, a clap for a mill. 8. It bears the attorney's requiring instruments. 9. It must bear, that these things were done upon the ground of the land, or other hereditament, and the hour of the day, before two witnesses at the least, required thereto, which witnesses must now subscribe with the notary, since the late act of Parliament 1685 [Subscription of Deeds Act, 1681, c.5; A.P.S. VIII, 242, c. 5; IV, 42, 9, *infra*]. And lastly, the attest of the notary, bearing the authority of his creation, and that he was present with the witness, saying, *vidi, scivi, et audivi,* that the things contained in the instrument, were so done as is expressed therein, and that he took a note thereof, and thereupon drew a formal instrument, and insert the same in his protocol, whereunto are adjoined his sign, his motto contained in his commission, relating to his faithfulness and trust, and his name or the initial letters thereof.

18. If any of these be omitted, the notary may be exauctorate and punished by the Lords, but the essentials are much fewer. Yet the seasin must contain the delivery of symbolical possession, by the superior or his bailie to the vassal, or his attorney, upon the ground of the land or other tenements, in presence of the notary and witnesses, with the date and subscription of the notary. But the delivery of the symbol of an office, having no particular place

or ground, is sufficient anywhere, as a baton for a military office, or a scroll, book, or cape for a civil office: but where the fee hath a particular ground or place, there it must be taken upon the ground, and it will not be sufficient to be in view of the ground; yet law or custom may otherwise order it in case of necessity; as the infeftments of lands in *Nova Scotia* were appointed to be taken at the castle-gate of Edinburgh. And when lands are rightly united or erected in baronies, seasin taken upon any part thereof sufficeth for the whole; and without union, seasin taken upon any part of the lands, will serve for all the lands in the infeftment lying contigue. Craig relates, [11,7,14] that a seasin was found null and false, where it bore, "These things were done upon the ground of the land," albeit the parties had but part of the ground of the land on which they stood within their shoes, but were not upon the fixed ground thereof.

The instrument of seasin must be taken by a public notary lawfully authorised, at the least so holden and reputed; for though the notary be deprived, it will not vitiate the instrument, taken *bona fide*, by persons who knew not his deprivation, till it be commonly known, or letters of publication intimated at the market-cross. But a seasin was found null, because it wanted these words, *vidi, scivi, et audivi*, Hope, Seasin, Primrose *contra*   [*Sub nom. Primrose* v *Duiry*, Hope, *Maj.Pr.* 111,6,32; M. 14326].

In ancient rights, or where there is not a more solemn infeftment, a seasin hath been sustained, though with considerable defects, as where the seasin bore not "delivery of earth and stone," but only "actual and real seasin," June 17, 1630, Earl of Wigton *contra* E. Cassils [Durie 518; M. 2246]. But not where the seasin wanted delivery of earth and stone, and the name of the attorney, Hope, Seasin, L. Lie *contra* Earl of Callander [*Sub nom. Lee* v *Lauderdale*, Hope, *Maj.Pr.* 111,6,39; M. 6637]. A seasin was sustained, though it did not repeat the precept, and did not bear "delivery of earth and stone," but only "of the ground of the land," yet was preferred to a posterior formal seasin, taken after the matter was litigious, where the seasin was sustained against the purchaser's author, Dec. 23, 1680, Lamberton *contra* L. Polwart [2 Stair 824; M. 14309]. And a seasin of land and a mill was sustained, bearing "delivery of earth and stone of the land and mill, with all solemnities requisite," March 15, 1631, L. of Smeitoun *contra* Vassals of Dumfermling [Durie 581; M. 14320].

19. Seasins being but the assertions of notars, do not prove nor instruct a real right, unless they be astructed by a warrant or adminicle in writ [IV, 42, 9, *infra*], except that it be against tenants at the instance of their master, who is known to be in possession: or that prescription hath run by one or more subsequent seasins, and forty years peaceable possession. And albeit the most ordinary warrant of seasins be the superior's precept ingrossed or related to in the seasin, yet after forty years' possession, there is no necessity to produce precepts of seasin, procuratories or instruments of resignation, even in the case of reductions of infeftments for want of these, Parl. 1594, cap. 214

[Declinature Act, 1594, c.212; A.P.S. IV,67,c.22]. In which there is not required peaceable possession, neither yet continued possession, as is required
in the act of prescription, so that interruptions as to this point will not alter
the case. But there is no necessity to produce any more for instructing an infeftment, but the seasin, and a warrant thereof, such as a precept of *clare constat*, a precept out of the chancellary, a disposition or contract of alienation,
according as the seasin doth relate to the one or the other; as if the seasin bear,
to proceed upon a precept contained in a charter, disposition, or contract of
alienation, these must be produced *specificè* as they are related; not only *passivè* to defend in reductions, but *activè*, as titles of reductions, declarators, and
all other processes, except against tenants or naked possessors, or where prescription hath run, because the charter when it is related to, is a part of the
investiture, making up the real right; and therefore, (as hath been now shown)
there is no necessity to produce a disposition, contract of alienation, or bond,
though the charter relate thereto. But if the seasin bear to proceed upon a precept contained in a disposition, contract of alienation, or bond, then these are
parts of the infeftment, and make up the real right, and so must be produced,
that the defender may except or defend upon any clause therein contained, in
favours of himself, his predecessors or authors; unless the infeftments be ancient, and clad with long possession, in which case it is like the Lords would
extend the foresaid statute, and would sustain a disposition, contract or bond,
as a sufficient adminicle of the seasin, though it related not thereto. And,
albeit this statute mentions only, that charter and seasin shall be sufficient,
under which a disposition or contract of alienation must be comprehended,
when the seasin is immediately taken thereupon, and not upon a formal charter, for then they are the real charter, yet it is not like they would reject a bond
obliging to grant such infeftment, albeit it do not *de præsenti* dispone, as a
sufficient adminicle to sustain a seasin, where they had been forty years in
possession, although prescription was not completed by immediate subsequent seasins or uninterrupted possession [11,12,20,*infra*], the party making
faith, that he did not keep up, or conceal any other part of the investiture;
which would sufficiently take off the presumption of fraudful concealing, or
away-putting the immediate warrant of the seasin, which might afford defences to the other party. For even in a recent case, of the infeftment of a wife
in liferent, her seasin was sustained upon production of her contract of marriage, albeit the seasin proceeded upon a bond granted for the same cause,
December 20, 1664, Mr. George Norvil, Advocate, *contra* Sunter, [1 Stair
244; M.12517], where nothing was alleged of long possession, and Nov. 22,
1628, Clappertoun *contra* Home [Durie 399; M.12512], where a wife's seasin
bearing in contemplation of marriage, was sustained without any adminicle,
but the marriage, against an appriser from the husband a year before his
death; Hope, Seasin, Murray of Philiphaugh *contra* Schaw [Hope, *Maj.Pr.*,
III,6,38; M.12510], Gray *contra* Finlayson [Hope, *Maj.Pr.* III,6,36; M.
12509]; but there could be less question if the seasin related to a precept apart,

and did not bear, whether the precept proceeded upon a charter, disposition, alienation or bond, for then the production of any of these would adminiculate the seasin.

Seasins within burgh, for serving of heirs by hasp and staple, by the immemorial custom and privilege of burgh, being given by the town-clerk, do prove sufficiently both the propinquity of blood, that the same was cognosced and seasin given accordingly, without necessity of any warrant or adminicle; but seasins of original rights, or conveyances to singular successors, will not be sustained by the town-clerk, without adminicles even as to tenements within burghs, as was found in an infeftment from a father to his son, bearing to be upon the father's resignation, Feb. 11, 1681, Irwing *contra* Corsan [2 Stair 859; M. 12522], June 21, 1672, Mitchel *contra* Cowie [2 Stair 87; M. 12520; 11, 3, 25, *infra*].

Seasins *propriis manibus*, when either the superior himself doth give seasin to his vassal's attorney, or when the superior's bailie by his precept gives seasin to the vassal, himself being present and accepting, or when the superior immediately gives seasin to the vassal; in these cases the notary's warrant is sufficiently instructed by the seasin, and by the disposition, contract of alienation, or bond, or when the seasin is *propriis manibus secundum chartam conficiendam*, if a charter thereafter made, be shown; as a seasin *propriis manibus*, by a father to his son, reserving the father's liferent, was found valid against a second wife's infeftment, granted for a competent tocher, being adminiculated by a bond granted by the father of the same date with the seasin, obliging him to warrant the same, Feb. 11, 1669, Buchan *contra* Tait [1 Stair 602; M. 12519]; yea, a seasin *propriis manibus* by a superior, containing resignation, accepted by the superior, and immediately seasin given *propriis manibus* was sustained, without any warrant subscribed by the superior, but by the vassal's disposition, containing procuratory of resignation, there being no more solemn infeftment in competition, Jan. 17, 1672, Young *contra* Thomson [2 Stair 47; M. 11207].

But as to seasins *propriis manibus* by husbands to their wives, in contemplation of marriage, either before marriage, where marriage followed, or after marriage, having no adminicle but the marriage; the Lords, according to the different cases, have sometimes sustained them when they were suitable to the parties, and not exorbitant, and where the question was only with the husband's heir, or with an appriser, Nov. 22, 1628, Clappertoun *contra* Hoome [Durie 399; M. 12512]; June 19, 1668, relict of Wallace of Galrigs *contra* his Heir [1 Stair 541; M. 12518], in which case it was instructed, that about that time, the wife had disponed to her husband her jointure by a former marriage: but such seasins are easily improven, if they be not asserted by the witnesses insert: as in the last case, the heir insisting in an improbation, there being four witnesses in the seasin, two of them deponed they were not witnesses thereto, the third remembered not, the fourth was positive for it, and the notary offered to depone, that it was true; yet having no adminicle, his oath was not taken, and the seasin was improven; but if there had been an adminicle, the notary and one of the witnesses being positive, the seasin would not have been improven: for where there is a warrant, mediate or immediate, providing a seasin be given, *Quod fieri debet facilè præsumitur ;* and therefore the witnesses not remembering or denial, would hardly improve such seasins, unless their testimony were positive, giving special circumstances of their denial, as being in such another country, or far distant place at that time, if the truth of that were otherwise astructed. But the general denial to be witnesses could import no more, but *non memini :* and therefore an adminicle in writ, with the protocol or oath of the notary, if he were alive, and especially if possession followed for some time; these would stronglier approve, than the not remembrance or general denial of the witnesses insert would improve. But this dipping upon a general question, *de fide instrumentorum,* we shall say no more of it in this place, nor of the admission and qualifications of notaries, as to which Craig [11,7,9] relates the customs of France, which were not then, nor have not yet been here allowed; but certainly more exactness ought to be in the admission of notaries, not only as to their skill, but as to their reputation of honesty and fidelity, and the least want or weakening of these should turn them out; and therefore the Lords, by a late act of sederunt, declare they will admit no notary of course as formerly; but upon testimonial of the person's education and reputation, and the trial and report of four of their number. For the introduction of the solemnity of the instruments of notaries, was not only because of old, few could write, and the impressions of seals were easily imitated: yea, so rude were subscriptions, even in Justinian's time, that some could so artificially imitate another's hand-writ, that himself could not know it, or durst swear it was not his writ. And therefore he introduced two remedies, 1. That private writs should not prove by the subscription of the party, unless there were three subscribing witnesses, knowing the parties-contracters; or that there were three witnesses who deponed anent the truth of the deed. 2. That otherwise, writs were made in public by a public person, which at first was only done judicially, but thereafter extrajudicially by a notary-public, *L.* 11, *C. et Auth. seq. qui potior. in pig.* [C.8,17,11]. But our custom hath returned to private writ, and trusteth not the instruments of notaries, but where they are adminiculated by writ, except in the case where parties cannot write: and then in matters of importance, two notaries and four witnesses are necessary by special statute. But this is not extended to seasins, but only to the subscriptions of notaries for parties, Feb. 11, 1669, Buchan *contra* Tait [1 Stair 602; M.12519], July 15, 1680, Bishop of Aberdeen *contra* Viscount of Kenmuir [2 Stair 786; M.3011]. Yet in some cases of small importance, instruments of notaries are probative: and in all cases where witnesses would prove, it doth much fortify the same, that they were witnesses required, and instrument of a notary taken thereupon; for then the instrument of the notary, astructed by the witnesses insert, make a strong probation.

To return to seasins *propriis manibus,* by husbands to wives without warrant or adminicle in writ, they are not generally probative, except in such cases as have been now expressed, Hope, Seasin, Bell and Morison *contra* Thomson [Hope, *Maj.Pr.* 111,6,30; M. 12508], L. of Coldingknows *contra* Dame Helen Herreis [*Ibid.*].

20. But for the further securing of infeftments and land-rights, that excellent statute which before was attempted, was at last perfected, Parl. 1617, cap. 16 [Registration Act, 1617,c.16; A.P.S. IV,545,c.16; II,10,5,*infra*], whereby all seasins, reversions, regresses, bonds or writs for making of reversions, and regresses, assignations thereto, and discharges thereof, renunciations of wadsets, and grants of redemption, not being registrate in a peculiar register, appointed for that end, or in case of consigning, renunciations, and grants of redemption in process, within sixty days next after the decreet, ordaining the same to be given up to the parties having right thereto, or at least within sixty days after seasin taken of the lands or rights, to which the reversions relate, it is declared, that the saids seasins and other writs shall make no faith in judgment by action or exception, in prejudice of a third party, who had acquired a perfect and lawful right to the saids lands and heritage, without prejudice to make use of these rights against the granter and his heirs: but there are excepted reversions contained in the body of the infeftment, and all seasins, reversions, &c. of tenements within burgh were excepted; but by the act of Parl. 1681, cap. 11 [A.P.S. VIII,248,c.13], they must now be inserted in the town-books, in the same way, as other seasins in the Clerk-Register's register of seasins, and are so marked by the town-clerk, without deputation from the clerk of register, for half price of seasins without burgh.

21. And to make land-rights yet more secure, because the former act did not require registration of instruments of resignation in the superior's hands *ad remanentiam*, whereby purchasers were not secure, but that the lands acquired by them might have been resigned or renounced to the superior, whereby their author's fee became extinct, without necessity of new infeftment, being consolidate with the superiority, whereby the superior's infeftment carried both superiority and property; therefore, instruments of resignation not being registrate, are declared null, yet with exception of tenements holding burgage, and therefore a seasin within burgh was sustained, though not found in the town-books, June 30, 1668, Mr. Robert Burnet *contra* Swan [1 Stair 547; M. 13550]; Feb. 11, 1681, Irwing *contra* Corsan [2 Stair 859; M. 12522]; which is yet good as to seasins, reversions, or resignations *ad remanentiam*, before the 6th of September 1681, which is the date of the said Act, at least before the act of sederunt; for upon consideration of this case, the Lords by act of sederunt, ordained the burrows to take sufficient caution of their town-clerks present and to come, to insert in their books all seasins given by them of the tenements within burgh, and all reversions, or bonds for granting reversions, assignations thereto, and discharges thereof, renunciations and grants of redemption, and that within sixty days after the giving of seasin, or presenting to them of the reversions, or others foresaids, and that under the pain of

the damage of any party acquiring *bona fide* for onerous causes by such latent rights though prior, declaring that they will hold all such seasins, reversions, &c. to be given hereafter, and not insert in the town-books in manner foresaid, to be latent and fraudulent, kept up of design to ensnare lawful purchasers.

22. And for the further security of land-rights, because apprising, or adjudication, with a charge of horning thereupon against the superior, maketh for some time, a real right; therefore an Abbreviate of Apprisings, contained in the allowance thereof, written on the back of the same, and signed by two of the Lords, was ordained to be registrate in a particular register for that purpose, within sixty days after the date of the apprising; with certification, that any other apprising, though posterior in date, yet first allowed and registrate, shall be preferred, Parl. 1661, cap. 31 [Registration Act, 1661, c. 31; A.P.S. VII, 229, c. 243], which is extended to adjudications, Parl. 1672, cap. 19 [Adjudications Act, 1672, c. 19; A.P.S. VIII, 93, c. 45; III, 2, 25, *infra*]. But this relates only to the new form of adjudications then introduced in place of apprisings; but for the old adjudications, upon the renunciations of heirs or for implement of dispositions, neither statute nor custom have yet cleared, whether these will be effectual against singular successors from their dates, or from the charge against the superior, or only from the seasins thereupon; which, as all other seasins, must be registrate. And if the Lords do sustain these from the charge, it will make a defect in the security of land-rights, till it be supplied by act of Parliament, or act of sederunt, ordaining the horning against the superior, to be registrate in the Register of Hornings, with the executions of the charge, though without denunciation, otherwise not to operate against singular successors purchasing *bona fide*, for causes onerous. And for further security of land-rights, because they might be reduced upon inhibitions, or interdictions; therefore these, if not registrate, are also null. And in respect, by rebels continuing unrelaxed year and day after the denunciation, the superior hath the fee, during the life of the vassal denounced, therefore horning, if not registrate, is also null: and the act of prescription excludes all prior rights, preceding forty years, unless they have obtained possession, or done diligence therefor by interruptions, which must be repeated every seven years, or else they are null, and must also be executed by a messenger; so, that where before, a citation made interruption, which continued for forty years, which might much insecure purchasers, they can now last but seven years, in which short time the noise thereof may readily reach purchasers; so that if a purchaser get a progress of infeftments for forty years, he may by the registers know if there be any real right that can affect the fee within that time, and hath no more to enquire, but as to interruptions within seven years, which if the Lords appoint to pass only upon bills, it may be found at the signet: so that upon the whole matter, no nation hath so much security of irredeemable land-rights as we have. It is true, redeemable rights are not so secure, because they may be evacuated by order of redemption, which proceeds by instruments of premonition and consignation, which require no reg-

istration; and therefore purchasers of apprisings or adjudications, during the legal reversion, are in hazard of any order of redemption, or summons for compt and reckoning; and likewise these who purchase wadsets or infeftments of property, or annualrent for security of sums, run the hazard of satisfaction and payment of these sums by intromission, or otherwise [II, 5, 15; II, II, 4; III, 1, 21, *infra*], wherein there is little inconveniency; for no man should purchase a redeemable right, without consent of the reverser, but upon his hazard; or if there be any reversion, reservation, or real burden in his author's right *sibi imputet*, it is his fault and negligence if he did not see to it, and secure himself against it when he bought it.

The question may occur here, if the keeper of the register of seasins do, according to the custom, mark the seasin registrate, and attest the same by his subscription, and yet, by negligence or fraud, shall not insert it in the register, whether in that case a purchaser *bona fide*, for causes onerous, though infeft thereafter, will be excluded by that prior infeftment, marked by the clerk, not recorded. Though nothing hath been observed in this case, yet if seasins marked registrate, though not found in the register, were found sufficient against singular successors purchasing thereafter, the design and tenor of this statute would be eluded; for the statute bears, "if they be not registrate," (which must import, their being insert in the register) "they are null;" and therefore, though the keeper of the register hath attested such seasins to be registrate, yet truly they are not registrate: and no purchaser could be secure by inspection of registers, if a false attest of a clerk could exclude him, who oft-times is insolvent. Yet by the 19th Act, Parliament 1686 [A.P.S. VIII, 600, c. 133], the contrary is statuted, which is declared to extend to former cases, yet there is a clause insert in this Act, that it shall no wise derogate from the Act 1617 [Registration Act, 1617, c. 16; A.P.S. IV, 545, c. 16], anent registration of seasins; which must either annul this Act, as reported in Parliament contrary thereto, or else it is inconsistent with the old Act; for a writ is not registrate by the clerk's attestation, but by being insert in the register. But because the keepers of registers are not able to book within the sixty days appointed by the act 1617, because the writs to be registrate are not presented till about the end of these days, therefore the Lords by an act of sederunt might declare, that the effect of that Act cannot be attained, so that parties may see their writs insert at the time appointed, unless they be presented with thirty days of their dates, that the keepers shall not receive them thereafter, and that they shall insert them within these sixty days, being so presented, and shall keep minute-books of the writs, wherein the presenter shall insert the writ and date of presenting, and sign it presented, whereby the keeper cannot change these minute-books.

23. Seasins, as all other instruments, must have the attest and subscription of the notary, giver thereof, bearing the names and designations of the witnesses insert. And a seasin was not found void, because taken in the night, nothing of latency or fraud being qualified, but possession conform,

Nov. 19, 1679, Arnot and Paton her spouse *contra* Turner [2 Stair 708; M. 14332].

24. If a seasin be only extracted out of the register of seasins, it will not be sufficient in improbations, but it proves in all other cases by the Act foresaid, because that register is chiefly for publication, as also the register of hornings and inhibitions, and not for conservation; for the keeper of that register doth not keep the principal seasins, but gives them back marked: but if the principal seasin marked as registrate, be wanting, if the notary who gave it be alive, he may renew it out of his protocol, and the keeper of the register of seasins may attest it registrate, upon the day mentioned in the register; and therefore the Lords, upon supplication, ordained the keeper of a register so to mark a seasin, Jan. 2, 1678, Sir Andrew Ramsay supplicant [2 Stair 587; M. 13553].

25. But if the notary who gave the seasin be dead, there remains yet this remedy, that a transumpt may be made upon production of the protocol and citation of the author, or his heirs, or any other party having interest; which transumpt is sufficient in place of the principal seasin, and may bear both the transumpt of the protocol, and of that part of the register where the seasin was registrate. But the instrument of a clerk, containing the tenor of a seasin, will not be sufficient without citation of the parties.

If both the principal seasin and the protocol be wanting, the tenor of the seasin may be proven, upon citation of the same parties; as in a transumpt, if there be sufficient adminicles in writ, and witnesses who saw the seasin, the extract of the seasin out of the register is a good adminicle therein.

Seasins taken out of the town-books, not by the town-clerk who gave the seasin, but by his successor, will not serve for a principal seasin, the town-book being but the protocol of the town-clerk; and therefore, either the town-book must be produced, that the seasin may be transumed, or commission granted for inspection or collation, which being returned, was found to suffice as a transumpt, Feb. 11, 1681, Irving *contra* Corsan [2 Stair 859; M. 12522; 11, 3, 19, *supra*].

There is another constitution of the property of lands or other heritable rights, by that excellent Act of Prescription, Parl. 1617, cap. 12 [Prescription Act, 1617, c. 12; A.P.S. IV, 543, c. 12], whereby it is statuted and declared, That whosoever shall show a charter of any land or other heritage, and can prove forty years uninterrupted possession, or shall show instruments of seasin, one or more continued and standing together for the space of forty years, proceeding upon retours or precepts of *clare constat ;* these rights are declared to be good, valid, and sufficient rights, for bruiking of the heritable right of lands or others, whereby these evidents are not only sufficient to defend, which was the only use of prescription as an exception, but are sufficient to pursue or compete with the most full and formal infeftments of lands, annual-rents, or other hereditaments.

26. Infeftments do sometimes express the meiths or marches of the lands and tenements, which thence is called a bounding infeftment, giving right to

all within the bounds, if the giver of the charter had right, or if the vassal by that infeftment has had peaceable possession till prescription: otherwise bounding charters prejudge not, Parl. 1592, cap. 136 [This should be c. 138; A.P.S. IV, 38, c. 54]. Yet prescription will adject that which is within the bounding to another tenement, which will not be elided by possessing the major part of that tenement; but no prescription can give right to what is without the bounding, as part and pertinent, November 17, 1671, Young *contra* Bailie Carmichael [2 Stair 3; M. 9636]. But where there is no bounding, possession clears the parts and pertinents of every tenement; and in competition, where any ground is claimed as part and pertinent of several tenements, witnesses are allowed to either party, for proving the possession and interruptions, unless it be alleged, that that ground is *separatum tenementum*, having a distinct infeftment of itself, which will exclude the alledgeance of part and pertinent, if the several infeftments be not excluded by prescription, as was found in the said case, November 17, 1671, Young *contra* Carmichael [2 Stair 3; M. 9636]. But though the one infeftment contain the ground in question, *per expressum*, in the enumeration of the parts of a barony or tenement, and though the other infeftment contain no enumeration, or in the enumeration mention not the ground in question, but the same is alledged to be part and pertinent comprehended under the common designation, or under some of the parts enumerated, if both flow from one common author, as original rights, the first is preferable, but both will be allowed witnesses for proving possession and interruption, *et in pari casu* the express infeftment will be preferable.

27. But the main question is here concerning infeftments holden of subjects, not being past upon the granter's resignation by the superior, or the superior's confirmation, or by his obedience upon decreets of apprising or adjudication; which therefore are called base infeftments, and private infeftments, because they proceed in a more private and ignoble way, being done by the granter and receiver thereof, without the interposition of the superior, and were latent rights before the Act for the registration, or being without clear possession, they are still accounted simulate rights.

The doubt is, whether such be complete real rights, carrying the property of the ground by the charter and seasin only, or not until possession of the hereditament be obtained. The ground of this distinction betwixt infeftments, and of the doubt as to base infeftments, is from the Act of Parliament 1540, cap. 105. [A.P.S. II, 375, c. 23] whereby it is clear, First, Before that Act, infeftments holden of the disponer, without resignation or confirmation, were valid without possession, and preferable to all posterior infeftments, though proceeding upon resignation, or by confirmation: for it is for remedy of this, that this statute is enacted, not upon the account of the manner of holding, but of the privacy and latency: for if the manner of holding were the motive, the basest infeftment might easily be made public by an infeftment upon resignation to a sub-vassal of the vassal who was last infeft; yet it were strange to think a sub-vassal of a base vassal should be less basely infeft, or more public, than his base infeft superior: and therefore an infeftment is base in opposition to a noble infeftment, holden of the king, of the kirk, or burgage, which are but administrators for the king of these parts of the public patrimony.

Secondly, By the letter of this statute, posterior infeftments upon resignation, or by confirmation, are only preferred to prior private infeftments, when the obtainer of the posterior infeftment bruiks the lands peaceably, by labouring, manuring, and uptaking of the mails, profits, and duties, and so are known heritable possessors thereof, year and day; or when such infeftments are for causes onerous, or do contain or import warrandice: neither is there any thing mentioned in the statute, as to the competition of infeftments, upon apprising or adjudication, with prior base infeftments, nor of the competition of one base infeftment with another: yet custom since that statute hath declared and determined the competition of public and base infeftments, and hath restricted this statute in some points, and extended it in others.

First, Custom hath preferred all public infeftments upon resignation or confirmation, or upon apprising or adjudication to base infeftments, though prior, if the base infeftment hath lain out of all kind of possession; and likewise hath preferred posterior base infeftments first clad with possession, to prior base infeftments without possession, especially in consideration, that such base infeftments are fraudulent or simulate, *retenta possessione ;* for the retaining of possession is a pregnant ground of simulation, not only of infeftments, but in any other rights [1, 9, 12, *supra*; 111, 3, 21, *infra*]; as when moveables are disponed and delivered, but presently taken back, and the natural possession continued in the disponer; though instruments be taken upon the delivery, yet other dispositions or legal diligences, attaining and retaining possession are preferable, because the other dispositions are presumed fraudulent and simulate; and gifts of single escheat or liferent escheat, are presumed to be simulate, if the rebel or his conjunct and confident persons be long suffered to retain the possession. And therefore, base infeftments *retenta possessione*, are also presumed fraudulent and simulate, and that not only *præsumptione juris*, by this and other statutes; but *præsumptione juris et de jure*, admitting no contrary probation: for certainly base infeftments may be, and oft-times have been, without simulation, and for onerous causes: and yet these have never been sustained or admitted to probation of the onerous cause which would exclude simulation, to validate such base infeftments: and albeit long retention of possession may raise *præsumptionem hominis*, that public infeftments are simulate or without a cause onerous, yet that presumption hath not been owned by law: and so is not *præsumptio juris*, but *hominis*, which with other evidences of simulation may reduce the right.

Secondly, Custom hath preferred posterior base infeftments, attaining possession or using diligence to attain it, to prior base infeftments, not attaining possession, nor using diligence to attain it: and albeit the supervening statute for registration of seasins be designed for publication thereof, that purchasers thereafter may not be ensnared or disappointed, whereby it might seem that the difference betwixt private or base infeftments, and public infeftments, might have been laid aside, since the said Act for registration of seasins, whereby the uncertainty of real rights, by proving base infeftments clad with possession, by witnesses (wherein our law is so justly jealous and cautious, that they are not admitted in cases where writ uses to be adhibited) might be avoided: yet the preference of public infeftments, to prior base infeftments, not clad with possession, being fixed by custom from this statute, before the Act for registration of seasins, by the space of threescore seventeen years, hath been still continued, to the great confusion and detriment of real rights; for if a base infeftment hath a subaltern infeftment, with assent of the person first basely infeft, that subaltern infeftment is a public infeftment by a superior, whose right is but base. Such infeftments as are without consent of the superior or order of law, have still retained the name and nature of base infeftments; and albeit this alledgeance useth sometimes to be proponed against base infeftments, that they are null, not being clad with possession, yet it is no simple nullity, but only a preference of a more solemn right; for pursuits for mails and duties, removings, yea, and reductions are sustained thereupon, and will not be excluded upon pretence of want of possession, as thereby being null, though they had lain long out of possession. So a base infeftment without possession was, found a sufficient title in a reduction to enforce production of all other infeftments, base or public, albeit the superior did not concur, Spots. Kirkmen, Douglas *contra* the Earl of Home [Spotiswoode 349]: and such infeftments do always exclude posterior arrestments: they do also exclude the terce of the granter's relict, Jan. 27, 1669, Bell of Belford *contra* L. Rutherford [1 Stair 594; M. 1260; III,6,12, *infra*]. But base infeftments do not exclude the liferent escheat of their author, unless they attain possession *in cursu rebellionis*, March 19, 1633, L. of Renton *contra* L. of Blackiter [Durie 680; M. 3662]; Feb. 21, 1667, Milne *contra* Clerkson [1 Stair 448; M. 3664].

Where there is no further ground of simulation than the want of possession, very little possession or diligence for possession will prefer base infeftments to posterior public infeftments, or to posterior base infeftments, clad with possession; as the lifting of one term's rent did prefer a base infeftment to a posterior public infeftment clad with many years possession, Hope, Alienation, Hamilton *contra* M'Adam [Hope, *Maj.Pr.* III,3,40 and 46]. And the payment of a small part of annualrent, far within a term's annual, was sustained to prefer a base infeftment of annualrent, which was also preferred, because there was a decreet of poinding of the ground, though not put to execution, February 26, and 27, 1662, Creditors of Kinglassie competing [1 Stair 105 and 109; M. 1283]. And a citation for attaining possession was found sufficient, Feb. 13, 1624, parties blank [Durie 109; M. 1276]; July 2, 1625,

L. Raploch *contra* Tenants of Lethem [Durie 169; M.1277]; June 26, 1662, Wilson *contra* Thomson [1 Stair 115; M.1289]; Jan. 24, 1679, Hamilton *contra* Seaton [2 Stair 679; M.1290]. Yea, a base infeftment of annualrent was preferred to a posterior base infeftment of property, which intervened before the first term at which the annualrent was payable, and clad with possession before that term, so that the annualrenter did not lie out of possession, but could attain none, July 26, 1676, Capt. Alison *contra* Carmichael [2 Stair 460; M.1285]. Yet a citation on a summons for poinding the ground, being only executed against the debtor, and not against the natural possessor, was found not to clothe the annualrent with possession, Mr. Fenton *contra* Lockhart of Carnwath, Nov. 11, 1690 [Possibly Harcarse 172; M.1290]. But if the annualrenter was in natural possession, citation of him were sufficient; as was found between Rule and the creditors of Langtoun competing, Feb. 1692 [Possibly Harcarse 627].

But an infeftment of property being base, will more easily be annulled as simulate, than an annualrent, because the infeftment of property gets warrant for present possession, which the annualrent doth not: and therefore a public infeftment intervening before the first term of the annualrent, would not be preferred thereto, but would be preferred to an infeftment base of the property, Nov. 6, 1691, Creditors of Langtoun competing [Possibly Harcarse 172; M.3033]. So an infeftment of annualrent, being out of discontiguous lands in several shires, was preferred as to both tenements, by getting payment of annualrents from the heritor or tenants, of either tenement, Nov. 6, 1678, Mr Milne *contra* Mr Hay [2 Stair 644; M.1341; 11,1,13, *supra*]. And possession by an infeftment for corroboration of an annualrent, did prefer the principal infeftment of annualrent, having no other possession, July 9, 1668, Alexander *contra* L. Clackmannan [1 Stair 550; M.1340]. And an infeftment of principal lands, and warrandice lands, being clad with possession of the principal lands, these being evicted, was found to make the infeftment of the warrandice lands effectual from its date, and preferred to a posterior public infeftment of the warrandice lands, though clad with long possession, Jan. 9, 1666, Brown *contra* Scot [1 Stair 335; M.1318]. Yea, base infeftments to wives upon their contracts of marriage, are preferred to all posterior infeftments, and the husband's possession is accounted the wife's possession, though he be common author to both, Nov. 23, 1664, Nisbet *contra* Murray [1 Stair 230; M.1303]. And though the husband did not possess himself, but wadsetters deriving right from him, July 18, 1667. Lady Burgie *contra* Strachan [1 Stair 475; M.1305]. And where the husband's mother did possess by a liferent flowing from the husband's father, to whom he was heir, it was found sufficient to clothe his wife's infeftment with possession, Feb. 21, 1672, Reid *contra* Countess of Dundee [2 Stair 74; M.1305]. But infeftments base to wives, not being upon their contracts of marriage, or in place thereof, are not holden as clad with possession by the husband's possession. And a base infeftment of a wadset, with a back-tack to the granter, is not held clad with

possession by the granter's possession as tacksman, till some further possession be attained.

Where there is any ground of suspicion or simulation, there must be a clear
possession; as a base infeftment by a father to his children was not sustained
by the father's possession, whose liferent was reserved therein, June 26, 1634,
Dury *contra* Bruce [*Sub nom. Bruce* v. *Durie*, Durie 721; M. 1310]; And an
infeftment by a father to his son was not found clad with possession by the
father's possession, though he had a factory from his son; but it was not alleged that the father had granted discharges, expressly relating to the factory,
July 10, 1669, Gardner *contra* Colvil [1 Stair 633; M. 1314]. Yet in the competition of two base infeftments, the former being granted to a stranger for
relief of cautionry, and the latter granted to a son and apparent heir for relief
of his cautionry, exceeding the value of the lands, the son's base infeftment,
though posterior, having first attained possession, and being without all suspicion of simulation, was preferred. And it was not found, that infeftments for
relief were in the same case with warrandice lands, where the possession of
the principal lands is *fictione juris* a possession of the warrandice lands; these
infeftments being less subject to fraud or uncertainty, than infeftments for
relief, which relate to personal debts, and oft-times generally to all debts or
cautionries, contracted or to be contracted, which debts may be retired and
kept up, and made use of by the infeftment for relief, June 26, 1677, Inglis
contra Tennents of Eastbarns [2 Stair 527; M. 1324]. The like was found after
full debate *in præsentia*, in the competition of the Creditors of Cockburn, as
to an infeftment of relief by Cockburn to the Lord Sinclair, July 1, 1691
[Harcarse 171; M. 1337]. It was also found, that an infeftment for relief,
though public, did not give right to the creditor for relief of him, for whose
debts it was granted, but only to the cautioner, who might renounce it at his
pleasure, in the competition of the Creditors of Langtoun concerning young
Langtoun's infeftment of relief [Harcarse 171].

28. Infeftments by confirmation, do not only require a charter from the
disponer, bearing the lands to be holden of the superior, and seasin thereupon, but require also the superior's confirmation, till which it is no real right,
but null; but whensoever the confirmation is added, the right becomes valid
from the date of the infeftment confirmed, both as to the right of property,
and as to the superior's casualities; and therefore an infeftment *a se*, not confirmed, was found null by exception, though clad with some years' possession,
December 4, 1623, Paton *contra* Stuart [Durie 85; M. 15040]; and found null,
though the confirmation was past the Privy Seal, Hope, Confirmation, Hunter *contra* Dalgliesh [Hope, *Maj. Pr.* III,8,12]. And also found null in an
annualrent, holden from the disponer not confirmed, Hope, Confirmation,
Lord Balmerino *contra* Lord Coatfield [Hope, *Maj. Pr.* III,8,13; M. 3007].
But if there were any mid-impediment betwixt the charter confirmed, and the
confirmation, it excludeth the confirmation and whole right, as an apprising
and infeftment thereupon; but confirmation of a right, not bearing to be

holden of the superior, but of a vassal, makes it not a public infeftment, nor takes it away the superior's ordinary casualities, as ward, but only recognition and forfeiture, Hope, Confirmation, Lady Cathcart *contra* vassals of Cathcart [Hope, *Maj.Pr.* 111, 8, 15; M. 4176 and 6461; 11, 4, 23 and 36, *infra*]; Nov. 17, 1627, L. of Clackmannan *contra* Burn [Durie 314; M. 1291]. Hence it is, that because confirmation constitutes rights holden of the superior, that the first confirmation makes the first right, though it confirm a posterior infeftment from the vassal, as is clearly determined in the case of double confirmations holden of the King, Parl. 1578, cap. 66 [A.P.S. 111, 98, c. 7], which is not introduced but declared by that Act, and holdeth alike in other confirmations.

It doth oft-times fall to be doubtful, whether a confirmation makes an infeftment public or not, when seasin is taken upon a precept of seasin in a disposition, which disposition contains obligements for infeftment, *de se et a se*, by confirmation; but the precept of seasin relates not specially to either obligement, and seasin is taken thereupon, and is afterwards confirmed: the question comes, whether this be only a confirmation of a base infeftment, to exclude forfeiture or recognition, or if it doth make the infeftment public? It was constructed as a public infeftment, as was found, July 15, 1680, Bishop of Aberdeen *contra* Viscount of Kenmure [2 Stair 786; M. 3011]. In this case, the confirmation was after the death of the obtainer thereof, and so could not relate to the precept, as *de se* to be holden of the disponer. Such an infeftment was found base without confirmation, and public after; so that it could not then be made use of as from the granter; but only as from the superior, July   1687, Deans *contra* L. Glencors [Possibly Harcarse 269; M. 10123].

29. Infeftments upon apprising or adjudication, when formally perfected, do require charters to be granted by the superiors of the apprised lands or other real rights, the tenor whereof is already set down in this title, and precepts and seasins thereupon, which have little peculiar differing from other infeftments, as to their tenors and effects, but that their *reddendo* is ordinarily general, when the appriser or adjudger cannot prove or instruct the tenor of his author's right; and therefore do bear such duties and services as were contained in the author's right, which the superior may be charged to renew and make special, so soon as the author's rights are produced; and if they be not so renewed, they are understood as ward-holdings: but for renovation thereof, the appriser or adjudger will get letters of horning summarily upon the allowance of the apprising or adjudication, which will not be excluded, although the superior have already granted infeftments in general terms, as aforesaid, but he must renew the same according to the special tenor of the author's right produced, and that without any new composition: yea, the appriser's heirs upon supplication, will obtain letters of horning summarily for renewing the same, and so will his singular successors, whether their title be apprising or adjudication against the former appriser or adjudger; in

which case he may make use of letters of horning, upon the allowance of his own apprising; and though his title be a voluntary disposition, he will get letters of horning, as succeeding in the place of the former appriser or adjudger, to renew and make special the former infeftment to his author, upon payment of a year's duty [11,4,32,*infra*]. But apprisings and adjudications being legal dispositions, and conveyances of the author's infeftment, we shall say no farther of them in this place, but leave them to the next book [111,2,13 *et seq., infra*], where they are considered amongst legal dispositions. We shall only add here, that before the year 1624, apprisings were left at the Great Seal, by warrant from the Lords, whence precepts were issued thereupon, against the superiors to infeft; which if they obeyed not, charters were granted by the King to supply their vice; but since, they are retained by the appriser, and he may have letters of horning summarily charging the superiors to grant charters and precepts of seasin, as is aforesaid.

30. This also is singular in apprisings and adjudications, that a real right of fee is constitute thereby, by a charge of horning against the superior, without charter or seasin [111,2,24,*infra*]: for such apprisings or adjudications are declared effectual by the Act of Parliament 1661, cap. 62 [Diligence Act, 1662,c.62; A.P.S. VII,317,c.344] ordering the payment of debts betwixt creditor and debtor: for after that charge, no infeftment upon voluntary disposition, or upon any other apprising or adjudication, can be granted by the superior, preferring any other vassal to the appriser, or adjudger, whom he hath unwarrantably refused to enter, if the appriser or adjudger insist in his apprising or adjudication for possession; but he may forbear to make use of the apprising or adjudication, and if he lie long out without further diligence, he will be presumed to have relinquished his apprising or adjudication, and posterior rights and diligences will be preferred; but if he enter into possession, no posterior infeftment or diligence will exclude him, although he insist no further but the charge of horning: and it hath not occurred to be determined, how long that right will subsist without infeftment; but it hath been found, that the superior will not be excluded from the casualities of superiority by his former vassal, if he have not been in the fault, in refusing to enter when the appriser or adjudger offered him a charter with a year's rent of the land or annualrent of the sum adjudged or apprised; this was in the case of ward, Feb. 9, 1669, Black *contra* Trinch [*Sub nom. Black* v *French*, 1 Stair 599; M.6911; 11,4,32; 11,4,36,*infra*]. Neither was a superior found to have interest to exclude an appriser from possession, till he paid a year's rent, but that he might possess during the legal, if he insisted not for infeftment [IV,35, 25,*infra*], which insinuates that, after expiring of the legal, the superior might hinder the appriser or adjudger to continue in possession till he take infeftment, and pay a year's rent,; but during the legal, the apprising or adjudication is but as a legal assignation to the mails and duties, so that the appriser cannot be forced to take infeftment till the legal expire, and the land become irredeemably his own, and then he is to pay a year's rent; in this case

there was no charge upon the apprising, Dec. 3, 1672, Hay *contra* L. of Earlestoun [2 Stair 123; M. 15043]. Albeit in the case of Johnstoun *contra* the Tennents of Auchincorse, July 22, 1665, [1 Stair 301; M. 15042] the appriser having charged the superior, though he did not then obey, yet appearing in the process of mails and duties, he offered now to receive the appriser; and therefore the appriser was excluded till he paid the year's rent, which being under consideration of the Lords, in the said case of Hay *contra* L. Earlestoun [2 Stair 123; M. 15043], they resolved to give the appriser his option within the legal to take infeftment or not, so that the charge doth only hinder others to preveen, but doth not exclude the superior from any casuality of the superiority, falling by his former vassal, unless he had been *in culpa*, refusing the appriser's entry, insisting orderly to be entered, which is a great advantage both to debtors and creditors, not to have the accession of a year's rent, till the ancient rights may be discovered, and that it may appear whether the apprising becometh an absolute right.

31. The main division of infeftments in relation to the holding, is in ward, blench, feu, burgage, and mortification. An infeftment ward hath its denomination from ward, which is the chief casuality befalling to the superior thereby; it is the most proper feudal right we have; and therefore, wherever the holding appeareth not, or is unclear, there ward-holding is understood; it is ordinarily expressed by "rendering service, used and wont:" and if the *reddendo* be not express in name of blench, or feu-farm, though it bear payment of some duty, yet ward is inferred, as by a charter, bearing, *sex denarios nomine canæ*, with a taxed marriage; so also it was inferred by a *reddendo*, bearing a particular duty, payable at Whitsunday and Martinmas, *cum servitiis in curiis nostris et alibi debitis, et consuetis*, Hope, *de feudi renovatione*, Williamson *contra* Thomson [Possibly *Watson* v *Thomson*, Hope, *Maj.Pr.* III,1,25; or *Williamson* v *Thomson*, M.16559; III,5,37,*infra*]. Of old, the main importance of a ward-holding was indefinite service to be performed by the vassal to his superior, and especially in war; but that being now little in use, the main effect of it is, the ward and marriage of the vassal, of which hereafter.

32. Ward-lands, according to the nature of proper feudal rights, might not be alienated by the vassal's granting any subaltern infeftment thereof; otherwise, not only the subaltern infeftments were void, but the vassal granter thereof his own infeftment became void by recognition; yet, by Act of Parliament, 1457, cap. 71 [A.P.S. II,49,c.15], all feus to be granted by the King, Prelates, Barons, or freeholders, are allowed and declared not to fall in ward, as being but heritable assedations, as the Act bears, paying to the superior during the ward the feu-duty; providing the lands be set to a competent avail, without prejudice to the King, which is [interpreted to be] the retoured duty, Parl. 1584, cap. 6 [A.P.S. III,349,c.5]. The same is repeated, Parl. 1503, cap. 91 [A.P.S. II,253,c.37], and extended not only to subaltern infeftments feu, but also of annualrents, so that it be without

diminution of the rental, which, in lands holden of the King by secular men, is the retoured mail, and in the King's property, and in kirk-lands is the full rental, they should happen to be at the time of the subaltern infeftments, which therefore the feus may not diminish, and the annualrent may not be so great as to exhaust the land, that the rental remain not free: this last act was temporal for that King's life, and therefore the extension as to annualrents ceaseth. Though the first Act expresseth, that the King will ratify all feus granted by the King's immediate vassals, yet the Act bears, "that the King" thereby "will give good example to the rest," viz. to other superiors; and therefore, a feu of ward-lands granted by a vassal, holding ward of a subject, before the Act of Parliament 1606, was found valid, though without the superior's consent, June 23, 1668, Stuart of Torrence *contra* Feuars of Earnock [1 Stair 542; M. 4169].

This privilege was taken away as to all superiors and their vassals, except the vassals of the King, who only might grant subaltern infeftments of their wardlands, Parl. 1606, cap. 12 [A.P.S. IV, 287, c. 11] whereby all such subaltern infeftments of their wardlands are declared null by exception or reply, unless the superior's consent were obtained; and therefore, the superior's consenting in the disposition by a vassal to a sub-vassal, was found to exclude the vassal's ward so far as concerns the subvassal, though it was a redeemable feu, July 1, 1672, Earl of Eglintoun *contra* L. of Greenock [2 Stair 94; M. 4178]. The same was extended to the vassals of the king and prince, who were thereby also excluded from setting of feus of ward-lands to sub-vassals, Parl. 1633, cap. 16 [A.P.S. V, 33, c. 16]: but the vassals of the king and prince were restored to their former privilege, and the said Act 1633 wholly repealed, Parl. 1641, cap. 58 [A.P.S. V, 499, c. 83] which now is rescinded, Parl. 1661, cap. 15 [A.P.S. VII, 86, c. 126]. Yet the lands set in feu, during the time of these several acts now repealed, are valid. So now ward-lands holden of the king or prince, may not be set in feu, nor of any other superiors, except bishops and their chapters for these might set feus for a feu-duty equivalent to the retour, Parl. 1621, cap. 9 [A.P.S. IV, 612, c. 9]. But this Act was only temporary for three years and therefore subaltern infeftments granted by vassals, if of the most part of the ward-lands, infers recognition thereof in the superior's hands [11, 11, 14-15, *infra*]; but if within the half, they are not null as to the vassal, but are null as to the superior, and exclude him from no casualities of his superiority, as ward, &c. But as the half may be sub-set, so any other right less than the value of the half, is sustained; as an infeftment of warrandice, Had. March 6, 1611, Cathcart *contra* Campbell [Not found]. The like holds of infeftments of liferent, but if the disposition or infeftment be granted to the vassal's apparent heir *in linea recta* it infers not recognition, because the superior is not prejudged by change of his vassal; but recognition was found incurred by a disposition and infeftment to the vassal's brother, though his apparent heir for the time, seeing there remained hope of issue in the disponer, and so his brother was not *alioqui successurus*, Spots. Recognition, King's Advocate and his son *contra* the Earl of Cassils and Lord Collane [Spotiswoode 251; M. 13378; 11, 11, 17–18, *infra*].

Feus of ward-lands granted by the king's ward-vassals, after the Act of Parliament 1457 [A.P.S. 11, 49, c. 15], and before the Act of Parliament 1633 [A.P.S. v, 33, c. 16], were found not only to be free from the ward, liferent-escheat, or recognition of the king's vassals; but also that the sub-vassal's feu did not fall by his superior the king's vassal's forfeiture, because the Act of Parliament expresseth a confirmation of such feus, which therefore needs not be past in exchequer, without which there is no doubt but ward and non-entry are excluded: and by a confirmation in exchequer, forfeiture would be excluded without question, even after the Act of Parliament 1633, and therefore the ratification and approbation of feus by the Act 1457, when it was in vigour, must also secure against forfeiture of the granter of the feu, as was found, February 12, 1674, and January 23, 1680, Marquis of Huntly *contra* Gordon of Cairnborrow [2 Stair 744; M. 4663], whose feu being granted after the Act of Parliament 1457, and before the Act 1606, was sustained against a donatar of his superior's forfeiture. The like though the feu was renewed upon resignation *in favorem*, not being *ad remanentiam*, November 16, 1680, Camp-bell of Silver-craigs *contra* L. of Achinbreck and Earl of Argile [2 Stair 796; M. 4171].

33. Infeftments blench are such, whose *reddendo* is a small elusory rent, as being rather an acknowledgment of, than profit to the superior; and therefore ordinarily it beareth, *si petatur tantum*, as a rose, a penny money, or the like, and these are not counted blench rights, unless they bear, "in name of blench farm;" or if they bear not, *si petatur;* or if it be a yearly growth or service, it is not due, and may not be demanded at any time, unless it be demanded within the year, at the term, as a stone of wax, or a pound of pepper, February 16, 1627, Lo. Semple *contra* Blair [Durie 276; M. 5447]. Where the like is observed to have been before, Had. June 18, 1611, Bishop of St. Andrews *contra* Galloway [Not found]. The like found where the *reddendo* bore *si petatur tantum*, Had. June 15, 1611, Bishop of St Andrews *contra* L. Tersons [Haddington, *Fol. Dict.* 11, 406; M. 15011]. So blench duties of lands holden of the king or prince, are declared only due, if they be asked yearly and no price can be put thereupon by the Exchequer, Parl. 1606, cap. 14 [A.P.S. IV, 287, c. 13]. Yet seeing by Act of Parliament, the king is not to be prejudged by neglect of his officers, who ought yearly to call for his blench duties, whereof many are considerable; therefore the exchequer continues to exact the king's blench duties, though not demanded within the year. There is another part of the Act excluding all liquidations of blench duties *in specie;* which therefore should be so exacted, though not within the year, unless the vassals voluntarily offer a price. In these blench farms there is no ward and marriage befalling to the superior, in which it differs mainly from ward.

34. Infeftments feu are like to the *emphyteusis* in the civil law, which was

a kind of location, having in it a pension, as the hire, with a condition of planting and policy, for such were commonly granted of barren grounds; and therefore, it retains still that name also, and is accounted and called an assedation or location in our law: but because such cannot be hereditary and perpetual, all rentals and tacks necessarily requiring an ish; therefore these feu-holdings partake both of infeftments, as passing by seasin to heirs for ever, and of locations as having a pension or rent for their *reddendo*, and are allowed to be perpetual, for the increase of planting and policy. But about the nature of *emphyteusis*, see §*3. Inst. de loc. cond.* [Inst., 3, 24, 3] *tit ff. si ager vectig.* [D. 6, 3] *et tit. C. de jur. emphyt.* [C. 4, 66].

35. In what cases feus are allowed of ward-lands, hath been now shown: in other cases they are ordinarily allowed, where they are not prohibited; so we shall only need to speak of cases, wherein they are prohibited and void; and that is, first, in the patrimony of the crown, which is annexed thereto, and cannot be set feu by the king, after the Act of Parliament 1633 [A.P.S. v, 33, c. 16], without consent of Parliament, by their Act of dissolution, bearing, "great, seen and reasonable causes of the realm, by sentence and decreet of the whole Parliament." But ratifications, which pass of course in Parliament, without report from the Articles, will not supply the dissolution of the annexed property, or validate infeftments thereof, even though the ratification bear a dissolution: upon which ground, the Earl of Mortoun's right to the Earldom of Orkney was reduced, February 25, 1669, King's Advocate *contra* Earl of Morton [1 Stair 614; M. 7857]. Neither can the annexed property be disponed by the king, but only in feu, even before the Act 1633, except by excambion without diminution of the rental, Parl. 1597, cap. 234 [A.P.S. IV, 131, c. 5]. And all infeftments, tacks, pensions, gifts, and discharges granted before lawful dissolution in Parliament, or after dissolution, yet contrary to any of the conditions of the same, are declared null of the law, by action or exception, as well as to bygones, as in time coming, Parl. 1592, cap. 236 [Probably Act 1597, c. 240; A.P.S. IV, 132, c. 11], which is confirmed and extended to feus, not only to be granted of lands, but to feus granted of the feu-farm-duties, which was a device invented to elude the law, Parl. 1597, cap. 239 [1597, c. 243; A.P.S. IV, 143, c. 14].

36. Secondly, Feus of the annexed property, after dissolution, may not be set with diminution of the rental, the feu-duty not being within the new retoured duty, Parl. 1584, cap. 6 [A.P.S. III, 349, c. 5]. And that it may appear whether the rental be diminished or not, before they pass the seals, they must be presented to the treasurer and comptroller, and registrate in his register, and the signature subscribed by him, otherwise they are null, Parl. 1592, cap. 129 [A.P.S. III, 561, c. 37]. And such feus set without consent of the comptroller, by his subscription, registrate in his register, are again declared null, Parl. 1593, cap. 171 [1593, c. 175; A.P.S. IV, 19, c. 18]. But the comptroller's office hath been of a long time adjoined to, and in the same commission with the treasurer's office, or commission of the treasury; and now no infeftment

passeth the seals, till the signature of it pass the exchequer, wherein the treasurer being also comptroller, or the commissioners of the treasury sign the signatures.

What lands and others are annexed to the crown, appeareth by the several Acts of Parliament made thereanent, consisting mainly of forfeited estates and kirklands, after the abolishing of the Popish religion; which because they were presumed to have been most part mortified by the kings of Scotland, therefore the intent of the granting ceasing by the abolishing of Popery, they returned to the Crown, as the narrative of the Act of annexation of the temporality of benefices, Parl. 1587, cap. 29 [A.P.S. III, 431, c. 8] bears; and therefore benefices of laick patronages, as having proceeded from these patrons, are excepted by the said Act: and though after the restitution of bishops and their chapters, the Act of annexation, in so far as concerned their lands was rescinded, Parl. 1606, cap 6. [1606, c. 2; A.P.S. IV, 281, c. 2] yet bishops being abolished, Parl. 1640, cap. 6 [A.P.S. V, 298, c. 7] their lands were again annexed to the crown, Parl. 1649, cap. 38 [A.P.S. VI(1), 408, c. 165] whereby all erection of kirk-lands in temporal baronies or lordships, by which the king interposeth any person betwixt himself and these who were formerly vassals of kirkmen, are prohibited and declared null; which Act is rescinded in the general Act rescissory, 1661, cap. 15 [A.P.S. VII, 86, c. 126] and now revived, Act 29. Parl. I. K. Will. and Q. Mary [Not found].

37. Feus of kirk-lands by prelates, or other beneficed persons, being granted by consent of their chapters, with all requisite solemnities, were esteemed legal securities, without any particular confirmation by the king or pope, there being no statute nor constitution obliging the subjects thereto, Parl. 1593, cap. 190 [A.P.S. IV, 20, c. 20] as appears by the narrative of the said Act. Yet it was the custom, that the king's or pope's authority was interposed to all feus of kirk-lands; therefore all feus not confirmed by the king or pope, before the 8th of March 1558, or being thereafter not confirmed by the king, are declared null by exception, Parl. 1584, cap. 7 [A.P.S. III, 351, c. 8; see Craig, II, 4, 19]. The reason hereof was, because in March 1558, the reformation of religion began to be publicly professed in Scotland, and the beneficed persons became hopeless to preserve their rights of their kirk-lands, and therefore endeavoured to dilapidate the same: but this was found not to extend to an infeftment of an office, as the office of forrestry, though it had lands annexed thereto, and a threave of corn out of every husband-land of the abbacy, seeing the statute mentioned only feus of lands, and this was but like a thirlage, January 20, 1666, Lord Rentoun *contra* Feuars of Coldinghame [1 Stair 341; M. 16473]. It is also declared in the 7th Act, Parl. 1584, that the old possessors were to have their confirmation, for payment of the quadruple of their silver rent, or the double of their farm; providing they sought the same within a year after the publication of that Act, otherwise they were to pay the eighth fold of the silver rent, and the triple of the farm, and the King was thereby obliged to grant confirmation to the old possessors

upon these terms; and being so confirmed, the same could not be questioned upon alleged diminution of the rental, or conversion in money, or any other cause of nullity, invalidity or lesion, or by any law, canon or statute, except improbation only. And it was declared, that confirmations by the King, of posterior feus should not prejudge the anterior feus granted by Prelates and their convents, with their common seals and subscriptions, at any time, being granted with consent of the King's predecessors, under their privy seal, though without farther confirmation by the Kings or Popes, Parl. 1593, cap. 190 [A.P.S. IV,20,c.20]. The reason hereof was, because in the time of the Reformation, most of the evidents of kirk lands were destroyed; and therefore the ancient possessors were presumed by their very possession to have right: and for clearing who were the ancient possessors, and what were kirk-lands, it is declared by act of sederunt, 16th of December 1612 [Printed in Spotis-woode, p. 190], that ten years possession before the Reformation, or thirty years possession thereafter, without interruption, should be sufficient to stand for a right of kirk-lands, the same being possessed as such; and feu-duty being paid to kirk-men before the Reformation, or to the King or others having right from them after the Reformation; therefore it was so decided, 5th of July 1626, Laird of Kerse *contra* Minister of Alva [*Sub nom. Kerse v Reid*, Durie 208; M. 5132]; though much stronger probation, of being part of a temporal barony for longer time, was alledged in the contrary, Hope, Earl of Home *contra* Earl of Buccleugh [Hope, *Maj. Pr.* III,21,27; M. 7972]; Spots. Kirkmen, Mr John Hamilton, Minister at Linton *contra* John Tweedie [Spotiswoode, 188; M. 5134]. This Act is correctory of the former Act 1584; for though confirmations were not obtained, as is there prescribed, under a nullity, yet by this Act, if the King's consent be obtained by his subscription and privy seal, the feus are base. Secondly, feus granted by Prelates were null, except they were expede by the consent of their chapters or convents, Parl. 1593, cap. 190 [A.P.S. IV,20,c.20]. Thirdly, Feus granted by the beneficed persons, as of themselves they ought to have been without diminution of the rental, seeing the property thereof was mortified to the kirk, and the incumbents were but as liferenters and administrators. It was also expressly declared and statuted, that any diminution of the rental, or change of victual for money, or any other disposition, making the benefice in a worse estate than at the kirk-men's entry, should annul the feu, Parl. 1585, cap. 11 [A.P.S. III,376,c.5].

38. Infeftments in burgage are these which are granted to the burghs by the King, as the common lands or other rights of the incorporation, and that for burgal service, in watching and warding within their burghs, &c. These can have no casualities, because incorporations die not, and so their lands can never fall in ward, or in non-entry. These infeftments in burgage are held by the incorporation, immediately of the King for burgal service, watching and warding within burgh, &c. And the particular persons infeft are the King's immediate vassals, and the Bailies of the burgh are the King's Bailies: and to

the effect that such infeftments may be known, it is declared, that all seasins of burgage-lands shall only be given by the Bailie and common Clerk thereof; otherwise the samen is declared null, (which seems to have given the rise to the exception in the act of Parliament, anent registration of seasins, that it should not extend to seasins within burgh), Parl. 1567, cap. 27 [A.P.S. III, 33, c. 34].

39. Infeftments of mortified lands are these which are granted to the kirk, or other incorporation having no other *reddendo* than prayers and supplications, and the like: such were the mortifications of the kirk-lands, granted by the King to kirk-men, or granted by other private men to the Provost, and prebendars of college kirks founded for singing; or to chaplains, preceptors or altarages, in which the patronage remained in the mortifiers.

40. Of all these mortifications there remains nothing now, except the manses and gleibs of ministers, which manses and gleibs are rather allodial than feudal, having no express holding, *reddendo* or renovation; yet are esteemed as holden of the King in mortification: and therefore the liferent of the incumbent, by being year and day at the horn, falls to the King [II, 3, 4, *supra*; II, 4, 63, *infra*].

Manses and gleibs did belong to parsons, vicars, and other kirk-men, before the Reformation, after which they were prohibited to set the same feu, or in long tack, without the royal assent, and the ministers were ordained to have the principal manse of the parson, or vicar, or so much thereof as should be found sufficient, whether the said gleibs were set in feu, or long tack, before or not, unless a sufficient manse be builded by these who have right to the feu, or long tack, Parl. 1563, cap. 72 [A.P.S. II, 539, c. 8] which was explained, Parl. 1672, cap. 48 [A.P.S. III, 73, c. 5] that the manse, either pertaining to the parson, or vicar, most ewest to the kirk, shall belong to the minister, and four acres of land lying most ewest to the said manse, to be designed by the bishop, or superintendent, at the visitation, by advice of any two of the most honest and godly of the parishioners: for want of this solemnity, a designation was found null, because it bore not two honest men by name, required to join with the presbytery, or their commissioners, though it bore that all the elders of the parish were present, and consented, but named none, Spots. Kirk-men, Minister of Lamingtoun *contra* Tweedie [*Sub nom. Hamilton, Atlington and Tweedie*, Spotiswoode, 188; M. 5134]. And though parsons', or vicars' manses, may be designed to be the manse of a minister, yet no other house can be designed, though it were in an abbey, but the parishioners must build one, February 11, 1631, minister of Innerkeithing *contra* Ker [Durie 568; M. 5125].

If there be no manse, nor gleib of old extending to four acres of land, then the designation is to be made of parsons, vicars, abbots, or priors land, and failing thereof, of bishops lands, friers lands, or any other kirk-lands within the parish, ay and while the four acres be completed, with freedom of foggage, pasturage, fewel, feal and divot, Parl. 1593, c. 165 [A.P.S. IV, 17, c. 8]. By which there is a clear order of designation; first, of vicars' and parsons' manses most ewest; and failing thereof, of parsons' or vicars' lands; failing these, of abbots, priors, bishops and frier-lands, or any other kirk-lands, as chaplainries and prebendaries: which order was found to be observed, 13th of July, 1636, Halyburton, minister *contra* Paterson [Durie 814; M.5138]. And therefore a designation of a manse, or gleib out of abbots lands was annulled, because there were parsons lands in the parish, though they were built with houses, and feued; for which the feuars were obliged to acquire a gleib, July 23, 1629, Nairn *contra* Boswell [Durie 467; M.5137]. The like, though the lands were feued all before the said Act of Parliament, January 25, 1665, Parson of Dysart *contra* Watson [1 Stair 254; M.5139]. Where there is not arable land near the kirk, the gleib is to be designed of pasture lands, sufficient for sixteen soums grass, most ewest to the kirk, Parl. 1621, cap. 10 [A.P.S. IV,612,c.10]. The designation of manses and gleibs, where they are not designed, or not a full quantity, or are become unprofitable by inundation, or other extraordinary accident, are ordained to be out of the kirk-lands most ewest to the kirk, according to the order in the Act 1593 [Probably Act 1593,c.165; A.P.S. IV,17,c.8], Burrows-town kirks being always excepted; yet a gleib was found competent to a minister of a burgh, having a land-ward part of his parish, Spots. Kirk-men, Mr. Ruch [*Sub nom. Roch* v *Keir*, Spotiswoode 192; M.5126]. The designation of gleibs was committed to presbyteries, Parl. 1644, cap. 31 [A.P.S. VI(1),221,c.225] which is declared to be by three ministers, and three elders, Parl. 1649, cap. 31 [A.P.S. VI(2),287, c.253] revived Parl. 1663, cap. 21 [Manses Act, 1663,c.21; A.P.S. VII,472, c.31] whereby designations were referred to the bishop, or such ministers as he shall appoint, with two or three of the most knowing in the parish: in which Acts the power of designation is extended, not only to kirk-lands, but where these are not, to other lands arable, or grass, ewest to the kirk, provided that the heritor thereof may offer other sufficient lands and grass, within half a mile of the kirk and manse. And by the Act 1649, there is added to the gleib pasturage for a horse and two cows, which is found to be regulated as the gleib before, which is also revived, Parl. 1663, cap. 21. with this alteration, that if there be not kirk-lands near the manse, or are not arable lands, the heritors shall be liable to pay yearly to the minister twenty pounds Scots, for his horse and kine's grass, and this Act is declared to be as if it had been made in March 1649, as to designations after 1649: that Parliament being rescinded without reservation contained in the Act rescissory, (as is in the Act rescissory of the other Parliaments,) "saving all private rights done thereby." But there is no warrant in any of these Acts to design temporal lands, where there are any church-lands; and therefore a designation was reduced, because temporal lands were designed, and kirk-lands past by, albeit the minister had been possessor *decennalis et triennalis*, which gave him a presumptive title, because his designation, which was the true title, was produced, February 6, 1678, Lord Forret *contra* Maters [2 Stair 610; M.5139].

A gleib designed, was found to carry a proportional part of the common pasturage following to the lands designed, February 2, 1630, Hamilton *contra* Tweedie [Spotiswoode, 188; M. 5134, and 5146]. Designation of a gleib was sustained, though it bore not the same to have been four acres measured, in respect it bore, "that the possessor's servants hindered the measuring:" and therefore it was designed according to the designer's estimate, July 5, 1626. Kers *contra* Minister of Alloway [*Sub nom. Kerse* v *Reid*, Durie 208; M. 5132]. And was so sustained, though there were lands nearer the kirk and manse, which were bishop's lands, seeing they were enclosed as a part of the king's park, February 13, 1629, Lady Dumfermling *contra* Minister of Dumfermling [Durie 425; M. 5137]. A designation was sustained, though there was only a notary's instrument without the subscription of three ministers designers, December 17, 1664, Paterson *contra* Watson [1 Stair 242]: here the ministers designers their testificate under their hand, was ordained to be produced before extract. A gleib being designed was sustained, though it was an united kirk, both kirks having gleibs before the Union, January 22, 1631, Ministers of Innerkeithing *contra* Keir [Spotiswoode 192; M. 5126]. A designation was also sustained, though it proceeded upon warning out of the pulpit, or at the kirk-door, after divine service, in respect of the custom so to do, though some of the most considerable heritors were out of the country, January 28, 1668, ministers of Hassanden *contra* the Duke of Buccleugh [1 Stair 515; M. 5135]. It was also sustained, though done but by two of the three ministers, named by the bishop, without a *quorum;* unless weighty reasons upon the matter were shown to the contrary, February 7, 1668, minister of Cockburnspeth *contra* His parishioners [1 Stair 521]. Manses and gleibs being designed, as said is, the feuars possessors and tacksmen have relief off the remanent parishioners, having kirk-lands *pro rata*, Parl. 1594, cap. 202 [A.P.S. IV,64,c.9] which was extended to a vicar's manse being designed; and the other kirk-lands, a part whereof were mortified to, and holden of a college, but were kirk-lands did bear burden, February 12, 1635, Cock *contra* Parishioners of Auchtergivan [Durie 754; M. 5150]. But where old gleibs of parsons are designed, there is no relief by other kirk-lands, except these, who had feus of other parts of the same gleib, seeing by the foresaid statutes, the feuars of old manses and gleibs are to suffer designation, or to purchase new manses and gleibs; so that these old manses and gleibs do not infer relief. This relief is not *debitum fundi*, affecting singular successors, as was found, June 24, 1675, Snow *contra* Hamilton of Monkland [2 Stair 335; M. 10167]. But when the designation is of temporal lands, the whole heritors of temporal lands are to contribute for a recompence thereof proportionally, Parl. 1649, cap. 131 [A.P.S. VI(2),288b,c.253], revived, Parl. 1663, Sess. 3. cap. 21 [Manses Act, 1663,c.21; A.P.S. VII,472,c.31]. Gleibs are teind-free, Parl. 1578, cap. 62 [A.P.S. III,98,c.6]. The like whether they are arable or grass, Parl. 1621, cap. 10 [A.P.S. IV,612,c.10]. And a gleib was found teind-free, though lately mortified, voluntarily without designation or process; and though not mortified to a parish-church, but a chapel, seeing divine worship was accustomed to be therein, June 9, 1676, Burnet *contra* Gib [2 Stair 425; M. 15640].

41. There is another division of infeftments, into these which are granted to one person and his heirs, and to more persons and their heirs, which are of divers sorts; sometimes as conjunct infeftments, and sometimes conceived in favour of fathers, and after their decease, to children or relations therein nominated.

Conjunct infeftments are called conjunct fees, whereby the fee is disponed jointly to more persons and their heirs, which may be to three or more persons, who by the infeftment become all fiars jointly and equally; whence there ariseth a communion by which they do possess the fee *pro indiviso*, until division thereof be made; which doth not comprehend an infeftment to an incorporation, as to a town or college, or to the use of the poor, who do not thereby become joint fiars, but have only a share of the benefit, according to the distribution appointed. These infeftments are not conceived to heirs, seeing incorporations are perpetual and die not, neither doth the public use thereof fail; therefore such infeftments require no renovation; and therefore superiors will not easily be induced to accept resignations from their vassals in favour of incorporations and public uses, by which all the casualties of their superiority cease; or to grant confirmations thereof, having the same effect; nor can they be compelled to grant such infeftments upon the vassal's bonds, granted of purpose, that adjudication may be used thereupon, that thereby the superior may be compelled to receive the incorporation; yea, though without design, an incorporation should become creditor to a vassal in a debt truly borrowed, either from the incorporation or their cedent, the question is, whether an adjudication thereupon might force the superior to receive the incorporation for a year's rent? Craig's opinion [11,22] is in the negative; and I have not heard such a case come to be debated. And though custom hath obliged superiors to receive man and wife in conjunct fee, which abate their casualties, during the life of two persons, the consequence would not be good, to stretch it to an incorporation that never dies; though the Act of Parliament introducing apprisings and adjudications, be generally in favours of all creditors. It were more just, that incorporations should pitch upon a person, and assign their debt to him expressly, to the effect that the lands might be adjudged to him and his heirs, for the use and behoof of the incorporation, or such other uses as were designed, which would be effectual against all singular successors, especially if the trust were expressed in the seasin; but the superior would have all his casualties by the death, neglect, or delinquence of the trustee and his heirs: however I shall not pre-determine myself or others in the case, but leave it to public determination.

Conjunct fees, by the custom of England are, always so understood, that the survivors have the whole benefit, so long as any of them are alive; but we do only extend this survivancy to conjunct infeftments to husband and wife, which bears ordinarily to the longest liver; but though that were not expressed, it would be understood as implied, and generally it resolves in the wife but as a liferent, and the husband is understood to be fiar, unless it be evident that the right was originally the wife's, and a liferent only designed for the husband; and therefore, if no heirs be expressed, or only generally their heirs, the husband's heir is understood in heritable rights, *Nam potior est conditio masculi;* and the wife is only liferenter, but with greater power than by a separate liferent, June 24, 1663, Scrymzour *contra* Murrays [1 Stair 194; M. 464]. And a wife having charged upon a bond granted to her husband and her, and the longest liver, was found not to have right to uplift the sum, or to insist therefore, without concourse of the man's heir, or he being called; that if the sum were insecure, it might be consigned to be re-employed to the wife in liferent, and to the heir in fee, December 10, 1671, Ross *contra* L. of Hunthill [*Sub anno 1661 et nom. Kinross v Hunthill,* 1 Stair 67; M. 8262]. Yea, a clause in a bond, bearing, "a sum borrowed from a husband and wife, and payable to the longest liver of them two in conjunct fee, and to the heirs betwixt them and their assignees, whilks failing, to the heirs and assignees of the last liver," was found to constitute the husband fiar, and the wife liferenter, albeit she was last liver; whereby her heirs of line (failing heirs of the marriage) became heirs of provision to the husband, and liable to his debts, January 23, 1668, Justice *contra* Barclay, his spouse [Possibly *Justice* v *Stirling,* 1 Stair 512; M. 4228]. And a clause in a contract of marriage, obliging the husband to take the conquest to him and his future spouse, and the heirs betwixt them, whilks failing, the heirs of the man's body, whilks failing, the wife's heirs whatsoever, was found not to constitute the wife fiar, but liferenter, and the husband fiar; whereby, failing heirs of the marriage and of the man's body, the wife's heirs of line were heirs of provision to the man, February 20, 1667, Cranstoun *contra* Wilkinson [1 Stair 444; M. 4227], for by this clause of conquest, it is evident the means were to come by the man. Yet an obligement by a man, bearing, "that whatsoever lands or sums of money he should purchase, during the life of him and his future spouse, (their present debts being first paid,) that the wife should be secured therein in conjunct fee; and in case of no issue, or children, the one half thereof to be disponed as the wife should think fit," was found to make the conquest divide betwixt the heirs of the man and the wife, and that her power to dispone the half was not a personal faculty, but did make her fiar in that half, and took off the presumption of the preference of the husband, seeing no mention was made of the heirs of either party, June 27, 1676, E. of Dunfermling *contra* E. of Callender [2 Stair 430; M. 2941; 11, 6, 10; 111, 5, 51, *infra*]. Conjunct fees to husband and wife, and the heirs of the marriage, by contract of marriage, do imply a restriction upon the man, not to alter the succession, without a necessary or just consideration, and so do exclude deeds fraudulent, or merely gratuitous, which might evacuate the effect, as to the heirs of the marriage; so that if there were heirs of the marriage, and also heirs of another marriage, the father could not alter the succession, in favour of the heirs of another marriage, because of the interest of the wife, and the tocher she brings: but it doth not hinder the father to give competent portions to the bairns of another marriage, June 19, 1677, Murrays *contra* Murrays [2 Stair 523; M. 12944]. Neither did such a clause, of conquest during the marriage, exclude a competent liferent, constituted to a wife of a subsequent marriage, albeit there were bairns of the first marriage, June 16, 1676, Mitchel *contra* Children of Littlejohn [2 Stair 426; M. 3190]. Yet where there survived no heirs of the marriage, a provision in a contract of marriage, that such a sum as the future spouses then had, and all they should acquire during the marriage, should be taken to themselves in conjunct fee, and to the heirs of the marriage; whilks failing, the one half to the man's heirs, and the other half to the woman's heirs; which failing, to a third person, found to constitute the man fiar of the whole, and that he might provide both the first stock and all the conquest to his children of a posterior marriage, which was found no fraudulent nor merely gratuitous deed, December 1 and 21, 1680, Anderson *contra* Bruce [2 Stair 808 and 820; M. 4232 and 607; II, 6, 3; III, 5, 52, *infra*]. Though there were no children of the first marriage surviving, neither had these children any children surviving.

42. Infeftments to more persons subordinate, are such as are taken to parents, and after their decease to such children and other persons named, whereby the parent is understood to be fiar and not liferenter, and the children or others to be heirs substitute, albeit both the father and the bairns named were infeft, July 23, 1675, L. of Lamingtoun *contra* Muire of Annistoun [2 Stair 360; M. 4252].

43. The third division of infeftments, is in respect of the succession, and they are either simple or tailzied. Simple infeftments are these which are taken to heirs whatsomever; for by that expression we express the lineal heirs, who, according to law, would succeed in any heritable right: but tailzied infeftments are, where the lands are provided to any other than the heirs of line, as when it is provided to heirs-male, or heirs-male of the fiar's own body, or to the heirs of such a marriage, or to the heirs of Titius, whilks failing, to the heirs of Seius, &c. Of these tailzies, there are many several ways, as the fiar pleaseth to invent, and ordinarily in them all, the last member of termination is to heirs whatsomever or the last branch or person substitute, or the disponer's heirs, and when that takes effect by succession, the fee which before was tailzied, becomes simple.

A tailzie [II, 3, 59, *infra*] must necessarily be a part of the infeftment, for no writ apart can constitute a tailzie, though bonds or contracts of tailzie, as personal or incomplete rights, may force the contracter or his heirs to perfect the same. They must also be constitute by the superior, being a part of the infeftment granted by him either originally in the first constitution of the fee, or thereafter by resignation or confirmation; and as a superior is not obliged to alter the tenor of the first investiture, or to accept a resignation, or grant a confirmation in any case, except where it is provided by law, whereby he is necessitate to receive apprisers and adjudgers; so neither in that case is he obliged to constitute a tailzie, but only to receive the appriser or the adjudger, and their heirs whatsomever; unless the debt and decreet, whereupon the same proceeded, be conceived in favour of heirs of tailzie; in which case, the apprising or adjudication, and infeftment thereupon, must be conform; unless it be otherwise by consent of parties; or at least, if the appriser or adjudger crave the infeftment to himself and the heirs of tailzie, the superior ought not to refuse it: for the apprising or adjudication being assigned to a stranger, he behoved to be infeft, much more the alteration of heirs is allowable.

Tailzies also being constitute, are broken or changed by consent of the superior, accepting resignation in favour of other heirs, whether the resigner resign in favour of himself, or his heirs whatsomever; or in favours of any other and their heirs: but most ordinarily by apprisings or adjudications the superior is necessitate to receive another vassal and his heirs, though perhaps he be substitute himself as an heir of tailzie; as if it be provided, that failing other heirs there mentioned, the fee return to himself. But infeftments holden of the King, have this privilege, that they are not refused, either upon resignation or confirmation, as the fiar purchaser pleaseth: yea, it is declared by several ordinances of the Privy Council, that the King or his commissioners ought not to deny his confirmation upon the reasonable expenses of the party; which ordinances are repeated in an Act of Parliament; and though the design thereof give not occasion to ratify the same, yet they are contained in the narrative, as motives of that statute; and therefore are not derogate from, but rather approven, Parl. 1578, cap. 66 [A.P.S. III, 103, c. 13] And though several Kings have revoked infeftments granted by them, from heirs of line to heirs male and of tailzie, yet the effect of such revocations hath never been tried by suit or decision.

Conjunct infeftments to husband and wife and their heirs, are tailzies, and though, if the heirs of that marriage be a son, and of a first marriage, he may be both heir of line, and heir of the marriage, yet may he enter as heir of the marriage: and if the defunct had other lands provided to heirs whatsomever, he may renounce to be heir in these lands, to the effect they may be first burdened with his father's debt and he or his lands provided to the heir of the marriage, can be but burdened in the second place, *in subsidium* of what is wanting by the executors, or heritage befalling to heirs whatsomever. Much more are infeftments tailzied, which are granted to husband and wife, and to the bairns of the marriage, whereby male and female come in *pari passu*. So bonds taken to parents, and after their decease to such a child *nominatim*, whereupon infeftment followeth, makes a tailzied fee; but these are rather called heirs of provision; and those are most properly called tailzied fees, where several branches are specially named and substitute, one failing another. But seeing heirs of tailzie fall under consideration in the transmission of rights by succession [III,4,33; III,5,17–18,*infra*], we shall insist no further thereon in this place, but shall proceed to consider the clauses which are adjected in infeftments, not being of the substantials or solemnities thereof, and how far such come in as parts of the real right, affecting singular successors, and how far they are only personal, affecting alone the heirs of the superior or vassal: and last, we shall consider the effects of infeftments themselves. And as to the first, beside the solemnities requisite in infeftments, there uses to be many clauses insert therein, all which we cannot follow, but shall insist in the most ordinary and important; these are Union, Erection, Warrandice, Reservations, Provisions, Conditions, and Clauses irritant.

44. Union is the conjunction, or incorporation of lands or tenements, lying discontigue, or several kinds, unto one tenement, that one seasin may suffice for them all; in which there is sometimes expressed a special place where seasin should be taken: and when that is not, seasin upon any part is sufficient, for the whole lands lying contiguous are naturally united, and need no union, so that seasin taken upon any one of them, extendeth to the whole: but where they lie discontiguous, other tenements being interjected, there must be seasin taken upon every discontiguous tenement, which must be all particularly so expressed in the instrument of seasin, whereof one will serve for all the tenements; or otherwise, when they are tenements of several kinds, as lands, mills, fortalices, and fishings, all which are several kinds of tenements, and require several seasins, and pass by several symbols or tokens, as lands by earth and stone, mills by the clap and happer; fortalices by the entry at the gates, and inclosing the person possessed, and excluding the granter of the possession solemnly, conform to the charter or precept.

Union can be constitute originally by no other than the sovereign authority conceding the same, January 16, 1623, Aitken *contra* Greenlaw [Durie 41; M. 16397]. And therefore union being constitute by a subject, not having the same from the King, was found null by exception, at the instance of the possessors, though pretending no right, December 16, 1628, Lady Borthwick *contra* Scot of Goldilands [Durie 410; M. 16399]. And when there is a place for the seasin of the union, a seasin taken elsewhere reacheth none of the lands lying discontigue, March 19, 1636, La Dunipace *contra* L of [Durie 802; M. 16581]. But if the lands united by the King be disponed wholly together by the vassal to others subalternly infeft, the union stands valid, July 12, 1626, Stuart and Douglas *contra* Cranstoun Home [Durie 213; M. 9060]; repeated January 5, 1627; which for the same reason ought to be extended to subaltern infeftments of an annualrent out of a barony or united tenement, which was found to extend to a mill, and to lands lying discontigue, though not taken in the place designed in the union, Spots. Executors, Lady Ednem *contra* tenants of Ednem [Not found; but see Durie 393; M. 1301].

45. Erection is, when lands are not only united in one tenement, but are erected into the dignity of a barony; which comprehendeth lordship, earldom, &c. all which are but more noble titles of a barony, having the like feudal

effects; and whensoever the tenements are granted as a barony, union is comprehended as the lesser degree, though not expressed; and therefore one seasin carrieth the whole barony, and all mills and fortalices thereupon, and fishings adjacent thereto. But erections can be only granted by the sovereign authority, and are not communicable by the subaltern infeftments, though the union implied therein may be communicated. Erection was found to be instructed by the King's confirmation of a charter, designing the lands a barony, though they were not a barony before, but the half of a barony, wherein the baron infeft his son *in libera baronia;* which infeftment being confirmed by the King, did constitute it a full barony, whereby an infeftment of annualrent taken upon a part of the land, affected the whole, Nov. 16, 1630, L. of Clackmannan *contra* Alardice [Durie 538; M. 16399].

Erections of kirk-lands in temporal baronies or lordships, whereby the Lords of Erection were interjected betwixt the King and the feuars, are prohibited, Parl. 1592, cap. 121 [A.P.S. III, 544, c. 13], and Parl. 1594, cap. 190 [1594, c. 198; A.P.S. IV, 63, c. 5], and the superiority of all these lands are annexed to the crown, Parl. 1587, cap. 29 [A.P.S. III, 431, c. 8], and Parl. 1633, cap. 10 [A.P.S. V, 27, c. 10]; the reason whereof is evident, that such erections are prejudicial, both to the King, who loseth his casualties of the feuars, and to the people, who must accept another superior instead of the King; and though they had formerly but subjects to their superiors, yet church-men were much more easy than secular persons, as requiring little service, and being ashamed to demand rigorous rates; but any man may obtain the lands he hath in property, holden immediately of the King, which were kirk-lands, erected in any dignity the King pleaseth to grant.

There are many exceptions in the acts of annexation of the temporality of kirk-lands, and in the acts against erections, by which the kirk-lands excepted are validly erected; and all the erections are so far allowed, as to give the Lords of Erection right to the feu-duties, or fruits of the property of kirk-lands feued, till they be redeemed by payment of ten per cent, and the infeftments granted to the vassals *medio tempore* are valid; but the casualities ought still to belong to the King.

It hath been sometimes questioned, Whether the union and erection of lands be dissolved, and loosed by an infeftment of a part thereof, from the vassal, holden of the superior by resignation or confirmation. Craig, *Lib. 2, Dieg. 7* [11, 7, 19] is for the affirmative, confirmed by the resemblance of a sheaf of arrows, bound with one ligament; for if one arrow be pulled out, all become loose, and so the union of the whole is dissolved, unless the superior give the new infeftment, but prejudice of the rest. But though such cases frequently occur, whereby infeftments of discontiguous lands would only be valid, as to the contiguous lands upon which they were taken; yet in no competition or other process, hath it been observed by any to be drawn in question or decided, so that we have ever rested in the negative: and the consequence from that resemblance is not sufficient; but on the contrary, he who unites many discontiguous lands, unites every part of them to every part, so that the taking off of one part dissolves only itself, the rest remaining united. But union or erection doth not change the jurisdiction of the lands united, as to the shires and bailliaries where they naturally lie, Vid. Tit. Confiscation, § Horning. [III, 3, 1, *infra*].

Baronies and united tenements, when they are originally granted, ought to express the several tenements, according to their proper designations, and so expressly unite them: but when these are acknowledged to have been baronies, or otherwise united, or are named, or designed as such by these who have power to unite, then the common name of the united barony or tenement, is sufficient to carry all that is holden and reputed, as parts and pertinents thereof; which was extended to lands, as parts of a common designation, though some particulars were named, and the lands in question had also proper names, and were expressed in the ancient infeftments, the right in question being an apprising, March 23, 1622, Gallowshiels *contra* L. Borthwick [Durie 23]. Union and erection are as qualities of the real right, and pass unto singular successors, who become vassals to the King or Prince; but ought not to be extended to subaltern infeftments, as is evident in baronies [But see II, 3, 44–45, *supra*].

46. Warrandice is either real, when infeftments is given of one tenement in security of another, or personal, when the superior obligeth himself to warrant the infeftment. As to the warrandice in dispositions and resignations, it is unquestionably personal, and cometh not within the infeftment; but though it be granted by the superior in the infeftment, yet it is but a personal obligation, nowise cohering, nor carried with the real right, and therefore the singular successor of the superior or author, is not obliged in the warrandice, neither doth the disposition or infeftment from the vassal, carry to his singular successor the right of the warrandice, unless it be assigned specially, or generally in the assignation of the rights and evidents.

Warrandice is a common obligement, both in infeftments and other rights, and it is sometimes expressed, and then it is regulated according to the tenor of it, whether it be absolute warrandice, or from fact and deed, or from future and voluntary fact and deed. But oft-times when warrandice is not expressed, it is implied; as rights are to be warranted, which are granted for an equivalent cause onerous: but in that case, where the disposition was only of all right the disponer had, the clause inferreth not absolute warrandice, but only from the disponer's future voluntary deed, Hope, Warrandice, Lo. Sinclair *contra* Creighton [*Sub nom. Sanquhar* v *Creighton*, Hope, *Maj.Pr.* VI, 22, 5; M. 16568]. Absolute warrandice is also implied, where the disposition or infeftment bears (*vendidit*), because that imports an equivalent price, Spots. Warrandice, Stuart *contra* Fivie [Spotiswoode 358; M. 1583]. But not so, if it were expressed under the terms of alienation, which is common to both gratuitous and onerous dispositions.

Warrandice from the future fact and deed of the disponer and his heirs, is implied in pure donations, Hope, Warrandice, Veitch *contra* Dauling [*Sub nom. Welch* v *Daling*, Hope *Maj.Pr.* VI,22,14; M. 16573], Schaw *contra* Durham [Hope, *Maj.Pr.* VI,22,15; M. 16573], and was extended to a legacy *rei alienæ scienter legatæ*, June 16, 1664, Murray *contra* the Executors of Rutherford [1 Stair 199; M. 13300; III,8,41,*infra*]; but ought not to be extended to future necessary deeds on causes preceding the gratuitous disposition, which the disponer is, or may be compelled to fulfil; neither upon any anterior deed; because, he who disponeth freely, is presumed but to dispone such right as he hath, but posterior inconsistent deeds are fraudulent. It is Craig's opinion in the forecited place, [11,4,1 and 2], that though warrandice from fact and deed be expressed, it doth not extend to prior deeds: and that in any case, if the cause of the disposition be for service done, for gratitude, or merit, that warrandice is implied: much more, if for future service, or for a feu-duty, or rent: yet if besides these, there be not an anterior cause in money, or value, such dispositions cannot be accounted onerous; for former merit or gratitude infer no civil obligation, and so no burden, which could receive legal compulsion. And as to annual prestation in future services, or duties, when there is eviction, the vassal is free of these duties, and hath no loss; and therefore they ought to import no more warrandice, but from future voluntary fact and deed; but whatever warrandice be expressed, it must be accordingly observed.

The effect of warrandice is, the up-making of what is warranted, in so far as it is evicted, and the ordinary procedure in it is, when any suit is moved whereon eviction may follow, intimation is made to the warrander of the plea, that he may defend; and if eviction follow, and distress thereby, declarator of distress, and action of warrandice for relief is competent. Also it is effectual for decerning the warrender to free the thing warranted of that which will undoubtedly infer a distress, though it hath not actually done it. In this case execution was superseded for a time, that therein the ground of the distress might be purged, July 1, 1624, L. Frendraught *contra* L. Balvenie [Durie 133; M. 16575]; the like July 17, 1666, Burnet *contra* Johnstoun [1 Stair 398; M. 16587]; Feb. 17, 1672, Smith of Bracco *contra* Ross of Balnagown [2 Stair 71; M. 16596]. Yea, warrandice will take effect where there is an unquestionable ground of distress, though the fiar transacted voluntarily to prevent the distress. And though no intimation be made of the plea inferring distress, yet the warrandice taketh effect, unless the warrander had a relevant defence, and could instruct the same.

Warrandice hath no further effect than what the party warranted truly paid for the right, whereby he was, or might be distressed, though less than the value of the right warranted, July 1, 1634, Glendinning *contra* L. Barnbarroch [Durie 723; M. 9225]. The like upon repayment of the sum given out, and the annualrent thereof, Hope, Warrandice, L. Craicklaw *contra* Lo. Harris [Hope, *Maj.Pr.* VI,22,9; M. 16571]; Jan. 26, 1669, Boil of Kelburn *contra* Wilkie [1 Stair 593; M. 16590]; February 28, 1672, E. of Argyle *contra* L. of Aitoun [2 Stair 81; M. 16598]. This will not hold in warrandice of lands, as to which lands of equal value, or the whole worth of what is evicted, as it is the time of the eviction, is inferred; because the buyer had the lands with the hazard of becoming better or worse, or the rising or falling of rates; and therefore is not obliged to take the price he gave. Neither is warrandice a full security, being but a personal obligement; and many times the price is not known: and if the warrandice be not absolute, the purchaser's hazard was the greater: but in warrandice of personal or redeemable rights, the matter is ordinarily liquid, and there is no design of hazard but an absolute relief. But warrandice hath no effect where there is collusion, by being holden as confest, or by suppressing the warrender's right, and receiving considerable sums therefor, whereby the right warranted fell in consequence, Feb. 18, 1679, L. of Wedderburn *contra* Sinclair [2 Stair 694; M. Supp. 90]; March 3, 1629, Murray *contra* L. Yester [Durie 431; M. 14026]. Neither where eviction falls through default of the party warranted when having a disposition of wardlands, with double infeftments, he infeft himself base without [having first obtained] the superior's consent and thereby the lands recognosced, Had. Feb. 1, 1610, Maxwel *contra* Mowbray [Haddington MS; M. 16567]. Neither was it inferred by the forfeiture of the disponer's apparent heir, seeing the fiar omitted to obtain the King's confirmation, which would have excluded the forfeiture, Hope, Warrandice, Hamilton *contra* L. of Nidderie [Hope, *Maj. Pr.* VI,22,8; M. 16571].

It is not so clear either in reason or practice, whether warrandice takes effect upon any other ground than what is, or may be a ground of eviction, to take away the right of the party by whom the warrandice is granted judicially; as when lands are taken away by inundation, or are become barren: or when a right assigned with warrandice becomes ineffectual, because the debtor is not *solvendo ;* or when any accidental or extrajudicial distress or damage befalleth to the party warranted, through occasion of the ground of warrandice, though not by legal eviction. *Secondly,* Whether warrandice takes place, when the right warranted is taken away or burdened by a subsequent law. *Thirdly,* Whether warrandice in general will extend to the forfeiture of the warrander's own superior.

As to the first, warrandice relates to the point of right, and not to the matter of fact; (unless the sufficiency of a thing be warranted, which will not extend to any visible or notour defect,) and therefore will not reach to accidents, the hazard whereof lies always upon the acquirer and the proprietor: yea, a clause of warrandice that lands should be worth so much yearly rent, was not extended to desolation by famine, March 10, 1636, Lady Dunipace *contra* L. Rouiston [*Sub nom. Dunipace* v *Lauriston*, Durie 802; M. 16581]. It was also found, that a cautioner being convened, and through occasion of compearance was made prisoner in a ship taken prize, had thereby no interest upon the clause of warrandice to distress the principal for this accidental damage, Maxwel *contra* Nisbet of Ladytoun [Not found]. So that unless somewhat more be concurring than the naked warrandice, either by the value of the onerous cause, for which the right is granted, or tenor of the assignation, it reacheth not the sufficiency of the debtor, or the like points of fact, which is Spotiswoode's opinion, Tit. *Assignation*. And it was lately found, that where a creditor had given a blank assignation to a cautioner, who had paid him with absolute warrandice, that as to the cautioner, to whom it was gratuitous for the creditor to give such a warrandice, it importeth not the sufficiency of the debtor, June 16, 1663, Hay *contra* Nicolson and Mitchell [1 Stair 198; M. 16586]. It was also found, that absolute warrandice in an assignation, bearing that the samen should be good, valid, and effectual, was not to be extended to the solvency of the debtor; but only that the debt could not be excluded by any legal exception, either from the cedent's deed or otherwise, as if the writ assigned had been false, the cedent not being accessory, or the debt null, or declared a public debt, Nov. 24, 1671, Barclay of Pearstoun *contra* Liddel [2 Stair 10; M. 16591], which quadrates with *l.4 ff. de hæreditate et actione vendita* [D. 18,4,4], where *venditor nominis tenetur præstare debitum subesse, debitorem vero locupletem esse, non tenetur præstare.*

As to distress by subsequent laws, when these are by way of declarator of an antecedent right, it is equivalent to a judicial eviction; but when the law is statutory, introducing a new burden, as taxes, augmentations of ministers stipends, &c.; it was Craig's opinion, *dieges. de evictione*, §6, [11,4,10] which he reports as the judgment of the Session, that in such cases the warrander should be liable *in quantum lucratus est*. But custom since hath cleared the contrary, that warrandice is never extended to subsequent statutory laws, but that these are always upon the purchaser's hazard: and therefore a general clause of absolute warrandice was not extended to a burden imposed by a subsequent law, though there was an anterior abrogated law to that same effect, July 12, 1667, Watson *contra* Law [1 Stair 472; M. 16588]. Neither was it extended to the making up of a gleib, though it was by virtue of a prior law, but the designation was after the disposition; because it was a burden the warranded might know, being notour that designation must be made of the land in question, July 1, 1676, L. Auchintoul *contra* L. Innes [Dirleton 88; M. 12055]. Yea, absolute warrandice in a lady's liferent, which is most favourable, was found not to extend to an augmentation of a minister's stipend thereafter though grounded upon a prior law, March 27, 1634, Lady Dunfermling *contra* her Son [Durie 717; M. 13408]. But where a clause of warrandice did bear, that a rental of a lady's liferent should be so much worth yearly, it was found effectual to make up an abatement of the rental by a minister's stipend modified thereafter, July 28, 1635, Lady Cardross *contra* her Son [Durie 776; M. 16580]; or to the making up a reader's stipend imposed by a posterior law. For in these cases it was the special tenor of the clause to uphold the rental, which would have been effectual not only as to eviction *in jure*, but as to distress *in facto* by inundation, devastation, or the like.

The intent of absolute warrandice being only against legal eviction, it doth not extend to every burden that may affect the land, as to a servitude of size-fish, Fotheringham of Pourie *contra* Lord Gray, Feb. 11, 1692 [Not found], or of pasturage, fewel, feal or divot, or to a thirlage of the land to the mill of the barony, paying the nineteenth corn, June 21, 1672, Sandilands *contra* E. of Haddingtoun [2 Stair 86; M.16599; 1, 14, 7, *supra*]. Absolute warrandice is sometimes general, and sometimes special, against ward, relief, and non-entry, &c. with a general clause, and all other danger, perils, and inconveniencies whatsoever, as well not named as named, &c. as to which, the general clause is not to be extended above the greatest of the special. But the question ariseth, if such clauses will reach subsequent wards or marriages of the superior, or to future forfeitures, or recognitions, non-entries, liferent-escheats, &c. It is certain that whatever of these burdens befal by the fault of the warrender, he must be liable therefor.

Absolute warrandice being much stronger than warrandice from fact and deed, which reacheth not only to facts of commission, but even to omission of duties; and therefore, if the warrandice be but by the author, and not by the superior, these subsequent distresses will not reach the author, unless the clause bear expressly, "such distresses past, present, or to come;" and so, though the fee were extinct by the forfeiture, or recognition of the superior, or burdened by his non-entry, or remaining at the horn; these occurring after the disposition will be upon the hazard of the acquirer, and not the author disponer: but if the warrandice be in the superior's charter, burdening himself, it will be extended to all subsequent distresses through his fault, and so to recognition, liferent-escheat or non-entry, but it will not extend to the forfeiture or recognition, or other fault of the superior's superior: neither will it extend to the ward, or the avail of the marriage of the superior bound in warrandice, falling thereafter, unless it be so expressed; for no provident man is presumed to guard against these, unless it be so expressed; and therefore there is little advantage by special clauses of warrandice; for the general clauses reaches all evictions from anterior causes, yea, the effect is the same, though there were no clause of warrandice expressed, if the right warranted be for causes onerous, viz. sums of money, or equivalent value; unless by the special warrandice, future deeds inferring eviction, or which would not infer it *ex natura rei* be expressed. But warrandice is never inferred from infeftments from the King as supreme superior, not acting *privato jure*, and though they were expressed, would have no effect; neither are the warrandices of infeftments by church-men effectual against their successors in office; yea, express warrandices of feus, or tacks of kirk-lands thereafter annexed to the Crown, after the said warrandice, doth neither reach the granters thereof nor their successors, Parl. 1587, cap. 29 [1587, c. 111; A.P.S. 111, 480, c. 77]. The reason whereof is there rendered, because the church-lands were annexed to the Crown by subsequent laws.

47. Infeftments do frequently bear conditions, reservations, provisions and exceptions, which give great ground of debate, which therefore must here be cleared. There is no question but infeftments may either be pure or con-

ditional, and some conditions are implied from the nature of the right, and are effectual, though they be not expressed; as in ward-holdings, the vassal cannot alienate without his superior's consent, which is as effectual as a resolutive condition, whereby, if the major part of the fee be alienated, the whole becomes extinct, and returns to the superior as he gave it.

48. Infeftments of warrandice imply this condition, that they should take no effect, but in the case of eviction of the principal lands. Infeftments for relief of cautionry, imply this condition, that they shall have no effect till distress, and that they shall cease by relief. Infeftments for satisfaction of sums, imply this condition, that the sums being satisfied, they are extinct, and the author's infeftments revives and stands valid without necessity of renovation.

49. Infeftment given for a particular office, and bearing not assignees or substitutes, as to be an ensign-bearer, advocate or chaplain, with lands and annualrents annexed, does imply this condition, that the heir be capable to exerce these offices; and therefore by his inability they cease, unless they be granted to assignees, with power of substitution, in which case they may be performed by another.

50. Infeftments by excambion do imply this tacit condition, that if the one tenement excambed be evicted, there is recourse to the other tenement with which it was excambed, for therein excambion or permutation differs from sale. This recourse is effectual, not only to the heirs, but to the singular successors of both parties, whether by voluntary or judicial rights; and therefore regress was sustained against an apprising, prior to the eviction, without necessity to instruct that the excamber had right when he changed, it being presumed that he delivered his rights to the other party; and therefore an old charter from the King, bearing, "the lands to have been disponed by his Majesty in excambion for the other party's lands," and expressing regress, but without mention of assignees, yet was found effectual to a singular successor, July 14, 1629, L. of Wairdess *contra* L. of Balcomie [Durie 461; M. 3678]. In this process it was found, that no person needed to be cited but the present proprietor of the lands excambed, and the heir, or apparent heir of the maker of the excambion, July 2, 1629, *inter eosdem* [1,14,1,*supra*]; and that regress was effectual against an appriser of the excambed lands, and was so decided, Dec. 21, 1623 E. of Montrose *contra* Ker [Durie 83; M. 3677].

51. The law doth also introduce conditions in infeftments, which do not arise from their nature, as in feus, by the common feudal law, and by special statute with us; whereby if the feu-duty be not paid by the space of two years whole and together, that the feu shall be extinct and lost, Parl. 1597, cap. 246 [Feu duty Act, 1597, c. 250; A.P.S. IV, 133, c. 17]. So the Roman emphyteusis by three years not payment, became void, *l. 2. C. de jure emphyt.* [C. 4, 66, 2]. It is therefore beyond doubt, that such clauses are effectual, whether expressed or not expressed in the infeftment.

52. It is also incontroverted, that liferents, one or more, may be effect-

ually reserved in infeftments, which will pass therewith as a real burden to all singular successors, and needs no other infeftment.

53. Infeftments are also sometimes burdened with the exception of other infeftments, which exceptions, if they be in the dispositive clause, as a burden upon the infeftment, they are effectual against singular successors.

54. Infeftments are also frequently burdened with faculties or powers to affect, or burden the lands, or others disponed, and that either absolutely at the disponer's pleasure, or for such sums to children or creditors; which clauses are frequent in dispositions by fathers to their eldest sons, and are very amply interpreted against them and their heirs, though the way of burdening might have been defective; as by a base infeftment, not clad with possession, or by bonds of provision, though no infeftment follow, as was found in the case of the relict of Robert E. of Carnwath *contra* Gavin, E. of Carnwath [1 Stair 456; M. 10436]. And a disposition by a father to his son, with a power to burden with such a sum, a bond granted thereafter to his daughter, without mention of that power, was found effectual against the son, in so far as was not satisfied with the father's moveables, June 24, 1677, Hopringle *contra* Hopringle [2 Stair 527; M. 4102], though these might be more strictly interpreted in the case of singular successors, acquiring for onerous causes. And in the case of the Creditors of Mouswal *contra* the Children of Mouswal [2 Stair 720; M. 934] Dec. 11, 1679, who having disponed his estate to his eldest son by his contract of marriage, reserving a power to himself to burden it with such a sum to his bairns, having given them bonds of provision with a base infeftment, the same was preferred without possession, by virtue of the reservation, to the posterior public infeftments of the creditors for prior debts, seeing he had then an estate sufficient for all his debts, and his bairns' portions. It is no less certain, that all the clauses contained in infeftments are not real burdens, affecting singular successors, such as warrandice, which only obligeth the warrander and his heirs, and is merely personal [11, 3, 46, *supra*]: so then the difficulty remains, what clauses insert in infeftments are real burdens, effectual against singular successors.

55. First then, if the infeftment bear a provision, that the person infeft shall pay such a sum, or do such deeds to a third party, this will import but a personal obligement, and will not affect singular successors. But the dispositive clause being expressly burdened with payment of such a sum, or bearing, "that upon that condition the infeftment is granted, and no otherwise," such a clause was found effectual against a singular successor, bearing only a provision in the dispositive words, "that the lands should be affected with such a sum," which was sustained against an appriser, Nov. 7, 1676, Caucham *contra* Adamson [*Sub anno* 1666 *et nom. Cumming* v *Johnstoun*, 1 Stair 404; M. 2727]. Here there was a clause irritant in the disposition, but it was not in the charter.

56. Provisions or conditions in infeftments, impossible or unlawful, if they be conceived as suspensive clauses annexed to the disposition, they annul

the same: But if there be provisions otherwise adjected, though they be in the terms of a clause irritant or resolutive they are void as not adjected.

57. Provisions also inconsistent with the nature of the right, are ineffectual, as if it were provided that the vassal should not owe fidelity to his superior, *Feud.* 2, *t.* 3, [*Libri Feudorum*, 2,3] or that the right should be valid by the charter without seasin, these provisions are inconsistent and null.

58. It is much debated among the feudists, about clauses *de non alienando*, with an irritancy or resolutive clause, or that the fiars should contract no debt, by which the fee might be alienated, or the tailzie changed; and they are generally for the negative, that clauses prohibiting contracting of debt, or simply not to alienate, are inconsistent with property, albeit they may be effectual if so qualified, that no alienation be made, or debt contracted to affect the fee, or alter the succession, without consent of the superior, or such other persons; but that being absolute, they cannot be effectual against singular successors; whereas these limited prohibitions resolve but in interdictions, and being contained in the seasins registrate, they are equivalent to interdictions, published and registrate. Though many such clauses have been in tailzied infeftments, yet none of them have come to be debated, but that which was in the tailzie of the estate of Stormont, tailzied to Annandale's heirs-male of his body, whilks failing, to Balvaird and his heirs, with a clause not to annailzie, or to contract any debt, or do any deed, whereby the lands might be taken from the heirs of tailzie, otherwise the contravener should *ipso facto* lose his right; and the next person who would be heir, should have right; which being at length contained in the original seasin, and all the subsequent seasins, was found effectual to annul the right of James Earl of Annandale, who contravened, and of all his creditors who apprised for his debt, Feb. 26, 1662, Viscount of Stormount *contra* Creditors of Annandail [1 Stair 106; M. 13966; I, 14, 6, *supra*; IV, 8, 6, *infra*]. By Act 22, Parl. 1685 [Entail Act, 1685, c. 22; A.P.S. VIII, 476, c. 26], clauses irritant in tailzies are approven as effectual against creditors and successors, being once produced before the Lords, and approven by them, and the original tailzie being registrate in a separate register for that purpose, and being repeated in all the successors' seasins, which if they omit, it shall infer a nullity of their right, but shall not prejudge creditors so contracting *bona fide;* which weakens the former tailzies, with clauses irritant.

And generally, all real burdens of lands contained in infeftments, though they give no present right to these in whose favours they are conceived, nor cannot give them any fee of the lands, yet they are real burdens, passing with the lands to singular successors, though they bind them not personally, but the ground of the land by apprising or adjudication; as if lands be disponed with the burden of an annualrent forth thereof, to such a person and his heirs, this will not constitute the annualrent, but may be a ground of adjudging an annualrent out of the lands [II, 10, 1; IV, 35, 24, *infra*]. In all these cases, purchasers by voluntary disposition are presumed, and ought to see their author's rights, at least a progress of forty years, whereby they may know such clauses, and consider them in the price, or otherwise secure themselves against them.

Clauses *de non alienando*, or *non contrahendo debitum*, are most unfavourable and inconvenient, especially when absolute; for first commerce is thereby hindered, which is the common interest of mankind; secondly, the natural obligations of providing wives and children, are thereby hindered, which cannot lawfully be omitted; thirdly, it is unreasonable so to clog estates, descending from predecessors, and not to leave our successors in the same freedom that our predecessors left us, whereby, though they have the shadow of an estate, yet they may become miserable, as if they shall happen to fall into captivity, or in any transgression that would infer a considerable fine, against which no clause can secure; then being disabled to borrow, they behoved to be denounced to the horn, and thereby their liferent-escheat fall to their superior, which no such clause can prevent; and therefore, if any man have ground to suspect the frugality of his successor, he may provide a part of his estate by a tailzie, disabling that successor to contract debt without the consent of such persons in which he confides, leaving some part of his estate to his discretion: for such a clause irritant being in the seasin, published by registration, may be sustained as equivalent to an interdiction; such clauses are also much more tolerable in lands acquired by the fiar's own industry, wherein if there be insert a tailzie with a clause *de non alienando*, to be insert in the original, and all subsequent seasins, and bearing "provisions for the wives of successors, not exceeding such a proportion of the fee, and for children only to affect such a proportion of the free rent:" or if persons having no near relations of value, prefer others of their name or kin to their estates: or in case of mutual tailzies, such clauses limited as aforesaid, may be much more tolerated. But clauses of that nature have never been attempted, but in proper tailzies where there are diverse nominate branches, which are neither heirs of line, nor heirs-male to one another, and where the main design is to preserve the tailzie; for when all the branches are of far relation, the preference of the first is not much above the rest; and therefore, the other branches have by such clauses *jus acquisitum*, and are not simply heirs, but partly creditors to the first branch: and therefore, though there were no clause irritant, they might reduce alienations merely gratuitous or fraudulent, especially when done, not by the heirs of line, or heirs-male of him who constitute the tailzie: for these are always in every tailzie in the first place, and while the fee continues in them, it is rather a simple fee than tailzied, as it becomes again, when all the branches of the tailzie fail.

The perpetuities of estates, where they have been long accustomed, have sufficiently manifested their inconveniency; and therefore, devices have been found out, to render them ineffectual: only the Majoratus of Spain hath been most reasonable and stable, that the King nobilitating a person of merit and fortune, either by the King's gift, or his own right, that estate can neither be alienated or burdened, but remains alimentary for preservation of the dignity of that family. But these perpetuities in England are now easily evacuated;

first, by warrants to sell, purchased in Parliament, which pass without much difficulty; and if they become frequent with us, it is like we will find the same remedy; they are also evacuated by a simulate action of fine and recovery, whereby the purchaser pretends, that he is unwarrantably dispossessed of such lands by the present fiar, who colludes and is silent, having received a price or other consideration, so that these sentences, though collusive, must be irrevocable. In tailzies the heirs-male, or heirs of line of every branch, being the issue of the first person of that branch, do succeed; and therefore there is a good caution by the law of England, that after the possibility of issue is extinct, the present fiar can do no more as to the fee, but what a liferenter could do; for the next branch being ordinarily altogether strangers to that fiar, little care will be taken to preserve the fee.

In the tailzie of Stormount, the whole estate was not comprehended, and it was distinctly provided, that in case any of the heirs of tailzie for the time should contravene, that the right should be devolved on that person who would succeed, if the contravener were dead: but in such tailzies, formerly it was not so clearly ordered, being only provided, that the contravener should lose his right, and the next heir of tailzie should have place, whereby it remained dubious, whether the next branch of the tailzie were meant, so that the contravener lost his own interest, and all descending of him; or whether he lost the interest of all descending of that branch; or whether he lost only his personal interest; wherein the design of the constituter of the tailzie might be dubious enough.

59. To sum up this important subject of tailzies, let us consider the effects thereof, according to the several ordinary tenors of the same, and how far the fiar or his heirs of tailzie is bound up thereby; we must then distinguish betwixt tailzies having clauses not to alter, burden, or alienate: and these that are simple without any express restrictive clause. Secondly, Betwixt tailzies made freely, and these that are made for onerous causes. Thirdly, Betwixt these that have clauses resolutive or irritant, and these that have only such clauses by way of obligation, provision or condition.

As to the first case, it is a general rule, that *quisque est rei suæ moderator et arbiter*, every man may dispose of his own at his pleasure, either to take effect in his life, or after his death, and so may provide his lands to what heirs he pleaseth, and may change the succession as oft as he will, which will be completed by resigning from himself and his heirs in the fee, in favour of himself, and such other heirs as he pleaseth to name in the procuratory, whereupon resignation being accepted by a superior, and new infeftment granted accordingly, the succession is effectually altered; yea, any obligement to take his lands so holden, will oblige the former heirs to enter, and to denude themselves for implement of that obligement, in favour of the heirs therein expressed; and if the superior refuse to accept the resignation, or to give confirmation, there will follow an adjudication for implement of the disposition, which is ordinary, and thereupon the superior must receive the adjudger; so that the first constituter of a tailzie, or any heir succeeding to him, may change it at their pleasure, unless the tailzie be for an onerous cause; as when tailzies are mutual, then the first constituters of the mutual tailzie cannot alter the same, although their debts may affect the same; yet no fraudulent or gratuitous deed can alter or evacuate such tailzies; and therefore a mutual contract betwixt two brethren, obliging them, that what lands they should succeed to, or acquire, should be taken to the heirs of their body; whilks failing, to the brother and the heirs of his body, &c. though thereafter either brother took their lands, otherwise to their heirs whatsomever, whereby sisters having succeeded to one of these brothers, they were decerned to denude themselves in favour of the other brother, Jan. 14, 1631, Sharp *contra* Sharp [Durie 553; M.4299,15562]. But this was declared not to hinder the fiar for the time to sell for a rational cause, only without fraud to evacuate the tailzie. But if the cause onerous be of less import, than to grant and continue a tailzie, it will import no more than once perfecting the infeftment by such a tailzie, whereby the hope of succession ariseth to these parties, in whose favours the fiar is obliged to take the tailzie; but he was not found obliged to continue the same, but that he might alter it thereafter, without refunding the money he got for granting it, being but of that value, as was equal only to the hope of succession, which behoved to be understood of alteration *sine dolo*, July 15, 1636, Drummond *contra* Drummond [Durie 815; M.4302].

Heirs of provision by contracts of marriage, are in part onerous, being granted for a tocher, and the interest of the wife concerned; therefore they cannot be altered by the husband at his pleasure, but do exclude all fraudulent or merely gratuitous alterations, as hath been shown, sect. 41. But if there be an express obligement not to alter the tailzie, albeit that will not give title to the heirs of blood of the present fiar, to quarrel his deed or alteration; yet it will give interest to any other branch of the tailzie, whether to the person nominated or his heirs, to quarrel and reduce such alterations; though it will not exclude alterations by apprising or adjudication, for debts truly borrowed by the fiar: and therefore, a tailzie of a sum of money, lent in these terms, "to be paid to the creditor and the heirs of his body; whilks failing, to the father and the heirs of his body; whilks failing, to a person named, and his heirs and assignees whatsomever," with a provision, "that the creditor and his heirs should do no deed hurtful to the tailzie, nor the debtor should not pay without consent of the heir of tailzie named," was found to give interest to that person as heir of tailzie, to declare that the sum was unwarrantably uplifted, or paid, without his consent, or order of law, by consigning it to be employed in the same terms; and that though he was heir of tailzie to the uplifter, that he was not obliged to fulfil his deed, or warrant his discharge, being contrary to the terms of the tailzie, as to which terms he was creditor; reserving always to lawful creditors, how far they could affect the sum for the fiar's debt, Feb. 3, 1674 Drummond *contra* Drummond [2 Stair 259; M.4306; III, 5, 18, *infra*]. And a clause in a bond, whereby a woman obliged herself to resign lands "in favour of herself and the heirs of her body, whilks failing, to the heirs of her father," and obliging herself to do nothing contrary to that succession, where-upon inhibition was used before her marriage, was found effectual against her and her husband whom she married thereafter, and disponed the lands to him and his heirs, as being a voluntary deed, without an equivalent cause onerous, albeit the father's heirs behoved to be the woman's heirs of tailzie, Jan. 28, 1668, Binnie *contra* Binnie [1 Stair 156; M. 4304]. Yet these restrict-ing clauses without irritancy, though conceived as provisions or conditions, if they be not in the investiture, albeit they be in prior obligations, dispositions, or contracts, there is no pretence thence to affect the fee as a real burden [11, 3, 43, *supra*], and even though they be contained in the investiture, seeing clauses irritant uses to be added thereto, they are understood to be but per-sonal obligements, whereupon no diligence having followed, they cannot be effectual against singular successors, whether by legal or voluntary disposi-tions; except in the case of reduction on the Act of Parliament 1621, against fraudulent alienations [Bankruptcy Act 1621, c. 18; A.P.S. IV, 615, c. 18].

Property being thus constituted by infeftment, it is to be considered what are the particulars it comprehends and implies, though not expressed, where-in this is a general rule, that lands being disponed with part and pertinent, all is carried thereby that falls under the denomination of the lands disponed, *a cœlo ad centrum*, and all that in the time of the disposition was accustomed to follow it, not only as servitudes, but even discontiguous parcels of land, which were not known as *distincta tenementa*, or parts of any other tenement, except what the law reserves, or the express provision of the superior.

60. The law reserves all these things which are called *regalia*, or *jura publica*, which the law appropriateth to princes and states, and exempteth from private use, unless the same be expressly granted and disponed by the king; and if the superior be a subject, if he have any of these *regalia* from the king, they remain with his superiority, unless he expressly dispone them to his vassal; and the superior may have them from the king, either expressly in a tenement holden of the king, or tacitly, when lands are erected by the king to him in a barony, or any higher dignity, whereby many of these *regalia* are comprehended, *baronia* being *nomen universitatis;* yet that will not compre-hend all; as first, mines and minerals of gold and silver, or lead of that fine-ness, that three half-pennies of silver may be fined out of the pound of lead, which mines are declared to belong to the king wherever they can be found, Parl. 1424, cap. 12 [Royal Mines Act, 1424, c. 12; A.P.S. II, 5, c. 13]. But mines of iron, copper, and lead of less fineness, belong to the proprietor and are not accounted with us *regalia*, though in some other countries they be [But see Act 1592, A.P.S. III, 556, c. 31]. *Secondly*, Neither do treasures found in the ground belong to the king's vassals, though their lands be erected in baronies, unless they were expressed. A treasure is money hid in the ground, the owner whereof is not known, *l. 1. C. de thesaur.* [c. 10, 15, 1] *l. 31.* §*1.ff. de acq.rer.dom.* [D. 41, 1, 31, 1]. *Thirdly*, Though all proprietors have the privi-

lege of fowling within their own ground, yet swans are particularly reserved to the king; and therefore, the privilege to kill swans is not carried under the name of barony, unless they were particularly expressed. *Fourthly*, Confiscated goods are not carried even under the name of barony, unless they be expressed.

61. Yet there are other *regalia*, which are carried under the name of barony, though not expressed; as jurisdictions and courts, fortalices, salmond fishings, forests and hunting of deer; and ports with their petty customs, established by the king's grant, or long possession, for repairing and upholding these ports; which therein differ from creeks and stations, which are natural; but ports are builded artificially, and need frequent reparation.

62. Jurisdiction and courts are comprehended in barony, in so far as concerns civil jurisdiction and blood-wits, or lesser crimes, but will not reach to capital punishment, unless the same be expressed, as it uses to be when the privilege of pit and gallows are expressed, or out-fang and in-fang thief, which seems to extend to the punishing of no more crimes but theft; and these who have only in-fang theft, can only punish thieves taken in the fact. And though courts be expressed, they will extend to nothing criminal, no not to blood-wits, unless these be expressed; but only to civil debates requisite for the proprietor, as to determine differences among his tenants, neighbourhood, multures, and smaller matters; or to constitute a baillie, who may judge betwixt the proprietor and his tenants, as to his rents, duties and services; and also may determine differences among his tenants. But all jurisdiction is cumulative with, and not exclusive of the superior's jurisdiction, so that there is place of prevention. The first attacher, if he proceed, is preferred: and if the superior and vassal attach together, the superior is preferred, unless custom or prescription have excluded the superior, which ordinarily takes place.

63. The courts of vassals, though they be barons, and have the privilege of capital punishment, are not of the same extent and importance, as the sentence of the judges ordinary of the kingdom; such as sheriffs, stewarts, baillies of royalty, regality and burghs. For first, the extent of their jurisdiction is not so ample. Secondly the jurisdiction of all barons and freeholders was of old subordinate to the sheriffs, and other judges ordinary, within whose jurisdiction the lands lay, Parl. 1503, cap. 95 [A.P.S. 11,254,c. 41]. And then there was place for falsing of doom, or appeal to the sheriff-court, who was to warn the parties upon fifteen days, and make the suitors of the sheriffdom ward thereupon. Whereby it appears, that the free-holders of the king, who owed suit to the sheriff-court, at least an inquest of them, were to concur with the sheriff in discussing the appeal from the baron or free-holder: but now these appeals, or falsing of dooms from any court to another, have been antiquated, and wholly in desuetude since the introduction of advocations, which is a far more excellent remedy; for thereby causes are not stopped at the choice or humour of parties: but the reasons of advocation are specially considered by

the Lords, whether they be relevant, and have such instructions as can be expected before discussing: and the subjects are further secured by the late Act of Parliament, that poinding cannot proceed without a charge be given and expired, which in all decreets, proceeding upon citation, requires fifteen days: in which address may be made to the Lords. Thirdly, Decreets of barons have no execution by horning, which goeth of course upon the decreets, precepts and executions of other judges ordinary; so that all the execution upon their sentences is only poinding, or corporal punishment. As to which, if there be any process for capital punishment, the Lords will very easily grant advocation, as they do advocate causes from inferior judges, not only upon incompetency, but upon intricacy and importance: so there being nothing more important than the life of man, they would easily advocate such process, wherein barons should not proceed summarily to execution. But both they and other inferior judges ordinary should after sentence at least abide terms of law by the space of fifteen days, that the Lords may give remedy by advocation, or suspension of execution: for though the Lords have not criminal jurisdiction, they do ordinarily advocate, and by the same reason may suspend criminal process, till the king's pleasure be known; but they ordinarily advocate, to the effect the same may be remitted to competent and unsuspect judges; so that if there were any doubtfulness in the case, the Lords would remit the cause to the Justices. Fourthly, The courts of barons or free-holders are not courts of record, in which writs use to be registrate.

64. As the courts of barons and free-holders have these restrictions more than the inferior judges, so they have this advantage ordinarily, that all the profits and issues of their courts belong to themselves; whereas sheriffs, stewarts and bailies of royalty are countable to the king, seeing these are the king's courts: but bailies of regality are not countable; because though they be the king's courts, yet the king hath gifted the profits of the court by the erection of the regality. If then an infeftment contain courts, the profits thereof are carried therewith, though not expressed; but ordinarily they bear *cum curiis earumque exitibus.* And therefore the amerciaments of courts, or their other issues, or their privilege on the breakers of arrestments, loosing their tacks to their masters within their baronies, are not comprehended within public confiscations reserved to the king.

65. Fortalices are also *inter regalia*, and are not carried by the fee, unless expressed, or at least the lands be erected in a barony. By fortalices are understood, all strengths built for public defence; whether that appear by common fame or reputation, such as all the king's castles, whereof many are now in private hands, as proprietors, or heritable keepers thereof, or constables of the same; such are the castles of Dunstafnage, Carrick, Skipness, and others belonging to the Earl of Argyle; the constabulary of Forfar belonging to the Earl of Strathmore; the constabulary of Dundee, &c. And when these castles are disponed, either in property or custody, the infeftments thereof carry therewith, not only the bounds of the castle, but the dependencies thereof, as

gardens, orchards, parks, meadows, and other ground possessed by the king or keeper, for the use of the castle, and all rents, annuities, jurisdictions and privileges thereunto belonging; which may be instructed by their charters, their court-books, or other writs or instruments, and even by witnesses, proving long possession: so, though an infeftment of constabulary bore only in general, *officium constabularii cum feodis et divoriis ejusdem*, yet it was found to extend to the proclaiming and riding of fairs, anterior to the constitution of the office, and exercing criminal jurisdiction in the town, where the fairs were held, during these fairs, but not to extend to other fairs recently granted by the king, or to any jurisdiction at other times, July 18, 1676 Earl of Kinghorn *contra* the Town of Forfar [2 Stair 452; M. 13100]. The like was done in the process betwixt Lord Hattoun and the Town of Dundee, Dec. 9, 1679 [2 Stair 718; M. 10272], wherein multitudes of witnesses were examined upon either part. And the emoluments, privileges, and jurisdiction of the constabulary, were decerned according to the probation; and particularly, twenty shillings sterling yearly, for which the town of Dundee counted in Exchequer, as belonging to the constable, which was found to belong to the office, albeit there was a discharge thereof granted to the town by Scrimzour, Constable of Dundee, which was not found effectual against Lord Hattoun, his singular successor in the office, by apprising.

66. The case is more doubtful as to other fortalices, which are not reputed to have been the king's castles. Craig's opinion is [11,8,3], that all strong holds are presumed to have been built for public defence, and not for private safety; wherein *turris pinnata* is comprehended, having turrets or rounds upon the angles, from whence shot may be directed alongst all the walls. And therefore much more may castles with bartizens or bands, that is, strong and high walls surrounding the castle: or if the castle be built upon a place naturally strong, which may give suspicion to the king to be an occasion of rebellion, and not to be patent and accessible at his pleasure; and most of all, if there were regular fortifications of stone or earth: certainly such fortresses or fortifications, whereby places are made of that strength, which is accustomed to secure against public enemies in war, may not be built without the king's warrant; and if otherwise built, may be demolished; and the builder punished: but long possession presumes a warrant. And as such fortalices may be presumed to have been at first the king's, from the very inspection of the fortalice, and its proper use; so long possession may take off that presumption, and that they have been built mainly for private use in times of trouble, with the king's consent. But we need not insist in these questions, seeing towers and fortalices do now pass in course in charters: Yet, though these were expressed, if it appear the fortress hath belonged to the king, and can be comprehended in the annexed property, the right of them will only resolve into an heritable keeping: so that the king, in time of war or insurrections, may make use of such strong holds, and put garrisons therein, seeing keeping doth not exclude the king's own necessary use: neither will the expressing of

fortalices generally, impower the vassal to build such strengths as are proper for public war; because the clause can only import such fortalices as then were built. But I see no ground to extend fortalices to all houses, with battlements, or with turrets, or rounds, which can only infer private safety against robbers, plunderers, or flying parties, but nothing proper for a siege or public defence of a kingdom: and therefore these may pass as houses or pertinents. And as to that ground Craig adduces, that it is treason to hold any fortalice against the King, or to deny him, or these commissioned by him, access, by armed force; and yet delivery of any other private right may be refused to the King without hazard; whence he inferreth, that the King must have greater right and interest in all such fortalices than in other things: this consequence is not good; for that which infers treason, is the holding out of the house, and denying access to the King by armed force, which will be treasonable in any house, whether it have battlements or turrets or not; but cannot infer that all houses with battlements or turrets, were built for public defence, and did once belong to the King; which recent custom doth further clear, there being nothing more ordinary, than to build houses with turrets or rounds upon the angles, without warrant, quarrel, or suspicion; these being rather for ornament than for strength.

67. Forests are likewise *inter regalia*, being places destinate for deer, for the King's use and pleasure in hunting, which cannot be extended generally to woods, but only to such where deer have been kept: for certainly woods are *partes fundi privati*, and are not *inter regalia*, in any nation, but forests for keeping of deer remain *inter regalia*, although the wood should fail: and wherever deer are kept as proper, and others debarred from hunting there, it is presumed to have been a forest proper to the King. And though the lands being *in baronia*, may carry the privilege and office of forestry, which gives the baron right to hunt, kill, and make use of the deer: yet he will be but held as keeper or forester, which will not exclude the King to hunt and kill the deer for his own proper use; for the property of the forest will never be understood, if it be not very expressly granted.

Forests have great privileges, and peculiar customs; for whereas no man is obliged to herd his cattle off other men's ground or corns, or to be answerable for the skaith they do, longer than in hayning-time, while the corns are upon the ground: so if any man have a mind to keep his neighbour's goods off his ground, he may do it; but he must herd his ground, and may turn off his neighbour's goods without wronging them, but could not put them in poindfold, before the Act of Parliament, 1686, cap. 11 [Winter Herding Act, 1686, c. 11; A.P.S. VIII, 595, c. 21] appointing winter-herding; yet generally if any man's goods be found in forests, they become escheat, and are confiscated two-thirds to the King, and one-third to the forester: and if any baron or landed man have hained woods, or forests of their own, they may escheat all goods that are found therein to their own use, Parliament 1535, cap. 12 [A.P.S. 11, 343, c. 9]; where private forests of subjects are only understood, such as are inclosed with a sufficient dyke: for the words of the statute bear, Hained woods or forests, which cannot be hained without inclosure; but the King's forests are large tracts of ground, which neither have been, nor can be inclosed: and therefore all the neighbouring heritors and possessors must either herd their goods off these forests, or lose them. Upon this account it was, that the King having by a signature under his hand, granted a forestry to the Laird of Fascally, the Exchequer, before passing thereof, desired the Lords of Session to consider and report what by law was the privilege, conveniency, or inconveniency of forests: and they having heard the obtainer of the forest, and the neighbouring heritors, did declare the privilege of a forest to be as aforesaid, June 21, 1680 [*Sub nom. M.Athol* v *L. Faskellie*, 2 Stair 775; M.4653]. Whereupon the Exchequer did represent to the King the inconveniency to grant new forests. Of old the comptroller had the inspection of the King's parks and forests; and it was lawful to the comptroller, or any having the King's warrant, to intromit with all goods in the King's forests, not put in by the comptroller and these having power from him, and to apply the whole to the King's use, Parliament 1592, cap. 138 [1592, c. 130; A.P.S. III, 560, c. 35]. And by the former statute the forester or keeper is prohibited to put in the forest any cattle belonging to himself; so that if the keeper first seize upon goods in the forest, he hath the third; but if the comptroller, or these having warrant from the King, do first seize, the keeper hath no share. And there are many more customs and privileges of the King's forests and chases in England, where the forester or keeper hath only the branches of trees, and the bark thereof, and such as are fallen or decayed: and as Skeen observes, that he may take a tree as high as his head; but now our heritable keepers have much more privilege, and may make use of the wood and deer, so as not to destroy either, and with a reservation of both for the King's proper use.

68. The hunting or killing of deer seems to be *inter regalia* with us, except these who have them within proper inclosures; for otherwise the King's forest having no inclosure, the deer by straying abroad, would easily be destroyed; and therefore, though every man may hunt them off his ground, by which they will be forced back to some forest, yet they may not kill them.

69. Salmon-fishing is also *inter regalia*, and therefore passeth not ordinarily as pertinent, and ought to be expressed in the infeftment; yet in some cases salmon-fishing hath been found constituted without special expression, but only by the common clause, *cum piscationibus*, and long possession, June 29, 1593, Lesly of Creik *contra* Forbes of Thainstoun [*Sub nom. Lesley* v *Ayton*, M. 14249]; in which case it was found, that salmon-fishing is only *inter regalia*, as it is a casuality *fluminis publici*, such as are navigable rivers; wherein there is a common use of passage and transportation; in like manner, where lands are erected into a barony, or any other dignity, salmon-fishing may be carried by the common clause, *cum piscationibus;* as when it bears fishing in salt and fresh water, though without mention of salmon-fishing, Hope,

Fishing, L. of Glenurchy *contra* Campbell [Hope, *Maj.Pr.* III,15,6; M. 14250]. So an infeftment to a burgh royal, bearing, *cum piscationibus et piscariis*, with immemorial possession, was found to give them right to a salmon-fishing and cruives, though none of them were expressed, January 26, 1665, Heritors of Don *contra* the Town of Aberdeen [1 Stair 305; M.14286]; January 13, 1680, Brown of Nuntoun *contra* the Town of Kirkcudbright [2 Stair 736; M.10845]. It was also found constitute by the infeftment of a sheriff-ship, and forty years possession, though the infeftments bore only emoluments in general, December 13, 1677, Earl of Murray *contra* the Feuars on the Water of Ness, the Marquis of Huntly and the town of Inverness [2 Stair 579; M.10903]. It was also found constitute by a Bishop's charter of lands, *cum piscariis*, bearing a *reddendo* of salmon, though the Bishop's right from the King was not produced, but presumed, and being a dignity, perfected by long possession of his vassal, January 13, 1680, Brown of Nuntoun *contra* the Town of Kirkcudbright [2 Stair 736; M.10845]. And likewise long possession by the space of forty years, was found to give right to a salmon-fishing upon both sides of the water, and drawing the same upon both sides, though the infeftment bore, "but fishing upon one side," Hope, Fishing, L. Monymusk *contra* Forbes of Barns [Hope, *Maj. Pr.* III,15,7; M.10840]. So a clause *cum piscationibus* was found to be a title for prescription *in baronia*, and that forty years uninterrupted possession constitutes the right of salmon-fishing, Feb. 7, 1672, Fullerton *contra* Earl of Eglintoun [2 Stair 64; M. 10843]. It is more dubious what the meaning of the clause, *cum piscationibus* simply, or of fishing in salt water, can import, seeing there are common freedoms of every nation to fish in the sea, or into brooks or rivers for common fishes; and therefore needs no special concession from the King or other superior; but the use thereof may be, first, that it may be the title or foundation of prescription of salmon-fishing, not only in fresh water, but in the sea, at the water mouth, where they are frequently taken: and also, that in other fishings, if a prescription run of interrupting and hindering others to fish whatsoever sort of fish, it will constitute a property thereof, which could not consist without this clause or the like, as a title; neither could it be comprehended as *annexis*, or *connexis* of lands, or as a servitude, being a distinct right, having so little respect to land.

70. There is a special way of fishing by cruives [Cruive: a box placed in a dam or dike running across a river to confine the fish that enter into it. A zair, or yair, is another name for the same thing.] or zairs, both in fresh water and salt, all which cruives are absolutely prohibited to be set within rivers, in so far as the tide flows, as being destructive to the fry of all fishes., Parl 1424, cap. 11 [A.P.S. 11,5,c.12], renewed Parl. 1477, cap. 73 [Act 1478,c.73; A.P.S. 11,119,c.6], Parl. 1581, cap. 111 [A.P.S. 111,217,c.15]. And as to other cruives in fresh water, they are also prohibited by the said last statute, except such as are infeft in cruives, lynes, or loups, within fresh water, who are to enjoy the same according to their rights, keeping Saturday's slop, and

the due distance betwixt the hecks [Heck: a toothed thing, like a comb], the distance of which hecks by the said Act of Parliament 1477, cap. 73 [Act 1478, c. 73; A.P.S. 11, 19, c. 6], is expressed to be three inches conform to the statute made by King David; but the Act of Parliament 1489, cap. 15 [A.P.S. 11, 221, c. 16], expresseth the distance to be five inches, conform to King David's Act; and in both these statutes, besides the distance aforesaid, Saturday's slop is appointed, and likewise that the mid-stream, by the space of five foot be always free: and that no cruives be made use of in forbidden time of year, when salmon may not be taken, which is declared to be from the feast of the Assumption of the Virgin Mary [13th August], unto the feast of St. Andrews in winter [30th November], Parl. 1424, cap. 35 [A.P.S. 11, 5, c. 12].

Few debates have occurred concerning cruives, notwithstanding the great notice thereof by so many of our Kings: one did lately occur, and was fully debated *in præsentia*, betwixt the Heritors of the water of Don and the town of Aberdeen, which was mainly decided on January 26, 1665 [1 Stair 255; M. 10840]. The case was thus: The town of Aberdeen having changed a cruive-dyke to another place within their own bounds, and built the same there again of new; whereupon the heritors, who had right to the salmon-fishing upon the water of Don, above these cruives, raised a declarator against them, wherein, after large disputes concerning Saturdays' slop, and the mid-stream, and the distance of the hecks, and the height of the cruive-dyke, and whether it ought to be built sloping or perpendicular, and whether it might be changed to the prejudice of the heritors; the Lords found, that the town of Aberdeen might change the cruive-dyke, keeping it within their own bounds, and having no more dykes but one; but found, that seeing they had a cruive past memory without interruption, which had determined the height and frame thereof, they found that the new dyke behoved to be built in all things conform to the old, and with no more detriment to the saids heritors fishing, than was formerly before the water had pooled at the old dyke; and so it was not determined how high a cruive-dyke might be, or whether it behoved to be sloping or not, where prescription had not determined it, which is very seldom: it was also found, that the distance of the hecks ought to be three inches, conform to the said act of King James III Parl. 1477, cap. 73 [1478, c. 73; A.P.S. 11, 119, c. 6], and not five inches, according to the act of King James IV Parl. 1489, cap. 15 [A.P.S. 11, 221, c. 16], which mentions five inches, which the Lords found to be a mistake in the transcribing, or printing of the Act of Parliament, in respect that both this and the former Act relates to the statute of King David as the pattern thereof, which mentions but three inches, and that hecks of five inches wide will be of no use, nor hold in any salmon; the Lords also found, that the Saturday's slop behoved to be observed, not only in one cruive, but in all the cruives of the dyke, and that by pulling up the hecks of each cruive by the breadth of an ell, to continue from Saturday at six o'clock, till Monday at sun-rising; and the Lords found, that part of the statute concerning the mid-stream, to be indeed distinct from

Saturday's slop; but they found that part of the statute concerning the mid-stream to be in desuetude, in all the cruives of the kingdom, and that it is not repeated by the Act of King James VI Parl. 1581, cap. 111 [A.P.S. III, 217, c. 15], and therefore found the same not obligatory, notwithstanding that in the late Act of Parliament 1661 [1661, c. 33; A.P.S. VII, 231, c. 245], there is an act ratifying all the old statutes concerning cruives, which was alleged to revive that point of the mid-stream, which the Lords did not respect as a general law, albeit the confirmation did run in these terms; because it past the Parliament without notice, as an ordinary confirmation, at the impetration of these pursuers, and did not pass the Articles, and was not appointed to be printed as a public law.

71. Mills are not carried as part and pertinent, because they are esteemed as *separata tenementa*, requiring a special seasin, unless the lands be *in baronia;* for then infeftment in the land carries the mills thereon: yet a mill being built upon a liferenters' land, after her infeftment, bearing *cum molendinis*, was found to belong to the relict, though mills was not in the dispositive clause; nor was she in conjunct-fee of a barony; but she was not found to have right to the astricted multures of any lands, but of her liferent lands, February 16, 1666, Lady Otter *contra* L. of Otter [*Sub nom. Campbell* v *Stirling*, 1 Stair 358; M. 8241].

72. The privilege of brewing being designed for public use, for common hostlaries, the inspection thereof is committed to the judges ordinary, magistrates of burghs, sheriffs, baillies, and barons, who are appointed to settle hostlaries in convenient places, and to visit their measures, if they be sufficient, and the goodness of their ale, Parl. 1535, cap. 13 [1535, c. 18; A.P.S. II, 346, c. 23]. And the said magistrates to burgh or landward are ordained to see reasonable prices taken for meat and drink in hostlaries, with power to deprive them of their privilege, if they transgress; so that a barony carries that privilege, though not expressed; but infeftments of other tenements carry it not, unless it be expressly granted by the King immediately, or by progress; that is, that all the superiors intervening betwixt and the King have that privilege, July 25, 1626, Stuart *contra* Brewers [Durie 226; M. 24]; but *in possessorio* the proprietor's infeftment bearing *cum brueriis*, will be sufficient, and presume the progress, unless that privilege be craved to be reduced, wherein the superiors must be called.

73. All other interests of fees are carried as part and pertinent, though they be not expressed; and albeit woods and lochs use oft to be expressed, yet they are comprehended under parts and pertinents; and therefore the master of the ground hath not only right to the water in lochs, but to the ground thereof, and may drain the same, unless servitudes be fixed to water-gangs of mills, or other works, and the ground of the loch, and all that is upon it, or under it, is a part of the fee: but if the loch be not wholly within the fee, but partly within or adjacent to the fee of another, then, unless the loch be expressed, it will be divided among the fiars whose lands front thereupon.

The parts of fees are only expressed in bounding-charters, but in all others the parts are only known by the common reputation of the neighbourhood, what they comprehend under the designations expressed in the infeftments, and by possession, as part and pertinent of the lands designed in the infeftment, whether they have but one common designation, as such a barony or tenement; or if there be an enumeration of their parts, by distinct names, which doth not exclude other parts, though belonging to none of the parts enumerated: there is only this difference, that express infeftments are preferable to these, which allege but part and pertinent, much more if it be alleged to be *separatum tenementum*, requiring a distinct infeftment; and yet prescription, as part and pertinent, will exclude an infeftment as a separate tenement: but where there are marchstones set, it is a great convenience to preserve peaceable possession; and though it cannot be proven when these marches were set, yet their being reputed as marchstones, will be sufficient to defend at any time, within prescription: but lands are oft-times so large, comprehending muirs and mountains, that march-stones cannot be set; for remeid whereof, the Lords of Session, by an Act of Sederunt, 1580, ratified in Parliament, 1587, cap. 42 [A.P.S. 111, 445, c. 23], "ordained all molestation in property or commonty, *in possessorio*, to be before sheriffs, baillies of regality, and other inferior ordinary judges, where the lands lie, and for that effect, the Lords will direct letters of cognition to proceed upon fifteen days warning, by an inquest of persons who best know the matter, the most part thereof being landed men, having at least four ploughs of land, or three hundred merks of irredeemable rent, and the rest substantious famous yeamen of the same parish; and failing thereof, of the parish nearest adjacent; and if both parties have cognitions raised, before litiscontestation on either, the half of the assizers shall be taken of these summoned for either party, or in case there be not a sufficient number of them habile, the judge shall supply the same, and the odd man to be chosen by lot: which inquest shall visit the ground, and shall return their verdict upon oath, both upon the claims and exceptions of the parties; and in case the judge ordinary be suspect, or that the lands lie in divers jurisdictions, the Lords are to appoint unsuspect judges, to be past under the quarter seal." There are only excepted the actions belonging to the members of the College of Justice, which are to be before the Lords; yet the Lords are accustomed to grant commissions to some of their own number, where questions arise concerning the parts or marches of tenements, to visit the ground, and there to receive witnesses, *hinc inde*, both as to possession and interruption, which the Lords do advise and determine without an inquest.

Parts of tenements *in possessorio*, are sustained by the present peaceable possession for some time: for seven years peaceable possession will sustain the right of the whole till reduction: and forty years possession as part and pertinent, is sufficient *in petitorio*, for the point of right, and will exclude an infeftment express, yea though it be an infeftment as *distinctum tenementum*, November 17, 1671, Young *contra* Carmichael [2 Stair 3; M. 9636]: but will not extend to bounded infeftments, which have no title to prescribe any thing without the bounds. If there be interruptions, and that either party hath had some possession, the express infeftment will be preferable, and any lawful interruption will preserve an infeftment of a separate tenement; but if neither party be expressly infeft in the lands in question, interruption by either party will not exclude prescription, because there is not a prior special right valid of itself, without possession; and therefore, if both parties have had mutual or promiscuous possession, each possessing when they could, and turning off the other, that part of the land so possessed will continue as a promiscuous commonty, which frequently falls out about the marches of large tenements, and was so determined betwixt the Lord Strathoord and Sir Thomas Stuart of Gairntully [Not found]; if neither party have an express or several infeftment, discontiguity will not exclude part and pertinent, though, if the question be with him to whom the land is contiguous, less probation will prefer him. Craig *Lib.*2,*Dieg.*3 [11,3,24], relates a case in his time betwixt the Earl of Angus and Home of Polwart [Not found], where discontiguity did not exclude part and pertinent, not being known as a distinct tenement.

Pertinents comprehend all the natural fruits; for corns are accounted as moveable, and as no part of the ground, as hath been shewn in the former title, section second [11,1,2,*supra*]. And also all servitudes; so a servitude of pasturage, in another heritor's wood, was sustained as a pertinent by long possession, Spots. Servitude, L. of Knockdolian *contra* Tenants of Partick [Spotiswoode 307; M.14540]. And part and pertinent being expressed in a minute of sale, it was found to carry common pasturage in a muir, which was a commonty to a barony, whereof the lands sold was a part, February 14, 1668, Borthwick *contra* Lo. Borthwick [1 Stair 523; M.9632]. And in the case betwixt the Laird of Haining and the Town of Selkirk, decided February 15, 1668 [1 Stair 524; M.2459], a barony of the King's *cum pertinentibus et cum pascuis et pasturis*, was found to carry common pasturage in the muir of the barony, and that the last forty years possession did presume the like possession in the feuars from the obtaining their feus; and that interruptions by the town, whose infeftment was but general, *cum communiis*, did not exclude the pasturage of the feuars, who had also made interruptions against the town.

74. Craig *Lib.*2,*Dieg.*8[11,8,17] debates this question, whether wood and coal be parts of the ground, or only pertinent as fruit thereof; for if these be parts of the ground, conjunct fiars or liferenters will have no share thereof, nor donatars of ward, non-entry, or liferent-escheat; so that the question is very important, wherein he relates two decisions, one betwixt the Lord Seatoun and his mother [Not found], who being served to a terce, was found to have right to the third of a coal-work, constantly going for sale in the defunct's time; and another betwixt Ramsay of Dalhousie and Mary Ballantine [Not found], his predecessor's relict, in relation to a wood which the fiar was found to have the only right to sell; and his opinion is, "that both are parts of the

fee, and that no conjunct-fiar, tercer, superior, or his donatar, hath any interest therein, as being no part of the fruits;" he pursues the same question as to
wadsetters, who are infeft in fee, but under reversion, to whom he attributes
a greater interest, that they may make use of the coal as their author did, yet
only for their proper uses: and as to an appriser, he relates [11,8,27] the
case of Sir James Hamilton [Not found], who having apprised the estate of
Camnethen, and cut down all the woods, he was found to have no right to
the woods during the legal; for then the apprising was not satisfiable by intromission: so that during the legal, they had nothing but the fruits, for which
they were not countable: but now the case is altered by the Act of Parliament
1621 [Diligence Act, 1621,c.6; A.P.S. IV,609,c.6], whereby the appriser's
intromission, in so far as exceeds his annual, is imputed to the principal sum;
and therefore he may continue in the profit of coals and woods, as his debtor
was accustomed.

But as to liferenters by terce, by distinct liferent, or by provision, where the
husband himself did not preserve the wood to be sold together, as *sylva
cædua*, but cut parts of it for his own and his tenants' use, for reparation of
their houses, liferenters and tercers may do the same. And where woods are
divided in so many haggs, that they yield a yearly profit, in that case the heritor hath rather used them as fruits than as parts; so that liferenters, tercers,
and donatars, may claim the same: yea, if a coal be a constant going coal, without apparent hazard of exhausting, it is like conjunct-fiars, tercers, or donatars will not be excluded therefrom, not exceeding the measure and method
accustomed by the fiar: but otherwise coal is to be considered only as a part,
and is carried as a part, though not expressed, nor in barony; as Craig in the
fore-cited place observeth, to have been decided betwixt the Sheriff of Ayr
and Chambers of Gadgirth [Not found]. And a party first infeft in land with
the pertinents, without mention of coal, was preferred to an express infeftment only of the coalheughs of that land, January 30, 1662, Lord Burley
contra Sim [1 Stair 88; M. 9630; 11,4,35,*infra*].

75. Let us now express the meaning of the specialities, ordinarily insert
in infeftments, as, *cum domibus, ædificiis, &c.* comprehends all houses and
buildings, as dykes of yards or parks, which though dry of uncemented stone,
cannot be altered by the seller, after the vendition. And there is a new privilege for encouragement of inclosing, that where the inclosure falls to be upon
the march of any other inheritance, the other heritor, though making no inclosure, shall be at equal expense of that part of the dyke which marcheth both,
Parl. 1661, cap. 41 [March Dykes Act, 1661,c.41; A.P.S. VII,263,c.284]
which was sustained, though the march was a stripe of water, being sometimes dry, July 21, 1669, Earl of Crawfurd *contra* Rig [1 Stair 642; M. 10475]
But how far this clause will be extended to fortalices, hath been now shown.
And though charters do frequently bear manor-places, yet both is carried
under the name of part and pertinent. As to the clause *cum molendinis, multuris et eorum sequelis*, mills have been spoken to already, sect. 71. But as to

multures, they are to be considered among servitudes real, Title 7, § Thirlage, infra [11,7,15,*infra*].

76. *Cum aucupationibus, venationibus, piscationibus,* signify privilege to kill fowls, fishes, and wild beasts, upon the fiar's own ground, from which he may debar others indirectly, by hindering them to come upon his ground, except upon the public high-ways, or such private ways only in favour of those to whom they are granted, which is seldom done, but ordinarily permitted; yet if lawborrows were used, they might infer a contravention; but by this clause the vassal hath no property in the wild beasts, fowls or fishes, which belong to none, but become proper to these who take them, except fishes inclosed in ponds, deer in parks, or fowls in vollaries; for these are proper, only by excluding of others to come upon their ground, the vassal having the sole occasion of taking such as are found there: neither doth this clause extend generally, for thereby swan or deer may not at all be killed or taken, nor salmon, or their fry, unless that power be expressed, or that the land be in a barony: nor can fowl or hares be taken in the time or manner prohibited by law; and albeit some do adject fishing in salt water, and in fresh, yet that imports nothing, no man being excluded from sailing and fishing upon the sea, which even in lochs and creiks is public to all the kingdom or nation; albeit other nations may be excluded from fishing, so far as any bounds can be perceived in the sea; for in so far kingdoms and nations have appropriated the sea, and made it public, peculiar to themselves, as to fishing and profits thence arising, though passage cannot justly be denied upon the land, as upon the sea, except to enemies: yet salmon-fishing in salt water and fresh, gives not only privileges within rivers, but at water-mouths in the sea. And the words *cum petariis, turbariis, &c.* signifies the privilege of fewel, by peats and turfs in mosses and muirs.

77. *Cuniculis, cuniculariis,* cunnings and cunningares, Craig [11,8,22] doubteth whether these may be made indifferently by all vassals, except a privilege be derived from the king, because of the great damage the cunnings do to the neighbourhood: but there is with us no restraint, but upon the contrary a command that every Lord and Laird make cunningaries, Parl. 1503, cap. 74 [A.P.S. 11,251,c. 19]

78. *Cum columbis columbariis,* doves and dovecotes, though they are carried as pertinents, yet they are restrained by Act of Parliament 1617, cap. 19 [Dovecotes Act, 1617,c. 19; A.P.S. 1v,549,c. 19], to such as have ten chalders of victual in rent or teind within two miles of the dovecote, and these can build only one dovecote there. *Cum fabrilibus, brasinis, &c.* are smiddies and kilns for making of malt. *Genistis, &c.* are whins or broom. *Sylvis, nemoribus, virgultis, lignis, &c.* are several kinds of woods or timber. And *cum lapidicinis, lapide et calce,* are all kinds of stone and quarries thereof.

As for courts and their issues, we have spoken thereto already, sect. 64, and likewise of blood-wits.

79. *Cum libero introitu et exitu,* doth not only signify the passage by the

high-ways, but such other passages as are necessary and convenient for the fiar, through the ground of the superior, or any other, where ways are not constitute by concession or prescription.

80. Herezelds [Herezeld or heriot: the best aught or beast of any kind, which a tenant died possessed of, due on his deathbed to his superior.] also being the best aught, as the best horse, ox or cow of the tenant dying upon the ground, is introduced by custom derived from the Germans, as the word of their language expressing the same, evidenceth; which signifieth the gratuity left by the labourers of the ground to their master, and which is now due by custom, whether left or not; and, therefore, rather from custom, than from the nature of the fee. And we have neither rule nor example for paying it by any, but by the labourers of the ground, so that though it be not expressed, it is not reserved to the superior, but belongs to the vassal, as Skeen [Skene, *De Verborum Significatione*, s.v. Herezeld.], observeth: but whereas he seemeth to make a herezeld only due, by tenants possessing four oxen-gang of land, to their masters going to the war, such poor tenants possessing only four ox-gate of land or less, not being able, by reason of poverty, to go in person with him; yet the constant custom layeth herezelds most upon tenants possessing more lands, and generally upon all who are not cottars, not paying immediately to the master, but to his tenant dwelling upon the ground, and there is no difference whether he be mailer or farmer, and is only due at the tenant's death. So the herezeld was found due to the Lady liferenter, though the defunct had the room in steel-bow, Hope, Herezeld, Lady Tochrig *contra* Baird [Hope, *Maj.Pr.* III,31,5; M. 5408]. But not where the defunct tenant was warned and decerned to remove, Hope, *ibid.* Callendar *contra* his tenants [Hope *Maj.Pr.* III,31,6; M. 5408]. And Craig observeth *Lib.* 2, *Dieg.* 8 [11,8,32] that a herezeld being taken, the tenant's successor is not to be removed for a year, and was so found, March 20, 1629, Affleck *contra* Mathie [Durie 439; M. 5409].

81. Steel-bow goods set with lands upon these terms, that the like number of goods shall be restored at the issue of the tack, do not pass by disposition of lands, as pertinents thereof, unless they were expressed, but do remain as moveables arrestable, December 4, 1638, Lady Westmoreland *contra* E. of Home [Durie 863; M. 14779]; January 28, 1642, Dundass *contra* Brown [Durie 889; M. 14780]; and so they fall under single escheat, and cannot be taken from the tenant till his tack run out, December 6, 1628, Lawson *contra* La. Boghal [Durie 406; M. 14778].

Title 4. Superiority and its Casualities,
Where, of Non-entry, Relief, Compositions for Entries, Ward, Marriage, and Liferent-escheat, &c.

1. *The Superior's* dominium directum.
2. *How Property is established in the King.*
3. *Superiors may exerce all acts of Property, except against their Vassals.*
4. *How the Property coming in the Person of the Superior, is established.*
5. *Superiors cannot interpose one betwixt them and their Vassals.*

HAVING now shown what is the interest of the vassal in the fee, it will be the more easy to find out what the superiors by his right of the superiority retaineth; for what is proper to the fee, and is not disponed to the vassal, is reserved to the superior, and it is either constitute as belonging to the superior constantly or casually.

1. The constant right of the superior standeth mainly in these particulars; First, superiority itself is *dominium directum*, as the tenantry is but *dominium utile*, (as before is shown) and therefore the superior must be infeft as well as the vassal, and that in the lands or tenement itself, without mention of the superiority, which followeth but upon the concession of the fee in tenantry, though sometimes, through the ignorance of writers, infeftments bear expressly to be "of the superiority."

2. Only the sovereign authority, as the common fountain of all rights of the ground, needs no infeftment, but hath his right founded *in jure communi*, and is not feudal but allodial. And when the right of lands fall to the king, by the casuality of his superiority, as by forfeiture, recognition, bastardy or last heir, if the lands be holden immediately of the king, they are *ipso facto* consolidate with the superiority, and the declarators required thereanent, do not constitute, but declare the king's right, without prejudice of what is consumed *bona fide*: but where they are not holden immediately of the King, the right thereof is perfected by gift and presentation, whereby the immediate superior is obliged to receive the donatar by infeftment, like to that of his former vassal; yet the King's right by this casuality, though it be not perfected, is real and effectual against all singular successors, whereby deeds of treason and recognition, being in fact are ordinarily proven by witnesses, and purchasers cannot be secured by any register; and therefore must secure themselves by the King's confirmation, or *novo-damus*. But where the King succeeds in any fee to a subject, as to property or superiority, before he can alienate the same, he

must be served heir in special thereunto; so King Charles I was served heir to Queen Anna his mother in the Lordship of Dumfermling, in which King James infeft her in fee, to her and her heirs, by a morning gift, the first day after his marriage with her; and Charles II was served heir to Charles Duke of Lennox, in the Earldom of Lennox: in which service, the chancellor and fourteen of the Lords of Session were the inquest, the youngest lord being left out, because there could be no more but fifteen: but the King needs no infeftment upon such retours; for if he acquire any lands holden immediately of himself, the instrument of resignation must be registrate; and if holden of a subject, there ariseth no real right to a donatar till he be infeft upon the King's presentation, and his seasin registrate, by both which the certainty of land-rights is preserved.

3. Secondly, Superiority carrieth a right to all actions following the land, against any other than the vassal; for seeing superiors are infeft in the lands, they can only be repelled from such actions, by the rights granted to their vassals, but by no others; and so may remove possessors who can show no right: this was found, though the superior's infeftment bore him only to be infeft in the superiority of the lands, November 19, 1624, Laird of Lagg *contra* his Tennents [Durie 149; M.13787]. Yet if an apparent heir produce his predecessor's right, it will defend him, except as to ward, or non-entry; or if a singular successor, though not received, produce his author's right, it will have the like effect.

4. If a superior become fiar by succession, or acquisition, for establishing the property in his person, he may either be infeft upon his own precept or the King's, Nov. 26, 1668, daughters of Mr. Robert Morton [1 Stair 567; M.6917].

5. But a superior cannot interpose one betwixt himself and his vassals, by infefting another in the lands to be holden of himself; for such an infeftment was found null by exception, Jan. 30, 1671, Douglas of Kelhead *contra* Vassals [1 Stair 710; M.9306]: but superiors must receive and infeft their sub-vassals upon the refusal, or incapacity of the vassal, and may at any time thereafter receive the immediate vassal, or his successor, or another, if the immediate vassal's right be extinct, or acquired by the superior, which is no unwarrantable interposition, which is repelled as contrary to the nature of the feudal contract and right, it being inconsistent that the superior should both give his superiority to another, and claim it himself, *dans et retinens nihil dat;* and if that were allowed, interposed vassals might be infinitely multiplied, Nov. 26, 1672, E. of Argyle *contra* McLeod [2 Stair 122; M.15013]; in which case the late Marquis of Argyle being forfeited, McLeod, who was Argyle's vassal, was retoured and infeft in the lands, as holden immediately of the King, which did not hinder the King to interpose the Earl of Argyle as donatar to his father's forfeiture, seeing the King had done no deed to accept McLeod as his immediate vassal, except that he was infeft by precepts out of the chancellary, passing of course.

6. Superiors nor their donatars need not instruct the superior's right; but the vassal must acknowledge it, or disclaim him upon his peril; so it was found in the casuality of a marriage, Feb. 25, 1662, Arbuthnot *contra* Keiths [1 Stair 104; M. 8528], which will not hold, if the right of superiority be newly acquired, and no infeftment given to the vassal, or his predecessors by virtue thereof. So the superior's infeftment gives him interest to pursue reductions and improbations against all parties, even against his own vassals, who will be forced to produce their rights, under the certification, to be declared null, or false and feigned, though, when they are produced, they may defend them [11,4,21,*infra*]. What hath not been allowed to the superior, should not be allowed to the vassal, which yet hath been frequently practised, when vassals make sub-vassals without any different *reddendo*, but with the same *reddendo* by the sub-vassal to the vassal, which is due by the vassal to his superior, and that sub-vassal doth frequently the like to his sub-vassal, whereby there are a great many superiors interposed between the first superior and the proprietor, and thereby great confusion is occasioned, and much trouble and expence, when ofttimes no more is intended than the transmission of the property to be holden of the first superior; as when lands are sold, and an obligement granted for infefting the buyer, by charters from the seller *à se* and *de se*, the charter *à se* is of no effect till it be confirmed, and lest another should be first infeft upon a posterior disposition, the buyer infefts himself on the charter *de se*, and never insists for a confirmation, but he or his sells the same lands to another in the same way.

The cause of this confusion is, that superiors are not obliged to receive the singular successors of their vassals, even though they should offer a year's rent for their entry: which privilege of superiors, by law and practice, is now evacuated, because superiors may be compelled to receive strangers upon apprising or adjudication for a year's rent; yea, if the vassal dispone the fee, and oblige himself to infeft, upon that obligement an adjudication is competent against the superior to grant the infeftment; which, though frequently practised, yet there is no express law allowing the superior a year's rent; there was indeed a law made for a year's rent, upon adjudications, when apparent heirs did renounce to be heirs, as well as upon apprisings, which doth not bear adjudications for implement of dispositions [11,4,32,*infra*].

Seeing then superiors may be compelled to receive singular successors by the course of law, it were far more convenient, both for superiors and vassals, that a law were made, that upon the vassal's disposition, letters of horning might be direct against the superior to receive him for a year's rent of the price, upon production of the disposition, whereby none would take such subaltern infeftments; and that if the disposition were redeemable as a wadset or annualrent, that the superior should only have the half of the annualrent of the sum, because his vassal is not totally excluded, and the other half whensoever the reversion became extinct.

It might also be statuted with greater advantage to real rights, that none should be capable to give subaltern infeftments, but the immediate vassals of the King, and that the proprietors by other subaltern infeftments, should all be ordained to take charters of the King's immediate vassals, from whom at first all subaltern infeftments behoved to flow, with this provision, that if the subaltern vassals were obliged any further to their immediate superiors, than they were to the first superior, as if they obtained a greater feu-duty, the superior being the King's vassal or his successor, should give to that subaltern interposed superior an irredeemable annualrent equivalent to the excresce which he had from his vassal, above what was due to the first superior, or if a ward or blench-vassal set the whole or a part of his fee in feu-ferm. By this means, there would be no sub-vassal but the immediate vassals of the King, or of the kirk, or of colleges and incorporations holding immediately of the King, not only to the benefit of proprietors, but of superiors, who by the multiplication of subaltern infeftments lose the casualities of their superiority; seeing the proprietor seldom returns to hold immediately of them, and frequently brook by prescription upon any title from their immediate superior, whereby the first superiors are utterly unknown very often and secluded.

7. Superiority carrieth a right to the service and duty contained in the vassal's *reddendo*, and that not only personally against the vassal, upon any personal obligation, or contract in writ, but also by virtue of the intromission, in meddling with the fruits and profits of the land; for all such intromitters may be pursued, and distressed personally for the duties contained in the *reddendo*, which being granted to masters of the ground, for their tack-duty against tenants, and all intromitters with the rents, is much more competent to the superior, for his feu-duty or other service in kind; how far this will be extended to blench-duty, hath been shown in the former Title [11, 3, 33, *supra*]. And as to services which are annual, as winning and leading of peats, &c. these are not due, if they be not required yearly in due time, whether they be due by vassals to their superior, or tenants to their master, Jan. penult. 1624, L. Carnowsie *contra* Keith [Durie 104; M. 14493]. So service of harrage and carriage in a feu-duty, was found not due, but when demanded within the year, June 27, 1662, Watson *contra* Elleis [1 Stair 116; M. 7975].

8. But also the superiority carrieth the right to the duty of the *reddendo* really against the ground of the fee, for which he hath action of poinding of the ground, against the vassal and all singular successors to him, whereby he may apprise the goods upon the ground, or the ground right and property of the lands, the saids duties being liquidate, upon re-payment whereof, the lands are redeemable as in other apprisings.

9. Superiority carrieth the right of jurisdiction over the vassal's lands and inhabitants thereof, if the same be granted to the superior in his own infeftment, either implicitly as being a barony, lordship or earldom; or expressly, having the power of courts and their issues; and though the superior grant the same to the vassal, yet that is not exclusive of his own right, but cumulative therewith. How far superiority carrieth the right of thirlage of the vassals'

lands to their superiors' mills, when the vassals have not granted to them the privilege of mills and multures, will appear amongst servitudes, of which hereafter, Title Servitudes.

10. Superiority carries all the casualities thereof, requiring declarator to heirs and singular successors, *hoc ipso* that they have the superiority established in their person, and do not fall to the executors of the superior, as to bygones, before his death, unless gifted or liquidate by sentence [11, 1, 4, *supra*], Had. March 5, 1611, Douglas *contra* Crawfurd [Haddington, *Fol. Dict.* 1, 367; M. 5460]; Feb. 19, 1635, Cunningham *contra* Stuart [Durie 756; M. 1738]; July 11, 1673, Fa *contra* Lo. Balmerino and L. Pourie [2 Stair 208; M. 5449]. But feu-duties, or any casuality may be separated from the superiority, by sentence or assignation; and therefore a disposition of the superiority was found to imply an assignation to the bygone feu-duties, which being to the vassal himself, needed no intimation, and was valid against a singular successor infeft in the lands in superiority, December 14, 1676, E. Argyle *contra* Lo. McDonald [2 Stair 478; M. 842].

11. A superior of kirk-lands pursuing his vassal for his *reddendo*, was not excluded till he instructed that he consented to the surrender, conform to the Act of Parliament 1633 [1633, c. 14; A.P.S. V, 32, c. 14], annexing the superiority of kirk-lands to the crown, reserving the feu-duties to the Lords of Erection, who consented to the surrender, which was presumed *in possessorio*, June 27, 1662, Watson *contra* Elleis [1 Stair 116; M. 7975].

12. Superiors are obliged to receive apprisers or adjudgers for a year's duty, albeit the superior allege a better right than the appriser; but the infeftment may bear *salvo jure cujuslibet et suo*, July 4, 1667, Shein *contra* Chrystie [1 Stair 469; M. 15066]. Yet a superior having received an appriser, was not found excluded from any right to the property, though he made no reservation thereof, seeing his receiving was necessary, July 19, 1664, Hospital of Glasgow *contra* Campbel [1 Stair 216; M. 6419; 11, 4, 36, *infra*]. But a superior being charged to receive an adjudger, was found to have his option, either to receive him for a year's rent, or to pay the sum adjudged for, getting assignation to the adjudication, being redeemable by the vassal from the superior, and without any year's entry to be paid at redemption, seeing the vassal was not changed, as is provided, Parl. 1439, cap. 36 [Diligence Act, 1469, c. 36; A.P.S. 11, 96, c. 12]; June 10, 1671, Scot of Thirlestain *contra* Lo. Drumlanrig [1 Stair 731; M. 15071].

13. And a superior is also obliged to receive a donatar upon the King's presentation gratis, and without present payment of the non-entry duties, till declarator, and if he refuse, he loses his superiority during his life, June 25, 1680, Lo. Blair *contra* Lo. Montgomerie [2 Stair 777; M. 15045].

14. A superior must also receive his sub-vassal, whom his immediate vassal refused to enter, without further instructing of the vassal's right, but by receipts of the feu-duty by him as a superior, wherein the mediate superior *supplet vicem* of the immediate *salvo jure*, June 28, 1672, Menzies *contra* L. of

Glenurchy [2 Stair 93; M.15067]. Yet a superior cannot exclude an appriser or adjudger within the legal, from the rent of the lands, till he pay a year's rent, December 3, 1672, Hay *contra* L. Earlstoun [2 Stair 123; M.15043; 11,3,30,*supra*].

15. And where a superior, or any to his behove, did take the gift of his own ward, he was found to have no interest to extend it further against his vassal infeft with absolute warrandice, than to a proportional part of the composition and expences, February 15, 1665, Boyd of Penkil *contra* Tennents of Carslooth [1 Stair 270; M.7758; 11,3,23; 111,2,2,*infra*]. The like where the ward had fallen after the vassal's right: for if it had fallen before, he could had nothing, December 1, 1676, Lo. Lindsay *contra* Bargallon [*Sub nom. L. Lindsay* v *Grierson*, 2 Stair 470; M.7761].

16. Superiors are not obliged to receive upon resignation, or by confirmation, and having accepted resignation, it did not exclude the marriage of the resigner's heir, there being no infeftment upon the resignation before the resigner's death, November 14, 1677, Purves *contra* Strachan of Kinadie [2 Stair 558; M.6890].

17. Superiority falling to more persons, doth not oblige the vassal to take infeftment of them all, but if heirs-portioners, of the eldest only, July 30, 1678, La. Lus *contra* Inglis [2 Stair 643; M.15028]. And by the same reason, if the superiority fall to many singular successors, by apprising, or otherwise, the vassal needs only take infeftment of the greatest interest.

18. The first and most common casuality of superiority is non-entry, whereby the fee being void, and no infeftment renewed thereof, through the vassal's neglect, being capable of entry thereto, the profits thereof belong to the superior. By the common feudal customs there was not only an investiture requisite at the constitution of the fee, but it behoved to be renewed, either at the change of the vassal, or at the change of the superior: Gudelinus, *de jure nov.* part 2. cap. 6, Zoesius, *de feudis.* cap. 12. But our custom requires no infeftment at the change of the superior, but only at the change of the vassal; for we require no oaths of fidelity, but fidelity itself is imported due without an oath: but elsewhere that oath is required, and being personal, it ought to be renewed, both at the change of the vassal and of the superior. But with us there being no fee without infeftment, *nulla sasina, nulla terra,* therefore the vassal must have the infeftment renewed. The renovation of infeftment to heirs in France and England is not requisite, but *mortuus sasit vivum,* as they express it, by which a special retour perfecteth the heir's right in his fee, with a great deal of ease, which is not consonant to the common feudal customs, whereby, if the vassal within year and day after his predecessor's death, require not to be entered by his superior, and offer his fidelity, he forfeits his fee, lib. 2, *Feudorum,* tit. 24; which severity we use not, for the vassal loseth not his fee by non-entry, nor the whole fruits of it during that time: but our custom is such, if by any means the fee be void, the vassal's right ceaseth during that time, and the fee is in the hands of the superior; and

therefore, in retours, to that article of the brieve it is answered, "that the lands are in the hands of such a man, Superior:" and though the infeftment of the predecessor, against others than the superior, be sufficient to maintain the right and possession of the vassal; yet as to the superior it hath no effect at all, after special declarator, till the vassal enter. And therefore the fee may be thus void, first by the minority of the heir, whereby he cannot enter by reason of ward; but this is expressed by the name of ward and non-entry, though it may signify the fee's being void, whether necessarily or voluntarily, yet it is appropriated to the latter, and contra-distinguished to ward [III, 2, 12, *infra*].

19. Or the fee become void by the reduction or nullity of the infeftment, or retour of any person formerly infeft, which is more rigorous, seeing the vassal had thereby a colourable title, and was *bonæ fidei possessor*, seeing reductions use not to be drawn back *ad præterita ;* so reduction of retours was sustained at the superior's instance, to give him the benefit of non-entry, July 12, 1625, L. Cathcart *contra* L. of Kerse [Durie 177; M. Supp. 23]. Feb. last, 1628, E. of Nithisdale *contra* L. Westraw [Spotiswoode 166; M. 5193]. Yet it is not determined, that the non-entry duties were competent from the beginning, but from the instruction of the nullity; therefore it must be considered what the nature of the right will import.

20. Non-entry taketh place whenever the fee is void, whether it be holden ward, blench or feu; but that which is holden in burgage, or is mortified, requireth no renovation of the infeftment, because societies and incorporations die not, which is extended to the particular tenements within burgh, holden burgage, which are thereby holden of the King, and the magistrates of the burgh give the infeftment as his bailies.

21. The effect of non-entry is attained by a declarator of non-entry, the style whereof beareth "that the tenement is void, and ought to be so declared, and that the fruits and profits thereof do belong to the superior, by reason of non-entry:" yet because the case of the vassal is favourable, decreet is only granted, declaring the non-entry, and finding only the feu-duties due in lands holding feu, July 19, 1631, E. of Kinghorn *contra* Strang [Durie 597; M. 96]; or the retoured mails in lands holding ward or blench, which have any such retour: or otherwise the whole duties of the fee are carried. The reason hereof is, because feus are locations, and the feu-duty is the rent or pension; and therefore *in favorabilibus*, that is interpreted to be the rent. So likewise in other lands, the retour was a valuation of the lands, as they were worth and paid at that time; the first whereof was called the Old Extent, and it is expressed by merk-lands, or pound-lands; the other is the New Retour, which though it be different in divers shires, yet being once a rent, in this favourable case, the general declarator reacheth no further. Yea, though there be no retour of the particular parcel of land in question, yet if there be a retour of the tenement or barony, whereof it is a part, that common retour will be divided according to the present rent, and a proportion thereof stated upon this parcel, as its retour, as was found in the former case, E. of Kinghorn

contra Strang [*supra*]. The like, Feb. 5, 1623, Ker *contra* Scot of Hartwood-mires [Durie 44; M. 9290]. Hence it is, that an annualrent, because it hath no retour distinct, but is retoured, *quod valet seipsum*, therefore if it be in non-entry, it is carried by the general declarator: and the non-entry was found to carry the whole profit of the annualrent by exception, in a poinding of the ground without any declarator, March 23, 1631, Somervel *contra* Somervel of Drum [Durie 585; M. 14320]: yea, though the annualrent be due by the superior's consent, yet it falls in non-entry, though it be due still by the personal obligement, where there is any, as in the case foresaid: but now by Act of Parliament 1690, cap. 42 [A.P.S. IX, 222, c. 96], the general declarator of annualrents carries only a penny or others expressed in the *reddendo*. In this declarator the superior producing his infeftment, needs not instruct the defender his vassal [11, 4, 6, *supra*]; and though the lands in question be not expressly in the superior's infeftment, but claimed by him as part and pertinent, he needs not instruct the same to be so, unless the vassal disclaim him as superior in that part [11, 11, 29, *infra*], Spots. Non-entry, Lord Yester *contra* his Vassals [Spotiswoode, 224; M. 16444]: neither needs he instruct that the lands were void since the time libelled, because that is a negative and proves itself, unless the vassal instruct that they were full.

The decreet of general declarator is not personal against the vassal, to pay the non-entry mails, &c. but is real against the ground of the tenement, for granting letters to poind and apprise, and so the calling of an apparent heir is sufficient, Spots. Escheat, Lo. Balmiranoch *contra* his Vassals [Not found]. But if the apparent heir be not called, but a person notourly known to have no relation, it is a relevant defence competent to any party called, though deriving no right from that defunct.

22. Though Craig insinuateth, that the action of special declarator is real, and the ground may be poinded for the whole duties, yet posterior decisions have upon good grounds cleared, that as to these, the superior is but as the master of the ground, and as he is in the case of ward; and therefore the ground cannot be poinded, neither is any liable but the intromitters with the fruits, Spots. Non-entry, Gray *contra* Murray [*Sub nom. Ogrie* v *Murray*, Durie 564; M. 9311]. Without this declarator of non-entry, the superior or his donatar cannot enter in possession of this void fee, and though he possess, he is comptable to the vassal for the mails and duties, Hope, Non-entry, Brown *contra* McCulloch of Barholme [Hope, *Maj. Pr.* III, 27, 32; M. 9303]; February 3, 1631, Ogilvie *contra* Murray of Halmyre [*Sub nom. Ogrie* v *Murray*, Durie 564; M. 9311]. But after declarator of non-entry is obtained, the superior may enter in possession any lawful way he pleaseth, and may dispose of the fruits and profits of the tenements, by himself or his donatar, and as if he were proprietor, and may out-put and in-put tenants therein, and hath the full profits and duties thereof, which may be pursued as other ordinary actions; though it useth to be pursued under the name of special declarator, which takes effect from the date of the summons, whereupon the general declarator

proceeded; because the decreet of the general declarator is only for the bygone mails, as aforesaid, and therefore reacheth not after the date of the summons, after which the whole mails and duties are due, not only in ward-
holdings and blench, but also in feus; and so it was found, that before general
declarator the feu-duty was only due, but that after general declarator the
whole profits, July 19, 1631, E. of Kinghorn *contra* Strang [Durie 597; M. 96];
July 25, 1666, Harper *contra* his Vassals [1 Stair 402; M. 9305]; July 11, 1673,
Fa *contra* Lo. Balmiranoch and L. of Powrie [2 Stair 208; M. 5449].

23. Non-entry is excluded [IV, 8, 7, *infra*], first by the entry of the vassal
and his infeftment, during the time thereof, even though the same was
granted by him, who was superior, after his predecessor was denuded four
ages before, which must be in respect the new superior's right was not known,
as neither being registrate, nor any intimation nor action thereupon, Hope,
Non-entry, Arthur *contra* Laird of Blebo [Hope, *Maj.Pr.*, III, 27, 30; M.
9334]. And if the vassal be infeft upon a charter from his predecessors, to be
holden of the superior, if the superior confirm it, the infeftment is valid, and
excludes the non-entry from the date thereof, and not from the date of the
confirmation, being simple, Hope, Non-entry, Bartoun and Harvie *contra*
Laird of Delspro [Hope, *Maj.Pr.* III, 27, 29]. 2. Non-entry is excluded *pro
tanto* by feus, terces of relicts, liferents of husbands surviving their wives by
the courtesy of Scotland. These are effectual by law, and are introduced
without the superior's consent. It is excluded also by his express consent, by
liferents or conjunct infeftments holden of him; for though the vassal may
enter to the fee, yet the liferent excludes the profits, and therefore, during the
simple liferent, the superior cannot obtain declarator of non-entry. 3. By the
superior's consent, it is also excluded by precepts of *clare constat*, which acknowledged the person who died last vest and seased, as of fee, during whose
time the non-entry cannot be claimed; and likewise, by receiving the vassal
with a *novo-damus*, renouncing expressly non-entry, if it was granted by the
superior, before the right was transmitted from him to the donatar. 4. It is
excluded by the superior's tacit, or presumed consent, by granting subsequent infeftments, for the space of forty years, March 19, 1629, Earl of Angus
and Douglas *contra* E. of Annandale [Durie 439; M. 9334]: June 29, 1629, Sir
Mungo Murray *contra* L. of Inchmartine [Durie 449; M. 9336]; Hope, Non-
entry, Arthur *contra* L. of Blebo [Hope, *Maj.Pr.* III, 27, 30; M. 9334]; for
thereby it is presumed that the non-entry is relinquished, not being claimed
nor reserved all that time; which Craig [II, 19, 17] observes to have been
found upon infeftments, continued by the space of thirty-six years; but the
best term, as being ordinary and known in law, is forty years; and this is not
by reason of prescription, which would only cut off profits of non-entry preceding the forty years, but this would take it away during and after the forty
years. The like is very rationally observed by Craig [II, 19, 16], to be inferred
by three subsequent seasins, having the same presumption as three subsequent discharges have, to infer exoneration of all bygones; but these must be

of three subsequent heirs, and not by receiving three singular successors. The non-entry returning to the vassal or his heirs, they cannot make use of it against the sub-vassals, especially if they be liable to warrant the sub-vassals as to non-entry, or by absolute warrandice generally; for thereby the right to the non-entry is *jus superveniens authori accrescens successori;* but the sub-vassals must pay their proportion of the expenses of the gift [11,4,15,*supra*]. But non-entry is not excluded, because it was gifted to the apparent heir of a superior of a sub-vassal, which superior was obliged in warrandice to his sub-vassal, seeing he was not heir, Spots. Non-entry, L. of Craichlaw *contra* Gordon of Barnernie and Mackie [Not found]. Neither is it excluded by any base infeftment, not being feu, though confirmed by the superior, if it hold not of the superior; for such confirmations import only a passing from recognition, as is shown in the last Title, concerning Confirmation [11,3,28,*supra*]. Feus exclude non-entry while they were allowed by the Acts of Parliament, as is there also shown. Non-entry is not excluded by tacks set by the vassal, which though they stand as real rights against purchasers by statute, yet have no effect against superiors, in prejudice of their proper casualities. Neither is it elided by charters, or precepts granted by the superior, though containing warrandice, till infeftment thereupon. Neither was it excluded by apprising and charge thereupon, without offer of a year's rent of the land, or annualrent of the money, February 3, 1681, Ker *contra* Hendryson [2 Stair 852; M. 6915]. Neither is it excluded because the vassal was not *in mora*, being hindered by a question of bastardy against him, Spots. Non-entry, *contra* Napier of Wrightshouses [*Sub nom. Mackalzean* v *Napier*, Spotiswoode 219]. Neither doth the vassal's minority stop non-entry of lands not being ward, nor restore the minor as leased; for as it hath been now shown, it is not the negligence of the vassal, but the nature of the right that infers non-entry: yet there is no doubt if it be by the superior's fault, it will be a personal exclusion against him.

24. Non-entry is most favourable, when extended to the retoured duties only: but as to the full rents, it is capable of many other exceptions, and doth not always run from the citation in the general declarator; as if a superior raise his declarator, and also reduction of the vassal's seasin, though he reduce the seasin, he will not have the full rents till the decreet of reduction and declarator, November 26, 1672, Earl of Argyle *contra* L. of Macleod [2 Stair 122; M.15013]: yea, if the superior do not insist, but only use citation, which may be at the vassal's dwelling-house, and never come to knowledge; or the vassal being a pupil without any tutor, it is not like the Lords would sustain the whole duties from the citation, but from the time the vassal becomes contumacious. And Earl Queensberry having interposed Kelhead betwixt him and his vassals, who thereupon pursued declarator of non-entry, though the infeftment was found null, yet the disposition was found to carry a gift to the casualities of the superiority, and the vassals were only found liable for the rent after the interlocutor sustaining the disposition as a gift of non-entry

[*Sub nom. Douglas* v *Carlyle*, 2 Stair 349; M.9320]; and where a tailzie was found to exclude a second branch, so long as there was hope of a former branch, the lands were found in non-entry, as to the retoured mail, but not as to the full rent, seeing the heir did not forbear to enter through wilfulness, but of necessity, July 24, 1677, Lord Melville and David Melville his son *contra* Bruce [2 Stair 545; M.9321]. And where a singular successor to the superior pursued non-entry, it was not sustained till he produced his progress from the acknowledged superior, the full duties were not found due from the citation, January 18, 1681, E. of Queensberry *contra* Irwin of Cove [2 Stair 835; M.3557]. And Craig [11,19,19] relates, that where the defunct died in battle for his superior, non-entry should have no place. The general declarator of non-entry is, for the neglect of the vassal's heir to enter; but the special declarator is only for his contempt, being interpelled by the citation in the general declarator. But the full rent is only where contempt appears, and so if there be different pretenders to the superiority, the apparent heir may call them all to discuss their rights: but though he do not, he will not lose the full rents, while that competition lasteth; yet if the superior be denuded by infeftment on a disposition, the pretence of not knowing the new superior will not be sustained, or if by an apprising expired: as in the case at the instance of the Duke and Duchess of Hamilton against Mr. John Elleis, February 17, 1691 [*Sub anno* 1684; Harcarse 207; M.9293], concerning the non-entry of the lands of Elistoun, albeit there was a decreet of general declarator *in foro contradictorio*, yet in the special declarator Mr. John was only found liable from the date of the decreet of the general declarator, because his author's infeftment was granted by his superior to his heirs-male, who would have been Abercorn, the duchess being only heir of line. And in the pursuit the Duke and Duchess against Kettlestoun, February 1692 [Not found], the infeftment by E. Mar, Lord of Erection, was not sustained, yet the full duties were neither found due from the citation on the summons of general declarator, nor from the decreet, because the author's infeftment was to the heirs-male of the superior, who was Earl Abercorn; but upon a decreet *in foro*, excluding Abercorn, the full duties were only found due since the production of that decreet. So much for excluding of non-entry: but we shall not here speak of the common exceptions, which extinguish all rights, as prescription, homologation, or the privilege of these who are absent *reipublicæ causa ;* of which in their proper places.

25. As to the question, Whether non-entry subsequent to ward whereby the superior or his donatar is in possession, requireth any declarator; Craig, and Skeen upon the word Non-entry, are for the negative; but since, Had. and Durie observe March 23, 1622, Lesly *contra* L. Pitcaple [Durie 424; M. 12604], that the lords found, that where the superior pursued both for the ward and subsequent non-entry, that he or his donatars, not being in possession by the ward, behoved to declare the non-entry, which would only carry the retoured mails till declarator; but if the donatar was in posesssion by the

ward, he might continue by the gift for three terms thereafter [11, 4, 36, *infra*].

26. The next casuality of the superiority is, the relief due by the vassal to the superior, for his entering him in the fee, as the lawful successor of the vassal. And though relief be only considerable in ward-holding, and uses to be subjoined to ward, yet all fees which require renovation, are liable to relief; and therefore relief is here immediately subjoined to non-entry. Relief is generally treated upon by the Feudists, the original whereof Cujace ascribeth to the constitution of the emperor Leo, extant in the Novels [Nov. Leonis, c. 13], bearing it to be the custom of several places, that the superior should have that year's rent, in which he receives a new vassal in his clientel, which therefore, by most of the feudal customs, is extended to singular successors of the vassals, who in some places, pay for their entry the fifth part of the price of the fee, and a fifth of that fifth; whereby if the price were 100 crowns, the composition for the entry would be 24 crowns.

27. But by the customs of England and France, the heir of the vassal, if he be minor, pays no relief, but he and his fee are in the hands of the superior, as in ward or custody, whereby the superior hath the whole profits, more than is fit for the education and entertainment of the minor vassal, which ceaseth with his majority, and there is no relief due: but if the vassal's heir at his death be major, his fee is liable to his superior for relief; which distinction is mentioned in the English *Magna Charta* [c. 3], and the quantity of the relief by heirs in England, is in ward-holdings or military fees 100 pounds sterling for an earldom, 100 merks for a barony, and 100 shillings for any other military fee, which is obliged to maintain one soldier; and if the fee be less, and liable only for a share of the entertainment of a soldier, it is liable proportionally for relief.

Relief, by the custom of France, is for a barony 100 franks, and for any other military fee 15. But if it answer not to the entertainment of one soldier, it pays for every acre 12 deniers; but if it be not a military fee, but that which the English call sockage, the *reddendo* whereof is not military service, but some other payment or performance, it is doubled the first year after the death of the vassal, the one half whereof is the relief, which is a real burden, for which the superior may poind or distrinzie all goods upon the ground. But as to singular successors, the most ancient feudal customs, making them only to descend to the issue of the first vassal, whose collaterals had no right, but were like our kindly tenants, by the propinquity of blood; yet by the favour of the superior, they were oft-times admitted in the fee, and were only liable for relief; so if the superior did receive a stranger, upon the resignation of his vassal, he was to pay a relief, which in some places was the fiftieth part of the price. And by the custom of France, it is the thirteenth part: therefore, from the original of relief, the reason of its name may be conjectured; and these who appropriate it to ward-holdings, interpret it to be called relief, from redeeming or relieving the fee out of the hands of the superior: but relief being a general feudal name, and many nations not allowing the superior the whole profits of the fee, in the minority of the heir, and giving a relief in the case of singular successors, that derivation must be too narrow; and therefore it seems most quadrant to the common feudal customs, that relief should import a subsidy or aid to the superior.

We have the more largely considered the rise and customs of nations concerning relief, because, though it frequently occurs with us, yet it hath been always kindly transacted betwixt the superior and vassal: and there is scarce a controversy or decision observed about it by any since the institution of the College of Justice, so that we must rest in the common custom used betwixt superior and vassal, the nature of this casuality, and the opinions of some few of our lawyers who have written upon it. Craig *Lib.*2, *Dieg.*20, [11,20,30], handles the matter of relief, and saith, "By our ancient custom, there was no relief due after ward;" but that it was the common opinion of lawyers at that time, that relief had only place in ward-holdings; and that it imported a year's rent of the fee, being the full profits thereof, when the superior or his donatar were in possession by the ward; but in other cases only a year's rent, by the favourable accompt, that is one year's new retoured duty of the fee, as it is retoured by itself, or the share of the retour of any barony or tenement, whereof it is a part. But Craig, with good reason holds relief to be due at the renovation of every fee, to the heirs of the investiture; for the duplication of the feu-duty in feus, is due at the entry of every heir; and that without an express clause in the *reddendo*, by the feudal custom, which is generally acknowledged: and even when the duplication is expressed, it doth ordinarily bear, *secundum consuetudinem feudorum :* and Sir Thomas Hope, in his title of Ward [Hope, *Min.Pr.*, IV,16], is of the same opinion, in respect that the precepts issued out of the chancellary, for infefting of heirs, even in feus or blench-holdings, bear *capiendo securitatem*, for the double of the feu, or blench-duty.

28. As to the quantity of the relief, Hope, in that title holdeth it only to be "the retoured duty, without exception, when the vassal or his donatar was in possession." And Sir John Skeen in his treatise, *De Verborum Significatione*, asserteth the same. It is also provided by Act of Parliament 1587 [1587,c.74; A.P.S. III,456,c.54], "That the full avail of the relief be taken and compted for in Exchequer, by sheriffs, stewards and baillies, without accepting any composition; and that charges be directed against persons, who have gotten precepts of seasin, or the sheriffs or their deputes, or both, to point for the sums contained in the book of Responde;" which is a book of record in the chancellary, drawn off the precepts of seasin to all heirs, and mentioning such a sheriff or baillie where the lands lie, *respondere*, that is to count in exchequer for the sums, which by the precepts of seasin directed to him, he is ordered to take security for, which sums would be liquid, and known according to the new retour, and the feu or blench-duty, but could not be known otherwise than by a process of liquidation, proving the full yearly rent of the fee, as to which the sheriff might not compone or transact; and it is generally ack-

nowledged, that when the full rent becomes due, there is no real execution, by poinding of the ground; but the superior hath the full benefit of the fee, as when it is in ward; and therefore the relief, which is *debitum fundi*, must only be the retour-duty.

29. Conform to this statute it was found, that the relief might be recovered, either by real action of poinding of the ground, or personally against the vassal, who had taken his precept of seasin out of the chancellary, though he had not taken infeftment thereupon, March 12, 1628, L. of Lauristoun *contra* the Sheriff of Mearns [Durie 359; M. 10163]; which was upon the personal security given to the sheriff at the infefting the heir, otherwise it is only a real burden on the ground.

30. If the fee be possessed by a relict conjunct fiar, the vassal's heir needs not enter during her life, for her conjunct fee doth exclude all casualities during her life; or if it be in possession of a husband by the courtesy of Scotland: yet these will not exclude the fiar to enter to the property burdened with these liferents, and it is oft-times necessary for him to secure his creditors; in which case it is most favourable, that the superior should have a year's retoured duty, as he would have gotten it, after the conjunct fiar's death, at least security for it to be paid after the conjunct fiar's death.

31. The clause *capiendo securitatem* will be in all precepts, notwithstanding these liferents, and it will not stop the seasin of the heir, till he pay the relief to the superior, whether king or subject; but security by sufficient caution must be received therefor.

32. In place of the relief to the superior by the vassal's singular successor, we have a composition introduced by statute 1469, cap. 36 [Diligence Act, 1469, c. 36; A.P.S. 11, 96, c. 12] whereby superiors are obliged to receive apprisers for a year's rent of the lands apprised [11, 3, 29–30, *supra*], for before that statute, no superior could be compelled to receive any other vassal than the heir of the first vassal provided by the investiture: for though in dispositions, lands are ordinarily disponed to the purchaser, his heirs and assignees; yet assignees use not to be repeated in the charters, and the meaning of that clause in dispositions hath been several times interpreted, that the disposition may be assigned or transferred. But infeftment being once taken, assignees have no further interest [11, 3, 5, *supra*], and that clause doth not save recognition, when the ward-vassal infefts any other in the fee than his heir apparent, as was found in the case of the Lady Carnegie *contra* Lo. Cranburn [Feb. 5, 1663, 1 Stair 172; M. 10375]. And though a disposition have no mention of assignees, yet before infeftment, while it remains personal, it is assignable; and a superior who granted a disposition by a minute, was decerned to receive the assignee to the minute, though he was not in friendship with him, Jan. 29, 1673, Ogilvie *contra* Kinloch of Bendoch [2 Stair 163; M. 10384]. This statute was by custom extended to adjudications, being the same in effect, but different in form from apprisings; for the design of the statute being to satisfy creditors by a judicial alienation of the debtor's lands,

ex paritate rationis, it was extended against the debtor's apparent heir, who being charged to enter heir, did not enter, and therefore lands were adjudged from him, to which he might have entered, either for his predecessor's debt or his own; whereupon the superior is decerned to receive the creditor-adjudger, whether for sums of money, or for implement of dispositions, and obligements to infeft. But the custom allowed not a year's rent to superiors for receiving adjudgers [111,2,49,*infra*], till the year's rent was also extended to adjudications by Act of Parliament, Dec. 3, 1669 [1669, c. 18; A.P.S. VII, 576, c. 39]. There is more reason for a year's rent to the superior receiving adjudgers for implement of irredeemable dispositions, and the like reason though they be redeemable [11,4,6,*supra*], but not for receiving liferenters adjudging upon their dispositions, because thereby the vassal is not changed, and the superior hath the accession of the liferenter's escheat. The superior hath the like composition for entering of adjudications now come in place of apprisings; but there is a great alteration by the Act bringing them in *pari passu*, for thereby a charge against the superior to enter is declared as effectual, as if infeftment had passed, and custom hath required no further diligence than that charge, so that it will be to the detriment both of debtor and creditor to urge actual infeftment, during the legal, and no unjust prejudice to the superior, seeing till then the adjudication is but *pignus prætorium*, and if it be redeemed or satisfied, the vassal is unchanged [11,3,30,*supra*].

The Lords of Session have always taken a latitude in the modification of the year's rent, especially if the sum apprised or adjudged for be small, and the lands be great [111,2,27,*infra*], and they have allowed the appriser or adjudger his option during the legal, to take infeftment or not, and yet not to be excluded from the rents of the lands, till he be satisfied, December 3, 1672, Hay *contra* L. of Earlstoun [2 Stair 123; M. 15043], *Vide hic Tit. 3 §29.* But the appriser runs that hazard, that if the debtor die before he be satisfied, if the land be holden ward, it will fall in ward, and relief, by the debtor's death, and in non-entry; for there is no reason that the casualities of the superiority should neither fall by the appriser nor by the debtor [11,3,30,*supra*]. But there is not the like reason, that the liferent-escheat of the debtor should exclude the appriser, if it fell after the apprising and charge; for the liferent-escheat falls to the superior with all the burdens which affected it by the vassal, even with the burden of his tacks; and therefore apprising with a charge must be as effectual as these [11,4,66,*supra*], July 24, 1632, Rule *contra* L. Billie [Durie 649; M. 3624]. Likeas the superior can have only one year's rent from all the apprisers or adjudgers. And now since apprisers and adjudgers within year and day come in *pari passu* where one needs only to be infeft or to charge, there is less reason to give an easy modification of the year's rent to the first appriser or adjudger, insisting for infeftment, than before; because one infeftment serves for all, and he who advanceth the same, gets relief off the rest, before they have access to the rents [111,2,27,*infra*].

33. The prime casuality of fees is ward, which is not competent to all

superiors; for ward is only competent in fees holden in military service, which have their denomination from this casuality, being therefore called ward-holdings, and that not by the tenor of the investiture, which seldom mentioneth ward, but by the nature of it; for, when the fee is holden for military service, or as the English better express it, by knight service, extending not only to following in war, but to council and assistance in peace, then, when the vassal is unfit for such service, the fee is open and remaineth in the hands of the superior, or his donatar; and though this capacity might be in some sooner, yet it is fixed in men to their majority, at twenty-one years complete; and in women, till they become fourteen years complete; for then they are capable of husbands, who may do the service required in the fee, Had. Dec. 20, 1609; and January 27, 1610, La. Kilbirnie *contra* the Heirs of Fairlie [Haddington, *Fol. Dict.* 1, 568; M. 8521]. What fees are holden ward we have cleared in the former title: it only now remains, that we hold forth the effect of this casuality.

34. Ward reacheth the custody of the person of the minor vassal, and of his lands holden ward, and hath its denomination rather from the former; for ward is as much as guard or custody: the superior or his donatar, is by the nature of this right, as a tutor to the vassal's heir; Craig observes [11, 20, 18], that he is preferable to all other tutors, except only the father of the heir whose fee descends from the mother, or some other person; and that he is obliged as other tutors, to pursue the rights of the heir. But the course of time having turned this right from its ancient institution, so that the superior hath less enjoyment of service, but more of profit of the fee, there is the less regard to the pupil's education, with, or by the superior to the effect he might be fitted for his service; and therefore other tutors, not only for the administration of the pupil's means, but even for the custody and education of his person, will be preferred [1, 6, 15, *supra*].

35. The main effect of ward then is, that thereby the superior or his donatar have, during that time, the full fruits and profits of the fee, and may remove tenants, and do all other deeds that the proprietor might have done, and was accustomed to do; as to continue the profits of a wood, if there be constant cutting; as being divided in so many hags, that the first is ready by the last be cut; or of going heughs, as they were accustomed by the vassal; but he cannot cut more than the accustomed yearly hags of wood, or put in more coal-heughers than the vassal had at his death, and ordinarily before [11, 3, 74, *supra*], and he may remove and in-put tenants, and that without any preceding declarator, or favourable accompt esteeming the retour mail for the rent, as in non-entry; but he may immediately pursue actions for mails and duties, removing, &c. unless the ward be taxed, and then the superior can have no more than the duties to which it is taxed: but for it, he hath not only the vassal, and all intromitters with the fruits, personally liable, but he may also poind the ground for the taxed duty.

36. Yet the extent of ward by the nature of the fee, cannot extend to the

alienation, or consumption of the substance of the fee, or any part or pertinent thereof, and this is cleared by the statute, Parl. 1491, cap. 25 [Liferent Caution Act, 1491, c. 25; A.P.S. 11, 224, c. 6]. Whereby donatars must find caution not to destroy the biggings, woods, stanks, parks, meadows, or dovecoats, but to keep them in such kind as they get them. Ward is also restrained by the statutes confirming feus, of which formerly; and these stand valid against the superior, during the ward; so do also all infeftments holden of him, either by resignation or confirmation: but not infeftments to be holden of his vassal, unless confirmed by him; for albeit confirmations by the king, which pass of course, do not take away the casualities of ward, &c. of the king's vassals, which affect the fee of the sub-vassals [But see 11, 3, 32, *supra*]; yet the confirmation of other superiors of sub-vassals' rights, doth take off from them the ward, seeing the Act 1606, cap. 12 [A.P.S. IV, 287, c. 11], doth only annul feus set by vassals, holding ward of subjects, without their superior's consent: which was so found that the superior consenting to a feu granted by his vassal to a sub-vassal, albeit the feu was under reversion, it was free of the ward and marriage of the vassal as to the sub-vassal feuar, but did only affect the vassal's interest, viz. the feu-duty, reversion and backtack, July 1, 1672, E. of Eglintoun *contra* L. of Greenock [2 Stair 94; M. 4178].

Ward is also restrained by the terce of wives, and liferent of husbands by the courtesy of Scotland, both which are introduced by law, and are valid without the superior's consent. But rentals and tacks set by the vassal, have only this effect against the superior or his donatar, that the tenants or labourers shall not be removed till the next Whitsunday, after the beginning of the ward, paying the old accustomed duty, Parl. 1491, cap. 26 [Leases Act, 1491, c. 26; A.P.S. 11, 225, c. 7] yet then the superior or his donatar may remove them, notwithstanding their tacks be unexpired, which therefore sleep during ward, but revive against the setter and his heirs, and endure as many years after the ward, as they were excluded by the ward, Haddington, July 4, 1611, L. of Couter *contra*   [M. 16559], where also the terce was found relevant to exclude the superior; yet ward is not excluded by annualrents holden of the vassal, March 21, 1629, Weyms *contra* L. Kincraig [Durie 440; M. 16561]. But now since the Act of Parliament 1606, prohibiting feus without consent of the superior, these did not exclude the ward, or other casualities of the superiority, as to fees not holden of the king, which was even extended to the fees holden of the prince, Hope, Ward, La. Cathcart *contra* Vassals of Cathcart [Hope, *Maj. Pr.* 111, 25, 28; M. 4176, 6461]. And, after the Act of Parliament 1633 [1633, c. 16; A.P.S. V, 38, c. 16], extending the foresaid Act to ward-lands holden of the king and prince; feus then granted till the year 1641, when the effect of that Act was taken away, and so feus of lands holden of the king or prince, were valid till the rescissory Act 1661, whereby the said Parliament 1641, was rescinded Parl. 1661, cap. 15 [A.P.S. VII, 86, c. 126]. So that now feus of lands holden of the king, prince, or any other superior, without their consent, do not exclude ward or other casualities of the superiority, except such feus as were granted the several times they were allowed by law [II,3,32,*supra*], but a charter upon an apprising did exclude the ward, though no infeftment was taken thereupon during the vassal's life, as Hope observes, title Ward, Hamilton *contra* Tenants of Newburgh [Hope, *Maj.Pr.* III,25,25; M.16443], because the superior's charter without seasin, did import a gift of the casualities, which might befal to the superior [III,2,20, *infra*]; and he there observes, that a ward was excluded by apprising and infeftment thereupon, whereby the defunct was denuded, albeit it was to the behoof of his heir, L. of Ley *contra* L. of Baro [Durie 401; M.7789].

During the legal, the superior or donatar, as before the infeftment upon the apprising, they might pay the appriser and take his right: so after, they may redeem him and exclude him, it being against reason, that by apprising (suppose of a great tenement) for a small debt, the superior should be simply excluded, and it may be upon design. If an appriser infeft possess, his ward falls, and not the former vassal's, though the legal be not expired; but after the ward is fallen, though the superior received an appriser apprising from the heir without protestation; yet it was found not to prejudge the ward by the death of the former vassal, July 19, 1664, Hospital of Glasgow *contra* Campbel [1 Stair 216; M.6419; II,4,12,*supra*; II,4,57,*infra*]. But a superior was not excluded from the ward by his vassal's death, because an appriser had charged him to enter him during that vassal's life, seeing that charge could not make the appriser vassal, by whose death ward would fall, and thereby make the superior lose his casuality by the death of both the old vassal and the appriser, unless the superior had been *in mora aut culpa*, which was not found, unless a year's rent of the land, or annualrent of the money, and a charter were offered with a bond to pay what further the Lords should modify, February 19, 1669, Black *contra* Trinch [1 Stair 599; M.6911; II,3,30,*supra*]. But a creditor apprising, though infeft, if he possess not, his ward falls not by his death, because his apprising is but a legal diligence, which he may renounce or relinquish, and insist by other diligence for payment.

If an apprising be satisfied or extinct by intromission, the ward-lands apprised become in the superior's hands by ward, till the majority of the heir, July 20, 1671, Lindsay *contra* Maxwel [1 Stair 761; M.10381]; in which case, the appriser was not found obliged to restrict to his annualrent, to the effect that the donatar of the ward might have the superplus, by the Act of Parl. 1661, cap. 62 [Diligence Act, 1661,c.62; A.P.S. VII,317,c.344], betwixt debtor and creditor, whereby there is a power given to the Lords of Session to cause apprisers restrict to their annualrent, which is only personal, in favours of the debtor, if he demand it.

The benefit of ward is also burdened with the maintenance and sustentation of the heir, by virtue of the aforesaid Act, 1491, cap. 25 [Liferent Caution Act, 1491,c.25; A.P.S. II,225,c.6], whereby a reasonable sustentation, according to the quantity of the heritage, is appointed to the heir, if he have not lands blench or feu to sustain him, and that [to be paid] by the superior and his donatar, and conjunct-fiars and liferenters of his estate; the quantity whereof is to be modified by the Lords, according to the quality of the heir. Hence it follows, that if the heir have only ward-lands of small value, which cannot exceed the heir's maintenance, the superior can have no part of the fruits; this modification takes place, not only when the heir hath no means; but though he had, if it was not sufficient to entertain him, the superplus is modified out of the ward-lands, and lands liferented proportionably. But here we shall say no more of the aliment of heirs by ward-superiors, or their donatars in this place; but you may see it in its proper place, Title Heir, §3 [III, 5, 3, *infra*].

Thus it appeareth in what way the casuality of ward is excluded, burdened, or restricted, being always by law, or by the consent and deed of the superior; but no private deed of the vassal without the superior's consent, or appointment of law, can burden the fee when it is in the hands of the superior, by ward, &c. So that servitudes introduced by the vassal, as thirlage, ways and the like, are not effectual against the superior or his donatar, when the fee is in their hands; unless such servitudes be introduced by prescription of forty years, or immemorial possession, whereunto all parties having interest, their consent is presumed; and therefore, in that case there is ground for sustaining of the servitude, even against the superior, who might at least have used civil interruption. Thus, marches set by the vassal of consent, or by cognition, whereto the superior is not called, hath no effect in his prejudice during the ward, February 8, 1662, Lo. Torphichen *contra*   [1 Stair 95; M. 2199], except in the case of prescription, as said is [11, 7, 3, *infra*].

As to the personal debts of the vassal, whether heritable or moveable, they do not affect the fee though in ward, albeit Craig, *Lib.* 2, *Dieg.* 20, [11, 20, 20], relateth, "that of old it was otherwise, and that the superior had the ward, with the burden of entertaining the heir, and with the paying of the annual-rents of his heritable debts [R.M. 11, 42, 6], and that the custom of wards in France is such:" for which there is a great deal of reason; ward being granted to superiors, when debts were not so many or so great as now, so that the superior in gratitude had what was then superfluous to the vassal; but now the vassal may, and many have been ruined by their heritable debts, running on in annual during the ward: but custom having given the ward to superiors simply, there is no remeid without a statute, correctory of this custom. So the casuality of ward may be enjoyed immediately by the superior, but is more ordinarily gifted to donatars, not only by the king, but by other superiors; which donatars may do whatsoever the superior himself might; because they act by his right, and are in effect his assignees: so that if gifts be granted to more donatars, the first intimation or diligence will be preferred [III, 3, 1, *infra*].

Gifts of ward and of non-entry were accustomed of old, to be granted by the Exchequer together, bearing, "not only for bygones, but for time coming till the entry of the righteous heir or heirs:" And albeit gifts of ward run still in the same style, yet by the acts and customs of exchequer, ward and non-entry are several casualities, and pass by several gifts; and notwithstanding the foresaid clause, the gift of ward reacheth only during the time of ward, and three terms thereafter, if the lands run in non-entry [Hope, *Min.Pr.*, Tit.IV,6]; but ward was not found to give right to three terms full rent, (here the donatar was not in possession during the ward) November 2, 1680, L. of Dun *contra* Vis. of Arbuthnet [2 Stair 810; M. 5120; 11,4,25, *supra*]. And albeit the gift contain relief, yet that casuality, as Hope observeth [Hope, *Min. Pr.* Tit. IV, 19 and 20], is always demanded by the exchequer, and counted for by the sheriff, being but a small duty of the retoured mail, as a gratuity to the superior at the vasssal's entry: and in that same place, he saith, "that under the gift of a simple ward, is not comprehended taxed ward, which being taxed is as a feu-duty, and rather as a part of the king's ordinary revenue, than a casuality:" upon which ground the Earl of Kinghorn, as tutor to the Earl of Errol, having gotten a gift of his ward, without mention of taxed ward, he was necessitate again to take a new gift for the taxed ward, and gave a considerable composition, and did not adventure to put the matter to debate before the Lords of Session, whether his gift would have been extended to taxt-ward or not.

37. The fourth casuality of superiority is called the marriage of the defunct vassal's heir, by which is understood the value of his tocher. There is nothing of this in the common feudal customs: it is in use in France and England; and Craig relates, that it was introduced in England in the reign of Henry III and from thence came to us; but it is more likely that we had it sooner; for King Malcolm Kenmore [1058–1093] gave out all his land to his subjects, reserving the ward and marriages of their heirs, which is long before Henry III of England [1216–1272].

38. Craig [11,21,4] states this casuality in a power of the superior, whereby he may marry the heir of his vassal who died last infeft at his pleasure, but without disparagement. By this supposition, the benefit of the heir's marriage would only be a penalty in two cases; the one, if the defunct's vassal's heir marry without obtaining his superior's consent, his fee should be burdened with a suitable avail of the tocher, which he did or might get; but if his superior did offer a suitable match, if he did marry another, he should pay the double avail of his tocher; yet in the common opinion the double avail is only penal.

39. And the single avail ariseth from the nature of proper fees, or ward-holdings, according as a fee is understood to comprehend, by the custom of this and other nations, who hold this casuality; and therefore it is *debitum fundi* as arising from the nature of the fee, or from the express tenor of the investiture, as is in several feu-holdings of the king.

40. And therefore the avail of the marriage being declared, an apprising, or adjudication on that decreet, is preferable to all other apprisings or ad-

judications, for the debts or deeds of the defunct vassal, his predecessors or heirs, albeit they were prior, as was found December 17, 1673, Hadden *contra* Moor [2 Stair 242; M. 10648].

41. But the avail of marriage doth not affect the apparent heir personally, January 5, 1681, L. of Dun *contra* Viscount Arbuthnet [2 Stair 825; M. 4175], and therefore cannot affect any other part of his estate but the ward-fee, or the feu *cum maritagio ;* though there be one decision in the case of Arbuthnet *contra* Fiddes, February 25, 1662 [*Sub nom. Arbuthnot* v *Keith*, 1 Stair 104; M. 8528], where the avail of the marriage was more worth than the ward-land, the heir was found liable personally, in so far as exceeded the same, which hath never been seconded, nor ought to be drawn in example [11, 4, 48, *infra*].

42. It is not the want of the superior's consent, which gives the avail of the vassal's heir's marriage, as was found in the case of the E. of Argyle *contra* L. M'Naughtan [1 Stair 720; M. 10791], where the superior being present at the marriage did not exclude him from the single value; yea, the superior's subscribing witness to the vassal's contract of marriage, was not sustained to exclude the single value, February 25, 1662, Arbuthnet *contra* Keiths [1 Stair 104; M. 8528].

43. The ground of the restriction of the avail of marriage ought chiefly to be taken from the rise and design of this casuality, which some do attribute to the superior's power, as tutor to his ward-vassal, whom he kept in his custody, and educate for his service in the war, which the name of ward insinuateth; for ward or guard is a fence or custody. But this cannot be the true cause of this casuality, seeing that tutorial trust behoved to be in favours of the vassal, directing him in his choice of a match, and could not be so far turned to his prejudice, as to make his fee liable to a double avail, if he refused the superior's offer of a match without disparagement, and married another.

44. Others therefore hold the cause of this casuality, to be for preventing the vassal's marrying with a family in enmity with the superior; but that would be too narrow a ground; for thereby the avail of a marriage would only be due, if the vassal's heir did actually marry with a family in enmity with the superior, and so would never be due, if the vassal's heir never married, or where he married with his superior's relation, or known friend, and yet neither of the said cases doth exclude a single avail.

45. We must therefore inquire for a more adequate and rational ground of this casuality, which appears very clearly to be thus; that by the nature of ward-holding as it was when first introduced, being for military service, and being a gratuitous donation, that service was not as an equivalent cause, seeing the occasions of war were uncertain, but was as a grateful acknowledgment of the vassal; and therefore when the vassal was not in capacity for service in war, the superior resumed his fee into his own hand, during the vassal's minority, and was not thereby obliged to aliment the heir, as appeareth by the 25 Act Parl. 1491 [Liferent Caution Act, 1491, c. 25; A.P.S. 11, 224, c. 6], ordaining wardators, that is, all having right to the ward of a vassal's heir,

whether superior or donatar or assignee, to give a reasonable living for sustentation of the heir, according to the quantity of the heritage, if the heir hath
no blench or feu-lands to sustain him on; so that before this Act, the heir had
no aliment out of his fee during his minority, and by the Act he had no aliment from the superior, if he had feu or blench lands to sustain himself; so
that formerly the heirs of ward-vassals were redacted to extreme penury in
their minority, if they had nothing else but their ward-fee. For remeid whereof, mutual burdens were introduced upon the ward-fee, viz. That the
superior should aliment his minor vassal, and yet in recompence thereof, he
should have the avail of his tocher; but being obliged only to aliment the heir,
and not to aliment him and his family when he were married, therefore his
tocher belonged to himself *ad sustinenda onera matrimonii*, till he came to
majority, and might enter to his fee, and have the full profits thereof.

46. The avail of which tocher, hath certainly been of old the tocher the
vassal got, wherein the superior had this just interest, that if his vassal should
imprudently marry, getting too small a tocher that therefore the superior
might offer him a match, with a better tocher; and if he refused it and
married the other, the avail should be esteemed as equivalent to the tocher he
might have had, and that in consideration not only of his ward-fee, but of all
other his estate, real or personal; which was very rational and suitable to the
time that the avail of marriage was introduced, when personal debts were very
rare; and therefore the vassal might well pay the avail of his marriage when
he came to his fee, without any excessive burden.

47. But since personal debts came to be so frequent, the avail of marriage
is only in relation to the free estate, real or personal, of the vassal, and custom
hath fixed the single avail about two years' free rent of the vassal, wherein
there is a latitude to the Lords, to modify according to the circumstances: and
as to the double avail, it never exceeds three years' free rent: But it is so little
favourable, and hath so many solemnities, that I never observed, since the
institution of the College of Justice, the double avail to be found due; the
method of obtaining it being so contrary to all the designs pretended for this
casuality: for therein the superior or his donatar, do never offer a match
which he believes the vassal will accept, but of design to get a double avail;
wherein nothing appears of tutorial trust, or of that strict confidence between
superiors and vassals; nor any thing to prevent marrying with an unfriendly
family.

But the single avail is favourable, as a real burden upon the fee, and hath
for recompence the aliment of the vassal's heir, and is a burden which the
vassal may bear, without hazard of ruin, or great distress, being oft-times
within the value of the tocher the vassal gets, and never above what by prudent management he might get, custom having fixed it to about two years'
free rent; so that though the vassal marry an heretrix of a great estate, and she
dispone the same to her husband, yet he pays no more, as was found June 14,
1673, Gibson *contra* Ramsay [2 Stair 188; M. 8534]. And there is no extension

upon the consideration of his personal qualifications, by his birth, beauty, vigour or reputation; but only in consideration of his estate, wherein the tocher is not accounted any part of his estate, because the avail comes in place of it.

48. There is one burden which may befal the vassal, and seems excessive when he hath a small ward-fee, and a considerable estate beside, two years of his free rent may be of more value than the fee itself, which he cannot avoid during the time of the ward; for the superior is not then obliged to accept a resignation *ad remanentiam;* [11,11,6,*infra*] and seeing fees are feudal contracts, having mutual prestations, if there be a contract in writ, the superior at no time is obliged to accept a resignation, and always there is such a tacit feudal contract. Yet if the vassal did first receive his fee, he ought not to complain, though he cannot avoid it, seeing it is by the increase of his fortune; and if he accept it after his other estate, he may blame his own imprudence. Yet he hath this remedy, that by acquiring a ward-holding of the king, who is the most benign superior, his marriage is only due to the king, though he be not the eldest superior, by his royal prerogative, who is always favourable, if application be made to prevent a rigorous donatar.

49. That the burden of the avail of a marriage may be easy, albeit a vassal have many ward-fees, holden of the same superior, or of different superiors, he is liable but for one avail, and that to the king if he be one of the superiors, or otherwise to the eldest superior. And on the other part, that superior, to whom the marriage is due, is only liable for maintenance of the heir, which is a further evidence of the true rise and design of this casuality, as hath been expressed.

50. Yea, though the marriage were taxed by the king, it excludes any other superior, as was found July 19, 1672, Earl Argyle *contra* McLeod [2 Stair 106; M.8533], where it is expressly determined, that one marriage can only be due for one vassal: and it was not respected, that a taxed marriage becometh like a feu-duty, so that if a vassal have several ward-fees with taxed marriages, he pays all the taxed duties; yet the king by his prerogative excludes any other superior. But where a vassal holds several ward-fees of the king, some taxed, some simple, he gets but one avail for the simple ward, wherein the duty of the taxed ward is deduced, as was decided, February 24, 1674, King's Advocate *contra* Stuart of Innernytie [2 Stair 328; M.8535].

51. When there is a prince, he being a subject, a ward-holding of the king excludes the avail of the marriage due to the prince; but when there is no prince, the marriage of the vassal of the principality is not excluded by an anterior superior; because then the king enjoys the principality, not as a subject prince, but as a sovereign prince, and so hath the same prerogative as in the royalty, albeit he gives his charters as Prince and Steward of Scotland; yet not as a prince subject as his son would be, nor as supplying the vice of the prince, for he is not comptable to a supervening prince, as was found, January 9, 1680, Purves solicitor *contra* L. of Luss [2 Stair 734; M.8542].

Yet if the king in the minority of the prince, infeft ward-vassals of the principality as administrator to the prince, he is comptable to the prince, and his royal prerogative doth not exclude anterior superiors.

52. Yea it is also consequent, that if the king acquire a superiority, by buying the same, it is *in privato patrimonio*, and therein *utitur jure communi*, and doth not exclude an elder superior.

53. There is no marriage due, if the vassal's heir apparent was married in his predecessor's lifetime, which gave occasion to think that the rise of this casuality was by the tutorial power of the superior, which being excluded by the lawful administration of the father, the superior could not claim his vassal's tocher for his neglect or contempt: but this is too narrow a ground; for though the vassal's predecessor be not his father nor grandfather, but a collateral, there is no tocher due; but the true cause is evident enough, that here the vassal's heir (while in ward) hath no tocher to expect, being married already, and ordinarily his tocher applied for his predecessor's debt; and therefore a superior cannot claim a tocher where the vassal can have none, nor could he claim a tocher, if it were known that his vassal were impotent and incapable of marriage.

The confidence between superiors and vassals, maketh the feudal contract to be *uberrimæ fidei*, most exclusive of all rigour and fraud; and therefore, if a vassal shall by precipitation, marry his apparent heir when he is *moribundus*, without treaty or public proclamations, the heir is liable for a marriage, although he was married before his predecessor's death as was lately found in the case of the Lord Colvil of Cleish, February 20, 1667 [*Sub nom. L. Treasurer* v *L. Colvil*, 1 Stair 446; M.8529]; much more if the vassal marry his apparent heir before he attain to the marriageable age, which in males is esteemed fourteen complete, and in females twelve complete: and although all formalities were observed, yet it were justly to be accounted a fraudulent design, to elude the avail of his heir's marriage; or if the heir were of that vigour that he did marry himself, or his tutors did marry him before he were fourteen complete, the avail of his marriage would be due; or if during the ward, the heir should acquire a ward estate holding of the king, it would not exclude his other superior, but would justly make him liable both to him and to the king, and might well be extended to two years' rent to either superior; whereas other double avails upon requisition are never to be extended above three years' free rent; for these are never without fraud, albeit they have been hitherto still excluded upon informality.

54. Let us now consider on the part of the heir, whether the superior can justly claim more avails of marriage than one by the death of one vassal, who died last infeft as of fee. It is beyond question, as hath been shown before, that one marriage only can be due, though the heir have many ward-fees, not only of different superiors, but of the same superior; nor is it to be controverted, that if several heirs apparent be married during the ward, that the superior may have a marriage for each of them, though they die during the

ward and not entered; for these cannot be accounted rigorous, seeing the several heirs either did get tochers, or it was their own fault if they did not; so the question only remains in case the apparent heirs die during the ward, and do not marry, whether any avail shall be due for them, or either of them, but only by the next heir that passeth the termination of the ward, who if not married then, is held as forbearing fraudfully in prejudice of the superior, and therefore is liable for a marriage, though he never marry.

This rigorous extension hath one decision for it, that every apparent heir of a ward vassal, attaining to the marriageable age, though dying during the ward unmarried, heaps as many avails of a marriage upon the fee; as was found, July 11, 1622, French and L. of Thorniedykes *contra* Cranstoun [Durie 30; M. 8524], which the Lords declared they would observe thereafter, in all such cases of marriage; yet they emitted no act of sederunt thereupon, to certify the lieges against mistakes of the just interest of superiors: but Durie declares it was never so decided before at any time, which sufficiently insinuates, that his judgment was contrary. It was again attempted in the case of Dickson of Headrig *contra* a Donatar, November 14, 1635 [Durie 778; M. 2169], where two apparent heirs had died unmarried, and the donatar of the marriage of the first having pursued the second, not for his own, but for the marriage of his elder brother, who dying *pendente processu*, the same donatar of the first brother pursues the third brother for the marriage of the first, wherein there was no more done but this dilator proponed and repelled, viz. no process, because the third brother was not charged to enter heir, and so there was no passive title against him for his brother's marriage, which the Lords did most justly repel; because an action for the avail of a marriage is *declaratoriè*, not *petitoriè*, and only for affecting the ground, and so is competent against any apparent heir: but there is no act or decreet sustained for the avail of the marriage of the first brother, who died during the ward unmarried; and as there was never a decision before that of French, so, for ought I could ever observe, there was never one since, and I hope never shall be; for it is no way consistent with the design of this casuality, that a foundation should be laid to ruin a vassal, and very incongruous to other cases; for if the vassal's heir should marry never so oft, he is but liable for one avail, even though he held several ward-fees of the same, or divers superiors: how incongruous then should it be, if the fee should be burdened for all the heirs that should happen to die unmarried during the ward: for in the said case of Headrig, there were three brothers succeeded unmarried, and there might been many more; for it is no rarity for a vassal to die, and leave many children, who may also die during the ward; so John Campbel of Skeldon told me, that he succeeded to his father in a ward-fee, being the seventeenth son.

55. But the great objection would be, that the vassal's heir is marriageable at his age of fourteen complete, and therefore he may be then required to marry, and if he doth not, but refuse a match offered without disparagement,

he is contumacious and he must be repute fraudulently to forbear to marry, in prejudice of his superior. I never found any example of an heir required to marry at his age of fourteen; and it were far rather to be accounted fraud in the superior *ad captandum lucrum*, being under the pain of paying the double avail; and on the other hand the vassal could pretend no prejudice, that if he did not marry before he were twenty one complete, he were made liable for the single avail; yea if he were required during the twentieth year of his age, and refused an offered match without disparagement, if he were made liable to the double avail. But if the rise and design of this casuality be considered, which at first was the real tocher, the vassal happened to get without fraud; or getting less, because it was no hurt to him, but to the superior, therefore the superior might, so soon as he could evidence the heir's suit, treaty or proclamation of marriage, offer him another; that so he might not only have that tocher which he got, but which he might have gotten; but now when custom hath determined the avail whatever the tocher were, there is no ground for requisition, till the last year of the ward.

But if a major succeed as apparent heir, unmarried in his predecessor's time, if he continue unmarried a year after his predecessor's death, though he be not required, his fee may be burdened with a single avail; or if at the ish of that year an offer be made of a match without disparagement, he might be liable for the double avail, because he may be presumed to forbear fraudulently in prejudice of his superior, in the same manner as a minor forbearing to marry till the ward be ended.

But this question yet remaineth undetermined, at what age of the ward-vassal the avail of his marriage may be declared, and in relation to what time his estate is to be counted? There was occasion for determination of this point in the declarator of the marriage of the Laird of Balmaghie, who succeeded to a ward-fee, first to his mother before he was fourteen complete, and then his father died at his age of seventeen or eighteen, and shortly after he married; the donatar insisted for the avail of his marriage according to the free rent he had when he married, at which time his father's estate fell to him, that was much more considerable. The defender alleged that his estate could only be considered at his marriageable age of fourteen, and there were several interlocutors sustaining that allegiance, but stopped again. The Lords inclined much to ease the vassal so far as law would allow, especially being a gift in *gros* granted to the donatar of the wards of several years; but certainly the general rule of estimation should be the time of the vassal's marriage; or being required in the current year before the termination of the ward; but seeing the first design was, that the superior should get his vassal's tocher, the value of it should be estimate when himself gets a tocher, or is supposed fraudfully to forbear to get it; for suppose the vassal's marriage be dissolved within year and day without a child, though he were married he would get nothing by it: and it can never be accounted fraud which is a virtuous prudence, that persons should not marry till they come to vigour, and are capable to rule a family; and therefore should never be accounted fraudulent, until the men come to twenty, and women to thirteen.

And now seeing the avail of marriage is determined to such a quantity, there is no reason for the superior to precipitate; because the marriage being *debitum fundi*, no other debt, real or personal of the defunct vassal, or his heir, can prejudge the superior; because the avail of the marriage is preferable to the same, or any other right, being a real burden upon the fee, and he can have no benefit by the marriage till the ward end; and process ought not to be sustained, till a year after the marriage, or a year after expiring of the ward; for if the vassal die unmarried, before the year that the ward terminates, there should be no avail, unless marriage actually exist, and be effectual by a year, or a child.

It may be pretended, that by this course the superior may be at the loss, if the heir become poorer at the time of the marriage, than when he was marriageable; which imports not; for minors are barred up by law from hurting themselves, and so they can sell nothing, but for payment of debt, whereby the superior has no loss; because the annualrent of the debt is more than the rent of the land: but on the contrary good curators do frequently increase their minors' estates; and seeing the ordinary avail comes now in place of the real tocher, it can never be so well declared, as at the time when the tocher was due.

56. The termination of the ward in males, is known to be the termination of their minority, but in females, it is determined to be their fourteenth year complete, for then they are capable of children, and governing their house, and they are never fit for war, and therefore a robust age for war is not required in them, nor can they otherwise serve but by a substitute, and their ward-fee is in so far improper, that women are capable to succeed. The termination of their ward is declared to be fourteen years complete, Parl. 1546, cap. 5 [Possibly 1547,c. 5; A.P.S. 11,599,c. 1], and Parl. 1571, cap. 42 [A.P.S. 111,63,c.19]. And albeit heretrixes get no tocher, yet their fee is liable for an ordinary avail, as if they were men, and that alike, whether there be more than one co-heir. In taxed marriage no aliment is due, because the vassal hath always the greatest part of the profit of the fee, exceeding the taxt-duty.

57. There is a great question, scarce yet cleared by custom or decision; in the case of apprisers being infeft in ward-fees, if they die within the legal, whether a marriage be due, seeing the apprising is then but *pignus prætorium*, consistent with the debtor's fee, and therefore the casualities should be due by the death of the debtor, and not of the appriser: or if it were due by the appriser, it behoved to return upon the debtor, seeing the appriser or adjudger should have his debt without damage: for it is beyond question, that the superior cannot have the benefit of the casualities, both by the death of the debtor and creditor, apprising or adjudging during the legal; but thereafter, if the creditor do not forsake his infeftment, which he may do, and seek other means

of payment, the dobtor's right becomes totally extinct, and the casualities fall only by the death of the appriser or adjudger; and though there were many apprisers of parcels of the ward-holding, each of them would be liable to all the casualities. There is one decision in the case of the King's Advocate *contra* Yeoman, July 13, 1680 [2 Stair 784], finding the appriser of a ward-fee dying within the legal, that his heir having proponed a defence, that the apprising was extinct by satisfaction within the legal, and his oath being taken upon the value of his estate, he succumbed in proving his exception; and his oath was found to prove his rent, but not his burden, as being a quality to be proven otherwise, and therefore he was decerned: but he acquiseced in that defence, and did not urge an answer to the objection, that his father died within the legal, which therefore yet remains entire. And there is much more reason, that during the legal, the casuality should only fall by the debtor's death [11,4,3 and 36, *supra*]. But now since by the Act of Parliament, bringing in all apprisers and adjudgers *pari passu*, a charge is declared sufficient to make the same effectual, if the adjudger will unnecessarily take infeftment within the legal, putting an unnecessary burden on the debtor, the casuality should justly lie upon himself, without relief, and no part of it should lie upon the debtor, or the other adjudgers coming in *pari passu;* but after the legal, the casualities will fall after the death of all the adjudgers.

58. There remains now to be considered, the addition made by the double avail of a marriage, which is most unfavourable, and hath quite deborded from the rise of it, which was, that the superior might not be prejudged, by the vassal's accepting too mean a tocher, therefore he was allowed to offer a match without disparagement, whereby he might get a better tocher; but none uses to be offered, but such as it is notour the vassal will not accept, that a double avail may be claimed; and therefore such offers should take no effect, till the last year of the ward of a minor-heir, or the first year of a major-heir. Although it hath been claimed at other times, yet there are many objections against it, both as to the matter and form: as to the matter, it takes only place, when a person is offered, when both the heir and that person is free of being otherwise engaged to marry; and therefore the double avail was not found due, when the heir was agreed in marriage with another woman before the requisition, though the contract of marriage was not subscribed; as was found, Feb. 22, 1678, Drummond of Machany *contra* Stuart of Innernytie [2 Stair 618; M.8541]: and much more where the woman is engaged in marriage to another man, the offer of her cannot infer the double avail, Had. Dec. 20, 1609, and Jan. 20, 1610, L. Kilbirnie *contra* the heretrix of Fairlie [Haddington, *Fol. Dict.*1,568; M.8521].

59. Secondly, The person offered, must be without disparagement, which is not to be accounted by means, but by quality and fame. There are only three degrees of quality that the law respects in this case; nobility, comprehending not only lords but barons, burgesses, and yeomen; and therefore a burgess offered to the heir of a lord, or baron, or gentleman of the like quality, though

he have little land-estate, may be refused, or a yeoman to a burgess. There is also a disparagement in the age of the person offered and the heir, which yet is with some latitude, that the person offered be not much older than the heir. 3. There is disparagement in the feature or integrity of the body, which may give a just aversion: in which more of beauty is required in a woman, offered to an heir being a man, than in a man offered to an heiress; but, in no case lame, or blind, or dumb, or deaf, or defective, or redundant in any member, or any conspicuous distortion, can be offered. 4. There is a disparagement in the qualities of the mind, as if an idiot, a fool, or weak person be offered, or a person of known evil humour, or evil fame, or the like.

60. As to the form of the offer, nothing is admitted to be proved, but by the solemnity of the instrument of a notar, which ought to be two. The first instrument must bear the superior, or his donatar's offering to the vassal's heir a person by name, and an equal and unsuspected place for interview and conference, and a lawful time, and an instrument taken thereupon, bearing the production of the donatar's gift, if it be made by a donatar, and the procuratory of a procurator, and the reading thereof: and the second instrument must bear the superior, procurator, or donatar's appearing on the day appointed for interview, and then requiring the solemnizing of the marriage to be at a convenient kirk, on a particular day, which ought not to be the Sabbath, not being the ordinary time of marriage; which instrument must contain the production and reading of the former instrument, that the superior, his donatar or procurator, with the person offered, came to the place of interview in due time, and waiting till mid-day was past; and therefore the double avail was not found due upon that defect, Hope, Marriage, the E. Angus *contra* Nisbet [Hope, *Maj.Pr.* III,26,24; M. 8523]. Nor where the instrument of requisition mentioned not the gift produced, albeit it was not called for, though it was offered to be proven by witnesses, that it was truly produced, Hope, *ibid.* Drummond *contra* Laird of Manner [Hope, *Maj.Pr.* III,26,25; M. 8523]; March 8, 1627, E. Rothes *contra* Balfour [Durie 286; M. 8526]. Neither where the place of interview was not an indifferent place, but the donatar's lodging, July 3, 1622, French *contra* the Heirs of Thornidykes [Durie 28; M. 2179,8524]; in which case it was not found necessary to require the curators, the heir being minor, for their consent is not necessary to marriage.

61. The last common casuality of superiors, is the liferent-escheat of the vassal, when the vassal is denounced rebel, for disobedience of the law, which because it is intimate by three blasts of a horn, is called horning, if he continue so unrestored, or unrelaxed year and day, his liferent is escheated, or forfeited unto his several superiors, of whom he held his fees. This may seem a penalty for disobedience to law, and is so as to fees holden of the king; yet if it had no other ground, the liferent could not befall to the superior, but to the king, whose command was disobeyed, as forfeiture and single escheat do; but the original of it is, that rebellion is like *capitis diminutio*, or *civitatis amissio* amongst the Romans, whereby such persons cannot stand in judgment, and they are

civiliter mortui, and thereby their fees become void, and return to their super-iors, and so is declared, Parl. 1535, cap. 32 [A.P.S. 11,349,c. 38], except in the case of treason or lese majesty, for then they fall to the king.

62. Liferent-escheat carries the profit of all fees and liferents [11,1,4, *supra*; 111,3,15,*infra*], whether constitute by conjunct-fee, infeftments, terce, or liferent-tack, during the life of the rebel, having remained year and day at the horn, (though thereafter he be relaxed), during his natural life, even though he be not infeft and entered as heir the time of his denunciation, if he enter thereafter; but if he renounce to be heir, or die unentered, there is no reason his liferent-escheat should prejudge another superior's creditors, July 3, 1624, Moor *contra* Hannay and the E. of Galloway [Durie 137; M. 3638].Yea, though there be no infeftment, if by contract or disposition, there be any heritable right or liferent provided, even though there were no infeftment required, as a terce by paction without service or kenning, Hope, Horning, Maxwell and Gordon *contra* L. Lochinvar [Hope *Maj. Pr.* VI, 27, 119; M. 3636]. So liferent-tacks of lands or teinds fall under escheat, without prejudice to these who have right to such tacks after the liferenters, Parliament 1617, cap. 15 [A.P.S. IV, 545, c. 15]. These tacks befall to the master of the ground; and liferents by terce or courtesy, fall to the superior of the land; for these liferenters are his vassals during life, and owe him fidelity and a *reddendo*.

63. Whensoever there is not infeftment actually expede, the denunciation makes not the liferent to belong to that person, of whom the liferent should have been holden, but to the king as an annualrent due by contract or dis-position, to be holden of the disponer, Had. December 20, 1609, Hay *contra* Laurie [Not found]; July 1, 1626, Halyburton *contra* Stuart [Durie 207; M. 3618]; July 22, 1675, Menzies of Castlehill *contra* Kennedy of Auchtifardel [2 Stair 358; M. 3639]. So likewise, liferent-escheat of a minister [11,3,4 and 40,*supra*] causeth his stipend and profit of his manse and gleib, though local-ly within a regality, to fall, not to the Lord of regality, but if there be infeft-ment, it falleth to the immediate superior. And likewise an annualrent due by an heritable bond, bearing a clause to infeft the creditor in an annualrent, without mention of particular lands or manner of holding, was found to fall in liferent-escheat to the King's donatar after year and day, July 1, 1626, Hali-burton *contra* Stuart [Durie 207; M. 3618]. And it was found, that a sum con-signed to redeem a wadset, was to be re-employed for the superior, during the wadsetter the rebel's lifetime, June 29, 1661, Tailzifer *contra* Maxtoun and Cunninghame [1 Stair 47; M. 5631].

64. Liferent-escheat of the vassal carries the liferent of the sub-vassal, falling after the denunciation of the vassal, and his being year and day at the horn, February 26, 1623, Sibbald *contra* L. Clunie [Durie 51; M. 3616]; July 24, 1632, Rule *contra* L. of Billie [Durie 649; M. 3624]; because then the sup-erior is in place of the vassal; but where the sub-vassal's liferent fell before the vassal's own liferent, it is carried by the vassal's single escheat. Liferent-es-cheat falleth by the vassal's rebellion, and the year and day subsequent is only

allowed to purge the rebellion by relaxation, which being used year and day
after the rebellion, hath no effect as to the liferent-escheat of such lands as
belonged to the rebel the time of the denunciation, though it hath effect as to
his moveables; therefore the vassal's voluntary deeds prejudge not the superior of his liferent-escheat, not only such deeds as are done after year and day
from the denunciation, but which are done at any time after the denunciation,
if relaxation be not used within year and day, which is to be extended to these
following cases.

65. First, No infeftment, proceeding upon a debt contracted by the rebel,
after the rebellion, though the infeftment be accomplished within the year,
will exclude the liferent-escheat, or prejudge the superior, if relaxation be not
used within year and day, whether the infeftment proceed upon the rebel's
own disposition, or upon apprising; because, in both cases, it is the voluntary
deed of the rebel that prejudgeth the superior: for albeit the apprising be a
deed of law and necessary, yet it proceeds upon a debt voluntarily contracted
after rebellion, which debts will not exclude the single escheat, and therefore
ought not to exclude the liferent-escheat. Secondly, The debts or obligements
of the vassal, though they precede the denunciation, yet no infeftment granted
by him *in cursu rebellionis*, for satisfying these anterior debts, will exclude the
liferent-escheat, unless he had been specially obliged to grant such an infeftment before the rebellion; for then the granting of it after is not a voluntary,
but a necessary deed, which he might be compelled to grant, January 23,
1629, Vallance *contra* Porteous [*Sub nom. Wallace* v *Porteous*, Durie 260; M.
8355]; in which case an infeftment for an onerous debt before rebellion, was
not found sufficient to exclude the liferent, seeing there was no anterior obligement to grant that infeftment; which is the more confirmed by the parity
of the case of inhibitions, which annul infeftments after the inhibition, though
granted for satisfying anterior debts: but if there were an anterior obligement,
the infeftment conform thereto, though after the inhibition, is valid, as not
being a voluntary, but a necessary deed.

Thirdly, Dispositions and obligements to grant infeftments anterior to the
rebellion, and infeftment thereupon posterior, do not exclude the liferent-
escheat, unless the infeftment be taken *in cursu rebellionis* [III,2,26; IV,9,6,
infra]; and so a contract of wadset long before rebellion, clad with thirty-eight
years' possession before denunciation, was not found sufficient to exclude the
liferent-escheat, December 3, 1634, Lindsay *contra* Scot [Durie 738; M.
3663]. Neither a charter and inhibition thereupon, seeing there was not seasin
taken within year and day, December 3, 1623, Harris *contra* Glendinning
[Durie 85; M. 3660]. Neither a base infeftment before denunciation, there being no possession thereon till year and day, March 19, 1633, L. Rentoun
contra Blackadder [Durie 680; M. 3662]; February 21, 1667, Miln *contra*
Clerkson [1 Stair 448; M. 3664].

66. Fourthly, Apprisings or adjudications, though for a debt anterior to
the rebellion, exclude not liferent-escheat, unless infeftment or a charge against

the superior be used thereupon within year and day after rebellion: for without infeftment or a charge, apprising is no real right [11,4,32,*supra*]: and therefore, though it were led before rebellion against a vassal, if infeftment or a charge follow not *in cursu rebellionis*, it excludes not the vassal's liferent-escheat to fall to the superior or donatar, July 24, 1632, Rollo *contra* L. of Kellie [Durie 649; M. 3624], albeit infeftment follow upon the apprising before the liferent was gifted, Hope, Horning and Escheat, Sir Patrick Murray *contra* Adamson [Hope, *Maj. Pr.* VI,27,104; M. 3658]. Neither did an apprising upon a denunciation begun *in cursu rebellionis*, but not perfected, exclude the liferent-escheat, February 16, 1631, Cranstoun *contra* Scot [Durie 569; M. 3661]. But if apprising or adjudication be led for sums prior to the rebellion, and be complete by infeftment or charge *in cursu rebellionis*, albeit they be deduced after rebellion, they exclude the liferent-escheat, as is insinuate in the limitations in the former decisions, and was so decided, Had. Feb. 13, 1611, Tenants of Lochauld *contra* Young and Areskine [Not found].

Liferent-escheat being one of the casualities of superiority, only introduced by statute or custom, there is this difference, from that which hath been said of non-entry, ward, or recognition, which are casualities arising from the nature of the feudal contract, that liferent-escheat flowing not thence, but upon the vassal's rebellion and disobedience to law, which is not against the superior, or any delinquence against the feudal contract, the vassal's liferent-escheat gives the superior no more than the vassal himself had the time of his denunciation; and so all real rights complete by possession, whether infeftments or tacks, are not prejudged by the subsequent liferent-escheat, as was found, January 19, 1672, Mr. William Beatoun *contra* Scot of Letham [2 Stair 51; M. 3664]. In feus, so far as is allowed by law, the vassal's liferent will reach no more than the feu-duties of feus set by the vassal before his denunciation; but any subaltern base infeftment, not clad with possession before rebellion, is excluded by the liferent, March 19, 1633, L. of Rentoun *contra* L. Blackadder [Durie 680; M. 3662]; February 21, 1667, Miln *contra* Clerkson [1 Stair 448; M. 3664]: in which case it was found, that possession, not being attained *in cursu rebellionis* during the year, it was not effectual. If a tack be set, without diminution of the rental, for the old tack-duty, it will not be excluded by the liferent, though it be set after denunciation, as was found in a tack after denunciation within the year, Hope, Horning, Charters *contra* M'Lelland [Hope, *Maj. Pr.* VI,27,87; M. 8371], Spots. Escheat, L. Tillibairn *contra* Dalziel [Spotiswoode 98; M. 8370]. The like of a tack set to a kindly tenant, Hope, Horning, Paton *contra* L. Drumrash [*Sub nom. Partoun* v *Drumrasch;* Hope, *Maj. Pr.* VI,27,124; M. 15183]: for in such cases, setting of tacks is a necessary administration for the good of both superior and vassal, and to shun debate concerning prejudice and unanswerable tack-duties; as in other cases of administration of beneficed persons, who, if their tacks be set without diminution of the rental, they are good.

67. Liferent-escheat extends itself to all fees, whether holden ward,

blench, or feu, but not to burgage and mortification, because the fiar is a society and incorporation, which dieth not; and therefore have no liferent-escheat: and though denunciation may be used against the persons administrating the same, even for that which is due by the incorporation, and as they represent it; yet that being supposed, their fault and negligence doth not prejudge the society; as magistrates of burghs, masters of colleges, incumbents in
common or collegiate churches, chapters or convents *sede vacante*.

68. But where a beneficed person having a distinct benefice, or a stipen-
dary, is denounced for his own debt, his liferent-escheat falleth, and therewith
the profits, during his life or incumbency; because though the fee be not in
him, yet he hath a distinct liferent thereof, which is not so in the former case,
where both fee and profits are in the society.

69. Liferent-escheat is made effectual by general declarator, finding the
vassal to be denounced, and year and day past, by production of the horning;
but there is no necessity to prove him vassal, unless he be a singular successor
in the superiority, not acknowledged by the vassal, or in case the vassal disclaim: herein is no mention of profits; but this declarator being obtained, the
fee is void from the denunciation, and the superior or his donatar have access
to the mails and duties thereof, and to set and remove tenants from the same,
and to do all deeds accustomed by the vassal himself, in the same manner as
in ward.

Title 5. Infeftments of Annualrent, Where, of Poinding of the Ground, and of Pensions

WHETHER annualrent by infeftment be a distinct right of property, or whether
it be only a servitude upon the ground, leaving the name of property to the
groundright, as Craig esteemeth, *Lib.* 1, *Dieg.* 10. § ult. is not worth much
debate; but in either case it falleth fitly here under consideration, after property and superiority, and before unquestionable servitudes.

1. Annualrent is so called, because it returneth to be paid every year, at
one or more terms. The English extend these rents to rents due by lease or
tack; but with us, annualrents are only constitute by infeftment; and though

the disposition or provision thereof may be sufficient against the constituent or his heirs, it is not effectual against their singular successors, and is no real right of the ground, without infeftment.

2. The rise of annualrents is from the prohibition of usury in the canon law, which they extend to the taking of any annual, or profit for money or any other thing; in lieu whereof those who were unfit for trading, or managing the property of lands, bought annualrents, either irredeemably, or under reversion, which had the same effect with the personal obligement for annualrent; and therefore it is still retained [with us] even where annualrent is allowed by personal obligation, and is not usury. Annualrents then may be constitute, either of money, victual, or other fungible, and that either in fee and heritage, or in liferent; and either by a several infeftment, or by reservation in infeftments of property: in which cases the proprietor's seasin serveth both.

3. Infeftments of annualrents in most things do agree with infeftments of property in the manner of constituting thereof, by charter or disposition and seasin; in which the symbol and token of the delivery of possession of the annualrent, when money, is a penny money; and when victual, a parcel thereof. Yet an old infeftment of annualrent was sustained, though it bore "only seasin to be given, according to the solemnities used in such cases;" albeit it was given thirty-six years before, and no possession thereby, March 23, 1631, Sumervel *contra* Sumervel [Durie 585; M. 14320]. Annualrent being once validate by possession, it was not excluded by the infeftment of property of the present heritor, though the annualrenter showed not the infeftment of him who constitute the annualrent; so that it did not appear whether both infeftments flowed from one common author; but seeing the infeftment of annualrent was prior to the infeftment of property, it was not excluded thereby, February 7, 1667, Smeiton *contra* Tarbet [1 Stair 437; M. 2855].

4. Annualrent may be either holden ward, or blench, or by mortification, and useth not to be holden feu or burgage, and is most frequently blench for a penny; but if no holding be expressed, it is held to be ward; and, therefore, the casualities of the superiority befall to the superior, according to the kind of the holding, as in property; so that being ward or blench, it falleth in non-entry, in the hands of the superior, without declarator, and so ceaseth during that time, even though the constituent as debtor be superior, though he may be liable personally, upon any personal obligement, for paying thereof, March 23, 1631, Sumervel *contra* Sumervel [Durie 585; M. 14320]. And because annualrents have no retour as lands, but is retoured *quod valent seipsum;* therefore the non-entry did carry it without special declarator; but by the late Act of Parl. [Act 1690, c. 42; A.P.S. IX, 222, c. 96], if the annualrent be blench for penny or the like, no more is due till declarator. Annualrents may be either base, or public by resignation or confirmation, and as to the requisites to accomplish it when base, it is fully shown before, Title 3, § Base Infeftments [II, 3, 27, *supra*].

5. So likewise annualrent falling in liferent-escheat, belongs to the sup-

erior during the annualrenter's life; and if it be redeemed, the profit of the money comes in place thereof, as followeth *a pari*, from a wadset redeemed, which was fallen in liferent-escheat; and, therefore, the money was ordained to be employed upon annualrent for the superior, during the life of the wadsetter, June 29, 1661, Tailziefer *contra* Maxtoun and Cunningham [1 Stair 47; M. 5631; 11, 4, 63, *supra*].

6. The English distinguish rent in rent-service, rent-charge, and rentseck. Rent-service is that which is due by the *reddendo* of an infeftment of property, as a feu or blench duty; this is as a part of the infeftment of property, but hath the same effect by poinding of the ground, as other annualrents. Rentcharge is that, which not being by *reddendo*, yet is so constitute, that the annualrenter may *brevi manu*, (his term being past) poind the ground therefor; we have no such annualrent, for we admit of no distress without public authority; but all execution must proceed by decreet and precept. Rent-seck is so called, as *redditus siccus*, because it is dry, having no effect without sentence; such are our annualrents.

7. There is a distinction of annualrents mentioned, Parl. 1551, cap. 10 [A.P.S. 11, 489, c. 30], in feu-annuals, ground-annuals, and top-annuals, which Craig [1, 10, 38] thinketh to quadrate with the English distinction of rents: but the consideration of that Act and ordinance, in relation to the articles there expressed, will make it appear, that the case being there of tenements within burgh, the feu-annual is that which is due by the *reddendo* of the property of the ground before the house was built; ground-annual is a distinct several annualrent, constitute upon the ground, before the house was built; and the topannualrent is out of the house: which is the more clear, that when such tenements were destroyed, the least abatement was of the feu-annual, or feu-duty; and, therefore, the proprietor repairing the tenement, was to pay the feu-annuals, with abatement of a sixth part; and the ground-annual as being more ancient than the top-annual, suffered an abatement of a fifth part, and the topannual of a fourth part.

8. The chief effect of annualrents, either by *reddendo* in property, or several infeftments, is by poinding of the ground, upon which the annualrent is constitute, and that by an ordinary action, whereby the annualrenter pursueth for letters to poind and apprise all goods upon the ground, for payment of his annualrent; and also for poinding and apprising the ground-right and property itself. As to the first member, the English custom extendeth it to all goods that shall happen to be upon the ground at the term, if they have but lain down thereupon. And our ancient custom extendeth it to all goods of the possessors, *et invecta et illata* by them, without retrenching it to what the tenant is due to the proprietor constituent of the annualrent; and the poinding in this case was extended to purge a spuilzie, Nov. 21, 1628, Watson *contra* Reid [Durie 398; M. 10510]; June 26, 1628, L. of Ednem *contra* Tennents of Ednem [Durie 377; M. 8128], where the pursuit was rather declaratory to establish the pursuer's right, than for present possession or execution.

9. But thereafter the Lords have been accustomed to interpose with chargers upon decreets of poinding of the ground, to restrict the same in favours of tenants, to their terms' mails, from the statute, 1469, cap. 37 [Diligence Act 1469, c. 36; A.P.S. 11, 96, c. 12], bearing, "that the cattle of poor men, inhabitants of the ground, shall not be poinded for the landlord's debt, where the mail extends not to the avail thereof" [IV, 23, 1–2; IV, 47, 24, *infra*]. And though the Act seemeth correctory of an evil custom, to poind the tenants' goods for the master's debt; yet the same reason, equity, and favour of their rusticity, craves the extension of it to these *debita fundi;* and, therefore, it was so restricted, the tenants producing their tacks, or offering to depone upon their rent summarily, without taking a term; but it was not found requisite that the annualrenter should either libel or prove the quantity of the rent, February 4, 1674, La. Pitfoddels *contra* the L. of Pitfoddels and Tennents [2 Stair 261], in which case it was found, that if the tenants the time of the poinding had compeared and produced their tacks, or had offered to make faith what the rent was, if more had been poinded than equivalent to their rent, it would have been a spuilzie; but they should not only depone what their rent is, but what is resting of it; for the poinding of the ground or the brieve of distress, is only restricted by the Act of Parliament, for remeid of that inconvenience, that was sometime in use; that where sums are to be paid by the brieve of distress against the Lord owner of the ground, the goods and cattle of poor men, inhabitants of the ground, were taken and distrenzied for the Lord's debt, where the mail extends not to the avail of the debt; and therefore, it is ordained, "That the tenant shall not be distrenzied for the Lord's debt, where the mail extends not to the avail of the debt, further than his term's mail extends to." And, therefore, in so far as the tenants' mails are resting, the poinding may proceed: and likewise for the current terms, though not yet come; that is, if the rent be victual, payable all at one term, the poinding may proceed for the value of the victual, according to the rate of the victual, *communibus annis*, in the several places of the country, as men use to buy, or wadset, or by the fiars of that place. Neither can tacks absolutely secure the tenants, if they be posterior to the infeftment of annualrent; in which case, if they be within the true value of the land, the annualrenter or others poinding *pro debitis fundi*, cannot be prejudged by collusive tacks, or such as are granted with considerable diminution of the true worth: so that the poinding may proceed for one year or term's mail, as the lands are worth the time of the constitution of the annualrent: but in this case the poinding cannot proceed summarily, till it be cognosced by declarator, or reduction of the tacks; which may frequently occur, tenants being oft accustomed to suspend in decreets for poinding the ground. Poinding of the ground was found to take no effect against corns standing upon the ground, having been poinded before by a third party, for a debt, Hope, Poinding, Paterson *contra* Adam [Possibly Hope, *Maj. Pr.* VI, 23, 6; M. 10543].

10. In a poinding of the ground, the proprietor the time of the summons

must be called, albeit his infeftment be base, but not the superior, January 19, 1636, Oliphant *contra* Oliphant [Possibly Spotiswoode 364; Durie 787; M. 2239]. And it is sufficient to call the wadsetter without the reverser, February 1, 1631, Williamson *contra* Cunninghame [Durie 562; M. 2238]. The tenants also must be called, in so far as concerns their goods, but the present heritors and tenants being once decerned, the decreet will be effectual against all singular successors, and subsequent tenants, without a new decreet of transference, Hope, Poinding of the ground, Forrester *contra* Tenants [Hope, *Maj. Pr.* VI, 23,6; M. 10543]; November 21, 1628, Watson *contra* Reid [Durie 398; M. 10510]; June 26, 1662, Adamson *contra* Lord Balmerino [1 Stair 114; M. 3346]. But a poinding of the ground upon annualrents, may proceed summarily, without declaring the right in a petitory judgment, though the annualrenter hath not been in possession for seven years; and a posterior annualrenter in possession seven years, was not found preferable, because annualrents being *debita fundi*, have neither prejudice not profit by possession, as in a possessory judgment, which is only competent upon infeftments of property or tacks, January 9, 1668, old Lady Clerkingtoun *contra* L. Clerkingtoun and the Young Lady [1 Stair 500; M. 10646]. And a poinding of the ground may proceed against the apparent heir, without a charge to enter heir, January 2, 1667, Oliphant *contra* Hamilton [1 Stair 422; M. 2171 or 2633; III, 5,23,*infra*].

11. As to the ground-right and property of lands, apprising upon infeftment of annualrent is not only effectual against the proprietor, but against any other apprising for personal debt, and infeftment thereupon, being after the original infeftment of the annualrent, though before the apprising thereon, Hope, Poinding and Apprising, Tenants of Clunie *contra* L. Tarachtrie, Slowand and Glendining [Hope, *Maj. Pr.* VI,28,44]. And it is the singularity of this right, that the infeftment of annualrent being once established, apprising thereupon will be preferred to all intervening rights and diligences, even though they proceed upon posterior infeftments of annualrents. And though by the late Act of Parliament [Diligence Act 1661,c.62; A.P.S. VII,317,c. 344] apprisings within year and day come in *pari passu*, there is an express exception of annualrents: and therefore, an apprising proceeding upon a personal obligement and requisition both for principal and annual, and within year and day of other apprisings, the appriser was allowed to pass from his apprising, as to the annualrents prior to the apprising; and these were preferred to all the apprisings: and his apprising was brought in *pari passu*, for the principal sum and annualrents after the apprising, December 22, 1671, Campbell *contra*   [2 Stair 33; M. 14106]. Yea, an infeftment of annualrent being betwixt the first effectual apprising, and the subsequent apprisings within year and day, was brought in *pari passu* with these apprisings, as to the whole right, as being in a matter dubious, upon a new statute, the annualrenter having rested thereupon, and not having apprised for his principal sum; which if he had done, he would clearly have come in *pari passu*, February 6,

1673, Brown of Colstoun *contra* Edward Nicolas [2 Stair 166; M. 2821; IV, 35, 30, *infra*]. But as to the competion of annualrents, adjudications, and inhibitions, and the preferences thereupon, vide infra, lib. 4. [IV, 35].

There is a case proposed by Sir Thomas Hope, [Hope, *Min. Pr.* XI, 4] viz. If one having right to some years of an annualrent by liferent, or otherwise, should apprise for these years, and that apprising expiring, whether that apprising expired will carry the right of property, not only from him who constitute the annualrent, but from the fiar of the annualrent himself, so that the infeftment of annualrent should become extinct? which seems to be resolved affirmatively, because of the nature of the right; for the infeftment of annualrent, being *jus sed ignobilius*, becomes extinct, if the annualrenter thereupon do apprise the property, and be infeft: and therefore, whoever appriseth for any years of the annualrent, the infeftment thereof, unless it be taken away by satisfaction or redemption, extinguisheth the infeftment of annualrent, without distinction whether the apprising be led for any years belonging to the fiar, liferenter, or any other: and whereas the difficulty seems to be, that the liferenter cannot prejudge the fiar of the annualrent, or apprise more from the fiar of the land than he had; it is answered, the fiar of the annualrent needs not be prejudged, because he hath a virtual reversion, and might thereby redeem from the liferenter of the annualrent, and so extinguish his right: neither doth the apprising exclude the annualrent itself, as to years posterior, by the tenor of the apprising, but by the nature of the right constitute to that very end, that an apprising for any years of the annualrent is drawn back *ad suam causam*, viz. the original infeftment of the annualrent; and so excludes all posterior infeftments; and therefore, extinguisheth not only these, but even the infeftment of annualrent itself ceaseth, by accession of the property, *ut juris nobilioris;* but if the fiar of the annualrent were neglective in so dubious a case, it is like the Lords would repone him, he satisfying the liferenter [IV, 23, 7, *infra*].

In the case of competition, the infeftment of annualrent itself will be preferred to the posterior rights, though no apprising followed, January 29, 1635, Hamilton of Brownhill *contra* Wilson [Durie 745; M. 14105]. For all infeftments of annualrent have that privilege and preference, though they be made use of by way of competition, without apprising thereupon: yea, though requisition was made, and an apprising led upon the sum, whereunto the annualrent was accessory, yet it was found the appriser might, *pro loco et tempore*, pass from that apprising, and upon the annualrent itself be preferred, January 24, 1663, Graham *contra* Ross [1 Stair 162; M. 237].

12. But as to apprising of moveables for rents, the Lords use in competitions to give so much time to the first annualrenter, and so to the rest, after each term, at which they only may poind: and so they decerned the first annualrenter to poind within twenty days of each term, and the second within the next twenty days, February 15, 1662, Ladies Mouswall elder and younger competing [1 Stair 101; M. 3486]. The like, allowing the first annualrenter

forty days after each term, July 26, 1662, Sir John Aiton *contra* Wat [1 Stair 138; M. 3487]. But as to the apprising of the property, the first annualrenter may apprise when he pleaseth, and then is preferable to all others; but the regulating of the poinding of moveables is in favour of the poor labourers. The like, June 26, 1662, Adamson *contra* Lo. Balmerinoch [1 Stair 114; M. 3346], where it was found, that the annualrenter might affect any part of the ground *in solidum*, albeit now belonging to several heritors; but so, as the heritor of the ground affected, behoved to have assignation to the decreet for obtaining and recovering his relief.

13. Annualrents long ago had no effect but by poinding of the ground, and could not come in to hinder arresters of the duties for the proprietor's debt, March 24, 1626, Gray *contra* Graham [Durie 197; M. 565]; but thereafter it was ordained to be a sufficient title against all intromitters with the duties personally, March 16, 1637, Guthrie *contra* E. of Galloway [Durie 836; M. 567]. Annualrents were found liable to public burdens, proportionally with the superplus rent belonging to the fiar, June 23, 1675, Bruce *contra* Bruce [2 Stair 334; M. 1185]. Yet this annualrent was not for security of a stock; the like was found of a liferent-annualrent, June 18, 1663, Fleming *contra* Gillis [1 Stair 191; M. 8273].

14. Annualrents, as to bygones, are moveable, and so arrestable, and belong to executors, Dec. 15, 1630, Ogilvie *contra* Ogilvie [Durie 548; M. 138; 11, 1, 4, *supra*]; yet it will be more competent and suitable to pursue it personally against intromitters with the rents, or possessors, than by a real action of poinding the ground.

15. An infeftment of annualrent redeemable, was found extinct by a renunciation registrate in the register of reversions, and that against a singular successor, though there was no resignation of the annualrent, Jan. 7, 1680, M'Lellan *contra* Mushet [2 Stair 732; M. 571]. An annualrent was also found extinct, by the annualrenter's intromitting with the rents of the lands, out of which the annualrent was payable, equivalent to the principal sum, for security whereof the annualrent was constitute; which intromission was found probable by witnesses, though it was silver-rent, Feb. 4, 1671, Wishart *contra* Arthur [1 Stair 714; M. 9978]: and therefore, singular successors succeeding in annualrents, either by voluntary disposition, or by apprising or adjudication, cannot be secure by inspection of registers, as they may be for lands; but they run the hazard of satisfaction of the principal sum for which the annualrent is granted, wherewith it falls in consequence: and no provident man will buy an annualrent given for security of a principal sum, but either upon necessity, for satisfying a prior debt, or upon great advantage; in both which cases, he should take his hazard, *nam scire debet cum quo contrahit*, as all purchasers of personal rights must do [11, 3, 22, *supra*; 111, 1, 21, *infra*]; for, as intromission with rents, doth more directly infer payment of the principal sum, so it extinguisheth the annualrent, as accessory thereto, even against singular successors. Annualrents also are suppressed by wadset of the land, or

other more noble right in the person of the annualrenter, unless that right were evicted.

16. Pensions resemble annualrents, or the *feuda ex camera*, or *ex cavena*, mentioned by the feudists; for thereby, a yearly rent is constitute to be paid out of the constituent's lands, generally or particularly: yet these pensions, not having infeftment, have but the nature of assignations, and so are not valid against singular successors; except only ecclesiastic pensions, constitute by prelates, which are valid against their successors in office; but not unless they be cloathed with possession or decreets conform, in the constituent's life. And so a pension granted by a bishop, with power to assign, was found valid to the assignee, after the first pensioner's death, against the succeeding bishop, and to be no dilapidation, July 23, 1625, minister of Kirklistoun *contra* White-law [Durie 180; M. 10060]; yea, though the pension bore a power to assign *etiam in articulo mortis*, and the dispute was with the assignee, Dec. 17, 1628, Chalmers *contra* L. Craigievar [Durie 410; M. 10062]: but in this case the pensioner granting assignation, reserving his own liferent, or to take effect after his death, whereby both might at once have interest therein, the assignation was found null by exception, though having decreet conform, and thirty years possession. The like, Hope, Assignation, Abernethie *contra* La. Drumlangrig [Hope, *Maj. Pr.* 11, 12, 23; M. 828]. But by the Act of Parl. 1606, cap. 3 [A.P.S. IV, 324, c. 71], archbishops and bishops are disabled to grant pensions to affect their benefices, further than themselves have right to the benefice, but do not prejudge their successors in office; yet pensions granted by beneficed persons, are not only due during their life, but out of their annat after their death, Feb. 28, 1628, Bairns of the Bishop of Galloway *contra* Andrew Cowper [Durie 351; M. 470].

17. Pensions granted by secular persons, though they contain assignations to the duties of lands specially, and have decreet conform, were found ineffectual against singular successors in the land, July 9, 1629, Urquhart *contra* the Earl of Caithness [Durie 459; M. 10063]; Dec. 11, 1662, Clapperton *contra* L. of Ednem [1 Stair 148; M. 10065]; neither against the lady tercer of the constituent, March 27, 1634, Countess of Dumfermling *contra* E. of Dunfermling [Durie 717; M. 13408]; yet a decreet conform being obtained against the granter of a pension, his tenants and chamberlains, is effectual against subsequent chamberlains, without new decreet or transference, yet must be transferred against the constituent's heir and his chamberlain, though it would be valid, being an ecclesiastic pension, against his successor, Dec. 7, 1630, E. of Carrick *contra* D. of Lennox [Durie 545]; Spots. *hic*, Weyms *contra* chamberlain of the D. of Lennox [Spotiswoode 227; M. 2194].

A pension, bearing for love and special service done and to be done, was found effectual, though the pensioner was removed, and did not that service, his removal being necessary by transportaiton, March 25, 1629, Doctor Strang *contra* Lo. Cowper [Durie 441; M. 6355]. The like of a pension granted to an advocate for services done and to be done, which was found valid during his life, though he left pleading, Dec. 3, 1662, Alexander *contra* Macleod [*Sub nom. Jamieson* v *McCleud*, 1 Stair 63; M.6356]. The like of a pension, for service done and to be done, though the service was not done, but not required: nor was it excluded by the pensioner's pursuing processes at his own instance against the constituent, upon a probable ground, though the constituent was assoilzied, July 26, 1678, Mr. William Weir advocate *contra* E. of Callendar [2 Stair 643; M.6363].

18. Pensions granted by the King are declared not arrestable in the Treasurer's hands. Act of Sederunt, June 11, 1613 [Printed in Spotiswoode, s.v. Pension, p.228]. The reason thereof must be, because such are ordinarily alimentary, and always for the King's special service, which would be impeded, if arrestable, by hindering payment of the pension [III, 1, 37, *infra*].

Title 6. Liferent-Infeftments, where, of Conjunct Fees, Terces, and Liferents by the Courtesy of Scotland

FROM the feudal rights of property, we proceed to servitudes, burdening the same; these are either personal or real: Personal servitudes are these, whereby the property of one is subservient to the person of another than the fiar: Real servitude is, whereby a tenement is subservient to another tenement, and to persons, but as, and while, they have right to the tenement dominant; as thirlage, pasturage, ways, passages, &c. and the like. Servitudes personal for term of life, are therefore called liferents; servitudes for an indefinite time are such, which either may or uses to be constitute for a longer or shorter time, such are pensions ecclesiastic, rentals and tacks, which, though they be in their nature but personal rights; yet by statute or custom, they have the effect of real rights, of which hereafter. Teinds also must come in as servitudes, though they are accounted as distinct rights.

1. The Roman law divideth personal servitudes into usufruct, use, and habitation. Usufruct is the power of disposal of the use and fruits, saving the substance of the thing, which if it be restrained to these persons, and their

proper use, without making profit or disponing to others, it is called the use, *l.12.ff. de usu et hab.* where the particular benefits are enumerated; but is without restriction of the proprietor, or usu-fructuar, who may make use of the fruits at their pleasure, and who, as he cannot molest, so cannot be molested by him to whom the use is granted, §1. *Inst. de usu et hab.* [Inst.2,5,1] *l.15, §1.ff. eod.* [D.7,8,15,1]. *Vid. l.10. §. ult. et. l.110 eod.* [D.7,8,10 and 11] and because of some special consideration in the law of that use of houses, habitation is a distinct servitude from other uses, §2. *Inst. de usu et habit.* [Inst. 2,5,5], *et tit.ff. de usu et habit.* [D.7,8,*passim*] *passim.*

2. All servitudes with us come under some of the kinds before named. Personal servitudes are either constitute by the deeds of men, or by the law, which provideth a competent portion to either of the surviving spouses, out of the lands and tenements of the other, during the surviver's life; as if the wife survive, she hath the third of her husband's tenements: and if the husband survive, he hath the liferent of the wife's whole tenements by the courtesy and that *provisione legis* alone, if the wife be an heiress. But other liferents constitute for surviving spouses, or otherwise, are *provisione hominis:* so may the terce or liferent by the courtesy be provided, and some things altered from the course of law: but oftener liferents are constitute by conjunct fees, and most ordinarily otherwise, which therefore retain the common name of liferents appropriated thereto, as distinct from conjunct fees.

3. Liferents are sometimes provided particularly, and sometimes generally, for the whole or such a share of the conquest, during the marriage, which though not fulfilled by the husband in his life, is effectual against his heirs, and is not accounted a fraudulent provision, though it be the whole conquest, even among merchants.

And where a husband purchased lands in favour of his eldest son, being then an infant, and not to himself, yet his relict was found to have right to her liferent thereof, as being a fraudulent deed in prejudice of the obligement of conquest, July 3, 1627, Countess of Dunfermline *contra* the E. of Dunfermline [Durie 302; M.3055]. But these provisions of conquest do not hinder the husband acquirer to denude himself without fraud, for any onerous or just cause; as selling for a price, or disponing to children, whether it be to the apparent heir by ordinary terms of contract of marriage, or to younger children, or to wives of subsequent marriages, June 16, 1676, Mitchell *contra* the Children of Thomas Littlejohn [2 Stair 426; M.3190]. And such a clause being of all sums acquired during a second marriage, was found to annul a universal legacy to the eldest son of the first marriage, but not to annul competent provisions to the bairns of the first marriage; June 19, 1677, Murrays *contra* Murrays [2 Stair 523; M.12944]. The like, January 3, 1679, Gibson *contra* Thomson [2 Stair 663; M.12946]. Yea, a clause providing the present stock, and all the conquest to the bairns of a marriage, which failing, the one half to the man's heirs, the other to the wife's heirs, was found to make the man fiar, and not to hinder him to provide his whole means, which were very great, to his bairns of a subsequent marriage, there being no bairns surviving of the former marriage, December 1, and 21, 1680, Anderson *contra* Bruce [2 Stair 820; M.607,4232,12890; II,3,41,*supra*]. But as to such clauses, conquest is only understood where the husband acquired more than he had the time of the clause, but not when he sold some lands and acquired others of no greater value, June 27, 1676, E. of Dunfermline *contra* E. of Callendar [2 Stair 430; M.2941]; yea a clause of conquest in a wife's contract of marriage, who was otherwise sufficiently provided, was found to be with the burden of the annualrent of a sum, which the husband declared under his hand to be a part of the price of the lands acquired, remaining due to the seller, December 20, 1665, La. Kilbocho *contra* L. of Kilbocho [*Sub nom. Dickson* v *Sandilands*, 1 Stair 328; M.3058; III,5,52,*infra*].

4. This is common to all kinds of liferents, and involved in the nature thereof, that they must be *salva rei substantia*, which by statute is especially extended to conjunct-fiars and liferenters, that they must be countable, and find surety not to waste or destroy the biggings, orchards, woods, stanks, parks, meadows or dovecoats, but that they hold them in such like case, as they receive them. Parl. 1491, cap. 25 [Liferent Caution Act, 1491,c.25; A.P.S. II,224,c.6], which is confirmed and declared to proceed upon twenty-one days'[charge] by sheriffs, bailies of burghs or regalities, under pain of confiscation of the liferent right to the King's use, Parl. 1535, cap. 14 [Liferent Caution Act, 1535,c.15; A.P.S. II,344,c.14]. And though the narrative of the statute expresseth conjunct-fiars and liferenters giving caution, as being most ordinary by provision of men; yet the statutory part is general, at least may be extended to terces and liferents by the courtesy. So a liferenter was charged summarily to uphold the tenement liferented, and to leave it in as good case as she found it, without precognition, how it was the time of her entry, March 23, 1626 Foulis *contra* Allan [Durie 196; M.8270]. By Act of Parl. 1594, cap. 226 [A.P.S. IV.71,c.36], "Anent ruinous tenements within burgh," they being cognosced by an inquest to be ruinous, as became, or which may become within a short time uninhabitable, the same must be repaired, by the liferenter, or the fiar may enter in possession, finding caution within the burgh to pay the liferenter the mail thereof, as the same gave, or might give the time of the precognition; but this Act was not found to derogate from the former Acts, nor that precognition was requisite before finding caution, except in tenements within burgh, decayed before the liferenter's entry, as was found in the foresaid case, Foulis *contra* Allan [Durie 196; M. 8270]. Neither was the liferenter freed from caution upon her offer to quit the possession to the heritor for paying of the rent, the tenement not being ruinous at her entry.

5. It is also common to liferents and conjunct-fees, that the liferent right is liable, as the superior of ward-lands or his donatar, for an aliment to the heir, to be modified by the Lords, by the said statute 1491, cap. 25 [Liferent Caution Act, 1491, c.25; A.P.S II,224,c.6] *Vide* Tit. Heirs §3 [III,5,3]. So

the said statute is extended to liferenters, to aliment the heir, though it doth not bear it, only *ex paritate rationis* it is so extended by custom.

6. Liferents are either constitute by way of reservation, in infeftments of property, or otherwise by a several infeftment; but it cannot become a real right, and be effectual against singular successors, without infeftment; though most servitudes may be constitute by disposition and possession.

7. Yea, though liferents being constitute by infeftment, may be conveyed by assignation [111,1,6; 111,3,15,*infra*], because there can be no subaltern or renewed infeftment of a liferent, which is only personal to the liferenter, and the right is incommunicable; yet the fruits and profits arising thence are communicable and assignable.

8. It is also common to liferents, that nothing done after their infeftment, by the constituent or his singular successor, can prejudge the liferenter: and so an appriser from the husband was found liable to the liferenter, for the true worth of the liferent lands, and not according as he set them, though they were never set before: except the appriser had set the lands, wholly or near to the worth, March 9, 1631, Lady Huttonhall *contra* Lairds of Moristoun and Touch [Durie 578; M. Supp. 63].

9. A liferenter's executors were found to have right to the Martinmas term, though the liferenter died upon the Martinmas day in the afternoon, Feb. 16, 1642, Executors of the Lady Brunton *contra* Heirs of the Bishop of Glasgow [Durie 894; M. 15885]. And they have right to the whole crop and profit of the land laboured and sown by themselves, or which was in mansing and not set to tenants, though the liferenter die before Martinmas, Dec. 14, 1621, Mackmath *contra* Nisbet [Durie 6; M. 15877]. A liferenter's executors were found to have right to the whole year's rent of a mill liferented by her, she having survived Martinmas, and that mill-rents were not due *de die in diem*, but as land-rents, not as house-mails; though the conventional terms of the mill-rent was after Martinmas, viz. one term at Candlemas after the separation, and the other at Whitsunday thereafter, July 20, 1671, Guthrie *contra* Laird of McKerstoun [1 Stair 762; M. 15890]. And a liferenter infeft in an annualrent of victual provided to be paid yearly betwixt Yule and Candlemas, her husband having died after Martinmas, and before Candlemas, she was found to have no share of her annualrent for that crop, Jan. 12, 1681 Katherine Trotter, Lady Craigleith *contra* Rochead, Lady Prestongrange [2 Stair 831; M. 2375; 111,8,57,*infra*].

10. A conjunct-fee, or conjunct-infeftment, is that which is granted to more persons jointly; which if it be provided to them and their heirs simply, it maketh them and their heirs to have equal right *pro indiviso*, and they are all equally fiars. But when conjunct-infeftments are provided to husbands and wives the longest liver of them two and their heirs; there the law presumes that the heirs are the man's heirs [11,3,41,*supra*; 111,5,51,*infra*]; and by that interpretation, the wife by the conjunct-fee is but liferenter: and generally heirs of man and wife in all things, except moveable rights, are ever under-

stood to be the man's heirs, *propter eminentiam masculini sexus;* so it was found in an assignation to a reversion, granted to a man and his wife and their heirs, that thereby the man's heirs (first, these of the marriage, and next, his other heirs whatsomever) were understood, Hope, Husband and wife, Collestoun *contra* L. Pitfoddels [Hope, *Maj. Pr.* II, 17, 29; M. 4198]: yet though this be *præsumptio juris*, it admits of contrary and more pregnant evidences; as a reversion granted to a man and his wife and their heirs, was found to constitute the wife fiar, because she was heretrix of the wadset lands, Hope, Liferent, Kincaid *contra* Menzies of Pitfoddels [Hope, *Maj. Pr.* III, 12, 36; M. 4220].

But to prevent this question, the provision ordinarily is to the longest liver of them two and their heirs, which failing, to such particular heirs exprest; whereby these are commonly esteemed fiars, whose heirs whatsomever are substitute: and yet a sum provided to a man and his wife, and the heirs betwixt them, which failing, to divide betwixt the man and the wife's heirs, was found not to constitute the wife fiar of the half, but only liferenter; and the wife's heirs of line to be heirs of provision to the man, and that the sum was disposable by him, and arrestable by his creditors, Jan. 29, 1639, Grahame *contra* Park and Gerdin [Durie 870; M. 4226]. So strong is this presumption, that there is no more meant to be granted to wives, but their liferent-right, and no part of the fee, unless the provision bear expressly, "a power to the wife to dispone;" and if it be adjected, at any time, during her life, the fee will remain in the man, and that power in the wife will rather be understood as a faculty, like to the power given to commissioners to dispone lands, than an act of property, unless that the provision bear, "a power to the wife and her heirs to dispone" as said is: but a conjunct-fee to a future spouse of the conquest during the marriage, in these terms, "the one-half thereof to be disponed upon as the wife shall think fit," being in a minute of contract, expressing no heirs, but being a short draught, the lady being of great quality, having about 22000 merks yearly in liferent, beside money and moveables; and the husband being a nobleman's son, having gained an estate of 7000 merks yearly, in the war, which he had left; the clause was found to be understood, and extended so, as to make both future spouses equal fiars, seeing the conquest was mainly to arise out of the wife's liferent, June 27, 1676, E. of Dunfermling *contra* E. of Callendar [2 Stair 430; M. 2941; II, 3, 41, *supra*].

If a conjunct-infeftment be granted to two or more, the longest liver of them, and express no heirs, but a liferent to them all, the same accresceth to the survivors, or if it be a right of lands or annualrents to a man and his wife, the longest liver of them two in conjunct-fee, and to their bairns named and their heirs; then the persons named are but as heirs substitute, and the father is fiar, even though the bairns were infeft with the father and mother, January 14, 1663, Bog *contra* Nicolson [1 Stair 155; M. 4251]; July 23, 1675, Moor of Arnistoun *contra* L. of Lamingtoun [2 Stair 360; M. 4252], where a sum was borrowed from a father, for himself, and for the use of his sons, and payable to the father, he being on life, and failing of him to his two sons, or the survivor, and his heirs, and all of them were infeft.

11. The main difference betwixt conjunct-fees and other liferents, is, that the conjunct-fiar, though by interpretation liferenter only, and so may not alienate or waste; yet by the nature of the right and custom, they have the benefit of all casualities befalling during their life, and may dispose thereof; which will not only be effectual during their life, but simply for that individual casuality. So conjunct-fiars may receive and enter the heirs of vassals, and have the benefit of their ward, non-entry, liferent-escheat, and may grant gifts thereof effectually, even as to the time after their death. So also a conjunct fiar, infeft with her husband in lands *cum sylvis*, was found thereby to have right to make use of the woods for her and her tenant's use, January 10, 1610, Hunter and others *contra* relict of L. Gadgirth [Haddington MS; M. 13523; 11,3,74,*supra*]. *Vide supra*, Lib. 2, Title 2, §41.

Simple liferenters have not these casualities of superiority; yet a fiar having disponed his barony, reserving his liferent, was thereby found to have right to receive the heirs of his vassals. And there is reason, that the fiar disponing with reservation to himself, whereby his own infeftment stands *pro tanto*, should have greater power than a liferent apart, or by reservation, to a person not being before infeft. Conjunct-fees, though public, as ordinarily they are, whereby, as to the superior, the fee is full, and the casualities of ward and non-entry excluded, yet the heir may enter to the property, and compel the superior to receive him.

12. Terce is the third of the tenements in which the husband died infeft as of fee provided to his wife surviving, by law or custom, though there be no provision or paction for that purpose. The original hereof, as hath been shown before amongst the interests of marriage [1,4,21,*supra*], is from that obligation upon the husband to provide for his wife; which therefore positive law hath determined to a third of his moveables, if there be children in the family, and if there be none, to a half: but in either case, she hath a third of his tenements. And though, as Craig observeth [11,22,28], by our ancient custom, terce extended only to a third of the tenements an husband had the time of the marriage, which if it were extended to all his tenements he then had, it would hinder him to dispose of any, and if only to these he had at his marriage, and at his death, it would be too narrow, and therefore now it extends to a third of those he stands infeft in, as of fee, the time of his death; and so, when he is denuded before his death, the terce is excluded. Yea, a base infeftment without possession, granted by a husband to his creditor, was found to exclude his wife from a terce of that land, January 27, 1669, Bell of Belford *contra* La. Rutherford [1 Stair 594; M. 1260; 11,3,27,*supra*]. This provision of law is more equitable and proportionable, than ordinarily their provisions by contract with the husband are, who being carried with affection, doth oft-times provide his wife to the prejudice of their children, and ruin of their estate; but this terce keepeth always proportionable, and maketh the

wife sharer of the industry and fortune of the man, and therefore more careful over it; and upon the contrary, husbands giving but small provisions to
their wives at their marriage, when they do but begin to have estates, they
increase not their wives' provisions according to the increase of their fortune;
but the law doth more fitly order the wife's provision to be increased or de-
creased, according to the condition of the man.

13. A terce taketh place ordinarily, where the husband died infeft as of
fee; and it hath effect by the widow's taking brieves [IV, 3, 11, *infra*] out of the
Chancellary, directed to sheriffs or bailies, to call an inquest of fifteen sworn
men, and thereby to serve the brieves; which have two heads, the one, "That
the bearer was lawful wife to the defunct;" the other, "That he died in fee of
such tenements." This is a pleadable brieve, and hath no retour; but service
alone is sufficient enough to give the wife interest as other liferenters have.
It was specially statute, That where the marriage was not questioned in the
husband's life, and the widow was holden and repute his lawful wife in his
time; no exception in the contrary shall be sustained in the service of the
brieve, but she shall be served and enjoy the terce, till it be declared in a
petitory judgment, that she was not a lawful wife, Parliament 1503, cap. 77
[A.P.S. 11, 252, c. 22].

14. The brieve being thus served, the sheriff or bailie must also, if it be
demanded, ken the relict to her terce, which is ordinarily done by the sun or
the shade; that is, whether the division shall begin at the east or the west, and
so the division of the tenements proceeds by acres, two befalling to the heir,
and one to the relict [Craig, 11, 22, 32], wherein there ought to be marches set,
and instruments taken thereupon, which is as a seasin; but this division being
most inconvenient, except the whole interest were used to be set in acre-dale,
it is not exclusive of other divisions by the worth of the lands or the rent, so
many rooms being designed for the tercer, the rest remaining for the fiar.
And this way of kenning would be valid, and much better. But it is not
necessary to divide, at serving the brieve, to constitute the terce; for the
service giveth sufficient title to the third of the mails and duties of every room,
March 15, 1632, relict of Veitch of Dawick *contra*   [Durie 630; M.
16087].

15. But she cannot remove possessors, because she brooketh the terce *pro
indiviso* with the heir, till it be kenned, or otherwise divided. The terce being
served, gives right not only to the years thereafter, but preceding, since the
husband's death, November 20, 1624, Tenants *contra* Crawfurd and Fleming
[Durie 153; M. 15837]: and so the tercer may pursue the heritor or other
intromitter, for all bygones of the third of the duty, not as they were at the
husband's death, but as they were bettered by the fiar, February 13, 1628,
Countess of Dumfermling *contra* Earl of Dunfermling [*Sub nom. Semple* v
Crawford, Durie 344; M. 14707], and that without deduction of factor-fee,
March 27, 1634, *inter eosdem*. The tercer being served, hath interest to pursue
for commission to cognosce pasturage lands, what soums they may hold, that

she may have the third soum, or else to divide, January 18, 1628, *con-tra* M'Kenzie [Durie 330; M. 15838]. The division of the terce from the two thirds, may be in the most convenient way, wherein all dwelling-houses, or kilns and barns, and other houses for service, will come in as they may be most conveniently divided. This is the most ordinary way of terces, by service as said is, when the husband died infeft in fee.

16. Terce takes place, not only in lands, but also in annualrents, wherein the husband died infeft as of fee, November 30, 1627, Tenants of Easthouses *contra* Hepburn [Durie 317; M. 15838]; but not to the terce of annualrents of bonds, whereupon no infeftment followed, June 24, 1663, Elisabeth Scrim-zeour *contra* Murrays [1 Stair 194; M. 464]. It is also extended to infeftments of teinds, February 13, 1628, Countess of Dumfermling *contra* E. of Dun-fermling [Durie 344; M. 14707]. But it is not extended to tenements or lands within burgh, or holden burgage; neither to superiorities or feu-duties, or other casualities thereof; nor to tacks, *ibidem;* neither to patronage or advo-cation of kirks; neither doth a terce extend to reversions.

If the fiar, whose land is liable to a terce, die, and his wife have right to another terce, which is called the lesser terce, though the husband died infeft as of fee of the whole tenement, she hath not a third of the whole but a third of these two thirds, which were unaffected with the greater terce, till the former tercer's death. Craig *lib. 2, dieges 22* [11,22,27], proposeth two cases, in which the relict will have a terce, though the husband died not infeft as of fee; the first is, if the husband infeft his apparent heir in his estate, if there be no liferent provided to the wife by a contract; in that case the relict will have a terce, which is most just, albeit it will not proceed summarily by a brieve, which bears only warrant for a terce of the tenements in which the husband died infeft as of fee: but it may proceed by declarator, and would not only have effect against the apparent heir, but against any gratuitous disposition made by the husband, reserving his own liferent; for such deeds would be found fraudulent, and contrary to the nature of the obligation of husbands to provide their wives, unless there remained tenements, out of which a reason-able terce might remain to the relict, according to her quality. The other case is, when a father, by his son's contract of marriage, is obliged to infeft his son in fee in certain lands; if the son's relict be no otherwise provided, she may claim a terce of these lands, though the father did not perform his obligement, which may be construed as fraudulent, and in her prejudice.

17. Terce is excluded by the wife's adultery or desertion; or by the death of either party within year and day, without children. And also, by whatso-ever way the husband is *sine fraude* divested, the terce is excluded: as by a crime inferring forfeiture or recognition by the husband or his superior, though not declared before his death, or by the ward and non-entry of his immediate superior, carrying the rent of the husband's estate. But there is one decision observed by Spotiswood and Hope [Spotiswoode 350; possibly Hope *Maj.Pr.* IV, 5, 52; M. 9853; III, 2, 20, *infra*], betwixt the Relict of John Cran-

stoun and Chrichtoun that an apprising without infeftment, did exclude a relict from her terce: yet it were hard to sustain that in all cases, even though there were a charge against the superior upon the apprising; which, as it would not exclude the superior from the ward, non-entry or relief, so neither could it exclude a relict from her terce, unless she had a conjunct-fee or liferent by consent, equivalent to a *tertia rationabilis*: and though our custom hath far deborded from the ancient design of terces, whereby a reasonable terce was appointed, and if any voluntary liferent were granted, Craig [11,22,8. cf. R.M. 11,16,77–78] observes, that it was ever understood to be no more, but for clearing and securing the tercer against the trouble and difficulty of recovering possession by a service, and therefore was always retrenched unto the terce: yet now, not only real voluntary provisions are sustained, though of the husband's whole estate and conquest, albeit granted *in æstu amoris*, with this temperament only, that if the heir have no other estate, the liferenter must entertain and educate him, according to his quality, by Act of Parliament, which is more extensive than a simple aliment; but she is also liable, *super jure naturæ*, to aliment her other children, if they have no provisions. Custom hath so far proceeded, as not only to allow voluntary provisions, how great soever, but therewith to add a terce of any other distinct tenement, unless the voluntary liferent were accepted in satisfaction of the terce; which indeed were reasonable in many cases, the voluntary liferent being oft-times small, and suitable to the estate the parties have when they marry, but cannot make a *rationabilis tertia*, if by conquest, their estate should grow great; neither is it reasonable that, though the voluntary provision be never so great, that a terce should be given, though little remained to the heir, only because by ignorance or negligence, the clause in satisfaction, were not adjected: which satisfaction may not only be proven by writ, but by presumption, from the design of parties, in the contracts of marriage, which are *uberrimæ fidei*: for suppose (which is ordinary enough) that a liferent of lands were provided by the contract of marriage; yet some lands were not mentioned, but there is a clause adjected for the liferent of the whole conquest, were it *rationabilis tertia*, to give the wife a third of that which is omitted, though she had a particular liferent of more, and the whole conquest, though never so considerable? Yea, it came lately to be controverted, whether a liferenter infeft in an annualrent, out of her husband's estate, consisting of one tenement, lying contigue, the annualrent being two thirds of the rent thereof, because it bore not, "in satisfaction of a terce." The relict did also claim a terce out of that same one tenement, and obtained it, till a statute was made in the contrary.

But so far as I can understand by former decisions, it hath not yet been determined whether relicts should have a reasonable terce, according to the terms of the ancient law, inducing terces, or whether she should have a terce, proportionable or suitable or not, though she be already suitably provided, if she have not expressly accepted her former provision, in satisfaction of her terce: which terce is most favourable when suitable; and therefore takes place in the two cases before mentioned, [11,4,16,*supra*] even beyond the letter of the law; and therefore, if it were unproportionable to the quality of the husband and wife, who might have a great estate in money, and little land, a voluntary provision out of any tenement, should not exclude a terce out of the remanent of the same tenement, or of any other tenement, unless the relict were sufficiently provided before. There is one interlocutor betwixt Jean Crichtoun and Kirkhouse her son, [*Sub nom. Crichton and Eleis* v *Maxwell*, 1 Stair 344; M.15843], wherein it was alleged, that she was sufficiently provided, to more than a terce of her husband's estate, which was repelled; but the case was *in possessorio*, where the relict was already served, and kenned to a terce, and was pursuing the tenants, so that the service and kenning being a standing sentence, doth not determine what might be done *in petitorio;* neither was that allegeance proponed, and offered to be proven, but only alleged informative; whereas the defence proponed was, that the relict's provision was but a minute of contract, bearing, "to be extended with all clauses requisite" whereof there was a process of extension depending, including the acceptance, in satisfaction of the terce, as being ordinary; but it was replied, that that clause was omitted in the full contract already extended: but now by the late Act of Parl. 1681. cap. 10 [A.P.S. VIII,247,c.12] there is no place for a terce, where there is a provision for the wife of liferent, unless a terce be expressly reserved.

Craig [11,22,27] proposeth another case, whether the relict would have a terce of lands competent in fee to her husband, and so possessed by him, though by fraud or negligence, he never infeft himself, which, he says, is the opinion of Littleton, and it is not without much ground, though it hath not come to be decided with us, voluntary liferents in satisfaction being so ordinary; for though the apparent heir not entering, cannot burden the fee with his debt, yet his *jus apparentiæ* gives him or his executors right to the fruits during all his life, [11,1,22; 11,3,16,*supra*; 111,5,2,*infra*] whereunto it would be suitable enough, that though his voluntary provisions to his wife could not affect the fee; yet the legal provision of a reasonable terce might, if the wife were not otherwise competently provided.

By the custom of England relicts lose their terces, by falling in public and atrocious crimes, as treason, murder, witchcraft, although they be restored by the King, by way of grace, because thereby the memory of their husbands, and fame of their children are disgraced; I know no such point to have been drawn in question with us. Craig in the forecited place [11,22,27] holds, that if the fiar transact for his own or his superior's forfeiture, or recognition, or obtain a gift thereof, it should accresce to the tercer, whose provision is onerous, importing warrandice, and therefore might be effectual against the fiar, if he represent the husband; and in all distresses, relief doth import what the party distressed truly paid out. A terce of wadset lands, wherein the husband died infeft, was not found elided, because the husband required, or charged for the money, not being denuded before his death, February 16, 1642, Veitch *contra* Veitch of Dawick [Durie 894; M. 14095]. But the wife's third continues as to the third of the annualrent of the money in lieu of the lands redeemed by the heir after his predecessor's death [11,4,63,*supra*]. A terce is not excluded by ward, non-entry, or liferent-escheat of the husband, as hath been more fully shown before, Title Superiority. [11,4,23,36 and 66, *supra*].

18. Terce is burdened proportionally by all *debita fundi* affecting the whole tenement, as annualrent, thirlage, pasturage, but with no other debts of the defunct, being personal, though they be heritable, and have a provision of infeftment.

19. Liferent by the courtesy or curiality of Scotland, is the liferent competent to the husband of the wife's lands and hereditaments: it is introduced by our common law, which is our most ancient custom, whereof no beginning is known, in the same way as the terce of the surviving wife, whereby, without any paction or provision, she enjoys the third of her deceased husband's heritable rights, wherein he died invested as of fee, during her life: so the husband liferents the whole lands and hereditaments of the wife, wherein she died infeft in fee, and that without any service or kenning, as in terces, but summarily, by virtue of his having been husband to the defunct; neither is there any difference, whether the defunct wife had a prior husband or not; or whether her hereditament be ward, blench, feu, or burgage.

The original of this liferent by the courtesy, as Craig observeth, *Lib.*2, *Dieg.*22 [11,22,40] is from the rescript of the Emperor Constantine [C.6, 60,1], whereby the father had the usufruct of the heritage of his children, befalling to them as heirs to their mother; and therefore, the courtesy takes no place but where there were children of the marriage, one or more, which attained that maturity as to be heard cry or weep; for then the law regardeth not how long the children live, or whether they do survive their mother, but *hoc ipso*, that they are born at maturity, they are heirs apparent of the fee; and the liferent is established in their father: in this the courtesy of husbands differs from the terce of wives; for the wife hath her terce, if either the marriage continue undissolved year and day, or though it continue not so long, if a child was born of the marriage, heard cry and weep, though the child had been begotten before the marriage, yea, though it had been born before the marriage, being legitimate by the subsequent marriage, how short soever it endured, the wife should have her terce. But the courtesy takes no place, unless a ripe child be born, though the marriage should continue for many years, so that the being of children procreate and born into maturity is the chief motive introductory of this law. And the law hath well fixed the maturity of the children by their crying or weeping, and hath not left it to the conjecture of witnesses, whether the child was ripe or not, both as to the courtesy, terce, and dissolution of the marriage within the year [1,4,19,*supra*]; in all which cases also, the law alloweth women witnesses, as being necessary in the case of the death of the children, at the time of their birth.

Skeen in his title *de verborum significatione*, upon the word *curialitas*, limiteth the courtesy to the lands or hereditaments, into which wives succeed as heirs to their predecessors, whether before, or during the marriage, which Craig in the foresaid place [11, 22, 27] doth likewise follow, and doth exclude the husband from the liferent of the wife's land, to which the wife had right by any contract, as *titulo emptionis;* which will not exclude the husband, where the wife's predecessor infefts her *per præceptionem hæreditatis;* as if a father should infeft his daughter, reserving his own liferent, with power to dispose, she is not thereby heir *activè*, nor is that estate accounted heritage but conquest; yet she is heir *passivè*, and there is more reason that the husband should enjoy his liferent of that estate, than if his wife had been therein heir of provision or tailzie, whereby failing her and her issue, another branch, not nearest of blood to her, might readily succeed; so that if her children were dead before herself, her heirs of tailzie would have much more reason to question her husband's liferent by the courtesy, than his own children as heirs of line would have to contravert his liferent of the estate, wherein she was infeft by her father or any of her predecessors, to which she was apparent heir; but there have been few debates or decisions, or limitations thereof, which would clear this and other points thereanent.

Liferenters were found free of the reparation of ministers' manses, by the Act of Parliament Sess. 3. Ch. 2. cap. 21 [Manses Act 1663, c. 21; A.P.S. VII, 472, c. 31], "Ordaining heritors to build or repair manses to the value of 1000 pounds;" whereof no share of relief was found due by the liferenters, they not being exprest, November 14, 1679, Minister of   *contra* L. & La. Beinston [*Sub nom. Morham* v *Buiston*, 2 Stair 706; M. 8499]. Yet if the whole estate were liferented by conjunct fee, the conjunct fiar might be liable as fiar in that case, when the heritor had no profit of the land; and if the whole were affected with a separate liferent, the effect would be the same, seeing what the heritor would be liable to, would diminish his aliment, which behoved to be made up by the liferenter.

Liferent by the courtesy hath the same extensions and limitations as terces; it affects all the wife's lands, not acquired by a singular title; it is not excluded by the ward, but it is excluded during the non-entry, or by the liferent-escheat of the wife: and also by the ward of the superior, or the forfeiture or recognition, either of the superior or wife: it is burdened with all real burdens by infeftment or tack, and with the aliment of the wife's heir, if he have not *aliunde;* it is also excluded by the dissolution of the marriage within year and day, by divorce, or by the husband's desertion of the wife, though divorce followed not; or by his adultery, or other atrocious crimes: but the courtesy excludes the ward, non-entry, or liferent-escheat of the heir of the wife, that they have no effect against the fee while the husband lives.

20. Amongst personal servitudes may be numbered public burdens, umposed by the King and Parliament for public use, such as taxations, which by the Acts imposing them, are declared real, affecting the ground, and that

thereupon the ground may be poinded; and so consequently do affect singular successors. The extraordinary burdens of maintenance and cess, imposed by the Parliament during the troubles, had not that clause therein of poinding the ground, and so were not found *debita fundi*, but *debita fructuum*, nor do they yet affect singular successors, July 13, 1664, Graham of Hiltoun *contra* the Heritors of Clackmannan [1 Stair 212; M. 10164].

Title 7. Servitudes Real, Where, of *Actus, Iter et Via*, Pasturage, and Thirlage, &c.

SERVITUDES are distinguished in real and personal, though neither of them be personal rights; yet these servitudes whereby one tenement is subservient to another tenement, and to persons only as having right to, and for the use of that tenement, are called real servitudes, as not being subservient directly to persons, but to things: and the other are called personal; because thereby the tenement is subservient directly to persons, and not with respect to any other thing, as liferents, &c.

Before we come to the particular kinds of these real servitudes, it will be fit to enquire how such servitudes are constitute; and next how they are destitute and extinguished.

1. As to the first, these servitudes require no infeftment, though they may be constitute by infeftments, yet there is no necessity of infeftment, to their constitution. 2. Real servitudes cannot be constitute by any personal right, as by contract, paction, testament or legacy, neither by disposition or assignation alone: the reason is, because they are real rights, and cannot be constitute by any personal right, which though they be oft-times the remote cause of real rights, yet there is more requisite to their constitution: and therefore though

such personal rights may be sufficient against the granters thereof, by a personal objection, whereby they cannot come against their own deed; yet they are not sufficient against singular successors, neither do they affect the ground 3. All real servitudes are constitute by possession or use; for things corporeal are said only to be possest; therefore incorporeal rights, as servitudes, have rather use than possession to consummate them, *l.3.* §*2.ff. de act. empt.* [D. 19,1,3] *l. ult. ff. de serv.* [D.8,1,20] *l.1.* §. *ult. ff. de serv. præd. rust.* [D.8, 3,1,2]; which though it be the last requisite to accomplish servitudes, yet it is not sufficient alone, but must have another title, either by the express consent of the proprietor, or by prescription. There is no difference in what way the consent be adhibited, so it be in writ; and the obligement to grant any servitude with possession, is equivalent to the formal disposition or grant thereof, as it is in the most of these rights, which do essentially require nothing else but consent alone, or consent with possession, and not any other solemnity; as obligements to grant assignations, discharges, renunciations, are equivalent to these rights themselves, when formally made [11,10,5,*infra*].

2. The civilians debate much, whether servitudes can be introduced by prescription, and whether in that case there be requisite a title, and the proprietor's knowledge; wherein we need not insist, seeing our prescription being only by statute upon the course of forty years, in most cases it presumeth both a title and knowledge: but theirs being upon ten years, against those who are present, may require more; yet many, even of the learnedest of them, account prescription sufficient, without a title, or any other than presumed knowledge.

With us, the servitude of a way to the kirk, was not found constitute by possession thirty years, but by immemorial possession, going and coming that way uninterrupted, without any writ [June 27, 1623, Haddington MS; M. 10880]; for here the way was claimed at the nearest to the kirk, whether the defender's lands were under crop or not: for though a way to the kirk be due to all parties in the parish, without consent or prescription, yet it must be with the least detriment to the interjacent lands, and so cannot always be the nearest way, but must go about corns; and though thirty or forty years *alternativè*, was not sustained to constitute a way through lands, even under crop; yet forty years is equivalent and always equiparate to immemorial possession: in the same case [June 27, 1623, Haddington MS; M. 10880], Haddington observes, "That a convenient way to the kirk, without going through corns, was sustained without prescription;" and the like would be sustained for passage to market towns, or public ports, till there be access to a high-way [11,1,5, *supra*]. A servitude of laying over a milldam upon another heritor's land, was found constitute by possession forty years, whereby the heritor of the mill was found to have right, that when the water did wash away the ground from the end of the dam, to lengthen the same upon the servient tenement, so that it might be made effectual with the least detriment, and that he was not liable for any damage by washing away the ground of the servient tenement, by occasion of his dam, July 20, 1677, L. of Gairltoun *contra* L. of Smeatoun [2 Stair 545; M. 14535]. *Vid. l. 11. ff. comm. præd.* [D. 8, 4, 11]. It must be adverted, that when such servitudes are said to be constitute by sole prescription, without writ, it is to be understood, without writ from the proprietor of the servient tenement; for ordinarily there is this much title in writ for these servitudes, that the party having right thereto is infeft in the tenement with the pertinents, under which servitudes are comprehended; or with common pasturage, by which he hath not only such pasturage as he hath been long in possession of, upon the lands of his superior or author; but forty years possession therewith, is sufficient against any other, who can be said in no case to have done any deed for the constituting of the servitude; and it was so found in the case of the town of Perth, concerning the Isle of Sleiples [Not found]. But this long possession is not estimate by deeds done by the proprietor of the servient tenement; as he who brings his grain to another man's mill, for never so many years, these deeds of his do not constitute a thirlage upon his lands, unless he suffer the proprietor or tenant of the mill, to cause him or his tenants either to bring their grain by process, or otherwise; and he who opens a window in his dyke or wall, whereby his neighbour hath a prospect, doth not thereby put himself under a servitude; but if he suffer his neighbour to break a window in his wall, and enjoy it till prescription be run, his suffering introduceth that servitude.

3. As to these who can impose servitudes, when they are constitute by express consent; yet they cannot be constitute without consent of the proprietor; and if the superior consent not, they will not be effectual against him, if the fee be open and return to him by right of superiority, for a time, or for ever. So liferenters cannot constitute a servitude, to have a real right against singular successors, or beyond the endurance of that liferent or wadset, much less can tenants; yet both can begin or continue to make up prescription. But when servitudes are constitute by prescription, the knowledge even of the superior is presumed, who though he had not the full right, yet might have interrupted [11, 4, 36, *supra*].

4. Servitudes are extinct by the proprietor of the tenement dominant his renunciation, or contrary consent in writ, without any other solemnity; and there needs here no other possession, than that possession the proprietor of the servient tenement hath of his tenement, whereby he may make free use thereof; for he who possesseth naturally or corporeally, possesseth to all effects and uses, unless there be impediment by any opposite standing right. Servitudes are also extinct by prescription of liberty: for as servitudes by prescription take away liberty, or the free use of the tenement servient; so liberty is recovered in the same way: for though in the short prescription in the civil law, simple forbearance of the servitude will not import prescription, unless some contrary acts that may hinder the use of it, were done by the proprietor of the servient tenement; yet in our long prescription of forty years, simple forbearance of the use may suffice, as presuming the will of the party

to be, to relinquish the servitude, and to suffer liberty to be recovered; and when the servitude is constitute by writ, the same will be the effect, seeing the writ and obligement prescrive, not being used, or acclaimed forty years.

5. To descend now to the kinds of servitudes; there may be as many as there are ways, whereby the liberty of a house or tenement may be restrained in favour of another tenement; for liberty and servitude are contraries, and the abatement of the one is the being or enlargement of the other. Servitudes, in respect of the subject matter, are either in reference to city tenements, such as houses for habitation, not for the use of agriculture or pasturage, whether they be in towns or villages, or not; and in country tenements are such as fields and grounds, and all houses for the use thereof, as stables, barns, byres, kilns, wheresoever situate in town or country. Servitudes upon city tenements are very many, whereof we shall point at the prime; they are either positive or negative. A positive servitude is that whereby the servient tenement is not only restrained of its liberty, but is constrained to suffer some things to be done to the behoof of the dominant tenement, contrary to its liberty. Negative servitude is that whereby the freedom of the servient tenement is only restrained.

6. The prime positive servitude of city-tenements is, the servitude of support, whereby the servient tenement is liable to bear any burden for the use of the dominant; and that either by laying on the weight upon its walls, or other parts thereof; or by putting in joists or other means of support in the walls of the same, which the Romans called *servitutem tigni immittendi;* or otherwise, this servitude may be, by bearing the pressure or putt of any building for the use of the dominant tenement, as of a vault or pend, or the like: such is the servitude of superstructure, whereby any building may be built upon the servient tenement. Like unto which is now frequent in Edinburgh, when one tenement is built above another at divers times, or divers stories or contignations of the same tenement are bought by divers proprietors, and thereby the upper becomes a distinct tenement, and hath a servitude upon the lower tenements, whereby they must support it.

The question useth to be moved here, whether the owner of the servient tenement be obliged to uphold or repair his tenement, that it may be sufficient to support the dominant tenement. There are opinions of the learned, and probable sons reaupon both parts; for the affirmative maketh the common rule, that when any thing is granted, all things are understood to be granted therewith that are necessary thereto: so he who constituteth upon his tenement, a servitude of support, he must make it effectual. And for the negative, servitudes are odious, and not to be extended beyond what is expressly granted or accustomed, to which we incline; and therefore it would be adverted how the servitude is constitute, that if it appear, the constituent had granted this servitude, so as to uphold it; or if by custom, he hath been made to uphold it, not upon the account of his own tenement, but of the dominant, he must so continue; and it is not only a personal obligation, but a part of the servitude passing with the servient tenement, even to singular successors: but if it appear not so constitute, it will import no more than a tolerance, to lay on or impute the burden of the dominant tenement upon the servient, which therefore the owner of the servient neither can hinder nor prejudge; but he is not obliged to do any positive deed, by reparation of his own tenement, to that purpose; but the owner of the dominant tenement hath right to repair it for his own use, by reason of his servitude, and the owner of the servient tenement cannot hinder him.

If it be objected, that within burgh, the owners of the inferior and supporting tenements are obliged to repair for the behoof of the superior tenements, the owners whereof may legally inforce reparation, yet it inferreth not this to be the nature of a servitude, but a positive statute or custom of the burgh, for the public good thereof, which is concerned in upholding tenements. But mainly, the reason of it is, because when divers owners have parts of the same tenement, it cannot be said to be a perfect division, because the roof remaineth roof to both, and the ground supporteth both; and therefore by the nature of communion, there are mutual obligations upon both, viz. that the owner of the lower tenement must uphold his tenement as a foundation to the upper, and the owner of the upper tenement must uphold his tenement as a roof and cover to the lower: both which, though they have the resemblance of servitudes, and pass with the thing to singular successors; yet they are rather personal obligations, such as pass in communion even to the singular successors of either party.

7. The next positive city-servitude is, stillicides, or sinks: stillicide is the easing-drop which falleth off any house or building, or the rain turned off a tenement either by dropping or by spout; concerning which, consider what may be done freely without any servitude, for thereby it will easily appear, what servitudes are competent herein. The main question is, whether the owner of any ground may build houses close to the march of his own ground, whereby his easing-drop will fall upon his neighbour's ground, or if by a spout he may make the rain that falls upon his own tenement, run over upon his neighbour's. And though it may appear from the common rule, *Cujus est solum, ejus est usque ad cœlum*, that thereby the owner may build upon any part of his own ground what he will, even though it be to the detriment of his neighbours' prospect or light; yet no man may dispose so upon his own ground, as to put any positive prejudice, hurt or damage upon his neighbour's; as if he should alter the course of any river or water running within his own ground, so that it cause an alteration thereof in his neighbour's ground, or by damming of the water make it run upon his neighbour's: and therefore he may not so build upon his own ground, as by gathering the water from its natural way, he should make it fall together upon his neighbour's ground: otherwise, any neighbour might take away both the profit and the pleasure of his neighbour's tenement or close, by spouts or kennels carrying the rain-water upon it

in abundance. And albeit it be not so palpable in the easing-drop as in spouts, what the neighbour's detriment may be, yet the very roof of the house is a considerable gathering of the water: and therefore every man ought so to build, as that the drops of the building may fall upon his own ground, which commonly in neighbourhood is counted two foot and a half within the march, according to the ancient Roman custom, *auctore Marciano*. If it were not so, but that the first builder might build to his march, no question the second might do the like; and so there should be no way to convey the drop, without much detriment to both. And though either might by a spout, keep the water from falling upon his neighbour's ground, yet that spout might fail, and at least his neighbour be put to the trouble of an action, to cause him keep it right, which his neighbour cannot enforce upon him. But as the Romans accounted it as a delinquence, *et damnum infectum*, a damage like to befall, though not befalling, when any thing was built, to hang over the highway, or whereby a neighbour might have probable damage, and therefore either caused the doer to demolish it, or to find caution not to damnify his neighbour; so from the same ground of equity and expedience, it ought to be in this case. There is an exception here of towns and villages, which for common conveniency, do allow houses to be built close together, which is tacitly imported in the incorporation of towns, or union of villages, in which the custom of the place must be the rule.

8. What hath been said of stillicides, holdeth more apparently in sinks either for conveying of water, filth, or any thing else, upon or through the neighbour's tenements, which cannot be done, unless there be a servitude thereupon either by consent or prescription.

9. Negative urban servitudes do chiefly concern the light, view, or prospect of tenements; for the owner of every ground may build thereupon at his pleasure, though thereby he hinder the view and prospect from his neighbour's tenement, or the coming of the sun-beams or light thereto, which being but in relation to the extrinsic benefit of that, which is not in, but without, the tenement, is not accounted a positive damage, from which the owners of neighbouring tenements must abstain, as in the case of stillicides and sinks: and so much the rather, that common utility would be highly impaired, if the first builder might hinder his neighbour to build upon his own ground, upon pretence that thereby his light or prospect were hindered; so that it is free for the owner to build what he will, though thereby he darken his neighbour's tenement. For helping the inconveniency that may ensue by this liberty of building, two servitudes use to be introduced, both restraining the owner's liberty; the one is, by giving light or prospect to the dominant tenement, whereby the building upon the servient tenement may neither be lifted higher, nor any building made where there are none, nor any window or in-let, whereby the prospect from the dominant tenement to or through the servient, be marred or altered: the other is, whereby the prospect or view of the servient tenement is restrained, in that there may be no building thereupon, or windows opened

therein, which may look to the house, close, or garden of the dominant tenement.

These servitudes of light or prospect cannot be introduced by the enjoyment and use thereof, though time out of mind: but there must be either consent or prescription, by hindering the owner of the servient tenement to use his freedom; for the first builder, though he have light or view for an hundred years through his neighbour's ground, doth not thereby put a servitude upon his neighbour, unless if he has been in use to hinder his neighbour to take away that prospect in any lawful way, by reiterate acts during the time of prescription. And, therefore, though two purchasers bought houses from the same owner, neither of them was found to be astricted not to build as high as they pleased, albeit to the prejudice of the light and view of the other, Hope, Servitudes, Sumervel *contra* Sumervel [Hope, *Maj. Pr.* III, 24, 6; M. 12769]. The predial or country-servitudes, whereby one ground or field is subservient to another, may be as manifold as the free use of the one may be restrained or impaired, for the profit or pleasure of the other; the chief of which in use with us are ways, watering, water-gangs, fueling, pasturage, thirlage.

10. Ways are a part of the reservation from property, and the necessary vestige of the ancient community of the earth: of which before, lib. 2. tit. 1. sect. 5. and which are understood as the common pertinents of all grounds; for free ish and entry are implied in the very right of property, though not expressed: but that doth not infer ways or passages from every part of the dominant ground, through every part of the servient, which would make both unprofitable, but it must be in the way least hurtful to either. And now by long custom it is everywhere determined, and can be no further claimed, than according to ancient custom: and it is a necessary effect of property, rather than a servitude, seeing it is mutual and equal to either ground, whereof the one cannot be called dominant and the other servient, until custom or consent have so determined that the ways which are constitute are more profitable to one tenement, and more burdensome to another, whereby this becometh the servient, and that the dominant tenement.

Ways are distinguished by the Romans, according to the measure or burdensomeness of them, in three kinds *l. 7 & l. 12. ff. de S.R.P.* [D. 8, 3, 7 and 12]. Of these the greater comprehends the lesser; our custom sticketh not to this distinction, but measureth the way according to the end for which it was constitute, and by the use for which it was introduced, as having only a foot-road, or a road for a horse to be led or ridden upon, or only a way for leading of loads upon horseback, or a way for leading of carts, or a way for driving of cattle, and is observed accordingly. There is another distinction of ways amongst the Romans, and with us, in public and private ways. Public ways are these which are constitute for public use, and which go from one public place to another, as from one burgh to another, or from a burgh to a public port; this is called a highway, and by the Romans, an imperial or pretorian way, and with us, the King's highway; for preservation whereof, there are express statutes, Parl. 1555, cap. 53 [A.P.S. 11, 498, c. 27], Parl. 1592, c. 159. [A.P.S. 111, 579, c. 78] and this is patent to all the lieges, without respect to any land, yea and to all strangers having freedom of traffic.

Private ways are these which are constitute by private parties, for private use, whereof both, or at least one end, is to a private place, and is a proper servitude to the use of that place for which it is constitute: so a way, the one end whereof is at a public place, may be a private way, if the other end thereof be from or for the use of a private place; as a way from a private place to a city or church, which doth not fall in to any public way; for in so far it remaineth private, and cannot be made use of, but for the behoof of the place or ground from which it comes; but it is not the largeness or latitude of the way, that makes a public or private way: for a private way may be as large as a public. Private ways are constitute as other servitudes by prescription, by going and coming that way uninterrupted, time out of mind, or forty years, without writ, or any other right [11, 7, 2, *supra*]. Private parties may repair these ways becoming difficult; so an heritor having a way to the church, and to a royal burgh, at a ford where there was an old bridge, was found (the ford becoming difficult) to have right to re-build the bridge, though the one end of it was but upon his land, and the other end upon his neighbour's who withstood it, Nicol. *de servitutibus*, Sir James Cleland *contra* Cleland [Nicolson, *Fol. Dict.* 11, 274; M. 12769].

11. Watering is a servitude of taking water, proper to one ground for the use of another, whether it be for the cattle of the dominant ground, which is most ordinary, or for other uses thereof; and it doth ordinarily carry a way for these cattle to come to that water through the servient ground; but if it be only a way to a public water in rivers or public lochs, it differeth nothing from the servitude of a way, unless with the way, there be also the making use of the private water in the fountains, ponds, or other places proper to the servient ground, *l. 3. §3, ff. eod* [D. 8, 3, 3, 3].

12. A water-gang is a servitude of conveying water through the servient ground, for the use of the dominant; and if the water be proper and belong to the servient ground, the servitude is the greater, but hath no different name; such are the aquæducts to mills and other uses; for without such a servitude, water may not be altered or diverted from its course, as was found, where the water-course was the march betwixt the heritors, that the one could not change its old channel (though it returned thereto again) without consent of the other, though he alleged no prejudice, but the want of the pleasure of the water, and fishing of trouts, and that thereafter he might make use of it upon his side, June 25, 1624, Ballantine *contra* Cranstoun [Durie 130; M. 12769]. It was also found, that an heritor might not divert the water from its own course upon his own ground, to the prejudice of others, having the right of fishing therein, Hope, *de actionibus in factum*, Bairdie *contra* L. Stonehouse [Possibly Hope, *Maj. Pr.* VI, 40, 6, *sub nom. Benned* v *Skartsouse ;* M. 14529].

13. Fueling is a servitude of suffering fuel to be taken from the servient ground for the use of the dominant and inhabitants thereof; and it is ordinarily in peats, turfs, and heather; and it doth necessarily import fields to win the fuel upon, and a way to bring it away, though these be not expressed. This servitude is sometimes constitute indefinitely upon a whole moss or muir, and sometimes upon a particular place thereof, and accordingly it is to be regulated by the consent or custom which did constitute it. The like is in the way for carrying the fuel, which sometimes is a cart-way, sometimes only a load-way.

Fueling is presumed to be comprehended under pasturage, though not expressed, as the minor servitudes are involved in the major; yet this presumption is taken off by contrary custom, or express paction; for they are not inseparable, as *iter et actus* are under *via*, there being no end nor interest to hinder a man to go or ride, where a cart or drove doth pass: but where common pasturage is constitute, it is a several and separable interest to break the ground for fuel, feal or divot, which in so far excludes the other party, and appropriates that part of the grass to the fueler; and so it was found, that a servitude of pasturage introduced by forty years' peaceable possession of the pasturage, was not to be extended to feal and divot, seeing the acquirer was interrupted in these, February 15, 1668, L. Hayning *contra* T. of Selkirk [1 Stair 524; M. 2459]. And even where the servitude was only constitute for feal, divot, clay, and stone, in a large muir indefinitely, it was not found to hinder the proprietor to rive out a part of the muir, leaving enough that might serve that servitude, for ever unploughed, and with condition, that if that sufficed not, more of the muir should be left lee again; wherein respect was had to the public utility of making a large muir to be profitable, June 21, 1667, Watson *contra* Feuars of Dunkennan [1 Stair 463; M. 14529]. The like was found in a servitude of fueling upon a muir of vast bounds, that it did not hinder the proprietor to plough: but the most convenient places for fueling were appointed to be laid aside, as they were adjacent to the dominant tenements; so that they might be secure of perpetual fueling, which the proprietor might never plough, Jan. 20, 1680, E. of Southesk *contra* L. Melgum and others [2 Stair 740; M. 7899]. But, in all these, by the nature of the servitude they should not be extended further than for the use of the dominant ground, and so are not applicable by the heritor of the dominant ground, to any other not inhabiting the dominant field: yet if custom and prescription hath been to the contrary, it overrules all; and so it was found, that an heritor or his tenants, having right to a common muir, not only might win fuel there for his own use, but sell it to others, Had. June 21, 1611, L. Monimusk *contra* L. Pitfoddels [Not found].

14. Pasturage is a servitude, whereby the grass of the ground servient is applied to the use of the ground dominant, and this sometimes reacheth to the full benefit of the grass; so that the proprietor hath no share thereof, but the benefit of the tillage and other pertinents besides the grass, whereby he may

till when he pleaseth, or open the ground for other effects of property, as to win coal or stone, unless by consent or custom it be otherwise regulated; but so much as remains grass, belongs wholly to the other. But must ordinarily pasturage is in common, either to the proprietor and him that hath the servitude; or to many having acquired the servitude promiscuously, though with exclusion of the proprietor from grasing; and that again is either for an indefinite number of soums, or definitely for a certain number exprest.

Common pasturage is ordinarily constitute by the charter of the dominant ground, expressing the clause with common pasturage, which, when general, hath no other effect than the common clauses of charters, to give the right of any pasturage belonging to the fee, if any be: but if it be clad with immemorial, or forty years' possession, by the Act of Prescription, it carrieth unquestionably the right of pasturage upon any ground belonging to the superior, and upon which he might the time of the charter have constitute a pasturage: yet it is more dubious, whether long possession can introduce pasturage upon ground not belonging to the superior, granter of the charter; and it hath been found that it hath been so constitute; yea though the clause of common pasturage be not in the charter, but only the land disponed with parts and pertinents, with long possession, Spots. Servitudes, L. Knockdolian *contra* tenants of Partick [Spotiswoode 307; M. 14540]. The like was formerly found in the case of the town of Perth anent the Isle of Sleiples [Not found]. Pasturage may also be constitute by a contract clad with possession, without any seasin, which is effectual, even against singular successors, Jan. 26, 1622, Turnbul *contra* L. Blanernie [Durie 11; M. 14499].

Pasturage being constitute in reference to the dominant ground, though it be indefinite and promiscuous, must be regulated and proportioned according to the use of the several dominant grounds, having right thereto proportional to the rent thereof, or the goods it may hold and fodder in winter. And though the pasturage hath been never so long promiscuously used, without any determinate soums, but that all have put to it what they pleased, that cannot be constitute by prescription as a right, being contrary to the very nature and substance of the servitude, whereby the pasturage would be destroyed and unprofitable to all, if not regulable and restrainable to what it might hold, and that by proportion: for though some have been in use to put more goods, and some fewer; yet unless the quantities had been determinate and fixed, others could not be excluded from their proportion; but such as by forty years' forbearance, are wholly excluded therefrom.

It is accustomed in some places, to regulate common pasturage by souming and rouming, which is the determining of the several soums it may hold, by particular proportion of every room of the dominant tenement; but none of the parties interested can compel the rest to divide, seeing it would be frequently to the disadvantage of severals of the parties interested: as when common pasturage is in a common muir, inclosed with a dyke, and so needeth none, at least but one herd for them all, which if it were divided, oft-times the several proportions of most interested, could not be worth a several herd: especially when the property remains in another, though burdened with this servitude: even though the proprietor retain a share in the common pasturage, yet he alone is proprietor; and if any stone or coal were found there, it would belong to him alone: but it is otherwise in the community of the full property, where, after division any party may till and use all acts of property. A servitude of pasturage of a definite number of sheep upon large muirs, was found not to give interest to cause the heritor or tenants soum the same, that the ground might not be overstocked, to the prejudice of the servitude, January 23, 1679, Mr. Alexander Dunlop *contra* L. of Drumelzier [2 Stair 678; 14531]. Where pasturage is constitute upon ground, a part of which hath been ploughed before the constitution, it doth not hinder the master of the ground to plough other places, than what was formerly ploughed, but he may plough as much as he pleaseth; yet so that whenever the ploughed ground lies lee, the pasturage will reach the same, January 20, 1680, E. Southesk *contra* L. Melgum and other heritors about the Muir of Munrewmount [2 Stair 740; M. 7899].

15. The chief and most frequent servitude in Scotland is thirlage, or a restriction of lands to mills, wherein the mill is dominant, and the lands astricted are servient: for as hath been shown before [11, 3, 71, *supra*; IV, 15, 1, *infra*], a mill is a distinct tenement from land, and is not comprehended under the name of part and pertinent thereof, unless there be an erection in a barony, lordship, &c. Mills at first were built, as sometimes they are yet, without any astriction or thirlage, but only to gain by the work thereof, an equivalent hire; and so it is a voluntary personal contract of location and conduction, none being obliged to grind their grain thereat; but such only come as please, and for such an hire as parties do accord: yet these who come to a mill without astriction, and without express paction, are understood thereby to agree to the ordinary multures of corns not astricted, which are called "Outen-town-multures." But now most lands are astricted to certain mills, and for a certain quantity of multure, far beyond the value of the work or grinding of the corns; but upon other considerations; whereby it is a part of the rent of the lands astricted; as when an heritor astricts his own tenants to his own or another's mill, it is a part of their rent; for the more multure they pay, they pay the less rent; and so it is alike to them, whether it be great or small; or otherwise, when a superior gives out lands upon condition of thirlage, the multures are a part of the *reddendo* or price; and it is a general rule, that none can thirle lands but he that is fiar, and hath power of disposal thereof; and therefore astriction, though it be not favourable, but hath the ordinary *odium* that other servitudes have, yet it is not to be accounted an unjust and intolerable bondage.

16. There are many questions about thirlage, which may be reduced to these two heads; first, How thirlage is constitute and instructed. Secondly, How far it is to be extended. As for the first, we shall proceed from the ways

more evident, to these which are more dubious: and first positively, and then negatively. The first and most unquestionable way of constitution of thirlage is, when an heritor thirleth his own lands to his own mill, by consent of his tenants, whereby the multure becomes a part of the rent. Secondly, When an heritor dispones his lands with express condition of thirlage thereof to his mill, or to any other mill. Thirdly, When the heritor of mills or lands feus and dispones the mill with the multure of his own lands *per expressum.* All these ways are uncontroverted constitutions of thirlage, whether they be in an infeftment, contract, bond, or other personal right; for these being clad with possession, are sufficient to constitute a servitude, though the right of the mill, being a separate fee, requireth infeftment. Fourthly, When the heritor of the mill feus or dispones the same with the multures used and wont, though he do not express out of what lands, it is sufficient to constitute a thirlage upon the lands, which were wont to pay in-towns-multure, being then his own lands; or to convey the right of the multures of other lands, being formerly astricted. But where a barony was principally disponed with the mill thereof, and the multures of the mill used and wont; it was not found to extend to the multures of another barony, holden of another superior, though in use to come to that mill, December 11, 1666, Tenants of Dalmortoun *contra* E. Cassils and Whiteford [1 Stair 410; M.5006]. Fifthly, Thirlage of a whole barony is inferred by infeftment in the mill of the barony, with the astricted multures of the said mill, being granted by the heritor, both of the mill and barony, whereby these parts of the barony that were not in use of astricted multures before, were thereby astricted, and that according to the use of the rest of the barony, Had. January 16, 1611, Wilson *contra* Warrack [Hadding-ton, *Fol. Dict.* 11,52; M.10022]; here the constitution bore not, "used and wont," but "multures of the mill generally." The like where the infeftment bore only, "the mill of the barony, with astricted multures," not repeating multures of the barony, Had. July 9, 1611, Moncreif *contra* Borthwick and Pittenween [Not found]. Sixthly, Thirlage is constitute without infeftment, or any writ subscribed by the heritor of the lands astricted, but only by an act or rolment of baron-court, bearing, "the heritor's consent, and forty years' possession conform," Hope, Mills and multures, E. Murray *contra* L. Earls-miln [Hope, *Maj. Pr.* 111,16,25; M.10851]. The like by decreet against the possessors, their master not being called, or consenting, but his bailie enacting them to pay multure with long possession, *ibid.* Mr. Andrew Miln *contra* Falconer [Hope, *Maj. Pr.* 111,16,22; M.10850]. Seventhly, A dry multure was found constitute and instructed by use of payment forty years, without any other adminicle; because it could not be constructed as a free or volun-tary deed, as other multures may be, Hope, Mills and multures, Dog *contra* Maxwel and the Tenants of Preston [Hope, *Maj. Pr.* 111,16,24; M.15963]; July 23, 1675, Sir George Kinaird *contra* Mr. John Drummond [2 Stair 360; M.10862]. Eighthly, Thirlage is inferred of lands within baronies of the King's property to the mills, holden and repute to be the mills of that barony, only as being in use past memory of man to do deeds of thirlage, as paying of multures, laying in of dams, February 5, 1635, Dog *contra* Mushet [Durie 749; M.10853]; January 8, 1662, Stuart *contra* Feuars of Aberlednoch [1 Stair 76; M.10855]; January 14, 1662, Nicolson *contra* Feuars of Tillicoutrie [1 Stair 80; M.10856]. Nor was it found relevant, that the feuars had right *cum molendinis*, in their *tenendas*, which was but past of course in exchequer, in the common clause, as was found in the foresaid case, January 8, 1662, Stuart *contra* Feuars of Aberlednoch [1 Stair 76; M.10855]. The reason hereof is, because the King's right is constitute *jure coronæ*, without infeftment or other writ, which is not requisite, or accustomed to be kept; and therefore, the presumption from long possession is sufficient. Craig, *l. 2, Dieges. 8* relateth it as the opinion of some "that immemorial possession is sufficient to instruct the thirlage of kirk-lands, in the same way as of the King's lands, to which he assenteth not;" and the reason seemeth much to be the same, especially after the Reformation, when the evidents of the Kirk were lost or destroyed: so that long possession hath been sufficient to instruct the right of property of kirk-lands; and may much more instruct this servitude, unless mills and multures had been granted to the feuars anterior to the feu of the mill. But, unquestionably, thirlage is easilier sustained in kirk-lands than others, as it was sustained, being by an infeftment of a mill *cum multuris* generally; and the Bishop's precepts to his tenants to pay their multures to that mill, with long possession, though without consent of the chapter, December 7, 1665, Veitch *contra* Duncan [1 Stair 324; M.15975].

17. As to the negative, 1. Thirlage is not inferred by the use of coming to the mill, and paying multures thereat, though immemorial, even though the multures paid were as great as the thirle multures, March 13, 1635, Gilchrist *contra* Menzies [*Sub nom. Menzies* v *McKay*, Durie 761; M.1815]. The reason hereof is, because such payment is but *voluntatis non necessitatis ;* and therefore, can no more infer a servitude, than they who (past memory) came such a way to a town, were astricted only to come that way: but infeftment in a mill, with the astricted multures of such lands *per expressum*, and forty years' possession of paying the insucken multures, was found to constitute the thirlage, though the feuars were infeft *cum molendinis*, before the feu of the mill, and sometimes went to other mills, which not being frequent, and for some whole years, was found but clandestine, and such as occurs in all thirlages, and no legal interruption, June 29, 1665, Heritors of the Mill of Kythick *contra* Feuars [1 Stair 291; M.11292]. 2. Thirlage is not inferred, because the lands are a part of the superior's barony, having a mill of the barony, where the vassal's infeftment contains *cum molendinis et multuris*, or a feu-duty *pro omni alio onere*, or such a feu-duty allenarly, November 26, 1631, Oliphant *contra* E. Marshal [Durie 603; M.15969]. But where the baron's disposition contained not these clauses his giving a subaltern infeftment of a party of his barony, which part was thirled to the mill before, it was not found liberate but continued thirled to the mill of the barony, though the mill and

multures of the barony were disponed thereafter to another, July 17, 1629, L. Newlistoun *contra* Inglis [Durie 464; M. 10852, 15968]. For, if the vassal had acquired that part of the barony with the multures, it would have been expressed particularly or generally, seeing thereby the seller behoved to diminish the rental of his mill [11, 7, 24, *infra*]. This decision is contrary to the former, for this charter bore a feu *pro omni alio onere*. 3. Thirlage of a barony or any part thereof, was not inferred by a disposition or infeftment of a mill granted by the baron, though it be the only mill of the barony, seeing he expressed it not to be so, nor expressed any lands nor the multures thereof, but only disponed the mill with the pertinents, July 12, 1621, Douglas *contra* E. Murray [Durie 2; M. 10851]. In this case, there were several acts of court thirling the tenants, and long possession; but the acts were only by a bailie, without warrant or consent of the heritor, albeit clad with forty years' possession. Neither was thirlage inferred by a charter of a mill with the multure used and wont, and long possession, though it was the mill of the barony, July 13, 1632, E. Mortoun *contra* Feuars of Muckart [Durie 646; M. 10853]. But a decreet against the tenants for astricted multures, and immemorial possession, was found to constitute thirlage to the mill of the barony, albeit the defender was infeft *cum molendinis*, prior to the infeftment of the heritor of the mill, and did sometimes go to other mills, but clandestinely, and sometimes was brought back by force, June 24, 1665, Coll. Montgomery *contra* Wallace and Others [1 Stair 286; M. 10857], which did not import interruption by clandestine abstraction, but by paying no multure, at least for a whole year. 4. Thirlage is not inferred by any deed of tenants, possessors, wadsetters, liferenters, or any other but the fiar; and therefore, there will be no process sustained against the tenants for multures, unless the fiar be called, February 9, 1628, L. Wardess *contra* L. Dunkincie [Durie 343; M. 2201]: or at least, that there have been prior decreets wherein he was called, constituting the thirlage; and all decreets and acts otherwise are null by exception, if quarrelled within prescription. 5. Thirlage of lands to another man's mill, doth not infer a thirlage of the teinds of these lands, though acquired by the heritor who thirled the lands, July 7, 1635, L. Innerweek *contra* Hamiltons [Durie 771; M. 15972]. The like *in molendino regio*, where no writ was shown, but possession, to constitute the thirlage, which was found not to extend to the teinds, January 8, 1662, Stuart *contra* Feuars of Aberledno [1 Stair 76; M. 10855]. The like where the clause of thirlage bore *omnium granorum crescentium super terris suis*: here the heritor of the lands thirled had no right to the teind, Spots. Mills and multures, L. Wauchton *contra* Hume of Foord [Spotiswoode 209; M. 15971]. The like where the clause in a charter, granted by an abbot to his feuars, bore the astriction *omnium granorum*, which was found to extend to the teinds which then belonged to the abbot; and the teind was found thirled, unless a feu-duty was paid both for stock and teind, January 21, 1681, Grierson *contra* Gordon of Spado [2 Stair 839; M. 10871]. Nor will the exception of teind be sustained in mills belonging to kirk-men, having right to both stock and teind.

18. The next point proposed, was the effect and extent of thirlage, being constitute, which is exceeding various; for clearing whereof, advert, that thirlage is either introduced and instructed by custom and prescription, or by paction and writ; when it is by prescription and custom, it is wholly regulate by custom, and the heritor of the mill and his tenant can get no more, and will get no less than they instruct to be their ancient custom; which holds though thirlage be constitute by writ generally, with the multures, sequels, and services used and wont, for then also custom must rule it; and the heritor of the mill will not be put to prove what the custom was before that writ, though it relate to custom past, but long custom present will be sufficient presumption and proof of what was that preterite custom, if the contrary cannot be proven; and though it should be proven, yet forty years' possession will alter the case, and either increase the servitude or the freedom. If the servitude be constitute by writ, special regard is had to the tenor of the writ, which therefore varieth thirlage accordingly; so thirlage simply expressed in writ, without mention of all grain growing upon the ground, was found to extend to all corns growing thereupon, abstracted to other mills, or sold, though they had paid no multure past memory for sold corns, June 26, 1635, L. of Wauchtoun *contra* Hoom of Foord [Durie 768; M. 11230].

19. A clause of thirlage bearing, *Una cum multuris omnium terrarum intra parochiam*, was found not to extend to other corns brought in, and not growing within the sucken, Hope, Mills and multures, Murray *contra* tenants of Drumsei [Hope, *Maj.Pr.* 111,16,20; M. 15962]. A clause of thirlage, thirling an heritor's tenants to another man's mill, and all the tenants' grain growing upon the land, found not to extend to that heritor's farmbear, whether delivered to him, or sold by him to his tenants or others, but that the same was multure-free, but yet was thirled, and behoved to come to the mill, and pay the small duties only, Hope, Mills and multures, Lo. Keith *contra* Keith [Possibly Hope, *Maj.Pr.* 111,16,22; M. 10850] which is also observed, with this further, that *invecta et illata* were not thereby thirled, Spots. *de servitutibus* [Not found]. A clause of thirlage *omnium granorum crescentium*, was found not to extend to the heritor's farms, who had so thirled his lands, not being ground at any other mill, but sold, or otherwise made use of: neither to corns not growing within the thirle, though tholing fire and water, or garnelled there, July 11, 1621, Keith *contra* Tennents of Peterhead [Durie 1; M. 15964]. A clause of thirlage granted by a town to a mill, expressing *invecta et illata*, found to be extended to all corns kilned or steeped within the thirle, though not brought to the mill, nor use made thereof within the thirle, Spots. *de servitute*, Ruthven *contra* Cuthbert of Drakies [Possibly *Cuthbert* v *Inverness*, Durie 840; M. 15973]. Thirlage of *invecta et illata* constitute by a town's charter, found effectual as to the grain that grew in the thirle of that mill, and was liable for a greater multure, as *grana crescentia*, so that these corns being bought by the town, fell to pay both the ordinary multure, as growing in the thirle, and a lesser multure by a several thirlage by the town's charter, thirl-

ing *omnia invecta et illata* in their town, to that same mill; seeing the town might shun the inconvenience of double multure, by buying only corns which grew not in the thirle of that mill, December 11, 1678, Sir Andrew Ramsay *contra* the Town of Kirkaldie [2 Stair 655; M. 15981].

20. In this case *invecta et illata* was found to import malt made within the liberties of the town, or brewed within the same, but not to meal where they did not buy the corn, but bought the meal, though it was baken in the town, in respect it was so proven to be the custom, November 24, 1680, *inter eosdem* [2 Stair 805; M. 15984]. But the quantity of abstract multures being referred to the townsmen's oaths, they were not found obliged to depone, that they had paid the whole multures of years long bygone, but only if they knew and remembered, that any part of it was not paid, and what that part of it was, December 12, 1679, *inter eosdem* [2 Stair 722; M. 9409]; but ordinarily, *invecta et illata*, or tholing fire and water, is only interpreted of steeping and kilning, but not of baking or brewing. A clause in feuars' charters thirling them to the superior's mills of such a parish, whereof there were four, was found not to put it in the option of the feuars to go to any of the four, but to keep to the particular mill, to which they were accustomed, in respect the mills had several suckens, and the feuars were in use forty years to pay multures, and do all services thereto, as was found   1663, as to the mill of Catharine [Not found]. And the like found as to the mill of Dalsangan, another mill of Mauchlein, about the same time [Not found]. Thirlage being constitute, or determined by custom, doth ordinarily carry, "Not only multures of the grain growing within the sucken, but those that thole fire and water within the same, by being kilned and steeped, and in some places brewn within the same." The quantity of multure, if it be not determined by writ, is determined by use of payment of the barony or sucken, though a part thereof in question paid less formerly, which did only liberate them from bygones, Had. January 17, 1611, Neilson *contra* Tenants of Innermesson [Haddington, *Fol. Dict.* 11, 468; M. 15961].

21. Besides the multures, thirlage is extended to sequels, which is understood to be the knaveship, bannock, or lock payable besides the multures, to the millers and their servants for their service, according to the use of the several mills, though these be not expressed, March 22, 1628, Adamson of Braco *contra* Tennents of Shallie [Auchinleck MS; M. 15966].

22. Thirlage also carries service to the mill, "as carrying home of mill-stones, upholding the dams, water-gates, and of the mill-house," which are diverse services and regulated according to the customs of the several mills. The thirlage constitute by infeftment of a mill, *cum multuris et sequelis*, found to give right to the ordinary mill-services to the mill-dam and mill-stones, [without proving possession,] unless by paction or prescription, the same were taken away, February 27, 1668, Maitland *contra* Lesly [1 Stair 537; M. 15978]. It was found, that an heritor of a mill being infeft, and in possession of the mill, with the multures of the lands in question, *nominatim*, he hath the

benefit of a possessory judgment, with seven years' possession, and so it will stand and be effectual, till it be reduced, notwithstanding an anterior infeftment, *cum molendinis* [IV, 3, 47; IV, 17, 2-3; IV, 22, 5 and 8; IV, 26, 3 and 15; IV, 45, 17, *infra*], June 28, 1636, Maxwel *contra* Maxwel [Durie 810; M. 10639].

23. Thirlage also is esteemed by some to carry this privilege, that the heritor of the mill may, *brevi manu*, cast down any other mill bigged within the thirle; (But Craig's opinion is in the contrary, in the forecited place [11, 8, 8],) and it was found that a mill might not be demolished summarily where the mill so bigged had gone fifteen days, Spots. Husband and wife, L. Ludquharn *contra* E. Marishal [Spotiswoode 154; M. 13982]. But it may be hindered while the new mill is in building, and may be civilly interrupted, *nunciatione novi operis*. In respect of the favour of going mills, which are not to be destroyed, for the public use of the country; from which ground it is, that the water-gang of a mill, passing through an heritor's land, was not suffered to be stopped, though it was without consent or prescription, not being to his prejudice, Hope, Mills, L. of Bass *contra* L. of Balgowan [Hope, *Maj. Pr.* III, 16, 23]. But though mills may not be stopped *brevi manu*, yet building a mill within the thirle on pretence to get voluntary multure, and that the builder will still bring his own corns to the other mill is unwarrantable, and contrary to the common custom of destroying querns, which might have the same pretence: nor could it be known what were clandestinely ground at the new mill, within the old thirle; but Halyards being building a mill near to Breast-mill, who craved summarily to stop him, by supplication to the Lords, they did refuse to stop, because it was not clear that his lands were thirled, July 29, 1673 [*Sub nom. Dundas* v *Skene*, 2 Stair 225; M. 5008].

Thirlage hath also this effect in some places, that when any person is apprehended abstracting corn, the horse and corn may be seized upon *brevi manu*, and the corns confiscated to the miller; and Craig relates in the forecited place [11, 8, 10], that it is the ordinary custom in France, that corns carrying out of the thirle are escheat to the Lord, and may be seized summarily. It is also related by Craig *l. 2. Dieges* 8, [11, 8, 9], out of the statutes of King William, that there ought to be a master and two servants in every mill, sworn to be faithful to the master of the ground, and his men, and that the common multure, not determined by infeftment, is the twentieth grain; and that all grain that shall be set down upon the ground of another thirle, shall pay multure there; and that when a horse carrying grain out of the thirle is taken, the grain is escheat to the miller, and the horse to the master; and that he who removes from the thirle, shall have his seed multure-free: these are most part over-ruled by custom, as hath been before shown. This far I find it amongst our customs, that the spuilzie of a horse was elided, because he was seized upon, taking corns out of the thirle to another mill, as was the custom of that place, and that after carrying back thereof, the horse was offered that same night, January 22, 1635, Menzies *contra* Mackie [Durie 743; M. 1815].

Thirlage *omnium granorum crescentium* upon such a tenement, found to extend to the mains, July 29, 1673, Dundas of Breast-Miln *contra* Skeen of Halyards [2 Stair 225; M. 5008].

24. It remains that we consider how thirlage being constitute, is destitute, or taken off; and that is in the like manner as it was constitute, either by prescription, whereby liberty is recovered to the thirled lands, which needs no positive act to deny the multures, but simply forbearance to lift or seek them is enough; or otherwise by any discharge or renunciation, without further solemnity, for in that way also it is constitute [11, 7, 4, *supra*]; but the most ordinary way of taking off thirlage, is by granting a charter, containing mills and multures in the *tenendas*, which was not found good as to the King's feuars, because passed in exchequer without notice, as the common style, January 8, 1662, Stuart *contra* Feuars of Aberledno [1 Stair 76; M. 10855], which is more evident, when mills and multures are in the dispositive clause: it hath the like effect when the mill and multure is disponed to one party, and by a prior disposition or infeftment, the same lands which were of old of the thirle, are granted to the vassals thereof, *cum molendinis et multuris;* for thereby the posterior infeftment of the mill and multures, is *a non habente potestatem*, and ineffectual, November 26, 1631, Oliphant *contra* E. Marischal [Durie 603; M. 15969]. Which is clear when mills and multures are in the dispositive clause, but if only in the *tenendas*, it is dubious whether the meaning be of mills, if any be on the ground disponed, as in all the other clauses, which are ordinarily repeated therewith, such as dove-cotes, cony-gairs, &c. and so the vassal having continued to pay astricted multures seven years after the charter, the clause *cum molendinis et multuris*, did not infer liberation, yet freed from bygones, as in a dubious case, January   1672, Lo. Newbyth *contra* La. Whitekirk [Possibly *sub anno* 1692; M. 15989].

25. [This section is omitted in the 1693 edition, but the substance of it is stated in the list of titles of sections and the next section is numbered 26. The omission was probably accidental and the text is, as in previous editions, supplied from the first edition.] In thirlage there is only allowance or deduction of seed and horse-corn, but nothing for expense of labouring, January 14, 1662, Nicolson [1 Stair 80; M. 10856].

26. Thirlage by a vassal was not found effectual against the superior, when the lands fell in his hands by ward, unless the superior had consented, December 11, 1666, E. of Cassils *contra* Tennents of Dalmortoun [1 Stair 410; M. 5006]. Thirlage by a vassal's charter, found not to make him liable for the abstraction of his tenants, but only the tenants themselves, December 10, 1667, E. of Cassils *contra* the Sheriff of Galloway [1 Stair 491; M. 15977].

27. If it be questioned whether multure be due when the mill is unable to work by frost, breaking of the dam, or otherwise, it must be distinguished, that if the insufficiency of the mill, or the want of servants be through the fault of the heritor, or his miller, these of the thirle may go to other mills, and they will not only be free of small duties, but they may retain for the repara-

tion of their damage, such out-sucken multures as they paid at the mill they went to; but if the insufficiency be by accident, without the miller's fault, they may go elsewhere with what is necessary for the *interim*, and will be free of the small duties thereof, but of no part of the multure; because, as hath been shown before, multures are now a distinct rent, and are not as the hire of the work, but besides the multure, the small duties are the hire; and therefore, the miller's failzie can only take away these small duties, and was so found, February 9, 1666, Heretrix of Johnsmill *contra* Feuars [1 Stair 352; M. 15975].

Title 8. Teinds, Where, of Benefices, Stipends, Presentation, Collation, Institution, Tacks, Annats, and Patronage

TEINDS being a burden, affecting lands and the profits thereof; and being also a distinct right from the lands, do most fitly fall under consideration here, and that, either as a servitude subjoined to the preceding servitudes, or as a several right, it requires the same order.

1. Teinds do affect all intromitters with the stock and teind jointly, or with the teind severally [1, 13, 16, *supra*; 11, 8, 23, *infra*], but though they be valued, they are not *debita fundi*, affecting singular successors, for which the ground can be poinded, Feb. 20, 1662, E. of Callender *contra* Monro [1 Stair 103; M. 15632]. Neither do they affect the present heritor, while a life-renter possesseth, June 24, 1663, Menzies *contra* L. of Glenurchie [1 Stair 193; M. 14788].

2. [In the 1693 edition there is no new paragraph, nor paragraph number,

between paragraphs 1 and 3. All editors concur in thinking that paragraph 2 should commence at this point]. Teind, as the word denoteth, signifieth the tenth of that which is teinded; and besides the civil decimations that have been imposed by sovereigns upon their subjects as a tribute for defraying of public charges, there have been anciently and frequently teinds granted for sacred and pious uses; so Abraham gave to Melchisedec the teind of the spoil of his enemies, Gen. xiv. 20. Jacob voweth to God also the tenth of all that God should give him, Gen. xxviii. 22. And it is evident that God appointed the tenths of Israel for the Levites, whom he had set apart for himself, who were to give a tenth thereof to the priests, who served at the altar, Numb. xviii. 26, and 28. The teinds did so continue till the alteration of the Jewish church. The heathens also did consecrate their teinds to their idols, and paid them to their priests: Thus Plinius, cap. 14. and 19. observeth, and Herodote observeth in his first book the like of Cyrus.

3. Aristus, Bishop of Rome, was the first who divided the ministerial charge by parishes, the church before not being so distributed to the several ministers; this order being so convenient, that by appropriation of a fixed pastor to a certain flock, no pastor might be idle, and no flock neglected, it hath run over the Christian world, and the teinds of these parishes have been paid to the pastors and ministers of the church.

4. From these and the like grounds, most of Papists, and some Protestant divines, have concluded teinds to be *jure divino*, as being institute and consecrate by God himself, having a moral and perpetual foundation, that these who are set apart from worldly affairs, to the service of God, should have a competent livelihood from these for whom they serve; but the determination of the *quota*, to be the tenth part rather than any other proportion, is a positive law that God manifested, and was observed before the written word; and was retained by the heathens, even after they had deviated from the true God: but most of the Protestant divines hold teinds to be the voluntary dedication and consecration of men for pious uses, and to have continued in a tenth part from the example of Abraham, the father of the faithful, and of the divine constitution, in the Judicial Law; but there is now no divine moral precept in the word for teinds, of which there is no mention in the New Testament, even where the maintenance of ministers is purposely spoken to; but only that these who "serve at the altar should live by the altar; that these who sow spiritual things, should reap temporal things;" which doth hold forth a moral duty of recompence, to provide a competent livelihood for these who are separate from the world for our cause, but doth not infer a tenth part, or any other determinate proportion but what is convenient.

5. Teinds are defined by the Canonists, to be a tenth part of all profits and increase; and they are of three kinds, personal, predial, and mixed: personal are the teinds of the profit of personal industry, as by trading, negotiation, artifice, science, &c. Predial are of the natural fruits of the ground or water. Mixed are of the industrial fruits of the ground only.

6. But our custom alloweth of no personal teinds, and of the predial and mixed, such only which have been in use, according to the custom of the several places: such are teind-fish, for which the buyers of the fish were found liable, because of that custom past memory, Feb. 15, 1631, Bryce, Semple and Schaw *contra* Brown [*Sub nom. Tacksmen to the Bishop of the Isles* v *Brown*, Durie 569; M.15631], but where the fishers were forty years in possession without teind, in such a bay, it was found sufficient to liberate them, Nov. 24, 1665, Bishop of the Isles *contra* the L. of Greenock and others [1 Stair 312; M. 10758]: also in other places, there is no teind of fishes; in some places, hay, staigs, swine, lint, hemp are teinded, in other places not, but generally victual is teinded, and stirks, lambs, wool and milk.

The vicarage teinds are local, according to the custom of the benefice or parish: and therefore, was sustained for the vicarage of salt, and so much out of each loom; but not upon thirteen years' possession, but only upon prescription by forty years' possession, Nov. 29, 1678, Birnie *contra* the E. of Nithisdail [2 Stair 649; M.2489]; yea in the same parish there was found diversity of the vicarage, some places having no vicarage of cows, and other places paying vicarage of milk, and wool for sheep; and other places paying vicarage of hay, geese and grice, July 7, 1677. Parson of Prestonhaugh *contra* his Parishioners [2 Stair 535; M. 10761].

7. Some lands also by long custom are teind-free, as temple lands, being out of use of payment of teinds for fifty years, were found free for all time thereafter, Hope, Teinds, E. of Wigtoun *contra* La. Torwood [Hope, *Maj. Pr.* III,18,26; M.15716]. Glebes and manses are also teind-fee. And the teinds of lands belonging to the Cystercian order, Hospitalers and Templars, were teind-free, and so continue in their feuars, though the privilege was only as to what these orders laboured themselves; yet the teind was found to belong to their many feuars, for what the feuars themselves labour, July 15, 1664, Crawford *contra* L. of Prestongrange [1 Stair 215; M. 15633].

8. Teinds were prohibited to be set in feu to laymen, by the Lateran council, or any way to be alienated from the church, though church-lands might be set feu; these being accounted but the temporality, and the teinds the spirituality, as flowing from a spiritual ground, or divine right.

9. Teinds are also acknowledged with us to be the patrimony of the kirk, Parl. 1567, cap. 10 [A.P.S. III,24,c.10], and they are not annexed to the Crown, as the temporality of benefices are. Parl. 1587, cap. 29 [A.P.S. III, 431,c.8].

10. Yet *decimæ inclusæ* are here excepted, for these are feued with the stock, and can be only such, as time out of mind, have gone along with the stock, and never have been drawn nor separate; and therefore are so ordinarily exprest, *decimæ inclusæ nunquam antea separatæ;* and therefore, such are presumed to have been feued out with the stock, before the Lateran Council, and so consistent with the canons: but if it can be proven that once they were separate by churchmen; though they had right both to stock and teind, and

were feued with teinds included, they are not true *decimæ inclusæ*, which no church-man could feu after the said council; neither can the king constitute feus *de novo, cum decimis inclusis;* so that these teinds included, are estimate as no teinds, long custom being sufficient to make lands teind-free; and therefore they have never come in with teinds or benefices, in any burden affecting teinds by law, as ministers' stipends, &c.

11. About the time of the abolition of Popery in Scotland, the Popish clergy did grant more frequently long tacks of their teinds: the king also gave donatives of teinds and erected them with church-lands into baronies and lordships, so that there remained little of them, no way able to entertain the ministers; and much controversy was like to arise about them, till all parties having interest submitted and surrendered the same to the king, 1. By the general surrender of erections and teinds, 2. By a particular surrender of some beneficed persons, 3. Of the bishops, 4. Of the burghs; Whereupon the king upon the 2d of September 1629, ordered the whole matter to this effect; that the whole teinds should be consolidate with the stock, being always affected with competent stipends to ministers, &c.; and that therefore, the titular or the tacksman of the teinds, having perpetual or heritable right, should sell the same to the heritors, at nine years' purchase; and where the right was temporary or defective, the price thereof should be made less accordingly.

12. And for that effect, a commission was granted for valuation of teinds, and for disposing thereof as aforesaid, and for modifying and localling stipends to the ministers: and his Majesty reserved to himself only a yearly annuity of ten shilling Scots out of each boll of wheat and barley, eight shilling of pease and rye, six shilling of oats, where the boll rendered a boll of meal, and proportionally less, where it rendered less: these decreets were ratified and prosecuted by several Acts of Parliament, 1633, cap. 8 [A.P.S. v, 23, c. 8], 15 [A.P.S. v, 32, c. 15], 17 [A.P.S. v, 34, c. 17], 19 [A.P.S. v, 35, c. 19], and 1641, cap. 30 [A.P.S. v, 470, c. 56], Parl. 1647, cap. 32 [A.P.S. vi, 272, c. 231]. Parl. 1649, cap. 46 [Probably c. 45; A.P.S. vi, 430, c. 221], Parl. 1661, cap. 61 [A.P.S. vii, 48, c. 67], but there was an exception in the Act 1633, cap. 19. [A.P.S. v, 35, c. 19] which ordained the teinds of all abbacies and other benefices [to be valued], except the teinds pertaining to bishopricks and other benefices, which fell not under the submission; in which there is a clause, that the saids bishops and beneficed persons should enjoy the fruits and rents of their several benefices, as they were possessed by them, the time of the said submission; and therefore, where they did draw the teinds by the space of fifteen years before the year 1628, or at least seven years of the said fifteen years, or had the same in rentalled bolls, they should so continue and not be valued; which provision is repeated, Parl. 1. Ch. II. Sess. 3. cap. 9 [1662, c. 9; A.P.S. vii, 386, c. 25]. But all this proved for the most part ineffectual for compelling titulars and tacksmen of teinds to sell their interest in other men's teinds to the proper heritors; because these commissioners allowing them their option to allocate whom they pleased, for the payment

of the minister's stipend, few ventured to pursue them for vendition, lest they might be excluded by allocation, which they were willing to avert by giving the dearest rates: but if the stipend had been laid proportionally upon all, the king's favour had been more effectual and equal. But buying of teinds being thereby retarded, the great work of these commissioners was to value, modify, and allocate stipends. When the tack-duties of the tacksmen were not found sufficient to make up the stipend, the commission did increase the tack-duties upon the tacksmen, and in recompense thereof, prorogated their tacks; whereby these, though at first being but slender rights, by many nineteen years' prorogations became little less than heritable rights; this alteration the commission made, as being a commission of Parliament, owning then a greater power than other judicatures.

13. The annuities of teinds not being annexed to the Crown, were disponed by King Charles the First to James Livingstoun, a groom of his bed-chamber, to be uplifted by him till he was satisfied of the sum of 10000 pounds sterling, which right was purchased by the E. of Lowdoun, and did receive many stops, and took little effect till the King's return, who gave a commission to the late E. of Lowdoun, to transact for the bygone annuities, and to dispone them with the full right thereof in all time coming; and his disposition with consent of two members of exchequer was declared sufficient rights to the buyers, and were appointed to be recorded in the books of exchequer, that the sums gotten therefore might be known, and imputed unto the sum for which the right to the annuity was granted; according to which, many have bought their annuities. That commission did also give power to value the teinds, that the annuity might be known, and to uplift and compone for the bygone and the current annuities until they were sold; and accordingly collectors were appointed by the E. of Lowdoun in several places of the kingdom. The like commission was renewed to James E. of Lowdoun, after his father's death, who did make some progress therein, in the same way as his father had done: but a stop was put thereto by the King's warrant, *in anno* 1674, which doth yet still continue; and with this stop, by a proclamation from the King, all the arrears of the annuity before the year 1660, were simply discharged.

14. The rule prescribed by the King, for valuation of teinds, to fix them to a constant yearly duty, was this; that where the teinds were severally known from the stock, and set by tack or rental, the same should be also valued severally, deducing a fifth part for the ease of the heritor; because frequently the churchmen had drawn the rate of the teind above the just value, by their stocked and rental bolls: but where the stock and teind were not severally known, the fifth part of the rent was decerned to be for the teind.

15. Teinds by the canon law, were all constitute into benefices, which follow the several offices in the Roman church, which were either prelacies or inferior to prelacies: prelacies were these who had chapters and convents, and therefore, one had the prelacy or preference amongst the rest of their col-

leagues, such were archbishops, bishops, abbots, priors, prioresses: Abbots and priors had the prelacy amongst the monks, of several monasteries, as the prioresses had over the nuns. There was also some few monasteries, which kept the name of monasteries or ministries, and the prelate was called minister, of which there are four in Scotland; the minister of Fale, Peebles, Scotland-wall, and the Trinity-friars of Aberdeen: next unto these, were the provosts of collegiate kirks, instituted for singing of mass, specially for their founders and patrons; these provosts governed their prebends, who were skilful in music, and had their several stalls in which they sat, for the more orderly singing of their parts of music, from which these prebends were designed of the first, second, or other stall. Some of the college-kirks were founded by the King and great families: the Chapel-Royal is a collegiate church, governed by the Dean of the Chapel; which office is now annexed to the Bishop of Dumblain, under whom are the prebends of the Chapel-Royal. The E. of Fife founded the college-kirk of Kirkheugh; the E. of March founded the college-kirk of Dunbar; the E. of Bothwel, the college-kirk of Crightoun; the E. of Lennox, the college-kirk of Dumbarton; the E. of Ross, the college-kirk of Tain. Other families erected chapels, officiated by one chaplain: inferior to these prelacies, were parsons, vicars, chaplains, prebendars; these had patrons whose advice and protection they used instead of a chapter and convent which prelacies had.

16. The general rule by the canon law was, that *decimæ debentur parocho de jure*, the parsonage teinds to the parson; the vicarage, or small teind to the vicar, and where no other appeared to instruct a right, the teinds were *ipso jure*, due to parsons and vicars: it was so found, that even the King's gift was not sufficient to carry the right of teinds from the incumbents, unless the mortification thereof to any other office or benefice, or possession thereof by another office, were instructed, June 27, 1665, Ferguson *contra* Stuart of Ascog [1 Stair 287; M. 7949]. The bishops and such prelacies as had *curam animarum*, had chapters; and the priors, prioresses, abbots, &c. had convents, whose consent in all matters of benefices being chapterly convened, was necessary; and in evidence thereof, the seals of the chapter or convent were appended. Vicars were either such as erew substitute by parsons and other clerks, or such as had a distinct office; and therefore were not changeable by their constituents, and were called vicars of cure *cum cura animarum*, or perpetual vicars: chaplains were clerks having *curam*, institute for their accommodation, who were far from ordinary churches; and therefore were erected upon the expenses of the founders, who were therefore patrons; and of all other patrons supposed to have greatest interest in these benefices; so that after the Reformation, these chaplanries and prebendaries were declared to return and be disposed upon by their patrons, to bursers of colleges, Parl. 1592, cap. 162 [Act 1592, c. 161; A.P.S. 111, 586, c. 89]. Likewise prebendars were such as had a *prebendam* or a benefice, which was at first a common name but was made special, by use to these clerks who had no other special name.

The intent of the constitution of these offices, as aforesaid, was mainly to secure the benefice and patrimony of the church against dilapidation, the incumbents being administrators, or at best liferenters, who might otherwise have wronged their successors, in favours of the friends and relations; and therefore prelates could do nothing of moment without consent of their chapters, or convents, or other beneficed persons, without consent of their patrons. Though these offices were abolished by the Reformation, there was no other way fallen upon for managing of benefices, but by giving secular persons the designations of these offices, who therefore were called Titulars; because they had the naked title without the office of bishops, priors, abbots, provosts, &c. who, in lieu of the consent of the chapters and convents, appended only the common seal thereof; and when bishops were set up again, and chapters appointed for them, the consent of the major part thereof was requisite, with the seal; yet it was not necessary that they should be chapterly convened, Parl. 1606, cap. 3 [A.P.S. IV, 324, c. 71].

17. Before the Reformation, according to the canon law, there were these restraints upon beneficed persons, in order to their benefices: as to teinds, they could grant no feus at all, neither could they grant tacks without consent of the chapter, or convents of prelates; the members whereof were found sufficiently proven by feus, and presentations granted by prelates, and subscribed by these persons as members of the convent, without necessity to show the erection or foundation, or these persons admission; and that there were no more members of the convent than these subscribing the several writs, June 24, 1623, L. Drumlanrig *contra* Maxwell of Hills [Durie 65; M. 7943]; Spots. Kirkmen, Parson of Kinkel *contra* L. Coulter [Spotiswoode 191]. The consent of most part of the prebendars was necessary, not reckoning the prebendars that were out of the country; this was also observed by the Earl Haddington, March 10, 1612, *inter eosdem* [Probably *Maxwell* v *Drumlanrig*, March 14, 1622; Haddington MS; M. 7941]. The consent of the chapter was found not only necessary to the deeds of the prelate, but to the deeds of the members of the chapter; and so a tack set by a dean, though of teinds mortified to a college, whereof the principal was dean, was found null for want of the chapter's consent, Spots. Kirkmen, College of Aberdeen *contra* Lord Frazer [Spotiswoode 186]; where he observes, that the same was found twice before; yet it was not found necessary to the tacks of the several members of the new-erected chapter of St. Andrews, whereof many ministers were of laick patronage, Hope, Teinds, Tenants of Craighall *contra* Mr. Walter Kinninmont [Hope, *Maj. Pr.* III, 18, 38]. But the old privilege of the Bishop of St. Andrews, which is yet continued, is, that the appending of his seal is sufficient, both for him and the chapter, without necessity of their subscription, Parl. 1606, cap. 3 [A.P.S. IV, 324, c. 71].

18. Secondly, Beneficed persons were restrained from setting tacks of their teinds, even with consent of their chapters, with diminution of their rental; and therefore ministers provided to benefices, granting pensions,

tacks or feus of their benefices, with diminution of the rental, as they found them at their entry, the same are declared null, and they to be deprived, Parl. 1581, cap. 101 [A.P.S. III, 211, c. 3]. And also all beneficed persons were ordained to find caution to leave their benefices in as good case as they found them; and all tacks, provisions, or changing of victual into money, in diminution of the rental which was at their entry, declared null, Parl. 1585, cap. 11 [A.P.S. III, 376, c. 5]. But by Act of Parl. 1606, cap. 3 [A.P.S. IV, 324, c. 71], it is declared lawful to the bishops to set as many tacks of the fruits and duties belonging to their benefice, either short or long tacks as they please, and for as many years as they think expedient; which may subsist of the law, without restraint or limitation of any time; which tack being once set, shall be accounted the rental, not to be diminished thereafter; but there is no restriction in relation to any rental, preceding the said act: but it is only recommended to the bishops to set to a competent avail, near the worth; but by the Act of Parl. 1617, cap. 4 [A.P.S. IV, 534, c. 4], bishops are prohibited to set tacks for longer space than nineteen years: and all pensions or tacks of the thirds of benefices, which then belonged to the Church, set in diminution of the rental, paid at the first assumption of the benefice, were declared null, Parl. 1597, cap. 244 [A.P.S. IV, 132, c. 11].

19. Thirdly, Inferior beneficed persons could set no longer tacks of any part of their benefice, than three years, without consent of the patron, Parl. 1594, cap. 200 [Act 1594, c. 203; A.P.S. IV, 64, c. 10], which was extended to deeds done by provosts and prebendars, though having a resemblance with prelacies, seeing the patron hath so great interest, Hope, Patron, L. Drumlanrig *contra* L. Cowhill and others [Hope, *Maj. Pr.* III, 14, 26]. And beneficed persons below prelates are discharged to set tacks of any part of their benefice, longer than their life, and five years after; and if these tacks be not registrate in a book kept by the Clerk-Register for that effect, within forty days after the date thereof, they are null, Parl. 1617, cap. 4 [A.P.S. IV, 534, c. 4]. Yet in these long tacks the consent of the patron is still necessary; and therefore a tack of teinds, without consent of the patron, was only found valid as to three years, and null as to the rest of the years contained therein, July 18, 1668, Mr. George Johnstoun *contra* Parishioners of Howden [1 Stair 555; M. 6848]. And a tack of teinds for more than three years without consent of the patron, was sustained by his subsequent consent, having accepted a right to the tack, and obtained prorogation thereupon, Jan. 19, 1669, E. Athol *contra* Robertson of Strouan [1 Stair 582; M. 7804].

20. A tack of teinds set by an university for a definite time with an obligement to renew the same in all time thereafter, was found not effectual after the definite time, though the same rent was received for years after, which was not sustained as an homologation, but as a tacit relocation, July 13, 1669, Old College of Aberdeen *contra* Town of Aberdeen [1 Stair 635; M. 2533].

21. To come to the condition of teinds, as they now stand; a great part of them is in the hands of the heritors, to whom the stock belongs; a part also is

in the hands of Titulars and Lords of Erection [11,8,35, *infra*], and tacksmen having right to other heritors' teinds, who have ordinarily prorogation of their tacks; the rest belongs to ministers, or royal burghs, for the maintenance of their ministers, colleges or hospitals. Of these teinds, which are not in the heritors' own hand, some are drawn in kind, or *ipsa corpora*, some are in old stocked rental-bolls, some are in tack or use of payment, and others under valuation. We need say nothing as to teinds that are in the hands of heritors to whom the stock belongs, about which there can be little controversy except in the case of new erections or augmentations; for teinds, through whatsoever hands they pass, carry always along with them, as a burden affecting them, competent stipends for the ministers who are, or shall be erected [11,8,30, *infra*]. Neither is there any other debate concerning teinds orderly valued, being thereby liquidate and clear; nor concerning these teinds which are in tack, during the tack, further than hath been said before of the requisites for setting such tacks. It remains to consider drawn teinds, and rentalled teind-bolls, and then to conclude with the present interest of ministers and patrons.

22. As to the drawn teinds, the manner thereof is prescribed, Parl. 1617, cap. 9 [A.P.S. IV, 541, c. 9], that the possessors may require the teind-master thrice, once for teinding of croft or in-field corn; next, for teinding barley; thirdly, for out-field corn, within eight days after the shearing of these three several kinds of corn, or at least, when the same are shorn till about a tenth part, to come and teind the same within four days; and the teind-master, if he dwell not within the parish, is ordained to have a servant for teinding, and to intimate his name publicly the last Sabbath of July, or first Sabbath of August: so that upon requisition to the teind-master personally, or at his dwelling-place in the parish, or to his servant designed, the possessor might proceed to the teinding of his own corns; and if the teind-master resided not in the parish, nor had any servant designed, or if upon intimation they appeared not, the possessor might, before witnesses, teind his own corns, and was only obliged to keep the teind skaithless for eight days after the separation; but if any meddled with the teinds any other way, he is liable for wrongous intromission.

23. Spuilzie of teinds is only competent in the case of violence, where the teind-master being in present possession and use of drawing the teind, doth orderly come to teind, and is debarred by force; or when the teind-master, being in use that same year, or the former year, to draw the teind, any other intromitted therewith. The former act is like ejection, and this is like intrusion, especially if the teind-master have used inhibition by public letters, published at the parish-church where the teinds lie, as an intimation to all parties having interest, to forbear meddling with the teinds, otherwise than by order of law, which may be executed by any person as Sheriff in that part, January 27, 1666, E. Eglintoun *contra* L. Cunninghamhead [1 Stair 344; M. 13092]. This inhibition is the competent legal way to take off tacit relocation, when teinds have been set in tack, and the tack expired, and when they are in

use of payment of certain duties; and hath then the same effect that warning hath in relation to tenants of lands; and being once duly used, it interrupts tacit relocation, or use of payment, not only for the years wherein it is used, but for all other subsequent years, March 18, 1628, Lo. Blantyre *contra* Parishioners of Bothwell [Durie 363; M. 6434]. But the titular may not by force draw the teinds after inhibition, but must pursue therefor, where there was any pretence of title, else it is a spuilzie in him, January 27, 1665, L. Bairfoord and Beanstoun *contra* Lo. Kingstoun [1 Stair 257; M. 1817].

Spuilzie upon inhibition was sustained against an heritor, receiving a joint duty for stock and teind, March 16, 1627, Inglis *contra* Kirkwood [Durie 291; M. 15629], but it is not effectual to infer spuilzie against tenants, continuing to pay their masters a joint duty for stock and teind, as they were in use before, though the inhibition was particularly intimated to the tenants; seeing they knew not how to distinguish the proportion of stock and teind, having still paid a joint duty promiscuously for both, December 13, 1627, Hepburn *contra* Tennents of Fairnieflat [Durie 320; M. 1779; 1, 18, 3, *supra*]. But the privilege of tenants paying to their masters for stock and teind jointly, was not extended to a merchant buying a whole crop together, who was found liable for the teind, though he paid before any diligence, June 24, 1662, Mr. Alexander Verner *contra* Allan [1 Stair 112; M. 14788]. In like manner, merchants buying the herring where they were taken in the isles, were found liable for the teind by immemorial possession, so to uplift the teind-fish from the merchants who bought whole boatfuls of the herrings green, December 13, 1664, Bishop of the Isles *contra* the Merchants of Edinburgh [1 Stair 240; M. 15633]. But as warning, so inhibition of teinds is taken off by accepting the old duty thereafter, or of the ordinary taxation, accustomed to be paid for the tack-duty, Hope, Teinds, Lo. Garleis *contra* Tennents of Whitehorn [Hope, *Maj. Pr.* 111, 18, 27]; or by a small part of the old tack-duty, *ibid*. Mr. Andrew Balfour *contra* Lo. Balmerinoch [*Ibid.*, 111, 18, 28; M. 6433], Glendinning *contra* Tenants of Partoun [*Ibid.*, 111, 18, 29; M. 13264].

24. Rentalled teind-bolls is, when the teinds have been liquidated and settled for so many bolls yearly by rental, or old use of payment which presumed a rental. By this means the beneficed persons gained an advantage of the possessors; and therefore, by the King's decreet-arbitral, such teinds which are separated, and severally set or known from the stock, had a diverse and dearer valuation; and therefore rentalled teind-bolls were found due by use of payment immediately preceding the debate, though exceeding the worth of the teind, till the teind in kind were offered, and intimation made that the party would not continue the use of payment of rentalled bolls, March 22, 1626, Lennox of Branshogle *contra* Tennents of Balfron [Durie 195; M. 15328]. Teind-bolls were found due according to the old rental, though a lesser quantity was received by a minister for several years: here the bishop to whose bishoprick the teinds of that parish were annexed, opposed the alteration of the old rentalled bolls, whereof a part only was allocated to, and received by

the minister, July 3, 1630, Mr. George Summer *contra* Stuart of Balgillo [Durie 525; M. 15330]. The like where there was a decreet formerly for the teind-bolls, but prejudice to offer the teind in kind in time coming, February 20, 1633, College of Glasgow *contra* Mr James Stuart [Durie 677; M. 15331].

25. The interest of bishops in their benefices, is much alike with ministers as to their entry, which is regulated by their consecration or translation, which if before Whitsunday, gives them the benefit of that year; and if after Whitsunday, and before Michaelmas, it gives them the half. During their incumbence, they have not only the fruits and rents of the benefice, but the power to set tacks for nineteen years, with consent of their chapters, *vide supra* §. 17, and to receive vassals, and to constitute commissars; all which are effectual after their death or removal. They have also the quots of testaments confirmed by all their commissars during their life, or within the time of their ann after their death; but they have no quots of testaments not then confirmed, although the persons died in their life, or during their ann; because the quot is due for the confirmation, as was found, July 6, 1676, Bishop of Edinburgh *contra* Captain Wishart [2 Stair 439; M. 15898]; and for the same reason they have not the compositions or duplications of heirs, apprisers or adjudgers, whom they do not actually receive in their life, which will not belong to their executors, or fall within their ann, but to the next entrant, who only can receive these vassals.

26. The interest of ministers in the teinds may be considered, either in their entry, during their incumbency, or after their removal. In all which, the minister's interest is of two kinds; for either he hath the benefice, parsonage, or vicarage, or hath only a stipend modified thereof; for these benefices did ordinarily belong to the incumbents of particular parishes, and followed the office of serving the cure there: and therefore, when these benefices were not erected in temporal baronies and lordships, or otherwise so affected by titles, tacks, or new erections, that the ministers thereby could not have a competency, they betook themselves to the benefice, and had the same right and privileges as to them, as beneficed persons formerly had, and might set tacks thereof in the same way, and with the same restriction, as is before declared. But more frequently the ministers had modified stipends, which were appointed by the King and Parliament to be modified out of the teinds, whatever the title or interest of any other person were therein; which they could not reach, if they took them to the benefice itself; as they might have done by the Act of Parl. 1581, cap. 102 [A.P.S. III, 212, c. 4], ordaining, "That all benefices of cure under prelacies, should be provided only in favours of able ministers."

27. The interest of ministers was according to the nature of the benefices whereunto they were to have right, or out of which their stipends were to be modified; for all kirks were either patrimonial, or patronate, and by clearing patronage, it will easily appear what kirks are [free or] patrimonial: for, this distinction is taken from that of persons in the civil law, into those who are *ingenui* or fully free, and *libertini* or become free, but with some acknowledg-

ments and services to the authors of their freedom, who were therefore called their patrons: so there stood the like relation betwixt patrons and kirks patronate, as betwixt patrons and libertines, the ground whereof was an eminent good deed done by the patron or his predecessor to that kirk, especially these acknowledged in law, *patronum faciunt dos, ædificatio, fundus;* signifying, the building of the church, or giving of the stipend, or of the ground necessary for the church, church-yard, manse or gleib, were the grounds for constituting the patronage, which were sufficiently instructed by the custom of the kirks, acknowledging such a patron: yet it was a voluntary agreement between the patron and congregation at first, till parishes were settled and all churches behoved to have a patron, except mensal and common kirks; then the interest of the parties pretending to be patrons, gave ground to determine the patronage, without the consent of parties.

It was lately contraverted who should be patron of a second minister, whose stipend was constitute, not out of the teinds, but by contribution and engagement of a town for the greatest part, and the heritors of the landward parish for the rest, whether the patronage and power to present that second minister, should belong to the patron of the kirk, having the unquestionable power of presenting the first minister, or to the contributors; in which competition, the patron of the kirk was preferred, because the contributors had never been in possession of presenting nor had reserved the patronage nor power of presenting in the erection of the second minister; which was only by an act of the bishop and presbytery, bearing the shares contributed for a second minister, but neither reservation nor protestation by them concerning the patronage or power of presenting the second minister; nor was any thing of custom or possession to show the meaning of the parties, November 18, 1680, Town of Haddington *contra* the E. of Haddington [2 Stair 799; M. 9901]. This case will not prejudge erections of second ministers in most of other towns in the kingdom, where the erection doth bear a "reservation of the patronage." For clearing of the derived right from the first patron, especially to singular successors, the patronage was ordinarily conveyed by infeftments, carrying expressly "advocation, donation, and right of patronage of such kirks." Such kirks then as acknowledged no patron are fully free; and these are provided, not by presentation, but the ordinary conveyeth *pleno jure*, whereby the incumbent hath right to the benefice, and full fruits: but in mensal kirks, the incumbent hath but a stipend, and these belong to the proper patrimony of prelates, who have right to the fruits thereof, as a part of their own benefice; and therefore are called "patrimonial or mensal." Patronage is also, either laic or ecclesiastic; laic is that which belongs to secular persons; ecclesiastic, that which belongs to churchmen; as when a bishop hath the right of presentation to a kirk, not in his own diocese; there he presents, but another must confer as ordinary, and so he is but ecclesiastic patron.

28. Kirks patronate required for the entry of ministers, a presentation of the patron, presenting a person to the church and benefice, to be tried by

churchmen having that power, and giving him the right of the benefice or stipend, being found qualified, and collation of the office and institution therein by churchmen upon trial, without which the incumbent could have no right; yet, where the bishop had the power of collation and institution and to confer *pleno jure*, a gift from the bishop conferring and admitting, was found sufficient without a distinct presentation or collation, July 4, 1627, Minister of Sklate *contra* Parishioners [*Sub nom. McKenzie* v *Parishioners of Sclait*, Durie 303; M. 14785]. But in kirks not patronate, institution and collation was sufficient. And of late the act of ordination or admission of ministers by presbyteries, served for all: but in benefices without cure, as prebendries or chaplanries, presentation is sufficient without collation and institution.

29. Ministers being thus entered, have right to their benefices or stipends during their incumbency, which they need not instruct by writ, but it is sufficient to prove by witnesses, that the minister, or his predecessors, have been in possession of that which is controverted, as a part of the benefice or stipend of that kirk, and that it is commonly holden and repute to be a part thereof; for there being no competent way to preserve the rights and evidents of the kirk amongst successors in office, as there are of other rights amongst other successors, the canon law attributeth much more to possession than the civil; for thereby *possessor decennalis et triennalis non tenetur docere de titulo* [11, 1, 25, *supra*]: which was not only extended to instruct that the thing possessed belonged to the benefice, but that the incumbent had sufficient right; and, therefore, liberated prebendars from production of their provisions, in the case of improbation, Hope, Improbation, Bishop of Galloway and Dean of the Chapel-royal *contra* the Prebendars [Hope, *Maj. Pr.* VI, 24, 80; M. 15627]: this presumption would not be elided by any extrinsic reversion, yea, it will liberate from production of any written right in reduction and improbation, where there is no right extant: but if a right be found by the oaths of churchmen or others, to be extant in their hands, the same will be presumed to be the right by which they possess, and it may be improven by a positive probation, but not by a presumptive probation, by way of certification, concluding it false, because the possessors declined to produce it, or to abide by it. When the right is produced, any exception may be proponed upon any thing contained therein; and, therefore, an annualrent of ten chalders of victual, mortified by the King to the chapel-royal, was excluded by a redemption thereof, granted by the King voluntarily upon payment, when the bishops were suppressed, in respect, the mortification bore "such a right mortified," which had therein a reversion; and, therefore, after redemption, thirteen years' possession could not establish the right, being redeemed: neither could the Act of Restitution of Bishops, restoring them to the rights and possession they had before 1637, do it; seeing that could not hinder another party to redeem, July 11, 1676, Bishop of Dumblane *contra* Kinloch [2 Stair 444; M. 7950; 11, 1, 25, *supra*]. A minister's stipend, as to the use of payment and quantity, was found probable by witnesses without writ, *in possessorio*, as was lately found, Minister's Relict *contra* E. of

Caithness [Not found]. As to the time sufficient to give a possessory judgment in benefices or stipends upon possession, without evidence in writ, but being holden and reputed as a part of the benefice, the canon law, *regula cancellariæ* 33, determines it to be three years' peaceable possession, which is rather as to the incumbent's right, that after three years' possession he cannot be questioned during his life. I find not our decisions so clear in it, but it cannot exceed seven years' possession, which gives a possessory judgment in infeftments of property, &c. and it was so found, Nov. 25, 1665, Petrie *contra* Mitchelson [1 Stair 314; M. 10640]. The like about that same time, Ferguson *contra* Agnew [Not found]. Ministers also during their incumbency, may set tacks according to the rule for setting of tacks by beneficed persons before expressed, which are valid and effectual, though the incumbent be deprived or transported, Parl. 1526, cap. 11 [Deposition of Ministers Act 1592, c. 117; A.P.S. III, 542, c. 9].

30. Ministers' stipends are ordinarily allocated out of the teinds of particular lands, and when they are allocated, all intromitters with the teinds of these lands allocated are liable for the stipend, not proportionally with other intromitters, but in so far as their whole intromission can reach, even though they made payment before they were charged by the minister, which they alleged was *bona fide* to the heritor or tacksman, Feb. 19, 1629, Kirk *contra* Gilchrist [Durie 427; M. 14786]. And if there be no allocation, the stipend is a burden affecting the whole teind, out of which it is modified; and the minister may take himself to the heritor intromitting, or the possessor, Spots. Kirkmen, Kirk *contra* Gilchrist [Spotiswoode 191; M. 14786]; December 3, 1664, Hutcheson *contra* E. of Cassils [1 Stair 235; M. 14788]; in which case it was found, that the minister might take himself to any of the heritors of the parish for the whole teind, in so far as his modified stipend went; seeing he had no locality, and that the heritor distressed behoved to seek his relief proportionally from the rest. And a minister was found to have right to pursue an heritor for his stipend payable out of his lands; and that accepting an assignation to a part of the tenant's duties, did not liberate the heritor further than what the minister received, unless the assignation bore, "in full satisfaction," Nov. 9, 1677, Rutherford *contra* Murray [2 Stair 556; M. 15333]. Yea, though an heritor was but an appriser of the stock and teinds, he was found liable personally, though he had not intromitted, and though he offered to assign as much of the rent, December 20, 1622, Prestoun *contra* Ker [*Sub nom. Crailing* v *Ker*, Durie 40; M. 14783]. And though the intromitter was but a wadsetter, both of stock and teind, having no more but his annualrent, and there being sufficient teind, beside [the teinds of] the wadset lands, March 21, 1633, Keith *contra* Gray and others [Durie 682; M. 14786]. But where a liferenter possessed, she was only found liable, not the fiar, June 24, 1663, Menzies *contra* L. of Glenurchie [1 Stair 193; M. 14788]. The reason why heritors are so liable for stipends is, that they set the lands for a promiscuous rent of stock and teind; but if there were not a valuation of a whole tenement together, but of

the several roums, the heritor would not be obliged to be the minister's factor.

31. But teinds before valuation are only due according to the crop and goods, without restraining the heritor in the free use of his ground, who may leave it all grass, though it had never been so long corn, and may stock it with yeld goods, which will yield no vicarage; and, therefore, having enclosed a parcel of ground, and sown it with kail, carrots, and herbs, the same was found teind-free, unless these were accustomed to pay teind in that place, June 9, 1676, Burnet *contra* Gibb [2 Stair 425; M. 15640].

32. Even after valuation, teinds are not *debita fundi*, nor do they affect singular successors, as to bygones before their right, Feb. 20, 1662, E. of Callender *contra* Monro [1 Stair 103; M. 15632].

33. The legal terms of benefices and stipends, whereby they are due to the incumbents, are Whitsunday, at which the fruits are held to be fully sown, and Michaelmas, at which time they are presumed to be fully separated; and, therefore, if the incumbent's entry be before Whitsunday, he hath that whole year; so if he be deposed, or transported before Whitsunday, he hath no part of that year; if after Whitsunday, and before Michaelmas, he hath the half, July 24, 1662, Weyms *contra* Cunninghame [1 Stair 135; M. 15885]. If after Michaelmas, he hath the whole; but if the incumbent die he hath further interest in his benefice, even after his death.

34. For ministers dying, their wives, bairns, or executors, have the annat of their benefice or stipends, which is acknowledged to be their ancient right, Parl. 1571, cap. 41 [A.P.S. III, 63, c. 18], whereby it is declared, "That beneficed persons dying shall have right to the fruits of their benefice upon the ground, and the annat thereafter to pertain to their executors:" But the question is, what the annat importeth. There is a letter concerning it written by the King to the General Assembly, and ratified by them. All do now agree, that if the incumbent die after Michaelmas, he hath right to that whole year by his service, and to the half of the next year by the annat; but if he die before Michaelmas, he hath right to the half of the stipend, if he survive Whitsunday, *proprio jure;* and to the other half as the ann, which his executors have right to; but all the question is, when the incumbent doth not only survive Michaelmas, whereby he hath the half of the next year, but if he survive the last of December, whether he hath right to the whole stipend of that year; as to which that rule hath been sustained, *in favorabilibus annus inceptus habetur pro completo;* and, therefore, the ann was the whole year, which was so decided, July 5, 1662, Executors of Fairlie *contra* his Parishioners [1 Stair 121; M. 472]; but the anns of bishops and ministers are now brought to a much more equal way by Act of Parl. August 23, 1672 [Ann Act, 1672, c. 13; A.P.S. VIII, 73, c. 24], whereby it is statute, "That the ann in all time thereafter, shall be half a year's rent of the benefice or stipend, over and above what is due to the defunct for his incumbency, viz. if he survive Whitsunday, he shall have the half of that year for his incumbency, and the other half for his ann, and if he survive Michaelmas, he shall have the half of the next year for his ann;"

whereas before, if he survived Michaelmas, and lived but till the last of December, his ann was but the half of the next year; but if he lived till the 1st of January, his ann was that whole year, whereby the next incumbent had nothing to expect for that year, during which the kirk was like to lie vacant. And there being no law, statute, or fixed custom of the extent of the ann, that Act gives the justest record and account of it, even for ministers.

The annat divides betwixt the relict and nearest of kin, if there be no bairns, and is extended to the profit of the gleib if there be no new entrant, July 19, 1664, Scrimzour, Relict of Murray *contra* his Executors [1 Stair 219; M. 463]; but where there is an entrant, the glebe belongs to him, and is not part of the ann, nor did belong to the former minister, unless it had been sown by him, and the crop upon it at the entry of the entrant, July 6, 1665, Colvil *contra* L. Balmerino [1 Stair 296; M. 464]; where it was also found, that the defunct had his ann, though he had neither wife nor bairns.

35. To conclude this title with the interest of patrons in benefices. We have already shown their original and kinds; their interest in the benefices or stipends is, first the right of presentation of a qualified person for the ministry, whom the presbytery behoved to try and admit, if he were qualified: whereanent the patron might appeal to the synod, and thence to the General Assembly; and if that person be still rejected, he must present another, which must be done within six months after the vacancy may come to his knowledge; but the six months may not run from the vacancy, but from the refusal or appeal discussed, which cannot be determined in six months: otherwise the kirk may admit a qualified person for that time, Parl. 1592, cap. 117 [Deposition of Ministers Act, 1592, c. 117; A.P.S. III, 542, c. 9]; Parl. 1606, cap. 2 [A.P.S. IV, 281, c. 2]; Parl. 1609, cap. 12 [A.P.S. IV, 439, c. 19]. And, by the institution of bishops, the presentation was directed to them in their several dioceses.

Secondly, During the vacancy without the patron's default, but by the default of the presbytery refusing to admit a qualified person, he had power to detain the whole fruits of the benefice in his own hands, as is clear in the said Act, Parl. 1592, cap. 117 [Deposition of Ministers Act, 1592, c. 117; A.P.S. III, 542, c. 9]. But thence it is not to be inferred, that while the patron presents none, he could enjoy the benefice.

Thirdly, Patrons are tutors and guardians to their church, without whose consent the incumbent can set no tack longer than for three years, Parl. 1594, cap. 200 [1594, c. 203; A.P.S. IV, 64, c. 10]. Patrons had also an indirect interest in their own benefices; where the ministers had an ordinary stipend, settled to them by long custom or modification, yet far within the worth of the benefice, patrons used to present them to the benefice, but withal took tacks of them to confident persons to their own behoof, carrying the superplus of the profit of the benefice, over and above the accustomed stipend of their predecessors, which hath not been quarrelled as a simoniacal paction or dilapidation. It seems also, that patrons for resemblance of personal patronages ought to be alimented out of the benefice, if they come to necessity, according as their benefice may bear, though there hath occurred no occasion to question or try this point; but by the Act of Parliament, July 23, 1644, Sess. 1, cap. 20 [A.P.S. VI, 128, c. 47], the power of disposing of the vacant benefice or stipend, was taken from the patron, and stated in the presbytery and parish, to be disposed upon for pious uses; and by Act of Parl. 1649, cap. 39 [A.P.S. VI, 411, c. 171], the power of presentation is also taken away: yet the title doth unfitly design that Act an abolition of patronage, for there is no more there taken away but the power of presentation; but on the contrary, where the patron could have no interest in the benefice or teinds, but indirectly as aforesaid, that Act declares the heritable right of the teinds, over and above the stipend, to be in the patron, but with necessity to dispone the same to the heritors, for six years' purchase: but these Acts are now rescinded, and patrons were returned to their ancient rights, but they were excluded from the fruits in the vacancy, which were applied to pious uses for seven years, and thereafter during his Majesty's pleasure, Parl. 1661, cap. 52 [A.P.S. VII, 303, c. 330], and the vacancies for seven years after the year 1672, were applied to universities, Parl. 1672, cap. 20 [A.P.S. VIII, 94, c. 46].

Ecclesiastical benefices were so ordinarily patronate, that there were scarce any free, but all were presumed to be patronate, and where the right of patronage did not appear to be established in any other, the Pope was presumed patron before the Reformation; and after the Reformation, the King is presumed patron, *jure coronæ*, where the right of another patron appeareth not. There are other patronages belonging to the King, *jure privato*, as when the King or his predecessors acquired any rights of patronages from any private person; or when the King or his predecessors founded or doted the benefice; or when any lands or baronies fall in the King's hand as superior, by recognition or forfeiture; all such baronies having annexed thereto, or comprehended therein, advocation, donation and right of patronage of any kirk, the King doth thereby become patron; and all those patronages are at the King's disposing, and transmissible to any subject by the King's proper deed, either annexing or incorporating the same in baronies or lordships, or by distinct gifts; for the patronage doth ordinarily pass as annexed to lands, by charters of burghs, baronies, or lordships; yet they may pass without infeftments, as *jura incorporalia*. All patronages or power of institution, which belonged to bishops, by the suppression the King becomes patron, though the bishops were not patrons of their mensal kirks; he is also patron of all common kirks, after the dissolution. But there were other patronages which, by Act of Parliament, are annexed to the Crown, either expressly, or when baronies, lordships, or benefices are annexed to the Crown, if therein patronages of any benefice were comprehended, they are annexed though not exprest; for barony or benefice are *nomina universitatis*, being united and erected; and therefore the barony or benefice, without expressing patronage, do carry the same by resignation, apprising, adjudication, recognition or forfeiture, as well as salmond-fishing or mills: but these patronages being a part of the annexed patrimony of the

Crown, cannot be disposed by the King, without a public law, or by a special act of dissolution for particular reasons of public good, anterior to the King's gift and ratifications in Parliament, which pass of course, and are accounted but private rights, which will not establish the same, though in the ratification there be a clause of dissolution, which is always understood to be as a private right and not a public law.

The patronage of all bishoprics did belong to the King, who designs the person to be bishop, and though the chapter might use the formality of election, they did not refuse the King's designation: the order of this election is prescribed, Parl. 1617, cap. 1 [A.P.S. IV, 529, c. 1]. Where the dean and chapter are ordained to choose the person, whom the King pleases to nominate and recommend, he always being an actual minister of the kirk, who being elected, hath sufficient right to the spirituality of his benefice, but not to the temporality, till he have a charter from the King, and do homage, and swear obedience to him; but the Archbishop of St. Andrews is to be elected by the bishops of Dunkeld, Aberdeen, Brichen, Dumblane, Ross, Murray, Orkney, Caithness, the principal of St. Leonard's College, the Arch-Dean of St. Andrews, the vicars of St. Andrews, Leuchers, and Cupar, or most part of them, Parl. 1617, cap. 2 [A.P.S. IV, 529, c. 2]. And by the same Act the Archbishop of Glasgow is to be elected by the bishops of Galloway, Argyle and the Isles, and the ordinary chapter of Glasgow, or most of them, the bishop of Galloway being convener of the electors; and now the bishop of Edinburgh, since that bishopric was erected, is by the erection made an elector and convener for St. Andrews.

The King is also patron of many laic patronages; and there are several other laic patronages belonging to subjects; ecclesiastic patronages belonged only to the bishops, who are patrons of some kirks; whereof some are patrimonial, or mensal, the fruits whereof are a part of the bishops' benefices, and the several parish-kirks are not distinct benefices, but *partes beneficii*, but must be served by the bishop himself, or a minister who is a stipendiary: and by the 19th Act, Parl. 1633 [A.P.S. V, 35, c. 19], all ministers are appointed to be provided with sufficient stipends, being eight chalders of victual, or eight hundred merks at least, except in singular cases, referred to the commissioners for plantation of kirks, who are authorised as commissioners of Parliament, to value teinds, modify stipends, and grant localities for fixing thereof upon particular lands. If a bishop did acquire any patronage of a kirk within his own diocese, that kirk cannot be patronate, but becomes free, and is conferred by the bishop *pleno jure;* for he cannot present to himself; yet by the collation, the person collated is not a stipendiary, but is parson or vicar, and hath the full benefit of the fruits, except in so far as they are restricted by tacks, set lawfully by them or their predecessors, or unless they were become stipendiars before the bishop's right.

Common kirks which were to be provided by the bishops and their chapters in common, were not properly patronate by presentations, but by nominations and collations; yet the incumbents were not stipendiaries, but enjoyed these kirks as benefices: but after the Reformation, when bishops and chapters were suppressed, these common kirks were declared to be of the same nature with other parsonages and vicarages, and to be conferred by presentations of the lawful patrons and collation, whereby they become then patronate, the King, or these whom he gave right being patrons; but after the restitution of bishops and chapters, Parl. 1617, cap. 2 [A.P.S. IV, 529, c. 2], these common kirks were restored to their ancient condition. College kirks were benefices, whereof the King was patron, except some few, which belonged to subjects: chaplainries and altarages were under patronage of the founders or their successors.

Before the Reformation there were but few inferior benefices below prelacies, viz. collegiate and common kirks, parsonages and vicarages, and may be found by the stent-rolls, whereby every parsonage and vicarage are taxed apart, as distinct benefices; the far greater part of all the teinds of Scotland did belong to prelacies, such as bishoprics and abbacies, and all the parish kirks which belong to them, are not distinct benefices, but a part of their patrimony, and were served by themselves, their vicars or their substitutes, without any fixed maintenance, but *ad placitum*; so that there was no patronages of all these kirks, and the ordinary provision thereof was the vicarage or small teind, and sometimes vicar pensions out of the parsonage teinds.

After the Reformation, all monasteries being suppressed, they returned to the King *jure coronæ*, as to their whole benefices, both teinds or spirituality, and lands and baronies, or other temporal rights; but the King gifted the most part of these benefices, both spirituality and temporality, to the nobility and gentry, and erected the same in temporal baronies and lordships; but with the burden of competent provisions to the ministers of all the kirks, which were parts of the patrimony of the said great benefices: whereby the Lords of Erection coming in place of these monasteries, had right to all the teinds of the kirks, which were the patrimony thereof; and as the abbots and priors did nominate their vicars in these kirks, so the Lords of Erection did nominate the ministers to the same, and presented them to the church-men, to be tried and admitted, and thereupon assumed the title of Patrons; because the ministers had no benefices, but were stipendiaries, having no rights to the fruits till the year 1587, when the temporalities of all benefices belonging to archbishops, bishops, priors, prioresses, or whatsoever ecclesiastical benefice belonging to any abbey, cloister, friars, monks, canons, common kirks, and collegiate kirks, were annexed to the crown, with several exceptions, Act 29, Parl. 1587 [A.P.S. III, 431, c. 8]; and though that Act seem only to annex the temporality then belonging to these church-men, and not to extend to the temporalities already erected to secular persons; yet by the exceptions of the many erections therein contained, it hath been ever held as an annexation of all the temporalities that did belong to these benefices, with inclusion of all others not excepted: but the spirituality or teinds, are declared not to be annexed; but by the Act 117 Parl. 1592, [Act 1592, c. 121; A.P.S. III, 544, c. 13] erections either of kirk-

lands or teinds in temporal lordships, after the said Act of annexation, are declared null, except such parts and portions of the kirk-lands, already erected
in temporal lordships, to such persons as, since the Act of annexation, have
received the honours of Lords of Parliament, and have sitten and voted in
Parliament, as temporal Lords: whence the question ariseth, whether that exception derogates only from this Act, or also from the said general Act of Annexation; but by the 198th Act of Parliament 1594 [A.P.S. IV,63,c.5], all
erections since the said general Act of annexation, not excepted in the said Act,
are declared null, which doth leave no doubt as to the erections, preceding the
said Act, not excepting the Act of Annexation; and by the Act 2 Parl. 1606
[A.P.S. IV,281,c.2], restoring bishops, it is declared for the better satisfaction
of his majesty's subjects and faithful servants, whom his Majesty hath reward-
ed with erections, feus, patronages, teinds and confirmations of teinds, patronages and other rights of abbacies, and that they may not be put in mistrust,
therefore ratifies the whole erections, infeftments, confirmations, patronages,
tacks, and other securities of benefices, not being bishoprics given, disponed,
and confirmed by his Majesty, during the Parliament 1587, before or sinsine,
agreeable to the said laws and Acts of Parliament; and faithfully promits *in
verbo principis*, never to quarrel the same: which seems to give farther ground
to erections, though qualified with that provision, that the said erections be
conform to the Acts of annexation, and laws made sinsine, whereby the same
might only extend to the erections, excepted and warranted in the said act of
annexation, which excepts several erections formerly made, and leaves some
kirk-lands to the King's disposal, by subsequent erections: in this case did
King James leave the condition of kirk-lands, teinds and patronages, when he
died *in anno* 1625.

King Charles I coming to the crown, and being informed of the great
benefit his father might have made by suppressing of popery and the popish
benefices, if he had not gifted them away before he did consider, did resolve
to recover the same to the crown; and therefore made a very ample revocation
of all deeds done in prejudice of the crown, or any of his royal progenitors;
and in the year 1627, there was a reduction intented of all erections of kirk-
lands, teinds, patronages, which did pertain to whatsoever abbacy, priory, or
other benefice, and Acts of Parliament ratifying the same, with all infeftments
of heritable offices or regalities: which revocation and process having made a
great noise, the King gave commission to several noblemen and others, to
endeavour an agreement with these who had right to erections, or any right to
kirk-lands or teinds; whereupon there was a submission made by many persons, who had right to kirk-lands and teinds, containing a procuratory of
resignation in the King's hands *ad perpetuam remanentiam*, of the superiority
of all lands and other temporal rights pertaining to whatsoever erection of the
temporality of benefices, reserving and excepting the property of all the saids
lands and others, whereunto they had right, before or after the saids erections,
they paying the ancient feu-duties to his Majesty, that were payable to kirk-

men; and that such demains and mensal lands of the saids benefices, as were never set in feu or rental by the ancient Titulars, before the Act of Annexation, nor by the King, and were then possessed by any of the Lords of Erection, should be feued to them and no others, for such feu-duties as his Majesty's Commissioners should appoint: they did thereby also submit to his Majesty, what satisfaction he should give them for the feu-duties, and other constant rent of the superiorities resigned; and all rights of tithes that they had, that his Majesty might appoint the quantity, rate, and price thereof, to be paid by the heritors to the saids Titulars of erection, with a burden of annuity to the King, excepting the teinds of the surrenderers' own proper lands, being always subject to his Majesty's annuity: which submission his Majesty accepted, and there followed thereupon an instrument of resignation at Whitehall, May 14, 1628. There was also a submission made by the bishops, of all teinds belonging to them, or their patrimonial kirks, provided they be not damnified in their benefices, as they were then possessed, either in quantity or quality, whether the samine were paid in rental-bolls or drawn-teind; so that their submission did only reach to teinds that were in tack, or other use of payment, and whereof the bishops or beneficed persons were not then in possession by rental-bolls, or drawn teind. This submission was *in anno* 1628. There is also a submission by the burghs of their teinds in the same year, and a fourth submission by several other persons having right to teinds at the same time.

The King did pronounce his decreet arbitral, upon the submission of the Lords of Erection, upon the 2d of September 1629, whereby he ordains the Lords of Erection to have ten years' purchase for the feu-duties, and all their constant rents, consisting of victual or money, the victual being reckoned at an hundred marks the chalder, deducing so much of the feu duties as were equivalent to the blench-duties, contained in the infeftments of erection, for which nothing was to be paid; and allowing the Lords of Erection to retain the feu duties until they were redeemed. His Majesty did also decern, that each heritor shall have his own teinds; that such as have right to other men's teinds, shall after valuation thereof, (whereby the fifth part of the constant rent which each land pays in stock and teind, is declared to be the teind) and where the teind is valued severally, that the heritor shall have the fifth part of the yearly value therof deduced, for the King's ease: and the price of the said teind for an heritable right was made nine years' purchase: And for other rights of teinds, inferior to heritable rights, proportionably according to the worth thereof, to be determined by a commission to be granted by his Majesty to that effect. There are also decreets by his Majesty upon the other submissions, to the same purpose; and by the 10th and 14th Acts, Parliament 1633 [A.P.S. v, 27, 32, cc. 10, 14], the superiorities of all kirk-lands are annexed to the crown, except these belonging to bishops, with the feu-duties of the said superiorities, reserving to the Lords and Titulars of Erections, who subscribed the general surrender or submissions, their feu-duties till they be redeemed at ten years' purchase, and reserving to them the property holden of his Majesty, for payment of the feu-duties contained in the old infeftments preceding the annexation.

By the 12 Act, Parl. 1652 [Act 1633, c. 12; A.P.S. v, 28, c. 12], the King restricts his general revocation in October 1625, registrate in the books of Secret Council, February 9, 1626 in a Proclamation then emitted, and in another July 21, 1626, to the annulling all pretended rights to the property of the crown, as well annexed as not annexed, whereof an account hath been made in Exchequer, and of the principality unlawfully disponed by his predecessors, against the laws and Acts then standing; and to the annulling of erections, and other dispositions of whatsoever lands, teinds, patronages, and benefices, formerly belonging to the kirk, and since annexed to the crown, and any other lands and benefices, mortified to pious uses, and of regalities, and heritable offices, and the change from ward to blench or taxt ward, since the year 1540. But since that time there hath been great alterations in the matter of patronage; for as to the rise and original of patronage, it hath been before there were Christian Emperors, Kings or States; and while congregations and their ministers were not under the protection of law, but might have been hindered and disturbed in divine worship. Then they obtained the protection of some potent neighbour, who might endeavour to defend them from violence, whom they owned as their patron; but when they came to be protected by law, and by Christian magistrates, they became judges who should be patrons; and not only according to consent, as before, but according to the greatest benefit; and there were no kirks without patrons, except patrimonial kirks of prelates, or common kirks, which were served by the prelates or monks, or other persons named by the prelates and their chapters, or by the plurality of the members of the collegiate or college churches: the churches also of deans were patrimonial, and named by the prelate and chapter; but when prelacies and monasteries were abolished, and the common kirks were dissolved, all kirks became patronate, and the King became patron wherever the right of another patron did not appear; and therefore no tacks of teinds could be set by incumbent ministers for longer time than three years, without consent of the patron, as said is.

The King having erected the kirk-lands (fallen to the Crown by the Reformation) into baronies, and gifted the same to secular persons, he did frequently therewith gift the patronage of kirks: and though their gifts bore not expressly the patronage, yet the Lords of Erection have always presented as patrons, which hath been controverted by the King, but hath never yet come to a determination. In *anno* 1649 [Act 1649, c. 39], patronage was totally abolished, and in recompense thereof the patrons had the benefit of the teinds, which were not disponed by the King, but with the burden of ministers' stipends, and augmentations, and also with the burden of tacks and prorogations; after the expiring of which, they would have the full benefit of the teind; but the Parl. 1649 being rescinded, patrons were restored to the same condition in which they were formerly; yet by Act 9 Parl. 9. Charles II

[Possibly A.P.S. VII, 48, c. 67] it is declared, that the ministers shall have no further right to the teinds, than they had before the Act 1649. But now episcopacy being abolished, the King is patron of all the bishops' patrimonial kirks, and the kirks of their deans; and likewise the power of presentation being taken from patrons, the way of now calling ministers is ordered by Act 23, Sess. 2. Parl. 1. K. William and Q. Mary [1690, c. 23; A.P.S. IX, 196, c. 53], whereby "it is statute and declared, that for supplying vacant churches with ministers, that the heritors of the parish being protestants, and the elders, are to name and propose a person to the whole congregation, to be approven or disapproven by them, and that the disapprovers give in their reasons to be cognosced by the presbytery; and if application be not made by the eldership and heritors, to the presbytery, for the call and choice of a minister, within six months after the vacancy, that the presbytery may plant a minister *jure devoluto*, for which the patron is to have six hundred merks, and right to the teinds of the parish which are not heritably disponed, they being obliged to sell the same to the heritors at six years' purchase: but any superiorities which did belong to the benefices of bishops or ministers, are declared to belong to the King, and the feu-duties to be retained till they be redeemed by ten years' purchase." Hence this Act is not purely ecclesiastic; for the call and presentation is not only by the session, but by the heritors, and magistrates of burgh; and therefore is directly under the cognizance of the civil authority: neither is it clearly expressed, whether the elders, heritors, and magistrates should consent severally, or as convened to a diet of meeting; nor is it determined who should convene them: but the kirk-session being an ecclesiastic judicature, should only act in their meeting, and the heritors cannot act in the same meeting, of which they are not members; so likewise the magistrates of burgh act in their council; and from the nature of the trust, the heritors should also act in a meeting of their own, consulting their reasons, and determining by the plurality of these present, upon an intimation to all concerned; yet there is nothing determined what shall be done in case these meetings differ; but doubtless any of them may appeal, and the civil authority may cognosce whether the Act of Parliament be rightly observed yea or not; all which a short time may easily adjust.

Title 9. Tacks, Where, of Rentals, Tacit Relocation and Removing

A TACK of itself is no more than a personal contract of location, whereby land, or any other thing having profit or fruit, is set to the tacksman for enjoying the fruit or profit thereof, for a hire, which is called the tack-duty; which therefore did only oblige the setter and his heirs, to make it effectual to the tacksman, but did not introduce any real right, affecting the thing set, and carried therewith to singular successors; but so soon as the thing set ceased to be the setter's, the tack could only defend the tenant till the next term of removing [1, 15, 4, *supra*].

2. Thus it was with us until the statute, Parl. 1449, cap. 17 [A.P.S. II, 35, c. 6], whereby purchasers and singular successors were disenabled to break the tacks set to the tenants: by this statute, tacks become as real rights, affecting the ground; and because they cannot come the length to be esteemed as rights of property, they are ranked here amongst servitudes personal; for as liferent rights are real rights, putting a servitude upon hereditaments to the person of the liferenter, during life, whereof a liferent-tack is a kind; so other tacks do subject the thing set to the tacksman for a time, and affect the same, though it pass to singular successors; albeit the statute only expresseth, "that buyers shall not break tacks," and is in favour of the poor labourers of the ground, for whose security it was chiefly intended; yet it is extended against all singular successors, whether by sale, exchange, apprising, adjudication, or any other way, as the statute bears, "that tackers shall remain with

their tacks, in whose hands soever the lands come;" and so in favours of all tacksmen, whether they be labourers of the ground or not, whereby tacks are now become the most ordinary and important rights; and if the great favour of this statute made them not in other things to be strictly interpreted, they would render infeftments of small effect.

That we may proceed orderly in this matter, we shall consider, First, The constitution of tacks. Secondly, The extent and effect of them. Thirdly, The kinds of them. Fourthly, The restrictions and defects of them. Fifthly, The avoiding and removing of them. As to the first, tacks are also called assedations, as a setting or settling of the tenant in the land; the English call them leases, as letting the tenement to the tenant; some tacks are also called rentals, as being the constitution of a fixed rent, and they are of longer endurance than ordinary tacks, being of one or more liferents, and have somewhat special in them, of which hereafter [11, 9, 15, *infra*].

3. As to the constitution of a tack, consider, First, Who may constitute it. Secondly, Of what. Thirdly, How. For the first, to the constitution of an effectual tack, the setter must not only have all the capacities requisite to contract, but he must have right to the thing set, and power to administrate; which being, tacks may either be granted by commission, if it be special, as to tacks, or at least as to matters of greater importance with a general clause for others; or otherwise by tutors, curators, or other administrators of the affairs of others, concerning whom Craig, *Lib.* 2, *Dieg.* 10 [11, 10, 1], moveth and removeth this doubt, whether tutors, &c. may set tacks for longer time than during their office, which he resolveth negatively, even though it were without the minor's detriment, continuing the ancient tackduty, seeing he is so far hurt as not to have the free disposal of his own. The subjects whereof tacks are ordinarily set, are lands; but it may be any other thing having fruit or profit, as a fishing, an office or a casuality.

4. As to the manner of constituting tacks, they must be considered in themselves, First, As personal rights. Secondly, As by the statute becoming real. As they are personal rights, the consent of the setter and tacksman, agreeing in the rent is sufficient: but as tacks are become real rights, there is a necessity of writ, except in a tack of one year, which may be verbal; but if the agreement be for more years, the setter may resile; and though the tacksman be in possession, if he resile, it will have no effect as to subsequent years, July 16, 1636, Keith *contra* his Tennents [Durie 816; M.8400]; the like though the setter had built houses conform to the agreement; yet the penalty of paying a year's rent by the failzier to the observer, was found to stand, July 15, 1637, Skein *contra*   [Durie 852; M.8401].

5. The writ requisite to constitute a tack, requireth not many solemnities; but if the thing set, the parties, the rent and the time, be clear, the tack will be valid: it was ordinarily granted by the setter to the tacksman for such a duty, without any mutual obligement upon his part, like unto a charter; but because the tenant not being bound, might at the end of any year before Whit-

sunday, renounce such a tack and be free, as being in his favour; therefore they are now ordinarily by way of contract, whereby the tacksman, as well as the setter, is obliged to stand thereto.

6. Craig saith in the fore-cited place [11,10,10], that *pactum de assedatione facienda, et ipsa assedatio parificantur, præcipue si possessio sequatur,* which is unquestionable as to the setter and his heirs; and was also found against a singular successor, by a personal obligement [of a father-in-law] in a contract of marriage, providing lands to the wife, and warranting the same free of all teinds, except such a quantity, which was in use to be paid; whereby a posterior assignation to the tack of these teinds was excluded, March 20, 1629, L. of Finmouth *contra* Wemys [Durie 440; M. 16463]. Here the obligement of the heritor was found equivalent to an assignation to his tack of the teind in question. The like of a decreet-arbitral, decerning a tack to be granted: this was in a spuilzie, Hope, Spuilzie, Crawfurd *contra*   [Hope, *Maj. Pr.* VI, 18, 73; M. 14737].

7. As a tack becometh a real right, it must necessarily be clad with possession, but requireth no seasin or instrument, or other solemnity, July 11, 1627, Wallace *contra* Harvie [Durie 307; M. 67]; Had. January 22, 1611, L. of Pitsligo *contra* L. Philorth [Haddington, *Fol. Dict.* 1, 432; M. 6425]. The like though the tacksman was in possession, yet not by virtue of the tack, but by virtue of a wadset, though the tack was renewed the time of the wadset, Hope, Removing, Ord *contra* Tenants of Fydie [Hope, *Maj. Pr.* VI, 16, 64]; and therefore a posterior tack being first clad with possession was preferred to a prior tack, June 23, 1627, M'Millan *contra* Gordon of Troquhen [Durie 299; M. 7018]

8. Yet a tack after redemption of wadset-lands, is valid against singular successors, as a part of the reversion; though it attain no possession before the setter be denuded, unless it be usurary; being far within the true value, whereby the creditor hath more nor his annualrent, Parl. 1449, cap. 19 [A.P.S. II, 35, c. 6; 11, 10, 10, *infra*].

9. As to the extension and effect of tacks, they are little less than of infeftments, for thereby the tacksman is maintained against all parties having interest till the tack be out-run, and he be warned; even though set by a liferenter, it will maintain the tenant against the fiar, either from removing till warning, or from paying more than the liferenter's tack-duty, though it be small, Had. June 26, 1610, Bruce *contra* Bruce [Haddington, *Fol. Dict.* 11, 427; M. 15314]. Yea, though the tack-duty was elusory, set by an appriser of a liferent, to a conjunct person being no labourer of the ground, February 1, 1631, Blaues *contra* Winram [Durie 563; M. 15881]. The reason why tacks by liferenters are effectual, for the year in which the liferenter died, is because by Act of Parliament, tenants can only be warned to remove forty days preceding Whitsunday; so that if the liferenters live till thirty-nine days before Whitsunday, their tenants cannot be removed, but brook *per tacitam relocationem,* till the new time of warning.

10. A tack hath also the benefit of a possessory judgment upon seven years' peaceable possession, as an infeftment, without necessity to dispute the setter's right, July 13, 1636, Bishop of Edinburgh *contra* Brown [Durie 814; M. 2719]; which was found where the tack did bear to be granted by the setter as heritable proprietor, otherwise, a tack by a liferenter, tenant or donatar might claim the benefit, December 1, 1676, Home *contra* Scot [2 Stair 470; M. 10641].

11. A tack set by an heritor for a tack-duty to be paid to his creditors, was found a real right effectual to the tenants; but whether it would be found a real right in favour of the creditors, in the same cause, it was first determined *negativè*, and thereafter *affirmativè*: but it is not like, the Lords would continue it, not being the habile way to secure creditors, and being a great mean of insecurity to purchasers, February 13, 1627, Samuel *contra* Samuel [Durie 271; M. 2813; 11, 9, 28, *infra*]. The negative is also observed by Spots. Tacks, Morison *contra* Brown [Spotiswoode 54; M. 2816]. A tack was preferred to an apprising, whereof the denunciation was six days after the date of the tack, though the apprising was led before possession upon the tack, March 25, 1628, Blackburn *contra* Gibson [Durie 370; M. 9211].

12. A tack is a sufficient title for mails and duties, and against all possessors, and it is obligatory against the setter's heir for the profit of the land, though the tacksman was never in possession, nor used diligence therefor during the setter's life, which was a long time, Had. July 13, 1610, Porterfield *contra* Ker [Hope, *Maj. Pr.* VI, 22, 4; M. 16568]; and in some cases, it is a good title for removing [11, 9, 41, *infra*].

13. A tack set by a husband and his wife, whereof the duty was payable to the longest liver of them two, was found to give her right to the tack-duty after his death against his heir, though she had no other right of the lands, and was otherwise sufficiently provided, February 14, 1637, Home *contra* Hepburn [Durie 825; M. 15171]. A tack set to a man and his wife for nineteen years, found to belong to the wife as liferenter, if she survive, and not to be disposable by the husband without her consent, Spots. Marriage, Gourley *contra* M'Gill [Spotiswoode 204; 1 B.S. 172].

14. As to the third point proposed, concerning several kinds of tacks, they are either verbal or by writ, liferent-tacks, or for certain years ordinarily, tacks or rentals, principal-tacks or sub-tacks, express tacks or by tacit relocation; and these which are set by wadsetters to the granters of the wadset, are called back-tacks, amongst which there are few specialities but what concerns rentals, sub-tacks, or tacit relocations.

15. A rental is a tack set to kindly tenants, which are the successors of the ancient possessors, or these who are received by the heritor, with the like privilege as if they were ancient possessors: and therefore, when tacks are set to persons, acknowledging or constituting them kindly tenants, they are equiparate to these that are set expressly under the name of rentals.

16. Such tacks are understood to comprehend more kindness and friend-

ship in the tenant to his master, than other tenants; and therefore the rentaller may not assign them, nor introduce a sub-tenant, unless the rental bear expressly that power; but must himself remain upon the ground as *colonus*, the same being in his own labourage. And rentals are strictly interpreted as to this point, but are more favourably extended than other tacks, as to any other point; because of the kindness and friendship designed to the rentaller thereby: and no tack is accounted a rental unless it bear so, or that the tenant is acknowledged as kindly tenant. And albeit after the expiring of rentals, their successors have no right to maintain them in possession; yet frequently of favour they are continued, and pay grassums at the renovation of their rentals, wherein they have ordinarily considerable ease. Ordinary tacks must contain an express and terminate endurance, otherwise they are null, not only as to singular successors, but even as to the setter and his heirs, because they are not constitute *habili modo*. And therefore, if they have no time, they last but for a year; and if they have no determinate time of ish, they last no longer; and they do not ordinarily give power of assignation or sub-tack, unless this be expressed: yet the granting of them does not annul the tack, but only the assignation or sub-tack, without warrant, annuls these, but they annul rentals, like to the alienations of ward-vassals [11, 9, 21, *infra*].

17. Rentals can be granted by none but the heritor of the ground; but if they be renewed by tutors for the accustomed grassums, it may be accounted as an act of lawful administration, much rather than that tutors should have power to expel the kindly tenants. It hath not come in controversy, whether donatars of ward, non-entry, or liferenters, may expel kindly tenants: or whether this title would not be relevant, to defend in removings against them, though not against the heritor; wherein this would make for them, that all these temporary possessors have not *plenum dominium*, and can but make use of the fee as the proprietors did, though they may out-put and in-put ordinary tenants, Nicol. Removing, La Lugtoun *contra* her Tenants [Durie 657; M. 9896].

18. Rentals do require writ, not only as a probation, but as a solemnity in their constitution; so a rental in the setter's rental book, was not found valid against a singular successor, July 5, 1625, L. of Aitoun *contra* Tennents [Durie 172; M. 7191]; yet such a rental was found valid against the setter, or a tacksman made by him, February 4, 1625, but inserted July 5, 1625, Maxwell *contra* Graham [Durie 173, note; M. 7192, note].

19. Some old decisions sustain rentals only for a year, when they mention no endurance, though they be set expressly as rentals, which doth not quadrate to the nature and design of rentals, whereby the rentaller being entered, is only to be understood to be for his life; and his successors ever to be in his master's power, to renew or not to renew, according to the rentaller and his successor's carriage, except the contract be very clear and express; and therefore a rental set to the rentaller and his heirs, without expressing a certain number of heirs, was found only to stand during the life of the setter and

rentaller living together, July 5, 1625, L. of Aitoun *contra* L. Wedderburn [Hope, *Maj. Pr.* III, 30, 12; M. 15187]; Hope, Rental, Lord Seaton *contra* his Tenants [Hope, *Maj. Pr.* III, 30, 12]. And where a rental bore to heirs indefinitely, the right of the first heir was sustained by the custom of the barony, March 15, 1631, Earl of Galloway *contra* Burgesses of Wigtoun [Durie 582; M. 7194]. And a rental bearing to the rentaller's heirs heritably, *ad perpetuam remanentiam*, was sustained as to the first heir of the rentaller, without necessity to allege custom so to set, March 13, 1632, Achannay *contra* Aitoun [Durie 629; M. 15191].

20. Grassums do presume kindliness, and in some baronies these are renewed, both at the death of the heritor, and at the death of the tenant; but more ordinarily at the death of the tenant only; yet in either case, if the grassum be received from the tenant, and thereby he be acknowledged by writ as a kindly tenant, he cannot be removed by the heritor or his heirs, even though he had not a formal rental; because the matter is not entire by receipt of the grassum; and therefore there is no *locus pœnitentiœ*, upon restoring thereof, especially as to the successors of old tenants, paying grassum before: and therefore rentals expressly so granted, or to tenants constitute kindly tenants, though they contain no ish, should not be annulled for want of an ish, which is implied in the nature of a rental to be a liferent; and it would be far contrary to that favour that in other cases is allowed them, to sustain them but as verbal tacks, lasting for a year: upon this ground it is, that a rental granted to a man and his wife, not bearing "the longest liver", nor any issue, was yet found to constitute them both rentallers during their life, and the wife surviving to enjoy the same, March 5, 1629, L. of Ley younger *contra* Kirkwood [Durie 433; M. 7195].

21. Rentals do ordinarily contain a clause, not to subset, assign, or annalzie, which if it be contravened, not only the assignation or sub-tack is void, but the rental itself, Had. Feb. 28 1610, Hamilton *contra* Boid [Haddington, *Fol. Dict.* I, 484; Hope, *Maj. Pr.* III, 30, 6; M. 7188]. The like being subset, as to a part, *pro tanto*, Hope, Rentals, Lord Douglas *contra* Walkingshaw [Hope, *Maj. Pr.* III, 30, 6; M. 7189]. Yea, though the sub-tack was only granted for certain years, and these expired before the pursuit, Hope, Rentals, Earl of Roxburghe *contra* Ker [Hope, *Maj. Pr.* III, 30, 9; M. 7189]. This is so far extended, as being in the nature of a rental without any such clause, that it falleth in whole in the same manner, as ward-lands recognosce by alienating or subsetting the whole, or major part, if possession follow, and that by exception or reply, March 15, 1631, Earl of Galloway *contra* Burgesses of Wigtoun [Durie 582; M. 7194]. Though the alienation was by excambion, and was conditional, "if the heritor consented," else to be null: the like where the rentaller had given a disposition of the rental, whereupon the acquirer was in possession, which was found to annul the rental, albeit it bore "assignees, and to exclude a sub-tack by the rentaller to that same party, granted before any controversy moved," February 21, 1632, L. Johnstoun *contra* Johnstoun

[Durie 622; M.7198]. The like by a sub-tack, though the sub-tenants offered to repone the rentaller, November 13, 1622, Bonar *contra* Nicolson [Durie 35; M.7190]. The like upon an assignation of a rental, though it contained a power to sub-set, and in-put and out-put tenants, March 21, 1623, L. of Craigie Wallace *contra* his Tennents [Durie 60; M.7191]. But this taketh no place, if the sub-tack be set to the rentaller's eldest son, who was to succeed, Had. March 19, 1622, Earl of Roxburgh *contra* Gray [Hope, *Maj.Pr.* 111,30, 9; M.7189]. It will also be elided if the heritor receive duty from the assignee as assignee, Hope, *hic*, L. of Craigie *contra* his Tenants [Hope, *Maj.Pr.* 111,30,11; M.6432]. But it will not be inferred by the rentaller's entering another in possession, without granting him a right in writ, July 5, 1625, L. of Aitoun *contra* L. of Wedderburn [Hope, *Maj.Pr.* 111,30,12; M.15187]; last of Jan. 1633, L. of Cleghorn *contra* Crawfurd [Durie 667; M.7199]; unless the rental contain an obligement to put no other in possession; and then it became null by granting tolerance, and that by exception against the person having tolerance, without calling the rentallers, July 15, 1628, La. Maxwel *contra*   [Durie 390; M.2228,15185]. A rental setting the keeping of a house, yard and others, to the rentaller and his heirs, as kindly tenants, was not found null by the rentaller's suffering the decay of the house and yard, whereby the rentaller failed in his duty, and in the cause of granting the rental, January 29, 1628, Duke of Lennox *contra* Houstoun [Durie 334; M.7201].

22. A sub-tack is that which is granted by the principal tacksman to his sub-tenant, who doth not thereby become tenant to the setter of the principal tack. This is competent to tacksmen, where lands are set to them or their sub-tenants, or that they have power to out-put and in-put tenants; and it is like a subaltern infeftment, and hath the same effect to defend the possession as the principal tack itself, if it be clad with possession, and cannot be taken away by any renunciation granted by the principal tacksman, though his tack bore not assignees, (but though it be not observed, it hath borne either assignees or power to in-put tenants or sub-tenants,) July 14, 1625, Earl of Mortoun *contra* his Tennents [Durie 177; M.15228]; yea, when the principal tack was reduced for not-production, the sub-tacksmen not having been called, the sub-tack was sustained as a defence, notwithstanding the reduction, seeing the heritor had consented to the sub-tack, December 13, 1626, Earl of Galloway *contra* McCulloch [Durie 245; M.7833]. This is the effect of a sub-tack *passivè*, but *activè* it is not a sufficient title to pursue without instructing the principal tack, unless it had been acknowledged by the defender.

23. Tacit relocation is that which is presumed to be the mind of both parties after expiring of a tack, when neither the setter warneth, nor the tacksman renounceth; for other significations of the alteration of their minds will not suffice, these being the habile way of voiding tacks, which is now much more strengthened by the statute, prohibiting tenants to be put out without warning before Whitsunday: but where warning is not requisite, other competent ways of evacuating the tack will be sufficient; as inhibition in teinds, or

actions for removing summarily from fortalices, coal-heughs, &c. Yea, though warning hath been used, if it prescribe by three years' not pursuing thereupon, it hath no effect even against tacit relocation, Had. June 26, 1610, Bruce *contra* Bruce [Haddington, *Fol. Dict.* 11, 427; M. 15314]. There is a kind of tacit relocation, by taking the rent before the hand, during which time, as Craig [11, 8, 32; 11, 10, 11] observeth in the fore-cited place, the setter cannot remove the defunct's successor for these years. Tacit relocation will be sufficient after a verbal tack, or where the tack is presumed upon use of payment, though none can be shown or proven: yea, tacit relocation was sustained for more years than the setter could expressly set; and is ordinarily, in the case of tacit relocation upon liferenter's tacks, which continue still after their death, till warning, and was so found in a patron's tack of teinds after the patron's right to set by the Act of Parl. 1649, was rescinded, January 16, 1663, E. Errol *contra* Tennents of Urie [1 Stair 158; M. 15318].

Tacit relocation can only defend the tenant, being natural possessor, but not possessing by his sub-tenant, nor to the sub-tenants alleging on the tenants' right, if he be warned; but he must allege, that he is sub-tenant to a tenant, who hath a tack for terms to run, December 2, 1628, Whitefoord *contra* Johnstoun [Durie 402; M. 13809]. Relocation is valid against the donatar of a ward, till warning or citation, which was sustained, though the tack-duty was elusory, and that the tack then slept, Spots, Removing, L. Lee *contra* Glen of Bar [Spotiswoode 355; M. 16560]. But tacit relocation is no relevant active title against any, but these who have right from the tacksman, though they had acknowledged the same by payment to him for years anterior, December 12, 1621, L. Lag *contra* Parishioners of Lintoun [Durie 6; M. 15315].

24. By what hath been said, it may appear, that the force and effect of tacks is so great, by reason of the foresaid statute and custom, extending the same, that it would swallow up all heritable rights, and make infeftments useless, unless tacks had their own retrenchments and defects, making infeftments necessary. As first, tacks not being liferent tacks, fall in single escheat, and these fall by liferent-escheat, Parl. 1617, cap. 15 [A.P.S. IV, 545, c. 15].

25. Secondly, Tacks have no effect against superiors in ward-lands, but sleep during the time of wards, non-entries, &c. for infeftments feu are then valid only in some cases: yet tacks are valid against liferent escheat, which is a casuality falling, not by the nature of fees, but by statute or custom. *Vide Title 4, Superiority, §61 Liferent-escheat* [11, 4, 61].

26. Thirdly, Tacks are *strictissimi juris*, and no further extended than is expressed; and therefore are not extended to assignees, unless expressed: and therefore tacks granted to women fall by their marriage, which is a legal assignation and cannot be annulled; yet may revive by the husband's death, being unexpired, *Vide* Craig, *Lib.* 2, *Dieg.* 10 [11, 10, 6]. Upon the same ground a tack not bearing "to assignees" was not found to accresce to a relict, as infeft with absolute warrandice, as *jus superveniens authori*, June 18, 1680,

Hume *contra* Lyel [2 Stair 772; M. 10391], which is to be limited thus, that it doth not exclude legal assignations by apprising and adjudication, but only voluntary assignations, Hope, *hic*, Lord Elphingston *contra* Lord Airth [Hope, *Maj. Pr.* 11,3,22; M. 15273]; November 16, 1680, L. Carlowie *contra* Dalrymple [Not found]. Liferent-tacks also may be assigned, not mentioning assignees, February ult. 1637, Hume *contra* Craw [Durie 832; M. 10371]; July 16, 1672, Duff *contra* Fowler [2 Stair 102; M. 10282]. The like when it is of more value than a liferent-tack, as being of many nineteen years, Spots. *hic*, Ross *contra* Blair [Spotiswoode 326; M. 10368]. The like holdeth in the power of making sub-tacks, or out-putting and in-putting of tenants, or re-movings, which are not competent thereupon, unless express, or unless it be against these who had the possession from the tacksman; except in liferent-tacks, and these of geater importance.

27. Fourthly, Tacks cannot be perpetual; and therefore necessarily must have an ish, or else they are null, July 17, 1688, Oswald *contra* Rob [Harcarse 270; M. 15194]. What privilege is herein granted to rentals, is shown before, § 16.

28. It hath been much controverted, and variously decided, whether a tack set for payment of the annualrent of a sum, be valid against singular successors, which were in effect a wadset-tack, which ought not to be sustained; seeing the habile way of wadset of heritable rights is only by infeftment, and it would make the security of land much more uncertain, if tacks which need not registration were valid against singular successors [11,9,11, *supra*].

29. Fifthly, Tacks are not valid as real rights against singular successors, unless they have a tack-duty; yea if they have one, but in the tack itself it be wholly discharged, yet the tack is valid; but the discharge of the tack-duty will never be valid against the setter's singular successor, January 31, 1627, Ross *contra* Blair [Durie 266; M. 15167].

30. But the want of an entry vitiates not a tack; for when there is no entry, the date or the next term is the entry, Dec. 4, 1629, Oliphant *contra* Peebles [Durie 472; M. 11535].

31. Sixthly, All tenants are burdened with necessity to enter and labour the ground, that the master may have ready execution, February 27, 1623, Samfoord *contra* Crombie [*Sub nom. Randifoord* v *Crombie*, Durie 52; M. 15256]; and not to rive out meadow or greens never ploughed, or destroy mosses, or deteriorate the ground worse nor he found it, February 6, 1633, L. Haddo *contra* Johnstoun [Durie 669; M. 7540]; and must leave the houses as good as at his entry, Had. February 27, 1610, *contra* [Not found]. All which are without express provision [1,15,6,*supra*]: neither may the tenant open the ground for winning of any mineral, coal, or clay for pipes, without that power be expressed, February 15, 1668, Colquhoun *contra* Watson [1 Stair 527; M. 15253].

It remains now to consider how tacks are destitute and taken off; and first, as to the point of right; next, as to possession. As to the point of right, we shall not speak of the nullities of tacks, by which they were never truly constitute, and so needs not be destitute: but when they have once a real being, they cease; First, By any deed contrary to the tenor or nature thereof, as hath been before shown in rentals, which is not so in ordinary tacks, unless there be a clause irritant, and that be declared, and so is not competent by exception, Spots. *hic*. Stevinson *contra* Barclay [Spotiswoode 327; M. 2725].

32. Secondly, They become void by not-payment of the tack-duty, in the same manner as a feu-right by the delay of two years, unless the tacksman offered payment in that time.

33. Thirdly, If the tacksman be pursued to find caution for the duties resting, and in time coming, if he find no caution, the tack becomes void, and he may be removed summarily without warning; this was also sustained against a back-tack in wadsets, though having no clause irritant, Hope, Confirmation, Dischingtoun *contra* L. of Pitmedden [Possibly *Dischington* v *Pittenweem*, Hope, *Maj.Pr.* III, 10, 31; M. 7181]; *idem*, Hamilton *contra* E. Argyle [Hope, *Maj.Pr.* III, 10, 34; M. 16518]. It was also sustained, though the duty was small, the ground plenished, and but one year resting, February 27, 1627, Lawson *contra* Scot [Durie 283; M. 15302]. But it is not sustainable where there are no bygones resting: neither was it sustained, unless a year were resting the time of the citation, at least at litiscontestation, albeit the tacksman was bankrupt, and in prison for debt, January 3, 1672, La. Binnie *contra* Sinclair [2 Stair 34; M. 10382].

34. Fourthly, Tacks cease by the expiring of the terms thereof, and the setter's warning, or other deeds, to take off tacit relocation, or the tenant's renunciation; the form whereof is, the tenant forty days before Whitsunday subscribes and delivers to his master a renunciation of his tack and possession, consenting that he enter *brevi manu*, without hazard of ejection; whereupon there must be taken an instrument of renunciation in the hands of a notar, as a solemnity requisite, which is sufficient to instruct the over-giving, as being the habile way approven in law; albeit in other cases not approven in law, instruments of notars prove not the deed of the party, in this case it avoideth the tack, and is probable by instrument, if the tack be expired; but during the tack the instrument will not prove the acceptance of the renunciation.

35. Fifthly, Tacks are taken off by the contrary consent of both parties, though they be not expired, as when they are really left by the tenant, and possessed by the master: or when by writ they are renounced and accepted; for verbal renunciations may be resiled from before they be perfected in writ, in the same manner as verbal tacks may, and much more promises to renounce; this way of renunciation is express and direct.

36. Sixthly, Tacks are taken away by tacit and implied renunciation, and by passing therefrom, as by taking a posterior tack for fewer years, and making use thereof; albeit but a minute, not by contract, nor subscribed by the tacksman, nor in his hand, but his acceptance proven by witnesses, and by

paying conform, January 17, 1632, E. of Lauderdale *contra* Wastertoun [Durie 612; M. 13797]. By accepting a posterior factory of the same lands, Hope, Action of reduction, E. of Tillibairn *contra* Dalziel [Hope, *Maj. Pr.* VI, 38, 22]. By paying a greater duty, Had. February 27, 1610, L. Gosford *contra* his Tenants [Not found]: L. Lethem *contra* his Tenants [Not found]. But not by paying of more presents, *ibid.* Hamilton *contra* tenants of Milburn [Not found]. Neither by sub-tenants paying a greater duty, without warrant of the principal tenant, Had. June 5, 1611, L. Pharnieherst *contra* Minister of Innerkeithing [Not found]. Also by taking an heritable right of the same thing; but it holds not, if the heritable right were reduced, for then the tack revives, Spots. Apprising, L. of Garthland *contra* Campbell [Possibly *Garthland* v *Jedburgh*, Spotiswoode, 232; M. 10545]. Neither was it taken off by a posterior apprising in the tacksman's person, seeing it was satisfied and declared extinct against him, Had. last of February 1623, Semple *contra* Tenants of Closeburn [Not found].

37. Tacks are taken off as to possession, by removing of the tenants, either voluntarily, as is before expressed; or more ordinarily, judicially by process of removing which is most frequent and important; and therefore is reserved to be spoken of together in this place, though there be diverse kinds of removings, having respect to diverse titles; for though removing be competent against all possessors, whether possessing without any title, or by an insufficient title, as an invalid infeftment, or the like, yet the rise thereof is for removing of tenants.

38. Removing is either summary without warning, or solemn upon warning; again summary removing is either by paction or law; by paction, when it is so agreed by the tack or other writ, that the tenant shall remove at such a term without warning, which will be sufficient at that time, Craig, *hic.* This will hold upon dispositions, whereupon the disponer may be compelled to remove summarily without any such express clause, which was also extended in favour of apprisers, against their debtors possessing a house, January 18, 1623, E. Lothian *contra* Ker and his Son [Durie 42; M. 13822]. But it is more questionable, whether it will be sufficient at any time thereafter, if the tenant be suffered to possess *per tacitam relocationem;* especially, seeing the statute for warning is a public law, introduced for the good of poor tenants, whose rusticity is excusable, if they advert not to anterior pactions; *nam pacta privatorum non derogant juri communi,* yet on the contrary, *cuique libet renunciare juri pro se introducto:* betwixt which, I conceive this temperament will hold, that such pactions, though recent, may be effectual at the precise term, or at any term or time thereafter upon intimation, if it be so agreed upon in writ; for promises in this case may be resiled from, (as before is shown) but in either case the tenant must have intimation before the term, which will suffice without the solemnities of warning; but it must be of that length, that the tenant may provide for himself, and remove his goods, which will be in the arbitriment of the judge; and I suppose that they will walk most

fairly and safely, who shall intimate the same to the tenant forty days before the term; or otherwise, all the effect is like to be, that he will be decerned to remove at the next Whitsunday after the process, without violent profits, as uses to be done when there is any probable excuse for the tenant's not removing.

Summary removing is competent by law without paction, in all cases where the statute appointing warning, takes no place; which is chiefly regulate by the reason of the statute, that tenants be not put at unawares to seek their habitations, at an unseasonable time of the year; and therefore, it is not necessary in several cases. First, Where the possessor is not tenant, but a vitious possessor; or where the possessor hath nothing but an insufficient infeftment, or tolerance; for the statute is only in favour of tenants, who are liable for mails and duties. Secondly, Warning was not found necessary for removing possessors from a tower or fortalice, though set in tack, Hope, *hic*, La. Saltoun *contra* Livingston [Hope, *Maj. Pr.* VI, 16, 60], or from a coal, *Ibid.* Wolmet *contra* L. Niddrie [Hope, *Maj. Pr.* VI, 16, 54], or from the possession of a liferenter's house or land, which was in the liferenter's possession, after the liferenter's death, and that upon supplication, it was obtained without process, Hope, Liferent, Prestoun *contra* L. Cockpen [Hope, *Maj. Pr.* VI, 16, 54; M. 13820]. And this was competent at the instance of a liferenter against these who continued the possession of a former liferenter, after her death, January 12, 1622, La. Kincaid *contra* her Tennents [Durie 9; M. 13821]. The like, but to take effect at Whitsunday after the process, against a liferenter's servant, possessing without a tack in writ, and also without violent profits, February 16, 1628, Thomson *contra* Merstoun [Durie 346; M. 8252]. But if the possession from the liferenter be by virtue of a tack, the possessor must be warned; as hath been shown amongst the effects of tacks [II, 9, 23, *supra*]. Removing is also competent by force of law upon a process, to find caution for the rent, or to remove, of which before [II, 9, 33, *supra*]. As to what is special in tacks of teinds, it hath been considered in that title.

The prime kind of removing is that which is solemn upon warning; for clearing whereof, we shall first consider the order pre-required. Secondly, The interest of the pursuer. Thirdly, The exceptions of the defender. Fourthly, The effects of removing.

39. The order of removing of old was thus [IV, 26, 6, *infra*]; the master of the ground did only verbally intimate to the tenant to remove at the next Whitsunday; and the only solemnity requisite was, that before the said term, he appeared before the door of the tenant, and broke a lance there, as a symbol of his breaking the tacit relocation betwixt them; whereupon the second day after Whitsunday, he came *brevi manu*, and expelled the tenant: or at least laid out some of his goods to complete the solemnity of his removing Craig, *hic.* [II, 9, 4]. Hence arose many quarrels, violences and breaches of the public peace; as when the tenant had any reason or pretence for which he

could not remove, or otherwise was unwilling, and not compelled by law or public authority, but by private force.

40. For remeid whereof, that excellent statute concerning warning and removing of tenants was made, Parl. 1555, cap. 39 [A.P.S. 11,494,c.12], prescribing the order of removing thus: "That the master of the ground give a precept of warning in writ, commanding his officer (which may be any person he pleaseth) for whose name a blank is left in the precept, to go forty days preceding Whitsunday, and intimate to the tenant that he remove himself, his family, sub-tenants, goods and gear, at the said term, and leave the tenement void and red, that the warner may enter in possession:" this may be done either personally, or at his dwelling-house.

Secondly, The precept must authorise the officer to make the said denunciation, forty days before the term upon the ground of the land, leaving a copy affixed thereupon; and by the same space, it must be done at the kirk-door, at the time of dissolving the congregation, from the first sermon, leaving a copy thereof affixed upon the kirk-door; all which must be done before two witnesses required for that effect, and executions made conform by the officer, which without any other instrument or solemnity doth sufficiently prove, unless it be improven. Upon this order the pursuer hath a privileged action upon six days' warning only, without continuation, Parl. 1555, cap. 39 [A.P.S. 11,494,c.12], and that because of the necessity of dispatch, that the new tenant, who hath taken, may be put in possession, and the land not left waste, both to public and private detriment. This order must be used, though the term of the tack be not at Whitsunday, but at Martinmas or Candlemas; and it will not suffice to be made forty days before these terms, June 15, 1631, Ramsay *contra* Weir [Durie 590; M. 13857]. The reason hereof is, because the warning is appointed that the tenants may timeously provide for themselves, which cannot be but before Whitsunday, the ordinary time lands use to be set. If the parties removed be out of the country, it will suffice to warn them upon the ground, and at the kirk-door upon forty days; but the citation [in the process of removing], must be upon sixty days, which is consequent from the statute, which prescribes nothing different from the ordinary course of law, in the case of parties out of the country, and it was so decided, January 11, 1622, L. Faldenside *contra* L. Bimerside [Durie 8; M. 13860]; February 20, 1666, M'Brair *contra* Crightoun, alias Murray [1 Stair 360; M. 13861]. This statute reacheth not warnings from tenements within burgh, which are regulated by the custom of burgh: where the town-officer by command of a bailie, though without writ, warneth only at the tenement, forty days pre-preceding Whitsunday, and in evidence thereof, useth to chalk the door, Craig, *hic* [11,9,9]; this was extended to a house within burgh of barony, July 18, 1634, Hart *contra* [Durie 729; M. 3783]. For there the reason of the statute for warning, that possessors may provide lands to go to, when fuel may be cast, holds not. Nor was warning before Whitsunday found necessary, for removing a tenant from a soap-work, November 21, 1671, Riddel *contra*

Zinzan [2 Stair 5; M. 13828]. Now in place of Whitsunday, the warning must be forty days before the 15th of May, because Whitsunday being a moveable term, it did oft run far in summer, when removing tenants did eat up the entrant's meadows, Parl. 1689, cap. 39 [1690, c. 39; A.P.S. IX, 222, c. 98].

41. We come now to the title, requisite for removing, which must be a real right of the ground, except the question be against a party who is personally obliged to remove; and therefore, First, There needs no title against such parties, who had the possession from the pursuer; for these can never question his title, whose interest depends thereupon, as to right or possession, unless they be decerned to acknowledge another. Secondly, A personal or incomplete right is a sufficient title for removing against the granter of it, or his heirs, if it contain a clause to remove, or put the pursuer in possession, expressly or by consequence. Thirdly, Infeftment of property or liferent is a sufficient title in removing, and that upon production of the seasin only; where the defender shows no better right; but the seasin must be both before the warning and the term, except in the case of heirs, this being a possessory judgment, and a continuance of the predecessor's possession; so that the tenant cannot be in doubt or hazard to quit the possession, as he may be in other cases, where he may be liable, both for the rent and rendering the possession to another party; and so it was sustained at the instance of an heir, though his retour and seasin were after the warning, Had. February 9, 1610, E. of Kinghorn *contra* Arbuthnot [Haddington, *Fol. Dict.* 11, 304; M. 13265]; Hope, Removing, Small *contra* tenants of Baltersaw [Hope, *Maj. Pr.* VI, 16, 55; M. 13266]; in the case of an appriser, whose apprising was before the warning, it was found valid, though the infeftment was after, against the debtor, from whom the lands were apprised, but to take effect at Whitsunday thereafter, and without violent profits, December 18, 1632, Dalrymple *contra* Douglas [Durie 659; M. 13276]. And removing was sustained, at the instance of an heir retoured and infeft, pursued upon a warning used by his predecessor, though his infeftment was after the term, July 28, 1637, E. of Haddingtoun *contra* His Tennents [Durie 855; M. 3173]. It was also sustained at the instance of a fiar, upon a warning made by a liferenter and fiar jointly, November 27, 1629, Ramsay *contra* Hume [Durie 470; M. 3173, 13792]. But a removing was not sustained upon a warning made by the fiar, before the liferenter's death, no not to take effect at the next Whitsunday, without a new warning, June 30, 1669, Agnew *contra* Tennents of Dronlaw [*Sub nom.* Agnew v E. Cassils, 1 Stair 628; M. 2232].

Though infeftment be the best title for removing, yet it must be limited. First, It takes no place being upon infeftment proceeding upon a precept of *clare constat*, Hope, *hic*, Stevinson *contra* Stevinson [Hope, *Maj. Pr.* VI, 16, 70; M. 13268]; and that in respect this precept is but the assertion of the granter: yet if either the predecessor of that heir was in possession, or the superior himself, it would suffice. And for the same cause an infeftment upon the owner's resignation, is not sufficient without possession. Secondly, it holds not in base infeftments, not clad with possession, (unless the author's right be instructed or acknowledged) if the defender have any title requiring reduction, to avoid it. Thirdly, A tercer's service and kenning to her terce, is a sufficient title in removing. Fourthly, The courtesy of Scotland is a good title for removing even after a wife's death, without any seasin or solemnity; or the husband's *jus mariti*, before her death, which will be effectual, though she die before sentence or process, to the effect, that the husband may get the benefit of the violent profits, for the time preceding her death, though he cannot attain the possession. Fifthly, An executor may insist for a removing upon a warning used by the defunct, to the effect he may obtain the violent profits, due before the defunct's death. Sixthly, A tack is a sufficient title for removing, if it contain expressly the power to out-put and in-put tenants, or if it be a liferent-tack, or for nineteen years or above, as hath been now shown amongst the effects of tacks [11,9,26,*supra*]; but this must proceed either upon the setter's right, or a possessory judgment in the setter or tacksman.

Removing was not sustained upon an incomplete right, as upon an apprising, though the superior was charged, and the letters had been found orderly proceeded against him, to infeft the appriser; and the objection only proponed by tenants, pretending no right, March 25, 1628, Lockhart *contra* His Tennents [Durie 370; M. 13790]. Which will not hold as to apprisings led since the year 1661, whereby the Act between debtor and creditor [Diligence Act, 1661,c. 62; A.P.S. VII,317,c. 344] declares an apprising with a charge effectual. The like holds in adjudications [111,2,24,*infra*], but in the case of the superior's pursuing upon the vassal's liferent-escheat, it must be declared, Hope, *hic*, Butter *contra* Harvie [Hope, *Maj.Pr.* VI,16,53; M. 13266]. And so consequently in all other rights of superiority, where declarator is required. And though the superior needs show no title, unless the vassal disclaim him, yet his donatar pursuing upon a liferent-escheat, was not admitted till the superior's seasin was produced, Hope, *hic*, M'Call *contra* Tenants [Possibly Hope, *Maj.Pr.* VI,16,56 or VI,16,67; M. 13787]: and it is so in all cases wherein the superior or the vassal are singular successors, and so have ground to doubt, and cannot be put to disclaim.

42. We come now to the exceptions against removing; to speak nothing here of common exceptions, or of the pursuer's want of a sufficient title, which are rather objections than exceptions, and are sufficiently cleared by what we have said upon the titles of removing. It must be adverted, that before the defender can have any exception admitted to his probation, he must find caution for the violent profits, if he succumb; and that by the said statute, Parl. 1555, cap. 39 [A.P.S. 11,494,c. 12], justly introduced in respect of the contentiousness of parties to keep possession; yet this will not hinder objections against the titles or other defences being instantly verified, and not making delay, it being the motive of that Act to prevent delays.

43. These exceptions, though they be many, may be thus marshalled; they are, First, Against the order and warning. Secondly, Upon deeds done

by the pursuer. Thirdly, Upon the interest of the defender's master. Fourthly, Upon the defender's own interest. Fifthly, Upon obedience. For the first, every point of the warning now related, is so necessary, that the omitting of any one affordeth a sufficient defence.

Removing may be excluded by deeds done by the pursuer, either by any personal obligement not to remove, or by any deed importing the same; as a disposition or obligement to infeft, which are sufficient against him, but not against his singular successors; or if he renounce, or pass from the warning or action either directly, or by deeds importing the same; as taking rents before the hand, or taking a herezeld as to the year ensuing [11,9,23,*supra*], March 20, 1629, Auchinleck *contra* Mathie [Durie 439; M. 5409]; or by accepting the old accustomed mails for terms after the warning, Hope, *hic*, Carnousie *contra*   [Hope, *Maj.Pr.* VI,16,69; M. 15315]; or by receipt of taxation for terms since the term of removing, *ibid.*; or by accepting services contained in the tack, for the terms after the warning; but this is not relevant, if the same be at the command of the pursuer's factor or grieve, without special order, March 5, 1629, L. of Lie younger *contra* Kirkwood [Durie 433; M. 7195]; neither by accepting presents, though accustomed, not being special in the tack, these being interpreted gratuitous, as before is shown [11,9,36, *supra*].

Removing is also elided by prescription, upon three years' forbearance to pursue; and that by the statute 1579, cap. 82 [A.P.S. III,145,c.20], for thereby the pursuer is presumed to pass from his warning; but these three years are not accounted *anni continui*, but *anni utiles* from the warning, without accounting the time betwixt the warning and term, but from the term to which the warning was made; because none can be said to delay to pursue, before he be necessitate to pursue, which is not till after the term; it was so decided February 6, 1629, La. Borthwick *contra* Scot [Durie 422; M. 11076]. But removing may be sustained before the term, that it may take effect precisely at the term; otherwise many tenants may be disappointed, who take upon the warning of other tenants, their roums, and renounce their own, or are warned therefrom; and so removing was sustained before the term, to take effect then, November 21, 1671, Riddel *contra* Zinzan [2 Stair 5; M. 13828]. But the process being once intented, it continues till the great prescription of forty years, except such as are not wakened every five years, for such prescribe in ten years by the Act 9, Parl. 1669 [Prescription Act 1669, c.9; A.P.S. VII, 561, c. 14].

The exceptions of removing on the interest of the master of the ground, are very frequent and various; for it is ordinarily proponed and sustained, that the defenders are tenants by payment of mail and duty to a third party, who is not warned nor called; neither are they put to dispute their master's right, to be valid, which holdeth, whether his right be an infeftment, liferent-right or tack; and though the tenant hath been put to condescend what the right is, and that in *specie*, it is a valid right, though he needs not dispute the particular defects of it, nor the competition of it with any other right. This exception is also elided by this reply, that the defenders had acknowledged the pursuer by payment of mail and duty. It is also elided by alleging, that the defender's master's right was reduced at the pursuer's instance, December 12, 1622, Spalding *contra* Fleming [Not found]. The like where his right was reduced at the instance of the pursuer's author, Spots. *hic*, Maxwel *contra* Tenants of Glassock [Spotiswoode 281; M. 13788], E. of Nithisdale *contra* his Tenants [Spotiswoode 284; M. 15184].

The exceptions against removing upon the defender's own right, are either in respect of his right to the lands in question, or to the other lands brooked by him *pro indiviso* with it; for the first, there are as many such defences as there are rights competent for defending possession; and they are either founded upon the benefit of a possessory judgment [II, 7, 22, *supra*; IV, 3, 47, *infra*], which how competent, may be seen at large Title, Infeftment, 13, §82, which needs not to be here repeated; or if that be not competent, the defender must found himself upon the point of right, which ordinarily infers a competition of rights; but in either case the defence will not be sustained upon any right, if the possession was not attained thereupon, but upon the pursuer's right; which possession must be restored, and the defender left to his action upon the other right, as accords; as if after redemption of a temporary right, whereby the defender entered in possession, he should defend upon another right, which will not be sustained in this possessory judgment, against him or his successor, from whom he had the possession, November 22, 1677, Stuart of Castlemilk *contra* D. Hamilton [2 Stair 561; M. 9222; II, 1, 27, *supra*: II, 10, 23, *infra*].

The exception *pro indiviso* [IV, 3, 12, *infra*] is very pregnant, and taketh not only place in solemn removings, but in the action to find caution for mails and duties, or to remove, though the excipient had taken tacks from the pursuer, December 6, 1623, *contra* Carmichael [Durie 88; M. 10599]. Yet it was not found relevant, to stop removing from the pursuer's part of a coalheugh in lands undivided, because the coals are divisible by measure as they are raised out of the coal-pit, Spots. Removing, Somervel *contra* Dickson [Spotiswoode 38]. Neither was it found sufficient to maintain a relict in possession of a house, which could not be divided. whereof she had a third part, and possessed the other two-thirds *pro indiviso*; but the fiar having the two-thirds, was to be preferred to the possession, paying her the third of the mail, upon condition that if he set the tenement, she should be preferred, giving as much mail as another, January 26, 1665, Logan *contra* Galbraith [1 Stair 257; M. 15842]. But if more tenants possess *pro indiviso*, if they have different dwellings, that defence will not be sustained, either as to that house, or the share of the possession.

The last exception against removing is, obedience by voluntary removing, conform to the warning, and leaving the land void and red at the term, without necessity of a renunciation in writ, March 2, 1637, Keith *contra* Simpson

[Durie 834; M. 5933]. But the allegeance of obedience was not found relevant upon an exception, bearing, "that the land was left void and red at the term," seeing that it bore not, "that the possession was offered to the charger:" in respect that at that time of his removing, another party entered in his vice. Here there was not only a warning, but a decreet of removing; but a party may pass from, and not insist in a warning; therefore the tenant's actual removing is not sufficient without renouncing or offering the void possession, that the warner may enter therein; for otherwise he is not secure, but another entering in the vice may put him to a new action, though not *de facto* entered Jan. penult. 1624, Greenlaw *contra* Adamson [Durie 103; M. 13888]. But the obedience must be full, according to the warning by the defender's removing himself, his family, sub-tenants and cottars, goods and gear, so that the pursuer may enter in possession; and therefore decreet would be obtained against the principal tacksman, and the letters still put to execution against him, till all these be removed; and if the pursuer please, he may pursue them to remove, without other warning than what was made to the principal tacksmen; so it was sustained against a son upon a warning against his father, even after his father's death, January 27, 1630, Hume *contra* Hume [Durie 486; M. 3173].

As to the last point, concerning the effects of decreets of removing, it is not only the attaining possession of the land itself, but sometimes also the corns growing thereupon, as being a part thereof, being a violent possession, Hope, Spuilzie, Elliot *contra* Lo. Buckcleugh [Hope, *Maj. Pr.* VI, 18, 72; M. 14761]. Yea, of the hay of that crop, though separated and stacked by the person removed, Hope, Spuilzie, Sir James Balmuir *contra* Williamson [Hope, *Maj. Pr.* VI, 18, 62; M. 14761]. But the main effect is, the obtaining the violent profits of the land, until the possessor's obedience; and that both against these who are warned, and against these who succeed in the vice of warned or removed tenants.

44. Violent profits [IV, 29, 1, *infra*] are so called, because they are such profits as are due by and for violent possession, whatsoever way it be, by warning and removing, ejection, intrusion, or succeeding in the vice, and they are opposite to ordinary profits, which were due by tacit relocation, or were formerly accustomed to be paid. Violent profits are pursued for by a several action, after the decreet of removing is obtained; wherein the decreet of re-removing is both a sufficient title, and probation of the violent possession against the parties removed therein, and their possession needs not again be proven, and their defences hindering the pursuer to obtain possession, would not be sufficient, unless they offer to prove the pursuer himself was in possession, or others by his warrant, Had. June 19, 1610, Monro *contra* L. Balnagoun [Haddington, *Fol. Dict.* II, 302; M. 13260, 16460]. Neither will any other thing but real obedience, by giving, or at least by offering the void possession, take them away, though the land lie waste. But violent profits were also found competent against these who were not warned, against whom

decreet of removing was not obtained, to wit, against any who suspended the decreet, and thereby hindered the defender's [pursuer's] attaining possession, Hope, Mails and duties, Ker of Fairnieherst *contra* Turnbull [Hope, *Maj. Pr.* VI, 19, 9]. Yea, a party obtaining possession by a decreet of removing, after litiscontestation in the reduction of the decreet, was found a violent possessor, and liable to violent profits himself, Hope, Possession, Gordon of Abergeldie *contra* L. Forbes [Hope, *Maj. Pr.* III, 21, 22; M. 14747]. As to the quantity of violent profits by the custom of burgh, it is the double mail of the tenements within burgh, Hope, Mails and duties, Buchan *contra* Seaton [Hope, *Maj. Pr.* VI, 19, 7; I, 9, 27, *supra*]. But in lands it is the greatest profits that the pursuer can prove he could have made. And though in cases of violence, the quantities and prices are ordinarily probable by the pursuer's oath, *iuramento in litem*, because he ought to have, not the ordinary value, but *pretium affectionis*, as that which themselves accounted to be their loss; yet here probation must be used: but if it be not full, the pursuer's oath may be taken. Violent profits are also sustained against all defenders *in solidum*, as in spuilzie [I, 9, 5, *supra*]; but when diverse compeared, and proponed partial objections against removings, and succumbed, they were found liable for the violent profits of the lands in the exceptions severally, Hope, Mails and duties, Wallace *contra* Blair [Hope, *Maj. Pr.* VI, 19, 8]; otherwise partial exceptions are not here competent, Hope, Exceptions, L. Balnagoun *contra* Monro [Hope, *Maj. Pr.* VI, 41, 12; M. 16460]. Neither will any exceptions be admitted, which was competent and proper in the decreet of removing, relative to right or possession, but suspension or reduction be obtained. The like as to violent profits against successors in the vice, March 22, 1623, L. Hunthil *contra* Rutherford [Durie 61; M. 13379].

45. Succeeding in the vice is a kind of intrusion, whereby after warning any person comes in possession, by consent of the parties warned, or their fault in not offering the void possession; but if the possession be taken without the master's consent any other way, it is an ordinary intrusion: or otherwise against such there needs no warning but a summary process, as in other intrusions, having the same probation; for in both, the possession must be proven, which with the warning is sufficient; but can have no effect till decreet of removing be obtained against the tenant warned. Though violent profits be the ordinary effect, both in removing and succeeding in the vice, these will proceed as to attaining possession, and no violent profits be obtained, when there is any colourable title, which might have made the warned party reasonably doubt of the pursuer's interest, or of his own right, Hope, Removing, Ord *contra* Tenants [Hope, *Maj. Pr.* VI, 39, 28; M. 9769]. But this useth ordinarily to be so provided in the decreet of removing, and will be hardly sustained thereafter, by re-canvassing the defences competent in the removing, that it may appear whether there were a probable ground in them or not; or at least the defender would protest for the reservation as to the violent profits; for if this were again sustained, it would bring over-head all the many

intricate defences competent in removings, of which formerly: therefore in the removing pursued by the E. of Argyle *contra* L. Macnaughton [2 Stair 278; M. 13889], the Lords repelled the defences, but declared that they would have consideration thereof, as having probable ground to debate, and would modify the excrescence of the violent profits, over and above the ordinary profits, July 16, 1674.

Title 10. Wadsets, Where, of Reversion, Regress and Redemption

A WADSET, as the word insinuates, being the giving of a wad or pledge in security; it falleth in consideration here as the last of feudal rights: for pledges are the last of real rights, as before in the title Real Rights is shown; where it was also cleared, what was the ancient custom of impignoration of moveables, which shall not be here repeated, but only what is proper to the impignoration of immoveables and heritable rights, by the feudal customs, and our own.

1. That which doth most properly agree to the nature of a pledge or wadset with us, is where any infeftment or security is granted in security of a sum of money, or for relief of cautionry, or any other sum, which bears expressly, "that the land or right is disponed for security or relief;" and therefore needs express no reversion; for it is necessarily implied that, so soon as relief or satisfaction is obtained, the infeftment granted in security ceaseth; so that if the granter of the infeftment, or any other bound in the principal obligation, either make payment, or the receiver thereof by his intromission be satisfied, *ipso facto*, the infeftment is extinct: yea, if the debtor, granter of the infeftment and security, should instruct compensation, as it would extinguish the principal bond, so would it in consequence the infeftment for security thereof. This infeftment being really a pledge, it is consistent with the infeftment of

property in the debtor, as two distinct kinds of rights; and thereby the debtor is not denuded, even although the infeftment for security were public by resignation; because it is not a resignation simply *in favorem*, but *ad effectum*, viz. for security; and therefore, when the debt is satisfied, the debtor needs not to be re-invested, but his former infeftment of property stands valid [III, 2, 38, *infra*]. It is also a wadset, when an infeftment of property, or any other real right is burdened with any sum of money: for thereby that right is impledged to the person to whom such sums are due, which differeth from the former in this, that the infeftment for satisfaction of sums, is immediately effectual for mails and duties, or removing, or for maintaining possession of the profits till the sums be paid: but sums wherewith a real right is burdened, have not these effects until adjudication be used upon the sums, and infeftment or a charge thereupon, which is drawn back to the date of the security burdened, and is preferable to prior adjudications upon personal debts [II, 3, 58, *supra*], in the same way as adjudications upon infeftments of annualrent have effect from the date of the infeftment of annualrent. These adjudications may be deduced at the instance, not only of the first creditor, but of his heirs and successors, or any his or their assignees, voluntary or judicial by arrestment, and decreets for making forthcoming; and, if the sum burdening be tailzied to diverse persons, or diverse heirs, in several cases, adjudications may proceed at any of their instances, having right for the time; and whatsoever way the sum burdening be paid or satisfied, the rights following thereupon are extinct *ipso facto*, and the proprietor needeth no resignation. But when a right is burdened with another real right, the right burdening hath immediate access, as if it were a right of property, and both it and the former right for sums burdening real rights, are preferable to the rights burdened; and even the real right burdening, doth imply a reversion to the owner of the right burdened, if they be for security of sums.

Like unto these in all points are infeftments upon apprising, which are truly *pignora prætoria*, whereby the debtor is not denuded, but his infeftment stands; and if the apprising be satisfied within the legal, it is extinguished, and the debtor needs not to be re-invested; and therefore, he may receive vassals during the legal; and if he die, the apparent heir intromitting with the mails and duties during the legal, doth thereby behave himself as heir, as was found, February 21, 1663, Hamilton *contra* Hamilton [I Stair 185; M. 9655]. Which holds also in adjudications, by the late Act of Parliament [Adjudications Act, 1672, c. 19; A.P.S. VIII, 93, c. 45], now come in place of apprisings.

But securities for sums have been of a long time taken frequently in another way, viz. by simple alienation, *titulo venditionis*, with a reversion, which is but *pactum de retro vendendo*, ordinarily taken apart; that if the creditor were not satisfied, he might force the debtor to pass from his reversion; and so his right stood absolute, which gave the occasion to these kinds of securities; and also because during Popery, all annualrents for the use of sums were discharged as usury; and therefore creditors bought annualrents, and gave reversions to the debtors, which was the same thing in another conveyance. As to these wadsets, we are to treat thereof in this place; and first, as to the constitution of wadsets; and next as to the destitution or extinction thereof.

2. As to the constitution of a wadset, it must be according to the thing or right impignorated; for a tack or liferent, or an assignation to these, or any other cessible right, may be given in wadset for security, and under reversion; but the ordinary wadset is by infeftment of property, or of annualrent; the conception whereof is not under the name of impledging, impignoration, hypothecation, or the like, but in the terms of disposition, or infeftment, whereby the property of the thing wadset passeth, and is established in the wadsetter, but under reversion to the constituent, whereby it hath two parts, the infeftment and the reversion. The infeftment in wadsets, is in all points like to other infeftments, whether they be infeftments of property or of annualrent, or whether they be public, holden of the constituent's superior, or base, holden of the granter himself; so that all the specialities of wadsets resolve in the reversion.

3. A reversion is a paction and condition, or provision for redemption of any thing alienated, upon such terms as are agreed upon [1, 14, 4, *supra*], which of itself is no more than a personal obligation, whereby the wadsetter is obliged; until by that excellent statute, Parl. 1469, cap. 27 [Reversion Act, 1469, c. 27; A.P.S. 11, 94, c. 3], it is declared, that the reversion shall be effectual, not only against the first wadsetter himself, but all his successors in the wadset lands; whereby reversions are accounted as heritable and real rights, effectual against singular successors, in the same way that tacks are made real rights, by the statute thereanent. The English by reversion, do not understand a right of redemption, but a right of survivancy or succession; as the reversion of an office, is a title to that office, after the removal of the present incumbent. And that which we call a wadset, they call a mortgage; for a gage is a pledge which is really engaged: and mortgage is a pledge, the redemption whereof dieth, or is extinct, if it be not used at the time, and in the manner agreed upon by the parties; so that with them in their mortgages, not only clauses irritant, or *pacta legis commissoriæ*, are valid; but if the provision for redemption be for a definite time, that being elapsed, the mortgage becomes irredeemable by their common law: what remeid may be had in the chancery upon equity, I know not.

4. Before we come to the solemnities requisite for constituting reversions, it is necessary to distinguish the several kinds thereof. Reversions are either legal, arising from law and statute, and not from consent of parties, as are the legal reversions of apprisings and adjudications; or they are conventional, by the consent of parties, which are either incorporate in the body of the wadset-right, or apart. They are also either principal reversions, or eiks to reversions; and they are either solemn and perfected, or only inchoate, such as promises, bonds, and conditions, for granting reversions.

5. Legal reversions require no other solemnity, than what is requisite to

the legal constitution of the right whereupon they follow. The common solemnities requisite for reversions and other writs of old, was only the seal of the granter, without necessity of his subscription. But, by the Act of Parl. 1555, cap. 29 [A.P.S. 11, 492, c. 2], it is required, that all reversions, bonds and obligations for making of reversions, be not only sealed, but subscribed by the granter's own hand, and if he cannot write, by his hand led at the pen by a notary; or otherwise, they make no faith, unless the same by consent of parties be registrate in the books of a judge ordinary, or that it be a reversion within burgh, contained in the instrument of resignation and seasin of lands by the bailie and town-clerk. And, by the Act of Parl. 1579, cap. 80 [Subscription of Deeds Act, 1579, c. 80; A.P.S. 111, 145, c. 18; 11, 3, 20, *supra*], reversions, assignations, and discharges thereof, and eiks thereto, or other writs of great importance, are ordained to be subscribed and sealed by the principal parties; or if they cannot write, by two notars before four witnesses designed, else to be null and of no faith. But the matter of reversions is perfected by the Act of Parliament, 1617, cap. 16 [Registration Act, 1617, c. 16; A.P.S. IV, 545, c. 16], ordaining all reversions, regresses, bonds or writs for making reversions, assignations and discharges of the same, to be registrate in the Register of Seasins and Reversions within sixty days of their dates, otherwise to have no effect, save only against the granters thereof, but not against their singular successors acquiring perfect and lawful rights: but this was not requisite in infeftments of burgage-lands within royal burghs, nor in reversions incorporate in the rights of wadset. Upon consideration of this inconvenience and insecurity of burgage-lands, the Lords by Act of Sederunt, ordained the burghs to take sufficient caution of their town clerks present and to come, to insert in their books all seasins given by them of tenements within burgh, and all reversions or bonds for granting reversions, assignations thereto, and discharges thereof, renunciations and grants of redemption, and that within sixty days after the giving of seasin, or presenting to them of the reversions or others foresaid, under the pain of the damage of parties, acquiring *bona fide* for onerous causes, that they may incur, by such latent rights; declaring, that such seasins and reversions, not insert in manner foresaid, to be esteemed as latent and fraudulent, kept up of purpose to insnare lawful purchasers; which Act of Sederunt is dated, February 22, 1681. So that, as by the first Act reversions are made effectual, by this last they are made evident, that acquirers may be secured against latent reversions; But now by Act of Parliament 1681, cap. 11 [A.P.S. VIII, 248, c. 13], a Register for Reversions is appointed, as well for these in burgh, as for these without burghs, and by the registration, or being in the body of the wadset, the necessity of sealing is taken off, and in desuetude. It is also consequent from this last Act, that not only formal and solemn reversions in the body of the wadset, or registrate, are effectual against singular successors; but also bonds and writs for making of reversions: otherwise there needs no ordinance to registrate these for the purchaser's security, if of themselves they could [not] affect purchasers [11, 7, 1, *supra*]:

but promises of reversion are nowise effectual against singular successors unless they have been brought into writ, at least by decreet before these successors' right; because being only probable by oath of party, the oath of the author will not prove against his singular successor. Neither will declarations, backbonds, or conditions of trust, be comprehended under reversions; but they remain obligements personal upon the person intrusted, unless they contain express obligements to redispone, which is a reversion, albeit it be not formal; or if it bear, to denude in favour of the disponer or any other; but if it be in trust to his behoof, though thereupon, *via actionis*, the trustee might be compelled to denude, yet it is no reversion; and however hath no effect against singular successors, unless they be registrate as aforesaid; except in so far as they may be grounds of reduction against the parties intrusted, or their singular successors, partakers of the fraud.

6. It is also frequently provided in reversions, that if the condition of the reversion be not performed betwixt and such a time, the reversion shall expire; and sometimes it is provided so to be, *ipso facto*, without declarator. This is a clause irritant, irritating or annulling the reversion, which in the civil law is called, *Pactum legis commissoriæ in pignoribus*, and is thereby rejected and void as an usurary paction, whereby the wadsetter getteth more than his just interest as a penalty; which therefore, as in other cases, ought to be modified to the just interest; especially seeing indigent debtors, through necessity of borrowing money, will be easily induced to such clauses [1, 13, 14, *supra*; IV, 18, 3; IV, 5, 7, *infra*]. And therefore a backbond for redemption of a tenement, bearing such a clause irritant, was found null two years after the term, and after a decreet of removing, all meliorations being satisfied, July 8, 1636, Cleghorn *contra* Ferguson [Durie 811; M. 7204]. Yet such clauses irritant are effectual upon the failzie committed, unless they be purged by performance, which is ordinarily received, when offered at the bar, in the declarator of the expiring of the reversion: so it was found purgeable at the instance of the reverser's creditors, March 19, 1631, Scot *contra* Dickson [Durie 584; M. 7203]. Yea, though the payment was not present, a time was granted before the extract of the decreet of declarator of the expiring of the reversion, that in the mean time, the failzie might be purged by interposition with the parties, February 7, 1628, Pringle *contra* Ker [Durie 341; M. 7203]; but no such time was granted where the requisition was upon ninescore days; but decreet was given, unless present payment were made, July 19, 1625, Nairn *contra* Napier [Durie 178; M. 7292]. But clauses irritant in reversions are only thus qualified in real impignorations: but when the reversion is of a true sale, not in security, but for an equivalent price, or where it is granted after the right related to, and not for implement of a promise or condition made at that time, it is valid; for only *pactum legis commissoriæ in pignoribus*, is rejected in law [1, 13, 14; 1, 14, 4, *supra*]. And therefore the irritancy was not found purgeable before the declarator, where the reversion was of lands disponed for a competent price by a true sale, January 17, 1679, Beatson *contra* Harrower [2 Stair 676;

M. 7208]. A bond bearing, that failing heirs-male of the granter, and of his brother's body, that the heirs-female should denude in favour of a sister's son, upon payment of a certain sum, being registrate in the Register of Reversions, was found valid against a singular successor, as a conditional reversion, and not as a substitution, albeit the bond was granted by an heritor, and that the land was never wadset, but became redeemable by this bond; and was not prejudged by a posterior liferent granted by that heritor in favours of his wife, which would have been effectual, if it had been a substitution; but the sum upon which the heir-female was obliged to denude, was ordained to be re-employed for the wife in liferent, January 16, 1679, L. Lambertoun *contra* La. Plendergaist [2 Stair 673; M. 10173].

7. As to the nature of reversions, they are *stricti juris*, and not to be extended beyond what is expressed, and so not to be extended to the assignees of the reverser, when not expressed, yea, not to his heirs, unless it be so expressed; but where heirs of the reverser were not expressed, without adjecting the ordinary clause of paying the debt to the wadsetter by the reverser, any time during his life, and so heirs were not found omitted *dedita opera*, but by negligence, they were not excluded, January 9, 1662, E. Murray *contra* L. Graunt [1 Stair 77; M. 10322; III, 5, 5, *infra*]. And a reversion taken by a father disponing to his son, found to be extended against the heirs of the son, though heirs were not mentioned, February 6, 1630, Muir *contra* Muir [Durie 490; M. 10339]. This was advised in absence. The like Spots. Redemption, Hamilton *contra* Hamiltons [Not found]. And the day of consignation being appointed eight days after the term, the consignation was not sustained at the term itself, though these days were introduced in the reverser's favour, July 12, 1634, Lo. Balmerino *contra* Eliot [Durie 725; M. 13460]; yet where the reversion bore the premonition to be at the parish church, it was sustained, being used only personally, December 11, 1638, Finlayson *contra* Wemys [Durie 866; M. 2170]. And where the reversion did bear consignation at the creditor's house in London, it was sustained, being at his successor's house in Edinburgh, Feb. 1, 1667, Creditors of Murray *contra* Murray [1 Stair 432; M. 13465].

8. The constitution or nature of wadsets being thus cleared, as to the kinds thereof, wadsets are either proper or improper; and they are either public or base.

9. A proper wadset is, where the fruits of the thing wadset are only given for the annualrent of the sum, and the hazard or benefit thereof, whether it rise or fall, is the wadsetters'; and there hath never been any case decided finding such proper wadsets usurary upon exorbitancy of profit: but by the Act of Parliament 1661, cap. 62, betwixt debtor and creditor [Diligence Act, 1661, c. 62; A.P.S. VII, 317, c. 344], all wadsets before that Act, though proper, are so altered, that if the person having right to the reversion offer surety and demand possession, the wadsetter must quit possession, or else restrict himself to his annualrent, and count for the superplus, and that not from the

Act of Parliament or citation, but from the offer of security; which was not sustained at the instance of a singular successor in the right of reversion, not having produced his right to the reversion at the requisition: and though it was produced in the process, the wadsetter was not found obliged to restrict or cede the possession, because he was in natural possession by labourage, till he were warned before Whitsunday, February 20, 1679, Bruce *contra* Bogie [2 Stair 699; M. 16530]; the restriction was also sustained, though there was a clause in the wadset renouncing the Usurper's Act, and all such Acts made or to be made; for that exception in the Act of Parliament relateth only to preceding clauses thereof, and not to the clause anent wadsets, which is posterior, January 29, 1662, L. Lamington *contra* Chiesly [1 Stair 88; M. 16520]; February 21, 1666, Lo. Borthwick *contra* his Wadsetters [1 Stair 361; M. 16524]; February 21, 1666, Ogilvie *contra*   [1 Stair 362; M. 16525]. In these cases it was considered, that there was no clause in the Usurper's Act for making proper wadsetters comptable, and therefore the renouncing that or the like Acts, did not hinder compting by this Act; only from the offer to find caution, made by instrument or judicially, in case the wadsetter choosed not to quit the possession, he became comptable.

10. But where in wadsets there is a condition of the reversion, that a tack should be granted for years after redemption, that tack was not found taken away by the Act Debtor and Creditor [Diligence Act, 1661, c. 62; A.P.S. VII, 317, c. 344]; but that if it were in the terms of the old Act, Parl. 1449, cap. 19 [Leases Act, 1449, c. 19; A.P.S. II, 35, c. 6], far within the true avail, it were usurary and null [1, 15, 7; II, 9, 8, *supra*], February 15, 1666, Lo. Ley *contra* Porteous [1 Stair 356; M. 16523]; February 17, 1672, Douglas *contra* and Verner [2 Stair 70; M. 16412]; in which case the tack was sustained, if it were not much within the worth of the land, as it was the time of granting the wadset, albeit it were much within the worth the time of the redemption; because there is a just design in such tacks to encourage the wadsetter to meliorate the wadset lands, and be at expenses therefor, seeing he will retain the same after the redemption, for the old rent they were worth when wadset, and the rent expressed in the tack will be presumed to be the true rent, unless the contrary be proven. But such a wadset granted to a brother for his portion, wherein the wadsetter was excluded from possession during a liferenter's life, the tack was sustained, January 21, 1662, L. Polwart *contra* Hume [1 Stair 84; M. 16408].

11. If there be a back-tack of the land, granted by the wadsetter to the reverser, or for his behoof, or a provision to compt for the profits of the land, or to hold the land at such a rent, it is an improper wadset.

12. A public wadset, which is holden of the constituent's superior, requireth, beside the reversion, a regress, which is an obligement upon the superior to receive and enter the reverser his vassal again upon the redemption: the necessity whereof is, because by the infeftment, though in wadset, the constituent is denuded, and the superior hath a new vassal, in whose place

he is not obliged to accept any other but by his own consent. Craig, *Lib.*2, *Dieg.*6 [11,6,25], moveth this question, whether a public wadset, being redeemed, and the reverser re-seased therein, it would be accounted heritage or conquest. And though it seem conquest, because it is a new infeftment, and not the old, yet he well resolveth, that if it return to the person, or the heirs of him, who was first infeft, if it was heritage before, it remaineth so; but if an assignee to the reversion and regress be infeft, it is truly conquest.

13. It remaineth, now to consider the destitution of wadsets, and how they cease, and this is either by consent or by law: by consent, either when the reversion is discharged, whereby the infeftment becomes irredeemable, and ceaseth to be a wadset; which discharge of the reversion is not effectual against singular successors, unless registrate conform to the said Act of Parl. 1617, cap. 16 [Registration Act, 1617,c.16; A.P.S. IV,545,c.16]; or otherwise by voluntary redemption of the wadset, which must be registrate by the said Act, or else it prejudgeth no singular successor in the wadset: yet it is not effectual to denude the wadsetter, who remains in the fee of the wadset, till the reverser get a resignation *ad remanentiam*, if a wadset holden of the granter himself, or be refused by the superior, if the wadset was public, Hope, Alienations, Kinross *contra* Durie [Hope, *Maj.Pr.* 111,3,41; M.13445 and 16519]; November 23, 1627, Dumbar *contra* Williamson [Durie 315; M. 570]. But if the reverser or his predecessor was infeft, a renunciation may exclude the renouncer's right, but will not establish it in the person of the reverser, but he must brook by his own right, Hope, Alienation, Hamilton *contra* M'Adam [Hope, *Maj.Pr.* 111,3,40]. Where wadsets are taken holden of the superior, regresses are also taken from the superior, and new infeftment thereupon to the granter of the wadset; but when reversions are carried by assignations, apprisings, or adjudications, to these who were never infeft, they must not only have a renunciation from the wadsetter, but a procuratory of resignation, that thereby they may be infeft; in which case the wadset right is not extinct, but conveyed, and the wadsetter is their author, and may not refuse procuratories of resignation, or charters for confirmation upon redemption of the wadset by the assignee, or adjudger, to put the wadset-right in the assignee; and a renunciation will not be sufficient, because the assignee to the reversion needs not be infeft to carry the right of reversion; but must be infeft by the wadsetter, being satisfied of his sum; who must grant precepts of seasin for infefting the reverser holden of the wadsetter; and if infeftments follow thereupon, and the seasin be registrate, there is no necessity of renunciation or grant of redemption. Yet renunciations or grants of redemption being registrate, exclude posterior deeds of the wadsetter, who yet continues in the fee, and the casualities will fall by his death, or deeds; but declarators of redemption do fully denude the wadsetter, and in that they differ from voluntary redemptions.

14. Wadsets are taken off legally, when the reversion is annulled, as by declarator of expiring thereof; for thereby the infeftment becomes irredeem-

able; but is chiefly by a legal redemption, which doth require an order of redemption, and a declarator thereupon, which must be diversely used in legal reversions, and in conventional reversions.

15. The order of redemption of apprisings and adjudications, by virtue of the legal reversion, is valid by premonition and consignation, and instruments taken thereupon, wherein there is not appointed a determinate time upon which the premonition must be made, or a determinate place where the consignation must be made, nor the person of the consignatar; but the premonition may be upon any number of days, sufficient for the consignation; yea, though it were the same day of the premonition, as Craig [II,6,4 and 24; III,2,22] observes: but if the creditor be personally apprehended, the consignation must be in the way most to his advantage, which therefore he may prescribe, being either near the place of premonition, or the lands wadset, or the parish church where they lie, which Craig accounteth competent places; or if he choose any other more advantageous to the consigner, it will be sufficient: but if he choose none, the premonisher must either consign that day where he finds the creditor: or if he used premonition at his dwelling-house, he must consign, either at the appriser's dwelling-house, or parish-kirk where the lands lie, as said is. If the creditor be out of the country, or have no certain abode, letters of premonition will be obtained from the Lords, *periculo petentis*, for premonition upon sixty days at the cross of Edinburgh, and for consignation to be made in Edinburgh: yea the order was sustained for redemption of an apprising near expiring, albeit the consignation was only at Edinburgh, and not at the parish-kirk where the lands lie, or at the debtor's dwelling-house, he being out of the country, February 22, 1631, Murray *contra* Lo. Yester [Durie 573; M.3711]; but where the party was in the country, this order, by summons of premonition and citation personally taken thereupon, not being by instrument of premonition, was found void, July 23, 1622, E. Desmond *contra* Hay [Durie 32; M.13446]; Had. July 11, 1623, Capt. Crafurd *contra* L. Covingtoun [Haddington, *Fol. Dict.* I, 431; M.6417]; where an instrument of premonition was found necessary, though no determinate time be requisite; in these cases the legal hath not been near expired; but that a new formal order might have been used, yet the exorbitancy of apprisings hath made the slenderest orders of redemption to be sustained, as if the appriser had been in possession, whereby a previous count was necessary, to know what sums were to be offered or consigned, a summons for count and reckoning, and for accepting what was resting, being used within the legal, hath always been sustained, as was found, July 2, 1625, Doctor Kincaid *contra* Haliburtoun [Durie 170; M.314,13447]. And a consignation of a sum for redeeming of several apprisings made by a singular successor, was sustained, because the instrument bore "an offer to consign the sums in all the apprisings, whereto the defender had then right," being performed in the process, February 12, 1631, Murray *contra* Lo. Yester [Durie 573; M. 3711,13457].

16. The redemption of wadsets upon conventional reversions, is by an order of redemption, consisting of premonition, or requisition and consignation, which is made effectual by an action of declarator of redemption thereupon.

17. Premonition is an act or deed, whereby the reverser or his procurator premonisheth the wadsetter, conform to the tenor of the reversion, to appear at the place of consignation, and receive satisfaction according to the reversion; and if it require the wadsetter to come to the place of consignation and receive his money, it is called a requisition: and in either case, it must necessarily be done by way of instrument: this instrument useth to bear, Production of the Reversion: yet a premonition was sustained without that, seeing the reversion was contained in the wadsetter's own seasin. And a premonition was not found null, though the procuratory was not produced, where the procuratory was not called for, January 18, 1662, Veatch *contra* Leyel of Bassendine [1 Stair 83; M. 12266]. But a requisition was found null, because it bore not "a procuratory produced the time of the requisition," albeit another instrument of the same notar did bear "a procuratory produced," and that in respect the question was not betwixt a wadsetter and reverser, neither party having damage, but betwixt a donatar of the single escheat, and the creditors of the wadsetter; so that if the Lords supplied the not production of the procuratory, the sum consigned would become moveable, and fall to the fisk; therefore the Lords refused to supply the procuratory, and found the requisition null, and the wadset unredeemed, January 12, 1677, creditors of Wamphray *contra* L. Calderhall [2 Stair 492; M. 8340]. Which for the same cause would hold, if the question had been betwixt the heir and the executor of the wadsetter; for in either of these cases, the formality of the requisition has the importance of the whole right; and where the reversion was in the wadsetter's own hand, and craved to be exhibited the time of the consignation, the premonition was found good without it, Hope, Wadsets, Lo. Yester *contra* Scot [Hope, *Maj. Pr.* iii, 10, 41 and 53; M. 13445]. The like in a redemption at an appriser's instance, who apprised the reversion, Feb. 19, 1662, Children of Wolmet *contra* Ker [1 Stair 103; M. 13463]. The like in a singular successor to a reversion redeeming, February 17, 1668, Montgomery *contra* Heirs of Haliburton [1 Stair 181; M. 13463]. Here the reversion was in the wadset right, which was in the defender's own hand.

Premonition may be done, either personally, or at the wadsetter's dwelling-house. But it was found null, when the dwelling house was not designed, Dec. 13, 1626, E. Buckcleugh *contra* Young [Durie 244; M. 13448]. Premonition must be used against the tutors and curators of minors, either generally at the Mercat Cross, or otherwise to the tutors and curators personally, December 17, 1629, L. Carnousie *contra* L. Techmuirie [Durie 475; M. 2181, 13454]. And a requisition was found null, because not made to tutors and curators by letters from the Lords, but only by an instrument taken at the market-cross, June 15, 1680, Gordon *contra* E. Queensberry [2 Stair 770;

M. 8235]. A premonition was sustained, though the reversion bore, "that it should be done at the parish-kirk," and it was done personally, which was accounted more, December 11, 1638, Finlayson *contra* Wemys [Durie 866; M. 2170].

18. Consignation [1, 18, 4, *supra*] must also be done by way of instrument, bearing the tenor of the premonition, and the production of the reversion and procuratory, in the same way as it is before said of the premonition, and the coming to the place and day, according to the reversion and premonition, which may be any time of the day, in the hour of cause; and therefore the wadsetter must attend that day, from mid-day to sun-set, because the reverser may come at any time of the day: and upon the wadsetter's not appearing, or not renouncing, the particulars contained in the reversion, are to be consigned according thereto, upon public intimation, by calling the wadsetter, if absent, at the most patent door, which must be done according to the reversion *in forma specifica*, and not *per æquipollens*, Hope, Wadsets, Lo. Frazer *contra* Crichton [*Sub nom. L. Sanquhar* v *Crichton*, Hope, *Maj. Pr.* III, 10, 32; M. 13443]. Yet it was sustained upon the consignation of a discharge of the like sum due by the wadsetter, in respect it was due by an article in the contract of wadset instead of money, January 2, 1667, Hog *contra* Hog [1 Stair 419; M. 13464]. Consignations use to bear, "the numeration of the money." Yet it was sustained, bearing "the production of all and haill the sum contained in the reversion," March 10, 1630, Grierson *contra* L. Troquhan [Durie 503; M. 13455]. Here the wadsetter did not appear, or at least did not require numeration. It must also contain an offer of what is generally in the reversion, and of what the defender can further condescend and clear, whereof the reverser was probably ignorant, as the dues competent in apprisings, and therefore a redemption of teinds upon consignation of the principal sum, and offer of what should be cleared to be resting of teind-bolls, [assigned for payment of the annualrent,] as the prices should be modified by the Lords, was sustained, being made good at the bar, February 21, 1623, Cunninghame *contra* Foster [Durie 49; M. Supp. 4]. Yea, the order of redemption of an apprising was sustained, though the bygone annualrent and penalty were not offered or consigned, the same being offered at the bar, as they were found due and modified, Hope, Wadsets [Hope, *Maj. Pr.* III, 10]. A consignation was also sustained, as made through the wadsetter's default, who offered not a sufficient renunciation, though the consigner did not offer the draught of a sufficient renunciation to the wadsetter to subscribe, albeit the wadsetter appeared, and was willing to receive the money, and offered a renunciation, which the Lords at discussing of the cause, found not sufficient, and found the consigner was not obliged, even in that case, to offer the draught of such a renunciation, July 12, 1634, L. Balmerino *contra* Elliot [Durie 725; M. 13460].

19. The order of redemption being lawfully used, the action thereupon is a declarator of redemption, because it is the order that constitutes the re-

demption, and the declarator but finds and declares it to be orderly proceeded, and decerns the wadsetter to denude himself conform thereto; and
therefore, though the reversion be personal, excluding assignees, if that person once use the order, he may assign it, and dispone the lands as redeemed;
and the assignee at any time, even after his death, will have interest to declare,
July 29, 1623, E. Marischal *contra* his Brother [Durie 78; M. 13539], March
3, 1630, Murray *contra* Myls [Durie 498; M. 10369]. Declarator of redemption was sustained upon an order used against a defunct, and the declarator
pursued against his apparent heir, without a charge to enter heir [III, 5, 23,
infra], or a new order, Dec. 11, 1638, Finlayson *contra* Weyms [Durie 866;
M. 2170]. But in the decreet of declarator of redemption against the apparent
heirs, they cannot be decerned to denude, unless they were charged to enter
heir; yet the declarator itself would be sufficient to extinguish the wadset even
against singular successors: but it would not convey the right of wadset to the
redeemer; and therefore, if he were not infeft, or heir to a person infeft in the
wadset lands, it would be necessary to charge the apparent heir to enter, to the
effect he might denude and dispone; and therefore a declarator of redemption against an apparent heir, did bear, " that the sums should not be given up
till the apparent heir were infeft and resigned," January 10, 1665, Campbel
contra Brison [1 Stair 247; M. 16521]. It was also sustained at the instance of
an appriser of the reversion, without calling him from whom it was apprised,
but only the wadsetter, ·December 17, 1629, Carnousie *contra* Techmuirie
[Durie 475; M. 2181, 13454]. In respect that the apprising was a legal assignation of the right of reversion granted by the wadsetter's author, and there
has been no intervening singular successors: but in redemptions against
singular successors in wadsets, whose rights do not instruct that they are derived from the granter of the reversion, the pursuer must instruct that the
granter of the reversion stood infeft in fee; otherwise that singular successor
will not be obliged to acknowledge the reversion; and because the successors
of the first wadsetter would have warrandice against the first wadsetter or his
heirs, if they had disponed the lands without reserving the reversion; therefore in that case, only the first wadsetter or his heir, if he can be condescended
upon, having any visible estate, have been of old accustomed to be called;
which is not necessary in other cases, and hath been the ground of that decision, July 9, 1630, Fisher *contra* Brown [Durie 527; M. 2205]; where it was
found necessary to call the heirs of the granter of the reversion, if the defender
could condescend upon them; for the ancient custom hath been to have more
respect to the heir of the granter of the reversion, than to the singular successor, present possessor of the wadset, as Craig observes, *Lib.* 2, *Dieg.* 6. so
that sometimes redemption hath been sustained upon premonition and citation, only of him who granted the reversion, or his heir: but ever since, the
present heritable possessor of the wadset must necessarily be premonished
and cited, and but seldom the granter of the reversion or his heir; as where
the granter of the reversion was immediate author to the singular successor,

against whom the order was used; as in the former case, his own rights behoved to acknowledge the right of the granter of the reversion, who was common author, and might intimate the plea to him: but could not be obliged so
to do, where his own right show no right from the granter of the reversion.

A redemption being voluntary without process, was sustained against a
sub-wadsetter's right, being a liferent by the wadsetter to his wife, albeit it
was registrate; yet the redeemer was not obliged to know it; but it was found
taken away without any order against her, or citation of her, July 27, 1665.
Hamilton *contra* her Tennents [1 Stair 303; M. 16522]. Redemption upon a
rose-noble used upon the Sabbath day, albeit the instrument of consignation
did not bear "the reversion was shown, nor read," was sustained, Spots.
Redemption, L. of Newark *contra* his Son [Spotiswoode 264; M. 13451]; but
this would not be drawn in example amongst strangers, where the wadset is
redeemable upon considerable sums. For though consignation upon the
Sabbath day by a father against his son be sustained *fieri non debuit, sed factum
valet :* yet the wadsetter cannot be obliged to attend and perform the requisites
of consignation, by numeration of money, perusal of writs, and subscribing
a renunciation upon the Sabbath day. Redemption was sustained without
necessity to the pursuer to uplift the sums consigned from the consignatar
and reproduce them at the bar, unless it were instructed he had taken them
up, December 7, 1631, Grierson *contra* Gordon [Durie 604; M. 10117], where
the extract was superseded till the consignatar was charged summarily upon
letters granted upon the instrument of consignation to exhibit the consigned
money, but no annualrent was found due after consignation. An order used
by an assignee was sustained, though he show not his assignation till the
process of declarator, yet so as the wadsetter was not comptable for the rents,
but from the production of the assignation, February 19, 1674 Lo. Borthwick
contra Pringles [2 Stair 267; M. 13473]. Yet redemption was not sustained at
the instance of an heir, not being entered at the time of the order, though
entered before declarator, January 19, 1672, Lo. Lovat and Kintail *contra* Lo.
McDonald [2 Stair 49; M. 13278]. But if the redeemer uplift the consigned
money, he must produce the same with the annualrent, and will have right to
the rent during that time, Hope, Confirmation, Baikie *contra*   [Possibly
Bruce v *Buckie*, Hope, *Maj. Pr.* 111, 10, 50; M. 10415, 13444]; December 8,
1671, Forest *contra* Brownlie [2 Stair 19; M. 13468]; November 29, 1672, D.
of Buccleugh *contra* Scot of Thirlestain [2 Stair 123; M. 13469]. Redemption
was not elided, because the sums were consigned in the hands of the redeemer's own servant, and taken up from him, seeing it was offered at the bar,
and no special provision in the reversion, anent the consignatar, Hope, Confirmation, L. of Drum *contra* Wishart [Hope, *Maj. Pr.* 111, 10, 47; M. 13447].
The like though there was an instrument of another notary contrary to the
order of redemption, Had. July 18, 1610, E. of Kinghorn *contra* Kincaid
[Not found].

20. The effect of declarator of redemption is, that it makes the redeemed

lands belong to the redeemer, and makes the sum consigned moveable, and to belong to the wadsetter's executors, if he have accepted the consignation, or if declarator do follow in his lifetime; but if declarator do follow after the wadsetter's death, the consigned sums will not belong to his executors, but to his heir, who remains proprietor of the wadset: but if declarator passed in the wadsetter's life, it did take away the real right of wadset, so the money came to be in the property of the wadsetter, as moveable, and fell to his executor, which till a declarator, was not so, seeing the order might be passed from, December 16, 1629, Laury *contra* Miller [Durie 477; M. 12499]; where it was found, that the consignatar was obliged to re-deliver the consigned money to the consigner, his heirs or assignees, passing from the order, though the wadsetter, to whose use it was consigned, was not called. The like was found, that till declarator the consigned sums remain in the property of the consigner, and belong not to the executor of the wadsetter, but to his heir: or where declarator of redemption was after the wadsetter's death, January 21, 1673, Nicol *contra* Laury [2 Stair 152; M. 14095]; June 18, 1675, L. Loy *contra* Forbes of Blacktoun [2 Stair 330; M. 286]. The like June 21, 1626, Murray *contra* Dishingtoun [Durie 203; M. 14093], though here the consigner entered in possession of the wadset lands before declarator, which is a sufficient owning of the redemption, and so to make the consigned sum moveable.

Upon declarator of redemption, letters will be obtained summarily against the consignatar, to re-produce the consigned money, December 7, 1631, Grierson *contra* Gordon [Durie 604; M. 10117]. But though the instrument of consignation will instruct the consignation against the wadsetter [IV, 42, 9, *infra*], yet it will not prove against the consignatar, without his oath, or writ subscribed by his own hand, January 14, 1630, Laury *contra* Miller [Durie 479; M. 12500].

21. Redemption was not elided by a singular successor, obtaining infeftment of the wadset lands after the order, or at least the infeftment being base, not clad with possession till after the order, though it was clad with seven years' possession before declarator, Hope, Confirmation, E. Errol *contra* Tenants and La. Seaforth [Hope, *Maj. Pr.* III, 10, 37; M. 13444].

22. Wadsets are also taken off by premonition or requisition, requiring the sums upon which the wadset is granted, which makes the sums moveable, and the infeftment of wadset void; yet so that the requirer may pass from his requisition, and the infeftment revives, January 29, 1635, Hamilton *contra* Wilson [Durie 745; M. 14105; II, 1, 4, *supra*]. But after decreet or charge for the sum, the requisition cannot effectually be past from, but the sum becomes moveable. The requisition may be also past from indirectly, by uplifting the duties of the wadset lands for terms after the requisition, Hope, Usury, Wallace *contra* L. Edzel [*Sub nom. Colley* v *Edzell*, Hope, *Maj. Pr.* II, 13, 19]; or taking posterior terms of annualrent from principal or cautioner. Requisition requires also the same solemnities that premonition requires; and therefore it was not sustained, where the procurator designed no time

nor place to pay the money required, though the instrument was mended at the bar, as to the reading of the procuratory, and the truth of it referred to the defender's oath, which the Lords admitted not, the instrument being otherwise when produced in judgment, February 7, 1628, Maxwel *contra* L. Innerweek [Durie 341; M. 13448]. The like where the requisition mentioned not the production of the procuratory, though it bore "not to be called for", November 13, 1622, L. Bass *contra* Wauchop [Durie 34; M. 13446]. This was in a requisition only to validate a charge: the contrary was found, where it bore, "that the procurator's power was known to him and the witness" January 18, 1665, Stuart *contra* Stuart [1 Stair 252; M. 5588]. Here there was an apprising deduced upon the requisition. The like where the procuratory was not called for, and was in the procurator's hand, and with it the writ which was the warrant of the requisition, which was shown, June 28, 1671, Hume *contra* Lord Justice-Clerk [1 Stair 741; M. 5688].

23. Declarators of redemption, or renunciations, or grants of redemption, do ordinarily bear, "that the wadsetter renounceth all right to the wadset lands;" and albeit he have a distinct right, it will not stop the declarator, nor oblige the redeemer to donate thereanent in that process: nor will it stop the entering the redeemer in the possession, in which he entered by the wadset [11, 9, 43, *supra*], but that right will only be reserved, November 22, 1677, Stuart of Castlemilk *contra* D. Hamilton [2 Stair 561; M. 9222]; and if the wadsetter condescend upon, and give evidence of any other right beside the wadset, it will be particularly reserved, or the renunciation will only bear, "all right by virtue of the wadset" Hope, Confirmation, Baikie *contra* [Possibly *Bruce* v *Buckie*, Hope, *Maj. Pr.* 111, 10, 50; M. 10415, 13444].

In the case of redemption of an apprising, the renunciation was restricted to the right in question, February 22, 1631, Murray *contra* L. Yester [Durie 573; M. 3711]. Declarators of redemption to decern the wadsetter to renounce, and resign all right to the wadset lands, unless a right distinct from the wadset could be instructed, which will be excepted, or an evidence given for such a right, which thereupon will be reserved: but a general reservation of other rights was not sustained, but a declarator of redemption was found a species of declarator of right; after which, no right competent and omitted, will be sustained, which was then known, February 2, 1676, D. Lauderdale *contra* Lo. and La. Yester [2 Stair 409; M. 9220].

Title 11. Extinction of Infeftments, Where, of Resignation *ad Remanentiam*, Recognition, Disclamation, Purpresture, and other Feudal Delinquencies

WE are not here to speak of the common ways of extinction of infeftments, and other rights, such as do extinguish the subject matter, as prescription, forfeiture, homologation, or acceptance of incompatible rights; neither, of these ways by which an infeftment is extinct as to one, but is conveyed to another, which falleth in consideration amongst conveyances of rights: but only of these ways proper to extinguish infeftments, and make the right to cease, and to return to the superior; and these are two, either by consent of the vassal, or by law.

1. Infeftments are extinct by consent, by resignation made by the vassal, who stands infeft in the lands, to his superior, *ad perpetuam remanentiam*, to which there is necessarily required as a solemnity thereof, an instrument of resignation in the hands of a notar: for in the same way that their constitution was perfected by an instrument of seasin, their destitution is consummated by an instrument of resignation, which no other writ nor acknowledgment of the vassal, of the being thereof, will supply, much less will the deeds done otherways prove; and, as in seasins there must be a tradition or delivery of possession by some token or symbol, as by earth and stone, &c. so in the instrument of resignation, there must be a re-delivery of the possession by an accustomed

symbol, which ordinarily is by delivery of staff and baston; yet in this they differ, that the delivery of the seasin must be upon the ground of the tenement, naturally or by union; but the resignation may be any where: and as seasin may be given, either to the vassal or his procurator; so may the resignation be either to the superior himself or to his commissioners, authorised to that effect.

2. And though instruments of resignation use to be by procurators, warranted by a procuratory of resignation; yet as there may be seasins given by the superior, *propriis manibus*, so may there be resignations by the vassal himself.

3. But in both, the instrument of resignation, alone is not sufficient as being but the assertion of a notar [11, 3, 19, *supra*], but they must have for their warrant a disposition, or other adminicle; and therefore, it is statute, Parl. 1563, cap. 81 [A.P.S. 11, 542, c. 19], that where such resignations are by procurators, the procuratories be subscribed by the party or notars; and if the resignation be *propriis manibus*, that the instrument be so subscribed, otherwise to be null; because the subscription of the instrument is in that case the only probation of the warrant thereof: but if there be a disposition or obligement to infeft, the instrument of resignation, though not subscribed by the resigner, will be sufficient, as warranted by the disposition or obligement. But seasins and resignations did formerly differ in this, that seasins must be registrate within sixty days after their dates, Parl. 1617, cap. 16 [Registration Act, 1617, c. 16; A.P.S. IV, 545, c. 16].

4. But so needed not instruments of resignation *ad remanentiam;* for though by that statute, renunciations of wadsets are to be registrate, it was not extended to renunciations of irredeemable rights *ad remanentiam*, these being either omitted by inadvertency or of purpose, in favours of superiors, that rights may be taken with their consent: yet in so far that excellent statute was defective, till the late Act of Parl. 1669, cap. 3 [Act 1669, c. 4; A.P.S. VII, 556, c. 4], whereby instruments of resignation are null, if not registrate within sixty days [11, 3, 21, *supra*]. By which, and others to that purpose, purchasers in Scotland, may better know the condition of these with whom they contract about infeftments, and be more secure of lurking rights, than any where (so far as I can learn) in the world [11, 3, 22, *supra*].

5. By this resignation so made, the property is consolidated as it was the time of the resignation, and is affected with all real burdens, or *debita fundi*, that validly affected it before; as feus, tacks, annualrents, servitudes: for though all such burdens as are not warranted by the superior's consent, or by law, cease when the fee returns to the superior, either for a time by ward, nonentry, &c. or for ever by recognition; yet when it returns thus by consent, it comes *cum suo onere*, which is very just and fit, seeing else such securities might easily be evacuated, by voluntary resignations in the superior's hand. There is another resignation, which is called *in favorem*, being for new infeftment to the resigner or some other; but thereby the fee is not extinct, but

either renewed or transferred, and therefore it shall be considered hereafter.

6. Craig upon this head [III,1,9], very fitly moveth and solveth this question. Whether the vassal may renounce and resign his fee to the superior, though he be unwilling, and instances two cases, first, in a vassal's holding a very considerable parcel of land ward, did thereby become obnoxious to his superior for the value of his tocher, having relation to the whole estate, which tocher did much exceed the worth of that tenement; and yet a resignation thereof being judicially offered, the superior was suffered to refuse it, unless the value of the marriage were first paid [11,4,48,*supra*]: the other of a burgess, offering to renounce his burgess-ship for shunning a great taxation put upon him: and therefore solveth the case upon the common axiom, *Cuique licet renunciare favori pro se introducto:* and therefore the fee of its nature being gratuitous in favours of the vassal, may be renounced; but that will not prejudge the superior of any casuality befalling to him before the renunciation, but will have only effect *ad futura :* and therefore a vassal judicially disclaiming his superior, was not admitted so to do, to exclude the liferent already fallen, March 26, 1628, Douglas *contra* L. Wedderburn [Durie 372; M.3556].

No contract, obligation or personal right, nor any less than an instrument of resignation, will take away infeftment; for though these may be sufficient against the granters thereof, by a personal objection, whereby they cannot come against their own deed; yet truly, the real right stands in the person infeft, and they are not denuded thereby; and so a renunciation, without the solemnity of an instrument of resignation, will not suffice to obliterate an irredeemable fee [11,5,15; 11,10,13,*supra*; III,2,38,*infra*], though it may be sufficient to evacuate any personal right; as servitude not requiring infeftment; yea, or a liferent, though constitute by infeftment, because it is communicable to no other persons by infeftment, and therefore passeth by assignation or resignation. The reason hereof is, because by the common custom of nations, real rights cannot pass by sole consent, without attaining possession in the way prescribed by law: and therefore this symbolical possession, which alone the law alloweth as sufficient, either in the constitution or destitution of fees, must be adhibited, and the real possession of the tenement itself will not suffice in either case, as is before instanced in seasins [11,13,16,*supra*; III,2,6,*infra*] by several decisions: so a renunciation without a formal resignation, was not found relevant to take away the infeftment renounced against a singular successor, November 23, 1627, Dumbar *contra* Wilson [Durie 315; M.570]. And resignation cannot be effectual, if the resigner be not infeft; for he who is not invested, cannot be divested.

7. Craig discusseth this question also in that place [III,1,29], Whether consent of one who is infeft, and thereby hath right, will validate the resignation of another, who is not infeft and hath no right [III,2,9,*infra*], which he determineth in the affirmative, with good reason; for though the consent alone would not be sufficient, yet seeing the form of the resignation is done,

though in the name of him who hath no right, yet by consent of him who hath right, here is both the substance and solemnity of the act; and it is alike, as if the resignation had been by the consenter, which I doubt not will hold, though the consent be but adhibited in the beginning of the disposition or contract: and though the consenter doth not dispone expressly for all right he hath (as is ordinary for further security,) yea, if the consent be not repeated in the procuratory of resignation, or mentioned in the instrument of resignation; for if it be expressed generally in the entry of the disposition or contract, it reacheth to every article thereof, and all done conform thereto. Consent hath the same effect in the constitution of fees; and so the consent to an annualrent, by a party having right and infeft, was found to validate the annualrent, though the disponer was not infeft; and so did exclude a tack set by that consenter afterward, December 15, 1630, Stirling *contra*   [*Sub nom. Stirling v Templeland Tennants*, Durie 548; M. 6521]. Yet, if more persons should dispone for their several rights, without consenting one to another, if any of them be omitted out of the procuratory or instrument of resignation, in whom truly the right standeth, nothing will be validly done, though that party be also in the disposition: and this is the reason, why when many persons dispone or resign, they do it all with one mutual consent; for thereby each of their rights doth contribute to the deed of the rest.

8. Infeftments are also extinct, when the superior adjudgeth or appriseth from his vassal; for thereby it was found, that the property was consolidated with the superiority, Spots. Apprising, Stevinson *contra* L. Craigmillar [Spotiswoode 41]. Or if the superior succeed as heir to the vassal; in which case, though the superior upon supplication obtained precepts out of the chancellary, to infeft him in the fee, it was thought, as superior, he might have infeft himself as vassal [11, 4, 4, *supra*; 111, 2, 23, *infra*]; but he would not have been so secure by a declarator of consolidation, upon the superior's special retour, as heir to his vassal in the lands; because that way would make a defect in the security of land-rights by the registers, in which decreets of consolidation are not required to be recorded; whereas the superior's seasin, either on the King's precept or his own, behoved to be registrate; and if the superior acquire the property by apprising or adjudication, the allowance thereof must also be registrate [11, 3, 22, *supra*]. The like effect will follow, if the vassal become heir, or singular successor to the superior, whereby, being infeft in the superiority, he may as vassal resign to himself as superior, *ad remanentiam*.

9. It is more disputable, how, and under what considerations fees are extinct, otherwise than by consent; some hold that they are extinct by the atrocious delinquency of the vassal against the superior, as the penalty or punishment thereof; and others conceive, that acknowledgment and fidelity being necessarily included in all fees, (as is shown before) though it be not expressed, so this is implied as a legal resolutive or irritant clause, that if the vassal fail in his duty, his fee becomes void. And others hold, that fees being

of their own nature gratuitous, even though there be a cause onerous, not being understood as adequate, yet they retain the nature of a donation, and as all donations are revocable *propter ingratitudinem*, so are these. Which soever of these be the ground, the consequences and effects are much to the same purpose. But I incline to the middle opinion; for unless it were evident by law, that the penalty of that delinquence were such and so applied, it would hardly be consistent upon the first ground; seeing otherwise, (as has been shown before of Delinquences,) the punishment is public, and would belong to the magistrate: and therefore, for several delinquencies, forfeiture of fees is introduced, without benefit to the superior, who as a private party, can have no more but a reparation equivalent to the damage sustained by him; and so the alienation of the fee, without his consent or encroaching upon the border of his property, would not infer for its reparation the return of the fee, how great soever. And for the last, though fees of their nature be gratuitous, yet they are oft-times for an equivalent price, and so the less ingratitude can be alleged; yea, though it be true, *Si ingratum dixeris, omnia dixeris*, yet fidelity and trust is a much stronger bond than gratitude; and the breach thereof hath the most powerful consequence, betraying of trust being most hurtful and hateful to mankind; and therefore, seeing fidelity is necessarily and properly in all fees, and is essential thereto, and inseparable therefrom, it looketh likest the surest ground from whence the eviction hereof may flow; and if it be truly gratuitous, it is an aggravating circumstance, making the deed more odious. But whatsoever it be, it is agreed by all, that the deed must be of knowledge, moment and atrocity. Though there be many such heaped up by the feudists, yet many of them have no place with us, where both such deeds are rare; and therefore the decisions thereupon are few: and certainly our fees being ordinarily onerous, are not evacuated but by such as are either named or known in law, or which are very atrocious. There be three such ways of extinction, which have peculiar names in law, recognition, disclamation, and purpresture. Of which therefore in the next place.

10. Recognition [IV, 14, *infra*] is the superior's returning to own the fee; and therefore may be extended to all the ways by which it returneth through the vassal's infidelity, as is hereafter expressed; but the least culpable, and yet most ordinary way of incurring recognition, is by the vassal's disponing irredeemably, or under reversion his fee holden ward: for by this he renders himself incapable to serve his superior and in a manner renounces and disclaims him. This kind of alienation makes recognition of ward-lands; but fees feu or blench do not recognosce by such alienations, but by the atrocious infidelity of the vassal. The nearest cause of recognition, is the vassal's alienation of the fee without consent of the superior, which is a legal clause irritant, implied in the nature of proper fees or ward-holdings, (though it be not expressed:) that if the vassal alienate the fee, without the superiors consent, it shall return to the superior. Whether the rise hereof be from the personal obligation of fidelity only, which the vassal oweth to the superior, or from

the obligement of gratitude and service, or from that peculiar choice of the person and race of the vassal, which the superior hath made, contrary to which, a stranger cannot be obtruded upon him; neither can the vassal withdraw himself from his fidelity, or render himself unfit for his service, or from all these; yet in this most do agree, that the nearest cause of recognition is the alienation of the fee. So then, the main difficulty is, what is meant by that alienation by which recognition is incurred: Craig *Lib.* 3, *Dieg.* 5 [111,3,25], declareth, that this alienation cannot be by naked contract or disposition, till seasin follow; for these being but personal and incomplete rights, do not alienate the fee from the vassal, but only constitute upon him a personal obligement so to do. It is also clear, that by infeftment granted by the superior upon resignation, there can be no recognition; because the superior's accepting of the resignation, importeth his consent; so that the question will only remain, when the vassal granteth disposition or charter *à se* to be holden of his superior, and before the superior's confirmation obtained, giveth seasin, unless the superior do confirm the seasin: or otherwise, while the vassal granteth a subaltern infeftment to be holden of himself.

11. As to the first case, it seems there can be no recognition incurred by infeftments granted by the vassal to be holden of his superior, because, if these be not confirmed, the right is null, and there is no alienation nor transmission of property, but the vassal, granter of the infeftment, remains still proprietor; and, therefore, such an infeftment is equivalent, as if the vassal did alienate upon condition that the superior should consent; and if he did not consent, the infeftment to be null: in which case, most feudists do agree, that by such infeftments there is no recognition; and this reason is the more fortified, that Craig in the fore-cited place relateth, that an infeftment null for want of registration, was not found to infer recognition, in the case of the King's Advocate *against* M'Kenzie and Bain [Not found]. For solution of this difficulty, it is not to be denied, that if a seasin be null by defect of any substantial or essential, necessarily requisite to seasin or symbolical delivery of possession, there would follow no recognition; as if there were no tradition of earth and stone, or symbol requisite, or not by the superior, or his baillie, or not to the vassal, or his procurator, or not upon the ground of the land naturally, or by union. But though seasin may be null, by defect of some accidental solemnity introduced by statute or custom, and not necessarily involved in the nature of seasin; as the indiction, or year of the Prince's reign, though law should declare the seasin null for want of these, yet the vassal performing the essential requisites, the feu falleth in recognition: and, therefore, there seemeth no ground to follow that decision adduced by Craig, excluding recognition upon the nullity of the seasin for want of registration. But as to the case proposed, the superior's confirmation is not essential to the vassal's seasin; neither is it so required by the common feudal customs, as with us: for thereby, if the superior did acquiesce, approve or homologate the seasin granted by a vassal to a stranger, the same would be valid without a formal

confirmation in writ; albeit by our custom, such infeftments till confirmed are null, not only as to the superior, but as to all other third parties, and so is become as a substantial of the infeftment; yet not being truly essential by the common feudal customs, it doth not exclude recognition; and as Craig in the fore-cited place rendereth the reason, that infeftments by the vassal, *à se*, not confirmed, infer recognition, is, because he hath done all that in him is to alienate the fee, there being no act remaining to be performed by him or his procurator; and, therefore, in the declarator of recognition, pursued at the instance of Hamilton, La. Carnegy *contra* Lo. Cranburn [1 Stair 166,172; M.7732,10375], upon the E. of Dirletoun's disponing of the lands of Inner-week, holden of the King ward, to Cranburn, and infefting him therein to be holden of the King; this defence was not found relevant, that the seasin was not confirmed, and so null, though done upon death-bed, accepted for a minor absent and inscient, and now recalling and reducing it.

12. For in such cases as rebellion or escheat, there is no privilege of minority, nor of deeds upon death-bed against the superior, though done by a minor, except the deeds upon death-bed be in prejudice of the heir, and be reduced by the heir *ex capite lecti*. But in this case, Dirletoun's heir did not quarrel the disposition made by him, as done upon death bed, but did take a gift of recognition from the King. But where the gift of recognition was not granted to the heir-male, who was heir in the investiture, but to an heir-female, the heir-male proponing, that the alienation was upon death-bed, and so null as to him, the Lords found, that if the disposition was upon death-bed, the defence was relevant and competent by way of exception, the declarator of recognition not being a possessory judgment: but where the disposition was in *liege poustie*, and was delivered with a precept of seasin simply, without reservation not to take seasin base upon the precept, which imported a warrant to take seasin thereupon, it was found, the taking seasin, when the disponer was upon death-bed, upon that precept subscribed and delivered in *liege poustie*, did infer recognition, July 20, 1669, Barclay *contra* Barclay [1 Stair 641; M.3241].

13. It is much debated amongst the feudists, whether by subfeudation recognition be incurred, or whether it be comprehended under alienation; because *in libris feudorum* albeit alienation of fees be expressly prohibited, yet in the same place, as Craig [111,3,22] observeth, subfeudation is allowed; because by subfeudation, neither the personal prestations betwixt superior and vassal are altered, seeing the vassal continues vassal, and liable to all these; neither is the real right and interest of the superior in the fee itself diminished; but he hath the same access thereto, as if there had been no subfeudation: yet subfeudation in all cases is accounted alienation; and where alienation is prohibited, subfeudation is understood, and so *emphyteusis* or feu-farm, which is at least a perpetual location. For solving this difficulty, it must be remembered, that *feuda* are *localia*, regulable according to the custom of the several places, and according to the nature of feudal rights, and com-

mon feudal customs, where special customs are not; and, therefore, there is no question of this point in France, or most places in Germany, where alienation of fees many ways is allowed: but in Italy and other countries, where the common feudal customs rule ordinarily according to the feudal books, the doubt remaineth, which may be cleared thus: *First*, Though in some cases alienation be extended to location, yet it is not so by the common feudal customs: *Secondly*, If the subfeudation be a real feu-farm, whereby the feu-duty is considerable, and competent to entertain the vassal, such subfeudation is thereby accounted only location; nor doth it infer recognition, being in effect no more than a perpetual location, whereby the antinomy in the feudal law is sufficiently reconciled, that such subfeudations are not alienations; but if the subfeudation be ward, blench, or in mortification, or though it be under the name of *emphyteusis;* yet for an elusory or an inconsiderable or unproportionable feu-duty, which by no estimation can be correspondent to the profit of the fee, but within the half of the true worth; in these cases the subfeudation is alienation, and inferreth recognition.

14. As to our customs in this point, they do agree to the common feudal customs, as to subaltern infeftments, blench, ward, or in mortification, or elusory, or unprofitable feus: but as to the feus, by which the major part of the ward or fee is not taken away, though such cases have not occurred to be controverted, they do not infer recognition, for if the major part be not alienated, subaltern infeudations, though blench, or in mortification, infer not recognition, when these rights are *disjunctim* of parts of the fee; there appears no reason that the subfeudation of the whole, with a feu-duty equivalent to the half of the true rent, whereby in effect the half is not alienated, seeing the *dominium directum* of the whole, and the profit of the half is retained, should infer recognition, especially now when generally fees are granted for causes onerous [11,3,32,*supra*].

15. And by the statutes allowing feus, Parl. 1457, cap. 72 [1457,c.71; A.P.S. 11,49,c.15], it is provided, that the feu be set to a competent avail, which, by the said statute, is cleared to be without diminution of the rental; which is commonly interpreted the retour-duty, because it was the public valuation and rate at that time. And by the said statute, such feus are confirmed and declared not to be prejudged by the ward, without mention of the hazard or recognition, as not being consequent upon such feus. But this statute being abrogated as to the lieges, Parl. 18, Ja. VI cap. 12 [Act 1606,c.12; A.P.S. IV,287,c.11], all sub-feus of ward lands, holden of subjects without the superior's consent, are declared null and void: but there is no mention of recognition to be incurred thereby. And feus are only prohibited, as being in prejudice of the over-lords, who are not prejudged, if the major part be not alienated, seeing all subaltern infeftments, not exceeding the half, are allowed by law: and albeit the narrative of the Act respects feus preceding it, yet the statutory part is only as to feus granted thereafter.

The like prohibition is appointed for the King and Prince's vassals, Parl.

1633, cap. 16 [A.P.S. V,33,c.16]. The effect of this Act, as to the vassals of the King and Prince, was suspended till the next meeting of Parliament, and the vassals exempted therefrom in the interim, Parl. 1640, cap. 36 [A.P.S. V,314,c.37]. And the said Act was wholly repealed, Parl. 1641, cap. 58 [A.P.S. V,499,c.83]. And so remained until all these Parliaments were rescinded, seeing the private rights of parties acquired thereby, by the general Act Rescissory are reserved, Parl. 1661, cap. 15 [A.P.S. VII,86,c.126; 11,3,32, *supra*]. But it hath been found, that alienations during these Acts now rescinded, and during the Usurpation, when wards were discharged, did infer recognition, if the vassal did not seek confirmation after the King's return, December 15, 1669, Maitland of Pitrichie *contra* Gordon of Gight [1 Stair 656; M.13382]. The like was found in the recognition at the instance of Sir George Kinnaird *contra* Vassals of the Lo. Gray [Not found]. The like, though the base infeftment inferring recognition was in anno 1643, when there was a statute then standing, allowing such infeftments, seeing after rescinding that statute, no application was made to the King for confirmation, January 7, 1676, Cockburn of Ryselaw *contra* Cockburn of Choustie [2 Stair 393; M.13389]; but recognition was excluded where the vassal required the superior to confirm the subaltern right *debito tempore*, and did purge the same, by procuring resignations *ad remanentiam*, to himself from the sub-vassals, February 11, 1674, Viscount Kilsyth *contra* Hamilton of Bardowie [2 Stair 266; M.13387]. But recognition was not found against a pupil upon his tutors granting infeftment for him during the Usurpation, July 15, 1669, Jack *contra* Jack [1 Stair 640; M.13381]. Whereby it is clear, that these feus have no effect against the superior, as to the ward or non-entry, more than tacks.

16. Whether the alienation be by infeftment, holden from, or of the vassal, there is no recognition with us, except in ward-holdings; yea, if the holding be dubious, and so a probable ground of error of the vassal, as being a payment of money in the *reddendo*, with service "used and wont;" which though truly ward, yet because the payment of money may render it dubious, Craig holdeth in the said *Dieg. Lib.* 3, [111,3,27], that it would not infer recognition; yet this will not give ground to think that alienation of lands, taxtward, would excuse from recognition, because ward is there more clear, and expressed *nominatim*, the casualities thereof being taxed as the marriage and ward-duties; which taxing is but a liquidation, or location of these casualities when they occur, and no alteration of the nature of the fee, and therefore in the said pursuit, at the instance of La. Carnegie *contra* Lo. Cranburn [1 Stair 166,172; M.7732,10375], it was not found relevant to exclude the recognition, that the ward was taxed.

17. It is also clear, that alienation, whether by infeftment holden of, or from the vassal, not exceeding the half of the fee, inferreth not recognition, so much being indulged to the vassal for his conveniency or necessity; but where together, or by parcels, or by annualrent, the major part was alienated, not only that which then was in the vassal's person falls under recognition; but

as Craig holdeth in the fore-cited place, *Dieges* 3, *Lib.* 3, even the whole fee; so that parcels alienated validly, but without the superior's consent before, become void and return, February 23, 1681, Hay *contra* Creditors of Muirie [2 Stair 865; M.6513]. Yet this seems very hard, that what once was secure, without the fault of the proprietor, should be lost, and may yet deserve consideration. But though the vassal grant infeftments exceeding the half of the fee, yet if some of them were extinct before others were granted, so that there was at no time rights standing together exceeding the half of the fee, recognition were not incurred. Deeds done by predecessors and their heirs, or authors, and their successors, are in this case conjoined. Upon the same ground an infeftment of the fee in liferent, would not infer recognition, because it exceeds not the half of the value. Yea, recognition was found not incurred by granting an infeftment in warrandice, for warrandice is but a hazard in case of eviction, not equivalent to the half of the worth of the lands granted in warrandice, unless the right of the principal lands were manifestly defective, Had. March 6, 1623, Cathcart *contra* Campbel [Not found].

18. Recognition is not inferred by an alienation to the vassal's apparent heir, by the ordinary course of law, as by a father to his eldest son; because the fee will befall to the son after the father's decease. Neither was it inferred by an alienation granted by a grand-father, with consent of his son to his oye, who was *alioqui successurus*, by the course of law, Hope, Recognition, Rae *contra* L. Kellie [Hope, *Maj.Pr.* III,28,14; M.6459]. Yet recognition was found incurred by a vassal's infeftment to his eldest son, his heirs and assignees, the son having disponed the major part to strangers; seeing the father who was vassal, did not bind up his son from disponing, by a clause irritant; neither did the son purge the alienations made by him, during his father's life, July 15, 1674, Sir Charles Erskine *contra* Forbes of Auchintoul [2 Stair 275; M.13387]. And recognition was found incurred by the infeftment of ward-lands, by a husband to his wife in fee, failing heirs of his body; albeit the wife did not accept or make use of the same, but bruiked by a prior conjunct infeftment, February 14, 1678, L. Knock *contra* La. Knock [*Sub nom. Know* v *Straiton*, 2 Stair 613; M.13390]. And recognition was found to be incurred by an alienation by the vassal to his brother, who for the time was his apparent heir, but not necessarily by the ordinary course of law, seeing the vassal might have had children of his own, and so his brother could not be called *alioqui successurum*, unless it were by accident, Spots. Recognition, King's Advocate and his Son *contra* E. Cassils and L. Collane [Spotiswoode 251; M.13378]. The like, July 29, 1672, Lo. Haltoun *contra* E. Northesk [2 Stair 111; M. 13384].

19. It is more questionable, whether recognition is incurred by a conditional alienation, bearing, "if the superior consent, or saving the superior's right;" Craig, following Baldus in the said third *Dieges*, *Lib.* 3, [III,3,26], declareth, that if such clauses be insert *bona fide*, they infer not recognition; but contrarywise, if they be done fraudulently, as when the vassal seaseth and

possesseth a powerful person, whom the superior cannot easily dispossess, or his enemy, concerning whom there can be no doubt of the superior's will; or if the superior have declared his will in the contrary. But for further clearing of this point, distinction would be made of the nature and tenor of the clause, which may either be suspensive or resolutive of the property or fee, in the former case; tradition is only made of the possession, but the property is suspended till the superior's will be known; as if the vassal dispone and possess another without seasin, there could be no recognition; or though he possess him by an instrument of possession, bearing expressly, "that he should have no right to the property till the superior's consent were obtained;" this were a suspensive clause, like to the *addictio in diem* in the civil law, by which only possession and not the property was transmitted for that time; and so till the purification of the condition, it could be no alienation: but when the clause is only resolutive, not hindering the transmission of the property, but resolving or annulling the same, though transmitted; in such a case, such clauses do not exclude recognition, because there is truly there an alienation, without the superior's consent, which is only to be disannulled by his disassent; much less can such general clauses as *salvo jure cujuslibet*, or *salvo jure superioris*, avoid recognition.

20. Recognition was found not excluded or burdened by inhibition against the ward-vassal, before the gift and declarator of the deed, inferring recognition, seeing the creditors inhibiting did not annul the infeftment simply, but in so far as it may be prejudicial to the ground of the inhibition, Dec. 16, 1680, Hay *contra* L. Bethaik and L. Balbegno [2 Stair 816; M. 7040], but now rectified by Act 15 Parl. 1686 [A.P.S. VIII, 598, c. 27].

21. Neither was recognition excluded, because the deed inferring recognition, was done when the disponer was drunk, not being to stupidity, impeding reason, July 29, 1672, Lo. Haltoun *contra* E. Northesk [2 Stair 111; M. 13384].

22. To come now to the superior's consent, it may be either antecedent, concomitant, or consequent to the alienation; and it may be either express or tacit, all which will be sufficient to avoid recognition, albeit many of them will not be sufficient to make a valid infeftment, if the same be granted by the vassal, to be holden from him of the superior, which by our custom is null till it be confirmed. Craig in the forementioned *Dieg.* 3. relates the opinion of the feudists, whereunto he agrees, that if the vassal's fee be granted to him, his heirs and assignees whatsoever, that thereby there is granted a general antecedent consent of the superior to his vassal, to alienate or assign to whom he pleaseth: But the contrary was found in the case of the La. Carnegie *contra* Lo. Cranburn, Feb. 5, 1663 [1 Stair 172; M. 10375], and that the disposition to assignees did only import a power to assign the disposition, before infeftment taken thereupon [11, 4, 32, *supra*].

23. There is no question but the superior's confirmation is sufficient; even the King's confirmation, though without a *novodamus*, albeit it may pass

in exchequer, without the knowledge and advertency of the recognition incurred, it was found sufficient, being done before the donatar of recognition
was infeft, Hope, Recognition, Rae *contra* L. Kellie [Hope, *Maj. Pr.* 111,28,
14; M. 6459]. Which confirmation doth secure against recognition falling by
that infeftment confirmed; but doth not secure against recognition upon
other subaltern infeftments not confirmed, which are not considered to be
known by the King or his officers, without a *novodamus;* and so imports but a
passing from recognition by the infeftment confirmed, but not to import an
absolute ratification *pro omni jure*, February 6, 1673, Lo. Haltoun *contra* E.
Weems [2 Stair 164; M. 6461]. The like was found February 23, 1681, Hay
contra Creditors of Muirie [2 Stair 865; M. 6513]. And a donatar of recognition, having granted precept of *clare constat*, acknowledging the vassal's right,
was found thereby excluded; albeit the precept did bear, to be in obedience
of precepts out of the chancellary, yet bore *quoniam clare constat*, &c. June 24,
1668, Gray *contra* Howison and Gray [1 Stair 542; M. 6413]. But the superior's consent is nbt inferred by granting charters for obedience upon apprising, though before any infeftment of the donatar, Hope, Recognition, L.
Lugtoun *contra* L. Lethindie [Hope, *Maj. Pr.* 111,28,15 and 16; M. 6416].

24. The superior's consent by homologation [1, 10, 11, *supra*], is as sufficient to avoid recognition, as if it were an express consent; so if the superior
require the new vassal or sub-vassal, to perform the services due out of the
fee; for thereby he acknowledges him vassal, as is observed by Craig [111, 3,
35], in the case betwixt the L. Calderwood and Maxwel of Calderhead. Or if
the superior should pursue the new vassal for the avail of his marriage, liferent-escheat, or other casuality of the superiority.

25. Recognition being incurred, so openeth and returneth the fee to the
superior, that no debt or deed of the vassal, doth burden the same, but these
only which before that time were established by consent of the superior; or
authority of law, as apprisings, adjudications, feu-farms, &c. conform to the
several Acts of Parliament. But even such being constitute after the alienation,
whereby recognition is incurred, albeit *bona fide*, for onerous causes, before
any diligence or declarator of recognition; yet they fall in consequence with
their author's right, Had. February 8, 1610, E. Buckcleugh *contra* Scot [Not
found]. Recognition excludeth all tacks set by the vassal without the superior's consent, whether prior or posterior, unless such as are set for the utility
and profit of all parties interested, having no advantage therein, as before hath
been shown in the matter of ward and non-entry; for though tacks be established by Acts of Parliament against purchasers, yet they are not so against
superiors.

26. Recognition doth also exclude servitudes upon the fee, by the vassal,
without the superior's consent, as thirlage, &c. yet this will not reach servitudes, introduced by long custom or possession, and strengthened by prescription, wherein the consent of all parties having interest, is presumed, that
they can never come in the contrary; for though it was most proper to the

vassal to look to his fee, yet the superior doubtless might have interrupted, which would have been sufficient for his own interest. And prescription being introduced to secure property, and put an end to pleas, will not be infringed but upon evident grounds, January 26, 1681, Edie *contra* Thoirs [2 Stair 842; M.6518; 11,7,3,*supra*].

27. Seeing recognition is exclusive of all interests depending upon the vassal; therefore all parties having interest may compear and defend, Hope, *de actionibus in factum*, L. Lugtoun *contra* L. Lethendie [Hope, *Maj.Pr.* VI, 40,3; M.6416]. But there is no necessity to call any save the vassal, seeing all other rights fall *in consequentiam*, as was found in subaltern rights in the said case, E. Buckcleugh *contra* Scot [Not found]. Though recognition be ordinarily by way of action, declaring the deed upon which it is incurred; yet a donatar of recognition being infeft thereupon, was found to have sufficient interest to pursue, succeeding in the vice, in respect of a prior decreet of removing, upon the donatar's infeftment upon the gift of recognition, without any preceding declarator, March 22, 1623, L. Hunthill *contra* Rutherfoord [Durie 61; M.13379].

28. In declarators of recognition, the superior's gift is a sufficient title, without instructing the superior's right, unless he be disclaimed, or the vassals be singular successors: but the King's gift is absolutely sufficient; and there will be terms assigned for proving the alienation of the major part, and incident diligences, against all havers, for production of their infeftments, *ad modum probationis*, February 17, 1671, Gordon *contra* Sir Alexander McCulloch [1 Stair 723; M.13383]. And whereas gifts of recognitions bear the particular deeds inferring the vacancy and return of the fee in the King's hands, because general gifts are not allowable, the extracts of seasins are sustained *in initio litis*, to instruct these deeds; but warrant was granted to the defenders to improve the seasins, or warrants thereof, and thereby to call for the principals, January 26, 1681, Edie *contra* Thoris and Dun [2 Stair 842; M.6518]. And diligence by horning was granted to the defenders in the recognition, for producing the seasins and warrants, February 23, 1681, Hay *contra* Creditors of Murie [2 Stair 865; M.6513]. And declarator was sustained upon production of the gift, though the donatar was not infeft; and though the heir whose right was in question, was minor, and though his authors bound in warrandice were not called: for the privilege of minority hath no effect as to the superior [11,11,12,*supra*], and the defender ought to intimate the plea to his author, January 28, 1681, L. Dun *contra* Scot [2 Stair 847; M.9098].

29. Disclamation is when the vassal denieth his superior to be his superior, which is diametrically opposite to that acknowledgment, which is necessarily implied in the nature of all fees, as there is in it the greatest ingratitude; and therefore disclamation, as being much more favourable upon the part of the superior, and odious upon the part of the vassal, than recognition, is not restricted to proper fees by ward-holdings, but taketh place in all fees; and

that not only when the vassal disclaimeth the superior as to the whole, or greater part; but if he disclaim him to be superior in any part of the fee, he loseth the whole.

Disclamation taketh no place if it proceed through ignorance upon any probable ground, which may several ways occur: First, as to the whole fee, when the case is not betwixt the first superior and the first vassal, but betwixt their successors; as if the vassal should deny a person to be his superior's heir in that superiority, through any doubtfulness of his being lawful heir, or of his being that heir to whom the superiority is provided, as being to heirs-male or of tailzie: but much more when the superior is singular successor to the first superior, or the vassal is singular successor to the former vassal; in all which there be frequent and probable grounds of doubt and mistake. Secondly, The same ground of doubt may be when the question is about some part of the fee, as whether such a piece of land, which is in question, be a part of the fee or not; or as when the fiar hath several conterminous tenements, holden of diverse superiors, if he affirm any parcel not to be a part and pertinent holden of the superior acclaiming, but of the other; in that case the vassal's not acknowledging the superior, will not be accounted disclamation, if the vassal have an infeftment, to which the ground in question may be referred; but if he have none, and yet possess, it is of no import to excuse from recognition: and therefore, though ordinarily it be held, that a superior pursuing his vassal for any duty or casuality, needs not instruct that he is superior, or that the defender is his vassal, but that it proves itself, unless he disclaim; as was found, Hope, Superior, Viscount of Stormont *contra* Grant [Hope, *Maj.Pr.* 111,7,37; 11,4,21,*supra*]: but that must be understood when the case is clear, and, when he is directly disclaimed, yet he may choose either to make use of the disclamation, or instruct his title, and so proceed, March 26, 1628, Douglass *contra* L. Wedderburn [Durie 372; M.3556]. The main question is, whether disclamation can be otherwise than judicially. Craig [111,5,3] answers the case, as to extrajudicial words, "that these are not ordinarily noticed in most cases; as extrajudicial confessions and the like; but as to extrajudicial deeds of the vassal," as if he should take infeftment from any other than his superior, it would be as real a disclamation as any verbal one judicially could be; but under the same limitation, if it were done of knowledge, and out of contempt of the superior.

30. Purpresture or purprision, is the vassal's going without his bounds, and encroaching upon the property of his superior; for purprises signify precincts and marches. The ground of it is from the fidelity and gratitude the vassal oweth to the superior; and therefore should not invade his inheritance; but this is not extended to encroachments upon the superior's commonty, as Craig [111,5,9] relateth the opinion of the lawyers in his time, in a purprision moved by the Constable of Dundee against the town of Innerkeithing [Not found]. But where the superior hath the right of property, burdened and barred with a right of common pasturage, acquired by the vassal by consent

or prescription, which though it marreth the effect of the superior's property, so that he cannot till or manure the same in prejudice of the pasturage, yet he remains direct proprietor; and if coal were found in that ground, it would be his alone: in which case, if the vassal should rive out and labour that ground, whereof he got common pasturage, it would be purprision, as is clear in the case of the common moors, disponed to none by the King in property; and therefore yet belonging to his Majesty in property, the riving out, or appropriating whereof, is declared purprision, Parliament 1600, cap. 5 [A.P.S. IV, 228, c. 13].

Purpresture must also be a known and manifest encroachment, as if a vassal should exclude a superior from a considerable part of a tenement; but when it is about marches it is not sustained, unless they be clearly manifest by march-stones; or that there hath been an antecedent cognition of the marches; and therefore, the action is either turned into a cognition, or at least before answer, a commission is granted to cognosce. Purpresture is thought to be incurred by encroachment upon the highways, and public rivers, as belonging to the King; but it could be inferred against no other than his vassal; and it being so ordinary by course of time to change the high-ways, or rather for the high-ways to change, when there becomes any impassibleness therein, there are other statutes appointed for securing thereof upon far less certification than purpresture; so that I conceive it could hardly be inferred upon that ground. Purpresture was only found competent to be cognosced by barons, comprehending superior dignities; but by none of their vassals or sub-vassals, Parl. 1477, cap. 79 [A.P.S. 11, 119, c. 11]. But now it belongs only to the jurisdiction of the Lords of Session, as all other recognitions do.

31. Craig hath largely and learnedly treated of other feudal delinquencies; adducing the feudal customs of the neighbouring nations, and the opinions of many learned feudists thereupon, both generally and particularly, enumerating the most ordinary delinquencies, for which they hold vassals to lose their fees: he doth also give his own opinion, how far these or the like would be sustained with us, but adduceth little what had been sustained. But this much in general, that *mitiores pœnæ nobis semper placuere:* and in conclusion, *Lib.* 3, *Dieg.* 6, [111, 6, 21], he makes superiors lose their superiority, and the same to befall to their vassals, for the same delinquencies, for which the vassals lose their fee, to their superiors, except what concerns the honour and reverence due by vassals to their superiors; which therefore will not consist with attributing the feudal delinquencies to ingratitude, which can hardly be understood to give rise to the superior's losing his superiority; and therefore it must be from that mutual friendship and fidelity betwixt the superior and vassal, arising from the feudal contract. Since his time there hath scarce any thing been observed in relation to recognition, or amission of infeftments upon feudal delinquencies, except what concerns alienations of proper fees, or ward-holdings, without the superior's consent; or what may concern recognition, as it is implied in forfeiture: so that we are yet much

left to infer the feudal delinquencies, resolutive of infeftments from the nature of these rights: and though Craig hath not gone near the length of foreign feudists, in assigning the specialities resolving fees; yet if we should go his length, there would be found few unquarrelable rights of superiority, or property in the kingdom, but which might, in a considerable time, give ground enough to extinguish the right, either of the superior or vassal: and since no such thing hath been moved upon either part, the general acquiescence of the nation must make these delinquencies resolutive of infeftments, much narrower, and much more upon the vassal's part than the superior's; for our custom hath never given the vassal the right of superiority, upon the delinquencies of the superior.

All fees, yea, and liferents by infeftments, do necessarily imply an acknowledgment of the superior, and fidelity to him, and thence only, and not from gratitude ought the causes of dissolving fees be deduced: for though pure donations are dissolved by atrocious ingratitude, yet the most proper fees were never pure donations, but were from innominate contracts, *do ut facias*, and the services due thereby were not by way of gratitude, but by way of special contract: and there is most of pure donation in the most improper fees, such as blench and mortification, which are almost allodial; and yet the fewest resolutive delinquencies are in these; and feu-farms were at first granted for cultivating barren grounds, and paying a feu-duty, or canon out of them; and where they have a considerable rent, they are far from being purely gratuitous, and are rather perpetual locations. And in most fees of all kinds there are not only casualities but profits; and therefore, the delinquencies resolving them, should neither be extended nor esteemed equal, but should be much more sustained in proper fees, or ward-holdings, importing personal or military service, than in improper fees. Yet all infeftments being in the terms and tenor of fees, they must have a *reddendo* and acknowledgment of the superior, and fidelity too, not only as obligements, but as resolutive conditions implied therein; and therefore, wilful and open disowning the superior by disclamation, or infidelity in breach of trust, should from the nature of the feudal contract resolve the same.

32. Though breach of trust be a general term, the extent whereof is not determined; yet certainly it must import the vassal's being actor or accessory in conspiring or in taking away the life of the superior, or mutilating or wounding him, or in taking away his right of superiority: under which accession, may be justly comprehended, the not revealing to him of these hazards; but this would not reach to the revealing of any loss or detriment the superior might have in his other estate, or the concurring or acting against him therein. It may also be extended to the conspiring, or acting, or not revealing these things which might infer upon the superior infamy, equiparate to death or wounds; but it seems not to import a duty in the vassal to give counsel to his superior, or not to reveal his secrets neither inferring life, limb, nor fame; for though these be acts of gratitude and friendship, yet they are not implied in

the fidelity of all vassals, but only such as owe military and personal service.

I shall not determine how far breach of trust in improper fees, could extend to the wife, children, and family of the superior. But proper and military fees by ward-holding, do not only import fidelity, but assistance and counsel to the superior, by which the vassal can be accessory to no atrocious deed against the life and blood of the superior, but against any infamy may befall him, or any great detriment in his estate: and so will reach to deeds of hurt or disgrace to his wife or children by adultery, fornication, or atrocious violence upon their persons, or attempts thereunto; and may also extend to the revealing of the superior's secrets, or not defending him against his enemies, or such as attack him, or deserting him in that case; and in case of a necessary flight, by over-powering, in not crying for help and relief; and in lawful war, in not concurring with him, or deserting him, while with any probability of prevailing, he stood in fight, if the vassal were then near him; but it will not import his concourse *activè* in private quarrels by force of arms, which are not warrantable.

33. In all cases the ignorance of the vassal not being affected, or his weakness, will excuse these delinquences, and whatever he acteth in self-defence, or upon provocation of the atrocious injury of the superior, or by public authority, or in the service of his prince, or any anterior superior in ward-holding: or unless the atrocious deeds be past from by the superior, by owning his vassal after the knowledge thereof, or by a considerable time's forbearance to quarrel the same; especially when in the mean time, either the superior or vassal dies: for, though death obliterates crimes as to the punishment; yet the right arising to the superior in the fee, from the delinquence, as a resolutive condition, is not excluded by the vassal's death, if the superior were ignorant of the fact, or not in capacity to vindicate the same through public calamity, or his pupilarity or absence: but by the mutual friendship and strict union betwixt superior and vassal, small evidences will import the passing by former delinquences, especially when not questioned during the life of both parties.

There are multitudes of specialities proposed by Craig, as delinquences resolving fees, not only in relation to the superior, his person and family; but also of invading his house, besieging the same, or entering it by force, or invading his property, which is the ground of purprysion, acknowledged by our custom, or by denying or refusing to show the superior the marches of the fee, or denying any part of it to be holden of him; or not showing him his holding and investiture, being solemnly called to that purpose (which takes no place with us; for our ordinary custom for superiors as well as others, is to pursue improbations of their vassal's rights, wherein the certification is not the loss of the fee, but the presumptive falsity of the writs) or the denying to do justice to superiors; but also in relation to the fee, if he waste or deteriorate it: yea, in relation to the vassal's own person, as if he fall in incest, or if he kill his brother, or commit any parricide, or if he contract friendship with the enemies of his superior: and generally, whatever may make him unfit or unworthy to attend his superior, or to be in his court: But none of these are implied in the fidelity of any vassal. There be also special grounds of resolution or extinction of fees by the particular nature or tenor thereof, as feus become extinct *ob non solutum canonem*, and other fees are extinct by resolutive clauses, as to both which we have spoken already, Title, Infeftments of Property, §58, [11, 3, 51, 58, *supra*].

Craig [111, 6, 15] doth hold, that by the delinquence of vassals, conquest, or *feuda nova*, become extinct and return to the superior; but heritage, or *feuda vetera*, do but become extinct as to the delinquent vassal, and his descendants, and is not returned to the superior, but devolved to the next collateral of the delinquent vassal descending from the first vassal, who would have succeeded, if the delinquent vassal had died without issue, and who must enter heir to the delinquent vassal's predecessor: but in this the interest of the superior is too far restricted; for we have no custom nor tenor to enter any person heir to a defunct, while a nearer heir is existent, whatsoever his delinquence be, except parricide. He doth also move this question [111, 6, 17], that if the vassal have committed a feudal delict against the superior, and a public crime inferring forfeiture, whether the fee would fall to the King, or to the superior, or if the first sentence of forfeiture, or recognition would prevail; but does not determine it. Yet the first delinquence is sufficient to extinguish the fee, if insisted in, and must give the preference; for the sentence of forfeiture or recognition is but declaratory, and hath effect, not from the sentence, but from the deed inferring it [11, 11, 25, *supra*]. There is no difference, whether the delinquence inferring recognition, was before the vassal was actually entered, or after; but it is more questionable, whether recognition would be incurred by the deeds of the apparent heir in his predecessor's life; which could have no effect as to collaterals, who are not *alioqui successuri*, seeing they may be excluded by a descendant, which in men is always in hope: and if the heir apparent die before his predecessor, it can have no effect to exclude either his collaterals or descendants; and it is more probable, that though the heir apparent should survive, he would not be excluded, seeing feudal delinquencies are now so little extended.

34. It hath been much and long debated, and is not yet decided, whether recognition can be incurred for any atrocious deeds done by sub-vassals, whereby the superior might claim the right of the sub-vassal's fee to fall to him by recognition; or, whether recognition can only be incurred by the deeds of the immediate vassal. There was a case in question, where a sub-vassal rose in rebellion against the King, whereby his fee, as all his other rights, were confiscated to the King by forfeiture, which could but confiscate them as they were in his person, with the burden of all real rights of liferent, annualrent, or other subaltern infeftments of the forfeited person: but if the forfeiture of the sub-vassal did also comprehend recognition, the sub-vassal's fee would fall to the King, and belong to his donatar, without any real right or burden contracted by the forfeited person, except such as were confirmed by the King, either by a special confirmation, or by that general consent of the King,

inviting all his subjects to set their ward-lands feu, by the Act of Parl. 1457, cap. 71 [A.P.S. 11, 49, c. 15], which would preserve such feus, being constitute before the Act of Parl. 1633, cap. 16 [A.P.S. v, 33, c. 16], rescinding that Act as to the vassals of the King and Prince, as was found, February 12, 1674, M. of Huntley *contra* Gordon [2 Stair 265; M. 4170], November 16, 1681, Campbel *contra* L. Auchinbreck and the E. Argile [2 Stair 796; M. 4171]. And therefore, if recognition were implied in forfeiture, in that case it behoved to infer a general rule, that recognition might be incurred by all atrocious deeds against gratitude and fidelity, committed not only by the immediate vassal, but by all subaltern vassals, and would not only be competent to the King, upon deeds of treason committed against him by his sub-vassals, but, by all deeds of atrocity done against any other superior by his sub-vassals; as if his sub-vassal should kill, wound, or betray his superior; so that the question behoved to return, whether there were any feudal contract or obligation of fidelity betwixt the superior and his sub-vassals; for if that were, then vassals might fall in recognition by such deeds, not only against their immediate superiors, but against all their mediate superiors, though never so many. For though the case in question be most odious and unfavourable, being rebellion; yet it hath its proper punishment introduced by law and statute; whereby the rebel loseth his life, lands and goods to the King, to whom all his subjects owe fidelity, as subjects, though all do not owe the feudal fidelity as vassals; and therefore, as in liferent-escheat, the fee returneth to the King, or any other superior, with all its hail burdens, it seems so to return in the forfeiture of sub-vassals: yet if recognition take place as to the King, it must likewise fall to all other superiors, whatever way the land be held, whether ward, feu, blench or mortification, if they have not a confirmation or consent of the superior, anterior to the deeds inferring recognition. We shall not therefore anticipate the public determination of this question [111, 3, 31, *infra*]; if custom hath determined it, that will take place: for all feudal rights are local, but there hath not yet appeared any case, by which a donatar by his gift and presentation, being infeft in the fee of the King's sub-vassal forfeited, has excluded these who had real rights from the forfeited person before the treasonable fact, though much hath been disputed upon the Act of Parl. 1584, cap. 2 [A.P.S. 111, 349, c. 6] concerning the quinquennial possession of forfeited persons, especially from the last clause thereof, bearing, that no person presented by the King to feu-lands forfeited, nor any vassal of any feuar forfeited, shall be compelled to produce their acquittances of their feu-mail, or annualrents of their forfeited lands of any year preceding the forfeiture; which doth clearly acknowledge, that when the feuar's right is forfeited, his sub-vassal's right is not forfeited.

Title 12. Prescription, Where, of Usucapion, Long and Short Prescriptions, &c.

PRESCRIPTION is the common extinction and abolishing of all rights, and therefore is reserved here to the last place; the name and nature whereof we have from the civil law, wherein prescription is sometimes largely taken for any exception, but hath been appropriated to the most common exception in all cases, whereby all actions and causes are excluded, by course of time; and so prescription had no further effect, than to maintain the possessor in possession by exception, but not to recover possession, being lost, and could not constitute the right of property.

2. And in this, Prescription did chiefly differ from usucapion, by the ancient Roman law, that usucapion did constitute property, and therefore is defined by Modestinus, *l. 3.ff. de usucapione* [D. 41, 3, 3] ; *adjectio, vel acquisitio dominii per continuationem possessionis temporis lege definiti.* To which description the name doth agree; for, *usucapere est capere ex usu aut possessione,* to

take or acquire by use or possession; but every possession was not sufficient, unless it were a possession as proprietor, or for the possessor's own use only: so detention of any thing in the name, and for the use of another, and for the possessor only in security, as a pledge or wadset, cannot constitute property.

3. As to the time appointed for usucapion, moveables are acquired by continual possession for one year, *l. 10.ff.* [D. 41, 3, 10] *de usucapion; Inst. eod.* [Inst. 2, 6, *pr*] *in principio*. And immoveables being in Italy by the space of two years: other immoveables by the space of ten years against these in the same province; and twenty years against these out of the same province, *Auth. malæ fidei* [Nov. 119, 7], *C. de præscript. longi temporis* [C. 7, 33]. From which common rule, some cases of greatest moment were excepted; as first, public rights belonging to emperors and kings, which (as all do agree) cannot be acquired by usucapion or prescription in less than thirty or forty years, and many think by no less than an hundred years, or immemorial possession. Secondly, Things belonging to cities, which in some cases could not be prescribed without an hundred years' possession, at least without thirty or forty years. Thirdly, Things belonging to the church, against which no other can acquire by prescription in less than forty years; and against the church of Rome by special privilege, by the space of an hundred years only. The recent Roman law hath taken off all differences betwixt usucapion and prescription, *tit. C. de usucap. trans.* [C. 7, 31] whereby in either case property is acquired: yet in the ordinary acceptation, prescription, which is short in moveables, is commonly called usucapion; but we make only use of the name of prescription for both.

4. In prescription or usucapion amongst the Romans, were required three things, continuation of possession uninterrupted, *bona fides*, and a title, besides the kind of possession, and time before-mentioned. As to the first, prescription is unquestionably interrupted by real interruption or discontinuation of possession; it is also interrupted civilly, by *litis-contestation*, process, &c.

5. As to *bona fides*, or innocent possession required in prescription, it is commonly agreed, that it is requisite at the beginning of the possession in shorter prescriptions, but that it is presumed in the longest prescription. The civil and canon law differ in this, that the civil law requireth only *bonam fidem* at the beginning, so that if any person acquire any thing from him, whom he believeth to be the owner thereof, and so believing beginneth to possess, though thereafter he understand that his author was not the true owner, yet prescription doth proceed; but by the canon law it proceeds not: but if at any time before prescription ended, he knoweth the thing belonged to another, prescription is impeded; yea, though prescription were ended, if the right of another appear, most of the canonists hold, that *in foro conscientiæ*, the possessor is obliged to restore, unless the knowledge and forbearance of the owner doth infer or presume a dereliction of the thing, or consent, which takes no place in the case of the ignorance, or error of the owner.

6. In either case it is controverted, whether he who doubteth of his or his author's right be *bonæ fidei*, or *malæ fidei possessor*. The common ground in which all agree, is that the possessor's credulity and belief of his own and his author's right makes *bonam fidem*, and his knowledge of the right of another, *malam*, which seemeth to infer, that he who doubteth, must be *in mala fide*, because he believeth not his author to have had right, doubt and belief being contraries: And upon the other part, he who only doubteth, cannot be said to know the right of another. The most rational conciliation is by this distinction, that doubting being like the dubious balance, when it inclineth more to the belief of the possessor's, and author's right, than of the right of the other; the denomination and effect is taken from the stronger, and he is said to believe his own right, and can no ways be said to believe the right of another, whose doubtful opinion doth rather incline to his own right than the others; and contrarywise, when his opinion inclineth more to believe another's right than his own.

7. These things being hidden acts of the mind, it is very difficult to know who is in *bona fide* or *mala fide ;* but *bona fides* is presumed, unless a contrary probation or vehement presumption be for *mala fides*, of which Menochius, *lib. 2, de arbitrar. Jud. quæst. cas. 225.* relateth many, whereof these are the chief: First, He who possesseth without a title is ever presumed *malæ fidei* possessor: Secondly, Common fame in the neighbourhood, that the thing acquired belongs to another: Thirdly, If it be intimated or declared to the acquirer, before he acquired it, that it was another's: Fourthly, The extrajudicial confession of the acquirer, or of witnesses that the thing belonged to another: Fifthly, If the acquisition be not with observation of the ordinary solemnities: Sixthly, If the acquisition be from a procurator, and the acquirer did not see his warrant, albeit he had one: Seventhly, If the acquisition be from a prodigal person: Eighthly, If the acquirer take unaccustomed ways of security: and lastly, By whatsoever the acquirer is obliged to know by law, *scire et scire debere æquiparantur in jure.*

8. As to the title requisite in prescription, thereby is not meant a sufficient valid title, which needeth not the help of prescription; but a colourable title is sufficient; as that which is acquired by emption: the emption is title enough for prescription, though the seller had no right; or that which descendeth from any other by succession, legacy, donation, &c. And generally, whatsoever way property useth to pass, is sufficient for prescription, though it be not sufficient alone to constitute the property, to which there is requisite the author's right, and the transmission thereof; but to prescription, the manner of transmission is enough; for *bona fides* and continuation of possession supplieth the rest.

9. Prescription although it be by positive law, founded upon utility more than upon equity, the introduction whereof, the Romans ascribed to themselves; yet hath it been since received by most nations; but not so as to be counted amongst the laws of nations; because it is not the same, but different

in diverse nations, as to the matter, manner and time of it; and therefore, nations under no common authority, do not prescribe properly against each other, albeit by long patience and not contradiction, their consent may be inferred, even by the law of nations.

10. The grounds and reasons of prescription, are first, public utility, *ne dominia rerum sint incerta, neve lites sint perpetuæ;* And also because the law accounteth it as a dereliction of the owner's right, if he own it not, neither pursue it within such a time, *L. 1. ff. h. t.* [D. 41, 3, 1] §*1 Inst. eod.* [Inst. 2, 6, 1]. In the civil law though prescription reacheth all kinds of things, moveable and immoveable, yet with these exceptions. First, These things that are not in commerce, as they are not capable of express alienation, so neither of prescription. Secondly, Things stolen, whereunto, for utility's sake, to repress that frequent vice, the law hath stated an inherent and real vitiosity, that passeth with the thing stolen to all singular successors; and therefore though such things be acquired by a just title, though for a cause onerous, and an equivalent price, and by continuation of possession *bona fide;* yet prescription taketh no effect because of the inherent vitiosity. The like is to be understood of rapine or violent possession: yet the fruits and profits of such things belong to the *bona fide* possessor, rather by that right that followeth possession, *bona fide,* (of which formerly in the title, *Real Rights,*) than by prescription. Thirdly, It runneth not against pupils by the civil law, though some think that it is not to be understood of their moveables: yet it runneth against other minors, but they may be restored if they pursue for restitution in the time and manner prescribed in law.

11. To come now close to our law concerning prescription, our common rule of prescription is by the course of forty years, both in moveables and immoveables, obligations, actions, acts, decreets, and generally all rights, as well against those absent as present: we have not these differences which we have shown were in the civil law; and because our prescription is so long, there is little question with us, *de bona fide.* But there must be continual possession free from interruption, and in lands and other fees, a title, of which hereafter.

12. By our ancient custom, there was no place for prescription in any case, which hath been corrected by our statutes, both as to long and short prescription. First, As to personal rights, in Parl. 1469, cap. 28 [Prescription Act 1469, c. 28; A.P.S. 11, 95, c. 4], and Parl. 1474, cap. 54 [Prescription Act 1474, c. 54; A.P.S. 11, 107, c. 9]. It is statute, That as to all obligations that should be pursued thereafter, and that were not then depending in law, before the making of that Act; "that if the creditor did not follow or pursue the obligation within the space of forty years, and take document thereupon, the same shall be prescribed and of no avail:" which statute, because it mentions only obligations, (that is to say, simple obligations) was not extended to others, as contracts of marriage, February 26, 1622, Hamilton *contra* Lo. Sinclair [Durie 18; M. 10717]: but afterward it hath been ordinarily extended

even to contracts of marriage, whereupon marriage followed, November 27, 1630, Lauder *contra* Colmiln [Durie 542; M. 10655]; December 23, 1630, Ogilvie *contra* Lo. Ogilvie [Durie 551; M.6541]. It was also extended to testaments, June 19, 1627, Lundie *contra* L. Balnagoun [*Sub nom. Lindsays* v *L. Balgony*, Durie 297; M. 10718]. And was also extended to pursuits for tutor-compts; Hope, Prescription [Hope, *Maj.Pr.*, VI,43]. It was also extended to all decreets, though *in foro contradictorio*, and this ordained to stand as a constant practick, July 26, 1637, L. Lawers *contra* Dumbar [Durie 854; M. 10719].

13. Prescription of forty years was found sufficient to constitute the right to a bell in a kirk-steeple against another kirk, pursuing therefor, without instructing a title whereby they had the bell, which is not necessary to be instructed, but is presumed from possession in moveables, December 7, 1633, Minister and kirk-session of Aberchirdo *contra* Parishioners and Kirk of Chanrie [Durie 695; M. 10972].

14. Prescription being odious, the forty years are accounted *de momento in momentum* : so that it is not the running, but the completing of the forty years that makes prescription; and therefore, a writ blank in the month and day, expressing the year, was reckoned from the last of December that year; and because there was three quarters wanting of forty years before insisting upon the pursuit thereupon, it was sustained as not prescribed, December, 23, 1630, Ogilvie *contra* Lo. Ogilvie [Durie 551; M.6541]. But in regard of the length of this prescription, it is accounted *ex tempore continuo, et non utili*, and so no abatement for the time of troubles, or surcease of justice, even in the case of mortification to bead-men, June 30, 1671, Bead-men of Magdalen chapel *contra* Drysdale [1 Stair 746; M. 11148]. Long after this statute there was no prescription of heritable and real rights; and therefore not of a decreet of poinding the ground, Hope, Prescription, Currier *contra* L. Louristoun [Hope, *Maj.Pr.* VI,43,26]. Only it was declared, that no person should be compelled to produce procuratories, or instruments of resignation, precepts of *clare constat*, or other precepts of seasin of lands or annualrents, whereof the heritors and their authors, or liferenters, having liferents reserved in their infeftments, were in possession forty years together, their charters making mention of the precepts, the wanting whereof shall make no reduction, the charters and seasins being extant, Parl. 1594, cap. 214 [Prescription Act 1594, c. 218; A.P.S. IV, 68, c. 24].

15. But prescription of forty years is introduced of all heritable and other rights, Parl. 1617, cap. 12 [Prescription Act 1617, c. 12; A.P.S. IV, 543, c. 12] where the heritors, their predecessors, and authors, possessed land, annualrent, or other heritage by themselves, their tenants, or others having their rights, (as by liferenters, wadsetters, tenants) for the space of forty years together, following the dates of their infeftments, without lawful interruption, that such shall not be troubled, pursued, or unquieted by his Majesty, and other superiors and authors, their heirs and successors, upon any

ground whatsomever, except upon falsehood, providing such heritors show a charter to them or their authors, preceding the said forty years possession, with the instrument of seasin following thereupon: or otherwise, instruments of seasin, one or more, continued and standing together for the said space of forty years, either proceeding upon retours, or precepts of *clare constat;* where, by standing together, it is not meant unreduced, but that either the vassal lived and brooked by one seasin forty years: or if he died, that the seasin was renewed to his heirs; and so continued not only the possession, but the seasin forty years; in which the continuation of seasins cannot be reckoned *de die in diem;* because there must necessarily be an interval betwixt the death of the person first seased, and the service of the heir to whom the law gives *annum deliberandi*, to consider whether the heritage will be beneficial or hurtful, and accordingly whether he will enter or not, February 15, 1671, E. of Argyle *contra* L. McNaughton [1 Stair 720; M. 10791]. And also all actions upon heritable bonds, reversions, contracts or others whatsomever, except reversions incorporate within the body of infeftments, used by the heritors for their title, or registrate in the register of reversions: which general clause was found to extend to actions of reduction of retours, though if no other heir had been retoured, the right of blood prescribes not, but any person may enter heir to his predecessor who died hundreds of years before; yet if any other were entered, he cannot after forty years, quarrel or reduce the same by the general Act of Prescription, though the retour was anterior to the special Act of prescription of retours, Parl. 1617, cap. 13 [Reduction Act 1617, c. 13; A.P.S. IV, 544, c. 13] whereby retours thereafter are irreducible, if not quarrelled within twenty years, Nov. 28, 1665, younger *contra* Johnstouns [1 Stair 315; M. 10925]. In the former statute it is declared, that actions of warrandice shall not prescribe from the date of the bond, or infeftment whereupon warrandice is sought, but only from the date of the distress.

16. But this prescription is not to be extended against superiors, upon their vassals' possession forty years, though no feu, blench, or other duty or casuality be demanded by the superior; because the vassal's right acknowledgeth the superior's right, and his possession is also the superior's possession: yet all duties and casualities thereupon, not pursued within forty years, prescribe, without prejudice to these due within forty years of the pursuit, December 15, 1638, Stuart of Gairntullie *contra* Commissary of St Andrews [Durie 867; M. 10750].

17. Which holdeth in tack-duties, which prescribe as to the years preceding forty, before the pursuit, but no other, March 10, 1627, betwixt two Glasgow men; Spots. Prescription, Stuart *contra* Fleming [Spotiswoode 235; M. 10749]. Yet prescription by possessing forty years, as part and pertinent, by an infeftment, was not elided; because, before these forty years the possessor's author had a tack of the lands in question, February 20, 1675, Countess of Murray *contra* Mr Robert Weyms [2 Stair 325; M. 9636]; though in this case the land in question was *separatum tenementum*, by a distinct infeft-

ment, but became part and pertinent by being so brooked forty years. By this statute, prescription of heritable rights doth not only exclude other infeft-ments in property, but also annualrents, pensions, and all other rights; and so an heritor possessing forty years was found free thereof, July 22, 1634, Forrester *contra* Possessors of Bothkennel [Durie 370; M. 10973], where the office of forester and the fees thereof were found prescribed.

18. From this prescription there are excepted the rights of pupils and minors, against whom prescription runs not during their minority, so that they need not seek restitution *in integrum*, as in the civil law; which exception is particularly expressed in the foresaid statute, and is extended to all other prescriptions of personal rights or others, Spots. Prescription, D. Lennox *contra* the Executors of Alexander Beatoun [Spotiswoode 236; M. 11147]. But there is no exception of rights mortified to pious uses, as bead-men, June 30, 1671, Bead-men of Magdalane chapel *contra* Drysdale [1 Stair 746; M. 11148]. Yet Heriot's hospital being founded to orphans and minors, and so in the case of the foresaid statute, the Lords found that prescription could not run against them, December 29, 1691, Thomas Fisher, treasurer of Heriot's Hospital *contra* Hepburn of Barefoord [*Sub anno* 1695, 1 Fountainhall 688; M. 10786].

19. In neither of the statutes introducing long prescription by forty years, is there any mention or provision, concerning the manner of the entry in possession, whether it was *bona fide* peaceable or lawful, but only that it have a title, and be continued without interruption.

20. The title in heritable rights, being ground rights of lands or annual-rents, is very well distinguished by the last statute, betwixt conquest and heritage; for heritage which hath descended by succession from a predecessor, is content with a more slender title, *viz.* seasins without the warrants or adminicles, but only bearing, that they proceed upon retours, or precepts of *clare constat*, providing that the possession hath been by virtue of these sea-sins; so that not only there must be possession for forty years together, but seasins consecutive, proper to the several possessors during that time: but purchasers must not only have for their title a seasin preceding the forty years prescription, but if they found upon their proper right, they must also produce a charter preceding the forty years. And therefore, though a pur-chaser should possess forty years, and show his seasin anterior thereto; yet would it not be a title for prescription, unless he produce a charter before that time, where, by charter must not be understood a solemn charter as it is dis-tinguished from a disposition or precept, but as it comprehends these; for many valid infeftments have no charter, but seasin proceeds upon the precept of seasin contained in the disposition. And though a precept of seasin were only shown as the warrant of the seasin, the same with forty years possession by virtue thereof, would perfect prescription; for the seasins of themselves, without warrant or adminicle, are but the assertions of notars, and not pro-bative; yet they are sufficiently probative, not only by the immediate warrant

or precept whereupon they proceed, but upon the mediate warrant; as if a seasin be produced with a bond or obligement to grant an infeftment conform to that seasin, *Vide Tit 3.* §*19.* But purchasers may well conjoin their own title and their authors'; so that if he can show in his authors' persons consecutive seasins for forty years, upon retours or precepts of *clare constat*, and possession conform, it will be sufficient: or if they cannot show such seasins and possession in their authors for the whole forty years, yet if they show the accomplishment of forty years by their own seasins and warrants thereof, and possession conform, these may complete the prescription.

21. This statute doth not only secure rights, and lands and annualrents, by forty years peaceable possession *cum titulo*, but also other heritable rights, such as wadsets; for registrate or incorporate reversions being expressed as exceptions, wadsets must be comprehended in the rule, and all infeftments for security or relief, which do imply a reversion incorporate. It will also extend to infeftments of teinds; for, though teinds be *separatum tenementum* from the stock, yet both are ground rights of the land. Infeftments of liferent, if possessed and unquarrelled for forty years, showing their seasin and the warrant or adminicle thereof, the same would make the liferent right irreducible, or might perfect prescription, being joined to the author's rights; yea, this statute hath been extended to long tacks of lands, teinds or others [11,12,23, *infra*], not to make them perpetual, but unquarrelable during their time.

22. A right to teinds may be prescribed, as well as other rights, by forty years' possession; but a right to bygone teinds, being founded in public law, prescribes not, except as to the bygones before forty years; and the possessor cannot prescribe an absolute immunity and freedom from payment within the forty years, and in time coming, seeing all lands in Scotland by law are liable in teind, except such as never paid any, being *cum decimis inclusis*, or belonging to the Cystertian order, Templers and Hospitallers, or gleibs, February 7, 1666, E. Panmure *contra* Parishioners of   [1 Stair 351; M. 10760].

23. This statute is also extended unto rights of patronage, or offices which are heritable rights, though they be not always constitute or continued by infeftment; yet forty years' possession by the original right in the first acquirer, or by the continuation in their successors, doth establish their rights against all quarrelling by reduction or declarator. Yea, this statute is extended to long tacks, which if clad with forty years' peaceable possession, either in the tacksman, or his assignees, or their heirs, who need no service, cannot be quarrelled, but stand valid, not only for these forty years, but for all subsequent years unexpired; as was found in a tack of teinds, though set without consent of the patron, and the bolls liquidate to ten shillings, July 7, 1677, Parson of Prestonhaugh, *contra* his Parishioners [2 Stair 535; M. 10761].

24. It is also extended to thirlage and multures, with any antecedent adminicle, as by enrolment of court [11,7,16,*supra*]; and generally to all servitudes, though there be no more antecedent title, but part and pertinent

of the dominant tenement, either exprest or implied; as was found in the case of a pasturage and sheilling, albeit there was produced an old tack, bearing, to be granted to the possessor, or his predecessor, November 27, 1677, Grant of Ballindalloch *contra* Grant of Balvey [2 Stair 566; M. 10876]. Whereupon it was alleged that a tenant possessing by tack from his master could not prescribe against him, which was not respected in this case, nor in that of the Countess of Murray *contra* Weyms [2 Stair 325; M. 9636], February 20, 1675. The like July 14, 1675, Colledge of Aberdeen *contra* E. Northesk [2 Stair 344; M. 7230]. But all annual prestations preceding forty years prescribe, though constantly paid for thirty-nine years, every year being a several obligement, though in one writ, prescribes severally, January 19, 1669, E. Athol *contra* L. Strowan [1 Stair 582; M. 7804]. It holds also in annualrents, July 22, 1671, and February 7, 1672, Blair of Balleik *contra* Blair of Denhead [1 Stair 765 and 2 Stair 64; M. 11235]. But it cannot be extended to prescribe against a superior, for not payment of the *reddendo* [11, 12, 16, *supra*], because a right of property cannot consist without superiority, unless there be a right taken from another superior.

25. Prescription doth not only exclude the preference of other better rights, which if insisted upon within prescription, would have been preferred as anterior, and thereby the posterior right reduced as *à non habente potestatem*. But all ground of reduction by the King, or other superiors or authors, is excluded, so that the neglect of the King's officers cannot be obtruded by the Act of Parliament declaring that their neglects shall not prejudge the King; neither any nullity in the titles of prescription, except it be in the essentials thereof: so, prescription cannot sustain a perpetual tack without ish, which is essential thereto; nor a seasin without a symbol, generally or particularly, or not given upon the ground of the land. But all requisites in rights introduced by custom or statute, and not essential thereto, are cut off by prescription.

26. The main exception or reply against prescription, is interruption, not only by the discontinuing the possession of the whole, but also of a part, which was found sufficient to interrupt the prescription as to the whole: as an infeftment of thirlage and possession of corns growing upon the lands, was found sufficient to exclude the prescription of the multures of all grain, June 26, 1635, L. Wauchtoun *contra* Hume of Foord [Durie 768; M. 11230, 15971]. So likewise, payment of annualrents within forty years, interrupts prescription of bonds, and that not only as to the party paying, but payment made by the principal debtor was found to interrupt prescription as to the cautioner, who never paid, nor was pursued during the space of forty years, December 18, 1667, Nicolson *contra* L. Philorth [1 Stair 497; M. 11233]. And an annualrent constitute out of two tenements, was found unprescribed as to both, by uplifting the annualrent out of either, though the one was now forty years in the hands of a singular successor, June 22, 1671, Lo. Balmerino *contra* Hamilton [1 Stair 738; M. 3350, 11234].

Prescription is ordinarily interrupted and excluded, by the dependence of any action, whereupon the right might have been taken away or impeded, Hope, Patronage, L. Glenurchie *contra* Campbel [Possibly Hope, *Maj.Pr.* III,15,6; M.14250]; *Idem*, Tacks and Tenants, Carnousie *contra* Keith [Hope, *Maj.Pr.* III,19,73; M.15315], even though there was only the first summons without continuation, or second summons, February 17, 1665, Butter *contra* Gray [1 Stair 272; M.11183]; yea, though the pursuer past from the summons *pro loco et tempore*, Hope, Removing, Douglas *contra* Lo. Herreis [Hope, *Maj.Pr.* VI,39,24; M.11228]; or by a transference, though reducible, because not proceeding upon the right title; seeing the right title was also in the pursuer's person, July 26, 1637, L. Lawers *contra* Dumbar [Durie 854; M.10719]. The like though the pursuit might have been excluded for want of solemnity, [in the executions of the summons], *in re antiqua*, where the custom was not clear, November 25, 1665, White *contra* Horn [1 Stair 314; M.10646]. Yea, an annualrent was found interrupted by a poinding of the ground, though therein the heritor was not called, June 15, 1666, Sinclair *contra* L. Howstoun [1 Stair 378; M.1289].

Prescription was also found validly interrupted by a charge of horning upon the bond in question, albeit proceeding only upon summary registration by the clause in the bond, and by no citation, July 21, 1629, Moris *contra* Johnstoun [Durie 465; M.11228]. But warning, whereupon nothing followed, was not found a sufficient interruption of an old tack-duty, Hope, Possession, Bruce *contra* Bruce [Hope, *Maj.Pr.* III,21,21; M.15314]; *Idem*, March *contra* Keir [Hope, *Maj.Pr.* III,21,25]. Neither was it found sufficient, to interrupt prescription of the first part of a mutual contract, that action was used upon the second, which saved the second from prescription; seeing the party concerned in the first, neither used action or charge thereupon, nor founded exception upon it, when pursued by the other party, November 27, 1630, Lawder *contra* Collmil [Durie 542; M.10655]. Interruption was also sustained upon a citation, at the instance of a party not then entered heir, being entered thereafter within the years of prescription. The like upon a summons of reduction upon minority, though it was not filled up within forty years, being insinuate in the title of the summons, that minors have interest to reduce deeds to their lesion, July 14, 1669, E. Marishal *contra* Leith [1 Stair 638; M. 10324].

But interruption was not sustained from the citation in a summons of re-reduction, not being *ex capite inhibitionis*, but from filling up of the reason which was after an inhibition, February 11, 1681, Kennuay *contra* Crafurd [2 Stair 858; M.5170]. And it was sustained upon citation upon the second summons, being only a day before the year was complete, albeit the first summons should be found null, and though the citation was at the market-cross upon a privileged warrant, purchased upon pretence that *non fuit tutus accessus*, past of course among the common bills, and the reason of the privilege was neither true nor instructed, and though the execution bore not a copy left at the cross, the party adding that, and abiding thereby as truly done by the executor of the summons, July 6, 1671, Mackbra *contra* L. McDonald [*Sub nom. McCrae* v *McDonald*, 1 Stair 749; M. 8338]. Interruption was also sustained upon a citation in a reduction in *anno* 1630, albeit the executions bore not the name of the pursuer or defender but "the parties within mentioned;" and were not written upon the back of the summons, but upon a loose schedule: and the citation was in the last of the thirteen years excepted from prescription, against a party of great quality, against whom many interruptions were like then to have been used; the user of the interruption deponing that he received the same from his father, or amongst his evidents, and knew not that they were the executions of any other summons, February 11, 1673, Muir *contra* Lawson [2 Stair 170; M. 11238]. But interruption was not sustained upon summary registration, without citation or charge, January 12, 1672, Johnstoun *contra* Lo. Balhaven [2 Stair 43; M. 11237]. And interruption by warning and citation thereupon, to remove from a salmond-fishing, was not found effectual in a competition betwixt two parties, both being then *in acquirenda possessione*, by prescription, and neither having a sufficient right constitute before, unless the party warned and cited, had discontinued his possession for a year at least, January 13, 1680, Brown *contra* Town of Kirkcudbright [2 Stair 736; M. 10845].

27. Prescription as to the King, was found sufficiently interrupted by the King's letters, published at the cross of the head burgh of the shire, where the lands in question lie, without citation or charge, March 29, 1630, E. Monteith *contra*   [Durie 515; M. 11290]. There was then an act of sederunt made penult of March 1630, upon a letter from the King to the Lords of Session, bearing, "that in respect by the Act of Prescription, 1617, all heritable rights clad with forty years' possession, are declared irreducible, unless they had been quarrelled within the space of forty years preceding that Act, and liberty granted to intent actions within the space of thirteen years after the date of the said Act, to interrupt prescriptions, albeit there had been no interruption for forty years before the said Act; and his Majesty resolving to use interruption within the space of thirteen years, of deeds done to the prejudice of the Crown, for preservation of his Majesty's right and actions competent to him and his successors, for that effect, seeing a multitude that may be concerned therein, cannot commodiously be summoned personally, or at their dwelling places, within the said thirteen years, which were to expire in June 1630: And it being necessary that some solemn act should be done, to testify the Knig's will and resolution, to prosecute actions, in his own time, which could not be more properly and conveniently done, nor by inserting and publishing as follows; therefore his Majesty appointed his declaration for prosecuting his rights, to be insert in the books of sederunt, and letters thereupon directed, to be published at the market cross of Edinburgh, and other places needful; and desired the Lords to declare the same, to have the force of a legal and lawful interruption." Which the Lords enacted to be done ac-

cordingly, as to the particulars therein contained; and issued letters of publication at the market cross of Edinburgh, and other market crosses of the kingdom, where the lands and baronies lie, or where the persons interested therein reside, and at the said market cross of Edinburgh and pier of Leith, for these without the kingdom: which act of sederunt was ratified, Parl. 1633, cap. 12 [A.P.S. v, 28, c. 12]. Which letter and acts, extended to his Majesty's annexed and non-annexed property, whereof the farms, duties, and feufarms were compted for in exchequer, since the month of August 1455, and to the principality, and to the erection of benefices, spirituality or temporality, patronage of kirks pertaining to his Majesty and his predecessors, regalities and heritable offices, any of the said particulars being unlawfully disponed against the laws and Acts of Parliament; and likewise against changing of ward in blench or taxt-ward, granted by the King or his predecessors in their minority, and not ratified by any King or Prince in their majority; and but prejudice to any person of their lawful defences in actions to be intented by his Majesty thereupon.

In prescription this is a general exception, *contra non valentem agere non currit præseriptio,* and therefore bonds prescribe not from their dates, but from the term of payment, February 17, 1665, Butter *contra* Gray [1 Stair 272; M. 11183]; June 23, 1675, Bruce *contra* Bruce [2 Stair 334; M. 11185]. And inhibition prescribes from the date of the last execution, and not from the registration, February 19, 1680, Lutefoot *contra* Prestoun [2 Stair 761; M. 11187]. So an obligement by a cautioner in a contract of marriage, obliging to employ a sum for a wife's use, found only to run from her husband's death, July 5, 1665, Mackie *contra* Stuart [1 Stair 295; M. 11205]. And likewise prescription was not found to run against a party to take away his infeftment, seeing he had given a liferent right, which would have excluded him from any action that could have attained possession, and that he was not obliged to use declarator or reduction in this case, more than in the prescription of bonds from their dates, February 28, 1666, E. Lauderdale *contra* Visc. Oxenfoord [1 Stair 370; M. 27]. The like, Jan. 17, 1672, Young *contra* Thomson [2 Stair 47; M. 11207]; Feb. 5, 1680, Brown *contra* Hepburn [2 Stair 752; M. 11208]. Yea, prescription was found not to run against a party forfeited, and sequestrated by the Usurpers, who possessed his right in question for eight years, which years therefore were deduced, January 25, 1678, D. Lauderdale *contra* E. Tweedale [2 Stair 602; M. 11193]. But where a party was not forfeited, but durst not appear during the Usurpation, he was not found *non valens agere,* seeing he might pursue by a procurator or assignee, July 24, 1678, Colonel Whitefoord *contra* E. Kilmarnock [2 Stair 642; M. 11196]. Yea, prescription was not extended to the liferent of a wife, in a sum payable to her, and her husband, the longest liver, though the stock was prescribed against the husband, who neither insisted, nor got annual for forty years; but not against the wife's interest for the annualrent, [during her life,] though the sum bore no annualrent, yet the wife was found to have right to uplift the sum, and to re-employ it for her liferent use, June 22, 1675, Gaw *contra* E. Weims [2 Stair 334; M. 11183].

28. Our statutes have introduced several short prescriptions, as the rights to which they relate do require, which we shall shortly represent, not according to the time they were introduced, but according to the time of their endurance, most of them occurring to be considered in their proper places, with the rights whereto they relate. And first, our law hath introduced the *annus deliberandi* in favour of heirs, because if once they enter or immix themselves in their predecessors' heritage, they become liable for their whole debts, though far exceeding the worth of their heritage; and therefore the heir apparent hath a year to deliberate whether the heritage will be profitable, during which he may not only inquire, but may pursue actions of exhibition *ad deliberandum* [111, 5, 1, *infra*], and if they forbear, they are free of all actions against them or the heritage during that year; and therefore, that privilege prescribes in a year and a day, after the defunct's death.

29. Secondly, By the Act of Parl. 1661, cap. 24 [A.P.S. VII, 63, c. 88], there is a preference granted to the creditors of defuncts, preferring them to the creditors of the heir or apparent heir; so that all diligences by the creditors of defuncts, against their estates, shall be preferred to the diligences, for debts contracted by apparent heirs, providing the said diligences of the defunct's creditors, be complete within three years after the defunct's death. Albeit the being complete be not expressed in the statute; yet by the design thereof, it must be so understood: for if diligences inchoated in these three years, though perfected thereafter, would be sufficient, the preference would not be for three years, but might come to be for forty years. Complete diligences are apprisings, or adjudications with infeftment, or a charge against the superior to infeft, poinding, and decreets for making arrested sums or goods forthcoming. And by the said statute, dispositions by heirs or apparent heirs of the defunct's estates, are declared not to be valid against their predecessors' creditors, unless made a full year after the defunct's death; therefore this preference of the defunct's creditors prescribes in three years, or rather in two years, because within the year of deliberation they cannot pursue, unless the heir enter or immix; and therefore this privilege prescribes in two years after the year of deliberation [111, 5, 13, *infra*].

30. Thirdly, There is a triennial prescription of spuilzies, ejections, intrusions, which comprehends succeeding in the vice of parties removed, Parl. 1579, cap. 81 [Prescription (Ejections) Act, 1579, c. 81; A.P.S. III, 145, c. 19]. This prescription by the statute, runs not against minors. And this prescription doth not take away the right, but only the privileges of the action as proceeding upon a short citation, and the oath *in litem*, allowed to the party injured, to declare his loss, and the violent profits; but hinders not the restitution, or recovery of the thing, with the ordinary profits. There is also a triennial prescription of merchants' compts, house mails, and the like, which is only as to the manner of probation, that if these be not pursued within three

years from the time they are due, witnesses shall not be admitted to prove the same, but only writ or oath of party: But in this prescription, minority is not excepted, Parl. 1519, cap. 83 [Prescription Act 1579, c. 83; A.P.S. III, 145, c. 21], which is not extended to rents of lands in the country, January 20, 1627, Ross *contra* Fleming [Durie 270; M. 12735]. In both these prescriptions (if actions be intented within the prescription of three years) custom did not limit these actions to three years; but they continued for forty years, which might have much more conveniently been cut off by three years; for thereby the action which is accessory, was more privileged, than the principal right, to which it is accessory, which is amended in part by posterior statutes, as to subsequent cases; for by the 9. Act Parl. 2, Cha. 2d [Prescription Act 1669, c. 9; A.P.S. VII, 561, c. 14] all short prescriptions wherein there was action intented *debito tempore*, the said action shall prescribe in ten years, except it be wakened every fifth year, minority being excluded: the like is extended to cases preceding the said Act, if not renewed, as is therein prescribed, Parl. 1685, cap. 14 [Prescription Act 1685, c. 14; A.P.S. VIII, 471, c. 14]. There is another triennial prescription in removings, that if they be not pursued within three years, they can never be pursued thereafter upon the same warning, wherein minority is not excepted, Parl. 1579, cap. 82 [A.P.S. III, 145, c. 20]. This prescription was not reckoned from the date of the warning, as being uncertain, but from the term, to which the warning was made, February 6, 1629, La. Borthwick *contra* Scot [Durie 422; M. 11076].

31. There is a quadriennial prescription against minors not possessing to reduce deeds done by them in their minority to their enorm lesion, from their age of twenty-one complete, to their age of twenty-five complete, but these actions being intented within that *quadriennium utile*, did last for forty years, till the said late Act of Parliament anent prescription and interruption [Prescription Act 1669, c. 9; A.P.S. VII, 561, c. 14].

32. There are several quinquennial prescriptions; as first, all arrestments upon decreets prescribe five years after the dates thereof; and arrestments upon dependences prescribe in five years after sentence, upon the dependence, if the said arrestments be not pursued or insisted upon, during that time, by the said Act [Prescription Act 1669, c. 9; A.P.S. VII, 561, c. 14]. Secondly, By this statute ministers' stipends and multures not pursued for within five years after they are due, and likewise mails and duties of tenants, not being pursued within five years after the tenant's removal, prescribe, unless the said stipends, multures, mails and duties, be proven resting by oath or special writ, acknowledging what is resting; and that all bargains concerning moveables, or sums of money, probable by witnesses, shall only be probable by writ or oath of party, if the samine be not pursued within five years after the making of the bargain, and all pursuits, and grounds thereof prescribe, unless they be wakened every fifth year. There is also a quinquennial prescription of the legal reversions of special adjudications, whereby lands are adjudged only equivalent to the sums, by the Act of Parliament

Sep. 6, 1672, cap. 19 [Adjudications Act, 1672, c. 19; A.P.S. VIII, 93, c. 45].

33. There was a seven years prescription of the legal reversions of app-risings; and there is a septennial prescription of interruptions, which, if they be not renewed every seven years, prescribed by the Act of Parliament Dec. 8, 1669, cap. 10 [Interruptions Act 1669, c. 10; A.P.S. VII, 561, c. 15].

34. There is likewise a decennial prescription of reversions of apprisings to which they were prorogued by the Acts of Debtor and Creditor, 1661, [Diligence Act, 1661, c. 62; A.P.S. VII, 316, c. 344] and of general adjudi-cations, when the adjudger cannot get a special one, by the said Act, Parl. 1672, cap. 19.

35. And by the said Act, Parl. 1669, cap. 9, there is introduced a pre-scription of twenty years of holograph-bonds and holograph-missives, and subscriptions in compt-books without witnesses, unless the verity of the said subscription be proven by the defender's oath; by which manner of probation there is action competent, till the long prescription of forty years.

THE END OF THE SECOND BOOK

BOOK III

Titles Contained in the Third Book

BOOK III

Title 1. Assignations, Where, of Arrestments, and Actions for making Forth-coming

HAVING now gone through all the several kinds of private rights, personal and real, both as to their nature and constitution, and as to their extinction and destitution; we are now come to the second part of our design proposed, which is the conveyance and transmission of these rights, which stand in force, and become not extinct; for the extinction of a right is no conveyance of it, seeing thereby it ceaseth to exist.

1. Rights are conveyed, or derived, either amongst the living, or from the dead; and in both, the conveyance is different, in personal and real rights; And in immoveable and heritable rights, the conveyance amongst the living, of personal rights, is by assignation, of real rights by disposition, and promiscuously of both by confiscation. Conveyance of right from the dead, is by succession; in moveables by executry, in heritable rights, by the succession of heirs and other like successors; of which in order.

2. Personal rights or obligations are sometimes incommunicable, and not assignable or transmissible, either by reason of the matter, such as most conjugal and parental obligations are, or where there is a singular consideration of the person, as in commissions, trusts, &c. Most of these are intransmissible, even by the consent both of debtor and creditor: yea, generally, all obligations are intransmissible, upon either part directly without the consent of the other party, which is clear upon the part of the debtor, who cannot, without consent of the creditor, liberate himself, and transmit his obligation upon another, though with the creditor's consent he may, by delegation: neither can a creditor force his debtor to become debtor to another, without his own consent, as when he takes him obliged to pay to him or his assignees [III, I, 16, *infra*].

3. Yet, that obligations may become the more useful and effectual, custom hath introduced an indirect manner of transmission thereof, without the debtor's consent, whereby the assignee is constituted procurator; and so as mandatar for the creditor, he hath power to exact and discharge, but it is to his own behoof, and so he is also denominated donatar; and this is the ordinary conception of assignations. The like is done amongst merchants, by orders, whereby their debtors are ordered to pay such a person their debt, which indeed is a mandate; but if it be to his own behoof, it is properly an assignation. And in favours of creditors, law hath introduced judicial assignations upon arrestment, and by apprising and adjudication. Assignations are more frequent with us than anywhere; there is scarce mention thereof in the civil law. Assignation is also called *cessio*, which, both there and with us, is most applied to *cessio bonorum et actionum*, whereby not only obligations, but property of things, and generally, all rights are ceded from the debtor to his creditor: from this term the assignee is called cessioner, as the assigner is also called cedent. Under assignations are comprehended translations, being transmissions from a prior assignee to a posterior; or retrocessions, which are the returning back of the right assigned from the assignee to the cedent, which are also called repositions.

4. For clearing the matter of assignations; *First*, Consider the requisites to make them perfect and valid conveyances. *Secondly*, What are the effects and extent thereof. For the first, an assignation doth necessarily require the clear expressing of the cedent, assignee, and thing assigned; and though the ordinary style of it be known, yet any terms that may express the transmission of the right assigned from the cedent to the assignee, will be sufficient, as if the cedent assign, transfer and dispone, make over, set over, gift, or grant the thing assigned to the assignee, or nominate or constitute him his cessioner, assignee, donatar, or procurator to his own behoof; and, therefore, an assignation to a bond was found valid, both against principal and cautioners, both being in the dispositive clause, though the cautioners were omitted in the clause, "with power, &c." which was not thought a necessary clause. Had. December 12, 1622, Johnstoun *contra* Jack [Not found].

5. The conveyance of bonds or other writs, wherein the name of the creditor or acquirer is left blank, have become of late very frequent, and have occasioned many debates, as to the conveyance of such rights, and the effects thereof: as first, whether the leaving the name of the creditor or acquirer blank be warrantable, or a fraudulent conveyance, to conceal and keep in the dark to whom the right belongeth, that creditors may not know to affect it by legal diligence: the reason ordinarily given for taking writs in that way, is to shun the trouble of assignations, translations, or intimations thereof, as they pass from hand to hand, according to that tenor of obligation, frequent in other places, whereby the debtor obligeth him to pay and perform such things *latori præsentium;* by which he is obliged to pay to none, but to him from whom he may get up the bond, and may safely pay to any that hath it.

There is another reason of taking blank-bonds, to shun compensation upon any debt due by the cedent; for the law alloweth compensation against the assignee, upon any debt due by the debtor to the cedent [This should probably read "to the debtor by the cedent".], before the assignation was intimated; but when the debtor gives a bond blank in the creditor's name, he is thereby understood to pass from compensation, which hath been sustained, *Vide Title 11,§6, Compensation,* [1,18,6,*supra*] for it is a just personal objection against him who granted the blank-bond, not to stop the effect or execution thereof, upon any other debt due by him to that party, to whom he granted the bond. And albeit such blank-bonds may pass amongst merchants, where intimations are not necessary upon bills of exchange, which are transmitted by the orders of merchants thereupon without intimation; and though such bonds may pass amongst persons of entire credit, yet such conveyances, if they should be encouraged, and pass currently without intimation, would be of dangerous consequence, and give occasion to much fraud; for thereby creditors should not know in whose person such rights stood, and how to affect them for just debts: and although the granter of such blank-bonds, or the haver, who so transmits them, may be excluded from compensation; yet others who may have interest to propone compensation in the same way, as they may found upon a discharge granted by the receiver of the blank-bond to the debtor therein, cannot be excluded from alleging compensation, there being no personal objection against them. And likewise, conveyances without a cause onerous, in prejudice of anterior creditors, by persons insolvent and ["and" should read "are"] fraudulent; so that, if either the first receiver of such blank securities, or the posterior receiver thereof be insolvent, and without an equivalent cause onerous, do transmit such blank securities, only by delivering the same, the intermediate havers can hardly ever be known, whose creditors might affect the right while in their hands.

Upon which consideration, the first occasion that occurred to the Lords being a blank-bond, granted by Marjory Sandilands, and delivered to Samuel Veatch, he did deliver the same to Marion Geddes, who filled up her name in the blank left for the creditor, and registered the bond against Sandilands the debtor: yet Tailziefer, who was Veatch's creditor, having arrested all sums in Sandiland's hands, due to Veatch, in the competition betwixt Tailziefer, the arrester, and Geddes, whose name was filled up in the blank, and the bond registered in her name before the arrestment, the sum remaining yet unpaid in Sandilands' hands, the arrester was preferred, in respect that, albeit Geddes's name was filled up in the blank-bond, and it so registered before the arrestment, yet the delivery of the blank-bond by Veatch to Geddes, being in effect an assignation, was found to require intimation; and, therefore, Tailziefer, the arrester, was preferred. In this case Veatch, who was first creditor, was insolvent [*Telfer* v *Geddes*, 11 Nov. 1665, 1 Stair 306; M. 1662]. And albeit the Lords in the competition betwixt David Henrison and Thomas George, decided January 18, 1668, preferred Henrison, whose name was in the bond as creditor, and who offered his oath for clearing, whether the bond was blank, *ab initio*, and when filled up, yet the Lords did not leave it to his oath, but took witnesses, *ex officio*, who proved that they saw the bond filled up with Henrison's name, before the arrestment laid on by Thomas George in the hands of the debtor, as due to Short, his creditor, before the arrestment; yet there was nothing adduced to prove that ever the bond had been blank or delivered to Short [*Sub nom. Brown* v *Henderson and George*, 1 Stair 509; M. 1665]. And likewise, a bond blank in the creditor's name, being delivered by the receiver of the bond to a creditor of his, in satisfaction of his debt, the same was found relevant to be proven that the blank-bond was delivered before the declarator of escheat of the party, to whom it was first delivered in satisfaction of a debt due by him before he was denounced, December 19, 1676, and January 17, 1677, L. Bamff *contra* Grant of Rosasolis [*Sub nom. Grant* v *Lord Banff*, 1 Stair 481, 495; M. 1654].

There hath been nothing done since to take off the necessity of a formal intimation to the debtor, of the filling up of the creditor's name, upon production of the bond itself, showing that name to be filled up; and, therefore, any arrestment upon the debt of the person to whom the bond was first delivered as creditor, or to his own behoof, or for the debt of any other person, in whose possession it came for his own behoof, before the said intimation, will prefer the arrester. As to the matter of probation, that the bond was blank *ab initio* in the creditor's name, it is a strong evidence that it is written with a hand different from the body of the bond; for though blank draughts of bonds be frequently drawn up by writers and notars, leaving the sums, the names of the debtor and creditor blank, which are filled up by any that makes use of the draught, yet at the subscription, the filler up of the sum, the debtor and creditor's name should be exprest; for these are more substantial than all the rest of the bond, so that if the creditor's name be not filled up with the hand that wrote the bond, or of him who insert the date and witnesses, it will be presumed to have been blank [IV, 42, 19 *infra*], in which case, the debtor's oath may be taken, to whom he did deliver it for his own use, and that person's oath to whom he did deliver the same, whereby the progress of it, till it come to him whose name was insert, will be found out; and upon this ground a disposition of lands bearing to be, "to two persons for themselves and other creditors of the disponers after-specified," after which, there were several lines written with another hand, inserting particular creditors and sums, without mentioning of the filling up thereof at the date of the writ; therefore an inhibition by a creditor of the disponers, was sustained to reduce the right of these creditors filled up in the blank, as presumed to be filled up after the inhibition, although the date of the disposition was before the inhibition; unless it were proven by witnesses insert in the disposition or others above exception, that the blank was so filled up before the inhibition, January 15, 1670, La. Lu. Hamilton *contra* Creditors of Monkcastle [1 Stair 660; M. 11550]. This ground is much cleared by Act 5, Parl. 1681 [Subscription of Deeds Act, 1681, c. 5; A.P.S. VIII, 242, c. 5], requiring the name of the filler up to be exprest, which, if wanting, will annul the writ.

These blank-bonds are so little favoured, that when the debtor depones that he is only debtor by a bond blank in the creditor's name, which he did deliver to such a party for his own use, but knows not now who hath the bond, and consequently to whom he is debtor, it will not liberate him from the debt of that party to whom he did deliver it; though it may make him liable to double payment to that party, and to him who hath the bond, it being his own deed in delivering the bond blank in the creditor's name, which infers that hazard: yea, if the debtor should depone that the bond was blank, *ab initio*, and delivered to such a party, but afterwards it was shown to the debtor, filled up in the name of such another party, before the arrestment, whereby he became debtor to that party, and not to the first; it is not like that quality will be respected, unless he depone that he had paid before the arrestment; for in Veatch's case [*Telfer* v *Geddes*, 11 Nov. 1665, 1 Stair 306; M. 1662], the filling up of Geddes's name was unquestionably offered to be proven, that the bond was registrated in Geddes's name before the arrestment, which is a much stronger probation than the oath of the debtor. And, therefore, in such cases, the debtor should get an instrument of intimation of the name filled up, or else suspend on double poinding. A blank-bond being lost, and referred to the debtor's oath, who confessed the same, and both parties agreeing upon the date, sum and witnesses, the debtor was decerned to pay the sum to the pursuer, to whom he had delivered the blank-bond upon caution to refund, in case he were distressed upon a bond, containing the same sum, date, and witnesses, June 27, 1676, Gibson *contra* Fife [2 Stair 434: M. 9980]. The like was done at the instance of the executors of the person to whom the blank-bond was delivered, January 4, 1678, Peebles *contra* Tennents of Rossie [2 Stair 588; M. 1668].

6. The assignation itself is not a complete valid right, till it be orderly intimated to the debtor, which, though at first, (it is like) hath been only used to put the debtor *in mala fide*, to pay to the cedent, or any other assignee; yet now it is a solemnity requisite to assignations, so that though the debt remain due, if there be diverse assignations, the first intimation is preferable, though of the last assignation, and that not as a legal diligence, which can be prevented and excluded by another diligence, but as a full accomplishment of the assignation, January 13, 1629, Finlayson *contra* Kinloch [Durie 413; M. 2923]; January 18, 1628, L. Halkertoun *contra* Falconer [Durie 329; M. 765]. But where both assignations were gratuitous, implying warrandice from fact and deed, the last assignation, though first intimated, was not preferred, because the cedent was debtor to the first assignee by the implied warrandice against future facts and deeds, July 15, 1675, Alexander *contra* Lundies [2 Stair 347; M. 940]. This behoved to be, because the last assignation was reducible, being gratuitous, on the implied warrandice of the first assignation.

7. Intimation may be by any legal diligence, as by arrestment, by a charge or process upon the assignation: yea, though the process be not sustained, because all parties having interest were not called, it will stand as an intimation; but it is most ordinarily by way of instrument, either by the assignee himself showing the assignation, or by his procurator, showing the same with his procuratory, wherein the like solemnities will be requisite, as are in instruments of premonition and requisition: of which, Title, Wadsets [11, 10, 17 and 22, *supra*]. So an intimation was found null by exception, because one person was both procurator and notar, July 3, 1628, Scot *contra* Lo. Drumlangrig [Durie 381; M. 846]. Neither was an intimation found sufficient by an inhibition, used by the assignee against the cedent upon the assignation, March 14, 1626, Nisbet *contra* Williamson [*Sub nom. Westraw* v *Williamson and Carmichael*, Durie 192; M. 859], where payment made thereafter to the cedent, was found valid. In this case it was also found, that intimation will not be supplied by a party's knowledge of the assignation. The like, June 15, 1624, Adamson *contra* McMitchel [Durie 128; M. 859]. Neither by the debtor's knowledge, though by a pursuit against him upon the writ, containing the assignation, but in relation to another matter therein; which was in shunning the committing a clause irritant Nov. 30. 1622,

Durhame and La. Wintoun *contra*   [*Sub nom. Murray* v *Durham and*
La. *Wintoun*, Durie 36; M. 855].

8. But assignations to annual prestations, as to mails and duties, teinds, or annualrents or assignations to rights, requiring possession to complete them, as tacks, are perfected by use of payment or possession, and need no other intimation; as was found in the case of the annualrent of an heritable bond, where getting payment of some years, preferred the assignee to a former arrester, though there was no instrument of intimation, January 18, 1628, L. Halkertoun *contra* Falconer [Durie 329; M. 765].

9. And any writ under the debtor's hand, acknowledging the production of the assignation, will be sufficient intimation, as if he gave a bond of corroboration to the assignee, or gave discharges of the annualrent, or any part of the principal sum [III, 1, 45, *infra*].

10. Where there are many *correi debendi*, principal or cautioners, intimation made to any will be sufficient as to all; yet this will not exclude payment made by another of the debtors, *bona fide*, to whom no intimation was made; to secure which it is safest for assignees to intimate to all the *correi debendi*.

11. Assignations to reversions or bonds for granting reversions, renunciations of wadsets, or grants of redemption, being registrate in the Register of Reversions, conform to Act of Parl. 1617 [Registration Act, 1617, c.16; A.P.S. IV, 545, c. 16], require no intimation, that register being designed, not so much for conservation of these rights, where the principals are not detained, but for publication thereof to all parties having interest, which is a sufficient intimation; as was found in the case of an assignation to the legal reversion of an apprising, December 5, 1665, Beg *contra* Beg [1 Stair 321; M. 6304].

12. Intimation being by our proper custom so necessary a solemnity, it holds not in the orders which stand for assignations amongst merchants, who act as oft with strangers especially, *qui utuntur communi jure gentium;* and therefore the first order by merchants, direct to their debtor here, to pay the debt to the obtainer of the order, was preferred to arresters and assignees, using diligence before them, though there was neither intimation of the order, nor acceptance by the debtor [1, 11, 7, *supra*].

13. Neither is intimation necessary to judicial assignations by apprisings or adjudications, March 25, 1635, Lo. Yester *contra* L. Innerweek, Hope, Assignations [Durie 764; M. 208]; *idem*, Apprisings, Bruce *contra* Buckie [Hope, *Maj. Pr.* 11, 12, 36; III, 10, 50; M. 207, 10415, 13444]: so that if the debt remain due, the first apprising or adjudication, without intimation, will be preferred; but seeing there is nothing to put the debtor in *mala fide*, payment made *bona fide*, will liberate the debtor; but will give repetition against the obtainer of payment, nor will his *bona fides* secure him, because it is no necessary act, as the debtor's is [1, 18, 3, *supra*; III, 1, 40, *infra*].

14. Marriage also is a legal assignation, requiring no intimation; for

thereby all the moveable rights of the wife are stated in the husband, *jure mariti*, without other intimation than the marriage [1,4,9,*supra*]: yea, intimation was not found necessary to a reposition of the assignee to the cedent, seeing the assignation was by a wife in her contract of marriage, which requires no intimation but the marriage; and therefore the husband's reposition to her needed no intimation, December 2, 1674, Craig *contra* L. Wedderly [2 Stair 287; M. 838].

15. Though in the cases aforesaid, intimation be a necessary solemnity to assignations, yet the assignation alone will be sufficient against the cedent, if he should quarrel it, because he is author thereof, and can do no deed contrary thereto: yea, it was preferred to an executor-creditor of the cedent's, even as to his own debt, July 27, 1669, Executors of Ridpeth *contra* Home [1 Stair 647; M. 2792].

16. As to the extent and effect of assignations, first, the same extends to all personal rights, whether moveable or heritable, as to bonds, liferents, tacks, reversions, mails and duties, annualrents, and to dispositions of lands and others, till infeftment follow; but it is no valid conveyance of any right completed by infeftment, except liferents, (which can have no subaltern infeftment) as to the ground right itself, though it may, as to the profits thereof, as to mails and duties of property, and to those no longer than the right by infeftment stands in the cedent's person; whence there ariseth to him and to his assignee, a personal obligement upon the possessors, which faileth as to all terms after the proprietor, Dec. 17, 1622, L. Kinbrauchmount *contra* Anstruther [Not found]; and an assignation to such a sum yearly out of teinds, was found excluded by an apprising of, or assignation to, the tack of these teinds, February 6, 1666, Watson *contra* Fleming [1 Stair 348; M. 2817]. But liferenters can be no other way denuded but by assignation, voluntary or legal, and so can never be excluded by any other, being possessor.

Assignations are effectual, not only of such rights as are granted to heirs and assignees, but generally to all rights, though not mentioning assignees, which by their nature are transmissible; and therefore, an annualrent by a father to his daughter, wherein his brother and sisters were substitute, failing the heirs of her body, without mentioning her assignees, and wherein the annualrent was redeemable, by a payment of a principal sum, which she had no power to require, unless she were married; the annualrent was found to belong to her assignee after her death, being principally constitute, and not accessory to the principal sum, June 24, 1679, Stuart *contra* Stuart [1 Stair 624; M. 30, 4337]: And albeit superiors be not obliged to receive singular successors without apprising or adjudication; yet before infeftment, assignees to the disposition, granted by the superior, may compel him to receive the assignee, which was so found, though the superior alleged that the assignee was not in good terms with him, December 24, 1673, Ogilvie *contra* Kinloch [2 Stair 246; M. 10384; 11,4,32,*supra*]. But reversions and tacks are in most cases unassignable, unless they be granted to assignees [11,9,26; 11,10,7, *supra*]; for albeit the assignation being a procuratory, may give them an interest to act *procuratorio nomine*, for the cedent; yet they cannot act *proprio nomine*, as procurators, *in rem suam;* therefore the oath of the cedent will always be competent against them, and they cannot obtain declarator of redemption, in their own name, or decreet for denuding of the wadsetter, in their favour: neither can assignees to tacks enter in possession, by virtue thereof: yea, liferent-rights by infeftment or tack, are so peculiar to the liferenter, that no assignation can state them in the assignee's person, but only the profits thence arising [11,6,7,*supra*]: so that in the assignee's person they are not liferents; and therefore the liferents of wives, which belonged to their husbands, *jure mariti*, as a legal assignation, fall not under the husband's liferent-escheat, nor longer than during the marriage; as they would fall under the liferent of the wife unmarried, but under the husband's single escheat only, *Vide Title Confiscation*, §*Escheat* [111,3,15,*infra*]. Upon which ground, Hope, upon Assignation, observes, that assignations to liferent-tacks, make them fall under the assignee's single escheat, in the case of Ker *contra* Ker [Hope, *Maj. Pr.* VI,27,111 and 120; M. 5071].

17. Thirdly, An assignation to a sum carries with it the inhibition raised thereupon, Hope, Assignation, Hay *contra* Ker [Hope, *Maj. Pr.* 11,12,34; M. 828,6302]. The like, where only "all actions following thereupon" were expressed generally, Had. June 28, 1610, Blair *contra* Gray [*Fol. Dict.* 1,422; M. 6301]. And an assignation to a bond was found to carry a bond of corroboration of the foresaid bond, though not mentioned therein, albeit the assignation bore not that ordinary clause, "with all that has followed, or may follow thereupon," which is but an explicatory clause of style of that which *inest de jure*, February 3, 1676, Cullie *contra* E. Airly [2 Stair 409].

18. Fourthly, The effect of assignations is, that the oath of the cedent cannot prove against the assignee, unless the matter had been litigious before the assignation or intimation, as in the case that arrestment had been laid on; and therefore a debtor having pursued the cedent to annul a bond, upon a reason to be verified by the cedent's oath, before the assignee had intimated, the cedent's oath was sustained, February 15, 1662, L. Pitfoddels *contra* L. Glenkindie[1 Stair 101; M.12454]. And an assignee pursuing in the cedent's name, and not in his own, albeit he produced his assignation in the process; yet there being no other intimation thereof, the cedent's oath was admitted against him, February 12, 1678, Frazer *contra* Frazer [2 Stair 612; M.844], July 26, 1628, Rule *contra* Aitoun [Durie 394; M.8349]. Or if the assignation be gratuitous without a cause onerous, the cedent's oath will be competent in all cases against the assignee, June 16, 1665, Wright *contra* Sheil [1 Stair 282; M.12455]; June 13, 1666, Jack *contra* Mowat[1 Stair 376; M.12456]. But the oath of the cedent will prove against the assignee in England, as to assignations made by residenters there, June 28, 1666, McMorland *contra* Melvil [1 Stair 382; M.4447], and uses so to be sustained against Englishmen, because the law there is such.

19. Fifthly, Assignations being intimated during the cedent's life, having summary execution, the assignee got protestation against a suspension raised against the cedent, after the cedent's death, without wakening or transference, and thereupon all execution did proceed summarily by horning, poinding, apprising, even after his death, Hope, Assignation, Stevenson *contra* L. Craigmillar [Hope, *Maj.Pr.* VI,2,6; M.837]: otherwise it would yield but an ordinary action, January 23, 1624, *inter eosdem* [Durie 100; M.836]. The same was found, and that there needed no confirmation, July 27, 1664, Muirhead *contra*   [1 Stair 223; M.14383]. Yea, though it was an assignation by a father to his son, of all his goods and debts; yet action was sustained thereupon without confirmation, June 25, 1663, Halyburton *contra* E. Roxburgh [1 Stair 195; M.16090]. But where there was no delivery, the assignation of all the goods was not found to give action without confirmation, June 23, 1665, Procurator fiscal of Edinburgh *contra* Fairholm [1 Stair 286; M.14386]. Or where there was a reservation to the disponer, to dispone otherwise during his life, July 4, 1665, Commissar of St. Andrews *contra* Hay [*Sub. nom Commissar of St Andrews* v *Balhousie*, 1 Stair 295; M.14387]. But since the restitution of Bishops, and reviving of the quots, actions are sustained upon assignations, not intimated in the cedent's life, if they be special, the pursuer always confirming before the decreet be extracted.

20. Except in the matter of probation, all exceptions competent against the cedent before the assignation or intimation, are relevant against the assignee, as payment, compensation, &c. which was found, even as to assignees to tacks, that the tacksman's back-bond was sufficient against his singular successor by assignation, Dec. 18, 1668, Swintoun *contra* Brown [1 Stair 574; M.3412,8408; 1,18,6, *supra*].

21. Assignations to incomplete real rights, as apprisings, dispositions of lands before infeftment, are affected with the assignee's back-bond, if the competition come in before infeftment, inhibition be used, or legal diligence that makes the matter litigious; and, therefore, the back-bond of an assignee to an apprising, was found effectual against his successors by translation, July 6, 1676, Gordon *contra* Skeen and Crafurd [2 Stair 440; M.7169]. But the back-bond of an assignee to a disposition of lands, not drawn in question till the assignee's singular successor was infeft upon his translation was not found effectual against the singular successor, June 20, 1676, Brown *contra* Smith [2 Stair 428; M.2844], for if assignations, back-bonds, or even discharges or renunciations of redeemable dispositions of lands, were effectual against singular successors in these lands, after the rights were perfected in their own persons, or their authors by infeftment, it might in a great part disappoint the design of these excellent statutes for registration of land-rights; therefore, unless inhibition were used, or the matter made litigious upon these personal rights before infeftment, they are not habile to affect a real right, or a singular successor therein; but because apprisings within the legal, may be taken away in the same manner as personal rights; therefore assignations,

discharges and back-bonds, by these who have right to the apprising, being made within the legal, are effectual, if thereupon the matter be made litigious before the expiring of the legal reversion, or inhibition used thereupon, they will be effectual against the singular successors, even after the legal is expired [11,3,22; 11,5,15,*supra*; 111,2,39,*infra*]; but after expiring of the legal, infeftments upon apprisings are in the same case as infeftments upon irredeemable dispositions; for they are the foundation of the rights of most lands in the kingdom, and if personal rights should make them insecure after the expiring of the legal, it would be of great inconvenience.

22. Assignees by tutors to their pupils' bonds, will have no execution till the tutors' counts be made by the cedent, December, 2, 1679, Cleiland *contra* Bailzie [2 Stair 713; M. 9983].

23. It is more dubious, and hath been diversly decided when the exceptions are personal against the cedent, as in mutual contracts, the contractor himself can have no action unless he fulfil his part; but whether his assignee will be in the like case is the question; which is at large cleared, Tit. 10, sect. 16 [1,10,16,*supra*], and therefore shall not be here repeated.

24. Judicial assignations are of two sorts, according to the matter conveyed thereby, which, if it be moveable, is conveyed from the debtor to his creditor by arrestment and decreet for making the arrested sums and goods forthcoming, and if it be heritable, by apprising or adjudication. As to the *first*, That the progress upon arrestment may be clearly taken up; we shall first consider the arrestment itself. *Secondly*, The loosing of it. *Thirdly*, The action for making forthcoming. Arrestment is a precept or command of a judge, ordaining the thing arrested to remain in the same case it is when arrested, till such things be done as are prescribed in the letters of arrestment: it is sometimes extended to any preparatory precept to judge, antecedent unto any further process; so the first citation, or securing of persons till trial were made, or surety found, is called an arrestment or attachment, as appears in the form of the crowner's arrestments of delinquents, Parl. 1487, cap. 99 [A.P.S. 11,176,c.4]; Parl. 1528, cap. 5 [A.P.S. 11,331,c.1]. But arrestment proceeds most ordinarily upon an interlocutory sentence, as when parties are contending for peats, turfs, or corn, upon debateable land; these use to be arrested till the matter be decided, whereby the thing arrested becomes litigious, and any thing done to the contrary hath the effect of breach of arrestment, and is of the nature of *innovata lite dependente*, which therefore must be summarily restored and put *in statu quo*, and brings no advantage but loss to the actor.

But arrestment which we are now about, is a precept by letters of arrestment, arresting debts or goods in the hands of any party haver thereof, at the instance of the creditor of him to whom the debts or goods belong, to remain under arrestment, until the debt whereupon the arrestment proceeds, be secured or satisfied; therefore arrestments may be granted by all judges ordinary, superior or inferior; but the arrestment of an inferior judge was only found effectual in process before himself, and before no other inferior judge, March 8, 1634, Smith *contra* Miller [Durie 710; M. 7484]. But upon occasion of this debate, most of the Lords thought an inferior judge might proceed upon the Lords' arrestment, passing in the king's name; and there is not wanting ground to think that an inferior judge may proceed upon the arrestment of another, seeing all of them proceed alone upon the King's authority; as if the defender change his domicile, an arrestment made by the inferior judge, where he dwelt before, ought not to be ineffectual, nor he necessitate to pursue before the Lords; for the Lords sustain process on arrestments by inferior courts, as was found in an arrestment before the Admiral, March 22, 1637, Finnie *contra* Gray [Durie 842; M. 3783]. Yet an arrestment upon the precept of an inferior judge was found null, because executed without the jurisdiction of that judge, although the party in whose hands it was made dwelt within the jurisdiction, Dec. 5, 1671, Miller *contra* Orsburn, Crafurd and L. Bishoptoun [2 Stair 18; M. 7293]. The reason hereof was, no execution is valid *extra territorium judicis*, which doth not conclude against the arrestment of an inferior judge, made within his own jurisdiction; but that it would be sustained against that party in any process before the Lords, or any superior having cumulative jurisdiction, or even before a co-ordinate or inferior jurisdiction, in which, if any question were made, the Lords, by letters of supplement, would readily authorise the same. Arrestment requires no other solemnity but the execution thereof, by him to whom the letters are directed, which requires the like requisites as other executions do; of which hereafter.

25. There hath been an extraordinary form of arrestment, sometime used and sustained, whereby creditors did arrest the goods of their debtors in the debtors' own hand, and thereupon did pursue such as bought from them, whereof there is an instance observed by Dury, January 10, 1624, betwixt the L. Innerweek, John Wilkie, and the La. Bothwel [Durie 96; M. 733]; wherein Innerweek having arrested a parcel of wool in the La. Bothwel's hand, upon a debt owing by her to him, and she having thereafter sold the wool to Wilkie, who paid the price, he was decerned to make forthcoming the true worth of the wool to Innerweek, although nothing appears instructed, that there was any collusion betwixt the La. Bothwel and Wilkie, but what may be conjectured from the Lords allowing the price of the wool. This kind of arrestment hath not been drawn in example, for I have found no instance of it observed by any since that time; and as the instance observed, is but the arrestment of one particular; if it were to be allowed, it might be extended to more particulars, even to all the moveable goods and means of the debtor, and certainly it would be ordinarily so used, as straitening the debtor more, that he could dispose of nothing, but to the use of the arresting creditor; and so it would become an inhibition in moveables, yet much more inconvenient, because inhibition must be published at the market-cross, and registrate; whereas arrestment may be done most privately before two witnesses: and though inhibi-

tions at first were designed to disable debtors, not only to dispone or dilapidate their lands or heritage, but their moveable goods, as the style of inhibition doth still express; yet experience did early show that there was a necessity for current course of moveables, and that it could not consist with traffic and commerce, that no man could securely buy moveables without inspection of registers; and, therefore, inhibitions have now no effect as to moveables; much less should arrestment of the debtor's moveables in his own hand, which could with no reason affect the moveables, when disponed for a just cause to third parties, much less could it infer breach of arrestment against the buyers after arrestment; and all the effect it could have, were only to superadd upon the debtor the penalty of breach of arrestment, thereby to confiscate all his moveables; whereas there are ordinarily liquidate penalties agreed upon, of consent of debtor and creditor. Such an arrestment might be sustained for the rents due to masters of the ground upon their hypothecation, or for *invecta et illata* for housemails; for the buyer might call for the master's discharge, and if he prejudged the hypothec, it were on his own peril; or, in the case of competition, the subject thereof might be arrested in the haver's hand, but only to make him liable not to sell or put it away, but not to make the buyer liable.

26. Arrestment being a personal prohibition, used against him in whose hands the arrestment was made, if he die, it is not extended to his successors, but they may dispose of the goods or sums arrested, unless it be renewed in their hands, in the same manner as an inhibition, which is also a legal prohibition, extending to heritable rights, as arrestment doth to moveables; but though the debtor, whose goods or sums were arrested, die, the arrestment ceaseth not; but the debt being established against his successors, process may proceed upon the arrestment, February 19, 1667, Glen *contra* Hume [1 Stair 443; M. 3645]; January 22, 1681, Riddel *contra* Maxwell [2 Stair 839; M. 783].

27. As to the effect and extent of arrestments, they can only be laid on, and affect moveable goods or moveable debts, and can only be made use of for satisfying of moveable debts (what rights are moveable, and what heritable, hath been shown in the title, Real Rights [11, 1, *supra*]) wherein by heritable, not only these are understood, which are properly so by infeftment, but also such sums and deeds, as are by destination such, as bearing obligement for infeftment or annualrent, even though the bond did bear no clause of requisition, yet, if it did bear annualrent, arrestment or apprising, had been found null thereupon, unless it had been made moveable by a charge, because the bond bore the sum payable at any time, upon a single charge of six days, July 20, 1622, Cranstoun *contra* L. Eastnisbit [Durie 31; M. 64, 8113]. The like, Hope, Obligations, Morison *contra* Creditors of Richardson [*Sub nom. Mowat* v *Richardson's Crs.*, Hope, *Maj. Pr.* VI, 37, 22; M. 695, 8113]; Cranstoun *contra* L. Lugtoun [Hope, *Maj. Pr.* VI, 28, 59; M. 8113]. Yet the contrary hath also been found in bonds, bearing annualrent, without a clause of requisition, that poinding, arrestment and apprising

might proceed without a charge, seeing it bore not to be paid with a charge, July 10, 1629, L. Clackmannan *contra* L. Barounie [Durie 460; M. 69, 8116]; January 25, 1642, Johnstoun *contra* Loch [Durie 888; M.8117; III,2,15, *infra*]. But the matter is now cleared by the act of Parl. 1644, cap. 41 [A.P.S. VI(1), 157, c. 85], renewed Parl. 1661, cap. 51 [Arrestments Act, 1661, c. 51; A.P.S. VII, 262, c. 283], declaring that all bonds and sums, though bearing annualrent, are arrestable at the instance of any creditor of that person, if infeftment hath not past actually thereupon; yet a sum whereupon apprising had followed, was found not to be arrestable by the appriser's creditor; and therefore an appriser, from that prior appriser, though posterior to the arrester, was preferred, February 22, 1666, Lockhart *contra* Lo. Bargenie [1 Stair 363; M. 701]. And though they do not so clearly determine upon what bonds arrestment may proceed, as against what bonds or sums it may proceed; yet it bears equally for satisfying of any debt, which, though it cannot be extended to an heritable debt, upon which actual infeftment is, till they be made moveable, yet ought to be extended to all other debts, upon which infeftment hath not followed, that *à pari*, as such debts are arrestable without a charge, so they may be arrested for satisfying the like debt, without a charge upon the debt to be satisfied, more than upon the debt arrested for satisfying thereof [III,1,37, *infra*].

28. Though no heritable right, upon which infeftment hath past, can be arrested till it be made moveable; yet the rents and profits thereof are arrestable and moveable, December 15, 1630, Ogilvie *contra* Lo. Ogilvie [Durie 548; M. 138]; and so are the bygones of an annualrent constitute by infeftment [II,1,4, *supra*], for these bygones are as to all effects moveable, though the right itself is heritable, as fruits falling from a tree are moveable, though the tree be not; yet they give a real action, by poinding of the ground, as well as personal against intromitters with the rents.

29. Yea, arrestment of annualrents, or mails and duties, is effectual, though laid on before the term, if the debtor to whom they belong were not denuded thereof before the term, the term being current when it was laid on, March 23, 1624, Brown *contra* Haliburton [Durie 122; M.765]; but it will not extend beyond the subsequent term, where the rent is paid termly, as in silver-rents, Hope, Arrestments, Mowat *contra* Dick [Hope, *Maj. Pr.* VI, 37, 32; M.765]: Otherwise it will extend to the whole year in which it was laid on, as in farms, which are paid together, Hope, Arrestments, Thomson *contra* Wishart [Hope, *Maj. Pr.* VI, 37, 21]. Yea, an arrestment of rent laid on before the term, was preferred to a posterior apprising, not having infeftment before that term, July 2, 1667, Litster *contra* Aiton and Slich [1 Stair 467; M.2765]. And an arrestment laid on *currente termino*, was preferred to a posterior assignation to that term, July 27, 1673, Creditors of Scot competing [2 Stair 223; M.702]. Arrestment is also valid, being laid on upon sums before the term of payment, February 21, 1624, Brown *contra* L. Johnstoun [Durie 112; M. 8127]; *eodem die*, Rentoun *contra* Acheson [Durie 113n; M.8127]. But in all

these, the execution was superseded till the terms of payment of the arrested sums were past, July 3, 1628, Scot *contra* L. Drumlanrig [Durie 381; M. 846]. Yet arrestments ought not to be laid on for satisfying of debts, whereof the term of payment is not come; therefore such an arrestment was excluded by an arrestment posterior, which was laid on for satisfying a sum, whereof the term of payment was come, when it was laid on, July 17, 1678, Lo. Pitmedden *contra* Patersons [2 Stair 636; M.813; III,1,34,*infra*]. The like, Steils *contra* Charters [Probably *Charters* v *Neilson*, 1 Stair 701; M.811]. Yea, it was extended to affect the price of lands, though laid on before writ, but after agreement, Hope, Arrestment, Lo. Dalhousie *contra*   [Possibly *Creich* v *L.Dalhousie*, Hope, *Maj.Pr.* VI,37,25].

30. Neither was arrestment effectual, being only laid on in the hands of the debtor's factor, and not in their own hands, for making the same forthcoming for payment of his debt to whom it was due; because factors are not debtors, but their constituents, Hope, Arrestment, Muirhead and M' Michael *contra* Wallace [*Sub nom. Muirhead and McMichael* v *Millar*, Hope, *Maj.Pr.* VI,37,17; M.732,2599].

31. Arrestments have never been extended to future debts or goods; for arrestments, both by their name and nature, do only stop the debtor's goods or debts arrested, to remain in the same condition they were in when arrested, till caution be found, or sentence be obtained for making forthcoming. But inhibitions do prohibit the party inhibited, and whole lieges to buy from the person inhibited till the debt be satisfied, which is absolute, and extends against all buying or blocking with the inhibited, whether *pro acquisitis*, or *acquirendis*.

32. Arrestment orderly laid on, renders the thing litigious, so that an assignation made thereto, though to a creditor thereafter, hinders not the arrester to prove the debt by the cedent's oath, December 10, 1623, Douglas *contra* Belshes [Durie 90; M.8347].

33. As to the second point proposed, concerning the loosing of arrestments, it hath been said before, that the intent of arrestment is the satisfaction of the arrester's debts, by the action for making forthcoming, which is a judicial assignation to him, of that which is arrested; or otherways by security, when he whose goods or sums are arrested, findeth caution, and thereby looseth the arrestment, which is done by supplication to the Lords, and their deliverance, which of old gave warrant to the messenger to receive caution, and loose the arrestment; but is well amended by the Act of Parl. 1617, cap. 17 [Arrestments Act, 1617,c.17; A.P.S. IV,546,c.17], annulling that way of loosing arrestments, and ordaining caution to be found in the Books of Session, before giving out of the letters, which are not effectual, when the arrestment proceeds upon a decreet; and, therefore, the letters express the arrestment to be loosed, unless it proceed upon a decreet. The same is to be extended to loosing of arrestments of inferior judges, by caution found in their books.

34. Arrestment is sometimes granted upon production of principal writs, but if the arrestment proceed upon production of the principal bond unregistrated, there being then no decreet of registration, it may be loosed, February 7, 1665, Graham *contra* Bruce and Doctor Martine [1 Stair 265; M. 792]. Or if the decreet be turned into a libel, June 30, 1675, Murray *contra* Hall [2 Stair 338, M. 794]. Or if the arrestment was laid on after the decreet was suspended: or if the term of payment of the sum for which it was laid on, was to come, November, 4, 1675, Mosman, Supplicant [2 Stair 363; M. 794]: or upon consignation of the sum arrested for, June 18, 1675, Hamilton, Supplicant [2 Stair 333; M. 793]. But when the arrestment was upon a dependence, though the decreet proceeded upon the dependence before the loosing of the arrestment; yet it was found, the arrestment might be loosed upon caution, June 9, 1674, Sibbald of Rankilor *contra* Sibbald his Son [*Sub die* June 9, 1677, 2 Stair 521; M. 796]. But in loosing arrestments, no juratory caution was admitted, July 16, 1661, College of St. Andrews, Supplicant [1 Stair 52; M. 791].

35. Arrestment being loosed, the party in whose hands it was made, may safely pay the sum, or deliver the goods arrested to the looser of the arrestment, June 21, 1626, Lo. Balmerino *contra* L. Lochinvar [Durie 204; M. 788]; Hope, Arrestment, Gordon *contra* Brown [*Sub nom. Gordon* v *Brody*, Hope, *Maj. Pr.* VI, 37, 28; M. 788]. But if the sum remain unpaid, the arrester may proceed against the person in whose hands he arrested, February 7, 1665, Graham *contra* Bruce [1 Stair 265; M. 792]. In this case the debtor who loosed the arrestment, had granted assignation to the debt arrested; yet the arrester was preferred to the assignee, in respect the caution is insufficient ordinarily, which comes in the place of arrestments.

36. Upon arrestment there ariseth two actions to the arrester, the one is against the cautioner, found in loosing the arrestment, the other against the person in whose hands the arrestment was made. This action for making sums or goods arrested forthcoming, is ordinary; and for understanding the requisites of it, it would be adverted, that arrestment may be raised upon production of the principal bond, without decreet or dependence, March 5, 1628, Binnie *contra* Ross [Durie 354; M. 675]; Feb. 7, 1665, Graham *contra* Bruce [1 Stair 265; M. 792]; Hope, Arrestment, Thomson *contra* M'Moran [*Sub nom. Thomson and McMurran* v *Philp*, Hope, *Maj. Pr.* VI, 37, 26; M. 675]. Secondly, It may be raised upon an action depending. Thirdly, Upon a decreet obtained against the debtor, whose sums are arrested: but there is no process for making forthcoming, till the debt be liquidated and established by a decreet at the arrester's instance, against him whose goods or sums are arrested, or against some representing him, which was so done, though the principal parties' advocate compeared and consented, March 13, 1628, Somervel *contra* Heriot [Durie 360; M. 781]; Hope, Transferring, L. Lamingtoun *contra* Durham [*Sub nom. L. Langton* v *Duirhame*, Hope, *Maj. Pr.* VI, 8, 18; M. 779]. And if that party die before the decreet for making forth-

coming, the decreet must be transferred against these representing him: but if none will enter to be heir, or executor to him, but renounce; yet the party that might succeed, must be called *cognitionis causa*; Spots., *de hæreditariis actionibus*, Murray *contra* Dalgleish [Not found]; and therefore, when the arrestment is upon a principal bond, or upon a dependence, the bond must be registrated, or decreet obtained thereupon, or upon the dependence, before the party in whose hands the arrestment was made, be obliged to answer. The party whose sums and goods are arrested, must not only be called *in initio litis*, but to all the diets of the process, March 17, 1637, Stuart *contra* Inglis [Durie 839; M. 2235]. In this process the arrestment was not found instructed by extracting the horning, containing arrestment and the executions, but that the principals of both must be produced, Spots. Arrestment, Boid *contra* Wilson [Spotiswoode 18; M. 676,12457]. For the act of Parliament for registration of hornings, &c. makes extracts probative, but that will not extend to the execution of the arrestment, though by the same letters, for that execution needs not be registrated.

37. As to the exceptions competent in this action; first, It is not competent to the party in whose hands the arrestment was made, to allege payment made by the party whose goods or sums are arrested, that being *jus tertii*, competent only to that party himself, who must be called, Dec. 21, 1621, Hamilton *contra* Durham [Durie 8; M. 7799]. Neither will it be relevant to either party to allege the debt, whereupon the arrestment is raised, is suspended; but the reason of suspension must be repeated by way of defence, Jan. 25, 1642, Stirling *contra* Aikenhead [Durie 888; M. 15140]. But it will be relevant to allege that the arrestment is null, as being executed upon the Sabbath day, Feb. 3, 1663, Oliphant *contra* Douglas [1 Stair 169; M. 15002]; or that the arrestment not being upon a decreet, was loosed, and that the sums are paid: it is also relevant, that the goods arrested were lawfully poinded by another creditor of the party to whom they belonged, because arrestment is but a begun incomplete diligence, and doth not transmit the right, till decreet be obtained thereupon: but others using more complete diligence, will carry the same, Had. June 5, 1611, Wright *contra* Thomson and Dick [*Fol. Dict.* 1,178; M. 2757], which was sustained, albeit the arrestment was laid on for excise, Dec. [4,] 1679, Forrester *contra* the Tacksmen of the Excise of Edinburgh [2 Stair 717; M. 2760]. Yea, though the party in whose hands arrestment was made, suffered the poinder to enter his cellars, and poind the goods arrested, March 11, 1635, Dick *contra* Spence and Thomson [Durie 760; M. 2758]. In this case the haver voluntarily opened his cellar by paction with the poinder, which was not respected, seeing he refused not entry to the arrester, if he had demanded it, Feb. 12, 1636, Lesly *contra* La. Ludquharn [*Sub nom.* Leslie v Nune, Durie 795; M. 2759]. But this exception was elided by this reply, that the party in whose hands the arrestment was made, colluded with the poinder, and voluntarily exhibited the goods arrested to be poinded, not being passive therein, but active to pre-

fer the poinder as was formerly relevant, Hope, Arrestment, Kinloch *contra* Halyburton [Hope, *Maj.Pr.* VI,37,24; M.2427]; White *contra* Blackater [Hope, *Maj.Pr.* VI,37,24]; Jan. 20, 1672, Bell *contra* Fleming and Watson [*Sub nom. Bell* v *Fleming and Williamson*, 2 Stair 52; M.12607]. It is also a relevant exception, that the ground of the arrestment, or the sum arrested was heritable [III,1,27,*supra*], before the Act of Parl. 1664 [Probably Act 1644; A.P.S. VI(1),248,c.272]; or since that infeftment hath passed upon either, unless it be made moveable; and therefore arrestment being laid on upon sums consigned, for a redemption, was not found effectual till declarator of redemption pass, which only makes the sums moveable; and, during the dependence of redemption, these sums cannot be arrested, as belonging to the user of the order; because they come in place of the lands redeemed, and can belong only to the wadsetter or appriser, or any having right from them to the lands wadset; but after redemption, the sum consigned may be arrested and made forthcoming for payment of the wadsetter's debt, Spots. Arrestment, Hepburn *contra* Hay [Spotiswoode, 16]. It is also a competent exception, that the thing arrested is a proper aliment, expressly constitute, and not exceeding the measure of aliment; Had. Nov. 29, 1622, Donaldson *contra* Kirkaldie and Barclay [Not found]. And the fee of a servant was not found arrestable, in so far as it was necessary for the service he was in, but only for the superplus, more than was necessary for his aliment in such a service, July 9, 1668, Beg *contra* Davidson, Preceptor of Heriot's Hospital [1 Stair 550; M.10380]. The like holds in the King's pensions and fees of his public ministers, Lords of Session, and others, which are not arrestable in the Treasurer's hands by Act of Sederunt, 1613 [A.S. 11 June, 1613; see Spotiswoode, 228; II,5,18,*supra*], and was so found in the case of Sir Robert Murray, Justice-Clerk [Not found], a part of whose salary was arrested.

38. When pursuits are for making arrested goods forthcoming, which are not liquid, the party in whose hands arrestment was made, will not be decerned for making forthcoming a liquid sum for the price: but if he offer the goods *ipsa corpora*, the decreet will contain a warrant to the magistrates of the place, to roup the goods arrested, that the price thereof may be delivered to the arrester, Nov. 12, 1680, Stevinson *contra* Paul [2 Stair 795; M.5405, 11348].

39. Apprising and adjudication of heritable sums, whereupon infeftment hath not followed, being little in use, though competent since the Act of Parliament 1644, which hath been continued by custom, though that Parliament be rescinded, we shall say no more of it in this place; but, as we have considered these several ways of transmission of personal rights severally, we shall now consider them jointly as they fall in competition, for preference amongst themselves, and each with others. In these competitions it must be considered that arrestment doth constitute no right in the arrester, but is only a legal prohibition to alter the condition of the thing arrested, nor to pay or deliver the same to the arrester's debtor; but that it may remain in his hand for satisfaction of the debt arrested for: and it is only general, arresting all

sums of money, or goods, in the hands of the party in whose hands it is laid on, due or belonging to the arrester's debtor, for satisfying of the debt, whereupon the arrestment proceeded; and therefore cannot be of more effect, than a denunciation of lands to be apprised, or a citation on a summons of adjudication; and therefore doth constitute or transfer no right, but is a legal diligence, rendering the subject matter arrested litigious, so that the party in whose hands the arrestment is made, cannot alter any sums or debts belonging to that debtor in prejudice of the debt arrested for, until the arrestment be loosed, and caution found for the debt or decreet absolvitor or declarator be obtained, excluding the arrestment: and if he do any thing on the contrary, it infers breach of arrestment, confiscating his moveables, and he is liable, as if the sums or goods remained in his hand, *pro possessore habetur qui dolo desiit possidere:* and though the arrestment have no intimation to the arrester's debtor, or any of his creditors; yet if any of them recover the sums or goods arrested, by the collusion or neglect of the party in whose hands arrestment is made, he will still remain liable; as if by collusion and gratification he or his procurator (whose deed will be presumed his) oppose the arrester, and procure delay, to compear and depone, and acknowledge the debt, or be holden as confest to another arrester; neither will he be liberated by offering his oath that he gave no such warrant; for the employing a procurator is a sufficient warrant for all the common course of process, and requires no special mandate; yea, if he pay or deliver to any other arrester, or even if by his collusion goods be poinded upon a decreet, he will not be liberated, seeing he ought to have raised a process of multiplepoinding, calling the debtor and all the arresters or assignees to dispute their several rights, that once payment to the party, found to have best right, might liberate him; yet if he have paid, he does thereby without a direct assignation, come in the place of the party to whom he hath paid; and if he can show that party's right is preferable to the arrester insisting, he will be heard thereupon.

40. And unless it be found that he proceeded warrantably, not only will he be decerned to make forthcoming, though it infer double payment; but he to whom he paid unwarrantably, will be compelled to restore and satisfy the arrester, the subject having been litigious by his arrestment, before the other party recovered the same, albeit he have recovered payment *bona fide*, without any fault in him, but by the litigiousness of the subject; for payment made *bona fide* with a preferable right, relieveth only the payer, who was or might have been compelled to pay, being conscious of no other right: for it is not relevant for the party obtaining payment *bona fide*, nor will that ground of law secure him, *qui suum recipit, licet a non debitore, non tenetur restituere*, which holds only in voluntary payments, *a non debitore*, and where the subject is not litigious [111,1,13,*supra*]. Upon the same ground, albeit the party in whose hands arrestment is made, collude not, but be equally passive, or equally oppose the competitors: yet if the debtor collude and propone defences against some of the competitors, and not equally against all, and there-

by procure delay, and terms to prove; if he succumb, though another pursuing in a several process, before the same or different judges, obtain decreet
and payment thereupon, yet he will be necessitated to refund, if he had not a
preferable right to whom he paid.

41. If the party in whose hands arrestment was made, appear and offer
to depone, if the pursuer suffer him to depone generally, that at the time of
the arrestment, he had neither goods nor sums belonging to the debtor in his
hands, the arrester will not *ex intervallo*, obtain him to be more particularly
interrogated, *ad vitandam perjuriam ;* but if before, or at his oath given in
general, there be special interrogatories offered by the party or the judge,
whether at any time there were in his hands sums or goods belonging to the
arrester's debtor, and how, and when he satisfied or delivered the same, he
will be holden as confessed, unless he depone particularly; that he be not his
own judge, as to the time when he was due, or when he ceased to be due; for
he may pretend or imagine, that, the time of the arrestment, he was not
debtor, because he had paid to an assignee, whose assignation was prior to
the arrestment, albeit intimation was not prior, though he had promised payment before intimation, yet he could not thereupon have been compelled to
pay, if before payment an arrestment had intervened; because his promise
could be but understood to be according to the party's right, to whom he
promised, which he could not quarrel; but if another did exclude that party,
he could not be liable to double payment, albeit he had given a bond of corroboration, unless the assignee had offered to intimate, and he had hindered
the same, as unnecessary, and promised payment; for then through his own
fraud or fault, he would be liable to pay both parties; and therefore, the
promise of payment was only found relevant to exclude an arrestment after
the promise, to be proven by the oath or writ of the arrester, and not of the
promiser, or party to whom he promised; yet if the promise were not so
proven, and thereby the arrester were preferred, the party promiser, in whose
hands the arrestment was made, was declared free of the promise, unless
there had been a transaction, or that the promiser had undertaken the
hazard; Elphingstoun *contra* Home and L. Stenhope, December 11, 1674
[2 Stair 292; M. 12462].

42. That which transferreth the right, is neither the arrestment, the citation, nor any thing in the process, but only the decreet for making forthcoming, which is in the same condition, as to subjects arrestable, as apprisings
or adjudications are to others, which do not import full satisfaction of the
debt, and do not fully liberate the debtor, but that other diligences may be
used for the same debt, unless he possess till the legal expire: and in the same
way after decreet, for making forthcoming, the arrester may use other diligences; but in competition with other creditors using diligence, he may not
exclude them, and keep up his own diligences, but hath his option thereof.
But seeing the arrestment maketh the subject arrested litigious, it hath the
common effect necessarily introduced by law *in re litigiosa*, that inchoat dili-

gence cannot be excluded, either by the voluntary deed of the debtor, or by any legal diligence posterior, unless the user of the first inchoat diligence become negligent, *nam vigilantibus, non dormientibus jura subveniunt.*

43. The application of these grounds will easily clear the preference in the competition of arrestments with assignations, or of arrestments with arrestments. And as to the competition betwixt assignations and arrestments, an assignation duly intimated, is a full and complete transmission of the right assigned, if by its nature it be assignable, and thereby the right of the cedent ceaseth, and the assignee becomes creditor, and hath no necessity of any farther diligence to complete the right: therefore no posterior arrestment will be preferred to an assignee if the intimation be before the arrestment, which is accounted, not only by days, but by hours: but if the intimation and execution of the arrestment be both in one day, and express no hour, if the arrester be not negligent, they will come in *pari passu*, because no priority doth appear, Spots. Debtor and Creditor, Ainsly *contra* Edward [*Sub nom. Inglis* v *Edward*, Spotiswoode 76; M. 2773], which will hold in the competition of diverse arrestments, or diverse assignations, where no priority doth appear; for we have little respect to the anteriority of debts in competition, but to the anteriority of diligence, as is evident in apprisings and adjudications; so if the hour be expressed in the arrestment, and not in the assignation, or contrary-wise, that which wants the hour, will prove no more but once that day, and the other will be preferred.

44. But if the arrestment be prior to the intimation, the arrestment is preferable, if it fail not in diligence; and therefore an arrestment was preferred to an assignation intimate the same day, but two hours thereafter, January 30, 1629, Davidson *contra* Balcanquel [Durie 420; M. 2773]. This distance was too narrow, for the executor and witnesses may mistake the present hours, so that three hours were a fitter distance to prefer: yea, an arrestment upon a dependence was preferred to a posterior assignation, though intimate half a year before sentence, upon that dependence, Hope, Assignation [Hope, *Maj.Pr.* 11,12]: but it must be in the discretion of the judge to determine, when arresters fail in diligence.

45. As to intimations, they are unquestionable if done by instrument, or by charge of horning, at the instance of the assignee upon the assignation; because the letters bear that the assignation was produced to the judge, passer of the bill: and there is little doubt that assignations attaining effect by possession, will be in the same case, as if intimated by instrument: or if a bond of corroboration be obtained upon the assignation, or discharges instructing payment of a part of the debt assigned: or if in process the assignation be judicially produced [111,1,7–9, *supra*]; but the case is not alike, nor have I observed it decided, if a citation before the assignation be judicially produced, will exclude an arrester, *medio tempore*, wherein the negative is more just and convenient; for a formal instrument of intimation will not instruct, if it bear not the production of the assignation.

46. As to the competition of arresters, the first arrestment, not failing in diligence, is preferable; and therefore the first arrester was preferred, though prior but by one day, though both obtained decreet upon the same day, and both used full diligence, February 1, 1666, Cunninghame *contra* Lyel [1 Stair 346; M. 809, 2872]. And likewise, an arrestment by letters from the Lords of Session, and first citation thereupon, being insisted in without negligence, was preferred to a posterior arrestment, though obtaining the first decreet before a sheriff; in respect that decreets before the Lords, cannot be so summarily obtained, especially, seeing they must abide the course of the roll, November 23, 1667, Montgomery *contra* Rankine [1 Stair 488; M. 809]. And a posterior arrestment was preferred to a prior, in respect the term of payment of the sum, for satisfying of which the first arrestment was laid on, was not come at the time of the first arrestment; but before the second arrestment was laid on, the term of payment of the sum, for which it was laid on, was past; albeit the terms of both sums were past before the competition came before the Lords by advocation, July 29, 1670, Charters *contra* Neilson [1 Stair 701; M. 811]; July 17, 1678, Lo. Pitmedden *contra* Patersons [2 Stair 636; M. 813]. And for the same cause, arrestment upon a decreet may be preferred to a prior arrestment upon a dependence; because the ground of the former hath *paratam executionem*, and not the ground of the latter: yet an arrestment upon a dependence was preferred to a posterior arrestment, obtained upon production of a registrable bond, before it was registrate, and so was not raised upon a decreet, Hope, Arrestment, Thomson *contra* M' Morran [*Sub nom. Thomson and McMurran* v *Philp*, Hope, *Maj. Pr.* VI, 37, 26; M. 675]. And arrestment laid on after the term of payment of the debt arrested, was preferred to a prior arrestment, laid on before the term of payment upon the debt arrested, January 23, 1673, Birnie *contra* Mowat and Crafurd [2 Stair 203; M. 812]. And an arrestment laid on verbally by a towns-officer was excluded by a posterior arrestment, having an execution before witnesses, albeit the verbal execution was the custom of the place, July 19, 1678, Warrock *contra* Broun [2 Stair 637; M. 686, 2617]. And a first arrester was not excluded for want of diligence, but was preferred to a posterior arrester, who had brought his cause to be concluded, at which time the prior arrester compeared, and produced an assignation, after his arrestment from the common debtor, whereby he needed no further diligence, July 19, 1673, Birnie *contra* Crafurd [2 Stair 217; M. 813]: This assignation was found no voluntary gratification, seeing it preferred the first legal diligence: and upon the same ground, an assignee by a bankrupt, was preferred to a posterior arrester, in respect the assignee had used the first diligence by horning, before the arrestment, Nov. 20, 1677, Bishop of Glasgow *contra* Nicolas and Broun [2 Stair 560; M. 1060, 8369].

Title 2. Dispositions, Where, of Resignations *In Favorem*, Apprisings and Adjudications of Real Rights, &c.

A DISPOSITION may, and sometimes doth, signify the alienation of any right, whether real or personal; so the style and translation ordinarily bears, the assignee to transfer and dispone: as assignation is sometimes extended to the disposal of real rights, which are frequently provided, not only to heirs, but to assignees; yet these terms are so appropriated and distinguished, that disposition is applied to the alienation of real rights, and assignation of personal rights.

1. In both dispositions and assignations, the disponer or cedent is called author, and the acquirer is called the singular successor, and in both, this common brocard takes place, *jus superveniens authori accrescit successori*, that is, whatever right befalleth to the author after his disposition or assignation, it accresceth to his successor, to whom he had before disponed, as if it had been in his person when he disponed, and as if it had been expressly disponed by him: whence ariseth the distinction betwixt dispositions and assignations, express and implicit, or tacit when the right is not expressly disponed, but tacitly or virtually; as he who dispones the property, *hoc ipso*, doth tacitly and virtually dispone any lesser right, as a reversion, servitude, liferent, though no particular mention be of these, according to another rule of law *majori inest minus;* so any person infeft in property, and his seasin registrated, will have right to a reversion, if no more was in the disponer's person; albeit assignations to reversions require special solemnities, as to be registrated in the register of reversions; yet the registration of this seasin be equivalent: so a liferent-right, granted by him who had only right of tack, was found to carry the right of that tack, during the liferenter's life, Hope, Liferents, L. Rosyth *contra* His Tenants [Hope, *Maj.Pr.* III, 12,40]. The like of a back-tack, *Ibid.* La. Boyd *contra* Her Tenants [Hope, *Maj.Pr.* III,12,49; M.6302], Stuart *contra* Fleming [Hope, *Maj.Pr.* III, 12,49; M.6302]. The like found of a liferent, which carried the right of a reversion *quoad* the liferenter's life, December 5, 1665, Beg *contra* Beg [I Stair 321; M.6304].

2. There is no question of this accretion, when the disponer disponeth for all right he hath, had, or shall acquire, which is a general assignation or disposition of any right supervening, if the debate fall betwixt the disponer and successor: there is also little question, if the right disponed have expressed or implied absolute warrandice, as being for a cause onerous; in which case, if the question be betwixt the disponer and successor, he who disponed for an equivalent cause, importing his acknowledgment of having an absolute right, cannot clothe himself with any posterior right, which would infer warrandice against him, if it were in another's person; and therefore, that personal objection excludes him, it being in his own person: neither is it questionable, that if the disposition or assignation be limited, as being only to a particular title, or generally, for any right the disponer hath, or bearing warrandice from his own fact and deed, then if he acquire a posterior right, he may make use thereof against that person to whom he dis-

poned, much more may any singular successor of his; and therefore, in the case decided, July 19, 1664, betwixt Dam Elizabeth Dowglas and Sir Robert Sinclair her spouse, *contra* L. Wedderburn [1 Stair 217; M.7748], anent the teinds of Kello and Kimmergem, whereof the Earl of Home, common author, gave a tack to Wedderburn's predecessor, with warrandice from his own deed; and any right the Earl then had, being reduced, he did thereafter acquire a new right from Coldingham, and thereupon granted a right to William Dowglas of Evla, to whom the said Dam Elizabeth Dowglas is heir, which supervening right was found not to accresce to Wedderburn, to defend his tack, seeing he had not absolute warrandice, but from his author's deed only. But the main question is, when the controversy is not betwixt the author and the party to whom he dispones, but betwixt the singular successor of that author, and that party to whom he had disponed before, in which case the personal objection upon the warrandice hath no place; and oft-times the right supervening requireth special solemnities, and cannot be transmitted without these; as resignation, confirmation, seasin; yet even in these cases, reason, and the Lord's decisions, extended the rule so that the supervening right *ipso facto* accresces without any new solemnities; but if the necessary solemnities have preceded when there was no right, whensoever the right supervenes, it is drawn back, as if it had been in the time of the former solemnities, *fictione juris;* and so, if a superior acquire the right of forfeitry of his superior, the same *ipso facto* accresceth to the sub-vassals, and cannot be made use of against them, Spots. Conjunct fees, Crawford *contra* L. Murdistoun [Spotiswoode 59; M.7756]. The like was found, February 15, 1665, Boid of Pinkel *contra* Vassals of Carsluth [1 Stair 270; M.7758]: in which case the vassals were ordained to pay their share of the composition of a ward [11,4,15,*supra*]; but where the supervening right befell to the author's apparent heir, and was by him disponed to another, before he was entered heir; in that case, the author's apparent heir, obtaining a gift of the liferent-escheat of lands disponed to vassals, the said liferent was not found to accresce to the vassals, because the apparent heir was denuded thereof in favour of another, before he was heir, Had. July 5, 1611, Skeen *contra* Vassals of Athol [M.7756]. This rule was so far extended, that a supervenient right, by decreet of reduction and improbation acquired by L. Swintoun, having right to the lands of Brimstoun, [by gift of E. Lauderdale's forfeiture,] was found to accresce to the Earl of Lauderdale, being restored, July 13, 1664, E. Lauderdale *contra* Heritor of Wolmet [1 Stair 213; M.26]. But this is not the accrescing of a new right, but declaring an old; yet, where a person having a disposition of lands, did infeft another in liferent, himself never being infeft, did assign the disposition to a third party, who was thereupon infeft, that disposition was not found to accresce to the annualrenter, because his author was never infeft thereupon, June 20, 1676, Brown *contra* Smith [2 Stair 428; M.2844].

It is the common opinion, that if a party grant infeftment, before he be infeft himself, and be thereafter infeft, it accresceth to that party whom he infeft before, if the question be betwixt them; but I have not observed it directly decided, *quid juris*, in these cases, if a person not infeft do give right to two parties, and thereafter be infeft, to which of the two his supervening infeftment will accresce: or if he infeft one, when he is not infeft, and thereafter another, when he is infeft, which of these will have right: yet if the common author's infeftment proceed upon the diligence of any party, the same will only accresce to him who is the procurer of it, if the preference be upon diligences, and not upon assignations: in that case it was found to accresce to the first right, with absolute warrandice, June 21, 1671, Neilson *contra* Menzies of Enoch [1 Stair 736; M. 7768].

3. But now to return to what is special in dispositions. A disposition is the transmission, or conveyance of real rights from the disponer to his singular successor, not in contemplation of the disponer's death, for such are comprehended among successions, from the dead, as legacies, donations *mortis causa*, &c. A disposition is said to be a conveyance, and so it is taken, not for the dispositive act of the will only, but whatsoever else is requisite to complete the conveyance, as tradition, resignation, possession, though a disposition is oft-times taken as distinct from these. For the more clear uptaking of conveyances of real rights; consider first, what is requisite to transmit them by the law of nature, without any positive law or custom; and next, what by these is requisite to transmit the several rights. As to the first, it hath been shown, in the title Real Rights [11, 1, *supra*], how far dominion and property is competent by the law of rational nature, and it cannot be doubted, but that though there were no positive law nor custom, that the rational creature is naturally instructed how to dispone and alienate his own, the power of disposal being the characteristic of dominion, which is natural to man, being created lord of the creatures. The question then is, by what act men may naturally exercise the power of disposal, which can be no act of the understanding, that being only contemplative, and nothing active nor operative for constituting or transmitting of rights; but it must needs be an act of the will, for by it, rights are both acquired, relinquished, and alienated. There may be three acts of the will about the disposal of rights; a resolution to dispone, a paction, contract or obligation to dispone, and a present will or consent that that which is the disponer's be the acquirer's. Resolution terminates within the resolver, and may be dissolved by a contrary resolution, and so transmits no right: paction does only constitute or transmit a personal right or obligation, whereby the person obliged may be compelled to transmit the real right. It must needs then be the present dispositive will of the owner, which conveyeth the right to any other, which is expressed by such words *de praesenti*, "Titius disponeth, alienateth, or annalzieth, gifteth, granteth, selleth, &c.;" which cannot properly import an obligation, having its effect in the future, though there may be obligations consequent as to delivery, warrandice, &c. but these terms do express something presently done, and not

engaged to be done, and so can be nothing else but the alienation or transmission of the right itself.

4. That the dispositive will of the owner alone, without any further, is sufficient to alienate his right, without delivery or possession, is evident in personal rights, wherein the dispositive clause of assignations or translations is sufficient; intimation or possession being introduced for expediency in some cases, by our custom. That the dispositive will is also sufficient to transmit real rights, it appeareth, because the will alone is sufficient to retain, not only rights, but even possession itself, though there be no corporeal act exercised therein; and therefore, the act of the will alone, as it retaineth, so may it relinquish that right or possession, whereby it ceaseth to be the former owner's; and therefore, if the will be not simply to relinquish but to remit or transmit the right to any other, *hoc ipso* that other doth become *dominus*: dominion being the power of disposal, which is a faculty, and no corporeal thing, it may be fitly constitute in the acquirer, by the will of the disponer, unless the acquirer reject it: for the disponer, before having the only power of disposal, and remitting that power to the acquirer, the thing cannot be said to be *nullius*, as being relinquished; and therefore, the dominion or disposal of it must either be in the disponer or the acquirer; not in the disponer, because by his will, which is sufficient to relinquish or quit it, he hath remitted it; and therefore that power must be in the purchaser, unless he reject it. This is the more evident, that positive law and custom, which requireth delivery or possession; resteth in symbolical or imaginary possession, as by delivery of earth and stone for land, of a penny for annualrent, and in some cases requireth no possession; so the fisk acquireth real right without possession; and the right of special legacies, and others from the dead, are transmitted without possession also.

5. But, for utility's sake, not only the Romans, but almost all nations require some kind of possession, to accomplish real rights, that thereby the will of the owner may sensibly touch the thing disponed, and thereby be more manifest and sure; so the law saith, *Traditionibus et usucapionibus, non nudis pactis, dominia rerum transferuntur*, with which our custom accordeth. It useth here to be debated, whether possession itself be sufficient to accomplish dispositions; or if there must be tradition, or delivery of that possession, by the disponer to the acquirer: the forecited law seems to require tradition, or at least usucapion, or prescription, which doubtless are the most proper ways to accomplish dispositions; yet *utiliter* and *equivalenter*, possession lawfully attained by virtue of the disposition, although not delivered by the disponer, will be sufficient; as if the disponer were not in possession himself, and so cannot deliver it; yet the acquirer may recover it from the detainer, or the acquirer might have been in possession before, by any other title, as by custody, conduction, &c.; in which case none require delivery: yea, it is more questionable, whether the possession would not consummate the disposition, though unlawfully attained; as if the disponer not being in possession, the

acquirer attained the possession from a third party, *vi aut clam*, though he might be obliged to restore that possession to the third party; yet whether it would not exclude a posterior disposition, though more legal possession; it is a question as probable in the affirmative, as in the negative, unless another having a disposition, were endeavouring to get possession, and were prevented by an irregular possession, albeit his endeavour were not by a legal diligence, but by requiring it.

6. It remaineth then that possession is the accomplishment of the disposition of real rights, so that not the first disposition, but the first possession, by virtue thereof, preferreth. This possession is not alike in all cases, for in some real, in others symbolical, possession is requisite, which cannot be supplied by real possession itself, as in property of lands or annualrents by infeftment, wherein the disposition and natural possession makes no real right without seasin, July 12, 1628, Bennet *contra* Turnbull [Durie 388; M. 2181]; November 25, 1628, Hall *contra* Wright [Durie 400; M.16477], December 16, 1629, Hunter *contra* Tennents of   [Durie 474; M.9443]. Possession is requisite, not only to the conveyance of the property of moveable goods, but also of liferent-rights, tacks, and rentals, servitudes, pledges, &c. which tacks, though they be truly personal rights of location, and constitute only as real rights by statute, yet intimation will not transmit them; but there is a necessity of possession: and though liferents be more properly real rights, because constitute by infeftment, yet seeing a liferenter cannot infeft another as a fiar can, assignation or disposition is sufficient, but it must be clad with possession: but reversions, though they be accounted as real rights by statute, require no possession for transmitting them, but an assignation duly registrated, according to the Act of Parl. 1617 [Registration Act, 1617, c.16; A.P.S. IV, 545, c.16], is sufficient as a public intimation.

7. In moveables possession is of such efficacy, that it doth not only consummate the disposition thereof, but thereupon the disposition is presumed without any necessity to prove the same, which was found sufficient to instruct the property of a ship from possession, without vendition in writ, July 26, 1673, Captain Hamilton *contra* the Master of the Ship Stetine [2 Stair 221; M.11925, 12774]. And the property of money was inferred, from having the key of the chest in which the money was found sealed, unless a contrary probation were adduced, June 18, 1675, Tailzior *contra* Rankine [2 Stair 333; M.9118]. And so a creditor having poinded goods from his debtor, was preferred thereunto, to a third party, who offered to prove these goods to be his own proper goods, bred upon his own ground, and set a grazing to that debtor, the poinder instructing that the goods were milked, wrought, and the offspring thereof enjoyed by the debtor for two years, without any possession by the other party, during that space, which so far presumed his right, that the Lords admitted not the contrary probation, November 24, 1624, Turnbul of Symountoun *contra* Ker of Cavers [Durie 151; M.11615]. The like upon two years' possession, June 17, 1625, Brown *contra* Huddelstoun

[Durie 163; M. 14748]. But restitution of a horse was not excluded, because the possessor offered to prove he bought him from one who then had him in possession, in respect the pursuer then offered to prove, that immediately before he had set the horse in hire for a journey to that person who sold him, November 18, 1680, Forsyth, Stabler *contra* Kilpatrick [2 Stair 801; M. 9120]: so that it will not be sufficient to any claiming right to moveable goods, against the lawful possessor, to allege he had a good title to these goods, and possession of them, but he must condescend, *quomodo desiit possidere*, as by spuilzie, stealth, &c., or that he gave them only in grazing and custody, and continued to use acts of property; the reason whereof is, because in the commerce of moveables, writ useth not to be adhibited, and it would be an insuperable labour, if the acquirers thereof behoved to be instructed by all the preceding acquirers, as if one should instruct that he bought or bred such goods some years ago, the present possessor behoved either to instruct a progress of them, through all the hands they passed from the first owner, or lose them, which being destructive to commerce, custom hath introduced this way, that possession being present and lawful, presumeth property without further probation, unless the pursuer condescend upon and clear the way of the goods passing from him, not by alienation, as if they were spuilzied, stolen, strayed, &c. February 3, 1672, Scot of Gorrenberry *contra* Eliot [2 Stair 59; M. 12727]: In which case, the libel was found relevant to be proven by the defender's oath, that he had not bought or acquired the goods *bona fide;* or that the goods were in a defunct's possession the time of his death, which is probable *prout de jure,* February 24, 1672, Semple *contra* Givan [2 Stair 78; M. 9117]; in which case a defunct's goods were restored, albeit they were long possessed after by his wife, and impignorated by her, and her second husband, without confirmation, the children of the defunct husband having recovered the same from the acquirer.

The passing of moveables from the proprietor must be so evidently instructed, that there may no probability remain of their being recovered, and thereafter alienated; upon this ground it was, that Sir John Scot pursuing Sir John Fletcher [1 Stair 258; M. 11616], for a book delivered to him, the Lords found the libel not relevant, unless it were condescended *quo modo* the pursuer delivered the same, viz. by loan, and would not put the defender to prove gifted, but presumed his title, unless the contrary were proven by oath or witnesses, January 27, 1665. And in a process for jewels, [December 12, 1665,] at the instance of Ramsay *contra* Wilson [1 Stair 326; M. 9113], who had them from Mr. Robert Byres, the Lords found, that the presumptive title of the defender and his author was elided, upon the contrary presumption, that jewels of such value could not be bought *bona fide,* seeing the seller was neither merchant nor jeweller, nor the jewels fit for his proper use; and because it was offered to be proven, he took them at his own hand out of the pursuer's possession, to whom they were impignorated by writ by the proprietor, who immediately went out of the kingdom [11,1,42,*supra*].

8. The most ordinary and important conveyances are of lands and annualrents, which pass by infeftment, for perfecting whereof, there must not only be a disposition, but also a resignation in the hands of the superior, and new infeftment granted by him to the acquirer thereupon, or by confirmation, or for obedience upon apprising or adjudication: for dispositions of lands to be holden of the granter, do not transmit the granter's right, because he continues superior in the direct dominion; but it becomes an original right, constituting a new subaltern infeftment. Resignation is either in favour of the superior himself, for consolidating of the property with the superiority; and therefore is called resignation *ad perpetuam remanentiam :* or it is a resignation in the superior's hands, in favour of the resigner himself; or in favour of an acquirer; and therefore is called resignation *in favorem.* The first of these is no transmission, but an extinction of the fee, and hath been spoken to in that title [11,11,1,*supra*]. The second is not properly a transmission, because it passeth not from, but returneth to the resigner; yet ordinarily under diverse considerations; as when he resigns from himself and such heirs, in favour of himself and other heirs, or when he resigns a wardholding, that it may be returned blench or feu. For the right understanding of resignations *in favorem*, consider the solemnities requisite thereto, and the effect which flow from the several steps thereof.

For the first, a resignation must proceed upon a disposition, or procuratory of resignation, having in it the effects of a disposition, which must be in writ; for the instrument of resignation being but the assertion of a notar, will not be sufficient alone, without an adminicle in writ: and though resignation *propriis manibus* can have no procuratory, yet the disposition whereupon it proceeds, must be shown as the warrant of the instrument of resignation. The second step in resignation, is the act of resignation itself, which necessarily must be by way of instrument of a notar, expressing the warrant of it, viz. the disposition, if it be done by the resigner *propriis manibus*, or the procuratory if it be done by a procurator, and that conform thereto, the resigner or procurator compeared personally before the superior or his commissioner, having special warrant to receive resignations, and that the resignation was made in the hands of the superior by staff and bastoun, delivered by the resigner or his procurator to the superior, as the token or symbol of the thing resigned, and that the same was accepted and received by the superior, or his commissioners, by taking the said symbol in their hands, for new infeftment, to be given to the acquirer: and though the resignation useth to be made by the vassal, or his procurator on their knees, and so is expressed in the instrument, either specially, or generally "with all humility," and that the superior or his commissioner, use to deliver the staff as the symbol of the fee to the acquirer, which is also expressed in the instrument; yet these are not so essential, but that without the being or expressing thereof the instrument will be valid. The last step of this transmission by resignation, is the superior or his commissioners giving new infeftment to the inquirer, the nature and re-

quisites of which infeftment hath been expressed before in the title Infeftments [11,3,*supra*].

The solemnities of resignation are so essential and necessary, that the
omission of them annulleth the resignation; and therefore renunciation without a formal resignation, though it may be sufficient against the renouncer,
yet it is not sufficient to take away the infeftment renounced, against singular
successors. Nor can it constitute any real right in the person of the acquirer,
unless he had *aliunde* another right standing in his person, in which case the
renunciation might exclude the renouncer, or his heirs, to quarrel that right,
Hope, Alienation, Hamilton *contra* M'Adam [Hope, *Maj.Pr.* 111,3,40 and
46; 11,11,6,*supra*]: the reason thereof is, because *jura eodem modo destituuntur
quo constituuntur;* and therefore, as infeftments cannot be constitute without
an instrument of seasin, so they cannot be destitute without an instrument of
resignation, or at least another instrument of seasin, with the superior's confirmation, or upon his charter for obedience; so that renunciation being personal, operates nothing, except in the case of wadsets, which are extinguished
by a renunciation registrate by the act of Parliament 1617 [Registration Act,
1617,c.16; A.P.S. IV,545,c.16]. But even wadsets cannot be transmitted
without resignation in favour of the wadsetter's singular successor.

9. But where it is said, that the resignation must be by the vassal or his
procurator, this question ariseth, if the resignation be made by him who is not
truly vassal, but with consent of the true vassal, *quid juris,* Craig, *Lib. 3, Dieg.*
1 [111,1,29], shows, That in his time this question was not clearly determined, nor is he positive in it, but this far, if the resigner had no title, no
consent could be sufficient: yet if he had a colourable title, the consent of the
true vassal might validate it, if the true vassal be consenter to the procuratory
of resignation, either expressly bearing, that the disponer, with consent, &c.
constitute his procurators, or if he be consenter to the disposition, by being
expressed in the entry thereof, which is holden as extensive to the whole disposition, and so as repeated in the same, will be as valid, as if the consenter
himself had granted the disposition or a procuratory; for the act of the disponer, though more express and amplified, is no more but his consent: and
so the other consenting, doth the same materially which he would do if he
were disponer formally; but if his consent be adhibited after the resignation
is made, it is merely personal, and cannot have influence on the resignation,
which was before it; or if he but permit or give license to the disponer, or,
which is alike, if he consent that the disponer dispone in so far as may concern the disponer's right, these will not be a sufficient warrant for the resignation; but if he give warrant or consent to the resignation, it is sufficient;
neither is there necessity to distinguish whether the disponer have a colourable title or not, seeing it is the consent of the true vassal, and the resignation
as flowing from, and warranted by that consent, which transmitteth the
right. And therefore an infeftment of annualrent, granted by a person not infeft, was found valid, because a consenter thereto was infeft; and so it did

exclude a valid right flowing from that consenter to a singular successor thereafter, viz. a tack, December 15, 1630, Stirling *contra* Tennents [Durie 548; M.6521]. *Vide Title* 11, §7.

10. Resignation how necessary soever to transmit an infeftment, yet because the procuratory and instrument of resignation may be lost, therefore the vassal possessing forty years, by virtue of an infeftment, mentioning such a resignation, the same will be valid without the production of the procuratory, or instrument of resignation; which therefore is presumed thence *præsumptione juris*, Parl. 1594, cap. 218 [Prescription Act, 1594, c.218; A.P.S. IV, 68, c.24; 11,12,15, *supra*].

11. As to the effect of resignation, there is no doubt, but when the same is truly made, and infeftment follows conform, the resigner is fully divested, and the acquirer is fully invested; and if there be conditions or provisions, whether bearing express clauses irritant, that the acquirer's infeftment shall be null, and the disponer's infeftment shall revive, or he have regress, how far these are effectual, until by resignation or judicial process, the same be recovered, is more fully cleared before, Title, Infeftments [11,3,58, *supra*]. It is no less evident, that before resignation be made, the disposition or procuratory operates nothing as to the real right, which notwithstanding remains fully in the disponer, though he be personally obliged to perfect it, albeit there be no such express obligement in the disposition, yet, by the nature thereof, the disponer is obliged to infeft himself, if he be not infeft, and to infeft the inquirer, Hope, Alienations, Gladstanes *contra* L. M� [Hope, *Maj.Pr.* 111,3,19]: the disposition of property being accomplished, carries all real right the disponer had of the land, or bonds for granting real right, in favour of the disponer, or his authors, though neither assigned nor mentioned in the disposition; yea, a liferent carrieth the reversion in the disponer's person, as to the liferenter's liferent use, that thereupon he might redeem a wadset: so likeways a disposition of lands immediately before a term, not expressing an entry, nor assignation to the rent, was found to exclude the disponer therefrom, though infeftment followed not, till after the term, Spots. Mails and Duties, Caldwal *contra* Stark [Spotiswoode 201; M.15880]. And generally, it carries mails and duties, as including virtually an assignation thereto, July 17, 1629, *inter eosdem* [Durie 465; M. 15880]: and though the disposition or procuratory cannot constitute a real right, yet it doth sufficiently exclude the disponer or his heirs, from troubling the acquirer's possession thereupon.

12. The main question then is, what is the effect of a resignation, when done and accepted by the superior, and no infeftment following thereon, where, in that case, the right standeth, whether in the disponer, acquirer, or superior, and whether the resigner be fully thereby denuded, or if he may not grant a second resignation, whereupon the first infeftment being recovered, will be effectual: this is very learnedly debated by Craig in the forementioned place [111,1,17], where he showeth, that the common opinion was, that the

second resignation with the first seasin will be preferred, though the Lords
had decided otherways, in the case of a citizen of Perth, who making a second
resignation in favour of his son, though after the first resignation by the space
of twenty years; yet Craig approveth the old opinion concerning the resigner,
never to be fully divested, till the acquirer were invested; this is clear, that by
the resignation, the fee falls in non-entry, and is in the superior's hands, and
while the resigner resigning in his own favour, be received, or the resignation
past from, or otherways, the acquirer be infeft, the superior hath the non-
entry duties of the lands resigned, if the infeftment be not delayed, through
his own fault. It is also clear, that, by the superior's acceptance of the resignation *in favorem*, there is upon him a personal obligation to infeft that person
in whose favour the resignation was made; and therefore, though the resigner die uninfeft, his heir by a single service, hath right to that as other
personal rights, and thereupon may compel the superior to infeft him; yea, as
Craig observeth in the fore-cited place [III,1,16], the Lords upon supplication, without citation, will grant letters summarily upon sight of the instrument of resignation, and warrant thereof, to charge the superior to infeft the
party, in whose favour it was made, who may not receive another resignation,
or infeft another party, or else his obligement may make him liable to the obtainer of the first resignation, *pro damno et interesse;* but the real right will be
carried by the first infeftment, though upon a posterior resignation; and so
posterior decisions go along with Craig's opinion, not only in the case of the
first public infeftment, upon a second resignation; but which is much more,
after a resignation is made, a base infeftment flowing thereafter from the resigner, and being but a short time before the public infeftment, upon the
resignation, yet was preferred thereto, as Dury observes, but expresses not
the parties, July 22, 1626 [Durie 225; M.6889]. As to the contrary decision
observed by Craig, it saith nothing, seeing the first infeftment upon the last
resignation, was in favour of the resigner's son, and so *inter conjunctas per-
sonas*, was fraudulent, which would not hold; so if that son had been a
stranger, acquiring *bona fide*, for a cause onerous, so then the resignation *in
favorem*, doth not denude the resigner of the real right, but is incomplete till
infeftment follow; and therefore a personal renunciation of him in whose
favour it was, will fully evacuate the resignation, and make the resigner's infeftment as entire as at first, which could not be without a new infeftment, if
the resigner had been divested; as in the case of a resignation *ad remanentiam*,
the superior's simple renunciation or discharge thereof, could not revive the
vassal's prior infeftment, but he behoved to be infeft *de novo*: and though
after the resignation, till it be past from, or infeftment follow, the lands be in
non-entry, it will not conclude that the resigner is denuded, and the fee is in
the superior, more than other non-entries, which give not the superior the
property, but a casuality of the fee [*Purves* v *Strachan* (1677), M.6890;
Dirleton, s.v. *Resignation;* Hope, *Min.Pr.* Tit. v, § 14]. Yet if the obtainer of
the second resignation first infeft, knew of the first, if it were given him as a

creditor, he were secure, but if it were merely voluntary buying, it might be reduced *ex capite fraudis*. And in what case dispositions of moveables or lands are holden to be simulate or fraudulent, hath been shown before, Title Reparation [1, 9, 12, *supra*], (upon circumvention or fraud) wherein retention of possession in moveables is a main ground for presuming simulation, especially in gifts of escheat: yet if the disposition of moveables bear expressly to take effect after the disponer's death, retention of possession will not annul it, neither will it be esteemed as a legacy, or *donatio mortis causa*, if death be the term, and not the consideration of it, and it was not found prejudged by the disponer's universal legacy, March 8, 1626, Traquair *contra* Bensheils [Durie 190; M. 3591].

13. So much for conventional conveyances of real rights; judicial conveyances of real rights are competent, not by the nature of the right, which cannot be alienated without consent of the owner, and in the case of infeftments, holden of the superior, without his consent, who is not obliged to receive any to be his vassal, but the heirs and successors of the first vassal, provided in the first investiture; and though the investiture bear also, the vassal's heirs and assignees, yet the superior cannot thereon be compelled directly to receive a singular successor, assignees being only meant such assignees to whom the dispositions should be assigned before infeftment thereupon, as was found in the case of recognition, La. Carnagy *contra* E. Cranburn, February 5, 1663 [1 Stair 172; M. 10375]. But law hath introduced in favours of creditors, judicial conveyances, requiring no consent, but the authority of law, which hath also its foundation in natural equity, by which, as obligations are effectual for exaction of what is thereby due, so if there were no positive law nor custom, the creditor might exact, either what is due *in specie*, or the equivalent: and therefore reprisals betwixt nations not governed by one common authority, are lawful; and by the custom of nations, extended not only against the party injurer, who is obliged to repair, but against all the subjects of his sovereign, if he do not cause reparation to be made. The judicial transmission of moveables is by poinding, which being a legal execution, we shall leave it to that place. Arrestment and the action for making forthcoming, do also transmit moveables; but is rather proper to personal rights, and so is competent against the havers of moveables, by reason of that personal obligation of restitution, which is upon the haver to the owner, besides his own property.

Of old, alienations of land for money were very rare in Scotland, or the contracting of considerable debts; for the nobility and gentry did then live in a plain and sober way, contenting themselves with that which their own estates did afford: and there was then known no legal executions for debt, against lands or heritable rights, but only against moveables, by the brief of distress or poinding [IV, 23, 1, *infra*], by which, not only the moveables of the debtor were poinded for his debt, but all the moveables upon his lands belonging to his tenants, as appeareth from Act 36, Parl. 1469 [Diligence Act, 1469,

c. 36; A.P.S. 11,96,c. 12], bearing this title, "That the poor tenants shall pay no further than their term's mail for their Lord's debt, by the brief of distress," which is correctory of the former custom, whereby the goods and cattle of the inhabitants of the ground were distrenzied for their Lord's debts, though their mails extended not to the avail of the debt, and that not only for real debts affecting the ground by infeftments of annualrent, feu-duties, or casualities of superiority, or other *debita fundi*, for which the moveables of the tenants and possessors may be yet poinded for the Lord's debt, not exceeding their terms mail, which is ordinarily in their hand, or if paid, may be allowed in the next term, but for the heritor's personal debt; for by the Act, the debtor's moveables in that, or any other barony or shire, are appointed to be poinded for satisfying of the debt; but *debita fundi* can only reach the moveables of the barony or tenement affected therewith; and though this Act, by its tenor, would yet extend to poinding of tenants' moveables for their master's personal debt, custom hath restricted it only to real debts, and it is entirely in desuetude, as to personal debts, which cannot burden tenants, but upon arrestment, in so far as they are then debtors to their masters [11,5,9, *supra*].

14. Before this statute in the year 1469 [Diligence Act, 1469, c. 36; A.P.S. 11,96,c. 12], there is no mention in our law or customs, of apprising or adjudication: but apprising was thereby introduced in this manner, that where the debtor has not moveable goods, but lands, the sheriff shall cause sell the lands to the avail of the debt, and pay the creditor, which shall be redeemable by the debtor within seven years, and if he cannot find a buyer, he shall apprise the debtor's land by thirteen persons of the best and worthiest in the shire, least suspect to either party, and assign to the creditor lands to the avail of the sum, and the superior shall receive the creditor, or any other buyer, for a year's rent, as the land is set for the time, or otherways shall take the land to himself, and undergo the debt. According to this Act, apprisings did proceed by sheriffs and bailies, who for satisfying of debts, liquidated by decreets, issued precepts for denouncing such lands to be apprised upon fifteen days' warning, conform to the Acts of Parliament, which denunciation was publicly read upon the ground of the land, before witnesses, and a copy thereof left affixed thereupon, and also at the market-cross of the head burgh of the jurisdiction, where the lands lie, and to the debtor whose lands were to be apprised, expressing the creditor, sum, day and place of apprising, that all parties interested might appear; persons of inquest and witnesses were also summoned to the same diet; and ordinarily the place was upon the ground of the lands, that the value and worth thereof might the more clearly appear, where, after discussing of the appriser's claim, the hability of the persons of inquest, and witnesses, so much land was apprised and adjudged as was worth the sum, the year's rent to the superior, and expenses of infeftment; and if the lands were burdened with any former annualrents, whereby a proportion of land could not be apprised, free of burden, there was ap-

prised an annualrent forth of the lands effeiring to the sums, and expenses foresaid, and redeemable in the same manner, which was sustained by the meaning and intent of the statute; and though by the words of it, apprising of lands was only mentioned, it was ever extended to all heritable rights.

Thus it continued until the Lords of Session, upon exceptions against the sheriff, upon his interest, relation, or enmity, or upon the lying of lands in divers jurisdictions, for preventing of expenses by many apprisings, where the lands in one jurisdiction sufficed not, did grant letters of apprising under the signet, direct not to the ordinary sheriffs, but to sheriffs in that part, which being frequent, did come to run in course to messengers, as sheriffs in that part, &c. And thereby the appriser, in respect the letters had a blank for inserting the messenger's name, did choose the messenger, who did denounce all lands and other heritable rights, which the appriser pretended to belong to his debtor; and in respect the letters bore a dispensation of the place, he did apprise at Edinburgh, all that the appriser claimed, in satisfaction of the debt, without knowledge or consideration of the value of the lands, or others apprised, or proportion to the sums apprised for, and thereupon was infeft in the whole, and paid to the superior for a composition, a year's rent of the whole, which was a considerable accession to the debtor's debt, and behoved to be paid by him; and by the said apprisings, the appriser might, and oftentimes did enter in possession of the whole lands, without being comptable for the rents thereof of what quantity soever: by this abuse, the intent of that excellent statute for apprisings, was enervated, and the same turned into a mere formality, until the Parl. 1621, cap. 6 [Diligence Act, 1621, c. 6; A.P.S. IV, 609, c. 6], which began to correct that exorbitant abuse, and declared apprisers comptable for their intromissions, in so far as exceeded their annualrents, to be imputed in their principal sums *pro tanto*, and that they being thereby satisfied of their sums, principal and annual, composition to the superior, and expenses of apprising and infeftments, that thereby the apprising should expire *ipso facto*; and it is also declared, that if the lands apprised be not worth of free rent, effeiring to the annualrent of the said sums, that before redemption, he shall be satisfied of the superplus. By which Act also it is declared, that minors may redeem lands apprised from them at any time within their age of twenty-five years complete; yet so, that after the first seven years, the appriser shall have the benefit of the whole mails and duties till he be redeemed; which hath always been extended to lands apprised from persons being major, if a minor succeed, during the legal; and if a person being major, succeed to him who was minor, he hath the benefit of reversion of seven years, in so far as was not run in the minor's life; and if less remain than a year at the minor's death, the major hath a full year to redeem after the minor's death [1, 6, 44, *supra*]; and by the Act 67, of the abrogated Parliament 1641 [A.P.S. V, 517, c. 110], apprisers were declared comptable for the rents of apprised lands intromitted with by them, during all the time of the legal, whether minors or others [III, 2, 39, *infra*].

Because of another great abuse, by the debording of apprisings from the first institution, that the first appriser apprising the whole estate, the other creditors had no more but the legal reversion, which did ordinarily expire, the subsequent creditors not being able to raise money to redeem the anterior appriser, whereby the first appriser carried the whole estate, and excluded all the rest, and being ashamed to take so great a legal advantage, and sometimes not daring to make use of it, did ordinarily compone with the debtor's apparent heirs, or some confident to their behoof, whereby the debtor's heir recovered his whole estate, by satisfying one creditor, and excluding all the rest; therefore the Parl. 1661, by their Act 62, anent Debtor and Creditor [Diligence Act, 1661, c. 62; A.P.S. VII, 317, c. 344], declared that all apprisings, deduced since the first of January 1652, or to be deduced in time coming, within a year after the first apprising, which became effectual by infeftment or charge, should come in *pari passu*, as if one apprising had been led for all the sums, and thereby the legal was extended to ten years; and it is declared, that whensoever the apparent heir, or any to his behoof, shall acquire right to any expired apprising, that the same shall be redeemable from them within the space of ten years after their acquiry, by posterior apprisers, upon payment of what they truly paid, in so far as shall not be satisfied by their intromission [III, 2, 41, *infra*]. This hath been so far extended by the Lords, that the words of the statute mentioning only posterior apprisers, might redeem expired apprisings, coming in the person of the apparent heir, yet that the samine was to be understood as the chief instances of this article of the statute; and therefore found, that any personal creditor had this benefit of redemption, because he might apprise, and there was no necessity to put him to the expense of actual apprising, Dec. 1683, Moll *contra* Craw [1 Fountainhall 242–3; M. 5322]. And likeways apprisings coming in the persons of the apparent heir, are ordinarily redeemable, for what was truly paid them within the legal, and the same is extended when the acquisition is by the apparent heir in the defunct debtor's time. But the apprising coming in the person of the apparent heir in his father's life, was not found redeemable by the father, nor by his other children, upon the bonds of provision, being granted after the expiring of the legal, Nov. 1681, Nasmith *contra* L. Posso [Pres. Falconer 1; M. 13479]. But these bonds being alleged granted during the legal, were found to give right to redeem, December 3, 1680, *inter eosdem* [2 Stair 811; M. 5316]. There is nothing in this statute, in case an apprising come in the person of the debtor himself, or to his behoof, after the expiring of the legal; nor hath decisions cleared, whether it will be redeemable from the debtor for what he paid, but there is no less reason to extend it to that case than the former, unless the appriser hath never taken possession, seeing as he might relinquish the apprising, so he might compone with the debtor, and so the apprising would become extinct, in the same way as if the apprising were disponed to the behoof of the debtor within the legal.

But neither did this statute cure the abuse of apprisings; and therefore the

Act of Parliament of the 6th of September 1672 [Adjudications Act, 1672, c. 19; A.P.S. VIII, 93, c. 45], upon consideration of the debording of apprisings from the first design, and of the great inconveniencies arising thereby, for the bringing in of all apprisers within year and day, did give way to break the credit, and ruin the interest of the most considerable heritors in the kingdom, creditors being thereby invited, under the hazard of being excluded to apprise within a year; and thereby one wilful, malicious, or necessitous creditor apprising, all the rest followed, and entirely broke their debtor's credit, unless they would pay all their debt in one day; therefore the Parliament did, in place of apprisings, ordain adjudications to proceed before the Lords of Session, for adjudging the lands and other heritable rights of debtors, effeiring to the sums apprised for, and a fifth more in place of the penalties and sheriff-fee, and allowed witnesses for either party, for clearing of the rental and rate of the lands, in the several places where they lie, and appointed the adjudger to have present possession of the lands adjudged, not being accomptable for his intromission during the legal, redeemable only within five years, whereby the creditor had easy access for his satisfaction, without all hazard of accompt, which had been the ground of many tedious processes of compt and reckoning for the intromission of former apprisers, and wherein the adjudger is to have the consent of his debtor, both as to right and possession, and delivery of the evidents; and it is declared, that if the debtor do not instruct, and deliver a good right, and consent, as said is, that the creditor might adjudge all the debtor's estate in the same manner, and to the same effect, as is appointed by the Act of Parliament 1661, betwixt Debtor and Creditor [Diligence Act, 1661, c.62; A.P.S. VII, 317, c. 344].

15. We shall not here speak of adjudications and apprisings, as they are legal executions, and of the order and solemnities requisite to them, as such; but only as they are conveyances of real rights, wherein we shall consider; First, Upon what ground apprising proceeds. Secondly, Against what rights it is competent. Thirdly, What is the effect of the process, or decreet of apprising, without further diligence. Fourthly, What is the effect thereof, when further diligence is used. Fifthly, What is the effect thereof when infeftment is obtained. And Lastly, In what manner it ceaseth and becometh extinct. As to the first, Apprising is an appreciation and judicial vendition of the thing apprised, from the debtor to the creditor: and as in all venditions, there must be *merx* and *prætium* or the price in numerate money, for if the matter consist in any thing else, it is not sale but exchange, therefore the ground of apprising must be numerate and current money, and if originally it be not so, it must be liquidate before apprising can proceed; neither can it proceed but upon a decreet establishing the debt by registration or otherwise in the person of the appriser, *activè*, and of the debtor *passivè*; yet an assignee, intimating before the cedent's death, may apprise summarily without action, establishing the debt in his person, as hath been shown. Title Assignations [III, 1, 19, *supra*]. Neither could apprising proceed upon heritable bonds, un-

less the same had been made moveable, by requisition or charge; and therefore was found null, proceeding upon an heritable sum, bearing a clause of
annualrent, though payable without requisition upon a single charge of six
days, seeing that charge was not given, July 20, 1622, Cranston *contra* L.
East-Nisbet [Durie 31; M.64,8113]; Hope, Obligations, Mowat *contra* the
Creditors of Richardson [Hope, *Maj. Pr.* VI, 37, 22; M.695,8113], Cranston
contra L. Lugtoun [Hope, *Maj. Pr.* II, 3, 22; M.64,8113]. But posterior decisions have run in the contrary, that if the sum were payable without requisition, apprising might proceed thereupon without a charge, as well as
poinding or arrestment; July 4, 1627, Edgar and Johnstoun *contra* Findla-
son [Durie 304; M.5536], July 10, 1629, L. Clackmannan *contra* L. Bar-
rounie [Durie 460; M.69,8116]; in which case the principal sum was payable
at a precise term, and no mention of any term or time thereafter, and yet was
apprised for, after that term [III, 1, 27, *supra*], January 25, 1642, Seatoun
contra Loch [*Sub nom. Johnston* v *Loch*, Durie 888; M.8117]. But if infeftment have followed, or requisition be requisite, the sum must be made
moveable before apprising [III, 2, 33, *infra*]: but other sums, though by destination heritable, yet having summary execution by the parties consent,
apprising is sustained thereupon.

16. As to the second point, against what rights apprisings extend: First,
though letters of apprising contain power to poind moveables, which must be
searched for; yet that which is properly called apprising, extends to no moveables, but only to heritable rights, as lands, annualrents, liferents, tacks, reversions, heritable bonds, July 25, 1623, E. of Errol *contra* L. Buckie
[Durie 77; M. 134]; and therefore it extends not to the mails and duties of the
apprised lands, before the apprising, February 14, 1623, L. Saltcoats *contra*
Home [*Sub nom. Saltcoats* v *Brown*, Durie 46; M.2763]. The like, though the
question was against the debtor himself, and that the style of the apprising
bore all right that the debtor had to the lands to be apprised, March 13, 1627,
Mackie *contra* Livingstoun [*Sub nom. McGhie* v *Livingston*, Durie 289; M.
136]. And where an annualrent is apprised, it extends not to the bygone
annualrents, which are moveable; but these being moveable, are arrestable,
neither doth it extend to the duties after denunciation, and before apprising,
February 16, 1633, Harper *contra* Cockburn and Johnstoun [Durie 674; M.
139; III, 2, 48, *infra*]. Apprising is extended to all heritable rights, though
they were not provided to assignees, but to the debtor and his heirs only, or
failing such heirs to return; and therefore public utility and the favour of the
creditor makes it more effectual than any voluntary disposition or assignation could be; so an apprising was found to carry a right, though not granted
to assignees, Hope, Apprising, Brown *contra* Essilmont [*Sub nom. Bruce* v
Buckie, Hope, *Maj. Pr.* VI, 28, 68; M. 10145]. And a husband granting right to
his wife, but with provision that she should renounce it, if he required it in
his own life allenarly, a creditor of his, apprising that land, and requiring the
wife to renounce, was found to have right thereto, Spots. Apprising, La.

Huttonhall *contra* Cranstoun [Spotiswoode 53; M.138]. An apprising of the ground-right and property of lands, and all other rights, &c. carrieth not only the property, but all other real right, or obligements for granting thereof; and though no infeftment follow, the apprising so conceived will carry any right, which requireth not infeftment, as if it had been specially denounced and apprised, June 19, 1635, Rule *contra* Home [Durie 767; M. 14374].

17. To come now to the third point concerning the efficacy of the process and decreet of apprising, without further diligence; and first, it hath the effect of an assignation, without necessity of intimation, and carries all rights which require not infeftments to transmit them, as liferents, reversions, tacks: and so an apprising was found to carry the legal of an anterior apprising, though the denunciation whereupon it proceeded, was anterior to the denunciation whereupon the first apprising proceeded, and thereby at the time of the denunciation of the second apprising; neither was the first apprising in being, neither the denunciation thereof, and so could not be denounced or apprised; yet the denunciation of the groundright, and all right competent, or that might be competent to the debtor, was found to carry the reversion of the said first apprising, November 18, 1624, Kincaid *contra* Halyburtoun [Durie 148; M.134].

18. Though second apprisings carry the legal reversions of anterior apprisings without infeftment; yet infeftment is frequently taken thereupon, that the posterior appriser may have interest thereby, to reduce or quarrel the anterior apprisings, and to pursue for mails and duties, or removing, if the anterior appriser should forbear.

19. The second effect of apprising is, that the debtor is thereby so far divested, that after his death, infeftment may be taken by the appriser, without transferring or infefting the debtor's heir, November 20, 1624, L. Lag *contra* His Tennents [Durie 150; M. 16083], and the cases there related. So likewise the heir of the appriser dying before allowance or infeftment, upon supplication obtained allowance from the Lords, and letters to charge the superior to receive him, Spots. *hic*, Frazer, Supplicant [Spotiswoode 51; M.6911]. The like was granted to the appriser's assignee, March 22, 1626, Collace *contra* Lo. Elphingstoun [Spotiswoode 340; M.16148]. Yea, an appriser did obtain allowance and warrant to charge the heir of the superior contained in the first allowance, December 5, 1628, L. Corsbie *contra* L. Kilsyth [Durie 405; M.6910]. From this ground it is, that an apprising excludes prior assignations, granted by the debtor, to the mails and duties of the lands apprised, as to terms after the apprising, Hope, Assignations, Meldrum *contra* L. Anstruther [Hope, *Maj. Pr.* 11,12,32; M.844].

20. And when an apprising was led before an husband's death, it excluded his wife from a terce, Hope, Apprisings, Crightoun *contra* Relict of Cranstoun [Hope, *Maj. Pr.* VI,28,51; M.15836; 11,6,17,*supra*]: where he doth also observe it to exclude a subsequent ward in respect the superior gave a charter upon the apprising, in his vassal's life, though no seasin followed

thereupon [11,4,36,*supra*], *ibid*. Hamilton *contra* Tenants of Newburgh [Hope, *Maj.Pr.* vi,28,53; M.16443]. And albeit Dury observes, that in the case betwixt the L. Covingtoun and the Lo. Balmerino, 7 March, 1633 [Durie 679; M.15065], it was not decided, but superseded in hopes of agreement, whether a superior could be compelled to receive the appriser, seeing he was not obliged to receive a minor himself till his majority; it seems the superior ought to receive the appriser upon his legal diligence, but prejudice of the ward, during the minority of his former vassal, and though he would not receive the minor, yet he would be necessitated to receive the appriser and his heirs whatsomever, though the lands were tailzied, and were to return to the superior himself.

21. The third effect of apprising is, that being a legal diligence, it renders the thing apprised litigious, not only from the date of the apprising, but from the date of the denunciation: so that no voluntary deed of the debtor, after the denunciation, can prejudge the appriser, if he be not *in mora*. Thus a tack set by the debtor after denunciation, was found null, Spots, Apprising, Blackburn *contra* Balvaird [Spotiswoode 52; M.8379]. Yet where the appriser was negligent, and obtained not infeftment, nor did diligence therefor for some years, a tack set by a debtor before the apprising, but having its entry after the apprising, was preferred thereto, Had. July 11, 1627, Wallace *contra* Harvie [Durie 307; M.67]. Yea, no infeftment or diligence being used upon an apprising for many years, an arrestment thereafter was preferred to the mails and duties of the lands apprised, February 14, 1623, L. Saltcoats *contra* Brown [Durie 46; M.2763]. But custom since hath always preferred apprisings to arrestments, although there were no infeftment or diligence upon the apprising, because it is a legal assignation, and needs no intimation unless the appriser had relinquished his right; and therefore, though that case of Saltcoats was adduced, an appriser of an annualrent was preferred to an arrestment, though the appriser neither was infeft nor used diligence, for nine years before the arrestment, February 23, 1671, Lord Justice Clerk *contra* Fairholm [1 Stair 727; M.2766; III,2,17,*supra*]. It is said, no voluntary disposition, or deed of the debtor after the denunciation, will prejudge the apprising, because if the deed done thereafter be necessary, and that thereunto the debtor was specially obliged before, and might have been directly compelled, such even after denunciation may be preferred; as an annualrent proceeding upon a bond, prior to the denunciation, containing an obligement to infeft in that annualrent, the infeftment thereupon though after denunciation was preferred, Hope, Apprising, Henderson *contra* M'Adam [Hope, *Maj.Pr.* vi,28,46; M.2818]. The like of an infeftment, whereof the charter was before denunciation, and the seasin before the seasin upon the apprising, *Ibid*. The like of an infeftment upon resignation, which resignation preceded the denunciation; and though the resignation was at first refused by the superior, being accepted thereafter, it was preferred, *Ibid*. Hope *contra* Henderson [Hope, *Maj.Pr.* vi,28,71; M.2818].

And so an infeftment upon a disposition for a cause onerous, which disposition was of the same date with the denunciation, and whereupon infeftment followed, before the apprising, was preferred to the apprising, Spots. Apprising, Hamilton *contra* Brown [Spotiswoode 44; M.2819]. Yea, an infeftment upon a disposition, posterior to an apprising, was preferred thereto, seeing the appriser did no diligence for six years, *Ibid.* Hamilton *contra* M'Culloch [Spotiswoode 43; M.1689]. And generally, voluntary rights are excluded, being granted after the denunciation of lands to be apprised, until infeftment be obtained, or a charge against the superior; all which is, the creditor being *in cursu diligentiæ :* but if he be supinely negligent, he will lose that privilege; and after a competent time for obtaining infeftment, or charging the superior from the decreet of apprising, any posterior voluntary right is preferable to the apprising, as was found in the competition of the creditors of Cockburn and Langtoun, January and February 1692 [Possibly Harcarse 172; M.1290], *vid. infra, Lib.* 4, *Tit.* 35. Competition of Real Rights.

22. In the competition of apprisings, being both legal diligences, the first appriser doing sufficient diligence, is preferred; as the first appriser, last infeft, but having first charged, was preferred, though the superior did voluntarily infeft a posterior appriser, January last, 1632, Ferguson *contra* McKenzie [Durie 616; M.2429]. Yea, a posterior apprising was preferred to a prior, where the debtor by collusion suspended the letters, and the denunciation of the one and not of the other, whereby the other apprised first, November 28, 1628, Borthwick *contra* Clerk [Durie 401; M.2427]. The like where the prior proceeded upon a citation of the party upon sixty days, as being out of the country, and the debtor was brought to the country of purpose that a posterior denunciation, upon fifteen days, by another appriser might give him the first apprising, and yet the other was preferred, Nicols., Tenants of Cockburnspeth *contra* Wardlaw [Not printed]. And upon the competition betwixt the L. Clerkintoun pursuing a reduction of L. Corsbie's apprising, as collusive, in so far as after his author Sir William Dick, had charged the superior with the first charge upon the letters of four forms, they gave infeftment to Corsbie before the days of the first charge expired; the Lords reduced the infeftment, but assoilzied him from bygones, as possessing *bona fide ;* and seeing the pursuer suffered Corsbie to possess without pursuit, till the legal was expired, they found that Corsbie, as now the second appriser, might redeem him, December 3, 1664, *inter eosdem* [1 Stair 234; M.2430].

23. The fourth effect of an apprising is, that being led by the superior against his vassal, it consolidates the property with the superiority, and is preferable to all posterior apprisings, whatever be their diligence, Spots. Apprising, Stevinson *contra* L. Craigmiller [Spotiswoode 41; M.836]. In other cases, apprising without further diligence, doth not transmit the real right, though it may exclude assignations to mails and duties or arrestments upon personal debts, yet it is no sufficient title for mails and duties, against

any other having any real title. Superiors may infeft themselves on their apprising, or may obtain precepts from the Chancellary to infeft them, and declarators of consolidation are inconvenient, not being in a special register, and so cannot come to the knowledge of acquirers [11, 11, 8, *supra*].

24. As to the fourth point concerning the efficacy of apprisings, whereupon diligence is used before infeftment be obtained; they have no effect to remove tenants, though the superior was charged, and the letters found orderly proceeded against him, and though only proponed by the tenants, and by no party pretending right, March 25, 1628, Lockhart *contra* His Tenants [Durie 370; M. 13790]; yet not against the person against whom the apprising was led, February 20, 1629, Galloway *contra* L. Bogmiln [Durie 428; M. 13791]: but since the Act of Parliament, bringing in apprisers *pari passu*, the first effectual apprising is declared to be, either by infeftment, or charge against the superior to grant infeftment, which is ordinarily sustained without further insisting, and therefore it must have the same effect as an infeftment, at least during the ordinary years of the legal, even for removing [11, 9, 41, *supra*]: but the apprising with diligence hath this effect; *first*, it is a sufficient title for mails and duties against the possessors; *secondly*, it excludes all posterior infeftments or diligences by the collusion, or voluntary deed of the superior, or any other; *thirdly*, it is effectual to compel the superior to receive and infeft the appriser, upon payment to him of a year's rent, which was formerly by letters of four forms, till the statute 1644, cap. 43 [Act 1647, A.P.S. vi(1), 823, c. 482], whereby one charge upon twenty-one days is sufficient; all which proceeds upon the allowance of the Lords, upon the back of the apprising; and albeit that Act is not revived in the later Parliaments, yet the Lords continue that custom.

25. This allowance of apprising is appointed to be registrated, and not the whole apprising, Parl. 1641, cap. 54 [A.P.S. v. 505, c. 90]. Yet neither the want of the allowance, nor the want of registration thereof, annulleth the apprising, till the last Act of Parl. 1661, cap. 31 [Registration Act, 1661, c. 31; A.P.S. vii, 229, c. 243], making the registration of the allowance necessary, otherwise posterior apprisings, first allowed, are to be preferred, unless without allowance the appriser hath obtained infeftment before the other's diligence [11, 3, 22, *supra*]; upon which grounds, the Lords upon supplication, without citation, ordained an apprising to be allowed and registrated, long after sixty days, and after the debtor's death, seeing it would be thereby preferable to all other rights, after the registration thereof, June 8, 1665.

26. There are many debates which arise concerning the entry betwixt apprisers and superiors, as whether the superior can be compelled to receive the appriser, without instructing that the vassal, from whom he hath apprised, was infeft, or specially charged, which hath been several times decided *negativè*, fifty years since. But now of a long time, charges against superiors for infefting apprisers, *salvo jure cujuslibet et suo*, have been still sustained, because it is unusual and difficult for the appriser to get his

debtor's evidents, unless it were the extract of his seasin, and the superior's receiving him upon obedience, cannot prejudge himself; and therefore the superior was ordained to receive the appriser, though himself was in possession, by virtue of a right, March 5, 1634, Black *contra* L. Pitmedden [Durie 709; M.15070]; the like, whatever right the superior might pretend, March 11, 1636, Scot *contra* Eliot [Durie 804; M.201].

27. The quantity of the year's rent by the Act of Parl. 1469, cap. 36 [Diligence Act, 1469,c.36; A.P.S. 11,96,c.12], is expressed to be a year's mail, as the land is set for the time, wherein consideration is had of such real burdens affecting the land, as are taken on, with the superior's consent: but in the case of a liferent so taken on, the year's rent was modified full, but delayed to be paid till the liferenter's death, July 18, 1633, Baird *contra* [Durie 686; M.15054]; and in the said case Scot *contra* Eliot [Durie 804; M. 201]. Consideration is also had of feus set by the debtor before the apprising, which while warranted by law, the superior will only get a year's feu-duty for receiving the appriser in the superiority, February 15, 1634, L. Munktoun *contra* L. Yester [Durie 705; M.15020]; Spots. Apprising, Cowan *contra* Mr. Elphingstoun [Spotiswoode 56; M.15055]; or if there be a sub-feu of lands holden feu at any time: but a subaltern blench-infeftment cannot make the blench-duty sufficient as a feu-duty, seeing a feu is an heritable location, for melioration of the ground, and is therefore presumed to be the rent at the time of the feu, which will not admit a contrary probation: but the superior will not be obliged to receive the appriser for a year's rent of the money apprised for, but of the lands apprised, March 23, 1622, Ramsay *contra* E. Rothes [Durie 23; M.199]; March 30, 1637, Paterson *contra* Murray [Durie 844; M.15055]. Yet in this last case the Lords modified the rent far within the worth of the lands, for the rent being worth eight hundred merks, it was modified to three hundred merks [11,4,32,*supra*]. A superior must not only receive the first appriser, but all others who charge, though one was infeft before any other charged, March 11, 1628, Ferguson *contra* Couper [Durie 358; M.15029]. And if more charge, he must accept a year's rent for all, providing that he, who shall be preferred, refund to the rest the proportions paid by them to the superior, July 22, 1628, Lord Borthwick and Hay *contra* L. Haystoun and Smith [Durie 392; M.15030; 11,4,32,*supra*].

28. If the superior be contumacious, and will not enter the appriser upon diligence, Craig, *lib.* 2. *dieg.* 2. [111,2,20] prescribes, that the superior may be thrice required, and if he refuse, letters may be obtained from the Lords to charge his superior, to receive the appriser, supplying his place, and so from superior to superior till he come to the King, who refuseth none; by which the superior would lose the casualities of his superiority, during his life, as is ordinary in the entry of heirs upon retour; yea, if the appriser offer a sum some way proportionable to the land apprised, or the sum apprised for, with a bond to pay what further the Lords shall modify, and offer a charter, it will stop the superior's casualities, February 9, 1669, Black *contra* Trench

[1 Stair 599; M. 6911]. But since the Act 1661, cap. 62, whereby apprisings became effectual by a charge against the superior, all inconvenience is avoided; the creditor is not put to trouble, the superior loseth no casuality, but all remains with the debtor, till the creditor be infeft, or the legal be expired, and the creditor possessed [11,3,30; 111,2,24, *supra*].

29. As to the next point, infeftment following upon an apprising, doth constitute a real right, but under reversion of seven years, being before the Act of Debtor and Creditor, Parl. 1661, cap. 62 [Diligence Act, 1661, c. 62; A.P.S. VII,317, c. 344], or since of ten years, which is counted from the date of the apprising, and not from the allowance or infeftment, November 11, 1630, L. Limpitlaw *contra* Aikenhead [Durie 538; M. 282], even against another appriser, alleging he could not know the prior apprising, till infeftment were taken thereon.

30. Yet it remains but as a security, which the appriser may renounce, or make use of other securities till he be satisfied, March 5, 1628, Lord Blantyre *contra* Parishioners of Bothwel [Durie 362; M. 217]. The like, though after the legal was expired, December 7, 1631, Scarlet *contra* Paterson [Durie 605; M. 218]. But here the appriser had attained no possession, and there was a preferable annualrent exhausting most of the rent [111,2,44, *infra*].

31. Remains the last point proposed, how apprisings become extinct, and are taken off; and that is, first, When the apprising is declared null, through defect of any essential solemnity. Secondly, When the sum whereupon it is deduced, is not due as when the half thereof was paid, Hope, Apprising, Blackburn *contra* Lamb [Hope, *Maj. Pr.* 11,15,8; M. 94], and Lamb *contra* Hepburn of Smeatoun [Hope, *Maj. Pr.* VI,28,49; M. 95]. Or being deduced for a term's rent, which was not due till after the apprising, albeit it was an assignee who apprised, seeing it was to the behoof of the cedent, it was found relevant to reduce the apprising *in totum*, June 20, 1678, Scot of Burnfoot *contra* Falconer and Edmonstoun [2 Stair 622; M. 98]; Jan. 31, 1679, Irving *contra* L. Drum [2 Stair 684; M. 98], where a term not due being apprised for, the apprising was retrenched to the principal sums and annualrents, without accumulation of annualrents, penalties or sheriff-fees. Yet an apprising for two sums, for one of which sums the decreet was loosed and turned into a libel, before the apprising was deduced; yet the apprising was sustained as a security for what terms therein were instantly verified, Nov. 23, 1677, Boid and Graham *contra* Malloch [2 Stair 565; M. 1782]. And an apprising was reduced, because one of the sums apprised for, was registrate *à non suo judice*, July 20, 1678, Moris *contra* Orrock of Balram [2 Stair 637; M. 7426]. In which case the Lords would have sustained the apprising as a security for the true sums resting, if the appriser would have past from the termly failzie. An apprising was not found null, though the inquest was only thirteen, albeit the custom hath been long of fifteen, nor because the seals did not appear, after twenty years, Dec. 3, 1690, Bennet *contra* Mackie [Not found]; the reason hereof was, because the Act introducing apprisings bears the inquest to be of

thirteen persons, Parl. 1469, cap. 36 [Diligence Act, 1469,c. 36; A.P.S. 11,96, c. 12]. The Lords do frequently supply defects in apprisings or adjudications, in so far as they may stand as securities of true debt, and real expense, especially when the question is betwixt the debtor and the appriser, but not in competition with more formal rights; and they are more strict against apprisings or adjudications, when they are insisted upon, as expired, or for penalties, sheriff-fees and the annualrents thereof; and therefore a posterior apprising being solemn and formal, according to the custom then in use, was preferred to a prior, not being so formal, July 15, 1670, La. Lucia Hamilton *contra* Boid of Pitcon [1 Stair 697; M. 12555]. And likewise, an apprising being led for penalties and termly failzies, was reduced as to these, because a part of the sum was not due at the date of the apprising, though it was deduced at the instance of an assignee: but if it were proved to the cedent's behoof, it was also found reducible, *quoad* the accumulation of the annualrents, and making them and the penalties principal sums. But seeing the appriser declared it redeemable, though the legal reversion was expired, it was sustained as a security of the first principal sum, and current annualrents thereof, Jan. 31, 1679, Irving *contra* L. Drum [2 Stair 684; M. 98]. And an apprising was sustained upon a bond, bearing a long term of payment, with a clause irritant, "That if two terms annualrent run together unpaid, the whole principal and annual should be payable, without abiding the first term," though there was no declarator of the irritancy, it not being penal, but taking away the favour of the creditor to the debtor, by delay of the term, June 20, 1678, Scot of Burnfoot *contra* Falconer and Edmistoun [2 Stair 622; M. 98].

32. Albeit the Lords do not ordinarily modify penalties after apprising, yet if they be exorbitant, they do modify the same, and all termly failzies, as they did in the said case of Orrock of Balram and Irving [2 Stair 637; M. 7426; IV, 3, 2, *infra*].

33. Apprising was sustained upon a sum payable without requisition, albeit there was no charge preceding the apprising, July 21, 1666, Thomson *contra* McItrick [1 Stair 400; M. 6893]. The like, though the bond bore annualrent before 1641, seeing there was no infeftment thereupon, or requisition therein, Jan. 14, 1679, Farquhar of Finian *contra* Stuart [*Sub nom. Farquharson* v *Stuart*, 2 Stair 669; M. 8118; III, 2, 15, *supra*].

34. And an apprising was sustained, though the lands apprised were not filled up in the letters of apprising, or special charge, nor in the executions, because the messenger who executed, was judge in the apprising, which relating the denunciation of the lands particularly, and charging the apparent heir to enter thereto in special, was found a more solemn execution than any execution apart, Jan. 16, 1680, Brown *contra* Nicol [2 Stair 739; M. 170]: for decreets of apprising, as they became to be by messengers, who apprised all which was claimed, and could admit no exception, was a mere executive sentence, as a poinding of moveables is.

35. An apprising was sustained without producing the letters of app-

rising, it being *in anno* 1636; but the instructions of the debt were found necessary to be produced, being within prescription, Feb. 11, 1681, Kenway *contra* Crafurd [2 Stair 858; M.5170]. Yea, an apprising was sustained upon a bond, payable upon requisition, though the apprising made no mention of the requisition, the instrument of requisition being produced.

36. And though the dispensation to apprise was neither at Edinburgh, nor at the head burgh of the shire, but a place upon the open fields, and upon account of a great rain, the messenger did not apprise that day, but adjourned the court of apprising till the next day, the apprising was sustained, July 12, 1671, Heirs of Lundie *contra* E. Southesk [1 Stair 752; M.71].

37. And an apprising of the ground-right of lands, and all right belonging to the debtor, the superior being charged thereupon, was preferred to a posterior appriser, who apprised particularly an annualrent out of the lands, which was the only right of the common debtor, November 21, 1673, Fairholm *contra* Rentoun and the Countess of Levin [2 Stair 230; M.182].

38. Apprisings are elided by payment, without necessity of renunciation, resignation, or reduction, as in the case of other infeftments, July 25, 1626, Lo. Lovat *contra* Frazer [*Sub nom. L. Lovit* v *Philorth*, Durie 226; M.296; II,10,1; II,11,6,*supra*]: the reason is, because apprising being but a legal diligence for security of the sum, which ceasing, it falleth without other solemnities; and the debtor's own infeftment stands valid, without renovation; which, with the infeftment upon the apprising, stood but as a parallel right for security, so that all returned *ad pristinum statum ;* and amongst the rest, the casualities of the superiority, if they were taken off by the apprising; and therefore an heir not entering, but being charged, if he satisfy and redeem the apprising, he will be in non-entry till he be received and infeft as heir.

39. Apprisings are excluded and qualified with the back-bonds and obligements of the appriser, as in personal rights, which are valid against singular successors; as a back-bond, that an apprising should not be prejudicial to another party's right, was found relevant against the appriser's singular successor, the King's donatar of the appriser's forfeiture, July 31, 1666, the E. Southesk *contra* Marquess of Huntly [1 Stair 402; M.10203; III,1,21, *supra*].

The last and most ordinary extinction of apprising is by intromission with the mails and duties of the apprised land, over and above the annualrent, for these are imputed in the principal sum, by the statute, Parl. 1621, cap. 6 [Diligence Act, 1621,c.6; A.P.S. IV,609,c.6] which is also extended to minors having the privilege after the ordinary legal of seven years: but it was not provided for in the said statute, that the appriser should be comptable for his intromission thereafter which is therefore provided for, Parl. 1641, cap. 67 [A.P.S. V,517,c.110], which, though it was neglected, and not revived, Parl. 1661, yet the Lords sustained the same, as now in custom twenty years and more, February 18, 1663, Ross *contra* McKenzie [1 Stair 182; M.298]. But the tenor of the said first statute being, that the quantities of the mails and duties shall extend to as much as will satisfy the whole principal sum, and annualrents thereof, composition to the superior, and annualrent thereof and expenses, in deducing the apprising, in that case the apprising is declared to expire, *ipso facto;* so that if any part thereof remain, and the debtor be so negligent as not to use an order, and count and reckoning within the legal, but suffer it to expire, the apprising will stand valid, and carry the right of the whole lands, and will not be extinct in so far as satisfied proportionally, Hope, Confirmation, Doctor Kincaid *contra* Haliburton [Hope, *Maj. Pr.* VI, 28, 64; M. 13447], which was so found, where a part of the sum was satisfied by payment, November 28, 1623, Craig *contra* Wilson [Durie 84; M. 293]. But if the remainder be very small, the Lords may be the more strict in modifying prices, and if that be not sufficient, a small remainder will not take away the right, *de minimis non curat prætor.* Intromission is not only extended to the rents and profits of the apprised lands, but to the price of any part thereof, sold by the appriser within the legal, January 14, 1669, M'Kenzie *contra* Ross [1 Stair 580; M. 299, 6792]. And an apprising was also found extinct, by the intromission of him to whom the appriser granted back-bond, declaring the apprising to be to his behoof, and that against a singular successor, who thereafter was infeft upon the appriser's resignation, July 12, 1670, Kennedy *contra* Cunningham and Wallace [1 Stair 692; M. 10205]. Yea, an apprising was found excluded, as being satisfied by the debtor, and retired by him, with a blank assignation thereto, lying by him at his death, though his son thereafter filled up his name therein, which was instructed by the son's oath and witnesses *ex officio*, February 27, 1666, Creditors of the Lo. Gray *contra* the Lo. Gray [1 Stair 369; M. 12311]. But an apprising was not found extinct by intromission, where the appriser paid to his debtor the superplus of the rent, above his annualrent, before the leading of any other apprising. Yet where an order of redemption was used before the expiring of the legal, the apprising was found extinct by intromission, after the course of the legal, July 7, 1676, Edgar *contra* Miln [2 Stair 441; M. 285]. The like was found in respect of an order used by a second appriser, and was sustained, though the first appriser had acquired right to an order of redemption by a third appriser, used against the second appriser, which was not found to hinder the second appriser to declare the first apprising satisfied by intromission during the legal, but prejudice to the third appriser, or to the first appriser, having right from the third appriser to redeem the lands from the second appriser, by satisfaction of the sums due to him, July 18, 1676, Gordon of Seaton *contra* Watson [2 Stair 451; M. 318]. Yea, an apprising being both against the principal and cautioner's estates, an order of redemption used by the principal debtor was found to keep the apprising unexpired, not only as to his own estate, but as to the cautioner's estate, February 10, 1675, La. Torwood-head *contra* Gardner [2 Stair 320; M. 284].

But the appriser hath it in his option, whether he will enter in possession of the mails and duties, or will uplift more thereof than his annualrent; yet if a

posterior appriser insist for possession, the first must either possess, do diligence, and be comptable, or suffer him to possess, February 11, 1636, Colquhoun *contra* L. Balvie [Durie 794; M. 3472]. But if the appriser possess, he
must do diligence for the rent of that land he possessed, and be comptable,
not only for what he intromitted with, but for what he might have intromitted
with; and if the lands were tenant-stead at his entry, he must compt accordingly at that rate, though thereafter given over and waste, if he neither set nor
laboured them himself, nor made intimation to the debtor so to do, February
9, 1639, Brownhill *contra* Cawder [*Sub nom. Hamilton* v *Lawder*, Durie 874;
M. 3391]. The like was found, that the appriser was comptable according to
the rental, allowing all reasonable defalcations, January 4, 1662, Seaton *contra*
Roswall [1 Stair 74; M. 297]. But where the appriser entered in possession of
the lands waste, he was not found comptable, according as he set them thereafter, for the first year of his proper labourage, seeing by the season without
his fault, he lost thereby, December 23, 1629, Dickson *contra* Young [Durie
478; M. 3471]. An appriser was found comptable for the rental of all the tenants of a small tenement, lying contigue, having taken decreet against all the
tenants, and yet refusing to count for some particular rooms, without showing
any hinderance to uplift from these, which, other apprisers calling to accompt,
could not know that he had forborn these, but nothing was determined as to
the common debtor's own labourage, January 14, 1681, Schaw of Grimmat
contra Muir [2 Stair 833; M. 301]. Yet where the appriser was disturbed in
his possession by the debtor, *via facti*, or *via juris*, he was not found comptable by a rental, but what he recovered, till he attained to peaceable possession, January 20, 1681, Burnet *contra* Burnet of Barns [2 Stair 838; M.
3478].

40. The Act of Parl. 1661, cap. 62 [Bonds Act, 1661, c. 32; A.P.S. VII,
230, c. 244], hath lengthened the legal of apprisings, and hath brought in all
who apprise within a year of the first effectual apprising *pari passu*. By this
Act these alterations are introduced as to apprisings: First, Whereas before
the first appriser being infeft, or doing diligence, had only access to the whole
apprised lands till he was satisfied; now the Lords are impowered to limit the
possession during the legal, as they shall see cause, the appriser getting his
annualrent, or security therefor; but the power granted to the Lords to restrict
apprisers, is only personal and peculiar to the debtor, and not to the posterior
apprisers, July 28, 1671, Murray *contra* L. Southesk and others [1 Stair 769;
M. 3477]. Secondly, all apprisings led since the first of January 1652, before
the first effectual comprising, obtaining infeftment or charging the superior
to receive, or within a year after the same, or to be led thereafter upon any
personal debt, within year and day of the first effectual comprising, come in
pari passu, as if they all had been contained in one comprising, the other apprisers paying to the first effectual compriser the expenses of his comprising,
and infeftment thereupon. But the year is not to be counted from the infeftment or charge, by which the apprising becomes effectual, but from the date

of the decreet of apprising, July 4, 1671, L. Balfour *contra* Dowglas [1 Stair 747; M.238]; and accordingly it was decided by the Lords, that those other apprisers behoved to pay the whole composition to the superior, Feb. 5, 1663, Grahame *contra* Ross [1 Stair 171; M.245]. Yet these apprisings that were prior to the act, were not found to come in *pari passu*, from the dates of the apprisings, albeit the Act bear, that they should come in as if they were in one apprising, but only from the date of the Act of Parliament; and as to what the first appriser had possessed *bona fide*, before the Act, if his intromission exceeded his annualrent, the same should be imputed to the expenses of the comprisings and composition, and in payment of the sums apprised for *pro tanto*, January 7, 1665, L. Blaitwood *contra* Browns [*Sub nom. Graham of Blackwood* v *Browns*, 1 Stair 246; M.262]. But in the said Act 1661 [Bonds Act, 1661, c.32; A.P.S. VII,230,c.244], apprisings on annualrent-infeftments, or other *debita fundi*, continue as before that Act.

Yet an apprising led before January 1652, though infeftment or charge were used thereon after January 1652, was found to exclude all apprisers after January 1652, whose infeftment or charge were posterior to the infeftment or charge upon the apprising led before January 1652, and that the said posterior apprising did not come in *pari passu* with that led before January 1652, though within a year of it; because the Act of Parliament relates nothing to apprisings deduced before January 1652, December 12, 1666, Home *contra* Creditors of Kello [1 Stair 411; M.236]. And albeit the first effectual apprising was satisfied, and so extinct; yet it doth stand valid as to the second apprising, within year and day; but a third apprising was not found thereby to come in *pari passu* with the second apprising, as being within year and day thereof, as if the second appriser became the first appriser, December 13, 1672, Street *contra* E. Northesk and Deans [2 Stair 133; M.248]; February 20, 1679, Tenants of Mortoun *contra* E. Queensberry [2 Stair 700; M.264]. And where the first appriser possessed but a part of the lands apprised, the second appriser not infeft, was preferred to the third appriser infeft, as to the remanent rents, because the second appriser needed no infeftment, but the infeftment upon the first apprising was sufficient for all the apprisings led within the year of the first, December 22, 1664, Ramsay and Hay *contra* Seatoun [1 Stair 244; M. 235]. There is also an exception from this clause, by another Act, Parl. 1661, cap. 21. Ses. 3 [Comprisings Act, 1663, c.22; A.P.S. VII,476,c.36], that second apprisers shall not be prejudged if they did acquire right to a former apprising, redeemed and satisfied by them, for their own security, before the said Act, albeit led since January 1652, which first comprising shall remain in the same case as apprisings were formerly; it was so decided, without necessity to allege that right was taken to the first apprising, to shun the expiring of the legal, or any other necessary cause, December 9, 1664, Veatch *contra* Williamson [1 Stair 237; M.11148; III,2,29,*supra*]. Thirdly, the extent of the legal is altered from seven years to ten years; so that where the legal was not expired the time of the Act, three years were allowed to redeem them from

Whitsunday 1661, which terminated at Whitsunday 1664; whereanent it being questioned, whether intromission during these three years should satisfy apprisings, which being deduced since January 1652, were expired according to the law then standing, and disponed to others, there being no mention of that point in the said Act, the Lords decided *affirmativè*, January 20, 1666, Clappertoun *contra* L. Torsonce [1 Stair 341; M. 298].

41. Fourthly, the benefit of redemption is competent to creditors against the apparent heirs of their debtors, acquiring right to expired comprisings, which was extended to apparent heirs, even during his father's life; seeing apparent heirs are generally expressed, and the design of the Act is alike whether the acquisition be before or after the debtor's death; but there is nothing provided in case a debtor acquire the apprised lands, after the legal is expired, and the debtor is infeft and in possession, and so is full proprietor; for though the reason and design of the law should rather be extended against the debtor than against his heir, yet there are no words capable of that addition; but it were necessary that it were added by Act of Parliament, June 19, 1668, Burnet *contra* Nasmith [1 Stair 540; M. 5302], or any person to their behoof, acquiring right to apprisings within ten years after the acquirer's right, for such sums only as they paid for acquiring thereof, and they were found extinct by the apparent heir's intromission by exception, which was so far extended, that it reached an apprising assigned to an apparent heir, though the assignation was before this statute, seeing the infeftment which made the apparent heir's right real and effectual, was after; and though the apprising was redeemable when acquired, but expired in the person of the apparent heir, July 21, 1671, Maxwell *contra* Maxwell [1 Stair 763; M. 5306]. This hath no ground from the statute; but the apparent heir getting right to the apprising *gratis*, it was not found to accresce to the creditors, but the Lords inclined that it should be redeemable within ten years after his right for the sum whereupon the apprising proceeded, February 13, 1673, *inter eosdem* [2 Stair 172; M. 5309]. An apprising acquired by the husband of an apparent heir, found not redeemable by what he paid, unless it were proven, that it was acquired by the wife's means, or upon her account, June 13, 1674, Richardson *contra* Palmer [2 Stair 271; M. 5312]; February 21, 1673, Richardson *contra* Lanmond and Skeen [2 Stair 178; M. 5310]; January 15, 1679, M'Dougal *contra* Guthrie and His Spouse [2 Stair 672; M. 5315]. But this ten years reversion was not found competent to the debtor himself, to redeem from his apparent heir, December 3, 1680, Nasmith *contra* Nasmith [2 Stair 811; M. 5316]. But a second brother acquiring an apprising upon easy terms, when his elder brother was out of the country, was not found redeemable by this Act, not being esteemed as apparent heir *alioqui successurus*, February 17, 1675, M'Lurg *contra* Gordoun [2 Stair 324; M. 5312].

And an apprising coming in the person of the apparent heir of the principal debtor, was found satisfiable by the sums payable therefore by the apparent heir, summarily without reduction, February 22, 1671, Dumbar *contra* Dick

[1 Stair 726; M. 5304]. The like was found by exception or reply, where the apprising was to the behoof of the debtor's eldest son, July 4, 1671, L. Balfour *contra* Dowglas [1 Stair 747; M. 238]. The like, though the apprising came in the apparent heir's person, within the legal, albeit the Act of Parliament expresseth only expired apprising coming in the person of the apparent heir, to be redeemable for what he paid, February 26, 1685, Campbel *contra* Campbel [1 Fountainhall 344; M. 5325]; this hath no warrant from the Act. Yea, it was found redeemable by any personal creditor of the defunct's, though the Act mentions only to be redeemable by posterior apprisers, December   1683, Moll *contra* Craw [1 Fountainhall 243; M. 5322]. Yet it was not found redeemable by children upon bonds of provision, granted after expiring of the legal, Nasmith *contra* Nasmith, Nov. 1681 [Pres. Falconer 1; M. 13479]. The like, where the apprising acquired by the apparent heir was found satisfied by intromission, equivalent to what was paid for the apprising; the said intromission being either within the ten years, or after the intenting a summons of declarator, offering to pay what remained after count and reckoning, it was found to prorogate the ten years reversion, without any other order, June 26, 1677, Kincaid *contra* Gordon of Abergeldie [2 Stair 531; M. 289; III, 2, 14, *supra*].

42. Apprisings deduced against apparent heirs, specially charged to enter heir, are not redeemable by the heir of the party charged to enter heir who was never infeft, but by the heir of the defunct, for whose debt the apprising was deduced, who died last vest before the apprising, February 6, 1668, January 19, 1669, Johnstoun *contra* Erskine [1 Stair 518 and 584; M. 213 and 317].

43. Minors have a special privilege as to the legal reversions of apprisings, and how far this is extended to majors succeeding to minors; *vid. Lib.* 1. *Title* 6. [1, 6, 44, *supra*] amongst the privileges of minors, and *vid.* Lib. 2, what hath been said of apprisings, *Tit.* 3. §29 and 30 [III, 2, 14, *supra*].

44. Apprising, while it is redeemable, is but a legal diligence for security; and the appriser may relinquish the same, though he be in possession, and may do any other diligence for recovering his debt; but if he continue to possess after the apprising becomes irredeemable, the debt is thereby satisfied and extinct, which was so found, albeit the apprising proved ineffectual as to a part of the lands apprised, the remnant being equivalent to the debt apprised for, correspondent to the lands that were evicted, should remain due to the appriser, June 18, 1675 L. Leys *contra* Forbes [2 Stair 330 M. 286]. The form and manner of procedure in apprisings will come in amongst legal executions, of which hereafter.

45. Adjudication upon renunciation to be heir, is *remedium extraordinarium*, introduced by custom, where apprising could have no place, when the debt to be satisfied is not a liquidate sum, or goods ordinarily liquidable, but is a disposition of lands, containing expressly or virtually, an obligation to infeft the acquirer, or some other: or an obligation consisting in some fact to be performed; or otherways, where the debtor's heir renounces to be heir,

whereby there is no party from whom the lands can be apprised; therefore *hæreditas jacens* is adjudged. This remeid is introduced by the Lords, who having ample power to administrate justice in all cases, and to make orders to that effect, do supply the defect of the law, or ancient customs, by such new remeids, as such new occurring cases do require, amongst which adjudication is a prime one, which Craig testifieth [111,2,8] to have been unknown to our predecessors, and being but recent in his time, and few decisions thereupon, the nature and effect of it was little known, but is now by course of time further illustrated. Adjudication hath place in two cases; the first and most ordinary is, when the heir renounces to be heir, in which case adjudication is competent, whether the debt to be satisfied be liquidate or not. The other is, when the obligement to be satisfied consisteth *in facto*, and relateth to a disposition of particular things; which disposition or obligement, not being fulfilled by the debtor or disponer, though all ordinary diligence be done, then adjudication taketh place to make the same effectual.

46. As to the first case, adjudication upon the apparent heir's renouncing to be heir, proceedeth upon these ways; if he be pursued as lawfully charged to enter heir, for satisfying of his predecessor's debt or obligement, he may renounce to be heir (if he have not meddled) either in the process against him, as charged to enter heir in the first instance, or some time thereafter, by suspension or reduction: if he renounce in the first instance, when the debt is not yet instructed and established, as when it proceeds not upon a clear bond or writ, but abides probation by witnesses, or otherways, then before the process of adjudication, there must be a process and sentence against the heir renouncing *cognitionis causa*, for establishing and proving the debt; in which, because there is a necessity in all processes to have a defender, the apparent heir renouncing, is only called to supply that place *cognitionis causa*, but without any effect against him, but only *contra hæreditatem jacentem*. But if the apparent heir renounce in the second instance, after decreet obtained against him; or, in the first instance, when the ground and title of the pursuit instructs the debt, then there needs no other decreet *cognitionis causa;* but the pursuer protesting for adjudication, the same will be admitted summarily [111,5,23, *infra*]. Adjudication itself is a most simple and summary process, whereby the heir renouncing, and the debt being established, as said is, the whole heritage renounced, or benefit whereto the heir might succeed, is adjudged by the Lords to the pursuer for satisfaction of the defunct's obligement, wherein the heir renouncing, is again called to sustain the part of a defender, which is only for form's sake; for he can propone nothing, and one single summons is sufficient without continuation; because it is accessory to a prior decreet, as Dury observes, but expresseth not the parties, February 26 1629 [Durie 430; M. 44]. And all is adjudged, *periculo petentis*, whatsoever the pursuer pleaseth to libel, alleging that it might have belonged to the heir entering: yea, though any party having interest, should compear and instruct that he hath the only right, and the defunct was fully denuded, it would be incompetent *hoc loco*,

Spots. Adjudication, Cairncross *contra* L. Drumlanrig [Spotiswoode 9; M. 43].

47. The reason is, because the adjudication is but *periculo petentis*, and can give no right, unless the defunct's right, competent to the heir renouncing, be instructed. Neither can the adjudger, who is a stranger to the debtor's right, be put to dispute the same, in obtaining the adjudication; yet the Lords admitted a singular successor to propone upon his infeftment, that the defunct was denuded, and adjudged not the property, but all right of reversion, or other right competent to the apparent heir, July 22, 1669, Livingstoun and L. Sornbeg *contra* Heirs of Line of the L. Forrester [*Sub anno* 1664, 1 Stair 221; M. 191]. In this case the matter was notour to many of the Lords, that the Lo. Forrester having no sons, did contract his estate with one of his daughters, to Lieutenant-general Baillie's son, who was thereupon publicly infeft. But the reason why apprisings and adjudications have past so much at random is, because apprisings have deborded from their ancient form, which was by an inquest knowing the lands, who therefore would never have apprised lands, but where the debtor was commonly reputed heritor, or heritable possessor: but when apprisings came to be deduced by sheriffs in that part, constitute by the Lords by dispensation at Edinburgh, where persons were made the inquest, who knew nothing of the lands, then all became to be apprised which was claimed; and though the appriser would not pay a year's rent for entering him in lands, where he had no probability of right in his debtor: the greatest inconvenience was as to the lands holden of the King, it was little addition of expenses, to pass one infeftment for all; and other superiors getting a year's rent, *salvo jure*, they were not suffered to controvert.

But now adjudications being in place of apprisings, and passing upon citation before the Lords, it is not like they will adjudge lands where the debtors are not, at least, reputed heritable possessors or liferenters; for now the Lords are in place of the inquest: and albeit as they suffer decreets in absence, to pass *periculo petentis;* so they will suffer adjudication to pass of all that is libelled; but if any other shall appear, and make it appear that they and their predecessors have been holden and reputed heritable possessors, and that there was no right reputed to be in the debtor, the Lords might readily supersede to adjudge, in the first adjudication, if there be any compearance, till some evidence be given of the interest of the debtor, seasins having been now registrated, since the year 1617: And likeways reversions, though adjudications of these might more easily pass, because no infeftment would follow: but where lands are adjudged, and infeftments follow, there arises thence grounds of pleas and pursuits, especially for reduction and improbation, upon which all the heritors of the lands contained in the infeftments, would be obliged to produce their rights, and open their charter chests, to parties having no pretence to their estates. Yet adjudication was sustained of all lands generally, without condescending, Dec. 19, 1638, Corser *contra* Dury [Durie 867; M. 44]; which is the last way, when none appear to object against putting their lands in the adjudication.

48. In these adjudications all is competent to be adjudged, which should have befallen the heir entering, as lands, annualrents, reversions, tacks, liferents, and all heritable bonds; yea, not only these rights themselves, but the bygone rents and duties thereof, preceding the adjudication, and after the defunct's death, may be adjudged and pursued against the possessors and intromitters in that same process, because these are competent to the heir renouncing, and there is no other way to attain them, as was found in the said case, Corser *contra* Dury [Durie 867; M. 44], Dec. 19, 1638; and likewise heirship-moveables, for the same reason are competent in adjudications, but not against other moveables of the defunct, which must be confirmed, Spots. Caption, Hagie *contra* Her Daughters [Spotiswoode 8; M. 135]; Nov. 24, 1638, Campbel *contra* Baxter [Durie 862; M. 139]; and so it was not competent against an heritable bond, made moveable by a charge, Jan. 30, 1627, Couper *contra* Williamson and L. Bogmiln [Durie 264; M. 135]: yet if an heritable sum should become moveable after the defunct's death, as by an order of redemption, it would be competent by adjudication, seeing it could be reached no other way. In this adjudication it is only competent to creditors to appear, having like process of adjudication depending, for all will be brought in *pari passu*, who are ready before sentence, with the first pursuer, Hope, Adjudication, Stuart *contra* Stuart [Spotiswoode 10; M. 9862].

49. If the adjudication be of lands or annualrents requiring infeftment, the superior will be compelled to receive the adjudger, though a stranger, his vassal, though he do not instruct his author's right, *salvo jure cujuslibet et suo*, Feb. 9, 1667, Ramsay *contra* Ker [1 Stair 440; M. 203; III, 2, 25 and 47, *supra*]. But as to the year's duty, payable by the adjudger to the superior for their entry, though the Lords thought it equitable, that it should take place, as well in adjudications as apprisings, the reason being alike in both, yet found not sufficient ground, whereupon to decern it, seeing the said year's rent is expressed in the act of Parl. 1469, cap. 36 [Diligence Act, 1469, c. 36; A.P.S. II, 96, c. 12]; and the composition of the superior, for receiving apprisers, Parl. 1621, cap. 6 [Diligence Act, 1621, c. 6; A.P.S. IV, 609, c. 6]. Yet in the next Act of the same Parliament, anent adjudications [Adjudication Act, 1621, c. 7; A.P.S. IV, 611, c. 7], there is no mention of composition to the superior, though the Act relateth to the former Act, anent apprisings; and therefore they thought it not competent to them to extend the said composition, *ad pares casus*, where it did so much appear, that the Parliament of purpose had omitted it; yet in the said case, Grierson *contra* Closburn upon the 21st of July 1636 [Durie 819; M. Supp. 85], they did forbear to intimate their decision, and desired the parties to agree [11, 4, 32, *supra*]. And no composition was found due by an adjudger, having charged before the late Act of Parliament, Dec. 23, 1669 [1669, c. 18; A.P.S. VII, 576, c. 39], whereby, like compositions are appointed for adjudication, as for apprising, June 10, 1671, Scot *contra* L. Drumlanrig [1 Stair 731; M. 15071]. In which case it was found that the superior might refuse to enter the adjudger, if he paid his debt; but

that he was to have nothing for composition if he did so, in the same way as in apprising, by the old Act of Parl. 1469, cap. 36 [Diligence Act; 1469, c. 36; A.P.S. 11, 96, c. 12], by which that option is given to the superior.

50. Craig observeth [111, 2, 21], that it was doubtful in his time, whether there was a legal reversion competent to any renouncing, and afterward returning to redeem adjudications as apprisings, wherein he favoureth the affirmative; but the said statute, Parl. 1621, cap. 7 [Adjudication Act, 1621, c. 7; A.P.S. IV, 611, c. 7] determineth the case, and granteth a legal reversion, in favour of those who have posterior adjudications, within the space of seven years, or ten years since the Act of Parl. 1661, betwixt Debtor and Creditor [Diligence Act, 1661, c. 62; A.P.S. VII, 317, c. 344], which is also competent to any renouncing in their minority, and being restored against the said renunciation, but it is not competent to any other heir renouncing; yet if the heir, though major, find that he hath prejudged himself, by renouncing a profitable heritage, he may grant a bond, and thereupon cause within the legal, adjudge and redeem the former adjudications, which, though to his own behoof, will be effectual, there being so much equity and favour upon his part, being willing to satisfy the whole debts.

51. It is clear by the said statute, the lands or heritage of a defunct may be adjudged, the heir renouncing, not only for satisfaction of the defunct's debt, but of the heir's own proper debt [11, 12, 29, *supra*]

52. Adjudications are taken off and extinguished in the same manner as apprisings are, by intromitting with the mails and duties of the lands adjudged, as is clear from the said statute. And though cases be not so frequent in adjudications, as in apprisings, to clear the other ways of their extinction; yet the reason being the same in both, there is no doubt but the determination will also be the same.

53. The other manner of adjudications, is for making dispositions or obligements to infeft effectual, whereupon when the acquirer hath used all diligence competent in law, against the disponer to fulfil the same, by obtaining decreets and horning registered thereupon, either against the disponer or his heir, law being there defective, and cannot make the disposition or obligement effectual, the Lords have allowed adjudication of the lands disponed, whether in fee or liferent, Had. July 19, 1611, Lo. Johnstoun *contra* Lo. Carmichael [Not found]; Spots. *hic*, [blank] *contra* Bruce of Airth [Not found]; and thereupon the superior will be decerned to receive the adjudger, as was found in the case of an obligement to infeft a woman in liferent, holden of the superior, wherein she having used horning, the superior was decerned to receive her, July 10, 1628, Harris and Cunningham *contra* Lindsay [Durie 385; M. 13273]; Feb. 24, 1675, Hamilton *contra* Chiesly [2 Stair 327; M. 53]. This manner of adjudication is extended no further than to the thing disponed, and hath no reversion, unless there be a conventional reversion in the bond or disposition to infeft; but this kind of adjudication comes not in with others of that, or any other kind: and there is more reason that the superior should have

a year's rent, if the disposition be of the fee, and irredeemable, than in other adjudications; but these adjudications do not become effectual by a charge, yet as a legal diligence it will exclude posterior voluntary rights: if the adjudication be for infefting a liferenter, no composition is due to the superior: it requires no charge to enter heir, or renunciation; but the adjudger must instruct his author's right, June 24, 1669, M'Dowgal *contra* L. Glenurchie [*Sub anno* 1663, 1 Stair 193; M. 51]. And these adjudications do not come in *pari passu*, with other adjudications within the year, nor any other with them, July 16, 1675, Campbel of Riddoch *contra* Stuart of Ardvorlick [2 Stair 350; M. 54]; Dec. 2, 1677, La. Fraser *contra* Creditors of the Lo. Frazer and La. Marr [2 Stair 577; M. 233].

54. By the late Act of Parliament, anent adjudications, September 6, 1672 [Adjudications Act, 1672, c. 19; A.P.S. VIII, 93, c. 45], there are introduced two new forms of adjudications; the one special of lands effeiring to the sum, and a fifth part more, in case the debtor produce his rights, and put the adjudger in possession of his particular lands adjudged: but if he do not, adjudications are to proceed, as apprisings did, generally, of all the debtor's lands, or real rights, *periculo petentis*, redeemable within ten years: these adjudications are come in place of apprisings, especially the general adjudications, which are declared to be in the same condition in all points as apprisings were by the Act of Parl. 1661, cap. 62 [Diligence Act, 1661, c. 62; A.P.S. VII, 317, c. 344], except as to the lengthening of a reversion from seven to ten years: so that what hath been said of apprisings, will have the same effect as to general adjudications; but special adjudications being equitable and favourable, will not meet with such strictness: this statute hath taken away the greatest reproach upon our law, which, for every debt, indefinitely apprised, every estate great or small, which had no excuse, but that the debtor might redeem within seven years: but all creditors being necessitated to apprise within a year, or to have no more than the legal reversion, paying the whole debts, the power of redemption came to be of little effect, few being able to pay all their debt in one day: but now if any debtor complain that his whole estate is adjudged, and no proportion kept betwixt the debt and his estate, it is altogether his own fault, seeing he might offer a proportional part, and liberate all the rest of his estate; which part is redeemable also in five years: and though a fifth part be added, it is no more than the ordinary penalty, being an 100 pounds for a 1000 merks, and 50 merks for the sheriff-fee, makes 200 merks, being the fifth part of a 1000 merks, and which was sustained in the most favourable cases of apprisings from the beginning, when the reversion was for seven years. After this Act 1672, there is no use for adjudications on the renunciation of apparent heirs, because there needs nor more for adjudication, but the liquidation of the debt, which is but declaratory, unless the creditor insist *petitoriè* against the apparent heir to pay, and if the heir in that case offer to renounce, the adjudication thereon will come in *pari passu*, as in other adjudications.

Adjudications being executive decreets, the Lords allow them the greatest dispatch; and to prevent collusion, whereby some debtors might be postponed by debate and probation till the year pass, which would exclude them; therefore the Lords do not suffer co-creditors to stop adjudications, that they may see for their interest, and put the pursuer to abide the course of the roll, unless they produce an interest, upon which the Ordinary will hear them immediately without going to the roll, January 22, 1681, E. Dundonald *contra* Dunlop and His Creditors [2 Stair 840; M. 12192]. Neither is the superior suffered to propone defences, Jan. 13, 1675, Kinloch of Gourdie *contra* Blair and Strachan [2 Stair 372; M. 193]. Yea, the Lords sustained the establishment of the debt in the same libel with the adjudication, July 26, 1676, Boyd *contra* Boyd of Pinkell [2 Stair 459; M. 188]. But if the debtor himself appear, the cause goes to the roll; and if there be prior adjudications instructed, defences proponed against the debt, or adjudication, which are not verified, the Lords adjudge and reserve these defences *contra executionem*, by suspension; in which suspension terms will be granted, because of the reservation; but there is this advantage, that how long soever the suspension be of expeding, the first decreet being within the year, brings the adjudger in *pari passu*. One adjudication being past, all others are called summarily by the Ordinary amongst the acts, after they are seen and returned, that they may pass within year and day: yea, the Lords give summary process in processes *cognitionis causa*, that adjudications may come within year and day, reserving all objections *contra executionem*. There is a clause in the Act for adjudications, that the citation shall have the same effect as the denunciation of lands to be apprised had, whereupon, in a competition between an adjudication and a voluntary infeftment, which was first completed by infeftment, the adjudger alleged, that though he was not infeft, he was preferable, because, after denunciation of lands to be apprised, voluntary rights used to be excluded, and so must citations in adjudications and [This probably should be "exclude"] voluntary rights; the Lords preferred the voluntary right; and found, that either in the case of denunciation in apprisings, or citation in adjudications, the effect is only that the common debtor may not grant voluntary rights *in cursu diligentiæ*, January   1682, Creditors of Enoch *contra*   [Pres. Falconer, 10; M. 8376]. But after the decreet of adjudication, and so much time as infeftment may be obtained, or the superior may be charged, the adjudication hath no such preference, February 18, 1692, Kilpatrick of Closburn *contra* Hunter [Not found]. In special adjudications, a fifth part adjudged for, is added in place of penalties, which are very unequal in bonds, and in place of sheriff-fees, which will hold though the right adjudged be a liquid sum, January

     1683, Man *contra* Ruthven [Possibly *Ker* v *Ruthven*, Pres. Falconer 22; M. 78]. Adjudication was sustained not only for liquid sums then due, but for other prestations, as for an obligement to employ a sum upon annualrent, Nov. 1681, Haliday *contra* Creditors of Bruce of Kenneth [Pres. Falconer 2; M. 2449].

     55. There is yet another kind of adjudication introduced by the 17th

Act, Parl. 3, Cha. 2. [Judicial Sale Act, 1681, c. 17; A.P.S. VIII, 351, c. 83], and by the 20th Act, Parl. 1 Sess. 2. K. Will. & Q. Mary [Judicial Sale Act, 1690, c. 20; A.P.S. IX, 195, c. 49], by the first of which Acts, "The sale of bankrupts' lands were to be by persons commissionated by the Lords, by a public roup, not being under the rate determined by the Lords, upon probation of the worth of the several lands, and after publication at the market-crosses of the head-burghs of the shire, stewartry, or regality, where the lands lie, and at the parish-kirks where they lie, and at six adjacent parish-kirks to be named by the Lords, at dissolving of the congregations, on Sunday after forenoon sermon, by letters of intimation under the signet, upon the Lords' deliverance specially expressing the time and place of the roup, and the creditors having real rights, and in possession, being specially cited upon twenty-one days, and all others having interest at the market-crosses of the head burghs where the lands lie; and these out of the kingdom, at the market-cross of Edinburgh, pier and shore of Leith, upon sixty days, expressing the lands to be rouped, and the price appointed by the Lords, and the time and place of the roup." But if there was a reversion running, the process could not proceed without consent of the reverser: but by the second Act it is declared, "That the buyers of bankrupts' estates, shall have a right thereto by the decreet of sale to be pronounced by the Lords, adjudging the lands sold to the buyer for the price decerned; and that the buyer shall thereupon be infeft, in the same way as upon other adjudications, and that the sale may proceed so soon as it shall be found that the debtor is bankrupt, and utterly insolvent, whether the legal be expired or not: and that if no buyer be found at the rate determined by the Lords, it shall be leisom for them to divide the lands, and other rights, among the creditors, according to their several rights and diligences; and because the sale may be obstructed by donatars of liferent-escheat, the Lords are empowered to determine the price and value of the liferent-escheats, and to sell lands for the price thereof, according as the said rights shall be found to have preference."

The order of procedure is continued as in the former Act, but with these material differences, that the sale is not by commissioners, but by a decreet of adjudication, and is competent, though there be legal reversions running without the reverser's consent; and there is added that necessary clause, that if buyers be not found, the lands shall be divided to the creditors, according to their rights and diligences, whereby apprisers and adjudgers, which come in *pari passu*, are to have shares of the price proportional to their sums; but in case there be a division, they have their choice of the lands effeiring to their share; but the Lords will not allow fractions, but whole rooms to be chosen, the excresce, to make up the price, being paid out, to be divided proportionally; and the choice to be made by the apprisers and adjudgers, according to the date of their apprisings or adjudications; but if there be more persons who have right to the same apprising or adjudication, they must have preference of their choice by lot, and none may choose in the middle of contiguous lands, but at a side.

There must be two parts of this process, first to prove the rental, and the rate of the several lands; in which rate are to be considered the benefit or convenience thereof, by houses, orchards, parks, coals, or other quarries, woods, fishings, servitudes upon other lands, &c. and likewise the burdens affecting the same, as servitudes to other lands, and likewise the manner of holding and warrandice: and for that effect the debtors must produce their rights, and must depone upon the having of any discharges, or grounds of compensation of the debts. Consideration also must be had of the tacks, or rentals of the teinds, and of infeftments of annualrents, and likewise of grassums, and what the land might pay of ordinary rent without grassums, which probation must be of every several roum, that in case of division, the price thereof may be known. The probation must also be of any casuality of superiority presently affecting the lands as non-entry, by general or special declarator, ward and marriage, and likewise the years of the person whose liferent-escheat affects the lands, and which must be estimated according to their age.

There is an Act of Sederunt February,　　　1692 [A.S. 24 February, 1692], declaring, that the like dispatch will be granted in these adjudications, as to others, without going to the roll, unless the debtor appear, and allege that he is solvent; but if he hath not sold his lands during the process, and paid his debt, it is not a sufficient defence, that his estate is better than his debt; for albeit the Act bear, that he is utterly insolvent, that is not the meaning, but that his estate is so incumbered, that none would buy unless he had sold the whole together, at least after the citation; for in the next part of the process, where the creditors are to be cited, it will appear whether he will be insolvent, for they must be cited to produce the instructions of their debts, and to depone what is truly due and resting of them; but if there be no common fame, or other evidence of the debtor's being broken, the process of the sale will not be sustained against him, as was found in the process of sale at the instance of Wallace of Inglistoun *contra* Lo. Forrester, February,　　　1692 [Probably 1 Fountainhall 556].

If the debtor before the roup can satisfy his creditors, by the sale of his estate, there will be no farther progress. Likeas, there needs no continuation of this adjudication more than others, but one citation serveth for the rental and rate, which being determined, there is warrant to be granted for a second citation against the debtor, and the creditors to appear at the day and place appointed for the roup, and to produce their rights to the lands, and the instructions of the debts, and to depone on both as aforesaid; which process must contain a clause for ranking the several creditors, for which there must be an auditor named, who must hear, determine, or report all alledgeances occurring; and if there be buyers for the whole estate, there is no necessity to proceed in the ranking of the creditors, if the price can satisfy them all; otherwise they must be ranked in the same process, and by the same auditor; *vid. Lib.* 2, Tit. 3, §85 [IV, 35, *infra*]. If there be no complete sale, the auditor must proceed to the division of the lands amongst the creditors in manner foresaid.

Title 3. Confiscation, Where, of Single Escheat, Liferent-escheat, Shipwreck, Waith-goods, Treasure, Forfeiture, Bastardy, and Last Heir

THE conveyance and transmission of all kinds of rights from private parties to the fisk, are here comprehended under one common term and title of confiscation. It is not proper in this place to treat of the fisk, or the privileges thereof, or upon the several causes upon which confiscation followeth, these being public rights; but we shall only consider the several kinds of rights, or things that befal to the fisk from private parties, and how they return to private parties again, by gifts and processes thereupon; and this is either in reference to moveables, liferents, or the property and stock of heritable rights and others. Moveables fall to the fisk either wholly and entire, and that is chiefly by denunciation and rebellion, or by some special statute, the penalty whereof is confiscation of moveables; such are breach of arrestment, or deforcement, wherein though the private party injured have an interest, yet in effect the whole is confiscated, and a part belongs to that party, by virtue of the statute thereanent, whereby they are constituted donatars: or otherwise some particular moveables befalleth to the fisk, either by custom or waith-goods, shipwreck, &c. or by statute. Liferents befal to the fisk by the denunciation of the owner, and his remaining un-relaxed year and day, or by such statutes whose penalty is the loss of the liferent.

The stock or property of heritable rights fall to the fisk by forfeiture, or becoming caduciary; the confiscation of the whole moveables is called the single escheat; and of the liferent, is called the liferent escheat. We shall only speak of the single escheat of moveables by denunciation; having spoken of breach of arrestment and deforcement, Tit. Reparation [1, 9, *supra*]: Secondly, Of liferent escheat: Thirdly, Of escheat of particular goods, as shipwreck, &c.: Fourthly, Of forfeiture: And, Lastly, Of things caduciary, especially by bastardy, and last heir, and of gifts and processes thereupon. Escheat being a common term, signifying any confiscation, yet it is restricted to moveables and liferents, and most properly to moveables, so that when it is simply expressed, it is ordinarily taken for single escheat, or escheat of moveables, which become confiscated to the King, upon not obeying a charge of horning, to pay or perform some obligation, whereupon the party is publicly denounced rebel, though there be no crime, but ordinarily an inability to perform; yet escheat falls also upon denunciation for a criminal cause, as when parties are declared fugitive by the Council or criminal court, and are thereupon denounced rebels.

1. Horning proceedeth thus, by letters executorial, giving warrant to messengers at arms, to charge any party in the King's name to obey what is contained in the letters, under the pain of rebellion; and if he obey not within the days of the charge, giving power to denounce him rebel by public proclamation at the market cross of the head burgh of the shire, stewartry, bailiary of royalty or regality, within the which the denounced dwells; and that by public reading of the letters of horning, and giving three blasts of a horn, for the clear manifestation and notice thereof, from whence it is called horning: and because of the certification the party denounced is called rebel, a term too harsh, such persons not being in hostility against the King, nor being public enemies, but only denounced upon causes civil, which they lie under frequently not through contempt, but inability to satisfy, as said is. The English do more properly call this execution Outlawry, whereby the party becomes outlaw, and hath not a person to stand in judgment activè or passivè: and if such should be called by us the denounced, it were smoother and more suitable than the odious term of rebel.

2. Seeing horning is the ground of single escheat and liferent escheat, it

will be fit to go through the several requisites thereof in order, and the nullities arising thereupon. First, The letters of horning must be signeted; and therefore, though the bill was past, and the matter small, and the parties indigent, a horning not signeted was found null, Had. June 1, 1610, M'Gill *contra*   [Not found]. Secondly, The executions, or indorsations thereof, must bear, that the party was charged personally, or at his dwelling house, designing the house; and therefore a horning was found null by exception, for not designing thereof, though the party was designed to be burgess of such a burgh, which might have presumed his dwelling-place to be there, July 14, 1626, Adam *contra* Bailies of Ayr [Durie 217; M. 3748]; yet a horning was sustained, though not designing the dwelling house *nominatim*, but by description of it; thus the messenger's execution did bear, that he charged the party, designed by such lands, at his dwelling house, it being proved, that he then dwelt there, Nov. 9, 1632, Montgomery *contra* L. Fergushill [Durie 651; M. 3749].

3. If the charge be in absence, at the party's dwelling-house, the execution must bear the messenger to have craved entry to give the charge to the party or his wife and family, and not getting entry, six knocks to have been given by the messenger at the most patent gate or door thereof; yet this being wanting in the extract, the same was sustained, it being proven by the keeper of the register, and his servant, that when the horning was offered to the register, these words were in it, and by the messenger and witnesses insert in the execution, that the knocks were used, the intent of the cause being alimentary and favourable, March 28, 1637, Scot *contra* Scot [Durie 343; M. 12265]. But this is not to be drawn in example: for the Register of Horning is that upon which the people ought to rest, and nothing omitted to be expressed in the register should be supplied by the principal hornings, messenger or witnesses: for executions of hornings cannot be proved by witnesses, and consequently no material point thereof.

4. Knocking at the door audibly is necessary, without which, executions might be clandestine, and never come to the party's knowledge. And therefore the messenger must express this as truly done, wherein he runs the hazard of being a forger, if the executions be improven, that either the knocks were not given, or were given fraudulently, that these within might not hear; as if the gate had been only struck with one's hand, a piece of earth or stick, which could not reach their ears that were within; for the affixing of a copy may be more easily evaded; seeing the party may send of purpose to take the copy off, being none of the witnesses in the execution; albeit sometimes, even the witnesses carry away the copy, and the messenger may imagine that his executions were true, when he said he left a copy affixed, because it was affixed when he began to move from the gate: yet if he saw it carried away, his executions would be found false, and he would not escape punishment. A horning was also sustained though it bore neither personally, nor at the party's dwelling-house, seeing it bore a copy to have been given, which necessarily imported to

have been personally apprehended, July 22, 1626, Stewart *contra* Hannai [Durie 224; M. 3803].

5. *Thirdly*, The execution must bear, that the messenger gave a copy of the letters to the party charged personally, or, in his absence, affixed it upon the most patent door of his dwelling-house; and therefore a horning was found null, because it bore not delivery of a copy, but only of a ticket bearing the tenor of the letters, Hope, Horning, Monteith *contra* Kirkland [Hope, *Maj. Pr.* VI, 27, 115; M. 3754]. But if the messenger get entrance into the house of the party charged, and deliver a copy to the party's wife, or some of his family; there the execution will be sustained, though it bear not knocks at the door, or affixing of copies thereupon, these being only required where entry is not gotten.

6. The charge must also be upon 15 days, being beyond the water of Dee, and six upon this side, Parl. 1600, cap. 25 [A.P.S. IV, 239, c. 38]. Yea, though fewer days be in the clause of registration, it was not found valid, February 14, 1625, Stewart *contra* Bruce [Durie 161; M. 6855]. The contrary was found, December 16, 1664, L. Philorth *contra* Forbes of Astoun and the L. Frazer [1 Stair 241; M. 6858]; January 20, 1675, L. Meldrum *contra* L. Tolquhon [2 Stair 306; M. 5737], where it was found, that the Act 1600 was not to be extended to hornings upon clauses of registration of consent; and that the meaning of the statute was both interpreted by the narrative, and subsequent consuetude, *Nam consuetudo est optima legum interpres*: and that the decision *anno* 1625, hath been upon this consideration, that the charger lived in Fife, and the debtor in Orkney, who could not possibly either come to the creditor and pay, or to the Lords and suspend on six days, and so was not contumacious, but free by the Parl. 1592, cap. 138 [Act 1592, c. 140; A.P.S. III, 571, c. 56], annulling impossible conditions in contracts: whereby there is sufficient ground of reconciliation of these decisions, for it is only contumacy that makes the escheat fall, which gave the rise to the Act of Parliament, to allow 15 days for all beyond the water of Dee. And though parties consent to less time, yet contumacy cannot be inferred, but where the party could by exact diligence come in time, either to satisfy the party, or to suspend, which some beyond Dee might do, if the charger were near, that they might offer just satisfaction, and if refused, they might have time to reach Edinburgh, and suspend: but in other cases that cannot be, as was evident in the said case, in *anno* 1625; and therefore consent in that case, can no more infer contumacy, than the express consent of parties, that charges and denunciations at the market-cross of Edinburgh shall be sufficient, which is declared null, Parl. 1592, cap. 138 [Act 1592, c. 140; A.P.S. III, 571, c. 56]. But the narrative of the Act shows, that it is only extended to hornings charging parties to appear at Edinburgh, to find caution in law-borrows or the like, and cannot be extended to parties beyond Dee, living near together, as in the said case of L. Philorth and L. Tolquhon [1 Stair 241; M. 6858; and 2 Stair 306; M. 5737], who lived in one shire or stewartry.

7. *Fourthly*, The executions must bear, that the party was denounced, conform to the charge, for not obedience thereof; and that either at the market-cross of the head burgh of the shire where the party charged dwells, or at the head burgh of the stewartry or regality or bailiary of royalty, if he dwell within these, Parl. 1597, cap. 264 [Act 1597, c. 268; A.P.S. IV, 139, c. 35]. Yea though the writ bear, that letters of horning executed at Edinburgh, should be sufficient against parties out of that shire, the same is declared null by the said Act [Act 1597, c. 268; A.P.S. IV, 139, c. 35]. When there was no head burgh of the regality known, the execution at the head burgh of the shire was sustained, Spots. Horning, Stirling *contra* Auchinleck [*Sub nom.* Stirling v *Abernethy*, Spotiswoode 146; M. 3723]; and the head burgh of the shire, where the denounced's dwelling lies locally, is sustained by the Act of Parl. though his dwelling be upon lands by annexation, in another jurisdiction, unless that be commonly known, and in use; therefore horning was not found null, not being executed at the head burgh of Renfrew, the dwelling being upon lands annexed to the Principality, January 11, 1677, Scot *contra* Dalmahoy [2 Stair 491; M. 3726]; neither, because the denounced dwelt in temple-lands within the regality of Torphichen, unless there were a known head burgh and register there, January 12, 1672, Scot *contra* Boyd of Temple [2 Stair 44; M. 3723].

8. *Fifthly*, The execution should bear, that the messenger at the denunciation did make three oyesses, before he read the letters of horning, that the people might thereby take notice of the intimation, which therefore ought to be with an audible voice, which, though it be not by any particular statute, yet is requisite by ancient custom, and should be expressed in the execution of all letters which require to be published at the market-crosses; the intent thereof being, that the publication thereof may come to the ears of the country, and be carried by common fame, that all parties concerned may look to their interest: and therefore such publications at market-crosses, and at the pier of Leith, have, by law and custom, as expedients to make them commonly known, three oyesses before reading of the letters, and affixing the copy of the letters upon these public places; and horning hath this superadded, that there must be three blasts of the horn after reading of the letters; but because executions do not always bear three oyesses, but generally lawful publication; the Lords did declare upon February 15, 1681, that they would sustain no executions of messengers, done in time coming, not bearing three oyesses, and public reading of the letters, upon a reduction at the instance of Gordon of Park *contra* Forbes [2 Stair 859; M. 3768], for the want of three oyesses, which came not to be decided, because the executions were improven: and an inhibition bearing only, that the messenger did lawfully inhibit, and not bearing three oyesses, nor the reading of the letters; the Lords found the same null, and would not supply it by witnesses, that these were truly done, July 11, 1676, Stevinson *contra* Innes [2 Stair 443; M. 3788].

9. The executions must also bear, that the messenger did give three blasts with his horn; and yet a horning was not found null, because it bore not

expressly the party to have been denounced rebel, or three blasts to be given, but only generally, that the rebel was denounced by open proclamation, and put to the horn, January 19, 1611, Hepburn *contra* L. Niddery [Haddington, *Fol. Dict.* 1, 266; M. 3765], and an execution was sustained, though it bore not three blasts, it being proven by the witnesses insert that these blasts were truly given, and the execution bore, orderly denounced, March 4, 1624, Drysdale *contra* L. Sornbeg and L. Lamingtoun [Durie 116; M. 3765]. But if these had been after the Act of Sederunt [Not found], the hornings would have been null; and even before they ought to have been annulled, for no part of a legal execution can be proved by witnesses.

10. *Sixthly*, The execution must bear, that the messenger, for more verification, hath affixed his signet, or stamp, and the stamp must appear, if the executions be recent, else it will be null, March 6, 1624, Commissary of Dunkeld *contra*   [Durie 118; M. 3778]. So the execution of a horning was found null, because it mentioned not the stamping thereof, Hope, Horning, Home *contra* Pringle of Whitebank [Hope, *Maj. Pr.* VI, 27, 73; M. 3777, 6687]; yet the executions were sustained though they bore not these words, seeing they were all written with the messenger's own hand, and were subscribed and stamped, as Haddingtoun observeth but expresseth not the party, February 19, 1611 [Not found]. But now by Act Parl. [Citations Act, 1686, c. 4; A.P.S. VIII, 586, c. 5], messengers being obliged to subscribe with the witnesses, stamping, which was when few could write, is not necessary.

11. *Seventhly*, Horning must not only be executed at the head-burgh of the shire where the party dwells, but must be registrated in the Sheriff-clerk's register of that shire within 15 days after denunciation thereupon, otherways the same is null, Parl. 1579, cap. 75 [Registration Act, 1579, c. 75; A.P.S. III, 142, c. 13]. Where the clerk is ordained to give an extract, and registrate it within 24 hours after receipt of the letters; and if he refuse it, the charger may registrate it in the next Sheriff-books, or in the Clerk of Register his books, which, upon instruments taken of his refusal, is declared sufficient, Parl. 1579, cap. 75 [*Ibid.* This is a mistake for the Act 1597, c. 269; A.P.S. IV, 139, c. 36], wherein the registration is ordained to be judicially or before a notar, and four famous witnesses, besides the ordinary clerk: but this part of the act is rescinded, and it is declared, that the registration in the Sheriff's, bailie's, or Steward's books by the clerk thereof, or by the Clerk-Register, and his deputes in the Books of Council and Session, shall be sufficient in itself, Parl. 1600, cap. 13 [Hornings Act, 1600, c. 13; A.P.S. IV, 230, c. 22]. And for this effect, there is a General Register of Hornings, Relaxations, Inhibitions and Interdictions kept at Edinburgh, and a particular clerk-depute having the charge thereof; but if the party live within stewartry, or bailiary of royalty or regality, the horning must be registrated there, in the same manner as other hornings must be registrated in the Sheriff-books, else it is declared null, Parl. 1597, cap. 268 [A.P.S. IV, 139, c. 35]. But denunciation against parties who have found security to underly the law, and compear not at the day appointed,

is declared sufficient, being at the cross of Edinburgh, within six days, though not at the head burgh of the shire, Parl. 1592, cap. 126 [A.P.S. III, 555, c. 30]. And likewise, denunciations against parties entering in the place of the criminal court, with more persons than their domestic servants and procurators, are declared valid, though executed only at the market-cross of the burgh where the justice-court sits for the time, and registrated in the Books of Adjournal, Parl. 1584, cap. 140 [A.P.S. III, 301, c. 17]. Executions of horning was also found null, because executed upon the Sabbath-day, Spots. Charge, Frenchman *contra* Lawder [Spotiswoode 35; M. 9380], but were not found null, because registrated after the rebel's death, being denounced before, December 20, 1626, L. Lie *contra* Executors of Blair [Durie 250; M. 3171]. *Vid.* Inhibitions, *infra* [IV, 50, *infra*].

12. Though the horning be orderly used; yet if the ground, or debt, whereupon it proceeded be not due, or be taken away before the denunciation, the horning is thereby null, and reduceable, though no suspension of the horning was raised before; but in this the officers of state must be called to prevent collusion, Spots. Escheat, Dowglas *contra* Creditors of Wardlaw [Spotiswoode 105; M. 2715]. So a horning upon Lawborrows was found null by exception, because caution in obedience was found before denunciation, November 29, 1626, Smeitoun *contra* Spear [Durie 239; M. 2714]; yea, horning was reduced, because, before denunciation, the charger had accepted a bond in satisfaction of the ground of the horning, which was found probable by the oath of the charger against the donatar, Hope, Horning, Mushet *contra* Forrester [Hope, *Maj. Pr.* VI, 27, 98]. The like where the charge was suspended before the denunciation, though the reason of suspension militated only against a part of the charge, Hope, Horning, L. Buckie *contra* E. Errol [Hope, *Maj. Pr.* VI, 27, 123]: but the rebel's oath, or holograph discharges before denunciation, were not respected as presumed collusive, February 10, 1663, Montgomery *contra* Montgomery and Lauder [1 Stair 175; M. 3615]. In this case it was found, that reduction of the decreet upon informality, not being upon material justice, did not annul the horning. Neither was horning taken away by compensation, by the like sum due to the party denounced equal to that in the horning, not having been actually applied by process or contract before the denunciation. Nor was any warrant required for using the execution, though for a party living in England, and done against a daughter and her husband: but the having the principal bond, was found sufficient warrant for registration of it, and execution thereupon. And the denunciation against the husband was not taken off, by dissolution of the marriage before declarator, December 23, 1673, Dalmahoy *contra* L. Almond [2 Stair 244; M. 5865].

13. Horning, though orderly used, proceeding only upon general letters by supplication against all and sundry, unless it be against a burgh, college, or community, not proceeding upon a citation, and for a special and certain duty, the denunciation thereupon hath no effect, as to escheat or liferent, though

caption usually follow thereupon, Parl. 1592, cap. 140 [A.P.S. III, 571, c. 56], which act doth declare such executions null: and therefore such a horning was not found sufficient to debar a party, as not having *personam standi in judicio*, January 24, 1674, Blair of Glasclun *contra* Blair of Baleid [2 Stair 256; M. 10159]; much less can these general letters make escheat to fall, or annual-rent be due; yet caption proceedeth upon it, and useth not to be quarrelled. But by the 13th Act, Parl. 1 Sess. 2, K. W. & Q. M. [Act 1690, c. 13; A.P.S. IX, 153, c. 16], general letters are discharged, except for the King's revenue, and ministers' stipends on decreets of locality, and poindings of the ground; but this Act excludes not charges of horning summarily, when the parties are named, for the charges of commissioners of Parliament, the Lords contribution-money which is a stent paid by known persons [IV, 47, 4–6, *infra*], or the like, as precepts out of the chancery, which are not summonses, but charges.

14. Horning is taken off, and ceaseth by relaxation, which requireth the same solemnities of publication and registration, as hornings doth, as is clear by the forecited Acts of Parliament thereanent; but it doth only operate to free the rebel relaxed, as to his goods and others, acquired after relaxation, February 14, 1635, Lockhart *contra* Mosman [Durie 755; M. 8365; 11, 4, 64, *supra*; IV, 47, 10, *infra*]; Dec. 23, 1673, Dalmahoy *contra* Lo. Almond [2 Stair 244; M. 5866]. It is also ordained, that all copies of summons, and letters delivered by the executor thereof, shall be subscribed by him, Parl. 1592, cap. 139 [Citation Act, 1592, c. 141; A.P.S. III, 573, c. 59]. I have not observed any exception founded upon this Act, which, though it expresseth not a nullity, yet ought to be a rule to messengers, especially in hornings and inhibitions, which may prefer any other to a more orderly diligence; and the want of subscriptions of the executor and witnesses, is now a nullity of the executions by Act 5. Parl. 3, Ch. 2. 1681 [Subscription of Deeds Act, 1681, c. 5; A.P.S. VIII, 242, c. 5].

15. The effect of horning duly used, and registrated in manner foresaid, is, that thereby the whole moveable goods, and debts of the parties denounced, are escheat and confiscated, and all that he shall acquire thereafter, till he be relaxed; whereupon the treasurer used to cause raise letters of intromission, for uptaking of the escheat-goods, direct to sheriffs and messengers; and in case they be deforced, or the sheriff not able or willing to execute the same, letters will be direct to noblemen and barons within the shire, to convocate the lieges in arms, and to make effectual the former letters immediately, Parl. 1579, cap. 75 [Registration Act, 1579, c. 75; A.P.S. III, 142, c. 13]; but this is long in desuetude. This is also an effect of horning, that the party denounced hath not *personam standi in judicio*, either as pursuer or as defender, yet the Lords would not hold him as confessed, if he appeared, and were hindered by the other party's caption, July 12, 1676, Purves *contra* Sharp of Gospetrie [*Sub nom.* Purves v Schaw, 2 Stair 446; M. 5740]. The same will hold in any thing requiring the personal presence of the denounced, as biding by a writ quarrelled of falsehood, &c.

For clearing the matter of escheats, it will be necessary to show, *first*, What falls under single escheat; *Secondly*, How far the same is burdened, or affected with the denounced's debts or deeds. For the first; single escheat extends to no heritable right, whether of land, annualrent, or heritable bond, but it carries the bygones of all these, preceding the denunciation and thereafter, till year and day [expire] July 1, 1626, Haliburton *contra* Stuart [Durie 207; M. 3618]; Hope, Horning, Wardlaw *contra* Dick [Hope, *Maj. Pr.* VI, 27, 105; M. 5070, 7871]. The reason is, because, the liferent-escheat begins but after year and day from the denunciation, so the intervening year belongs to the single escheat. What rights are heritable, and what moveable, hath been shown before, Title, Real Rights [11, 1, *supra*], so that all which is there moveable, except moveable bonds bearing annualrent, falls in the single escheat, and some things are moveable in relation to escheats, which are not moveable in relation to the succession of heirs or executors, as tacks not being liferent tacks, Parl. 1617, cap. 15 [A.P.S. IV, 545, c. 15]. It carries also the office of a Sheriff clerkship, Hope, Horning, Kinross *contra* Drummond [Hope, *Maj. Pr.* VI, 27, 92; M. 3636]: and likewise the *jus mariti* of a husband, and therewith *per consequentiam*, the liferent-right, or other right of the wife belonging to the husband *jure mariti*, Spots. Escheat, Dawling *contra* Cochran [Not found]. It carrieth also all casualities befalling to a rebel denounced before the denunciation, as the liferent-escheat of his vassals, Had. February 13, 1611, Simpson *contra* L. Moncur [Not found]. But if the casuality fall to the superior, after the superior's own liferent had fallen by his rebellion, year and day, it would be carried with the superior's liferent-escheat, February 26, 1623, Sibbald *contra* Clunie [Durie 51; M. 3616]. And if the liferent-escheat, or any other casuality be gifted, the gift makes it moveable, and so to fall under the donatar's single escheat, March 10, 1631, Stewart *contra* La. Samuelstoun [Durie 579; M. 3623]. Assignations to liferent-tacks, and other liferents have been found to fall under single escheat, because the direct right is incommunicable; for no liferenter can put another liferenter in their place, but can only assign the profits befalling to the liferenter by the liferent right; so that it is no liferent in the assignee, but is as the *jus mariti* in a husband, which is a legal assignation [11, 6, 7, *supra*] likewise, clauses of relief in heritable bonds fall under single escheat, because there is no heritable clause adjected to the clause of relief; but assignations to heritable bonds makes them not to fall under single escheat, because the creditor's right is directly transmitted and stated in the assignee's person. The single escheat of ministers carries the melioration of their manses, but the escheat of an executor carries no more than what is his own interest, and not the share of the wife, bairns, creditors, legatars, or nearest of kin, which is escheat by their own rebellion only, even though the testament were executed by decreets, at the executor's instance against the debtors, December 21, 1671, Gordon *contra* L. Drum [2 Stair 31; M. 3894; II, 1, 14, *supra*; III, 8, 71, *infra*].

16. As to the other question, how far the denounced's debts or deeds

affect his moveables fallen in escheat: It is clear, that the debt contained in the horning affects the escheat [IV, 10, 2, *infra*], whether in the hands of the treasurer or donatar, Parl. 1551, cap. 7 [A.P.S. II, 483, c. 1]. Parl. 1579, cap. 75 [Registration Act, 1579, c. 75; A.P.S. III, 142, c. 13]. And likewise all intromitters with escheat goods, by gift, assignation, or otherwise, upon a single summons of six days, Parl. 1592, cap. 147 [A.P.S. III, 573, c. 63]. It is doubtful whether the debt in any horning whereon a gift is taken, should burden the escheat; because the first horning is only that which makes the rebellion, and so the debt therein should only burden the escheat; and though whatever horning is produced, is presumed to be the first, yet where more gifts are presented on diverse hornings, whoever be preferred, he should be preferred with the burden of the debt of the first horning. 2. It is clear, that no assignation, disposition, or other deed done by the denounced, after denunciation, not being for fulfilling an anterior obligement before denunciation, for a cause onerous to a lawful creditor, can affect the moveable goods or debts of the denounced: but when the denunciation is upon a criminal cause, the escheat takes not only effect from the denunciation, but from the committing of the fact. Therefore a donatar of escheat recovered a sum due to the rebel, though assigned before the fact, and paid before process, seeing intimation was not before the criminal fact, Hope, Horning, Chalmers and Gordoun *contra* Gordoun [*Sub nom. Gordon and Chalmer* v *Gordon*, Hope, *Maj. Pr.* VI, 27, 83; M. 12048]. Thirdly, these debts, or deeds of the denounced, do not simply affect the escheat goods, unless they be consummated, or lawful diligence done before the uptaking of the escheat goods by the treasurer or donatar, yea, before general declarator; for that being the intimation of the donatar's gift, it renders it to him a complete valid right, after which no creditor not having a real right, or legal diligence before, can have any access; and therefore a donatar, having obtained general declarator, was preferred to a lawful creditor arresting after declarator, Feb. 22, 1628, Anderson *contra* Gordon [Durie 348; M. 3643].

But the question remains, how far lawful creditors, whose debt is before the denunciation, or criminal fact, using diligence thereafter, but before declarator, or obtaining assignations intimated, or dispositions clad with possession before declarator, may thereby affect the escheat goods? For answer hereunto, though, in *rigore juris*, the goods and debts of the denounced fall to the fisk, as they are the time of the denunciation, or criminal fact: and the declarator, according to the nature of all declarators, doth not constitute the fisk's right, but declares the same to have been from the denunciation, or criminal fact, (albeit as an assignation it doth not constitute the donatar's right) therefore the real right passing to the fisk without possession, or at least the privilege of the fisk might in the full extent thereof exclude all posterior diligences or deeds; yet such hath been the royal benignity of our Kings, and their favour to lawful creditors, that in this they accounted *id solum nostrum, quod debitis deductis, est nostrum ;* for which the treasurer hath been accustomed to prefer creditors, giving gifts of escheat to them before others, and in taking back-bonds from them, in favour of other creditors; yea, by long custom, creditors whose debts were anterior to the denunciation, or criminal fact, doing diligence before declarator, are preferable to the donatar, Spots. Escheat, Nisbet *contra* Fullartoun [Spotiswoode 104; M. 3643]; Feb. 24, 1637, Pilmure *contra* Geggie [Durie 830; M. 3644]. In this case the escheat belonged to a Lord of regality, and the arrestment was laid on before the gift of escheat: but where the donatar's gift was in payment of his own debt, he was preferred to an arrester, arresting the rebel's goods after the gift, but before declarator, February 27, 1623, Thomson *contra* L. Murckil [Durie 52; M. 3641]; but voluntary assignations not intimated before declarator, for satisfaction of debt due before denunciation, or a criminal fact, are not preferred to the donatar; but assignations or other rights, for which there were special obligations before rebellion, are not voluntary but effectual, being complete before declarator, Hope, Assignation, Stuart *contra* Wardlaw [Hope, *Maj. Pr.* VI, 27, 88]; Clerk *contra* Naper [*Sub. nom Stark* v *Naiper*, Hope, *Maj. Pr.* VI, 27, 85; M. 3652], and Crafurd *contra* McAul [Hope, *Maj. Pr.* VI, 27, 97]. And though an assignation not being intimated before rebellion, was preferred to the donatar, yet it was in consequence of a decreet of council decerning that assignation to be made, and so not voluntary: so a donatar was preferred to an assignee, whose assignation bore a cause onerous, and was before declarator, but after rebellion, December 6, 1631, and February 26, 1633, L. Conheth *contra* L. Earlstoun [Durie 678; M. 8357]; December 18, 1629, L. Capringtoun *contra* Cunninghame [Durie 476; M. 8356]. In like manner a disposition made by the rebel for a just debt, before the gift or declarator, was preferred to the donatar; here it is not expressed, that the debt was before the rebellion, February 10, 1635, Mosman *contra* Lockhart [Auchinleck, *Fol. Dict.* I, 556; M. 8365].

Dispositions and delivery of goods, because moveables, are more easily transmissible in favour of commerce, have always a presumptive title upon possession, so that if the goods be bought in a market, there is no question, or if bought out of market from a rebel, getting the price, which accresceth to the fisk, unless the buyer was in *mala fide ;* or getting the goods before declarator, in satisfaction of a debt due before the rebellion. 2. Legal diligences upon arrestment being complete before declarator, are valid, though after rebellion; yea, the decisions favour even the inchoate diligence, if the arrestment was before declarator upon a debt before rebellion; and it was so found, February 19, 1667, Glen *contra* Hoome [1 Stair 443; M. 3645]. But voluntary assignations are not effectual, if they be not complete by intimation before rebellion, and though they be where payment or satisfaction either in money or renewed bonds, innovating the rebel's bond, was not obtained before rebellion, the donatar was found preferable; but otherwise the creditor, by precept, assignation, or otherwise, for payment of his debt, prior to the rebellion, obtaining payment before declarator, was found secure against the donatar, Feb. 11,

1675, Veatch *contra* Executors of Ker [2 Stair 321; M. 1073]. But though actual payment were obtained by assignation after declarator, it will not secure the creditor, December, 20, 1676, *inter eosdem* [2 Stair 482; M. 2874].

17. The matter of escheat being thus cleared, we come to the gift thereof, and declarator thereupon. A gift first sealed, was preferred to another first signed in Exchequer, albeit so near in diligence as coming that same day to the seals, December 6, 1662, Stuart *contra* Nasmith [1 Stair 148; M. 5098]. Gifts of escheat [11, 4, 36, *supra*] are in effect the assignations thereof by the fisk, whereof the intimation is the declarator; so that a posterior gift, with a prior general declarator, is preferable to a prior gift, with a posterior declarator: but where there is yet no declarator, preference is by the first citation if the same was followed with lawful diligence; and therefore a posterior gift, whereupon the citation was prior but three days, was preferred to a prior gift, January 31, 1635, L. Renton *contra* L. Wedderburn [Durie 748; M. 5097]. Here both donatars were creditors, competing for preference, but other donatars could not claim the preference, for the prior gift before decreet of declarator would be preferred, though posterior in diligence; neither could the possession of a second donatar, not being creditor, prefer him to a prior gift, or require no declarator. If there be no citation or declarator, the donatar's possession is sufficient alone, and will prefer a posterior gift, though granted to the rebel himself, being before any diligence upon the prior gift. And if two gifts be produced as interests, without any diligence on either, the first gift is preferable.

18. Gifts of escheat, as all other gifts by the King, are null, if granted before the casualty fall, as an erection of kirk-lands in a temporal lordship was found null, because a commendatar stood then in the right, and did not resign or consent: and therefore a posterior erection to that commendatar, upon his own demission was preferred, February 24, 1666, Sinclair *contra* L. Wedderburn [1 Stair 366; M. 7972]. And so a gift of escheat before denunciation was found null, by exception, because it mentioned no particular horning whereupon it proceeded, though done by the King's own hand at court. And though anterior hornings were produced in the process, and no other donatar nor officer of state quarrelled the same, November 20, 1628, Waston *contra* Stuart [Durie 397; M. 5069].

19. Gifts of escheat not bearing expressly "goods to be acquired," extend no further than to the goods the denounced had the time of the gift, February 2, 1627, Somervel *contra* Stirling [Durie 267; M. 5074]. And though the gift bore expressly, not only the goods the rebel had, but which he should acquire thereafter during his rebellion; yet the same was only extended to what he had the time of the gift, and what supervened within year and day, November 25, 1626, E. Kinghorn *contra* Wood [Durie 237; M. 5072].

20. Escheats of persons living within regality, belongs to the lord or bailie of regality, infeft with that privilege: and therefore gifts by the King reach not these escheats, but only gifts by the lord or bailie of the regality,

which was found to comprehend all moveable goods, and sums belonging to the party denounced, as well within the regality as without the same, June 26, 1680, Young *contra* L. Raploch [2 Stair 778; M.3635]. But these gifts differ from the King's gifts, that they are effectual according to their tenor, both as to goods before and after the gift, and are valid, though granted generally, or though before the casualty fall, if a special gift, after the casualty fell, be not in competition; for the prior limitations of the King's gifts, are only in favour of the King, that he be not prejudged by the default of his officers; but private parties ought *sibi invigilare;* and albeit the diligence of creditors be preferred to donatars, chiefly by the King's benignity; yet a creditor's arrestment being prior to the gift, though after the horning, was sustained against a donatar of escheat, by a lord of regality, February 24, 1637, Gilmore *contra* Hagie [*Sub nom. Pilmuir* v *Guthrie of Gagie*, Durie 830; M.3644]. This decision insinuates, that escheats within regality are burdened with the denounced's debts, and diligence after the horning before the declarator, as in the King's gifts.

21. The main difficulty anent gifts, is, when they are simulate, and to the behoof of the denounced, which is much cleared by that excellent statute, Parl. 1592, cap. 145 [A.P.S. III,573,c.63], declaring it a sufficient evidence of simulation, of any assignation or gift of escheat, if the rebel himself, his wife, bairns, or near friends, remain in possession of his tack and goods, to their own uses and behoof: yet it is not declared how long their possession must be, seeing the rebel ordinarily, for some time is in possession, till the donatar use diligence: but where the rebel retained possession till his death, a gift though declared was found null by exception, July 12, 1628, Morison *contra* Frendraught [*Sub nom. Cranston of Moriston* v *Crichton of Frendraught*, Durie 389; M.522]; Had. June 26,1611, Gairdner *contra* Lo. Gray [Not found]: yea, it was found simulate, where the rebel possessed nine years, June 26, 1622, Inglis *contra* L. Capringtoun [Durie 27; M.11592]; and other circumstances concurring, four or five years possession by the rebel was found sufficient, the donatar having consented to several tacks, and wadsets granted by the rebel: and yet the same gift was found valid in part, in so far as concerned heritable rights, acquired by the donatar from the rebel, December 23, 1623, Ballantyn *contra* Murray [Durie 94; M.11594]; so four or five years possession of the rebel were found sufficient to infer simulation, though the donatar was a creditor, and the rebel's lands apprised, seeing the appriser possessed not, but the rebel, January 6, and 9, 1666, Oliphant *contra* Drummond [1 Stair 334; M.11597]; so that the time of possession sufficient to infer simulation, remaineth *in arbitrio judicis*. The next ground of the simulation of gifts of escheat, and presuming the same to the rebel's behoof, is, when it is taken in the name of the children in his family, which was found relevant, without mention of the rebel's possession, June 25, 1622, Lo. Borthwick's Bairns *contra* Dickson [Durie 27; M.11591]. But the presumption was not found sufficient, that the gift was to the behoof of the rebel's son: here it was not alleged that he was then in his father's family, March 20, 1623, Keith

contra L. Benholme [*Sub nom. Dalgarno* v *Earl Marischal*, Durie 59; M. 11593].
The like where the son was not in his father's family and was a creditor, and
made faith it was to his own behoof at passing the gift, though the party denounced did remain in possession some time after declarator, December 4,
1669, Jaffray *contra* Jaffray [1 Stair 655; M. 11599].

    The third presumption of the simulation of gifts is, when the same is pro-
cured, and passed by the rebel's means, which was sustained, though a part
was by the donatar's means, and a part by the rebel's, though the donatar was
then a creditor, June 26, 1622, Inglis *contra* L. Capringtoun [Durie 27;
M. 11592]. The like found probable by members of the Exchequer, as witnesses, November 28, 1626, E. Kinghorn *contra* Wood [Durie 237; M.5073];
Hope, *Cessio Bonorum*, L. Clunie *contra* L. Blandine [*Sub nom. Cluny* v
Bandain, Hope, *Maj. Pr.* VI, 30, 12]; Cant and Porterfield *contra* Stuart
[Hope, *Maj. Pr.* VI, 30, 12]. The like against an assignee, constituted by the
donatar, Hope, Horning, Hamilton *contra* Ramsay [Hope, *Maj. Pr.* VI, 27,
103; M. 7832]. Simulation of a gift of liferent to the rebel's behoof, was found
probable by the rebel's oath, and the witnesses inserted in the gift, June 19,
1669, Scot *contra* L. Langtoun [1 Stair 620; M. 5100, 12316]. This ground of
simulation is found relevant, not only against the donatar, but against a singular successor, not partaking of the fraud, whose assignation was after the creditor's diligence, December 10, 1623, Douglas *contra* Belshes [Durie 90;
M. 8347; III, 1, 32, *supra*]. And though there was no diligence, the gift being
expede blank in the name, and filled up thereafter, in the donatar's name, it
was found simulate even as to him, though obtaining it for his true debt,
December 17, 1670, Langtoun *contra* Robison [1 Stair 703; M. 11600]. Simulation is not otherwise valid against singular successors; yet it was not found
relevant to exclude the donatar, and to prefer another donatar, in so far as
concerns the first donatar's debt, truly owing to him, though the gift was
given at the rebel's request, and passed at his own charges: so that the exclusion, by this presumed simulation, was only inferred as to the profit of the
gift, above the donatar's own debt, *in quantum lucratus est*. For that was found
no fault in the debtor-rebel, to concur in desire and moyen to get a gift to his
creditor, in so far as concerned that creditor's debt, March 11, 1624, Douglas
contra L. Eastnisbit [Durie 119; M. 3638], which decision is contrary to that
Inglis against L. Capringtoun [Durie 27; M. 11592], but is posterior thereto
and juster; so the donatar having made faith, the gift was to his own behoof,
showing his debt and back-bond, December 12, 1673, Dickson *contra*
McCulloch [2 Stair 239; M. 11600]. This must be understood, if the rebel
was relaxed; for if unrelaxed, a gift, though taken expressly in his name, returneth and accresceth to the fisk, and next donatar, July 6, 1627, E. Annandale
contra L. Coockpool [*Sub nom. E. Annandale* v *Murray*, Durie 305; M. Supp.
41]: yea, though he was thereafter relaxed before any other gift, November
28, 1626, E. Kinghorn *contra* Wood [Durie 237; M. 5072]; Had. June 2, 1610,
Lennox *contra* Turnbull [Not found]. But if the denounced were relaxed, the

time of the gift, as it would be sufficient in his own person expressly, so it is valid in another's person, though to his behoof, yet it will exclude none of the creditors. These nullities are not only competent to posterior donatars, but also to the rebel's creditors using diligence.

22. To come now to the declarators of escheat; they are two, first general, the next special. In the action of general declarator, the rebel or his bairns, or nearest of kin (if he be dead) must be called, Hope, *Cessio Bonorum,* Frazer *contra* McPherson [*Sub nom. Frazer v McFinzean,* Hope, *Maj. Pr.* VI, 30, 18; M. 2207]; but the declarator hath no effect against moveable heirship, unless the rebel's heir were called. As to the other moveables, though there uses seldom to be executors confirmed to defunct rebels, and therefore the wife and nearest of kin are ordinarily called; yet if the wife was only called, she being executrix confirmed, it will be sustained. And though summons of general declarator bear all parties having interest, who must be cited generally at the market-cross of the head burgh where the rebel's residence is, that is but *stilus curiae,* and the want of it hinders nothing, the rebel being cited particularly, June 27, 1666, Massoun *contra* Black [1 Stair 381; M. 2209].

23. The title in the general declarator is the gift, and the horning whereupon it proceeds, the extract whereof does as sufficiently prove as the principal, Parl. 1579, cap. 75 [Registration Act, 1579, c. 75; A.P.S. III, 142, c. 13]. The tenor of the general declarator is, that the rebel was duly and orderly denounced by the horning libelled, and that thereby the whole moveable goods and gear, &c. became escheat, and belong to the pursuer by virtue of his gift; all which is instantly verified by the titles: and therefore, if no relevant exception be proponed, decreet is instantly given.

24. No exception will be here competent against the horning, not being instantly verified; for all others will be reserved to reduction: so it was found, it being alleged, that the rebel dwelt in another shire than where he was denounced, Had. June 12, 1611, Mr. Ocheltrie *contra* L. Symontoun [Hope, *Maj. Pr.* VI, 27, 75]. Yet if the reduction be depending, it may be sustained as prejudicial, and be first discussed, Had. December 12, 1622, Dalmahoy *contra* Scot [Not found]. Neither will any exception be sustained against the ground of the horning, as not due or satisfied; and that it proceeded upon a null bond, subscribed only by one notar, Had. January 12, 1610, Durham *contra* Cleland [Not found]; or that payment was made before denunciation, November 30, 1630, Douglas *contra* Wardlaw [Durie 544; M. 2714]; Hope, Horning and Escheat, Lord Douglas *contra* Lord Carmichael [Hope, *Maj. Pr.* VI, 27, 74]. The reason is, not only because the alledgeance is not instantly verified, but specially, because the King's officers are not called, that they may defend the King's interest, and obviate collusions upon forged discharges, or otherwise; for ofttimes the donatar hath but a small interest, in respect of his back-bond, and so may readily conclude: and therefore, though the defence be instantly verified, it is not received by exception; though it might justly be without multiplication of processes, intimation being made to the Treasurer and Ad-

vocate, that they might appear for the King's interest: but if it be a visible nullity in the horning, or an exception wherein there can be no appearance of collusion, it is sometimes admitted, as this exception, that the horning was suspended before denunciation and was false, it was sustained, Hope, Horning, Sheriff of Murray *contra*   [Hope, *Maj. Pr.* VI, 27, 82]. Exceptions of any party compearing for their interest, and alleging assignation, or disposition of the goods or diligence done, use not to be received in the general declarator, but reserved to the special, because the general is but an intimation, and so proceeds summarily.

25. The action of special declarator, though it hath the name of declarator, yet hath little in it declaratory, but it is petitory of the goods specially libelled in it. There is no necessity to call the rebel, or any representing him, but the haver or intromitter with the escheat goods. The title in this action, is the decreet of general declarator, and there is no necessity to produce the gift or horning, February 10, 1627, Creditors of Stuart of Coldingham's escheat *contra* a Debitor of the Rebel [Durie 271; M. 12012]; November 20, 1629, Lundie *contra* Lundie [Durie 468; M. 14026]; where another donatar was admitted for his interest, in the special declarator, though he had no general declarator: nor is any exception competent against the same, or ground thereof, but only by reduction; unless exceptions proponed in the general declarator be repelled as incompetent there, but reserved to the special declarator. Special declarators may be pursued any other way, as upon arrestment or particular libel, for restitution and delivery of the escheat goods. It is also consistent in the same libel with the general declarator; but, before the pursuer insist in the other member for the special declarator, he must pursue that member for the general declarator, and extract his decreet.

26. Liferent escheat, though it be a penalty of contumacy and rebellion, and so is properly a confiscation; yet seeing it doth not befall only to the fisk, but is a common casualty of superiority, and hath been handled in the title Superiority; we shall not here repeat, but only touch some differences between liferent escheat, and single escheat. First, Single escheat is only a legal penalty, and therefore belongs alone to the King, and his ministers of justice, who are comptable to him therefor as sheriffs, &c. or to their own behoof by their infeftments, as Lords and bailies of regality: but liferent escheat is not only penal, but is a legal consequence of the condition of the rebel, whereby he being outlawed, and having no person in judgment, is excluded from the possession of all his rights, and is esteemed as *civiliter mortuus*, whereby his fees become open, and are in the hands of his superior, whether the King, or any other superior, by his continuing unrelaxed year and day: and therefore the diligences done against, or the deeds done by the rebel, for satisfying of his lawful debts contracted before rebellion, do not affect his liferent escheat, as they do his single escheat, though they be done before year and day expire, being after the rebellion: and so arrestments, or assignations, even though before rebellion, have no effect after year and day is run; because these being

but personal, and liferent escheat a real right by the superiority, whereby the vassal is denuded of the liferent, therefore the effect of these personal rights ceaseth; but all real rights flowing from the vassal before the rebellion, as feus, annualrents, tacks, apprisings and adjudications, whereupon there was a charge [11, 3, 30; 11, 4, 32 and 66, *supra*], are effectual, and not excluded by liferent escheat, though these are excluded by ward, which is a casualty following the nature of feudal rights; whereas liferent escheat ariseth not from the nature of fees, but is introduced by law or custom; and therefore the fee falls in the hands of the superior, as it was in the hands of the vassal, with all the real burdens he had fixed upon it [IV, 9, 2, *infra*]: neither does posterior voluntary infeftments, though for debts prior to the rebellion, and granted before declarator, exclude the liferent echeat, Had. January 18, 1611, Ord *contra* L. Craigkeith [Haddington, *Fol. Dict.* 1, 554; M. 8353]. The like, where the infeftment was granted after rebellion, but within year and day, January 23, 1627, Wallace *contra* Porteous [Durie 260; M. 8354]. Where there is an exception insinuated, unless there had been a prior obligement before the rebellion to grant the infeftment, as if in that case (though *in cursu rebellionis*) it would be sufficient to exclude the liferent. The like was found, that infeftment upon a voluntary disposition made *in cursu rebellionis*, within the year, and for a debt due before rebellion, excluded not the liferent escheat, March 19, 1628, Raith *contra* L. Buckie [Durie 364; M. 8356]; Hope Horning, L. Frendraught *contra* Meldrum [Hope, *Maj. Pr.* VI, 27, 94], Gordon of Lesmoor *contra* Gordon of Haddo [Hope, *Maj. Pr.* VI, 27, 79]. But infeftments *in cursu rebellionis* upon special obligements to grant the same before denunciation, are valid. *Vide Lib.* II. Tit. 4. §53.

As to legal diligences of creditors, whether apprising and infeftment thereupon, being after rebellion, will exclude the liferent escheat, was declared the last Title in the second effect of apprisings, [11, 4, 32 and 66], the sum whereof is, that they are thus preferable to voluntary dispositions, that being done *in cursu rebellionis*, for a debt before rebellion, there being infeftment, or charge in *cursu rebellionis*, they exclude the liferent. Secondly, Single escheats require general and special declarator: liferent escheats require but one declarator for all, wherein the title is the horning, the gift, and the superior's seasin, without farther instructing the superior's right, and without continuation, July 2, 1622, Carmichael *contra* Lermont [Durie 28; M. Supp. 2]; March 6, 1624, Douglas *contra* L. Eastnisbit [Durie 118–119; M. 3637]; June 23, 1625, Viscount of Stormont *contra*   [Durie 165; M. 5731]. And there is no necessity to instruct the lands holden of that superior by the defender [11, 4, 69, *supra*]. The reason, is because that is presumed, unless the defender disclaim, or that the superior be a singular successor, never acknowledged by the vassal, or his predecessors.

27. Shipwreck, and waith-goods, or treasures in the ground, whose owner appeareth not, are confiscated as caduciary, whereby the owners are presumed to relinquish, or lose the same. And so *a jure suo cadunt*, and the things become

nullius, and yet belong not to the first possessor, as things relinquished do, by the common law, but do belong to the king, by his royal prerogative, or to others having right from him. We have spoken of these before in the title, Real Rights [11, 1, *supra*]; and shall only add this, that by that just and noble statute, Parl. 1429, cap. 124 [A.P.S. 11, 19, c. 15], it is declared, that where ships are wreck in this country, the ship and goods shall be escheat to the king, if they belong to such countries as use the like law anent shipwreck in their own land, otherways they shall have the same favour, as they keep to ships of this land broken with them. It is also declared amongst the statutes of king Alexander II. cap. 25 [Not in A.P.S.], That if any living man, or beast, as dog, cat, &c. come quick out of the vessel, the same shall not be accounted shipwreck, but shall be preserved to the owner, claiming and instructing his right within year and day, or otherways it shall belong to the king; so it was found, where an ox escaped alive out of the ship, and the Admiral's decreet, finding the same escheatable as shipwreck, was suspended *simpliciter*, December 12, 1622, Hamilton *contra* Cochran [Durie 39; M. 16791]. In which case nothing was alleged but this old statute, the genuine meaning whereof seems only to be, where any person came to land, the ship and goods should not be confiscated as wreck; but the posterior act, Parl. 1429, cap. 124 [A.P.S. 11, 19, c. 15], repeats not that provision, but regulates the matter according to the custom of other nations, to do to them as they do to us, without any other limitation. And therefore where some persons came to land, the ship being broken, the same with the goods dispersed were confiscated, if confiscation in the like case should be proven to be the law, or custom of that place, to which the ship belonged, January 20, 1674, Jacobson *contra* E. Crawford [2 Stair 254; M. 16792]. But except by the law of reprisals, that we might treat other nations as they treat us, wherever the true owner claimeth and instructeth his right, he ought to have it, and the confiscation should only be where there is nothing upon the wreck showing the owner, which is the reason of the old statute; for an ox can be known whose it is, and so where the wreck ship is, the owner may be known by writs in the ship, and if writs or other evidences make the owner appear, it is relevant and just.

28. Forfeiture is the great confiscation, comprehending all other penal confiscations; and is extended to the taking away of life, lands and goods, Parl. 1424, cap. 3 [A.P.S. 11, 3, c. 3]. For it is the penalty of the highest crime, to wit, treason; which at first, and by its native signification, it expresseth crimes against the life of any party under trust: so the slaughter of any person under trust, credit, or power of the slayer, is declared treason, Parl. 1587, cap. 51 [A.P.S. 111, 451, c. 34].

29. Thence it is also called treachery, and the committers thereof traitors. And because of that trust betwixt the king and all the lieges, as their superior and sovereign, the chief point of treason is against the king's person, as appeareth by the act first cited: these also who, without cause, wilfully raise a fray in the king's host, commit treason, Parl. 1455, cap. 54 [Probably Act

1455, c. 49; A.P.S. 11, 44, c. 3]. Upon the same ground, because of the trust betwixt the superior and his vassal, and such crimes against the superior, are also called treason, and thereby the committer loseth for ever, all lands and heritage he held of that superior, *Quoniam Attachiamenta,* cap. 19 [Q.A. c. 19; A.P.S. ed. c. 15]. But this treason infers not a simple forfeiture, but only is a ground of recognition; but as now the terms are taken, treason, and forfeiture of life, lands and goods are adequate; and, wherever the one is expressed in any Act of Parliament, the other is understood; so the striking or slaying of any person, within the Parliament-house, during the time of Parliament, within the king's inner chamber, cabinet, or chamber of presence, the king being within his palace, or within the inner tolbooth, the time of session sitting; or within the privy council-house the time of the council sitting; or, in his Majesty's presence any where, is declared treason, Parl. 1593, cap. 173 [Act 1593, c. 177; A.P.S. IV, 28, c. 34]. So impugning the dignity or authority of the three estates of Parliament, or procuring any innovation, or diminution of their power, is prohibited under pain of treason, Parl. 1584, cap. 130 [A.P.S. III, 293, c. 3]. And also the declining the King and his council, in any matter to be inquired before them, Parl. 1564, cap. 129 [Act 1584, c. 129; A.P.S. III, 292, c. 2]. Purchasers of benefices at the court of Rome, are ordained to be denounced as traitors to the King, Parl. 1471, cap. 43 [A.P.S. 11, 99, c. 4], Parl. 1488, cap. 4 [A.P.S. 11, 209, c. 14], Parl. 1540, cap. 119 [A.P.S. 11, 377, c. 39]. So forgers of the King's coin and homebringers thereof incur the loss of life, lands and goods, Parl. 1563, cap. 70 [A.P.S. 11, 538, c. 5]. Saying of Mass, resetting of Jesuits, seminary priests, and trafficking papists; and these themselves are liable to treason, Parl. 1594, cap. 196 [A.P.S. III, 63, c. 6], Parl. 1607, cap. 1 [A.P.S. IV, 371, c. 2]. Raising of fire wilfully, or burning of houses, or corns, whether folk be therein or not, is declared treason, [[Parl. 1528, cap. 8 [Act 1526, c. 8; A.P.S. 11, 316, c. 10], Parl. 1540, cap. 118 [A.P.S. 11, 377, c. 38], Parl. 1567, cap. 32 [A.P.S. III, 34, c. 39] and 33 [A.P.S. III, 34, c. 40]]; and wilful setting coal-heughs on fire is declared treason, Parl. 1592, cap. 148 [A.P.S. III, 576, c. 70]. Landed men committing or resetting riot or robbery, incur the pain of treason, Parl. 1587, cap. 50 [A.P.S. III, 451, c. 34]. And generally all resetters, maintainers, and assisters of declared traitors, commit treason, Parl. 1592, cap. 149 [Act 1592, c. 146; A.P.S. III, 575, c. 68]. Accusers of others of treason, if the accused be acquit, commit treason, Parl. 1587, cap. 49 [A.P.S. III, 450, c. 33].

30. Forfeiture confiscateth the forfeited person's whole estate, without any access to his creditors; yea, without consideration of dispositions, infeftments, or other real rights granted by the forfeited person, since or before the committing of the crime of treason, for which he was forfeited, which fall and become null by exception, Hope, Forfeiture, Viscount of Rochester *contra* Tenants of Carlavrock [Hope, *Maj.Pr.* III, 32, 15]; Had. July 14, 1610, Campbell *contra* Lifnories [Haddington, *Fol.Dict.* I, 314; M. 4685]; Spots. Conjunct-fee, Crawford *contra* L. Murdistoun [Spotiswoode 59; M. 7756];

unless these rights have been confirmed by the King as superior, or consented to by him.

31. It hath been much controverted, whether feu-infeftments granted by forfeited persons, before committing of the crime, be also annulled by the forfeiture; and if the act of Parliament anent feus, Parl. 1457, cap. 71 [A.P.S. 11,49,c. 15], should not only defend them against recognition, and the casualties of superiority, but even against forfeiture itself, it being therein declared, that the King will ratify the said feus. The like is to be understood of other superiors: so that, though *de facto* they be not confirmed, yet the declaration and obligement of the statute standeth as a confirmation thereof, or at least as an obligement upon all superiors, against which they, nor their donatars, cannot come. This is to be understood, while feus are allowed by law: *vide Title Infeftments*, §34 [11,3,34]. It was so decided, February 12, 1674, M. Huntly *contra* Gordon of Cairnborrow [2 Stair 265; M. 4170]; November 16, 1680, Campbell of Silvercraigs *contra* L. Auchinbreck and the E. Argyle [2 Stair 796; M. 4171]; not only because the said Act of Parliament imports a confirmation of feus granted thereafter, but also because forfeiture is by statute penal, and not by the feudal right, like unto liferent-escheat, which returneth the fee to the superiors, but with the burdens put thereupon by the vassal, whether feu, blench, ward, or by annualrent or tack. And therefore, when any person is forfeited, that is not the King's immediate vassal, his estate, both property and superiority, falls to the King, but with the burden of all real rights constituted by the vassal [11,11,34,*supra*]; yet forfeiture of the King's immediate ward vassal proceedeth upon crimes which infer recognition, and therefore returns his ward lands to the King, as they came from the King free of all burden. So that the Act of Parl. 1457 [Act 1457,c. 71; A.P.S. 11,49,c. 15], which secures against ward and recognition, must also secure feus against the forfeiture of the vassal granter of the feus, but will not secure any other subaltern right, without the superior's consent, as a blench infeftment, January 13, 1677, M. Huntly *contra* L. Grant [2 Stair 493; M. 4689]. But forfeiture, which is not by the nature of the ward-holding, as done against the King, who is supreme superior, and so infers recognition, gives the King no more right than the forfeited person had, as treason for raising fire, or burning coal-sinks, or for accusing another of treason unjustly.

32. Tacks also being necessary and profitable, are not excluded by forfeiture, Maitland, Dec. 14, 1570; Home of Manderstoun *contra* Tennents of Oldhamstocks [Maitland, *Fol. Dict.* 1,313; M. 4684]; Leslie of Wachtoun *contra*   [Not found]. The like as to tacks for a competent duty, but not in tacks for grassums, January 28, 1674, General Dalziel *contra* Tennents of Caldwal [2 Stair 258; M. 4685].

33. But by the Act of Parl. 1644 [A.P.S. VI(1),223,c. 229], forfeiture was declared to be without prejudice to all persons not accessory to the crime of the superior, of their rights of property of any lands, wadset, or others holden by them, of the forfeited person, or of the payment of their just debts,

or relief of their cautionries out of the forfeited estates, which was rescinded by the general Act Rescissory, Parl. 1661, cap. 15 [A.P.S. vii, 86, c. 126]. But this Act is now repealed by the Act of Parl. 1690, cap. 33 [A.P.S. ix, 225, c. 104], K. William and Q. Mary, as to posterior forfeitures.

34. Forfeiture could not be pronounced in absence of the forfeited person by the Justice-General, but only by the Parliament: so that no certification of the Justices could reach lands, but only moveables, July 30, 1662, Yeoman *contra* Oliphant [1 Stair 139; M. 4773]. Neither could it extend to heritable bonds, November 31, 1671, Hag *contra* Moscrop and Rutherford [2 Stair 15; M. Supp. 9]: but now the Justices may proceed to forfeit absents, in case of open rebellion and rising in arms, Parl. 1669, cap. 11 [A.P.S. vii, 562, c. 17].

35. Because of the difficulty the King or his donatar might have, in knowing the rights of forfeited persons, by labouring the same with their own goods, setting the same to tenants, and uplifting the mails and duties, as their heritage, and so being reputed heritable possessors for the space of five years immediately preceding the process of forfeiture, the lands so laboured or possessed pertain to the King, and his donatar, though they can produce no heritable right, or title thereof in the forfeited person: for trial whereof, commission may be granted under the testimonial of the Great Seal, to such persons as shall be thought fit, by the advice of the secret council, to take cognition by an inquest, what lands were bruiked by the forfeited person as heritable possessor thereof, so commonly reputed and esteemed by the said five years space, with power to call before them all parties pretending interest, which being returned to the chancellary *ad perpetuam remanentiam*, shall be a sufficient right, Parl. 1584, cap. 2 [A.P.S. iii, 349, c. 6]. This right was sustained to a donatar though there was no precognition of the five years' possession, July 14, 1623, Maxwell *contra* L. Westeraw [*Sub die* July 19, Durie 72; M. 10599]. But here the donatar was made to depone, that he had just reason to affirm, that the rights were wanting, Hope, Possession, *inter eosdem* [*Sub nom. Lord Nithsdaill* v *Westerhall*, Hope, *Maj. Pr.* iii, 21, 31; M. 4710]. This was not elided, though it was offered to be proven that the forfeited person's right was reduced *in foro contradictorio*, upon recognition before his forfeiture, Had. February 20, 1611, L. Hairstones *contra* Rambel [Not found]: so the said five years' possession, being reputed heritable possessor, infers *praesumptionem juris et de jure* of the forfeited person's right, which admits no contrary probation, as to the forfeited person's right, if the quinquennial peaceable and lawful possession be proven; but the probation thereof by inquest will not exclude a contrary probation by reduction upon the possession of others, within the five years: and if the possession be not lawful and peaceable, but interrupted or vitious, the statute takes no place; for by possession, lawful, peaceable possession of the forfeited persons must be understood: and if any person have moved action within the five years, for taking away the rebel's right and possession, they will be heard after the forfeiture, as before; yea,

citation before the five years, and inhibition within the five years, with a subsequent security, were found sufficient to take off the benefit of this Act, July 23, 1666, E. Southesk *contra* M. Huntley [1 Stair 400; M.4712]. This privilege is not competent by exception, offering to prove five years' possession, but by a retour upon a commission served by an inquest, June 13, 1666, Hume *contra* Hume [1 Stair 375; M.10620]. In this statute it is also provided, that where there were tacks, or possessions of lands, or teinds possessed by the forfeited person, in respect that the rights thereof might also be abstracted, that the King and his donatar should continue in that same possession for five years, without any account for the profits thereof, and longer, if a right be instructed of the forfeited person: and if a feuar be forfeited, the land is not liable for the feu-duty preceding the forfeiture; because the discharges thereof might have been abstracted. Possession of the rebel for fewer than five years by the forfeited person, was found sufficient to continue for five years, though no tack nor temporary right was instructed, January 24, 1667, Hume *contra* Hume [1 Stair 429; M.4721].

36. It is also declared in this statute, that the forfeiture of the apparent heir carries therewith the right of the lands, to which he might succeed, though he were never entered heir, nor infeft, whereof Craig mentions a case, *Lib.* ii. *Dieg.* 8 [11,18,23; *sub nom. Bisset* v *Bisset* (1564) M.4655], that the daughters of the Laird of Laisindrum were excluded from their succession to their goodsire, because their father was forfeited, though he was never received, nor infeft in these lands.

37. Craig, in the forecited place [11,18,23; *sub nom. Bisset* v *Bisset* (1564) M.4655] moveth, but determineth not this question, whether the forfeiture inferreth a corruption of the blood of all the descendants of the forfeited persons, whereby, till they be restored, they are incapable of any succession, though descending to them by the maternal line. This corruption of the blood is frequently in England, where persons are specially attainted and convict of treason; and sometimes with us it is called Dishabilitation, and is a part of the doom or sentence, that the successors of the person convict shall be incapable of lands, estate, honour, or office; yea, their fame and memory is sometimes condemned, and their sirname abolished, as was done in the forfeiture of the Earl of Gourie [In consequence of the so-called Gowrie Conspiracy. See A.P.S. 11,192–3,195–9,203–12; Arnot, *Criminal Trials*, 83; Pitcairn, *Criminal Trials*, 11,146; Lang, *James VI and the Gowrie Mystery*]: but it is not consonant to our customs, that forfeiture in other cases should infer this corruption of the blood: First, Because of the multiplication of cases to which forfeiture is now extended, as to theft in landed men, and false coin, &c.: Secondly, If none of the descendants of forfeited persons were capable of succession to any person, that could not be by reason of any specialty in the matter of succession, but of something in their person by reason of the forfeiture, excluding them thence, which would not only take place in heritage but in moveables; yea, the oye, or further offspring of the forfeited person,

could not succeed to their own immediate parents, which would infer, that they could be capable of no goods or means, but the same would be instantly confiscated: Thirdly, Though forfeitures in Scotland have been very frequent, the offspring of such have ordinarily acquired lands and goods, and their children succeeded them therein, without obtaining restitution of their blood; so that this corruption of the blood is rather to be thought a specialty in some atrocious treasons, by the tenor of the doom of forfeiture, than a general consequence thereof.

38. But whereas it hath been said, that the apparent heir being forfeited, the King hath right to the heritage, to which he might succeed; it may be questioned, whether that may be extended to the apparent heir, if he be forfeited during his predecessor's life, or if it be only in the case that the heir apparent is forfeited after the death of his predecessor, where *de præsenti* he may be heir. There is no doubt if the person forfeited should be fugitive, and survive his predecessor, but the heritage accrescing to him, wherein he might *de præsenti* be infeft, would fall under forfeiture, though he were not actually infeft; and it seems no less clear, that being forfeited, if he should die before his predecessor, that his brother, or collaterals, might succeed to their father, or any other to whom the forfeited person, if he had survived them, would have succeeded. It is more doubtful whether his descendants could, if any were; for these would exclude the collaterals: and there seems no reason to exclude them from their grandfather's heritage, not being dishabilitated; and seeing I have not found it extended further, I conceive it more favourable, that the heir apparent dying before his predecessor, should not hinder his descendants to succeed to that predecessor. But unless the forfeiture did incapacitate the predecessor to dispose upon his own estate, the forfeiture in that case would be improfitable; yet seeing we have no complaints of exheredation in Scotland, but that parents may freely dispose of their estates at their pleasure, it would be hard to bind up the parent more in relation to the fisk, than to his own child, unless fraud, to prevent the effect of the forfeiture, without a rational cause, do appear.

39. For the further security of the King and his donatar, it is provided, Parl. 1594, cap. 205 [Act 1594, c. 202; A.P.S. IV, 64, c. 12] that no letter of pension, factory, bond or assignation, granted by any forfeited person, shall be valid, unless it be confirmed by the King, or authorised by decreet of an ordinary judge, obtained before citation in the process of forfeiture; which seems to insinuate, that creditors should be satisfied out of the forfeited estate: but it will reach no further than the moveables fallen by forfeiture, which seem to be affected in the same way, as falling by single escheat, the full dominion in both being the King's, but with the burden of admitting the diligence of lawful creditors before the declarator; but I have not observed this practised in moveables of forfeited persons. The reason of this statute appeareth by the Act immediately preceding, whereby a former Act of Parliament [A.P.S. III, 539, c. 3], in favour of the vassals of forfeited persons, is

rescinded, and appointed to be delete out of the books of Parliament; which rescinded act, though it be not extant, but delete, as aforesaid, hath affected forfeited estates with the debts of the forfeited persons, and with the subaltern infeftments, granted by forfeited persons not confirmed; and therefore such rights being constituted by a law then standing, could not be derogated from by a subsequent law: and therefore it was necessary to caution, by the foresaid Act 202 [A.P.S. IV,64,c.12], that simulate or antedated rights, might not affect estates forfeited before the said Rescissory Act. Yet by the statute 205 [A.P.S. IV,64,c.12], though that which was in favour of vassals of forfeited persons, was delete out of the records of Parliament; yet letters of pension, bonds or assignations, granted by forfeited persons before citation on the process of forfeiture, being authorised by the sentence of an ordinary judge, shall be valid, viz. to affect the forfeited estate; for, as to other effects, there would be no question; therefore the Act 1644 [A.P.S. VI(1),223,c.229] was not without ground nor precedent, even as to heritable rights, whereunto pensions are only relative; and likewise the 33d Act, Parl. 1, Sess. 2, K. Will. and Q. Mary [Act 1690,c.33; A.P.S. IX,225,c.104], though more extensive in prejudice of the royal prerogative, wants not ground and example, that nothing should be forfeited which could not have been alienated by the forfeited person; and therefore it is statute, that no forfeiture thereafter shall prejudge tacksmen, creditors, superiors, vassals, heirs of entail, husbands or wives of forfeited persons; which shall defend tacksmen possessing before the treason, it being open and notour, or before the process if the treason were latent; and that the forfeited estate shall be subject to all real actions and claims, though they be not raised within the five years preceding the forfeiture, excepting feu-duties, annualrents, and annual prestations not insisted for within the five years; and shall be subject to all creditors, real or personal, contracting prior to the treason, being notour, or to the citation in the forfeiture, being latent, the debts being always upon record by being registrated, or diligence done thereupon, excepting debts contracted during open rebellion, and rising in arms; and that no heir of entail shall profit [Probably "forfeit"] more than what he could affect his estate with, so that the infeftment of tailzie be registrated, conform to the Act of Parliament 1685 [Entail Act, 1685,c.22; A.P.S. VIII,477,c.26]. And all the sub-vassals' rights are confirmed: yet this will not import, that the ordinary casualty of recognition is hereby taken from the King more than from the subjects, by decreets against the King, which, without forfeiture, would recognosce.

40. Sentence of forfeiture being pronounced, it is declared irreducible upon any nullity in the process upon which it proceeded, till the crime be remitted by the King, or the party tried and acquitted thereof: but restitution shall only be granted by way of grace to the party forfeited, or their posterity, Parl. 1584, cap. 135 [A.P.S. III,297,c.11]; which was not found to extend to dishabilitation of the son of the forfeited person, but that it might by Act of Parliament be taken off, without citation of any party, who had acquired right

upon the dishabilitation from the donatar, which fell in consequence, February 24, 1665, Douglas and Sinclair *contra* L. Wedderburn [1 Stair 276; M. 14058].

41. The doom or decreet of forfeiture, when passed in Parliament, gives immediate access to the mails and duties of the estate possessed by the forfeited person, and needs no declarator; because it is a decreet of Parliament, and hath the like effect as ward, which requireth no declarator, January 6, 1681, Home *contra* Home [2 Stair 827; M.2142]. The like though the doom of forfeiture was by the Justices in absence, seeing it was ratified in Parliament [Act 1669, c. 11; A.P.S. VII, 562, c. 17], not by ratification passing of course, but by a public law, ratifying that forfeiture by the Justices, as if it had been done in Parliament, and all such forfeitures by the Justices being for open rebellion and rising in arms against the King, December 15, 1680, Gordon of Troquhen *contra* a Wadsetter of Barscobe [2 Stair 816; M. 4722].

42. Bastardy and last heir makes things befal to the fisk, as caduciary, because such things can be lawfully claimed by none; and therefore are applied to the fisk [IV, 12–13, *infra*]. Before we can conceive the effects of bastardy, we must understand the efficient that makes a bastard, which being relative and defective, is best taken up by the opposite, viz. a lawful child begotten of persons lawfully married: so then a bastard is a child whose parents were not lawfully married; and therefore such are bastards; First, whose parents were not at all married; secondly, those whose parents were married, yet were not in degrees capable of marriage; thirdly, those who were married, and in capable degrees, yet the marriage was inconsistent, because of some impediment, as if either party were married before, and the other spouse on life, whether that were solemnly, or privately, by promise of marriage, and copulation following; in which last case, if the impediment be secret, and not known to both parties, Craig observeth [II, 18, 18–19], as his own opinion, and the opinion of the Canonists, that the said impediment, though it be sufficient to annul the marriage, yet not to take away the legitimation of the children procreated *bona fide* by any of the parties before knowledge of that impediment.

But, because who are the parents, is sometimes dubious, procreation being secret both in the act and effect: for clearing thereof, it is the common rule in the civil law, and with us, *Pater est, quem justae nuptiae demonstrant*, L. 5. ff *de in jus vocando* [D. 2, 4, 5]. So he is presumed to be the father, who the time of the conception was married to the mother; but in this case, lawful marriage is not opposed to clandestine, or irregular marriage, as not being after proclamation in the church, or by a person having power to marry by the canons of the church, or statutes of the country; but that is only understood as unlawful marriage in this case, which materially is unjust and inconsistent, where marriage could not have subsisted, albeit it had been orderly performed, as being by persons in degrees prohibited by divine law, or where either party had another lawful spouse then living, and undivorced: yea, marriage betwixt the adulterer and the adulteress, after dissolution of the former marriage, doth not infer bastardy of the children of the subsequent marriage, though it may debar them from succession [1,4,7,*supra*], The presumption that the children born in marriage are the husband's, requires such time as they might have been lawfully procreated, when both parties were free and unmarried, which, if it was nine months before the birth it is sufficient; but if less, the presumption will not suffice, unless it appear the child was unripe, and born before the time, otherways the child will be presumed to be the former husband's. This is *praesumptio juris*, and admits contrary probation; as first, if the father were absent, or impotent, the time that the conception could be, which absence is not necessarily beyond sea, as the English require the father's absence; and therefore if he be within the four seas during the time the birth is in the womb, this presumption prevaileth against his absence with them: but with us it will be sufficient, that his absence be special and circumstantiate, that there remaineth no doubt, that he could not have been present. As if the father were in prison, or at a very great distance, so that a short time of his escape might not suffice him to be present. This presumption will also be taken off, by the testimony of both parties agreeing that the child belongs to another father, and so is a bastard: but the testimony of either of them will not suffice, as Craig relates [11,18,20], of a lady, that having controversy with her son, she was accustomed to confess that he was a bastard: and of a queen, related by the doctors, whose name they forbear, who at the time of her death, declared to her son, that he was not the king's son, yet he was received as king, in his father's place. It hath been more frequently seen, that the father hath disowned the child born of his wife, which, though it might infer suspicion and reproach, yet not bastardy, unless the mother also, of consent, or by process, were made to acknowledge it.

It will not be sufficient to elide the foresaid presumption, though the wife's adultery should be proven, yea, though at a time answering to the time of conception, which hath an ordinary course of nine months, yet hath had such variations, that the child hath been accompted belonging to the father, by reason of the marriage, though it preceded the birth of the child, only by the space of eight, seven, or the beginning of six months; especially if, by the judgment of physicians, the immaturity of the child concurred; yea, this presumption will attribute the child to the father, though the child be born nine, ten, or eleven months after the father's death: but, in these cases, the probability of the circumstances may make the mother's testimony alone sufficient to instruct the bastardy of the child. Neither is marriage here accounted, by the solemnization thereof in the church, which, in some places, is ordinarily without that: and though with us, it be a requisite solemnity, yet it is not of the being of marriage. And therefore cohabitation, as man and wife, supplieth the solemnity of public marriage, which, being a transient act, and having no record, could seldom be proven; yea, though it could be proven by the oath of both parties, or otherwise, that there was never a formal marriage, if the parties were capable of marriage, cohabitation would supply; for after contract, or promise of marriage, or *sponsalia*, if copulation follow, there is thence presumed a matrimonial consent *de præsenti*, which therefore cannot be passed from by either, or both parties, as having the essential requisities of marriage. If diligence be used for performing that solemnity, though it take no effect, the contract of marriage will make the child lawful as when, in the time of proclamation thereof, the one party died, whereof Craig [11,18,19] relateth a case; yea, in the case of Edward Younger there mentioned, who having begotten children under promise of marriage, but refusing to acknowledge or perform it, the woman having obtained sentence of the Commissars (who are judges of matrimony and legitimation) against the said Edward, for solemnizing the marriage, which, though he obeyed not, the children were accounted lawful, and capable of succession.

Marriage, as is before shown, Title, *Conjugal Obligations* [1,4,6,*supra*], is proved by cohabitation of the father and mother as married persons, which was sustained upon ten years cohabitation as man and wife, though it was offered to be proven the child was reputed bastard, July 7, 1626, Somervel *contra* Halcro [Durie 210; M. 12635]. And there being a mutual probation, whether a defunct was lawful, or a bastard, and six witnesses being examined on either side, though several of the witnesses on the one side proved, that the defunct was reputed bastard, and that his mother gave signs of repentance publicly in the church, for fornication with his father; but others proving that they were in their house, and saw them cohabit as man and wife, but did not mention how long, the defunct was found to be no bastard, but a lawful child, January 15, 1676, Swintoun *contra* Kaills [2 Stair 400; M. 12637]; yet this was elided by contrary probation, that the father had then another wife, and a lawful child thereby, and that the person in question was reputed bastard, Hope, Bastardy, Chirnside *contra* Grieve and Williamson [Haddington, *Fol.Dict.* 11,263; M. 12635]. Bastardy is also elided, by proving the person in question, to be holden and reputed lawful, unless the pursuer condescend, and instruct the contrary by particular circumstances, Hope, Bastardy, Hog *contra* Hog [*Sub nom. Roy* v *Roy*, Hope, *Maj.Pr.* IV,8,16; M. 12635]; Chirnside *contra* Hume [Sinclair, *Fol.Dict.* 11,261; M. 12629]. The like where the person in question was fifty years old, Hope *contra* Scot [Probably *Hirpet* v *Scot* (1618) M. 2197]: the like being 80 years after the bastard's death, who died an old man, the Lords would not grant process *de statu defunctorum post tantum tempus*, February 25, 1642, Crafurd *contra* Russels [*Sub nom. Crawford* v *Pursels*, Durie 894; M. 12636].

43. Bastardy hath no effect till declarator, which proceeds upon a general citation against all and sundry, at the market-cross of the shire where the bastard dwelt, at the instance of the King's advocate, or donatar, because the bastard can have none to represent him; but if the bastard's debtors be called specially, there will not only follow a general declarator, that the person was bastard, but a decerniture against the debtors, which is a special declara-

tor, though these may be disjoined in several processes: but if any party appear, as nearest agnate, he would be admitted to defend, December 11, 1679, Somervel *contra* Stains [2 Stair 720; M. 2197]. It was also found, that a declarator of bastardy was not relevantly libelled, that the father and mother were not married, unless it were added, that the defunct in his life was holden and reputed bastard, which was found and instructed, by his taking legitimation from the King, February 19, 1669, K. Advocate *contra* Craw [1 Stair 609; M. 2748]; June 15, 1672, Livingston *contra* Burns [*Sub anno* 1670, 1 Stair 680; M. 11973]; January 6, 1680, Somervel *contra* Stains [2 Stair 731; M. 12638].

44. As to the effects of bastardy, from the former principle, *Pater est quem justa matrimonia monstrant ;* children not begotten of parents lawfully married, are called *vulgo quæsiti*, and are counted in law, to have no father, agnates nor kinsmen on the father's side, and therefore they cannot succeed to their father, or any of their agnates; neither can any of these agnates succeed to them, either in heritable or moveable rights, but only their own succession, by lawful marriage: so then bastards dying without lawful issue, their goods become caduciary and void, and so fall to the fisk; yea, if the lawful issue of the bastard at any time fail, for the same reason, their goods become caduciary, and return to the king, either by reason of the bastardy, or as *ultimus hæres*, July 13, 1626, Haltro *contra* Somervel [Durie 215; M. 1348]. Though bastards can have no ascendent or collateral heirs of line, yet they may have heirs of tailzie, in lands which did exclude the fisk, when the same was provided to the bastard, and the heir of his body; which failing, to any other person and his heirs, Spots. Bastardy, Weir *contra* King's Donatar [*Sub nom. Muir* v *Wallace*, Spotiswoode 28; M. 1344]. They may also be heirs of tailzie specially nominate, as Craig observeth [11, 16, 19; 11, 18, 11], in the case of E. Errol *contra* Hay of Cockstoun [Spotiswoode 28; M. 1344], who, and the heirs of his body, made a member of tailzie, which was sustained, though he was bastard. Bastardy hath only effect against succession to the bastard, but doth not incapacitate the bastard, to dispose of his own estate, heritable or moveable, in his *liege poustie :* and likewise the bastard's wife hath her share of his moveables, as other relicts have; but if the bastard have no issue, he hath no power of testing, and can neither nominate executors, nor leave legacies, unless he obtain legitimation from the King [see Craig 11, 18, 16]. A bastard's wife having a disposition of all he had, was found to have right thereby to the half of the moveables, though the marriage was dissolved by the bastard's death within year and day, which was not found to give the benefit of the moveables to the fisk, as they would have returned to private parties, November 28, 1691, Stuart of Noll, &c [Not found].

45. Legitimation, though it hath many ample clauses, yet the main effect of it is, that the bastard having no lawful children, hath thereby power to test, June 18, 1678, Commissioners of the Shire of Berwick *contra* Craw [2 Stair 621; M. 1351]. But it hath no effect as to his heritable rights, which his testa-

ment cannot reach: it will have the like effect, if the bastard obtain from the king, the power of testing; and therefore a bastard's legatar was preferred to the donatar of bastardy, July 7, 1629, Wallace *contra* Muir [Durie 457; M. 1350]. In which case it was found, the relict had her half: and if the bastard had lawful children surviving, he may test without any gift, none being concerned but his children, to whom also he may name tutors, as was found, March 8, 1628, Mure *contra* Kincaid [Durie 356; M. 1349]; and these will succeed him as heirs, or executors. The effects of bastardy, in hindering their succession to others, falleth to be considered in the subsequent titles, concerning Succession [111, 4, *infra*].

46. It remains to be cleared, whether the bastard's debts follow his estate, and what diligence of lawful creditors will exclude the donatar or fisk: it was so found, that the bastard's creditor, arresting before his death, had access notwithstanding the bastardy, Had. February 26, 1611, Clerk *contra* E. Perth [Haddington, *Fol. Dict.* 1, 58; M. 778]. The difficulty will be of the diligences competent after the bastard's death, seeing he hath none to represent him; yet bastardy is but a species of *ultimus hæres*, the ground in both being the same, that the King is heir, because there can be no other heir, and so is last heir. And therefore in both cases, the estate is liable to the debt, which may affect it, *contra hæreditatem jacentem* by adjudication, calling the officers of state and donatar: Craig is of the same opinion, *Lib.* 2, *Dieg.* 17 [11. 17, 12 and 16], and was so found, July 25, 1560, King's Donatar *contra*   [Not found]. It was also found, that the donatar of bastardy pursuing for payment of a bond due to the bastard, was liable to fulfil the bastard's back-bond, June 20, 1671, Alexander *contra* L. Saltoun [1 Stair 735; M. 9208].

47. *Ultimus hæres* [IV, 13, *infra*] may seem to be a succession from the dead, and to come in amongst other heirs; yet though it hath the resemblance of an heir, because it hath effect, when there is no other heir, and makes the heritage liable to pay the defunct's debts, it is only a caduciary confiscation of the defunct's estate, with the burden of his debt, but no proper succession to him therein, which appeareth thus; the heir is one person in law, and is therefore personally obliged for all the defunct's debts, so is not the fisk, against whom or the donatar there lieth no personal action for payment, but for restitution, if he have intromitted, and of real action *contra hæreditatem jacentem*, which is most proper by adjudication, being the supplement of ordinary actions, or executions competent by law. For there being no party to represent the defunct debtor, there can be no decreet, but *cognitionis causa*, and adjudication following thereupon, in which the fisk or donatar is to be called passive, as the party having interest, to see that the debt be due, which will affect the defunct's caduciary heritage, to the detriment of the fisk, or donatar. So then *ultimus hæres*, and bastardy, are of the like nature, which being caduciary confiscations, fall to the fisk, because no other can have right. There may be this difference betwixt them, that in the case of the last heir, creditors, for their satisfaction, may confirm the defunct's moveables, and so

recover the same, for their own satisfaction; in which case they would be liable, as other executors, to the remanent creditors of the defunct, and to the fisk, or donatar, for the superplus, as in the place of nearest of kin, and to the relict also for her part; but this being only for obtaining their own satisfaction, and for shunning a more extraordinary way, by adjudication (which also they may use at their option,) they ought not, in prejudice of the fisk, to have the third part of the defunct's part, as other executors: but in the cases of bastardy, confirmation of executors is not competent; because the bastard, being excluded from the power of making a testament, can have no executor.

Concerning Last Heir, the greatest doubt is, who they are, and in what cases they take place. As to the first, Craig, *Lib.* 2, *Dieg.* 17 [11,17,11] is not positive, whether superiors be last heirs of the defunct, in the fees held of them, or if the King be the last heir for all: and according to the ancient feudal customs, there is no doubt, the feus return to the several superiors; for thereby none could succeed, (without express provision in the contrary,) but the lawful issue, or the descendants of the first vassal, whose person and race was peculiarly chosen and confided in by the superior. But now fees not being gratuitous, as at first, but for onerous causes, besides the *reddendo and service ;* they are ordinarily granted to the vassal, and his heirs whatsomever; which failing, the King by his prerogative royal, excludeth all other superiors, who are presumed to retain no right, nor expectation of succession, unless by express provision of the investiture, the fees be provided to heirs-male, or of tailzie; which failing, to return to the superior, in which he is proper heir of provision.

As to the other doubt, in what case the King is last heir, Craig, in the forenamed place [11,17,11] relateth, that some were of opinion, that if the defunct had no heirs within the seventh degree, the king taketh place as last heir: and that others thought it to hold in collateral successions; but his own opinion is in the contrary, that any heir, of what degree soever, hath right, which suiteth with the ground now laid down, that the King hath right, as last heir, to the heritage becoming caduciary; because no other party can be instructed lawful heir: so he reporteth, it was found in the case of the Earl of Marr, who was served heir to Lady Elizabeth Dowglas Countess of Marr, beyond the tenth degree. And that the Lord Seatoun, that he might have a title to the redemption of the lands of Longnidrie, against Forrester, served himself heir to the granter of the wadset, beyond the seventh degree, whereof several degrees were collateral. And the French King Henry IV succeeded to Henry III [in 1589] though not within the fifteenth degree. The gift, or right of *ultimus hæres* hath no effect, till decreet of declarator be obtained thereupon, in the same way as in bastardy, July 20, 1662, L. Balnagowan *contra* Dingwal [1 Stair 139; M. 3409]; July 31, 1666, Crawford *contra* Town of Edinburgh [1 Stair 403; M. 3410]. Where a general summons against all and sundry was found sufficient, but if there were a relict or executor, they ought to be particularly cited.

Title 4. Succession by the Civil and Feudal Law, and Our Law, Where, of Deathbed, *Annus Deliberandi*, and Kinds of Heirs in Scotland

SUCCESSION to defuncts is the most important title in law; for thereby the rights of all persons do necessarily pass once, and frequently oftener, in every generation; and therefore the rule and course of succession ought to be accurately searched out, and followed: and because the channel of succession is with us divided in two currents, by the one whereof all heritable rights, and by the other all moveable rights, are conveyed from the dead to the living, the first passing unto heirs, the second unto executors; we shall in this title consider that which is common to succession, and in the subsequent titles, that which is proper to the several kinds thereof. As to the common consideration of succession, we must severally inquire; First, What natural equity holdeth forth of succession: Secondly, What the judicial law: Thirdly, What the civil Roman law: Fourthly, What the feudal customs: And lastly, What our own law and consuetude provideth concerning succession.

1. For the first, It may seem that succession hath little foundation, far less a competent regulation, in equity, or by the law of nature; because the

matter of succession is so variable, that every nation, yea, almost every province, and many cities, have their several constitutions and customs for succession, arguing it to be wholly in the arbitriment of people, and authority over them. Yet this will not follow, that succession hath no rise, nor rule in equity: for, as hath been oft-times shown before, most of the rights of men are ordered in equity; yet so, as they are put in the owners' power, who may alter the same by their will. So it will be found in the matter of succession, which appeareth thus: 1. Succession was before constitutions or customs: of constitutions, there will be no doubt, these are but rare to this day, succession being yet ordinarily by custom, and custom necessarily implieth antecedent acts of succession, inductive thereof, which therefore behoved to have some other rule than the custom thereby introduced. 2. Where there is neither law nor custom concerning succession; as when people from divers countries do gather into new plantations in America, and live not severally, as parts of their mother-countries, but jointly, such have goods, which by their death become not caduciary or *nullius*, to be appropriated by the first occupant. If therefore they remain in the property of some persons, which needs must be by some law, it can be by no other than natural equity, or the law of rational nature. 3. It is not to be thought that God, who hath allowed property, would leave man destitute of a natural rule, whereby to regulate it after the owner's death, though there were no human law nor custom about it.

2. But it is not so dubious, that there is a rule of equity in succession, as what it is; for clearing whereof, we shall parcel it out thus: First, Every right, being a faculty, or power of exaction or disposal, it is a chief interest and effect of it, that the owner may dispose thereof not only to take effect presently, but, if he please, to take effect after his death; and, by the law of nature, the sole will of the owner is sufficient to pass or transmit his right, if communicable, to take effect when he willeth in his life, or after his death. So then the first rule of succession in equity, is the express will of the owner, willing such persons to succeed him in whole, or in part. It may be objected, that the will of the owner is not the rule of succession; because there lieth upon the owner a natural obligation to provide for his relations, not only during his life, but after his death; as it is said, 1 Tim. v. 8. "He that provideth not for his own, especially these of his own family, hath denied the faith, and is worse than an infidel;" which importeth, that infidels have naturally that principle; and therefore the first member of succession in equity must be those of the defunct's family, and not those of his institution or choice. This doth indeed well conclude a natural obligation on all men to provide [for] their own; but first. It will not extend so far, as to incapacitate the owner to dispose of his own, either in his life, or after his death; so that there remain a competent provision for his own, otherwise he might not even gift in his life; but he may gift, both to take effect in his life, and after his death, and is not necessitated to institute his own as heirs, but to provide them: 2. The duty of provision is a personal obligation, but the power of disposal, and succession thereby, is a

real right, which are *toto genere* different rights: now real rights are not hindered, nor altered by personal obligations, though the disponer hath failed and remains debtor; as an obligement to dispone is no disposition; but the present dispositive act of the will doth only constitute or convey the right; which, though it be posterior to an obligement in favour of any other, that doth not annul the disposition, though it oblige the disponer. If there be no express will of the defunct, the main difficulty is, what is the second member of natural succession, wherein the presumed will of the defunct takes place, which hath this rule, *quod naturaliter inesse debet, præsumitur.*

And therefore the defunct's will is presumed to institute his own, whom he is naturally obliged to provide in the first place; so that it is not the obligement to provide, but the defunct's will presumed thence, which disposeth upon his succession; for the obligement to dispone, and the actual disposition, are different *toto genere;* and if the obligement to provide were the rule, the express will of the owner could not over-rule it. Where there is a custom of succession, the defunct's will is presumed to be according to that custom; which being a law by the common authority where the defunct lived, importeth his will or consent, at least by submission. The presumed will of the defunct to provide his own, is not indefinite of all his own; but it hath a natural order, or substitution standing in the nearest degree of consanguinity: for natural reason sheweth, that as there is not an equal relation, so there cannot be an equal division to all; and there being no natural rule of proportion, the nearest degree must exclude the further degrees in succession; which is clearly held forth in the foresaid text, having an explicatory and applicatory term, "especially these of his own family;" and as the proportion is unknown, so the benefit, being extended to all degrees, would evanish; therefore whatever natural affection, or charity, might oblige the defunct to have done expressly, his presumed will hath no rule beyond the first degree.

3. Fourthly, Therefore the first degree of succession, by the conjectured will of the intestate, is of children, according to that, Rom. viii. 17. "If children, then heirs": which consequence doth necessarily import, that all children are heirs: neither can this be an allusion from the Judicial law, by which all children were not heirs, but the male excluded the female; therefore it must needs be a consequence from the law of nature: and seeing there is no different proportion held forth by this text, or by the light of nature, the succession of all children must be in equal shares, whether male or female; for in all communions, and partnerships, an equal division takes place, except an unequal be expressed.

4. It is more dark, whether by the law of nature, there be competent the right of representation, whereby the issue of the defunct children represent them, and come in with the surviving children, to get that share which their defunct parent would have got, if alive; whereby they would not succeed *in capita*, the whole successors getting equal share, but *in stirpes;* whereby the issue of the defunct child, though they succeed equally among themselves,

yet unequally with the surviving children, because the whole issue of the defunct, get but an equal share with each of the surviving children: as if a father having three children, the eldest dying before him, leaves one child, and two oyes by another child; if there be place for representation, the heritage would divide in three, the two surviving children will have two third parts, the other third will divide in two, whereof the child of the defunct will get one half, and the other half will divide equally betwixt the two oyes: so then the question is, whether the descendants will thus succeed, or if the survivers will wholly exclude the issue of those deceasing.

This right of representation taketh place with us, and most other nations, in the right of immoveables, which we call heritable rights, whether it be of descendants or collaterals: but doubtless in that the course of the law of nature is altered for the preservation of the stock or stem of the family: so that it is clear, that there is no right of representation in collaterals, by the law of nature; as that the child, or grandchild of a brother should come in with a brother, because the propinquity of blood, natural affection, and so the presumed will of the defunct, is diminished: but it is not so clear in descendants, neither shall we be positive in it; but it seems most suitable to reason and the text adduced, that if the issue of defunct children remain in the family, that they should come in by representation in the place of their defunct parent; for these that are in the family extendeth to all that are not foris-familiated, whether children or grandchildren, to whom there remaineth the like affection in the common parent: but when the defunct child was foris-familiated, and so presumed to have been provided, and to have gotten a share, and therewith put out of the family, to live in a distinct family; in that case there seems no ground for representation, which doth agree to our custom in the succession of moveables, wherein there is no right of representation; but the nearest of kin exclude the issue of the defuncts, which were of the same degree, which succession is certainly more near unto the natural succession: so what hath been said, may sufficiently clear the natural succession of the descendants, whether children or grandchildren, and while there are any descendants, there is place for no other.

5. The third branch of natural succession, failing the express will of defuncts, and their descendants, or the issue of their bodies, is of parents; among whom these in the nearest degree are preferable, as father and mother: and if the father be dead, there seems to be place for representation to his father to come in with the surviving mother equally; but other parents of, or by the female line, who are in another family, from the ground laid in the text, "Of providing these in the family," seem not to come in to exclude brothers and sisters, and other collaterals in that family; as the grandfather and grandmother on the mother's side. It will not be opposite to this, which is said, "Children are not to lay up for parents, but parents for children:" [2 Cor. xii, 14] which is not to be understood absolutely, but comparatively, and according to the ordinary course of nature.

6. The fourth link of natural succession is brethren and sisters, among whom brethren and sisters-german, being related by both bloods, exclude these who are only of one blood by the father's side: the reason is, because the presumed will of the defunct, being from the interest and relation, these of double relation, by both bloods, are preferable to these of single relation.

7. The last degree of natural succession is, of uncles, aunts, nephews, nieces; all which being in equal propinquity to the defunct, come in together, and failing these, the succession would befall equally to the nearest degree of cousins, among whom the nearest degree excludeth the [further], without right of representation: and these conjoined by both bloods, exclude these conjoined by one: husband and wife do not succeed properly, either to other, but having a communion of goods, there is a division by the death of either.

8. The main question is here, whether there be naturally any difference in succession, betwixt the collaterals on the father's side, who are called agnates, and the collaterals on the mother's side, who are called cognates. Justinian in his Novel Constitutions, cap. 4. No. 127 [Nov. 118, 4] took off all distinction of agnates and cognates in succession [111, 4, 19, *infra*]: for which he is generally reprehended by interpreters, who hold such a difference, even in equity, cognates being conjoined by women, who ordinarily are under the power of others, even naturally by marriage; and so being of another family, they are not of the defunct's own family, as the agnates are, (amongst these the mother, father's mother, or other ascendants on the father's side in his family, are not hereby excluded) and so neither these or others, by their express nor presumed will, can transmit any goods or estates. Yet this point remaineth more dark; and I conceive what hath come by the mother's side, or by the grandmother, &c. therein the cognates of her blood would naturally succeed, because there are two grounds of presumption joined, propinquity of blood and gratitude, or remuneration to that lineage, by whom such things by succession came; so that *paterna paternis, materna maternis*, ought to take place in equity, as the presumed will of the defunct, unless the express will, or the law or custom of the place, be to the contrary [111, 4, 34, *infra*]. If the propinquity of degrees be alike, gratitude may cast the balance. And so much for the natural course of succession, which hath been the more insisted in, not only to show the goodness and righteousness of God, instructing man with an inbred law, written in his heart, though he were destitute of any human constitution or custom, so that he might walk justly in this important matter of succession, albeit all the lines of this divine impression be not clear to our sin-dimmed eyes; but also that, where positive law or custom is dubious, in the matter of succession, or is defective therein, emendation and extension may be fetched thereto, from the law of nature; therefore we shall now proceed to the positive law of God given to Israel, concerning succession.

9. The Judicial law, in the case of the daughters of Zelophehad, Num. 6, 27 [Num. xxvii, 8], determineth the order of succession, in lands or immoveables, to stand as a perpetual statute to the children of Israel. Thus the

first degree of succession is of all the sons, whereby the daughters and their descendants are excluded; but the sons do not succeed equally, for the first-born had a double portion of all that the father had, Deut. xxi. 17. by which the eldest son had twice as much as the other sons: so that the heritage being divided in one portion more than there were sons; of these the eldest had two, and each of the rest one; as if there be two sons, it divides in three, whereof the elder hath two third parts, and the younger one third part; if there be three, the heritage divides in four parts, whereof the eldest hath two fourth parts, which is the half, and each of the rest hath one fourth part.

10. This right of primogeniture was so secured, that the father could not prefer any other son thereunto, Deut. 24, v. 16 [Deut. xxi, 16]. Failing sons, the inheritance passeth to the daughters equally; for though the text expresseth it to pass to the daughter, in the singular number, yet it is cleared by the context, that all the daughters are therein included; for the daughters of Zelophehad, though more in number, are found to have the same right, and to get an inheritance among their father's brethren; by which it appeareth that the right of representation had place there; for all the daughters of Zelophehad were but to have that share which their father would have had, if he had been alive among his brethren; for they claimed the right of their father, whom they show not to have been in the company of Corah [In the Authorised Version, Korah], thereby forfeiting his right: so then the right of representation must take place amongst all descendants; so that the children of the sons, though these sons survive not their father, would exclude the surviving daughters, or would come in with the surviving sons, not equally and *in capita*, but *in stirpes*, whereby they would succeed to the shares of their pre-deceased fathers, by right of representation.

11. The third degree of Jewish succession is, failing descendants, the inheritance passeth to the defunct's brethren; and these failing, to his father's brethren; and these failing, to the nearest kinsman of his family, that is, the nearest agnates on his father's side, where all the male-agnates of the same degree are understood. It doth not appear whether in this collateral succession there be place for representation; and though there be no mention of the succession of women, or their issue, but only of daughters, some have thought, from the parity of reason, in every degree, failing the males, the females are to succeed, and to exclude further degrees of males, as if there be no brothers but sisters, these should exclude the father's brother: it may be also thought strange, that in all this course of succession, there is no mention of the succession of parents.

12. In answer to these doubts;—as to the first, I conceive, that in collateral succession there is also place for representation; so that the brother's sons, as representing the defunct brother their father, would exclude the father's brethren, and so of the rest; because it is said, if there be no brethren, the inheritance shall pass unto the father's brethren; which failing, unto the nearest kinsman; and, if there be no right of representation, the cousin-

german, or father's brother's son, would exclude the nephew, or brother's son; for uncle and nephew are never understood by the name of cousins or kinsmen; but have that special nominate relation of uncle and nephew, or father's and brother's son; and therefore the brother's son, as representing the brother, must succeed and exclude the father's brother; secondly, *Caeteris paribus*, succession will certainly descend to the brother's son, and not ascend to the father's brother.

13. As to the second doubt, I hold, that only daughters and their issue do succeed, and no other females or their issue; the reason is, first, from the text, where failing sons, daughters are expressed, but failing brothers, sisters are not substitute, but uncles: second, the division and succession of the land of Canaan was typical, and was not to pass from tribe to tribe; and therefore daughters succeeding are appointed to marry in their own tribe; because ordinarily they were to be married when their father's succession did probably appear; but this could not have been if father's sisters, and these of further degree, had succeeded, these being ordinarily married before their succession.

14. As to the third, concerning succession of parents, it is sure, mothers and all cognates by the mother's side, being ordinarily of other tribes and families, were, for the reason now adduced, excluded from the succession. The text is clear, that only kinsmen in the family, that is, on the father's side, succeeded; but the reason why there is no mention of fathers, &c. [III, 4, 35, *infra*] may be because the land of Canaan being typical, it is fixed to tribes and families, and uses not to pass by testament or provision, or to be acquired further than by wadset, to return at the Jubilee; therefore among the Jews lands passed by the ordinary course of legitime succession, and so came from the fathers to the children, which pre-supposes the father to have been predeceased, and could not succeed. By this tract of the Jewish succession it is clear, that God, by his positive law, altered the effect of equity, and of his moral law, in succession: for it hath been now shown from that place [Rom. viii, 17], "if children, then heirs," that all children must needs be heirs, not by the Judicial law, but by equity; and yet by the Judicial law, not all children are heirs, but sons exclude daughters, and other females are excluded by males of a far distant degree, which necessarily infers, that for expediency, the course of succession may be altered. The like must also be in other effects of equity, which are in our power.

15. The order of succession in the civil law, did exceedingly vary, being in many points different, in the ancient law of the Twelve Tables, in the honorary law, introduced by the edicts and customs of the Pretors, who had authority to supply and correct the ancient law, and in the imperial constitutions, especially in the Novel Constitutions of Justinian. They did all agree in this, that the chief mean of succession, is the will or testament of the defunct, which they held so sacred, that all pactions or provisions, which might any way hinder the free liberty of testing, or any act whereby defuncts might be restrained, or constrained in the free disposal of their estates, were not only

null, but exclusive of such persons from having any interest in the defunct's inheritance; yet were the Romans so sensible of the natural obligation of parents to provide their children, that their middle laws, necessitated fathers either to institute their children, or expressly to exheredate, or disherish them, expressing their delinquency of ingratitude, the kinds and measures whereof the law did determine; so that if the children were passed by in silence, and neither instituted nor exheredate, the law declared the testament void; and if they were exheredate without a due and true offence, it did allow the children *querelam inofficiosi testamenti*, that is, complaint against the testament made *contra officium*, which is the natural obligation, or duty of parents to provide their children; for the like reason, the same complaint was competent to the fathers, against the testament of their children; but because that remeid might have been elided, by exhausting the heritage by legacies, whereby the institution of the children might prove ineffectual for their provision, therefore the law allowed children a legitime portion, being the fourth part of the heritage; which, that it might extend to all heirs, Falcidius was the author of that noble law, restraining legacies, so that there might remain a portion to the defunct's heirs, which law and portion, in honour of his name, was called the Falcidian Law [40 B.C. See Gaius 11,227; Inst. 2,22; D. 35,2], and *Portio Falcidia*, whereby the fourth part of the free goods of the testator, remained always secure against legacies, and when a new subtilty was invented, to frustrate the Falcidian law, by taking away the heritage, not directly by legacies, but indirectly by trust or *fidei commissas*, Trebellianus procured that ordinance of the Senate, called *Senatus-consultum Trebellianum* [56/57 A.D. See Gaius 11,253; Inst. 2.23; D. 36,1; c. 6,49], whereby that portion called also *Trebellianica*, should remain safe against fidei-commissary trusts: and though it be the common opinion of the Doctors, that if the defunct expressly prohibit the heir, to take the benefit of his *Falcidia* or *Trebellianica*, they will be thereby excluded [Nov. 1,2, §2], yet the common opinion is also, that it cannot be extended to children, as to their legitime, whom the law hath fully secured, either by ordaining them to be instituted heirs in whole, or at least in a fourth part, which is their natural or legitime portion: and if they be instituted in less, they have right to the supplement of their legitime portion, or otherwise they must be expressly and justly exheredate, and they have the common benefit of other heirs, of their *Falcidia*, or *Trebellianica*, which the testator cannot frustrate without express prohibition.

16. If there be no lawful testament, by the law of the Twelve Tables (which is the ancient Roman law, and in comparison of the Pretorian or Imperial law, is only called the law, or the civil law) the succession of the defunct falleth, in the first place, to the defunct's children, or nearest descendants, without distinction of any lawful children, though adopted or posthumous, or though of divers lawful marriages, whether male or female, so that they remain in the defunct's family, and in his paternal power; for these who are emancipated, and demitted from the family, and from under the

paternal power, they are either really or presumptively provided, and so have no share of the succession: (of this paternal power and emancipation, see before, Title, Obligations of Parents [1,5,11-13,*supra*]) these in the family were called *haeredes sui et necessarii*; because they were *ipso facto* heirs without solemnity or entry; among these, the right of representation had place, so that for example, the grandchildren succeeded with the children, but not equally, and *per capita*, but *per stirpes*; for the grandchildren had but the share of their defunct parent equally among them, and so of all other descendants being in the family. The Pretors did in a part alter this, and brought in the children or issue emancipated with those of the family, without distinction; providing the emancipated brought in their goods, and adjected the same to the inheritance, *per collationem bonorum*; yet because only the law, that is, the ancient law, could make heirs, the emancipated were not called heirs, but *bonorum possessores*. The Pretorian law did also take off the necessity and damage of the succession, that none might be necessitated to be heirs, yea, all heirs had the benefit of an inventory, being timeously and duly made, beyond which they were not liable for the defunct's debts.

17. The next degree of succession, by the ancient Roman law, was failing descendants in the family, the nearest agnates of the same degree succeeded; but there was no succession of parents, nor of cognates related by the mother's side; (here mother comprehends grandmother and all other ascendants of that kind); so the next degree was of brethren and sisters, &c.

18. The Pretorian law did also emend this, and first brought in the fathers, with the brothers and sisters-german, or of both bloods: and thereafter the Tertullian Senatus-consult, failing the father, brought in the mother with the sisters in their share, but not with the brothers-german, who, if there were no sisters-german, excluded their mothers totally; as if, for example, there were a brother-german and a sister-german, the father being dead, the brother had the half, and the sister's half was divided equally betwixt her and her mother, and so the mother is preferred to the father's father, and to the defunct's brethren, and sisters of one blood; failing those of this degree, the brothers and sisters by the father's side; and these failing, the nearest degree of agnates, in which the parity of reason inferreth, that as in brothers and sisters, so in other collaterals, these of both blood make a nearer degree, than these of one blood; failing all these, the Pretorian law admits spouses to be heirs, each to other, the husband to the wife, and the wife to the husband; and lastly, the fisk takes place as last heir.

19. But the Emperor Justinian, by the Novel Constitution, 118. cap. 4, took off all distinction of agnates and cognates, and brought in the mother equally with the father; with what reason or approbation, we have touched before [111,4,8,*supra*]. This is the sum of succession by the Roman law, wherein there is no distinction of moveables or immoveables, and which takes up no small part of the body of the civil law, and writings of lawyers; wherein to insist particularly, would raise a great bulk, unnecessary for our purpose;

whereunto, we conceive this summary may suffice. But while the Roman empire and laws were trampled down by the Northern nations, the feudal law arose, and doth yet continue with the civil law of the Romans, and other nations, by which there is a great distinction introduced, in the succession, in moveables, and in lands or immoveables, which are now of a feudal nature: we shall therefore go on to the common feudal customs.

20. The feudal customs are local, and it is hard to find a common rule therein for succession, which is variable, according to the diversity of place; only, if we call to mind what was formerly said, Title, Infeftments [11, 3, 5–6, *supra*], of the distinction of ancient and proper fees, and of declining and improper fees; the nature of proper fees will hold forth the matter of succession therein; for a proper fee, being freely granted by the superior to his vassal, for military service, the vassal's person being chosen by the superior, and a special trust reposed in him, and the like hope of his issue, *Patrem sequitur sua proles*: it was at first so simply done, that entering the vassal in possession, in presence of his peers, was a sufficient constitution of his right, and the investiture signified then, not so much the act constituting, as the writ evidencing the fee; in the which case, from the nature of the right it is consequent, first, that none should succeed in the fee, but such as were fit for the military services; and so women and their issue were utterly excluded, and all the males succeeded equally: 2, in proper fees, none could succeed but the lawful issue of the first vassal, whose person and issue was specially chosen; among which, first the male issue of the vassal who died last infeft, according to their nearness, do succeed with the right of representation; next unto the descendants among the collaterals, brothers, and their male issue; and among these, the brothers-german, and their issue, exclude the brothers by one blood; and after brothers, father's brothers, and their male issue; and so other agnates of the last deceased, being always of the male issue of the first vassal, which being extinct, the fee ceaseth and returneth to the superior, not as the vassal's heir, but by virtue of that *directum dominium* which still remained in the superior. In this course of feudal succession, there could be no place to the vassal's father, or other ascendants; because, if the fee were a new fee or conquest by the son, his father nor his brethren could not succeed, as not being of the issue of the first vassal; and if it were an old fee, not purchased by the son, but whereunto he did succeed, it doth necessarily presuppose the death of the father, and other ascendants, to whom the son could not be heir, nor succeed, till they were dead: but if the superior receive the son upon the father's resignation, it is not to be held as *feudum novum*, whereby both the brothers, father, and father's brothers, would be excluded; and therefore if the son die without issue, and have no brother, the father ought to be preferred to the father's brother, being still of the blood of the first vassal. But when by the course of time, fees declined from the proper nature of ancient fees, and the investiture did express the tenor and special nature thereof, the tenor of the investiture became the first rule of succession in such fees, and came in place of the testa-

ment or will of the defunct; for, seeing the vassal could not alter the succession, without consent of the superior, he could not effectually test thereupon.

21. In the next place, what is not the express will of the vassal, and the superior by the tenor of the investiture, is regulated by their conjectural will, from the nature of the fee, and propinquity of blood: so if the fee be originally granted to a woman, her issue female succeed, as well as the male; or if the *reddendo* be not military service, but money, grain, or services competent to a woman, or manual services, wherein there is no choice of persons, &c., and so generally fees holden blench or feu, in all these women may succeed; because they are not excluded by the nature of the service. 2. If the fee be granted to heirs whatsomever, not only doth the issue of the first vassal, but all other his lawful heirs, or the lawful heirs of the last deceasing vassal, whether of the issue of the first vassal, or not, do succeed: and now fees being ordinarily acquired by sale, excambion, or the like onerous titles, *feuda ad instar patrimoniorum sunt redacta ;* heirs whatsoever are commonly expressed, and if they were not, they would be understood; for that which is ordinary is presumed.

22. The course of feudal succession hath given the prerogative to primogeniture to the eldest male of the nearest degree to the defunct vassal, who excludes not only the females of that degree, but the males also, and their issue, not only among us, but in England, France, and most other nations, which is more consonant to the nature of feudal rights, that the fee be not made insufficient to maintain the vassal, and that many vassals be not substitute in place of one. Before we descend to our own customs, it will be fit to consider the justice and expediency of this common custom in feudal succession. The lawfulness of primogeniture will be easily evinced from what hath been said already upon succession, wherein the will of the proprietor is the rule even in equity; and though he be naturally obliged to provide for his own, that personal obligation reacheth him, but not the inheritance, nor doth it oblige him to make these to succeed, but to give them competent provisions; and therefore the Judicial law, which is the positive law of God, evidenceth sufficiently the lawfulness, and in some cases the expediency of altering the natural course of succession; and therefore, not only the male issue is thereby preferred to the female, but all the females are utterly excluded, except daughters, that the inheritance may remain within the tribe; and the preference of males is, because females are less fitted for management of lands, and therefore are to have a portion, which the Judicial law calleth the Dowry of Virgins.

The expediency of primogeniture is partly public, and partly private: the public expediency is, that the estates of great families, remaining entire and undivided, they, with their vassals and followers, may be able to defend their country, especially against sudden invasions; for with us, in France, Poland, and many other places, the great families are the bulwarks of their country; having means to maintain themselves, and their followers, for some time, without standing armies, constant pay, and subsidies. The private expediency is, for the preservation of the memory and dignity of families, which, by frequent division of the inheritance, would become despicable or forgotten. Primogeniture taketh place in Germany and France, in proper fees like unto our ward-holdings, but not in allodials and lands holden freely, or for cane or rent: Gudelinus, *de jure novissimo*, lib. 2. cap. 13. relateth, that, in many of the German and French provinces, the male gets two third parts, and the females one; in other provinces the children of the first marriage succeed in all the lands the parents had, during that marriage, and so in order the children of after-marriages; and in other provinces and cities, the youngest son succeedeth in all, excluding the rest; and generally, bastards are not admitted, even to the succession of their mothers; and in England, though primogeniture have the prerogative by the common law, yet it hath an exception of the custom of Kent, where primogeniture hath no prerogative, and therefore that custom is called the Gaball kind of Kent,[1] which is as much as "to give to all the kind." The customs of England and Germany are contrary in this; that, in Germany, parents come in the next place after descendants, and exclude brothers and sisters, and all other collaterals; but in England, parents do never succeed; so if the defunct have no issue, brothers nor sisters, nor their issue, the father's brother succeeds, and excludes the father, though his relation be by the father, and much further distant than the father; and it sometimes falls out, that the uncle succeeding, dying without issue, the father succeeds his brother, and so accidently and mediately succeeds to his own son.

23. To return to our customs in succession, in respect of the matter, it is divided in two branches, the one is of moveables, the other of immoveables, which do as much differ, as do the customs of divers nations; the successor in immoveables doth only retain the name of heir, and therefore immoveables are called heritable rights, and that part of the moveables which belongs to the heir, is called heirship moveable. The successor in moveables, from the office of executing the defunct's will, express, or presumed, is called executor. We shall here summarily, at one view, set forth the whole matter of succession with us, which we shall more fully and distinctly follow in the ensuing titles. Heirs in law are called universal successors, *quia succedunt in universum jus quod defunctus habuit*, they do wholly represent the defunct, and are as one person with him, and so they do both succeed to him *activè*, in all the rights belonging to him, and *passivè*, in all the obligations and debts due by him; and when they do not orderly enter, they become successors *passivè*, liable to the defunct's debt, but not heirs *activè*, having power to claim his right, till they be entered according to law: other successors are called singular successors, as assignees and purchasers, but heirs only are universal successors: and now, when heirs are of divers kinds, as some in moveables, some in lands and other heritable rights; and of these, according to the investiture, some succeed to lands provided to heirs of line; some to lands provided to heirs-male; some to lands otherwise tailzied; in all which some heirs succeed alone, and *in solidum*, some succeed *in parte et pro rata :* yet all may be said to suc-

ceed *in universum jus quod defunctus habuit :* By *universum jus,* the whole right, not simply, *et in solidum ;* but the whole rights of such a kind, either *in solidum,* or at least *pro rata parte,* as he who succeeds in a half, or third part of all the defunct's rights *active et passive,* succeedeth *in universa et singula jura,* in all and every right, though not *in totum et solidum,* in the whole or every part of every right.

24. As to moveables, we shall not repeat, what hath been said, Title, Real Rights [11, 1, 2 *et seq., supra*], of the distinction of heritable and moveable rights, whether goods or moveable debts; but shall only hold forth, what becometh of moveable rights, after the owner's decease. And, first, if the defunct be married, there was thereby a communion of goods, betwixt the defunct and the other spouse, which, being dissolved by death, the surviver may withdraw their share, which share is estimated by the condition of the family at that time; for if, in the family, there were a husband, a wife and children not forisfamiliated, the wife's share is the third; but if there were no child unforisfamiliated, the wife's share is the half, which is not properly a succession, but a division. The first degree of succession in moveables, with us, is by the will of the defunct, by his testament, or codicil, whereby the defunct may name executors, and dispose of his moveables, either in part, by particular legacies, or in whole, by an universal legacy, whereby, in effect, the universal legatar is instituted heir in the moveables; and if the executor nominated be not also universal legatar, he hath but one office, and is not heir for himself, but in name, and to the behoof of the legatar, and hath but a *fidei commissum* of the moveables, and so is but *hæres fidei commissarius,* obliged to restore to the wife, bairns, their nearest of kin, and to pay creditors *secundum vires inventarii,* and what remains free, to the legatars. These legacies, whether particular or universal, do immediately transmit the right to the legatars, and their successors: the solemnities of testaments or legacies, are very plain with us, but we shall leave them to the title Executry [111, 8, *infra*].

The will of the defunct is restrained with us, in three cases: the first is, Bastards cannot at all test, or leave legacies, unless they be legitimated, or have power from the king of making testament, or have lawful children: 2dly, A father is bound up in respect of his children in his family, which are not forisfamiliated and provided for, these having necessarily their portion natural, and bairns' part of gear, wherefrom their father cannot exclude them by legacies, or otherwise, as by donations, in contemplation of death, or any other gratuitous deed done on deathbed; so an assignation to a moveable bond granted on deathbed, was found null as to the relict and bairns' part, Spots. Assignations, Pyrie *contra* Ramsay [Spotiswoode 8; M. 2069]. Yea, it was found, that the gift of money by the defunct, out of his own hand, on deathbed was null as to them, *Ibid.* Moncreiff *contra* Moncreiff [Not found]. The like of an assignation to a confident person, to the behoof of the defunct's bairns, which was found not to prejudge the relict's third, July 10, 1628, Cant *contra* Edgar [Durie 386; M. 3199]. And therefore a father hath only power to dispose upon such a part of his goods, which are thence called dead's part, whereof, if he have a relict, and bairns in the family, the bairns' part is the third, the relict's part is also a third, and so the defunct's part is only a third; but if there be no relict, then the bairns' part is the half, and the dead's part is the other half; but if there be neither wife nor bairns, the defunct may dispose of the whole, as persons never married, or wives upon whom there is no restriction, though they have husband or children: for they may dispose of their share of the husband's moveables; or if they acquired or succeed to any moveables, in viduity, they may entirely dispose thereof, though they have children; if legacies exceed the defunct's own part, then they abate proportionally, unless there be a preference granted by the testator, or a privilege, whereof I know none with us, for even a legacy *ob pias causas*, viz. a mortification to a kirk, was found to have no privilege, but it and other legacies suffered proportional deduction, seeing they exceeded the dead's part, July 6, 1630, Monro *contra* Scot's Executors [Durie 526; M. 8048]. The reason of this restriction is that the natural obligement for provision of children, of which before, it is extended only to the immediate children and not to grandchildren, neither doth it restrict the mother but only the father. The third restriction of the defunct's will is in favour of their heirs of line: for heirs having the sole interest in heritable rights, are, by our custom, justly excluded from coming in with other children in moveables, except that which is called heirship-moveables, which is the best of every kind of moveable, wherein the defunct's will cannot prejudge the heir.

The second member of succession in moveables is, from the intestate; so that failing the defunct's will, with the restrictions aforesaid, the nearest of kin have interest, both in the defunct's moveables and office of executry; and though they claim not the office, yet they have a right to the goods, leaving a third of dead's part to the executors, for administration of the office. These nearest of kin take place in order: all the nearest degree, male or female, come in equally, and there is no right of representation in moveables. The first degree is children, male or female, with whom grandchildren come not in by right of representation, in place of their defunct parents: so children have an interest in their father's moveables, viz. their bairns part, wherein their father cannot prejudge them, and their interest as nearest of kin, whereby they succeed to the dead's part, in so far as intestate. Next unto children are grandchildren, or any descendants of the nearest degree. Next unto these are brethren and sisters, wherein brethren and sisters-german, or by both bloods, exclude these by one blood. Next unto brethren and sisters are their descendants, in the nearest degree, without representation. And last are the nearest degree of agnates, male and female jointly, without representation [III, 8, 32, *infra*]. If there be no descendants, or agnates, as in the case of bastards, who can have none, or others, who happen *de facto* to have no children or agnates, their goods become caduciary, and are confiscated to the king as last heir, or by reason of bastardy; of which before, Title Confiscation [III, 3, 42 *et seq.*].

In the succession of moveables the same goods or debts are not in all cases accounted moveable, since the act of Parliament 1641, cap. 32 [Bonds Act, 1661,c. 32; A.P.S. VII,230,c. 244], whereby bonds bearing annualrent, which before in all respects were heritable, by the destination of the annualrent (which, being perfected by infeftment, is an immoveable and heritable right) are declared to fall under executry, and so to be moveable; and yet by the said statute, the relict and fisk are excluded. The reason expressed in the statute is, because the obligement upon the debtor to pay annualrent, is for the profit of the creditor; and not a destination of infeftment of annualrent in favour of the heir, to exclude the bairns: and therefore such clauses make not such sums heritable as to the bairns and nearest of kin, unless they bear an oblige-ment to infeft the creditor in land or annualrent; in which case they are properly heritable, and belong only to the heir; but if not, the same belongs to the bairns and nearest of kin, *excludendo fiscum et relictam;* whereby there arises a different division of moveable sums, falling under executry: and of such as were moveable before the said act, which, if there be a wife and children, are divided in three; whereof the bairns' part is a third part, and the dead's part a third, [and the wife's part a third]. Another in the testament, of bonds bearing annualrent, which, if there be bairns, is divisible in two parts, whereof the one half is the bairns' part, and the other half the dead's part, and the relict hath no part being excluded; so that in case of escheat, such sums are not moveable, and fall not under escheat.

Yet, if such debts become simply moveable by a requisition or charge, or by the death of the debtor or creditor, before the term of payment of annual-rent, or otherwise, they remain in the ancient condition; and the statute doth not exclude the fisk and relict. But where a charge could not be given, through the debtor or creditor's death, and there was no requisition provided, a decreet for payment was not found to make the same moveable, as it would have been if the bond had been heritable, by a clause of infeftment; and that because, by a posterior bond of corroboration for the same sum, executors were excluded, which no charge nor requisition doth alter; but it is still pre-sumed, that the debtor would re-employ the sum in the same way, to his heirs excluding executors. And therefore a process and decreet for payment was not found to make it moveable, though these would make it moveable as well as a requisition or charge, if it had been heritable, by a clause of infeftment, July 12, 1676, Chrystie *contra* Chrystie [2 Stair 447; M. 5580]. It is also con-sequent from the said statute, 1. That such bonds bearing clauses of annual-rent, may be exhausted by the debts due by the defunct, bearing a clause of annualrent: 2. It is consequent, that the executor will get no relief against the heir, of debts bearing a clause of annualrent, without a clause of infeftment, in so far as there are such debts in the executry; but the heir will have relief thereof against the executor: 3. It followeth, that debts bearing a clause of annualrent, and no clause of infeftment, will not exhaust the relict's part; because, as she is excluded from any share of such debts due to her husband, so she must be free of any such debt due by him, as was found, December 23, 1668, M'Kenzie *contra* Robertsons [1 Stair 576; M. 5784; III, 8, 47, *infra*].

25. Succession in immoveable and heritable rights, proceeds wholly in a different manner: for succession in moveables is more near to the course of natural succession, and to the civil law of the Romans, especially their ancient and middle laws; but the succession in heritable rights agreeth more to the recent feudal customs of most nations, whereby primogeniture is established, for the honour and preservation of noble families, and in them for the good and safety of their kings and countries.

26. Succession in moveables and heritables do mainly differ; First, That in moveables the express will of the defunct, by his testament, legacies and donations, in contemplation of death, have the first place, but in heritable rights they have no place at all; yea, no personal contract, or obligement of the fiar, can have any effect in prejudice of his heir, to take from him any part of the heritage, directly or indirectly, by legal pursuits thereupon, if the foresaid personal right or contract was done *in lecto ægritudinis* upon the fiar's death-bed. And though the same disposition or contract were made in the fiar's health, or *liege poustie*, it doth not alter the succession, unless it be in the investiture, though, as being of itself, or having in it virtually a personal obligation, it may by process compel the fiar, or his heir, to denude themselves, and to obtain new infeftments conform thereto; as if by contract a party may be provided to be the contractor's heir, in whole or in part; this provision doth not make that party heir in any right, whereupon infeftment hath followed, which only properly are heritable rights; neither can that party be served heir of provision to the contractor thereupon; yet the contractor may be compelled to take his right accordingly to himself, and these heirs of provision; which if he have not done, his other heirs may be compelled to enter, and to denude themselves in favour of that party provided to be heir, conform to the contract: but dispositions, obligations, or contracts of any heritable right, on death bed, are null and reducible, in so far as may prejudge the heir. If the disponer's apparent heir be not entered heir, as charged to enter heir, he will be liable, and after horning against him the right may be adjudged from him; but if he cannot enter heir, upon his renunciation the right will be adjudged, whereupon infeftment will follow.

27. The privilege of heirs, not being prejudged by their predecessors' deeds done on deathbed, is, (as most of our laws) by ancient custom, time out of mind, and not by statute or written law [IV, 20, 37, *infra*]; for though the books called *Regiam Majestatem* treat thereof [R.M. (Skene's ed.) II, 18; (A.P.S. ed.) II, 15; (Stair Socy. ed.) II, 18], yet does not introduce it, and it hath been compiled by some stranger, who hath not fully known our law, but, by mistake, hath resolved most cases by the customs of other nations, especially of England. The reason of this custom may be conjectured, not only from the nature of feudal rights, not disposable by testament but only by investiture, but also for public utility; because persons on deathbed are weak, the

mind being easily affected with the trouble of the body, and so is easy to be wrought upon by insinuations or importunities, to do deeds contrary to their interest and former resolutions, especially by the popish clergy, who having, for their own corrupt ends, forged purgatory and prayers for the dead, the power of indulgence and pardon of sins, did thereby deceive the Christian world, and obtained upon deathbed, so large donations to their clergy, to the prejudice of the donatar's lawful heirs; which therefore our ancient custom hath wisely provided against.

28. The main difficulty is, in what cases the law accounteth parties to be on deathbed, or when they are in health, and *liege poustie;* for these are the two opposite terms of law, *liege poustie* or deathbed: for clearing whereof, these points must be considered; 1. Whether it be necessary to prove, that the defunct before the deed in question, had contracted disease, or become sick; and whether it be necessary to condescend and instruct the special kind of sickness, as that it was *morbus sonticus*, or a disease affecting the whole body and brain; or if the keeping the house, and the party's dying before he went abroad, be sufficient to infer *presumptivè*, that he had contracted the disease whereof he died so soon as he kept the house: 2. Whether a contrary probation of the party's being in health be sufficient; as that he was of a sound judgment and memory, and kept the ordinary time of putting off and on his clothes, and of eating and drinking, as when he was in health; or if writing securities that require clearness and distinctness of mind be sufficient; or if doing his ordinary affairs, making bargains and accounts, trysting for others or himself, playing at cards or other games within doors, giving evidence of being merry, be sufficient to instruct health and *liege poustie*: 3. If sickness contracted be presumed or proven, whether there be necessity to prove the continuance of the sickness till death, or that the defunct died of that sickness, or if the sickness once contracted be presumed to continue, unless convalescence and recovery of health be proven: 4. Whether *liege poustie* by convalescence be sufficiently proven by the defuncts' going to kirk and market freely, without help: and whether it be sufficient to go to the market-place, or to the kirk, though there be no convention nor congregation there; or whether it be requisite, that going to kirk and market be when there are meetings convened there, or in market-time: 5. Whether in that case supportation being proven, it is more pregnant and preferable to the probation of walking freely, and by what acts supportation is inferred, whether by helping the defunct by the oxter, by his elbow, or by his hand, be sufficient, or if helping up stairs, or down stairs, to and from his horse, or upon a ragged way, or whether being helped by a staff, will infer supportation: 6. Whether going freely to kirk and market unsupported may be taken off by any probation, that notwithstanding thereof, the sickness did continue whereof the defunct died: 7. Whether convalescence and *liege poustie* may be proven by any other acts, than going unsupported to kirk and market, or if equivalent acts may be sufficient; and if going abroad about the house unsupported be sufficient.

Deathbed is of so great importance with us, as reaching the estate and heritage of parties, that the Lords have been very careful for clearing and fixing the same, that it may not be under uncertain conjecture or probation; and whereas, by an ordinary act of litiscontestation, the pursuer might prove his reason of deathbed by any two habile witnesses, or the defender might in the same manner prove the going abroad to kirk and market, or acts equivalent in defence; or the pursuer might prove supportation by way of reply, and all by any two habile witnesses: yet the Lords have taken a far more secure way to allow probation to be adduced by either party, concerning the condition of the defunct, as to his sickness or health, and concerning his going abroad thereafter, and the manner thereof; whereby neither party hath the choice of the witnesses, to be in a capacity to influence them, but either party adduces witnesses, and there is scarce any one unexamined, who knew any thing of the matter; so that the truth comes to clear and evident light, and the probation stands in place of litiscontestation: for albeit it bear to be before answer to the relevancy, and that after the probation is closed, they are permitted to resume the debate as to the relevancy, as to such points as they desire chiefly to be noticed, and wherein they do believe that sufficient probation is adduced, which probation was closed, and might not be debated upon, how far any point is proven, which was only proper to the Lords to consider; but since the Act of Parliament for publication of testimonies, the advocates pitch upon the witnesses for each point, which they suppose proven, so the Lords need read no more, as they do in advising writs, but consider the clauses pitched on; yet no new litiscontestation can be made, or any new fact admitted to be proven, after the probation before answer is concluded and advised or renounced, unless the Lords, *ex officio et proprio motu*, for clearing of any part of the probation that remains dubious, require further, as they may do at the advising of any cause, even upon litiscontestation; as was found, December 5 and 6, 1662, Clelands *contra* Cleland [*Sub anno* 1672, 2 Stair 126, 128; M.3305,3307].

To come then to the points proposed to be cleared: for the first point, whether keeping the house presumeth sickness contracted, or if sickness must be proven, and what kind of sickness. Albeit the ordinary style of the reason of reduction bear, that before the deed in question, the defunct contracted the mortal disease whereof he died; yet it is not necessary to allege or instruct, that it was *morbus sonticus*, January 7, 1624, Schaw *contra* Gray [Durie 95; M.3208]. Neither that the defunct was bedfast when the deed was done, February 1, 1622, Robertson *contra* Fleming [Durie 13; M.3290]. And albeit the presumption of the contracting of sickness from his keeping of the house, be not always sufficient alone, yet it is of great importance, and a small probation of sickness with it will suffice, otherwise it were easy to keep all access from the defunct of indifferent persons that might prove his condition, and none be admitted but contrivers and concurrers in the deed: and therefore a deed done by a man enclosed for the plague, was found reducible as done on deathbed, as being done after the defunct was enclosed on suspicion of the plague, and dying before he came out; without necessity to prove he was sick or infected when the deed was done, seeing there was no further access for a fuller probation, February 23, 1665, Jack *contra* Pollock and Rutherford [1 Stair 275; M. 3213]. This presumption doth withstand a far stronger opposite probation of health, when the defunct went abroad, as was found in the said case, Robertson *contra* Fleming [Durie 13; M. 3290], where it was not found relevant to elide deathbed, that the defunct was in strength and ability, to have come to kirk and market; not that the defunct put on his clothes daily, and that any disease he had was but lent [Mild, from Latin *lentus*], and not *impedimentum rebus agendis;* as was found in the said case, Schaw *contra* Gray [Durie 95; M. 3208]. Neither that the defunct lived a year and a half after the deed in question, and was only hindered to come abroad by a palsy, which troubled his walking, and made him not come abroad, albeit he did all his affairs within doors as formerly, July 1, 1637, Cranstoun Riddel *contra* Richardson [Durie 847; M. 3212]. And albeit there be remembered a case of a disposition, made by David Graham, merchant in Edinburgh, for a pious use to the kirks, that his having on his clothes, the contriving and writing the whole disposition himself, was sufficient to elide deathbed, and to instruct health: yet the circumstances of that case are not fully known, not being observed by any of the Lords, and the decision hath ever been decried since: but, in the case of the creditors of the Lord Balmerinoch *against* the Lady Cowper, for reducing of the disposition of his estate to her, which was decided, June 25, 1671 [1 Stair 742; M. 3292], it was not found relevant to instruct *liege poustie;* that after the disposition, my Lord made bargains and counts, seemed to be merry, and laughed, kept on his clothes, kept the table, came from his chamber to the hall, whistled to himself, and danced, albeit no particular disease, but only sickness was proven. In this case it was found, that convalescence was sufficiently probable by going to kirk or market freely. And, in the foresaid case, Clelands *contra* Cleland [5 and 6 Dec. 1672, 2 Stair 126, 128; M. 3305, 3307], health was not found proven, albeit soundness of judgment and memory was proven; and that the defunct did not only all his own affairs, but trysted for others, and that he lived two years and a half after the disposition, and was in like condition as he had been seven years before; so that it seems, that if the contracting of sickness be proven, no contrary probation of any acts within doors will be sufficient to elide the reason of deathbed; by all which decisions, the second point proposed is sufficiently cleared.

As to the third point proposed, Whether sickness being proven once contracted, the continuance thereof till death must be proven. It is commonly held, that if it be proven sickness was contracted, and that death followed, *probatis extremis praesumuntur media;* and sickness once being proven, is presumed to continue, otherwise it were scarce possible by a positive probation to instruct the continuance of the sickness till death, and this is only *praesumptio juris*, laying the burden of probation upon the party that alleges convalescence. The fourth point for proving *liege poustie ;* either that there was no disease, or convalescence: if there had been a disease, by going freely to kirk and market unsupported, is the ordinary and unquestionable defence against deathbed, upon which law and custom hath pitched, as the most public and sure evidence of health and convalescence: so that, albeit the going to kirk and market were but of design to validate the deed, yet if the attempt be perfectly made out, it would be sufficient; and much more will it be allowed, when the going abroad is principally to hear sermon, or for devotion, or about affairs to the market: in which case, taking the party by the hand, or helping him at a ragged ground, would not infer supportation, there being no design of cautiousness in the party, but using his ordinary way; as if a gentlewoman accustomed to be led by the hand, should go so led to the kirk or market, by reiterated acts it might be sufficient for inferring health or convalescence; but if it did appear to be upon design, she behoved to forbear the prerogatives of her quality, and go freely alone without being led; or if an old man, infirm by age, or any defect in his legs or feet, not arising from inward sickness, should be helped in difficult places, in reiterated acts in going to kirk and market, without design. And as to that qualification, whether it be sufficient to go to the kirk or market-place, or at the congregation, or gathering at the market, I have not observed it particularly debated or decided, but that parties, when they went to the kirk, ordinarily went to the prayers, and certainly it is the most secure way, that the going be to the congregation, or meeting at the market, otherwise pickt out witnesses may be chosen to wait upon the party to the kirk or market-place, which, in many cases, will be very private, and will not expose the party to public view. Therefore the Lords published an Act of Sederunt, February 29, 1692, of which the tenor follows [IV, 20, 42, *infra*]: "The Lords of Council and Session, taking to their serious consideration, that the excellent law of deathbed, securing men's inheritances from being alienated at that time, may happen to be frustrated and evacuated, if their coming to church or market be not done in such a public and solemn manner, as may give some evidence of their re-convalescence, without supportation, or straining of nature: and seeing some may think it sufficient, if parties, after subscribing such dispositions, come to the church at any time, and make a turn or two therein, though there were no congregation at the time; and likewise, if they make any merchandise privily in a shop or crame, or come to the market-place, when there is no public market, and all this performed before their own pickt out witnesses, brought along by the party, in whose favour the disposition is made, that the state and condition of his health or sickness may be as little under the view and consideration of other indifferent persons, as can be: the occasion of which mistake might have been, that formerly there were public prayers, morning and evening, in the church, in many places, to which those who apprehended any controversy might arise upon the validity of their dispositions, were accustomed to come at the time of prayer, and some thought they might come to the church, though there were no public meeting thereat, since these public prayers were not accustomed, and to take instruments of their appearing there. For remeid whereof, the Lords declare, they will not sustain any such parties going to church and market, where it is proven that he was sick before his subscribing of the disposition quarrelled as done *in lecto*, unless it be performed in the day-time, and when people are gathered together, in the church, or church-yard, for any public meeting, civil or ecclesiastic; or when people are gathered together in the market-place, for public market: and further declare, whensoever instruments are taken, for the end foresaid, that the said instrument do expressly bear, That it was taken in the audience and view of the people gathered together, as aforesaid; otherwise the Lords will have no regard to the said instrument."

The fifth point concerning supportation, is the ordinary reply against going abroad; and as hath been said, it is ever to be considered, whether the act appear to be of design or not; and that, if the acts be reiterated and of course, nothing that was ordinary for the defunct in taking of help, when he was in unquestionable health, will import supportation; and therefore in the case, Pargillais *contra* Pargillais [1 Stair 615; M. 3304], decided, February 26, 1669, it having been proven that the defunct was a very old man, and that after the disposition quarrelled, he had several times come to Calder, and done affairs there; and that he went up from the market-place, in the market-time, to the place of Calder, being a steep way, borrowed money from the Lord Torphichen, told and received the same, which was found sufficient; albeit he was helped up stairs and down stairs, and was helped to his horse, and from his horse, and his man led his bridle, and that he had a staff in his hand. But when the going to kirk and market is upon design, the least defect in the exact performance, will render it ineffectual; and so in the case of the disposition made by the Lord Couper [Probably *Balmerino* v *Couper*, 28 June 1671, 1 Stair 742; M. 3292], it having been evident, that it was of design to validate the disposition, that the next day after the disposition my Lord went to the market at Couper, the laying his hand upon Thomas Ogilvie's hand, who walked by him, and that only at some times, and in ragged places where he was accustomed to take any walking by him by the hand before: yet seeing he put nature to the utmost reach, to manifest health by that act, and could not fully perform it, it was not found sufficient; but he was found to be supported. And in the case Clelands *contra* Cleland of Faskin [5 and 6 Dec. 1672, 2 Stair 126, 128; M. 3305, 3307], the defunct finding that his disposition was quarrelled, and stopt at the exchequer, as being done *in lecto*, immediately after he caused make a chair, with a fixed footstool to bear his feet, in which he was carried with men, till he came within two pair or thereby, to the kirk, and thence he walked to the kirk, but there was no congregation, and returned to the chair, and so was carried home; and the witnesses that were about him being examined, whether he walked freely or with help, many deponed, that several persons having walked close about him, they could not distinctly know;

and several witnesses having deponed, that he walked freely without help, and two having deponed that he was helped by themselves, his so going abroad was not found sufficient; neither was his being carried in the chair found equivalent, as if he had ridden upon his horse; because a sick man might have required help even upon horse-back, and would not have been able to have ridden freely without help, and yet might have been able to sit in a chair: in this case also it was found, that supportation was more positively proven, albeit by fewer witnesses, the witnesses themselves being supporters.

As to the sixth point proposed, whether going to kirk and market unsupported inferreth health, or convalescence *præsumptione juris et de jure ;* so that a contrary probation that even then he was sick, and so continued till death, hath not yet been distinctly decided: albeit in Pargilleis's case it was not regarded, that the witnesses deponed, that Pargilleis, when he came to the market appeared sick, and continued sick thereafter; neither can any conjectural probation in such case be respected; because *squalor morbi* doth ordinarily remain after convalescence, which, if it were sustained, would render that defence uncertain and conjectural; so that there can be no question, unless the probation of the being then sick, were positive, and pregnant; as if a person in a hot fever, wherein there is ordinarily strength enough, should come abroad to market, the foam and fury of the fever continuing in his face, or if the party did groan, and bemoan himself, as sick persons use to do; or if positive acts importing sickness be proven, as fainting, or vomiting, which was sustained in the process between Graham of Garvock and Drummond, February   1692 [Not found], in which case it was proven, that the disponer signed in his bed, and was sick, but immediately after rose, and went to the kirk, and returned unsupported, the apparent heir being present, which was sustained, though there was no congregation, seeing the heir might have called unsuspect witnesses; yet his vomiting in his return was sustained, to prove the continuing of his sickness and deathbed.

For the last point offered to consideration, whether convalescence can be proven otherwise, than by going unsupported to kirk and market; I have seen no decision, whereby deathbed hath been elided, upon such equivalent acts; but, on the contrary, it was found, in the case of the Lord Salton [Not found], that his coming to a green, near his house unsupported, and standing there, till he saw men play at foot-ball, was not sufficient: and, in Couper's case [Probably 1 Stair 742; M. 3292], his coming frequently with strangers to their horse, and sometimes going up and down stairs unsupported, and oft-times going out and walking in his garden, and once to a house a quarter of a mile off, and all unsupported, were not found equivalent to going unsupported to kirk and market. And, in Cleland's case [Probably 2 Stair 126, 128; M. 3305, 3307], his going several times to his barn, and to some trees, a pair from his gate unsupported, were not found equivalent to going to kirk and market; yet it cannot be doubted but there may be acts equivalent, as if any person should go a far journey; but the equivalence must not stand in this, that the defunct did acts, requiring as much strength as going to kirk and market; in respect of this difference, that going to kirk and market exposes the party to public view; whereas other private acts about his house may be proven by a few persons prompted for that purpose; which probation cannot be balanced with any other for clearing, that there was support or help, as in the case of going to kirk or market, or going a long journey, where there may be had many unprepossessed witnesses. Deathbed was not found elided by riding on horseback a journey of about sixteen miles, seeing the party had a man who rode behind him, and for some part of the way he was tied to the man; which was found to be supportation. Nor was it respected, that, long before his sickness, he had in his testament left the same things in legacy, and therefore was not prevailed upon with importunity, seeing his purpose might have altered after that testament, December 11, 1677, Lockhart *contra* Lockhart of Lie [2 Stair 576; M.3297, 3328].

29. As to the extent of deathbed, it doth not only annul dispositions of lands but assignations to heritable bonds, February 24, 1624, Donaldson *contra* Donaldson [Durie 113; M.5571]; or to a bond, moveable in itself, becoming heritable, by a posterior obligement, to employ it for annualrent, Spots, *Juramentum Calumniae*, Arthur *contra* Watson [Not in Spotiswoode]: Yea, it will annul any bond, though moveable, in so far as thereupon the heritage may be apprised or adjudged, January 7, 1624, Schaw *contra* Gray [Durie 95; M. 3208]. But an heritable sum being paid to the defunct on deathbed, his discharge thereof was not reduced, *ex capite lecti*, though the money was instantly given away, after it was received, which was found valid as a legacy, out of the dead's part, March 15, 1634, Brown *contra* Thomson [Durie 713; M. 3200]. Deeds on deathbed will not prejudge the relict, or bairns' part, but are null as to them, as well as to the heir, as hath been now shown. Deathbed was extended against bonds, though granted by a father to a son, having no other provision, which were not sustained, though offered to be restricted to a competent portion, due naturally by parents to children, July 1, 1637, Riddel *contra* Richardson [Durie 847; M. 3212]. Yea, deathbed was found relevant to reduce a disposition in favour of the disponer's only daughter, in prejudice of the brother and heir-male; though the disposition contained a power to alter the tailzie, or dispone at any time in his life, but bore not *etiam in articulo mortis*, February 25, 1663, Hepburn of Humbie *contra* Hepburn [1 Stair 186; M. 3177]. But where the disposition was neither to an heir-male, nor of line, that clause was sufficient to capacitate the disponer on these terms to burden, though it mentioned not deathbed, or *in articulo mortis*, June 22, 1670, Douglas of Lumbsdean *contra* Douglas [1 Stair 684; M. 329]. And deathbed was not sustained, to reduce a disposition by a father to a son, seeing the father reserved such a sum, to be at his disposal, in his disposition to his apparent heir, though it mentioned not, at any time in his life, June 28, 1662, Seaton of Barns *contra* Seaton [*Sub nom. Hay* v. *Seaton*, 1 Stair 116; M. 3246]. And now, since the Lords have frequently decerned aliment to bairns, against

the father's heirs, having competent estates, it is like the Lords will allow all provisions on deathbed, in so far as they may be competent aliments.

Holograph writs without witnesses, prove not their own dates to have been prior to the subscriber's deathbed, and therefore they are presumed to be on deathbed, without which that privilege would be evacuate, it being as easy to induce a sick person to antedate a writ, as to prejudge his heir: but if it be proven by witnesses, that the writ was seen and delivered, before the granter contracted the sickness whereof he died; or if it was subscribed before his sickness, though not delivered; if it was in favour of his children, or had a clause dispensing with delivery, or did reserve his liferent; the presumption to have been done on deathbed, will be thereby elided. But a disposition to nieces, having been proven to be subscribed, before the subscriber's sickness, but blank in the name, was reduced as upon deathbed, because the name was not filled up; albeit the writer did depone, that it was delivered to him to fill it up with the niece's name, seeing he filled it not up till the granter's sickness, July 22, 1678, Birnies *contra* Polmais and Birnies [2 Stair 624; M. 3242]. But deathbed was not found to hinder the recalling of a disposition made by a grandfather to his oye, and delivered to a third party in *liege poustie;* if it should appear, that the delivery was not simply to the behoof of the oye, whereby it became irrevocable, but conditionally, that the disponer might re-cal it; for evidence whereof, it was proven, by that third party's oath, that the defunct on the deathbed called for it, and he delivered it; and that the defunct on deathbed delivered two blanks for dividing the right in the first disposition, which he delivered, with his said first disposition to a notar, and ordered the filling up of the one half to the heir, the other half to a second son; but for further clearing, the party to whom the first disposition was first delivered, was appointed to be re-examined, what the defunct expressed, when he delivered the first disposition to him, December 9, 1676, Ker *contra* Ker [2 Stair 474; M. 3248]. But thereafter, the third party not being found to be examined, the Lords found, that there being nothing proven, expressed at the delivery, the re-calling, and the re-delivery did import, that the delivery was not simple to the behoof of the oye, making it irrevocable; but that it was conditional to be delivered to the oye, if the disponer did not recal it; and that his recalling of it for a special effect, to divide the same betwixt his heir and the second son, was effectual, both against his oye to whom he first disponed, and effectual against his heir as to the one half, albeit the revocation was on deathbed, seeing thereby the heir had no prejudice, but benefit, being formerly excluded by the disposition to the oye, delivered in *liege poustie*, January 25, 1677, *inter eosdem* [2 Stair 499; M. 3249].

30. Only free deeds on deathbed are thus reducible; for if there were an equivalent cause onerous, which was truly employed upon the defunct, or might affect the heir, it is not to the heir's prejudice, and so not reducible; thus the reason of deathbed was elided, because the bond quarrelled was offered to be proven for furnishing truly delivered to the defunct, July 13,

1632, Pollock *contra* Fairholme [Durie 645; M. 3209]. The like of a discharge granted by a bastard, after he was infected of the plague, against the donatar of the bastardy, November 23, 1609, Mar *contra* Auchinleck [Not found]. In all these, witnesses are sustained to prove the cause onerous in the writ. And likewise a bond granted on deathbed, being proven for a cause onerous in part, viz. drugs, and service to the defunct on his deathbed, was sustained *pro tanto*, and reduced for the rest, January 7, 1624, Schaw *contra* Gray [Durie 95; M. 3208]. But a liferent granted to a wife on deathbed, and a liferent-tack of teinds of the lands liferented, were not reduced, Hope, Teinds, La. Dunlop *contra* L. Dunlop [Hope, *Maj. Pr.* 111,18,32; M. 3208]. The reason whereof is observed to have been, because the husband before sickness was bound to infeft his wife in lands, or annualrent equivalent, Nicol., *de hæreditariis actionibus, inter eosdem* [Not found].

31. As deeds on deathbed prejudge not the heir; so deeds in Testaments, though done in *liege poustie*, have no more effect than on deathbed. And it is not *habilis modus*, by testament to dispone any heritable right, December 14, 1664, Colvin *contra* Colvin [1 Stair 241; M. 15927]: deathbed is not competent by exception, but by reduction, January 11, 1666, Seatoun *contra* Dundass [1 Stair 336; M. 2736]; but in declaratory or petitory actions, as recognition, it is receivable by exception, July 20, 1669, Barclay *contra* Barclay [1 Stair 641; M. 3241]; or in a reduction it is competent by exception or reply, February 3, 1672, Home *contra* Bryson [2 Stair 60; M. 881]. A third difference is, that successors in moveables, or executors, are not liable *passivè* for the defunct's debt *in solidum*, but heirs are, though they far exceed the value of the inheritance, without the benefit of an inventory; and though Craig's opinion [11,13,14] is, that heirs may renounce, even after their entry, if the heritage appear overburdened, the course of decisions since his time hath cleared the contrary.

32. Because heirs entering cannot renounce, there is *annus deliberandi* allowed to them by law, in which they may abstain from entering, and immixing themselves with the heritage, and then they are not convenable for the defunct's debt, upon charges to enter heir, or otherwise; but if they enter, or meddle sooner, they are liable; this *annus deliberandi* is ordinarily accounted a year from the defunct's death, which was so accounted, though during a great part thereof the heir remained unborn; Had. February 7, 1610, Knows *contra* Menzies [Not found]. But the contrary was found thereafter, that the year was accounted from the birth of the posthumous heir, that the benefit of deliberation might be profitable to his tutor in his name; Spots. Heirs, Livingstoun *contra* Fullertoun [Spotiswoode 137; M. 6870]; yet a summons on a charge to enter heir, the day of compearance being after the charge to enter heir, and after the year, it will be sustained, June 26, 1667, Dewar *contra* Peterson [1 Stair 464; M. 2171; III,5,22,*infra*]; in which case it was found, that even actions real, as reductions, declarators, &c. which require no charge to enter heir, are not competent within the year of deliber-

ation; because in these the heir cannot defend, without the hazard of behaving as heir.

33. Succession in heritable rights in Scotland are either by the will of the fiar, or by law, *provisione hominis* or *legis*. Heirs by the course of law are called heirs of line, as befalling by the line of succession appointed, and known in law; all other heirs do cross or cut that line, and therefore are called heirs of tailzie, from the French word tailzer, to cut; whence Craig [11,16,4] conceived this tailzied succession hath been first denominate amongst the French and Normands, and thence being brought into England by the Normand conquest, both in custom and name, hath been derived to us; yet it is liker to have come to us immediately from France, with which we kept greater intercourse than with England of old; and our tailzies, at least to heirs-male, are ancienter than the English, which begun but from the famous law, called the second statute of Westminster [1285, the first chapter of which is known as the Statute *De Donis Conditionalibus*, and was the basis of the English equitable interest in tail], in the reign of Edward the first of that name of the Normand line.

Heirs of tailzie are also called heirs of provision; which terms are equiparate, both comprehending all heirs, which are not according to the line or course of law; and among others, heirs male and heirs of marriage: yet our style doth ordinarily distinguish them so, that where there is no alteration from the lineal heirs male; and where there are several substitutions of certain persons or lines, failing others, by the tenor of the infeftment, they are specially called heirs of tailzie; but when there is an alteration of the lineal succession, yet not simply to heirs male, nor to divers members of tailzie, they retain the common name of heirs of provision, as is most ordinary by contracts of marriage providing lands to the heirs of the marriage, whereby the heirs lawfully procreated betwixt the married persons, whether male or female, do succeed; so that daughters of that marriage will exclude sons of another marriage or heirs of the body of the members of the tailzie, whereby their collaterals, or ascendants, are excluded: and in proper tailzies there are always divers lines or persons, male and female, substitute as members of the tailzie; as when infeftments bear lands to be granted to the fiar, and to the heirs of his body, or to the heirs male of his body, or to his heirs of such a marriage; which failing, to such another person named, and to the heirs of his body, or to the heirs male of his body, &c. and so to a third and fourth; which all failing, to the first fiar and his heirs whatsoever, or to return to the superior, or to any other person, and to their heirs whatsoever: and where such persons and lines are not substitute, it is not properly called a tailzie; but if it be simply to heirs male, it is so specially denominate. All other heirs which are not heirs of line or heirs whatsoever, retain the name of heirs of provision, the chief whereof are heirs of marriage, which failing, the husband's, or wive's heirs whatsoever, in which case there is but one blood or line, and not divers persons, and different lines substitute; in these tailzies the person nominate may succeed, and be served heir of tailzie, though otherwise incapable of succession as bastards,

as hath been shown in the former title [111, 3, 44, *supra*]; but the persons nominate are never the immediate and first heirs in lands, but always the fiar's
heirs of his body; which failing, the persons nominate: for if the heritage
should be granted, for example, to John, and after his decease to William and
his heirs, John would be thereby naked liferenter and William fiar, who could
not be served as heir to John: but if it were granted to John, and the heirs of
his body, which failing to William, these failing, William would be served heir
of tailzie to John: but this holds not in bonds, or securities for sums of money;
for parents do frequently take their bonds, and infeftments for security thereof, to themselves, they being on life, and after their decease to such children
nominate; yet the parents are fiars, and the children are but heirs substitute.
So then all succession with us is either of heirs of line, male, tailzie or provision: heirs of line are also called heirs general, so also are heirs male, and of
conquest, and these may be served heirs by a general service: but other heirs
of tailzie or provision by investiture, cannot be served heirs but by a special
service, serving them to such particulars, whereunto they succeed by infeftment or provision: heirs of line are also called heirs whatsoever, because they
are absolute without limitation; and in all cases, where heirs whatsoever is
not specially altered by the infeftment, rights follow the lineal succession; as
among heirs male, the same course taketh preference, except that female heirs
are excluded, as that first descendants, then brothers, &c. do succeed; and
amongst heirs of marriages, the eldest son doth exclude the rest, and so in the
members of tailzies.

We shall not need here to debate the lawfulness or expediency of constituting heirs male, or of tailzie, or of provision, having already cleared, that the
first ground and rule in equity, is the will of the proprietor, though he be personally obliged to provide competently for his own, especially those of his
family; and therefore, though several of our Kings, in their general revocations,
have revoked tailzies, it can infer no more but a scruple in them, and a preserving of their power, against the course of prescription; but doth not infringe such rights being lawful in themselves. The expediency of tailzies is the
the same with primogeniture, to preserve the memory and dignity of families:
but as primogeniture, for that end, excludeth females of nearest degree, heirs
male excludeth them simply; and heirs of tailzie have had their rise from
dissatisfaction with some of the fiar's race, or preference of them, otherwise
than by the propinquity of blood: some have also tailzied their lands, so as by
infeftments to introduce a primogeniture among females, as the law hath done
among males; as if the land were granted to the fiar, and the heirs male of his
body, which failing, to the eldest heir-female of his body, without division,
and their heirs carrying the arms and name of the family. To come now to the
heirs of line, the law hath ordered them thus: First, The eldest lawful son,
and his descendants in order, by right of primogeniture, excludeth all other
descendants, male or female; failing sons, the daughters, and their descendants do all succeed equally, except in rights indivisible, which fall to the eld-

est: failing descendants, the next degree is of the next immediate brother-german, and his descendants, and among middle brethren, the immediate elder brother succeedeth in conquest, whereunto the defunct did not, nor could not succeed as heir; but in all others the immediate younger brother succeedeth, and therefore is called the heir of line, and the other the heir of conquest: if the fiar be a woman, her brother-german excludeth sisters-german, and of her brothers, the immediate elder brother succeedeth in conquest, and the immediate younger in heritage; failing brothers-german, sisters-german, and their descendants, exclude both brethren and sisters by the father's side only, July 2, 1629, Cunningham *contra* Multray [Durie 454; M. 9664]; failing brothers, or sisters-german, brothers by the father's side succeed to the defunct, whether male or female, the immediate elder in conquest, and the immediate younger in heritage. Failing all brothers and sisters, the father, or other masculine ascendant of his line succeed to the defunct, whether male or female, and exclude the brothers or sisters of that ascendant, as a grandfather excludes his brethren, father's brethren to the defunct. Failing ascendants, the father's brothers, and father's sisters, and their descendants, succeed in all points as brothers and sisters, the double blood excluding the single blood, and the immediate elder brother succeeding in conquest, and the immediate younger in heritage; and all failing, the grandfather; and failing him, his brothers and sisters the same way: and so upward, till there can be any propinquity of blood proven; which all failing, the King taketh place as last heir.

34. In this line of succession observe, first, That there is no place for adoped children, or their issue, but only for the natural issue of the vassal, which cannot be changed by a voluntary act of adoption, without consent of the superior in the investiture; neither is adoption in use with us in any case. 2. These natural heirs must also be lawful, whereby bastards are excluded; and who are such, appeareth by the former title. 3. There is no place for cognates, as to the mother, grandmother, or other feminine ascendant, or these of their side, but only to agnates conjoined by the father, grandfather, &c. which holdeth, even though the heritage descended from the mother, or these of her side; for in the service of heirs the nearest lawful heirs are only inquired, and retoured either by the lineal succession aforesaid, or by express tailzie, or provision in the infeftment, without respect from whence the inheritance flowed, for which we have no statute nor custom: but in England it is otherwise; for *paterna paternis* and *materna maternis* takes place [111,4,8,*supra*]; but with us the contrary was found in the case of Gilbert, as Craig observeth, Lib. 2. Dieg. 17 [11,17,9]. And he there relateth that many afterwards changed their opinion therein; and though there be equity in it, yet no law nor practique since hath favoured the maternal line; but the father was found heir to his son, even in the lands where the son was infeft as heir to his mother, and did exclude his brother-uterine by that mother, February 5, 1663, Lennox *contra* Lintoun [1 Stair 172; M. 14867]. 4. In all this line of succession there is place for representation of descendants, in place of their defunct parents: so that

females of a further degree, by the right of representation, exclude males of a nearer degree; as the eldest son's daughter will be preferred in the grandfather's inheritance, to his other sons in private rights, though that be controverted by the more common feudal customs, as is largely and learnedly disputed by Tiraquellus.

35. In this lineal succession the father, grandfather, or other ascendants of the paternal line, succeed in heritable rights, next unto brothers and sisters, and before all other collaterals or agnates. We have shown before [III,4,14, *supra*] why there is no mention of ascendants in the Jewish succession, because such a case could hardly occur among them. Craig, *Lib.* 2, *Dieg.* 13 [II, 13,46–47] affirmeth, that it was doubtful in his time, whether ascendants could succeed in heritable rights, and that he had heard the opinion of some learned men in the contrary, and that he had not found the Lords decide in it, and that it is contrary to the feudal law, and also to his own opinion; yet he brings both evident reason and example in the contrary; the reason is, that no inquest can justly retour, that the father's brother is nearer than the father: he bringeth also the example of the E. of Angus, served heir in the Earldom of Angus to his own son, whom he had infeft therein; and the Lo. Colvil in the like manner, having infeft his son in all his estate, though some affirmed, that his was by provision in the infeftment; yet that the service was, is sure; but that provision, is uncertain: and though some also were doubtful, whether the E. of Angus was served and infeft as heir to that same son, which well inferreth, that the father was not infeft as heir to his son, but not that he was not served heir to him therein; for he might have been served and not infeft, whereby the service as incomplete became void, and the next Earl behoved to serve of new to the son, who died last vest and seased as of fee. The custom and common opinion since is for the ascendants; and so the Earl of Roxburgh was served as heir-male to his son the Lord Ker, and many others, which ought to be the more favoured, as more conform to equity, and the law of nature, which *in dubio* ought to take place, where there is no law nor custom to the contrary, as with us there is none; neither did I ever hear of one who attempted to exclude a father by the father's collaterals: and though there had been no decision upon it, neither have there been upon many other uncontroverted customs, especially in succession; but the acquiescence of all parties, having interest in matters of so great moment, is a strong evidence of the national consent by custom: but it hath also been so decided by the Lords, Hope, Succession, Burnet *contra* Mauld [Probably Hope, *Maj.Pr.* IV,3,36]; yea a son being infeft as heir to his mother dying without issue, his brother-uterine by the mother was not found heir to him, but his father, February 5, 1663, Lennox *contra* Lintoun [1 Stair 172; M. 14867]. As to the alleged opposition of the feudal law, as hath been oft-times said, it is local; and therefore, as in England, all ascendants are excluded, so in Germany, they succeed in the next place after descendants, and are preferred to brothers and sisters, according to the natural course of succession. The reason why brothers and sisters

of the defunct are preferred to the father with us, may be, because such fees do commonly proceed from the father, and, therefore, by the continuance of that same fatherly affection, are derived to the brothers and sisters, and because they stand in more need of provision than the father, who commonly reserves his own liferent.

¹ [Gavelkind, a custom which applied from the Norman Conquest to 1925 to socage land situated in Kent whereby land descended on intestacy to all sons equally, a widow was entitled to dower in half of her husband's land till her remarriage, a widower was entitled to a life estate in half of his wife's land, though no issue had been born of the marriage, and the land was devisable, all respects in which the custom differed from that applicable to England generally.]

Title 5. Heirs, Where, of Apparent Heirs, Heirs-male, Heirs-portioners, Heirs of Conquest, Tailzie and Provision, and their Brieves and Services, &c.

BY the former title it appeareth who are heirs: let us now consider what their interests are by being heirs: and that is either active by the benefit, or passive by the burden whereunto they do succeed: for heirs being successors *in universum jus quod defunctus habuit*, they do fully represent the defunct, both in the rights belonging to him, and in the debts due by him. First, then of the interest common to all heirs; and next of the interest special to the several heirs.

1. The interest of heirs is most properly competent, when they are entered heirs according to the due course of law, of which afterwards; yet some things are competent, not only to heirs entered, but to apparent heirs: as first, they have interest to pursue exhibition of all writs made by their predecessors to their wives, children, and others *in familia*, but not of writs made by them *extra familiam*, December 6, 1661, Forrester and Schaw of Sornbeg, her Spouse, *contra* Tailfer [*Sub nom. Telfer* v *Forrester and Sornbeg*, 1 Stair 65; M. 4007]; or to their predecessors simply, to the effect they may know the condition of the heritage, and may deliberate whether they will enter heirs or not [IV, 33, *infra*]; seeing if they do enter, they are liable for all the defunct's debts, though they far exceed his estate, and have no benefit of inventory, as in moveables; and therefore they are allowed to pursue for inspection of all writs, importing a debt of the defunct; yet not so as to open the charter-chests of strangers, who have purchased lands from the defunct, on pretence of the burden by the warrandice; for in that case the stranger's infeftment will exclude them, and only dispositions made to these in the family hinder not inspection of the heirs, whose rights flow from the defunct or his predecessors: but I doubt not but all will be obliged to produce bonds, or personal obligements, which might burden the apparent heir if he enter; as was found in the case of dispositions, and bonds granted by the defunct to strangers, February 26, 1633, L. Swinton *contra* L. Westnisbet [Durie 677; M. 4005]. But if infeftment had followed upon the disposition, the defender would not be obliged to produce the disposition, because the apparent heir might, by the registers, find his predecessors denuded. This inspection is competent during their *annus deliberandi;* and it was so found in favour of the apparent heir pursuing exhibition within the year, February 26, 1633, L. Swinton *contra* L. Westnisbet [Durie 677; M. 4005], where the writs pursued for were likely to be the ground of a plea against the defender himself. This exhibition *ad deliberandum* is competent at any time before the heir enter, even after the *annus deliberandi*, which is granted to apparent heirs, that they may be free of all actions on charges to enter heir, reductions, or declarators during that time, if they do not enter, or behave as heirs. But on this account the apparent heir

hath no interest to put parties to count and reckon *ad deliberandum*, June 22, 1671, Leslies *contra* Jaffrey [1 Stair 738; M. 3998]: albeit to count was once sustained *ad deliberandum*, March 16, 1637 [*Sub nom. Home* v *Blackader*, Durie 838; M. 3996], which was not followed, it being unreasonable to cause a party count, who thereby could not be exonered. In these exhibitions the relation, or propinquity of blood of the apparent heir, passeth without probation as *notorium*: so as if the defender be absent, the decreet will not be null, for want of probation of the title. Yet a Scots woman's son, born of parents residing in Holland, was found to have no interest to pursue exhibition, as apparent heir to his mother's father, till he produced an authentic declaration and trial by the magistrates in that place, that he was the eldest lawful son of his mother, December 17, 1627, Fleming *contra* Brown [*Sub nom. Donaldson* v *Brown*, Durie 322; M. 4647].

2. Apparent heirs may defend all rights competent to them, upon production of their predecessor's infeftments, whether they be called, or compear for their interest, January 19, 1627, L. Rosline *contra* His Tennents and George Fairburn for his Interest [Durie 258; M. 5233]. They may also continue their predecessor's possession [IV, 28, 4, *infra*], and pursue for mails and duties of their lands, finding caution, in case of doubtfulness, to make these forthcoming to any other having interest, Spots. Heirs, Oliphant *contra* his Tenants [Spotiswoode 142; M. 5244]. Yea, the rents of lands were so far found to belong to an apparent heir, that, though he died unentered, the next heir not entering to him, was found obliged to pay the former apparent heir's aliment, in so far as he intromitted with the rents of the years, during which the former apparent heir lived, December 20, 1662, La. Tarsapie *contra* L. Tarsapie [1 Stair 150; M. 5206]; and consequently the rents might be confirmed by his executors, or arrested for his debt. The like was found of moveable heirship, wherewith the apparent heir was entertained by his mother, June 27, 1629, Robertson *contra* Dalmahoy [Durie 452; M. 5402]. They may also pursue the liferenters of their estate for aliment, February 12, 1635, Hepburn *contra* Preston and Seaton [Durie 755; M. 381].

3. The aliment of heirs, out of their lands, being liferented, or in ward, is constitute by the Act of Parliament, 1491, cap. 25 [Liferent Caution Act, 1491, c. 25; A.P.S. 11, 224, c. 6; 11, 4, 36 and 11, 6, 5, *supra*; IV, 22, 10, *infra*], bearing a reasonable living to be given to the sustentation of the heir, after the quantity of his heritage, if the said heir have no blench or feu-farm to sustain him, as well of ward-lands fallen in the King's hands, as in the hands of any Baron, spiritual or temporal: whereby it is clear; 1. That the quantity of the aliment is indeterminate, and therefore is modified by the Lords, according to the quality of the heir, and his estate: 2. It takes no place, if the heir have blench, or feu-lands, sufficient to sustain him; but if these be not sufficient, the same will be made up by the liferenters and wardatars proportionally, Had. March 16, 1622, Heir of Miltoun *contra* Calderwood [Haddington, *Fol. Dict.* 1, 29; M. 386]. Yea, where the minor had any other means sufficient to entertain him-

self as the heir, being a writer, and thereby able to aliment himself, he was found to have no aliment from his mother's liferent, who brought 8000 merks of tocher, and had but 10 chalders of victual in liferent, July 21, 1636, L. Ramorney *contra* Law [Durie 819; M.388]. The like, where the heir was not minor, but designed himself preacher, and so having a calling, February 11, 1636, Sibbald *contra* Wallace [Durie 794; M.388]. Here the relict was infeft in no land, but had an annualrent of 400 merks, out of land, and the heir was not minor; whereas the Lords thought the Act of Parliament was not in favour of majors, who ought to do for themselves; but all must be considered complexly in this decision, some heirs, by their quality, not being bound to follow callings; but the liferent was a mean annualrent, no more than an aliment to the relict, the pursuer major, and having a calling; and certainly, where the liferent is but an aliment, the apparent heir must rather want, than the person provided for a cause onerous.

Though the Act mention only ward-lands, yet it was extended to a minor having no ward-lands, against a liferenter of all his estate, being houses, and annualrent of money, February 22, 1631, Finnie *contra* Oliphant [Durie 573; M.406]. In this case, it was not found sufficient, that the liferenter offered to to maintain the minor, her own child, upon her own charges, she being married to a second husband; but the tutor obtained modification, with consideration of the moveable heirship: the contrary was found, where the mother was married, yet her offer of entertainment was received, July 14, 1627, Noble and his Tutors *contra* his Mother [Durie 310; M.407]. Neither was the modification excluded, because there were free lands at the defunct's death, seeing they were apprised thereafter for the defunct's debt, Hope, *de hæred.*, White *contra* Caldwell [*Sub nom. Whyt* v *Calderwod*, Hope, *Maj.Pr.* IV,5,68; M. 386]. The like, the debt being great, and the annualrent thereof equivalent to the rent of the lands not liferented, February 13, 1662, Brown *contra* her Mother [*Sub nom. Birnie* v *Rossie*, 1 Stair 99; M.392]; but aliment was not found due by a father, liferenter to his son, on this act, but only *super jure naturæ*, July 21 1636, L. Ramorney *contra* Law [Durie 819; M.388]; nor by a grandfather to his oye, who had disponed his estate to his son, reserving his liferent of a part, the rest unsold by his son, being liferented by his wife, July 7, 1629, Hamilton *contra* his Goodsire [Durie 457; M.392]: but where the heir's mother brought a great tocher, and the grandfather fell to a plentiful estate by his brother, the heir was found to have aliment of his goodsire, though he disponed the land to the heir's father, burdened with his mother's liferent, June 27, 1662, Heir of Gairn *contra* L. Gairn [*Sub nom. Ruthven* v *Gairn*, 1 Stair 115; M.393]. This behoved not to be from the statute, but *ex debito naturali*. Aliment was found due by a liferenter to her daughter, the apparent heir, though she renounced to be heir, July 16, 1667, Hamilton *contra* Symonton [1 Stair 474; M.382]. But, where a father disponed to his son a part of his estate, reserving his liferent, and another to his son, and his wife in conjunct fee after the son's death, his apparent heir got no part of his aliment from his goodsire, but only from his mother, February 26, 1675, Whiteford *contra* L. Lamington [2 Stair 328; M. 394]. Aliment was found due to the heir by an assignee to a gift of ward, without necessity to prove that he intromitted with the ward-lands, unless he had been legally excluded, which was modified by the Lords: and it was not found sufficient to entertain him in the assignee's family; but nothing was modified for that time that the minor's mother alimented him gratis, February 19, 1679, Sibbald of Cair *contra* Falconer [2 Stair 696; M. 407].

4. Heirs also not entered have the benefit of such obligements or provisions conceived in favour of heirs, which, by their nature or meaning, require to be fulfilled before the heir's entry; as when a party was obliged to employ a sum upon land, and to procure himself, and his umquhile spouse, infeft therein in liferent, and the heirs procreate betwixt them in fee, the bairn of the marriage who would fall heir, was thereby found to have right to crave his father, to employ the money accordingly, though he never was, nor actually could be heir, his father being alive, December 16, 1628, L. Collington *contra* Granton [Durie 410; M. 12974]. In this case the Lords inclined so to decide, but decided not; but that day Durie observes a like case decided, July 7, 1632, Young *contra* Young [Durie 410,n; M. 12974,n]. The like was decided, February 13, 1677, Frazer *contra* Frazer [2 Stair 503; M. 12859]. In which case a father, by his contract of marriage, being obliged to employ a certain sum upon security, to him and his wife in conjunct fee, and to the heirs of the marriage, and likewise to take all conquest during the marriage, the one half to the wife in liferent, and the other to the heir of the marriage in fee, after the wife's death, process was sustained at the instance of the apparent heir of the marriage against his father, who was decerned to employ the special sum to himself, and after his decease, to the heir apparent of the marriage; albeit thereby the father would remain fiar, and might dispone or burden the sum so employed for reasonable considerations, but not by deeds merely gratuitous to evacuate the obligement: and if he did deeds prejudicial, he would be obliged to purge the same, or re-employ *de novo*: but it was not so found, as to the conquest before the marriage, which might be altered during his life; for that only could be accounted conquest, that he had more at his death, than at his marriage. And so heirs of a marriage, in an obligement in case a wife deceased without surviving heirs of the marriage, these were interpreted bairns of the marriage, who survived their mother, but died before their father, and so could never be served heir to him, January 27, 1630, Turnbul *contra* Colinshlie [Durie 486; M. 2938]. The like, where a father was obliged to infeft himself and his spouse in conjunct fee, and the heirs procreate betwixt them, &c. the apparent heir was found to have interest to pursue the father for fulfilling thereof, and of the obligement adjoined, not to dispone in their prejudice, Hope, *de hæredibus*, Hamilton *contra* L. Silvertounhill [Hope, *Maj. Pr.* IV, 5, 73]. Tacks set to heirs require no service, but being notour, to be the person who might be served heir, they have right

without service, July 9, 1675, Home *contra* Johnston of Oldwells [2 Stair 343; M. 14375].

5. As to the benefit of heirs, they have right, not only to obligements concieved in favour of the defunct and his heirs; but though there be no mention of heirs, unless, by the nature of the obligement, there be a specialty, appropriating the same to the person of the defunct only, as in commissions, trusts, &c. So heirs were found to have the benefit of a promise, made to their predecessors, for disponing of lands to him acquired for his use, though it mentioned not heirs, Had. February 22, 1610, Heir of Robertson *contra* Livingstone [Not found]. The like of a reversion, not mentioning heirs, which was thought to be omitted by neglect, seeing it bore not redeemable to that party during his life, as is ordinarily adjected when that is meant, January 9, 1662, E. Murray *contra* L. Grant [1 Stair 77; M. 10322; 11, 10, 7, *supra*]. The like of an annualrent, though it bore only to be paid yearly, and not perpetually, or heritably, or to heirs, February 2. 1667, Pourie *contra* Dykes [1 Stair 434; M. 11648]. And a substitution, mentioning only a person substitute, without mention of heirs, was found competent to that person's heirs, January 6, 1670, Innes *contra* Innes [1 Stair 657; M. 4272].

6. Heirs have the benefit of heritable rights, not only whereupon infeftment hath followed, but which by destination are heritable, as requiring infeftment to their accomplishment, as heritable bonds bearing clause of infeftment; for these bearing only clause of annualrent, are declared moveable, by and since the Act of Parliament 1641, cap. 57 [A.P.S. v, 414, c. 107] revived Parl. 1661, cap. 32 [Bonds Act, 1661, c. 32; A.P.S. vii, 230, c. 244] of which in the last title [iii, 4, 24]. So also are reversions, pensions, tacks, without necessity of being entered heir, June 17, 1671, Boyd *contra* Sinclair [1 Stair 735; M. 14375]; July 9, 1675, Home *contra* Johnstoun of Oldwells [2 Stair 343; M. 14375]; and all rights having a tract or course of time after the defunct's death. In these cases, where the defunct's right is temporary, and runneth out by a certain course of time, that time runneth, whether the defunct's heir be entered, or do possess or not, as tacks, pensions, or annual prestations, during so many years, and therefore these require not service or solemnity; but that person, who might be served, may continue or recover the defunct's possession, and his possessing makes him liable *passivè*, as representing the defunct. Neither needs there any service of children *nominatim*, substitute immediately to their parents; but if they be substitute in the second place, a service must be used to instruct, that the heirs appointed in the first place did fail, July 21, 1676, Hay of Drumelzier *contra* E. Tweddale [2 Stair 445; M. 12857; iii, 5, 25 and 51, *infra*]. What rights are heritable, and what moveable, vide title Real rights [ii, 1, 2 *et seq., supra*].

7. Heirs have also right to moveable heirship, and to all obligements, though the matter be in moveable rights, if executors be expressly secluded; otherwise, if the matter be moveable, and heirs only be expressed, but not executors, yet executors will not be excluded, because heir is a general term,

comprehending executors, Hope, Ejection, Balmure *contra* Tennents [Hope, *Maj. Pr.* VI, 15, 27].

8. The special interest of heirs are, according to their several kinds, viz. heirs of line, and of conquest, heirs-portioners, heirs-male, and heirs of tailzie and provision. The interest of heirs of line is, that they are heirs generally, not only because they may be served by a general service, but chiefly because they most generally represent the defunct. So that, what cannot be claimed by a special title, either as being conquest, or specially provided by the tenor of the infeftment, befalleth to the heirs of line: and therefore, in dubious cases, what doth not appear to belong to other heirs, appertaineth to these, in respect of whom heirs-male, and of tailzie and provision, are accounted as strangers, and may come against the defunct's deeds, in favour of the heirs of line; but the heirs of line cannot come against such deeds in favour of others; because, as heirs of line, they are reputed as one person with the defunct, and so are obliged to maintain and fulfil his deeds not done on deathbed: and it was so found in the case of an heir of tailzie against an heir of line, Spots. Tailzies E. of Home *contra*   [Spotiswoode 332]: and as heirs of line have generally the benefit, so they have more effectually the burden of the defunct's debts, which ordinarily reach them in the first place, so that oft-times the heirs of line have little or nothing free. We shall not need to be special, what befalleth the heirs of line, being to show particularly what befalleth to the other heirs; for what remaineth, belongeth to the heirs of line only. Heirship-moveables belong only to heirs of line, and not to heirs of tailzie, January 27, 1666, Colonel Montgomerie *contra* Stuart [1 Stair 345; M. 5396].

9. Heirship-moveables is the best of every kind of moveables belonging to the defunct, which the heirs of line may draw from the executors, whereof there is an ordinary list [Hope, *Min. Pr.* (1734 ed.) Appx. 11]: the reason of this heirship-moveable is, because, by our law, primogeniture excludeth the defunct's other nearest of kin in heritage, whereas the nearest of kin succeed alone in moveables; and as they have no share with the heir in heritable rights, so most fitly the heir hath no share with them in moveables, but hath only the best of every kind, which therefore is called heirship-moveable; in which the defunct cannot, in his testament, or any other deed done on deathbed, prejudge his heir, as was shown last title; but if the nearest of kin be all females, they are both heirs and executors, or if but one male, he is both heir and executor, in which cases there is no heirship-moveable drawn.

Heirship-moveable is established by the act of Parl. 1474, cap. 53 [A.P.S. II, 107, c. 8], ordaining the heirs of prelates, barons, and burgesses, to have the best of every kind, according to the burrow laws, and so was found not to belong to the heir of a defunct who had only heritable bonds, being neither prelate, baron, nor burgess, Hope, *de hæred.*, Todorig *contra* Purdie [Hope, *Maj. Pr.* IV, 5, 55; M. 5390]. But the heirs of prelates was extended to other beneficed persons, as was found in the case of the heirs of the parson of Dingwal, November 28, 1623, Rig *contra* McKenzie [Durie 84; M. 5391]: and likeways the heirs of barons was extended to any person's heirs dying in fee of lands, though not erected in a barony, Hope, *de hæred.*, Keith *contra* M'Kenzie [Hope, *Maj. Pr.* IV,5,67; M.5891]; Todorig *contra* Purdie [Hope, *Maj. Pr.* IV,5,55; M.5390]. Heirship-moveable was found competent to the heir of a person, who died only infeft in an annualrent, July 19, 1664, Scrimzeor *contra* the Executors of Murray [1 Stair 219; M.463,5396]. But heirs of a burgess was found not to extend to an honorary burgess, who died not trading or working in the burgh, Spots. Heirs, Leslie *contra* Dumbar [Spotiswoode 138; M.5394].

Heirship-moveable is not always a single thing, but goeth sometimes by pairs, and sometimes by dozens, as in spoons, &c.; so the heirship of oxen was found to be a yoke and not a single ox, Nicol., *de hæreditatis petitione*, July 20, 1610, Black *contra* Kincaid [Not found]. And heirship taketh place only *in corporibus*, but not *in quantitatibus;* as in money, cloth, metal, &c. And so the shell of a salt-pan, which was out of use, was accounted but iron, and not to fall under heirship-moveable, Had. January 19, 1611, Reid *contra* Thomson [Haddington, *Fol. Dict.* 1,365; M.5387].

10. Heirs of conquest, though they be also heirs of line, as befalling by the course of law, and not by the tenor of the infeftment, therefore they were set down as lineal successors in the preceding title; yet because heirs of conquest have only place where there is an elder and younger brother, or an elder and younger father's brother, &c. and their issue to succeed: in which case the law alloweth two heirs, the immediate elder succeedeth in conquest, and the immediate younger in heritage: therefore the one is specially called the heir of conquest, and the other retaineth the common name of the heir of line. Conquest is *feudum novum*, whereunto the defunct did not succeed as heir to any person, or whereunto the defunct could not succeed as heir; for if that were disponed to him by the defunct, whereunto he would have succeeded, it were but *præceptio hæreditatis*, and so remained to be reputed as heritage to descend to the younger, and not to ascend to the elder, as Craig observeth, *Lib.* 2., *Dieg.* 15 [11,15,17]. Such heritages are rare, and befall only by tailzie, or provision amongst middle brethren; because the eldest by primogeniture excludeth the rest from being heirs of line; but it may befall in case of the heirs of line, when the nearest successor is the father's, or grandfather's brothers, or their issue, there being elder and younger brothers: but conquest is frequent, because not only that which is acquired properly, by the means and industry of the defunct, but that which is by gift of the defunct's parents, or any other, or whatsoever the defunct could not succeed to, is conquest: yet if the heir of conquest succeed, that which was conquest becomes heritage, and descends, as if there were four brothers, and the third acquiring lands, died without issue, the second would be his heir therein, who, if he died also infeft, the lands would fall downward to the youngest brother, and not upward to the eldest brother. The custom of England is contrary; for thereby the eldest brother succeedeth to all his brothers, failing the issue; but with us, the im-

mediate elder or younger doth always succeed, though of different marriages, none of them being brothers-german: and therefore, in the case proposed by Craig, *Lib.* 2, *Dieg.* 15 *in fine* [11,15,19] of a brother by a second marriage, dying without issue, and having three brothers of a former marriage, no doubt, the youngest would succeed, according to the opinion of Oliphant and King, there related, albeit that Craig's opinion be, that the eldest would succeed; but it was decided contrary to Craig's opinion, July 20, 1664, L. Clerkingtoun *contra* Stuart [1 Stair 220; M. 14867].

Heirs of conquest succeed, not only to lands conquest by their immediate predecessors, but in other heritable rights, passing by infeftment, as annualrent, or such as are heritable by destination, and which are accomplished by infeftment, as dispositions of lands or annualrents, apprisings, or adjudications, &c. The like, where an annualrent was first disponed, and a clause of requisition and reversion subjoined, July 7, 1675, Robertson *contra* Lo. Halkerstoun [2 Stair 338; M. 5605]; and in reversions, Hope, *de successionibus*, Heirs of Pitcairne [Hope, *Maj.Pr.* IV,3,32; M. 13442]. But in this case it is not cleared, whether the lands given in wadset were heritage or conquest; but it seems, if the lands had been heritage as they were wadset, the reversion would also belong to the heir of line, as the lands whereto it was accessory would; yea, heirs of conquest succeed in heritable bonds, bearing a clause of annualrent, as was found amongst the heirs of Dr. Craig [Not found]. But the heirs of line, and not the heirs of conquest succeed in tacks acquired by the defunct, Hope, Succession, E. Dumbar's heirs [Hope, *Maj.Pr.* IV,3,35; M. 5605]; and June 23, 1663, Ferguson *contra* Ferguson [1 Stair 193; M. 5605]. The heirs of line do also succeed in pensions, or any other right not requiring infeftment, as in these which having a tract of time, after the defunct's death, do thereby exclude executors, and do belong to the heir of line and not of conquest, though they be acquired. The heir of line, and not the heir of conquest, falleth to be tutor, as nearest agnate of the pupil, to whom the heir of line might succeed. The heir of line hath right to the heirship-moveables, and not the heir of conquest.

11. Heirs-portioners are amongst heirs of line; for when more women or their issue succeed, failing males of that degree, it is by the course of law that they succeed; and because they succeed not *in solidum*, but in equal portions, they are called heirs-portioners; and though they succeed equally, yet rights indivisible fall to the eldest alone, without any thing in lieu thereof to the rest: as, 1. The dignity of Lord, Earl, &c. 2. The principal mansion, being tower, fortalice, &c. which doth not extend to houses in burghs, nor to ordinary country-houses, the former being divisible, the latter fall under division, as pertinents of the land whereupon they stand, and are not as *separata jura*, or distinct rights. 3. Superiorities are accounted indivisible, and befall only to the eldest daughter and her issue, and thereby all the casualties of the superiority, either preceding or following the defunct's death, as ward, relief, marriage of the vassal's heirs, non-entry, liferent, escheat, &c. The reason is, be-

cause the vassal's condition ought not to be worsted, and they made subject to many superiors by such successions. Craig, *Lib.* 2, *Dieg.* 14. excepteth the superiority of feu-lands, the feu-duties which are divisible amongst all the heirs-portioners, yet the former reason of indivisibility of the superiority, in respect of the vassal's interest, reacheth feu-superiorities as well as others; and it is hardly conceivable how superiorities should belong to the eldest, and yet the feu-duties divide to the rest, seeing the superiority, as being the *dominium directum*, is the only title for poinding the ground, or pursuing the possessors or intromitters with the fruits thereof. It seems, for the reason adduced, the superiority, and therewith the feu-duty, befalleth to the eldest; yet so, because the feu-duty is constant and liquid, and is not like the other causualties of superiority, which are illiquid and accidental; therefore the other heirs-portioners ought to have compensation for their parts of the feu-duty, in or off other proper lands: or if there were more superiorities of feu-lands, so that some of the superiorities might befall one heir, and others to other heirs, no particular superiority being divided, or the vassal made vassal to many superiors, I conceive it would be allowed; or otherwise the eldest co-heir would be decerned to infeft the rest in annualrents out of the fee, correspondent to their share of the feu-duty. A vassal's heir, though the defunct had taken infeftment of more heirs-portioners, was not found obliged to take infeftment of some of them severally, but either of all jointly, or of the eldest, July 30, 1678, La. Luss *contra* Inglis [2 Stair 643; M. 15028]. How far heirs-portioners succeed *passivè*, and are liable for the defunct's debt, shall forthwith appear.

12. Heirs-male, and of tailzie and provision, succeed not by law, but by the tenor of the infeftment or provision; and therefore have that benefit and no more, which is so provided to them, or which is accessory thereto; whereby any right or security, of lands or others, befalling to these heirs, which is thereafter acquired by their predecessors, though the same be acquired to him and his heirs whatsoever, yet the same will befall with the principal right, to which it is accessory to the heir-male, or of tailzie or provision: as if a proprietor infeft himself, or his heirs-male, or of tailzie or provision, in lands or annualrents, and thereafter acquire reversions, apprisings, tacks, or other further or better security of the same lands to himself, and his heirs whatsoever; these will accresce to his heirs-male, or of tailzie or provision, whether the infeftment in their favour be anterior or posterior, which is the more dubious case. For it cannot be thought that the defunct having before provided such lands or annualrents to his special heirs, doth by acquiring new rights mean to set his heirs by the ears to debate upon their several rights: neither can his posterior deeds be reputed an alteration of the former provision; which can only be done by resignation, unless the defunct debarred expressly his former special heirs, and obtained his heirs whatsoever infeft. And though heirs whatsoever do ordinarily signify heirs of line, who are heirs general, and take place, when the right of no special heir appeareth; yet the adequate signification thereof is not heirs general, but heirs generally, whether of line, male,

tailzie or provision; as is more clear *passivè* in the defunct's obligements: as if he obliged himself and his heirs whatsoever; by heirs whatsoever will be understood all kind of heirs in their order; yet in some cases only his special heirs, if the obligement relate to lands or others so provided, as will shortly appear: and therefore heirs-male, or of tailzie and provision, in respect of the heirs of line, are as strangers, and may come against their predecessor's deeds in favour of his heirs of line; as if any person provide any lands or annualrents to his heirs-male, or of tailzie, and thereafter dispone the same to his heirs apparent of line, his heirs-male, or of tailzie, will in several cases not be obliged to fulfil that provision; and if such express provisions be ineffectual to the heir of line, it seems a general heir taking a new right in favour of heirs whatsoever should be less effectual: but the difficulty is, how special heirs can be served heirs in such rights supervenient, conceived in favour of heirs whatsoever, which will be loosed, if the heirs special may be comprehended, and so served under the common title of heirs whatsoever. How far heirs of tailzie or provision may alter the tailzie of the fee, or affect or burden the same, is largely considered, *Lib.* 2. *Tit.* 3. §58 [11,3,58] which therefore needs not here be repeated.

13. The common interest of heirs *passivè* is, that they are liable for their predecessor's debts, for they are reputed in law as one person with their predecessors, and so represent them, not only *activè* in their estates and goods, but also *passivè* in their debts and burdens, *Quem sequuntur commoda eundem et incommoda sequuntur* [1,7,13,*supra*]; and this is common also to executors as being heirs in the moveables, but as the executors succeed only in moveable rights *activè*, so they succeed only in moveable debts *passivè*, yet the creditor hath his option to pursue either, or both of them, whether the debt be heritable or moveable, and the heir hath relief against the executor, in so far as he is distressed for moveable debts; so hath the executor relief against the heir of the heritable debts, March 7, 1629, Falconer *contra* Blair [Durie 434; M. 12487]; Spots. Executors, L. Carnousie *contra* Meldrum [Spotiswoode 121; M. 5205; III, 8, 65 *infra*]. But heirs and executors differ in this, that the executor is only liable *secundum vires inventarii*, according to the inventory of the confirmed testament, unless he disorderly intromit with more; but the heirs are liable *in solidum*, though the debt far exceed the value of the estate. Heirs are liable for their predecessor's debts, which are preferable to the heir's proper debts, if they be decerned within three years after the defunct's death; neither can the heir dispone in their prejudice within a year after the defunct's death, Parl. 1661, cap. 24 [A.P.S. VII,63,c. 88] but not all the same way. First, Heir-portioners, though jointly they be liable for their predecessor's debts *in solidum*, without benefit of inventory; yet severally, each heir-portioner is regularly liable but *pro rata parte*, though the proportion whereunto they succeed be more than the whole debt, February 7, 1632, Home *contra* Home [Durie 619; M. 14678]; Spots. Improbation, L. Lawers *contra* Dunbars [Durie 619; M. 14678]; Duncan and the Heirs of Ogilvy [Spotiswoode 143;

M. 14680].

14. Yet one heir-portioner was found liable *in solidum*, as successor in his whole estate by disposition *post contractum debitum*, though there were other two sisters, the one of whom being called, renounced, the pursuer condescending upon nothing, unto which she could succeed; and the other having no means, but being called *passivè*, February 15, 1634, Orr *contra* Watson [Durie 704; M. 9767]: Neither did it avail that the other sisters had received portions of money near to the value of the estate, by the father in his life, but action of relief was reserved against them, as accords, March 21, 1634, *inter eosdem* [Durie 714; M. 9768]: The reason thereof adduced is, that the getting portions in money, could be no *præceptio hæreditatis*, and so could not make the receivers lucrative successors, *post contractum debitum*, as the disposition of the lands doth. Yea an heir-portioner being convened without the other, was found liable *in solidum*, because the other was found not *solvendo*, and had disponed all right to the defender, January 24, 1642, Scot *contra* Hart [Durie 888; M. 14681]. But here the matter was but of small moment, and this was a doubt in the first decision; in this case, if some of the heirs-portioners should be *insolvendo*, whether or not recourse might be had against them that were *solvendo*, at the least, to the value of their proportion; which, though it seems equitable, and is favoured by this last decision, yet it is not decided in the former, neither have I observed it decided since; but in the pursuit, December 23, 1665, at the instance of Dame Rachel Burnet, now Lady Preston, *contra* the sisters of her first husband [*Sub nom. Burnet v Lepers*, 1 Stair 329; M. 5863], the Lords only decerned against the heirs-portioners *pro rata*, but with reservation to the pursuer to insist and dispute her right against any of them for more, if any of them proved insolvent: but it seems the portion of the insolvent would not reach the solvent above the value of their succession; because the only ground they could be liable on, for more than their part, would be *in quantum lucrantur*. For, as heirs they could not be liable *in solidum*, neither by our law nor the civil law. And if the creditor's taciturnity, whereby the other heirs became insolvent, did appear, it would prejudge the silent creditor, and not the co-heir, who did not know the debt, and so could not prevent the other's dilapidation.

15. There is a case occurreth oft-times amongst heirs-portioners, when several obligations and provisions are granted in their favour by the defunct, thereby, after his decease, they become mutual debtors and creditors, and sometimes these provisions exceed the estate; *quid juris*, whether do these obligations evanish and become extinct *confusione*, because the same persons become debtors and creditors? or whether they do all stand? and, in that case, whether the first in order will be preferred, or if they all will be abated proportionally to the value of the heritage? Thus Maitland observes, December 20, 1550 [Not found], that a father infeft himself, and the heirs of the first marriage, and thereafter resigned and infeft himself and the heirs-male of the second marriage, which failing, his nearest heirs whatsomever: these heirs-

male of the second marriage failed; and, therefore, not the daughter of the first marriage only, but she, and the daughters of a third marriage succeeded by the second infeftment, as his heirs whatsomever, substitute to be his heirs of the second marriage. Craig hath the same case [*Aikman Sisters*], but otherwise observed, *lib.* 2. *dieg.* 14 [11, 14, 11]. where a person had provided his lands to the heirs of three several marriages, of each whereof there survived a daughter: the question was, which of the daughters should succeed? Whether the first, as having the first provision, or the last having the last provision? The parties were three sisters, Aikmans. In which the Lords admitted all the three sisters as heirs-portioners, and so confounded the provisions, being all equal and about the same thing, which must be the reason, and not that which is there rendered, viz. because the defunct, notwithstanding of these provisions in favour of heirs, might have disponed effectually to a stranger, and so likewise to his own children of another marriage; for that reason would have excluded the daughters of the first marriage, and preferred the daughter of the last marriage; and as hath been shown, tailzies of provisions, upon an antecedent onerous obligation, such as marriage is, hinder the fiar to dispone, or provide the same to his heirs of line, representing him simply, who must fulfil his obligement; albeit his disposition to strangers, not so representing him, will be effectual: And therefore Craig, in the same place [11, 14, 11] observeth, in the case of Isobel Baron, who being heir to her father of his first marriage, by which it was provided that the heirs of the marriage should succeed to all lands conquest during the marriage; and thereafter, having a son of the second marriage, who was his father's heir of line, to whom his father disponed, or provided a tenement acquired, during the first marriage; yet the said Isobel, as heir of that marriage, recovered that tenement from her brother as heir of line [III, 5, 19, *infra*].

But the main difficulty remaineth, when the obligement in favour of the heirs-portioners are unequal; for, when they are equal, whether they become extinct by confusion or not, it is alike. But if they be so extinct when they are unequal, there will not be an equal abatement; but the greatest obligement will be extinct, as well as the least: neither can such obligations be wholly extinct by confusion, but only *pro rata*. So that, if there be three heirs-portioners, for example, the obligement granted to every one of them can only be extinct for a third part, because they are but heirs in a third part; and as to two third parts, each two of them are debtors to the third: and if the obligation exceed the value of the heritage, such of them as find themselves losers if they enter heirs, may abstain and renounce, and they, or their assignees, may pursue any of the rest that shall enter for fulfilling of the defunct's obligements; but if they be considerate, when all the obligations jointly exceed the value of the estate, they will all renounce and assign their obligements, and their assignees will be preferred, according to their diligence, without consideration of the priority or posteriority of the obligements; but if they happen to enter, or when their provisions are not personal to themselves, *nominatim*, but as they are heirs of provision, and therefore necessarily require that they must be heirs, before they can obtain their provisions, then the obligements or provisions of each heir-portioner are extinct, as to their own proportion; but they have like action against the other heirs-portioners, for their proportion, as other creditors have: the point will be clear by example, if three sisters were provided by their father to unequal portions, the first to 15,000 merks, the second to 12,000 merks, the third to 6000 merks, and the defunct's whole estate had only been worth 18,000 merks. All of them entering, the case would be thus: the eldest would succeed to 6000 merks of the heritage for her part, and the second would be liable to her for 5000 merks, as the third of her provision, to whom she would also be liable for 4000 merks, as the third of the second's provision, which being compensed, the second would be liable to the first in 1000 merks *de claro*. In like manner, the first would be liable to the third in 2000 merks, and the third would be liable to the first in 5000 merks, which being balanced, the third would be debtor, *de claro*, to the first in 3000 merks: so the interest of the first would be 6000 merks, as her own portion; and one out of the second, and three out of the third's portion, being in all 10,000 merks. The second falleth 6000 as her share, out of which she is liable in 1000 merks to the eldest, and the youngest is due to her *de claro*, 2000 merks, whereby her interest will be 7000 merks, the youngest's portion will be 6000 merks, out of which she is due to the eldest 3000 merks, and to the second 2000; so there will remain only free to her 1000 merks.

This may clear the case as to liquid sums, but as to dispositions, or provisions of lands, or other obligements *in facto*, these, or the interest, or value, will be the same way effectual amongst the heirs-portioners, as if they had been made to strangers; except where the same disposition or provision is made to divers of them: for then either being equally obliged to others, as representing the defunct, the same became void and ineffectual *pro tanto*, as was found in the said case of the sisters Aikmans; but since the Act of Parliament 1621, against fraudulent dispositions [Bankruptcy Act, 1621,c.18; A.P.S. IV,615,c.18], the first disposition, or provision, constituting that party creditor, may give ground to reduce a posterior disposition of the same thing to another of the heirs-portioners, as being without a cause onerous, after contracting of the first debt: but that will not hold in bonds for sums of money, all which will have their effect, as is before said: neither will it hold, when the provision of lands provideth the party destinate to be heir, for thereby the party cannot quarrel that predecessor's deed: otherwise the first obligement, or disposition to any of the heirs-portioners *nominatim*, may reduce any posterior disposition to others of the heirs-portioners. Two daughters being served both heirs-portioners to their father in some teinds, but one of them succeeding to her brother, who was infeft as heir to his father in lands, excluding the other sister, who was not sister-german to her brother by both bloods, and both being pursued for their father's debt, they were not found liable equally, but proportionally, according to the interest they succeeded to; the one being only immediate heir to her father, in a right of teinds, wherein her brother was not served and infeft, the other being equally and immediately heir to her father in these teinds, and mediately heir to her father, by being heir to her brother, who was heir to his father, being infeft in the lands by precept of *clare constat*, without service, June 10, 1673, White *contra* White [2 Stair 183; M. 5207].

16. Other heirs not being heirs-portioners, are liable for the defunct's debt *in solidum*, except heirs substitute in bonds, who are only liable *quoad valorem* in the sums in these bonds, July 3, 1666, Fleming *contra* Fleming [1 Stair 386; M. 13999; III, 5, 51, *infra*].

17. Heirs are not convenable at the creditor's option, as in the case of heirs and executors, but they have the benefit of an order of discussing. Thus, first, debts and obligements relating to any particular lands or rights, and no other, do, in the first place, affect the heirs, who may succeed in these lands or rights before the heir general: so an obligement obliging the defunct's heirs of line or tailzie, so soon as he should come to his estate, was found to affect the heir of tailzie who came to that estate, without discussing the heirs of line, Hope, *de hæredibus*, Lyon *contra* Scot [Durie 50]. So an obligement, obliging a debtor and his heirs-male, succeeding in such an estate, which was provided to heirs-male, and all other heirs succession, was found to burden the heir-male, before the heir of line or executors, July 22, 1662, Anderson *contra* Andersons [1 Stair 132; M. 14879]. So likewise an obligement to infeft a party in an annualrent out of lands designed, to affect the heir of provision in these lands, without discussing the heir of line, was the opinion of the Lords, though there was no decision in it, Had. February 19, 1611, L. Blair *contra* Fairly. [Haddington, *Fol.Dict.* I, 176; M. 2746]. And in these cases the heir of tailzie or provision will have no relief against the heir of line, or other nearer heirs of blood, who otherwise, and also executors, must be discussed before heirs of provision or tailzie. General obligements not relating to particular lands, do, first, affect the heirs of line, who are heirs-general. 2. The heirs of conquest, July 21, 1630, Fairly *contra* Fairly [Durie 533; M. 3560]. 3. Heirs-male must be discussed before heirs of tailzie or provision, not being so near of blood, Hope, *de hæred.*, Dunbar *contra* Hay of Murkill [Hope, *Maj.Pr.* IV, 5, 69; M. 3559]. The like must follow as to heirs of marriages, who are also heirs of blood, and must be discussed before other heirs of provision or tailzie, who therefore are only liable in the last place, the rest being discussed, unless they be obliged to relieve the heir of line, November 22, 1665, Scot *contra* Boswell of Auchinleck [1 Stair 310; M. 3571].

18. But an heir of tailzie was not found to represent the defunct in obligations contrary to the terms of the tailzie, as to which heirs of tailzie are as creditors and strangers; as when the security of a sum was by way of tailzie payable to the creditor, and the heirs of his body, which failing, to a person named, his heirs and assignees whatsoever, the creditor being obliged to do no deed hurtful to the tailzie, and the debtor obliged not to pay without the

consent of the person named; that person was found to have interest to obtain declarator that the sum was unwarrantably paid by the debtor, without his consent, or order of law, by consigning it to be employed in the same terms; and therefore the debtor was ordained to make up the security again as at first, reserving to creditors how far they could affect this sum for the first fiar's debt, or whether the terms of the tailzie would exclude the fiar's debts or deeds for his necessary use, or only unnecessary and voluntary deeds, February 3, 1674, Drummond *contra* Drummond [2 Stair 259; M.4306; 11,3,59,*supra*]. And in like manner, a father having granted two bonds of provision to his two daughters, payable to them and the heirs of their body, which failing, to return to the father and his heirs, the one of them having died without heirs of her body, but having assigned her bond to her sister, the assignation was found ineffectual, as being done on design to disappoint the tailzie made by the father of the return of the provision, in case the daughters had no heirs of their bodies, and so was done without any onerous cause or just consideration, January 31, 1679, Drummond *contra* Drummond [2 Stair 686; M.4338].

19. Heirs of marriage are heirs of provision, and partly creditors, and therefore may quarrel deeds fraudulent, or merely gratuitous, done by the defunct whom they represent, in prejudice of their provisions, as was found in the forementioned case of Baron, observed by Craig [11,14,12; 111,5,15, *supra*], who being heir of a marriage, to whom all lands conquest during the marriage were provided, the father having disponed a tenement acquired during that marriage, to his eldest son by another marriage, yet that heir of the marriage did recover the same from that son, albeit the heir of the marriage did represent her father, yet not simply, but according to the provision by the contract of marriage; which being an onerous contract, *uberrimæ fidei*, the father, contractor, can do no deed contrary thereto, but upon an onerous cause or just consideration; and therefore, if he sell any thing falling within such provisions, the heir of provision cannot quarrel that stranger, but is obliged to fulfil to him, but might quarrel the same, if it were merely gratuitous; much more might heirs of a marriage quarrel deeds prejudicial to their provision in favour of the children of other marriages, without which the great trust of these contracts would be eluded, whereupon parties rely, and make matches and give tochers, and therefore take provisions to the heirs of the marriage, either of definite sums, or of all, or a part that the contractors have, or shall acquire during the marriage, by which the whole estates of citizens are ordinarily conveyed; or otherwise, contracts of marriage bear particular lands, or sums to be provided to the heirs or bairns of the marriage, and also the conquest during the marriage; which clause of conquest will reach only to what the father had more at his death than the time of the contract, and is ordinary both in the contracts of citizens and others, which therefore should not be elusory, but effectual, according to the true meaning of the parties, which is not to bind up the father, that he cannot do deeds for causes onerous,

or rational considerations, but that he can do no other deeds merely gratuitous and arbitrary, in prejudice of such provisions; for though by such provisions, when fulfilled, he himself must become fiar, and so may dispone, yet
he is also debtor, and so cannot effectually dispone against the import and
meaning of the provision: and therefore a father by his contract of marriage
having provided certain tenements to himself, and his future spouse in conjunct fee, and to the bairns of the marriage, &c. and the wife having restricted
herself to the half of the liferent of these tenements, after which the father
having infeft her of new in the second half, the said last infeftment was found
reducible at the instance of the bairns, as heirs of the marriage, and that they
were not obliged to fulfil their father's deed in favour of their mother, who
was competently provided, in respect the same was contrary to the provision
in the contract of marriage, July 10, 1677, Carnagie and Clark *contra* Smith
and Baird [2 Stair 536; M. 12840]. Yea, a father by his contract of marriage
having provided a definite sum to the eldest heir-female of the marriage, and
thereafter having disponed his estate to her, she marrying a person that would
assume his name and arms, wherein if she failzied, providing the same to his
second daughter upon the same terms, &c. the said eldest daughter having
married suitably before she knew that disposition, and her husband refusing
to take her name, she was found to have right to take her to her portion by
her mother's contract, and so the right of her father's estate was devolved to
her second sister, upon the terms therein contained, who was found liable to
pay the provision to her eldest sister, contained in her mother's contract, July
26, 1677, Stevinson *contra* Stevinson [2 Stair 550; M. 15475, 17000]. But
these provisions do not hinder just and rational deeds of the father, as providing a jointure for a posterior wife, as was found in the case of Mitchel
contra the Heirs of Littlejohn, June 16, 1676 [2 Stair 426; M. 3190]. Nor will
they hinder fathers to provide children of another marriage with competent
provisions according to his condition, though thereby the conquest during
the marriage will be affected; yea, where in a contract of marriage the husband's present means, and his wife's tocher, were provided to be employed
for the man and wife in liferent, whilks failing, the one half to the man's heirs,
and the other half to the woman's heirs; there being no bairns of the marriage,
the husband was not found liable to employ that sum, and the conquest in
favour of himself and the wife's heirs, but that he might employ the whole in
favour of the child he had by a posterior marriage, December 21, 1680,
Anderson *contra* Bruce [2 Stair 820; M. 607; 11, 3, 41, *supra*].

20. The exception that all parties having interest are not called, will be
sufficient to sist process against such heirs as have the benefit of discussion,
without necessity to condescend or instruct any right they may succeed to,
January 24, 1672, L. Luss and Glendening *contra* E. Nithsdale [2 Stair 53;
M. 3565, 13255].

21. But the exception of the order of discussing will not be sustained,
unless the defender condescend on, and clear an heritage to which the anterior

heir may succeed, which being a dilator, must be instantly verified, as where it is notour; and where that cannot be, sometimes process will be sustained against both heirs of line and tailzie together, superseding execution against the heirs-male or of tailzie, till the heir of line were discussed, July 13, 1626, Edgar *contra* Heirs of Craigmiller [Durie 216; M. 8124]. And heirs of line and provision being pursued jointly, the heir of line renouncing, was assoilzied, and protestation admitted for adjudication against the heir of line, which the pursuer was ordained to assign to the heir of provision, and was not found obliged further to discuss the heir of line, or to put him to his oath upon any other passive title, seeing the heir of provision required not the same, when the heir of line renounced, nor showed any visible estate which might befall to the heir of line, June 22, 1678, Crawfurd *contra* the Heirs of the L. of Rater [2 Stair 624; M. 3578]. The question is here, what is meant by discussing, which is not understood by that heir's renouncing to be heir, January 26, 1672, Cowan *contra* Murray [*Sub anno* 1622, Durie 10; M. 3577]; but in that case the renounced heritage must be adjudged. Discussing therefore is by horning, caption, and apprising, March 22, 1627, Edgar *contra* Heirs of Craigmiller [Durie 293; M. 3576]; or otherwise by adjudication in case the heirs renounce; but the other heirs may exclude the renunciation, by alleging his behaving as heir, as was found in the foresaid case, January 15, 1630, Cleghorn *contra* Fairlie [Durie 481; M. 9664]. This passive succession of heirs in their predecessor's debts and obligements, making them personally liable thereto, befalleth in three cases: 1. When the heir is entered heir. 2. When he is not entered, but immixeth himself, by meddling himself as heir, or becoming lucrative successor, after the debt contracted. 3. When the heir is lawfully charged to enter heir, though he hath neither entered nor meddled, if he do not renounce, he is personally obliged; and if he do renounce, his person and proper estate is free, and only the heritage is liable, and the creditor hath action *contra hæreditatem jacentem*. The first case is most ordinary and orderly, the second inferreth the vitious passive titles, *gestionem pro hærede*, or *præceptionem hæreditatis;* of which in the ensuing titles. Let us here consider, first, the charge to enter heir, which is antecedent to the entry; and then the entry of heirs itself.

22. The charge to enter heir is founded upon the Act of Parliament 1540, cap. 106 [A.P.S. 11, 375, c. 24] and it is of two kinds, a general charge, and a special charge: the general charge to enter heir proceedeth thus; the creditor, upon supplication, without citation, obtaineth from the Lords of course letters passing under the signet, to charge the party complained upon to enter heir to the complainer's defunct debtor, within forty days after the execution of the charge, with certification, if he enter not, such process will be granted against him as if he were actually entered heir: the reason of this charge with us is, because heirs are not liable *passivè*, if they enter not, nor immix themselves in the heritage; and therefore, that the creditor may not lie out beyond the year and day granted to heirs to deliberate, the law hath introduced this

remeid, that the creditor may charge the debtor's apparent heir to enter, whereupon he hath personal action against him, if he renounce not, and thereupon may reach not only his heritage, but his own proper goods belonging to him *aliunde ;* and if he renounce, he hath action *contra hæreditatem jacentem* [III,2,46,*supra*].

The general charge to enter heir may be executed against the apparent heir, after the defunct's death, even within the *annus deliberandi ;* but the summons thereupon must be after the year and day is expired, not only from the defunct's death, but from the heir's birth, if he be posthumous, Spots. Heirs of Livingstoun *contra* Fullertoun [Spotiswoode 137; M. 6870]; and therefore a summons executed after year and day expired upon a charge to enter heir within the year, was sustained, June 19, 1628, Maculloch *contra* Marshall and Reid [Durie 376; M. 2168,6870]; Had. July 10, 1610, Montgomery *contra* L. Langshaw [Not found; III,4,32,*supra*]. There is also an Act of Sederunt in *anno* 1613, allowing general charges to enter heir within the year and day, or within the days of the charge, if the heir renounce and omit that defence, the decreet *cognitionis causa*, and adjudication thereupon, were found valid, and that alledgeance proponed by another creditor, was repelled; because it was free to the heir as well to renounce when he pleased, as to enter when he pleased, July 10, 1631, Blair *contra* Brown [Durie 596; M. 6870]; but it is like the posterior creditor hath been negligent, otherwise that *præmatura diligentia* of pursuing and renouncing within the year, would have been accounted collusive and fraudulent, and so would not prejudge the other creditor doing diligence in the ordinary way. General charges to enter heir do evanish, as incomplete diligences, if the party charged die before litiscontestation or sentence; and though the forty days be expired before the death of the party charged, yet the charge useth not to be transferred, or made use of against any subsequent heir apparent; but it is not consequent, that if the charger die before litiscontestation or sentence, that the same should also become void, because the charger doth not necessitate the party charged to enter or renounce in favour of the charger's heirs, but of himself. Yet it was found, that an assignee might insist upon a charge at the cedent's instance, after the cedent's death, though nothing followed thereupon during his life, June 18, 1631, Prior of Archattan *contra* Captain of Clanronald [Durie 591; M. 10370].

23. A special charge to enter heir differeth from the general charge in this, that the general charge is in lieu of the general service: for thereby the creditor reacheth the person of the apparent heir of his debtor, and his estate or goods established in his person, unless he renounce: and so the general charge is the ground of a process and decreet for payment: but thereby the creditor cannot reach the lands and annualrents, which are not as yet established in the person of the apparent heir, he not being specially served thereunto, or infeft therein. And therefore, that the creditor may reach these, he must use a special charge, which supplieth the special service and entry. This special charge, though it proceedeth upon supplication without citation, yet it

must be upon production of a decreet at the creditor's instance, not only *cognitionis causa*, but for performance. And it is competent in two cases; first, upon the proper debt of the party to be charged: for if the debtor be un-entered to some of his predecessors, and so their rights not established in his person; in that case the creditor must charge his own debtor specially to enter heir in the rights competent to him by that predecessor, with certification if he enter not, the creditor shall have such process and execution against that land and heritage to which he might enter, as if he were actually entered therein, whereupon apprising doth proceed. In this case there is no necessity of an antecedent general charge, which only is used to the effect that the debt may be established against the person of the debtor's apparent heir *passivè*, by a decreet upon the general charge. The other case is, when the debt is not the proper debt of the party charged, but of some predecessor to whom he may be heir; in which case the debt must first be established against him *passivè*, and then followeth the special charge: in this case the special charge cannot be till after year and day, because it presupposeth not only the summons, but also the sentence upon the general charge, both which must be after year and day [111, 2, 46, *supra*]. When the debt is the proper debt of the party charged, if the special charge may not be at any time, even within year and day, or if it must be after the *annus deliberandi* : this makes for the negative, that it needs not abide the year of deliberation, because the intent of the deliberation is not so much whether the party charged will be heir, as whether he will personally subject himself to the ground of that charge: for albeit he renounce not, that will not make him liable to any of the defunct's debts, except it be by his fraud and collusion with one creditor in prejudice of another. And therefore, seeing he cannot deliberate, whether he will be subject to his own debt, he ought not to have the benefit of year and day before the special charge be effectual. Yet before the late Act [1661, c. 24; A.P.S. VII, 63, c. 88] preferring the diligence of the defunct's creditors to the heir's proper creditors, there was no reason to allow special charges for the apparent heir's own debt, but more summar execution than other charges, so to prefer the apparent heir's proper creditors to the [defunct's] creditors. This preference of the diligences of the defunct's creditors to the diligences of the heir's proper creditors, is only if the same be complete in three years after the defunct's death, wherein the *annus deliberandi* is not contained; but in that year the heir can make no valid voluntary disposition, Parl. 1661, cap. 2 [Act 1540, c. 106; A.P.S. 11, 375, c. 24; 11, 12, 29, *supra*]. The Act of Parliament, which is the ground of the charge to enter heir, and is only the rise of the special charge, insinuates an exception, if the heir be major: But the custom of the Lords hath introduced the general charge to constitute the debt, and allows both charges against minors. There is no necessity either of a general or special charge, as to real actions, which may proceed against apparent heirs; as poinding of the ground, January 2, 1667, Oliphant *contra* Hamilton [1 Stair 422; M. 2171; 11, 5, 10, *supra*]. Neither are they necessary in declarators or reductions [11, 10, 19, *supra*].

24. The remedy against both charges to be heir, is a renunciation to be heir, whereby the renouncer's person and his proper estate will not be liable for his predecessor's debt, but only his predecessor's heritage. This renunciation useth to be offered by way of exception in the process upon the general charge; and if the defender be not absent, it is not ordinarily admitted by suspension, except in favour of minors, who, though being apparent heirs, they take a day to renounce and fail therein, yet they will be restored against the same by suspension without reduction, January 25, 1628, Kennedy *contra* Mackdougal [Durie 331; M. 2699]; Spots. Minors, Nisbet *contra* Nisbet [Spotiswoode 301; M. 13899]. But if the minority were controverted, and not instantly verified, it must be by reduction, Spots. Minors, Craig *contra* Cockburn [Spotiswoode 212; M. 8980]. A renunciation to be heir was admitted *rebus integris*, though the decreet and charge were sixteen years before, July 20, 1626, Harvie *contra* Baron [Durie 221; M. 9038]. Yea, it was admitted, though there was an adjudication and the decreet suspended, which was declared to stand, and the apparent heir's person and proper estate were only freed, Spots, *Restitution in Integrum*, Oliphant *contra* Blackburn [Not found]. A renunciation to be heir was not admitted with this quality, excepting to the renouncer certain lands whereinto he was appointed to be infeft by his father's contract of marriage, and whereupon inhibition was used before contracting of the charger's debt, to the effect he might enter heir to those lands, January 23, 1627, La. Ogilvie *contra* Lo. Ogilvie [Durie 261; M. 13898]. But in the like case, Hope, Inhibition, Thornton *contra* Bailie [Hope, *Maj. Pr.* II, 15, 14; M. 6944], Had. June 15, 1615, and the like Had. Nov. 30, 1620, Adamson *contra* Hamilton [Hope, *Maj. Pr.* II, 15, 14; M. 13897], the apparent heir was suffered to renounce to be heir to his goodsire, except as to those lands which his goodsire had disponed to his father in his contract of marriage, whereupon inhibition was used: which the Lords found a singular title consistent with a renunciation of the heritage *ex titulo universali*. The exception upon renunciation to be heir is elided, if the defunct's estate be burdened with the heir's proper debt; which is taken off by the duply of purging the same, as appears in the decisions before adduced [III, 5, 23, *supra*]. The said exception is also elided by the reply of behaving as heir, albeit the same were libelled as a several passive title, March 18, 1631, Bennet *contra* Bennet [Durie 582; M. 12218].

25. The entry of heirs is either of heirs general or heirs special. The former requires only a general service, which is necessary to all heirs, except heirs in tacks, pensions, and heirs *nominatim*, immediately substitute in bonds [III, 5, 6, *supra*]. But heirs of tailzie or provision must be served, that it may appear that the heirs to whom they are substitute are failed; and therefore the only child of a marriage was found to have title to pursue implement of the contract of marriage, he serving heir of the marriage *cum processu*, July 21, 1676, Hay of Drumelzier *contra* E. of Tweeddale [2 Stair 455; M. 12857]. The general entry of heirs proceedeth thus: a brieve is taken out of the

Chancery of course, without citation or supplication, for serving such a person nearest and lawful heir to such a defunct. It may be directed to any judge ordinary at the party's option, albeit the defunct nor the heir never lived within that jurisdiction, March 6, 1630, L. Caskiben, Supplicant [Durie 501; M. 14420]. The Lords may, in cases where an ancient or important service is required, choose the judge most fitting for the affair; and when brieves pass of course, they are obtained to any judge desired; but they are easily advocated, and remitted to the macers, with assessors in cases of difficulty.

The tenor of the brieve, is by way of precept from the King to the Judge to inquire *per probos et fideles homines patriæ,* that such a person died at the faith and peace of our Sovereign Lord; and that the user of the brieve is the nearest and lawful heir: So this breive hath only these two heads; and thus not only heirs of line may be served generally, but also heirs of conquest, being to succeed to reversions, heritable bonds, or the like rights, not having an infeftment, nor requiring a special service: Hope, Succession, Earl of Dumbar's Heirs [Hope, *Maj. Pr.*IV, 5, 69; M. 3559, 5605]. And, no doubt, heirs-male may be served generally, that they may succeed to the like rights which may be conceived in their favour, and whereunto they can have no other access. And, for the same reason, heirs of a marriage may also be served, and heirs of provision in bonds.

General services use to be included in special services, as members thereof: and a retour to an annualrent, bearing to be granted to heirs whatsoever, and that the persons retoured heirs in the said annualrent, was found to instruct him general heir, though it did not bear *per expressum,* that he was heir generally, but only in that annualrent, Feb. 9, 1676, Drummond *contra* Stirling [2 Stair 413; M. Supp. 50]; the general service of heirs being retoured, doth so establish rights not having infeftment (as dispositions, heritable bonds, reversions, apprisings, and adjudications) in the person of the heir served, as that no posterior heirs can have right thereto, unless they be served heirs to the person last served heir, though the right stood in the name of the first acquirer, and not of the last heir; as an heritable bond or reversion remaining in the name of a father, to whom his eldest son was served heir generally, who, dying without issue, the second brother must be served heir to his brother, and not to his father therein, as was thought by all the lords after dispute *in præsentia,* albeit the matter was agreed without decision, Spots. Heirs, Captain Rollo *contra* Stewart of Gairntullie [Spotiswoode 144]; the reason is, because the general service is a complete establishing of the right in the person of the heir: and therefore, as in special services, the heir is served to him who died last vest and seised as of fee, whereby that right is established; so, in the general service, the heir must be served to him in whose person the right stood last. And though, in special services, the heir cannot be served to him who is last served special heir, unless he had been also infeft; the reason thereof is, because the special service, as an incomplete right, evanisheth, and the next apparent heir must be served again to the same defunct; but it is not so in general services.

26. The entry of heirs to lands or annualrents, the fee whereof is by infeftment, is either by consent of the superiors voluntarily, or by law. The former is by the superior's precept, which, from the initial words thereof, *Quia mihi clare constat*, &c. is called a precept of *clare constat* [11,3,14,*supra*], by which the superior acknowledgeth, that the defunct died last vest and seized in such lands or annualrents, and that the same are holden of him by such a tenor, and that the obtainer of the precept is nearest and lawful heir to him in the said lands, &c. and that he is of lawful age for entering thereto; and therefore commands his bailiff to infeft him therein. Infeftment being past accordingly, giveth that party the real right of the lands or annualrents, if done by the right superior. It doth also constitute the receiver thereof heir *passivè*, and makes him liable to his predecessor's debts: but it will not constitute or instruct him heir *activè* or give him an active title to pursue as heir. Yea, it will not be a sufficient title as to the real right of the ground against any other party, than those who acknowledge the giver thereof to be superior, and the receiver to be heir. For if, upon any other colourable title, they question any of these, the infeftment and precept of *clare constat* will not be sufficient alone, unless it have obtained the benefit of a possessory judgment or prescription.

27. Like unto this is the entry of heirs, within burgh-royal, by hasp and staple [11,3,19,*supra*], according to the custom of burgh, which is instructed by the instrument of seasin only, without other adminicles, Nov. 13, 1623, Mershal *contra* Mershal [Durie 79; M.6839]; July *penult.* 1629, Wilson *contra* Stuart [Durie 468; M.12514]. In which case, though a seasin by hasp and staple was sustained to instruct an heir *activè*; yet it was only because this pursuer had been proved heir *passivè* thereby, at the distance of that defender.

28. The securest entry of heirs specially, in lands or annualrents, is by law. The procedure whereof is in this manner: any person may summarily obtain a brieve out of the chancellary, in the same manner as the general brieve, which is directed by way of precept from the King, or lord of the regality, having chapel and chancellary; whereby the judge, to whom it is directed, is ordained, by an inquest upon oath, to inquire "who died last vest and seized, as of fee in such lands or annualrents, and if, at the faith and peace of our sovereign lord; and who is his nearest and lawful heir therein; of whom it is holden in chief; by what service, and what the value of it is, now, and in time of peace: and if the said heir be of lawful age, in whose hands the same now is, from what time, how, by what service, by whom, and through what cause." It is needless to be curious concerning the number of the heads of this brieve, some parts thereof not being distinct, but explicatory of the former.

29. These brieves are accordingly directed to the judges ordinary, where the land or annualrent lies, as to sheriffs, bailies of royalty, or regality, or bailies of burghs-royal. But, if there be just exception against the judge ordinary of the place, or if the lands or annualrents lie in divers jurisdictions,

and be so represented, warrant will be granted, upon supplication to the lords, that the director of the chancellary issue brieves to other persons, and frequently, in the case of divers jurisdictions, they are directed to the macers.

30. By virtue of this brieve, the judge ordinary, or delegate to whom they are directed, citeth persons to be members of inquest, upon 15 days; and proclaimeth the brieves at the market-cross, unless they be served at the Michaelmas court, when all the freeholders are obliged to be present, and then the brieve may be served, without further delay, conform to the act of Parl. 1429, cap. 127 [A.P.S. 11,19,c. 18]. and Parl. 1503, cap. 94. [A.P.S. 11,253,c. 40] where it is left arbitrary, to summon the inquest on what days the judge, server of the brieve, pleaseth; or presently, if they be persons of inquest present in the tolbooth, unsummoned. But, in all cases, the brieves must be proclaimed publicly at the market-cross, in plain market, where most confluence of people is gathered, so as it may come to the knowledge of all parties having interest. And then that the said brieve be thrice cried plainly together; which is by three several oyesses, with a loud and audible voice, before the reading of the brieve and the sheriff's precept thereupon; and each oyes to be at as great distance from other, as the time required to give the said oyes thrice: and that the officers of the town be present. But if the brieve come to be served so near Whitsunday or Martinmas, that there does not intervene a market-day, the brieves may be proclaimed upon any week day, the officers and six others of the town being present: yet, either the day of compearance, or the day of citation is numbered as one of the fifteen, July 27, 1626, Mackulloch *contra* Mackulloch [Durie 229; M. 6856]. There is no necessity to summon any defender: in lieu whereof is the publication of the brieve, by proclamation at the market-cross. Yet, upon the supplication of the party interested, warrant was granted by the lords to the director of the chancellary, that no brieves should be issued for serving heirs to such a defunct, unless they contained a clause to cite the supplicant, who was donatar to the defunct's bastardy, Spots., *de hæreditariis actionibus*, Mackculloch *contra* L. Martoun [Spotiswoode 30].

31. The inquest being called, consisteth ordinarily of fifteen persons, against whom like exceptions are competent, as against witnesses. And though Craig, *lib.* 2. *dieg.* 17 [11,17,23] regretteth that any person is admitted to be one of the inquest, whose rent exceedeth not 40 *lib.* though they be not *pares curiæ*, nor convassals with the party to be served, neither of the vicinity, or neighbourhood, contrary to the intent and ancient custom of these services; yet he acknowledgeth, that it was so ordinarily, especially in the service of noblemen, and custom hath continued the same hitherto. But those of the neighbourhood were fittest, because, as Craig observeth in that place, inquests are in the middle, betwixt Judges and witnesses, partaking part of them both; for two or more of them, of their proper knowledge, will be sufficient for witnesses, in the matter of fact; and, upon their declaration, all the rest will serve *affirmativè*, without any other testimony. And it is like they have

been of old, sole judges in brieves, the Judge Ordinary having no more power but to call and order them: and they are yet with the Judge Ordinary or delegate, as Judges; for they must serve, and do sometimes seal the service with him.

32. The inquest being settled, the heir apparent gives in his claim, craving to be served heir to his predecessor, in such lands or annualrents; and therewith the brieve and executions thereof, together with the instructions of the same.

33. The brieve and claim are as a libel, against which any party compearing, and found to have interest, may propone their exceptions, which are many more than those contained in the said last act of Parliament 1503, cap. 94 [A.P.S. 11,253,c.40]. And first, against the executions, as being blotted in the date, or other substantials, and so null; which thereby may not be mended, as other executions; as the name and sirname of the follower, and of the defender; the name of the land, and cause upon which the brieve was purchased, which was found, not only to extend to the blotting of the brieve, but to the executions thereof, July 27, 1623, Mackulloch *contra* Martoun [Durie 224; M.2703]. Or, as not proclaimed upon fifteen days, which also will be relevant, by way of reduction: Or, that the defunct was bastard, and had no lawful issue: Or, that the pursuer of the brieve is bastard, and so incapable of succession; wherein, if the proponer be more special and pregnant than the apparent heir, in his allegeance of being nearest and lawful heir, he will be preferred. Exceptions also are competent as to the point of right, by proponing and instructing, that the defunct was denuded of the fee; but exceptions upon parallel rights, that the defunct had not a good right, are not competent here. And also exceptions upon the age of the apparent heir, or his being forfeited, or rebel, &c. are here competent: and likewise objections and debates, upon instructions and writs adduced, for proving of the claim and heads of the brieve. In which cases, if there appear difficulty or intricacy, the Lords, upon supplication, will constitute assessors, or grant advocation of the service; and after discussing of the points *in jure*, will remit the same, either to the same, or to other Judges delegate. But no objection or exception will be admitted, unless it be instantly verified, because this brieve is no brieve of plea, Parliament 1503, cap. 94 [A.P.S. 11,253,c.40] and therefore cannot admit of terms to prove exceptions.

34. The debates upon the brieve being discussed, the pursuer thereof must prove, and instruct sufficiently the heads of the same: As first, that the defunct died last vest and seised, as of fee, at the faith and peace of our Sovereign Lord; which comprehends, first, the death of the defunct, which is ordinarily proven by the knowledge of the members, notoriety, or common fame, without necessity to instruct the same, by ocular witness who saw the defunct die, or buried. But, in case of the defunct's death out of the country, or if it be dubious or controverted, the testimony of witnesses, or proper knowledge of two at least of the inquest, or testificates from abroad, especially

from the magistrates of the place where the defunct died, or was buried, are requisite; or common fame, as to persons who perish, or are killed. The second point of this head is, that the defunct died last vest and seised, as of fee; which must be instructed, by production of the infeftment, especially the instrument of seasin, and warrant thereof, or ground of the same: for though *in antiquis* the very precept cannot be shown; yet the charter or disposition will be a sufficient adminicle to corroborate this seasin, that it be not accounted only as the assertion of a notar: yea, there is no doubt, but since the Act of Prescription [Prescription Act 1617, c. 12; A.P.S. IV, 543, c. 12], consequent seasins having the course of forty years, may instruct this point, being sufficient, even in the case of competition, which is much exacter than this [11, 12, 20, *supra*]. And Spotiswood [*Sub tit.* Brieves, p. 30] observeth upon retours, that *in anno* 1547, a negative service was reduced, upon production of a transumpt of the defunct's seasin, out of a protocol transumed before a commissar, with a decreet against the superior, bearing to have confessed, that he had infeft the defunct. But here the instructing the defunct's being once infeft, will infer a presumption that he so continued, and so died infeft, unless the contrary be proven, that he was denuded. The third point in this head, that the defunct died at the faith and peace of our Sovereign Lord is also presumed, *quia quod inesse debet praesumitur*, and therefore needs no other probation, but layeth the burden of probation upon the alleger in the contrary, viz. that the defunct died rebel, or that he was forfeited, or his blood attainted; which may be elided by the replies of relaxation, dispensation, or restitution. But there useth no notice to be taken of rebellion upon civil debts; but only open rebellion of war, or upon treasonable causes, whereupon the defunct was declared fugitive; which makes the defunct, as to this point, not to die at the faith of our Sovereign Lord, November 21, 1626, Seatoun, Supplicant [Durie 234; M. 2208].

35. The second head of the brieve is, That the pursuer is nearest and lawful heir to the defunct in these lands, which resolveth in two points; first, that the fee was provided to such heirs as are contained in the claim, whether they be heirs of line or of conquest, heirs-portioners, heirs of marriage, heirs-male, or of tailzie and provision: and this can only be instructed by the defunct's infeftment, and other ancient evidents, where, *in dubio*, the presumption is always for the heir of line. So that, if it be not sufficiently instructed, that the fee was provided to special heirs, it will belong to the heirs-general of line or conquest, according to law; as if it be instructed by three consequent seasins, which ordinarily do not express the several kinds of heirs. The other point of this head is, that the pursuer of the brieve is nearest lawful heir, which sometimes also is instructed by the infeftment; as when the person to be served is a member of tailzie nominate; as if the infeftment bear land, or annualrents to be granted to the fiar, and to the heirs of his body; which failing, to George his brother, &c. George pursuing a special service, needs no further instruction; because that he is George, the defunct's brother,

passeth without probation as *notorium*. But ordinarily the propinquity of blood to the fiar who died last infeft, or to some member of tailzie substitute, must be known to the inquest, or proven. For proving whereof, the relation must be particularly condescended on, according to the line of succession, mentioned in the former title; as that the pursuer is the defunct's eldest son, or the eldest lawful son of that son, or that they are the daughters of that son, &c. or the lawful daughters of the defunct, &c. And it will not be sufficient to instruct, or serve the pursuer nearest lawful heir, without condescending. Here also the propinquity of blood being condescended on and proven, it is sufficient, in whatsoever degree it can be proven, though it were beyond the tenth degree. Yea, any degree being presumed to be the nearest degree, unless a nearer degree be instructed; for it resolves in this negative, that there is no other nearer degree, which, as other negatives, proves itself: and that the pursuer is not only nearest heir, according to lineal succession, by course of law; but that he, nor none of the intervenient blood, were bastards, or unlaw-ful children, (which is instructed sufficiently by common fame, or being so holden and reputed in the intermediates) it will be sufficient, that nothing is known to the inquest on the contrary, unless bastardy be on the other part alleged and instructed. This propinquity of blood is proven, either by writ, or by retours, infeftments or designations, or acknowledgments of the fiar for the time, bearing such a person to be of such a degree, or relation to him. And, *in antiquis*, writs bearing such designation and acknowledgment, even by others of fame, will be sufficient; for there is not equal evidence of fame required in all cases. And therefore, when the fee is to fall caduciary, and to cease from the fiar's proper blood, less probation will serve, than when the competition is betwixt divers persons of the same blood, or, at least, members of the same tailzie; amongst whom the pregnantest probation will take place. So the service and retour of the Earl of Airth, then designed Earl of Strathern, was reduced, because the propinquity of blood was not sufficiently instructed, which could not be known by the inquest, or witnesses, the progress thereof being far past memory of man, and hear-say or common fame was not found sufficient; neither were the writs produced sufficient to prove the said Earl's propinquity of blood to David, Earl of Strathern, son to King Robert II or to Eupham, only daughter to the said David, and Patrick Graham her spouse, which progress not being sufficiently instructed, the right remained with the King, as the unquestionable descendant of King Robert III and so the heir of his brother, the said David Earl of Strathern; so that no other lawful issue being proven of the said David's own body, nor of any other nearer brother, all his right remained with the King, as descending from King Robert III who was brother to the said David Earl of Strathern, March 22, 1633, the King *contra* E. Strathern [Durie 683; M. 6691]. There is another exception against this head, that the pursuer hath slain his father, mother, goodsire, grandsire, &c. whereby he, and all his issue, are excluded from the heritage of the party slain, if he be convict thereof by an assize, and the next agnate may be served, Parl. 1594, cap. 220 [Parricide Act, 1594, c. 224; A.P.S. IV, 69, c. 30], which was not sustained, where the slayer was only declared fugitive, for not appearing to underly the law, in a dittay for slaying his mother, February 3, 1674, Oliphant *contra* Oliphant [2 Stair 261; M. 3429].

36. The third head of the brieve is, of whom the fee is holden in chief, or who is immediate lawful superior thereof, and this must also be instructed by the infeftments; whereby the giver of the last infeftment will also be presumed to continue superior, and the inquest will serve accordingly, unless another superior be instructed or acknowledged by the pursuer. Which acknowledgment, in respect of the pursuer's hazard of disclamation, and that the subsequent superior's rights are in his own hand, and he cannot be prejudged by the service; therefore that point will be so served *periculo petentis*.

37. The fourth head of the brieve is, by what service the fee is holden, whether it be ward, blench, feu or burgage; which also must be instructed by the evidents. And if nothing else appear, the fee is presumed to be ward, because that only is the proper fee, and all others are improper, declining from the nature of fees, and therefore are not presumed, but must be proven. And as Craig observes, lib. 2. dieg. 17 [11, 17, 33] it will not instruct the fee not to be ward, though it contain a particular *reddendo*, of a cane or duty; yea, though it bear *pro omni alio servitio et quæstione seculari;* unless it express the said *reddendo* to be in name of blench-duty, or in name of feu-duty: so an infeftment, bearing a particular duty, payable at Whitsunday and Martinmas yearly, *cum servitiis in curiis nostris debitis et consuetis*, was found to be a wardholding. Hope, *de feudi renovatione*, Williamson *contra* Thomson [M. 16559; 11, 3, 31, *supra*]. And an infeftment bearing *sex denarios nomine canæ*, with a taxed marriage, was found ward, February 7, 1610; as was resolved by Oliphant the King's Advocate, in a consultation with the Bishop of St. Andrews, for entering the Lord Lindsay to the lands of Struthers.

38. The fifth head is, the value of the fee now, and in time of peace. The reason of inserting of this article, is, because there is due to the superior a year's rent of the fee, for the entry of the heir, which is called the relief, of which formerly, title, Superiority [11, 4, *supra*]. And that it might be constant, and liquidate, there was a general valuation of the whole kingdom, which is called the Old Retour, or Old Extent. Thereafter there was a second retour, called the New Retour, or Extent; whereby the new retour of some shires was made the triple, and some the quadruple of the old; yea, different new retours were in the same shire, but there is no new retours in southern shires upon the border, which were frequently wasted with war, and little addition in the northern shires. So the meaning of the article is, what the fee is worth now, that is, what the new retour, or extent thereof is, and what it was worth in the time of peace, or what is the old extent thereof. Craig [11, 17, 36] declares, he could never find clear satisfaction in the reason of these expressions, especially, why the old retour is called, that which was in the time of peace. And he conjectureth, that because our forefathers are said to rest in peace; therefore,

by the same peace, is meant the time of our predecessors: but I conceive the matter may be better cleared thus. The casualties of the superiority were of old, the chief patrimony of the Crown of Scotland, and were further extended than of late; and therefore it seems, that the time of the making the new retour, and cause thereof, was the frequency of war, requiring an addition of the royal revenue. And though, through the alteration of the rate of money, neither of the retours be now considerable; yet doubtless they were very considerable in those times. So that by *quid valet nunc*, is to be understood in the time of war, at which time the new retour was made; which is the more evident, by the opposite member, what was the value in the time of peace. So that the old retour being that value which was before the necessity of heightening thereof by the war, it is fitly said to be that which was in time of peace; and the new retour, that which was made in time of war. And immediately after the constitution thereof, the brieve was made to express it by the then present time, *nunc*, which hath been always so continued, because the style of brieves is not to be altered. This is the more evident, that the bordering shires, which were frequently wasted by incursions, were not altered in their extent, so that it hath been made in a time of war. The new extent is not only the rule of relief, but of non-entry, in lands holden ward and blench; for the new retour mail is only due till general declarator. But, in feu-lands, there is only regard to the extent; for, during the non-entry thereof, at least before general declarator, nothing is due but the feu-duty, and the duplication thereof for the relief. Annualrents had no difference before or after declarator, and therefore were always retoured to the full value of the annualrent, and was thus expressed, *quod valet seipsum*, which is well altered by the Act 42. Sess. 2. William and Mary [Act 1690, c. 42; A.P.S. IX, 222, c. 96], that the whole annualrents shall only fall to the superior by the special declarator.

39. The sixth head is, Whether the pursuer be of lawful age; wherein we must distinguish betwixt ward-holdings and other holdings, blench, feu, or burgage; for in these any age is lawful age: but in ward-holdings, because the superior, by virtue of the ward, hath the profit of the land, during the heir's minority, therefore they cannot enter till their majority, at which time only the heir is of lawful age, which in men is twenty-one years complete, and in women fourteen years complete, Had. January 27, 1610, L. Kilbirny *contra* Fairlie [Haddington, *Fol. Dict.* 1, 568; M. 8521]. Yet if the King, or any other superior, give dispensation of the age, the service will proceed; but the benefit of the ward continueth with the superior, by the dispensation in the disposition. The heir's age must also be instructed to the inquest, either as being notour by inspection of the persons, for it would be ridiculous to prove a grey-headed heir to be major; but *in dubio* witnesses, or other sufficient adminicles, must be adhibited.

40. The seventh head of the brieve is, in whose hand the fee is; that is, to whom the profit and benefit thereof doth now belong. For ordinarily the fee is

retoured, to be in the hands of the superior by reason of non-entry; but some-times it is retoured, to be in the hands of the superior's superior, when the superior hath lost the casualties of the superiority during his life; and some-times it is in the hands of the liferenters, by conjunct fee, or liferent holden of the superior, which doth not hinder the entry of the heir to the fee, yet excludeth non-entry. The remanent articles of the brieve, "from what time, how, by what service, by whom, and through what cause," are but circum-stances relative to the last head, that thereby it may appear, 1. How long the fee hath been in non-entry, or in the hands of the immediate superior or life-renter: 2. How it came to be in that condition; as if it became in non-entry by the vassal's death, and in the hands of the mediate superior, by the contu-macy of the immediate superior, in not entering his vassal; and in the hands of the liferenter, by the infeftment of liferent granted by the superior: 3. The kind of service which relateth to the fee being in the hands of the liferenter, in respect that the liferent is oft-times a different holding from the fee, and is ordinarily blench; and therefore it is the superior's interest to know what such service is, and also to know by whom, and through what cause, the fee is in the hands of such a person. These circumstances, therefore, do not make distinct heads of the brieve, and are not always necessary to be retoured, as the former heads are.

41. The points aforesaid being cleared, and instructed to the inquest, the service is the sentence or decreet, which ought to be sealed with their seals, and with the seal of the Judge to whom the brieve is directed, and is so returned to the Chancery, whence it is called a retour, being registrate there, and extracted; till which it is not complete: neither doth the service ordinarily instruct the active title but only the retour. The service is kept in the Chan-cery, for warrant of the retour: yet it was found, that services before the year 1550, were sufficient to satisfy the production in improbations or reductions, without producing the retour itself; because at that time the books of the Chancery were destroyed by war, February 17, 1624, Lo. Elphinstoun *contra* E. Marr [Durie 111; M. 2218].

42. Retours are easily annulled, or reduced, because no defender is called thereto, and the probation in most part is by presumption, as hath been shown; and by the proper knowledge of the inquest, or witnesses, whereof there seldom remaineth any testimony *in retentis*. The Lords would not reduce a retour for want thereof, but ordained the whole inquest to be examined upon oath, upon what evidence they served, February 24, 1665, Mercer of Aldie *contra* Rowe [1 Stair 276; M. 14424]. A retour being found null on one head, was found null *in totum*, Hope, Retour, L. Lugtoun *contra*   [Possibly *L. Lugtoun* v *Lethindie*, Hope, *Maj. Pr.* 111, 28, 15; M. 6416 or 6847]. A retour of a sister as heir to her brother was found null by exception, upon production of another brother's retour, though posterior, who thereupon was preferred, albeit an excommunicated Papist, February 16, 1627, Lo. Colvill *contra* Herds [Durie 276; M. 2704]. And a retour of a second brother served heir to his

father, where the elder brother was absent, and reputed dead; but returning home again, and granting bond to a creditor, who charged him to enter heir, and apprised and possessed; the retour of the second brother was thereupon found null by exception, albeit twenty years after the date thereof; though by the Act of Parliament 1617, cap. 13 [Reduction Act, 1617, c. 13; A.P.S. IV, 544, c. 13] retours are not quarrellable by reduction, or summons of error, unless the same be intented, executed, and pursued within twenty years after the service and retour, in respect of the apprising and possession within these years, which imported an interruption, and that the second brother's retour was null by exception, and needed no reduction, January 11, 1673, Lamb *contra* Anderson [2 Stair 148; M. 10984]. A retour was also annulled by exception, by referring to the party's oath, that he had no contingency of blood with the defunct, February 10, 1636, Murray *contra* Sinclair and Meikle [Durie 793; M. 14084]. The like in the case of a woman retoured sole heir; it being instantly verified, that there was another sister, Hope, Retour of Idiotry, Fairly *contra* Fairly [Hope, *Maj. Pr.* V, 14, 58]. The like was found by reply, referring it to the party's oath, that he was a bastard, Spots. Retours, Murray *contra* Murray [Spotiswoode 30].

43. Retours are ordinarily annulled and reduced by a great inquest, of forty-five members, who do inquire, not only concerning the verity, and sufficiency of the retour, but also concerning the ignorance and malice of the *jurantes super assisa*; which is not always inferred when the retour is reduced; as if it be found, that the defunct died not last vest and seased, as of fee, by instructing that he was denuded, July 7, 1663, Mow *contra* Dutchess of Buccleugh [1 Stair 196; M. 2705]; or that he died not at the faith and peace of our Sovereign Lord, by instructing that he was forfeited; or that he was not nearest and lawful heir, by instructing a nearer heir, is no error in the first inquest, seeing these points were presumed, and needed no probation. And in like manner, if by reduction, there be a more pregnant condescendence and probation for another party than for the heir served, it will be no wilful error, unless competition had been at the time of the service. But it must be an evident and gross error in the positive probation, specially concerning the death of the defunct, and his being once infeft; the special relation, and degree of blood of the heir, his age, and the extent of the fee, which though the point of least moment, yet will annul the retour. But if there be a probable cause for the inquest, as by production of writs containing wrong extents, they will be declared free of wilful error, Spots. Retour, Ker *contra* Scot of Hartwoodmires [Spotiswoode 30]. The manner of reducing of retours, is by a summons of error against the assizers before the king's council, which is now the Lords of Council and Session, Parliament 1471, cap. 47 [A.P.S. II, 100, c. 9].

44. Though it be the ordinary way to annul retours by a great inquest, yet the Lords do sometimes sustain reductions thereof as erroneous by witnesses before themselves, without a great inquest, July 7, 1663, Mow *contra* Dutchess of Buccleugh [1 Stair 196; M. 2705].

45. The reduction of retours being of such hazard to the members of inquest it is statute, Parliament 1494, cap. 57 [Act 1496, c. 57; A.P.S. 11, 238, c. 6] that they shall not be reducible, but within three years after the date, so as to infer error against the inquest; albeit they may be reduced, so as to render the retours null in themselves at any time within twenty years after they were deduced, Parliament 1617, cap. 13 [Reduction Act, 1617, c. 13; A.P.S. IV, 544, c. 13] which Act reacheth only retours after it, but not retours before, and actions against the same; which prescribe by the general Act of Prescription, Parliament 1617, cap. 12 [A.P.S. IV, 543, c. 12] as was found, November 28, 1665, Younger *contra* Johnstoun [1 Stair 315; M. 10925].

46. The heir being thus specially served and retoured, if the fee immediately hold of the king, he doth thereupon obtain precepts out of the Chancery of course, without citation, commanding the judge ordinary of the place where the fee lies, Sheriff or bailie, to give seasin to the person retoured *capiendo securitatem*, taking security for the non-entry and relief due to the king; for which the judge ordinary is comptable in exchequer, unless the profits belong to himself as bailie of regality. If the said judge ordinary do not grant seasin accordingly, the Lords, upon supplication and instruments of his disobedience, will grant warrant to the director of the Chancery to issue precepts to another person as Sheriff in that part, specially constitute, without first using horning against the Ordinary disobeying, Spots. David Balfour, Supplicant [Not found]. These precepts, because of the clause *capiendo securitatem*, were found to make both the person of the heir, and the ground liable for the sums due thereby, though infeftment was never taken, Spots. Sheriff, L. Stobs *contra* L. Lowristoun [Not found; 11, 4, 29, *supra*]. These seasins are appointed to be given by the ordinary clerk of the jurisdiction, Parliament 1540, cap. 77 [A.P.S. 11, 359, c. 12]; Parliament 1567, cap. 27 [A.P.S. 111, 33, c. 34]; Parliament 1587, cap. 64 [A.P.S. 111, 455, c. 50]. If the fee be holden by any other superior than the king, if he do not willingly grant infeftment upon sight of the retour, the heir will of course get precepts out of the Chancery to charge the superior to enter and infeft the heir so retoured; with certification if he fail, he shall lose the benefit of the superiority during his life; containing also this clause in favour of the superior, *faciendo vobis quod de jure facere debet.* And upon instruments of the superior's refusal or delay, being thrice required, he loseth the non-entry during the life of that vassal, but loseth no other casualty of the superiority, December 18, 1630, Stark *contra* L. Airth [Durie 549; M. 6900]; Had. March 24, 1632, Hay *contra* L. Achnames [Durie 633; M. 15023; 111, 5, 48, *infra*].

47. For preventing of the loss of the superiority during life, the superior being charged, if he obey not, must suspend the precepts; which is done most ordinarily upon this reason, that the heir hath not satisfied the relief and non-entry duties due to the superior, conform to the clause of the precept *faciendo vobis*, &c. which Craig, *lib. 2. dieg.* 17 [11, 17, 43] shows not to have been sustained by the Lords, seeing the superior had poinding of the ground com-

petent therefor; yet the custom since hath been contrary, July 29, 1624, L. Capringtoun *contra* L. Keirs [Durie 142; M. 6897]: in which case Keirs being pursued to receive Capringtoun in place of Capringtoun's immediate superior, Foulshiels, who being charged to enter heir within forty days to the superiority, that he might receive Capringtoun his vassal, obeyed not; and therefore Keirs, Foulshiel's superior, supplying his place, was ordained to receive Capringtoun, he always paying the non-entry; neither was Capringtoun the subvassal put to take out charges against Keirs, as he had done against Foulsheils; but this action was summarily sustained. The like March 12, 1630, Somervel *contra* Downie [*Sub nom. Somerville* v *Somerville*, Durie 306; M. 13580], where the annualrenter craving entry, was not found liable to pay the full annualrent during the non-entry, but the blench duty only. And though in the case of Peebles *contra* Lo. Ross, January 23, 1630 [Durie 485; M. 15019], Peebles, as superior, craving the non-entry duties for three terms subsequent to the ward, to be paid to him by the heir craving entry, not according to the new retour, but according to the full duties, as being subsequent to the ward, was ordained to enter the heir without payment of those duties, without prejudice of his right thereto *prout de jure :* the reason is rendered, because the duties were not liquid as the new retour is; neither was the case itself clear and unquestionable, and therefore was only reserved. If the superior himself be not entered, he may be charged to enter within forty days, with certification if he fail, to lose the superiority during his life, conform to the act of Parliament 1474, cap. 57 [A.P.S. 11, 107, c. 13], and if he fail, his superior may be pursued *via actionis*, to supply his place, and receive the sub-vassal with the same certification, without necessity of charging him with precepts out of the Chancery: as was found in the said decision, Capringtoun *contra* Keirs [Durie 142; M. 6897].

48. The certification of loss of the superiority during the superior's life, though it would seem to extend to all the casualties of the superiority befalling after contumacy; yet it was found only to extend to the non-entry, which was purged by [the entry made by] the mediate superior, who supplied the place of the immediate superior: but that subsequent wards and liferent-escheats did notwithstanding belong to the immediate superiors, Had. March 24, 1623, Hay *contra* L. Achnames [Durie 633; M. 15023]; in which case it was also found, that the feu and blench-duties contained in the *reddendo*, did no ways fall by the said certification: which is clear, because these are not casualties of the superiority. But whether these casualties will not be lost during the life of the contumacious superior, as the certification would import, and will belong to the mediate superior supplying his place, is not so clear; because, if the negative hold, the certification which seems so great, signifies nothing [Hope, *Min. Pr.* Tit. 4, §16–33].

49. The next reason of suspension of these charges for entering of vassals, is, That the heir retoured doth not produce the ancient evidents, that the new precept of the superior for obedience may be made conform thereto.

This reason was repelled, Had. November 14, 1609, L. of Drum *contra* L. of Ley [Not found]. And though that might have been admitted, because of old infeftments were simple; but now since they are clogged with many provisions which fall under the service of the brieve, there is reason that the ancient evidents should be shown with the retour, and those provisions in the precept offered to the superior, otherwise the said provisions may become ineffectual; because these precepts and infeftments thereupon, will be sufficient rights, without showing any elder. And seeing it is the vassal's duty to show his holdings to the superior, there can be no time so fit as at the entry. A third reason of suspension of these charges useth to be upon the superior's right to the property by recognition, or upon improbation of the heir's retour; which, if decreet be not passed thereupon, will be repelled, and only reserved as accords, but will not be sustained upon a reason of prejudiciality of a reduction at the superior's instance, Spots. Sheriff, L. of Taich *contra* Hume [Not found]. Craig, *Lib.* 2, *Dieg.* 17 [11,17,42] moveth this question, when one person is the fiar, and another liferenter of the superiority by reservation of his frank-tenement, or liferent; and the like is, when liferent is by conjunct-fee; of whom in that case ought the heir to crave to be entered? In which he relates, that the Lords, in favour of the vassal, found, in the case of Cranstoun, brother to the L. Cranstoun, that the heir might enter by any of them he pleased, being without detriment to either of them. As to the casualties of the superiority, how far such casualties belong to liferenters, vid. Tit. Liferents [11,6,*supra*].

50. There is another weighty and subtile question in the entry of heirs, Whether that person who falls to be nearest heir at the time of the defunct's decease, may not then be entered, though there be a nearer in possibility, or in hope? There is no question, but when a nearer heir is really or probably in being, in the womb, though unborn, that the service must be stopped till the birth. For in all things tending in favour of those unborn, they are accounted as born: and that not only for presuming that there is a living child, not a false conception, but presuming that it is a male child, not a female. And therefore daughters of a defunct cannot be served heirs, if there be a probability of a posthumous child, who is presumed to be a son; whereby they will be excluded till the contrary appear. It was so amongst the Romans, who therefore sent the womb in possession for the child. But with us the fee of necessity must remain in non-entry; and the friends, or nearest agnates of the birth, as pro-tutors, may continue the possession. But the difficulty is, when the nearest heir is in possibility, but neither conceived nor born: and this occurs specially in two cases; First, in the case of heirs ascendent, as when the father succeeds to the son, having no issue, brother or sister; for in that case, though at the defunct's death there be neither sister nor brother gotten or born, yet the father may have them after: So that the question will be, Whether the father may enter immediately upon the death of his son, having no children, brother nor sister, born, nor in the womb; or if he must attend

the future possibility of a supervening brother or sister? The other case is in heirs of tailzie, whereof there was a notable instance, long debated in *anno* 1647 and 1648, on this occasion. The L. of Blackwood married his natural daughter Marion Weir, having no other children, to Major James Bannatine; and in contemplation of the marriage, and for a sum advanced by the major for satisfying his debts, he disponed his estate of Blackwood "to Major Bannatine, and the heir to be procreate betwixt him and Marion Weir; which failing, to the heirs of the said Marion Weir by any other lawful husband; which failing, to the heirs of Bannatine." The major died without issue: so the question was, Whether Bannatine's heirs should succeed, or if the succession behoved to be pendent, till it appeared whether there would be any lawful heir of the body of the said Marion Weir, who was no member of the tailzie herself, but only the heirs of her body. The whole question resulted in this point, Whether "whilks failing" was to be understood failing *de præsenti* at the time of the fiar's death, or failing simply, as being existent at no time. The matter was not decided, but transacted, whereby Marion Weir being married to William Lowrie, and having children during the dependence of the plea, the matter ended by transaction betwixt the L. of Corehouse, who was Major Bannatine's heir, and William Lowrie taking burden for his heirs with Marion Weir, thus: that the tailzied estate should belong to Marion Weir's heirs; that William Lowrie for them should pay to Corehouse 20,000 pound Scots, as the sum which the major his brother had contracted for payment of Blackwood's debts, and had paid out upon contemplation of the marriage. This was a very equitable transaction to the same effect, as if the clause in the tailzie had been interpreted thus: that, failing heirs of Marion Weir, that is, so long as the heirs failed, the major's heirs should succeed to him in the tailzied estate: So that, where there became to exist heirs of Marion Weir, both that they should succeed to Major Bannatine's heir, to wit, Corehouse who was served heir of tailzie to his brother Major Bannatine, and should exclude Corehouse his heirs of line; whereby the fee should never be *in pendente* at the death of the last fiar, but that person should be entered as heir of tailzie, who, at the death of the defunct fiar, or at the time of the service, was nearest heir of the tailzie, whereby Corehouse should succeed as heir of tailzie to his brother; because, at his death, neither of the two former branches of the tailzie were existent, viz. the heirs betwixt the major and her, and Marion Weir's heirs by another husband. And therefore a judicious and just inquest, serving a brieve for the heirs of tailzie of Major Bannatine, could not but find that he died last vest and seased as of fee, in a tailzied estate of Blackwood; and that the major's heir of line, to wit, Corehouse, his immediate elder brother, was the nearest heir to the major by the tailzie, there being no heir of Marion Weir then existent, conceived or born, she being unmarried: for, if she had then had a lawful child, the inquest behoved to have served that heir as nearest heir of tailzie to Major Bannatine, then his heir of line. Neither would that child be excluded, because the child could not be heir to

Marion Weir, while she was on life; for heirs in that case were only meant, such as might be heirs if she were dead. Suppose then there had been a son betwixt the major and Marion Weir, who had been infeft as heir to his father, and died without issue; Marion Weir at her death having then a daughter by a second husband; that daughter would have succeeded as heir of tailzie, albeit a son of Marion Weir were in possibility, and in the nearest hope, and to whom the title of her heir would be most proper, as being her heir of line, or heir *simpliciter;* yet the fee would not remain *in pendente*, and vacant till the event of that possibility, but the daughter would be served as nearest, at the last fiar's death. And therefore the inquest could not justly swear but that Major Bannatine's heir of line was his nearest heir of tailzie the time of the service. For if it should be objected, that there were a nearer heir in possibility or hope, the inquest could not demur thereon; because an heir in possibility is not, but only may be. And therefore the major's heir is the nearest heir of tailzie, who needs not be served heir of line to the major. If the major had an untailzied estate, his brother might renounce to be heir of line to him in that estate, and yet might be heir of tailzie to him in the tailzied estate, as being still his heir of line demonstrative; that is, the person who might be his heir of line. And therefore, after Corehouse his death, if he had died infeft as heir of tailzie to his brother; if the question again had arisen betwixt Corehouse his son as his heir of line, and Marion Weir's son being then existent, an inquest could not justly serve Corehouse heir of tailzie to him in the estate of Blackwood; because then Marion Weir's son was a prior branch of the tailzie, and so behoved to exclude Bannatine's heir of line, which was the posterior branch. Therefore, in lieu of this temporary succession of Corehouse resolving in his liferent, as the branches of tailzies frequently do, he accepted 20,000 pounds, which was his brother's true interest, and denuded himself in favour of Marion Weir's son, the prior branch; so we are left in both to a rational debate, without decision. As to the first case, we have already shown, both by reason and practice; that failing the fiar's children, brother and sisters, his father and grandfather succeed, and exclude their collaterals. So thence it necessarily followeth, that these ascendants may be served without delay, otherwise they could never be served, there being ever possibility of the issue of men. Yet, if they should not be entered before the superveniency, even though but in the womb, the same would take place; but, if the ascendant be actually entered, the law affordeth no remedy, reversion, or restitution. Neither can this difficulty be a reason against the succession of ascendants, because the question is only betwixt them and their own children, and nothing operates in favour of their brothers and sisters, or their descendants. As to the other case, in the instance proposed, it seems the succession ought to have depended, till the event of the lawful issue of Marion Weir: First, Because that had a determined time, by the course of nature, viz. the fiftieth or fifty-second year of her age; at which time, the issue of women is reputed extinct, which is not so in the case of men:

Secondly, In tailzies upon contracts, and for onerous causes, respect is to be had to the meaning and interest of the parties-contracters; and *in dubio, pars mitior est sequenda*. And that sense is to be embraced, by which the provisions can have some effect, and not that by which they can have none. Whereby it may seem, that it was Blackwood's meaning, that the succession of his own natural daughter should be substitute, in the second member, to the heirs betwixt the major and her; and that, while these were possible his heirs should have no place, otherwise the second member had been elusory: For if, by failing of the heirs of the major with the said Marion, at the time of the said major's decease, Marion's heirs, by another lawful husband, should take place, her other heirs could never take place; for she could not have another lawful husband at the time of the major, her first husband's death.

Yet the reasons on the contrary are no less pregnant; as well in this case, as in the case of heirs ascendent, that the heirs nearest at the time of the fiar's death, should have right immediately to succeed; because the fee necessarily must belong to some person, and it cannot hang in the air on a future possibility; which is a principle, whereof mention and use hath been made frequently before: Secondly, If that were the meaning, then at the time of the major's death, the lands were truly *nullius;* and so, as caduciary, behoved to the King, as *ultimus hæres*. But if it had been so expressed, that no place should be to the heirs of the major's other heirs, till there were no possibility of heirs of Marion Weir; the difficulty seems the same, that the fee should be pendent, and *nullius*. It may be answered, That even in that other case, the major's other heirs would succeed, notwithstanding that provision, which doth but resolve in a personal obligation to those heirs to forbear: yet they were heirs; and if contrary the provision, they should enter, it would give interest to the heirs of Marion Weir, to compel the major's heirs having entered, to denude themselves in their favour; but there was no such thing in this case. And as to the reasons upon the contrary, though it may seem Blackwood's interest, that the heirs of his natural daughter should be in the second place; yet *non fuit habilis modus*, to make the fee pendent and *nullius*. But to that which is the main reason, viz. otherwise the second member behoved to be elusory;—it is answered, That it is not elusory, because the most ordinary and hoped case was, that there should have been heirs betwixt the major and Marion; who, if they had died without issue, the lands would have fallen to Marion's heirs by another lawful husband, and not to the major's other heirs. So that the case which fell out, that there was no children procreate betwixt the major and Marion was not feared, and so not provided for, as it oft-times fares in such cases. Therefore we conceive it more probable, that, in all cases, that person, who, at the time of the defunct's death, is in being, born or unborn, may be heir, and immediately enter, so soon as by the birth it appears who may be served.

There hath a later case occurred, and been determined on this occasion. The late E. of Leven tailzied his estate and dignity to the heirs-male of his body; which failing, to the eldest heir-female, without division; which failing, to the second son of the E. of Rothes, which failing, to the second son of the Lo. Melvil, who had married the E. of Leven's sister; which failing, to the second son of the E. of Wemyss, who had married his mother. The E. of Leven left three daughters after him, who died all unentered. The E. of Rothess having no second son, David Melvil, second son to the Lo. Melvil, took a brieve out of the Chancery, to serve himself heir of tailzie to the E. of Leven. The E. of Rothess took a gift of the non-entry, in the name of Sir William Bruce, who raised an advocation of the brieve, with a declarator, that while there was hope of a second son of the E. of Rothess's body, Davib Melvil, nor no son of a subsequent branch, could be entered: or declaring, that the lands were in non-entry. Both members of the said declarator the Lords did sustain, and stopped the service; albeit many inconveniencies were represented thence arising: as that there could be no active title for pursuing the rights of the family, or for receiving vassals; nor any access to the estate *passivè* by creditors. But the Lords did reserve to the special declarator, how far the non-entry would reach, whether to the retoured duties only, or to the full rents. But many of the Lords were of opinion that David Melvil should enter as heir of tailzie; yet so that if the Chancellor had a second son, he or his issue would succeed as heir of tailzie to David Melvil, and neither his own heirs of line, nor the E. of Wemyss's second son; because, at the time of David Melvil's death, the Chancellor's second son would be a nearer heir of tailzie to David than his own son, as being of a prior branch of the tailzie, February 22, 1677, Bruce *contra* Melvil [2 Stair 510; M. 14880]. But the Lords found, that the non-entry by the special declarator, could not reach to the full rents, but only to the retoured duty; seeing the apparent heir was neither in *culpa* nor *mora*, which doth only infer the full duties: and therefore found the donatar had only right to the retoured duties; and that the remainder continued *in hæreditate jacente*, to be managed by the Lo. Melvil, as curator *datus bonis* of the estate of Leven by the King, and having power to manage the affairs of that estate as a tutor, as if an heir had been entered, July 24, 1677, *inter eosdem* [2 Stair 545; M. 9321; 14896].

51. It cometh oft-times to pass, that, through the unclear conception of clauses of provision, it becomes dubious who is thereby constitute fiar, and who liferenter; as is ordinary when sums of money are lent, and the obligement to repay is conceived thus; "To be paid at such a term to the lender, and in case of his decease, or failing him by decease, or after his decease, to such a person." Whence these questions result; First, Whether the lender be fiar of the sum, and the person substitute heir of provision; or if the person substitute be heir [This word probably should be "fiar", as in MSS]; whether he may succeed at any time, or only if the lender die before the term of payment? As to the first question, the person substitute is not fiar but heir, and the lender is not liferenter but fiar; and therefore may dispose of the sum at pleasure, by assignation, legacy, or otherwise, as other fiars may do, February

22, 1623, Leich *contra* L. of Balnamoon [Durie 49; M. 14845]; July 28, 1626, L. Tulliallan *contra* L. of Clackmannan[Durie 231; M. 4253]; where the clause did bear, to be paid to Clackmannan and his spouse, the longest liver of them two; and in case of their decease, to Alexander Bruce their son in fee, with an obligement to infeft the spouse in liferent, and the son in fee, in an annualrent effeiring thereto; yet the father was found to have right to dispose of the sum. The like was found, February 20, 1629, L. Drumkillbo *contra* Lo. Stormount [Durie 429; M. 4254]; where the father surviving the term of payment, though he freely, and without a cause onerous, discharged the sum provided to be paid to him, and failing him to his son, though it bore a clause of infeftment to the father in liferent, and to the son in fee, but no infeftment followed. The like, though the father and the son substitute were both infeft in one seasin, July 23, 1675, L. of Lamington *contra* Muire of Annistoun [2 Stair 360; M. 4252].

As to the second question, the more ancient decisions have interpreted such clauses strictly, thus, that the sum payable at such a term to the first persons, and failing them by decease to a person substitute, should only belong to the person substitute, if the first person died before the term of payment, so that it should be payable at no term thereafter to the person substitute; but if the first person survived the term of payment, though he did nothing to alter the substitution, the same should not belong to the person substitute, but to the first person's heirs, Hope, Succession, Spots. Assignations, L. Bonytoun *contra* Keith [Not found], Feb. 22, 1623 Leich *contra* L. Balnamoon [Durie 49; M. 14845] where it was found, that such sums came under the first persons surviving the term, their testament, and belonged to their executors. But more frequent decisions, with better reason, have interpreted such clauses on the contrary, that the person substitute is heir of provision whensoever the defunct dies, whether before or after the term; because the constitution of heirs is simply, and not *ad diem* : but mainly because the ordinary intent of such clauses is to appoint portions for the bairns named therein, who therefore are substitute heirs of provision to their father; so that if he do not expressly alter, or prejudge the substitution, his intent is, that they succeed him whensoever, Spots. Assignations, Currie *contra* Nimmo [Spotiswoode 63]; Relict of Thomson *contra* Johnson [Spotiswoode 63]. The like in a legacy left to a person, and failing her by decease to another; which was not found a *fideicommissum*, to be restored by the first person to the second at her death; and therefore the assignee of the first person was preferred, Spots. Disposition, Reid *contra* Downy [Not found]; January 18, 1625, Wat *contra* Doby [Durie 157; M. 14846]; June 26, 1634, Keith *contra* Innes [Durie 721; M. 14846]. Therefore such sums bearing no clause of infeftment, yet fall under testament, neither hath the relict a third thereof, Hope, Successions. In these substitutions, though the person be substitute as heir, yet he is not properly heir, and so needs not to be entered by any service, because he is nominate, and there is no other heir. But in tailzies, though some of the members of the tailzie be nominate, yet because in lands, as is before said, the person nominate is never the first heir; therefore there must be a service, to inquire whether the first heir fails or not, which is unnecessary where there is one person only nominate to be heir, concerning which there needs be no inquiry. Though the persons substitute be as heirs, it followeth not that they must be liable as heirs of provision to the first person's debt, contracted before the substitution; because they are not properly heirs, not requiring any service; but they are *interpretativè* like to heirs; because the nature and intent of such clauses is not to constitute the first person as a naked liferenter, but that they are understood as if they were thus expressed, "With power to the first person to alter and dispone at his pleasure during his life." So thereafter only the heirs substitute take place, though in these respects as heirs, yet in reality as secondary, conditional, or substitute fiars: but the substitute is liable, other anterior heirs and executors being discussed, unless the person substitute abstain; because the substitution is a gratuitous deed in prejudice of creditors, *post contractum debitum*, and so annullable; and the substitute meddling is liable to repay *quoad valorem* only, but never by an universal passive title, July 3, 1666, Fleming *contra* Fleming [1 Stair 386; M. 13999; III, 5, 15, *supra*].

The next difficulty is, who is fiar in provisions, or tailzies of sums, annualrents, or lands in conjunct-fee; wherein these rules do ordinarily take place. First, That the last termination of heirs whatsoever, inferreth that person of the conjunct fiars, whose heirs they are, to be fiars, and the other liferenters. 2. When that is not expressed *potior est conditio masculi*, the heirs of the man are understood [II, 3, 41, *supra*]. But these have their own limitations; as first, in moveable goods, and sums provided to a man and his wife, and their heirs, without mentioning; which failing, to whose heirs the same should be due, were found not to fall to the man's heirs, but to divide equally betwixt the man and wife's heirs, February 2, 1632, Bartholomew *contra* Hassingtoun [*Sub nom. Bartilmo* v *Hassington;* Durie 617; M. 4222]; February 18, 1637, Mungle *contra* Steill [Durie 827; M. 6087]. Yea, a clause in a reversion redeemable by a man and his wife, and their heirs, was found to constitute the wife fiar of the reversion, because she was fiar of the land wadset, Hope, Liferent, Kincaid *contra* Menzies of Pitfoddels [M. 13441]. But an assignation to a reversion provided to a man and his wife, the longest liver of them two, and their heirs, was found to make the man only fiar, Hope, Husband and wife, Collistoun *contra* L. Pitfoddels [Hope, *Maj.Pr.* 11, 17, 29; M. 4198]. A clause in a charter providing lands to a man and his wife, the longest liver of them two, and the heirs betwixt them; which failing, to the heirs of the man's body; which failing, to the wife her heirs whatsoever: though the last termination was upon the wife, yet the husband was found fiar, Had. July 24, 1622, Ramsey *contra* L. Conheath [M. 4226]. The like in a clause providing a sum, being a wife's tocher, to the man and wife, and the longest liver of them two in conjunct-fee, and to the heirs betwixt them; which failing, the wife's heirs; yet the husband was found fiar: and therefore the creditor apprising excluded the wife and her heirs, January 29, 1639, Graham *contra* Park and Jarden [Durie 870; M.4226]. And a bond providing a sum to a man and his wife in conjunct-fee, and the bairns procreate betwixt them; which failing, to two bairns of a former marriage *nominatim*, containing a precept for infefting the spouse and the two bairns named, whereupon all the four were infeft: yet the father was found fiar, and all the bairns of the family, male and female equally, were found heirs of provision; and the two bairns named were found heirs substitute, failing the bairns of the marriage, January 14, 1663, Beg *contra* Nicolson [1 Stair 155; M.4251]. And a bond bearing a sum borrowed from, and payable to a man and his wife, the longest liver of them two in conjunct-fee, and to the heirs betwixt them, and their assignees; which failing, to the heirs and assignees of the last liver, found to constitute the husband fiar, and the wife liferenter, albeit she was last liver, and that her heirs of line were found heirs of provision to the husband, January 2, 1668, Justice *contra* Barclay his Mother [Probably *Justice* v *Stirling*, 1 Stair 512; M.4228]. A tocher provided to the husband and wife, the longest liver in conjunct-fee and liferent, and to their bairns in fee, was found to make the husband fiar, and that the father might alter the substitution, December 12, 1665, Pearson *contra* Martine [1 Stair 325; M.4249]. And generally in all infeftments in conjunct-fee betwixt man and wife, the husband is always interpreted to be fiar, and the wife liferenter, albeit the last termination be upon the wife's heirs, who are heirs of provision to the husband, unless the right flow from the wife originally; as if she should resign her lands in favour of her husband, and herself in conjunct-fee, and the heirs of the marriage; which failing, her heirs: or if the right did flow from the wife's father by a gratuitous deed. But by contract of marriage a father obliged himself to infeft the husband-contracter, and his daughter, in conjunct-fee and liferent, and the heirs betwixt them; which failing, the daughter's heirs and assignees whatsoever: and by the same contract the husband was obliged to provide all lands that he should acquire or succeed to, to himself and his wife, the longest liver of them two in conjunct-fee, and the heirs betwixt them; which failing, the one half to the husband's heirs, and the other half to the wife's heirs, and their assignees: by both these clauses the husband was found to be fiar, and the wife liferenter; albeit the tenement disponed by the father was not *nomine dotis*, yet there was no other tocher, July 2, 1671, Gairns *contra* Sandilands [1 Stair 753; M.4230]. Yet a clause in a minute of a contract of marriage, obliging the husband to infeft his wife in conjunct-fee and liferent in such a barony named, and obliging him and his heirs and assignees, that all and whatsoever lands, or sums of money, should be purchased by him during the marriage, that security should be made in liferent thereof, as of the foresaid barony, to his future spouse, in case of no issue of children, the one-half of the said conquest to be disponed upon as the wife shall think fit, the conquest was found to be equally to the husband and wife, and that she was liferenter of the whole, and fiar of the half, in respect the minute did not bear whose heirs should succeed; and that the conquest was all to be expected by the wife's means, therefore she being conjunct fiar, that the one half of the conquest should be disponed as she pleased, she was found fiar of that half as not being a faculty, but a power of disposal importing property, June 27, 1676, E. Dumfermling *contra* E. Callendar [2 Stair 430; M.2941, 4244; 11,6,10,*supra*].

52. There do many questions arise as to the succession o heirs of provision, by clauses of conquest in contracts of marriage. The main question is, What is accounted conquest; whether that which is acquired, and thereafter disponed, be accounted conquest, either as to the wife, or to the heirs, or bairns of the marriage? As to which, it hath been shown before, that such provisions infer not only a succession to the heirs, or bairns of the marriage, as heirs of provision; but thereby the wife or heir, and bairn of the marriage, have an interest as creditors; that the husband or father cannot, *ad arbitrium*, do deeds prejudicial to that which is once acquired; but the husband is not thereby bound up from disponing to strangers, for causes onerous, or to other wives or children, for competent provisions. But he may not otherwise intervert the design of those provisions, by taking the rights to wives, or children of another marriage, unless he have not means *aliunde* to provide them [11,3, 41 and 11,6,3,*supra*]. And therefore the husband being obliged to take all sums acquired during the marriage, to himself and his wife in conjunct-fee; having taken a sum acquired during the marriage, in the name of his second son; his relict was found to have right to the annualrent thereof, July 16, 1625, Knox *contra* Brown [Durie 178; M.3065]. The like, where the bonds were taken originally in the name of the bairns, leaving out the wife, March 14, 1623, Graham *contra* Representatives of her Husband [*Sub anno* 1623, *et nom. Graham* v *Finnie's Heirs*, Durie 361; M.5481]. But clauses of conquest, of all lands acquired during the marriage, do not extend to lands acquired and disponed during the marriage. Yea, conquest of lands was extended, where there was a disposition without infeftment, with a burden of a part of the price upon to the disponer, January 24, 1629, La. Rentoun *contra* L. Rentoun [Durie 417; M.3056]; Spots., Husband, Countess of Dumfermling *contra* E. Dunfermling [Spotiswoode, 155; M.3056]. And, where the clause of conquest bore lands or annualrents, the same were extended to bonds bearing annualrent, though without clause of infeftment, February 20, 1629, Douglas *contra* White [Durie 423; M.3049]. And these clauses are interpreted strictly according to the tenor thereof; for sometimes they only bear lands conquest, sometimes lands or annualrents, sometimes lands, annualrents, or sums of money, and sometimes also goods or gear; in which case the executors will be obliged to employ moveable goods and sums, for the wife in liferent, and for the bairns and heir of the marriage in fee. These clauses of conquest do never extend to any thing, whereunto the husband succeeds as heir or executor, unless succession be expressed. A clause of conquest, obliging the husband to take all lands, annualrents, and sums, conquest during the marriage, to himself, and the heirs and bairns of the marriage, one or more, found to constitute

all the bairns of the marriage, male and female, heirs-portioners; and that it was not alternative, that the husband might either take the conquest to himself, and the heirs of the marriage, or to himself and bairns of the marriage, at his option. And, therefore, having taken a considerable sum in favour of himself and the heir of the marriage, who was his only son; yet, after his death, his four daughters of that marriage obtained decreet against their brother, to denude himself of their shares, January 29, 1678, Stuart *contra* Stuart [2 Stair 604; M.3052]. But conquest is only understood, of what the husband acquired more after his contract of marriage, than what he had before. And, therefore, if he acquired lands, annualrents, sums or goods; if he instruct that he had as much, or a part thereof, before, as he sold, the superplus will only be counted conquest. And though he have not disponed on any thing he had before, yet if he contract debt for purchasing the conquest, it will be burdened with the annualrent of the debt, as was found in the former cases. And the like, December 20, 1665, La. Kilbocho *contra* L. Kilbocho [1 Stair 328; M.3058]; June 27, 1676, E. Dumfermling *contra* E. Callendar [2 Stair 430; M.2941, 4244]. The like was found in a provision of conquest, of all the husband's goods and gear acquired during the marriage, to the wife for her liferent-use, which was found to be with the burden of the husband's debt contracted before or after, and so to import only liferent of the free gear, December 23, 1660, Smith *contra* Muir [*Sub anno* 1668, 1 Stair 576; M.9858]. And where a husband was obliged to employ a definite sum for himself, his wife and bairns of the marriage, and also his conquest; and having acquired a tenement during the marriage, to himself and his heirs whatsoever, that tenement was applied to the definite sum, *primo loco*, and the superplus as a conquest, January 4, 1672, Beaty *contra* Roxburgh [2 Stair 34; M.3067].

So much for the being and interest of heirs. As for the proving and instructing who are heirs, the most ordinary way is by retour, or infeftment as heirs, or by a service though not retoured; but those instructions must be repeated in every several process; for, so an heir *activè*, was found not to be instructed by a decreet at his instance, as heir, against the same defender, and in the same matter, without re-production of the instructions, February 11, 1629, Stuart *contra* Wilson [Durie 423; M.Supp.54]: neither was it instructed *passivè* by a decreet of the Commissars, by production of the defender's seasin without reproduction thereof, Had. Neither was it instructed *passivè*, by the King's gratuitous restitution of the apparent heir, of a forfeited person, which made him capable of his father's rights, but not heir nor successor to him, Hope, Forfeiture, Halyburton *contra* Lo. Balmerino [Hope, *Maj. Pr.* IV, 7, 10; M.4656, 9649]. Neither by a bond, wherein the party designed himself heir, or at least apparent heir, which relateth nothing to the benefit of succession, January 24, 1627, L. Glenkindie *contra* Crawfurd [Durie 261; M.6869]. Neither by an award of a town-court, recognoscing a burgess, heir to his predecessor, Spots. Heirs, Gudelet *contra* Adamson [Spotiswoode 139; M.9738].

Title 6. Behaving as Heir, Where, of *Gestio Pro Hærede*, and the Exceptions against this Passive Title

GESTIO pro hærede, is the apparent heir's disorderly entry, and immixing himself with the heritage, without order of law; and therefore it gives him no right nor active title as heir, but makes him only heir *passivè*, whereby he represents the defunct in all his debts and burdens, and is liable for them all.

2. This passive title, as Spots. observes, was but introduced by the Lords of Session, and was not before the institution of the College of Justice, the apparent heir being only liable for restitution of the single value formerly; as was found in the case of an heir's intromission with the heirship-moveables, November 14, 1546, Seatoun La. Dirleton *contra* Dumbar [Not found].

3. The reason of introducing this passive title, is in favour of creditors, [111,7,1,*infra*] that they be not unsatisfied, or shifted by the heirs of the defunct debtors; who, if they might continue possession of their predecessor's means and estate, and be but comptable, would rarely enter, and huddle up their intromission, and with time ascribe it to singular titles, abstracting their predecessor's rights. And therefore it is an expedient custom, that they should either enter legally, and for good and all, or that they should wholly abstain; especially seeing the law allows them a year to inquire into the condition of the defunct's heritage, whether it will afford them loss or gain, during which time they may deliberate, and if they abstain, can be troubled by none. So that, though it may seem rigorous for a small intromission to make the intromitter liable for all the defunct's debts, how great soever; yet it being so easy to abstain, and the hazard known, the expediency and favour of the creditor preponderateth the wilful disadvantage of the debtor's heir.

4. In this title the Lords have always taken great latitude, and some-

times have found small intromission not relevant, to infer this title, in odious cases, November 6, 1622, L. Dundas *contra* Hamilton [Durie 33; M.9658]. Where a decreet of spuilzie of teinds being obtained against Peill's goodsire, and never insisted in, till, in his time, he was convened as heir to his father, who had behaved himself as heir to the goodsire, in so far as he had entered and dwelt in the house of Peill; and there being in the house, the goodsire's best board, standing bed, and brewing caldron, he used the same, by eating at the board, lying in the bed, and brewing in the caldron; and delivered the goodsire's beef-pot to a flesher, for flesh furnished to the defender's father; the defender's mother having kept possession of these heirship-goods for five years before.

5. Yet this condescendence was not found relevant in this case, where the passive title was not established before the defender's father's death. As the Lords lately found, that these passive titles, *quæ sapiunt delictum*, should not be competent after the intromitter's death [III,9,14,*infra*]. It was also thought by the whole Lords after dispute *in præsentia* upon this title, that it takes only place, where the apparent heir's *animus immiscendi, et adeundi hæreditatem*, did appear, and not where he hath any probable or colourable title, Spots. Heirship, Corser *contra* Durie [Spotiswoode 145]. Yet, in favourable cases, a small intromission was sustained, as making use of the defunct's chief bed and board, though standing in the defunct's house, seeing the heir entered the house before he obtained inventory of the moveables made by authority of a judge, though the house belonged to himself *proprio jure*, Had. March 8, 1610, Bailzie *contra* Home [Haddington, *Fol. Dict.* II,27; M.9658]. Or by intromission with a mazer-cup [A drinking cup of maple] of the defunct's, and drinking therein; entering into the house where he died; lying in his bed, and bed-clothes standing there; and wearing his silk stockings, though all these were undisposed upon; and that the defunct's mother, who had given them to her son, had meddled therewith, who died in a chamber belonging to his mother, and her name was upon the mazer, January 15, 1630, Cleghorn *contra* Fairly [Durie 481; M.9664].

6. There are two cases of behaving as heir, viz. Intromission with the moveable heirship; and Intromission with the lands, teinds, tacks, or other rights which might have belonged to the intromitter as heir. In both which cases the intromission will not infer this passive title, unless the intromitter might succeed in the same particulars. And therefore the apparent heir of line, and no other, can be liable by intromission with heirship-moveables, because the same can only belong to the heir of line. So the intromission with rents of lands, teinds or tack, will not infer *gestionem*, unless by the apparent heir, who would succeed therein, according as they are provided to heirs of line, of conquest, heirs-male, or of tailzie or provision [III,6,13,*infra*]. Neither will any other intromission be relevant, but what is immediate, or by express warrant, command, or ratihabition.

7. A tutor or curator's intromission will not infer *gestionem* upon his

pupil, unless he accept the same from the tutor in his accompts, nor the intromission of one having a general commission, as factor, &c. It was so found in the case of a tutor's intromission with the rents of the pupil's predecessor's lands, for the restitution whereof he was only found liable, November 3, 1665, Boyd *contra* Tailzifair [*Sub die* Nov. 30, 1 Stair 317; M. 16275].

8. Behaving as heir by intromission with the moveable-heirship, is most unquestionable, when the said moveable is chosen, drawn, and separated by the heir from the remanent moveables; in which case the apparent heir will not be admitted to allege, that the defunct could not have an heir or heirship-moveables when he formerly drew the same, July 13, 1631, L. of Gadgirth *contra* L. of Auchinleck [Durie 595; M. 9709]. But it seems very hard, where the apparent heir's choice of such particulars as the best of every kind for heirship, doth not evidently appear; for that must be accounted the best, which is such in the opinion of the apparent heir: and yet, in favourable cases, intromission with any kind of moveables, out of which heirship may be drawn, will be found sufficient, and reputed as the heir's choice. As the apparent heir's making use of his father's board, lying in his bed, though he disposed not thereof; and though the same were standing in a house disponed to him by his father, before contracting of the debt pursued on, seeing he continued two years in possession, and got no warrant from the Lords, or made any inventory thereof, July 14, 1626, Johnstoun and Masson his spouse *contra* Masson [Durie 218; M. 9659]. The like, by making use of the defunct's bason, silver spoons, timber beds and boards, without alienation thereof; though the beginning of the intromission was, when the intromitter was not apparent heir himself, but was tutor to another heir who was idiot, seeing he continued five years after the idiot's death, himself being then apparent heir, January 17, 1627, Fraser *contra* L. Monimusk [Durie 256; M. 9661]. Yet the contrary was found, where the intromission began before the intromitter was apparent heir, there being a nearer apparent heir, though it continued after that nearer apparent heir's death, when the intromitter was apparent heir, July 2, 1629, Cunninghame *contra* Moultry [Durie 454; M. 9664]. Yea, behaving as heir, was sustained by intromission with certain goods of the defunct which might have been heirship, though they were confirmed promiscuously by an executor, and bought from him by the apparent heir. But this executor was his own domestic servant, and confirmed to his own behoof, December 16, 1630, Weir *contra* Ker [*Sub nom. Ker's relict* v *Ker*, Durie 549; M. 9682]. The like, where the heirship-goods were sold to the apparent heir by a stranger, seeing they were not delivered to that stranger, but possessed by the defunct till his decease, but his possession continued by the apparent heir, Had. Feb. 9, 1621, Melvil *contra* Melvil [Not found]. But the contrary was found, the goods being disponed by the defunct to the apparent heir, albeit not delivered before his death, otherwise than that the defunct being unmarried, came to his son's house, and lived with him till his death, January 30, 1630, Calderwood *contra* Porteous [Durie 488; M. 9681]. Neither was the same inferred by a disposition

of the defunct to his apparent heir of certain moveables, in satisfaction of his heirship-moveables whereunto he might succeed, February 24, 1636, L. Meidhope *contra* Hepburn [Durie 797; M. 9691].

9. The ordinary objections and exceptions against behaving as heir by intromission with the heirship-moveables, are, first, That the defunct was neither prelate, baron, nor burgess, to whose heirs only heirship-moveable is competent by the Act of Parliament [A.P.S. 11, 107, c. 8], the extent whereof is shown in the former title. And therefore the pursuer must condescend, and instruct that the defunct was either baron, prelate, or burgess, which would be sufficiently instructed by the defunct's infeftments of lands or annualrents at any time; for thence it would be presumed, that he continued undenuded till his death, for *semel baro semper baro præsumptivè*. And this will be elided by this exception, that the defunct was denuded before his death. For, though some have been of opinion, that *semel baro semper baro* is meant, that though a person once infeft were denuded, yet his heir would have heirship as a baron. For which I find neither reason nor decision, but it is most reasonable that he who is once proven to be a baron, should be presumed so to continue, unless the contrary were proven, that he was denuded. It was so found, January 27, 1636, Straiton *contra* Chirnside [Durie 791; M. 5395]. But if the legal was not expired at the defunct's death, he is not esteemed denuded; and therefore his heir hath heirship: February 26, 1663, Cuthbert of Draikies *contra* Munro of Foulis [1 Stair 188; M. 9666]; July 8, 1628, Dumbar *contra* Lesly [Durie 383; M. 5392]. Neither will it be sufficient that the defunct was once burgess, but it must be proven, that, when he died, he was acting as a burgess. So that, neither the heirs of honorary burgesses, nor they who once were trafficking burgesses, and take themselves to a country life, their heirs, will have heirship-moveables. And therefore *semel civis semper civis* is not presumed; neither *semel prælatus semper prælatus ;* for, if a beneficed person were deprived or demitted before his death, his heir would have no heirship-moveables.

10. The second defence against intromission with heirship-moveables, and which is also competent against vitious intromission, is, That the defunct died rebel, and his escheat was gifted and declared before intenting of the creditor's pursuit, June 10, 1663, Gordon of Lismoir *contra* Keith [1 Stair 190; M. 9667]; June 10, 1674, La. Spenserfield *contra* Hamilton of Kilbrachmount [2 Stair 270; M. 9762]; Dec. 22, 1674, Heirs of Seaton of Blair *contra* Seatoun [2 Stair 295; M. 5397]. And it is not necessary to allege, that the apparent heir had any right or tolerance from the donatar; for the exception is equiparate to executors confirmed against vitious intromission; whereby vitious intromission is excluded, albeit the intromission was before another was confirmed executor, if the confirmation was before intenting of the creditor's cause. But it is no relevant defence that the defunct died rebel, and so had no moveables, but that they were confiscated. Neither was it sufficient that the escheat was gifted, not being also declared before the creditor's pursuit: as was found in the said two first cases.

11. The third defence is, That the apparent heir intromitted by a gift to himself, or to his behoof; or by a right or tolerance from a donatar. These being prior to the creditor's pursuit, although posterior to his intromission, albeit not declared, are relevant; because the donatar thereby is in possession, and needs no declarator, Feb. 26, 1663, Cuthbert of Draikies *contra* Munro of Foulis [1 Stair 188; M. 9666]; July 10, 1663, Gordon of Lismoir *contra* Keith [1 Stair 190; M. 9667]; July 4, 1665, Innes *contra* Wilson [1 Stair 294; M. 9874]; June 10, 1674, La. Spenserfield *contra* Hamilton of Kilbrachmount [2 Stair 270; M. 9762]; Feb. 10, 1676, Grant *contra* Grant [2 Stair 413; M. 9763].

12. The fourth exception is, When moveables belonging to a defunct remain in his house, whereunto his apparent heir hath right by infeftment, wherein the defunct had his liferent or tolerance: if the heir enter in possession of the house, if at his entry he represent to any competent judge, that there are moveables in or about the house belonging to the defunct, which he desires to be inventoried, or that such as cannot be preserved may be sold, that the price may be made forthcoming to all parties having interest. If inventory or sale be made by warrant of that judge, the continuing of these moveables in the house, or the sale of those which cannot be preserved, will not infer behaving as heir. Yet the making use of the things in the inventory, or the sale of that which is not warranted, yea, the omission out of the inventory, of moveables of any considerable value, was found to infer behaviour, Jan. 25, 1632, Scarlet *contra* Paterson [Durie 614; M. Supp. 65].

13. The other ordinary member of behaving as heir, is by intromission with the rents of lands, or teinds, whereunto the defunct had right by infeftment, or entering in possession of these lands and teinds, unto which the apparent heir would succeed, which is the most direct behaviour as heir, and is only competent against such persons as might be heirs, in that whereunto they immix themselves. And so an heir of line possessing or intromitting with the rents of lands provided to heirs-male, or to heirs of tailzie or provision; or the intromission of these with the profits of lands or teinds befalling to heirs of line, will only infer restitution or reparation, but will not infer a general passive title, making the party liable to all the defunct's debts [III,6,6,*supra*].

14. There are many defences which use to be proponed against this species of behaviour: as first, It was an ordinary custom to shun this passive title, that the apparent heir granted a bond of purpose to adjudge the defunct's right, upon the apparent heir's renunciation, and then take right to the adjudication, till the Lords, by an Act of Sederunt, February 28, 1662, did declare, that if apparent heirs should, in time coming, take right to any apprising or adjudication of their predecessor's rights for their own debt, and did possess thereby, whether before or after expiring of the legal, they should be liable as behaving as heirs [1,18,9,*supra*]: and therefore no defence for such rights will be sustained, albeit it were a true debt of the apparent heir's,

and not a simulate bond granted of design to adjudge or apprise. This is only if the apparent heir take right to the apprising or adjudication led upon his own debt, real or simulate, within the legal; for then the acquirer being both debtor and creditor, the debt becomes extinct by confusion: but there is then no ground to conclude, that, after the land apprised becomes irredeemable, the apparent heir, or the heir entered, may not buy that land as well as any other; for though the act 62, Parl. 1661 [Diligence Act, 1661, c. 62; A.P.S. VII, 317, c. 344], makes all apprisings coming in the person of apparent heirs, led against their predecessors, to be redeemable for the sums they paid therefor, it doth not extend to apprisings led against the apparent heirs themselves.

Neither is it a relevant defence, that the lands or teinds were apprised, or adjudged from the defunct, albeit infeftment had followed thereupon, if the heir apparent intromit without right, or warrant from the appriser or adjudger, within the legal, February 21, 1663, Hamilton *contra* Hamilton [1 Stair 185; M. 9655]. But it is a relevant exception, that the apparent heir's intromission or possession was by right from an appriser or adjudger, though the legal was not expired, unless the sum were fully satisfied by intromission or otherwise, January 10, 1662, Barclay *contra* L. Craigievar [1 Stair 78; M. 9684]. The like, though the apparent heir continued to possess for some time after the apprising was satisfied by intromission, February 26, 1663, Cuthbert of Draikies *contra* Munro of Fowlis [1 Stair 188; M. 9666]. Yea, intromission with the rents of the defunct's land by his apparent heir, was elided by a tolerance from a donatar of recognition, albeit not declared till after his intromission, the apparent heir paying the single value of his intromission, July 17, 1666, Ogilvie *contra* Lo. Gray [1 Stair 397; M. 9684]. But a tolerance from apprisers after the intromission, was not found relevant, July 11, 1671, Maxwell *contra* Maxwell [1 Stair 751; M. 5306]. Yet the apparent heir's intromission was elided, because the defunct's rights were improven, though after the intromission, March 22, 1628, Farquhar *contra* Campbell of Kingingcluch [Durie 367; M. 9022]. And an apparent heir's intromission was elided by a colourable title, though not valid, whereby the heir of a marriage being entered and infeft as heir to her mother, yet her infeftment being reduced, and her father being found fiar in a dubious provision of conjunct-fee, the heir so served was not found liable, as behaving as heir to her father; but only *quoad valorem* of her intromission, July 12, 1671, Gairns *contra* Sandilands [1 Stair 753; M. 4230]. But it was not elided, because the apparent heir passed by his father, and was infeft as heir to his good-sire, though his father was infeft; that colourable title was not sustained, the apparent heir being *in mala fide*, having the evidents in his hands, Nov. 23, 1671, Rorison *contra* Sinclair [2 Stair 8; M. 9687]. Yet behaving as heir was not inferred by the heir apparent's intromitting with the rents of lands which his predecessor had disponed in trust to a third party, for the behoof of the apparent heir, and whereupon the intrusted was infeft, Jan. 14, 1662, Nicol *contra* Hume of Plandergest [*Sub nom. Nicol Harper v Home*, 1 Stair 80; M. 9774]. But intromission by the apparent heir was elided by a disposition by a defunct to the apparent heir's son, his oye, though without infeftment; or by a tack to the apparent heir's husband, though expired before the defunct's death, as being continued *per tacitam relocationem*, Jan. 16, 1667, Reid *contra* Salmond [1 Stair 427; M. 9656]. Behaving as heir was inferred by the apparent heir's entering in possession of a coal-heugh, whereof the defunct had tacks for terms to run, albeit the apparent heir took a new tack, Had. June 26, 1610, Aitchison *contra* L. Cockpen [Not found]. The like though the apparent heir took a gift of the defunct's escheat, who had an unexpired tack of the lands, and pretended to possess as donatar to the single escheat, Had. June 28, 1610, Crawford *contra* L. Cockpen [Not found].

15. Behaving as heir was also inferred by the apparent heir's giving a receipt of the defunct's charter-chest, and keeping it two years without protestation or inventory, June 28, 1670, Ellis of Southside *contra* Carse [1 Stair 686; M.9669]. But it was not proponed, that the person behaving was dead, which purgeth vitious passive titles.

16. Behaving as heir will also be inferred by uplifting or discharging sums, principal or annual, which would befall to the party as apparent heir; or by doing any deed that might transmit the defunct's right. But it was not found inferred by the apparent heirs renouncing to be heirs, in favour of the heir-male, to whom their father had disponed, seeing they gave no right thereby hurtful to creditors, though they got a sum for their kindness and willing renunciation, July 5, 1666, Scot *contra* Heirs of Auchinleck [1 Stair 389; M.9694]. Neither by the apparent heir's getting benefit by a transaction with a party having right from the defunct, granted on death-bed, and being obliged to acquire the defunct's debts, and apprise thereon, and to communicate the benefit of the apprising, unless a deed had been done communicating any right of the defunct, July 19, 1676, Nevoy *contra* Lo. Balmerinoch [2 Stair 454; M.9694]. But behaviour was not inferred by the apparent heir's taking out of brieves, seeing the same were not served, June 28, 1670, Ellis *contra* Carse [1 Stair 686; M.9669]. Neither was it inferred by proponing payment of the defunct's debts, and succumbing, which is only effectual as to that process, Jan. 21, 1675, Tailzifer *contra* Corsan [2 Stair 307; M.9712]. Neither was it inferred by the apparent heirs' voluntary payment of their predecessor's debt, Jan. 26, 1628, Commissar of Dunkel *contra* Abercromby [Durie 333; M.3502]. Neither by taking a day to renounce and failing, which hath only effect as to that process, July 16, 1629, Murray *contra* Ross [Durie 463; M.9708].

17. There is the same ground for excluding this passive title, unless it were established against the apparent heir in his own life, as to exclude vitious intromission; which hath frequently been repelled when not established in the intromitter's life [111,6,5,*supra*; 111,9,14,*infra*].

18. It remains now to consider, whether behaving as heir, being a vitious passive title, will import more than if the apparent heir had been actually

entered, which may occur in two cases: First, Where heirs-portioners behave themselves as heirs whether they will be liable *in solidum*, or only *pro rata?* 2. Whether those who behave themselves as heirs, will have the same benefit of the order of discussing and relief, as if they were actually entered? As to the first case, the behaviour of heirs-portioners cannot oblige them *in solidum*, but in so far only as if they were actually entered heirs; which is always *pro rata parte*, according to the number of the heirs-portioners, *non per capita, sed per stirpes:* but as it hath been yet undetermined, whether heirs-portioners may be liable for more than their share of the debt, not exceeding their share of the benefit to which they have succeeded, there is no question but if heirs-portioners behave as heirs, they would be made liable *quoad valorem* of their intromission, if it did exceed their share.

19. As to the other case, behaving as heir being a vitious passive title, they will not have the benefit of discussing; which is only competent to heirs lawfully entered. Yea, they will not have relief from the heirs who are liable before them; because they have in their person no active title. Yet it is *in arbitrio judicis* to ordain the creditor, on satisfaction, to assign his right, by which the heir behaving may indirectly attain relief, as assignee by the creditor. This favour will not be refused, unless the manner of behaviour be very odious; as when it is fraudulent, by concealing the immixtion; or that the creditor himself having another interest, may be prejudged by his assignation: and therefore heirs behaving, if distressed for moveable debts, they have no direct recourse against executors. And if the executry be mean, so that there be small provisions for the wife and children, the creditor will not be ordained to assign; and it may so fall out in other cases, the same reason may occur, where heirs of conquest, or heirs-male, of tailzie or provision, behave, if the prior heirs, who are nearer of blood, have little benefit.

Title 7. Lucrative Successors, How this Passive Title is Extended, and How Limited, by our Practice

THERE is no nation hath been more favourable to creditors, or more studious of their satisfactions than this [111, 6, 3, *supra*]; which hath anticipated all conveyances, devices and frauds prejudicial to creditors, either in favour of singular successors by simulate assignations or dispositions, without equivalent onerous causes, or in favour of apparent heirs, that they might in no way enjoy their predecessor's estates without satisfying their debt; which hath given the rise to this passive title, whereby apparent heirs, accepting dispositions from their predecessors of their heritage, wherein they would have succeeded, or any part thereof, are made liable to all their predecessor's debts, contracted before such disposition or right. And the acceptance thereof is accounted *præceptio hæreditatis*, and as an immixtion with the inheritance, makes the apparent heir to represent the defunct *passivè;* yet with this temperament, that he shall be liable only to the debt contracted before the disposition or right made to him by the defunct, in which right he might have succeeded; wherein apparent heirs are most expediently differenced from the other singular successors without onerous causes, that these are not personally liable, except in so far as they have disposed of such rights as were fraudulently disponed to them in trust, and in which they were interposed persons to the behoof of the disponer or his children; but these rights are always reducible at the instance of anterior creditors. But because such fraud is more incident to apparent heirs, therefore these are personally liable for the whole anterior debts, and the right granted by them may also be reduced upon the statute 1621 [Bankruptcy Act, 1621, c.18; A.P.S. iv,615,c.18]; yet the personal obligement doth remain, and both are compatible, Hope, Successor Lucrative, Gray *contra* Burgh [Hope, *Maj. Pr.* iv,7,13; Durie 176].

2. This passive title is not only extended to dispositions of lands bearing expressly a lucrative title, as "for love and favour," &c. but though the narrative thereof bears expressly a cause onerous, which being betwixt the disponer and his apparent heir, proves not; and therefore the cause onerous must be proved *aliunde; Vid.* Title, Reparation upon Circumvention [1,9,15,*supra*], where the narrative of writs amongst conjunct and confident persons, proves not the cause to be onerous. And though there be a cause onerous instructed, it will not be sufficient, unless it be equivalent to the worth of the lands, to sustain it against reduction: but if the cause onerous be considerable, the heir will not be liable simply, or personally, but the right may be reduced, in so far only as concerns the anterior debt reducing, and the heir may be liable *in quantum est lucratus*. And therefore an apparent heir having accepted the benefit of a disposition and infeftment, granted by his predecessor to a third party, but to the apparent heir's behoof; the Lords, before answer, ordained the cause onerous of the disposition to be instructed, reserving to their consideration how far the apparent heir should be liable personally thereby, January 14, 1662, Harper *contra* Home [1 Stair 80; M.9774]. The like of a disposition of lands by a mother to her apparent heir, though it did bear a sum of money, which did not prove betwixt mother and son, February 15, 1676, Hadden *contra* Halyburton [2 Stair 416; M.9794]. The like was found of a disposition by a father to his son and apparent heir, though the son offered to prove it was for equivalent onerous causes, seeing the disposition itself did bear, "for love and favour and other good considerations," November 22, 1671, Beaty *contra* Roxburgh [2 Stair 8; M.9794]. But bonds of provision by parents to children, infer no passive title, though the children be heirs apparent, as when the bonds are granted to the eldest son, or bonds of provision to younger sons, or a tocher to daughters, when there are no sons, though in

that case the daughters might be esteemed heirs apparent, although truly they be not; for a man is ever understood to be capable of having a son, and therefore daughters are little more heirs apparent than brothers; yet bonds of provision or tochers are reducible by anterior creditors, if the defunct had not a visible estate sufficient for these portions, and his whole anterior debts. And therefore accepting a tocher did not make a daughter liable as lucrative successor, though there was no son; yet the daughter and her husband were found liable to the father's anterior creditors, for what was above a competent tocher suitable to the parties, December 23, 1665, Burnet *contra* Lepers [1 Stair 329; M. 5863; I, 9, 15, *supra*]. Neither will the taking bonds in the name of the daughters, or assigning bonds to them, make them liable as lucrative successors; and yet the accepting of assignations to heritable bonds by a father to his eldest son, in which the son would succeed as heir, may infer this passive title, December 2, 1665, Edgar *contra* Colvil [1 Stair 319; M. 9777]. But, where the father in his contract of marriage, provided his son to several bonds, which, before any creditor pursued, were paid and cancelled; and it did not appear by the contract, whether they were heritable or moveable; the Lords did not sustain the passive title, but found the son liable *in quantum lucratus*, and did presume the bonds to be heritable, unless they were proven to be moveable, Jan. 7, 1679, Hamilton *contra* Hay [2 Stair 688; M. 9780]. But a disposition of lands to the eldest son, was found to make him lucrative successor, although by his father's contract of marriage with his mother, his second wife, the father was obliged to infeft the eldest son of the marriage in the said lands, which did import a succession, seeing the obligement contained no determinate time, and so might be performed by the father any time in his life, November 29, 1678, Higens *contra* Maxwel [2 Stair 648; M. 9795]. The like was found in a disposition of lands and annualrents to the eldest son of the marriage, seeing these were provided to the heir of the marriage, February 22, 1681, More *contra* Ferguson [2 Stair 863; M. 9781]. The disponer's bairns' portions are not a cause onerous, being granted after the creditors' debts, albeit undertaken and secured by the apparent heir, *bona fide*, before any diligence at the creditor's instance, not being paid before the pursuit; *Ibid:* because the heir may suspend upon double poinding, and will not be made to pay both the bairns and creditors.

3. This title is extended to dispositions granted in apparent heirs' contracts of marriage, which, in many respects, is accounted a cause onerous, July 8, 1625, Gray *contra* Burgh [Durie 176; M. Supp. 22]. Where the son was not liberated, though he offered to renounce the lands he had by contract. And it was found, that lands being disponed and resigned by the father in favour of the son, by his contract of marriage, though they were for the present wadset and disponed with that burden, and thereafter redeemed by the son by his own means, so that there remained nothing in the father, but the superiority and the reversion, yet the contract of marriage was found onerous as to the wife's liferent: and, in respect the son was minor, and presently

revoked the disposition, and renounced all other rights, except that of the wadset which he had redeemed; he was liberate of the passive title, and the lands declared redeemable by any creditor anterior to the contract, January 14, 1634, Courtney *contra* Weems [*Sub anno* 1637, Durie 822; M.9790]. In the like case, where lands were disponed by a father to the son in his contract of marriage, for a tocher paid to the father, for some debts and bairns' portions, far within the worth of the land; the son was not found liable *in solidum* as lucrative successor, nor yet the pursuer put to a reduction; but the son was in *hoc processu* put to compt, and pay the superplus of the true price of the land, June 17, 1664, Lyon *contra* Bannerman [1 Stair 203; M.9792]. Yet the common rule is, that contracts of marriage are only gratuitous, when they exceed the just proportion for such parties.

4. This title takes place, not only in universal dispositions of the predecessor's whole estate, but a disposition of any part thereof is sufficient; seeing the least, as well as the most, is *præceptio hæreditatis*.

5. This title is extended also not only to dispositions made to, and accepted by the immediate apparent heir, but also to the mediate apparent heir, so that he be *alioqui successurus*, by the course of law necessarily, as what is granted to the eldest son of the apparent heir, because the ground of this title being to prevent deeds in favour of the disponer's successors, prejudicial to the disponer's creditors, whose debts are anterior, the reason holds as much where he dispones to his oye, who, by the course of law, is to succeed to him, as to his son. 2. It is *præceptio hæreditatis* in the oye as well as in the son. And therefore the rule in this title is not, that the accepter be that person who would succeed at the time of the disposition, and so may seem to be immediate apparent heir *pro tempore :* for so a disposition by one brother to another, or to a brother's son, the disponer for the time having no children, will not infer this title, November 22, 1665, Scot *contra* Boswell [1 Stair 310; M.3571]; December 22, 1674, Heirs of Seatoun of Blair *contra* Seatoun [2 Stair 295; M.5397]. The like, though the disponer was an old man, the time of the disposition, and had little hope of issue, December 17, 1632, La. Spenserfield *contra* L. of Kilbrachmont [*Sub anno* 1672, 2 Stair 136; M.9779]. The reason is, because the brother or brother's son is not *alioqui successurus* by the course of law, while the brother's children are in *spe*, and therefore such are never called apparent heirs; neither is the presumption in them, that the defunct would, in prejudice of his creditors, adventure simply to dispone to such, while he had hope of issue, but all this holds in oyes. And it was so decided, January 29, 1639, La. Smeatoun *contra* Richardson [Durie 870; M.9775]; where an infeftment was granted by the goodsire to the oye, reserving his son's liferent. And, in the like case, the father who was but liferenter, and his oye fiar by the grandfather's disposition, were both found lucrative successors, February 23, 1637, Lightoun *contra* L. of Kinaber [*Sub. nom. Forbes* v *Fullerton*, Durie 828; M.9772]; but this decision was stopped to be further heard.

6. But here occurreth the question, if the disposition be anterior to the debt contracted, but the infeftment posterior to the said debt, *quid juris?* The ground of doubt is, that though the defender had a prior disposition, yet, by the infeftment only, he was successor, seeing lands pass not by dispositions, but by infeftments; and therefore he was clearly successor *post contractum debitum*, and also *ex causa lucrativa*. 2. If this were not the meaning, the intent of the law would be frustrate: for it were easy to make dispositions and to keep them up, and in the mean time to contract debts, when the creditors could not know the debtor's condition, and so contracted *bona fide*. This case was decided *negativè*, that the infeftment, though posterior to the debt, did not infer this title, being upon a disposition anterior to the debt, February 23, 1637, Lightoun *contra* L. of Kinaber [*Sub nom. Forbes* v *Fullerton*, Durie 828; M. 9772]. The like was found, where there was an obligement in a contract of marriage, to dispone lands, prior to the debt contracted, albeit both the disposition and infeftment were posterior to the debt, and did not bear expressly "in implement of the contract," which was presumed, seeing no other cause was shown, July 23, 1678, Ferguson *contra* Lindsay [2 Stair 638; M. 9803]. For answer to the contrary reasons; the first is, upon misapplication of the words, *post contractum debitum*, which are not to be referred to successor, thus, *successor post contractum debitum ex causa lucrativa ;* but *successor ex titulo lucrativo, qui titulus est post contractum debitum*. So that, if the lucrative title be not after the debt, this title takes no place. As to the other reason, the same inconveniency will be of dispositions to strangers, which, being kept up, creditors may contract *bona fide*. And yet inhibition before infeftment will not be effectual, unless it precede the infeftment and the disposition, which will also be effectual against the apparent heir. But if there be fraud in keeping up such dispositions, which will be easier presumed in the person of the apparent heir, than a stranger, it will be sufficient upon the common reason of fraud, to reduce the infeftment, though the general passive title be not inferred.

7. This title can take no place, first, where the party to whom the right is granted is not *alioqui successurus* in that same right, because it cannot be *præceptio hæreditatis*, where there can be no *hæreditas*. And so a disposition to an heir of tailzie, of lands not provided to that heir of tailzie, cannot infer this title, though it may be reducible, as without a cause onerous. Neither will a disposition of tailzied lands to an heir of line, infer this title; for, in that case, it cannot be *præceptio hæreditatis*, albeit the disposition will be reducible, as without a cause onerous. But there is more reason, that rights acquired originally by predecessors, in name of their apparent heirs, cannot infer this title, because the predecessor himself never being fiar in that right, the apparent heir could not be his heir therein. Neither can such rights be reducible by the Act of Parliament 1621 [Possibly Bankruptcy Act, 1621, c. 18; A.P.S. IV, 615, c. 18], because the failing thereof will not make the fee return to the predecessor who never had it; but the same can only be reached by a declarator, that it was acquired by that predecessor's means, after the debt contracted,

and therefore ought to be affectable, as if it were in the person of the debtor, or his heir; which hath frequently been found relevant, and sustained.

Title 8. Executry, Where, of Testaments, Codicils, Legacies, Relict's Part, Bairns' Part, Dead's Part, Confirmations, and Office of Executry

THERE remains now the other branch of succession, viz. in moveables, which is of two kinds; the one of executors, which is the only lawful succession in moveables, and therefore is both an active and passive title, the other illegal and vitious, and is therefore called vitious intromission, and is only a passive title. Of the former in this title, and of the latter in the next. The whole interest of the moveable goods and rights of defuncts, is comprehended under the term of executry, wherein, not only that which is proper to the executor by his office, or succession, is contained; but also that which befalleth to the defunct's relict, children, and nearest of kin, and to his legatars and creditors. We shall not here repeat what hath been said of succession in general, of which at large in its proper place, *supra, tit.* 4; where the rise and rule of succession, both according to equity and the law of nature, and according to the positive law, and custom of this and other nations, is held forth. This much only in general, that the will of the owner is effectual in equity to dispose upon his rights, either to take effect during his life, or after his death; the former being complete, constitutes a present right, irrevocable by the disponer; the latter is ambulatory, and dependent upon the owner's will, and hath always implied in it the condition of his death; and therefore may be altered, abrogate, and derogate by a posterior will. And thence it is called the latter will of the defunct, because the latter will is always effectual, and preferable to the former will. It is also more favourably interpreted and extended, than contracts or dispositions amongst the living. And if there were no positive law, the express or presumed will of the defunct would be the adequate rule of his whole succession; but succession being of great consequence, whereby all the rights of men are at least once, and many times oftener, transmitted in every generation; therefore positive law for utility's sake, hath justly and fitly prescribed the forms and solemnities thereof, that it may be clear and sure, and hath applied remedies to make it effectual, and hath restrained the power of the defunct's will in some cases, especially in favour of the defunct's wife and children, whom, by the law of nature, he is obliged to provide; and hath also declared the degrees of succession, meaning, and presumption of the will of defuncts.

1. The Romans, of all nations, were most solicitous in this matter, and accounted it a public interest, *reipublicæ interest, voluntates defunctorum effectum sortiri:* and therefore they did exactly guard the power of testing, not only against violence and fraud, by severe punishments, and exclusion from all benefit of succession, but also they rejected and annulled all pactions, restraining the power of testing, as *pactum Corvinum de hæreditate viventis;* which was not only extended to pactions made by persons, disposing of the heritage of persons to whom they might succeed, but even to pactions in relation to their own heritage. They did also clearly determine what persons had not the power of testing, and in whose favour testaments might not be made; and the manner of all kinds of testaments, institutions, and substitutions of heirs, legacies, *fideicommisses,* and the sense of most ordinary clauses in all these; and also the succession of the intestate: which hath made the matter of succession swell into a mighty bulk, and to make the chief integral of the civil law; wherein to insist here would neither be necessary nor profitable for our purpose: but, as in other cases [111, 4, 15, *supra*], a short sum, without ampliations or citations, may suffice.

2. Succession amongst the Romans was either by testament, or from the intestate. The ancient way of testing amongst the Romans was either in peace and solemn, which was done in presence of the people being convocated *collatis comitiis,* or otherwise by a simulate sale, *per æs et libram* [Gaius 2, 103]; wherein the testator, in presence of five witnesses Romans, did hold a balance, and weighed money therein, and under that form, as it were, sold his inheritance for the money, and asked witnesses. Or otherwise testaments were made *in procinctu* [Gaius 2, 101], when they were standing in battle before the fight, without other solemnity than three or four witnesses. This was the ancient form of testing. The matter and power of testing was very absolute, according to equity: concerning which this was the law of the Twelve Tables, *uti quisque rei suae legasset, ita jus esto.* But the after-course of the civil law changed both this ancient manner and power of testing, and redacted testaments into three kinds, solemn, nuncupative, and military.

3. Solemn testaments were so called, because they required the most solemnities; as, First, That the testaments were in writ, the name of the heir at least being written by the testator, or one of the witnesses. Secondly, There behoved to be seven witnesses, being Romans, specially required, all present, and subscribing by themselves or another, and sealing the testament at the foot thereof; none of which might be women, pupils, servants, prodigals, or furious persons; neither the heir himself, nor any of his domestics; each sub-

scription bearing, "I Titius, &c. being called and required to be a witness to this testament, which is contained in this schedule, have subscribed it with my hand, and sealed it with such a seal." Thirdly, The testator also behoved to subscribe thus, "I Mevius, &c. declare this schedule to be my testament, and I have tested as is contained therein;" or by another if he could not write, who stood as the eighth witness. Fourthly, The testament behoved to be made by one continued act, without intervention of any extraneous act, lest by extraneous acts the mind might be diverted, or inconsiderate in so solemn an act. So the testament was closed up and sealed; and if the testator opened the testament, it was presumed he changed his mind: but after his death, the witnesses were called together, to acknowledge their seals and subscriptions, at the opening thereof. Or otherwise, it was opened by the authority of a judge, before other honest witnesses. And if any of the witnesses acknowledged not their subscriptions, the testament was held suspect.

4. A nuncupative testament is that which was by word only, before seven witnesses qualified as aforesaid; yet two witnesses were sufficient in a father's testament amongst his children; and a woman might be witness therein. Or in a testament for pious uses five witnesses did suffice, where there was any penury of witnesses.

5. A military testament was that which was made by the soldiers in war; wherein they had these privileges; First, When they were *in procinctu*, ready to join battle, any declaration of their mind, by word or writ, though it were written in the sand, was sufficient. It was also valid, if made during the expedition, with such solemnities as can be had for the time; yet so, if the testator lived a year, in which he might make it more solemn, it became void. Military testaments have this further privilege, that the testator may institute for a time, and may institute in a part, and so die partly testate and partly intestate; which is against a principle of their common law.

6. The ancient absolute power of testing was, by the subsequent course of law, cleared and restrained, not only by the declaratory laws, finding testing and other acts invalid, as done by furious persons out of their lucid intervals, and by idiots, and by pupils, who have not the use of reason; or those made by fraud, or error in the substantials, or by extortion; but more particularly it is limited in these particulars.

7. First, *Filii familias*, persons in the power and family of their fathers, could not test upon their goods, whether profectitious from their father, or adventitious *aliunde*, even though their father consented; but only on their own *bona castrensia*, acquired in war, or *quasi castrensia*, as in *militia togata*.

8. Secondly, Captives with public enemies, or persons given in pledge to them, or persons condemned to capital punishment, whose goods were confiscated, or those condemned of infamy, could not test.

9. Thirdly, By testament some persons can neither be institute nor substitute heirs, such as the spurious children of the defunct, to put a restraint upon such unlawful procreations. But children begotten on concubines, while

those were tolerated, could not be institute or substitute, there being lawful children, in more than a sixth part of the heritage. Only there could be left to spurious children legacies for their necessary aliment. Neither could persons guilty of, or condemned for treason, be institute or substitute heirs.

10. Fourthly, The power of testing is restrained in those who have lawful children, who were necessitated, either to institute their children their heirs, or expressly to exheredate or disheirish them, expressing the cause of so doing. For if these instituted others, and passed over their children in silence, the testament was void. And if they unjustly exheredated them, they had *querelam inofficiosi testamenti*, to annul the testament, as done against the natural duty of fathers, without a just cause.

11. Fifthly, The power of testing was restrained in favour of lawful children, that the testator could not by legacy, or *fideicommissum*, abate from the children their portions natural, due to them by the law of nature, obliging parents to entertain their children; which their law defined to be the fourth part of the inheritance, debts deduced, when there were fewer than four children; a third part when four; and a half when more. If there be no children, this *legitima* is due to the parents, grandfather and grandmother; but not to brethren, unless a base person be institute; which portion natural the testator could not prohibit the children to withdraw from the heritage.

12. Sixthly, The Falcidian law [Inst. 2,22; D. 35,2,1] did restrain legacies, that they might not exceed three fourth parts of the inheritance; so that there behoved to remain one fourth part to the heir; which therefore was called *portio Falcidia*. And therefore, if the legacies did exceed three quarters of the free inheritance, debts being deduced, they were abated proportionally, that the *Falcidia* might remain to the heir.

13. This *portio Falcidia* differs from the natural portion in this, that the testator could not prohibit the heir to take the benefit of the portion natural; but he could effectually prohibit the heir to take his *Falcidia*. The reason whereof was, because the *Falcidia* was introduced, to the effect that the wills of defuncts might be executed, which could not be if the legacies left nothing to the heir considerable, but trouble, as oft-times it falls out: so that this being a remedy in favour of the testator, to make his will effectual, he might prohibit it; and could not be presumed so irrational as to prohibit it, if he had not good ground to know that his heirs would enter without it. Or indirectly, if the testator prohibited the alienation of the heritage, the law esteemed it as a prohibition of the *Falcidia*. But the *Falcidia* had no place in military testaments, or in legacies left to pious uses, or left to the relict of the testator, *nomine dotis;* the reason of these exceptions being in favour of soldiers, pious uses, and tochers. And if the heir omitted to make inventory, he lost the benefit of his *Falcidia*.

14. When the fiduciary succession became in use, whereby heirs were institute or substitute to the use and behoof of others, to whom they were to restore the inheritance, or some part thereof, or thing therein, which therefore was called *fideicommissum* [Inst. 11,23], as being committed to the trust

and faithfulness of the heir, the *senatus consultum Trebellianum* [Gaius 2,253; D. 36, 1, 1] did introduce the reservation of a fourth part to the heir, institute or substitute, by these *fideicommisses*, in the same way that the *Falcidia* was a reservation from legacies; and therefore this fourth part was called *Trebellianica*: which therefore hath the same exceptions with the *Falcidia*; of which in the former paragraph. And this further; if the heir were forced by law to enter, or if within a year thereafter he do not fulfil the will of the defunct, he lost the benefit of his *Trebellianica*. And if he had either legacy or portion of the inheritance, it was reckoned to him as a part of his *Trebellianica*.

15. The use of these fideicommissary trusts was, when the testator designed his inheritance, or some of his goods, either for persons that were not capable to be heirs, or not fit to manage, as through pupilarity, prodigality, or some other defect, then he institute other heirs fit for the present management; and desired, or required them by his testament, to restore the inheritance, or some part of it, to such persons; and that either simply to a day, or conditionally: and ofttimes the day of restitution was after the heir's own death, whereby he had his liferent or usufruct thereof. At first this was wholly left to the trust and faithfulness of the heir, without any legal remedy or compulsion: which afterward were adhibited, with the reservation of the *Trebellianica*, as hath been shown. But where the persons in whose favour the trust was, were such as could not be heirs, or succeed, as spurious persons, &c. then those heirs were not compelled to restore.

The essential and chief point of a testament is the nomination of an heir [Inst. 11,14; C. 6,24], either by institution or substitution, without which it was not allowed the name of a testament, but only a legacy, or, at best, the name of codicils; which is called by some an imperfect testament.

16. Codicils might be made before five witnesses, either in writ or nuncupative; and they were ordinarily additions to testaments: yea, because, if when testaments, through want of solemnity, became void, the legacies failed; therefore there used to be adjoined this clause, "If this be not valid as a testament, let it be valid as a codicil;" which thence is called *clausula codicillaris* [C. 6, 36, 8].

17. The form of institution of heirs was, in plain and short terms, thus, *Titius hæres esto*. These were either institute solely or jointly, and that either equally or indefinitely, which is understood equally; or otherwise by certain portions. No institution can be conditional, or to a day; or if it be, it is presently effectual; because the heritage cannot hang in the air, and belong to none, else it would prove caduciary. Yet in military testaments this privilege is indulged, as hath been said.

18. Substitution is the nomination of substitute heirs, who take place failing the institute [Inst. 11,15; D. 29,2; 38,16]. There may be as many subordinate members of substitution as the testator pleaseth. The institute, or prior substitute, is found to fail, when either he cannot, or will not enter; but if once he enter, the substitution for ever evanisheth. And if he or his should

be extinct who was institute, the heritage becomes his patrimony, and no more the first defunct's heritage; and so falls not to the substitute, who is heir of the first defunct, but to the heirs of the institute. It is otherwise with us in tailzies, or other substitutions, as hereafter will appear.

19. Substitution was of two kinds, vulgar and pupillar. Pupillar is that [D. 37, 5], whereby fathers were allowed in their testament, having named their children, being pupils, to be their heirs, to substitute heirs to them; which substitutes had not only the father's heritage, but the son's, dying in pupillarity; under which is comprehended that which is called *substitutio exemplaris*, whereby parents having institute their children, being idiots, their heirs, did substitute other heirs to them, if they entered not, and died idiots or furious. And in military testaments the pupillar substitution is not only effectual, if the testator make his own will, and institute his children; but though he only substitute, and though the children survive their pupillarity, yet if they enter not, the substitution is valid. All other substitutions are ordinary, or vulgar [Inst. 11, 15; D. 28, 6; C. 6, 26], when the testator institutes heirs, and substitutes others; but hath only effect as to the testator's own goods, if those institute enter not, but not as to the goods of the heirs institute.

20. The matter of next moment to the institution, or substitution of heirs, is the leaving of legacies, which may be left in testaments, or codicils, and without either in some cases. Any thing may be legated, which is in the defunct's goods, alienable, except in so far as is restrained in the *Legitima, Falcidia, et Trebellianica;* of which formerly. Yea, though the thing legated be not the testator's, the heir is obliged to purchase it to the legatar, or the value of it, if the testator knew it was another's; for then his mind is followed, to make it effectual, at least by the value. But if the testator legate any thing, thinking it to be his own, which is not his own, the legacy is ineffectual. For legacies being donations, they are understood to be given only in so far as the giver hath right: and therefore there is no warrandice of them as to the testator's right. But if the heir deliver any thing not specially legated, in satisfaction of the legacy, if that be evicted upon defect of the heir's right, he is liable for warrandice; as if an heir were appointed to give in legacy a horse worth such a price, not being in the heritage, but delivered by the heir to satisfy the legacy; if the horse be evicted, the legatar hath warrandice against the heir, because it is not the defunct's right, but the heir's right that fails. Legacies, and particular *fideicommisses*, not being for restitution of the whole heritage, or any special part, or quota thereof, are equiparate, as *fideicommisses* of the heritage, or a quota thereof are equivalent to the institution, or substitution of heirs. And either legacies, or *fideicommisses* may be general, whereby a quantity is left; or special, whereby an individual body is left, as such an horse, &c. so may they either be left purely, or conditionally, or to a day.

21. This is common to all legacies, that, if the legatar die before the testator, the legacy becomes void, and is not transmitted to the heirs and successors of the legatar. Neither doth the legacy belong to the legatar ordinarily, if

the testament wherein it is left be void, for want of the requisite solemnities, of which formerly [111,8,16,*supra*], unless it have the codicillar clause, or if the heir do not enter, or if the codicils in which it is left, or the testament, having the codicillar clause, want the solemnities requisite to codicils.

22. If the legacy, or *fideicommisses* be conditional, the lagatar dying before the existence of the condition, loseth the legacy, and doth not transmit it to his heir if it be a casual condition, but if it be a potestative condition depending upon the power of the legatar, and not upon accident without his power; or if left to an uncertain day, which is equivalent to a casual condition; if so the condition be in the legatar's power, unless he did all diligence to satisfy the same, he loseth the legacy. But if the condition fail not through his fault, as being offered and not accepted, or being impeded by any third party; the legacy is thereby transmitted to the legatar's heirs, who are only liable for the interest of the condition. Legacies pure, or to a certain day, are transmitted by the death of the testator; especially if the heir be entered, though the day be not come; *quia cessit dies, sed non venit.*

23. In the several cases, by which legacies are established, and transmissible, the property thereof is in the person of the legatar, if it be a special legacy; but the possession thereof remains in the heir, against whom the legatar hath not only a personal action, for payment or delivery of the legacy; but hath also a real action of vindication against him, and all other havers thereof, for delivery of the same. So *fideicommisses*, which are not conditional, are not alienable by the heir, but are recoverable from every singular successor.

24. Conditions adjected to legacies, or *fideicommisses*, are of divers kinds, of which shortly observe; 1. That when conditions are copulative, they must all be jointly performed; or, when divers conditions are severally set down in several places of the testament. But if they be disjunctive, the performance of any of them is sufficient. 2. If the condition be divisible and performable by more persons, each performing his part, hath access to his legacy. But if it be imposed upon one person, the performance of a part thereof doth not give access to a proportionable part of the legacy; but the condition must be wholly performed, otherwise there is no part of the legacy due. 3. Conditions impossible *in facto*, as not being lawful, regularly are void, and as not adjected. Among which that is accounted one, if marriage be absolutely prohibited, which the Authentics restricted only to maids, and found it lawful in the case of widows to adject such a condition, *si Titia nubat ;* and therefore, if the legatar married not to that person, the legacy was not due. In legacies and *fideicommisses*, a false narrative vitiates not, as when the efficient cause, mentioned therein, was not true. For example, if a legacy be left, bearing to have been for services done, generally or particularly; albeit these were not done, it is valid. But the expression of the final cause implies a condition: and if it be not performed, the legacy ceaseth, *causa non secuta ;* as when legacies are left for such uses, services, or deeds to be done. Legacies being gratuitous,

are of the nature of donations; and therefore are revoked by ingratitude, *ipso facto*, not only in reaching the defunct, as if enmity rose betwixt him and the legatar; but even after his death; as if he curse him, or endeavour to make him infamous; yea, those things against the heir will be sufficient to take away the legacy. So much may serve for a summary of the Roman law, in the matter of testaments. As for the succession of the intestate, it being one, without distinction of heritable and moveable rights, we have spoken thereof before, title, Succession. We shall therefore only touch on these points which are common, in all successions, by the Roman law, viz. of the inventory, collation of goods, and right of accrescence, or *collatio bonorum*, and *jus accrescendi*.

25. The inventory of heritage, was a repertory of every particular contained therein, and was contrary to the rules of the Roman law, *l. si dotis nomine*, 33. *ff. soluto matrimonio* [D. 24,3,33], by which there was neither a duty nor benefit to the heir by an inventory. But the use thereof was introduced by Justinian in favour mainly of heirs, and in some cases of creditors and legatars. Of heirs, that they might not be liable for the defunct's debts *in solidum*, but *secundum vires inventarii*, according to the value of the inheritance; and this much in favour of the creditors and legatars, that the inheritance might not be embezzled. And therefore the making of the inventory was appointed to be with great solemnity before a judge, upon citation of the creditors and legatars, so far as they were certain, and public proclamation for the rest, and before famous witnesses. And, in place of the absent legatars and creditors, three persons were to be present, besides the witnesses, of good fame and means. The inventory behoved also to be made within thirty days, after the heir knew and could enter to the heritage, and behoved to be complete within sixty days after the beginning thereof. The inventory not being thus made, the heir was liable to the creditors for their whole debts, and to the legatars for their legacies, without deduction of his *Falcidia*. Neither could the testator dispense with, or prohibit the making of the inventory, in prejudice of the creditors; but he might in prejudice of the legatars, so as the *Falcidia* would be due, in that case, though the inventory were not made.

26. Collation [D. 37,6; C. 6,20] is the obligation of the nearest heirs descending, to communicate what the defunct parent bestowed upon them by donation, or tocher, unto the inheritance, that an equal proportion or division might be of the whole amongst the co-heirs. The reason of this collation was, the equality of interest and affection of parents to their children of the same degree, and thence their presumed will, that these should enjoy equal benefit by their parents. And therefore, if it appeared not to have been the parent's will, collation had no place; as if the thing were bestowed, with express exemption, or prohibition of collation, or if it were left as a legacy, or donation *mortis causa ;* for thereby the parent's purpose appeared, to prefer that child to the rest, even after the parent's death. Collation was competent amongst no other heirs, than descendants in the same degree, and not amongst extraneous heirs, institute, or substitute, or amongst ascendants, or collateral heirs;

but only when the co-heirs were by testament, or from the intestate, who are in the same degree, as being all children, or all oyes, &c. But if children, or grandchildren were institute or substitute together, there was no collation. Amongst things bestowed upon children by their parents, their peculiar provisions and tochers were comprehended, but not their entertainment or expense of their education. And therefore, though one child were elder, or longer entertained than the rest, or though more sumptuously; or though educated with more noble accomplishments, and at a greater rate, as being bred at schools, trades, exercises, &c. neither the instruments requisite for these, as books, clothes, or the like, came under collation, or was there any estimate or consideration thereof. The reason is, because entertainment and education is presumed to be according to the fitness and capacity of the persons, whereunto a proportion is observed in all societies and communions. And therefore the parents are presumed to have expended upon their children proportionally, according to the capacity and excellency of their spirits, and to render them fit to the services of their generation; which, as they have a benefit, so they have with them a large burden, and oft-times hazard. Neither do donations to children for any special service done to their parents, come under collation; because these are not properly donations, but remunerations.

27. The right of accrescence, is that whereby the portion of an heir, legatar, or fidei-commissar befalleth to another [D. 32, 80]; not by a new and several succession, but by the first succession, and as a part thereof. We have little use of this; and therefore I shall be the shorter, in the many and subtile debates agitated amongst the Doctors thereupon. For taking clearly up this right, we must take notice, that co-heirs by testament, or legatars, or fidei-commissars, are either appointed conjunct by the words of the testator, or by the matter, or conjunct as to the words, but disjunct as to the matter, or wholly several, both as to words and matter. As if the testator say, "Titius and Mævius shall be my heirs," there the copulative conjunction joins them in the same sentence, and they are joint in the same inheritance, without expressing their distinct portions, in which the law interprets them equally institute. The like is, if he leave a legacy, or *fideicommissum*, in the like terms. But where the proportion is express, equal, or unequal, thus; "Let Titius and Mævius be my heirs equally;" or, "let Titius be heir in one half, and Mævius and Caius in another half:" here Caius and Mævius are conjunct in words and matter; but they are several from Titius both as to words and matter. Or, in the first case, Titius and Mævius are joined in one sentence, but separate as to the matter, because their portions are severed and expressed. But if the testator say thus; "I leave Titius my dwelling-house," and say after, "I leave Mævius the same dwelling-house," there is no conjunction of words, because to both severally the same thing is left. In all these cases there may be substitutions; we shall then set down the right of accrescence in the several cases thereof.

First, In the institution or substitution of heirs directly; there is place for accrescence, whether the co-heirs be conjunct or disjunct. The reason is, because of that principle of the civil law, that no man can die partly testate, and partly intestate, except in military testaments. And therefore, if any of the co-heirs will not, or cannot enter, the inheritance accresceth necessarily unto the other co-heir, with its own burden, whatever it be. Neither can the heir reject that portion, for the same reason: and if he enter before the other heir be excluded, he hath no remedy, and can neither reject the whole, nor a part; because he might, and should have seen to the other's entry with him, or else he enters on his peril. This takes no place in legacies, or *fideicommisses*; because, in these, the ground of law proceeds not. And therefore, if any heritage be ordered to be restored to such persons, severally in distinct portions, if one of them will not, or cannot accept, that portion accresceth not to the other, but returns to the heir. And so in legacies, if there be a substitution to any of the heirs, the portion accresceth not, because there is place for the substitute, who becomes co-heir with the other institute. This accrescence is so necessary, that the testator cannot prohibit it, because he cannot die testate, *pro parte;* and therefore *provisio hominis non tollit provisionem legis*, being as to the necessary requisites, essentials, and solemnities of law. Secondly, In the institution or substitution of heirs, or in legacies, and *fideicommisses*, if there be more persons, and some of them joint as to both matter and words; the rights of those so conjunct do accresce (if any of the persons so conjunct do not, nor cannot accept) to the rest of the conjunct, and not to those that are disjunct in the matter, though they be conjunct in the words. As if the testator say, "Let Titius be my heir", and thereafter say, "Let Seius and Mævius be my heirs;" if Seius or Mævius cannot, or will not enter, their portion accresceth to the other, and not to Titius. And therefore this conjunction is called a tacit substitution, because the law presumes, that the testator did not inconsiderately, or in vain, join Seius and Mævius in one sentence, and put Titius in another by himself; and so construeth that these two should be more conjunct, and their portions accresce to one another, and not to Titius. Thirdly, This proceedeth where the conjunction is only in words, if there be any disjunct both in matter and words: for then the conjunction makes the portions of the conjuncts to accresce each to other, and not to those who are wholly disjunct. As if the testator say, "Let Titius be my heir in the half, and let Seius and Mævius be my heirs equally in the other half." Here Seius and Mævius are conjunct in words, and not in the matter, because their portions are severed, and yet their portions accresce to other, and not to Titius, who is wholly disjunct; and that from the presumed will of the defunct, as having considerately put them in one sentence for that purpose. But this takes place only in institution and substitution of heirs, that the testator die not partly testate, but not in legacies and *fideicommisses*; for in these the portion of the conjuncts only in words not being accepted doth accresce to none, but returneth not to the heir. Fourthly, In all cases where there is conjunction in the matter, and not in words, there is place to accrescence: as if the testator say, "I leave my dwelling-house to Titius, I desire my heir to restore the same dwelling-house to Mævius; the portion of either party not accepting accresceth to the other, and returneth to the heir. But if the testator say, "I leave my house to Titius, I leave the same house to Seius and Mævius," either indefinitely, or expressing their portions; Seius and Mævius their portions accresce each to other, and not to Titius; because if they and Titius be conjoined in matter only, yet they are also conjoined in word; and so the more conjunctions prevail by the presumed will of the defunct. This kind of accrescence, is called by the Doctors *jus non decrescendi;* because each party being provided to the whole, which cannot be effectual, therefore *concursu partes faciunt*, and the deed is made effectual to them in part, equally; if the will of the defunct appear by the provision, not to take away the former wholly, as in many cases it falleth out. And therefore in this accrescence, if any burden be adjected, if that party accept not, his portion accresceth to the other without that burden; because the other enjoys his own right, which was total, and becomes now effectual as to the whole, the impediment that retrenched it being wholly taken off. But in all other conjunctions the portion accresceth with its burden; and therefore the accrescing portion, as being special, may be rejected in legacies and *fideicommisses*: but it cannot be rejected in institutions or substitutions, lest the testator should be intestate in part; but *in jure non decrescendi*, when portions accresce amongst those that are conjoined in the matter only, the accrescence is necessary, and the portion accrescing cannot be rejected; because it befalleth by one integral right, which either must be accepted wholly, or rejected wholly; and therein *approbans non reprobat*, no man can both approve and disapprove of the same individual thing.

28. The law and customs of Scotland have reduced the matter of testaments, and succession in moveables, much nearer to natural equity, and made it much shorter and plainer than the Roman law. For first, the civil law did lay the greatest weight upon the free power of testing; which our law hath so far abridged, that all contracts, pactions and provisions, in relation to the heritage of persons living, are valid and ordinary, in contracts of marriage, &c. And even *pactum Corvinum*, in the worst sense, is valid; as when one being provided by contract of marriage to be a bairn in the house, sells that proportion in the lifetime of the contracter; which was sustained July 6, 1630, Aikenhead *contra* Bothwel [Durie 525; M. 9492]. So an obligement to leave a legacy was found valid, and to stand as an irrevocable legacy; yet only to be taken out of the defunct's part of his free goods, January 13, 1631, Houstoune *contra* Houstoune [Durie 552; M. 8049].

29. Secondly, Not only may the power of testing be restricted by paction, but it is actually restricted by law, to extend to no immoveable or heritable right, which cannot be alienated, or affected upon death-bed, or, which is equiparate, by testament, though the testator were in his *liege poustie*, or perfect health; and that on good considerations; because persons are ordin-

arily, and still presumed to be weak when affected with sickness, and so not fit to alienate, or affect things of their greatest concernment, as their lands, heritage, &c. And because it is the great interest of persons to be free of all importunities when they come to their death-bed, at which time they are only capable of their dead's part, which is seldom considerable; and so they cannot affect their lands, nor can they further dispose of their goods upon the solicitation of churchmen, which is very powerful in the popish church, where indulgences and prayers for the dead, to bring them out of purgatory, are believed, and cannot but be forcible upon dying men, who then are more concerned for the safety of their souls than preservation of their estates. And everywhere the pressing desires of wives for themselves, or for such of their children as they most affect, or of children, relations and friends, may have great impression upon the sick, for preserving their peace and quiet: so there remains nothing testable with us but moveable rights. What rights are moveable, and what heritable, see in the beginning of the title, Rights Real [11, 1, *supra*], which shall not be here repeated. Thence it is, that there is a total separation of the succession in heritable rights, which are only competent to heirs, and in moveable rights; as to which, because they were intrusted to prelates, and their officials, as being presumed most careful of widows and orphans, and that the will of defuncts should be effectual, who did appoint persons to execute defuncts' wills, the persons so appointed were called executors; and the whole moveable rights of defuncts, whether tested on, or from the intested, are comprehended in executry.

30. The whole interest of executry with us, is in the office of the executor, the division of the communion of goods betwixt man and wife, (whereby the relict hath her part) the succession of children, and nearest of kin, or legacies. There is with us, properly, no institution or substitution of heirs: for albeit the nomination of executors be in the defunct's power, in the first place, and doth resemble the institution of heirs, and may receive substitutions in the same way, yet it is not properly a succession, but rather an office, which therefore hath a part of the goods. Executors are heirs in moveables, and when heirs only are expressed, executors are comprehended *quoad mobilia*. If there be a nomination of executors, with a material legacy to another, it is fideicommissary succession, to be restored to the universal legatar. And executors-dative have also a fideicommissary succession, which they must restore to the wife, and nearest of kin of the defunct. So must executors nominate, not being also universal legatars, and being strangers, retaining only a third of dead's part to themselves, for executing their office. The greatest power of defuncts, either by testament or otherwise, is the power of legating by particular or universal legacies. The interest of the wife is not so much a succession as a division of that communion of moveable rights, which the law stateth betwixt the husband and her, *stante matrimonio*, and which is dissolved by the dissolution of marriage; and so she taketh her share of the free goods by way of division.

31. The succession in moveables from the intestate belongeth to the

nearest of kin [111,4,24,*supra*], who are the defunct's whole agnates, male or female, being the kinsmen of the defunct's father's side, of the nearest degree, without primogeniture, or right of representation; wherein those joined to the defunct by both bloods, do exclude the agnates by one blood.

32. The line of succession in moveables is, first, the nearest descendants, male or female, in the same degree, equally, whether sons or daughters, without right of representation. So that if the defunct, the time of his decease, had two daughters, though he had an oye by a son, the daughters will exclude the oye, albeit the defunct had nothing but moveables. The next degree of the nearest of kin is brothers and sisters german; and failing these, brothers or sisters by the father's side only, or their nearest descendants of the same degree, without right of representation. As to the third degree of succession in moveables, failing descendants, and brothers and sisters, and their descendants, the question is, Whether the father surviving will exclude his own brother, or if there be any place for ascendants in the succession of moveables? Such cases occur rarely: and I have not observed it debated or decided. It is but of late since the like case hath fallen in the succession of heirs, and heritable rights; wherein our custom hath, according to the course of the law of nature, found the father to be heir to his son, and not the father-brother, or any of his descendants; and in that we have differed from the custom of England [111,4,35,*supra*]. And there is no reason why, if the question should occur, that the like should not be done in moveables. The next degree is of the father's brethren and sisters-german; which failing, the father's brethren and sisters by the same grandfather, and their descendants in the next degree; in all which both bloods exclude one blood: and if there be no agnate or kinsfolk found, who can instruct their propinquity of blood, the goods become caduciary, and confiscate, and belong to the King as *ultimus hæres*, who, and his donatar, have the same interest that the nearest of kin would have had; *Vide* title, Confiscation, Section *Ultimus hæres* [111,3,47,*supra*]. Children *in familia* have not only the common right, as nearest of kin to dead's part, but have their legitime portion, called the bairns' part; in which their father cannot, by testament, legacy, or donation *mortis causa*, prejudge them; or by any other deed on deathbed [111,4,24,*supra*]. So by the premises it appears, that the whole power of defuncts, as to the succession in their moveables, is to nominate executors, and give legacies.

33. The nomination of executors is properly called a testament. Additions thereto, or alterations thereof, are called codicils. Legacies may be left whether there be testaments or not, and either in the testament, codicils, or apart; but all is ambulatory during the defunct's life, and may be taken away expressly or implicitly, by posterior or derogatory deeds, unless the defunct be obliged by contract *inter vivos*, not to alter the same; in which case contract and paction doth so far overrule the power of testing, that posterior deeds, whether expressly or implicitly altering, would be ineffectual, like to that obligement to leave a legacy, which was found an effectual legacy with-

out further solemnity, January 13, 1631, Houstoun *contra* Houstoun [Durie 552; M. 8049; III, 8, 28, *supra*].

34. The effect of testaments being so small, the solemnities thereof are no other than what are requisite to accomplish any other writ; for two witnesses suffice, and if the testament be holograph, it is valid; or if the testator cannot, or be not able through sickness to write, a testament will be sufficient by a notar and two witnesses, notwithstanding of the Act 80, Parl. 1579 [Subscription of Deeds Act, 1579, c. 80; A.P.S. III, 145, c. 18], requiring to writs of importance two notars and four witnesses, which holds not in testaments, though containing matter of great importance. For ministers are authorised as notars in the case of testaments, Parl. 1458, cap. 133 [Disqualification of Ministers Act 1584, c. 133; A.P.S. III, 294, c. 6]. The reason hereof is, because ministers are ordinarily with sick persons the time of their death. Nuncupative testaments are not of force in Scotland; for though legacies left within an hundred pounds may be nuncupative without writ [III, 8, 36, *infra*], yet the nomination will not so subsist, nor be respected by the Commissaries. And therefore a verbal testament, taking away a formal legacy, was not sustained, though made at sea, and so in a case of necessity; and not admitted to be proven by witnesses in the ship, February 18, 1631, Houstoun *contra* Houstoun [Durie 571; M. 12307].

35. The effect of testaments is no greater, though made in England, the testator residing there, and so extends not to an heritable sum due in Scotland, left in legacy by the testator, being a Scotsman, July 3, 1634, Melvil *contra* Drummond [Durie 723; M. 4483]; Hope, Testaments, Purves *contra* Chisholm [Hope, *Maj. Pr.* IV, 1, 13; M. 4494]; Executors of Colonel Henrison, *ibid.* [Hope, *Maj. Pr.* IV, 1, 15; M. 4481, 4482]. Neither do nuncupative testaments of Scotsmen, though residing *animo remanendi* abroad, and dying there, have any effect with us, albeit nuncupative testaments be valid according to the law and custom of that place. For albeit the custom of the place may supply the solemnity of any writs or evidents, for instructing a right, as writs made abroad by notars, or tabellions, are valid, though not done according to the law of Scotland, which requires two notars and four witnesses in writs of importance; yet the custom of those places cannot constitute any right of succession, not allowed by the law of Scotland. And therefore William Schaw, factor and residenter in London, having lived and died there, in the house of one Mary Lewins, who had confirmed in England a nuncupative testament, whereby he had designed her as executrix and legatrix; and the nearest of kin of the said William having confirmed themselves executors to him in Scotland, and the competition being betwixt them, the Lords preferred the executors confirmed in Scotland, and had no respect to the nuncupative testament, as having no effect by the law of Scotland, January 19, 1665, Schaw *contra* Lewins [1 Stair 252; M. 4494; I, 1, 16, *supra*; III, 8, 55, *infra*].

36. The like solemnities will be sufficient for codicils and legacies. Yet a

nuncupative legacy within an hundred pounds is probable by witnesses, Had. November 24, 1609, Russel *contra*   [Haddington, *Fol.Dict.* 1, 159; M. 2546]; July 7, 1629, Wallace *contra* Mure [Durie 457; M. 1350]; where a greater legacy, left by word, restricted to an hundred pounds, was found so probable.

37. The power of testing is competent to all persons who have the use of reason, though minors, having curators not consenting [1, 6, 34, *supra*]; wives clad with husbands, without their consent; persons interdicted, without consent of the interdictors: but not to pupils, idiots, furious persons in their furiosity: neither to bastards, not having lawful issue, or *testamenti factionem* by the king's gift; as in the former case, Wallace *contra* Mure [Durie 457; M. 1350]; *vide* Tit. Confiscation, sect. Bastardy [111, 3, 42, *supra*].

38. Legacies are either particular or universal, general or special. Universal legacies are when the whole moveables, in so far as is in the defunct's disposal, and not left by particular legacies, is legate, and so it is *legatum per universitatem*, and like to the succession of an heir. Special legacies are where some individual is left, as such a horse, clothes, &c. or such a sum due by such a person, whereby the property is stated in the legatar, and, at most, but the possession or custody in the executor [111, 4, 24, *supra*]; and therefore the legatar may pursue for delivery, or payment of the special legacy, against the havers or debtors: but he must call the executor, that his interest may be preserved, lest the debts exhaust even the special legacy. Upon which consideration the Lords sustained not a pursuit upon a special legacy, leaving a sum due by such a person in such a bond, pursued against the debtor, the executor not being called, March 10, 1627, Forrester *contra* Clerk [Durie 288; M. 2194]. And before, the pursuit against the debtor, at the legatar's instance, was simply repelled, not being against the executor, February 4, 1623, L. Balnamoon *contra* L. Balcomy [Durie 43; M. 3844]. Yea, a process was sustained at the instance of the universal legatar against the debtor, the executor being also called. Here there was malversation betwixt the executor and the debtors. But ordinarily legatars have no immediate action against the debtors of the defunct, but only against his executor, Hope, Legacy, Bannatine *contra* Eliot [Not found]. Legacies may be left, not only in testaments or codicils, but where there is none, or where there is, in contracts, letters, or tickets apart; though the legacies were not in the confirmation, December 1, 1629, Executors of Scot *contra* Rae [Durie 472; M. 6847].

39. Legacies and donations in contemplation of death, or done on deathbed, albeit as *inter vivos*, yet being of moveables, as bonds, assignations, or gifts of money, or goods on death-bed, have the like effect, and are only effectual as to the defunct's free goods at his disposal, which is called the dead's part [111, 4, 24, *supra*]. And if the whole legacies exceed the dead's part of the free gear, regularly they are abated proportionally; wherein there is no preference nor privilege granted to legacies left *ad pias causas*: as for building of a kirk, delivered by the defunct long ere he died, which suffered proportion-

able defalcation with the ordinary legacies, July 6, 1630, Dr. Monro *contra* Executors of Scot [Durie 526; M. 8048]. But if the defunct express his will, to leave a legacy without defalcation, it will not be defalked with the other legacies.

40. Whether a special legacy, without such express will of the defunct, will be abated proportionally with other legacies, I have not observed it oft decided; but I conceive it will not bear a proportional deduction, because, though not the express, yet the tacit and presumed will of the defunct seems to be so, else why should he leave that legacy more specially than the rest? which is more clear in things left in legacy; as when a horse, sword, clothes, &c. are left, and the other legacies are not special, there seems no reason, upon failing of the other legacies, to burden the special legacies, and abated they cannot be directly, not being quantities but bodies. The same reason is in sums specially legated; for though it may appear, that the defunct's reason may be to leave such a special debt to such a legatar, not as a favour, but because the debtor is less *solvendo*, yet with that hazard, the other advantage is consequent, that as he will get no benefit with the other legatars, so he should bear no abatement with them; and it was so decided, July 21, 1665, Spruel *contra* Murray [*Sub nom. Spreul* v *Miller*, 1 Stair 300; M. 8052]; where the question was between a special legacy left, not with other particular legacies, but with a general legacy.

41. *Quæritur*, Whether, as in the civil law [Inst. 2, 20; D. 22, 3, 21], so with us, if the testator leave a special legacy of that which he knows is not his own, it will be valid *quoad valorem?* It was found, that a special legacy left of an heritable bond, which fell not in executry, was valid to affect the dead's part of the moveables *pro tanto*, January 22, 1624, Drummond *contra* Drummond [Durie 99; M. 2261]. A legacy by a wife, ordaining an executor to discharge a bond to the legatar, was found valid, and to be made up by the wife's executors, albeit the half of the bond belonged to the husband *jure mariti*, as being *legatum rei alienæ scienter legatæ*, and the wife was presumed to know that common principle in law, and not to be ignorant thereof, June 16, 1664, Murray *contra* Executors of Rutherfoord [1 Stair 199; M. 13300; 11, 3, 46, *supra*]. It was also so decided of a bond left in legacy, which bond had been assigned by the defunct to another shortly before his death, whereof he was presumed not to be ignorant, June 24, 1664, Falconar *contra* Dougal [1 Stair 205; M. 13301]. The like was found of a legacy left by a defunct, of a sum he had upon such lands, which sum he could not but know was heritable, and could not be legated; where the executor, who was also heir, was decerned to make good the legacy, December 2, 1674, Cranstoun *contra* Brown [2 Stair 287; M. 8059]. Yet a legacy being special, bearing such a bond to be confirmed, and communicate to the legatar, was not found due, or to be made up, in respect that, after the legacy, the defunct made that bond heritable, by a supervening security, which did import the revocation of the legacy, July 8, 1673, Edmondstoun *contra* Primrose [2 Stair 205; M. 13304]. But where the testator gives a special legacy, of that which he supposeth to be his own, he

giveth it only as he hath it, without any warrandice, being merely gratuitous, and the executor is not obliged to make it good; as if he legate a sum which he supposeth moveable, and yet is truly heritable, February 21, 1663, Wardlaw *contra* Frazer of Kilmundie [1 Stair 186; M. 5703].

42. Legacies are sometimes left together in one writ, and sometimes by posterior writs, which do not derogate to the prior legacies; but all come in together. If they exceed the defunct's part, they suffer all proportional abatement, except such as are special legacies. For if one thing, or sum, be specially legated to one person, and by a posterior writ be legated to another, the posterior legacy takes place, and is a revocation of the former; and they do not come in together, *concursu partes facere;* as they would do, if left in one writ, by the Roman law, and each legatar would have but a half; but we have no such custom, or style, to legate the same thing entirely to different persons, in the same writ. And if that should happen, it is like that the posterior legacy, though in the same writ, would exclude the prior, as an alteration of the testator's mind, while his testament was a framing; for it is ordinary in the same writ, to alter prior clauses by posterior. Bonds of the tenor, as debtor and creditor *inter vivos*, or assignations to moveable bonds, they only affect dead's part, and neither the heir, the wife, nor the bairns, yet they are preferable to legacies; so bonds of provision to children on deathbed, though they have but the effect of legacies, yet they do not come in with prior legacies, to suffer a proportional abatement, but are perferred thereto, December 14, 1676, Mitchel *contra* Littlejohn [2 Stair 479; M. 3216, 8056]. And a defunct having, on deathbed, given assignation to one of his children to some of his bonds, and thereafter by his testament, nominate that child, and another his executors, and universal legatars; the universal legacy was not found to take away the prior assignation, though the same was not delivered, nor did contain a clause dispensing with delivery; but that child had both the assignation, and the half of the remainder of dead's part, January 29, 1679, Aikman *contra* Successors of Boyd [2 Stair 684; M. 11347]. A legacy by a husband to his wife, was found not to be understood to be in satisfaction of her third, but to be wholly out of the defunct's third, January 12, 1681, La. Craigleith *contra* La. Prestongrange [*Sub die* January 25, 2 Stair 840; M. 6450]. And a legacy left for building a bridge, being a definite sum, the executor having built the bridge with less expense, the superplus was applied to build another bridge in the same shire, June 18, 1678, Commissioners of Berwickshire *contra* Craw [2 Stair 621; M. 1351].

43. Legacies, donations in contemplation of death, or deeds on deathbed, may affect the defunct's whole free moveables, debts being deduced, except only as to the relict's part and bairns' part [III, 4, 24 and III, 8, 39, *supra*], which were found not to be prejudged by an assignation to a moveable sum made by the defunct on deathbed, July 10, 1628, Cant *contra* Edgar [Durie 386; M. 3199]. The reason of this limitation of legacies will easily appear, when the nature of the relict's part, and bairns' part shall be considered. The relict's

part of her husband's executry, or moveables, hath its rise from that communion of goods, betwixt man and wife *stante matrimonio*, of which, title, Conjugal Obligations, sect. 12 [1,4,17,*supra*]. The communion of goods, betwixt husband and wife, is competent *ipso jure*, without contract, as a part of that individual society, wherein marriage consists; and therefore, by the dissolution of the marriage, the communion is dissolved: so that, if the husband die first, the wife hath her share of this executry; and if the wife die first, her executors, legatars, and nearest of kin, have a share of the free moveables the husband hath, the time of her death; in which the children of that wife, though of other marriages, will have part of her share, with the children procreate betwixt the present husband and the wife, both being in a like propinquity to her.

44. The bairns' part is their *legitima*, or portion natural, so called, because it flows from that natural obligation of parents to provide for their children, which is not extended, to restrain the parent to dispose of any part of his means, but only so, as to leave a portion thereof to his children; which, because the law orders, and determines it, it is called the legitim. The bairns' part is only competent as to the father's means, and is not extended to the mother, or grandfather; nor is it extended to any but lawful children. Neither is it extended to all lawful children, but only to those who are not forisfamiliated; and it carries a third of the defunct's free moveables, debts being deduced, if his wife survived, and a half, if there was no relict.

45. But here the question ariseth, What is forisfamiliation, whether being actually out of the family be sufficient, as if the child exercise a trade apart, or be married, without the father's consent, at least without a portion or tocher from the father? Or whether it be sufficient that the child be forisfamiliat, and provided by the father, albeit the said provision be not accepted expressly "in satisfaction of the portion natural, and bairns' part?" Or whether none be accounted forisfamiliated, to exclude them from the bairns' part, unless they discharge the same, or accept a provision "in satisfaction thereof?" There be probable reasons for all the three parts; but the main doubt is, upon the last two, Whether provision be sufficient, as being presumed to be given and accepted, "in satisfaction of the portion natural." So much the rather, that, in contracts of marriage, fathers oft-times use to adject a clause; that the child contracted shall be "a bairn in the house;" which would be superfluous, if the child would be a bairn of the house, unless the bairns' part were expressly discharged: and therefore tochers and provisions being neither expressly "in satisfaction of the bairns' part," nor yet with provision, "That that child shall be a bairn in the house;" must be holden to be given and accepted, "in satisfaction of the portion natural." Which is confirmed by a decision observed by Dury, February 1, 1622 [*Smith* v *Elleis*, Durie 14; M. 4777], where Janet Eleis having pursued the executors of umquhile Patrick Eleis her father, for her share, with the rest of the four bairns, in the said Patrick's house; and that by a clause, in her contract of marriage with John

Smith, afterwards Provost of Edinburgh, providing her to be portioner of her father's free gear, with the rest of his bairns, provided the rest were forisfamiliated, and provided likewise by their father: in which case, the said Janet was found to have her share, albeit two of the bairns were not married, but only provided: whereby it appears, that the Lords accounted provision as forisfamiliation.

Yet the contrary opinion is more probable, viz. That nothing can take away the bairns' legitim, unless it be discharged. And that a presumption, of accepting a tocher, or portion, in satisfaction, will not be sufficient, unless it bear "in satisfaction of the portion natural and bairns' part." 1. Because the legitim is so strongly founded in the law of nature, and positive law, that presumption or conjecture cannot take it off. 2. This is more suitable to the civil law, which we follow in this case, whereby the difference betwixt children, being emancipated or forisfamiliated, or *sui juris*, under the paternal power, and in the family, is taken off as to the succession and legitim. And therefore there is introduced *collatio bonorum*, whereby all that the emancipated or forisfamiliated received from their father, must fall in under the accompt. So their tochers, gifts, provisions, &c. are imputed in a part of the legitim, but are never presumed to be the whole, unless it were expressed. 3. *Collatio bonorum* is ordinary with us, by which the tocher of the married children comes in the accompt of the bairn's part, which could not take place, if those tochers were presumed to be in satisfaction of the bairns' part, unless the clause "to be a bairn in the house," were expressly added. Which was so found, February 27, 1627, Ross *contra* Kellie [Durie 282; M. 2366]. Where the pursuer being married and tochered, was not excluded from the bairns' part, there being no other bairns of the family. Yet there was a wife in the family, and so the executry was tripartite. Neither was the pursuer made to bring in her portion, *collatione bonorum*. But here the contract bare, that the tocher was in satisfaction of that daughter's right to her mother's third, who was her father's first wife. If then it be urged, that the clause, "to be a bairn in the house," signifies nothing: It is answered, That the clause may be *propter majorem evidentiam et securitatem ;* but also as to the clearing of this question, Whether that clause hath not this effect, that that child should not only come in to have a share of the portion natural with the bairns of the family, as if that clause had not been adjected, but the child had come in only *provisione legis ;* in which case, the child forisfamiliated behoved to have brought in the tocher, or portion, *collatione bonorum ;* but when the child comes in also *provisione hominis*, the effect is, that it be without collation. Which is so much the more evident, that oft-times children are provided to be bairns of the house, after the rest are likewise provided. So that, when that condition is not adjected, the meaning is, that without consideration of the tocher, or former provision, the children by that clause should have equal share. And it was found, Spots. Test. Carsen *contra* Carsens [Spotiswoode 339; M. 2367].

46. Collation then hath only place amongst children, where it is not pro-

hibited, expressly or implicitly by the father, providing that child to be a bairn in the house. But collation hath no place as to the wife; because tochers in such provisions, being, as *inter vivos*, of its own nature, it is no part of the executry, but is done by the husband *in legitima potestate*, who is *dominus omnium bonorum*, at least hath *plenam administrationem*, notwithstanding the communion of goods in the wife; but *collatio* is only a remedy introduced in law, to keep equality amongst the children, who have an equal interest in their father and his moveables; but it is not introduced, to keep an equality betwixt the wife and them. Neither doth it design an equality in all things, but in provisions or tochers in money, which must be accounted to those who got the same. But land disponed to a second son for love and favour, not bearing for his portion, or in satisfaction thereof, was not found to exclude him from his share of the bairns' part, with his sister; nor to require him to collate what he got in land, February 14, 1677, Duke and Duchess of Buccleugh *contra* E. Tweddale [2 Stair 504; M. 2369]. Hence ariseth another branch of the former question, Whether, if all the children be forisfamiliated and provided, but have not discharged their portion natural or bairns' part, or accepted the provision in satisfaction thereof; if in that case they will have access to a portion natural, in prejudice of the relict and legatars? I say, if they be all provided, because if some of them be in the family unmarried and unprovided, the relict and legatars will be no more prejudged, if all the bairns come in, or only some of them, because many, or few, they will have all the bairns' part, and no more. The former case, Ross *contra* Kelly, seems to bring in the children, though all forisfamiliated, to a legitim with the relict, because there was but one child, and she married, and tochered. Only it is observed, that her provision was in satisfaction of her mother's part; so that, albeit she was married, yet it appears that she was not provided, *ex bonis paternis*, but only *ex bonis maternis*. And therefore it remains yet unclear, and there seems much reason, that the wife's interest being a division of her communion of goods, she should not divide with them who are out of the family and provided, unless they had a provision to be bairns in the family [Contrast 111, 8, 45, *supra*]. By the common practic also, Commissaries divide the executry in two, where there is a wife, and the whole children married, and so presumed to be provided. And it was so found, where there was but one child married and provided, though not expressed in satisfaction, but the child was admitted to a third, offering to confer, February 18, 1663, Dumbar of Hemprigs *contra* Frazer [1 Stair 181; M. 2367]. And where a defunct had only two daughters, besides his heir, the one in her contract of marriage, getting a tocher in full satisfaction of her portion natural and bairn's part, and the other in her contract, being provided to be a bairn in the house, was found to have the whole right to the bairns' part, and to the dead's part, and office of executry, excluding the other, who was found to succeed to no part, as being renounced in favour of her father, and returning back from him by his succession; but that it accresced to the other, though she was not executrix nominate, but dative: and therefore the confirmation of her sole executrix was sustained, January 27, 1680, Sandilands *contra* Sandilands [2 Stair 748; M. Supp. 99]

47. There is another considerable difference between the condition of the wife and children, introduced by the act of Parliament 1641, revived, Parl. 1661, cap. 32 [Bonds Act, 1661, c. 32; A.P.S. VII, 230, c. 244] whereby bonds and provisions bearing clauses of annualrent, which before were heritable, and so fell not within executry, now are moveable as to the bairns, nearest of kin, executors and legatars, only excluding the relict, and are disposable by legacy, or nomination, and at the defunct's disposal, by testament, or any deed on deathbed; and they are exhaustible by debts of the same nature: which debts of that nature do not exhaust the relict's part; which is inferred by a necessary consequence from the foresaid act of Parliament 1641 [III, 4, 24, *supra*]. For seeing thereby wives have no share of their husbands bonds bearing annualrent, as they have not the benefit, so they ought not to be burdened with such bonds, unless the husband or wife die before the term of payment of the annualrent, or that the bonds become moveable *simpliciter*, by a charge, or pursuit thereof for payment, whereby the creditor's mind is presumed to make the sum simply moveable: in which case the wife hath both the benefit and burden of such bonds in her share, July 19, 1664, Scrimzeor *contra* Murrays [1 Stair 219; M. 463]. Yet the wife hath her share of the annualrent of all bonds, though heritable, due before dissolution of the marriage: but no share of the said annualrents after, nor of the stock, June 24, 1663, *inter eosdem* [1 Stair 194; M. 464]. In this case a bond being payable to the husband and wife, the longest liver of them two, but bearing no annualrent, the relict was found to have her option, either to lift the whole, and re-employ it for her liferent use, or to have the half of the stock, seeing it bare not annualrent; but not to have both the annualrent of the whole, and the half of the stock. But bonds which exclude executors are heritable *quoad creditorem*, but moveable *quoad debitorem;* because the creditor excludes his executor: whereas the debtor's executor is not excluded, but liable. But bonds bearing clauses of infeftment are simply heritable, both as to the debtor and creditor: for by these the mind of the creditor appears, to exclude all others but his heir, except as to the bygone annualrents [II, 1, 3–4, *supra*].

48. Heirs are excluded from the bairns' part, though in the family, because of their provision by the heritage, except in two cases. First, if the heir renounce the heritage in favour of the remanent bairns; for then the heir is not to be in a worse case than they, but they come in *pari passu*, both in heritable and moveable rights, which is a kind of *collatio bonorum;* which will hold when there is no bonds but heritable bonds.

49. Secondly, it was found, if there be but one child *in familia*, and so both heir and executor, that child hath not only the heritage, but the whole bairns' part, and so abates the relict's part, and dead's part, without collation of the heritage, January 12, 1681, La. Craigleith *contra* La. Prestongrange [*Sub die* Jan. 25, 2 Stair 840; M. 6450].

50. In the division of executry, respect is had to the time of the defunct's death, as to the relict and children, though before confirmation, or any one's owning of the succession: for then, if there be a wife surviving, and children, the executry is tripartite, whether the bairns be of the same marriage, or some other marriage; as was found, June 17, 1631, Chapman *contra* Gibson [Durie 591; M.8163]: in which case there was but one bairn, who, if the father had been dead, would have been heir. The like, July 18, 1624, Henrieson *contra* Sanders [*Sub nom. Henderson* v *Sanders, et anno* 1634, Durie 728; M.8164]. So the wife and children surviving, transmit their parts to their nearest of kin *ipso jure*. And legatars have right to, and do transmit legacies to their executors, though they have not insisted or recovered them in their own life, unless the legatar die before the testator, for then the legacy is not due, or that the legacy be conditional, and the legatar die before the condition be purified. And if any of the children, who survive the defunct, die before confirmation, they transmit.

51. Yea the nearest of kin surviving, transmit their right by the Act of Parliament 1540, cap. 120 [A.P.S. 11,377,c.40] whereby it is clear that the nearest of kin have a proper right, and not solely by the office of executry: but it is more clear by the Act of Parliament 1617, cap. 14 [Executors Act, 1617, c.14; A.P.S. IV,545,c.14] which maketh *jus agnationis* to the nearest of kin, due by executors, though the nearest of kin be not confirmed executors, and so have interest only by the office. And so it was found amongst the executors of umquhile Patrick Bell in Glasgow, whose three sisters having confirmed his testament, one of them was found to transmit her share to her children, though she died before execution; for the son of that sister was found to have his share, albeit the office of executry accresced to the two sisters surviving, and with the office the third of the dead's part, February 12, 1662 [*Sub nom. Bells* v *Wilkie*, 1 Stair 96; M.9251]. The like was found since betwixt Agnes Maxwel and the E. of Wintoun [Not found]. And, after full debate, it hath been determined, that the interest of the nearest of kin is only extended to those who are existent nearest of kin the time of the confirmation of the defunct's testament, which is *aditio hæreditatis mobilium;* and the executor is *hæres fideicommissarius*, who must restore to the relict and bairns their part of the free gear, debts deduced; and to the nearest of kin, whether bairns or any other *in proximo gradu* the time of confirmation, the dead's part, the legacies deduced, reserving to the executors nominate, if they have no proper interest, a third of the dead's part unexhausted by legacies; so that the executor *adit hæreditatem*, not for himself only, but for all parties having interest, which is suitable to the entry of heirs in heritable rights, and whereby *jus sanguinis* of the nearest of kin is not prejudged, seeing immediately after the defunct's death edicts may be served, and the nearest of kin will be confirmed executors, if a nomination be not produced. And though any of the nearest of kin should die before a confirmation can be expede, it is an extraordinary contingency, which law regardeth not. And the Act of Parliament 1617 [Executors Act,

1617, c. 14; A.P.S. IV, 545, c. 14], which establisheth the right of the nearest of kin, by making executors countable to them, pre-supposeth a confirmation before the interest of the nearest of kin be established. But though the executor die before the testament be executed, there must be an executor *ad non executa*, who will be countable to those who were nearest of kin at the time of the first confirmation. And if any of them die before they attain their share, the bairns or nearest of kin will have no right, till they confirm the testament of the nearest of kin deceased, and give up an inventory of what will be due to the defunct's nearest of kin, by the executors of the prior defunct. Neither will the share of any bairn, or nearest of kin, deceasing without children, belong to the survivor *jure accrescendi*, who will not represent them *passivè*, and be liable to the debts; and therefore must be confirmed as executors to them, and thereby have both an active and passive title [111, 8, 61, *infra*]: all which was found, February 14, 1677, Duke and Duchess of Buccleugh *contra* E. Tweeddale [2 Stair 504; M. 2369].

52. By the premises it is evident how executry is to be divided, what dead's part is, and how it may be affected with legacies, or deeds of the defunct in testament, or on deathbed. For first, all persons who have no wife, or children unforisfamiliated, without husbands, and wives though they have children, have the whole disposal of the executry, and may leave legacies and donations of their moveable estates, and do other deeds on deathbed, equivalent to their free goods; so that dead's part is the whole. But if the defunct had a wife and children unforisfamiliated, then the executry is tripartite; and dead's part is a third, the wife's part is a third, and the bairns' part a third. But if the defunct have a wife and no children unforisfamiliated, the executry is bipartite, the dead's part is a half, and the wife's part another half; or if he have children unforisfamiliated, and no wife, the executry is also bipartite: and in either case, his legacies or deeds on deathbed, may be equivalent to the half of his free gear. And if the Commissaries, by error or mistake, make the division otherwise, none are prejudged thereby who are not called and compearing, but may summarily, without reduction of the confirmation, be admitted to claim their share; which was so found, Feb. 27, 1627, Ross *contra* Kello [Durie 282; M. 2366]. Children have a threefold interest in their father's executry. First, their bairns' part, wherein their father cannot prejudge them. Secondly, their interest in dead's part, whereby they have title to the office of executry, if the defunct nominate none: or thirdly, if he die, they have all that is free of dead's part, not exhausted by legacy, or by the executor's allowance for his administration, which is the third of the dead's part. And that when he nominates executors, unless they be also universal legatars, or though the children appear not to claim their office, when executors-dative are confirmed by the Commissaries.

53. This interest is common to all other nearest of kin. This is clear by the Act of Parliament 1617, cap. 14 [Executors Act, 1617, c. 14; A.P.S. IV, 545, c. 14], as to executors nominate, that the nearest of kin may pursue them

for the free gear, even for dead's part, except a third to the executors for their administration. So that if they have any legacy, it is imputed as a part of the third, and the executor nominate hath not both *separatim*, and he hath but the third of dead's part, debts and legacies being deduced. So that if there be an universal legacy to another, the executor nominate hath nothing, November 29, 1626, Forsyth *contra* Forsyth [Durie 239; M. 3923]; July 9, 1631, Wilson *contra* Tinto [Durie 593; M. 3924]; where the reason is rendered, because before the Act of Parliament 1617, defuncts might exhaust all their dead's part by legacies; and that Act was not to better executors, but to restrict them. The like, January 15, 1674, Patoun *contra* Leishman [2 Stair 253; M. 3925]. The like Spots. Executors of Moncrief *contra* Moncrief [Not found]. And seeing the said Act bears, strangers being nominate shall have but a third of the dead's part; therefore the wife will have no more but her third; or if one of the children should be nominate, or the nearest of kin: for none of these are strangers, and so have nothing for their administration but their expenses, November 28, 1676, Ker *contra* Ker [2 Stair 467; M. 3926]. But concerning executors-dative, this statute gives them no share of dead's part. The heir being executor nominate as to the executry, is a stranger, and retains a third, December , 1690 [Not found].

54. The order of confirmation is, that the Commissaries having emitted edicts, affixed on the church door where the defunct died, calling all persons having interest to confirm, then according as parties compear and compete, they prefer the greatest interest: first, the executor nominate; then the nearest of kin; thirdly, the relict, legatars, and creditors; and all failing, the procurator-fiscal, or such who are surrogate by him, who enjoyed the whole dead's part till their right were reduced on a better title. But since, not only the wife and bairns, who may call all executors to accompt for their parts, but also the nearest of kin, have been admitted to call the ordinary executors-dative to an accompt without reduction. But before the said statute all executors had the whole profit of dead's part, as the narrative of it bears. And yet of old it appears the executors had little benefit, if there was any debt, heritable or moveable; for they were only liable for a year, and thereafter to find caution to relieve the heritor, Parl. 1503, cap. 76 [A.P.S. 11,234,c. 15]. But these executors-dative have not a third of dead's part, for their administration, though they be strangers: for the statute gives that only to executors nominate, being strangers: but the fiscal, by the trust committed to Bishops to have a care of defunct's executry, and the *quota*, which is the twentieth penny of the free gear, should execute the executry, where none are nominate by the defunct; and therefore executors-dative are his assignees, surrogate in place of the fiscal, November 28, 1676, Ker *contra* Ker [2 Stair 467; M. 3926]. The Commissaries' horning had general letters, to charge all concerned to confirm, and if none appeared, they confirmed their fiscals, or datives in their place. But by the late Act of Parliament 1690 [Act 1690,c. 13; A.P.S. IX, 153, c. 16], general letters are taken away, and none can be confirmed but bairns,

wives, nearest of kin, legatars, or creditors [III,8,61,*infra*]. This interest of children, as nearest of kin, is never taken away, unless they renounce or discharge, not only the bairns' part, or portion natural, but all that they may succeed to by their father's death; but if they die before confirmation, the bairns' part is transmitted to their executors or assignees, yet not their share of dead's part. To come now to the office of executry, and what power executors have *active*, and how far they are liable *passive*, we must distinguish: executors they are either nominate, or dative, constitute by the Commissaries, and these are preferred according to their several interests in the executry; and these who are creditors of the defunct, preferred *hoc nomine*, are called executors-creditors. Executors are also principal, or *ad omissa, et male appretiata*, or *ad non executa*. And all these may be either sole executors or co-executors. All executors are obliged to give up inventory upon oath, bearing, that they have omitted nothing known to them, nor have misappretiate the same, and must find caution to make the executry forthcoming to all parties having interest. They use also to protest, that what further comes to their knowledge they may eik or add to the inventory; which they may still do before another do diligence to confirm a dative *ad omissa, et male appretiata*, or before they be pursued for super-intromission.

55. An executor nominate in England was admitted to pursue in Scotland, upon a confirmation there, without inventory, in respect of the custom there, not to make inventory, February 16, 1627, Lawson *contra* Kello [Durie 277; M.4497; I,1,16 and III,8,35,*supra*]. But in that case an executor-dative, confirmed in Scotland, having found caution, was preferred to the executor nominate and confirmed in England, Spots. Executors, *inter eosdem* [Spotiswoode 338]. An executor being decerned, though not confirmed, may pursue not only the defunct's wife and bairns to give up inventory, but also strangers, Had. November 11, 1609, Heriot *contra* Heriot [Not found]. But till he be confirmed, or have licence to pursue, he cannot pursue for payment, Had. December 12, 1622, Cathcart *contra* Cunninghame [Not found].

56. Executors intending to confirm use to get a licence to pursue; which ordinarily bears *excludendo sententiam* : which was sustained though general, to pursue for all the defunct's debts, naming none, Hope, Executors, Farquhar *contra* Law [Hope, *Maj.Pr.* IV,4,47; M.16083]. But the obtainer must be first decerned executor; for till an edict be served and an executor confirmed, there can be no title given to pursue; yet before confirmation the licence may be granted. A decreet being extracted on such a licence before confirmation, the decreet found null, Hope, Executors, Aitken *contra* Richardson [Hope, *Maj.Pr.* IV,4,34]. Licences use not to be granted after the principal confirmation; and therefore was not sustained as a title, December 14, 1621, Haliday *contra*   [Durie 7; M.3871]; yet it was sustained for pursuing a debt particularly expressed therein, being *dubii juris*, January 21, 1624, Carnousie *contra*   [Durie 99; M.16084]. The like where the licence was granted to a creditor, surrogate as executor-creditor *ad omissa*, June 30,

1665, Stevinson *contra* Crafurd [1 Stair 292; M. 16092]; February 21, 1668, Scot *contra* L. Clerkingtoun [1 Stair 529; M. 16093]; where the reason is rendered, that there is more reason to give licence after confirmation, when the worst or most doubtful debts are omitted. Executors confirmed have right to call for, and uplift all the defunct's moveables confirmed. The executor of a donatar of a liferent-escheat, was found to have right to the bygones of that liferent, before the donatar's death, and his heir to the profits of the liferent after the donatar's death; albeit there was no declarator in his life, January 28, 1671, Keiry *contra* Nicolson [1 Stair 709; M. 5448]. Sums secured by a condition in a reversion, that no redemption should be till these sums were paid, (where the disposition was not granted for these sums, as the cause thereof,) though they affect the ground disponed, yet remain a moveable right befalling to executors, February 18, 1676, Wauch *contra* Jameson [2 Stair 417; M. 5526; II, 4, 1, *supra*].

57. It useth to be controverted betwixt the heir and executor, about the rents of lands, and others, which run according to the legal terms, and decided thus [11, 6, 9, *supra*], if the heritor or liferenter survive Whitsunday and Martinmas, their executors have that whole year, albeit it be victual payable at Candlemas, because the last legal term is Martinmas. And it was so decided even in the case of a mill, February 21, 1635, L. Westnisbet *contra* L. Swintoun [Durie 757; M. 15883]. The like was found, albeit the entry of the tenant was at Whitsunday, and the conventional terms of payment of the mill-rent were, the first half at Candlemas, and the second at Whitsunday, that a liferenter surviving Martinmas, being the last legal term, had the rent of the mill, both payable at Candlemas and Whitsunday, after that Martinmas, July 20, 1671, Guthry *contra* L. Mackerstoun [1 Stair 762; M. 15890]. But if they live only till Whitsunday, then their executors have the half of the rent, victual or money; if they live till the term-day, though they die that day, their executors have the term wherein they died. And it was so found, that the defunct dying on Martinmas day, at eleven hours, his executors had the whole year's rent, Hope, Executors, Tenants of Merchistoun *contra* Napier [M. 15877]. The like where the defunct died on Martinmas day, in the afternoon, the executor got the whole year, February 16, 1642, La. Brunton relict of the Bishop of Galloway *contra* his Executors [Durie 894; M. 15885].

58. Steelbow goods (being recently set) belong to executors, after expiry of the tenant's tacks, as presumed to be the same which were set; but not to the heir, or his relict for her part, December 4, 1638, Countess of Westmoreland *contra* Countess of Hume [Durie 863; M. 14779].

59. Co-executors cannot pursue unless the rest be concurring, or called, March 8, 1634.   *contra* L. Lag [Durie 710; M. 14689]. Yet if any of the executors confirmed will not concur, and contribute equal pains and expense, the pursuit will be sustained without him; and he may be excluded by a process before the Commissaries on that ground, June 26, 1629, Young *contra* Murray [Durie 451; M. 3880]. But when co-executors have obtained sentence,

and so execute the testament, every one may pursue for their shares severally, without concourse or calling of the rest, January 25, 1665, Menzies *contra* L. Drum [1 Stair 254; M.3881]. One executor cannot discharge a debt wholly, seeing the other executors have equal share in all, March 17, 1630, Semple *contra* Mackie and Dobie [Durie 507; M.2739]. An executor's discharge was sustained, though she died before the testament was registrate, she having confirmed, made faith and found caution, Hope, Executors, Lawson *contra* La. Humby [Hope, *Maj.Pr.* IV,4,30; M.5798]. Amongst co-executors the office accresceth to the survivers, who are in the same case as if the defunct-executor had not been named: only in so far as the testament was executed before that executor's death, his share is transmitted to his executors, and accresceth not; but is transmitted *cum onere debitorum defuncti, pro rata* [III, 8,79,*infra*].

60. Assignations granted by executors have only the effect of procuratories, and cease by the death of the executor, unless they have attained effect by sentence or satisfaction, whereby alone the testament can be executed. And if all the executors die before the testament be executed, then, in so far as it is not executed, the goods remain *in bonis defuncti;* and the assignee cannot pursue, but there must be an executor *ad non executa.*

61. If all the executors be dead, and any part of the testament unexecuted, then there is place for executors *ad non executa.* A testament is executed when the debt is established in the person of the executor *activè,* and of the debtor *passivè,* either by a new security, or by a decreet: for albeit the wife's part and bairns' part befall them, rather as a division of the defunct's moveable estate, than as a succession, and so fall due to their executors, though the testament was not confirmed before their death, yet the goods are esteemed as *in bonis primi defuncti,* and must be confirmed so, as *non executa;* and yet the nearest of kin to the wife or bairns must also be confirmed executors to them, to establish the obligement of the first defunct's executors in their persons, for payment of their shares, the goods and estate being *in bonis* of the first defunct. But the bairns' interest as nearest of kin, falls not to them unless the testament be confirmed ere they die: for there is no right of representation in moveables as to the dead's part, whether befalling to bairns or others nearest of kin, though living the time of the defunct's death, but only to those who survive the confirmation [III,8,51,*supra*].

62. Executors *ad omissa et male appretiata,* ought to call the principal executor to their confirmation, else their confirmations are null, February 14, 1622, Bain *contra*   [Durie 17; M.2187]; March 12, 1631, Duff *contra* Alves [Durie 581; M.2188]. But this holds not in executors-creditors *ad omissa,* June 28, 1623, White *contra*   [Durie 68; M.2187]. These having a more favourable interest for satisfying their own debt. It may be questioned here, whether these things can be called *male appretiata,* which are appretiated by the defunct himself? Doubtless *modica differentia* is not to be regarded; but if the price be considerably to the lesion of creditors, lega-

tars, or others as being a half or third within the just price, they may be repretiated, February 1, 1662, Belshes *contra*   [1 Stair 90; M.3873]. Otherwise it stands, though both the quantity and price were known to be greater, the difference not being exorbitant, February 2, 1672, Nimmo *contra* Martin [2 Stair 59; M.3875]. Otherwise executors are comptable, according to the ordinary prices; seeing *id non agebatur* by the price, to gift to the executor; unless it had been expressed that the price should not be questioned, and then it is as a legacy to the executor, and to be imputed in part of the benefit of his office; and prejudges none but legatars. For the defunct can do no deed on deathbed, or in testament, further than extends to the dead's part.

63. Executors-creditors must instruct their debt before the Commissars; and therefore, if they have no writ to instruct it, they must pursue the nearest of kin *cognitionis causa;* and, having obtained decreet, it will instruct their interest to get confirmation as executors-creditors. Nevertheless they must instruct their debt to the defunct's creditors, or others, but the confirmation is not alone sufficient, though the debt were produced as the ground on which the Commissars preferred the creditors to be executors-dative, Spots. Testaments, Reid *contra* Lochier [Spotiswoode 338; M.13262]. Yet no objection against their title or debt, or that they are satisfied by the executry or otherwise, will exclude them, as that the debt was a bond on deathbed, though proponed by other executors-creditors, confirming within some days after, February 16, 1628, Creditors of Marshal *contra* Byres [Durie 347; M.Supp. 47]. And therefore they may confirm, and uplift much more than the debt due to them, but are liable for the superplus; but their confirmation prejudgeth not other creditors, who used diligence before their confirmation.

64. So much for the office, power, and interest of executors *activè.* Let us now consider their duty and burden *passivè.* And that is, first, all executors are liable for diligence in executing the testament, but not all equally; for those who have a profitable office, are liable for more diligence, than these who have not; as executors nominate, where dead's part is not exhausted with legacies, are most obliged for exact diligence. But if there be an universal legatar, whereby the executor hath no benefit, the executor is only liable *quoad dolum et latam culpam,* and for supine negligence, but not to use horning and poinding, but to assign whenever the legatar insisteth, June 11, 1629, Nivin *contra* Hogs [Durie 444; M.6533]. The like as to a special legacy, whereof the executor had no benefit, and the legatar might have pursued for it himself, December 2, 1628, Pool *contra* Morison [Durie 403; M.3493, 3847]. The ordinary diligence required of executors, is sentence and registrate horning against the defunct's debtors; but how soon this must be dispatched, is according to the difficulty and length of the process, *quod est in arbitrio judicis.* Executors are liable, in the first place, to the defunct's creditors, *secundum vires inventarii,* and no further. And that not only to the creditors to whom moveable debts are due, but also to the creditors in heritable debts, or obligements prestable by the executor not consisting in facts proper

to heirs, as to dispone lands, &c. Had. December 14, 1609, Gray *contra* Craig [Haddington, *Fol. Dict.* 1,246; M.3562]; February 24, 1627, Carnegie *contra* Lermonth [Durie 281; M.3564]; Hope, Executors, Adam *contra* Gray [Hope, *Maj. Pr.* IV,4,45; M.3564]. And so were found liable to employ a sum on land or annualrent for a wife's liferent-use. Hope, Executors, Trad *contra* Jackson [*Sub nom. Traill* v *Jackson*, Hope, *Maj. Pr.* IV,4,28; M.3563]. And also for warrandice of an infeftment being liquidate, July 22, 1630, Salmond *contra* Orre [Durie 533; M.14688]. And an executor was found liable to pay a creditor of the defunct, the price of lands sold to the defunct by a minute, without restricting the creditor to the heir, who only would get the right of the land by the minute, which remained incomplete; or without causing the creditor dispone the land to the executor, in lieu of the moveables exhausted by the price, reserving to the executor relief against the heir as accords, July 1, 1662, Baillie *contra* Henrison [1 Stair 118; M.3564]. And generally, creditors have their option, to pursue the heirs or executors of their defunct debtors. Yet executors were not found liable for an annualrent not accessory to a stock, for years after the defunct's death, but only his heir, February 5, 1663, Hill *contra* Maxwell [1 Stair 171; M.5473]. But if there had been no heritable right to affect, the executor would have been found liable.

It was long dubious whether executors-creditors were liable for any diligence, seeing they confirmed for payment of their own debts; and therefore were only obliged to assign to creditors after the executors themselves were satisfied, or at least that they had sufficient time to recover satisfaction. But the Lords, by Act of Sederunt, 14th of November 1679, declared executors-creditors liable for what they confirm, as other executors-dative, but that they are not obliged to confirm the whole inventory; and that they might have licence to pursue, to find out the most solvent debts of their defunct debtors, making faith that they doubted of the existency, probation, or solvency of these debts, and finding caution to confirm what they found good debt; and that other executors might be confirmed *ad omissa*, who should be liable to all parties as principal executors. The reason whereof was, because the means of orphans might be neglected by the confirmation of executors-creditors, who were obliged to give up and confirm a full inventory upon oath, though far exceeding their own debt, whereby other executors that were obliged to diligence, were excluded and hindered. Executors-creditors are liable for the defunct's privileged debts; as funeral expenses, servants' fees for a year or a term, as the servants were feed, which are preferable to the executors-creditors' own debt, November 25, 1680, Crawfurd *contra* Hutton [2 Stair 805; M.11832], where servants' fees for a year current, were found privileged, unless they were feed for a lesser time.

65. Executors have relief of all heritable debts against the heir, as the heir hath of moveable debts against the executor, July 30, 1630, Carnousie *contra* Meldrum [Durie 536; M.5205]; December 11, 1632, Shaw *contra* Shaw [*Sub nom. Shaw* v *Crawford*, Durie 657; M.5482; III,5,13,*supra*; IV,22,22, *infra*].

66. Executors may not prefer one creditor to another, and so may not make voluntary payment, but upon sentence without collusion. And if before payment, any other creditor use citation, they may not pay securely, till in a double poinding the creditors be called, and dispute their preference, December 2, 1628, Lyel *contra* Hepburn [Durie 403; M. 3867]; December 16, 1629, White *contra* Relict of the Master of Jedburgh [Durie 475; M. 3868]; July 8, 1634, Prestoun *contra* Executors of Hepburn [Durie 724; M. 3881]. Unless the creditor citing, pass from that instance, December 5, 1623, Rochead *contra* Manderstoun [Durie 87; M. 2190]. And therefore the ordinary defence is, That the inventory is exhausted by payment made upon sentences before intenting of the pursuer's cause. Yet if the executor have paid, he may allege, that the creditor to whom he hath paid, had done more timeous diligence, and so was preferable; in which case he will be heard, as if that creditor were competing. And executors may pay creditors whose debts are acknowledged in testament, without process, if the same be paid before intenting of any other creditor's pursuit; but, after citation, debts may not be paid, though given up by the defunct in testament, March 31, 1624, La. Curriehill *contra* Executors of   [Durie 125; M. 3864]. Neither may the executor pay any other debt, though before citation, in prejudice of the debts in the defunct's testament, which puts the executor *in mala fide*, and in necessity to suspend, on double poinding, even though these debtors testamentary insist not, March 8, 1631, Duff *contra* Alves [Durie 577; M. 3869]. Yea, executors may not safely pay any creditor of the defunct, not being a testamentary or privileged one, but upon sentence. Otherwise executors might before pursuit prefer what creditors they pleased, June 7, 1677, Andrew *contra* Anderson [2 Stair 521; M. 3854].

67. Executors may be pursued immediately after confirmation, before they can have time to do diligence, but the decreets against them ought to be qualified by superseding execution for a competent time, that they may do diligence.

68. Because creditors at distance may be excluded, not knowing of the defunct's death; therefore the Lords, by Act of Sederunt, February 28, 1662, did declare that all creditors of defuncts using legal diligence at any time within half a year of the defunct's death, by confirming themselves executors-creditors, or by citation of the defunct's executors, or vitious intromitters with their goods, shall all come in *pari passu*, without respect of the priority or posteriority of their diligence.

69. After the six months from the defunct's death, creditors pursuing thereafter, are preferable according to their diligence; and the collusion of executors cannot prejudge them, by defending against one and not against another, or preferring creditors obtaining decreets in inferior courts, before decreets of the Lords, (which require longer time) the citation thereof being prior to the other citation.

70. If the executor make payment *bona fide* to the relict, bairns, or legatars

of the defunct, before intenting of any creditor's clause, he will be secure against creditors intenting posterior process; for he could not hinder the payment of these, upon unknown creditors. But voluntary payment, without sentence at the instance of the relict, bairns, and legatars, will not secure him. By the Roman law, legatars were obliged to find *cautionem Mucianam*, obliging them to refund their legacies, in case posterior creditors did pursue, *l. si cujus es, ff. de jure deliberandi* [Possibly a mistake for L. *Scimus* §5 *C. de jure deliberandi*, i.e. C.6,30,22,5], which hath not been accustomed with us. But there is competent to such creditors action of repetition against the relict, bairns, or legatars, which will be instructed by their discharge to the executors.

71. Testaments or confirmations are executed, when the inventory is established in the person of the executor, either by obtaining payment, bond or decreet; yet thereby the executor becomes not to have the full property of the defunct's goods and debts so established; but he remains *fideicommissarius*, and is obliged to restore to the defunct's creditors, before his own creditors. Yea, the decreets or bonds granted to him for the defunct's estate, may be affected for debts due by the defunct. And in competitions betwixt the creditors of the defunct, and the creditors of the executor, the defunct's creditors are preferable; though the creditors of the executor *proprio nomine*, have done more diligence. And for the same cause the rebellion of the executor, or his delinquency, doth not confiscate the executry, although established in his person by decreets, in prejudice of the defunct's creditors, but only the executor's own interest therein, December 21, 1671, Gordon *contra* L. Drum [2 Stair 31; M. 3894; III, 3, 13, *supra*]; Dec. 16, 1674, L. Kelhead *contra* Irving and others [2 Stair 293; M. 3124].

72. But executors may safely pay funeral expenses, comprehending medicaments to the defunct; because these have a privilege, from the common obligation of humanity to the dead [III, 8, 64, *supra*; IV, 35, 3, *infra*], and therefore are preferable to all other debts of the defunct, and so may be paid at any time, December 16, 1674, L. Kelhead *contra* Irving and Borthwick [2 Stair 293; M. 3124]. Servants fees for a year or term as they are hired, and a term's house-mail, or drugs to the defunct on deathbed, have the like privilege.

73. Arrestment was found to put the executor *in mala fide* to pay the creditors, not calling the arrester, who being a cautioner, arrested all sums in the executor's hands due to the creditor, though he had not used diligence thereupon to make forthcoming, June 14, 1625, Cowper *contra* La. Haltoun [Durie 161; M. 3865]. Yet without legal diligence or intimation, exhausting as aforesaid, was not found relevant against a creditor, whom the executor had acknowledged by paying annualrents to him, Spots. Executors, Tailfer *contra* Moffat [Spotiswoode 120; M. 3868]. The executry is likewise exhausted, by debt due to the executor himself, without any process, but merely by exception of compensation, though he be not confirmed executor *qua* creditor, but executor otherwise.

74. The defunct's debtor will not get compensation, upon an assignation to any debt of the defunct's, taken after the defunct's decease, whereby that debtor would be preferred to other creditors doing diligence, February 8, 1662, Crawfurd *contra* E. Murray [1 Stair 95; M. 2613; 1,18,6,*supra*]; Feb. 14, 1662, Children of Mowswell *contra* Lawrie [1 Stair 100; M. 2614].

75. The old custom was, that executors behoved to get exoneration before the Commissars, calling the creditors and all having interest and counting to them. And it was not relevant to allege exhausting, by exception, but there behoved to be a decreet of exoneration obtained, which is the only full and general liberation. But it was not valid against creditors having put the executor *in mala fide*, as being creditors testamentary, or acknowledged by the executor, or using citation or arrestment, June 14, 1625, Couper *contra* La. Haltoun [Durie 161; M. 3865]. Neither was exoneration valid being general, not containing a particular account, March 10, 1632, La. Ludquharn *contra* La. Haddo [Durie 628; M. 3872].

76. But now for a long time, the Lords have been accustomed to admit the exception of exhausting, albeit there hath not been a decreet of exoneration obtained. For instructing exhausting, executors may found upon payment of the privileged debts at any time; upon the expense of confirmation; upon debts due to themselves before confirmation, (but not upon debts assigned to them after confirmation); upon payment of testamentary debts, though without process; upon payment of other debts thereafter, according to the priority of diligence; upon absolvitors by process or execution for recovery of the defunct's debts not recovered; and upon expenses of process or executions, seeing executors get no expenses modified against the defunct's debtors, who are not obliged to pay without sentence.

77. All these being allowed, if any thing in the inventory remain unrecovered, the executor will either get time to do further diligence, or will be liberate on granting of assignations to the creditors, according to their diligence. Executors are not obliged to make faith upon the defunct's debts, except in so far as may concern the executor, without prejudice to creditors, legatars, wife, bairns, and nearest of kin, Spots. Executors, Monteith *contra* Smith [Spotiswoode 113; M. 12477]; March 6, 1627, Scot *contra* Cockburn [Durie 285; M. 12477]; March 13, 1627, Ker *contra* La. Covingtoun [Durie 289; M. 12478]. And therefore they cannot exoner themselves by decreet, upon their oath, or holding them as confessed, without having other probation.

78. Executors are not convenable severally, nor liable *in solidum*, but *pro virili parte*, unless they have intromitted with as much as will satisfy the debt in question, July 22, 1630, Salmond *contra* Orre [Durie 533; M. 14688]; July 23, 1625, Atkin *contra*   [*Sub nom. Aitken* v *Hewart*, Durie 180; M. 3878]; July 12, 1626, Turnbull *contra* Mathison [Durie 212; M. 7574]; Hope, Legacies, M'Michael *contra* Mewharie [Not found].

79. If any of the executors be dead, the office accresceth to the survivers, and they are liable and convenable alone. But if the deceased hath intro-

mitted with, or done diligence for any part, in so far as the testament was executed before the executor's death, it liberates the survivers, and the pursuers must have access to those representing the deceased. But for what is wanting through negligence of the whole executors, the survivers are liable. And so where the deceased had intromitted with their share, the survivers were only found liable for their own parts, Hope, Legacies, Haliday *contra* Haliday [Hope, *Maj.Pr.* IV,4,37; M.14687; III,8,59,*supra*]; July 18, 1628, Peacock *contra* Peacock [Durie 391; M.2189]; July 23, 1625, Aitken *contra* Ewat [*Sub nom. Aitken* v *Hewart,* Durie 180; M.3878].

80. Executors are liable for the inventory, without necessity for any to prove that they intromitted therewith; which is presumed unless the executor show his diligence, and how he was excluded; which was sustained as to the moveables of the defunct, confirmed by an executor-creditor, February 7, 1679, Pearson *contra* Wright [2 Stair 689; M.3497]. And an executor was found liable for sums confirmed, due by bonds whereof the dates were expressed in the confirmation; which were presumed paid to him, seeing the bonds were not produced, January 29, 1681, Gray *contra* Brown [2 Stair 847; M.3933].

81. Executors are to be confirmed *ubi defunctus habuit domicilium;* and as to these who had houses, or residence in divers commissariots, the chief residence is the domicile, and that Commissary only confirms the whole, though in other jurisdictions, Had. June 25, 1611, L. Abercromby *contra* [Haddington, *Fol.Dict.* I,330; M.4846]. But as to defuncts residing out of the country, their testaments are confirmed at Edinburgh; yet if they die in Edinburgh, or elsewhere, not *animo remanendi,* their testaments are not to be confirmed at Edinburgh, but where they had their domicile. So albeit a defunct had dwelt in Edinburgh half a year, in a house taken for a year, and furnished for himself, it was found, that his testament behoved to be confirmed in the country; because he had his principal domicile there, with some children and servants, and attended at Edinburgh on law-affairs, Procurator Fiscal of the Commissariot of Edinburgh *contra* the Relict and Children of the deceased Earl of Panmure, February 7, 1672 [2 Stair 67; M.4847].

Title 9. Vitious Intromission

1. *Vitious Intromission is only a Passive and not Active Title, even against other Vitious Intromitters, without Assignation from the Creditor.*

2. *Vitious Intromission is the most extensive Passive Title, reaching not only those who might represent the Defunct, but all other Intromitters.*

3. *The Reason of the Large Extent of this Title.*

4. *All Vitious Intromitters are Liable* in solidum, *and Convenable severally.*

5. *Whether Vitious Intromission be competent by way of Exception.*

6. *Vitious Intromission when sustained generally.*

7. *Vitious Intromission is only Competent to Creditors.*

8. *Vitious Intromission is Excluded, if Executors were Confirmed before Citation, though after the Intromission.*

9. *Whether an Executor-creditor, being Confirmed, excludes Vitious Intromission pursued thereafter.*

VITIOUS intromission is only a passive title, making the intromitters liable to all the defunct's debts *passivè;* but is not an active title, whereby the intromitter can call and pursue *activè.* For thereupon there is no ordinary action competent at the instance of the intromitter, against his complices for mutual relief; but the intromitter paying must only make use of the creditor's name to give him a title, upon the creditor's assignation, which will necessitate the other intromitters to satisfy, but only *pro rata,* they proving that it is to the behoof of another intromitter, whose part at least must be abated.

2. This is the largest passive title, extending not only to those who have relation to the defunct, and have a title to be his heir or successor in moveables, but to any stranger intromitting without any interest; whereas *gestio pro hærede,* and successor *titulo lucrativo post contractum debitum,* can be incident to none but apparent heirs *qui præcipiunt hæreditatem.* But not only the children, and nearest of kin intromitting are liable *in solidum* for the defunct's whole debts, but any other person having no legal interest of succession; which is peculiar to this and no other nation, and not without ground.

3. The rise and reason of this passive title is, because moveables are more easily abstracted from creditors of defuncts than their lands, or profits thereof, which every one will not attain without a title, at least without being apparent heir therein. But if defuncts' moveables might be meddled with without confirmation, or making inventory upon oath, and no further hazard than single restitution, there would never be a confirmation; but both creditors and orphans would be highly prejudged, by abstracting and concealing the moveables of defuncts. And to remedy this, our law hath introduced this passive title, that without confirmation, or other title, the meddler shall be liable *in solidum* to creditors.

4. Vitious intromission is so far extended, that one intromitter may be convened singly *in solidum,* and his alleging other intromitters will not liberate him *pro tanto,* July 12, 1628, L. Moristoun *contra* L. Frendraught [Sub nom. *Cranston v Crichton,* Durie 389; M. 522]. But where more intromitters are convened, and decerned together, they are only decerned equally, though their intromission were unequal, it not being alleged that any of them were insolvent.

5. Vitious intromission is hardly competent by exception, but only by action, Yea, vitious intromission may always be purged by confirmation, before intenting of the pursuer's cause. To which it is more consonant, that they who allege vitious intromission should not be permitted to do it by exception,

but by pursuit, that before the pursuit the intromitter may have liberty to purge.

6. Vitious intromission is also sustained generally, without necessity to the pursuer to condescend on particulars, if the intromission be referred to the defender's oath, who knows his own intromission, and must either adject a quality which is competent, or propone a defence to purge the vitiosity.

7. This passive title being so large, wants not its own limitations and exceptions; as first, it is only effectual to creditors, and not to legatars, or any other party, who cannot pursue upon this ground, nor for any further than is truly intromitted with, in such cases where those can pursue intromitters, as in special legacies, &c.

The intromission must be universal; not that the intromitter must meddle with all the defunct's moveables, but must meddle *quasi per universitatem*, because heritage is *per universitatem*: and he that meddles with a flock of sheep meddles *per universitatem*; yet many of the flock may be meddled with by others, but what remains being still the flock, he is only said to meddle with the flock. And so intromission with one thing, or some small thing, will not infer this passive title.

8. It is a legal defence against vitious intromission, that there are executors confirmed to the defunct, whether it be the intromitter or any other, though the intromitter derive no right from these executors: for the confirmation gives the executor the property of the goods. Even though the intromitter caused a person wholly insolvent be confirmed, and find a cautioner *insolvendo*, and the intromitter paid the quote, and was at all the expense, July 28, 1626, Tenent *contra* Tenent [Durie 230; M. 9866]; Spots. Universal Intromitters, Stevenson *contra* Paterson [Spotiswoode 352; M. 9849].

9. Some have questioned, Whether confirmation of executors-creditors could purge vitious intromission, seeing creditors do only confirm for their own satisfaction, and not to execute the defunct's executry, and so need confirm no more than will satisfy themselves. But I have not observed it repelled, nor is the difference convincing.

10. Confirmation of executors, whether by the intromitter, or others proponed by exception or reply, to purge vitious intromission, is relevant: But not in so far as concerns those creditors who had used citation and diligence against the vitious intromitters before confirmation, whose sentences are drawn back to their citation; especially *si non sint in mora*, and so *est jus iis quæsitum*, at least *inchoatum*, before confirmation, Had. December 12, 1609, Durie *contra* Clark [Not found]. But this must be limited thus, If the creditor had used citation shortly after the defunct's death, there being no competent time to confirm, neither any time limited in law other than year and day, after which the executor must be comptable to relieve the heir; and therefore, unless the intromitter were merely *prædo*, having no interest, as neither being wife, bairn, nearest of kin, nor having a disposition without delivery, it is sufficient to confirm after the intenting of the creditor's cause, being within

year and day; in which case the intromitter confirming will be liable *secundum vires inventarii*, albeit only convened as intromitter, not as executor, without necessity of a new process. It was so found in the case of the defunct's son, who intromitting, and being cited, yet confirming within year and day, was only liable as executor, January 24, 1628, Aldie *contra* Gray [Durie 330,332; M.9867]; Hope, Executors, Bald *contra* Hamilton [*Sub nom. Bard* v *Hamilton*, Hope, *Maj.Pr.* IV,4,41; M.9865]; Spots. *eod.*, Thomson *contra* L. Rentoun [Spotiswoode 120; M.9869]; January 28, 1663, Stevenson *contra* Ker and others [1 Stair 164; M.9873].

11. The exception of confirmation of executors is elided, by alleging that the intromitter, though having confirmed, yet hath fraudently concealed some part of the goods and means, not put in the inventory; which super-intromission *dolosè*, is relevant to elide the defence on confirmation, Hope, Executors, Raeside *contra* Cathcart [Hope, *Maj.Pr.* IV,4,27]; Spots., *eod.*, Cleland *contra* Baillie [Spotiswoode 112; M.9849]. Super-intromission was also sustained without a dative *ad omissa*, to elide exhausting proponed by an executor, January 14, 1639, Inglis *contra* Bell [Durie 870; M.2737].

12. Declarator of escheat hath the same effect to exclude vitious intromission, as the confirmation of executors, which is not only competent to the donatar intromitting, but to any other intromitter, both being universal titles, reaching the defunct's moveables, every intromitter therewith is liable to him, Dec. 15, 1638, Ogilvie *contra*   [Durie 867; M.9856]. But the defence was elided by continuing possession, the gift being holden simulate. It is not relevant to allege, that the defunct died at the horn, and thereby had no moveables, they having become escheat to the King; nor that the defender had a gift, *post litem motam*, without declarator, February 7th, 1662, Gray *contra* Dalgarno [1 Stair 92; M.9850].

13. Vitious intromission was also restricted to the single value, when it is by virtue of a disposition from the defunct, albeit the disposition was found null by reply, as done in defraud of creditors, by a husband to his wife, June 16, 1671, Bonar *contra* La. Couper [*Sub nom. Bowers* v *Couper*, 1 Stair 734; M.2734]. And a disposition of moveables, with an instrument of possession, being for a cause onerous, granted while the defunct was on deathbed, though there was no natural possession till after his death, was sustained to purge vitious intromission, July 6, 1664, Brown *contra* Lawson [1 Stair 209; M.9857]. But if the disposition were shortly before the defunct's death, his continuing in possession will not infer simulation or fraud, but the same will purge the vitious intromission, at least restrict it to the single value.

14. Vitious intromission being penal, *sapiens naturam delicti*, is not to be sustained against any as representing the intromitter, when no action is intented against the intromitter in his own life [III,6,5,*supra*]; after which no other can be able to clear the title of his intromission with moveables *quæ transeunt per commercium;* and so the defunct might have bought them *bona fide*, July 10, 1666, Cranstoun *contra* Wilkison [1 Stair 391; M.10340]. Yet

though decreet were not obtained before the intromitter's death, if litiscon-testation were made against him compearing, when it was proper to him to purge his intromission by any competent defence, if the same were proven after his death, it might overtake his successors.

15. Vitious intromission is simply excluded by those who acquire, by way of commerce *bona fide* for a just price, albeit in some cases executors may re-cover defunct's goods *rei vendicatione*. But where *bona fides* doth not appear, but collusion or fraud, the buying of defunct's goods will not be sustained: as was found in the case of a party deponing that he bought a defunct's goods within ten days after the defunct's death, when he knew there could be no confirmation of the same, or lawful title thereto, albeit he deponed that the seller had a disposition from the defunct, but did not produce it, and his oath was not found to prove it, but the acquisition was found to be by collusion, the buyer being the defunct's good-son, pretending to buy from a stranger, November 29, 1679, Irving *contra* Kilpatrick [2 Stair 712; M. 13229].

THE END OF THE THIRD BOOK

BOOK IV

TITLES CONTAINED IN THE FOURTH BOOK.

BOOK IV

Title 1. The Authority of the Lords of Council and Session

THE Institutions of the Law and Customs of Scotland, as to the constitution and transmission of the several kinds of private rights, in all matters civil, having been printed and published *anno* 1681, and the copies being all sold; and now a second edition being also printed, with many corrections and additions, I would not longer disappoint the desires and expectations of many, to add the last part of the Institutions proposed in the former edition; which I did the rather forbear till now, that I might know how the former part did satisfy, and that, if any objections were made as to the former parts, they might be amended in this, where I found reason for it; and that if any had written against the matter and method I had followed, I might be able to give them a reply in this. For the matter is the same in this, and in the former parts, though here it is to be set in the form of process, pleadings and decisions. And the good acceptance the former parts have had, obliges me the more to consummate the matter, by the new edition of the former parts, and the addition of this. And in this edition I have added what alterations have occurred by law since the former, or what hath been further cleared or altered by posterior decisions, so far as I could find them, which are but very few, before I was restored, having found none observed by any of the Lords in that time.

I had not so soon published the former edition, if I had not seen evidently enough, that I could not continue to enjoy that station (to which I had right during my life,) as things then stood; for if I had continued, my modesty would not have allowed to hear any thing of mine cited, while I was present; nor had it been fit to have given any appearance of being predetermined in my judgment, in points that had not come the length of a fixed custom; and therefore I did still forbear to be positive in such points, but rather held forth what had been decided by the Lords. And in the Decisions observed by me, I have been so tender of their honour, as not to express my own particular judgment. But in this last edition, I have proposed my opinion, what emendations were just and fit to be made by Acts of Parliament, or of Sederunt. And

I do declare, that I will not esteem it my honour nor my credit, to be tenacious upon my own opinion, but ever to be ready to concur with what I shall be convinced to be just. And certainly a just inclination is best seen, and with least suspicion, by giving opinion when there is least interest or influence of any party, but the case stated as between Titius and Mævius. I have resolved very seldom to use citations of law, or of our decisions; for, in the former parts, I endeavoured rather to hold forth what had been decided by the Lords, than to give my own opinion, which now I resolve more freely to give, much of form occurring in this part; wherein I will offer my opinion, in what I think might be amended. And I may say, without vanity, that I know no man that ever had so much opportunity of experience, in this judicature, as myself, so that I should need the less to urge my opinion by decisions.

1. The first point necessary to be cleared, in judicial decision of private rights, and making the same effectual by legal execution, is to clear the jurisdiction and authority of the judicature, which is to determine the same. The authority of the Lords of Session was requisite to be known at all times, and never more than now. Some few had appealed from them to the Parliament (as is expressed in the Decisions observed by me) but when they became more calm, they did pass from their appeals, or disowned the same, as without their warrant. This was taken notice of in the Claim of Right, whereby appeals were disclaimed; yet Protestations for Remeid of Law, from the Session to the Parliament, were claimed, and very justly. But there was neither determined the time when, nor the cases in which they were competent, which yet, there is no doubt, the king and estates of Parliament will in due time determine. There is no question the Lords of Session may exceed their authority, and there is no other judicature that can control the same, or warrantably judge therein, save only the Parliament. And therefore parties grieved may protest, that they acquiesce not in such sentences, and may protest for remeid of law by the Parliament, albeit such protestations are never mentioned in our law before. But though it is not to be imagined, that by that part of the Claim of Right, it was meaned, that all the sentences of the Session might thereby warrantably be brought into the Parliament; yet of late, several persons have been so litigious, and so far mistaken in that design, that some have directly appealed, and others have protested for remeid, both against the interlocutors, and definitive sentences of the Lords.

For clearing this matter, which is of the greatest importance, on which depends much of the security of every man's right, and the quiet of their minds, by knowing how the same may become unquestionable, without the hazard of sustaining any process or plea against them; it will be necessary to show what course this nation hath followed, for obtaining this great end, which all the nations of the world (in any measure civilized) have most carefully endeavoured to establish inviolable. We shall therefore begin with the most ancient establishment for the final determination of pleas in this kingdom, by our statutes of Parliament; and thence shall proceed to the alterations made for curing any inconveniences that did appear in that establishment.

2. The establishment of this last resort of pleas and process is clearly settled, Parl. 1424, c. 45 [A.P.S. 11,8,c.24] by King James I, who was one of the most excellent and best experienced kings we ever had. He had most of his breeding among the English, by whom he had been taken while he was on his voyage to France, and detained prisoner eighteen years [1406–24]; and he was likewise for some time in France, being brought thither by Henry v, King of England, of design to influence the Scots in his favours, they having about that time fought in France with singular valour and success against the English. So that he had opportunity to learn and understand the order of the administration of justice in both these kingdoms. He did fix most of our forms, by erecting of the Chancery, and the brieves thereof, which were the fixed tenors of all summonses before the ordinary courts, as they yet are in England, and without them no suit can be commenced in the Court of Common Pleas, which is the most proper judicature of the common law of England, which brieves they enlarge by declarations, extending the same to the several special matters; and it behoved also to be so with us, till the erection of the College of Justice, wherein the Clerks or Writers to the Signet were intrusted with the forms of summonses and diligences: yet there have still remained with us some brieves of the chancery, of the greatest importance and utility, such as the brieves of mortancestry, for entering all heirs of defuncts, the brieve of idiotry, for cognoscing the furiosity or fatuity of persons, and the brieve of division, for dividing of lands, &c.

3. The narrative of that statute, *anno* 1424, is in these terms: "As anent bills of complaint, whilks may not be determined by the Parliament, for divers causes belonging the common profit of the realm." The statutory part is in these terms: "It is ordained, that the bills of complaint be execute and determined, by the judges and officers of the courts, whom to they pertain of law, either justice, chamberlain, sheriffs, bailies of burrows, baronies, or other spiritual judges, if it effeirs to them." The recourse from these ordinary judges is determined in these words: "If the judge refuse to do the law evenly, the party complainand shall have recourse to the king, who shall see rigorously punished sik judges, that it shall be example to all others." The statute also clears what is meant by doing the law evenly, viz. "That but fraud or guile they do full law and justice."

4. By this statute it is clear, that whatever the course of the final determination of process were before in Parliament, yet both king and Parliament did then determine, that it was for the common profit of the realm, that bills of complaint may not be determined by the Parliament, but that they be determined and executed by the judges ordinary of the courts which then were: As first, The Justice General, who had an universal jurisdiction, both civil and criminal through the whole kingdom, and held justice-airs through the country twice in the year, Parliament 1440, cap. 5.[A.P.S. 11,32,c.2], once on

the grass, and once on the corn, Parliament 1483, cap. 94. [Act 1485,c.94; A.P.S. 11,170,c.4]. The Chamberlain's jurisdiction is also universal, in relation to the towns, "That their common goods be observed, and kept to the common profit of the town, to be spent in common, and necessary things of the burgh, by the advice of the council in the town, and deacons of crafts, where they are, and inquisition yearly to be taken in the chamberlain-air, of expenses and dispositions of the same, and that all tacks set thereof for longer than three years, thereafter be null," Parliament 1491, cap. 36. [Common Good Act, 1491,c.36; A.P.S. 11,227,c.19]. The jurisdiction of the Justice General was restricted to criminal causes by several statutes thereafter; and the chamberlain and justice-airs came to be in desuetude, as now the whole office of the Chamberlain is neglected.

5. By this statute of King James I there is recourse to the king, but not for altering the sentences of the judges ordinary, but for punishing of them, if they had not administrate justice *without fraud or guile;* which can go no further than manifest and palpable injustice against law, which doth always infer fraud by wilful injustice, but reacheth not to dubious cases, where just and rational men may be of different judgments, unless there be corruption by bribe, or bias: otherwise no man but a beggar, or a fool, would be a judge.

6. Albeit the said establishment mentions only recourse to the king, for punishment of the malversant judges ordinary; yet the statute of the same king the next year, Parliament 1425, erecteth the Session, to which the last resort was to be had, cap. 65. [A.P.S. 11,11,c.19]. The title of this Act is, "Of the Session to be holden: of their power and expenses." The Act is in these terms: "Our Sovereign Lord the king, with consent of his Parliament, has ordained that his Chancellour, and with him certain discreet persons of the three Estates, to be chosen and depute by our Sovereign Lord the king, shall sit frae then furth, three times in the year, where the king likes to command them, which shall knaw and examine, conclude and finally determine, all and sundry complaints, causes and quarrels that may be determined by the king and his council."

7. By this statute it appears, that, before the establishment in the former year, all causes might be determined by the king and his council; so that the lieges had their option, to pursue either before the judges, or before the king and his council. But that wise king found this an unsupportable burden for the king, and insufficient for the subjects, the king's council following his court, and so neither being certain when to be found, nor able to determine all causes that might come before them, even in the first instance, did therefore ordain all causes, to be first determined by the judge ordinary, conform to the foresaid establishment. But nothing being thereby provided for a remeid, against the malversation of the judges ordinary; therefore, by this statute, the Session is erected, with power finally to determine all complaints, causes, and quarrels that might be determined before the king and his council, to wit, at that time after the establishment; whereby there was only re-

course to the king himself, without mention of his council, and only upon complaint against the judges ordinary; and therefore these complaints are committed to the Session only, to be finally determined by them, without mention of any recourse from them to any other judicature, whereby they were judges in the second instance.

8. This Court was called the Session, because it was to sit at such places as the king appointed, but was not to follow his court, as his council did before, nor to go through the kingdom as the Justice General, and Chamberlain did; by that title it was also distinguished from the ecclesiastic courts, which were called consistories, where the judges did stand in administering justice.

9. But the power of the Lords of Session is cleared and enlarged by King James 11, Parliament 1457, cap. 61. [A.P.S. 11,47,c.2] whereby it is again put in the option of parties, to pursue before the Lords, or the judges ordinary, in these terms: "And the parties complainand to have full freedom to follow their actions before the said Lords, or their ordinary judge:" but if the question concern fee or heritage, and not the matter of possession only, "The Lords shall gar the sheriff restore the party to the lawful possession, and recognosce the lands in the king's hands:" but if there be no question of right, but only of possession; "The judge ordinary should only judge thereon for a year after that Act." And by the next Act of the same Parliament [A.P.S. 11,48,c.3], the manner of bringing causes before the Lords, is determined thus: "The sheriffs of the shires where the saids Lords shall sit, shall be warned to proclame in ilk ane of the places, three months before the Session; and if any person has any action to follow, he shall wairn them to pass to the king's chapel, and raise summons, upon fifteen days at least, after the citation; and if any action pertaining to the saids Lords knowledge, be continued in the time of the Session, in the shire where the Session sits, these persons to be arrested forthwith by a macer, and justice to be done thereupon as effeirs; and all other causes pertaining to the knowledge of the saids Lords, shall be utterly decided and determined by them, but any remeid of appellation to the king or Parliament."

10. But by the next Act, viz. the 63d of the same Parliament, *anno* 1457, [A.P.S. 11,48,c.4] it is declared, "That the time of the lords sitting was but forty days, and peradventure in seven years not to come again to them;" whereby it is evident, that neither the time nor place of their sitting, when and where it was to begin and end, nor the continuance of their persons in authority were settled, but both were ambulatory, at the king's pleasure.

11. But in the reign of King James 111 the Parliament 1469, cap. 27. [Act 1469,c.26; A.P.S. 11,94,c.2] altered the former establishment, and parties were ordained "to come first to the judges ordinary of temporal lands," which there are named to be "the justices, sheriffs, stewards, bailies, and barons, provost and bailies of burrows; and if they failzie him, he shall come

to the king, and his council; or, if the judge do wrong in administration of justice, the party shall also come to the king and his council, and get letters to summon the judge ordinary; who, if his office be heritable, shall be put therefrae, for three years, if he be found in the wrong, and for ever, if it be not heritable."

12. In this statute there is no mention of remeiding the party lesed; but, on the contrary, if he get justice duly executed, and ministrate to him, "he must be content:" so that the final determination of the judges ordinary is thereby insinuated.

13. And by the same King James III Parl. 1471, cap. 42 [Act 1471,c.41; A.P.S. 11,101,c.o] it is statute, "That in time thereafter, where any brieves pleadable happens to be followed, before whatsoever judge and doom given be falsed and gainsayed, by any of the parties, and thereafter discussed in the Parliament; if it happens the doom to be determined for the party follower, baith parties shall pass again to the next justice–air, where the party defendant may take ane or mae other exceptions, dilator or peremptor, as they follow in order; but it sall not be leisume to them, to take any exception that they pre-termitted or let pass by at that time." This statute alters the first establish-ment in bringing exceptions before the Parliament, but does not appoint the cause to be determined by the Parliament, but to be remitted to the Justice-General.

14. By the same King in his Parl. 1475, cap. 63. [Act 1475,c.62; A.P.S. 11,111,c.3]. "Anent the administration of justice in civil actions and com-plaints, through all the realm", it is statute and ordained, "That all parties com-plaining shall first pass to their judge-ordinar, and pursue justice, and that the ordinar shall minister them justice without partial means or sleuth. And if the judge fails in his office and administration of justice, the party shall come and pleanzie to the King and his Council upon the judge, and likewise on the party; and in that case they shall have summons baith on the judge and on the party to compear before the King and his Council, and there have justice and reformation."

15. By this statute it is clear, that the establishment by the Session was altered, and returned to the King's Council; but there is no mention or pro-vision of any remeid against sentences of the King and his Council.

16. But the same King, in his Parl. 1487, cap. 105. [A.P.S.11, 177,c.10], statutes, "That all civil actions, questions and pleas, moved between what-somever parties, be determined and decided before their judge-ordinar, sua that na action shall be deduced, called nor determined before our Sovereign Lord's Council, except allenarly actions pertaining in special to our Sover-eign Lord, actions and complaints made be kirk-men, widows, orphans, and pupils, actions of strangers of other realms, and complaints made upon offi-cers for fault of execution of their office, or where the officers are parties themselves."

17. All that hath been formerly said of the King's Council, is not under-

stood of the Privy Council; the first mention whereof in the Acts of Parliament, is in Parl. 1489, cap. 12. [A.P.S. 11,220,c.12].

18. By King James IV in his Parl. 1503, cap. 58. [A.P.S. 11,249,c.2], the King's Daily Council, so called in distinction to the Privy Council, "is ordained to sit continually in Edinburgh, or where the King makes residence, or where it pleases him, to decide all manner of summons in civil matters, complaints, or causes daily, as they shall happen to occur, and shall have the same power as the Lords of Session had." And so their decreets became final, without appellation to King or Parliament.

19. The recourse that was before from the judges-ordinary to the King and his Council, or to the Session, was by way of complaint, wherein, if just ground was found for remeid, the party and judge-ordinary were called to answer. But because in France and other nations, appeals were in use; therefore King James I introduced appeals, Parl. 1429, cap. 116. [A.P.S. 11,18, c.6]. The terms used to signify appeals is, Falsing of Dooms, in a very rude and peremptory way; whereby a party, when the doom was given and pronounced, if he would appeal, might not remove out of the place he stood in, nor advise with any man, and behoved to assign a reason of his appeal, and protest for more reasons; but he had not any time of deliberation, whether he would appeal or not. This was remeided by King James IV. and the matter and order of appeals is clearly determined in his 6th Parl. *anno* 1503, cap. 95. [A.P.S. 11,254,c.41] "If the appeal be from sheriffs, stewards or baillies, or their deputes, the party appealing was to come within fifteen days to the Justice-Clerk and present his process of the falsing of doom, and, with advice of our Sovereign Lord or his Justice there, shall incontinent thereafter be set a justice-air, for the discussing and ending of the said doom falsed: and if the said doom be falsed in the justice-air, or if there be any other brieves pleadable presented to the Justice, and in the pursuit of them happens the doom to be falsed, within fifteen days thereafter, the party that falses the doom shall come to the Clerk of Register, who shall shaw the same to the King, who shall depute thirty or forty persons, more or fewer as pleases him, whilk shall have power as it were in a Parliament, to decide and discuss the said doom. And if the appeal be from the bailies within burgh, the party shall likewise come to the Chamberlain, who shall set a court of the burrows upon fifteen days, and make the said doom to be discussed. And where there is an appeal from a freeholder to any immediate superior of that court appealed from, he shall set his court upon fifteen days, and make the said doom to be discussed. And if it be falsed in the said court of Four Burrows, or in the Sheriff-court, to have siklike process to the court immediately superior."

20. Here is no mention of any appeal from the King and his Council to the Parliament, but only from sheriffs and bailies of royalty and regality to the Justice. And if there be an appeal from the Justice, in the second instance of that which was appealed to him, or in the first instance of processes begun before him, the discussing of that appeal from the Justice, is to be by persons

nominate by the King, who are declared to have power to determine, as it were, "in a Parliament;" which must also be done in the appeals from the court of the Four Burrows, or from the Chamberlain in the second instance upon the decreets of burrows. Neither is any appeal to be discussed by the Daily Council, who are only to determine summons in causes civil begun before them, wherein they have the same power as the Lords of Session had; from whom there was no appeal to King or Parliament.

21. This is the full and just account of the manner of discussing all civil processes, from the second Parl. of King James 1 *anno* 1424, till the fifth Parl. of King James v *anno* 1537 [Act 1532,c.36; A.P.S. 11,335,c.2]. At which time King James v having institute the College of Justice before, the same was then ratified and established in Parliament. The tenor of the institution is thus, "Concerning the order of justice, because our Sovereign Lord is most desirous to have a permanent order of justice, for the universal well of all his lieges; and therefore intends to institute a college of fourteen persons, with a President, to sit and decide upon all actions civil; and the Lords are to sit constantly at Edinburgh, and to be sworn to minister justice equally to all persons, in such causes as shall happen to come before them; with such other rules and statutes as shall please the King's Grace to make, and give to them for ordering of the same: providing always, that the Lord Chancellor when present, shall have vote, and be Principal of the said Council; and siklike, other Lords as shall please the King's Grace to join to them of his Great Council, to have vote, siklike to the number of three or four. This constitution the Estates of Parliament approves, and has chosen the persons *named after that Act*, whose processes, sentences and decreets, shall have the samin strength, force, and effect, as the decreets of the Lords of Session had in all times bygone." The same King, in his seventh Parliament, *anno* 1540, cap. 93 [A.P.S. 11,371,c.10]: "After his perfect age of twenty-five years, with the advice of the Estates, ratifies and approves, for him and his successors, the institution of the said College of Justice, to remain perpetually for the administration of justice to all the lieges of this realm, and to be honoured siklike as any other College of Justice in other realms. And attour, gives and grants to the President, Vice-President, and Senators, power to make such Acts, Statutes and Ordinances, as they shall think expedient, for ordering of processes and hasty expedition of justice."

22. By this institution of King James v this judicatory hath been ever since called the Session, or College of Justice; and the members thereof have frequently been called the Senators of the College of Justice, or Lords of Council and Session; because they have all the authority and powers of the Session institute by King James 1, or of the Daily Council erected and regulated by King James 111 and 1v.

23. It is a great mistake in some, who pretend that the Session at first was a committee of Parliament, because it bears "the Chancellor, and with him certain persons of the three estates;" but they advert not to the words

that follow, viz. "to be chosen and depute by our Sovereign Lord the King." And these also are mistaken, who think, because the king, with advice and consent of the three estates, did choose the first nomination of the Session, that therefore any total nomination must be by the king also with consent of the estates; for that nomination was a part of the first institution, which, being a law, required the consent of the estates; and yet often the king acts with consent of the estates, some things, which he might act by his own particular authority, and which require no statute, but for the greater solemnity, and satisfaction of the kingdom.

24. Some also may imagine, that that part of the institution of the College of Justice in the said Parliament 1537, cap. 68. [Not in A.P.S.], entitled, "The King's good mind anent the Lords of Session," is not an Act of Parliament, because it does not repeat the words of the consent of the estates of Parliament; which imports nothing: for whatsoever is recorded amongst the Acts of Parliament, was certainly with consent of the king and three estates, though some bear only the king, and some only the estates, and some only the Lords of Articles.

25. By this Act the king promises, "That he shall not, by any private writing, charge, command, or desire the Lords to do any thing otherwise in any matter that shall come before them, but as justice requires; or to do any thing that may break statutes made by them: and that he shall authorise, maintain and defend their persons, lands and goods, from all harm, wrong and hurt, and injury to be done to them by any manner of person: and who does in the contrary, shall be punished with all rigour. And because they present his person, and bears his authority in doing of justice, that he shall have them in special honour and maintenance, and shall give no credit to any man that will murmure them, or any of them, by doing wrong or inhonesty; but they shall be called before him, and gif they be found culpable, to be punished therefor, after the quality of the fault and demerit; and if they be found clean and innocent, the person complaining shall be punished with all rigour, and never have credit with him again. Likeas, he exeems them frae all paying of taxes, contributions, and other extraordinar charges, to be uplifted in any time thereafter: And grants to them, that gif any person dishonours and lightlies them, or any of them, any manner of way, that they command and charge, and put the person or persons in ward in any of his castles they please, till they have made satisfaction of the fault, at the Lords' consideration, if the fault be small and injurious; and gif it be great, till the king be advertised, that he may cause the same be amended, and punishment made thereof as effeirs." This Act bears to be subscribed by the king, at the castle of Stirling, the 10th June, and of his reign the nineteenth year, which was in order to put the same in the Books of Council, with the statutes made by the Lords of Session; which does not import, that it was not signed as other Acts of Parliament when it was passed.

26. The privileges of the College of Justice have been confirmed by all

the subsequent kings and queens, and without doubt, will be confirmed by their present majesties in this current Parliament.

27. The Lords of Session are declared to be judges competent to the reduction of infeftments, albeit confirmed in Parliament, Parliament 1567, cap. 18. [A.P.S. III,29,c.22]. They are also declared judges in interpretation of Acts of Oblivion, Parliament 1587, cap. 44. [A.P.S. III,448,c.27]. And it is declared, that nine ordinary Lords are sufficient at the pronouncing of decreets and interlocutors, as in all other causes, *ibid.* which alters the *quorum* in their institution, that requiring ten.

28. It is implied in, and necessarily consequent from the office of the Lords, to interpret all Acts of Parliament, without which they were not capable to determine all civil causes: they must also interpret the decreets of all courts produced before them, as the titles or interests of parties, or means of probation, in so far as they are adduced in the saids causes, without exception of decreets of Parliament: which interpretations have no other effect but in relation to the saids causes, without prejudice to other judicatories, to interpret the same as they are convinced.

29. By the 59th Act, Parliament 1661 [A.P.S. VII,305,c.336], the Lords of Session are declared to be the only proper judges, in discussing the validity or invalidity of infeftments of his majesty's property, or any other infeftments, which may not be discussed nor decided in Exchequer, neither by way of exception, action or reply; reserving always to the Exchequer to judge in all other business concerning his majesty's rents and casualties, as they might have done before the year 1633. This Act, though it bear to be an explanation of the 18th Act, Parliament 1633 [A.P.S. V,35,c.18], anent the Exchequer, yet in effect it is an abrogation thereof, stating the power of the Exchequer as it was before the said Act 1633.

30. The Lords of Session are declared the king's great Consistory, Parliament 1609, cap. 6. [A.P.S. IV,430,c.8] which is only in relation to advocations from the Commissars, or reduction of their decreets; but they are not judges in the first instance, in confirmation of testaments, or in the matter of divorce. They are also declared judges in the presentation of ministers, and in the pactions of ministers with their patrons, whether they be symoniacal or not, Parliament 1612, cap. 1. [A.P.S. IV,469,c.1].

31. After the institution of the College of Justice, all appeals or falsing of dooms, did entirely fall in desuetude and ceased; and in place thereof, came advocations of processes from other courts, suspensions of their own decreets, or of these of other courts, and reduction of their own decreets, or of the decreets of inferior courts, and of all other rights; whose forms became fixed and known. And there is no other term nor tenor of action, by way of nullity, complaint, or review, which have been introduced in other countries, by the importunity and obstinacy of parties, when they had lost the benefit of appeals; which were the ordinary remedies for superior courts to rectify and redress the sentences, interlocutory or definitive, of inferior courts.

32. When appeals were in force, they had no effect after parties did acquiesce in the sentences of judges, interlocutory or definitive, which was necessary for that great interest, the final sopiting of pleas, and ascertaining of rights: and therefore, by the Roman law, appeals were not competent, not being brought in within ten days after the sentence appealed from; for then parties were presumed to acquiesce in the sentence *præsumptione juris et de jure*, unless a clear ground for reponing them were instructed, as death, captivity, sickness, or the like. And if they did not bring in their appeal to the judge appealed to, within thirty days after their appeal, they were in the same way understood to have passed from the appeal, and to have acquiesced in the sentence. Yet they had recourse to a superior judge, upon nullity of the sentence of the inferior judge, but not upon injustice: yea, appeals were not only from interlocutory, or definitive sentences, but from acts of execution thereof. But our appeals had no time in proponing them, but behoved to be instantly, and had only fifteen days to bring them to the court appealed to.

33. Though appeals were very universal, and are yet retained in our church assembly, (the order thereof in case a laick pursued an ecclesiastic is prescribed Parliament 1426, cap. 87 [Act 1427,c.87; A.P.S. 11,14,c.5]) be cause they have no constant and continued superior judicatories, from whom they might procure advocation, nor is their time of sitting ascertained, to be so long as were necessary for appeals; yet, without vanity, it may be said, that the order instituted by King James v hath introduced a far more excellent way, in the remedies of law for obtaining justice, than by any kind of appeal. For appeals did frequently stop the course of justice, and had their rise from the prejudices and passions of parties, and their litigiousness, and had great inconveniencies; for parties are ordinarily biassed by their own interest, and when they have advice of their lawyers, and have heard them plead probable and favourable alledgeances, they are apt to trust their opinion, or their reasons, more than the deliberate sentences of indifferent judges, whom conscience and honour oblige to be signally just, justice being their peculiar character: and yet parties, upon the most mean and remote conjecture, will apprehend them to be carried another way, though they have remedies against any just suspicion from consanguinity, affinity to parties, or any interest in the cause, which might bias them. And parties, when they lose interlocutors, are frequently in fervor and passion, and therefore interpose appeals, which after some time, when they were cooled, they would not have proposed; but being engaged, and supposing they had offended the judges appealed from, they were not willing to insist further before them. And, on the other part, though judges appealed from, were not obliged to sist process, unless the case were at least dubious, importing no injustice in their sentence, but requiring the highest skill in a more solemn judicatory, where ordinarily there were more experienced judges and pleaders; yet because they were censurable, if they refused to sist process in a dubious case, they were apt to ease

themselves of litigious persons, by sending them to the superior court, and so from court to court, till they came to the last resort.

34. How much more rational and convenient is it, that the reasons against the sentences of any court should be presented unto the superior court, who were not offended nor suspected? For they, by considering the relevancy of these reasons, and by production of the process, seeing that the case truly is, as it was represented in the reasons, do advocate or call the process from that court, that the reasons of advocation may be heard and determined before them. And yet this remedy hath no place after a definitive sentence; for then the only remedy is by suspension, where the reasons and verifications are considered before the suspension pass and stop execution. But yet, though suspension be refused, and that execution goes on, reduction is competent upon nullity of any decreet or sentence; and, upon material justice, which doth not always import iniquity of the other court, because the case might be so dubious, that neither side can be esteemed a wilful and fraudulent iniquity, and yet may be over-ruled by more full consideration upon the debate of the more eminent judges and lawyers.

35. Our custom doth allow no court to advocate causes but the Session, who therefore advocate in many cases, where they cannot determine the cause, but only the reasons of advocation; and so they advocate from all the criminal courts, and have oft advocate from the Justice-General, when that court was in one person, as if the matter in question were not competent to his jurisdiction, as not being criminal but civil, or as being in the prohibited degrees of affinity or consanguinity to either party, or as interested in the cause, or as having shown enmity against the party, or as having shown partiality. So the Lords did advocate a cause of theft from a sheriff, and remitted the same to the Justice-General. And if they advocate from any criminal judge, they do either remit to the Justice-General, or name another as sheriff or bailie to determine that cause advocated, February 21, 1666,   *contra* Sheriff of Inverness [*Sub nom. McIntosh* v *Sheriff of Inverness*, 1 Stair 362; M.7411]; yea, they did suspend a decreet of assythment of the Justice-General, as being merely civil for damage, and having nothing in it of punishment, December 16, 1664, Innes *contra* Forbes of Tolquhon [1 Stair 241; M. 7415].

36. The Lords do advocate from any of the commissaries. And albeit the commissaries of Edinburgh have a superiority over the other commissaries, and may reduce their decreets, and all of them have peculiar powers, which the Lords cannot judge in the first instance; yet they can judge in the second instance by advocation, suspension, or reduction, even in their peculiar cases, but so as to remit to themselves, either simply or qualifiedly, directing the point in question. They do also reduce the decreets of inferior commissaries immediately, or the decreets of reduction of the commissaries of Edinburgh, reductive of the decreets of inferior commissaries.

37. The Lords do also reduce the decreets of the High Court of Admiral-

ty, and suspend the same. And albeit they cannot in the first instance judge a maritime cause; yet they can, in the second instance, judge of the sentence of any admiralty: and when the Judge of Admiralty did that which is only competent *ex nobili officio*, they did cognosce the same: and therefore the Judge of Admiralty having in the process of adjudication of ships, appointed an act before answer, for mutual probation; the Lords required him to proceed upon the evidences adduced, and to adjudge or assoilzie; and, because he did not, they advocate the cause from him, June 12, 1673 and July 9, 1673, Captain Gilles *contra* the Owners of the Bounder [2 Stair 185 and 207; M.11907 and 11909]; December 17, 1673, Captain Stuart *contra* Owners of the Seal-fish [2 Stair 241; M.11926]. But by the 16th Act, Parl. 1681 [A.P.S. VIII,351,c.82], advocations from the Court of Admiralty are discharged, and suspensions are to pass only *in præsentia* in time of Session, or by three Lords in the vacance; and any bill of suspension or stop, is to be discussed upon the bill summarily, without abiding the course of the roll. It is also thereby declared, that the High Court of Admiralty may review their own decreets and sentences, which no other ordinary court of law can do, nor could the Judge of Admiralty have done it before; neither is there before any mention of review in our law, but in the statute approving the judicial proceedings during the Usurpation; wherein it is provided, that the Lords may review the decreets of the Commissioners for Administration of Justice, summarily, upon complaint, without suspension or reduction, within the space of a year of that Act, or within a year of the majority of minors.

38. The Lords do judge the point of right, as to gifts given by his Majesty under his own hand, or by the Exchequer, and likewise the gifts given by the Lords of Privy Council, as of vacant stipends, which lately have been frequent.

39. Yea, the Lords may, and sometimes must suspend decreets of Parliament, as when they are fulfilled, or when full obedience is offered and refused; and that either when there is no Parliament, or in the intervals between sessions of a current Parliament; but they cannot suspend *simpliciter*, but only until the Parliament may determine. And, *in anno* 1661, they did pass a bill of suspension of a decreet of Parliament, upon this reason, that the decreet contained in the decerniture, a person who was not in the libel, process, nor citation, and yet was not decerned upon notoriety, without requiring citation; which being represented to the Earl of Middleton then Commissioner, as being an encroachment upon the Parliament, he was desired by the Lords to come and hear the dispute, which he did, and was well satisfied, seeing it was only a suspension till the Parliament should determine.

40. By this course parties are not excluded from remeids of law, upon their acquiescence, and not quarrelling for ten days; or, upon their not insisting within thirty days, as was in the most favourable appeals; but they have far greater latitude to redress themselves. Yet acquiescence in the decreets given in the Outer House *in foro contradictorio*, if the decreet be orderly ex-

tracted, makes them as effectual as if they did proceed upon dispute *in præsentia ;* because, upon consignation of a dollar (as an amand, to be forfeited to the poor, if the party be found to be litigious) [IV,1,63,*infra*] or upon a bill to the Lords, any point may be represented and determined by them all: for, if any such distinction were made of decreets *in foro*, it were impossible for one court to determine all the pleas of a nation; and therefore this acquiescence is much more favourable, just, and convenient, than these acquiescences, which exclude remeid, where appeals are in use.

41. If this course be compared with the former order, which we had by appeals, it will be evident how much more convenient it is: for most vassals in the kingdom, though they had courts, yet being vassals of a barony, they behoved to appeal first to the baron-court; and if they thought themselves lesed there, there behoved to be a second appeal, to appeal to the sheriff; and if not redressed there, there behoved to be a third appeal, to appeal to the Justice-General; and if yet unsatisfied, a fourth appeal, to appeal to delegates appointed by the King. Whereby every party might have different judges, as the King pleased. What expense of time and money behoved this procedure to require? Whereas now there is immediate application to the Session, by all, either in the first or second instance.

42. There is indeed an Act, Parl. 1. Sess. 3. Ch. 11. c. 9. [Act 1663,c.9: A.P.S. VII,451,c.3] against advocations for sums not exceeding 200 merks, which were very fit to be observed; but parties do rarely insist on that ground, knowing that it may come before the Lords at last; so the Lords do only proceed *secundum allegata et probata :* but if it were proponed, the Lords might not repel it, and the clerk of the bills ought to be ordered to present no bill for ordinary summons, where the sum claimed exceeds not 200 merks, unless it be in favour of the members of the College of Justice, whose privilege is not taken away by this Act; for their attendance upon the Session exeems them from other courts.

43. The Lords have no jurisdiction in the first instance, in these causes which proceed by brieves out of the chancery, which can only be directed to, and served by the inferior judges, such as brieves for serving of heirs, brieves for serving relicts to terces; brieves for serving tutors of law; brieves of idiotry for cognoscing furiosity or fatuity; brieves of division of lands bruiked *pro indiviso* by several heritors, except in the case of bankrupts' estates, by the late Act of Parliament; whereby, in case buyers be not found at a competent rate, the Lords are impowered to divide the bankrupt's estate, or what remains unsold, to be adjudged to the creditors.

44. The Lords do easily suspend their own decreets in absence, albeit they have proceeded upon probation by writ or witnesses, or by presumptions, and other evidences in law. And albeit compearance be made, and the most litigious debate betwixt a major and a minor; yet they do reduce their own decreets *in foro ;* not only when matters of fact then competent were omitted, but there hath been no decision yet to exclude further reasons and

arguments of law: yea, the Lords suspend sometimes, and more frequently reduce their own decreets upon compearance, by proponing new matter of fact, either emergent since the decreet, or truly come to the proponer's knowledge thereafter, although it was competent to have been proponed in the decreet, if evidence be given, that it was not *dolosè* omitted, to protract the plea. Yea, the Lords do oft-times repone parties against several certifications, they paying the expenses of the parties delayed thereby, and giving evidence of a rational excuse, and that there was no fraud in the case.

45. If any complaint be made of the unwarrantable extracting of decreets *in foro*, or that they were inconform to the interlocutors; the Lords do ordinarily call in the decreet, without reduction, if the alledgeance be relevant, and instructed, if it be questioned *de recenti*, even without suspension or reduction. And the Lords do frequently, upon new application, resume in consideration, their former interlocutors, even upon the point of material justice; whether in relation to the relevancy, or the probation, before the final sentence be pronounced and extracted. The Lords do also reduce their decreets *in foro*, upon reprobatures protested for, against the hability of the witnesses, and the truth of their preliminaries, when at the time of their examinations, reprobatures are protested for; otherwise parties are presumed to acquiesce in the witnesses, and cannot reduce upon their inhability, or upon the falsehood of their preliminaries; but in no case can they reduce upon the falsehood of their concurring testimonies.

46. But the Lords have never reduced or altered their decreets upon alledgeances, either in fact or law, which were proponed and repelled therein; and if they should so do, there could be no end of pleas. For if they could alter the first time, by admitting that which they did repel, or by repelling that which they did sustain; there is nothing could secure the lieges, but that they would return again to their first judgment, and back from that to the second, without end; and thereby no man could, with security and confidence, call any thing his own; therefore custom hath so secured that point, "proponed and repelled," that it is an unbrangable foundation of all the securities of the nation. All nations have been earnest and anxious, that there might be a known termination of pleas, *reipublicæ interest ut sit finis litium ;* it would mar the quiet of any nation, if they could have no rights, but what might be brought in question; but if there were a sentence attainable, which, without dispute, might be opponed to all that might be said against it, without another answer; then might they say, *hic murus aheneus esto.*

47. The strongest objection that can be adduced is, That wrong can have no warrant, and that it is against moral honesty to adhere to that which might be convinced to be materially unjust. But this bugbear will import nothing, when rightly considered: Can there be any doubt, but decreets with consent of parties, are more solemn and strong than private contracts, which yet are liable to the same objections? It might be more strongly objected against prescription, whereby rights are cut off by the course of time; that the finding

out of no evidents can recal, although thereby the right cut off may be as evident as the meridian light: and in long prescriptions there is no retreat upon pretence of fraud, either at the entry, or endurance of the possessor, if the possession be not interrupted. All which is maintained, *Ne dominia rerum sint incerta, ne lites sint æternæ*. And though some few may have prejudice by this necessary sopiting of process; yet, according to the English axiom, Better a mischief to a few, than an inconvenience to all.

Divine authority asserts, than an oath interposed is the end of all strife, especially when it is referred, or deferred by the parties pleading; and though the clearest proof by writ should instruct the contrary, yet the strife is ended, *Lis est sopita, lis est finita, res judicata pro veritate habetur, præsumptione juris et de jure*, which admits no contrary probation. A fixed custom of a nation is a common consent of all and every one, and cannot be altered without the same common consent, or by a law, wherein also the common consent of all the commonwealth is implied.

48. This termination of pleas is not founded upon the honour and authority of the Lords of Session, but upon the most eminent and evident common interest of the nation: and therefore, as an oath terminates pleas, though perjury were proven, yet the perjury may be punished; so may the Lords of Session, if they do by fraud, or wilfulness, give an unjust decreet, yet the decreet will stand; and they will be the more tender of solemn decreets, that they cannot reduce them. It is not the Lords' tenaciousness for their honour and reputation of their justice, that makes them stand to this: for, if a decreet be found null through want of a necessary point, the Lords have frequently recalled the same interlocutors, which they neither would nor could recal, except in the case of nullity, and yet the point of honour is alike in both. And they do of course hear, and consider again, all alledgeances and decreets in absence, because both parties have not been heard, although the case hath been clearly enough proposed and unanimously determined.

49. The reason why the Lords reduce decreets upon nullities, is, because these points which infer nullity come not to be considered, nor determined by the Lords; but are to be noticed, and observed, by parties and lawyers.

50. There is another requisite for termination of pleas, and securing of rights, viz. That decreets of the Lords *in foro contradictorio*, cannot be loosed nor reduced upon alledgeances, which were competent before final sentences, and were omitted, and not proponed. The reason of this is, because litigious parties might draw pleas to a great length, by forbearing to propone all that they might propone in law, or fact, before sentence, and might again suspend upon new grounds, and so make as many processes and decreets as they could have defences; whereby the litigious would overthrow the innocent, and the rich, the poor, by wearying them out, and making then unable to attain their right. This defence against quarrelling decreets *in foro*, was accustomed only to be extended, for defence of decreets in the first instance by ordinary actions, but not in decreets of suspension: and therefore parties were accus-

tomed to be absent in the first decreet, and to spin out as many suspensions and decreets thereupon, as they could adduce, or pretend reasons in law, or fact; and that, because reasons of suspension behoved to be instantly verified, and so as they got new instructions, they might raise new suspensions. To obviate which inconveniences, the Lords, by Act of Sederunt, *in anno* 1649, declared that they would not sustain reasons of suspension, which were competent and omitted, either in the first decreet, or in subsequent decreets of suspension; which did not exclude reasons of suspension that required a course of probation, because these were not competent in suspensions, to stop the execution of decreets, but by reduction, unless it had been in the first suspension of a decreet in absence: and if new instructions were found after the decreet, and that it did appear by sufficient evidence, that they were not *dolosè* omitted, they were receivable against decreets, as well in the first instance, as in the second. And as for alledgeances *in jure, ignorantia juris neminem excusat;* and if parties do not employ skilful advocates, it is their own fault, and ought not to prejudge others, but "competent and omitted" is not sustained against strangers, July 23, 1667, Hans Jurdan *contra* Capt. Logan [1 Stair 477; M.12222]. Neither is it sustained against the decreets of inferior courts, *ubi non est copia peritorum,* unless it did appear to be *dolosè* omitted in cases obvious to every capacity, January 31, 1677, Gardin *contra* Paterson [*Sub nom. Garden* v *Pearson,* 2 Stair 501; M.6664]; February 13, 1677, Baggat *contra* Caldwell [2 Stair 504; M.12228]. But it was sustained in a decreet *in foro,* proceeding upon an act before answer, as well as upon an ordinary litiscontestation, June 4, 1674, Cockburn *contra* Halyburton [2 Stair 268; M.12164].

51. This defence, competent and omitted, is not only necessary for termination of pleas; and innocent, because it takes no place where it is purged of fraud; but it hath also been established by the 42nd Act, Parl. 1471, [Act 1471,c.41; A.P.S. 11,101,c.o] bearing, "That if any doom be falsed, and discussed in Parliament, if it happens the doom to be determined for the party-follower, baith parties shall pass again to the next justice-air, where the party-defendant may take an or mae other exceptions dilator or peremptor, as they follow in order; but it shall not be leisom to them to take any exception, that they pretermitted, or let pass by at that time;" whereby not only "competent and omitted" is established, when it is absolutely omitted, but even when it is omitted to be proponed in its due order: and so dilators are not competent after peremptors. Also in the Act of Regulation competent and omitted is established by Act of Parliament [Courts Act, 1672, c.16; A.P.S. VIII,80,c.40].

52. The authority of the most solemn sentences of Session being thus cleared, it comes next to be considered, how far protestations for remeid of law, from the Session to the Parliament, ought to be extended; that is, how far now there is law or custom for extending such protestations, and how far it would be to the common benefit of the nation, by a statute to extend the

effect of such protestations. As to which, consider, 1. That certainly there is no custom for bringing causes unto the Parliament on such protestations, though the narrowest inquiry were made, both by the records of Parliament and Session. 2. There is no statute, nor Act of Parliament, for bringing processes from the Session to the Parliament, in any of all the constitutions, or orders of government before related: for before the erection of the Session, "it is ordained, that the bills of complaint be execute and determined by the judges and officers of the courts whom till they pertain of law, viz. justice, chamberlain, sheriffs, bailies, and spiritual judges; and if the judge refuse to do the law evenly, the party complaining shall have recourse to the King, who shall see rigorously punished sik judges"; Parl. 1424, cap. 25. [A.P.S. 11,8, c.24]. And when the Session was erected, their power is expressed in these terms, "That they shall know, examine, conclude, and finally determine all and sundry complaints, causes and quarrels that may be determined before the King and his Council": Parl. 1425, cap. 65. [A.P.S. 11,11,c.19].

53. There is neither expression nor insinuation in either of these constitutions, for bringing causes from the Session to the Parliament, but on the contrary, "That it was for the common profit of the realm, that bills of complaint may not be determined by the Parliament, but that they be determined and execute by the judges-ordinar." Yea, it is expressly statute [A.P.S. 11, 48,c.3], "That all causes pertaining to the knowledge of the Lords, shall be utterly decided and determined by them, but any remeid of appellation to the King or the Parliament."

54. And when the Daily Council was set up again, and appeals brought in and ordered, as hath been before shown, the last resort was to delegates to be named by the King, to determine as if it had been determined in Parliament, without any mention of an appeal, or of a complaint to the Parliament, except once in relation to pleadable brieves [A.P.S. 11,101,c.0], which yet doth not bear, that the Parliament should determine the cause, but that when an exception was brought to be considered in Parliament, it was provided, "That it should return and be determined by the next justice-air," which is wholly hetroclite from the order then established. So that it cannot, with any congruity, be otherwise interpreted, than when the Justice-General being doubtful of an exception, referred it to the Parliament to be cleared, and whether any more exceptions should be received: for in the ordinary course, the King's Council had the same power as the Session had, and so might determine without appeal to the King or Parliament; which was in relation to causes brought before themselves in the first instance; but there lay no appeal to them, as is clear by the Act ordering appeals.

55. There is as little ground of bringing processes from the Session to the Parliament, by the institution of the College of Justice; for thereby the Senators of the College of Justice had the same power and authority that the Lords of Session and the Daily Council had before; and so their final sentences were ultimate, without appeal to King or Parliament, appeals then be-

ing in vigour and observance, but did absolutely become in desuetude and cease, by the institution of the College of Justice.

56. Yet protestations for remeid of law are not in all cases against law, but are sometimes just and necessary, as when the Lords of Session determine without, and beyond their authority and jurisdiction committed to them. But this is not peculiar to the Lords of Session; for it is competent against the sentences and decreets of all sovereign courts ordinary, when they exceed their proper jurisdiction; for no other court can redress what they so do, but only the Parliament. And though the Estates in the Claim of Right [1689, A.P.S. IX,38,c.28], did particularly declare against appeals from the Session, and did declare for protestations for remeid of law, because some had attempted to appeal from the Session, for protesting against the sentences of the Lords, more than against the sentences of any other supreme judge-ordinary; yet this being *remedium extraordinarium*, which hath not occurred in any memory, but of late, it is no wonder that in our written law there be no mention of it. But of late, since the Claim of Right, many have made use of such protestations, as if it had been designed that every one, at their arbitriment, might thereby bring their actions from the Session to the Parliament, which cannot be thought to have been the meaning of the Estates, seeing it were impossible for the Parliament, which sitteth but seldom, and hath no determinate time, to discuss all these protestations, which every litigious person might bring in: therefore, till the King and Estates of Parliament determine in what cases such protestations may warrantably be used, and in what cases they ought to be punished, as murmuring against the Lords, it is fit to consider and propose in what cases the lieges may ensnare themselves, and become liable to punishment for murmuring against the Lords, contrary to the institution of the College of Justice, and the authority and privileges thereof.

57. First then, This protestation is not an ordinar, but an extraordinar remeid, which the Lords are not obliged to admit of in all cases: and particularly, an extraordinar remeid is never to be allowed, where an ordinar is competent; and therefore is never to be allowed where the Lords, by their authority, can give remeid of law. In what cases the Lords may give remeid against their own sentences, hath been before expressed. Therefore such protestations ought not to be used against interlocutory sentences, except declinators of the Lords' jurisdiction, where they have not authority, neither against decreets in absence, neither against decreets of suspension, upon allegeances not instantly verified; because there is a remeid for such by way of reduction, without stopping execution in the mean time. And in very many cases the Lords admit not exceptions, or allegeances in the first instance, where they are not instantly verified, but reserve the same to another instance; as in general declarators they refer many exceptions to special declarators: and other allegeances they reserve *contra executionem*, as is ordinary in adjudications, because these only come to have a share who adjudge within the year after the first effectual adjudication. The Lords are also very apt to

repone parties against circumduction of the term, when recently proposed, upon reasonable excuses against contumacy, and upon competent evidence; or to repone parties holden as confessed to their oaths.

58. And on the other part, there is no doubt that the lieges have right to protest for remeid of law, from the Session to the Parliament, whensoever the Session determines beyond, and without the authority given them by the King and Estates in Parliament, for they have but a limited jurisdiction.

And therefore, first, No decision passed in Parliament betwixt party and party, by process after cognition of the cause, shall be called in question by any inferior judge, Parl. 1587, cap. 39. [A.P.S. III,443,c.16]. This does not hinder the suspending of the decreets of Parliament, upon obedience, by the Lords, when the Parliament is not sitting, which does nowise call in question the sentence of the Parliament.

Thence it is also clear that the Parliament may decide causes upon cognition before themselves, which will not warrant parties to raise process before the Parliament, even in the first instance, as they do before the Session, which must determine every cause that is brought before them, but warrant should be obtained from the Parliament for processes to be decided before them, that no more may be admitted than they see reasonable, otherwise a great inconvenience would follow, that parties by intenting process before the Parliament, might propone declinators of the Session in the same cause; unless it were remitted to the Session, as the Parliament did in the reduction of the forfeiture of James Wood, apparent [heir] of Boningtoun, as appears by the fifth unprinted Act, Parl. 1604 [A.P.S. IV,273,c.6], and thereby parties who found themselves to be most in danger, and to have least right, might intent a process before the Parliament, declaratory of their right, that the Session might not be in capacity to cognosce the same, if there were not an antecedent warrant of Parliament for that process.

The Parliament of old did ordinarily name a committee of their number to determine causes before them, who were called *Domini ad querelas*, as the Lords of Articles were called *Domini ad articulos*: but since the institution of the College of Justice that hath not been ordinary, except in extraordinary cases, as after revolutions: and so in the Parl. 1661, (being the first after King Charles 11's restauration) there was a committee of the same kind, but termed the Committee of Bills, which judged in causes brought before them, in the first instance, not generally, but upon account of oppression, or of necessity of a present remedy, the Session then not having been re-established after the Usurpation.

The Commission for Valuation of Teinds was instituted by several Acts of Parliament, not as a committee of Parliament, terminate with the Parliament, but as a standing commission, continuing as an ordinary judicature until another commission were named, with a parliamentary authority, in some points extraordinary, which were necessary for the end for which it was erected. They are the only ordinary judicature having power to value teinds, to modify stipends to ministers, to allocate the same upon the teinds of particular lands, to sell teinds in the hands of titulars or tacksmen to the heritors; and because the teinds were generally under tacks, having less tack-duties than could be sufficient for the ministers' stipends, therefore the Commission hath an extraordinary power to heighten the tack-duties, and, in recompense thereof, to prorogate the tacks. They have also power to divide or unite parishes, and to alter the situation of kirks. But these things being done, the rights arising therefrom belong not to their jurisdiction, but to the Lords of Session.

The Privy Council hath also its proper jurisdiction as to matters of state, and preserving of the public peace, and determining and punishing all riots and violent encroachments upon lawful possession. The Lords of Justiciary are the supreme ordinary judges in criminals. The Admiral is the only judge of prizes, and some maritime causes, in the first instance; and by the forementioned Act of Parliament the Lords of Session are excluded from advocating such causes. And the Commissaries are the proper judges in the confirmation of testaments, and in the matter of divorce. And inferior courts are the only competent judges, in the first instance, of sums not exceeding 200 merks.

In these things, therefore, there may be a protestation for remeid of law from the Session to the Parliament, if they shall decide and determine these proper subjects of the other courts.

59. There may be likewise a protestation for remeid of law from the Session to the Parliament, if they shall reduce or alter their own decreets *in foro contradictorio*, upon iniquity, wherein they have no jurisdiction, because they are *functi officio* : their decreets are declared final and ultimate, without any remeid by appellation to the King or to the Parliament, appellation being then the ordinar remeid. And if there be no appeal to the King, or to the Parliament, but that their solemn sentences be final, there is no pretence for themselves to reduce the same; for then their sentences should not be final, neither could there be any termination of pleas; which would be contrary to one of the greatest interests of mankind, which hath been endeavoured to be prevented by this and all other civil nations. For if, upon allegeance of iniquity, the solemn sentences of the Lords should come again to be determined in Parliament, pleas would be unavoidably perpetuated, as will forthwith appear. Yea, if the Lords of Session should recal or reduce their solemn decreets, upon new arguments, pleas would never end, so long as human invention can continue: for new pretences will never be wanting, if they were receivable upon new arguments. But if new matter of fact, competent and known, before solemn decreets *in foro* were admitted, the rich and litigious might thereby weary out the innocent, and there could not be that termination of pleas that is necessary and requisite for the quiet of men's minds, and the security of their rights. No nation doth allow fraudulent deeds, much less such fraud as hath so pernicious consequences.

60. The extremes on either hand being equally thus cleared, there remains no more in controversy, but as to protestations for remeid of law, upon allegeance of injustice or iniquity committed by the Lords; as to which there is difference to be made of their sentences out of the sphere of their jurisdiction, and these within the sphere thereof.

Their sentences without their jurisdiction may be questioned in two cases, 1. In declinators, refusing their jurisdiction, in things not proper thereto; which if they repel, and sustain themselves competent where they are not, if the party repelled protest for remeid of law to the Parliament; in so far the justice of that sentence repelling the declinator must be discussed in Parliament, and can be nowhere else determined; yet it will not stop their procedure, unless they voluntarily do the same, but it will annul the sentence upon incompetency.

But, 2. It is more doubtful what should be said, if parties called before the Lords, in causes not competent to their jurisdiction, shall not decline, or, having declined and being repelled, shall yet proceed in their defences: for, in either of these cases, the defenders do prorogate the jurisdiction, and so do consent thereto, and consequently cannot quarrel these sentences, unless they be allowed to quarrel all their sentences upon iniquity, not only as to the competency, but as to the material justice of the cause. Yet, even in these cases, there is a great difference between their sentences, which have only vigour by the consent of parties, and these which have force by their proper authority; for the prorogation of their authority states them but as arbiters, whose decreets are quarrellable, not only upon incompetency, but upon enorm lesion, by iniquity.

61. But that the meaning of the Estates in the Claim of Right [1689, A.P.S. IX,38,c.28] should be understood to be, that parties in their humour, at their pleasure, might protest for remeid of law by the Parliament, upon allegeance of injustice, in matters proper to the Lords' jurisdiction, can hardly be supposed, for many reasons.

First, If protestations be admitted in this case to any one, it must be equally to all, seeing there is no ground of distinction; and then farewell all honour, deference, or respect to that judicature, which hath been in great reputation, both by natives and strangers, since the institution of the College of Justice; so that, in that case, no murmuring against them can be the least fault, albeit they represent the King's person, and bear his authority, and have been acknowledged as the supreme judicature in all cases civil, Parliament 1661, cap. 23. [A.P.S. VII,240,c.260], and the supreme judges under his majesty in all causes civil, Parliament 1661, cap. 50. [A.P.S. VII,250,c.270].

Secondly, If, upon pretence of iniquity, the sentences of the Lords be all recognoscible in Parliament, it would require perpetual Parliaments: for all causes behoved to be pleaded of new before the Parliament, which yet have no fixed time of their sitting; and if they should, would make an untolerable burden of expenses upon the nation.

Thirdly, It will be obvious to every capacity, to consider whether the rights and interests of the nation will be more secured by the determination of judges, who have devoted their lives and studies to meditate on and understand, not only material justice, the common rule of the world, but also the particular statutes of this and neighbouring nations, and who are censured if they go out of the bounds of discretion, than if they were to be determined by the Parliament, the greatest part of the members whereof, (without the least derogation to their honour, natural abilities and faithfulness,) cannot be so qualified, nor are they censurable for any thing they shall do.

Fourthly, If the sentences of the Lords of Session be recognosced in Parliament, then it is impossible to terminate pleas, and so no man can say that any right he hath, or can have, may be secure: for they can never be without question and debate, what is just and what is not; and that to any process that shall be intented they may at last say, there can be no further process, because, what is alleged, is already proponed and repelled, without necessity to make further answer. In this all ordinary judicatures are at an end in determining rights, and are punishable if they bring the matter again in question, which is not possible to be in the decreets of Parliament; because the Parliament can never exclude the full liberty of themselves, or of their successors; no more than persons can by one resolution secure that they cannot resolve the contrary; and therefore the same Session of Parliament may judge that to be unjust, that it judged to be just, and contrariwise, as oft as they will; and much more may different Parliaments: for, whatever a Parliament can do at one time, in making of laws, or determining of causes, may be at their pleasure abrogate or derogate.

Fifthly, Such protestations upon account of injustice, would at once unhinge the most solemn sentences of all the judicatures of the nation; for there was no anterior law, more in relation to the Session, than to any other judicature; and much more was established by express law for the Session, than for any other judicature, their sentences being declared final, and without remeid by appellation to the King or Parliament: yet the same is the right both of the Privy Council and Justiciary, who are supreme ordinary judges in their proper jurisdictions. So, whatsoever hath been said before, of that common interest of mankind for termination of pleas, is much more evident in the decisions of Parliament.

Sixthly, It is another great and common interest, that men's rights ought to be determined, not alone by the laws standing when the determination is, but by the laws that were standing when the rights were acquired, or the deeds done, although thereafter these laws were abrogated: so the rights of teinds, benefices, and patronage, that were acquired in the time of popery, are to be judged by the canon law: the rights of land before King James 1 were sufficiently established by charters, and being entered in natural possession, without seasin; and these acquired after that, were sufficiently established by charter, precept, and symbolical possession by the instrument of a notar, without necessity of being registrate; but now, since the Act for registration of seasins, rights of lands cannot be established against singular successors, without such an instrument of seasin being registrate. And therefore, seeing the sentences of the Lords of Session, at the first institution, were declared to be final, without appeal to King or Parliament, and the same power was given to the King's Daily Council, and again the same power was given to the Senators of the College of Justice: Can the sentences given conform to these laws, be altered or reduced, while these laws are standing?

It would be a pitiful evasion to pretend, that albeit the sentences of the Lords were without remeid by appeal, yet now appeals have ceased, which hinders not but that they may be reviewed or reduced in Parliament; for the meaning of statutes is not to be measured by words, but by the sense and intent, which is evident to be, that there might be an end of pleas; and they would have been plainly elusory, if there had been remeid by review or reduction, which might have been used when appeals were in vigour; but both the words and meaning of the statute is, that the sentences shall be final, without remeid; and though appellation, which was then the ordinar remeid, be named; yet the remeid is not by the appeal, but by the reduction following upon the appeal, as now it would be upon the protestation: the difference of which is only this, that, in appeals, sometimes the judge appealed from, sisted, but was not obliged to sist, unless the case had been at least dubious; whereas protestation doth not sist process or execution in any case; and though in that it be easier than an appeal, yet in this it is more inconvenient, that if an appeal was not brought in, and insisted in before the judge appealed to, in a few days, it was deserted, and no further remeid was allowed; but there is nothing determined to regulate those protestations, either when they shall be taken, or when they shall be insisted in.

62. The jurisdiction of the Lords is exercised thus. At the first institution of the College of Justice, ten of the ordinar Lords made a *quorum*, but thereafter it was brought to nine, as hath been before shown. This *quorum* must be present at all interlocutors, and sentences upon dispute *in præsentia*, upon report, and upon deliverances on bills: and there is no difference of power, whether the *quorum* be more or less, providing they be always nine.

63. One of the Lords hears causes disputed in the Outer-House, and determines the same, where he finds the case clear; but if it be dubious, he doth either of his own proper motion declare, that he will advise with the Lords; or if any Advocate press for the Lords' answer, if there be any dubiety, the Ordinary will not refuse it, upon consigning of a dollar as an amand, to be forfeited to the poor, if the proponer by found litigious. But if the case be fully clear, the Ordinary may refuse an amand, and yet the proponer may give in a bill to the Lords with his reasons, which will cost him more, and he may receive a reprimand if his bill be found impertinent, which these who are ingenuous and tender of their credit will not do. So the Ordinary in this case judges as a *quorum* doth, and not by delegation only, but by the institu-

tion, whereby the sentences interlocutory or definitive of the Ordinary, have the same effect as these of a *quorum*, and as acquiesced in. But the Ordinary may stop the same to hear the parties further, being in his own week, when he sits without, or within six days after the interlocutor: and for discussing any such stops as he hath given in his own week, he sits without the next week thereafter, before the Ordinary of that week come out; and if he cannot reach all in that week, he hath an hour at the side-bar weekly, till he dispatch all that he stopped in his week.

64. When any point is to be reported to the Lords, the parties are allowed inspection of the minutes, and if either party find any thing not minuted as it was proponed, upon application to the Ordinary, he will order it, and will allow either party to add reasons in law for the same, being in his own week, or the week following: and that either party may be ready, the Ordinary affixes upon the wall, a roll of these causes he is to hear again in the subsequent week, or at the by-bar.

65. The Ordinary, in discussing of causes, must exactly follow his roll, and may not continue, or pass by any cause, unless he decline himself, or be declined upon a relevant ground; in which case the next Ordinary goeth out before him the next day, to hear and determine the same.

66. The Ordinary may not give a stop, until he receive a note of the points desired to be heard, whether the same be new matter of fact, or new reasons of law, against his former interlocutor; whereof there should be two doubles, one to be detained by the Ordinary, and the other to be delivered to the sub-clerk to give up to the party concerned, that he may see and be ready to answer the same; with which note the double of the former interlocutor should be given to the Ordinary by the party; whereupon the Ordinary must put the same in his particular roll, either for the next week after he was Ordinary, or for the by-bar.

67. No bill should be given in to the Lords, or read, which hath a remeid by the Ordinary; unless the bill bear, that the Ordinary repelled, or refused to hear upon the application as aforesaid; for an extraordinary remeid by a bill to the Lords, should not be used while there is an ordinary remeid by the Lord Ordinary.

68. Another of the Lords doth weekly serve upon the Bills of Advocation and Suspension, both in the time of Session and of vacance, to whom only in their weeks these bills are to be presented, that there be not clashing nor confusion. And if the Ordinary give any bill to be seen, or give a stop of execution; the passing, or refusing, or the hearing and determining that bill, albeit it were presented on Saturday, and so cannot be answered till Tuesday thereafter, yet it returns to the Ordinary to whom it was first presented. And the Ordinary ought to give an answer to every bill of suspension or advocation offered in his week, and sign his deliverance thereupon. But if it be a bill of suspension against a decreet *in foro*, if it be in Session time, the Ordinary cannot pass it, but must report it to the Lords; or if it require a charge to set

at liberty. But if such a bill be presented in the vacance, it may be refused by the Ordinary alone; but it cannot be past, but by a meeting of three of the Lords, and that by the next preceding and subsequent to the Ordinary, if they be in town. If the Ordinary hear parties upon a bill, either as to passing thereof, or as to the discussing of the cause upon a bill of suspension, or even the cause advocated being so referred; the Ordinary hath privilege, at any time to intimate at the by-bar, that he is to hear such a bill, having given competent time to the other party to see the same; and to appoint the time, when he will hear the same, which must be at the by-bar, before the hours designed for hearing of causes, which came from the Outer-House; otherwise their time would be confounded, and none would be secure when to be heard. Also he only passeth all the ordinary bills of horning, caption, summons and diligences, the deliverance being written on the back thereof by the clerk of the bills, whose trust it is, that nothing pass but what is ordinary, until he obtain special warrant; the rest pass of course without the Ordinary's observation; for one of the Lords were not able to read them, in the time he is to attend, hundreds being oft-times presented together, yet all are past *periculo petentium*.

If a bill hath been presented and refused, the clerk of the bills ought to retain the bill; and if another bill be presented, he ought to show the Ordinary the refused bill, that if the new bill contain new matter of fact, he may pass or refuse it; but if it only contain arguments of law or reason, urging the former points, he may not pass, but by a meeting of three, or by a report to the Lords; for *par in parem non habet imperium*.

69. There are other two Lords that serve weekly on the witnesses, who do both attend in the afternoon each Sederunt day, except Saturday; and do examine witnesses severally; or, if the case be of great importance, as tenors or improbations, they must concur in examination. They must examine no witnesses, but such as have been produced at the bar and have made faith, and unless there be in the minute-book the same day, a minute bearing *avisandum* and *witnesses* upon the process; which, being once called, needs not a new calling, unless the witnesses be brought to the bar on Saturday, in which case the *avisandum* must be till the next Tuesday. The Ordinaries on the witnesses must discuss the objections against the hability of the witnesses, and in case of dubiousness, must report to the Lords.

Title 2. The Order of Discussing Processes

NEXT to the authority of the Lords of Session, which hath been spoke to, both as to the whole Lords and their *quorum* jointly, or by the Ordinary Lords, who serve severally in the Outer-House, on the bills and on the witnesses; the order of exercing this authority comes fitly here to be considered, and that as to the order of calling, hearing, reporting, and determining of causes, from their first dependence, till the final decreets concerning them.

1. It had bred intolerable confusion and inconvenience, if there were not

a fixed and known order, whereby every point falling under the Lords' jurisdiction, or pretended to fall under it, were to be heard and determined; so
that all concerned might know when to attend. For the Session is not a court
of peremptory diets, such as are other courts, that have not a fixed and continued time of sitting, as the Privy Council, Justice Court, &c. which no man
is obliged to attend, but on the day to which they are cited, or by an Act of
Continuation to another fixed diet, which is also peremptory: but the Session
being a court that hath a continued and fixed time of sitting, all points of processes before them are with continuation of days.

2. There was a necessity of a particular continuation of certain summonses of great importance, which behoved to be called and continued by an Act
of Continuation, whereupon letters were issued for a second citation, which
letters were called the second summons; but that order hath been with good
advantage changed, by Act 6. Parl. 2. Sess. 3. Ch. 11. [Summons Execution
Act, 1672,c.6; A.P.S. viii,64,c.6]. So that now summonses which before
were to be continued, have two diets; and the citation to the first diet may be
by any person that can write his execution, whose name is held as insert in
the blank of the summons, which are always direct to "sheriffs in that part;"
because of old, all executions were by the ordinary sheriffs, but since the institution of the College of Justice, the Lords direct to "sheriffs in that part,"
that is, to sheriffs constitute by them to that effect. And the second citation is
only given by messengers, and not until the diet of the first citation be passed.

3. Without this fixed order of hearing and determining, all parties that
were cited behoved constantly to attend every day of the Session, till the
cause were determined, unless the same were not called in a year after the
diet in the summons, or after the last calling by a clerk: for then there is necessity of a new Summons of Wakening, for the cause is holden as sleeping;
which will not occur but by the interruption of the sitting of the Session, or
by the negligence of the party which may call.

4. The Lords are obliged to sit during the time appointed for the Session
by Act of Parliament, unless there be a warrant from the King or Parliament,
or Privy Council to the contrary, except in solemnities warranted by law or
custom. They sit every week-day except Monday; that day being free, because causes heard upon Saturday could have no time for drawing informations, if the dispute were to be decided on Monday in the forenoon; yea,
every Ordinary Lord is obliged constantly to attend, and if he be absent,
without an excuse admitted by the Lords, he loses so much of his salary, as is
correspondent to the sederunts while he is absent. And likewise parties and
pleaders would be confounded and surprised, if they could not know when
they might be called, or when their disputes might be reported and advised.

5. For shunning these inconveniences, in the institution of the College of
Justice, there was appointed a Table, in which all summonses to be called
were to be set down: but the kingdom was divided in four quarters, and the
time of calling their causes was only in that quarter of the year appointed for

them; and such particular causes were to be called upon Monday; and Friday was for the King and Queen's causes, and for strangers; but all other causes any day of the week.

But the inconvenience that followed upon this method made it fall in desuetude; so that no causes were to be called or discussed upon Monday, for the reason now adduced: and it was very inconvenient that no party might call any cause but in their own quarter of the year, so that for three quarters they could have no justice; therefore causes were called promiscuously, at the option of the Ordinary for the Outer-House, or at the option of the Chancellor or President for the Inner-House. By this the whole nation became in dependence and clientel of the Chancellor and President, and such Ordinaries as went to the Outer-House, whereby every one might call their own friend, so that the defenders were all in diffidence, surprise and confusion, supposing the causes to be called upon particular respect of persons, and when they were not in the advocate's recent memory; so that they wrangled upon every frivolous pretence, and did not acquiesce in the interlocutors.

6. The Lords became sensible of the great inconvenience by surprise, and therefore by Acts of Sederunt began to give remedies, which were perfected by the Act of Regulation [Courts Act, 1672,c.16; A.P.S. VIII,80,c. 40], till which the Lords would not pass from their privilege of calling their friend in their own week; and, after much debate, it was yielded, that they should have Saturday privileged, to call what causes they would on that day, which gave great offence and suspicion, that when so good a remedy was fallen upon, it should have an exception; therefore the King gave a commission under the Great Seal, 21 August, 1669, for regulating the manner of procedure in all judicatures; whereupon the commissioners did frequently meet, and in March 1670, did return to his Majesty certain Rules and Articles of Regulation which his Majesty did approve. But because this way could not be effectual without authority of Parliament, therefore the saids rules were confirmed in Parliament, August 30, 1672, by Act 16. Parl. 2. Sess. 3. Ch. 11. [*Ibid.*]. By this Act of Regulation this general and just ground was laid, "That all processes should be discussed and determined, as the parties are in readiness, and do call for justice, after the process have been seen by the defender's advocates, and are returned by them; and that according to the date of the returns which are set down and signed by the defender's advocate, upon the process itself, that no parties be preferred in obtaining justice, to any other who was ready and calling for it before. And it was appointed that Books of Inrolment be made, for inrolling of processes, according to the dates of their returns: and that no cause be called but according to these rolls, except only the King's causes, which may be called at any time when His Majesty's Advocate pleaseth, upon either of the two next sederunt days after the processes are returned, or at any time thereafter, upon fifteen days advertisement to the defender's advocates, that they may acquaint their clients to be present."

7. But because there was necessity to give dispatch to some causes more

than others, therefore there were appointed two Books of Inrolment for the Outer-House: in the one were inrolled suspensions, advocations, removings, ejections, and recent spuilzies; and in the other were inrolled all other causes, according to the date of their returns.

8. And for preventing of the miscarrying of writs produced in processes, in respect copies, although attested by notars, are not sufficient, because the other parties must see the principals, that they may consider whether there be any ground of suspicion of forgery or vitiation, and that they may by their clients, and by other writs, consider whether the subscriptions be the subscriptions of the parties, that they may propone improbation as they shall see cause; and that it might be known how long the defenders kept up the process unreturned: therefore the leader of the process causes write upon the back of the process the writs given out therewith, and subjoins thereto "given out by" him subscribing the same; and when the process is offered to the leader of the process for the other party, he may compare the writs with the list, and if all in the list be not given therewith, he may refuse to receive the same.

By this means two great inconveniences are shunned, which did before exceedingly endanger parties, and trouble the Lords; to wit, the forcing of defenders to give back processes, for which advocates were frequently called, and much altercation about the time they had the process, which is now evident by the date of the out-giving. And likewise debates are shunned concerning writs that were a-missing, which now is cleared by the list on the back of the process.

9. There were likewise appointed two Books of Inrolment for the Inner-House: the one for ordinary actions proper to the Inner-House, viz. reductions of heritable rights of lands or annualrents, after the production is satisfied in the Outer-House, and avisandum made for disputing the reasons; declarators of rights of lands or annualrents, probations of tenors, *cessiones bonorum;* wherein, after the dilators are discussed in the Outer-House, a great avisandum is made: and of such causes where the Lords, upon report of the dispute from the Outer-House, shall, for the importance, intricacy, or preparative of the points reported, ordain the cause to be heard *in præsentia*. In which book the causes shall be inrolled, as they are offered to the keeper of the book, in the Session-house, each Saturday from two till three o'clock in the afternoon, according to the dates of the great avisandums, or of the interlocutors for hearing of the causes in presence. The other Book of Inrolment for the Inner-House, is for concluded causes only, to be insert as aforesaid, according to the date of the acts concluding the cause, wherein a great avisandum is made. These great avisandums are so named, in distinction from avisandums for reports, or for witnesses.

The causes presented every Saturday are to be set down according to the dates of their returns.

10. The Lords, both in the Outer-House and Inner-House, are ordained

by the said Act "to proceed to the discussing of processes, in order as they stand in the saids rolls *respectivè*, without passing over, or anticipating any cause. And it is appointed that each process shall be still called in its order, until it be brought to an act, protestation, or decreet; and if it be delayed till something be produced or done, which requires not an act extracted, then, after the day to which it is delayed, the same shall be called till it be discussed. And where, at the calling of any cause in the Inner or Outer-House, the pursuer insists not, the process shall be delete out of the roll, and protestation shall be granted if it be demanded:" but if no protestation be demanded and extracted, the pursuer may enter the cause again in the Books of Inrolment, as it shall be offered, as before is expressed, but after all that were entered before, though the return be of a prior date. And that it may appear what causes are discussed, and what delete, or delayed upon something to be done not requiring an act to be extracted, it is appointed, that it be written upon the margin of the roll at every cause, "discussed," "delete," or "delayed" till such a day; after which day the cause must be put in the roll as it stood before, without a new inrolment in the books. Yea, to make all secure, "If any cause be called out of its due place, the pursuer's advocates may refuse to insist, or the defender's advocate to answer: and the clerks are prohibited to write upon any process called out of its own due course, or to extract any act or decreet thereupon."

11. Thus the calling and hearing of all causes is so ascertained, that the most powerful or most favourable person of the nation, yea, the King's Advocate for the King's proper causes, cannot obtain the meanest or most unfavourable person in the nation to be postponed or delayed: so that none have reason to complain that they get not equal hearing and dispatch in justice as they are ready, and call for it.

Not only is the equal hearing of causes secured, but lest any might be surprised in reporting the points at interlocutor, when they could not know the time of the report, that they might have given timeously their informations to the whole Lords; therefore the Lords have done all that is possible, to ascertain the time of the reports to be made to them, in this manner:

First, The Ordinary in the Outer-House doth first report, after notice given by him to either party, and that before the reading of any bill; and while he is reporting, the Ordinary of the preceding week goeth out to the bench of the Outer-House, and heareth any cause, wherein he gave interlocutor in his week, and stopped the same; but he is to call no other cause: he is to go out half an hour before the Lords sit down, and so to continue (if he have need) till ten o'clock. If he hath then any point to report, the same must be reported on his day of report from the by-bar.

Secondly, If any point hath been disputed *in præsentia*, that the Lords have thought fit to allow informations to be given on, the President reports the same upon the day appointed for that report.

Thirdly, The Ordinaries upon the witnesses report any dubious point, occurring at the examination of parties or witnesses, which may least admit delay, because of the attending of parties and witnesses.

Fourthly, The Ordinary upon the Bills reports what occurs, immediately on perusal of the bills, which requires no information; but when the Lords by deliverance appoint advocations or suspensions to be heard upon the bill, the Ordinary on the Bills must go out to the by-bar and hear the same, before the Lords sit down, that he may not hinder the rest in their course at the by-bar; and what reports he is to make, must be made before the reports of the rest from the by-bar.

Fifthly, Reports from the by-bar are made in this order. The necessity of calling causes at this bar is, because of controversies that arise upon the minutes of the clerks in the Outer-House, or upon allegeance of new matter; therefore the Lords were accustomed to go to this bar as they had occasion, whereby more than one came together, which bred confusion, and the noise troubled the Ordinary on the bench; advocates also were uncertain what was to be called at the by-bar: whereupon much complaint was made against hearing at that bar, which was not of old known. But these did not consider, that formerly any Ordinary (upon such occasions as now bring them to the by-bar) went to the bench, and stopped the Ordinary, the prejudice whereof was not then perceived, when none could know what causes had no hearing at all, while it was at the option of the Lords to call whom they pleased.

But, to remedy the inconveniences arising from the by-bar, the Lords ordained, that none should go to the by-bar but one at once, and that in order as they sit; so that three go out every day, if they have need: the first from nine till ten, the second from ten till eleven, the third from eleven till twelve; whereby every week every Ordinary may have an hour to hear at that bar, and none report that week, but they report the weeks thereafter, in the same order as they went out to hear. They must also affix upon the wall a roll of the names of the parties whom they are to hear at the by-bar, and the time they are to hear; so that none can be taken tardy, either in hearing on reporting. These reports from the by-bar are made last; because they occur frequently upon the neglect or litigiousness of the parties, who procure stops, which, with the multiplicity of bills, is the ground that causes fall behind in dispatch. And it were most just, that if the parties delayed to attend, they should have their expenses from the parties, who by their neglect or litigiousness do delay them. But the Lords have done all that is possible to make little and regular hearing at the by-bar, having of late ordered every Ordinary to go to the bench the next week after he sat, before that week's Ordinary come out; and after five sederunt days, they are not allowed to give any stop, but parties must in that case suspend if they have cause.

Yet after all these remedies, parties do frequently importune the Lords with bills, containing long narrations of matters of fact; and frequently a repetition of the same matter of fact, without distinct proposing thereof, and the manner how they would prove the same, which oft-times is nothing but a repetition of what hath been heard and determined, which doth unnecessarily consume a great part of the lieges' time, by reading thereof; and that oft-times, when the matter formerly determined is forgot. And therefore the Lords do strictly enjoin the clerks, to give out acts, protestations and decreets, within   days after they are pronounced in the Outer-House, and within   days after they are pronounced in the Inner-House, if the same be demanded by either party; and after these days they will receive no more bills (unless new matter of fact do emerge, or come to knowledge) without expenses to the party delayed, and amands to the poor. If this course were not followed, the bills of wilful persons could not be brought to an end.

12. The order of dispatching bills is thus: By the institution of the College of Justice, Parl. 1537, cap. 52. [College of Justice Act, 1532,c.36; A.P.S. 11,335,c.2], it is statute, "That all parties, or their procurators, deliver to the Chancellor or President their bills." And to the effect that not only they, but the remanent Lords, may have time to read bills, before they be presented; the Lords have appointed boxes for every Lord, to be standing upon a table in the waiting-room of the Inner-House, from three of the clock till six, that all who have bills to offer, may put them into these boxes, by a slit in the cover of them; whereby bills may be put in, and cannot be got out, till the Lords open their several boxes. By this the lieges are eased of the trouble to go to the Lords at their several dwellings through the town; and the occasion of solicitation is prevented: for further preventing whereof, the Lords do at the beginning of every Session declare, and engage upon their honour, that they will admit of no solicitation, by word or letter.

For preparing the dispatch of these bills with as little consumption of time as may be, the President causes write a list of all bills, except such as pass in course; and if he conceive them to be groundless, causes write on the list, that they be "reported by the clerk," that they may be rejected without an answer; wherein there is no hazard, seeing all have received the copies, and if any desire a reported bill to be read, it will be done. And where there is any doubtfulness in the matter, the President causes write upon such bills, "The party to see;" whereby much time is gained; by which means there is no bill rejected till it be reported or read. The clerks make intimation of what bills are to be seen, and the time appointed for returning answers: and if the answer be not returned as aforesaid, he doth ordinarily intimate again, "with certification, that the Lords will advise the bill without an answer."

13. If bills and reports be so multiplied that they cannot be overtaken in the forenoon, or, if any cause be to be advised, wherein there are many points, writs, and witnesses, the Lords, according to the Act of Regulation, do meet in the afternoon for dispatch of the same.

14. Whereas formerly no interlocutors were signed by the President or the Ordinary; now all interlocutors and bills which are past in the Inner-House, upon hearing there, or upon report, are signed by the Chancellor or President; and all that are passed by the Ordinaries are signed by them.

15. Acts are called in the Outer-House weekly, upon Wednesday and Saturday, after they have been called twice by the clerks, who, at the third calling, are publicly to report what is to be proven, that certification may be granted, or the term circumduced, or second diligence granted.

16. Whereas formerly the Lords advised all causes, wherein probation was by witnesses, with close doors, calling no advocates; now parties are present at the examination of witnesses and oaths of parties; and the advocates are called at the advising thereof by the roll of concluded causes, except plain oaths which go not to the roll, but are read by the clerks, and advised by the Lords as they are offered. And when parties are called in concluded causes, they are heard upon the oaths, and also they are allowed to call for the testimonies of the particular witnesses, that they suppose to make for them, in relation to the several points to be proven, in order, as they are stated in the acts, without necessity for the Lords to read over all the witnesses, more than they need read over large writs adduced for probation, whereof they have always been accustomed to read the clauses pitched upon by either party, and therefore they must mark these clauses with figures or letters, and likewise the testimonies or parts thereof ought to be marked, and called for by the number of the witnesses adduced; whereby parties do also know, that no depositions can be abstracted, or neglected by the clerks.

17. Probation adduced by acts of litiscontestation, or acts before answer, is only advised by the Lords *in præsentia;* yet the Ordinaries may hear and determine any writs produced *ab initio* before litiscontestation: and if any plain and single point be referred, or deferred to an oath of calumny, or verity, they may take and instantly advise the same; but the Ordinaries may determine reasons of reduction, upon iniquity, or upon nullity of decreets of inferior courts, on that ground that there was not sufficient probation, and may hear parties debate upon the testimonies of the witnesses, and find proven, or not proven, being done before litiscontestation; in the same way as they may determine writs produced *ab initio :* as was found, June 21, 1677, Sir Andrew Ramsay *contra* Auchinleck [2 Stair 526; M. 12241]. But they cannot advise writs produced after litiscontestation, Feb. 21, 1678, Oliphant *contra* Coupar [2 Stair 617; M. Supp. 79]. And if writs be produced to satisfy the desire of an act of litiscontestation, if the writs do not concern the matter in question, but are only produced, to stop the circumduction of the term, to get delay, till the cause come into the roll of concluded causes; the Ordinary ought to reject the same, and circumduce the term.

18. By what hath been said of the office and duties of the Lords of Session, it will easily appear, that this court is brought to as distinct and accurate methods, for equal and expedite administration of justice, as should be desired; and, that if it be compared with the supreme courts that have been, or are in other nations, there will be found no reason to repent or be ashamed of that great deference that this nation hath always had to the Session since the institution of the College of Justice; and that they are not the best friends to

the nation, who would diminish or derogate from the authority or honour thereof. It is also very visible how much the weight and toil of the Lords of Session are increased above what they were.

First, Before the Act of Regulation, it was not known what causes the Lords had upon hand, and were obliged to discuss and finish; for when they called what causes they pleased, and left others uncalled, these who could not get their causes called, and who for obtaining the same, were necessitated to a long, expensive, and anxious attendance, behoved to leave them, and endeavour by references to bring their pleas to an accord; wherein arbiters must drive the going nail, and advise these, who might worst sustain the present prejudice, to purchase the remedy, by ceding a part of that, which, (if they were authoritative judges,) they would determine in their favours: but now, by the Books of Inrolment and the rolls, which are every day on the wall, it is evident how far at any time the Lords are behind with their work; which, though it exceedingly benefits the nation, and excites the Lords to extraordinary diligence, yet it triples the toils they took before.

Secondly, Formerly when parties obtained calling, if the Ordinary brought the cause to an interlocutor, and reported the same, unless he had particular favour, he went no further, but left the parties to make their application to the next Ordinary: by this, matters of any length or perplexity came to have interlocutors by divers Ordinaries, not very quadrant, whereby the cause was rendered more perplext, than if nothing had been done, and others scarred to meddle with it; this is now amended, and the Ordinary is obliged to continue to hear, according to the roll, until the cause be brought to a decreet, protestation, or act, which doth also prevent that great inconvenience, that what the Ordinary in his week had stopped his successor behoved to enter upon.

Thirdly, Formerly there were no interlocutors signed by the Chancellor, President, or Ordinary, but only bills were signed; now all interlocutors must be signed not only upon report in the Inner-House, but by all the Ordinaries, of all that passeth upon summons or acts; whereby the President is obliged to sit after the rest a long time, for signing all bills and interlocutors that are past that day, while they are fresh in remembrance; and the Ordinaries must revise every thing that is past, and sign the same, which is very useful to the lieges, but very troublesome to the Lords.

Fourthly, Formerly the oaths of witnesses and parties were taken by the Lords when no other were present, but each severally as he was to depone; but since the Act of Parliament for publishing of testimonies [Evidence Act, 1686, c. 18; A.P.S. VIII, 599, c. 30], parties are all allowed to be present, and have a great advantage by offering verbal interrogatories, arising from the answers to written interrogatories; yet the altercation of parties and pleaders, arising therefrom, is very burdensome to the Lords.

Fifthly, Formerly the testimonies of witnesses were advised with close doors; but now parties and procurators are called, [Court of Session Act, 1693, c.26; A.P.S. IX, 305, c.42] whereby these that are wilful breed the

Lords a great deal of trouble, and consume much time, debating upon the import of the testimonies, not only at the first, but by several bills thereafter; whereby the Lords are necessitated several times to revise and advise the same testimonies.

By all these, and other superadded burdens, the Lords are necessitated to have long Sederunts, every week in the afternoons, which formerly was very rare; but without these the Lords could not now overtake their work.

Title 3. Ordinary Actions Generally

F R O M the authority and power of the Lords of Session, jointly in their *quorum*, or severally by the Ordinaries in the Outer-House, on the Bills, and on the witnesses, and the order of their hearing, determining or reporting; we come now to the exercise of that authority, as to the matter and manner thereof. And from justice, in the several private rights thence arising, in their nature and constitution, and in their transmission from the living, by assignation of personal rights from private parties, or by gifts of rights confiscated, or by disposition of real rights by consent, or by law, or rights arising from the dead by succession; we come now to the application of justice by judgment, which comprehends the cognition, trial, and determination of all manner of private rights, and the execution of what is determined, by making the same effectual so far as can be.

We are not to insist in the cognition or execution of justice, competent to the inferior courts, but only so far as is competent to the Lords of Session, who are the supreme judges-ordinary in all civil causes, either in the first, or in the second instance: and so, whatever is cognosced by inferior courts, may be recognosced by the Lords, whose decisions regulate all the inferior courts. And their subjects and form of procedure being known by the former title, the law that inferior judges are to be ruled by is the same.

It were of great advantage to the nation, that all who attend the inferior judicatures were first advocates, who, for a considerable time, had attended the House, and practised; which would be a great mean to keep all the courts superior and inferior uniform, for preventing the trouble and expense of the lieges. And where the inferior magistrates do not themselves ordinarily attend, they might elect their deputes of such. This would also encourage the study of law, to which many of our youth are inclinable, whereby they arise to a greater number, than that the affairs of this nation can afford suitable provisions to their spirits and parts.

 1. This general difference between the Lords, and the inferior courts is to be observed, That the Lords have privilege *ex nobili officio*, which is competent to no inferior court. The distinction and import of *nobile officium* with us, hath its rise from the Roman law, whereby all causes were judged by the Prætor, under whom there were not such inferior courts as we have, where causes might be first determined without the Prætor's authority, who could not possibly dispatch all the causes, even of the city of Rome; though, when

it increased to a great bulk, many Prætors were appointed, yet all these could not dispatch the causes of the city personally; and therefore they delegated judges in such causes as they thought fit, reserving matters of the greatest import to themselves. These delegates were not arbiters; yet sometimes, by consent of parties, they named arbiters, who had a greater latitude in judging according to equity, than the *judices dati*, who being at that trouble and attendance, had a legal allowance from the parties for their pains; and therefore their office was called *officium mercenarium;* but the proper office of the Prætor was *judicium nobile*. This distinction hath been retained, under the same signification, where the Roman law hath any respect, but not under the same terms; and therefore with us, the properer terms are *officium nobile* and *officium ordinarium:* so that the jurisdiction of inferior courts is not mercenary, but yet hath not the *officium nobile*, which is extraordinary; and therefore they must keep their ordinary form of process, and if they do debord, their sentences do become null.

The Lords of Session have both the *officium ordinarium* and *nobile*. For it is only in some cases, that they may proceed, not according to the ordinary forms, which custom hath determined, for any case which hath formerly occurred: But in new cases, there is necessity of new cures, which must be supplied by the Lords, who are authorized for that effect by the institution of the College of Justice. And if they might in other cases extend their *officium nobile*, it would render the subjects unsecure, and the power of the Lords too arbitrary. But, in many cases, it is necessary wherein they may have recourse from strict law to equity, even in the matter of judgment; and in more cases they may recede from the ordinary form and manner of probation, whereof there are many instances commonly known.

Every sovereign court must have this power, unless there be a distinct court for equity, from that for law, as it is in England, where the judges of the Court of Common Pleas judge all according to the rigour of law, and so they cannot modify the most exorbitant penalties, nor give remedy but by the tenor of their known brieves; which being found highly inconvenient, their Kings at first assumed to themselves, to remedy the inconvenience, which they found the common law defective in, either by want of forms, or want of power to qualify these exorbitances, that were inconsistent with equity, and a good conscience: but these cases multiplying, and many pretending unwarrantably to them, the King could no longer dispatch them in his own person, but gave that power to the Chancellor, with the assistance of twelve masters of the Chancery. And there are since several courts of equity and conscience, set up by authority of Parliament. Other nations do not divide the jurisdiction of their courts, but supply the cases of equity and conscience, by the noble office of their supreme ordinary courts, as we do.

2. The Session comes nearest to the praetorial power, which did supply what was wanting by their common law of the Twelve Tables, or by their recent law, made by the suffrage of the people, or by the suffrage of the Ple-

beians, or of the Senate, or by their strict forms of actions at first, or there-after by their strict observance of the kinds of actions, though not of the precise words; yea, they had power to correct the extremity of these laws, and so they accounted *summum jus, summam injuriam.* We shall only give some instances of the *nobile officium* of the Lords of Session.

First, They modify exorbitant penalties in bonds and contracts, even though they bear the name of liquidate expenses, with consent of parties, which necessitous debtors yield to; these the Lords retrench to the real expenses and damage of parties: [111,2,32, *supra*] yet these clauses have this effect, that the Lords take slender probation of the true expenses, and do not consider whether they were unnecessary or not, so that they exceeded not the sum agreed upon; whereas, in other cases, they allow no expenses, but what is necessary or profitable.

Secondly, When the advantages of legal execution are exorbitant, especially in apprisings and adjudications, when the question is in that which may make the legal expire, the Lords do strictly judge the nullities and informalities, and extend the profits received by these rights, to this equitable effect only, that they be not perpetually redeemable, or require a new legal; but they determine a lesser time, in which the same may be redeemable. And if there be no hazard of the legal, they sustain these diligences as redeemable securities, although there be many nullities and informalities therein, if there be not a more formal right in competition.

Thirdly, The Lords, in the reduction of their own decreets *ex nobili officio*, do pass over nullities or informalities, where they see nothing wanting in material justice: but if any defect be in material justice, they do most strictly judge all informalities and nullities for opening the decreet, that any thing escaping in material justice may be amended, as is more ordinary in interlocutors.

Fourthly, By our most ancient custom there was no legal remedy for payment of debt, but by poinding of moveables, whereby creditors had warrant to poind the goods of their debtors, yea all the goods upon their ground, though not belonging to themselves, but to others, till that excellent statute, Parl. 1469, cap. 37. [Diligence Act, 1469, c. 36; A.P.S. 11,96,c. 12], which both shows the disease, that tenants' goods were by the brief of distress or poinding, taken for their Lord's debt, without limitation, and also provides a cure; for by that statute it is limited only to their moveables, where their mail extends to the avail of the debts, or at least to their current term's mails or duties, albeit the term be not come. By this statute apprising of the debtor's lands is introduced; which thereafter was not only made effectual against the debtor infeft, but also against his apparent heir not being infeft, but being charged to enter heir, if he did not renounce to be heir: yet no statute did provide a remedy in case the apparent heir renounced; which therefore the Lords, *ex nobili officio*, supplied, by adjudging the lands, either for the debt of the defunct, or for the debt of the apparent heir.

Fifthly, When dispositions were granted of lands or annualrents in property or liferent, but without precept of seasin, or procuratory of resignation, so that such dispositions became ineffectual, the Lords introduced another kind of adjudication, adjudging the lands or annualrents from the disponer to the purchaser, he having first used the ordinary remedy by horning.

Sixthly, The Lords, by their ordinary office, cannot take away writ by witnesses; yet where there are many concurring evidences, though not full probation, the Lords *ex officio* examine witnesses *ad rimandam veritatem*, without discussing the relevancy till probation were ended; and if, at advising of the probation and other evidences, they find them pregnant, they do sustain them probative; and so trusts are discovered, and retiring of writs lying by defuncts uncancelled, and oft-times with blank assignations or dispositions: and all manner of frauds are found out this way, which cannot otherwise be found out.

Seventhly, The Lords do frequently make acts for probation before answer to the relevancy, which is only *ex nobili officio*, and may alone be used, when there is eminent hazard to carry away most important rights by two pickt-out witnesses; as when the question is of deeds done on deathbed [IV,20,48, *infra*]. For the ordinary exception is health or convalescence, evidenced by going to kirk and market; and the reply is, that these evidences were done of design, and nature violented, and could not fully make out the attempt, but that the party was supported, or that it was evident the sickness was continued; in this case two witnesses chosen by the defender, would carry to him the greatest estate; or two witnesses chosen by the pursuer, might both prove the sickness and support, and so carry the estate to him: To prevent which, the Lords do not allow contrary probations in these points, to be adduced by the several proponers, but do allow either party to adduce a certain number of witnesses, not exceeding such an equal number, to be examined upon these points, "What was the condition of the defunct, when he subscribed the disposition in question? Whether he went to kirk and market after? And whether he went freely, none touching him? Or if he was helped or supported? And what evidence there was of the continuance of his sickness upon him?" The like is done when the question falls concerning deeds *in confinio majoris ætatis*, being questioned upon minority and lesion, and in such others. Upon the same grounds the Lords did prohibit the Judge of Admiralty to make any act before answer in a process of adjudication of a ship, for clearing who was the owner, and what was the port, June 12, 1673, Captain Gilles *contra* Owner of the Bounder [2 Stair 185; M.11907]; December 17, 1673, Captain Stuart *contra* Owners of the Seal-fish. [2 Stair 241; M.11926]

3. Let us now return to the exercise of the jurisdiction of the Session, wherein is to be considered, the matter of their jurisdiction and the manner of it. As to both, it will be fit to consider the most ancient manner of cognition of causes in this kingdom, and what alterations were therein, till both matter and manner were finally settled by the institution of the College of Justice.

First, By the 45th Act, Parl. 1424 [A.P.S. 11,8,c.24], it is clear that all complaints were to be decided before the Judge-Ordinary, as they then were, in these terms: "Anent bills of complaint, whilk may not be determined by the Parliament, for divers causes belonging to the common profit of the realm, it is ordained, that the bills of complaint be execute and determined by the judges and officers of the courts whom to they pertain of law, auther Justice, Chamberlain, Sheriffs, Bailies of burrows, Barons, or other Spiritual Judges: and gif the judges refuse to do the law evenly, the party complaining shall have recourse to the King, who shall see rigorously punished sik judges." But by the 65th Act, Parl. 1425, [A.P.S. 11,11,c.19] the Session was erected to "examine, conclude, and finally determine all and sundry complaints, causes and quarrels, that may be determined before the King and his Council." The power of the Lords of Session is further cleared, Parl. 1457, cap. 61. [A.P.S. 11,47,c.2], and the manner of bringing causes before them by the same Parl. cap. 62. [A.P.S. 11,48,c.3]. But all actions were first to be pursued before the Judges-Ordinary, Parl. 1487, cap. 105. [A.P.S. 11,177,c.10]. The way of bringing actions from the Judge-Ordinary to the Session, was by a summons of error, which is the same with a reduction; but it mentions the quarrelling the verdict of the inquest, and so relates not to civil causes, but to criminal, wherein the great inquest of forty-five recognosced the verdict of the ordinary inquest. But because the Session was not appointed to sit constantly, a Daily Council was erected, with the same power that the Lords of Session had, Parl. 1503, cap. 58. [A.P.S. 11,249,c.2]. And the way of bringing processes before that Council, was only in the first instance; for appeals, or falsing of dooms, and the order thereof in all cases, is determined in that same Parliament, cap. 95. [A.P.S. 11,254,c.41] but they come never to that Council, but to other delegates to be named by the King: and thus it continued till the institution of the College of Justice by King James V after which all appeals ceased, and in place thereof came advocations, suspensions, and reductions of decreets.

4. King James I having been eighteen years prisoner in England, being taken as he was going to France, he understood the course of justice in both these kingdoms, and was the instituter of the Session, and of instruments of seasin: he did also institute the forms of all summonses, which, for their comprehension of much in few words, were called brieves; and he erected a chapel or chancery, and gave them the *formula* of all these brieves, as the same were used in England, which every one took out in course, without any special warrant. The chief brieves were the brieve of right, whereby, the right both of property, superiority, annualrent, and liferent were determined; and the brieve of disseasing, whereby the point of possession was decided, and secured against all attempts of dispossession. The same course by brieves doth yet continue in England, in the courts of law, and are directed to the sheriffs to be executed; but because it was not possible to reach all special cases by these brieves, pursuers were allowed to join therewith declarations

of their own, extending the general heads of the brieves to their particular circumstances, which must also have been so with us. But by the institution of the College of Justice, clerks to the signet, now called writers to the signet, were instituted as a part of the said College; and then all the brieves of the chancery fell in desuetude, except those which yet remain, which are still directed, and only to be served by sheriffs, stewards, bailies of royalty or regality: and in place of the rest of the brieves, ordinary summonses were introduced by the styles accustomed by the writers to the signet, and sustained by the Lords, and were directed to sheriffs in that part, having a blank for inserting the name of any person the pursuer pleased, who thereby was substitute in place of the sheriff; and they behoved to be continued, and entered into a roll or table dividing the several causes for every day in the week, and for the four quarters of the kingdom. And because some summonses required more speedy dispatch, therefore the writers could make no alteration in these points, but did address to the Lords by bills, and did obtain warrant from the Lords for summons, dispensing with some or all of these requisites, which therefore were called privileged summonses, and they bear at the end of the summons, *Ex deliberatione Dominorum Concilii*. And likewise such summonses passed upon bill, as were of a special nature, not comprehended in the ordinary style; which at first were perused and considered by the Ordinary on the Bills, and passed if they were found relevant; but being exceedingly multiplied, they passed in course upon the trust of the writers and clerk to the bills, that no bill pass but what is accustomed; and therefore they pass only *periculo petentis*.

5. The brieves which are now taken out of the Chancery are of two sorts, retoured and not retoured. The brieves for serving of heirs are returned to the chancery, after they are served by the judge-ordinary, and are registrate and kept there, and extracts thereof granted, which are therefore called retours. These brieves require no citation of particular parties, but are served by a public citation at the market-cross of the head-burgh of the shire, or other jurisdiction, upon fifteen days' warning. The heads and meaning of these brieves are explained, Tit. Heirs, [111,5,28 *et seq., supra*]. And there must be called an inquest, whose sentence is called a service, which is retoured to the chancery. The tenor of the brieve is this "CAROLUS, &c. vicecomiti et balivis suis de, &c. Salutem, Mandamus vobis et praecipimus, quatenus per probos et fideles homines patriae, per quos rei veritas melius sciri poterit, (magno sacramento interveniente) diligentem et fidelem inquisitionem fieri faciatis, de quibus terris et annuis redditibus cum pertinen. quondam A. B. de G. pater C. D. latoris praesentium, obiit ultimo vestitus et sasitus ut de feodo, ad fidem et pacem nostram infra balliam vestram? Et si dictus C. D. est legitimus et propinquior haeres ejusdem quondam A. B. sui patris de dictis terris et annuis redditibus cum pertinen.? Et si sit legitimae aetatis? Et quantum valent dictae terrae et annui redditus nunc per annum? Et quantum valuerunt tempore pacis? De quo tenentur? Per quod servitium tenen-

tur? Et in cujus manibus nunc existunt? Qualiter? Per quem? Ob quam causam? Et a quo tempore? Et quod per dictam inquisitionem diligenter factam, esse inveneritis, sub sigillis vestris et sigillis eorum qui dictae inquisitioni intererunt faciendae, ad capellam nostram mittatis, et hoc breve. Teste meipso. Apud Edinburgum, decimo quarto die mensis Julii et anno regni nostri decimo quarto, 1662."

6. The second retourable brieve is the brieve for serving tutors of law, which is retoured to the Chancery, and thence there is a nomination taken out designing the tutor of law [1,6,9,*supra*]. The tenor of this brieve is as follows: "Vicecomiti et ballivis suis de, &c. salutem, Mandamus vobis et praecipimus, quatenus per probos et fideles homines patriae, per quos rei veritas melius sciri poterit, (magno sacramento interveniente) diligentem et fidelem inquisitionem fieri faciatis, quis sit propinquior agnatus, id est consanguineus ex parte patris dilecto nostro B. filio legitimo quondam A. sui patris? Et si ille propinquior excessit aetatem viginti quinque annorum completam? Et si sit sui rei providus, et potens cavere idoneè de administratione rei alienæ? Et si ille propinquior sit immediate successurus ipsi B. si ipsum contigerit in fata decedere? Et si sit; quis tunc ex parte matris idoneor, apud quem, usque ad ejus legitimam aetatem, possit et debet educari? Et quod per dictam inquisitionem diligenter factam, esse inveneritis, sub sigillis vestris et sigillis eorum qui dictae inquisitioni intererunt faciendae, ad capellam nostram mittatis, et hoc breve. Teste meipso. Apud Edinburgum, &c."

7. The third retourable brieve is the brieve of idiotry, which is a special kind of brieve of tutors of law; for thereby such tutors are served to idiots, or furious persons, as are their nearest agnates, past twenty-five years of age. The tenor of this brieve is as follows: "Vicecomiti et balivis suis de E. salutem, Mandamus vobis et praecipimus, quatenus per probos et fideles homines patriae, per quos rei veritas melius sciri poterit, (magno sacramento interveniente) diligentem et fidelem inquisitionem fieri faciatis, si B. sit incompos mentis, fatuus et naturaliter idiota, sic quod timetur de alienatione tam terrarum suarum, quam aliarum rerum mobilium et immobilium? Et quamdiu sustinuit istam fatuitatem? Et si sit, quis sit tunc propinquior consanguineus dicto B? Et si ille propinquior sit suae rei providus, et potens cavere idoneè de administratione rei alienae? Et si sit legitimae aetatis? Et quod per dictam inquisitionem diligenter factam, esse inveneritis, sub sigillis vestris et sigillis eorum qui dictae inquisitioni intererunt faciendae, ad capellam nostram mittatis, et hoc breve. Teste meipso. Apud Edinburgum, &c."

But if the party be furious, the brieve bears to inquire, "Si sit incompos mentis, prodigus et furiosus, viz. Quod neque tempus neque modum expensarum habet, sed bona et possessiones dilacerandas et dissipandas profundit, et quamdiu sustinuit illam furiositatem?" &c.

This brieve is retoured to the chancery, and thereupon a nomination of the tutor is given out.

8. On these three retourable brieves there are issued decreets of the

chancery. On the first brieve the retours of heirs are decreets of the chancery, and upon them follow precepts commanding the superior to receive and infeft the heirs conform to their retours, when the retours contain lands or annualrents. And upon the executions thereof, if obedience be not given, there are subsequent precepts for making the first effectual, as is explained, Tit. Heirs. [111,5,*supra*].

9. The nominations of the tutors on the brieves of tutory and of idiotry, are the decreets of chancery, but have no precepts following thereon; these nominations being the titles whereby these tutors act. In all these decreets and precepts, the King himself decerneth and commandeth immediately, without a subordinate judge.

The difference between the brieves and nominations of ordinary tutors of law, and these of idiots or furious persons, are these; the ordinary tutory inquires, "Who is the nearest agnate of twenty-five years complete? And if he be fit for administration, and to find caution?" which is the first head of the brieve. The next is, "If he be nearest to succeed, and who is the most fit person on the mother's side, with whom the pupil may be educated?" But in the brieve of idiotry, the first head is, "Whether the person be *compos mentis*, *fatuus*, or a natural idiot, and that there is ground of fear that he may alienate his lands or goods?" Whereby not only idiots, but any uncapable to manage their affairs, as persons dumb or deaf, are to be understood. The next point of the brieve is, "How long the party hath been under that incapacity?" For deeds only done in that time are void. The third point is, "Who is the party's nearest agnate of lawful age?" (which is not to be understood by his majority, but by his being twenty-five years complete) "and if he be fit to administrate the affairs of another, and able to find caution?" Therefore the nominations are not to be given out to either of these tutors, till sufficient caution be found. But in the brieve of idiotry, that article is not expressed, "Whether the tutor be nearest heir; and that if he be, a person be nominate for custody;" which therefore the Lords ought to supply, as having the Praetorian power.

10. The brieves not retourable are four, which are not decreets, but precepts directed to sheriffs, &c. who thereupon cite parties, and hear and determine: and therefore they are called pleadable brieves; because particular parties are called specially, and not only generally at the market-cross, as in the other brieves; wherein yet parties may appear though not called, and may plead so far as they can instantly verify, either by objections against the brieves and executions, or by exceptions instantly verified; but though none appear, they are not contumacious, neither doth an executorial follow by horning and poinding, as in other decreets.

11. The first of these unretourable brieves, is the brieve of terce, whereby a relict is to be served to a third part of the tenements, wherein her husband died last vest as of fee [11,6,13,*supra*]: it is a warrant to the sheriff, steward, or bailie, where her husband's lands lie, to call an inquest, and therewith to cognosce what lands or annualrents the husband had the time of his death;

and to assign her a reasonable terce thereof, which she may either crave to be kenned, that is, to be divided from the two thirds belonging to the heir, or otherwise she may bruik the third of the rent, until the division be made. The tenor of this brieve is as follows: "Vicecomiti, &c. Salutem, Mandamus vobis et praecipimus, quatenus dilectae nostrae B. relictae quondam A. latrici prae-sentium, haberi faciatis rationabilem tertiam partem suam, de omnibus et singulis terris et annuis redditibus cum pertinen. quae et qui fuerunt dicti quondam A. sui mariti haereditarie, infra balliam vestram, quas et quos de nobis tenuit in capite, et de quibus obiit ultimo vestitus et sasitus ut de feodo. Tantum inde facien. quod pro vestro defectu, amplius inde justam queri-moniam non audiamus. Teste meipso. Apud, &c."

In the serving of this brieve, all must proceed according to what was holden and reputed, viz. That the relict was holden and reputed as lawful wife in the husband's lifetime, and that the matrimony was not accused in their life-times, Parl. 1503, cap. 77. [A.P.S. 11,252,c.22] yet the contrary may be proved, by way of declarator or reduction before the Lords. The service must also bear, that the husband is reputed to be dead, and at what time; that there-by the relict may have right to the profits of the terce, from the next term af-ter her husband's death; it is also sufficient to instruct, that the husband died in possession of the lands in question, and was holden and reputed heritable possessor thereof, albeit it will be securer against reduction, that the seasin be produced; yet his possession as heritable possessor must be known.

12. The second unretourable brieve is the brieve of division, whereof the tenor follows: "Salutem, Mandamus vobis et praecipimus, quatenus totas et integras terras de, &c. cum pertinen. jacen. infra balliam vestram; inter A. ex parte una, et B. ex parte altera, portionarios dictarum terrarum, juste et se-cundum assisam terrae contingentem, partiri faciatis. Tantum inde facien. quod pro vestro defectu amplius inde justam querimoniam non audiamus. Teste meipso, &c."

The portioners are such as bruik *pro indiviso*, whether they be heirs-por-tioners, or portioners by apprising or adjudication, or if there be divers ter-cers, who have not been kenned to a particular division; for, in that case, the brieve of terce is not the competent way of division, for that is only competent between the tercer and the heir.

13. The third unretourable brieve is the brieve of lining, which is of this tenor: "Praeposito et Ballivis burgi de, &c. Salutem, Mandamus vobis et praecipimus, quatenus per duodecim de melioribus et fide dignioribus bur-gensibus dicti burgi, per quos rei veritas melius sciri poterit, (magno sacra-mento interveniente) juste et secundum leges burgi, lineari faciatis tenemen-tum terrae Jacobi A. jacen. in dicto burgo ex parte Boreali viae Regiae ejus-dem, inter tenementum terrae Joannis B—— ex parte orientali, ex une parte; et tenementum terrae Davidis C. ex parte occidentali, ex altera parte; et sicut dictum tenementum terrae per dictos lineatores lineatum fuerit, ita illud de caetero firmiter faciatis observari. Tantum inde facien. quod pro vestro

defectu amplius inde justam querimoniam non audiamus. Teste meipso, &c."

14. The fourth unretourable brieve is the brieve of perambulation, which is for clearing controverted marches, and is of this tenor: "Vicecomiti, &c. Salutem, Mandamus vobis et praecipimus, quatenus per probos et fideles ac antiquiores homines patriae, juste et secundum assisam terrae, perambulari faciatis rectas metas et divisas, inter terras de, &c. cum pertinen. quae sunt A. ex parte una; et terras de, &c. quae sunt B. ex parte altera, jacen. in baronia de, &c. et infra balliam vestram. Et sicut dictae divisae et metae juste et secundum assisam terrae perambulatae fuerint, ita eas de caetero firmiter faciatis observari. Tantum inde facien. &c. Teste meipso, &c.

But though the brieve bear generally *per probos et fideles homines patriæ*, which might extend to any men of the kingdom; yet it is statute, Parl. 1579, cap. 79. [A.P.S. III,144,c.17]. That in all time thereafter, in causes of perambulation, no persons be received upon the inquest thereof, but those who have heritage of their own, and dwell maist ewest the same, to wit, within the sheriffdom where the lands lie; or (if they may not be had within that shire) then within the four next adjacent shires, unless the marches be instructed by bounding charters, or other evidences in writ.

15. All these brieves must be served with inquests, and so cannot be served before the Lords in the first instance; and though the brieves may be advocated, yet they must be remitted unto Sheriffs, to wit, the Ordinaries, if the reasons of advocation be not sustained; or to others in their place, if the reasons be sustained: in which case brieves for serving heirs, are accustomed to be remitted to the macers and assessors, if any difficulty arise; and so may the brieves of idiotry.

16. There remains yet in the Chancery a brieve for calling the Parliament, which was the ordinary way of calling the same; but since, it hath been accustomed to be called by public proclamation. The tenor of that brieve is this: "Jacobus Dei gratia Rex Scotorum, Vice-comiti, et ballivis suis de Argyle, Salutem; Quia ordinavimus Parliamentum nostrum tenendum apud *Edinburgh*, et inchoandum die Sabbati, octavo die mensis Julii proxime futuri, cum continuatione dierum; Vobis praecipimus et mandamus, quatenus summoneatis, seu publicè summoneri faciatis, omnes et singulos episcopos, abbates, priores, comites et barones ac caeteros libere-tenentes totius balliae vestrae; et de quolibet burgo, tres vel quatuor de sufficientioribus burgensibus sufficientem commissionem haben. quod compareant coram nobis, dictis die et loco, in dicto nostro Parliamento, una cum aliis regni nostri praelatis, proceribus et burgorum commissariis, qui tunc ibidem propter hoc intererunt congregati; ad tractandum, concordandum, subeundum et determinandum ea quae in dicto nostro Parliamento, pro utilitate regni nostri et reipublicae, tractanda fuerint, concordanda, subeunda et determinanda: et vos vicecom. sitis ibidem dicto die, haben. vobiscum summonitionis vestrae testimonium, et hoc breve: et hoc sub poena quae competit in hac parte, nulla-

tenus omittatis. Datum sub testimonio nostri magni sigilli, Apud *Halie-rude-house* decimo quinto die mensis Maii, anno regni nostri vicesimo 1587.—Vicecomiti et ballivis suis de Argyle. Pro Parliamento."

17. There is another distinction of brieves into these that are pleadable, and these that are not pleadable. Pleadable brieves are these that require particular citation, as is the brieve of division, and as was the brieve of right and disseasing; for there the defenders were specially cited, and might propone defences, and get terms to prove: but there are other brieves which now remain that are called not pleadable, because they admit no terms to prove; yet any concerned may propone any objection against the brieves and executions, or any exception that can be instantly verified.

18. If the judges, to whom these brieves are ordinarily to be directed, be concerned in the cause, or in near relation to the parties concerned, or in enmity against them, the Lords will advocate the brieves to the macers, or others as sheriffs in that part; or if brieves be to serve heirs to lands in divers shires, they will cause the brieves to be directed to the macers; and in case of intricacy therein, or in other brieves advocated, they will appoint some of their own number to be assessors, who will report any difficult point to the Lords, and proceed by their direction.

19. Before we come to ordinary actions before the Lords, it is fit to explain what is meant by those terms which ordinarily occur, viz. a cause, an action, a process, an instance, and a plea. A cause is the right to be discussed and determined, so called, because it is the cause of all the rest; for thence an action doth arise, a process doth proceed, or an instance, and a plea.

20. An action is defined by Justinian, to be *jus persequendi in judicio quod sibi debetur ;* about which there are many debates, especially why an action should be defined a power to prosecute, it being rather a prosecution of a power; for all right is comprehended in some kind of power: or how it should be said to be for prosecution of that which is due, which would rather import personal actions only, and can hardly be stretched to all real actions: neither doth an action extend only to what is done in judgment; for he who useth citation of course, without any particular warrant, is in action, but is not in judgment, till the defender be called by the judge to appear. But an action may be more plainly described, to be "a prosecution by any party, of their right, in order to a judicial determination thereof:" and so it is begun by taking out a summons or brieve of course, or an application by bill for obtaining a summons, and is not terminate till a final sentence be obtained, and execution thereupon, when the sentence is condemnatory.

21. A process is, "an action sustained by a judge, that thereupon either an act or definitive sentence may follow;" for all dilatory exceptions are proponed in these terms, no process for such a cause; and therefore an action not sustained cannot be a process; though in vulgar acceptance, any summons when but called by a clerk, and appointed to be seen, is called a process.

22. An instance is, "that which may be insisted in at one diet or course of

probation," whether it be instantly verified at the first calling, or a term be assigned to prove: for whatsoever cannot be proven at that term, cannot be in
that instance, seeing there cannot be more acts of litiscontestation than one,
for obtaining one decreet: and if there be in the same summons more points
which cannot be proven at the same diets, the libel doth contain many actions
upon which many acts and decreets will proceed at divers times.

23. A plea contains more than one process, viz. all that is done until the
parties do fully acquiesce and insist no further: therefore if a decreet be suspended, or reduction intented, the plea is not ended, but is still depending
from the first judicial act, where the defender doth, or should appear, till the
parties acquiesce. But a supplication or citation doth not make the dependence of a plea, but the intention thereof; and so an action is said to be intented
and depending.

24. Actions before the Lords of Session, are either in the first or second
instance. An action in the first instance, is either summary or solemn. A solemn action is that which proceeds expressly in the King's name, and hath no
execution till parties be heard, or be contumacious. And so a summary action
is that which wants these solemnities.

25. A summary action is of two sorts; the first is that which passes by a
bill and a citation thereupon by an order of the Lords, without passing the
signet; such are complaints against members of the College of Justice, especially in that which concerns their employment and trust. Such also are
complaints upon contempt of the Lords authority; as when parties proceed
to execution, where there is a stop or suspension given, or where an inferior
judge proceeds after an advocation duly intimated; or when the Lords appoint reasons of advocation, or the principal cause to be discussed upon the
bill; or when a cause is ordained to be discussed upon a bill of suspension.
These, and generally all complaints *super attentatis aut innovatis lite dependente*, proceed by bill and deliverance, without a signet summons, and go not
to the roll; nor is there any further time to see, but, upon the sight of the bill
and deliverance, the party is to answer at the next calling; and so the matter
is discussed by the Ordinary upon the Bills, or summarily *in præsentia*, if the
matter be important or atrocious.

The other kind of summary action is when a charge of horning is obtained upon a bill without citation or sentence; such are hornings granted
summarily by statute or custom. By statute, several Acts of Parliament ordain
letters of horning to be direct summarily; so horning is direct against liferenters, to uphold the liferent lands and tenements, in the case they received
them; so heritors of a parish are summarily charged to meet and stent themselves for building or repairing kirks, or kirk-yard dykes. By custom, charges
of horning are granted in several cases; as, 1st, for the King's revenue of whatever kind; 2d, for payment of the commissioners to Parliament; 3d, for payment of the Lords of Session their contribution-money out of the several
benefices.

These hornings are called General Letters, because the particular persons which may be charged are not particularly expressed *nominatim* but under a general designation. But such as are not authorized by statute, or ancient custom, had no effect but for obtaining caption, for thereby escheat did not fall. And because too many of these general letters were surreptitiously obtained, they are discharged by several Acts of Parliament, and most strictly by the 13th Act, 2d Sess. Parl. 1690 [A.P.S. ix,153,c.16]; wherein the King's revenue, and ministers' stipends upon decreets of locality are only excepted; and decreets of poinding the ground are left as before. Yet there may be letters of horning summarily granted for commissioners' charges, upon production of the attest of the clerk register of their attendance, and of the attest of the collectors of supply, of the valuation of the particular heritors and liferenters in the shire. Letters may be also summarily directed, for the contribution-money, against the particular persons accustomed to pay the same [111,3,13, *supra*]: neither can the late Act annul the general letters, warranted by the particular statutes to which this late Act bears no derogation.

26. The ordinary solemn summonses are such as are intented before the Lords, in the first instance, and these are called ordinary actions, in distinction from the causes which come before the Lords, in the second instance, by advocation from inferior courts before decreets, or by suspension or reduction, after decreets either of the Lords themselves, or of inferior courts, or of causes first intented before the Parliament, and by them remitted to the Lords, or of actions remitted by the Privy Council to the Lords, which are found to concern the point of right wherein the Lords of Council decline themselves, and therefore oblige not the Lords to discuss them; yet, where the Council in matters of riot doth demur, till the matter of right be first cleared, the Lords use summarily to discuss the point of right, upon recommendation of the Council.

27. Ordinary actions proceed not by brieves, but by larger summonses, which therefore are called Libels. They are called summonses, *à summonendo*, because the executions thereof advertise the defenders to appear and answer thereto, at the terms therein prescribed. These executions are also called citations, *à citando*, because they hasten the defender's appearance; which name arises from the ancient Roman way of citing parties; when the complainer, without authority from a judge, required his party to appear before a judge, who might hear and determine their controversy; and if he refused he might compel him, if he had sufficient strength and assistance for that effect. But this course hath been long since laid aside, as being apt to beget breaches of the peace; and, in place thereof, summonses by apparitors have succeeded, wherein there must be some certification, which may rather induce the person summoned to appear, than to fall under these just penal consequences upon their contumacy. These penal consequences being declared by the tenor of the summons, are therefore called certifications, because the judge doth ascertain the party called, and not compearing, what he will do in that case.

28. A certification is necessary in all summonses, for it is the sting that gives them efficacy, without which they would be elusory; yet the certification is not always the equivalent of what is demanded by the summons, but is partly penal, exceeding what is demanded in this, that summonses do always bear or import, that the party is cited to hear and see it found and declared, or sufficiently instructed, or to be proven, what in fact is alleged, and whence the conclusion in law is inferred, but yet the certifications do oft-times proceed without any probation.

29. The great certification in the Roman law, in real actions, was by their *primum decretum*, whereby the pursuer was put in possession of the right he claimed, without any probation, and did enjoy the fruits thereof, till the contumacious party did recover the same by way of action; wherein if he succumbed, the second decreet excluded him for ever. The common certification in summonses or brieves, by the custom of England, is, that the party cited, and not compearing, shall be outlawed, whereby he has no more benefit of law, till the contumacy be purged: but no sentence in the cause can proceed, by their common law, till the party pursued be sisted in judgment before the judge and jury.

30. The course which our custom did of old follow against contumacious parties, was this. By the first citation they were condemned in the pursuer's expenses, and amerciated in a fine to the King: and by contumacy at the second summons, they were again condemned in the pursuer's expenses, and a greater unlaw to the King, viz. the double of the first. And if they continued contumacious at the third citation, they were condemned in the expenses to the pursuer, and the quadruple of the first amerciament to the King: and then did the judge proceed in the cause to do justice, and the pursuer was put in possession of the lands in question, till he were satisfied of his expenses, and the King's unlaws were paid; or in the possession of moveable goods for year and day; but if the contumacious person had not land nor goods, he was to be outlawed, and put to the horn, Parl. 1449, cap. 29. [Act 1449,c.30; A.P.S. 11, 37,c.18]. This hath been introduced in imitation of the custom of England; but by the statute it was only temporary.

31. Our custom, now past memory, hath come to a course far nearer material justice in civil causes; but the Secret Council and Justiciary sustain no process against absents, but do only grant certification against them, declaring them to be fugitives; whereupon they are denounced, and are to be taken by caption, and then the principal cause ceases, till they be brought personally to the bar. But the Session proceeds to do justice against parties absent, [IV,38,27–28,*infra*] and determine the relevancy of summonses or bills, and admits instructions thereof, or gives terms to prove the same by writ or witnesses, and decerns, and puts the decreets to execution; whereby the pursuer enjoys the profits, till by reduction he be put *in mala fide*, by production of a clear probation of the contumacious party's right. But if probation be by oath, whatsoever point is referred to oath by the summons, if the contumaci-

ous party be cited by a messenger of arms, personally apprehended, or if latent, vagrant, or in a place where there is no safe access, being cited at the market-cross, and if out of the country, at the market-cross of Edinburgh, and at the pier of Leith; in any of these cases, if the party cited be absent, and the days of compearance be passed, he is holden as confessed; that is, the law presumes he is conscious of the truth of the matter of fact referred to his oath, and therefore forbears to appear and depone; and so he holden as if he did depone and confess that which is referred to his oath. Hence it appears that in these summonses there are two certifications; the one is, that if the party cited appear not, the Lords will proceed to do justice, as if he did appear, which is understood when the summons bears "with certification," and when there is no mention of certification it is implied; for it is rather an act of exact justice, than a penal certification. The other certification is special, according to the nature of the summons.

There is a third certification of great import, in summonses of reduction and improbation, by which parties call for all writs whereby their rights may be questioned, with this certification, that if they be not produced, they shall be reputed and holden as false and feigned, upon this presumption of law, that they are kept up fraudulently; for that if they were produced, they would be proven to be false and forged, which is *præsumptio juris et de jure*, and admits not of a contrary probation, that thereby men's rights may be secured, and an end put to pleas. But this certification operates only as to the effect such writs may have against the pursuer's rights, whereupon the process proceeded.

There is a fourth important certification, whereby when parties pursue, and do not insist, the defenders take protestation against them, that no effect may follow upon that summons or charge, till a new citation or charge: but because that would not sopite the plea, therefore the defenders raise a process against the former pursuers, to insist; with certification never to be heard thereafter in that plea.

32. The first division of summonses with us, is in privileged and not privileged. Privileged summonses are accounted all such, as require a bill to be passed by the Lords upon some speciality. All these summonses bear at the end of them, *Ex deliberatione Dominorum Concilii*. The writers to the signet are comprehended in the institution of the College of Justice, and are authorised to expede summonses which had not the accustomed brieves of the chancery, wherein their styles by custom came to be known: and they are every year publicly called, and commanded to keep the accustomed styles, and are censurable if they do it not, the matter and order being always the same, though they be not tied to particular words, as they are tied in the brieves of the chancery. But if any new case be proposed to them, whereof they have not an accustomed style, they ought to present the same by bill, that the Lords put not parties to trouble, upon grounds altogether irrelevant. These summonses are like the Roman actions, *præscriptis verbis*, for which there was no

name nor form acknowledged in the law, but from special matters of fact and circumstances, inferences of law or equity, were deduced, although the same could be ascribed to none of the titles of actions in that law; such also were their *actiones extraordinariæ*: and therefore, in such cases, the writers ought always to begin with a deduction of the matter of fact, and thence infer the point of right, and thereto subjoin the authority and command. But in unprivileged summonses, the writers ought to begin with the authority and command, as they do in all reductions, and many other summonses. This is too much neglected by long deduction of writs, though the matter of fact be clear, and may be short; as when there is a progress of assignations, intimations and translations, whereby summonses become so large, that it is troublesome and expensive to give full copies, much to the prejudice of defenders: for thereupon, and upon the defective relations and deductions, where fact is premised, summonses come oft to be cut by the advocates, and altered before they be discussed; whereby the Lords are necessitate to admit short copies, and to sustain these alterations, which, in strict law, ought not to be admitted: and therefore advocates were accustomed, at the calling of processes, to accept the same as proponed, protesting against any alteration, as being either unnecessary, or as making in effect a new summons, seeing, as to the alterations, defenders had not time to prepare their defences. But the Lords are so careful not to protract processes, that they were accustomed to permit executions to be altered, if the alterers would bide by the same, as truly done, which now is not to be admitted, when the executors and witnesses do subscribe, and no alteration can be without all their subscriptions: yea, the Lords do sometimes turn summonses from one state to another; as actions of contravention are oft-times turned into actions of molestation, where the cases inferring penalties of contravention are not clear: they do also sustain charges defective in any formality, as ordinary summonses.

The next ground of privileged summonses passing by bill, is where the king hath interest; as in all gifts flowing from the king, and in improbations. But the chief ground of bills is, when the ordinary requisites in summonses, as to diets and tabling of them, conform to the times of the year and quarters of the kingdom, and the days of the week, upon which the several kinds of processes did proceed, were craved to be dispensed with. There is now no necessity of a bill on that account, because a new order is introduced by the Act of Regulation [Courts Act, 1672,c.16; A.P.S. viii,80,c.40]. By bill, warrants were craved for summonses without continuation, and for fewer days than is ordinarily required; and seeing these bills passed of course, almost all summonses came so to be passed, wherein the Secretary's servants did concern themselves, that many bills might remain at the signet, upon which summonses were oft renewed.

33. For remedying these inconveniences, the Lords, by an Act of Sederunt, June 21, 1672, did determine what summonses were to be privileged as to the diets, declaring that none should be privileged, either by the Lords' de-

liverance, or otherwise, excepting "removings, recent spuilzies, and recent ejections," where, by recent, is understood such summonses as are executed within fifteen days after committing of the deeds, "intrusions, and succeeding in the vice of persons removed, causes alimentary, exhibitions, summonses for making arrested goods forthcoming, transferrings, poindings of the ground, wakenings, special declarators, suspensions, preventos, and transumpts." Of which recent spuilzies and ejections, intrusions and succeedings in the vice, (which in deed are all spuilzies, though not of moveables) are privileged on fifteen days' warning, and the rest on six days. But they did prohibit any shorter diet for the first citation, declaring that all other summonses should abide twenty-one days' warning. And further declared the second summons to be always on six days, except in processes against the inhabitants of Edinburgh and its suburbs, who may be summoned for the second citation upon twenty-four hours. And they declared all these to be privileged, whether there were any privilege contained in the summons or not; and declared all other privileges passing in course, *periculo petentium*, to be null.

Since this Act, adjudications are by Act of Parliament [Adjudications Act 1672,c.19; A.P.S. VIII,93,c.45] introduced in place of apprisings, which pass upon one citation, and are privileged upon six days, where parties are near; as likewise the adjudication of the estates of bankrupts, to such as upon roup, do buy the same; or to the creditors by division, if buyers be not found to offer a competent price.

34. Before we come to special kinds of actions and summonses, with their forms by our customs, it is fit to give a general view of the divisions of actions by the Roman law, and their particular actions may come in, as they may confirm or clear the reasonableness of ours. It will be needless to say any thing of their actions, which relate to such rights as we have not; as the whole matter of servitude, libertinism, manumission, and patronage, or other succession, which was not by their law, but by the Praetor, whereby the successors were not called heirs, but *bonorum possessores*: or of that irrational extension introduced by Justinian in the Novels, whereby all cognates of the maternal line were equally brought in with the agnates of the paternal; which, with the actions arising thereon, make a great part of the Roman law.

35. The most general division of actions by the Roman law, is expressed in these words, *Omnium actionum, quibus inter aliquos, apud judices arbitrosve, de quacunque re quæritur, summa divisio in dua genera deducitur: aut enim in rem sunt, aut in personam.* §2, *Inst. de actionibus* [Inst.4,6,2.]; *L.25ff. de Obligationibus et Actionibus* [D.44,7,25]. This division is taken from the rights upon which actions are founded, which they divide into Dominion and Obligation. And to the same purpose they divide actions in vindication of things, and in condiction of what is due by obligations.

36. They have another division of actions from the authority whence they are allowed or institute; and so all actions are either Civil or Praetorian. Civil actions are these which arise from their civil law, as distinct from the

Praetorian law. The civil law was the law of the Twelve Tables; and their *actiones legis* had all exact forms, and there could be no other action but under these forms. But these were very defective of what was necessary, and therefore the Praetor supplied the same by addition of new actions, which were established by the *Edictum Perpetuum;* yet the forms continued both of the old and new actions, until at last they were abolished, *Cod. lib. 2. tit.* 58. Yet though the rigour of words was removed, the species and tenor of the actions remained, and have particular titles and names, except the action *præscriptis verbis,* which is a general name.

37. But because both the civil and praetorian actions were too narrow, another distinction arose *inter actiones directas et utiles:* these *actiones utiles* arose from the parity of reason, and were founded upon the reason of the law, but not upon the words of it; such are all the *actiones contrariæ;* for instance, *actio tutelæ* is *directa* against the tutor, to compt and pay, but *actio contraria tutelæ* is for the tutor, against him who was his pupil, for his necessary and profitable expenses.

38. They had also another division of actions, viz. into these which are *rei persecutoriæ,* and those which were *pænales* [Inst.4,6,16]. The former reached only to the true interest of the pursuer, but the latter extended it above the true interest, such as are the actions *in quibus inficiando lis crescit,* in which the double value, and others in which the quadruple value of the true interest is decerned.

39. They have another division of actions in temporary and perpetual; and into these which are competent to heirs, and not competent to heirs, and in these which are competent against heirs, and not competent against them. They have also a distinction of actions in ordinary and extraordinary. They distinguish also between ordinary actions, and interdicts which concern possession only, and do not proceed wholly upon citation and cognition, but by way of command or prohibition, the disobedience whereof infers contempt and punishment, and the deeds done contrary thereto are annullable.

40. Of all these divisions and distinctions of actions, there is very little use by our customs, except the first; and that some actions which are of a criminal nature, reach no further than the actors, as vitious intromission which is a general passive title, or behaving as heir by intromission with heir-ship-moveables, or with the rents of lands, whereunto they might have succeeded and which are to be proven by witnesses, should not give action against the intromitter's heirs or successors, any further than in what the defunct was profited.

41. The Romans had another distinction of actions, into these which are *bonæ fidei,* and those which are *stricti juris* [Gaius 4,62]. *Actiones bonæ fidei versantur in tutelis, fiduciis, mandatis, rebus emptis venditis, actionibus locati conducti, negotiis gestis, actione depositi, commodati, pignoratitiâ, familiæ erciscundæ, communi dividundo, præscriptis verbis, quæ de æstimato proponitur, et eâ quæ ex permutatione competit, et in hæreditatis petitione* [cf.Inst.4,6,28]. The

rest are *stricti juris*. The rise of this distinction was from the *formulæ*: all actions which had an exact *formula*, were *stricti juris*, and these which had not, were *bonæ fidei*, according to the account given by Seneca and Cicero. But afterward the *formulæ* being taken away, it was much questioned wherein the difference then stood. It was clear that in *actionibus stricti juris* no exception was competent, but that which was proponed in litiscontestation; but in *actionibus bonæ fidei*, exceptions were competent thereafter, and might be supplied by the judge; thereby also annualrent was due from delay, but in *actionibus stricti juris*, only from litiscontestation. Yet the controversy remained in the other differences, which is commonly determined, that *in bonæ fidei judiciis*, there are mutual prestations between both parties, and therefore either party ought so to insist, as he would allow his party in the opposite action, whereof the judge acted *ex bono et æquo*, as an arbiter; and therefore these actions were also called arbitrary actions; but he could not so proceed *in actionibus stricti juris*, which agrees with all the former actions, except *in petitione hæreditatis*, where there are no mutual prestations, save *in familia erciscunda*; yet Justinian added that action generally rather by his authority, than by the suitableness of the nature of the actions.

42. The Romans had another special kind of actions, which they called prejudicial actions, whereby questions were moved and determined, whether any person was free, or a servant, or a libertine; or when the question was, who was the father or mother of a child, as when a husband denies the child born by his wife, to be his, or denies her to have been his wife; or contrary-wise, when a woman contends her birth to be lawful, gotten of her husband; wherein, if the woman made intimation that she was with child, and the husband, nor any other in his name, denied not that it was by him, the husband could not thereafter refuse the same; or, if after divorce, the question so arose, which was only competent to the husband, denying the divorced wife was with child by him; in that case, unless the woman had intimated, the husband might have action to prove the child was not his. The like action is betwixt a child claiming to be the child, or lawful child of a father; and a father, contending the child not to be his child, or lawful child. It is also competent to the mother, or other relations of the child, in name of the child. These actions were called prejudicial, because they were not controvertible by any other persons, and therefore no collateral interest could give ground to allege a person to be a servant, a libertine, or a wife, or a child, albeit the consequence thereof were prejudicial to them, because the law allowed them not to be lawful contradictors in these points; but what was holden and reputed was sufficient. But, in many cases, one action or question may be prejudicial to another, that is, may be first determined; but all parties having interest may controvert the same.

Albeit these prejudicial actions have not, by our custom, been brought in question; yet there is no ground to doubt but they would be followed for their equity and expediency. And albeit we allow no annualrent, but where it is specially appointed by statute, or by consent of parties, or in way of penalty, neither make we difference of exceptions, as to the time of proponing the same; yet judges should have a greater latitude, and the Lords may the more exerce their *officium nobile*, in actions *bonæ fidei*, than in those which are *stricti juris*.

43. To come now to the kinds of action competent by law and custom with us, they are very few which have special names, when compared with actions in the Roman law: for even, after the taking away of the strict terms of the *formulæ*, all their ordinary actions had known names, many whereof arose from the rights whereon they were founded, as *rei vindicatio* in property; *actio confessoria et negatoria* in servitudes; and upon obligations and contracts, as *actio ex stipulatu, empti et venditi, locati et conducti, mandati et contra, depositi et contra, pro socio, actio tutelæ, &c.*, also many peculiar forms of actions were denominate from their authors, as *actio ex lege Aquilia, actio Publiciana, Pauliana, ex Senatus-Consulto Macedoniano ;* and severals had their names from the name or initial words of the *Edictum Perpetuum :* yet we have actions sufficient for attaining the same ends.

44. It were to be wished, and not difficult to be obtained, that summonses did more expressly relate unto the rights whereupon they are founded, under their legal names and titles; and that the styles were accommodated thereto, whereby they needed not so long narrations of matter of fact, but the very mention of the right would give ground for inferring the conclusions desired, which hath not been accustomed in personal actions, but those generally have been libelled as *actiones præscriptis verbis*, wherein the matter of fact is first deduced, and then the matter of right is thence inferred; after which follows the will of authority, commanding the parties pursued to appear, to hear and see the premises verified and proven, and then decerned, conform to the points of right inferred.

45. The first distinction of actions with us, is in personal and real, but not as these terms are taken in the Roman law, for that division, as is before expressed, is stretched to all actions; but with us, Real Actions are only such, wherein the ground of lands, or the profit of teinds are craved to be poinded; such as actions for poinding of the ground upon infeftments of annualrents, for feu-duties, for non-entry-duties in general declarators, or for avails of marriages, or upon ecclesiastic pensions, for affecting teinds and benefices. But we make not use of the name or nature of Vindication, whereby the proprietor pursues the possessor, or him who, by fraud, ceases to possess, to suffer the proprietor to take possession of his own, or to make up his damage by his fraud. This part of the action is rather personal than real, for reparation of the damage by the fraudulent quitting possession; yea, the conclusion of delivery doth not properly arise from vindication, which concludes no such obligement on the haver, but only to be passive, and not to hinder the proprietor to take possession of his own; wherein the Romans were so precise, that none could vindicate, but he who proved his right of property; and it was

not sufficient to recover his possession, till the Praetor gave action to him that pretended that he had acquired by usucapion, though the time was not complete: but they did not own any personal obligation upon the haver. We have shown before (*Lib.* 1, *Tit.* Restitution) that there is a real obligation upon possessors, not having a title sufficient to defend their possession, to restore or re-deliver, not only to the proprietor, but to the lawful possessor, which is also consonant to that common principle of the Roman law, *suum cuique*. Yet in our real actions by poinding of the ground, there is nothing decerned against the possessors personally, but only not to impede the poinding of the ground; therefore, in all other cases, we proceed upon the personal obligation. But we have other actions, which we neither account personal nor real, such as are all declarators, wherein there is nothing concluded, inferring any positive deed of the defenders, but only declaring the right to the pursuer, upon which he may insist by petitory or possessory judgments.

46. There is also a division of actions, in principal actions, and actions accessory. Of the last sort, are exhibitions, transferrings, transumpts, actions for division of what is common.

47. The more full division of actions with us, is in actions declaratory, petitory, and possessory. Declaratory actions are these, wherein the right of the pursuer is craved to be declared, but nothing is claimed to be done by the defender; but the effect is, that in petitory or possessory actions, the defender is excluded from any defence that might have been proponed in the declaratory action. Petitory actions are these which proceed without a declarator for establishing an entire right in the pursuer, whether it be real or personal; such as the restitution or delivery of moveables, and all poindings of the ground. These actions are also called petitory judgments, not from this, that something is claimed from the judge, but that something is claimed to be done or permitted by the defenders; and they extend to all personal actions upon contracts, and obligations of all sorts, wherein no regard is had to possession. Possessory actions or judgments are these, wherein an absolute right is not insisted for, but possession is claimed to be attained, retained, or recovered; such as actions of spuilzie, or wrongous intromission with moveables; where the pursuer needs not prove an absolute right but a lawful possession; or, though the possession at the first was *vi, clam*, or *precario*, yet it is a good title against any dispossession, except by law or consent: such also are actions for mails and duties by persons infeft; or by dispositions, assignations, apprisings or adjudications without infeftment, or upon arrestment; for all these proceed upon the right of the person infeft; but actions for making arrested goods forthcoming, affecting personal debts, are not possessory, but petitory. These possessory actions require a title in writ; but there are others that require no title, but only possession, such as ejection, intrusion, and succeeding in the vice of parties removed.

The summons on actions declaratory are called declarators; and such actions may be pursued for instructing and clearing any kind of right relating to liberty, dominion, or obligation; but they use not to be raised or insisted on, where there is no competition or pretence of any other right: yet parties may call any whom they please, the conclusion being to hear and see it found and declared, that the party had such a right; and if the parties cited please, they need not appear, if they conceive not themselves to have any pretence of right; for they will have no other prejudice, than that they cannot pretend to have had any right to the matter in question at that time, till they reduce the declarator, which they may easily do if they had lawful defences, the declarator being in absence.

As declarators may be in all points of right or possession, so, in some cases, they must be before possessory judgments can proceed, as declarators of right of property, or declarators of redemption of wadsets, &c.

In all declarators, the pursuer's title must be libelled and instructed before process, if it be in writ, even though the writs were in the defender's hands: for regularly the pursuer should have first pursued exhibition of the writs, on which he was to found, if in the hands of a third party, or even in the hands of the defender in a principal cause: yet, if he libel that the writs are in the defender's hands, and cite him personally by a messenger, or instruct his having, by writ, the Lords may sustain the same. Amongst declaratory actions, rescissory actions are comprehended, by reduction (not of decreets, for these are not ordinary actions, but come in only in the second instance).

We shall not here insist in the nature or tenor of all these declaratory actions, but shall only touch these that are of a more simple nature and common style. This is to be observed of all declaratory and rescissory actions, that the will of authority, commanding the appearance of the defenders, and the title of the pursuer, ought to be in the first place, without premising relations of fact.

48. There are other summonses that vulgarly are called special declarators, which are not declaratory but petitory, viz. special declarators of escheat, or non-entry; because the denunciation of the defender having been instructed in the general declarator, all his moveable rights are thereby declared to belong to the King or his donatar; after which he may pursue for exhibition and delivery of moveable goods, or of the writs instructing the same, or of other moveable rights, or for payment of the moveable sums falling under escheat, before any judge competent. And likewise after general declarator of non-entry, the superior or his donatar may pursue in all possessory judgments, as if he were proprietor, until the heir be entered; in all which there is nothing declaratory.

Title 4. Declarators of Property and Superiority

DECLARATORS of right proceeded of old by the brieve of right, which is now out of use; and even the actions of declarator of right or property of lands, is little in use; but in place thereof, reductions and improbations are accustomed, wherein it is not only declared, that the pursuer hath right, but also that the defender hath no right, and any pretence he hath is rescinded and declared null or false. The difference of which is, that in declarators of right, terms are competent to the defenders, upon anterior or more formal rights than the pursuers, which may bring the cause as soon to a conclusion as by reduction: but in reductions containing improbation, all the defender's rights must be produced, and there is ordinarily no litiscontestation, but only a discussion and determination of the rights produced by both parties; for there is in the summons of improbation a certification that whatever rights are called for, against which there is a reason libelled, are to be declared false and forged, if they be not produced at the terms assigned for production thereof; which certification by our constant custom is so strong, that though the defenders be absent, it cannot be recalled; and thereby it is much preferable to a declarator, against which parties absent are easily reponed; and though they do compear and be decerned, yet upon new evidence without fraud, the decreet of declarator may be reduced.

2. In this summons of declarator of property, the pursuer's title must be libelled, and albeit a charter and seasin clad with possession will be sufficient, yet the eldest progress the pursuer hath is most convenient to be libelled; and if the progress be not full and sufficient of itself, if the pursuer or his author's possession have continued forty years, by virtue of the titles required by the Act of Prescription [Prescription Act, 1594,c.218; A.P.S. iv,68,c.24], the same must be libelled accordingly, and the continuance of possession by the pursuer, his predecessors and authors must, in that case, be particularly libelled, viz. that it is either by labouring or pasturing, or by uplifting of mails and duties, which must be accordingly proven; and a citation must be at the market-cross, against all and sundry having, or pretending to have interest, and any that are suspect to have pretence of interest, must be particularly cited, or else a declarator will operate nothing against them. Albeit the possession be libelled to be without interruption, yet that being negative, is presumed, unless the contrary be proven, and therefore needs no other probation, but yearly possession of the fruits or rents by virtue of the titles libelled.

3. This declarator is very plain, and the style obvious, if the pursuer's infeftments, and the infeftments of his predecessors and authors be holden of the King, and be in the pursuer's own hands, needing no assistance by possession; for then the will is premised, and the rights are deduced as the pursuer's title, and the conclusion thence deduced, that the pursuer hath the only and irredeemable right of property. But if the pursuer's right be holden of a subject, the title must only be the infeftment he produceth; and it must be added, that he or his authors were in possession, by virtue thereof, and that thereby it became a complete right of property. And it must be added, that thereby he hath good right to prove, that he, his predecessors and authors, from whom he derives right, had the heritable and irredeemable right of the lands and others in question, anterior to any right the defenders could pre-

tend; whereby the pursuer will get a term to prove, and incident diligence against his authors and others, havers of the evidents.

4. Declarators of the right of superiority differ nothing from declarators of property, but in so far as concerns the vassals; against whom also it will proceed, whereby they will be obliged to produce their rights. These declarators being so clear, and yet so rare, for the reason mentioned, there needs no style thereof.

5. The defences competent, beside the objections of the informality of the pursuer's rights, are the defender's prior or more formal rights, or that the pursuer's rights proceeded *a non habentibus potestatem*, as being inhibited or interdicted, or being fraudulent, or *in cursu diligentiæ* of the defenders their predecessors and authors, or upon any disposition or personal right granted by the pursuer or his predecessors, to whom he is heir or apparent heir, all which are competent by exception, although they would not all be competent in a possessory judgment. Replies and duplies are competent on the same grounds.

Title 5. Declarators of Redemption

DECLARATORS of redemption are founded upon the right of reversion, legal or conventional, and the order of redemption; which in conventional redemptions is by an Instrument of Premonition, premonishing the wadsetter to receive the money at a certain time and place, conform to the reversion; which is *stricti juris*, and must be punctually observed, whether the same be done by the reverser or his procurator, whose procuratory must be known to the notar, and shown to the party if required, which must be insert in the instrument of premonition. And the Instrument of Consignation must be exactly according to the premonition, and the procuratory known, and shown if called for; wherein the liquid sums of the reversion must be offered; and if the wadsetter appear not, he must be waited for from mid-day to sun-set; for one hour is too punctual a term for consignation; and whether he compear or not, the liquid sums must be shown to be in bags, which, at the view, may carry some proportion to the reversion: but it is safest to sort and place the money on a table, that it may quickly be told, lest the wadsetter come not till sun-set. If any thing in the reversion be not liquid, an obligement to fulfil the same, at the sight of the Lords, must be offered with the money, upon a renunciation sufficient to denude the wadsetter, and to re-invest the reverser; which renunciation the wadsetter must offer, because it is his deed; and he is obliged for no more than what is sufficient: and if the wadsetter have not the renunciation, and grant of redemption ready before sun-set, or if he refuse to deliver it, or to accept the money and obligement for what is illiquid, the liquid sum must then be numerate and consigned, and thereupon instruments must be taken, relating to the reversion, the premonition, and all the points foresaid at the consignation.

2. The tenor of a summons of declarator of redemption of a wadset may

be thus: "Our will is, and we charge you, that ye lawfully summon B. to compear before the Lords of our Council and Session, upon the   day of   next to come, in the hour of cause, with continuation of days, to answer at the instance of A, as having right to redeem the lands of, &c. by virtue of a letter of reversion granted to him, or whereto he has right by progress; whereby the saids lands are provided to be redeemed upon payment or consignation of, &c. in the hands of, &c. upon the peril of, &c. and upon performance of the other conditions contained in the said reversion, viz. &c. as the said reversion dated, &c. more fully imports: That is to say, the said defender to hear and see it found and declared, That the said lands, &c. were lawfully redeemed, loosed, and out-quit from the said defender, by offer made to him by the said pursuer, of the liquid sums contained in the said reversion, and of a bond for performance of the conditions and provisions contained in the said reversion, which are not liquid and special, but general or penal, as the same should be liquidate and determined by the saids Lords, summarily upon supplication made to them by either party, upon the   day of   next to come; he always subscribing and delivering a valid grant of redemption and renunciation containing procuratory of resignation, for reseasing the said pursuer: and because the said defender did not accept the said offer, and resign accordingly, therefore the said liquid sums and bond aforesaid, were consigned in the hands of C, for the use of, and to be forthcoming to the said defender, as appears by authentic instruments taken thereupon in the hands of N, notar public, dated, &c. and that conform to the said reversion, and conform to lawful premonition made to the said defender, according to the said reversion, at the time and place contained in an instrument of premonition, bearing certification, that if the said defender compeared not, or delivered not the said renunciation, and received not the saids sums contained in the reversion, the samine should be consigned in manner foresaid; which instrument of premonition is under the hand of N, notar public, and is dated, &c. And therefore the said defender ought to be decerned to subscribe the said grant of redemption, whereof the tenor is herewith produced and repeated, as a part of this libel *brevitatis causa ;* and ought to be decerned to remove himself, his wife, bairns, cottars and servants, forth and from the saids lands, and to enter the said pursuer in the peaceable possession thereof, conform to the laws and daily practick of this realm, in all points, &c. According to justice, &c."

This form contains all that is necessary for a decreet of redemption: and the summons being of a fixed order, requiring no relation of circumstances, should not be libelled as a circumstantiate action *præscriptis verbis,* first deducing a long narration of writs, and then repeating the conclusion both before and after the Will. There uses to be added in summonses commonly these words, "That ye summon, warn, and charge the defenders, personally, or at their dwelling places; and in case they be furth of the kingdom, at the market-cross of Edinburgh, pier and shore of Leith; and the tutors and curators of such of them as are minors, at the market-cross, &c. But the first words are superfluous and improper, and the remanent words are not necessary, because, to lawfully summon comprehends them all; so that the adjection thereof is only to direct the messenger how to summon lawfully, in case he be ignorant; and therefore they shall not be repeated in the subsequent forms.

3. If this declarator be against a singular successor in the wadset right, then to the tenor of the reversion must be added, either that it is contained in the body of the wadset, or that it is duly registrate in the Register of Seasins and Reversions, expressing the place of registration in the General or Special Register, and the date thereof; otherwise the reversion is but personal, and will not be effectual against a singular successor; but will still be effectual against the granter and his heirs, or lucrative successors after the date of the reversion, being infeft upon their lucrative title: and the declarator may proceed against apparent heirs, without a charge to enter heir, which is not necessary in declaratory actions, unless they contain a petitory or possessory conclusion, or that the wadsetter was not infeft, or heir to him that granted the reversion; for, in that case, the apparent heir must be charged, and decerned to grant redemption, renunciation and resignation, and to remove and enter the reverser to the possession: or if the wadsetter was infeft upon a disposition from his author, holden *a se* of his superior; for then he must be decerned to deliver a grant of redemption, with a procuratory of resignation; yet if this superior have granted a regress, he may thereupon be compelled to enter the reverser, either by a separate petitory action, or by a conclusion in the summons of declarator; in which case the superior must be cited.

4. No exception will be competent against this declarator, upon any right of the defender's, if the reversion be in the body of the wadset, or duly registrate, as aforesaid; because the conclusion of repossession is a possessory judgment, and therefore the wadsetter must restore the possession, reserving any other right competent to the wadsetter, by way of action in a petitory judgment; even though the right he pretends to were prior to the reversion: but if the reversion be merely personal, a singular successor may defend himself by any real right.

5. If the wadsetter hath continued in possession after the order, there uses a conclusion to be added for payment of the mails and duties, so far as possessed or intromitted with by the wadsetter: but unless the quantities be proven by writ, or referred to the wadsetter's oath, it must abide terms of probation, which delays the decreet of declarator: and therefore it is much more formal to have a distinct summons of mails and duties going on with the declarator; for incongruous actions should not both be contained in one libel, to the prejudice of the writers, and of the signet.

6. This declarator is competent, either for redeeming of lands, annualrents, fishings, or any casualty: and it is competent, not only upon a written reversion, but upon a bond or condition of reversion in writ, or a promise of reversion; and in either of these cases, the title must be deduced accordingly.

7. Exceptions upon clauses irritant in reversions, which in the Roman law are called, *Pacta legis commissoriæ in pignoribus* [D.20,1,16,9], and which by that law are reprobated and void, do not impede consignation with us [11,10,6,*supra*; IV,18,3-5,*infra*]: yet of old they were not found null, but being penal, they were reduced to the just interest, and commonly a term was granted to instruct the damage through the not punctual performance. But since, there hath been little regard to these clauses in wadsets, albeit they do bear to be of consent, and renouncing all exceptions and objections in the contrary, and to be valid *ipso facto*, without declarator; for still these are exorbitant penalties, which necessitous debtors yield to. But if the reversion were gratuitous, such clauses irritant, of whatever tenor, are not penal; and therefore are valid exceptions against the redemption: or if there be not a real impignoration, but a true sale for a competent price, clauses irritant are also valid, albeit there be a reversion. And if there be a true impignoration, a temporary reversion imports a clause irritant; and being penal, the Lords will prorogate the same. But if the reversion be granted only to the reverser during his life, custom hath sustained the same; and if he use the order of redemption, though he obtain not declarator in his life, his heirs have right to obtain the same, because the order did extinguish the wadset, and the declarator doth only declare that it was extinct by the order; so that whosoever would have been heir to the reverser before he granted the wadset, hath the title and right of the declarator.

8. Reversions being *stricti juris*, should only be performed *in forma specifica;* and therefore consignation should only be in current money, and not in consignation of assignations, or the equivalent sums upon like wadsets, which require an order; nor even upon personal sums, though the Lords, *ex nobili officio*, have sometimes sustained compensation, when the reverser uplifted the consigned sums: and likewise they have sometimes sustained the order, against the defence of simulate consignation, when the sum consigned was not numerate; or being made in the hands of an insolvent person, when the reversion did bear the consignation to be upon the peril of the consigner, providing the reverser produce the money at the bar, with the annualrent since the consignation; and the deeds which are not liquid or penal, being modified by the Lords, or determined *in forma specifica.*

9. If the consignation was made through the absence, or faulty refusal of the wadsetter, and if the sum consigned was put in the hands of the clerk of the bills, or was put in the hands of the clerk of the process, the expense due to the clerk for the custody and delivery must be upon him: but if any favour be *ex officio* granted to the reverser, he must bear the expense. If the reversion bear a particular person, in whose hands consignation should be made, the reverser is not obliged to produce the money at the bar; but the Lords grant letters of horning upon the instrument of consignation, against the consignatar, to produce the sum, (although there be nothing under his hand to acknowledge the receipt of the money) in respect of the instrument adminicula-

ted by the reversion, which therefore proves unless the contrary be proven, wherein the oath of the consignatar will take off the probation by the instrument of consignation; but his successor will not be burdened thereby, unless the truth of the instrument be further instructed; yet it fully proves the using of the order: but if the consignatar do on oath deny, the reverser must produce the consigned money at the bar.

10. Declarators of redemption of apprisings have been much assisted by the Lords *ex officio*, in respect of the exorbitant advantage apprisings had. And therefore, if the appriser entered in possession before the legal expired, the rents of the land are imputed in his annualrent in the first place, and his principal sum in the next; unless he be impeded by law or force, or by the debtor's own intromission: and therefore, if an action of compt and reckoning of the intromission be raised and executed before the legal expire, the Lords sustain the redemption, upon consignation of what is found due after compt and reckoning, albeit there be no order used: and if there be no intromission, yet if the appriser do within the legal dispone a part of the apprised lands, the price will be imputed in his sum, seeing his sum is thereby truly paid, although he could communicate no more right than what he then had, and the legal cannot expire as to the rest, but it may expire as to that part of the lands or others disponed; and therefore in the declarator, the singular successors must be called; yet a summons of compt and reckoning will be sufficient against them, because it is not clear how much was paid. The compt and reckoning may be elided by protestation for not insisting, or by sentence upon a summons to insist, with certification not to be heard thereafter; or upon an opposite declarator of right upon the apprising: for by no compt of intromission with the rents or price, doth the apprising become always redeemable; but the Lords will assign a short time to produce the remainder of the sum at the bar.

If the appriser have intromitted with no part of the rents, or price of the lands apprised; an order must be used, and a declarator thereupon, of the like tenor with the former: but seeing there is no consignatar, nor time or place of premonition, as there is in conventional reversions; therefore the premonition may be upon any days sufficient for the appriser or his successor's attendance, and in any public place: and in case of absence or refusal, consignation may be made in the hands of any person, upon the peril of the consigner.

11. Declarators of redemption of infeftments granted for satisfaction of sums, or for relief of cautionries or other distresses, whereby the person infeft hath right to the whole duties, though they exceed his annualrent, to be imputed in his annualrent in the first place, and his principal sums in the next, do proceed in the same way, as in redeeming of apprisings.

12. Adjudications which proceed upon renunciations of heirs, are redeemable by creditors, in the same way as apprisings.

13. Adjudications since the Act of Parliament, stating them in place of apprisings, when they are general, are redeemable in the same way as appri-

sings. Special adjudications redeemable within five years, are redeemable in the same way as wadsets; for there is no account of intromission therein, more than in any wadset, and therefore there must still be an order; but the time of premonition, and place of consignation, and the consignatar, and hazard of his sufficiency, is the same as in apprisings. Both these adjudications have effect since the Act of Parliament introducing the same, which is dated September 6, 1672 [Adjudications Act, 1672,c.19; A.P.S. VIII,93,c.45].

Title 6. Declarator of Trust

DECLARATORS of redemption have been subjoined to declarators of property, because they relate to property redeemable, and are seldom under the terms or tenor of impignoration; and therewith there are consigned [probably "conjoined"] all declarators, which are under reversions or obligements to denude, whereby the creditor may declare his right to the subject in question, and may render it litigious, that albeit the obligement be but personal, yet singular successors thereafter cannot exclude the effect thereof. And for the like reason, declarators of trust are next considered, which differ from declarators of redemption, or declarators on bonds to denude, that, in proper trust, there is neither bond, condition, nor promise of reversion, or obligement to denude.

2. Trust, in the vulgar acceptation, comprehends all personal obligations for paying, delivering, or performing any thing, where the creditor hath no real right in security; for thereby he trusts more to the faithfulness of his debtors, that they did not engage to what they were not able to perform, and that they would not disappoint their performance, by disposing of their means in the creditor's prejudice. There are in the Roman law, several titles *de rebus creditis:* but trust properly so called, and here meant, is the "stating a right so far in the person of the trustee, as it can hardly be recovered from him, but by his faithfulness in following that, which he knows to be the true design of the truster." Such were the *fidei commissa* at first among the Romans, especially in testaments, when heirs or legatars were named to the behoof of others, by the express or presumptive will of the testator, yet without any efficacious obligement to apply the same according as was designed; and oft-times even without so much as a naked paction.

3. Trust is sometimes taken for the act of the truster, whereby he commits that which is his own to another, in confidence that he will restore the same, or dispose thereof, as the truster requires. And this is a kind of faith or confidence in the person trusted. But more properly, trust signifies the faithfulness of the trustee, to perform that which is intrusted to him. And the acts of both, make up a tacit mandate or *depositum*, whereby they mutually agree, that the thing intrusted shall be kept and preserved by the trustee, and shall be disposed of at the pleasure of the truster. The design of the truster may be either express, when he so declares by word or writ to the trustee; or it may be, when his meaning and design appeareth from the deed done, whereof

there have been many examples, and may be many more; as when a creditor takes a bond from his debtor, in name of a third party, but doth not deliver to him the bond, if that third party should pursue exhibition and delivery of the bond, as being his, the truster behoved to prove that he procured the bond by his own money and means; seeing, by our custom, there is no necessity to prove the delivery of writs, but that is presumed to have been done to, or for the person in whose favours the writ bears to be granted; but this presumption may be elided by the debtor and witnesses, unless he in whose name it is, adduce stronger evidences for it; or if a party should dispone his estate to another, who is not his apparent heir, or of near relation of blood, although the disposition were delivered, yea, though it did bear a pure donation for love and favour, or for onerous causes; yet, if it did appear that he, in whose name it was granted, had no means nor credit to purchase it, not only his oath acknowledging that he paid no money for it, nor performed any cause onerous suitable to it, but even witnesses *ex officio*, and other evidences might instruct, that it was to the behoof of the disponer, or some third party. There are many examples of proving trust, amongst Mandates, *Lib.* 1, *Tit.* 12.§ 17.

4. Trust may be of any kind of right, whether of things moveable, or heritable. And therefore the delivery of goods, or disponing or assigning of moveable rights on deathbed, where the receiver cannot instruct a reasonable cause, are interpreted as in trust, to be retained if the disponer die, but to be restored if he recover; for such deeds use not to be done, but when there is little hope of life.

5. The proper way to recover such rights given in trust, or to apply them to the design of the truster, is by a declarator of trust: this declarator, though it may be libelled as an action *præscriptis verbis*, by premising the whole matter of fact, and all the circumstances and evidences to infer the trust; yet, in effect, it is a reduction of the pretended right of the unfaithful trustee, and a declarator of the right that the truster had; and therefore ought rather to be libelled as other declarators or reductions, premising the will or command of authority, and may be in these terms: "Our will is, and we charge you, that ye lawfully summon B. to compear, &c. to answer at the instance of A. as he who did intrust the defender, and took the right underwritten in his name, to the behoof of E., and the defender knew, or might know, that the design and purpose of the pursuer was not to alienate or gift the said right, but that he might make the same forthcoming to the behoof of the said E, viz. (here insert the right intrusted) that is to say, the said defender to hear and see himself decerned to exhibit and produce before the saids Lords, the said right granted in his name by the said pursuer; and to hear and see it found and declared, by decreet of the saids Lords, that the said right was granted in trust to the behoof of the said E. for the reasons and causes after following, viz. &c. And therefore the said defender to hear and see himself decerned to denude himself of the foresaid right, in the terms and tenor of the deed herewith repeated and produced, as a part of this libel; and decerned to subscribe

before famous witnesses, the foresaid deed, and to deliver the same with the foresaid intrusted right, with all that has followed thereupon, to be used and disposed upon by him as his own proper evidents in all time coming. And als the said defender, to hear and see himself decerned, to make compt, reckoning, and payment of all profit and benefit received by him, or any deriving right or warrant from him, by virtue of the said intrusted right, or which he might have received by doing the diligence of a faithful trustee, conform to a particular account thereof produced herewith, and repeated as a part hereof. Conform to the laws and daily practick of this our realm, &c. According to Justice, &c."

If the pursuer's title be not granted to himself, but to others, from whom he hath right thereto by progress, the same must be libelled accordingly; or if the pursuit be against a singular successor of the trustee, it must be libelled, that he was conscious that the right acquired by him, was truly to the behoof of the party libelled, the samine having been so declared to him by his author, or appearing by the matter of fact, whereby he was partaker of the fraud of the trustee assigning or disponing fraudulently, contrary to his trust.

6. The proper exception in this declarator, is, on the expenses wared out necessarily or profitably upon occasion of the trust, which is competent, albeit the trustee were denuded before intenting of the declarator of trust, and is not excluded, but falls into the accompt, albeit he was fraudulently denuded, whereby the performance of his trust was imprestable *in forma specifica*, but by damage and interest; in respect that, by the necessary or profitable expense, the truster was *lucratus*, which, in all cases, is effectual, by action, or exception, unless as a penalty, it be expressly excluded by statute.

Title 7. Declarator of the Superior's Tinsel of Non-Entry, by Failing to Receive his Vassal

WE come now to declarators relating to superiority and its casualties. The first of which is, the declarator of the superior's losing the benefit of the superiority during his life, in case he obey not the precepts directed out of the chancery, for infefting his vassal. For by our feudal custom, the infeftments of vassals' heirs are to be renewed at the death of every heir, but not at the death or change of the superior: and the superior cannot compel the vassal to enter, but hath the benefit of non-entry until he enter. And on the other part, if the superior receive not his vassal, he loses the benefit of his non-entry, which falls in two cases. The one is, when the superior is infeft in the superiority: for then the vassal being retoured special heir, holding of such a superior, he gets, of course, precepts out of the chancery, to charge that superior to infeft him as heir, and upon the disobedience of that precept, he gets a second, and a third; and if all be disobeyed by the superior, the Lords give horning against that superior's immediate superior, to supply his place, and receive the vassal, whereby the superior loseth the non-entry of that vassal during his life: to evite which, superiors use to obtain from the Lords suspensions of these precepts; wherein, if the superior succumb, he loses the non-entry and is liable for the vassal's damage, which is modified by the Lords. The other case is, when the superior himself is not infeft, for which there is a remedy provided, Parl. 1474, cap. 58. [Act 1474,c.57; A.P.S. 11,107, c.13]. "Whereby the superior is ordained to do diligence to enter to the superiority, within forty days after requisition made by the vassal, and if he fail, incontinent thereafter the vassal is to be entered by the King, or by that superior's superior, and shall hold of him: and the vassal's immediate superior shall tine the tenant for his lifetime, and satisfy the vassal's skaith." Whereupon the Lords ought to give a summary charge against the superior's superior, if a subject, or a warrant to the director of the chancery, if the superior hold of the King; but, in neither case, doth the superior lose any more but the non-entry during that vassal's life, and no other casualty of the superiority.

2. The tinsel of the non-entry by the superior's disobedience, is competent by way of exception against the superior, or his donatar, pursuing for non-entry. And it may be pursued by way of action and declarator against the superior, his heirs, or successors in the superiority, for freeing that vassal or his singular successors from non-entry upon the superior's disobedience. This action is necessary, because the precepts out of the chancery have not the effect of charges of horning, either for caption or escheat, and therefore the superior was to be convened by way of action, to hear and see it found and declared, that he had lost the benefit of non-entry; and that the vassal ought to be received by his superior supplying his place for that time. In which declarator his superior is to be called, that it may be declared against him, that he ought to supply the place of the immediate superior if he be a subject. But now, when actions must abide the course of the roll, and the process having been so tedious against the superior by the three precepts, letters of horning should not be denied, to charge the superior's superior, if a subject, to supply, by receiving the vassal, unless the immediate superior have suspended the precepts, in which case he would be charged upon the decreet of suspension [11,3,29,*supra*].

3. The proper exception in this declarator, or reason of suspension of the charge is, either a reduction of the retour, thereby excluding the pretended vassal from being a true vassal, which is receivable by way of exception, or reason of suspension, because the service passeth without citation of parties; or otherwise the competent exception is, that the non-entry-duties preceding the precepts, were not paid, nor offered and consigned; but this will not be sustained further than for the retoured duties: for if a general declarator have passed, the vassal will not be excluded upon non-payment of the full duties, because they are not *debita fundi*, and therefore the vassal is no further obliged than any other intromitter. But the exception will be relevant for the relief, not exceeding the retoured duty, which only occurs in ward-holdings.

4. But seeing it is like, that the Lords will not put vassals to an action, but will grant summary charges, it is not necessary to propose the tenor of this declarator.

5. If the fee be holden feu, it hath been controverted, and not yet clearly determined, whether, during the non-entry before summons of declarator, the superior should have no benefit by the non-entry? (For if the feu-duty serve for the non-entry duty, he can have no benefit before the citation in the general declarator.) Or whether the feu-duty should be doubled, the one half being superadded in place of the retoured duty? If the feu-duty serve for both, the contumacious superior should lose it during the vassal's life: but, if the superior have pursued for the non-entry, whereby the vassal became contumacious in not entering, it affords a relevant defence or reason of suspension, against losing of the non-entry-duties; unless the vassal had not a competent time to be served and retoured.

6. I have not known it determined, whether the *annus deliberandi* be competent to vassals, before they be obliged to raise brieves, for their service? For which there appears to be the same reason, as to defend them against creditors; in which case they cannot be contumacious for not entering, till they have a competent time after their year of deliberation. But there is no doubt, that if then they be negligent, the superior's contumacy will not exclude him from the non-entry, for all the terms from the defunct's death. It is also a competent exception or reason of suspension against the entry of vassals, that they have not fulfilled that article of the precept, *capiendo securitatem, &c.*

Title 8. Declarator of Non-Entry

W E come now to the casualties of superiority. The first whereof is the non-entry duties of the fee, while it is void, the vassal not being infeft therein; which occurs in divers ways (as hath been explicated, *Lib.* 2, *Tit.* 4. [11,4,18, *supra*]). For the superior having the *dominium directum* of the fee, nothing excludes him from the full benefit thereof, but the right of the vassal, which is not complete until he be infeft, *nulla sasina, nulla terra :* yet, while the vassal is not contumacious in lying out uninfeft wilfully, the superior or donatar hath only the rent by the favourable account, by the new retoured duties, which was the old rent, by a valuation of the whole temporal lands of the kingdom, as they were then esteemed worth, all burdens deduced; which retoured duties are *debita fundi*, and thereupon the ground may be poinded, which cannot proceed till there precede a declarator of non-entry: and though a poinding of the ground be not a declaratory, but a petitory action, and it is more formal that they should be in two several summonses, going on together, that so soon as the declarator is decerned, the poinding of the ground may immediately be also decerned, seeing there is nothing more to be proven, but what is contained in the declarator, yet both use to be sustained in the same libel, whereby it is a complex action. It is not proper to say any thing here of the nature or tenor of poinding of the ground, till its proper place amongst petitory actions [IV,23,*infra*].

2. The declarator of non-entry may and doth proceed, either at the instance of the superior, or at the instance of his donatar, who in effect is his assignee, and therefore the action proceeds in the name, and upon the right of the superior; yet there is no necessity to express the superior's right, unless it be a liferenter in conjunct-fee who pursues, and whose right the vassal is not obliged to know: yet it is more convenient and effectual, that in the pursuer's title both the superior's right, and the donatar's be libelled, and at least the superior's seasin and the donatar's gift be produced: for without the gift no process will be sustained. And albeit the vassal may deny the superior's right, which would infer disclamation, and loss of the property, yet the superior cannot make use of both; and, therefore, if he make use of the disclamation, the non-entry must cease: for no man can be both superior and proprietor at once of the same fee; yea, disclamation will not follow, if the vassal had just ground of doubting, whether the party claiming the superiority was truly superior, even though he might find his seasin in the Register; as if the vassal were infeft upon apprising or adjudication, and had not recovered his author's infeftment, whereby he might know of whom he held; or if his predecessor's or author's seasin were held of another kind of heir than he who now claims it, seeing the service of heirs proceeds without calling of parties, and thereby if a wrong heir were served, the vassal owning him might hazard disclamation: or if the superior had acquired right by apprising or adjudication, he were obliged to produce a complete title, and not his seasin only.

3. Non-entry also uses to be pursued, for declaring that the superior or his donatar has right to the full rents and duties. But it is not convenient so to libel it: for although the vassal were absent, he will easily recover in the second instance, by [?the] restricting to retoured duties. If there be not a special retour, but the right of a part of a barony, which hath one retour for the whole, yet the non-entry may proceed; but in the poinding of the ground the pursuer must libel and prove the rent of the whole barony, that the retour of the whole may be divided proportionally. And albeit the declarator will be sustained, though it bear not that the lands are holden ward, because that is presumed, as being the nature of a proper fee; yet it is safest to libel, that the fee was holden ward or blench. Kirk lands were not retoured; and therefore the retoured duty is the feu-duty. Annualrents had no retour; and therefore the whole annualrent was carried by the general declarator, till the late Act of Parliament [Act 1690,c.42; A.P.S. IX,222,c.96] ordaining, that in time thereafter general declarators should only carry the *reddendo* of the annualrent.

4. The tenor of the most ordinary declarator of non-entry is at the instance of a donatar; and therefore it is fittest to express the same: for there is no difference when it is at the instance of a superior, but that the donatar's interest is left out. And if the King be superior, the Treasurer, or Commissioners of Treasury, or the Advocate, are pursuers. And in the king's non-entry

the Advocate must be libelled, as concurring for the king's interest. The tenor of such a declarator of non-entry may be as follows: "Our will is, and We charge you, that ye lawfully summon C, heir to B of, &c, and also O, P, Q,,R, tenants and possessors of the saids lands, to compear, &c. to answer at the instance of A, donatar to the non-entry of the said defender, by a gift of non-entry, granted by S, immediate lawful superior thereof, by virtue of his infeftment of the samine, by charter or precept, dated, &c. and seasin following thereupon, under the hand and subscription of N, notar-public, dated, &c. duly registrate in the Register of Seasins, &c. upon the day   of   , &c. which gift of non-entry is dated the   day of, &c. That is to say, the said defender to hear and see it found and declared, that the saids, &c. have been in non-entry in the hands of the said superior thereof, since the death of the said B, who died last vest and seased of the samine, and who deceased in the month of   , *anno*, &c. Or by a nullity of the heir's infeftment; Or by the acquirer's neglect to insist for infeftment, upon the resignation of his author; Or by the vassal's neglect to renew his infeftment, upon his own resignation: And that the retour-mails, or feu-duties of the same, yearly and termly, since the time foresaid, did belong and pertain to the said pursuer as donatar, and in time coming, ay and while the entry of the righteous heir or heirs: and that the said donatar, by virtue of his said gift, hath good and undoubted right to poind the ground of the saids lands, &c. for the saids non-entry duties, bygone and in time coming, until entry of the righteous heir to the samine; together with a year's duty foresaid, for the relief of the samine, after the entry of the saids heirs, conform to the said gift, laws and practicks of this realm in all points, &c. with certification, &c. According to justice, &c."

5. The effect of this declarator is, not only the poinding of the ground, if the fee be of land, by poinding the goods on the ground, not exceeding the tenants their term's mail, as the samine shall be declared by them upon oath; but also the full rents from the citation in the general declarator, become due. But if the fee be an annualrent, a mill or a fishing, that hath not goods on the ground, the ground-right and property thereof (and also of the land, failing goods thereon) is to be apprised or adjudged; and the full annualrent or profit of the mill or fishing, is to belong to the donatar, until the entry of the lawful heir, which needs no other declarator, but an ordinary action before any judge competent, superior or inferior, which is improperly called a special declarator.

6. But seeing heirs have a year to deliberate after the defunct's death, albeit during that year the declarator may proceed; yet neither the action for poinding of the ground, nor for the full profits, ought to proceed till the year of deliberation be ended: yet the citation may be within the year, so that the day of compearance be after it.

7. Beside the objections against this declarator, and the general exceptions against this and other rights, there are several special exceptions against

non-entry [11,4,23,*supra*]; as first, that the fee is full by a conjunct-fiar, or by the reserved liferent of the fiar: but any other liferent will not afford a relevant defence. The second exception is, that the heir himself is infeft. But neither of these exceptions will exclude the non-entry, for any terms after the defunct's death, and before the infeftment, unless the heir be infeft with a *novodamus*, renouncing all casualties of superiority in general, or in particular, non-entry: the heir's entry also must be voluntary, as by precepts of *clare constat*: for if the heir be entered upon obedience, there is yet place for the donatar to reply upon any relevant ground, that in an ordinary action might have excluded the entry of the heir; as that the heir did not give caution, conform to the clause *capiendo securitatem;* or that being required, he did not pay the retoured duties, feu-duties, or blench-duties of annualrents due before the charge: and therefore these or the like may be repeated as replies, to stop the declarator, or to exclude the exception, until the samine be satisfied. The third exception is, upon the consent of the superior, by confirmation of infeftment granted by the defunct vassal, confirmed by the superior, which is effectual from the date of the charter confirmed: but the superior's confirmation of a charter to be holden of his vassal, doth not exclude the non-entry of his vassal's heir. The fourth exception is, upon three subsequent seasins voluntarily given, as having the same effect with three subsequent discharges, importing a liberation from any thing prior. The fifth exception is, if the superior or his donatar have not insisted for his non-entry, for the space of forty years, during which time the fee hath been full, in whatever way; for thereby not only the duties preceding the forty years are excluded by common prescription, but the non-entry itself is understood to be past from, though the infeftments, whereby the fee was full, were not voluntary, but upon obedience. Craig [11,19,17] holds this exception sufficient, though the fee were but full for thirty-six years, which is not a legal term. He doth also hold [11,19, 19], with very good reason, that if the vassal died in the service of his superior, he ought to receive his heir *gratis* unless contempt appear by not taking infeftment, when cited by a declarator of non-entry: for though the superior give a precept with warrandice, yet if the vassal neglect to take seasin, the fee is in non-entry from the date of the precept. The sixth exception is, the superior's contumacy in not infefting the vassal's heir, upon the precepts out of the chancery, or if being required himself to enter to the superiority, he did not the same. The seventh exception is, upon the preference of real burdens on the fee, such as terces of relicts, or the liferent of the husbands of heiresses by the courtesy of Scotland, or any other feu-duty, annualrent, or real burden.

8. The minority of the heir affords no defence against the retoured duties, or full duties; because this casualty arises from the nature of the fee; yea, the non-entry takes place for the terms after the defunct vassal's death, though his apparent heir was not born, or though he was only in hope; as it may occur in several branches of tailzies, if the entry of the nearest heir existent be suspended, in hope of the existence of an heir of the body of a prior branch,

though not yet begotten. But all things that excuse the contumacy, or contempt of the apparent heir, do exclude the full duties.

9. Gifts of ward and non-entry by the King, passing in exchequer, do bear as the common style, the "non-entry ay and while the entry of the lawful heir;" but though the style be continued, yet custom hath restricted it to three terms after the expiry of the ward, which doth also comprehend the year of relief; which would not so hold in the gifts of subjects: for these would be extended according to their tenor. It were a rigorous extension of non-entry subsequent to a ward, to extend it to the full duties, even though the superior or his donatar were in possession; seeing in that time the heir may be retoured, and the superior charged by precepts out of the chancery: and therefore the superior could not justly refuse to enter the vassal's heir, even though his year of deliberation were running, he could not be said to be contumacious, or to contemn his superior, having that privilege by the law.

Title 9. Declarator of Liferent-Escheat

DECLARATOR of liferent-escheat is congenerous with declarator of non-entry; and therefore is subjoined thereto. For the vassals being denounced rebels, and at the horn, they have not person to stand in judgment, and are as *civiliter mortui*, whereby their fees are open, and in the hands of their several superiors. And though it is called liferent-escheat, as being confiscated as a penalty of that civil rebellion, yet the true original of it is the fee's being void through the incapacity of the vassal to enjoy it, otherwise all liferent-escheats would belong to the King, as do the liferents of forfeited persons, as being truly penal for the crime of treason; but other liferents belong to the several superiors, and are amongst the casualties of superiority: yet when a liferent is not by infeftment, but by personal obligement, as is the annualrent of an heritable sum, where infeftment has not followed, the same belongs to the King, and also liferent-tacks; neither of which are casualties of superiority, or belonging to vassals as such. Liferent-escheat is rather *inter bona vacantia*, through the vassal's incapacity, than amongst those which are properly called escheat.

2. Liferent-escheat doth not arise from the nature of fees, or from the general feudal customs, but by our particular statutes and customs; and therefore it befalls to the several superiors *cum suo onere;* whereby whatsoever did affect the same, while in the hands of the vassal, the same doth affect it in the hands of the superior [111,3,26,*supra*]: in which it differs from the common casualties of superiority, as ward and non-entry; for these return to the superior as he gave them, with such burdens only as he gave it with, or whereunto he consented, or such as were introduced by statute, as terces of relicts, and liferents of husbands by the courtesy.

3. Declarator of liferent may either proceed in name of the King or other superior, or at the instance of their donatars, as being their assignees. If it be

at the instance of the King or his donatar, it must contain the concourse of his Advocate. But the most simple declarator is at the instance of the superior, being a subject, wherein all the necessary requisites must be libelled; and though the superior's title be sometimes omitted to be libelled or produced, because, if the vassal deny the same, it may infer disclamation; yet it is safest to libel his title, for the reasons given in the declarator of non-entry, which hold alike in this case.

4. This declarator should not be libelled as an action *præscriptis verbis*, not falling into a known style; but the will should be premised, and the tenor may be as follows: "Our will is, and We charge you, that ye lawfully summon B to compear, &c. to answer at the instance of A, who stands infeft in the lands of, &c. by precept, charter or disposition, and seasin following thereupon, dated, &c. and thereby having right of property of the samine, at least of the superiority thereof, and thereby hath right to the rents, duties, and profits of the samine; That is to say, (in case the said B shall produce and intrust his right to the property or liferent of the said lands, as vassal therein) to hear and see it found and declared, That the said defender was lawfully denounced upon letters of horning, raised at the instance of   for the causes therein contained, which letters are dated, &c. and the denunciation thereupon is dated, &c. duly registrate in the Register of Hornings, at E, conform to the Act of Parliament; and that he hath contemptuously remained unrelaxed therefrom, for the space of year and day, from the time of the foresaid denunciation: And that thereby the saids lands are become in the hands of the said pursuer, as lawful superior thereof; and that the rents, profits and emoluments of the samine belong to the said pursuer, and that of all years and terms since the said denunciation, and yearly and termly in time coming, ay and while the said defender be lawfully relaxed from the horn, conform to the laws and daily practick of this our realm, in all points. Or else to allege a reasonable cause in the contrary, with certification, &c. According to justice, &c."

5. With this declarator, the petitory part of the mails and duties uses sometimes to be joined; and then the tenants and possessors must be called, and the quantities must be proven, and so the summons must have double diets. But this is not the regular way; yet, for speedy attaining to possession, the summons of mails and duties may be raised with the declarator, and proceed therewith; and so soon as the said declarator is extracted, the possessors will be obliged to answer in the action of mails and duties.

6. The proper exceptions against this declarator, are founded upon the burdens affecting the liferent, or the estate liferented, while it was in the vassal's hand [11,4,65; 111,3,26,*supra*]; whereby, not only infeftments of annualrent, but even tacks clad with possession, are relevant exceptions; yea, arrestments, if diligence have followed; but all must be prior to the denunciation. 2. There is another kind of exceptions more proper, that where vassals were obliged to grant infeftments, or other rights before the denunciation, if they

be perfected within year and day after the denunciation, the same are relevant against the declarator, whether the obligement be express by bond, or by disposition importing an obligement to infeft. But a base infeftment, though before denunciation, will not be effectual, unless it obtain possession within that year. Neither hath inhibition any effect against this declarator, though prior to the denunciation, unless infeftment be upon the ground of the inhibition within the year. Neither is apprising or adjudication relevant, though prior to the denunciation, unless infeftment follow thereupon within year and day thereafter.

7. The law has indulged a year and day after denunciation to relax; but the rents and duties from the denunciation are due, in so far as they are not exhausted by the burdens aforesaid; yet the rents within the year have been found to fall to the donatar of single escheat. Defences upon objections against the horning, are not receivable by exception, because the King being concerned in the effect of horning, as to the single escheat, it cannot be taken away, until the Officers of State be called by way of action; and therefore, if there be any ground of reduction, the vassal, so soon as he is cited, may raise reduction, which thereby may be brought in by way of exception, if the production be satisfied.

Title 10. Declarator of Single Escheat

DECLARATOR of single escheat hath the nearest resemblance to the declarator of liferent-escheat, so that the differences only betwixt the two are necessary to be observed. As that, single escheat belongs only to the King, or to his donatars; amongst which are the Lords of Regality, or the heritable bailies thereof, having the benefit of escheat in their charters. And this declarator of escheat is always at the instance of these, or of other donatars, all being the King's assignees, with whom the King's Advocate concurs for his Majesty's interest. But liferent-escheats belong to all superiors, and use to be declared in their names, as well as in the names of donatars.

2. Liferent-escheat is only burdened with real burdens affecting the same before denunciation, or for which there was an anterior obligement, or inchoate right perfected within year and day, by infeftment or charge. But single escheat is burdened with the debt in the horning whereupon it fell, Parl. 1592, cap. 145. [A.P.S. 111,574,c.66; 111,3,16,*supra*]. Which therefore is proper to the first horning; but any horning produced is presumed to be the first, if a prior be not shown: and therefore the gift given upon any horning, if it bear with the burden of the ground of that horning, doth become so burdened by the tenor of the gift.

3. Single escheat is also burdened with the preference of lawful creditors, whose debts are before denunciation, and who have obtained payment *bona fide* from the party denounced, or by poinding, arrestment and decreet for making forthcoming, before decreet of declarator obtained by the donatar, whereby the escheat-goods and rights are established in his person, and the

King is denuded of the right thereof: for, till then, the King allows prefer-ence to lawful creditors for moveable debts. But there is no limited time in that preference, as in liferent-escheat: for the decreet of declarator, whenso-ever obtained, terminates the preference. Creditors obtaining satisfaction of debts due before denunciation, by assignations or dispositions of moveables, albeit voluntarily granted by the rebel, and satisfaction being obtained before declarator, are secure against gratuitous donatars, but not against donatars, who, upon their own horning, obtain gifts, as to the debt in the horning, be-cause that is a legal diligence for payment of that debt, but it will not be so extended to other debts due to the donatar. There is no necessity here to de-termine what falls under single escheat, or what are the specialities in the pre-ference of creditors, because this declarator is only general, declaring the party to be duly denounced, and thereby all his escheatable goods and rights to belong to the King and his donatar. And thereupon the donatar having de-clared his right, hath interest to pursue for, and intromit with all his escheat-able goods and rights, before whatever judge competent; and these actions are called special declarators, but very improperly. The particulars both of the right and burden of single escheat are handled amongst confiscations, *Lib.* 3.[111,3,*supra*].

4. The tenor of this declarator may be thus: "Our will is, and We charge you, that ye lawfully summon B, or his wife, bairns, and nearest of kin, he being deceased, to compear, &c. to answer at the instance of A, Lord or bailie of the regality of   or our or their donatar, by virtue of our or their gift of single escheat, dated, &c. That is to say, the said defender to hear and see it found and declared, That he was lawfully denounced rebel, and put to the horn, upon a decreet obtained against him at the instance of E, by virtue of letters of horning duly executed against him, which denunciation is of the date, &c. and the said horning is registrate in the Register of Hornings, &c. And that there-through all moveable goods, and all other moveable and es-cheatable rights, which did belong to the said defender, the time of his de-nunciation, or that accresced, were acquired, or did belong to him, at any time thereafter, before he be duly relaxed from the horn, doth belong and ap-pertain to the complainer, as his own proper goods and rights, to be intro-mitted with, and disposed upon at his pleasure, conform to the the laws and practick of this our realm, in all points, &c." Note, The King's Advocate's concourse must be mentioned, if the action proceeds upon the King's gift.

5. No defence is receivable against this declarator, on any objection against the horning, which is only competent by way of reduction, albeit the Advocate be pursuer; because, in the same horning, the King's interest in the liferent-escheat may be concerned.

Title 11. Declarator of the Avail of Marriage

THERE uses to be no declarator of ward; because the vassal, during the ward, was in the custody of the superior of old, and was educated and alimented by him; and therefore he needed no more declare his right than any tutor, but did immediately enter to the possession of his vassal's ward-fees.

2. But the casualty of the avail of his vassal's marriage hath no effect till the ward be ended. And the avail not being liquid, it must be declared what the true avail is, whether the marriage be due in ward-holding by the nature of the fee, or in feus *cum maritagio* by the tenor of the investiture, which is regulated according to the marriage in ward-holdings, unless the infeftment bear any express alteration; and that, albeit the nature of the rights be very much different; for in ward-holdings, the vassal hath no benefit but his aliment, till the ward be ended; but in feu-holdings the vassal hath the full benefit from his predecessor's death, if he timeously enter.

3. The avail of the marriage of a ward-vassal is introduced by our feudal customs, and not by express paction, and had its rise from the nature of proper fees granted for military service; and therefore while the vassal was minor, and was accounted unfit for that service, the superior enjoyed his military fee fully; and thereby the vassal's apparent heir, if he had no other estate, was in distress: and therefore our custom introduced a mutual obligement upon the superior and the vassal, to this effect, that the superior should supply the vassal's aliment, so far as he had no other estate during the ward; and that he should have the vassal's tocher, as a real burden affecting the fee after the ward, and that *optima fide;* and therefore, if he did by any precipitation, or collusion, diminish the value of his marriage, or exclude it, the superior should have such an avail of his marriage, as were suitable to his estate when he married; or at least that he should not forbear to marry till the ward ended, to delay his superior's casualty; and therefore the superior was allowed to declare the value of his marriage when he married, or at any time after he became marriageable during the ward; his marriageable age being accounted fourteen years complete; so that, if he married before that age, and died before he attained to it, his fee should be free of the marriage.

4. Though the avail of a marriage doth not burden the apparent heir personally, nor his other rights, but only the fee, by poinding of the ground [11, 4,41 and 48,*supra*], yet it is modified with respect to all his free estate, and is ordinarily modified to two years' free rent or thereby. But if the superior offer him a suitable match, keeping the formalities appointed, and he refuse the same; in that case, the avail is heightened a year further, and is therefore called the double avail. Both have been explicated amongst the casualties of superiority, *Lib.* 2, *Tit.* 4. The petitory part for poinding of the ground, uses to be joined with the declarator in the same libel; but it may be more regularly carried on with it, in a distinct libel.

5. The tenor of this declarator may be thus: "Our will is, and We charge you, That ye lawfully summon B, as holding the lands of   of C, at the least as heir apparent in the saids lands, holden ward, or feu *cum maritagio*, to compear, &c. to answer at the instance of the said C, or at the instance of B, his donatar, by virtue of his gift of the avail of the marriage, of the near-

est lawful heir of the last deceased vassal, which gift is dated, &c. That is to say, the said defender to hear and see it found and declared, That the avail of a marriage is due out of the saids lands, to the said superior or his donatar, by modification of the Lords of our Council and Session, according to the condition of the estate of the heir, or apparent heir: and that the said defender is apparent heir in the said estate, and that he is of age marriageable, being past fourteen years complete; and that the saids lands ought to be poinded for the avail of the marriage, at the expiring of the ward. And to hear and see it verified and proven, that the defender hath an estate, whereof the particular lands, annualrents, and sums of money, render of rent and profit the sum of   yearly, conform to a particular account thereof produced herewith, and repeated as a part of this libel *brevitatis causa*, according to which rent the avail of the said marriage ought to be modified, conform to the laws and daily practick of this our realm, &c. According to justice, &c."

6. The proper exceptions to be proponed here, are the burdens upon the estate of the vassal, at the time he is pursued for declaring the avail, for which the same term that is to be assigned for proving of his rent and annualrent, will be assigned to the defender to prove the debt and burdens, that the free rent may appear. Defences are also competent against the instruments of offer of a match without disparagement, which have been spoken to in the fore-mentioned place, with the other exceptions, which have been sustained or repelled in this declarator.

7. This declarator requiring probation of the free estate of the vassal, by witnesses, or oath of party, must have a double diet of compearance.

Title 12. Declarator of Bastardy

BASTARDS are accounted *vulgo quæsiti*, where polygamy or concubinate are not allowed; and therefore they are esteemed to be *incerto patre*, which no contrary probation can avoid, so that it is *præsumptio juris et de jure ;* therefore bastards have no agnates, and neither can have heirs, nor can be heirs to any other agnates, unless it be by a tailzie, in which the bastard is named as a branch of the tailzie. I have not observed it controverted, whether they may be heirs to their mothers, or cognates of her line; but, unless statute or custom have otherwise determined, in favour of lawful marriage, there is no ground to seclude them from their mother's succession, or these of her line; but as to the paternal line, they can neither be heirs, nor have heirs, except those of their own bodies by lawful marriage; and therefore all their means and estate, are *bona vacantia nullius ;* and yet they do not fall to the first possessor, but do belong to the King as Sovereign, or to any other sovereign power, as a part of the public revenue. But the King's officers, or his donatars, have no petitory action for meddling therewith, till first declarator of the bastardy precede.

2. In this declarator there is no necessity to call any person specially, because none do represent bastards but the lawful issue of their own bodies, if

any such be: this declarator hath no place, so long as they or their lawful issue continue; but, whenever they fail, the King has action to declare their estates, real and personal, to belong to him or his donatar, which extends not only to that person who had no succession, but to the means of any of his predecessors, intervening betwixt him and the bastard [IV,12,6,*infra*].

3. The means and estate of bastards comes to the King *cum suo onere*, with the burden of all that could have affected the same in the bastard's hands, as the terce and third of the bastard's relict, whereby she may be served to a terce, and may recover the half of the free goods, from the donatar or any intromitter, and may defend her possession thereof, without hazard of being vitious intromitter: for a bastard can have no heirs in rights heritable or moveable, nor can grant legacies, unless he had a gift of legitimation, or a power to test from the King: and, by parity of reason, the bastard can do no effectual deed on deathbed, at least the King may reduce the same *ex capite lecti*.

4. Albeit the King's donatar be liable to suffer the bastard's estate to be affected with his debt or disposition in *liege poustie*, yet he is not personally liable; but must be called *cognitionis causa*, for declaring and establishing the debt, whereupon adjudication may follow, either of the bastard's moveables, or heritable rights, or the moveables may be arrested and made forthcoming.

5. If the bastard had infeftments of land or annualrent, the King uses to dispone the same to a donatar, and then the declarator is a kind of declarator of property, and a special declarator of bastardy. It were convenient that the disposition should bear a clause not to take infeftment, till the declarator were first past; otherwise any man's estate might have the burden and affront, by an infeftment of his estate, under pretence of bastardy.

6. Law doth not allow bastardy to be declared after the death of the bastard, and therefore the declarator must bear, that the bastard was so holden and reputed during his life. Yet, when the issue of the bastard's body fails, the bastardy may be declared after the bastard's death: for, in that case, the pursuit may be, as upon the title of *ultimus hæres;* for, if the issue of the bastard's body be extinct, all his means fall to the King as *ultimus hæres*, because none of them could have an heir.

7. The tenor of the declarator of bastardy may be thus: "Our will is, and We charge you, that ye pass to the market-cross of the head-burgh of

where B bastard did reside at the time of his death, and to the head-burghs of the shires where his lands and annualrents, or other rights by infeftment, lie, and there, by open proclamation, lawfully summon all and sundry having, or pretending to have interest, in the estate of the said B, to compear, &c. to answer at the instance of D our donatar, as having right by disposition from us, to the lands, annualrents, or other heritable rights by infeftment, &c. or by gift: That is to say, to hear and see it found and declared, that the said B was holden and reputed bastard, and that his mother was never lawfully married, or at least never lawfully married to A, who was commonly reported to be his father; and that thereby the lands, annualrents, heritage, debts, sums of money, goods and gear, belonging to the said bastard the time he contracted the sickness whereof he died, did fall and belong to us by his death, without lawful issue of his own body, and now belongs to our said donatar, as having a gift of bastardy, or disposition of the lands, or others wherein the bastard died last vest and seased, as of fee, viz.　　　And that Our said donatar has good and undoubted right thereto, by virtue of the said disposition; and that he may lawfully take infeftment thereupon, as his own proper heritage, conform to the laws and daily practick of this Our realm, &c. According to justice, &c."

8. If a bastard die without issue, within a regality, having the benefit of bastard's goods, the declarator must proceed at the instance of the Lord or Bailie of Regality, or their donatar, with concourse of the King's Advocate, because the right is only founded upon the royal interest; the Lord or Bailie of Regality being only the King's donatar, and pursuing in his right.

9. Albeit no person needs be specially cited to this declarator, yet any concerned may appear and defend upon the general citation.

10. This declarator must have two diets; because witnesses are to prove that the bastard was in his lifetime so reputed: and if there be any disposition of his heritable rights, the property cannot be declared, without some evidence of the bastard's title; for the quinquennial possession is not in this case as in forfeiture.

11. The proper exception against this declarator is, that the party pretended to be bastard, was lawfully begotten, and that his father or mother were lawfully married: at least lived and cohabited together as man and wife; at least were so holden and reputed at the dissolution of the marriage: or that the bastard was legitimated by the King's gift, anterior to the donatar's gift or disposition. How the being lawfully begotten may be instructed, and the other instances against bastardy, may be seen upon that head, *Lib.* 3, *Tit.* Confiscation [111,3,42 *et seq., supra*].

Title 13. Declarator of the King's Right, as Last Heir

THE King's right, as last heir, befalls when a defunct dies, to whom none can be entered heir of line or blood, or executor upon that title; and therefore such a defunct's whole estate and means are *bona vacantia*, and belong to the King, or any other sovereign authority, as a part of the public revenue. But the King is not truly heir, but as heir; and therefore his donatar is not personally liable, as the defunct's heir would have been, but is only liable to suffer sentences and execution against the defunct's estate. But in any mutual contract, if the donatar crave the benefit of it, he must perform the mutual obligements as the cause of it, not as a personal obligement, but as a quality of the right; otherwise it were *causa data causa non secuta*.

2. There is little difference in the declarator of *ultimus hæres*, from the declarator of bastardy. The tenor thereof may be thus: "Our will is, and We

charge you, that ye pass to the market-cross of the head-burgh of the shire of E, where B dwelt when he died, and also to the market-cross of the head-burgh of the shire of F, where the lands and others wherein he died last vest and seased, lie, viz.   and there lawfully summon, warn, and charge all and sundry having, or pretending interest, as heirs, successors, or creditors of the said B, to compear, &c. to answer at the instance of Our Advocate, for Our interest, and also at the instance of D our donatar, as having right to the saids lands of   wherein the said B died last vest and seased, as of fee, by virtue of Our gift or disposition, dated, &c. That is to say, to hear and see it found and declared, that all lands, heritages, debts, sums of money, goods and gear, which belonged to the said B the time of his decease, or the time of contracting the disease whereof he died, do belong to Our said donatar, by virtue of the said gift or disposition granted by Us to him; and that Our said donatar, by virtue thereof, has good and undoubted right to the lands, and others above-written; and that he may lawfully take infeftment thereon, and dispose of the same as his own proper heritage, in all time coming, conform to the laws and daily practick of this our realm, &c. According to justice, &c."

3. If any person appear, and condescend upon his propinquity of blood, it will found a dilator during the year of deliberation, that he may have competent time to deliberate, that he may enter himself heir; in which case the Lords will easily advocate the service to the macers and assessors [111,3,47, *supra*].

Title 14. Declarator of Recognition, Disclamation and Purpresture

THESE declarators are competent to all superiors, in the several cases wherein they occur; and they are founded upon the nature of fees, which necessarily imply the fidelity of the vassals to their superiors: and therefore it is as a clause irritant in the investiture, if the vassal act any thing atrocious against that fidelity in any fee. But if, in a proper fee or wardholding, the vassal alienate the fee, or the major part thereof, or if he disclaim his superior wittingly, or if he invade his superior's adjacent property, by adjecting it to his own, these deeds do resolve his fee, and make it return into the hands of his superior; whereby he recognosceth it, or owneth it to become again his own property, albeit there be no mention of any of these in the vassal's infeftment. But the superior cannot possess himself of the fee, or pursue any possessory judgment, until the recognition of the fee be first declared [11,11,10–28, *supra*].

2. Albeit disclamation and purpresture have these proper names and titles, which use to be handled apart, yet they are but particular kinds of recognition; and therefore the tenor of the recognition is one in them all, though the particular acts inferring the recognition, whether one or more, must be specially libelled: as if in blench or feu-holdings, the deed inferring recognition be the killing, wounding, or beating the superior, or an atrocious

deed importing infamy against him; or in ward-holdings, the disclaiming him as superior directly, or indirectly by owning another as superior wittingly, or by alienating or burdening the fee above the half of the value, without the superior's consent, whether by infefting another to be holden *à se* of the superior, or holden *de se*, or granting infeftments of annualrent exceeding the value of the half of the fee: in all which cases the tenor is the same; but these specialities are left blank.

3. The recognition may be either in the name of the superior himself, or in the name of a donatar, who ordinarily gets a charter which he founds on, expressing the special cause of recognition: for in declarators of recognition there is no general clause, neither uses there to be a gift, but only a disposition and charter, whereby the obtainer thereof becomes vassal to the superior, in place of the former vassal, according to the tenor of the charter.

It were regular and convenient, that such charters contained a clause not to take infeftment before declarator, because they may be given without just cause, and the donatar is in no hazard to be prevented by any other, if he timeously and diligently insist in the declarator.

4. This declarator is ordinarily at the instance of donatars, and may be more easily and simply at the instance of superiors. The tenor may be thus: "Our will is, and We charge you, that ye lawfully summon B, as having been vassal to C in the lands of   at least apparent heir therein, who, or his predecessors or authors, have committed the deeds of recognition underwritten, to compear, &c. to answer at the instance of D, as having right by charter from the said C, superior of the saids lands, and others foresaids, as fallen in his hands by recognition, for the causes specially contained in the foresaid charter, viz.   which charter is dated, &c. That is to say, the said defender to hear and see it verified and proven, that he hath wittingly and wilfully committed the saids deeds of recognition: and therefore to hear and see it found and declared, that therethrough he has amitted and lost the right of property of the saids lands, and others foresaids; and that the same did recognosce to the said superior of the samine, and that, from and after the committing of the saids deeds of recognition: and that the said pursuer, by virtue of the foresaid charter, hath good right to take infeftment thereof, and to bruik and joyse the saids lands, and others foresaids, by virtue of the said charter and infeftment to follow thereupon, as his own proper heritage, in all time coming; and to intromit with, claim and pursue for, the rents and profits of the samine, since the saids deeds of recognition, against all possessors and intromitters therewith, conform to the laws and daily practick of this Our realm, &c. According to justice, &c."

5. This declarator must have double diets, unless the vassal's infeftment be produced. And albeit it bear not the deeds of recognition, to be wittingly and wilfully done, that will be presumed upon the deeds, unless the vassal condescend and prove, that he did the same by ignorance or mistake, without any wilfulness or contempt; as if the superior or he were singular successors,

or that the fee was by the investiture provided to other heirs, than he who now claims the same as superior, or that the deeds against the superior's person were for necessary self-defence, *ex inculpata tutela*, or in obedience to lawful authority, or in defence of a more ancient superior; or that words importing his infamy were in obedience, upon judicial examination as a witness.

6. But minority affords no exception in this matter, which of its nature is criminal. Neither will it be a relevant exception, that these deeds were done by him who had curators or interdictors, without their consent: nor that the infeftment *à se* was null, not being confirmed, and so could import no alienation; if it did contain precept of seasin, and that thereupon seasin was taken, albeit the charter or precept of seasin did bear a provision, that the infeftment should not be effectual, unless the superior consented or confirmed: but if it did bear, that seasin should not be taken till the superior confirmed, it would be relevant; for this clause were suspensive, whereas the former were only resolutive.

Title 15. Declarators of Astriction

MILLS at first were built only to procure hire for grinding of grain; but afterwards there were agreements between the proprietor of the mill and some of the neighbourhood whereby such a proportion of the grain grinded was agreed on to be given and taken, for the hire of that service; without which agreement, or a particular agreement upon several occasions, those who came to the mill were understood to be obliged to pay the ordinary hire or multure. In either case, there was no more but a personal contract of location: but now of a long time, mills have become feudal fees, and separate tenements, requiring special infeftments, except in the case of infeftments in barony, which is an universal title whereby mills are carried as part and pertinent without a special seasin; yet still some come to mills without astriction, and pay a less duty than those who are astricted ordinarily; though there may be an astriction for so small a duty, as is only equivalent to the service, which all must pay that come, without special agreement. But agreement for a definite time doth infer astriction.

2. Astriction or thirlage is a perpetual burden upon the lands astricted, for paying a certain multure and services to the mill; and thereby it becomes a servitude, wherein the mill is the dominant tenement, and the lands thirled are the servient tenements; and it is a real burden affecting these lands, passing therewith to all singular successors [11,7,15–27,*supra*]. Yet there doth not thence follow a real action by poinding of the ground, but a personal action against the possessors, and is rather a burden upon the fruits than upon the ground. Nor doth it affect singular successors buying the fruits, but only the possessors to whom the crop belongs, and not the master of the ground, if he be not possessor by labourage. It is also in the power of the possessors to labour more or less as they please, or nothing: if they labour none, even though they inclose a part of these grounds, never to be laboured, there is no

multure due, unless there be constitute a stocked multure, which is called a dry multure, which can only be so constituted by the heritor, and therefore is constantly due by him and by the possessors, though they labour none.

3. Heritors do astrict their own tenants most ordinarily to their own mills; and then the multure and mill-service becomes a part of the tenant's rent, and there is no ground of complaint, how great soever the multure be, for the rent must be the less. Yea, the multure becomes a real burden upon the several rooms; and although *res sua nemini servit*, yet there being a proper interest of the millers, and of the tenants, this thirlage is consistent, notwithstanding that rule.

4. There needs no other probation of astriction of tenants, but their use of going to their master's mill. Yea, though some pay less multure and services than others, yet all are astricted; and whosoever acquires the mill by disposition, apprising, or adjudication, carries the multures of those tenants that were accustomed to come to that mill, even though the lands astricted be not a barony; and that, though the disposition of the mill do not bear expressly "with the thirle multures of such lands," or generally, "with thirle multures," but only, "with the multures used and wont." And, albeit purchasers should be so uncautious as to buy the mill, without mention of multures, or that the mill be adjudged or apprised without mention thereof, yet the astricted multures will follow the mill, unless it were otherwise expressed, or did appear by the nature of the sale; as if an heritor should sell a mill and mill-lands, lying adjacent to the buyer's lands, without getting a price, suitable both to the mill and mill-lands, and to the multures, sucken, and sequels of the mill.

5. Thirlage of lands to mills of the King's property, is sufficiently instructed, by use of coming to the mill, and paying the insucken multures, though the thirlage be not founded upon, nor adminiculated by writ, which is a royal prerogative, necessary for the King, because he is not prejudged by the neglect of his officers, in keeping any writs.

6. Thirlage also of mills which did belong to kirk-men, as parts of their benefice, is more easily instructed than the thirlage of other subjects; because, in the time of the Reformation, their evidents were destroyed and lost. And that albeit the question be of thirlage of lands, which were not of their own property or superiority; but much more, if the question be of such lands; for therein they are in the common case with other heritors, as to the multures of their own lands accustomed to be paid to their own mills.

7. Thirlage, in other cases, cannot be constitute or instructed by mere use of coming and paying such a multure, and such services and sequels, unless there be other concurring evidences importing a thirlage, as if there were use of payment of a dry multure (unless it were proven to be by a temporary agreement) or if the multure-service and sequels were so great, that these who were accustomed to come, might have them elsewhere much more easy and convenient; in that case, immemorial, or forty years ordinary coming to

the mill, and paying such duties, would instruct thirlage: for it is a strong presumption that none would so long pay so heavy a duty unnecessarily; yet it is but a presumption, that may be elided by a contrary presumption, as if the mill belonged to a near relation, which might give a probable ground, that the continuance at it was by gratification.

8. The ordinary way of constituting thirlage of other men's lands is, by bonds of thirlage, granted by the heritors of the astricted lands, to the heritors of the mill. Yet these bonds alone will not make it a real burden, affecting singular successors, unless there were use of payment after such bonds. 2. Also acts of court, whereby heritors enact their own tenants to come to another mill, and coming accordingly, makes the astriction real; but if it be only an act by a bailie, except his warrant be instructed, it will not make a constitution, but will be a title for prescription. 3. Decreets for multures or mill-service, though they be but by inrolments of baron-courts, without formal extracts, if they be on compearance, they are more effectual than the acts of bailies; for they are not only titles for prescription, by subsequent possession, but also they are evidences that the anterior possession was not voluntary.

9. Thirlage is sometimes the ground of a possessory action, sometimes of a petitory action, and sometimes of a declaratory action. When the thirlage is special both as to the lands, and as to the liquid quantities of multure, which hath been so possest within seven years; then a possessory action is competent to continue the same. But if there hath not been so long continuance of possession, yet if the constitution hath not been seven years since, albeit it was clad with some years possession the multures may be acquired without a declarator, by a petitory action. But if there hath been no possession within seven years, there must be a declaratory action, to declare the right of the thirlage, before there be a petitory or possessory judgment; in which the heritor of the astricted lands must be called, and likewise in the petitory judgment; but, in the possessory judgment, it is sufficient to call the possessors.

10. The tenor of the declarator of thirlage may be thus: "Our will is, and We charge you, that ye lawfully summon B, heritor of the lands of   or liferenter, or wadsetter of the samine, to compear, &c. To answer at the instance of A, heritor, liferenter, or wadsetter of the mill of   with the multures, sucken, sequels and services thereof, conform to their infeftments of the samine, dated, &c. And als at the instance of T, tacksman, or tenant of the said mill, That is to say, The saids defenders to hear and see it found and declared, That the saids lands of   were astricted and thirled to the said mill, in payment to the pursuers of the quantities of multure, sucken, and sequel after specified, viz.   For the reasons and causes following. (Here must be insert the particular ways of astriction and instruction thereof before mentioned.) And that the pursuers have good and undoubted right to the saids multures, sucken, sequel and services, since the said astriction, and in all time coming; and ought to be answered and obeyed therein by the defenders, their tenants and possessors, and the saids astricted lands, conform

to the quantities of the grindable corns growing thereupon, grinded at any mill, or gifted or sold, and not grinded at the pursuer's mill, and also of all grains *invecta et illata*, tholing fire and water within the saids lands thirled as aforesaid, conform to the laws and daily practick of this our realm, &c. According to justice, &c."

11. *Invecta et illata* will be sufficiently proven by custom, though it be not express in the constitution of the thirlage, unless the thirlage be special and particular in all things.

12. It will be a relevant defence, that the bond or act of thirlage did not attain possession before the defender's infeftment of the lands in question, he being a singular successor to him who granted the bond of thirlage, or made the acts of astriction, if these be the causes of astriction. But if possession anterior be instructed or offered to be proven, it will be relevant. 2. It will be a relevant defence against astriction by prescription, that there was interruption by process for declarator of liberty from thirlage; or by interruptions *via facti*, by grinding of corns growing upon the lands pretended to be astricted, for several whole years; yet, if the pursuer libel and offer to prove ordinary coming to the mill, during the prescription, and paying the duties acclaimed, though he prove not every year, the libel will be relevant, unless the defender positively offer to prove the interruption, as aforesaid, wherein he will be preferred as more pregnant. 3. It is a relevant exception against this declarator, that the defender being singular successor, did *bona fide* possess the lands in question, and consumed the fruits thereof, without the knowledge of any thirlage: but the reply of his being *in mala fide*, by instructing the thirlage by writ *ab initio*, or by a decreet of astriction, will elide that defence.

Title 16. Actions to Insist with Certification not to be heard thereafter, and Actions of Double Poinding

LAW hath provided two remedies for freeing defenders from the hazard of pursuers, that do, or may insist against them, that they may not at discretion be obliged to attend, for defence of their processes. The one is, when they are cited to a certain day, and receive a copy of the summons; they appear the next Session-day after the term to which they are cited, and produce the copy, and cause call the same, and crave protestation, that seeing the pursuer appeareth not to insist, they may be declared free from that instance, and not to be called till they be cited of new. This is not competent at the first diet, because they are to be cited to the second diet, after the first is elapsed; so that the instance cannot fall by the first citation, seeing they are to be cited again by the second citation.

2. This protestation being obtained and extracted, the defender lies still under the hazard of the same cause in another instance; for remedy whereof, law allows him to raise a summons against the pursuer to insist with certification, that if he insist not, he shall never be heard thereafter, in that cause; whereby this certification is peremptory, not only excluding the summons

till new citation, but excluding the cause, whereupon the summons was founded.

3. The other remedy is, when parties are, or may be pursued, by different pursuers, upon distinct rights; in which case, they cannot found upon a third party's right. And therefore the law allows that they may cite all parties, that do or may pretend right against them, for that which they do acknowledge they may be liable to, either by a personal or real action, to the effect that they may dispute their rights and preferences, and that the pursuer in this action may be only liable in once and single payment or performance; and that he, nor no right of his, may be liable to double distress, but that he may safely pay or perform to the party that shall be preferred, and found to have best right. Whereby a decreet of preference, and performance, secures the performer for ever; and that, albeit the decreet of preference were in absence, or though thereafter it were reduced, whether it had been in absence, or upon compearance; so that the party thereafter preferred, will have access against these who were formerly preferred; for as payment made *bona fide*, secures the payer, when no other party is called, so much more are these secured, who pay or perform, *auctore prætore*.

4. Both these actions are declaratory, and neither petitory nor possessory, albeit they have these special names, and are not under the general name of declarators.

5. The action for insisting, is not competent after litiscontestation; because then, either party is master of the process: for as the pursuer may insist to prove, conform to the act; so the defender may call upon the same act, and circumduce the term, for the pursuer's not proving, and so may be assoilzied *simpliciter*, and not only from the instance; and therefore this action cannot proceed till the forementioned protestation precede and be extracted; which may be obtained, although the pursuer appear and give out his process to be seen; for if after it is returned, he do not inrol it, the defender may again call upon his copy, and will get protestation, simply, or conditionally to be extracted if the pursuer do not inrol the next inrolling day. And when the cause is called by the roll, if the pursuer insist not, the defender will get protestation.

6. If the defender in this action to insist, do appear, if he have any probable ground for it, he will get a time to prepare himself to insist.

7. The tenor of the action of double poinding may be thus: "Forasmuch as it is humbly meant and shown to us by our lovit A, That whereas the complainer, or his lands and goods, are distressed and troubled at the instance of B and C, as pretending right, by several arrestments, and actions for making forthcoming, of certain sums of money addebted by the complainer to D, or wherewith his lands of   are affected and burdened, and may be poinded by the saids parties pretending different rights and titles thereto: and it being most just and reasonable, that the complainer, or his lands and goods, should only be liable to once and single payment and performance, to the

party who shall be found by decreet of the Lords of our Council and Session, to have best right thereto, and should be freed of any trouble or distress, at the instance of any of the other parties pretending right, as is alleged. Our will is herefore, and We charge you, that ye lawfully summon the said B and C, pretending right as aforesaid, to compear, &c. To answer at the instance of the pursuer, That is to say, The saids defenders to produce before the saids Lords their several rights, titles, and interests, whereby they pretend to be preferred in the matter above written. And to hear and see it found and declared, by decreet of our saids Lords, who hath the best and preferable right thereto; and that the others may be decerned, to cease and desist from troubling or molesting the complainer thereanent; and that payment or performance to the party found to have best right, shall liberate and free the pursuer at all hands; with certification, that if they compear not, or produce not sufficient titles and rights to the subject in question, or that compearing and producing, they shall not be preferred; they shall never be heard thereafter, to pursue, molest, or trouble the pursuer in any sort; at the least, that payment or performance to the party who shall be preferred, shall absolutely liberate and assoilzie the pursuer from all instance, action, and execution, for the matter in question, bygone, present, or in time coming, conform to the laws and daily practick of this our realm, &c. According to justice, &c."

8. The tenor of the action for insisting, may be thus: "Forasmuch as it is humbly meant and shown to us by our lovit A, That whereas the complainer was pursued at the instance of B, to appear before the Lords of our Council and Session, upon the   day, &c. in the hour of cause, with continuation of days; alleging that, &c. According to which citation, the complainer appeared and produced a copy of the summons; which copy being oft-times called in presence of the saids Lords, the said B not compearing, the saids Lords admitted protestation, declaring that the complainer should not be obliged to answer, nor the said B have any further process in the said cause, till the complainer were of new summoned for that effect. And seeing the said B doth not yet insist in the said cause, having had sufficient time to do the same, and that the complainer ought not to lie under the hazard of plea, in the said matter, at the option of the said B, that he may take advantage of the complainer, or of his successors, in their minority, and ignorance of the affair, or when the means of probation of the complainer's defences may be lost: therefore, in all law and reason, he ought to be decerned to insist in the said cause, with certification, that if he failzie, he shall never be heard therein thereafter, and that the complainer shall absolutely be assoilzied therefrom for ever, as is alleged. Our will is herefore, and We charge you, that ye lawfully summon the said B to compear, &c. To answer at the instance of the said complainer; that is to say, The said defender to hear and see the premises verified and proven; and being so verified and proven, to hear and see himself decerned to insist in the said cause, with certification, that if he insist not, he shall never be heard therein thereafter; and that the complainer shall be

simpliciter assoilzied therefrom, conform to the laws and daily practique of this our realm, &c. According to justice, &c."

Title 17. Declarators of Servitudes

THE Roman law had two special actions in relation to servitudes; the one confessory, whereby parties did insist to obtain a servitude to be decerned in their favour [D.7,6,5,6; 8,5,2,1]; the other negatory [D.8,5,2,*pr.*; 44,2], for obtaining a decreet, declaring them free of such particular servitudes.

2. The same actions are competent with us, but in different ways, and by distinct kinds of actions: for when parties insist for servitudes, having been in recent use of enjoying the same, they may insist in a possessory action for that effect; because it is the continuation of their possession, and they have no need to declare their right of the servitude. But if they, or their authors, have not been recently in use of enjoying that servitude, a possessory action is not competent to them, but they must first declare their right: the reason whereof is, the same which makes the difference betwixt possessory and petitory, or declaratory judgments; whereby those who are out of possession cannot pursue from the constitution of their right to their citation, for profits or damages, though they should sufficiently instruct their right to have been complete from the beginning, but the defenders do enjoy their fees *bona fide*, without any such burden, till they be constituted *in mala fide* by a process, or that they have known the pursuer's right, and have hindered him to enjoy the same. The time of enjoying the privilege of a possessory judgment, in defence of actions of mails and duties, or removing, did vary for some time; but now hath been long fixed to seven years' peaceable possession, without interruption; so that, till reduction or declarator, they had a dilatory defence upon the privilege of a possessory judgment [II,7,22,*supra*; IV,22,5 and 8,*infra*]. And though the same question hath not frequently occurred in servitudes, yet no less time should be required for that privilege in them.

3. The privilege of a possessory judgment is not competent against poinding of the ground upon annualrents, feu-duties, or other real burdens, which appear by infeftments, whereby they may be known, and which are several distinct fees, neither in actions for teinds, for the same reason; because the rights thereof are notour. But this is not to be extended to servitudes, against which proprietors, wadsetters, or liferenters, have the privilege of a possessory judgment, till the servitude be declared.

4. The tenor of a confessory action, or declarator of servitude, may be thus: "Our will is, and We charge you, that ye lawfully summon B, heritor, wadsetter, liferenter, or possessor of the lands of S, which lands are burdened with the servitude under written, to compear, &c. to answer at the instance of A, as having right to the servitude of   , as part and pertinent of the lands of F, belonging to the pursuer, his predecessors or authors, by continual possession, and use of the said servitude, as a pertinent of their saids lands, and to the behoof thereof as the dominant tenement, by frequent and ordin-

ary use and possession, as they had occasion, past memory, at least during the space of forty years, at least as having right to the said servitude, by a bond of servitude, or disposition thereof, from the heritor of the said servient tenement, for the time; which bond or disposition is dated, &c. by virtue whereof the said pursuer, his predecessors or authors, have been in possession, and use of the said servitude: That is to say, the said defender to hear and see it found and declared, that the said pursuer hath good and undoubted right to the said servitude, in manner above-written; and the said defender to be decerned by decreet of the saids Lords to desist and cease from troubling him in the peaceable enjoyment of the said servitude, and to pay and satisfy to him the damages sustained through his unjust hindering his enjoyment thereof, and through his detaining the profit of the said servitude, as shall be modified by decreet of the saids Lords, conform to the laws and daily practick of this realm, &c. According to justice, &c."

5. The negatory declarator of servitude is seldom used, because servitudes have not proper possession, but use in place thereof; and therefore parties concerned may stop that use, if they find any ground of doubt of the right thereof, without hazard of ejection or intrusion: for thereby the party having right to the servitude, may pursue a petitory or possessory action upon the servitude, if he be not long silent, as aforesaid; yet the negatory declarator is requisite, to liberate the pursuer's tenement of any pretence of right or possession, whereby another may claim a servitude, as pertinent of the pursuer's tenement, by long possession, or by an insufficient title, accomplished by prescription; especially lest his probation of interruption may fail by the death of his witnesses. This declarator requires no more but the denial of the servitude, which is negative and proves itself, unless the contrary be proven; and thereupon concludes declarator of liberation from such servitude, decerning the defender to desist and cease from troubling the pursuer therewith.

6. In the confessory declarators defences will be competent upon anteriority of the defender's infeftments, before the constitution of the servitude, or upon interruption thereafter; or that the servitude was constitute *a non habente potestatem*, he who constitute the same, either not being infeft in the tenement pretended to be servient, or being denuded in favour of the defender, his predecessors or authors, before the constitution attained possession; whereby the pursuer will be obliged to reply and instruct, that the constituter of the servitude had right by infeftment, and that the servitude was clad with possession before he was denuded, which he needs not libel and instruct *ab initio;* but he cannot exclude the defence, as not competent in this judgment, because it is not possessory but declaratory.

7. In the probation of the continuance of possession, it will be sufficient to prove, that frequently and ordinarily the servitude was made use of. An interruption will not be inferred by one year's forbearance to possess, unless there were actual debarring, or instruments taken upon interruption.

Title 18. Declarators of Clauses Irritant

HITHERTO declaratory actions of the rights of pursuers have been handled. There remains yet rescissory actions, whereby the rights of defenders are rescinded, and declared to be null or void, or to be resolved, or false, or holden and reputed as false; whereby the rights of pursuers do by consequence revive, and therewith also clauses declaratory of the pursuer's own rights are joined; so that they are not only preferable to the rights rescinded, but also declared to be absolutely valid rights; in which case there must be citation at the market-cross, against all and sundry having, or pretending right to the right in question.

2. These rescissory actions are all declaratory, and neither petitory nor possessory, concluding nothing to be done by the defenders: for though they may conclude that they should desist and cease, yet that is only negative, prohibiting to do.

3. Clauses irritant are so called, because they are designed to make void the rights in which they are contained, in the events therein expressed. They are also called resolutive clauses, because in these events they do resolve the rights wherein they are contained; and sometimes they bear, that in the cases therein mentioned, the rights shall thereby become null, *ipso facto*, without declarator; but notwithstanding of this, clauses irritant are not effectual till they be declared, where they are exorbitantly penal: for the Lords *ex officio* have power to modify exorbitant penalties, albeit they bear to be liquidate of consent of parties; and, for the same cause, they have power to qualify these clauses irritant, and to allow time for purging the same [1,13,14; 11,10,6; IV, 5,7,*supra*]; yet only if they be truly exorbitantly penal: for such clauses contained in gratuitous rights take their full effect, because then they are not penal, but are conditions and provisions qualifying the right; and therefore they need no declarator: but if the right wherein they are, be founded upon by way of defence or reply, the allegeance of the right's being gratuitous, will be relevant.

4. These clauses irritant may be contained in any right; but they use most ordinarily to be contained in wadset-rights, bearing, that if redemption be not made conform to the reversion, within such a time, or in such a way, then the reversion shall become void: or in case the reversion be only made temporary, the effect is the same, except it be in a true sale for a competent price, wherein both clauses irritant, and temporary reversions are valid, because there is nothing penal in these cases.

5. The Roman law doth absolutely reject such clauses in impignorations, which they call *pacta legis commissoriæ in pignoribus* [D.20,1,16,9]. Our customs did formerly sustain such clauses, but modified the exorbitancy thereof, by giving competent time to redeem, albeit the time contained in the reversion was elapsed; but did not sustain the reversion to be perpetual. But since, our custom hath more closely followed the Roman law in this point, if that

which was done was truly an impignoration, and not a sale for an equivalent price.

6. The next case most ordinary for clauses irritant, is in tailzies [11,3,58, *supra*]; whereby the heirs of tailzie are burdened with certain provisions and conditions, sometimes by potestative conditions, in the power of the heir to perform; sometimes accidental, not being in the heir's power. These clauses irritant in tailzies are not properly penal, because it was in the power of the constituent to assume or not assume these heirs of tailzie to be his heirs; and therefore they are effectual, and established by an Act of Parliament [Entail Act, 1685,c.22; A.P.S. VIII,477,c.26], not only against the heirs of tailzie, and their successors, but also against singular successors, even though they be creditors apprising or adjudging for the heir's proper debt; but they will not defend against the constituent's debt, in prejudice of which no posterior tailzie could be made. Such clauses irritant in tailzies do not well quadrate with the right of property: for thereby these heirs have not the power of disposal of these tailzied rights, and therefore such clauses use not to be put upon heirs of line, nor heirs-male, nor heirs of provision by contracts of marriage; for all these are heirs of blood: and if, in such cases, heirs were so bound up, that they could neither sell, nor effectually contract debts that might affect these estates, commerce of lands would thereby be taken away, and proprietors would frequently be rendered miserable; because, though the fee of their estates could not be affected for their debts, yet no tailzie could hinder their rents to be arrested, and made forthcoming.

7. Albeit clauses irritant in tailzies be not penal, and upon that account require not declarators, yet there must be declarators before the tailzied infeftment can be annulled or resolved; because such clauses are against the common course of law, and therefore are odious, and should not take effect before they be declared; for if they were effectual by a petitory action, claiming the whole profits since the act contravening the clause, the heirs of tailzie would be miserable; and those in whose favour the right were reducible, should impute it to their own negligence, that they should not sooner declare the clause.

8. Heirs of tailzie are sometimes the nearest male of blood, when fiars bring in their sons, or other nearest relations, *nominatim*, as branches of a tailzie, who otherwise would have been heirs-male; against such these clauses irritant ought not to be extended, nor against the heirs in the last termination of the tailzie: for if the estate come to the last branch of the tailzie, and his heirs whatsomever, it ceases to be a tailzied estate.

9. Clauses irritant are so many and various, that a common tenor cannot be framed for them; but as they may be pursued by declarator, so may they also by reduction, the style whereof is more fixed and uniform than of any other process.

Title 19. Actions *Cognitionis Causa*

ACTIONS *cognitionis causa* are declaratory, because they do not conclude payment, or any thing to be done by the defender; and therefore are competent against apparent heirs without a charge.

2. The effect of the decreet is only to declare what debt was due by the defunct, that it may affect his heritage or moveables.

3. In this the apparent heir, or nearest of kin are called; because, though they have not entered, nor owned their succession, yet they may do it thereafter; and therefore they may object against the interest, order, relevancy, or instructions produced *ab initio*. But they can propone no exception, which if admitted would make them behave: nor can they propone it, because they have no title in their person sufficient to make litiscontestation.

4. There is little need of these actions now, since adjudications are come in place of apprisings except it be for deducing the first adjudication: for if one adjudication be past and extracted, all posterior adjudications within the year will pass as acts, and need no decreet *cognitionis causa*, unless the ground thereof be altogether illiquid, and then it may be an article in the process of adjudication, and will obtain summarily an act for probation, to make it liquid, if it be necessary.

Title 20. Reductions and Improbations

REDUCTIONS of decreets are not here to be considered, for these come in in the second instance, and are to be spoken of after decreets; but reductions of other rights, which come in the first instance, and improbation of writs necessary for these rights, which being found or declared forged, do annul the right whereof these writs are evidents, are proper in this place, amongst declaratory actions, which comprehend rescissory actions.

2. Rights are declared two ways; *affirmativè*, declaring the right itself to be good and valid, and sufficient to exclude any other right; or *negativè*, by reducing and annulling any pretended right, whereupon action or exception might be founded, in prejudice of the pursuer's right. Both these ways may, and ofttimes used to be joined in the same summons, reducing opposite rights, and declaring the pursuer's own right; which require divers grounds; for a pursuer on his right may remove a posterior right, or a less formal, which will not infer that his own right is absolutely valid and secure; and therefore, if a declarator of the pursuer's be libelled, all having interest must be cited at the market-cross: and no right of land can be declared absolutely valid and secure, without instructing a clear progress from the King, who is supreme superior, or by another progress secured by prescription, and uninterrupted possession, during the space of forty years; for albeit reductions may contain a clause declaratory of the validity of the pursuer's right, upon less grounds, which will be sufficient against the defenders, who have no bet-

ter right, yet an absolute right can no otherways be declared, than by the two *media* now mentioned.

3. Summons of reduction may either be alone, or joined with an improbation in the same libel. A single reduction proceedeth in the same form as a reduction and improbation: for in both, the writs craved to be reduced, are called for to be produced, with certification that if they be not produced, they shall be holden to be null, and no ways to prejudge the pursuer's rights and titles, whereupon the reduction proceeds: and if they be not produced, certification is granted against them, or any of them. This certification is a decreet to be extracted by itself, but it bears only the writs called for and not produced, to be reduced, ay and while they be produced: the meaning whereof is, not that the production of them any way, will annul the decreet of certification; but they must be produced *legitimo modo, i.e.* in a process of reduction of the decreet of certification. Yet the decreet of certification has this effect, that whatever the reducer obtains possession of, by virtue of the certification, or by any action following thereupon, whereby the reducer's own right takes effect, by removing the opposite right by the certification, he is not accountable therefor, whether it be the profit of lands, or of sums, or of other rights, albeit the intromission be after a summons of reduction of the certification, and still until the reducer be put *in mala fide,* by producing writs sufficient to reduce the certification.

4. Single reductions have also this effect, that when writs are produced and reduced, by reasons founded upon better rights, the decreet of reduction is a decreet *in foro contradictorio,* and hath all the privileges of decreets *in foro.* But, because single reductions in matter of land-rights are seldom used, without an improbation, the certification whereof for not production (albeit in absence) is not reducible, there is no necessity to insist further in a single reduction. Only this must be observed, that no certification can be granted against any writs, but such against which there is a relevant reason of reduction libelled. And therefore, general reasons against all writs are at first libelled, as not being subscribed before famous witnesses, &c. And after production, the pursuers are allowed to add special reasons against the writs produced.

5. Reduction and improbation needs no other general reason to be libelled before production, but that the writs called for are false and forged, and that the summons contain a certification that they shall not only be declared null, but also shall be holden and reputed false and forged, and to make no faith in judgment or outwith. And yet the certification hath only effect, as to the rights and titles, whereupon the process proceeds; for the writs, though not produced, are valid as to all effects, either against any other party, or against the same party, as to other rights besides these libelled.

6. A decreet of certification upon this summons, is of all other decreets most difficile to be reduced, even though in absence; yea, harder to be reduced than the decreet of reduction against the writs produced, though it be *in foro contradictorio.* The reason is, because this certification is the most com-

mon and greatest security of all rights by infeftment, and is much more effectual than a declarator of right; wherein, if the defenders be absent, they will easily be heard in the second instance, but will not so be heard against this certification, which I never observed to be recalled, except in the case of a certification against a person, who, in the whole time of the process, was out of the country, a soldier of the Scots forces then in Ireland, and in prison; where there was a great number of privileges concurring.

7. This process hath also this advantage of a declarator, that a term will be granted to prove exceptions upon writs not produced, and if they be the writs of authors, there will be incident diligences sustained: there may be also replies upon rights anterior to the rights in the defender's defences, and duplies upon rights anterior to these, or what further plies parties please to allege. All of which, of old, was founded on a brieve of the chancery, called the brieve of right.

8. But since the erection of the College of Justice, this process of reduction and improbation was invented and sustained, which is peculiar to this nation, and is a more absolute security of men's rights, than any form of process in the Roman law, or in any neighbouring nation: for thereby all the rights that can be pretended to, must be produced before there can be any dispute in the cause, except dilators against the interest of the pursuer, and order of the process; and so there is rarely litiscontestation made in this process, unless the pursuer libel upon possession and prescription; wherein present or recent possession must be proven; but being proven as far as memory doth ordinarily reach, ancient possession will thence be presumed, and the continuance thereof, unless interruption be alleged and instructed, or that the defender allege he hath produced sufficiently, to exclude the pursuer.

9. This certification being of so great import, the Lords give large time for production. And before the Act of Regulation [Courts Act 1672,c.16; A.P.S. VIII,80,c.40], there were three terms for production assigned in this process, and two in a single reduction, wherein there is now but one term, and two in an improbation and reduction. And whereas formerly incident diligence by way of exhibition was allowed, during the progress of which the principal cause was superseded, until the incident ended; wherein, not only the oaths of parties havers of writs, but witnesses were sustained to prove the having, and thereupon a decreet of exhibition, and horning and caption, all which behoved to be ended before the principal cause were resumed: yet now, by the Act of Regulation [Courts Act 1672,c.16; A.P.S. VIII,80,c.40], horning is granted against all havers to produce at the first term, and caption for the second term, in the same way as against witnesses. For there is the same reason obliging parties to exhibit writs that may prove, and to give their oaths for that effect, as to give their oaths of verity in any other point as witnesses.

10. There may be acts extracted for either of the said terms: but these are not acts of litiscontestation, but acts of production, which are peculiar to

reductions; so that it is so far from having two litiscontestations therein, that there is seldom one.

11. This certification being so hardly reducible, the Lords are careful that the same be orderly extracted; yea, they will recal certifications, if further writs of importance be recently produced: and if any formality be omitted, or if there be improbation or reduction of the executions, whereupon the certification proceeded, the Lords will sustain the same, even *pendente processu*, to reduce the certification, or at any time thereafter, while parties are obliged to produce executions.

12. If there be a declarator of right libelled in this reduction, when the reasons come to be discussed, though the defender can have no term to prove; yet the pursuer may still reply on other titles, till rights are produced prior or better than his titles, and will get terms to prove the same, which I have not seen sustained in other reductions; but that, if the defender produced a better right, he was assoilzied from that libel; yet the pursuer might raise a new libel upon other better rights, or other more relevant reasons; for in this case there is no ground for "competent and omitted"; and it were hard to bind up the defender from any further production, and yet to allow the pursuer to reply upon other rights than those libelled; unless the defender may produce more writs, at the term assigned to the pursuer.

13. After so long dependence upon the acts for production, there is no incident ordinarily competent for recovering writs, because horning is allowed against all havers; yet if the defender be positive, upon special witnesses, to prove the having of the writs called for, he ought also to have horning against these witnesses for proving the having, that he be not necessitate only to prove by the haver's oath or writ, which doth in all points supply the incident that was formerly allowed by way of action of exhibition.

14. In this summons there useth to be called for, not only particular writs but also there is a general clause, "calling for all other writs and evidents of the lands, and others in question, granted to the defenders, and their predecessors to whom they may succeed *jure sanguinis;* or which are granted to their authors called, or which were granted to their predecessors, to whom, they may succeed *jure sanguinis:*" for this process being declaratory, it proceedeth against apparent heirs, without charges to enter heir; and therefore it proceedeth not only against these who were actually heirs, but against these who might have been actually heirs. But I find that the general clause hath been ordinarily restricted to the writs only granted by the pursuer and his predecessors, to whom he is actually heir; or granted by his authors, whose rights he produceth, or by their heirs actually served as heirs to them in the right in question. This restriction is upon this account, that the pursuer hath no interest to reduce or improve any writs, but these granted by him, his predecessors and authors, which doth too much enervate this useful process: for, seeing the pursuer's title gives him interest to call for removing of all writs, that may trouble him in the peaceable enjoyment of the lands and other rights, where-

in he stands infeft, upon this ground that the rights called for are false; there is no reason to hinder him, to call for any right granted by whomsoever, whereunto the defenders have, or may have right by succession, to the effect they may be improven, and thereby removed from troubling the pursuer in his right or possession. Yet there is good reason, that the pursuer should not insist upon any title, to which he might have right by succession, until he be actually infeft on that right: and for the same reason, he cannot insist to reduce and improve, upon a disposition, or any other right but an infeftment, if the reduction be for reducing infeftments.

15. Any infeftment will be a title for founding a reduction, and improbation, even though it be base, and without possession: but if the defender produce a public infeftment, or a base infeftment clad with possession, although it were posterior, it will stop certification; because it is a better and preferable right.

16. It is a great prejudice to this useful process, that pursuers are not masters of their superiors' or their authors' infeftments, and have no title to get exhibition of them, except in the way of incident, to instruct or astruct the pursuer's title. But since it is a necessary requisite for infeftments, that the seasins be registrate, since the Act of Parliament 1617 [Registration Act, 1617,c.16; A.P.S. IV,545,c.16], it ought to be sufficient to extract the seasins of the pursuers' authors, and libel thereupon: and the pursuit should not be excluded for want of the principal seasins, or warrants thereof, upon production of an infeftment of the defenders, prior to the infeftments produced by the pursuer; but the defenders ought to take terms to produce all rights they can pretend to the lands or other infeftments in question; and the pursuer ought to have the same terms to produce his authors' and predecessors' infeftments, whose seasins he produces, and to have diligence by horning and caption, against the havers thereof; that so all the rights that either party may pretend, may be *in campo*, before they come to dispute the reasons.

17. Not only the obtainers of infeftments called for to be reduced, must be cited, but also the author's granters of these infeftments, or their heirs, or apparent heirs, must be cited; because there are ordinarily clauses of warrandice in the infeftments, and therefore the authors have interest to defend the rights granted by them.

18. These processes are first called in the Outer-House; and if there be no compearance certification is granted. But if the pursuer himself can satisfy the production in a single reduction, he will rather do it, than take certification, that he may get a decreet upon his reasons repeated; which, though it be but a decreet in absence, yet it is better than a certification in absence. But if there be improbation with a reduction, he will readily rest in that certification, which is so strong.

19. If the defender appear, and produce the writs in question, he must abide by the verity thereof, under his hand, with certification if he do not, the same will be holden as forged. This certification is on the same ground with

the certification for not production, viz. That the defender dare not own the writ in question as true. The Lords do sometimes allow the *Abiding by qualificatè*, that the user did not immediately receive the writs in question, but had them by assignation, or by succession; in which case he must abide by the verity of the assignation, and must give evidence that the writ was by the defunct the time of his death, in case the samine be found false; so that his sole assertion of using them *bona fide*, is not sufficient.

20. The defender may not only propone defences against the interest of the pursuer, and the order, but also, that all persons having interest are not called, especially the defender's authors: and likewise, if he produce rights relevant to elide the pursuer's titles, as being prior or preferable, the Ordinary may hear him thereupon, which will stop certification, or taking of a term to produce: and if the defence be found relevant, the defender will be assoilzied. But if there be an interlocutor of the Lords repelling the defence, the defender may make a further production, and will be heard again upon the whole writs produced: but after that second production, he will not be heard to dispute upon any further production, till the full production be closed, or certification granted *contra non producta*. And so the process goes on in the Outer-House by calling the first and second act for production, until the production be closed; which may either be by the pursuer's holding the production satisfied, or by a certification *contra non producta :* after which the Ordinary can proceed no further, but makes a *great avisandum*, for discussing of the reasons of reduction *in præsentia ;* unless the Lords have granted warrant to discuss the reasons *extra*, which they use not to refuse in single reductions of small moment. This is called a great *avisandum*, in distinction from the ordinary *avisandums*, to be reported to the Lords. According to the date of the great *avisandum*, the cause is enrolled in the roll of the Inner-House, and is set in order of the processes produced that Saturday in which it is produced, according to their dates. The Ordinary doth also allow the defender to see his own production in the clerk's hands, that accordingly he may be ready to dispute when he is called.

21. It is a relevant defence against certification, or taking a term to produce, that the writs called for are *in publica custodia*, that is, in the Registers of Session, or in the chancellary: but extracts of seasins, hornings, or inhibitions, will not stop certification, because the principals are not left at the register. Yet the defender must condescend upon the date of the registration, and if the writs be not found accordingly, certification will be granted: and therefore the clerks of Session, and the director of the chancellary use to be called; yet, though they be not, the Lords will appoint them to search and produce, or certify that the writs are not found. 2. Certification will not be granted against executions, warnings, or minutes of process, if the reduction be not very recent after pronouncing of these decreets; seeing such minute small papers cannot be long preserved. Yet if they be extant, they must be produced by the clerks, that it may appear whether the decreet was extracted according

to the warrants. But if these be not extant, all is presumed to be orderly done, especially seeing defenders are allowed to see the scrolls of decreets, and to compare the same with the minutes, and to complain by bill, if the clerks do not frame the decreets accordingly. 3. In the reductions of apprisings deduced before the year 1624, certification will be refused; because apprisings then were left as the warrant of the signatures for infeftment thereon, and so are *in publica custodia*. But as to writs registrate in other courts than the Session, the clerks of these courts must be called, and the hazard of not production lies upon the defender, who, or his authors, choosed that court to registrate in.

22. Reductions with improbations must proceed at the King's Advocate's instance, for the King's interest; and therefore it must proceed upon a bill. The reason of the Advocate's concourse is, because the improbation is criminal, if the writ be produced; and the Lords' decreet of improbation is the chief ground of capital punishment for forgery.

23. When the writs called for to be improven are produced, if the pursuer find ground to insist to the improving of any of them, he has two ways to proceed: the one is by the witnesses insert, who when called, if seeing their subscription, they do deny that to be their hand-writ, as they then were accustomed to write, and deny that they were witnesses to the subscription, or to the subscriber's owning of his subscription, the writ will be improven; and this is called the direct manner of improbation. But if the witnesses be dead, or be not found, or do not remember of their having been witnesses, or how they used to subscribe at the date of such writs, the writ will not thereby be improven. If there be but two witnesses, if the one improve, though the other witness do affirm, the writ will be improven rather as null than forged. But if there be more than two witnesses, of whom some are dead, these are presumed to prove: so that if two dead witnesses remain, the living witnesses denying their subscriptions will not improve, in the direct manner of improbation, though their testimonies may concur as adminicles in the indirect manner.

24. The other, called the indirect manner, is by comparison of the hand-writ of the parties and witnesses, with their other subscriptions, or holograph writs, and by other evidences, as that the subscriber or witnesses were *alibi* at the date the writ bears, or that they could not subscribe, &c.

25. If the witnesses be not sufficiently designed, that they may be known how to be called, as if they be of a very common designation, whereof it is known there are many agreeing in the same, the defender must condescend upon a further designation, that they may be known; and if he do not, that witness will not be a proving witness.

26. The indirect manner is not competent while the direct manner is competent. And the indirect manner must be by articles improbatory in writ, which must be seen by the defender, to whom there is allowed articles approbatory: and before the advising, witnesses will be allowed to the pursuer to

prove his articles of improbation, and to the defender to prove his articles of approbation: at the advising of which, the parties are to be heard as in a concluded cause; but there is no formal act of concluding the cause, as in other processes, according to the common rule, *nunquam concluditur in falso*, i.e. there is never a formal conclusion, but all evidences may be still offered before sentence be extracted.

27. Reasons of reduction may be as many as there can be defences, exceptions, replies, duplies, &c. For whatsoever is relevant for either party in the first instance in ordinary actions, is also relevant by way of reduction. But some points are only competent by reduction, and not by exception, and most of these reasons of reduction are competent in competitions; of which hereafter.

28. The most frequent reason of reduction is *ex capite inhibitionis :* for inhibition is a legal remedy for securing of rights, especially of debts and obligations, and it passeth of course by a common bill, the deliverance whereof is signed by the Ordinary on the Bills, upon the trust of the clerk of the bills, without special consideration of the contents thereof: and the tenor of it is a representation that the party craved to be inhibited is like to disappoint the complainer of the performance of his obligation, by dilapidation of his estate, directly by alienation, or indirectly by unnecessary contracting of debt; and therefore craving that he may be prohibited to sell, annailzie, or contract debt till he satisfy the petitioner's debt contained in his bill; and that the lieges may be prohibited to accept alienations, or to contract with him till the foresaid debt be paid. Inhibition being a legal execution, it will be explicated hereafter in its proper place. And there needs no more to be said of it, but whatever is done contrary to it, is *spreta auctoritate ;* and therefore gives a relevant reason of reduction.

29. The proper exceptions against the reason of reduction *ex capite inhibitionis*, are, 1. That inhibition (although it pass of course by inadvertence) cannot be extended to secure any obligement, but that *quæ habet paratam executionem ;* and therefore it is no contempt to alienate or contract, where there is a term of long endurance, before the obligation to be secured can take effect, as if a debt be payable after the debtor's death, or after many years; much more if the obligement to be secured be only conditional: for when obligations are to a day, they are presently obligatory; *nam dies cessit, licet non venit :* but conditional obligations are but obligations in hope, or rather the hope of an obligation, and so begin not to oblige till the condition exist [1,3,8,*supra*]: and therefore inhibition upon them is not effectual, and if that objection were offered to the Lords, the inhibition would not be passed. Amongst conditional obligations are obligations for warrandice, the condition whereof is distress; and so, though inhibition pass of course, upon clauses of warrandice, yet, if the case were represented to the Lords, it would not pass, except there were a distress, or an evident ground of distress instructed; and the clerk of the bills ought not to pass such inhibitions otherwise. 2. That inhibitions

ought not to be granted, nor sustained, when passed of course at the instance of wives upon their contracts of marriage against their husbands, for performance of these obligements, which are against their common interest; as when the husband is obliged to employ the tocher, and so much of his, upon land or annualrent. If the husband be a trading merchant, the employing of his stock so, doth ruin his trade; and therefore inhibitions should not pass thereon, except the husband be *vergens ad inopiam*, or do not providently follow trading. 3. That inhibition can reach no further than lands or annualrents, in the jurisdictions where it is published and registrate. 4. That the right craved to be reduced was not voluntarily granted, but that there was an anterior obligement, whereby the granter might have been compelled to grant the same, at least by a general obligation, as to grant an infeftment in wadset, annualrent, security or warrandice: and although particular lands be not expressed, yet the granting of any of these or the equivalent, out of any of the granter's lands, or other heritable rights, is secure. But if there be diverse obligements granted for the same cause, as principal bonds, and bonds of corroboration, the bond of corroboration is reducible upon inhibition prior to it, although posterior to the principal bond, unless the principal bond contain an obligement to grant such corroboration.

30. The second common reason of reduction is, *ex capite interdictionis*, which in effect is but a special kind of inhibition: for it is the prohibition that makes the interdiction effectual. And therefore all the exceptions that are competent against inhibitions, are competent against interdictions. The rise of interdictions is from positive law; for by pure equity every man is master of his own, and may gift or alienate as he pleaseth; but the positive law of most nations hath provided a remedy against levity and weakness of judgment; so minors, if they be enormly lesed, are restored; and if they have taken curators, their deeds without the curator's consent are null by exception: but their lesion is only annullable by reduction; for when they have curators not consenting, they need not allege lesion. Positive law hath also restrained the liberty of lavish persons though majors; and the Roman law gave curators to prodigals, as well as to minors: and in both lesion behoved to be proved. But though deeds by minors having curators be null, yet deeds by lavish persons having interdictors are not null, but reducible upon lesion: for though the interdictors have a resemblance with curators, yet they are not obliged to manage the minor's affairs, by themselves or their factors, but only to consent with them, that their deeds be not reducible upon lesion.

31. Interdictions are most secure which are made *causa cognita*, when lavish persons instruct their levity, and name provident persons to be interdictors. But frequently persons interdict themselves to such other persons, either simply, in which case the plurality is required, or by a *quorum*, or *sine quibus non*; in which case, though the *sine quibus non* accept not, die, or be excluded for malversation, or albeit a *quorum* remain not, the interdiction remains while any interdictor remains, because the levity, which is the cause of

the interdiction, remains; but if the levity cease, the interdiction may be annulled *causa cognita*.

32. Interdictions voluntary *sine causa cognita* are valid, although there be not a just cause, if there be any particular interest of parties for the interdiction; as if heirs be prohibited to act without the consent of such persons, this will not be effectual, unless a clause irritant be adjected, or that the provision be published as an interdiction; but if it be published, it will not be relevant to allege, that the party was *rei suæ providus*, because there is a particular interest of a third party secured by the interdiction: otherwise it is a sufficient defence against voluntary interdiction, that the person interdicted was *rei suæ providus*, when the deed was done [1,6,39,*supra*], or that he was not lesed thereby. But the renunciation of the interdiction with mutual consent is elided, if the party remained lavish; for as curators and their minors cannot by consent take away curatories, so neither can interdictors and lavish persons take away interdiction, *nisi causa cognita ;* wherein the authority of the judge secures contractors, albeit the person remain lavish: nor will the reduction of the decreet, upon probation of the levity, endanger the deeds after that decreet; because, as positive law gives authority to the interdiction, so positive law may take it off.

33. There is a common exception both against inhibition and interdiction, that albeit the style thereof be expressly against the alienation of moveables, as well as heritables, and albeit that style be so continued, yet they reach only heritable rights, consuetude having so restricted them, that there may be a free course of commerce in moveables.

34. The third reason of reduction is, minority and enorm lesion; which being largely treated, *Lib.* 1, *Tit.* 6. Tutors, &c. [1,6,44,*supra*] it needs not here be repeated. But deeds being done without consent of curators, (where they are) is competent by exception, as a nullity; whereas minority and lesion without curators, is not competent by exception, but by reduction.

35. The fourth reason of reduction, which is not competent by exception, is, when a right is craved to be reduced, as flowing *a non habente potestatem ;* which is, either when the granter of the right never had power to grant it, or had not that power when he granted it, as not being entered and established in that power, or as having been in that power, but denuded of it. But this is only competent to the party that hath a better right, otherwise such allegeances are *super jure tertii*, and are only competent when the other parties pretending right are called by double poinding or in competition.

36. The fifth reason of reduction is, upon nullities which are not instantly verified, but following upon facts requiring declarator; as if the case be for annulling of rights upon clauses irritant, if these clauses be not instantly verified, they cannot be proponed by exception, but will be repelled, and reserved till reduction. This case falls frequently, in clauses irritant in tailzies, bearing, that in such cases the tailzie shall become void; and albeit it bear *ipso facto*, or without declarator, yet custom rejects these additions, as contrary

to the current course of process, and the necessary requisites thereof; otherwise all possessory judgments would be retarded by such clauses: as if an heir of tailzie were pursuing for mails and duties, and any defender having a title should propone that nullity of the tailzie, it would not be relevant, though the clause irritant did bear to be "competent by exception", or "without necessity of declarator". Yea, these clauses irritant are so unfavourable, that though the condition be instantly verified, sometimes they will not be admitted by exception, but will be reserved to reduction and declarator, that during the dependence of these processes the clause irritant may be purged.

37. The sixth reason of reduction, which is not competent by exception, is, *ex capite lecti*, or upon deathbed. This is founded upon the proper law of this kingdom, whereby deeds done on deathbed, are not effectual against heirs, to affect their heritage, or against bairns to take away their legitim. This point being largely treated, *Lib.* 3, *Tit.* Succession [111,4,27 *et seq.,supra*], there needs the less to be added here.

38. This law of deathbed is diametrically opposite to the Roman law, which did by all means secure the freedom of testing, whereby all rights were transmissible by nomination of heirs, by legacies, and *fideicommissa*. But since the feudal law came in, whereby vassals cannot dispose of their wardfees without consent of their superiors, it was a fit and just consequence, that they could not dispose of such fees by their testaments, or appoint other heirs than the heirs in the investiture. And therefore they might not use indirect ways of alienation of these fees, by granting obligations, or doing deeds on deathbed, whereby the vassal might be changed. But the main reason of this law hath been, for the quiet and security of dying persons, against the importunity of husbands, wives, children, or other relations; and especially against the importunity of the Romish priests, who pretended a far greater interest and duty of mortification to pious uses, than of leaving to heirs, not only as meritorious to expiate the sins of the donors' lives, especially of the more vicious persons, but also for obtaining constant prayers and supplications for delivering their souls out of purgatory. And therefore this is a most convenient and just law, when men, through any indisposition, continue in or about their houses, and are not seen to indifferent and unsuspect witnesses; that thereby they may be free from all importunity, seeing they can do no more but dispose of their share of their moveables, which is rarely of considerable value, moveable debts being deduced.

39. Deathbed is not competent by way of exception; for if the allegeance thereof were so competent, it would impede the course of most possessory judgments.

40. There is also competent a declarator of *liege poustie*, "bearing that such deeds were done when the author thereof was in *liege poustie*," that is, in the posture and condition of a liege able to serve his lord in the war, not excusable by indisposition or sickness; "and that therefore the right granted in that state, is to be declared valid."

41. There have been many debates upon this law; as particularly, when persons were to be accounted in *liege poustie*, and when not, but that they had contracted disease, after which they did never convalesce? And albeit at first it was much contended, that there behoved to be proven *morbus sonticus*, a mortal sickness, or a sickness affecting the brain, inducing weakness and instability of judgment, yet these debates are now all laid aside, and there being so many bad examples of dispositions about the time of death, it hath been sustained sufficient, that before the signing and delivering of the writ constituting the right, the granter thereof became sick, and never came abroad thereafter, to the public view, where it might be evident, whether the party was without suspicion of sickness, or that he had so far convalesced, as to be capable of unsuspected witnesses of his convalescence.

42. The common defence against this reason of reduction, is, That after the deed quarrelled, the defunct went to kirk and market, when there was confluence of people. And therefore to validate such deeds, parties went ordinarily to the kirk in the time of public prayer, when there was sermon, or when there was reading, singing, and prayers, which was ordinary during the time of popery, and a considerable time after the Reformation: for under popery no prayers (but such as were secret) were allowed, except in consecrated churches and chapels, but none was allowed otherwise in families; yet, after the Reformation, devotion in families was generally urged, and therefore was more followed than the morning and evening prayers, which came to be dishaunted, and fell into desuetude: yet people, to validate controversed dispositions, went to the kirk, though there was no public meeting in it; and to the market, albeit not in time of market: and therefore convalescence or *liege poustie* by going to the kirk, albeit no public exercise, or appearance thereat, or to the market, though not in market-time, were sometimes sustained. Which proceeding upon mistakes, the Lords were unwilling to call in question deeds so done before that mistake was cleared; but they did clear the same for the future, by an Act of Sederunt in February 1692, declaring, "That they would not sustain going to kirk and market, to validate dispositions to be made thereafter; unless it were proven, that the granter went to the kirk when there was a public meeting in it, or in the kirk-yard for burying; or to the market, unless a confluence of people were there in market-time" [111,4,28,*supra*].

43. Declarator of *liege poustie* is competent against the allegeance of contracting of sickness, as well as for proving convalescence from sickness contracted.

44. Small evidence sufficeth to instruct the contracting of sickness; yea, the presumption of sickness was sustained, a party being sequestrated upon suspicion of the plague, and dying in that condition, though nothing could be proven that the party was actually infected before sequestration. So that, if a party were detained by a sore, which doth not commonly pass under the name of sickness, or a wound or bruise, if he kept in or about the house, and went

not abroad, it is sufficient, seeing it is difficile to know when fevers arise from such causes.

45. The defence of kirk and market is not exclusive of other evidences of *liege poustie ;* as if a man should go a voyage, though it cannot be proven he was at kirk and market.

46. The defence of public appearance presumes convalescence, unless the contrary appear; as if there were evident tokens of the continuance of the sickness, by the view of the party's countenance, or by fainting, or vomiting in going or returning; or not being able to go and return, without resting or support, for such distance as men ordinarily walk a-foot to churches; or if a man should be carried in a chair to the kirk-yard, going and coming free, that length would not prove *liege poustie*, if the deed were done of design to validate a controvertible right; but if a party came riding to the kirk-stile, or rested in walking, or had some support for conveniency or point of honour in other occasions, it would do no prejudice; but when designed, it is a strong presumption of continuance of sickness, when it cannot be done freely without help; and therefore in that case, ladies behoved to forbear from being led for honour.

47. Many domestic acts in and about the house, will not be sustained as equivalent to kirk and market, to prove *liege poustie :* because favourable witnesses may be chosen of purpose; but, in public view, there can be no suspicion.

48. The defence of kirk and market, and the reply of the evidence of the continuance of sickness, by fainting, vomiting, stopping, resting in the way, or support, used to be sustained in the ordinary terms of litiscontestation sustaining the reply, without acknowledging the defence, which therefore the defender behoved to prove; and if he proved it not, there was no necessity to prove a reply; neither did the defence acknowledge the libel, that sickness was contracted, but that behoved to be proven, or otherwise the defender would be assoilzied: so that two witnesses could prove any of these points, and carry the greatest inheritance thereby. Upon occasion of these contrary allegeances, the one party offering to prove health, and the other sickness; the one offering to prove support in going to kirk and market, the other offering to prove, that the party walked free, there being none near him in all the way; the Lords resolved to prefer neither party in probation, but before answer to the relevancy, allowed witnesses to be adduced by either party, to be examined upon the condition of the defunct, when he delivered the disposition in question: for if he did retain it till he was sick, it is alike as if he had then signed it; nor will the clause of dispensing with delivery suffice in that case, unless his liferent be reserved, or that it be a tailzie competent to his heir, in which cases he had interest to retain it. And next the witnesses are to be examined, whether the defunct went to kirk and market or not? Or how he went, supported or free? And if there were evidences of sickness, and what they were? Whereby witnesses are deterred from false testimonies, and great

interests are not carried by two witnesses, which, in other cases, where writ uses to be adhibited, could not prove above an hundred *Lib.* [IV,3,2,*supra ;* IV, 39,4 and 5,*infra*] This form goes of course now of a long time; and the Ordinary in the Outer-House, when the reasons of reduction are referred to him, may order it, though, in most cases, he can do nothing which requires to be done *ex nobili officio* [III,4,28,*supra*].

49. The seventh reason of reduction is, the incapacity of the granter of the right, by being insensible by drink, disease, or otherwise, when he granted the same; which is not to be sustained by way of exception.

50. The eighth reason of reduction is the priority, which is largely explicated, *Lib.* IV. *Tit.* Competition [IV,35,*infra*], with all the exceptions thereof, which are many.

Title 21. Petitory Actions upon Personal Rights

ACTIONS before the Lords of Session, were formerly divided into actions, declaratory (comprehending rescissory actions) petitory, and possessory actions. We are now come to petitory actions, which are not so called, because something is sought to be done by the judge; for so all actions are petitory, but they are called petitory, because something is demanded to be decerned by the judge, to be done by the defenders, which doth not arise from possession. And so possessory actions are those, whereby something is to be done by the defender, not alone upon the point of right, but upon the point of right and possession, or upon sole possession. And petitory actions are sometimes taken more largely, as they comprehend all actions, but such as are possessory, according to the ordinary division of judgments, into petitory and possessory.

2. Petitory actions as here properly understood, are very many. But for order sake, they may be distinguished into these actions that are founded upon personal obligations, and these which are founded upon the right of moveable goods, and these which are founded upon the rights of property of lands, and these founded upon infeftments of annualrent, and these founded upon the right of superiority, and these founded upon hypothecation. This order is according to the method of rights followed, *Lib.* I. and II. of these Institutions: there being no different action founded upon the third book, wherein is handled the conveyance of rights among the living by assignation, disposition, or confiscation; or from the dead, by active succession; for passive succession affords no action, but is only a passive title.

3. The first kind of petitory actions, according to this order, is upon personal rights. It would make the style and tenor of summonses much shorter and clearer, if difference were observed between ordinary petitory actions, which have a known special title in our law, and these actions, which are involved in various circumstances and matters of fact; which therefore, in the Roman law, are called *actiones præscriptis verbis ;* in which the matter of fact is to be first deduced, and the matter of right thence inferred, and then the

will and conclusion subjoined. But in ordinary petitory actions, the will may be premitted, and the title of the pursuer libelled particularly, whereby the natural consequences from such titles are known, and determined in law; and are not at the conjecture of the formers of libels, as in the actions *præscriptis verbis*.

4. This will appear as we go through the several titles, in the order they are explained in the two first books of these Institutions, from *Lib.* 1. *Tit.* 2., of Liberty. If any person be in restraint, the Lords, upon supplication, give charges to set at liberty, wherein there is not an ordinary action: but these charges come in with decreets, and executive actions. What else concerns liberty is rather declaratory than petitory, unless it be the damages by unwarrantable imprisonment, or restraint. The 3d Title, of Obligations in General, contains only general considerations upon obligations, but no special obligation. The 4th Title, of Conjugal Obligations, foundeth actions at the instance both of husbands and wives, arising from the nature of marriage, and the laws and customs relating thereto; but as to the actions upon the several tenors of contracts of marriage, they must be *præscriptis verbis*, according to that tenor. From Title 5th, of Obligations between Parents and Children, there arise ordinary actions for all their mutual obligations, flowing from the law of nature, and the statutes and customs clearing and establishing the same. From Title 6th arise the ordinary actions between tutors and pupils, curators and minors, interdictors and persons interdicted; and consequently actions of compt and reckoning in all these cases, which are competent to either party, or to both; but he is accounted to be pursuer that first provokes to judgment. All these compts are articulate libels, where every article is a several libel, but being so many, they cannot be discussed at the bar, but by auditors. From Title 7th, of Restitution, there arise mainly actions for delivery of moveable goods, which will come in their own place; but here there comes in actions for restitutions of things *quæ cadunt in non causam*, or *ob turpem causam*, or of *indebite soluta*, or *causa data causa non secuta*. From Title 8. arise actions from the obligations *negotiorum gestorum*, and the diligence required therein; the actions *de in rem verso*, and *quantum locupletiores facti sumus ex damno alterius;* and the actions of relief of those who are jointly bound with, and do pay for others, as *correi debendi*, and conjunct cautioners. From Title 9., Reparation, there arise petitory actions for damage by delinquence, by extortion, circumvention, simulation, collusion. From Title 10. there is no special action, it containing only general observations upon the nature of promises, pactions, and contracts. From Title 11. arise petitory actions upon loan, and upon bills of exchange. From Title 12. arise actions on mandates or commissions, and the diligence of mandatars; and the contrary action for the mandatars' expenses. From Title 13. there arise the actions for custody or *depositum*, sequestration, consignation, deposition, and the actions on the Edict *nautæ, caupones, stabularii;* the diligence of all these, and the contrary actions for the expenses of depositars. From Title 14. arise the

actions upon permutation and sale. From Title 15. arise the actions from location and conduction. From Title 16. arise the actions from society and the
duties of partners. From Title 17. arise the actions against cautioners; actions
upon transactions, and promissory oaths of parties. The 18th Title affords no
actions, but only exceptions, upon liberation from obligations.

5. The action for delivery of moveables, is also upon the personal obligation of the haver, which is distinct from the right of property, which is rather
a declaratory action, as *rei vindicatio* in the Roman law did chiefly declare the
pursuer's right of moveables; the action for delivery of moveables, may be
from all title and interest in them; but the prime action is, from *Lib.* 1, *Tit.* 1.
Real Rights [11,1,*supra*], where, besides the general observations on real
rights, the special ways of appropriation of moveables are handled, whether
by occupation of that which belonged to none, accession, alluvion, specification, or conjunction: the remainder of that title, though it much considers
possession, yet these actions are not possessory actions; possession being rather the probation of the right of moveables, than the cause of it; for thence it
is presumed, that the moveables possessed belong to the possessors: yet it admits contrary probation, if he that claims the same can prove that he once possessed these moveables, and that they did not pass from him by any right of
alienation, but by impignoration, custody, loan, or by being stolen, or taken
by violence, or having strayed, or having been lost, or that they were in possession of a defunct the time of his death. And as these are competent exceptions, so they are sufficient titles for petitory actions, for recovery of these
moveables as well as for detaining them.

6. The property of prizes taken by letters of mart, from public enemies,
or by reprisal, afford adjudications of ships and loadings, which are more declaratory than petitory, and are properly *rei vindicationes;* but the recovery
thereof by reducing these adjudications, are more petitory. These adjudications cannot be begun before the Lords of Session, but before the Admiral;
and come only before the Lords in the second instance; and so are not ordinary actions by the jurisdiction of the Lords.

Title 22. Petitory Actions upon Infeftments and Equivalent Rights

FROM the third Title, *Lib.* 11. treating of Infeftment of Property, there arise
many actions both petitory and possessory. The petitory actions are competent to those who have not been in recent possession, but insist upon the
point of right by infeftment. Unto which, by Act 62. Parl. 1661 [Diligence
Act, 1661,c.62; A.P.S. VII,317,c.344], are joined apprisings, whereupon
there is a charge against the superior to infeft the appriser, which, in case of
his disobedience, is accounted equivalent, during the legal, as if he had given
infeftment, seeing, during that time, there is no absolute change of the vassal;
but thereafter it becomes an irredeemable right, and then the superior or
others concerned may stop all action until the appriser be infeft, and pay a
year's rent. And adjudications being now come in place of apprisings, they

have the same effect; as also adjudications upon renunciations of apparent heirs, or adjudications for implement of dispositions of property or liferent. The heirs of vassals, albeit not infeft, have a petitory action for a competent aliment according to their quality, to be paid by donatars of ward, and life-renters, which doth not extend to the reserved liferents of parents, or others disponing the property with reservation of the disponer's liferent.

2. The udal rights of Orkney, by the peculiar customs of the isles of Orkney and Zetland, give the same right as infeftments, and thence arise the same petitory actions.

3. Manses and glebes, being mortified to the kirk, have the same effect.

4. Wadsets of property by disposition and reversion, and infeftments for satisfying of sums, being redeemable rights of property, have the same effects against the possessors of the lands, as if they were irredeemable, until they be actually redeemed.

5. These rights, as they are the ground of declaratory or rescissory actions, when they have not had possession within seven years [11,7,22,*supra*], and so cannot have action for mails and duties, or for removing, against the possessors, who possess by infeftment or equivalent right, if they or their authors have been seven years in uninterrupted peaceable possession, by interruption by way of action, or real intermission of possession, so they give petitory actions against others, for mails and duties or removing. But if the parties infeft, or their authors, or these having equivalent rights, have possessed within seven years, then they have possessory actions for mails and duties, without necessity of an antecedent declarator. The title of these actions upon infeftments must be seasins, with the warrants and adminicles thereof; such as obligements to give infeftments, which suffice in old infeftments, or charters, precepts, or dispositions in new infeftments.

6. In these petitory actions, any party compearing for his interest, and producing an infeftment, or equivalent right, will be admitted; whence arises a competition wherein the same grounds of preference are competent, as in the case of reductions.

7. Actions for mails and duties are not only competent to persons infeft, or having rights equivalent, but likewise to others, who found upon these rights, as to assignees to mails and duties; or to apprisers or adjudgers without infeftment or charge; or to these having dispositions without infeftment: for in all these cases an assignation to the mails and duties is virtually comprehended, though not formally expressed. But these cannot insist, except against tenants or possessors who pretend no right, unless they produce the infeftment of their authors, or that the rights have been acknowledged by the possessors, as deriving possession from the pursuers, or having paid mails and duties to them.

8. Infeftments in liferent or equivalent rights, do found the like actions for mails and duties, and removing, as are competent to the proprietors, in

whose right they pursue: so that if the proprietor was in possession, and the liferenters continued that possession for seven years, the liferenters have the benefit of a possessory judgment; but if not, they have only the benefit of a petitory judgment, proceeding upon their author's right and their own; in which case it will not be effectual to call the tenants and possessors only, unless they have acknowledged the proprietor or liferenter.

9. Liferenters by terce, or by the courtesy, have the same actions as liferenters by infeftment, either apart or by reservation in the infeftments of others.

10. The tenor of actions for a suitable aliment, at the instance of apparent heirs, against their superiors, in ward-lands not being taxed, may be thus [11, 4,36; 111,5,3,*supra*]: "Our will is, and We charge you, that ye lawfully summon D, superior or donatar of the lands of, &c. holden ward of him by A, who died last vest and seased as of fee in the saids lands, to compear, &c. to answer at the instance of B, heir or apparent heir to the said deceased vassal in the saids lands, as having right to a competent aliment conform to his quality, out of the rents and profits of the saids lands during the ward: That is to say, the said defender to hear and see a competent aliment modified by the saids Lords, and allocate upon certain lands, being parts and pertinents of the saids ward-lands: and, for that effect, to hear and see the rental of the saids lands verified and proven, conform to the laws and daily practique of this realm, &c. According to justice, &c."

11. The proper exceptions against this action are, *first*, That the apparent heir has other lands or estate, sufficient to aliment him according to his quality; at the least, the said other estate ought first to be allocated, and the remainder only to be taken out of the ward-lands. If it be replied, that the apparent heir's quality ought not to be the rule of the quantity of the aliment, but the quantity of the rent of the ward-lands, making a just proportion between the vassal and the superior's interest in the ward-lands, this reply ought not to be sustained, because the aliment of heirs and the value of the marriage of the heir are mutual causes; and therefore, as the value of the marriage is due according to the whole estate of the vassal, and his quality, yet so as only to burden the ward-fee; so likewise the aliment of the heir must have respect to his quality.

The *second* exception is, That the apparent heir hath right to an aliment from the liferenter of the ward-lands, or of other lands, who therefore must be called, either to bear the burden in the first place, or at least a proportional burden. This exception is not clearly determined by law or custom: for, though it is certain that both superiors, donatars and liferenters, are liable for an aliment to the heir, yet how the burden affects them is not determined. And it seems just, that the superior, or donatar of ward-lands, should only be burdened, if the rent of the ward-lands be sufficient for an aliment to the heir, conform to his quality; because an aliment is in compensation of the value of the heir's marriage. And as to liferenters, they are liable for an aliment to the heir, whatever the tenure of the fee be; and therefore they ought only to supply what is required above the rent of the ward-fee, proportionally to the rent of the life-rent.

12. The tenor of a summons of aliment, at the instance of the heir, or apparent heir, against the liferenters, may be thus: "Our will is, and We charge you, that ye lawfully summon L, liferenter of the lands of, &c. wherein A died last vest as of fee, and who thereby is obliged to aliment the heir, or apparent heir of the said fee, To compear, &c. To answer at the instance of B, heir, or apparent heir of the said fee: That is to say, the said defender to hear and see an aliment modified by decreet, &c. to the said pursuer, out of the profit of the liferent of the said fee, to be allocated upon certain parts of the saids lands, during the liferenter's life; and to hear and see the samen proportioned between the superiors or donatars of the ward-lands, and the several liferenters of the other lands: and, for that effect, to hear and see the rental of the saids lands to be allocated, verified and proven, in presence of the saids Lords, conform to the laws and daily practique of this Our realm, &c. According to justice, &c."

13. It is a proper exception against this process, that the apparent heir has a sufficient estate of his own, or a calling sufficient to aliment him.

14. The tenor of the petitory action for mails and duties, and the possessory action for the same, differ in this, that in the petitory action the pursuer ought to deduce his title upon the point of right, as high as he can; otherwise, if any having a prior right (though not in possession) appear for his interest, he may exclude the pursuer; and he must also cite not only the tenants and possessors, but the heritors, tacksmen, or liferenters, who are in possession by uplifting the mails and duties. But in the possessory action the pursuer ought expressly to libel, that he, his predecessors and authors, have been in uninterrupted possession for the space of seven years; and thereby have the benefit of a possessory judgment: and therefore he needs produce no more but a right warranting that possession: for no other party that produces another right, will be sustained to compete, unless he have the benefit of a possessory judgment, but his right will be reserved to reduction. Nor needs the pursuer call any but the present tenants or possessors, because he himself is in possession by his tenants, from whom he uplifted the duties of the former years; and if the tenants pretend any other master, they ought to intimate the plea to him.

15. The tenor of the petitory action for mails and duties may be thus: "Our will is, and We charge you, that ye lawfully summon B and C, tenants and possessors of the lands of   , To compear, &c. To answer at the instance of A, as having right to the mails and duties of the saids lands, by virtue of his title herewith produced, viz. &c. That is to say, the saids defenders to hear and see themselves decerned to make payment to the pursuer, of the mails and duties of the lands libelled for the years following, viz. &c. and in time coming, during the pursuer's titles produced, and the defender's pos-

session, the terms of payment of the same being always first come and by-gone: and, for that effect, to hear and see all lawful probation adduced for proving of the worth and value of the yearly rent of the saids lands, and others foresaids, as the same may pay for a constant rent in stock and teind, the de-fenders being always freed and liberated of any teind-duties payable forth of the same, according to the holding and sowing of the saids lands, and the meadows, parks, and inclosures therein, conform to the rate and custom of the country, where the saids lands lie, and according to the rent of mills and fish-ings, as the saids mills are worth conform to their thirle, and according as the saids fishings are worth conform to the rates of the country: at the least, to make payment of the bygone rents conform to the last use of payment; and in time thereafter from the citation hereon, to pay the full duties, which the saids lands and others foresaids are worth; conform to the laws and daily prac-tick of this our realm in all points, &c. According to justice, &c."

16. The proper defence in this process is, that the defender hath a prior and better right to the saids lands and others, and duties thereof libelled; or that the defenders have the benefit of a possessory judgment, by seven years possession, upon a valid title, which must be specially condescended on, wherein not only infeftment, or other rights requiring no infeftment, with the foresaid possession, are relevant, but also tacks are relevant both for the time bygone, and payment made conform thereto, and also for time coming, viz. in respect the same is granted by the setter having an anterior right, or the benefit of a possessory judgment. Yea, the defence upon a tack clad with seven years' possession is relevant *in possessorio*, to maintain the tack in time to come, until it be reduced, without instructing the right of the granter of the tack. A reply upon a prior possession by the space of seven years, by a sufficient title, will not be relevant, if the pursuer have ceased to possess by a tack, which cannot recover possession *activè* by a possessory judgment, as an infeftment may.

17. The petitory action of removing is seldom competent; because, if the pursuer thereof, or his author, have not been in constant possession for the space of seven years, before intenting of the cause, he cannot pursue a remov-ing until he declare his title, if the defender by a valid title be in possession; albeit he hath not attained the privilege of a possessory judgment, yet being in present possession, though for a shorter time; yea he hath that competent defence against the pursuer, that he cannot insist to remove, until he declare his right; which doth not so hold in actions of mails and duties, wherein the defenders may intimate the plea to their masters, and if they be not defended, and pay *bona fide*, they are secure for these years: but when parties are re-moved, they can have no benefit either as to years past, or in time coming; yet all may be removed at the instance of these from whom they had posses-sion, but it is not sufficient that they have acknowledged the pursuer by pay-ment of mails and duties, thereupon alone to be removed.

Seeing removing is so rarely competent by a petitory action, it is fittest to refer the tenor thereof and the exceptions against the same, to be handled amongst possessory actions.

18. All actions for mails and duties, and for removing, at the instance of superiors, against the tenants and possessors of ward-lands, or against the tenants and possessors of other lands, after declarator of non-entry, or liferent-escheat, are petitory actions, proceeding upon the right of superiority, without respect to possession, and they do not require the libelling or proving of possession in themselves or their vassals: neither are defences upon possessory judgments relevant against superiors, or their donatars, but only against the vassals who are proprietors, wadsetters, or liferenters.

19. The action for mails and duties, at the instance of the superior or donatar, against the possessors of ward-lands, require no further title but the superior's infeftment, which nothing can elide but the infeftment of the vassal; or these rights that are introduced by law, such as are liferent by terce, or by the courtesy; or otherwise rights granted by the vassal, with the superior's consent, to be holden of the superior, which, though they have not attained infeftment, will exclude the superior, upon the personal exception of his own consent. But if his consent be only to an infeftment, to be holden of his vassal, albeit infeftment follow, yet it will not exclude the actions of mails and duties, and of removing, but will only exclude recognition.

20. But when superiors, or their donatars, pursue for mails and duties, upon non-entry, they must libel upon a decreet of general declarator: for till that be passed, they cannot insist even for mails and duties, and much less for removing. And the same holds in the like actions, upon liferent-escheats; wherein the general declarator must precede the same: and in these actions not only the exceptions founded upon rights constitute by law, as liferents by terce or courtesy, or by consent of the superior, but all defences are competent against the superior or his donatar, which would be competent against the vassal; because liferent-escheat is not a casualty of superiority, by the nature of the feudal right, but by our particular customs, whereby vassals, being rebels civilly by denunciation for not obeying the charge, if they do not relax within the year, they are holden as *civiliter mortui*, and their fees are holden as void and open to their superiors; yet still with the burden of all rights that did affect the same, when the vassal was denounced.

21. There is also a petitory action, at the instance of an heir, against a liferenter, for reparation of the liferent lands and houses, at any time of the liferenter's life, that they may be put in as good condition as they were at the liferenter's entry. And also it is competent against the heirs and executors of the liferenter, after the liferenter's death, wherein must be libelled the condition of the liferent-lands and houses at the time of the entry, and how they are at the time that the liferenter is quarrelled; for which letters of horning are summarily granted to charge the liferenter to repair, and an action against the representatives for the same effect.

22. There is likewise a petitory action, founded upon the mutual obliga-

tions of heirs and executors, for relief of the moveable debts whereby the heir is distressed, and of the heritable debts whereby the executor is distressed [III,8,65,*supra*]: for creditors have action against either, or both of them, for any debt of the defunct. But creditors have not the same access against heirs of line, male, tailzie and provision, there being an order of discussing amongst them, that the posterior heir cannot be distressed, till the heirs prior in order be discussed; unless the defunct have burdened one special heir only [III,5, 17,*supra*].

23. There is also a petitory action, at the instance of fiars against cutters of wood growing upon their fee: this differs from spuilzie or wrongous intromission; because the growing wood was part of the fee, and therefore doth not belong to any other but the fiar; nor doth it fall under ejection, or intrusion, or wrongous intromission, but it ought to be libelled upon the special title of the fiar.

Title 23. Poinding of the Ground

POINDING of the ground is a petitory action, founded upon many several titles and interests, and is of great importance; and deserves to be handled by itself [II,5,8–10; III,2,13,*supra*; IV,47,24,*infra*]. And by our ancient custom, after recovery of decreet against any landlord, there was a brieve of the chancellary passing of course, for poinding the readiest goods upon that landlord's lands; which therefore was called the brieve of distress. But this was an irrational custom, as if every landlord had taken a letter of mart against his neighbour, not only to seize upon his own goods, but upon his tenant's goods; and that not only for the landlord's real debts by infeftment, but for his personal debts. And therefore, by the 37th Act, Parl. 1469 [Diligence Act, 1469,c.36; A.P.S. II,96,c.12], a very just alteration was made, whereby the brieve of distress became no more in use.

2. By this Act; 1. The goods of the inhabitants of the ground were no more to be distressed, except for their term's mail; and even that is out of use, but the rents of tenants may be arrested for their master's debt, and made forthcoming, not only for the bygone rents, but for a current term's duty, though the term be not come. 2. All execution became competent against the landlord's proper goods, which were to be poinded according to the avail of the debt; and, failing of moveable goods within the shire where the landlord lived, or if these were not sufficient, the King gave letters of poinding to other sheriffs, wherever the debtor had moveable goods or rents. But, 3. There was no access to the property of his lands, till his moveables were first discussed, and then letters were direct to the sheriffs where the debtor had lands, or if the sheriff gave the decreet himself, he was (without any other warrant, but his own executorials) authorised to sell the debtor's land, to the avail of the debt, which necessarily required a public intimation at the head-burgh of the shire, upon a market-day, and in market-time, to all parties that pleased to buy; and it behoved to resolve in a roup, that it might not be in the discretion

of the sheriff, to sell at what rate he pleased, but at the best rate offered. Of the lands so sold, there was no reversion. But if there was no buyer found, the sheriff, or other judge-ordinary was ordained to choose the best and worthiest in the shire, and least suspect to any of the parties, to the number of thirteen persons, to apprise lands, and assign the same to the creditor to the avail of the debt, and that within six months after recovery of the decreet. And the superior is thereby obliged to receive the creditor, or any other buyer, to be his vassal, he paying a year's mail, as the land was set for the time; unless he take the land to himself, and undergo the debt.

3. The alteration of the course established by this excellent statute, has brought much trouble and mischief to the nation. For the Lords of Session did grant letters of poinding and apprising upon decreets for personal debts, directed to messengers, as sheriffs substitute by the Lords, for that effect; and bearing dispensation with apprising upon the ground of the land, within the shire, and by the worthiest and least suspect of the shire; with power to apprise at Edinburgh, by any inquest that the creditor pleased to call; whereby all that was claimed as the debtor's lands, without any evidence, that they were his lands, or that he was holden and reputed heritable possessor thereof, were apprised at random, for the least as well as the greatest debt. And for a long time the appriser enjoyed the whole rents, without imputing the same in his principal sum, till that was in part amended, by Act 6. Parl. 1621 [Diligence Act, 1621,c.6; A.P.S. IV,609,c.6]. And since divers alterations have been made. And by Act 62. Parl. 1661 [Diligence Act, 1661,c.62; A.P.S. VII, 317,c.344], all apprisings were brought in, to have proportional shares according to their sums, if they were deduced within a year, after the first apprising, whereupon there was infeftment, or charge against the superior to grant infeftment; and likewise all apprisings before the said first effectual apprising, and the same was ordained in all adjudications: this was not extended to real debts by infeftment. Also the legal reversion was lengthened from seven to ten years. But this did not cure the inconvenience; and therefore, by Act 19. Parl. 1672 [Adjudications Act, 1672,c.19; A.P.S. VIII,93,c.45], adjudications before the Lords, were introduced in place of apprisings by messengers. And it was put in the option of the creditor to adjudge land, effeirand to his debt, and a fifth part more, in place of penalty, the lands being redeemable within five years; providing the debtor produced the evidents, and gave at least transumpts of them, and consented to the adjudger's possession: or otherwise to adjudge all lands in general, redeemable in ten years, and coming in *pari passu* as before. But very few creditors made use of the special adjudication, and few debtors restricted them to it, to the great prejudice of both parties, whereby a great part of the nation has become bankrupt [IV,51,12, *infra*]; whereas the reviving of the old statute would have cured all these inconveniences.

4. Albeit the foresaid statute 1469 allows the tenant's goods to be poinded for their master's debt, not exceeding a term's mail; yet the Lords have

always interpreted it, to be for the master's debt due by infeftment (and not for his personal debt) and that by an action for poinding the ground. The effect of this action is only for granting letters of poinding and apprising, that thereby the goods upon the ground may be poinded, not exceeding the term's mail, in the first place; and if these do not satisfy the term's annualrents insisted for, that then the ground-right and property of the lands may be apprised, in satisfaction of the whole annualrents resting, if there be no moveables poinded, and of the remainder if moveables be poinded. But creditors do frequently pass by moveables, though they be upon the ground; and custom hath sustained apprisings, albeit they bear, that search was made for moveables, and none found; when it was not so truly done; which is a bad custom, and contrary to the foresaid statute, prohibiting lands to be apprised, so far as the moveables on the ground can satisfy, which is not required in adjudications.

5. Poinding of the ground is competent; first, for the bygone annualrents of an infeftment of annualrent, which is most ordinary: but there can be no poinding for the stock or the principal sum, for which the annualrent is granted, yet the annualrents apprised for are not as mortified, that they could not be redeemed: for it is declared by Act of Parliament, that wherever an annualrent relates to a stock or principal sum, it is redeemable upon payment of that principal sum, without any conventional reversion. But frequently there is a personal obligement to pay the sum: and sometimes it bears, "That execution upon the personal obligement shall be but prejudice of poinding the ground upon the real right." In which case, the creditor may poind the ground for the bygone annualrents, and may apprise the same for the stock; but this apprising will not be effectual against singular successors, as the apprising on the annualrent will be, which is effectual as if it were of the date of the infeftment. The apprisings by the real right for the bygone annualrents do not come in *pari passu*, with the apprisings or adjudications for personal debts; but have effect from the date of the infeftment of annualrent.

Secondly, Poinding of the ground is competent for all feu-duties, for which the ground of the lands (where these feu-duties are in the *reddendo*) may be apprised, for all the bygone feu-duties unpaid.

Thirdly, Ward-lands may be apprised for the non-entry duties, due to the superior after general declarator; which are preferable to all annualrents constitute by the vassal, albeit with the consent of the superior; that consent only importing that recognition shall not follow upon such annualrents; but it doth not import that these annualrents shall be preferable to feu-duties, or the non-entry duties, by decreets of general declarator.

Fourthly, The ground of lands may be apprised for the avails of the marriages, after they are declared.

Fifthly, The ground of any lands may be apprised by poinding of the ground, for any sum wherewith the vassal's infeftment is burdened, or the land may be adjudged for the same sum: and neither the apprising nor adjudication will come in *pari passu*, with apprisings or adjudications for personal debts, but will be ranked according to the date of the infeftment, wherein the burden is expressed; especially if it be not only expressed in the disposition and charter, but in the seasin; and the apprising or adjudication will not only be effectual for the annualrents, but for both principal sum and annualrents, wherewith the infeftment is burdened; yet still the feu-duties and non-entry duties by general declarator are preferable thereto, as well as to the apprisings on annualrents; because the real burden is not a burden upon the superior's right, but upon the vassal's.

6. These apprisings and adjudications upon real rights, as they do not come in *pari passu* with these upon personal rights, so neither do they come in *pari passu* amongst themselves, though they be deduced within the year; but they are preferable in manner foresaid; yet the posterior apprising imports a right to redeem the prior within seven years, all which is clear by the exception contained in the Act 62, Parl. 1661 [Diligence Act, 1661,c.62; A.P.S. VII,317,c.344], which beareth, "without prejudice always of ground-annuals upon infeftment and other real debts, and *debita fundi*, and of comprisings therefore, of lands and others affected therewith, which shall be effectual and preferable according to the laws and practique of this kingdom now standing," viz. as the law was on the first of January 1661, which was the date of that Parliament.

7. There is a very intricate question, whether an apprising deduced on the bygone annualrents, due by infeftment of annualrent, if the same should expire unredeemed, would not only extinguish the right of the proprietor of the land, but also the right of the annualrent itself, so that there could be no poinding of the ground for any subsequent annualrents? This question hath been resolved *affirmativè*, *Lib.* 2, *Tit*, Annualrents [11,5,11]. But there remains yet this question, whether an appriser for the bygone annualrents due by an infeftment of annualrent, can apprise the whole fee, or only so much thereof as is correspondent to the value of the bygone annualrents apprised for? The affirmative is much more just and consonant to this right, that a branch should not defeat the stock; and I have seen no decision to the contrary, but that the ancient statute stands unalterable as to this point; whereby there will never arise a question betwixt the fiar of the annualrent, and these that have only apprised for some bygone years' annualrents: for though the proprietor of the annualrent may redeem within the legal, yet he is not obliged to search registers, that he may know what apprisings were upon bygone annualrents, and when expired; these being only designed to secure purchasers that they be not excluded by prior real rights.

8. It is questionable whether poindings of the ground may now be by apprising, since the 19th Act, Parl. 1672 [Adjudications Act, 1672,c.19; A.P.S. VIII,93,c.45], whereby adjudications are introduced in place of apprisings? or whether adjudication doth thereby only come in place of apprisings for personal debts? The reason of the doubt is, Because the narrative

of that Act bears, that messengers, or ignorant persons of inquest, should not be judges in matters of importance: and yet in the same statute, it is ordained, "That, upon processes raised before the Lords, at the instance of any creditor against his debtor, principal or cautioner, the Lords shall adjudge, and decern to the creditor in satisfaction of the debt, such a part of the debtor's estate, consisting in lands and other rights, which were in use to be apprised, as shall be worth the sum, principal and annualrent, then resting to the creditor, and a fifth part more, in respect the creditor wants the use of his money, and is necessitate to take land for the same; beside the composition to the superior and expenses of the infeftments;" which doth not well quadrate to annualrents or other real burdens which have no penalties, and should not have a fifth part more upon that account. Both these objections are satisfied if poindings of the ground be by apprising, according to the foresaid ancient statute, by an inquest of the worthiest and least suspected to any of the parties, in the shire where the lands lie; and not by messengers (as sheriffs substitute) apprising at Edinburgh, but upon the ground of the land, and upon particular inspection of the worth thereof; whereby such a part of the land may be apprised, as may be equivalent to the bygone annualrents, or other real burden, for which the apprising doth proceed; and that upon inspection of the land, and choosing such a part thereof as may be conveniently separated from the rest, having a reversion for seven years after the apprising, conform to that old statute, which is much confirmed by the said exception in Act 62. Parl. 1661 [Diligence Act, 1661,c.62; A.P.S. VII,317,c.344], providing, that apprisings for annualrents and *debita fundi* remain as before that Act, and are not altered thereby. And therefore, though the legal reversion of other apprisings for personal debts be lengthened to ten years, yet these apprisings for real debts are only redeemable in seven years. And there ought to be no composition to the superior for the entry of these apprisers, when the same proceed for his own feu-duty; or for the non-entry duties by the general declarator of non-entry; or for the avail of marriages, as being in favour of himself or his donatar; or even for annualrents holden immediately of himself; for thereby his vassal is not changed; and composition ought only to be for annualrents holden of the vassal, or for sums wherewith the vassal's infeftments are burdened.

9. In competitions with infeftments, the bygones of annualrents by infeftment, feu-duties, non-entry duties, or avails of marriages are taken in and preferred in their due order as aforesaid, albeit there be no apprising thereupon deduced. And albeit these burdens that flow from the right of superiority, be preferable, not only to apprisings on personal debts, but to apprisings on annualrents or other *debita fundi*, yet it doth not hinder apprisings to take effect for any of them, seeing the whole lands are not apprised, but an equivalent portion thereof, effeiring to the ground of the apprising.

10. The tenors of summonses for poinding of the ground are different, according to the several rights, whereon they proceed. Summons for poin-

ding of the ground for a feu-duty, may be thus: "Our will is, and We charge you, that ye lawfully summon B, proprietor of the lands of   (whose infeftments are granted with a *reddendo* of an yearly feu-duty of payable to A, his immediate superior) and also C and D, tenants and possessors thereof; and all others having, or pretending to have interest, by open proclamation at the market-cross of   To compear, &c. To answer at the instance of the said A, superior foresaid, &c. That is to say, the saids defenders to hear and see letters of poinding and apprising direct by decreet of the saids Lords, for poinding the readiest goods and gear upon the ground of the saids lands, in payment and satisfaction of the bygone feu-duties resting unpaid, extending to the sum of, &c. not exceeding a term's mail of the tenants and possessors of the saids lands *respectivè;* and in so far as the saids feu-duties are not satisfied thereby, and by the goods on the ground belonging to the said B, heritor thereof; then, and in that case, for apprising the ground-right and property of such part and portion of the saids lands, as is equivalent unto the saids resting feu-duties; whereby the right of the said B vassal, in the said portion of land, shall be extinct, and the samen shall be consolidated with the superiority to the pursuer, to be bruiked and joysed by him as full proprietor thereof in all time thereafter, redeemable always, as accords, &c. conform to the laws and daily practique of this our realm, &c. According to justice, &c."

11. Summons of poinding the ground for non-entry duties differ from the former only in this, that non-entry duties are in place of the feu-duties, and that the decreet of declarator liquidating the same, must be specially deduced; but if it be at the instance of a donatar, there must be no mention of the consolidation.

12. If the summons of poinding the ground be for the avail of marriage, the title of the superior, or his donatar, must be deduced, and the declarator of the avail of the marriage: and it must have the article of consolidation, if it be at the superior's instance; but is without it, if it be at the donatar's instance.

13. The summons of poinding the ground for the bygone annualrents, due by infeftment, may more conveniently be as a summons *præscriptis verbis,* deducing the infeftment of the proprietor granter thereof, and the annualrenter's infeftment constituting the annualrent.

14. If the summons be upon a sum burdening an infeftment, the same tenor must be followed, and the conclusion is the same, "being only to hear and see letters of poinding and apprising direct against the proprietors, wadsetters, liferenters, tenants, and possessors of the lands and others affected, for poinding the moveables upon the ground thereof, not exceeding a term's mail of the lands possessed by the several possessors, or the hail moveables so far as the proprietor is in natural possession, by labourage or pasturage;" because the foresaid old statute, restricting the poinding of the moveables to the term's mail, is only in favour of tenants, against whom it is effectual, although

the term be not come, the poinding being *currente termino ;* for thereby the tenants are secure, that they may retain from their masters the price at which their goods were apprised.

15. There are very few exceptions competent against actions for poinding the ground, unless it be by production of preferable rights, which turns into a competition; for thereby any preferable right is receivable, as if there were a reduction depending thereupon, because annualrents and other *debita fundi* are always sustained without declarator or deduction, and without respect whether they have had recent possession or not: and, therefore, if an annualrent, or a real burden on an infeftment, were constitute *à non habente potestatem*, the same would be reducible upon that ground, and these who had right would be preferable without reduction. 2. Upon the same ground a defence upon an infeftment and seven years' possession, is not relevant against a poinding of the ground, which hath neither benefit nor detriment by possession.

16. It will not be a sustainable defence for tenants, that they are only liable for such a duty by use of payment, or by tack, to restrict the poinding to that, if it be not a competent duty, but collusive, if it be replied, that the just rent of the lands is more. But this will be a relevant duply that the tack was set, and clad with possession before the constitution of the annualrent: which will not be relevant against poinding of the ground at the instance of the superior, or his donatar, against whom no tack is effectual, albeit the superior were a purchaser of the superiority after the constituting of the annualrent; because the Act of Parliament securing tenants against purchasers [Leases Act, 1449,c.18; A.P.S. 11,35,c.6], is only against the purchasers of the property, wadsetters or liferenters. 2. It is not a relevant exception for tenants, that they can only be poinded for the half of their yearly rent, (unless it be alleged that the same is payable termly, and not for the whole year together), for in that case their goods may be poinded for a year's rent, seeing they may retain from their master, as well for a year's rent in that case, as for a term's rent in the other, because it is presumed that they have paid their masters, when the term is past: yea, though they have not paid, the statute secures them to be distressed for no more but their term's mail; but they are not secured if they pay before the hand. 3. It used to be alleged, and sometimes sustained for annualrenters, that the old statute restricting brieves of distress to a term's mail, was only in relation to personal decreets for the landlord's rent: but now, of a long time, the landlord's debt is understood both of real and personal debt: and by the Lord, is not only to be understood the proprietor, who is the immediate Lord, but the superior, who is the Over-lord; seeing the words of the statute may bear that interpretation, and the reason expressed therein is alike for all; but there is no rent due to superiors but in feus.

17. If the pursuer do not specially libel the rent when he comes to poind, he cannot make the rent as he will then allege; but the oath of the tenant

must rule the same, though he should depone upon a tack, and doth not produce it; because poinding of the ground doth not require an antecedent charge, as poinding upon personal debts doth; so that the tenant cannot be presumed to have always his tack about him; and therefore it is safest in poindings of the ground, to libel and prove the rent, if the pursuer intend to insist against the moveables on the ground.

18. If the tenant's rent be not in money, but in kind, the messenger (who is a kind of judge in the execution, as sheriff constitute for that act) may determine the price by the oaths of the apprisers, as it is current the time of the apprising, aud so proceed to apprise the tenant's moveables: and likewise he may take the oaths of other persons, pretending the goods on the ground not to be the tenant's goods, but theirs, and may pass by the same. And albeit it is not so cleared by custom, whether the oath of any party will exclude the poinding in this real action, as it is clear in personal decreets, yet *in dubio sequendum quod tutius est* [IV,30,6,*infra*]. The English, indeed, upon these annualrents, which they call rent-charge, do indifferently poind the goods on the ground, to whomsoever they belong, if they find them but lying on the ground; and that by the tenor of their leases or tacks, which frequently bear that clause: and that in case no distress or poinds be found, the landlord may re-enter to the possession, and expel the tenant without the authority of any judge. But then it is only competent upon the very term of payment, whereby all that have goods on the ground not belonging to the tenant, may drive them off. But we have no such summary poinding of the ground, nor are our poindings restricted to any terminate time, but at any time when the annualrent is due, and the term of payment thereof come.

19. The decreet obtained upon this process, is effectual against all singular successors, proprietors, wadsetters, liferenters, tenants, or possessors, without transference, or any other action against these succeeding, both as to the moveables on the ground, and as to the ground-right and property, or other heritable right; because it is a real right whereupon the same is grounded, and needs but one sentence; whereas decreets on personal rights must still be transferred, because the lands or goods are only poindable, as pertaining to such persons.

20. In actions of poinding the ground, not only proprietors having prior rights may appear, and be preferred, whereby the action is totally excluded, and the ground is assoilzied; but likewise other annualrenters, or these having right to *debita fundi*, may appear, and be preferred. As, 1. The superior for his feu-duties, non-entry duties, or avails of marriages, although they be due, after, not only the constitution, but the terms of the annualrent; because these are due from the date of the infeftment of the first author of the annualrent. And, 2. Annualrenters, or these who have right to real burdens, which are prior to the constitution of the annualrent instructing the same, will be preferred, and will have decreet for poinding of the ground; whereby it is poindable by all who instruct their rights, prior to the pursuer's right in their due

order. But posterior annualrents, or terms of annualrents posterior to the date of the summons, will not be comprehended in the decreet, but will be repelled in that action, without prejudice to insist in another action. Yet prior annualrenters cannot stop the execution upon posterior annualrents, by any pretence that can be moved to the messenger, who can be no judge in the competition, and can have little inconvenience, if only a parcel of the lands suitable to the annualrents resting be apprisable. Only if the burden on the land be greater than the value of these who are cut off by poinding of parcels, they must impute it to their own negligence, that did not pursue when they might, *vigilantibus non dormientibus jura subveniunt*, not only in personal, but in real rights, which holdeth as to the bygone annualrents. And if this did not hold, there could be no apprising of a part but of the whole land, for which there was no warrant by the ancient statute; and that custom of apprising came in upon personal decreets, in respect that the apprisers were not able to instruct the right of their debtor, and therefore were admitted to apprise all they pretended to be the debtor's, *suo periculo :* which doth not hold in poindings of the ground, which extend only to the particular right expressed in the pursuer's own title, and can be extended to no other ground of the debtor: and therefore, in the remedy by the Act 19, Parl. 1672 [Adjudications Act, 1672,c.19; A.P.S. VIII,93,c.45], for poinding a part, the defender must produce his rights; or otherwise the whole must be yet apprised or adjudged, as before; because in these summary executions the pursuer cannot know who hath the last and best right.

Title 24. Petitory Actions for Teinds or Teind-Duties

TEINDS are introduced by law and custom, and do burden the fruits, not the fee of lands. Neither do they affect any but the intromitters with the fruits; nor all intromitters: for tenants paying a joint duty for stock and teind, are not liable for the teind (but their masters are) in so far as they have paid *bona fide*. Neither doth a citation put them *in mala fide*, if it be not presently insisted in, because of their rusticity, and subjection to their masters, who will take decreets in their own courts and poind: much less will merchants buying for a price be liable for the teind [11,8,22,*supra*]. Nor is the heritor liable, but as he is intromitter with the whole rent for stock and teind, or with both the rent and teind when separate. But because heritors in the valuation of their teinds do value whole baronies or tenements together, that the fifth of the rent of the whole may be the teind of the whole, thereby they become liable for the teind, and not the tenants, because it is not divided upon their rooms; yet if it be so divided, their masters are not liable for the teind, unless they intromit with the whole crop, or receive payment of the teind apart, or a joint duty for stock and teind.

2. The right of teinds affords both a petitory and a possessory action in diverse cases. And in no case there is necessity of a declarator; but the petitory action is competent upon the right being instructed: and then there uses

no more to be insisted for, but use of payment or tack, or tacit relocation. But the possessory action is only competent for drawn teind, when the teind-master hath been in possession to draw the same the year immediately preceding: for then he has a possessory action for spoliation of the teind. But if he was not in possession the year immediately preceding the year in question, he will only get use of payment till he use inhibition, which is the legal way of interrupting tacit relocation of teinds, or use of payment: but the inhibition will reach no further than that year in which it was used.

3. There is an annuity due to the King out of teinds, the same being valued; which being a part of the revenue, letters of horning are granted for the same summarily against the teind-master, the heritor, or possessors, so far as the teinds are in their hands, unless the heritor have acquired right to the annuity, which, not being annexed to the Crown, is at the King's disposal. These actions for teinds may be pursued against all intromitters with the whole crop, or against the heritors, where the teind is not divided upon the several roums. But if the land come to be divided by distinct infeftments, or equivalent rights, either of property, wadset, or liferent, they can only be pursued for their proportional parts of the total valuation; yet the favour of the stipendiary ministers for their stipends, which are but alimentary, allows them to have action against any of the heritors, who come to have divided rights after the valuation for the whole, so far as the teind of their possession can reach; and these have action of relief against the rest. And if these stipendiaries have no locality, they have access to the whole teinds of any part of the parish, so far as their stipend goes; and these who are so made liable must seek their relief.

4. Teind-masters are those who have right to teinds, wherein the common rule of the canon law is, that the parsonage teind is due to the parson, and the vicarage to the vicar; and that without showing any title but their incumbency, and their title to the benefice; which is not needful to be shown by these where there is *decennalis et triennalis possessor, qui non tenetur docere de titulo*, albeit it were in competition with other church-men, where the question is only who hath right to the benefice, and not to particular teinds; and therefore, if ministers be in possession of the parsonage and vicarage, or of either of them, they may pursue upon their collation and institution, or upon their act of admission, without any other title.

5. But if the teinds have been otherwise applied or mortified, as to bishops, abbots, priors, provosts, chaplains, or to colleges or universities, the same must be pursued upon these titles, at the instance of such as derive right from these beneficed persons, or from the King, or other patron, when the benefice is vacant, or when it is suppressed.

6. The right of teinds which belonged to popish prelates, did, after the Reformation from popery, fall to the King, as *bona vacantia*, and were derived from the King by erections and temporal lordships; but with the burden of ministers' stipends. And inlike manner, the rght of teinds was derived

from kirk-men by tacks; and when the tack-duty was not sufficient to pay the minister's stipend, the Commission for Plantation of Kirks had committed to them a parliamentary power, to burden these tacks with ministers' stipends, and in compensation thereof, to prorogate the tacks for such time as they saw convenient. By these erections and prorogations, most of all the teinds of Scotland are carried: and the same must be libelled and produced in the petitory actions, pursued at their instance, or at the instance of such as derive right from them.

7. In benefices patronate, the patron had right to the teinds *sede vacante.* But several Acts of Parliament have restricted the right of patronage; and now the patron has only the application of vacant stipends, to pious uses within the parish.

8. All those who have right to teinds have one common name, by which they are called teind-masters; and the pursuits at their instance proceed in the same way as actions at the instance of heritors, wadsetters, or liferenters, against tenants, possessors, or other intromitters. And the petitory action runs in the same terms, except as to the variety of the active title, or of the passive title, by being possessors or intromitters. And because now most teinds which belong not to ministers, do belong to the Lords of Erection, or to those deriving right from them; therefore the tenor of one action at the instance of a Lord of Erection, will suffice for all actions for teinds, altering only the active title, which action may be thus: "Our will is, and We charge you, that ye lawfully summon B, possessor or intromitter with the crop of the lands of
To compear before the Lords of our Council and Session, upon the
day, &c. To answer at the instance of A, who stands infeft in a barony erected by us, comprehending the teinds of the saids lands, conform to his infeftment, dated, &c. whereby the pursuer hath good and undoubted right to the teinds, parsonage, and vicarage, of the saids lands, and ought to be answered and obeyed of the samen. Which teinds of the saids lands extend in value to the fifth part of the rent thereof: likeas, the saids lands pay, or are worth to pay, the sum of   reckoning the payments that are in kind to the ordinary rates of the country, where the land lies; extending in haill to the sum of   yearly; and the saids lands are possessed, or the fruits and profits thereof are intromitted with by the said B, the crops and years of God 1690, 1691, &c. That is to say, the said defender to hear and see the premises sufficiently verified and proven, and being so verified and proven, to hear and see himself decerned by decreet of our saids Lords, to make payment to the pursuer, of the teinds of the saids lands, extending to the fifth part of the fruits and profits thereof in manner above specified, conform to the laws and daily practique of this our realm, &c. According to justice, &c."

9. The proper exceptions against this action are, 1. That the defender or his master is infeft, or at least is heir apparent to the person last infeft, in the lands in question, *cum decimis inclusis.* For instructing of this, it will not be sufficient to produce a charter of the stock and teind of the lands jointly, even

though it bear *cum decimis inclusis;* unless there be instructed a progress of such rights bearing to be originally from kirk-men, and bearing *cum decimis inclusis,* which frequently is cleared by these words, *nunquam antea separatis;* which charter, with seven years' possession, gives to the heritors and possessors a sufficient defence *in judicio possessorio;* for the possessory judgment may be competent *passivè* to the defender, albeit the pursuer have no necessity of a declarator for his active title. 2. There is a proper defence upon the lands, which did belong to the Cistertian order, which were teind-free still, by a privilege of that order, which is continued to their singular successors, albeit they be not church-men. 3. There is also a proper exception of the teinds of Temple-lands, (which were the glebes of the Templars) and of all glebes of kirk-men, that were in time of Popery, or that have since been, or shall be designed for glebes. There are many other competent exceptions and defences in this cause, which are common with other causes, for the defender, or for competitors producing and defending upon a better right, or by payment made *bona fide,* which are not to be mentioned at the several actions, but hereafter when litiscontestation is to be explained.

The possessory actions for teinds upon present possession, or inhibition, are to be found amongst possessory actions.

10. If teinds be pursued for *separatim,* viz. the parsonage teinds, which are only due out of the crop, then there must be particular libelling of what was sown, and what is the ordinary increase of the lands in question, or what was the quantity of the crop, as it was proved and delivered by taskers or servants; whereof the tenth part is only due.

11. If the vicarage teind be separate from the parsonage, and belong to another benefice, then the same must be particularly proven, by all the particulars carrying a vicarage teind, which is only according to the custom of the place; for many more things are teindable in one place, than in another; wherein the tenth part is due for the teind. But in vicarage, it is a sufficient defence upon tack, or use of payment, or tacit relocation, until interruption, which does not require inhibition, as in parsonage teinds, but the citation makes interruption.

12. There is also both a petitory and possessory action for vicarage. But the possessory action is, where the teind-master was, immediately before, in possession of drawing the teind, and was hindered by the possessor or other intromitter, to continue the drawing thereof; for thereby there is a spuilzie for vicarage teinds, as well as for parsonage; but with this difference, that it is a spuilzie in parsonage, if the teind-master was in immediate possession, although he were not hindered to draw the teind; unless the possessor did himself separate the teind from the stock, and preserved it conform to Act 9. Parl. 1617 [A.P.S. IV,541,c.9], anent the Teinding of Corns.

Title 25. Actions upon Hypothecation

OUR law doth allow of no hypothecation of moveables by consent of parties, without delivery, and real possession, though it was competent by the Roman law; because thereby the current commerce in moveables would be hindered. Neither doth it allow of many hypothecations competent by the Roman law, but only of the hypothecation of the fruits and goods on the ground, belonging to tenants or possessors, for the rent; and the *invecta et illata* in houses, for the mails of the houses. Which hypothecations extend only to one year, that commerce be not thereby hindered: for buyers or other acquirers may and should see that the present year's rent, when they buy, be satisfied, and then they are secure.

2. These hypothecations have very different effects. The master of the ground hath no hypothecation upon *invecta et illata*, as is competent for house-mails; because houses have no fruits, and therefore the goods brought in are hypothecate in place of the fruits. But lands or other tenements which have fruits, may be secured by the fruits. By the fruits, are not only to be understood the grain growing on the ground, out of which the parsonage teind is taken; but likewise all things out of which vicarage teind can be taken in that place, as stirks, lambs, wool, and the product of milk, butter and cheese, staigs, the birth of swine, herbs and roots; which may not only be detained upon the ground, at the term when the rent is to be paid, during that year, but may be recovered by action from all intromitters, albeit they were poinded upon personal decreets, or at the instance of donatars; unless there remained sufficient fruits on the ground, at the terms of payment. And it is not enough that there were other goods upon the ground, sufficient to pay the rent at the terms; because the poinders might have poinded these other goods, and likewise the master of the ground might poind the same for prior rents: but still the fruits of the ground should remain, so as to be sufficient for a year's rent when the terms come. This hath not been extended against buyers in public market, which were too great a hinderance to commerce [1,13,15 and 29,*supra*]; for in the market none is obliged to inquire whether he that sells the goods was tenant in the lands, whereon they grew; neither could his assertion of the contrary secure the buyer, if the fruits sold in the market were hypothecated.

3. The hypothecation of *invecta et illata* for the rent of houses, ought to be extended against all tenants, and possessors of tenements, which have no natural fruits, as against millers, colliers, salters, and the like. Our custom hath not made it so clear, what is meant by *invecta et illata*. There is no question but it is extended to all the proper goods of the possessor, which are brought into the house, close, or gardens, for the use thereof; as all household-furniture, ornaments, and utensils. But it is more questionable if other goods, which were brought in not to remain for any time, but to be removed, or sold out, so soon as possible, can make the intromitters liable: for thereby, these

who buy from merchants, out of their shops, would be liable for the rent. There is no ground to make the goods of others, beside the possessors, to be hypothecated, if they were carried out again before the term of payment: but if they be there when poinding is used for the rent, there seems reason enough that they may be poinded, because they might remove them in time, and not put the landlord to the necessity of their oaths; which I have not heard hath been made use of, to stop the poinding of goods in houses for the rent thereof; but only for exeeming goods from poinding for the rents of lands.

4. These actions are petitory actions, because masters of the ground or landlords require no possession of the goods recoverable by these actions.

5. The action against intromitters with the fruits of the ground, for the rent, may be libelled thus: "Our will is, and We charge you, That ye lawfully summon B, as he who intromitted with the fruits underwritten, extending to the prices after mentioned, which grew upon the pursuer's lands of   in the year   and which by the law were hypothecated for the rents of the said year, in which the saids fruits grew, To compear, &c. To answer at the instance of A, master of the ground, to whom the rents of the saids lands were due and payable; which fruits so intromitted with by the defender, extend to the particular quantities and prices after following, viz. &c. That is to say, the said defender to hear and see the premises verified and proven, and being so verified and proven, to hear and see himself decerned, by decreet of our saids Lords, to pay the price of the saids fruits, at the rates and quantities libelled, conform to the laws and daily practique of this our realm, &c. According to justice, &c."

6. The proper exceptions against this action are, 1. That the rent was paid. 2. That at the time of intenting the cause, there remained sufficient fruits upon the ground for payment of the rent, in whole or in part; but not that there were other goods upon the ground, sufficient for payment of the rent; for to this it will be relevant to reply, that the other goods on the ground were necessary for the stocking and labouring of the ground, and therefore the landlord was not obliged to waste the ground, but might pursue the intromitters with the fruits. 3. Another exception is, that the defender intromitted by buying in public market, at least, acquired from those who so bought. 4. The goods in question were poinded by letters for poinding the ground, which is a preferable right: for if such poinders were not secure, they could not safely apprise so much of the land as would be sufficient for the remainder. 5. The goods in question were restored to the possessors, before intenting of the cause.

7. The action against intromitters with *invecta et illata*, for house-mails, differs little from the former; and the proper exceptions are much the same.

Title 26. Actions Possessory in General, and Removing in Special

HAVING gone through actions petitory, there follows now (according to the method proposed) actions *in judicio possessorio;* which differ from the former mainly in this, that actions petitory proceed upon the point of right complete in itself, at least prior and preferable to any right of the defender: and albeit sometimes possession be requisite to accomplish the right, as in base infeftments the right is not complete without possession; yet the actions thereon are petitory. But the possessory actions are such as need not debate the point of right, but must continue possession, as it was at the intenting of the action. These actions are like the interdict in the Roman law, *uti possidetis* [D.43,17, 1]; whereby lawful possession is continued, until the point of right be determined, and what is enjoyed *medio tempore*, is secure, until the obtainer thereof be put *in mala fide*, by a better right, either by way of reduction, declarator, or in competitions of many rights, where there is a necessity to allow all parties to adduce all their reasons of preference, as in a reduction.

2. These possessory actions are of two sorts. Some require a special title in writ, not for probation of the right, but for constitution of it, which therefore must be libelled and instructed: others proceed upon sole possession, and require the production of no title in writ. Of the former sort are actions for mails and duties, actions for removing, actions against molestation: of the other kind some relate to moveables, to wit, spuilzie, and wrongous intromission: others relate to lands, to wit, ejection, intrusion, and succeeding in the vice of removed tenants or possessors.

3. The distinction of the petitory and possessory judgments, as to lands and other heritage by infeftment, ariseth from the feudal customs of this kingdom; where there are many subaltern infeftments of the same heritage, and every party keeps in their own hands their own right; so that, if the proprietor were to instruct his progress, by insisting for mails and duties, or by recovering the natural possession by removing of tenants and possessors, his right would be very lame and ineffectual, if any person should produce a prior right, or the possessors should say they possess in the right of another, who had a prior right; so that the proprietor behoved to found upon all his superior's rights, prior to that right, whereupon the defence were founded, which are not in his hand, and he had no title to get them into his hand, but by an incident diligence, if the proprietor possessing might be excluded by any right prior to his own infeftment. For remedy of which inconveniencies, our law hath wisely introduced this remedy of a possessory judgment, whereby proprietors of lands and other heritages, pursuing for rents or removing, or defending their present possession, need allege and instruct no further than seven years' lawful and uninterrupted possession, by virtue of an infeftment; whereby they do not only secure the profits they have made as *bona fide possessores*, but may continue to enjoy the future profits, till they be put *in mala fide*, by judicial production of a better right, by way of reduction, declarator or competition.

4. The most ordinary possessory action is, for mails and duties; whereby the rents and profits are claimed, as a yearly rent payable at one or more terms. The pursuer in this action doth ordinarily produce no more but his

seasin, against tenants that have acknowledged him, and have no other right sufficient to defend them: but if any other compear to defend them, and produce an infeftment, the seasin will not be sufficient; and therefore, when any such title is suspected, the pursuer should more prudently libel upon infeftments of seven years' standing in himself, his predecessors or authors; for an apparent heir may continue his predecessor's possession, upon production of his predecessor's infeftment.

This action for mails and duties may either be petitory or possessory. It is petitory, when the pursuer founds not upon a course of possession, but upon a title sufficient to attain possession, and in that way it hath been handled before, *Lib.* 4, *Tit.* 22. But if the proprietor, his predecessors or authors, have been seven years in possession before the years pursued for immediately; at least, there hath not seven years intervened, since he or they were in possession seven years; then it is a possessory action, whereof the tenor needs not be expressed, because it differs nothing from the petitory action, but that the title is libelled, of seven years' continuance of possession, by virtue of it; and it is often pursued simply by production of the pursuer's seasin; and if a contradictor appear, the privilege of the possessory judgment is replied upon.

5. But removing is an action, by which not only the tenants and possessors must be called; but if they be tenants and possessors who have paid mail and duty to another as their master, the action will not be effectual until that master be called, if he have had a lawful possession, by uplifting of mails and duties by infeftment, or by a tack, whereof there were terms to run. Therefore, removing being more frequently pursued, as a possessory action, it was not treated of amongst petitory actions, but was reserved to this place. And, albeit it may be also pursued as a petitory action, against any who hath not been in possession seven years, by virtue of any infeftment or tack unexpired, yet the tenor in both is much the same.

6. Removing in Scotland, anciently was thus. The master of the ground did verbally intimate to the tenant, to remove at the next Whitsunday, after expiry of his tack; and at the second lawful day after Whitsunday, he expelled the tenant *brevi manu*, without sentence [11,9,39,*supra*]; and thus it was till the 39th Act Parl. 1555 [A.P.S. 11,494,c.12] prescribed the order of removing thus: "Lawful warning being made forty days before Whitsunday, to the tenant; and on the ground of the lands, leaving a copy of the precept of warning and executions thereupon; and the precept of warning being read at the parish kirk where the lands lie, upon a Sabbath-day in the forenoon, the time of preaching or prayers," (which custom hath interpreted to be at the dissolution of the first preaching, or at the time when it uses to be dissolved, if there be no preaching) "and a copy left affixed upon the most patent door of the kirk; upon this, action for removing is competent, on six days. But if the party warned compear, and shows nothing, but offers to improve the indorsation; in that case, he shall not be heard in judgment, but if he find suffi-

cient caution to the warner instantly, that if he prove not his allegeance being found relevant, the profits, damage and interest, that the warners or others having interest, have sustained, or shall sustain, by the delay of the foresaid allegeance, shall be refunded."

7. This statute is still in vigour, but because Whitsunday was a mutable term, running oft-times far in summer, whereby the removing tenants did eat meadows, and haining; therefore the fifteenth day of May is now the term of removing, by Parl.1 K.W. and Q.M. Session 2, c.39, Anno 1690 [Act 1690,c.39; A.P.S. IX,222,c.98]. Whatever the term of removing be, the warning must be forty days before the same term, (and albeit tenants or their masters being out of the country, must be summoned on threescore days, yet the warning needs only be upon forty days) because the same term is the competent term for taking lands, and providing fuel, which is ordinarily peats, to be casten and win about that time. This ground doth not extend to tacks or houses in burghs-royal, or other burghs, nor to any other tack, which hath not that special consideration.

8. Removing may proceed on a great variety of titles. 1. If the possessor have been introduced by the pursuer, he cannot require any title for the removing at the pursuer's instance, unless he hath been forced by process to acknowledge another master. But receiving of mails and duties will not be a sufficient title, where the defender received not the possession from the pursuer; because if he desert the possession unwarrantably, he will be liable for the rent, as possessor, *nam pro possessore habetur qui dolo desiit possidere.* 2. A disposition, though without infeftment, is a sufficient title to remove the granter of it. 3. An apprising or adjudication with a charge, being since the Act 62, Parl. 1661 [Diligence Act, 1661,c.62; A.P.S. VII,317,c.344], is a good title for removing; because it is holden equivalent to an infeftment during the legal. 4. The terce of a relict being kenned, is a sufficient title for removing the tenants of her share. 5. The courtesy of Scotland is likewise sufficient. 6. A tack containing a power to remove tenants, expressly, or by the nature of the tack, being a liferent-tack, or a rental, if it hath attained possession, or that the setter thereof was in possession when he set it. But an apparent heir hath no title to remove, till he be infeft, though he may pursue for mails and duties; because he may renounce to be heir, and so the tenant will be liable as if he had continued to possess: yet if he warn, when he is apparent heir, and be infeft before the time of warning, his title will be sufficient; because the former reason holds not in that case, if his predecessor died in possession. 7. Any infeftment of property or liferent, or the superior's infeftment during the ward, or after declarator of non-entry, or liferent-escheat, are valid titles of removing: but infeftments upon the pursuer's own resignation are not sufficient titles for removing; unless the pursuer have been in possession by mails and duties; because infeftments pass of course in Exchequer, upon any person's own resignation (except it be of the King's property) seeing the King receives all his subjects in any other rights of property, whereof the

casualties only belong to the King; though for knowing the progress of rights by infeftment, the King be the supreme superior.

9. The tenor of a summons of removing may be thus: "Our will is, and we charge you, that ye lawfully summon B, tenant or possessor of To compear, &c. To answer at the instance of A, as having right to in-put and out-put tenants, in the saids lands, by virtue of, &c. (here is to be mentioned the particular title) That is to say, the said defender, to hear and see himself decerned by decreet of our saids Lords, to flit and remove himself, his family, subtenants and cottars, forth and from the saids lands, &c. and to offer the void possession thereof, that the pursuer may enter thereunto, brook and enjoy the same, conform to his right, and that at the term of, &c. conform to a warning made to the said B, forty days before the said term for that effect. Conform to the Act of Parliament made anent warning and removing of tenants, laws and daily practique of this our realm, &c. According to justice, &c."

10. There are many proper defences against this summons, and not only as objections upon the insufficiency of the title and interest of the pursuer, or against the legality and order of the warning: as, 1. This dilator defence is relevant, that all parties having interest are not called, especially the defender's master, to whom he is tenant, by payment of mails and duties preceding the warning, and who stands infeft, or hath tack for terms to run. This defence not being peremptory of the cause, must be instantly verified, unless other distinct defences be sustained to be proven; for then this also will be admitted to probation: but otherwise there must be at least produced discharges of the rent, bearing the master's title, which the tenant is not obliged to dispute, nor could he be master of his landlord's title, who hath been in possession by lifting of mails and duties; which being so evident a possession, he ought to have been cited.

Secondly, That the defender is tenant to another, who is his master by a sufficient title to defend the possession, by payment of mails and duties to the said master, who was not warned. This exception is not merely dilatory, as only exclusive of the instance by this summons, but is exclusive of any summons for removing at this term; and therefore it ought to have a term for proving, although there were no other defence, in which it differs from the former exception: for though the tenant's master were not called, yet if he were warned, a new summons would remove the tenant at the same term. And though this reply hath been sustained against this defence, that the pursuer has reduced the right of the person whom the tenant pretends to be his master, yet the tenant is not obliged to dispute his master's right, when he is not called: but it would be relevant against the exception of not warning that person, that warrant be granted to cite him, for proving of the reply. But the production of it *instanter*, without calling the master, ought not to remove the tenant.

Thirdly, Another exception against removing, is upon prescription by Act

82, Parl. 1579 [Prescription Act, 1579,c.82; A.P.S. III,145,c.20], bearing, "that all actions of removing be pursued within three years after the warning, with certification, that the warner shall never be heard thereafter, to pursue the same upon that warning." Or, though the action begin within the three years, yet it must be renewed, according to Parl. 1669, cap. 9. [Prescription Act, 1669,c.9; A.P.S. VII,561,c.14], whereby it prescribes in ten years, if it be not wakened every five years.

Fourthly, Another defence is, the pursuer's passing from the warning expressly or directly, or by deeds importing the same; as by taking of rent before the hand, or for terms after the warning; or by requiring or accepting services or presents expressly due by the tack, or by taking the herizeld [heriot] of a defunct tenant, whereby his wife and bairns cannot be removed for the year thereafter.

Fifthly, Another defence is, upon any personal obligement, or incomplete right, importing a right to the tenant of his master, to retain or attain the possession; which is not relevant against singular successors.

Sixthly, Another exception is, that the defender possesseth the lands in question *pro indiviso* with other lands. But this is not relevant for removing from any subject, whereof there are daily profits divisible, as a coal-heugh, or fishing. Neither is it relevant for a liferenter on her terce, against the fiar of an indivisible tenement: for there the greatest interest must carry the natural possession, and be liable to the lesser for its share. So likewise, if a possessor by virtue of a right coming in *pari passu* with another greater right, (as is now frequent by concurring adjudications) or if a tenement have several tenants possessed *pro indiviso*, and having different houses, any of these tenants may be removed, and another put in his place, or the master of the ground may possess the same.

Seventhly, This is also an exception, that the defender or his master hath the privilege of a possessory judgment, by virtue of a valid right, capable thereof, condescended on, and seven years' possession by virtue thereof, in the person of the defender, his predecessors or authors. This will not be elided by an allegeance of its being clandestine, or having a vicious entry. But it will be elided by the reply of interruption, either by intermission of possession, or by process of removing, or of mails and duties. But if the action be not possessory, that the pursuer, his predecessors or authors, have been seven years in possession, by virtue of a competent title; the defender's possession, though it be not for seven years, will yet defend him till the pursuer's right be declared, or the defender's reduced: yet if the pursuer had been in possession by a competent title, for seven years, albeit not immediately before the warning, it will be sufficient for removing the defender, unless, after the pursuer's seven years, he hath possessed peaceably for seven years, otherwise his shorter possession will not defend him against the prior seven years' possession, being *in possessorio*.

Eighthly, The last defence against removing, is obedience, that the defender hath removed at the term, conform to the warning, and left the tenement void, and delivered the void possession to the pursuer, or at least offered the same. But it is not relevant that the tenant left the possession void and red, if before he offered the same, any other entered in his vice, or if any that was in his family continued to possess, or if he did not remove his cottars who require no particular warning.

11. None of all these defences, not being instantly verified, are competent, until caution be found for the profits, and the warner's damage and interest, in case the defender succumb; as is provided in the foresaid statute.

12. It is not a relevant defence against the removing, that it is pursued before the term, if it be after the warning: for though in personal obligements, actions be not competent before the term, yet removings have been so sustained, and justly; because, if the ground be not red at the term, the intrant tenant can have no access, and so may protest to be free, and the land will be left waste.

13. Albeit removings be in the roll of causes that are summarily discussed; yet the term falling in the vacance, this great inconvenience follows, that the warning cannot be made effectual at the term: and therefore warning may be made in the beginning of January, that the removing may be discussed before the end of February.

14. There is another kind of removing, which is called summary, in distinction from the former solemn removing by warning. Summary removing without necessity of warning, is competent in several cases: 1. By the nature of the possession, which if it be vicious, violent or clandestine, removing is competent at any time without warning, as against those who succeed in the vice of persons removed, whether they remove by consent or by process; for their entry is by intrusion; and all others that so enter may be summarily removed; much more those who enter by ejection of the natural possessor; and all who possess precariously, may be so removed. Yea, if any have entered in possession and have never paid mail and duty to any, albeit the possession was altogether void and deserted, so that the possessor will not be liable as an intruder, yet he may be summarily removed: thus the bairns, servants, or others that were in family with removed tenants and others; or those who were in family, or servants, or cottars to liferenters, in what was in the liferenter's natural possession, may be summarily removed.

Secondly, Summary removing is competent *ex pacto*, even against tenants, if by their tack they be obliged to remove at the ish thereof, without warning. But if they be not removed precisely at that time, by an antecedent charge of horning, they are understood to be continued by tacit relocation; and therefore must be warned ere they can be removed.

Thirdly, Those who dispone lands or other hereditaments, with an obligement to enter the acquirer in possession, may at that time be summarily removed. But if there be only a disposition, with an obligement to infeft, although there be expressed a term of entry, which gives access for mails and duties, and implies a tacit obligation to remove; yet the disponer's not re-moving, will not infer violent profits; nor is there reason to remove him from his natural possession, without warning; at least he will only be decerned to remove at the next Whitsunday, without violent profits; and much more, if the pursuer's title be but apprising or adjudication, whether with charge, or with infeftment; for these are but legal dispositions, and ought not to remove the debtor summarily; yea, though he be warned, the Lords may restrict the appriser or adjudger's possession to his annualrent, being within the legal, Parl. 1661, cap. 62. [Diligence Act, 1661,c.62; A.P.S. VII,317,c.344].

15. There may be an objection made against what hath been said of re-moving, by the privilege of a possessory judgment; that a possessory judg-ment hath been accustomed only to be made use of, in way of defence, so that any having a prior right, may remove a possessor having but a posterior right, without necessity for the pursuer to allege any possession. It is true, that any infeftment may remove a naked possessor, but cannot remove a possessor by infeftment, though posterior, unless the pursuer instruct his right immedi-ately, or by progress from the King; or at least, that it is perfected by pre-scription, or that it hath continued in possession for seven years, and so hath the privilege of a possessory judgment, whereby the possession must be con-tinued; unless the defender, who is actually in possession, have acquired a possessory judgment, which will defend, though the possession be posterior to the other, if it hath had seven years' peaceable possession without interrup-tion: for any man may infeft another, which will not give action against a pos-sessor infeft, unless a progress be shown from the King, or from a common author to the pursuer and defender, whose right neither party can quarrel: and even in that case, the pursuer must instruct, that his or his author's right was once clad with possession, otherwise it is understood as a continued base infeftment, holden of the common author, which cannot exclude him that is in actual possession, though his infeftment be of the same kind; because it has the advantage of possession. But this will be further cleared in the title Com-petition. [IV,25,*infra*].

17. [Thus in second edition, there being no section 16.] If, in removings, there be any defect in the order, or any probable defence, whereby the de-fender appears not to be *in mala fide*, or litigious; the Lords are accustomed to decern in the removing, only to have effect at the next removing term after the sentence.

It were proper here to treat of violent profits. But it is more proper to be treated in an action by itself, after Ejection and Intrusion [IV,29,*infra*], whence violent profits are consequent, as well as from removing, unless the pursuer have set the land.

Title 27. Molestation

MOLESTATION [I,9,28,*supra*] is a possessory action, having the like re-quisites as removing. And though the name, in the vulgar acceptation, might comprehend molestation in moveable goods, as well as in heritage; yet as a law-term, it relates only to conterminous tenements, where some part or pertinent is controverted, to which of the two it pertains, or if it be common to both. And so it is competent, chiefly in rural tenements; though it may also, and doth sometimes occur in tenements in towns, where there are gardens, or closes, or waste ground, wherein either party may claim right, and attempt to labour or sow, or to throw dung thereon. In this action, as well as in removing, there must both be possession, and a sufficient title of that possession; whereas Ejection and Intrusion, which are also possessory actions, require the production of no title, but are founded upon mere possession.

2. Molestation is almost the same with that action in the Roman law, *finium regundorum*. And by this the marches of adjacent tenements were determined and regulated; yea, and not only were the parts and marches of either tenement declared; but they were so regulated, that if they might be better ordered by exchange of parts, which reached into either tenement, or whereby there might be a more defensible march, it was accordingly ordered: and it were a very just conclusion in our molestations, which is already ordered by the Act of Parliament, for inclosing upon marches [Act 1685,c.39; A.P.S. VIII,488,c.49].

3. Regulating of marches may be by perambulation, for preventing of molestation; which is by a brieve of the chancery yet in vigour, which passeth of course, and is the most proper remedy, whether there be molestation and contention, or not; yet the Lords of Session are authorized by Act 42. Parl. 1587 [A.P.S. III,445,c.23], to order molestations upon complaint made to them, conform to an Act of Sederunt of their own, then ratified in Parliament, bearing, "That they were much hindered in expedition of other weighty causes, by complaints of molestation, which cannot be so conveniently determined as upon the ground. And therefore it is statute, That whensoever any party shall mean themselves to the Lords, upon troublance or molestation, committed upon properties or commonties; the Lords, by their deliverance, shall direct letters, ordaining the inferior judges-ordinary, to take cognition therein, upon summons or precepts to be directed upon fifteen days' warning. Whereupon the defences of parties shall be first discussed, where the judges use to sit, or where the Lords appoint: and, after the production of the parties' rights, consisting in writ, the judges shall put the points probable by witnesses, to the knowledge of an inquest, the most part being landed men, having four ploughs of land, or three hundred merks of yearly rent unredeemable, and all the inquest shall be of the parish where the lands lie, or the next adjacent parishes. And if there be mutual molestations, then before litiscontestation, the witnesses on both shall be remitted to the inquest, who shall visit the ground, and examine the witnesses, and return their report. And the judge-ordinary, or other judge delegate upon suspicion of him, shall, at acceptation of their commission, make faith to minister justice duly, and that they have not taken, nor shall take reward, profit or good deed from any of the

parties, nor have made, nor shall make any paction or contract with any of them, for any certain sum before the plea be intented, or during the dependence thereof. And in case of mutual molestations, the equal half of the assize shall be taken of the persons summoned for either of the parties. And if there be any wanting, the judge shall supply them, of landed men, or famous and honest yeomen, and the odd man shall be chosen by cavel or lot. And if the judge-ordinary be suspect, or if the lands be in divers jurisdictions, the Lords shall name judges by commission. And in case of error by the inquest, they are punishable *pœna temere jurantium super assisam*. After the verdict of the inquest, the judge-ordinary or delegate is to give his decreet. There is only exception of molestations for, or against the members of the College of Justice, who shall use their privilege to pursue before the Lords, or other judges-ordinary as was formerly accustomed."

4. This Act determines nothing of the election of the inquest, except in mutual molestations. So that, in other cases, the pursuer hath too great advantage, having the power or influence of citing all the persons for the inquest, out of which the judge must name the whole inquest, being qualified as aforesaid: and therefore the Lords ought to give so long a term, and so many days for citation, that both parties may have mutual actions of molestation; and they ought to give injunctions to the director of the chancery to give the like time.

5. Albeit there be an exception of the actions of molestation of the members of the College of Justice, that the same may be before the Lords; yet that ought to be extended no further, than to the making litiscontestation, and decreet; but the probation should be by an inquest and commission direct for that effect, which may be in the vacance; seeing their privilege is founded on their attendance on the Session.

6. In this action, whosoever first provokes to judgment, is pursuer, and the other is defender. But where there are mutual actions, either party may insist.

7. It hath been variously decided, whether the superior of either, or both parties ought to be called in molestations. But the case is not alike in all infeftments: for in ward-holdings, the interest of the superior is far greater than in other holdings, not only for his casualties, but for the ordinary cause of returning of the property by recognition, upon alienation of the major part; and seeing parts of either tenement may be adjudged to the other, it is just in ward-holdings that the superior should concur or be called, but not other superiors.

8. The tenor and nature of brieves of perambulation are explained before, *Lib.* 4, *Tit.* 2. Ordinary Actions, &c. The summons of molestation may be thus:—"Our will is, and We charge you, That ye lawfully summon B, heritor, wadsetter, or liferenter of the lands of   and   tenants and possessors thereof, To compear before the Lords of our Council and Session, &c. To answer at the instance of A, heritor, liferenter, or wadsetter

of the lands of   as being molested and troubled in the possession of
the saids lands by the said B, or by the tenants and possessors of the said B,
his saids lands of   at the least, who may be troubled or molested
therein, by reason of the unclearness of the marches and possession thereof:
That is to say, the said defender to hear and see letters direct to the judge-
ordinary, where the lands lie, or other judges delegate, to take cognition, and
to determine the marches and possession of the saids lands, Conform to the
Act of Parliament made anent the order of cognition in cases of molestation,
laws and daily practique of this our realm, &c. According to justice, &c."

9. The only proper defence is upon a prior cognition, or bounding charter; and yet immemorial possession altering the same, will be a relevant
reply.

Title 28. Ejection and Intrusion

THESE two actions are here joined, because they differ in very little, save in
this, that ejection is by some kind of violence, when the possessor of lands or
other tenements, or his family, servants, or goods on the ground are dispossessed, and turned away, or not suffered to enjoy the benefit of the ground, so
that the ground is not void. But intrusion is, when, though there be neither
family, servant, nor stock of goods upon the ground, yet the possession is detained *animo*, the natural possession having been lately before, by dwelling,
labouring, or pasturing, and is not presumed to be relinquished [1,9,25–27,
supra].

2. These actions require no active title to be produced or proven,
but only possession. For one of the first principles of government is, the preservation of each person in their possessions, not to be put therefrom, but by
their own consent, or order of law; yea, though the possession itself had been
violent, or clandestine, it will not warrant a dispossession any other way: for
though, in some cases, there be compensation in crimes, yet not in this, because it is the chief basis of the public peace. But there must be libelled and
proven natural possession, by dwelling, labouring or pasturing, to have been
recently before intrusion, or to have been at the time of the ejection. Inter-
verting of the landlord's possession, by payment of mails and duties, will not
be a title for these actions, but both the tenant paying will remain liable,
though it infer double payment, and the intromitter will likewise be liable for
payment.

3. It hath been commonly held, that ejection is not competent to the
master of the ground, when his tenant is ejected. But in this, the case must be
distinguished, that the tenant will have the benefit of the violent profits; but
there is no reason to exclude the master of the ground to pursue the ejection,
as to repossession, and the ordinary profits; and albeit his tenant would not
insist, yet the master may use his name for these effects.

4. Ejection is not only competent to the party ejected, but if he die, it is
competent to his wife and bairns, without representing him by entering heirs

or executors; seeing possession is only in the question, which is continued with these to whom the right would befal [111,5,2,*supra*].

5. The tenor of a summons of ejection may be thus; "Our will is, and we charge you, that ye lawfully summon B, to compear, &c. To answer at the instance of A, for the defender his wrongous, violent and masterful coming by himself, his servants, complices and others in his name, of his causing, sending, hounding out, command, reset, assistance, or ratihabition, upon the   day of, &c. to the lands of   pertaining to the pursuer, at least, in his possession, by labouring of the same, and pasturing of his goods thereupon, and by other deeds of possession: and then and there wrongously, violently, and masterfully ejecting the pursuer, his family, tenants, cottars, goods and gear, and intruding himself in the possession of the same, by himself and others as aforesaid; and also violently and masterfully continuing and maintaining the said violent and masterful possession, by the space of   That is to say, the said defender to hear and see the premises verified and proven; and being so verified and proven, to hear and see himself decerned by decreet of our saids Lords, to repone and restore the complainer, his tenants, cottars, and servants, to the possession of the saids lands, in the same state and condition they were in, the time of the foresaid ejection: and to make payment of the violent profits since the ejection, till the pursuer be repossessed; with the other damages arising from the ejection. And also to hear and see himself decerned to desist and cease from troubling the pursuer therein, in any time thereafter, otherwise than by due order of law. Conform to the laws and daily practique of this our realm, &c. According to justice, &c."

6. The summons of intrusion differs only from that of ejection, in this, that the intruder did wrongously enter in the possession of the lands, and violently and masterfully detains the same, by himself, his complices, and others, &c. as in the former summons.

7. The proper defences against these actions, are, 1. That the defender restored the ground, and relinquished the possession, within twenty-four hours after the intrusion or ejection; which will assoilzie from the same, but not from the expenses and damages sustained thereby, wherein the pursuer will have his oath *in litem*. 2. That the defender entered the possession by authority of a competent judge. 3. That the defender entered in possession by consent of the pursuer or others, who were in lawful possession of the lands; which will not be sustained, unless a more pregnant evidence of that consent be condescended on, than the acts of violence which shall be condescended on by the pursuer; such as delivering of keys, removing of goods, renunciation of possession subscribed by the renouncer. But if the condescendences be not evidently more pregnant, and witnesses offered of greater fame and faith, the Lords will *ex officio* admit witnesses of equal number, to be adduced by either party to be examined on these points, viz. who were present at the entry of the possession? And what way it was entered? To the effect that if other persons

were present, which neither party adduce, the Lords may ordain them to be cited, as witnesses most unsuspect, if they be not in degrees defendant to one or other of the parties; that upon the whole testimonies the Lords may determine. 4. Another defence is the particular prescription by Act 81, Parliament 1579 [Prescription (Ejections) Act, 1579,c.81; A.P.S. III,145,c.19], bearing, "That all actions of spuilzies, ejection and others of that nature (which comprehends intrusion) be pursued before the ordinary judge, within three years after committing thereof; otherwise, the pursuer's alleged hurt never to be heard thereafter. Providing this Act extend not to minors, but to be pursued within three years after their perfect age." Yet custom hath allowed to insist in the action, even after these years, for restoring the possession, and the ordinary rents; but not for violent profits.

8. No defence will be admitted against these actions, without it be instantly verified; unless caution be found the first diet of litiscontestation, as in removing, Parliament 1594, cap. 217. [Ejection Caution Act, 1594,c.217; A.P.S. IV,68,c.27]. But custom hath required caution to be found, before acts of litiscontestation be extracted.

9. No disposition or obligement to possess, express or implied in dispositions conventional or legal, will be relevant against ejection; unless it bear a warrant to enter in possession summarily: and even then, it will not be sufficient, if resistance be made: for it will not import to allege, *frustra petis quod mox es restiturus*, which hath many exceptions, and will be elided, because *spoliatus ante omnia restituendus*, which hath no exception, save ratification of the possession. Yet these will be sufficient defences against intrusion, where the possession, though not deserted simply, was yet deserted as to corporal possession; so that here the defender may defend upon obligements to possess; or upon voluntary dispositions, having present entry, expressed or implied. But a defence will not be sustained, upon apprising or adjudication, there being a power reserved to the Lords to restrict these; neither do they contain any warrant for summary possession.

Title 29. Actions for Violent Profits

WITH these actions of ejection, &c. there are sometimes added clauses for violent profits, which is not so regular: for the decreet of repossession is the title for the violent profits, which therefore should be expede before the other can be insisted in: yet a distinct process may be carried on therewith for the violent profits, to be insisted on immediately, and not to begin thereafter and go to the roll. And there is the more reason to admit the conjunction, since the course of the roll, than before. And where these are not distinct processes, there must be a new dispute, and new terms taken to prove the violent profits. But because violent profits arise not only from intrusion and ejection, but from removing and succeeding in the vice, which is a kind of intrusion; therefore they shall be here considered as they are insisted for in a several action.

2. Violent profits are so called, because they arise from violent attaining

or retaining of possession, and are partly persecutory, partly penal, comprehending not only the ordinary profits of a tenement, which it would be worth, as a constant rent, but such profits as the greatest industry could procure, allowing nothing for the expense of the labour: for he that sets these violent possessors a work must pay their charges [11,9,44,*supra*].

3. The extent of violent profits hath not been fully determined. It is true, in house-mails, the double mail is ordinarily sustained for the violent profits. Neither is it oft controverted, whether the tack-duty, or use of payment accustomed, be the full rent that the tenements might yield as a constant duty: but certainly, if the ease were considerable, the double of the full rent would make the violent profits, otherwise the penalty would be very unequal: for sometimes houses are set too high, upon special considerations of the fancy and pleasure of the taker, and sometimes too low. But the violent profits of other tenements are much more unclear, especially of lands, where there is reason that he, who is injured by violence, should have his oath *in litem* as much, if not more, in violence in lands than in moveables, if he depone what he esteems the true rent of the land, as it might pay as a constant rent, and that he should have the double thereof, as well for these as for tenements in burgh; which were far more summary, than that which is frequently used, by libelling and proving what the lands could sow, and what the increase might be by the best industry: what cattle it might feed, and what profit might thence arise by buying inland beasts to be fatted, or by stocking only with milk-cows, and the profit of the stirk and milk, and the profit of the wool, lambs and milk-ews [1,9,27,*supra*], which is more conjectural and expensive.

4. Violent profits arise not only from ejection and intrusion, and succeeding in the vice of persons removed, but from continuing of possession after decreet of removing, which is still a violent possession against the will of the obtainer of the decreet.

5. The tenor of this action may be thus: "Our will is, and We charge you, that ye lawfully summon B, against whom the decreet for possession after-mentioned was obtained, To compear, &c. To answer at the instance of A, who obtained a decreet against the said B before, &c. upon the
day of, &c. for quitting and renouncing the possession of, &c. to the effect the pursuer might enter in, and to, the natural possession thereof, where nevertheless the said B continued in the violent and wilful possession, after as before the said decreet: That is to say, the said defender to hear and see the premises verified and proven by production of the said decreet, and by probation of the said violent possession: and being so verified and proven, the said defender to hear and see himself decerned by decreet of the saids Lords, to make payment to the pursuer of the violent profits of the saids, &c. not exceeding the double of the ordinary constant rate the samine were worth, according to the estimation of the said complainer upon oath; and that for all years and terms since the term of   , which was the said term of the violent profits. And siklike yearly and termly in time coming, until the com-

plainer be put in the peaceable possession of the same, conform to the laws and daily practique of this Our realm, &c. According to justice, &c."

·* Title 30. Action of Spuilzie and Wrongous Intromission

THE action for spuilzie of moveable goods [1,9,16–24,*supra*] differs very little from the summons of ejection, save in this, that ejection is dispossession of the possessor in heritable rights by infeftment, and spuilzie is the dispossession of the possessor in moveables; so that the tenor of the summons is much the same, except as to the subject.

2. The oath *in litem* in spuilzies hath this effect, that if a part of the moveables be proven to be spuilzied, the pursuer hath not only *juramentum in litem pro pretio affectionis*, but for the whole particulars libelled, unless the defender prove by the pursuer's oath or writ, that these particulars which were to be proven, were not spuilzied.

3. Spuilzie is not only extended against the principal party, but against all accessories, who are all liable *in solidum*, and have no relief against their complices, unless the pursuer assign the decreet of spuilzie to them; and even in that case, they will only have effect against their complices *pro rata*, except against the principal actor. But in ejection none can be decerned to restore the possession, but the party that took it.

4. The exception of prescription in not pursuing within three years, is relevant against spuilzie, as well as against ejection, by Act 18, Parl. 1579 [Prescription (Ejections) Act, 1579,c.81; A.P.S. 111,145,c.19]. But that exception doth not exclude wrongous intromission; so that, albeit the Act of Parliament bear, that the pursuer shall insist within three years after the spuilzie, otherwise the pursuer's alleged hurt never to be heard thereafter, yet custom hath interpreted it only in relation to spuilzie as such, that is, for the violent profits, and the oath *in litem;* but in that process the pursuer may insist for restitution of the goods, or the ordinary values, which hath not been so interpreted in ejections, wherein none can insist on the prescribed summons of ejection, for restoring the possession summarily: yet he may warn the ejector, and insist in a removing or repossession.

5. This is also peculiar in spuilzie, that the exception of lawful poinding hath this reply, that the goods poinded were plough-goods, which are not poindable the time of ploughing the ground, where any other goods are, that may be apprised or poinded, according to the common law, besides the horses, oxen or other goods pertaining to the plough, that labours the ground the time of the ploughing, if the other goods were in view, or offered to be brought in view, of the messenger.

6. There is also a peculiar exception against spuilzie, that the time of the poinding a party compeared and offered to depone, that the goods were his own, and not the party's against whom the letters of poinding were direct; which oath the messenger, as judge in the execution, is allowed by custom to receive: but he ought to examine the party upon any pertinent interrogatory

proponed by the creditor poinding, or that occurs to himself; as, how the goods alleged became his who claims them ? Whether by a natural possession, or only by a simulate possession from the debtor, *retenta possessione ?* Or whether they were delivered in trust, or for the behove of the debtor ? And whether the mutual cause of disponing and delivering them by the debtor, was performed ? And accordingly he may proceed or stop. But if all points of doubt be clear by the oath, the poinder must pass by these goods. Or if the wife, bairns, or domestic servants, of him that claims the goods, offer their oath, it will stop the poinding; because the owner himself could not know the time of the poinding, that he might attend; and because he might by way of action recover these goods, though poinded for another man's debt; whereby the creditor would be at more inconvenience. And albeit these persons should so depone, the creditor would not be excluded from proving the goods to be his debtor's; because such oaths not being oaths of verity, could not absolutely establish the right, being against the presumption of property by possession; and therefore the deponent must clear by his oath, when and how he possessed the goods he claims, and how he ceased to possess the same, that it may appear if by any alienation from or to the debtor, or if he put them a-grasing to the debtor, or that they strayed upon his ground. But this will not be relevant against any execution upon a decreet of poinding of the ground, which can go no further than the possessor's term's mail, against whom, any other whose goods was in his possession, may recover the price from him: for poinding of the ground has much more privilege than poinding on personal debts. See *Lib.* 4, *Tit.* Executorials on Decreets, §26 [IV,47,26,*infra*].

7. Wrongous intromission is here joined with spuilzie, because it differs not from a spuilzie, save that in a spuilzie, restitution is craved by the oath *in litem*, and the violent profits of the spuilzied goods, which use not to be extended further than to the profits of cattle, and these things which, by their proper use, render a profit; and so corns, or other such goods, have not violent profits; but oxen or horse, though they have not a natural profit by themselves alone, yet they have by their masters using them, in riding or ploughing, &c. But the profits which are merely natural, as of mares, sheep, goats, &c. are competent even where there is no spuilzie, *in quantum* thereby the possessor was *lucratus :* but if he had a colourable title, he is secure, as to the fruits *bona fide* consumed.

8. Wrongous intromission by the meaning of the term, would seem only to be extended, where the entry of the possession was by wrong: but though there were no injury in the entry, yet so soon as the owner claims his goods, and they are refused, the possessor becomes a wrongous intromitter; and therefore, by this action, all parties may recover their goods, where there is not another special title; as if the goods were delivered by location, custody, society, trust, &c. which accordingly ought to be libelled as the title of repetition. And though there were no wrong in attaining or retaining possession, yet, by a natural obligation, all men are obliged to restore to the owner that

which is his, by that general precept of the law *suum cuique*, as well as to permit the owner to intromit therewith by vindication. This action is competent for recovery of all goods to the true owner, when there is no special title competent for recovery thereof.

9. But because moveables pass from hand to hand, by all titles of alienation, without writ, and frequently without witnesses; therefore there is necessarily introduced a *præsumptio juris*, that he who is possessor is proprietor [11,1,42; 111,2,7,*supra*]; so that he who would pursue for recovery of the same, must exclude the presumption, by a stronger probation that the goods do not belong to the possessor, but to the pursuer; and therefore he must condescend and prove, that these goods could not pass from him by alienation, as by donation, sale, exchange, solution, &c. As, 1. He may prove by the defender's oath, that he knows the goods are the pursuer's, and did not pass from him by any alienative title. 2. He may instruct that the goods were spuilzied from him, or poinded for another man's debt, or that they were stolen, robbed, strayed, hired, or that they were the goods of a defunct in his possession the time of his death, or the like: and so these grounds must be specially libelled, that the pursuer was in possession of the goods in question, and that they passed from him, not by any alienative title, but by the ways aforesaid; and therefore ought to be restored with the natural fruits thereof, at the least, in so far as the possessor, or he who, by fraud, ceased to possess, was profited thereby.

10. Against this, it will be a competent exception, that, albeit at first the goods did so pass from the pursuer, as is libelled, yet he did thereafter recover the possession, and that the defender offer to prove from whom he acquired the same, and is not obliged to prove any other intermediate author, without prejudice to the pursuer to pursue that author, who must instruct his author, whereby at last, though with many processes, and much expense, the pursuer may find out the wrongous intromitter, and have damages against him for all, if he was *in mala fide*.

Title 31. Actions Accessory, and Specially Transumpts

IN the third title of this book [1V,3,47,*supra*], treating of actions generally, according to our customs, there were proposed several distinctions of actions; and first, that of actions declaratory, petitory and possessory, which now have been expended; and we are next to come to the division of actions in principal and accessory. These actions are called accessory, which can have no effect alone, but as they are accessory to other actions, which therefore are called principal actions, such as are all the actions preceding.

2. The first of these accessory actions, is the action for granting transumpts of writs, which is always a *medium* for other actions, by the writs transumed, which are to be used, either by way of action or defence.

3. The rise of this action is, because oft-times writs are common evidents to several parties, and have not clauses of registration, or parties are not

willing to publish them by registration; and therefore any concerned must pursue the havers of them to exhibit them, and to hear and see transumpts thereof granted and delivered to be made use of as authentic writs, having the same effect as if they were registrate.

4. This action doth most ordinarily arise upon obligements to grant transumpts; as when a part of any barony or tenement is disponed in property, wadset or liferent, the disponer retains the evidents, or a part thereof in his own hand, and obliges himself to give transumpts to the purchaser. By this he is obliged to exhibit the writs, to be transumed before the Lords, and so must suffer them to remain in the clerk's hands, till doubles thereof be formed, which doubles the Lords ordain to be collated and signed by the Clerk of Register, or the principal clerks of Session, as his deputes. But although there be no express obligement to grant transumpts, yet the interest in common evidents is a sufficient title to cause them be produced, to be transumed; but a collateral interest will not be a sufficient title, but only when the writs are a part of the pursuer's progress of any right, personal or real. Lesser interest gives only title for exhibiting writs *ad deliberandum*, or *ad probandum;* but will not give ground for a decreet of transumpt. Yet parties concerned may take instruments on the production, and may crave that the tenor of the writs may be contained in the instrument; which hath not the full effect of a decreet of transumpt, for that instrument will only prove against the parties who were in the process, and did produce these writs, and against these representing them, but will not prove against their singular successors; but a decreet of transumpt proves as fully as a decreet of registration, against all parties having interest; with this difference, that, in case of improbation, the extract of a registrate writ will not stop certification, but unless the writ be registrate in the public and common registers of Session, or Chancery, if the date of the registration be condescended upon, and be found by the Register books to have been so registrate, which being found, the extract is sufficient to all effects, because the principal is left with the register, as in public custody, for which these who give them to be registrate, are not answerable, but the keepers of these registers; but when decreets of transumpt are quarrelled, as to the verity of the principal writ, the user of the transumpt must produce the principal, because there is nothing left in the record to instruct; and therefore he will obtain incident diligence against the havers, to produce the same.

5. In the action for transumpts, the granter of the writ, or these who do or may represent him, or their assignees, must be called, as well as the havers, and all others having or pretending interest, at the head burghs of the shires where the granters of the writs, or these representing them, or their assignees do reside; to hear and see the writs inspected, as unvitiate and unsuspect, and to be transumed. And, therefore, though there be an express obligement to give transumpts, a transumpt upon that obligement will operate no further than against the person obliged, and these representing him; unless the

granters of the writ, and these to whom it was granted, and the representatives of both, were also called.

6. The tenor of this action may be thus: "Our will is, and We charge you, that ye lawfully summon B, granter of the writ underwritten, or heir, or apparent heir to him, or assignee to the said writ, and all others having, or pretending to have interest, at the market-cross of the head-burgh of
where the granter thereof doth reside, To compear, &c. To answer at the instance of A, as now having right to the said writ, in manner after specified, viz. &c. And thereby having good and undoubted right and interest, to call and pursue for an authentic transumpt of the same, of which writ the tenor follows (here the full tenor is insert) That is to say, the said defenders to hear and see themselves decerned to produce the said writ; and being so produced, to hear and see the said tenor above insert, ordained by decreet, &c. to be exactly collationed with the principal, and to hear and see it found and declared, by decreet foresaid, that the principal is unvitiate and unsuspect of forgery, and that the transumpt thereof foresaid shall be as effectual, to all intents and purposes, as if the same were registrate in the Books of Council and Session; except in the case of certification, for not production of the same in an improbation. Conform to the laws and daily practique of this our realm, &c. According to justice, &c."

7. There is no exception against this action, except improbation upon the forgery of the subscription, or vitiation *in substantialibus*. Yet there may be objections against the interest of the pursuer, or that all parties having interest are not called.

Title 32. Actions for Probation of the Tenors of Writs

THIS action is not a principal action, but accessory, for thereby a writ lost or destroyed is only made up by witnesses, and no right is claimed thereby, either declaratory, petitory or possessory, but only the making up of the tenor of the writ; upon which writ actions may be intented, or defences proponed.

2. The rise of this action is from two grounds. 1. Some writs are essential solemnities, and not only evidences of probation. And therefore, though the deeds in such writs were truly done, yet if they be not done in such a form, they are null. 2. By our law, witnesses are not admitted to prove, in cases where writ may, and uses to be interposed. For, albeit probation by witnesses be sufficient in all cases by the moral law, yet the memory of witnesses being lubrick, and their apprehension of what is said or done being uncertain, whether they adverted or not, or whether they rightly conceived what was done or said; therefore positive law hath justly and fitly rejected witnesses in some cases, unless they had been particularly required to have been witnesses, and the special points repeated to them: and, in other cases, though they had been required, they will not be admitted, because the law hath required parties to take writ in cases of importance, and as the penalty of their neglect rejects witnesses. Yet, when writ hath been adhibited, and without the party's

fault hath been lost or destroyed, in such cases, witnesses cannot be rejected, either to prove the fact, where the writ is only for probation, or to prove the tenor of the writ, that it may remain for probation, or to prove the tenor, where the proving of the fact will not suffice, in respect the writ is a necessary solemnity.

3. This action, in divers cases, requires divers points to make it relevant. For, 1. There is a great difference in probation of the tenor of writs; for some writs are designed to remain constantly, as dispositions of lands and heritable rights, which, though they may be retired before infeftment or possession, yet that was not the design of granting them: but other writs are not designed to remain constantly, as bonds of borrowed money, which are not designed so to remain, but to be paid; and therefore the debtor making payment, uses to retire his bond, and needs not require a discharge. Hence it is that the law doth presume, that *chirographum apud debitorem repertum præsumitur solutum.* Yet this is not *præsumptio juris et de jure :* for it admits a contrary probation, that the writ came to the debtor's hand in another way, than can infer payment, or quitting the right; as if it were given to the debtor to see, and he refused to return it; or if he found it, or intromitted with it any unwarrantable way: therefore the tenor of bonds for borrowed money, is relevant to be proven by the oath of the debtor, or by such a special *casus amissionis* as necessarily proves the writ was in the creditor's possession; as if it be proven that the writ was in the creditor's possession when he died, found among his writs, or in the hands of his advocates, or in the clerk's hands, produced by him; or if the witnesses prove that his house was burnt, and that they knew the bond was there, and that no writs were gotten out safe; or that they knew the writ was stolen, or taken away by violence from the creditor, or any intrusted by him: in these or the like cases, the tenor even of bonds may be proven, albeit there be not adminicles in writ, relating to them; because the witnesses do only take away the presumptive probation, that the sum was satisfied, and the writ retired, by the debtor. And therefore it will be a relevant exception, for the debtor to offer to prove by witnesses, that, after the time at which it is libelled to be proven by witnesses that the writ was burnt, stolen or taken by violence, the same was in the creditor's hands, or that it was in the debtor's own possession: yea it will be sufficient to prove by witnesses, that the sum was paid or satisfied; for here the debtor cannot be excluded from using witnesses, because this is a case in which writ uses not to be adhibited, neither do witnesses take away writ which requires no witnesses: but, as witnesses are competent in an extraordinary case, for the creditor, so they cannot be refused in the like case, for the debtor.

4. This doth not so hold as to the probation of assignations, translations, retrocessions or repositions, and the writs conveyed thereby; because no prudent man will rest satisfied with the retiring of such writs, that neither being ordinary nor safe: for in all assignations, &c. Instruments of intimation are requisite to make them effectual, and a prior intimation with a later assigna-

tion is preferable; and therefore a more general *casus amissionis* is relevant in the probation of the tenor of these; unless the contrary be offered to be proven by the creditor's oath, either of calumny, knowledge, or verity.

5. The *casus amissionis* must always be libelled; because the pursuer's design may be to prove the tenor of the writ to be other and better than the writ truly was; and also because of the frailty of the memory of the witnesses, who if they privately said they did remember the writ to be of such a tenor, (though that being said to the pursuer, will not exclude them from being witnesses, except he had prompted them so to say). It unsecures men's rights when they are put upon the memory of witnesses, and not *de recenti*, and in plain cases: and therefore if the *casus amissionis* be not special, adminicles in writ must be produced, relative to that tenor; or otherways, no article extraordinary should be sustained to be so proved by witnesses: for the tenor of a writ may be proven as to some articles, and not as to others pretended to have been in it, even though there be adminicles of the writ; unless they mention these articles: as if in bonds of borrowed money there be alleged tailzies or extraordinary substitutions or irritancies, or cases in which the sums shall not be due or payable, or the like, in contracts of marriage or other writs.

6. But where there are adminicles relating to the tenor produced, the *casus amissionis* will be sufficiently libelled, that the writ was lost. But without these, some proof should be of the *casus amissionis;* as if the Lords require the pursuer to depone that the writ was lost. But if the defender require his oath of verity or calumny, his oath may utterly exclude any further process.

7. So then in probation of tenors, there must still be libelled a *casus amissionis*. But if that be specially proven, there needs no adminicles. And if there be adminicles as to the ordinary articles, there needs no further probation than what has been said of the *casus amissionis*. But the oath of party is sufficient without both.

8. If the witnesses depone that they were witnesses insert, or that they remember who were the witnesses insert; the names of the witnesses and their designations, which are a part of the tenor, and even their subscriptions, should be contained in the decreet. And if they depone that they were witnesses insert and subscribing, they should subscribe a duplicate of the tenor. And in both these cases, the witnesses are not only witnesses of the existence of the writ, but *de rei gestæ veritate*, or if they saw the writ subscribed and delivered, or saw the deed performed mentioned therein; all which make the strongest evidence against improbation.

9. The witnesses in probations of tenors do prove, if they depone that they saw the writ, and that they took notice of the subscription thereof, and that they did not see any vitiation or appearance of forgery therein; and that they remember the tenor of the principal articles therein, and that they were to the same effect as now they are drawn in form; which is sufficient, although they do not depone that they were in the same words.

10. Tenors of writs may be proven, without the oath of party or witnes-

ses, by writs relating the same, subscribed by the same party, his heirs or assignees, in so far as they are related; yea though they be not related, it is a sufficient presumptive probation, if there be authentic writs presupposing the writs, whereof the tenor is to be proven: for instance, if a charter be granted originally to a vassal, bearing for implement of a disposition or contract; though it bear not the tenor thereof, yet the tenor may be made up according to the tenor of the charter: or if a precept of *clare constat* be granted, it is a presumptive probation to make up the tenor of the defunct's charter: or if in a charter upon resignation, a procuratory of resignation be mentioned apart, or in a disposition, thence the tenor of the disposition or procuratory may be proven, in so far as may arise upon the clauses in the charter.

11. But improbation will always be competent against tenors, by the indirect manner of improbation; unless two witnesses insert prove the tenor, and subscribe the duplicate: in which case the defender must insist in the direct articles by way of defence, against the proving of the tenor; because the probation of the tenor will be equivalent to a declarator of the verity of the writ, wherein if the defender compear, he will be excluded from insisting in an improbation. But in all other cases, the indirect manner of improbation is still competent, yet without hope in many of the cases before proposed.

12. By what hath been said, it is evident, that this action is so various, that it must be pursued as an action *præscriptis verbis*, and hath not one common definitive form.

Title 33. Exhibition *ad Deliberandum aut ad Probandum*

Exhibition and delivery is an ordinary principal action, whereby the owner of a writ craves the same to be exhibited and delivered to him; so that it is a petitory action, when he claims it as his own by right, and a possessory action, when he claims it as having been unwarrantably taken from him, being in his possession, or that it was in his custody, &c.

2. But there are other two kinds of exhibition, which are only accessory actions, as when an apparent heir pursues the havers of his predecessor's writs, to exhibit them, that he may have inspection, to the effect he may deliberate whether he will enter heir to that predecessor or not [111,5,1,*supra*].

3. The other exhibition is *ad probandum*. For when any party hath a point to be instructed, or proven by a writ, which is not his own writ, but belongs to another, the law, from the common duties of society in the same common-wealth, obliges the haver to produce, although it be his own writ, and though the claimer hath no other interest, but to instruct or prove some point competent to him to instruct or prove. And this is only in the dependence of a process, whence this exhibition is sustained *incidenter:* and therefore it is called an incident diligence, which was only competent by way of action, till the Act of Regulation of Judicatures [Courts Act, 1672,c.16; A.P.S. VIII,80,c.40; IV,41,4,*infra*], whereby warrant is granted for letters of horning, to charge those who are alleged to have such writs, to compear and

depone anent the having, and to exhibit what they acknowledge, in the same way, and upon the same ground, as they might be summarily charged to compear and depone as witnesses: yet the action will not be excluded, if no more time be protracted but what would be necessary by horning and caption; because the having of writs is probable by witnesses. But it is not proper here to say more of this action, till its proper place in processes.

4. The rise of exhibition *ad deliberandum* is, because, by our law, an heir entering is liable to all his predecessor's debts, though they do far exceed his heritage, and that in favour of creditors, that they be not put to compt and reckoning upon the value of the estate and debt of their debtors, as in other nations: and therefore we allow the heir a year to deliberate, during which time he has the benefit of this action, that he may call for all writs which might infer debt on him if he were entered, or might exclude him from the benefit of any right, wherein he finds his predecessor infeft. And though sometimes this action hath been restricted, as to dispositions granted to strangers *extra familiam*, yet that is only to be understood where these strangers produce the evidents, denuding that predecessor, or at least condescend on the dates where they are *in publica custodia*, if they be so found there, which is competent to all parties called to produce writs *ad deliberandum*, if they be in the Session-records at Edinburgh, for thereby the apparent heir may have inspection, but he is not obliged to go to all other registers, not being able to know the clauses of registration, or in what courts the writs are to be registrate. But if the defender instruct, that the pursuer's predecessor was denuded, he needs not produce any anterior writs of that right [III,5,1, *supra*].

5. This action is competent not only within the year of deliberation, but thereafter, till the heir be entered: yet so, that creditors may charge him to enter heir, and obtain decreets thereupon. But it will not be a relevant defence, that he hath behaved as heir, or is lucrative successor; for these are passive titles, only competent to creditors. Neither needs the apparent heir prove his propinquity of blood, but that is presumed as notour in the vicinity, against which no man would come, being under the hazard of great expenses, if he come in the contrary, to the trouble of any other.

6. The tenor of this action may be thus: "Our will is, and We charge you, that ye lawfully summon C and D, as these who have in their hands the writs underwritten, necessary to be seen by B, that he may deliberate whether he will enter heir or not to A, his predecessor, To compear, &c. To answer at the instance of the said B, nearest lawful heir apparent, of line, male, tailzie or provision to the said A, and thereby having good interest to call for inspection of all writs, by which it may appear, whether the heritage will be profitable or hurtful: That is to say, the saids defenders to hear and see themselves decerned, by decreet of our saids Lords, each of them for their own parts, to exhibit and produce before the saids Lords, all bonds importing debt, granted by the said umquhile A, or any of his prececessors whom he did represent,

and whereby the pursuer might be liable: and likewise to produce all writs and evidents of lands, wherein the said A, or his predecessors, died last vest and seased as of fee; and also all dispositions of lands, heritage, or servitude, granted to, and in favour of the said A, by any person or persons whatsomever, whereunto the pursuer would have right as heir foresaid; as also all writs and evidents, whereby the lands and others foresaids were provided to other heirs; and siklike all writs and evidents granted by the defunct and his predecessors, to whom he was or might have been heir, whereby they were not totally denuded: and all heritable obligements, in favour of the defunct, and his predecessors or authors, or whereto they had rights by progress: To the effect the complainer may deliberate, whether he will enter heir to his said predecessor or not; the having of which writs the pursuer refers to the oath of verity of the saids defenders *respectivè*, in so far as shall not be proven by writ, conform to the law and daily practique of this Our realm, &c. According to justice, &c."

7. The proper defences against this action are, 1. That the pursuer is already actually entered heir, and so has no place for deliberation. 2. That the pursuer's predecessors were totally denuded; which will not be competent by way of quality, but must be instructed by writ. 3. That the writs are *in publica custodia* at Edinburgh, and the dates being condescended on, and so found.

Title 34. Action of Transference and Wakening

THE action of transference is necessary, when either the pursuer or defender dieth *pendente processu :* for then the process must be transferred in the person representing that defunct *activè*, if the pursuer die; or against the person that doth or may represent the defender *passivè ;* or both *activè* and *passivè*, if both pursuer and defender die. But if the libel bear several pursuers, and also several defenders, and if there be separate interests, wherein the others needs not be called or concur, in so far the process may proceed without transference. By this it is evident, that this is not a principal, but an accessory action; whereby the process in the principal cause is put in the condition that it may proceed in the same state and place in the roll as before.

2. The active title will not be relevant, that the pursuer of the transference is apparent heir, but he must be actually heir. But it is sufficient for the passive title, that the defender is apparent heir: and therefore there can be no process, unless the pursuer's active title be actually instructed.

3. Transferences were required formerly, not only when the persons were changed as predecessor and successor, but also when they were changed as author and purchaser; and so assignees, or singular successors, could not proceed in their author's process, till they transferred the same in themselves *activè*, or in the defenders *passivè*, if they became denuded in favour of singular successors. And in the libel and decreet of transference, all the process was *verbatim* insert. The former was chiefly in favour of the bishops, for the quots; whereby moveable rights remained *in bonis defuncti*, unless the assignations

were intimated in the defunct's life; and therefore there behoved to be a confirmation. The posterior ground was *propter commodum curiæ,* that there might be many sheets in the libel and decreet of transference: but both are now well altered; for the process is only expressed by a breviate, and confirmation is but seldom required; and there is no necessity of transferring, except in the case of the death of the pursuer or defender: so that there is no necessity of mentioning a tenor of this action which is obvious.

4. Summonses of wakening are necessary, when a process hath once been called, and is superannuated, not being called in a whole year, through the pursuer's negligence. For though all actions before the Lords are with continuation of days, whereby the parties must attend till their tours of calling come; yet it were unreasonable that they should be obliged constantly to attend, without being called: and therefore, if the pursuer at any time neglect to call them for a whole year, he can have no process till the defender be cited again, which is called a wakening, because the principal process became to be (as it were) asleep, after that year. But frequently the clerks call the process in the Outer-House, at least put upon it a *partibus,* expressing a day when the process was of new called. But if a cause be inrolled, although, with the multiplicity of business, the Lords fall so short of the roll that a year intervene, there is no need of a wakening, because the parties are not obliged to attend at uncertainty as before, but they may be advertised by their advocates, when their causes come near in the roll.

5. Concluded causes are not excluded for want of a wakening, because then regularly there is no need of the client's informing upon new matter of fact; for nothing is to be advised but the probation. The tenor of this process is also so very obvious, that we shall not mention it.

6. Both these actions are so far accessory, that whenever the day of compearance passes, the principal cause is called, as it stood in the roll, and the transference or wakening is only to take off the objection of the death of the parties, or sleeping of the process.

Title 35. Competition

ALL ordinary actions with their accessories, which are competent by our customs before execution on decreets or summary execution, have been hitherto explained. There are other actions executive, which come to be considered after decreets; such as actions for making arrested sums forthcoming, actions for breach of arrestment, and for deforcement, actions for adjudication of real rights, and actions for contravention of lawborrows, which are to be handled in their proper place. It remains now before litiscontestation, to consider the competition of rights, which implies as many different actions as there are competing rights. In which also both declaratory, petitory, and possessory actions are comprehended: for, whatever parties may allege in declarations, reductions, or improbations, they may allege the same in competitions, when many several rights contend for one common subject, and do insist for preference; which ordinarily are referred to an auditor, if the competition be about real rights by infeftment or equivalent titles, who considers all the titles and evidents produced, and reports any difficulty in the preference of them, whereupon a decreet of preference or ranking followeth.

2. Our custom regards not the priority or posteriority of personal rights, but only the priority or posteriority of diligences, except what concerns the royal prerogative, especially that the King is not prejudged by the neglect of his officers.

3. There is also preference amongst the creditors of defuncts, for those debts which are expended for medicaments for the sick and funeral charges, wherein humanity hath given them the privilege to be preferred to other debts, though having prior diligences [111,8,64 and 72,*supra*].

4. Special legacies are also preferable to general legacies, that if the defunct's part be not sufficient to satisfy all the legacies, special legacies suffer no abatement with the general legacies. But there is no privilege for legacies to pious uses, but they suffer abatement with other legacies, unless they be special, or that they be preferred expressly by the defunt.

5. The Roman law gives privilege and preference to the tochers of women, in competition with the creditors of their husbands: for by that law their tochers return to themselves at the dissolution of the marriage. In place of which, our custom gives them infeftments in liferent or provisions in money for their liferent-use; which used to have preference to the husband's other creditors, in case the money had not been employed, nor infeftment taken for the liferent of lands: but the Lords of late have rejected this preference, in respect that these provisions to wives became exorbitant; whereby it was presumed, that they were designed for the children, to exclude the creditors.

6. There hath been a frequent competition amongst arresters and assignees; wherein arrestments come in according to their dates, if the arresters have not been negligent, in procuring decreets for making arrested sums forthcoming: and therefore arrestments, whereupon actions were pursued before the Lords, are not postponed to posterior arrestments pursued before inferior judges, though obtaining the first decreet; if the pursuer before the Lords was only kept off by the course of the roll, and not by his negligence. But if both pursuits were in the same court, the prior decreet is preferable, albeit upon the posterior arrestment; because the arrestment doth not give the arrester right, but process thereupon excludes posterior voluntary rights by dispositions or assignations, as being *in cursu diligentiæ* of the arrester: yet if he be supinely negligent, the voluntary right will be preferable, if perfected, by intimation of the assignation, and by possession on the disposition.

7. In competition of assignations amongst themselves, they are preferable, not according to the dates of the assignations, but of the intimations. In competitions between arrestments and assignations, if the intimation by prior to the arrestment, the assignation is preferable: if both be of one day, and

express different hours, the preference is according to the hours, if so many hours intervene, as the messenger or notary may not be mistaken in the latitude thereof; so that three hours will be sufficient, otherwise they come in *pari passu.*

8. The great grounds of competition are upon infeftments, upon which many competitions have, and will always arise, and much more now than before, since the Act 62, Parl. 1661 [Diligence Act, 1661,c.62; A.P.S. VII,317, c.344], bringing in apprisings *pari passu,* &c. which doth likewise extend to adjudications, which are come now in place of apprisings. And the general rule of preference of rights by infeftment, is, *prior tempore, potior jure.* The rule doth not only extend to rights of property, but also to rights of wadset, and to infeftments granted for satisfaction of sums, whereby the parties infeft have right to the haill duties, to be imputed first in the annualrent, and then in the principal sum till it be paid, which have the same extensions and limitations as general apprisings or adjudications. This rule is also extended to apprisings or adjudications general or special, and likewise to rights equivalent to infeftments (as the right of courtesy of husbands, and terces of wives) and to infeftments granted for security of sums, whereby these sums become *debita fundi,* or to other *debita fundi,* and also to infeftments for relief, or for warrandice of principal lands. In this, these real rights differ from personal rights, wherein respect is not had to the priority or posteriority of their dates, nor to any diligence for obtaining decreets thereupon; but are preferable according to the priority of real diligence by arrestment, and decreets for making forthcoming, or by apprisings or adjudications of heritable sums, while they were not arrestable, or of incomplete voluntary rights without infeftment. The rule is also extended to infeftments for annualrents.

9. The priority and posteriority of infeftments is not only when they are upon different days, but when they are upon different hours of the same day, the distance being at least three hours, that thereby it may be evident that the notary could not so far mistake the true hour; and this is the reason why in seasins the notary mentions the hour of taking the seasin, which, if he omit, though it will not annul the seasin, yet any other seasin on the same day, expressing the hour, will be accounted prior; and no probation by the oath of party, by the notary and witnesses, or even by writ, will determine the hour; because it is a solemnity no other way probable but by the tenor of the seasin, and not otherwise probable, than the other contents of the seasin itself.

10. The priority and posteriority of infeftments is to be reckoned according to the last act necessary for accomplishing the right, which is the date of the seasin, except in charters for confirmation: for dispositions or charters granted by vassals *a se,* i. e. to be holden of their superiors by confirmation, are accounted null, as incomplete, until the charter of confirmation be granted; and though the vassal's charter contain a precept of seasin, whereon seasin is ordinarily taken before the confirmation; yet it is the charter of confirmation that makes the infeftment valid from the date of the seasin confirm-

ed; unless there were a *medium impedimentum*, by the superior's granting a prior confirmation, albeit of a posterior seasin, or by his granting a charter upon resignation, whereof the seasin is taken before confirmation, or by receiving an appriser or adjudger before the charter of confirmation. In this a charter for confirmation is better than a charter upon resignation, that if the superior or the vassal resigner die before seasin be taken, seasin cannot be taken on that charter upon resignation.

11. Charters of confirmation granted by the King, as to priority, are reckoned by appending the Great Seal. And therefore the servant intrusted to append the Seal, writes upon the charter, the day of sealing, and ought to express the hour of that day, and ought not to prefer or postpone any party who offers a charter to be sealed, and the parties who so offer, may take instruments thereupon; or if the matter be recently questioned, the Lords will examine the appender or witnesses on the true time of the offer, and will declare the charter to be of that date. But if seasin have not been taken till after the confirmation, the date of the seasin is the rule.

12. The main reason why there is no preference of personal obligements by their dates, but only of diligences and infeftments, is, because it is a great interest of a nation, to know with whom they may contract, which were utterly impossible, if the dates of obligations, or yet the dates of dispositions incomplete, should give preference. But infeftments must necessarily be taken upon the ground, which therefore the tenants or neighbours may easily give account of to parties concerned: and the knowledge of the priority or posteriority of them is now much better attained by the Act 17, Parl. 1617 [Registration Act, 1617,c.16; A.P.S. IV,545,c.16], ordaining seasins to be registrate; "Whereby it is declared, that seasins not being registrate within threescore days, shall be null in prejudice of third parties, acquiring perfect and lawful rights to the lands and heritage contained in the unregistrate seasin." Another reason of the preference of infeftments, by the dates of the last solemnity accomplishing the same, is, because thereby the granter was, or was presumed to be, so far divested of the right conveyed; and therefore any posterior infeftment was *a non habente potestatem*, the granter being before denuded. And albeit the same deed may be due by several obligations; yet the right of property can only be conveyed by one conveyance: for he who had the property before, can have it no further, and he cannot be divested until another be invested: yet he who hath the real right of superiority or property, may defend himself by many conveyances against several parties; because all the conveyances may be exclusive of their several rights, and so he avoids his trouble or peril from them, and no other can pretend that his right is not founded upon that conveyance.

13. This general rule of preference of infeftments by priority, hath very many exceptions. And, 1. If there be any nullity by reason of the want of any necessary solemnity, required in the constitution of the right, it is thereby simply null, and can have no effect, even against the granter, further than an

incomplete disposition would have; which is, that it would be a ground to compel the granter to give a valid infeftment, and might defend the possession against him, as implying an assignation to the fruits or rents. And, albeit in controversies between a possessor by infeftment and a petitor, *in possessorio*, even nullities would not be receivable without reduction, yet when there comes many competitors to insist together, whatsoever might afford a relevant reason of reduction, is receivable as in a reduction: for instance, a personal obligation with an inhibition, being prior to all the competing infeftments, not only prior to the seasins, but to the dispositions or obligements to dispone, will so far prefer the ground of the inhibition, as if an apprising or adjudication were actually deduced thereupon, with an infeftment or charge; though these must be used thereafter for other effects. What solemnities are requisite in infeftments of property or of annualrent, without which they will be simply null, will appear in these titles, *Lib.* 2, *Tit.* 3, 4, 5. But the priority of infeftments doth always prefer *in petitorio*, when the question is alone as to the titles, abstract from possession: as when none of the parties competing is in present possession, and cannot instruct that they or their predecessors or authors were ever in possession. And yet in that case, neither party instructs a perfect and full title, unless they instruct the progress of their right, from a common author to the parties; in which case neither of them may quarrel their common author's right, on which their own is founded: and consequently the common author being divested by the first infeftment, the posterior infeftments are *a non habente potestatem*. And if a common author do appear under the King, who is the supreme superior and first author of all infeftments, albeit the progress upward to the King be not instructed, it is still presumed *præsumptione juris et de jure* : for the King claims not the property of any land, but of the annexed property, and of the property of lands falling to him by forfeiture, recognition, or as last heir (whereof bastardy is a species) or by acquisition, wherein the King *utitur jure communi;* hence it is that the King gives charters of confirmation, or upon resignation, without exact instruction of a full progress from the King, the same being always given *periculo petentium*, even though the fullest warrandice were expressed in the King's charter, which imports no more but protection by law. If therefore the progress of the competitors come up to one common author, if none appear to own that common author's right, the first infeftment may without hazard of disclamation take infeftments of the King as superior. And if by the competitor's progress a common author appear, albeit all the progress be not complete by the infeftments of every heir, yet the first original right will be preferred in competition: for therein apparent heirs are as well preferred as heirs entering: and it is *jus tertii* to the other competitors having posterior rights from the same author, whether the heirs *successivè* were entered and infeft or not; because the present vassal, if any part of that progress were wanting, could yet serve to the last that he shows to have been infeft, and thereupon may be infeft. But if, in the progress from the nearest common author, there be singular titles, if

the one competitor show a progress all along from the common author by predecessors, and not by singular successors, and the other show a progress by
singular successors, the transmission from the heirs to these singular successors, if recent, must be instructed, and if ancient, must be adminiculate,
wherein ancient possession, or common fame in the vicinity of the singular
successors of their being holden and reputed heritable possessors, will be
sufficient.

14. Secondly, If a posterior right from the common author instruct long
possession, and the prior infeftment cannot be instructed to have attained
possession before the posterior; then arises the *præsumptio juris* acknowledged
by cap. 105, Parliament 1540 [A.P.S. 11,375,c.23], whereby a posterior infeftment, where warrandice may fall, clad with peaceable possession, at least for
year and day, by labouring, manuring, and uptaking of the profits, and so
kenned heritable possessor thereof, year and day, is preferred to a prior base
infeftment not clad with possession; for in that case, the first infeftment is
presumed to be fraudulent *retentâ possessione*. All original infeftments granted
by, and holden of the first common author as superior, were base infeftments;
and the first clad with real possession, was preferable: and, albeit singular
successors obtained right to that original infeftment, by resignation or confirmation, apprising or adjudication, yet the original right being base, if it
attained not possession before the other competing original right, the rights
by progress (however acquired) fall with the original right in consequence.
And in the competition of posterior rights by singular titles, that which is
upon resignation or confirmation, will be preferred to a prior right from the
same superior, being base.

15. Thirdly, These were the grounds of preference of infeftments, before
that excellent statute of prescription, Parl. 1617, cap. 12. [Prescription Act,
1617,c.12; A.P.S. IV,543,c.12] and continues so as to infeftments whereupon
there were interruptions, for pursuing of which there were thirteen years
allowed next after the date of that Act; in which time actions or competitions
were to be regulated as before the Act: "otherways these who have infeftments with forty years' continual possession following and ensuing the date
thereof, and that peaceably, without any lawful interruption made to them
therein during the said space, such persons, their heirs and successors, shall
never be troubled, pursued nor unquieted in the heritable right and property
of their saids lands and heritages foresaid, by his Majesty or others their
superiors and authors, their heirs and successors, not by any other person
pretending right to the same, by virtue of prior infeftments public or private,
nor upon no other ground, reason, or argument competent of law, except for
falsehood. Providing they be able to show a charter and seasin to them or
their predecessors, by their superiors and authors preceding the entry of the
said forty years possession; or that they produce instruments of seasin, one
or more, continued and standing together for the said space of forty years,
either proceeding upon retours or upon precepts of *clare constat*, which are

declared to be valid and sufficient rights (being clad with the said peaceable and continual possession of forty years, without any lawful interruption) for bruiking of the heritable right of the same lands and others foresaids: but the years of minority is not to be accounted in the course of the said forty years." And because infeftments might still be uncertain by interruptions within the said thirteen years, or as to infeftments prior to the Act of Prescription, or within the forty years possession as to rights posterior, which might not easily come to the knowledge of the proprietors, or false executions might be made up; therefore by the cap. 10. Parl. 1669 [Interruptions Act, 1669,c.10; A.P.S. VII,561,c.15], it is statute, that all executions of summons for interruption, be only by messengers. And if the execution be not personally, it must be at the parish kirk of the defender in time of divine service, or immediately thereafter. And that all citations for interruption, whether in real or personal rights, be renewed within seven years, otherways to prescribe. In which seven years minority is not to be counted. And likewise all executions of summons must bear expressly the names and designations of the parties, pursuers and defenders, and shall not only relate generally to the parties in the summons, without naming and designing them, unless the execution be indorsed on the back of the summons, cap. 6. Parl. 1672 [Summons Execution Act, 1672,c.6; A.P.S. VIII,64,c.6], and must be subscribed by the witnesses, cap. 6. Parl. 1681 [Subscription of Deeds Act, 1681,c.5; A.P.S. VIII,242,c.5]. Albeit these statutes have done much to secure purchasers, and to order the preference of infeftments, yet there are many cases, in which the competition must be upon the former grounds, which were before the Act of Prescription; as not only interruption by citation, but also interruption by intermission of possession, or of the continuity of seasins; which cannot be understood by every discontinuity, for no seasin can follow another, till the party to be infeft gets his infeftment renewed by charges upon his retour, or by precepts of *clare constat*, which must take a time; and if the superior be unwilling, they may take a long time, and yet the seasins must be reckoned as continued.

By the Act of Prescription, no other seasins are sufficient without their warrants, but these which proceed on retours or precepts of *clare constat;* in all which cases the competition must be upon the former grounds.

In these competitions, no special privilege is respected by seven years' possession, which takes only place *in judicio possessorio;* but in these competitions, all parties are as *in judicio petitorio.*

In competitions, all parties will be admitted for their interest, who produce an infeftment to themselves or to their predecessors, to whom they are, or may be heirs in that right, or to their authors; if therewith they show a title voluntary or legal, from these authors, to them or to their predecessors, to whom they are, or may be heirs.

In competitions, all persons who produce the foresaids infeftments, will upon supplication obtain ordinary and incident diligence by horning and caption, against all the havers of writs, that may instruct their progress, as high as they can: and albeit ordinarily incident diligences are not granted till after litiscontestation, yet seeing they are granted in reductions, so soon as terms are taken to produce, that they may be able to satisfy the production, they ought also so to be granted in competitions.

Prescription was only an exception to defend possessors; but this statute 1617 makes it an active title, to attain or recover possession, and to exclude all other rights.

16. Fourthly, The priority of infeftments is not the rule of preference, where the competition is upon infeftments by or from the heirs of defuncts; for in that case the 24th Act, Parl. 1661 [A.P.S. VII,63,c.88], "doth annul any right or disposition made by apparent heirs, within a year after the defunct's death, in so far as may prejudge their predecessor's creditors. And declares, that the creditors of the defunct shall be preferred to the creditors of the apparent heir, after that Act, as to the defunct's estate: providing the defunct's creditors do diligence against the apparent heir, and the real estate belonging to the defunct, within the space of three years after the defunct's death." By this statute, posterior infeftments for the defunct's debt are preferable as to the defunct's estate, to prior infeftments for the heir's debt, as aforesaid. By the creditors doing diligence within three years, must be meant complete diligence by apprising or adjudication, whereupon infeftment or charge hath followed to the party himself, or to any other appriser or adjudger, with whom he comes in *pari passu*: for if incomplete diligence within these years were sufficient, it might keep the preference uncertain for forty years.

17. Fifthly, Any voluntary infeftment being granted *in cursu diligentiæ* of a creditor, that creditor's right is preferable, and in competition will be preferred, though it be not completed[1,9,15, *supra*]; but *cursus diligentiæ* is taken away, if negligence intervene; which must not be reckoned by what diligence possibly might be done, but by such diligence as prudent men would have done in such circumstances. By diligence in this case, is not understood a personal action, which could not be known, but a real diligence for affecting the subject in question, and not the person of the debtor only; whereof the law hath determined several cases; as, diligence by apprising runs from the denunciation of the lands to be apprised; and diligence by adjudication, now come in place of apprising, runs from the citation upon the summons of adjudication, which must so hold in adjudications upon the renunciation of heirs, or for completing of dispositions. But so soon as decreets of apprising or adjudication are obtained, and such time as a charge may be given to the superior, that diligence is then complete, and the infeftments are preferable according to these seasins or charges. In like manner, an inchoate diligence of inhibition is preferable to a voluntary infeftment, albeit granted before the inhibition was complete: for inhibitions require executions against the parties inhibited, and also against the lieges at the market crosses of the head burghs of the jurisdiction where the person inhibited dwells; and therefore, during the course of this diligence, the debtor may not give a voluntary right, which

may frustrate that inhibition; so that the voluntary right is not only reducible upon the inhibition, when complete, but when inchoate, if diligently insisted in.

18. Sixthly, When any debtor becomes bankrupt or insolvent, no voluntary right after he is charged with horning, will be preferred to the debt whereupon the horning was raised, and that, by the Act of Parliament 1621, against fraudulent dispositions of bankrupts [Bankruptcy Act, 1621,c.18; A.P.S. iv,615,c.18], bearing that clause expressly, in these terms: "That in time thereafter, if any dyvor, or interposed person partaker of the fraud, shall make any voluntary payment, or right, to any person, in defraud of the more timeous diligence of another creditor, having used horning, &c. The prior creditor shall be preferred to the con-creditor, who being posterior in diligence, has obtained preference by the partial favour of the debtor, or his interposed confident." But this preference by horning, hath only effect, when the common debtor is insolvent: whereas the former diligence prefers, though the debtor be not insolvent.

19. Seventhly, Any ground of fraud is a sufficient reason of reduction, or preference, against the committer of the fraud, or these who are partakers of the fraud, but not against singular successors, who are not partakers of the same.

20. Eighthly, There is yet no determination by statute or custom, whether infeftments obtained by illegal violence or concussion are reducible, not only against the purchaser or his heirs, but against singular successors: yet the parity of reason in fraud or force, should secure the innocent purchaser, who neither was accessory to the force, nor knew of it when he purchased, which requires a statute; for force, as well as fraud, are *labes reales* by common law.

21. Ninthly, All infeftments voluntarily granted after inhibition, are reducible *ex capite inhibitionis*, not only as to infeftments voluntarily granted, but even as to infeftments upon apprising or adjudication, if the debt whereupon they were deduced, be posterior to the executing of the inhibition, at the market-cross of the head-burgh of the jurisdiction, where the inhibited person dwelt; which ought not to be extended to the market-crosses where the lands lie: for the law having provided, that the inhibition must be executed at the market-cross where the person inhibited dwells, both against him and against the lieges, and that by open proclamation in market-time of day, by three Oyesses, and affixing a copy on the cross, prudent men ought to have some intrusted for them, to give notice of that publication; for it is for that end these solemnities are used, and they may know where their debtor dwells, but it were unreasonable to oblige them to inquire, wherever he has lands, and to have some to attend for them at the crosses where these lands lie, seeing the inhibition is null, if not done at the cross where the debtor dwells [iv,50,10,*infra*]. Yet the inhibition will be effectual against a voluntary disposition, preferring a creditor; but not to the borrowing of money, and

granting bond therefore, which an inchoate diligence of inhibition cannot exclude, but only an inhibition complete.

Inhibition is only effectual against posterior voluntary rights; but if there was a prior obligement to grant that right, it is not reducible, because not voluntary; seeing the granter might have been compelled by law to grant it. Inhibitions being complete, are not only relevant to reduce voluntary infeftments being posterior, but even infeftments on apprising or adjudication, if the debt whereon they proceeded was posterior to the completing of the inhibition.

Interdictions are a kind of inhibitions, whereby a weak or lavish party obliges himself to do nothing in prejudice of his heritage, without consent of such persons who are called interdictors, and who thereupon procure letters to inhibit him to act contrary to that interdiction: so it hath the same effect as another inhibition, if the party was truly weak or lavish.

22. Tenthly, Seasins, inhibitions, and interdictions, are ordained to be registrate, as before is expressed, or otherwise they are null as to any who have a complete right, who thereby are preferable, if they be prior to the registration; and even after the days required for registration, for they may be registrate after these days by warrant of the Lords, and will exclude rights after that registration, according to the custom which hath been used, which ought not to be continued: for when a purchaser waits forty days after his agreement, and then searches the registers, and goes on in confidence to perfect his securities; if, when he is gone, an exclusive right or diligence may be put in the register, before he complete his right, if it exclude him, the register is of no security.

It is a great weakening of this excellent statute for registration, that the Keepers of the Registers do not book and insert so soon as they receive the writs to be registrate; and that upon pretence that they cannot do it, because many may come together, and parties will not attend till they be filled up; so that there is nothing to instruct when they were presented, and upon this pretence the keepers may prefer those who were last presented to those who were first, and thereby evacuate the security of purchasers; wherein their gain, or other grounds of partiality, may instigate them. And therefore, as the Act of Regulation [Courts Act, 1672,c.16; A.P.S. VIII,80,c.40] has appointed them to keep minute-books, so the Lords, by Act of Sederunt, in July 1692, published by proclamation, ordained the keepers to cause the presenters immediately as they present, to sign the minute: so that now they can neither alter the minute-book, nor wrong any party by the booking; whereas formerly they might write over the minute-book, yea, a whole register, which now they cannot do without the concourse of all the presenters. This was so much the more necessary, that by a late decision and statute following thereon [Act, 1686,c.19; A.P.S. VIII,600,c.33], parties getting seasins marked on the back, and signed by the keeper, are preferred accordingly, although the seasin be not found in the register; whereby all security by the registers terminates in the solvency of the clerks, and their cautioners, which hath enervate the whole design. To prevent this mischief, the Lords, by the foresaid Act of Sederunt, have appointed all keepers of registers for publication, upon the first application, to insert the substance of what is offered to be registrate, in their minute-books, to be signed by the presenter, which minute-books they cannot be able to alter as before.

23. Eleventhly, Apprisings and adjudications are appointed to have a minute on the back thereof, signed by two of the Lords, which must also be registrate for the security of purchasers: and therefore, if they be not so registrate, a posterior valid right will be preferable thereto; and the allowance ought not to be registrate after the time appointed, for the foresaid reason [111,2,25,*supra*].

24. Twelfthly, All *debita fundi et onera realia* are excepted from the general rule of preference by the dates of the infeftments on personal rights. These real burdens are many, and to be differently ranked; 1. What is due to the superior by the tenure or nature of the investiture, is preferable to all; such as the feu-duties in feu-holdings; the non-entry duties in ward-holdings; and the avails of marriages, whether by the nature of the fee in ward-holdings, or by the tenure of the investiture in feu-holdings *cum maritagio :* for all these the ground is poinded, and the apprising thereupon is preferable to all voluntary or legal rights affecting the vassal's right. 2. In the next place, infeftments for warrandice, if they be in the same investiture with the infeftment of the principal lands, albeit neither the infeftment of the principal nor warrandice lands be public, but base, holden of the granter, and that there be no other possession of the warrandice lands, but the possession of the principal lands; yet thereby both are valid: but the infeftment of the warrandice lands can take no effect till distress, and then they are drawn back to the date of the infeftment. 3. In like manner infeftments reserved in the infeftments of vassals are preferable to the vassal's infeftment, and to all infeftments flowing from him. 4. Infeftments granted for security of sums, are real burdens upon the fee of him that grants the said infeftment for security. These are not infeftments of property, but they are as servitudes upon the infeftments of property, and as real impignorations: for they cannot take possession, but the sum they secure may be the ground of an apprising or adjudication, which will not be preferable according to their dates, but according to the date of the infeftment for security; wherein this infeftment differs from a wadset, which is an infeftment of property, under reversion, which can take possession: it differs also from an infeftment for payment or satisfaction of a sum, which doth not only possess for the annualrent, but likewise for the principal sum, and ceases so soon as both are paid in the same way as an apprising or adjudication ceaseth. Albeit there be no apprising or adjudication upon the sum, for which the infeftment for security is granted; yet, in competition, that sum will be preferred according to the date of the infeftment; and whosoever obtains right to the sum by assignation, arrestment, or otherwise, carries the right. 5. If an

infeftment be granted with the burden of a sum, it makes that sum a real bur-den, whereupon the fee may be apprised or adjudged, and the apprising or adjudication thereon will be preferred, as of the same date with the infeftment burdened; whereby a purchaser proceeds on his own hazard, if he buy with-out sight of his author's infeftment; and if he get but right as a creditor, the party having right to the sum burdening, will be preferred as an anterior real creditor, and not personal only.

25. And lastly, The general rule of preference of infeftments and equiva-lent rights is exceedingly altered by c.62. Parl. 1661 [Diligence Act, 1661,c. 62; A.P.S. VII,317,c.344], which brings in apprisings before the first effectual apprising by infeftment or charge, and all posterior apprisings within a year of the first effectual apprising, to be *pari passu*, as if one apprising had been deduced for all; which holdeth in adjudications come in place of apprisings; and also must so hold in adjudications upon renunciation to be heir. So that there is no need to repeat apprisings, seeing adjudications are now the ordin-ary course. So then the first effectual adjudication is the adjudication for all, as if all were pursuers in that adjudication; and therefore the adjudger cannot renounce that adjudication simply, but for his own share: and though he were paid or satisfied by intromission, yet the adjudication stands good for the rest of the adjudgers; and any of them have interest to call for production and transuming of that adjudication. The adjudications coming in *pari passu* doth not import equality of shares, but proportionally according to the sums in the several adjudications: and if the penalties be too great and unequal, the Lords will modify the same.

Albeit the foresaid Act of Parliament mention diligence, upon the charge against the superior, yet custom hath required no more but the charge; it being incongruous for an adjudger, who designs to be a vassal, to use caption against his superior; and therefore the adjudication, with the charge, hath (during the legal) all the effects, as if infeftment were expede: for during the legal, the adjudication is but *pignus prætorium*, not denuding the vassal. And the superior cannot compel the adjudger to take infeftment; so that, during the legal, he is free of a year's rent, which he behoved to pay, while infeft-ments were necessary [11,3,30, *supra*].

26. This concourse of adjudications hath bred several questions amongst adjudgers competing with annualrenters, or competing amongst themselves, when any of the competitors have ground of reduction against any of the rest, upon any of the grounds of preference before mentioned; and that as to sev-eral effects: as, 1. Though the estate affected be fully sufficient to satisfy all adjudgers and annualrenters, yet still there must be a ranking of them, to the effect it may be determined who shall first have access to the tenants, or to distress the ground: for if they may promiscuously distress the tenants, the lands may be laid waste. And therefore, where there are but two competitors for annualrents, the Lords allow some days to the first annualrenter to use execution, and supersede execution by the second annualrenter till that day:

but if there be many, and if the parties agree not among themselves upon a common factor, the Lords will appoint a factor upon their application, and intimation to all parties concerned, albeit there be no process depending amongst them.

Secondly, If the estate affected be not sufficient to pay the annualrents of all the annualrenters and adjudgers, the question is, How the common factor shall pay them their shares of the rent? Or, in case there be a judicial sale, how they shall share of the price? Or, in case there be not buyers found, but that there must be a division of the estate to the creditors, how they shall have access to what shall be their share of the land, corresponding to their sums? As to which the annualrenters, prior to the first effectual adjudication, do not come in with the adjudgers *pari passu*, but are preferred according to their dates, and so must choose accordingly, with the least detriment to the rest, taking off at a side, and taking off a whole roum distinct, and not *pro indiviso;* which, if it exceed their proportion of the sum, the Lords must determine the rate of the roum, and they must pay in the superplus, which the next annual-renter must accept as a part of his satisfaction, and take land for the rest in the same way. And as to the adjudgers, though they come in *pari passu*, as to the proportion of their shares, yet the first adjudger hath still so much preference, as to choose the roums corresponding to his interest, and so the rest in order. And if there be one adjudication in favour of diverse creditors, they must have their preference in choice by lot.

27. As to the division of the rents till a sale be made, or of the price after the sale, both of these proceed by the same rule, which hath been in a great part determined in the competition of Langtoun and Cockburn's creditors. [There are many decisions under the name of Cockburn of Langtoun's Credi-tors.] These having been mutual cautioners each for other, did suddenly break, and upon the first suspicion, gave infeftments of annualrent to many of their creditors, and all the rest adjudged within the year, and so came in *pari passu;* and some of the annualrenters did likewise adjudge, whereby they had two titles. At the first hearing of the competition of these annualrenters who had adjudged, with the other adjudgers, the Lords inclined to give them their option of either title, but not of both; because it was so determined by the common custom, when annualrenters or wadsetters did apprise, they were necessitated to charge for their sums, and thereby to make them liquid and moveable, which was a passing from their first infeftment for the time, yet so as they might pass from the apprising, and return thereto: but afterward creditors did in their securities provide, that they might make use of their infeftments, or of apprisings on their sums, the one but prejudice of the other; and thereby in competition they made use of their apprisings, in so far as they were upon their annualrents, whereby these annualrents, being *debita fundi*, were preferred to any other apprising for personal debt only; and they made also use of their apprising as to the stock of their sums. But since adjudications came in place of apprisings, the making sums moveable by a charge hath not

been required: yea, albeit in apprisings against apparent heirs, there behoved first to be a decreet against the apparent heir, as lawfully charged to enter heir, and after that a special charge to enter heir in such lands, or heritable rights; yet this is not necessary in adjudications, which are mainly declaratory actions *contra hæreditatem jacentem*, wherein the heir needs not be charged to renounce, if the adjudication have no personal conclusion against him to pay. And to the effect creditors may come in within the year, if there be one adjudication extracted, neither the debtor nor his apparent heir, nor the concreditors, can postpone any creditor from adjudging, upon any exception not instantly verified: and therefore, though they should propone payment, or compensation to be proven, they will be repelled *hoc loco*, but reserved *contra executionem ;* and so compensation in that case will be allowed *post sententiam*, in the second instance, because it was proponed, and not admitted to probation in the first instance. And therefore an adjudger, adjudging for bygone annualrents, and for the stock, may crave preference by his adjudication for the bygone annualrents in his adjudication, as being *debita fundi ;* and for the annualrents thereof, as becoming a stock by the adjudication, and may insist for the principal stock to come in *pari passu pro tanto*.

It were neither just nor fit, to put annualrenters to a poinding of the ground by apprising, for their bygone annualrents: for the adjudication ought to be sustained as a poinding of the ground, where it is not only for the stock, but for the annualrents due by infeftment of annualrent; yea, seeing adjudications are put in place of apprisings, annualrenters may adjudge for the annualrents rather than apprise; and to the same effect as if they did apprise; and therefore, in adjudications, where poinding of the ground is competent, if the creditor adjudge not both for principal and annualrents, but only for bygone annualrents, he may libel his action of adjudication "for poinding the moveables on the ground, not exceeding the tenant's term's mails, and also for adjudging the ground-right and property, and all other right of the land, or other heritable right, for satisfying the said annualrents, in so far as they shall not be satisfied by poinding the goods on the ground:" which is a far more ready process than a poinding of the ground, which hath only a warrant for letters for poinding the ground, whereupon an apprising with all its formalities must follow: whereas here the decreet of adjudication hath immediate access for both.

28. To return then to the division of the rent, or price of incumbered estates, there is no difficulty if the free rent exceed the annualrent; for then all will be paid of their current annualrent, and of their stock by a sale. But if the free rent come short of the annualrent, the method of division ordered by the Lords was thus: That the adjudgers were to be accounted as joint proprietors, and the annualrents as servitudes on the property: and therefore, 1. The annualrents affecting the property, and every part thereof, behoved first to be satisfied in order according to their dates; so that if the rent did not satisfy the whole annualrenters, these who were prior would carry all, and the whole

adjudgers would be excluded. 2. If the free rent exceed the annualrent of all the annualrenters, then the superplus is to be divided proportionally to the adjudgers, in respect the annualrents being all prior to the first effectual adjudication, the adjudgers could have nothing till the annualrenters were satisfied.

29. This is the rule of division; but all the former grounds of reduction are exceptions from the rule. So that if any of the competitors could reduce the right of another, in a process of reduction, they may make use of the same reason in the competition. For instance, if any of the competitors had used inhibition against any others, in that case they would draw out of the share of these whom they could reduce, so much as to make up the share they would have had, if that reducible right did not exist: and yet that reducible right, albeit prior to the other rights, could not recur upon them, to make up what the reduction had carried from it, in favours of the reducing right; because the ground of reduction is always upon the fault or defect of the right reduced; as in the present instance, a right reducible *ex capite inhibitionis* is faulty and defective, as proceeding against the King's authority, prohibiting to take any such right; and therefore it cannot claim to be made up out of any other right, which is not faulty; which holds in the other grounds of reduction, as the being *in cursu diligentiæ*, &c.

If then the inhibition be against some of the annualrents, in favour of another annualrenter, then the reducing annualrent, if by its order it would fall last, would carry from the reducible annualrents its share: but if both annualrents by their order fall to be satisfied, and are not cut off by their posteriority, then the reducing annualrent can claim no more but preference to the reducible annualrent, in the choice of lands in the case of division.

If any of the adjudgers have inhibited before the constitution of any of the annualrents, these adjudgers would draw from the shares of these annualrenters, as much as will make up the adjudgers' share, to that quantity they would have got, if these annualrenters were not existing. For instance, suppose there were two adjudgers, and one annualrenter prior to both, and suppose that one of the adjudgers had inhibit before the constitution of the annualrent, and the other had not; suppose also that all the three had equal annualrents, as if each of them were upon a sum whose annualrent were 400 pound, and yet the free rent of the estate they affected were only 600 pound, the question is, How should this 600 pound be divided amongst them? The annualrenter would claim his full annualrent, being 400 pound, as being prior to both the adjudgers, whereby there would remain to the adjudgers but 200 pound, which would be equally divided betwixt them, because they are equal; so each of them would carry 100 pound; yet the adjudger who had the inhibition, would claim as much of the 600 pound, which is the common stock, as he would have had if there were no annualrenter, and so he would draw 300 pound; so that the annualrenter would have only remaining 200 pound, but could not return upon the other adjudger, as being prior to him: and therefore the first adjudger would retain his 100 pound: which will so hold if the annualrent had been reducible upon the other grounds before expressed.

If the ground of reduction be for one adjudger against another, as if there were three adjudgers, whereof each claims a yearly annualrent of 400 pound, in all 1200 pound, and yet the free rent were only 600 pound; if there were no ground of reduction, each adjudger would have 200 pound. But suppose the second adjudger had used inhibition against the common debtor, before the contracting of the third adjudger's debt, in that case the question is, How should the 600 pound be divided amongst the three adjudgers? The first adjudger would have 200 pound, because the inhibition struck not against him, so that he would have his share, as if there had been no inhibition, which should neither profit nor prejudge him. The second adjudger having the inhibition, behoved to have his share, as if the third adjudger were not existing, in which case the 600 pound would have been equally divided betwixt him and the first adjudger, and so he must have 300 pound, but he can claim no more, to abate the last adjudger's share, seeing his reduction does not simply annul the last adjudication, but only in so far as it is prejudicial to the second adjudication; and therefore the first adjudger having drawn 200 pound, and the second 300 pound, the third hath 100 pound.

This will hold, whatever be the number of the annualrenters or adjudgers, who have inhibitions, or other grounds of reduction against any of the rest.

30. There is another case that hath not been determined, viz. suppose an annualrent be after some of the adjudications which come in *pari passu*, and before others of them, the question is, what should be the share of that annualrent? There occurred a case of this kind, Brown of Colstoun *contra* Nicolas, decided February 6, 1673 [2 Stair 166; M.2821], wherein the statute bringing in apprisers *pari passu*, being new and dubious, the annualrent was brought in as if it had been an adjudication *pari passu* with the adjudications [II,5,11, *supra*]. I know no decision since to second this, and so there is no formed custom in the case. It is certain, that the statute leaves annualrenters as they were before, and so they can never come in *pari passu* with adjudications, unless the date of the first effectual adjudication and the annualrent were the same: and therefore, there is much more reason that the annualrent, which was constitute *in cursu diligentiæ* of the first effectual adjudication, should be postponed to all the adjudications. Albeit some of them were before the first effectual adjudication, because the real right of adjudications is only by the infeftment of the first effectual adjudication, or charge thereupon. But if the infeftment of annualrent be after the infeftment or charge upon the first effectual adjudication, all the adjudications within the year, before or after the annualrent, should be preferred thereto; because the first effectual adjudication is, as if all the prior and posterior adjudications within the year, were contained in it, and so the diligence for obtaining of that adjudication is for them all: and therefore, if the annualrent were after the citation, whereupon the first effec-

tual adjudication did proceed, the annualrent is reducible as *in cursu diligentiæ*, unless the adjudger have been negligent, not obtaining infeftment, or giving a charge, so soon as by ordinary diligence he could do it: for where diligence prefers, it must be continued diligence.

It were also very inconvenient, if the common debtor might, by voluntary infeftments, prefer one creditor, by constituting an annualrent, to the diligence of other creditors, who, by adjudication within the year, are, *fictione juris*, stated as if their sums were in the first effectual adjudication; which is more than any presumption.

Title 36. Actions Extraordinary

HITHERTO ordinary actions of all sorts have been explained; all which had an ordinary form of process, and must be inrolled and discussed according to the order of the roll. Besides these, there are extraordinary actions, which proceed summarily, without the course of the roll; whereof these following are the prime. 1. Adjudications being brought in place of apprisings, and all adjudications within the year of the first effectual adjudication by infeftment or charge, or before the same, coming in *pari passu*, as if they were all contained in the first effectual adjudication; therefore so soon as any adjudication is extracted, all other adjudications within the year, are called amongst the acts without inrolment. And all defences and exceptions are repelled *hoc loco*, and reserved *contra executionem;* that is, these summary adjudications are not only liable to suspension or reduction, but, even in any process founded upon them, all defences and exceptions which might have been proponed in the first instance, are competent against them. This is admitted by the Lords, upon account of the extraordinary prejudice that creditors would sustain, if they were necessitated to abide the course of the roll; for then they could not expect to come in within year and day of the first adjudication. Yet the first adjudication must have all the formalities of other processes, wherein not only the defender who is called, but con-creditors will be admitted for their interest, they producing the same.

2. Processes of sale of broken estates, being a kind of adjudication, having an extraordinary and proper form by statute; whereby, in the first instance, the evidences of the debtor's being *obæratus*, must first be instructed, either as notour, or by competitions of many creditors, whom the debtor cannot satisfy, unless he could sell all his estate at once; and then a term is assigned to prove the rental of the lands and casualties thereof, and the ordinary rate of lands of such holding and casualty in the shire where they lie: after which the probation being advised, and the lowest rate determined by the Lords, there is a second instance and a new citation and intimation. Now, if both these should abide the course of the roll, it would be a great detriment to creditors; therefore the Lords, by Act of Sederunt, have ordered these processes of sale to proceed summarily without inrolling, reserving all defences to be proponed before the auditor of the sale by roup. And it is only competent to the defend-

er to object against his being alleged insolvent; for in this case, bankrupt is an improper term, being proper only to merchants, and others whose estates are in moveables; but as to heritors, if they be *obærati*, so that by the real diligence of creditors they cannot sell their estates, except all be sold together, this process is not to their discredit; since it only ariseth from the bringing in apprisers or adjudgers within the year *pari passu ;* but it was their fault, that they did not offer their evidents, and possession of lands proportional to the sums; in which case only a partial adjudication could proceed, redeemable in five years.

3. All incident actions are extraordinary, and need no inrolment; as sequestration of charter-chests; inspection thereof; nomination of factors in competitions of many creditors, whether the ranking be past or not; processes for tutors nominate to accept or be excluded, and the like. And when reductions of acts are insisted in, they are summarily discussed: for the reason why they must be raised, is, because parties are not obliged to attend but at the diets of processes; and therefore, if at any other time bills be given in to alter acts, if they proceed upon informality of process, or that acts are not conform to the minutes, in these cases there needs no reduction, if the complaints be in due time before the acquiescence of parties is presumed by law. But, if the complaint be upon matter of fact, which ought to be consulted with the clients, the Lords should not admit of the same upon bill, unless the party were in town; but there must be reduction to oblige the party to attend at the term in the reduction, which therefore is summarily discussed. Also, when any party is appointed to be called *incidenter*, and the process continued against that party, then that citation is discussed summarily.

4. Transferences of processes, upon the death of either party, are summarily discussed, albeit probation must proceed; as when the passive title cannot be instantly verified, but proceeds upon behaving as heir, lucrative succession, or vitious intromission, both the relevancy and probation of these proceed summarily; because they are accessory to the principal cause, which remains in the roll as it was, and is marked by the Ordinary to continue till these incident processes be discussed.

5. The king's causes proper to the crown, and not belonging to donatars, are, by the Act of Regulation [Courts Act, 1672,c.16; A.P.S. VI I I, 80,c.40], to be summarily discussed; the King's Advocate intimating to the defenders a fourth-night before he insist, that they may be ready.

6. Actions upon invasion of either party in process, against the other, proceed summarily without inrolment; and that by bill, if the party-injurer be present, or by citation under the signet, if he be absent.

7. All complaints upon contempt of authority, proceed summarily by bill, if the party be present, or by citation if absent; as when execution proceeds after suspension, or sist duly intimated, either *apud acta*, or by instrument of citation.

8. All incident penal actions for vindicating the Lords authority, are to be

discussed summarily, whether the penalty be by amerciament, imprisonment, or corporal punishment. For though the Lords are not criminal judges, yet all sovereign courts have implied in their jurisdiction, these penalties, without which the same cannot be explicated; and therefore all affronts or contempts of the Lords, or any of them, may be so punished. And where parties are found accessory to malversations in process, they are so to be punished. Thus in prevarication, or excusable accession to forgery, or false testimony, parties are frequently set upon the pillory, or have their ears nailed to the trone, with papers upon their brow, showing their crime, when yet the Lords do not find reason to commit the offenders to the criminal judges.

Title 37. Advocations

ACTIONS ordinary and extraordinary, which are competent to be discussed before the Lords of Session, in the first instance, having been explained in the former titles, the proper method leads us now to actions competent before the Lords in the second instance, by advocation, suspension of their own decreets, or of the decreets of other courts, and reduction of the same: of which in order: and first, of advocations, these being before decreets. As for suspensions and reductions of decreets, these being after decreets, are to be explained after decreets.

2. Advocation, as the name imports, is an action craving a cause to be removed from another judicature unto the Lords, to be discussed by them, or to be remitted to another competent and unsuspected judge.

3. The Lords may advocate causes, where, though they cannot be judges in the cause advocate, yet they are competent judges in the advocation: for, as they are the king's ordinary council in matters of law, they have that amplitude of jurisdiction, that whatsoever hath not an ordinary judicature to determine it, is at the Lords' determination.

4. The subject matter of every jurisdiction is commonly known. All matters of state, and for maintenance of the public peace against riots or violence, are proper to the Privy Council, which was instituted for these effects, and so distinguished from the King's ordinary council, whereunto the College of Justice hath succeeded: and therefore the Lords are denominated Lords of Council and Session. All crimes which occur not in the explication of the jurisdiction of the Session, or other courts, are proper to the criminal judges, chiefly to the Justice-General, Justice-Clerk and five of the Lords of Session, associated to them, by the Act of Regulation of Judicatures [Courts Act, 1672,c.16; A.P.S. VIII,80,c.40]. All actions criminal committed at sea, or within the seamark, are proper to be judged by the Lord High Admiral of Scotland, and his deputes, and the civil actions accustomed in that court, as the adjudication of prizes, and actions among seamen. All actions for confirmation of testaments, or adherence, or divorce, are proper to the Commissaries. All actions for debt not exceeding two hundred merks, are by statute [Act 1663,c.9; A.P.S. VII,451,c.3; Courts Act 1672,c.16; A.P.S. VIII,80,c.40]

only competent to the ordinary judges in the first instance, and are not to be advocated by the Lords, unless the parties be members of the College of Justice, who are obliged to attend the Lords, which statute was made, that the Lords might have more time to decide matters of greater importance. All actions for valuation of teinds, plantation of kirks, modification, augmentation and locality of stipends, are proper to the Commission for Plantation of Kirks, and that not only in the first instance, but in the second instance by suspension or reduction. There is ordinarily a commission for criminal causes upon the border, which is proper to them according to the tenor of the commission. Bailies of regality are competent judges of crimes committed within their regalities, unless the same be first pursued before the Justice-General, in which case the bailies of regality cannot repledge from, but sit with the Justice-General, and have a vote decisive, as is statute in relation to church-men's regalities, in the act of annexation of the temporalities of kirk-lands to the crown. It is not determined by the Act of Regulations [Courts Act, 1672, c.16; A.P.S. VIII,80,c.40], adjoining five of the Lords of the Session, whether the bailies of regality are restricted in their jurisdiction, from having a vote with the Justices either in the ordinary or circuit-courts: but it appears more rational, that these bailies should have a vote, when there are many criminal judges, than when there was but one. All sheriffs, stewards, bailies of royalty, bailies of burrows, barons and their bailies, have criminal jurisdiction, unless they be prevented by superior courts; but they cannot repledge and are restricted as to the kind and order of procedure.

5. It would not be consistent with the justice and security of the kingdom, that there were no remedy to stop the course of any of these criminal judges, albeit they were never so partial and suspect; and, therefore, upon complaints to the secret council, the execution of sentences of criminal judges can be stopt; yet they can neither be advocated nor reduced by the Privy Council, who have no such form. So that it is both necessary and accustomed, that the King's ordinary council, the Lords of Session, should advocate all these causes proper to particular jurisdictions, which cannot begin before the Lords, nor be determined by them, if there be just ground of advocation, viz. upon the point of competency of jurisdiction, as if one court proceed in that which belongs to another, or if the crime be not committed within their jurisdictions, or if the parties be not liable thereto; or if they be declinable by reason of relation to either party, or of enmity against either party; or if they have given partial counsel, while they were judges; or if the crimes be peculiar crimes of the Crown; or of such moment or difficulty, as requires the pleading of the learnedest lawyers, and determination of the skilfulest judges, or the like. Yet the advocation is to this effect, that the Lords may appoint competent unsuspect and impartial judges; and, therefore, they do remit such causes if they be of moment or intricacy, unto the Justice-court; or otherwise name delegates in place of the Judges-ordinary, for these particular causes remitted to them: but where there is a collegiate court, so long as there

remains a *quorum*, against whom there is no exception, there ought no advocation to be passed.

6. It were of great importance for the security of the lieges, if the time of citation and execution were determinate in the matter of crimes. For some courts cannot judge in some crimes, unless it be within three suns from the commission of the crime. And the law hath secured the lieges' moveables, and other smaller interests, that execution may not be done within term of law, which is fifteen days. How necessary then were it, that there should be a fixed time for capital execution of criminal sentences, or these of like import, for the right of parties, and for preparation for death, and that access might be made to the Privy Council to stop execution, that the King might give pardon, if he found cause, and that the justices and their conjuncts might give their judgment, whether all things had legally proceeded, as is contained in the criminal process, or that they might reduce the sentence upon nullity or injustice; which were much more safe and fit than the accusing criminally the inquest.

7. The ordinary advocation is of civil processes, in matters which may be judged by the Lords in the second instance. It was introduced in place of appeals, and is a far more excellent remedy.

8. Appeals were accustomed, and in vigour with us, as in most other nations, but more peremptory than in any nation: for there was no time to appeal, but instantly at the pronouncing of the sentence; and there was a long train of appeals from court to court, and at last to delegates appointed by the King, before the institution of the Session. But of a long time there hath been no appeals allowed, or admitted in this kingdom; but, in place of appeals, advocations were introduced, stopping and removing processes, not at the humour or pleasure of parties, but by the judgment of the Lords, thus.

9. The manner of passing advocations is by bill presented to the Ordinary upon the Bills, and containing the reasons of advocation: which bill doth not pass of course, but upon special consideration of the reasons, by the Ordinary, and competent instructions produced; all which do appear from the copy of the process craved to be advocated, which ought to be produced, and which may not warrantably be refused by the clerk of the process, if required to give a double of the libel and minutes; or at least there ought to be produced an instrument bearing these duplicates to have been required, and either refused, or a competent time proposed by the clerk to transcribe them, and an instrument at that time, bearing, that a copy was not delivered, signed by the clerk. If the signed copy be produced, advocation should not be granted upon any alledgeance, but what was proponed and repelled, otherwise it would evacuate the jurisdiction of all inferior courts: for, albeit when advocations are passed and come to be disputed, the Lords may remit, yet the party delayed hath no more ordinarily but the protestation-money for his expenses and prejudice: and if the cause were remitted, there were too much probability, that the inferior judge would be too severe against him who did advocate, and few

persons against whom advocations are passed, will refuse to advocate of consent, if the other party will instantly insist in the principal cause before the Ordinary.

10. For eviting these inconveniencies, the Lords do of course grant warrant to the Ordinary on the Bills, to discuss the reasons of advocation on the bill: for if the advocation pass the Signet, it must abide the course of the roll; and albeit the roll of suspensions and advocations never be so far behind as the roll of ordinary actions, yet it would be too great a delay of justice, if the advocation behoved to go to the roll.

11. If no reason of advocation were sustained, but what was sustained or repelled, or where a copy of the process was not delivered, advocations now would make little delay. But the pretence of unskilfulness in procurators before inferior courts, and of parties being unwilling to propone declinators of the judges, is the ground that other reasons of advocation are admitted; which should not be sustained, seeing there is still a remedy by suspension.

12. The most ordinary reason of advocation is, upon the incompetency of the judge; which is elided by a party's prorogating the jurisdiction by proponing defences, without proponing declinators: for *primus actus judicii est judicis approbatorius;* yet if the defender propone declinators with other defences *simul*, these will not prorogate the jurisdiction, but will be understood as a vindication of the defender, that he is not litigious. But by the nature of the defences, the declinator must be first answered; and if it be repelled, it will be a relevant reason of advocation, if the verity of it be notour; as if the matter of the process be not under the jurisdiction of the judge; or the defender not dwelling within his district; which ordinarily are notour, and need no further probation. But if it be incompetency upon relation to the parties, which must have probation, if it be not notour, the proponer ought to come *paratus*, instantly to verify the same, by the oath of the party, the knowledge of the judge, or by witnesses ready to prove, who will not be rejected as ultroneous; because it being a dilatory defence must be instantly verified; so that, if witnesses without citation were not admitted, that just defence could not be proven, though it be matter of fact probable by them.

13. The relation declining the judge, is the same with the relation declining particular Lords of Session, which is lately [Declinature Act, 1681,c. 13; A.P.S. VIII,350,c.79], extended to uncles and aunts, nephews or nieces, by consanguinity; but as to affinity, only to brothers and sisters, and not to good-brothers marrying two sisters or good-sisters marrying two brothers. *Vide Lib.* 4, *Tit.* 39, §14.

14. Declinature upon enmity must also be instantly verified, and may be referred to the judge himself generally; but if it be otherwise proven, the facts inferring enmity must be particularly condescended upon; which may be proven by oath of the judge, by writ, or by witnesses, though not cited before.

15. The next reason of advocation is the judge's interest in the cause; or if it be instructed that *fovet consimilem causam*, having a cause in the same cir-

cumstances depending before another court; which also must be instantly verified, as aforesaid. This is not a reason of incompetency, but of suspicion of prejudice.

16. The fourth reason of advocation is the exemption of the defender from that court; which some have obtained by way of action, upon frequent acts of injustice; or otherwise by exemption upon privilege, as the members of the College of Justice are privileged by statute. But, in either case, if the parties propone other defences, they cannot return to their exemption.

17. The fifth reason of advocation is, upon the intricacy and importance of the cause, as if it come to a competition of heritable rights, or to a discussion of the nullity of decreets: for inferior judges have not power of reduction; except the Commissaries of Edinburgh, who can reduce other commissaries' decreets, and the Judge of Admiralty, who can reduce the decreets of other judges of admiralty. This will not exclude manifest nullities of original writs, as wanting of witnesses or designation of them. And as inferior courts cannot reduce, so neither can they improve any writ, that being proper to the Lords, either by certification, or by probation of the forgery, which uses to be remitted to the criminal court, if the Lords inflict not a lesser punishment than that of forgery.

18. The sixth ordinary reason of advocation is, that probation appears to be requisite *ex nobili officio*, which is not competent to any inferior court: and therefore, where there is reason to give acts before answer, for adducing evidences on the part of one party or more, from whence the point in question is to be inferred, it is a sufficient reason of advocation; as if old bonds be quarrellable upon circumstances or matters of fact, to prove their payment, or retiring, or if matters of trust be in question, no inferior judge can use such probation.

19. After litiscontestation, there is no relevant reason of advocation, except upon iniquity in the material justice of the cause, by sustaining an irrelevant libel, or an irrelevant defence, reply, duply, &c. or by rejecting a relevant libel, or repelling a relevant exception, reply, duply, &c. or by determining an incompetent manner of probation; which must also be instructed by a copy of the process, as aforesaid, or by instruments for not obtaining of the said copy subscribed.

20. There are three statutes limiting the Lords' jurisdiction in advocations. The first is in the end of c. 39. P. 1555 [A.P.S. 11,494,c.12], anent the warning of tenants, in these terms: "That no advocation of causes be taken by the Lords, from the judge-ordinary; except it be for deadly feud, or the sheriff-principal or judge-ordinary be party, or the causes of the Lords of Council, their advocates, scribes, and members." Which, though it appears to be general, yet, being an article in the act for warning of tenants, it is not to be generally extended, but in the advocation of removings. And yet even in these actions, it is in desuetude in several points, which, by custom, are sustained; as if the deputes have interest in the cause, unless the principal judge

sit, or another depute; or in the case of iniquity: but the Lords use to order that advocations of removings in the vacant time, be only passed by three Lords met together. The second statute restraining advocations, from competent judges, is, where the action is for sums within 200 merks, or whereunto the inferior judges are by law expressly appointed to be judges, c. 9. P. 1663 [A.P.S. VII,451,c.3], which is to be understood, where the inferior judges are by law appointed to be proper judges, as the Commissaries in confirmations and divorces. Yet even in these, inquity is a competent reason of advocation. The third statute limiting advocations, is, c. 16. P.1681 [A.P.S. VIII,351,c.82], whereby advocations are excluded in causes intented before the Admiral, even upon iniquity, because of the necessary dispatch of causes before that court; and therefore they are only remediable by suspension or reduction.

21. There is no necessity to offer a tenor of advocation, because it is uniformly observed amongst the writers.

Title 38. Preliminaries of Process

WE have now gone through the several kinds of actions, which precede litiscontestation and decreet; after which, only actions presupposing decreets do remain; such as reductions of decreets, or suspensions thereof, (under which are comprehended suspensions *super cessione bonorum*) diligences or executory actions, as inhibition, arrestment, actions for making arrested sums forthcoming, and adjudications. We come now to consider actions as they become processes; that is, till they receive further progress by sentences interlocutory or definitive; so that an action, though depending, is not yet a process, till there be an interlocutor upon it. Yet the summons, with the instructions thereof, either for the title passive or active, or for probation, is called a process, albeit properly it be not, until an interlocutor be upon it: for the first defence, and the most general in all actions, is dilatory, in this form, "No process for such a reason;" that is, there can be no further procedure in favour of the pursuer, whether by an interlocutory sentence, or by a decreet.

2. An action imports more than a cause, viz. That there is a warrant granted to cite parties, which should not be granted, unless the grounds of it be relevant, *i.e.* such as being proven, would infer the conclusion claimed; and therefore actions which have a fixed form go of course, and are expede by the Writers to the Signet, as they were before by the brieves out of the chancery, which are unquestionably relevant. But when they proceed upon bills, it would be too laborious a task, narrowly to consider what bills are just, but they are passed of course, *periculo petentium*, except in the case of bills of advocation and suspension, which pass not of course, but are read before the Ordinary, and passed upon consideration if the reasons be relevant, and have competent instructions. Yet a warrant for citing is not properly an action, till actual citation be added thereto; for a summons is so named *a summonendo*, because it advertises the party to appear before the judge; and a citation is *a*

citando, because it hastens the defender to compear at the term contained in the summons. But seeing the defenders may compear any moment in the hour of cause that day, they are not called till the next Sederunt day, or any day after; seeing summonses before the Lords are with continuation of days, which lasteth for a whole year; yet so, that the defenders are not obliged to attend all that time: for they may produce the copy of the summons which they received, the next day after the term, or any day thereafter within that year, and thereon crave protestation, bearing that, seeing the pursuer insists not, he can have no process till a new citation: but because the pursuer needs not then be present, seeing his advocate can do all that is then needful without information, the defender gets no expenses or protestation-money, upon the admitting of such protestations; and if any advocate appear and produce the summons, the clerk marks upon the margin thereof, the pursuer and defender's advocates, and appoints the defenders to see the summons, executions, and instructions: and though none appear for the pursuer, the protestation is not admitted that day, but the summons is called the next day, with certification; and the third day protestation is admitted and extracted; which formerly was passed of course by a clerk, but now must be signed by the Ordinary.

3. The executions do ordinarily bear, that such persons were cited to compear, "day and place within contained;" because, executors of summonses adventure not to determine upon what days the citation should proceed: and therefore the defender's advocate should not call upon the copy, to obtain protestation, till the competent days for such a summons be past, of which formerly. See *Lib.* 4, *Tit.* 3. §33. But if the summons be privileged as to the days of compearance, the term may be six days on this side of Dee, or fifteen on the other.

4. When the pursuer's advocate produces the summons, to exclude the protestation, the day of compearance is oft-times left blank, that the pursuer's advocate may fill in what day he pleaseth; but he should not fill up a longer day from the giving the execution, than the law requires; for thereby the defender would be obliged to an uncertain attendance: and therefore he may crave the incompetent day to be changed, as it should have been; which the clerk may do at the calling of it.

5. Sometimes the process is given out with the day of compearance blank. And, though the defender's advocates score the blank, or make it to a wrong day, it may be mended at the bar; seeing there is a rule as aforesaid, which, upon neither side, should be transgressed, and it deserves no new sight upon that alteration.

6. If there be many defenders, and different advocates, the clerk marks the process to be seen in such an advocate's house, who is answerable for the return of it; and unless the rest come to his house and advise, he should send it with a servant to be seen in his hand. But the pursuers do most prudently, who cause take it up, and give it to the several defenders apart.

7. Before the Regulations [Courts Act, 1672,c.16; A.P.S. viii,80,c.40],

there was great contention and trouble to the Lords, anent the getting back of process, and concerning the writs in the process: but by that Act, the pursuer sets down an inventory of his production, and under it a minute, bearing, "Given out by such an advocate, to such an advocate, such a day;" which being signed by the out-giver, prevents all questions about the production, and the time of returning; which is now little controverted, because the cause cannot be suddenly called, but must come in by its course in the roll; whereas, before the Regulations, it might have been called the same day on which it was returned; and this inventory of the process is a great security for the writs produced, which the defender's advocate is answerable for, seeing he may refuse to take in the process, if the inventory answer not the production. This inventory is also a mean to instruct what writs came to the clerk's hands; whereas, before this regulation, there was no remedy for recovering writs, but the oath of the receiver.

8. When a process is returned, the advocate who returns it must write thereon, "Seen and returned by me," and sign the same. But if, upon inspection, he find his clients not concerned he then writes, "Returned, as not being for the defender," and signs it. And when several advocates compear, for several parties, they should all write their returns upon the process when they have seen it; whereby, at calling of it in the roll, they cannot pretend they have not seen it, as ofttimes they do, and delay process, nor can they disclaim their appearance afterward.

9. After a process is returned, it may be offered to the keeper of the books of inrolment, upon any Saturday, at the hours appointed; and the producer may then see it insert according to the dates of the returns of these that are presented that day, in the book that is proper for that kind of process; for there is one book for suspensions, advocations, removings, ejections, and recent spuilzies, which are to be called upon Tuesdays and Wednesdays weekly; and another book for all other causes, except concluded causes, which have a particular book for the Inner-House; and there is another book for actions to be discussed in the Inner-House; yet these actions must first be inrolled for the Outer-House, and are thereafter inrolled for the Inner-House, not by the date of the returns, but by the great avisandum made in the Outer-House; as when great avisandum is made in the Outer-House for discussing the reasons of reduction of heritable rights of lands or annualrents, after the production is closed; or in probation of the tenors of writs destroyed or lost, after the adminicles are discussed; or in *cessiones bonorum :* or for determining of any point, which, upon report from the Outer-House, the Lords, for its importance or intricacy, have ordained to be heard in their own presence. Yet, before it be inrolled, the Lords *in præsentia* may call the cause then in debate, while it is recent in the minds of the pleaders, and makes no uncertain attendance; which cannot extend to more than a single point at once. But if once the cause be inrolled in the Inner-House roll, it cannot be called again, till it come in, in its course.

10. The execution of summonses, and all diligences, was of old done by the sheriffs, while processes proceeded upon brieves out of the chancery, as they do yet execute these brieves which remain. But since the institution of the College of Justice, though any person was sufficient to execute summonses, wherein there was no special certification, yet the old style was so far retained, that the summonses are still directed to sheriffs in that part specially constitute by the Lords, for whose name there is a blank left to be filled up by the pursuers at their pleasure. But, if the certification in the summons be, that if the party cited to give his oath, appear not, he shall be holden as if he did appear and did confess the verity of the points referred to his oath, then the execution must be by a messenger at arms, against the party personally apprehended, unless the party be out of the country; for then the messenger must execute the summons at the market-cross of Edinburgh, and pier and shore of Leith [IV,3,31,*supra*; IV,47,4,*infra*]; and in either case, the summons must bear the certification "To be holden as confessed." The reason of this certification is, because Edinburgh is *communis patria*, and every provident man is supposed to have an ordinary procurator there, who may take notice of public citations at the cross; and when the process is called, if he be still out of the country, he will either get a long term, or a commission to depone.

11. If parties be latent, vagabonds, or have no domicile, or if they dwell or haunt where there is not *tutus accessus*, the summons bears special warrant upon the notoriety thereof, to cite them at the nearest market-cross to the places where they dwell or haunt, to which there is safe access; wherein there may be certification to be holden as confessed, as against persons out of the country.

12. The executions of summons do properly signify the acts done by the executor thereof; but, because these acts are expressed in the attestation of the executor, that attestation is called the execution, or the indorsation, because the same uses to be written on the back of the summons. These executions of old were called "the rehearse of the summoner made in court by writ or word, having sufficient witnesses of diverse baronies, who shall swear in court that they by-stood, saw and heard, and for witnesses were tane, where the summoner made the summons, &c. cap.113. Parl. 1429 [Act 1429,c.112; A.P.S. 11,15,c.2]." And thereafter executions of summonses did only require that the same were stamped or sealed by the officer, otherwise to make no faith, cap. 33. Parl. 1469 [Act 1469,c.32; A.P.S. 11,95,c.8]. The signet or stamp must have upon it the first letter of the executor's mane, or surname, or some other thing that shall be universally known to be his signet, cap. 74. Parl. 1540 [A.P.S. 11,359,c.9]. The reason hereof was, because at that time few executors could write. But little notice was taken what was upon the stamp, and any vestige of a stamp in old executions was sufficient. But now all executions must be subscribed by the executor, and the witnesses; so that there is no necessity of a stamp: for wherever the executor does subscribe

and design himself, it is more effectual than the stamp; for thereby there is a better mean to improve the executions, than by the stamp, cap. 4. Parl. 1686 [Citations Act, 1686,c.4; A.P.S. VIII,586,c.5].

13. Executions of summonses are of diverse tenors: for if the parties cited be personally apprehended, or if he be cited at his dwelling-house, or at the market-cross nearest his dwelling or haunt, or if at the market-cross of Edinburgh, and pier of Leith, as out of the country, the executions must differ accordingly. But in all executions the executor's name and designation must be expressed, and the letters which are his warrant; as also the names and designations of the parties, pursuers and defenders, must be expressed, and not related generally, as they used formerly to bear only, "the persons within written," cap. 6. Parl. 1672 [Summons Execution Act, 1672,c.6; A.P.S. VIII,64,c.6]; yet if the executions be written on the back of the summons, and not in schedules apart, though the execution bear but "the persons within written" generally, it may suffice. The executions must also bear the day of compearance, which is ordinarily left blank till the summons be called, as hath been said. They also use to bear the place of compearance, "at Edinburgh, or where it shall happen the Lords to be for the time;" because of old the Session had no fixed place: but being now fixed, the mention of the place is not necessary, unless the King should command the Session to sit elsewhere.

14. The days of compearance at first were very long, but were settled to be on twenty-one days' warning, cap. 6. Parl. 1466 [A.P.S. II,85,c.7], which is to be understood of the first summons: for the second summons is upon six or fifteen days. See §3, *hoc. Tit.* But executions at the market-cross of Edinburgh, and pier of Leith, must be upon sixty days for the first summons, and fifteen days for the second. But second citations against parties within Edinburgh, or the suburbs, pass upon twenty-four hours. Privileged summonses are ordinarily upon six days. But as to this, the Lords made an Act of Sederunt, of the 21st June 1672, of which we have already spoken, *Lib.* 4, *Tit.* 3. §33. The executions must also bear, "for the cause, to the effect, and with certification contained in the summons."

15. Executions of summonses against parties personally apprehended, must bear so: and it were very fit, that they bear the place where, which would be a mean of improbation, if there were stronger evidence of the parties being *alibi*. They must also bear a copy delivered, or at least offered and refused: which copy must be subscribed by the executor thereof, cap. 139. Parl. 1592 [Citation Act, 1592,c.141; A.P.S. III,573,c.59]. The giving of a copy is the most essential part of the execution, which contains all the other points which use to be expressed, and may supply the defect of them, especially where the party cited is personally apprehended; but in other executions the manner of leaving the copy is necessary, and is prescribed by cap. 75. Parl. 1540 [Citation Act 1540,c.75; A.P.S. II,359,c.10], bearing, "That if the executors cannot apprehend the person, they shall pass to the gate or door of

the principal dwelling-house, where he actually resides for the time, and there shall desire to have entrance, and shall show the letters to the servants of the house, or other famous witnesses, and offer the copy thereof to the servants; but if they refuse, he shall affix the same upon the gate or door. But if they get not entrance, they shall first knock at the gate or door six knocks, and shall affix the copy upon the said gate or door." These knocks are not to be given if there be access to the rooms where the servants are. And certainly the giving of the copy to the wife or bairns is more effectual than to servants. But these who design to steal through sentences, without lawful executions, do either give no knocks, or not such audible knocks as may be heard in the rooms of the house; and sometimes they cause carry away the copy after they have affixed it, whereby their executions will not only be a falsehood, but a forgery.

16. All executions at market-crosses, or at the pier of Leith, must be by messengers, and must bear his going to the market-cross in due time of day, when people may take notice; and before he read the summons, he must, with audible voice, cry three Oyesses: the design whereof is to convocate people, to hear and give notice; and then he must read the letters, and require the witnesses being present, and must affix a copy upon the cross or pier. All which must be expressed in the executions.

17. Before executions were subscribed by the executor and witnesses, if objections were made against them at the bar, the pursuer was allowed to amend the same, abiding thereby as true, which cannot be now done. Yea, if an execution be once produced, another execution of a different tenor will not be admitted, though subscribed by the executor and witnesses; because it is not safe to fix the verity of the execution upon their memory: and therefore the executor and witnesses should sign the execution when it is done.

18. In all summonses there must be pursuers, one or more, and defenders one or more. There must also be an active title of the pursuers, and a passive title of the defenders, expressed or implied. And if these titles require writ, the same must be produced before decreet. The active titles must be anterior to the day of compearance, at least before calling of the process in presence of the judge: yet in accessory titles the judge will allow them to be produced *cum processu*; as when an heir pursues for an heritable debt, and claims likewise the bygone annualrents, he must produce his retour as heir: but he may confirm the annualrents, and produce the confirmation *cum processu*. If the pursuer expect a decreet without litiscontestation, he must instruct the passive title when the process is called by the judge: but if he take a term to prove, it is sufficient to prove the passive title at that term.

19. Active titles are either original or by progress. Original titles are where the right is originally in the pursuer. But titles by progress are either retours on services of heirs, or confirmation of executors, or assignations, or translations, or gifts to donatars, or dispositions voluntary or judicial,

or a collateral interest from whence the conclusion of the summons is justly and legally inferred.

20. Passive titles are these wherein the defenders must be passive, either by being decerned to pay or perform, or to suffer, permit, or not repugn; which is in all declaratory actions, wherein parties cited must not hinder the effect of the summons, except by way of reduction upon just reasons.

21. When there can be no special defender condescended on, citations are allowed to be at the market-cross against all and sundry, to the effect that if any have interest, they may appear and defend. And in some actions citation must be upon the ground of the land, and a copy left there; which is also to give notice to any possessors, that they may defend. Yea, if any other have interest, though neither called generally nor specially, and that interest be evident from the process, or otherwise be produced, they will not only be admitted to defend, but to compete and crave preference.

22. In summonses *cognitionis causa*, the apparent heirs must be called, though they have renounced to be heirs. And they are called in declaratory actions though they be not entered. And likewise the nearest of kin must be called in summonses *cognitionis causa*, for obtaining confirmations, if the debt be not liquid, that the pursuer may be confirmed as executor-creditor. And summonses of adjudication proceed against apparent heirs.

23. When pupils and minors are pursued, their tutors and curators must be cited; but it will suffice that they be cited at the market-cross without naming them, but only that the minor is cited "with his tutors and curators, if he any have, for their interests."

24. The passive titles by progress are, as heirs, executors, wives, bairns, legatars, or as behaving as heirs, by intromitting with the heirship-moveables, or rents of lands, or the stock, or annualrents of sums, whereunto they have right as heirs; or by lucrative titles after contracting of the debt in question; or as vitious intromitters with the moveables of defuncts. All these special titles, active and passive, are largely explicated, *Lib.* 3. of these Institutions.

25. The implied titles are oft-times without writ; thus in pursuits for debt the pursuer's title is as creditor, and the defender's is as debtor, which needs not be so expressed; but in progressive titles they must be more particularly expressed, especially the active titles, as having right by progress, or as having good and sufficient interest to pursue the action.

26. In all summonses there must be a certification expressed or implied. In special certifications the same must be expressed; and other certifications are but generally expressed: as that "the Lords will proceed to do justice," which is sufficiently expressed when the summons bears "with certification, &c." Or, though no certification be mentioned, yet it is implied when the summons bears to cite the defenders "to hear and see it found and declared," or "to hear and see the premises verified and proven, and them decerned:" for thereby it is implied, that the Lords will proceed to do justice against them, as well when they are contumacious in not appearing, as when they do

appear: or when parties are cited to depone, it imports the certification of being holden as confessed.

27. It is an useful point in the law of this kingdom, that all civil judges do proceed to do justice, although defenders compear not, if they be lawfully cited; and that because of their contumacy: and therefore, if the summons bear, that the pursuer refers any point to the defender's oath, either simply or in so far as shall not be proven by writ, he will be holden as confessed. And if the pursuer pursue for improbation of any writ, the certification is, that if the writ be not produced, it shall be holden and reputed as false and forged; and therefore can never be made use of against that pursuer, his heirs or successors, as to that cause only. Or if the pursuer produce writs to instruct his summons, the Lords will advise the summons and writs, and decern as if the defender did appear. Or if the pursuer libel relevantly, the Lords will assign a term to prove. Upon all such processes all execution proceeds, as well as upon decreets wherein the defenders have compeared. But if the relevancy of probation be dubious, the same is represented to the Lords before they give act or decreet; and yet, in the second instance, they will hear the parties thereupon, as if the decreet had passed of course; but they so advise processes in absence, that defenders be not put to trouble where there is no relevant cause, albeit they be absent.

The law of many civil nations hath been defective in this: the Romans did seldom so proceed; but in possessory judgments they put the pursuer in possession, much to the same purpose as we do in single reductions, wherein the implied certification is, that the defender's rights shall be reduced, ay and while they be produced; whereby the pursuer enjoys the fruits till he be put *in mala fide* by a reduction, and by production of a better right in that reduction: and, therefore, the Romans did compel defenders to compear, and did give warrant to the pursuers to bring them by force before the judge, which sometimes they might do without a special warrant: but that is not in use with us, as being the occasion of resistance and breach of peace. Likewise the law of England gives no judgment against defenders absent, as to the cause, (but only gives an out-lawry against them, whereby they lose the benefit of law till they appear) except in cases of treason, wherein they proceed to condemn absents, but give them a year thereafter to appear and vindicate themselves [IV,3,29-31,*supra*].

But though our law proceed against contumacious absents in civil matters, yet not in criminals: for there must be more caution, in decerning against the life, members, fame, or freedom of persons, than against their estates; and therefore the Secret Council, and all criminal judges, must stop till parties be present. But criminal libels contain a certification that parties cited shall be declared fugitives, and denounced rebels; and thereupon caption is granted. And sometimes they are commanded to appear under the pain of treason, and letters of fire and sword are given out against them. Yet the Parliament proceeds in matters of treason against absents. And the criminal judges are, by a

late statute, authorised to proceed against absents in treason for open rebellion, and bearing arms against the King, cap. 11, Parl. 1669 [A.P.S. VII,562,
c.17].

28. The reason justifying the certification of being holden as confessed,
is, that it is a presumption of law, that the defender absents himself, because
upon his oath he dares not deny the libel. And the like reason is for the certification against writs to be declared false and forged; for there the law presumes that the defender keeps them up, because he knows that if they were
produced, they would be proven to be false, and he would be remitted to the
criminal judges, to be punished as a forger. This certification is the great
mean to secure the rights of the people, especially land-rights: for all who by
the records, or by fame, or any suspicion, may be feared to pretend right, being called, are excluded for ever from making use of the writs against which
such a decreet of certification is extracted; which is the strongest certification, and is scarce capable of reduction, or being reponed against, if there be
no nullity, or forgery of the executions, and that recently questioned, for
thereafter none are obliged to produce executions. But there are more easy
remedies against other certifications, viz. by suspension or reduction: for if
probable excuses of the contumacy be adduced, parties will be reponed to
their oaths recently, before other rights proceed upon the decreet. And parties are heard against other decreets in absence, of course, and are not put to
pay the expense of the decreet or attendance before they be heard, even
though they pretend no excuse for contumacy: but the consideration of expenses is reserved to the event of the cause.

29. By what hath been said, it will be evident what is the reason of the
name certification, viz. that thereby it is made known to the defender for certain, what the judges will do against him if he do not compear.

30. Formerly summonses were continued, and act and letters granted
for a second citation, till by cap. 6, Parl. 1672 [Summons Execution Act,
1672,c.6; A.P.S. VIII,64,c.6], it was appointed, that instead thereof, there
should be two diets in all summonses, which before used to be continued.
Summonses were not to be continued which were instantly proven by writ.
But if they were to be proven by witnesses, or oath of party, they were to be
continued, and so required two citations. The second citation may not be
made till the term of compearance in the first be past [IV,2,2,*supra*].

Title 39. Processes in so far as discussed without Litiscontestation

WE come now to the discussing of processes, wherein the chief duty of the
judge, and the interest of parties is concerned; for what was done before,
passed for most part of course. But now the process is considered, as it is called before the judge, to determine either the relevancy or probation, or both.
And here is to be explained, the discussing of processes without litiscontestation; which frequently occurs. And in this, our forms differ from the Roman
law, in which no sentence could be without litiscontestation: for by that term,

they understood the pursuer's deducing his cause before the judge, in presence of the defender, who had power to answer and dispute if he pleased, there being no sentence in the cause till the defender appeared; and therefore they by litiscontestation, and by the *etymon* of the word, understood the parties controverting or contesting in a plea. But our law understands not the term in that sense: for by litiscontestation, with us, is meant a judicial act of process, for proving such points by either party, as the judge determines to be relevant, the proving whereof, or the failing in proving of the same, will give a decreet condemnator or absolvitor, without further dispute on the relevancy, or manner of probation, (for both are determined by that act.) Unless some point be emergent, or new come to knowledge before conclusion of the cause.

2. By acts of litiscontestation sometimes one, and sometimes both parties have terms admitted to their probation. And therefore contestation of pleas with us, is to be understood by its *etymon ;* importing a warrant for either, or both parties, to adduce *contestes ;* and *testes* by their native signification, comprehends not only witnesses, but writs, whereby parties testify the truth of things contained in the writ, as well as by their depositions. Instead of this term, the English use the term of joining issue; that is, of settling the points, whereupon the issue of the process will follow.

3. Processes with us, are said to be discussed, when the relevancy thereof is determined; for the whole office of judges is in determining the justice and truth of pleas, or the point of fact, and the point of right arising from that fact; *ex facto enim jus oritur.*

4. The English do commonly join the point of fact and right, and so allow witnesses for either party upon any point they think fit, and then judge what point of right there ariseth from the fact proven by either party. Our ancient custom did not allow this way in any case, being tenacious in this axiom, *frustra probatur quod probatum non relevat*, and with very good reason, that people should not be put to the trouble and expense to adduce witnesses, before it were determined what points would be effectual if they were testified; beside that oaths should not be taken in vain. And therefore a great part of our debates were, which of the parties should have the benefit of probation, or be burdened to prove; for sometimes it is a benefit to have the choice of the witnesses, and oft-times it is a burden to be necessitated to prove: for what the law or the judge presumes to be true, needs no probation, and sometimes admits no contrary probation; but where it admits contrary probation, it burdens that party to prove, against whom the presumption lies. For instance, it is a common brocard, negatives prove themselves; that is, they are presumed, and need no probation: but on the contrary, *affirmanti incumbit probatio.* As to the burden or benefit of probation; whenever allegeances to be proven were contrary, the dispute ran who should be preferred to prove; as in reductions upon minority, if the defender offered to prove the party when obliged was major; or if in spuilzies or wrongous intromission, the defender offered to prove voluntary delivery or lawful poinding, or a warrant for intromission, these alle-

geances were contrary to the libel [1,9,19–20, *supra*], or when in reductions on death-bed, the pursuer offered to prove that the defunct when he granted the right in question, had contracted sickness, and the defender offered to prove *liege poustie* and health [IV,3,2; IV,20,48, *supra*]; in which contest, the most strong and pregnant probation offered, was preferred; as that which was by writ or instrument, against that which was by oath or witnesses; or that which was offered to be proven by witnesses above all exception, and persons of great reputation, was preferred to ordinary witnesses. And unless there were great odds in pregnancy, the pursuer was preferred to the defender in allegeances contrary to the libel; and the defender was preferred to prove his defence, contrary to the reply of the pursuer; and he in his reply was preferred to the contrary allegeance of the defender in his duply.

5. But by more recent custom, the Lords have of a long time, *ex nobili officio*, preferred neither party to the proving of contrary allegeances; but before answer for determining the relevancy, they have allowed either party to adduce so many witnesses, to be examined upon such points as the Lords found fit to be cleared, for instructing of the cause; but did not allow contrary probation, but only allow the choice of the witnesses to either party, and in that case they admitted witnesses, though not above exception, when the point of fact was of difficile probation. These acts are therefore called acts before answer, and have the same effect as acts of litiscontestation; for in both, the parties must propone all their allegeances, and will ordinarily get no more witnesses but what are in the first diligence. And there may be in the same act some points to be proven before answer, and some to be proven *peremptoriè*, the relevancy being before discussed.

6. There are several cases, in which decreet may be obtained without litiscontestation. As, 1. When the cause proceeds upon special certification, as to be holden as confessed, if the advocate for the defender compear, and produce his client to depone, who instantly doth depone at the bar, if the oath be plain and clear without doubtfulness, the Ordinary will instantly take the oath and advise it, and condemn or absolve accordingly. Here there is no act of litiscontestation, nor any term taken to prove. But if the defender's advocate take a term to produce his client not appearing, there is a term assigned, and litiscontestation made.

7. The second case is, in improbations, wherein the certification is, that if the writs called for be not produced, they shall be holden as false and feigned; if none compear for the defender, a decreet of certification is pronounced of course: or if there be compearance, and some writs be produced, the defender may allege that he hath produced sufficiently to exclude all that the pursuer hath produced, which the Ordinary may presently determine, and if he find the production sufficient, may assoilzie, or give the Lords answer; whereby if that defence be repelled, the defender may produce more writs, and the Ordinary may in the same way determine thereanent: but the defender can make no further partial productions, otherwise he might debate so

long as he had a new document to produce; unless he declare he will produce no further: for then he may dispute upon the third production; and though he do not so declare, yet he will get a term to produce, as if he had not produced, and yet that term is not accounted as litiscontestation, but it is called a term for production, albeit if nothing be produced, decreet of certification will follow. And if production be made, so that the reasons of reduction come to be disputed, there rarely follows litiscontestation; because the defenders can allege upon no other writ, seeing certification is extracted *contra non producta* although production be made, unless the pursuer hold the production satisfied, or the defender declare he passeth from any more. But the pursuer is not excluded from offering to prove by other writs than his titles produced, and thereupon litiscontestation may be made: otherwise the decreet is without litiscontestation; unless, in the discussing of the reasons of reduction, there occur points which are probable by oath or witnesses, as prescription, part and pertinent, &c.

8. Thirdly, In simple reductions without improbation, the certification expressed or implied is, upon the general reasons libelled; as that the writs called for are vitiated, or are null as wanting witnesses, or wanting the designation of witnesses: and therefore, if there be no compearance, or sufficient production to exclude the pursuers, there follows a decreet without litiscontestation.

9. Fourthly, If the pursuer verify his summons by writ, the defender being absent, the Ordinary alone can advise and determine; but, in case of difficulty, he will represent the case to the Lords, whereupon decreet will follow without litiscontestation. But if the defender compear, and do not propone a relevant allegeance, decreet will also instantly follow.

10. Fifthly, In the action to insist, with certification not to be heard thereafter (of which formerly, *Lib.* 4, *Tit.* 16.) if none compear, or compearing do not take a term to insist; certification is admitted, and it is declared that the defender shall never be heard again in that cause. Which also is a decreet absolvitor without litiscontestation.

11. Lastly, In processes where all is proven, by writ produced at first, by either party, there is no term, nor litiscontestation, and little dispute concerning the relevancy; because the defender, before he produce any writs for his defence, will dispute first the relevancy; and if that be sustained, will then produce; and in the dispute, there is no mention of relevancy, but the ordinary terms are the points alleged, or the writs produced are not to be respected, for such reasons.

12. Relevancy is only disputed, when acts of litiscontestation are craved, and terms to prove. The meaning of relevancy (which is more accustomed with us than elsewhere) imports, the justice of the point that is alleged to be relevant. But under the allegeance that such points are not relevant, the meaning is, that though the points alleged were proven, they would not justly infer the point deduced from them: for relevancy imports the relieving or

helping the alleger: and the English mean the same thing, when they say, the plea is not good; for by goodness, that special kind of goodness, viz. justice, is meant.

13. It will be proper here to consider dilatory defences; the effect whereof, when they are just, terminates the instance, and gives an absolvitor from that instance, without any term to prove; for all dilators must be instantly verified, and have no acts of litiscontestation, unless they be proponed *peremptorie;* in which case they cease to be dilators, and become peremptors; as when improbation is proponed against executions, if it be proponed *peremptorie,* a term will be assigned to improve; and therefore dilators being common to actions that are without, and with litiscontestation, they are most proper to be handled here: so that there will remain for the next title, the relevancy of summons, exceptions, replies and duplies, and the species of them which are common to many actions: for these which are proper to the several actions have been considered with their proper actions; as also their proper dilators are insinuated in the requisites of every action, implied or expressed.

14. The first common dilatory defence comprehends all declinators, according to that common axiom in all nations, *primus actus judicii est judicis approbatorius.* This defence extends to all judges supreme and subordinate; but not to arbiters, who have no authority, and whose sentences have legal execution, only by virtue of the clause of registration in the submission, and at the end of the blank on the other side thereof, wherein the decreet-arbitral is to be filled up: and so it is effectual for compelling the parties to attend the diets of the arbiters, and to obey their orders; wherein the certification is, the penalty in the submission. But a judge-ordinary having authority, albeit it be limited, yet if the defender decline not, he becomes competent for that action; and therefore advocations ought not to be granted, where parties have proponed defences peremptory or even dilatory, if the same be not proponed before, or at least with declinator. But here we are only to consider declinators against the Session, or members thereof. Declinators from the members of the Session are not competent upon account of the clerks; because they are but servants, and must be under the command and over-ruling of the Lords, and even under command of the Ordinaries, in that which is proper to their charge. There is more reason of declinator of clerks in inferior courts, where there is but one judge, and commonly the clerk has a great influence; and therefore, if he be declined, the judge may substitute another for that action.

The declinators against particular Lords of Session are determined by two statutes, as to affinity or consanguinity. The first is, cap. 212. Parl. 1594 [Declinature Act, 1594,c.212; A.P.S. IV,67,c.22], bearing, "That no Senator of the College of Justice shall sit or vote, in any action or cause, where the pursuer or defender is either his father, brother, or son, but be declined therein." The other statute is, cap. 13. Parl. 1681 [Declinature Act, 1681,c.13; A.P.S. VIII,350,c.79], whereby declinators of the Lords are extended to these degrees of affinity, as well as consanguinity, so that a Lord cannot sit or vote, where the pursuer or defender is either his father-in-law, brother-in-law, or son-in-law; nor yet where he is uncle or nephew. And these declinators are extended to all other judicatures. But affinity to the wives or husbands of uncles, aunts, nephews or nieces, affords no declinator, but under father is comprehended grand-father, or great-grand-father, &c.

It is a competent reply against all these declinators, that the judge declined is of equal relation to either party; for then the ground of suspicion upon inequality of affection ceaseth.

Declinators are also competent against a particular Lord, upon other common grounds; as if he be interested in the cause, or even *si foveat consimilem causam*, if he have the like cause depending; or if he hath given partial counsel in the cause, by instigating the plea, giving positive advice in law, or being present at consultations in the cause. But it doth give no ground of declinator, if a party inform any of the Lords before intenting the cause, and he dissuade him from intenting it, and tell him that it is not just, legal, or not honourable; or if judicially in exercing his office, he do positively offer what may be sustained, though it be not proposed, whether it be *in jure* or *in facto*, by showing that the allegeance as proponed is not relevant, but might be relevant in such other terms.

Declinators are not competent against any of the Lords upon pretence of enmity, hatred, or prejudice against either party: for the Lords are supposed to be men of greater virtue, than to entertain such: for they must speak to any of the King's lieges, who come before them in their office; and none may refuse to speak to them in exercising the same, or show any token of disrespect or prejudice, by murmuring against their judicial actings, which is punishable by the Institution of the College of Justice.

Declinators are also competent against several Lords, ordinary or extraordinary, by Act of Sederunt [A.S. 6 Nov.1677], if they have received or heard any solicitation, or verbal information in the cause, during the dependence thereof; or if any missive letter be offered, if they read the same before they present it to the Lords; if they did not use all means they could to stop or withdraw from hearing any further thereof, except in the verbal informations of parties, or other persons for them, required or allowed judicially; or before auditors in diets appointed for both parties to be heard; or before Ordinaries upon the Bills in passing of bills; or in case of accommodation by consent or order of the Lords. And likewise the Lords, by a late Act of Sederunt [A.S. 11 Nov.1690], have obliged themselves upon their honour, to observe that Act, though they be not declined; and this they do subscribe every Session; which now is much more easy to be observed, seeing all informations and bills relating to interlocutors given, or to be given, are conveyed to the Lords, by boxes placed in the Session-house, having slits, at which the same may be put in, but cannot be taken out, but by the several Lords themselves.

Declinators against the whole Lords, is upon the limitations of their jurisdiction, which are all set down at large, *Tit.* 1. of this fourth book.

15. The second branch of common dilators is, upon the incompetency of discussing the cause *hoc ordine*, which differs from the defence against relevancy: for a process may be just, and yet not competent in the way proposed; as in all causes where declarator must precede an action petitory, all petitory actions thereupon are incompetent, till declarator precede. All the titles upon declarators above explained do show, what are these actions petitory, which declarators must precede; and therefore there are as many dilators upon incompetency, as are the declarators in these titles. In these titles there is no declarator insisted in, but what must precede a petitory action, and not other declarators: for there is no right but is capable of declarator.

16. The third branch of dilators is, upon the executions, and upon all the formalities required therein. And, 1. Upon the common formalities of ordinary summons, which are contained in the preceding title; any of which being omitted, affords a dilatory defence. As if the executions of summons have not witnesses designed; it is a dilatory excluding process; or if the designation be too general, it must be made more special, that it may be capable of improbation, which is of that moment, that if the verity of the executions be improven, it will annul the decreet following upon such executions, albeit it be a decreet *in foro contradictorio :* or if the executor and witnesses subscribe not, after the act appointing the same to be so subscribed: in which the witnesses must be so designed, as they may be found out.

And, secondly, any of the solemnities requisite in executions, being proven not to be true, it is a forgery, and is not only a false assertion, which many times is no forgery: for what is asserted in writs, though it be not true, makes not the writ false as forged; but it is not so in executions; for thereby the messengers, or other executors forge or make up executions, which they never did act; as if their executions bear the defenders to be personally apprehended, or a copy given; or if executions bear to be done at the dwelling-house, because the executor could not find the party personally, if it be proven, that there was patent access to the party without close doors or gates, or that upon the knocking they were opened, and yet the execution was not made by giving a copy to the party, or to some of his domestics; or if it bear that the party was personally apprehended, and a copy given, or offered and refused; or if it bear that the executor knocked, when yet the doors or gates were patent; or if it bear six knocks given, when yet so many were not given, or if they were not audibly given; or if it bear a copy left and affixed upon the most patent door, when yet it was not so affixed and left, but that either it was not affixed, but put in the hole of a lock, that there might be no vestige of it, or being affixed, it was not left, but taken away in the view of the executor and witnesses; or if the day of executing be not true; or if the oyesses at the market-cross be not audible; or if the reading of the summons, and affixing copies on the cross be not true, and so at the Pier of Leith; these, or any of these being found not true, make the executors forgers, and the witnesses accessory, and do turn the decreets albeit *in foro* unto libels; wherein the reply of competent and omitted is not receivable, unless they be proponed and sustained *peremptorie;* because, being proponed *dilatorie*, they could not then be proven.

But, thirdly, If the competent days be not given by the execution, till the day of compearance, it is a sufficient dilator. But if it be passed over, it cannot annul the following decreet, because it was competent and omitted; and when parties do appear, albeit the days be not full, they do not stick at it, if the difference be small, or if they do, the Lords may over-rule it; and yet it will be no nullity: for these formalities in process, make only nullities, when the Lords give no interlocutor, but they pass of course, and are left to the diligence of parties and their advocates, as when any point necessary to be proven, is not proven, or when the extracted decreet is not conform to the minutes, when recently questioned. The competent days are not to be reckoned by the privilege of summons, unless they have a competent privilege: for any other privilege of time is *periculo petentium*, as was formerly shown.

And, lastly, dilators do arise from the number of citations, viz. Where all is proven by writ or by presumption, there needs but one citation; but if the probation be by oath, or witnesses, there must be two citations.

17. The fourth branch of dilators is, upon the not production of the titles requisite to be produced *in initio litis*, as is declared in the former Title; wherein is shown what may be produced *cum processu*, which therefore affords a reply to that dilator.

18. The last branch of dilators is, that the date of these titles that must be produced *ab initio*, is posterior to the citation; for the design of citations is not only to give time, that parties may come to the place of judicature, but that they may prepare themselves to defend, and consider whether they will satisfy or plea; for if they offer due satisfaction, though it be refused, they escape expenses of plea.

Title 40. Discussing of Ordinary Actions, till Final Sentence, or till Litiscontestation

ORDINARY actions are here meant, in opposition to suspensions or reductions of decreets, which are to be considered after decreets; and so advocations are here to be comprehended. The reasons of advocation, and the exceptions against the same, are treated of *Lib.* 4. *Tit.* 37. which relates only to them, as the cause is advocated, but not as to the cause itself, for when it is once advocated, it proceeds as any other action in the first instance.

2. The manner of discussing advocations is thus: when an advocation is called by the roll, the defender in the advocation produces the copy of the advocation, formerly called by the clerk; and craves a protestation and remit; that is, that he may have a sentence of the Lords, remitting the cause to the court from which it was advocated. And if there be no appearance for the raiser of the advocation, protestation and remit is granted of course, without consideration, whether the reasons of advocation were relevant and instructed,

or not; which is a kind of decreet-absolvitor. And this protestation contains fifteen pounds Scots to be paid, which is the ordinary expenses; but if there be extraordinary litigiousness, and no probable ground, the Lords may, and sometimes do, add further expenses.

3. If the raiser of the advocation compear, he repeats his reasons of advocation, which must be in writ, and if they be not in the body of the advocation, they are added in a paper apart. And he ought to mention what reason he insists on, for he may choose what order he will follow in his reasons. If the Ordinary find not the reasons insisted on relevant, and instructed, he will remit the cause. But he will allow no term to instruct the reason: for in this part of the process, there are no terms to prove, but all must be instantly verified. And albeit testificates will not prove in the principal cause, they will instruct reasons of advocation; where the suspicion of the inequality of the judge, on any account, is ground enough to call the process from him. And so the Ordinary proceeds in the several reasons, and should not allow the other party to answer such reasons as he sees clearly are not relevant. And when he finds any reason relevant and instructed, he requires the other party to answer, and so determines; and he seldom reports, the matter being so ordinary, and of so small moment. If he sustain a reason as relevant and instructed, he then advocates the cause; whereupon there used an act to be extracted, before the Act of Regulations [Courts Act, 1672,c.16; A.P.S. viii,80,c.40]; and till that were done, there was no further process: but now, the Ordinary ought immediately to proceed to the principal cause, in the same way, as if the principal cause had been raised before the Lords in the first instance. So there is no more specialty in discussing of advocations.

4. By the discussing of causes, is here understood the bringing them to a decreet, or act of litiscontestation; by which act the points to be proven by either party are fixed and determined, that according as these points shall be proven or not proven, decreet condemnator or absolvitor will follow, without any further dispute as to relevancy, unless some point emergent or new come to knowledge be represented by bill. But if the Lords find not the bill to be relevant and competent, it ought to be instantly rejected without an answer; yet if the point proposed be dubious, or do contain pregnant grounds of law, though no new point of fact, with some excuses of not proponing these allegeances before extracting the act of litiscontestation, and which do, at least indirectly, debate against the justice of the interlocutor, (wherein there is ordinarily much keenness and clamour expressed, and if there be any impertinent reflection, the Lords will call and censure the drawer of the bill, and will appoint such words to be expunged) the Lords will either refuse the bill, or pitch upon the points they think deserve hearing, and will remit to the Ordinary who heard the cause, to hear the parties on these points. But now they do not admit written answers, which take up so much time, and so swell decreets with impertinent clamour, unless the bill relate to interlocutors upon hearing *in præsentia*, and then they ordain the other parties to answer: but

they either refuse the bill, if they see cause, or pitch on the points they think deserve hearing, and appoint the parties to be heard *in præsentia* thereupon; but do not change the interlocutor till new hearing. But if, upon the new dispute, the Lords be not generally convinced, they will not alter by the mere plurality; otherwise there could never be certainty in acts of litiscontestation. For suppose one *quorum* have determined *pro*, and another *quorum* of different members determine *contra*, carrying the point by a vote or two, parties would ever watch their opportunity, as they conceived the Lords of the several Sederunts to favour them, and would never miss to press new clamorous bills, to obtain an alteration, and so a third sederunt might make a second alteration, and so forth; so that justice could not be dispatched: and therefore the first vote, when no party could make a choice, is always to be sustained, unless a new *quorum* do generally alter; which will rarely occur, but when it doth occur, the Lords ought to concur in it; for they do not own an infallibility of their judgment, nor should they ever prefer their honour (in that they saw not so much at first as at last) to justice, which should still have place till the last stroke of justice be given, by a formal decreet *in foro contradictorio*, which the Lords have no authority to recal, because of that great and universal law, absolutely necessary for the security and quiet of nations, that, in every well-governed commonwealth, there must be some definitive sentence, which must seclude all fear or suspicion of being alterable, or even to come to a new dispute upon the matter, but that the opponing of that sentence, without saying further, must be *hic murus ahæneus esto* [IV,1,46,*supra*].

5. To prevent the inconvenience of altering interlocutors, the Lords are accustomed, immediately upon the hearing of a cause in the Outer-House, to call in a dubious and nice debatable point to be determined in their presence. And if, after interlocutor, they find probability of alteration, upon representation by bill, they do also call the same in their presence. And if, after all, the matter be very dubious and important, as a leading case, whereof full informations have been given to all the Lords, they determine it when all are present, except the Ordinary upon the bench. But after the second hearing in presence, there having been a former hearing in the Outer-House, they will not permit lawyers to urge for an interlocutor of the whole house, but only when it is *ex proprio motu*, lest a difference of decreets *in foro* should on that head be introduced, whereby few would acquiesce, but in such a determination; which could not possibly dispatch the affairs of a nation.

6. Therefore the Lords ought not to admit any alteration of acts of litiscontestation orderly extracted, upon new arguments of law, unless at a diet of process when the other party is obliged to attend, that the party may furnish the best lawyers he pleaseth to choose. But if new matter of fact be represented by bill, after the act of litiscontestation is extracted, the Lords will reject the same in that way; yet if they find the point proposed relevant, they will allow that party to raise reduction of the act of litiscontestation, that the other party may be obliged to attend, and inform his advocates of the matter of fact;

which reductions are always taken in so soon as they are called, after the term of compearance, and do not go to the roll, because they are but incidents accessory to the principal cause.

7. When the Lords see fit not to prefer one party, in choosing the witnesses for probation, they do, *ex officio*, before answer to the relevancy, allow witnesses to be examined *hinc inde*, upon such points as the Lords think fit to be proven, and then there is extracted an Act before Answer, and the dispute upon the relevancy is reserved till the advising of the probation. Such acts have the same effect as acts of litiscontestation, and are only to be determined *in præsentia*: but they should not be inrolled amongst concluded causes by ordinary acts upon litiscontestation, for which Saturday is proper; and the determining one act before answer might consume several Saturdays, if both relevancy and probation were to be determined together: and therefore such actions ought to be inrolled in the ordinary roll for the Inner-House, so soon as the probation is closed, and a great avisandum made for that purpose.

8. Litiscontestation is accounted as a judicial contract betwixt parties, when it is upon compearance; yea, it is esteemed as a transaction, whereby parties agree, that the cause shall have its event, according as the points contained in the act shall be proven or not proven: and therefore there can be no more litiscontestations but one, or terms for probation in the same cause. And to prevent alterations upon emergencies, diligences are given out before the acts be extracted, that any alteration occurring may be insert therein. This is requisite to terminate pleas, because defenders, or parties appearing for their interest, may pass from their compearance, before they enter into litiscontestation, if they please, as well as they may forbear to appear upon citation, and suffer a decreet in absence, wherein litiscontestation is made *parte non comparente*: and therefore they may propone all dilatory defences, or may dispute against the relevancy or competency of the libel; but with this difference, that when they do not appear in the first instance, they may in the second instance propone all defences dilatory and peremptory, but when they do appear, they cannot again propone the defences which were repelled before they passed from compearance; and therefore the Act of Regulations [Courts Act 1672,c.16; A.P.S. VIII,80,c.40] appoints these points which were decided, to be insert in the decreet, albeit the parties pass from their compearance.

9. Litiscontestation is made, not only when the defender appeareth, but also when he appears not. And if the pursuer do not instantly prove his libel, he takes a term to prove the same, which by our style is called litiscontestation *reo absente* or *parte non comparente*. So litiscontestation does not import with us a contesting or debating, but a taking a term to prove by the testimony of witnesses, writ, or oath; all which come under the name of testimony.

When litiscontestation is thus made, if it be in an action that hath a fixed tenor, it passeth of course at the first calling by the clerks; but if it be a circumstantiate action *præscriptis verbis*, the clerks ought to report it to the

Lords, who, if they find it not relevant, will give no decreet upon it: and though they find it relevant and instructed, yet in the second instance they will allow the relevancy to be disputed again, and the probation to be reconsidered, because it passed *parte inaudita ;* and therefore may be altered, either upon matter of fact, or arguments of law.

10. Nothing does more retard justice, and bring the Lords and lieges greater trouble, than the multiplicity of bills: for there be few things to be done, but what have an ordinary course to be dispatched *viva voce.* But the inadvertence of some, and the litigiousness of others, make them forbear to acquiesce in, and extract acts of litiscontestation, of design that the matter may be forgot, and then they bring all over by bills; whereby the Lords are necessitated to read what hath formerly passed, and upon what grounds, as contained in the minutes; especially where the parties in their bills and answers differ in their relation of the case, as to what hath preceded; whereby they become so large, that they require far more time, than if nothing had been said or done, and are very expensive to the lieges, by causing write over so many large informations. But which is yet worse, bills are oft-times drawn by unskilful agents, mendicating the hands of advocates thereto, wherein such undigested stuff is multiplied, as none would have impudence to offer at the bar, wherein fact and law is jumbled together, without distinct proposal of points of fact instructed, or to be proven, as they behoved to propone at the bar: so that the Lords are necessitated to gather the matter out of that mass, wherewith there are mixed long narrations and allegeances, neither true nor competent to be proved. And beside this, when an Ordinary gives the Lords' answer to a point, both the informations before the interlocutor, and the bills after, repeat all pretended to have been said at the bar, repeating interlocutors unfaithfully.

For preventing these inconveniences, the Ordinary ought to cause write distinctly, the point whereupon he gives the Lords' answer, and the clerk of the process should be strictly prohibited to read any bill, but that which hath been delivered to him the night before; and no other clerk should read bills relating to processes, except the clerk of the process, who should peruse the bill the night he receives it, and should be peremptorily injoined, that if the bill be for altering any interlocutor, and if the interlocutor be not expressed truly therein, he should not read it till that be amended: for it makes a great stop in the Lords' procedure, to call for the process, and read the interlocutor, which the clerk alone may do. And if there be any new matter of fact proponed in the bill, that was not determined by a prior interlocutor, the clerk should not read the bill, but return it back to be amended, until the point of fact be set down by itself, in greater characters, bearing expressly, that the alleger either shows that the same is instructed by the writs produced, and marked by figures or letters at the clauses instructing the same, or otherwise offer to prove the same, condescending upon the manner of probation; adding to the point of fact the arguments to inforce it: and if there be more points, that they be set down severally, with their reasons as aforesaid. By this order the clerk suffers no prejudice, having the same benefit for reading the bill, when orderly, as when disorderly, and the Lords can much sooner and clearlier determine the points of fact proposed.

11. By these means, the loss of time and trouble by bills may be much prevented. And by the Acts of Sederunt, November 7, 1686, and July 7, 1691, the Ordinary in the Outer-House, and he only, is not only allowed, but ordained, to sit in the Outer-House the week immediately following his proper week, from nine o'clock in winter, and from half nine in summer, till that week's Ordinary come out, that he may hear any parties, who make application for stopping or altering any sentence, given by him in his week; providing the allegeances be delivered to him in writ, that if he find them altogether irrelevant, he may refuse the same; and if he resolve to hear them, he is to give the copy of them to the clerk, to be shown to the other party, that he may be in readiness when called. And the clerks are ordained to affix a roll of these orders given to them for hearing of the saids causes. And after that week, the Ordinary is allowed to hear parties at the side-bar, upon the allegeances presented, as aforesaid, being presented within six days after the date of the sentence craved to be stopped or altered, a copy being given to the other party, and the cause affixed on the wall as aforesaid, conform to the Act of Sederunt, November 7, 1690, whereby all stops thereafter are prohibited to be granted by the Ordinary: albeit these acts do not exclude the Lords *in præsentia*, the chancellor or president to stop sentences after these days are elapsed, that there might be place for extraordinary cases. But, after the Ordinary's time of sitting in the Outer-House is elapsed, and six sederunt days after any act, protestation or decreet, the Ordinary cannot then help the parties, unless upon a bill, the Lords remit a point to him to be heard; or if any allegeance be inconsistent with the Lords' interlocutor upon report, the Ordinary cannot hear nor report; unless it be remitted to him upon a bill. And there is no injury can be pretended, though after elapse of these days, there were admitted no further hearing: for, by the general custom of most civil nations, there is no place for interposing appeals, if they be not offered within ten days after pronouncing the sentence appealed from, whether definitive or interlocutory; for then the law presumes, that parties have acquiesced. And by our ancient statute, allowing appeals or falsing of dooms, they were only allowed immediately at pronouncing of sentences. Upon which grounds, decreets by Ordinaries have the same effect as decreets *in præsentia ;* because acquiescence is presumed, if application be not made as aforesaid, within six days after pronouncing of the sentence craved to be altered. Yet the Lords do rather amerciate the parties in fines, to be applied to the poor, for not proponing their allegeances in due time, and do then hear them.

12. To come now to the particular points, upon which litiscontestation may be made, which is only where some point is admitted to probation: If the pursuer instruct his libel *instanter*, or if the defender do instantly instruct his

exception, &c. there is no litiscontestation, albeit the exception doth not import the verity of the libel; but if any point be admitted to probation, for any party, litiscontestation is made, even though it be by an act before answer, which may be many different ways.

First, if the defender be absent, or pass from his compearance, and if the pursuer crave a term to prove his libel, litiscontestation is thereby made. But, if the defender compear and propone only dilators, or objections, but doth not pass from his compearance, and either propones no peremptory exception, or the same is not found relevant and competent, the decreet following is a decreet *in foro contradictorio*, as well as when peremptory defences are sustained, and the defender hath succumbed in not proving the same. But if he pass from his compearance, before he propone a peremptor, albeit he cannot in the second instance make use of peremptors, which he then had in his power, and *dolosè* omitted; yet albeit he knew of a relevant defence, but had not the writs for proving thereof in his power, he might prudently and innocently rather pass from his compearance, than propone a relevant exception, whereof he was not secure in the probation; because he could not obtain an incident diligence for production of his own writs, which for the present might be amissing, or out of his power; and therefore he might give way; and let the pursuer attain his intent, whereby he might be necessitated to pay, or by suffering the pursuer to attain or retain possession, lose the profits for a time, rather than succumbing in probation, lose the cause for ever; in which case his passing from his compearance is sufficient evidence of his not acquiescence.

Secondly, If the defender propone a relevant exception, importing the verity of the libel, but yet eliding and excluding the same, and for which he gets a term to prove, litiscontestation is made upon the exception only, which, if proven, will assoilzie the defender. And there are many such exceptions, as if the defender propone payment, he acknowledges the debt, which the pursuer needs not prove; unless the defender do expressly propone that he paid *indebitè per errorem*, which if he do not instantly verify, that it was *indebitè solutum*, or at least by the pursuer's oath, the allegeance of *indebitè solutum* should be repelled, and only reserved to reduction; because it might make a general pretence of delay: and therefore improbation by exception is not admitted without consigning a considerable sum for an amand, in case the proponer succumb; and the allegeance of *indebitè solutum* should not be otherwise received by exception. And, in a pursuit of spuilzie, the exception of lawful poinding acknowledges the libel, in so far, that the defender intromitted with the goods in question; yet defenders do frequently deny the libel *quoad* the prices and quantities, which therefore the pursuer must prove. And it hath been sometimes contended, that even where the defence imports not the verity of the libel, unless the defender deny the libel, he is understood not to controvert it; yet of a long time that hath not been sustained, but the decreet hath been found null for want of necessary probation. But if the defence acknowledge the verity of the fact libelled, and if the defender deny not the prices, he is understood to acquiesce in them, and the pursuer's not proving thereof will not annul the decreet; but if he deny the same expressly, the pursuer must prove it.

Thirdly, If the defender propone a relevant exception, which doth not import the verity of the libel, a term is assigned to the pursuer to prove the libel, and the same term to the defender to prove the exception; and if the pursuer take a long term to prove the libel, he cannot refuse the same for proving the exception. For instance, if the defender propone compensation, or a general discharge; these, or the like, do not acknowledge the verity of the libel, nor are they contrary thereto, but both are consistent to be true.

Fourthly, If an exception be proponed acknowledging the libel, the pursuer may propone a relevant reply, importing the verity of that defence, and then litiscontestation is only made upon the reply, and the event of the cause depends upon the proving or succumbing in it, and the pursuer may take as long a term to prove his reply as he pleases: yea, many points will be competent to him by reply, which would not be competent to the defender by exception; because the pursuer is not presumed to reply *animo differendi*, as the defender is suspected to do: and therefore inhibition, interdiction, and other reasons of reduction, will be sustained by reply, though not by exception; yet not always, for where there must be a production satisfied, and superiors and authors cited, it cannot be by reply.

Fifthly, As many defences may be relevant, and do not acknowledge the libel; so replies may be relevant, which do not acknowledge the verity of the exception: and therefore a term must be assigned to the defender to prove the exception, and to the pursuer to prove the reply. But if the exception acknowledge the libel, if the defender succumb in probation thereof, the pursuer will prevail, though he neither prove the libel nor reply; yet the same term is assigned, for proving both the exception and reply: because otherwise it would protract the process, and disorder the form of litiscontestation. But if the term be circumduced against the defender, the pursuer prevails, and the defender cannot urge the circumduction of the term against the pursuer, unless he adduce some probation of his defence.

Sixthly, If neither the exception acknowledge the libel, nor the reply the exception, then a term will be assigned for proving all the three: but if the term be circumduced against the pursuer for not proving the libel, the defender will be assoilzied; or if the pursuer adduce probation, and the defender succumb, he will be decerned, though the pursuer's reply be not proven; and if the defence and exception be proven, yet if the pursuer succumb in the reply, the defender will be assoilzied.

Seventhly, Litiscontestation may be made upon the duply only, if the exception acknowledge the libel, and the reply acknowledge the exception. But litiscontestation may be so made, as neither the exception acknowledgeth the libel, nor the reply the exception, nor the duply the reply; and then a term will be assigned to the pursuer to prove the libel and reply, and to the defender to prove the exception and duply: but if the pursuer succumb in proving the libel, by circumduction of the term, the defender is assoilzied by the Ordinary; but if he adduce probation, if the term be circumduced against the defender for not proving the exception, he is in the same manner decerned; and if both prove, yet if the pursuer succumb by circumduction of the term for not proving the reply, the defender is assoilzied; and if all the three be proven, yet if the defender succumb in the duply, he will be decerned; and the like holdeth, if there be a triply and quadruply. If probation be adduced, the Ordinary cannot advise it; but if writs having no contingency or probability to prove, be offered, the Ordinary may reject them, and circumduce the term.

13. Having thus cleared the form of litiscontestation, it remains that we consider the matter thereof, which would be almost insuperable, if we should condescend upon all the relevant exceptions, replies and duplies, which might be admitted, and the irrelevant which might be repelled: but it will be necessary to consider these, which are common to all or many actions; for we have already considered the prime peculiar exceptions and replies, with the particular actions wherein they are competent, which precede decreets, and shall consider the same as to actions executive of decreets, and suspensive of them.

14. Exceptions are so termed by the Roman law [Gaius 4,115; Inst.4, 13], from the formulæ of actions in that law, and the Edicts of the Praetors, which, if they did bear conditions, not to hold in such cases, these conditions were thence called exceptions. They were also called prescriptions; because they were not competent, but when they were prescribed by the law, or by the Praetor; but that term is now otherwise restricted. But still the term exception is retained, though not for the former reason, but because all processes proceed upon the rules of law, which have many fallacies and exceptions; and therefore, whensoever the presumption of verity is on the part of the pursuer, he needs not otherwise prove, but obtains his decreet upon presumption; as when declaratory actions proceed upon negatives, which prove themselves, that is, are proven by presumption alone; yet there is place to a stronger probation on the part of the defender, which therefore is the exception of that general rule. And as the exception is to the libel, so is the reply to the exception, and the duply to the reply: for still the presumption or probability of the allegeance, being stronger for the one party than the other, doth either exclude the other from any probation, or at least lay the burden of the probation upon the other.

15. A defence is a general name, comprehending all allegeances, which may defend defenders, whether they be dilatory or peremptory defences. And they comprehend both objections against libels and exceptions. Objections do reject the libel, and consist only in negatives, showing something to be wanting, for attaining the conclusion libelled: such as these; the want of a

sufficient title; or the want of a legal order of citation; or that all parties necessary to be called are not cited; or that the libel is not relevant; that is, that the premises do not infer the conclusion to be just according to law; or that the matter therein contained is not competent to be pursued in that way. But exceptions are always positive allegeances, supposing the sufficiency of the libel.

A reply doth in the same way differ from objections against the relevancy or competency of an exception: for it must be a positive allegeance, supposing the exception to be relevant and competent, if it were not excluded by a positive probation eliding the same: and so is the duply in respect of the reply, &c. but though in other ordinary disputes, any answer is called an exception, and any answer to that answer is called a reply (and so unskilful pleaders or clerks argue or conceive disputes in that way) yet legal disputes require another accuracy; and therefore nothing should be called an exception, but what is a positive allegeance eliding a libel, nor should any thing be called a reply, but a positive allegeance eliding the exception; but all other arguings should be expressed by the terms of allegeances and mutual answers.

16. The first and most common exception in all processes, is *exceptio rei judicatæ*, that the controversy is already decided, by a competent judge; which is relevant, albeit it were a decreet of an inferior court, which, if it have no evident nullity, is relevant till it be reduced. Neither is the nullity a reply, but an objection arising from what appears in the decreet; for if it be a nullity appearing from the process and minutes, it cannot be insisted in till these be called for and produced in a reduction.

Res judicata is relevant, not only being a decreet between the pursuer and the defender; but it is sufficient, if it was between their predecessors or authors.

But the exception *rei judicatæ* must not only be, that the decreet had the same conclusion; but also, that it proceeded upon the same *media concludendi*, if the decreet was an absolvitor: for though absolvitor was pronounced against a pursuer, it could not hinder him to insist for the same conclusion upon a different medium, in which case competent and omitted takes no place, but only in decreets condemnatory *in foro contradictorio*. So he who pursues a reduction of any decreet or other right, may raise as many actions as there are relevant reasons [IV,52,3,*infra*]: but he cannot multiply suspensions upon different reasons, which were competent the time of the decreet. This might be a reasonable ground for a statute, to exclude pursuers from multiplying processes, upon mediums competent and known the time of the first process; and to appoint that all the mediums might be libelled in the first process, and insisted in together, as well as many defences or reasons of suspensions must be insisted in together; or else what was competent and omitted should be lost. But now there is no other remedy, but that if there be such multiplication of actions upon different *media*, the pursuer succumbing should be condemned in large expenses.

17. It is a relevant reply against the exception *rei judicatæ*, that the decreet whereby the matter was judged, is reduced or renounced. But if it be alleged only to be under reduction, unless the production be satisfied, so that the reasons of reduction may be repeated, it will not be sustained by reply.

18. The second common exception is *exceptio litiscontestatæ*: for litiscontestation being as a contract or transaction between parties, either party hath the benefit of it; and neither party can resile from it; and therefore, if either party insist in another action, the other may except upon the litiscontestation, whether made in the same court or another, even though inferior. And albeit iniquity had been committed therein, yet the habile way of remedying it, were by advocation or reduction. But the defender in the new cause, may at his option use this exception or not; because the other party having disowned that mutual contract by litiscontestation, he cannot be obliged thereby, and yet if he please, he can compel the other to stand to it.

19. This exception may rather appear to be a dilatory than a peremptory defence, and so not to have a term to prove: and indeed it is not *peremptoria litis et causæ*, because it hinders not the party to insist in that litiscontestation; neither yet is it only *peremptoria instantiæ*, which is proper to dilators, whereby there must be new summons, but no new summons can in this case be used without mutual consent, but only the old, wherein litiscontestation was made.

20. The third common exception is prescription, which is largely treated, *Lib.* 2, *Tit.* 12. Prescription, to which there needs no more here be added, but that which is proper to be in litiscontestation, as a common exception against all pursuits, viz. the prescription of forty years, which is our longest prescription. And it hath a two-fold consideration; the one is, as it excludes all title and action upon rights, if there hath been neither possession nor process within forty years; and therefore may be proponed negative without alleging forty years' possession in the defender, and so it proves itself, unless the pursuer propone interruption, which doth elide the prescription; so that, in neither case, there is a term to be assigned to prove the prescription. The other consideration of prescription is, as it establisheth and completeth a right by forty years' possession uninterrupted; and being so proposed, the possession must be proven to have been so long. And though it be not proven to have continued every quarter, month, or year; yet ordinary possession will be sufficient *ad victoriam causæ*, albeit it be proponed in the terms of a continual possession, *quia probatis extremis præsumuntur media* [IV,45,22,*infra*], if the distance be not great; yet so, that interruption of any considerable time being positively proven, will afford a reply. The Act of Prescription, Parl. 1617, cap. 12. [Prescription Act 1617,c.12; A.P.S. IV,543,c.12] maketh prescription not only sufficient to defend against other rights prescribed, but also to pursue and recover possession, when it is lost; and to declare an absolute unquestionable right, not only of moveables, or of obligations, but of heritable rights of lands and annualrents.

The shorter prescriptions are proper for the several cases to which they relate, and to the actions and processes concerning the same.

21. The fourth common exception is, *ex capite doli mali*, viz. That the pursuer's title and right was obtained by fraud [cf.D.4,3,1]. But this is not relevant against all actions, as the former exceptions were. For if the title be rights of lands or annualrents, fraud is not competent by exception, but by reduction. Neither is it competent, to be proponed as a reply or duply; because superiors and others having interest must be cited, and the production must be ended before debating of the reason of fraud. This ariseth from the special nature of feudal rights, and likewise fraud being of a criminal nature, it is not relevant against singular successors, not partakers of the fraud, but only against the committers of the fraud, and these representing them, especially as to feudal rights: for so it is expressly provided by the fore-mentioned statute; the reason whereof is, to secure land-rights, and that purchasers be not disappointed; and therefore no action can be effectual against them, upon the fraud of their authors, unless they were accessory thereto, at least by knowing the same when they purchased: but supervenient knowledge will not prejudge them. Yet if a decreet were obtained against the author upon fraud, before the purchaser's right, it would be relevant against the purchaser; because his author's right was thereby annulled; and as to this point and other nullities, purchasers must run their hazard, and lean to their warrandice, there being no register appointed for publishing such decreets: yet by the minute-books of decreets of the clerks of Session, accurate diligence may discover such decreets, if pronounced within forty years, before which time they prescribe, unless there be interruption, which, by the late Act, must be so oft renewed, and only by messengers, that little more can be done to secure purchasers.

But in personal rights the fraud of authors is relevant against singular successors, though not partaking nor conscious of the fraud, when they purchased; because assignees are but procurators, albeit *in rem suam:* and therefore they are in the same case with their cedents, except that their cedents' oaths, after they were denuded, cannot prejudge their assignees.

Yet in moveables, purchasers are not quarrellable upon the fraud of their authors, if they did purchase for an onerous equivalent cause. The reason is, because moveables must have a current course of traffic, and the buyer is not to consider how the seller purchased, unless it were by theft or violence which the law accounts as *labes reales*, following the subject to all successors, otherwise there would be the greatest encouragement to theft and robbery.

22. By what hath been said upon the exception of fraud, it doth appear what may be the replies and duplies of the case: for if the defender do except, that the pursuer's right was acquired by fraud, it is a relevant reply that it is a land-right, and the pursuer is a singular successor, or that it is a purchase of moveables, by commerce, for an equivalent cause: to which the relevant duplies are, that the defender was partaker of the fraud, and at least knew of

it before he purchased; or that a decreet was pronounced upon the fraud before his acquisition. Each of these allegeances acknowledges the former; so that the duply is only to be proven, and litiscontestation is made upon it alone.

23. It is not to be expected that the ways how fraud may be committed, should here be determined, and how *dolus bonus* is innocent, and different from *dolus malus*, which is *hydra multorum capitum;* upon which there are large treatises [cf.D.4,3,1]. Only in general, it is never *dolus bonus* that doth hurt or prejudice to the parties, who are induced by acts altering their judgment or inclination. But if they be induced for their own good (either by word or other signs) so to change, albeit these words or signs do not truly infer the conclusion designed, it is *dolus bonus:* but still these acts must be without lying. Thus all stratagems of war are justified, as *ex dolo bono*. Jacob's putting the peeled rods before the sheep and goats [Gen.xxx,37–41] could not escape to be accounted *dolus malus* to the prejudice of Laban, if he had not a divine warrant for it, which is insinuated in the context of that history, that GOD gave Jacob the cattle of Laban by that means. Grotius [*De Jure Belli ac Pacis*, III, 1,17–20] holdeth lying to enemies to be lawful, because speaking of the truth becomes only a duty of love; and therefore is not due to enemies. But GOD having absolutely prohibited lying, and having declared truth a distinct virtue from love, the reason is of no moment: but the rule of the Gospel doth not only prescribe love to all men, but even to enemies, who may only be punished, or put out of capacity to do hurt, either by plain force or stratagem.

24. The fifth common exception is that of *errore lapsus:* for generally lawyers treat these two as congenerous allegeances, *errore lapsus et dolo circumventus*. But the exception upon error is seldom relevant, because it depends upon the knowledge of the person erring, which he can hardly prove. Neither will error have any effect, if it be not *in substantialibus*. For it will be no defence for a purchaser to allege, that he was deceived in the value of the thing bought, or that the thing bought was insufficient, by a visible fault: for in these the answer will only be, *caveat emptor;* and if it be a latent insufficiency, it will rather be esteemed that he was *dolo circumventus*, than *errore lapsus;* for it will rather be presumed, that the seller knew that fault and concealed it, than that the other was ignorant of it. Yet certainly there are many cases in which a defence may be, that a party was *errore lapsus*, and that either on the part of a purchaser, or of his author: as if one should sell a barony, and the enumeration of the lands should include distant lands, that were never united in the barony, nor in the rental by which it was sold; if the seller were pursued to perfect the bargain, or on the warrandice, he would have the exception of *errore lapsus*. It were a hard thing to determine whether Jacob were *errore lapsus*, or *dolo circumventus*, when Leah came into his bed instead of Rachel [Gen.xxix,21–30]; but certainly he might have repudiated Leah, as not being his wife, if he had not ratified the marriage by continuing therein: and no doubt he was not only *dolo circumventus* by Leah or her

father, but he was also *errore lapsus*, yet it was by his own fault; for although she came to him in the dark, yet if he had but spoken to her, her voice could not but have discovered who she was, to him who had so long conversed with her.

25. The sixth common exception is, that the right in question was yielded to by the defender *ex justo metu*. For though a true assent, whatever were the motives, is of itself effectual, yet positive law doth justly annul such consents as are obtained by just fear; just on the part of the sufferer, but unjust on the part of the actor; which consent is justly rendered ineffectual, as the penalty of the injury, in the same way as he who consents being *dolo circumventus*, his assent is of itself effectual, but positive law hath taken away its effect, for the common interest; and therefore there are two excellent edicts in *Edicto Perpetuo*, as to both, *quod dolo malo factum est, ratum non habebo* [D.4,2,1 *et seq.*]; as well as, *quod vi metuve factum est* [D.4,2,3].

But it is not any other fear that gives this exception, but such fear *quæ cadit in virum constantem*, as it is commonly described, but too narrowly: for certainly that may be a just fear to a woman that will not be to a man; and to a weak person that will not be to a resolute; so women's consent to the alienation of their liferent, if it be total, the very deed imports, that it was for the reverence of their husbands, and for fear of offending them, if they were the movers; or though it be the alienation but of a part of their provision, if their husbands were *viri feroces*, and used to keep them in terror, though no menaces were proved, it would be sufficient: and therefore our custom hath well provided, that a wife's consent should be judicially, *et extra præsentiam mariti*. There was an eminent case of James Stuart of Minto [1677, 2 Stair 489; M.16489], who being taken prisoner by Sir John Whitfoord, with another man's caption, was carried in the night, from place to place, in muirs far from neighbourhood, till he disponed his estates for a very unsuitable cause; the Lords reduced the disposition *ex capite metus*, in respect of the person, albeit a man of ordinary resolution would have resisted it.

It is not *justus metus* relevant to reduce a disposition, or other deed, that it was granted to persons of power and interest, by mean persons, or these that were capable of being in danger of crimes, although the same was desired by persons in power, unless threatenings were used, or insisting against the party upon refusal in criminal matters, which might reach life, members, or estate; yea, though the circumstances may infer presumption of just fear; yea, if the party upon oath depone, that what he did was voluntary, and not upon account of fear, it would be a sufficient reply, even against wives and weak persons.

26. There are variety of cases of just fear; as, 1. When the deed is done by compulsion, or concussion, *ex vi majori*, by positive acts of force, as by wounding, or beating to the hazard of life, especially with weapons invasive, which will not reach to switching, unless it be long continued; for vexation may be more intolerable than death, although the single acts be inconsider-

able; as by tickling, some have been made laugh to death. It is too well known that the French dragoons, by vexation of Protestants with quartering, reproaching, affronting, straitening in the conveniences of life, and in the requisite acts of religion, have made Protestants do more to dissemble, and counteract their religion, than fire or gibbet, or any other sudden death could ever do; yet every single act would not infer just fear. 2. Just fear is inferred not only by positive acts inferring constraint but by restraint; as by long and unlawful imprisonment, or by hindering of necessary food, sleep, rest, clothing, or by affording only corrupt meat and drink, which the extremity of hunger would make the injured person take, though it were known to infer the hazard of life. 3. Violence upon the chastity infers just fear, as when men are abused with sodomy, or women with rapes or sodomy. 4. It is inferred by disgrace; as by cutting off members, slitting up noses, cutting out of tongues or eyes. 5. It is inferred by threats to do such things, by those whose inclination, custom, and opportunity befitted them to do the same: so frequently persons have drunk up poison offered unto them, without any actual violence, but knowing that if they did it not, they would be compelled by violence and torture to do it, and so behoved to endure both: and others have dispatched themselves, to prevent cruel deaths or torture. Yea, there be innumerable such acts which the malice and cruelty of men can invent.

27. But legal execution, though by force, affords not the exception of *justus metus*, if it be not upon a capital cause: and therefore bonds or dispositions granted by persons incarcerated upon caption, are not reducible upon that head, and yet may be quarrelled upon other relevant grounds: for if payment were made, it will not hinder reduction of the decreet and repetition of the sum. Yet if a person were taken by caption, being sick and unable to travel without hazard of life, and to prevent the same did give bond or other right; it would afford the exception of *justus metus;* because it were not truly a legal execution, seeing it ought not to be done in that case.

28. Fear and fraud have much the same effects, as to singular successors, except in the case of robbery, which, as well as theft, is *vitium reale* in moveables: and therefore what hath been said of fraud in that point [IV,35,19 and 21, *supra*], needs not here be repeated.

29. The seventh common exception is, the pursuer's acknowledging or approbation of the defender's right, directly and expressly by consent thereto, or ratification thereof, or indirectly, and tacitly by doing deeds importing the same, which is called homologation, from a mathematical term, by which one figure doth quadrate with another, having like angles thereto; so homologous triangles are these which have equal angles, severally, each of them being of equal wideness to the angles of the other.

This exception is only relevant against the parties consenting or homologating, or those representing them; unless the consent be adhibited in the investiture, for then it is relevant against singular successors, as being a part of the real right; or being a judicial consent in process, whereby the matter became litigious before the pursuer's right.

Homologation arises from many several deeds, and is largely treated, *Lib.* 1, *Tit.* Obligations Conventional, §11. [1,10,11,*supra*] wherein many decisions are adduced importing homologation, which may be seen in that place.

30. The eighth common exception is, renunciation of all pretence of interest to the defender's right, which is only effectual against the renouncer, his heirs or successors representing, but not against singular successors, which holdeth not in wadsets, which are habilely extinguished, as well by renunciation, as by grant of redemption, or resignation. Reduction or declarator are comprehended under the first exception, viz. *exceptio rei judicatæ*.

31. These are the common exceptions in all actions. There are also several exceptions common to actions upon personal rights and obligations. As first, *pactum de non petendo*, when the pursuer has obliged himself not to insist for payment or performance: which, if it be absolute, importeth a renunciation of the right pursued on; but if it be only temporary, for a short time, it is not a peremptory but a dilatory exception, and doth not exclude a decreet, but only the present effect thereof, whereby the decreet is granted conditionally, to pay or perform at the time to which the delay is granted. But it maketh the pursuer liable to the expenses of plea, *plus petendo tempore*. And being dilatory, it must be instantly verified, yet if it be a long delay, it will procure a term to prove it, and will absolve the defender from that process; seeing he is not obliged to lie under the process for so long delay; and therefore a new citation will not revive that process: yet it will not hinder a new process to be raised, after the time of delay is past.

32. The second common exception in personal actions is, payment or performance made to him who had the full right to discharge.

33. The third common exception in personal actions is, payment made *bona fide* to him who had not the true right, but where there was another preferable right, which the defender neither did, nor was obliged to know: and therefore the law secures the payer, without prejudice to the pursuer to insist against the obtainer of the payment [1,18,3,*supra*].

Of this there are many cases: for instance, tenants are secure, by paying to their master, albeit there be citation against them, much more when against him and them also, upon a better right; unless there were arrestment upon their master's personal debt: for even arrestment upon dependence of real actions will not make tenants liable for double payment, so long as their master's right is not fully discussed and excluded: it doth also defend them against teind-masters, when they pay a joint duty for stock and teind. Also, if a sum due by many debtors, co-principals or cautioners, be assigned, and intimation made to one of the debtors, it becomes a right preferable to the cedent's right, as to them all; and yet, if the cedent charge any of them to whom the assignation was not intimated, and he make payment, not knowing of the intimation, he will not be liable to double payment. Which also takes place in arrestment, though decreet for making forth-coming be obtained against a principal debtor, which carries in consequence the right as to the cautioners, yet if they be distressed and pay, they are secure. Or if a debtor pay to a person denounced, before citation in a special declarator, he is secure: for he is not obliged to search the register of hornings. A main ground of these and the like, is that common brocard in law, *bona fides non patitur ut idem bis exigatur*, which yet takes only place, when the first payment is made *bona fide*.

34. The fourth common exception in personal actions is, a Discharge or exoneration, whether it be special or general, and that without necessity to prove payment or performance. But if the general discharge be with special discharges, it is not relevant for any greater cause, than is the greatest contained in the special discharge.

35. The fifth common exception in personal actions, for annual payments or prestations, is, upon Three Subsequent Discharges of three subsequent years or terms: for thence the law presumes, that all prior years or terms are paid or renounced, unless they be reserved. Against which, this reply is relevant to be proven by writ or oath of party, that the prior years or terms are yet resting unpaid.

Under this exception is comprehended Acceptilation, whereby the pursuer hath accepted any thing in satisfaction of the obligement, which is equivalent to a discharge or renunciation.

But partial receipts, albeit they exceed three terms, or three years, are not relevant to exclude bygones; because they import only to be to an accompt of all bygones.

36. The sixth common exception in personal actions is, Confusion, when the defender comes to succeed in the pursuer's right, whether by a general or special title. This exception is not always total; because though the defender succeed in the right as heir, yet if he render the same moveable, it will not belong to his heir, but to his executor, and so the action revives against that executor. Yet it is not a dilatory but a peremptory defence, and that separation is as a new right supervenient.

37. The seventh common exception in personal actions is, upon Compensation, which takes only place, where both the pursuer's and defender's titles are liquid, and of the same kind. And it hath the same effect as a discharge; and it operates from the concourse of the two liquid debts, so that though the defender's debt bear not annualrent, or be not registrable, yet it will elide the pursuer's debt from the time of the concourse, from which no annualrent will be due. But by statute, compensation is not competent in the second instance, by suspension or reduction: Parl. 1592, cap. 143. [Compensation Act, 1592,c.143; A.P.S. 111,573,c.61].

That which was not liquid, may be liquidated by the pursuer's oath, but will have only effect from the time of that liquidation. And since the Act of

Regulation, if there be any distinct defence, for which a term is granted, compensation is sustained to be liquidate by witnesses, being proven within the term assigned for the other defence, albeit the foresaid statute require that compensation be instantly verified, seeing the Act of Regulation [Courts Act, 1672,c.16; A.P.S. VIII,80,c.40] is a supervenient law, therefore the favour of ending pleas may allow the liquidation by witnesses, as aforesaid; or if witnesses be at hand, and may be called by a macer; or if the pursuer take a term to prove.

Recompensation is a relevant reply against compensation, as is particularly explicated, *Lib.* 1, *Tit.* Liberation, § 6. [1,18,6,*supra*] wherein also the former exceptions in personal rights are largely treated.

38. This is peculiar in personal actions, that the common exceptions of fraud or force are not competent by exception, if the personal action proceed upon a registrable writ, the nature whereof is to give ready execution by a decreet without citation: which must also hold in bills of exchange, these by a late statute having the effect of registrable writs: and likewise in other cases, where summary charges are granted by law or custom.

39. The last of all exceptions is Improbation, offering to prove the pursuer's title or instructions to be false and forged; after which no exception is competent, either in real or personal actions, or in declarators. And therefore, if defenders intend to propone improbation, they must propone all the prior exceptions with reservation of improbation, at least in such as do import the verity of the libel; seeing what the defender acknowledges as true, he cannot improve as forged, except he reserve improbation: for though of its own nature he might propone it in any order, yet our custom excludes all exceptions after improbation; and therefore protesting for reservation of improbation is not *protestatio contraria facto*.

Improbation being tedious, and requiring much delay, our law esteems it as suspected to be proponed *animo differendi litem;* and therefore admits it not by exception, unless the proponer consign such a sum as the Lords appoint, according to the importance of the cause, as an amand, in case by the event it appear, that improbation was proponed *animo differendi.*

Seeing registrable writs, and these of like nature, have *paratam executionem*, improbation ought not to be sustained against them by exception, but ought only to be reserved by way of action. Yet so, that if the pursuer be not very solvent, he may be put to find caution, in case the sum be recovered by improbation.

40. All these points which are competent by exception, are also competent by reply. And in several cases they are competent by reply, when they are not competent by exception or duply; because the pursuers are never presumed to delay themselves; and therefore improbation by reply ought always to be sustained without an amand.

41. In all acts of litiscontestation the manner of probation must be determined, especially what is to be proven by witnesses; for all things may be

proven by oath of party or writ. But as to the particulars, they will be expressed when we come to treat of probation.

42. In like manner incident diligences are not competent, unless they be sustained in the act of litiscontestation, or in acts before answer. For albeit formerly it was sufficient to protest for the same, yet the Act of Regulations [Courts Act 1672,c.16; A.P.S. VIII,80,c.40] hath very fitly appointed it to be proponed and determined in these acts. Likeas the same may be proponed and sustained either for the defender, or the pursuer, or both.

43. The last point in acts of litiscontestation is, the term assigned for probation. Ordinary diligences for probation pass of course, and are not expressly mentioned in the act. Extraordinary diligences cannot pass but by the Lords *in præsentia*, upon bills.

44. When points are admitted to be proven by writ, parties do ordinarily protest for reservation *contra producenda*; that is, that what allegeances emerge from the writs produced, may not be excluded; which protestation is not necessary, because it will reach no further than to such allegeances as the proponer could not know when litiscontestation was made, otherwise it would give occasion to unnecessary delay; as if a defence of compensation were proponed, this reservation would not allow a term to prove recompensation, or a general discharge which would take away that compensation, because it was competent and omitted at the time of litiscontestation; yet what is instantly verified will be received even at advising of the cause: and this is the difference of "competent and omitted" against acts of litiscontestation, and against decreets *in foro contradictorio*. And though that protestation be omitted, allegeances that could not be foreseen, arising from the writs produced, cannot be excluded, especially these which arise from the inspection of the body of the writ, as vitiations or nullities.

Title 41. Diligences *Pendente Processu*

ACTS of litiscontestation would have no effect if law had not prescribed the way to make them effectual, by the authority and warrant of judges competent, whereby they are put to execution by precepts direct to messengers at arms, commanding parties, witnesses, or havers of writs, to compear before the Lords, upon the day assigned as the term of probation, with continuation of days, to depone upon the points contained in the act, and found relevant therein. The precepts against parties to whose oath of verity any point is referred, do only command them to compear at the term, with certification,that if they compear not, they shall be holden as confessing the point referred to their oath; but precepts against witnesses cannot have that certification,but all that can be done against them, or against the havers of writs, is to compel them to appear, and depone; and therefore these precepts are called executorials, because they are for putting the acts to effect by execution: they are also called compulsators for the same reason. And they are called diligences, because they excuse the users thereof from negligence, whereby posterior

diligences being exactly followed, are preferable to prior diligences being neglected, *vigilantibus non dormientibus jura subveniunt*, which is founded upon
that great interest to hasten pleas to an end. They are also called diligences,
because though the effect do not follow, yet the user thereof hath endeavoured
what he could, and so is held as in the same case, as if he had obtained the
command of the precept. These precepts are called executorials before executions be thereupon; but they are only called diligences, when they are executed in due time.

2. Diligences are of three sorts, being either upon precepts before decreets, upon acts, or upon decreets.

The last sort of diligences and executorials, viz. these after decreets, which
serve for putting of decreets to execution, and making them effectual, are ordinarily horning, caption, poinding, charges to remove, and thereupon
letters of possession, which are granted on all decreets in petitory and possessory actions, (but declaratory actions need none) together with the executory
actions upon arrestments, and of adjudications of lands and annualrents.

3. Diligences before decreet are either ordinary or extraordinary. The
ordinary diligence against parties to depone, to whose oaths points are referred with certification, are only by citation to compear under that certification.

4. Diligences upon acts are these, against havers of writs requisite to
prove, or to produce writs for eviting certification *contra non producta*, and
they are partly ordinary and partly extraordinary. Their form is much altered
by the Act of Regulations [Courts Act, 1672,c.16; A.P.S. VIII,80,c.40], before which the ordinary diligence was only a summons, to cite the havers of
writs, which might have been done by a summons of exhibition, at the instance of the defender, so soon as he was cited, or even before citation,
whereby he might call for production of any writ belonging to himself; but if
he neglected the same till the act of litiscontestation, then he might take out a
summons to cite parties to produce his own writs, or the writs of others, who
were obliged to produce the same on such occasions. But if he behoved to
prove with any other men's writs, in that case he had no title or interest to
force them to produce writs, other than by occasion of the act; which he
could not do, unless the time of the act he had protested for incident diligence, which was a summons of exhibition against the havers of writs requisite for probation, wherein the defender had no other interest, but the
common duty of all in the same society, to assist the dispatch of justice by
their oaths, or by the writs in their hands. But this protestation used neither
to be admitted nor repelled, until the term of probation, when the pursuer
insisted for circumduction of the term, and then the defender did produce
that exhibition, with the executions thereof, which is called an incident diligence, as every action that is only competent *incidenter* in a principal action, is
called an incident action: as when a process is continued against a party,
necessary to be called, and not called in the principal summons: as if a

woman be cited, and she marry *pendente processu*, the summons must be continued against her husband, before it can have further progress against herself.

This incident diligence was necessary in many cases: as if a cautioner were pursued for payment of a debt, most exceptions competent to the principal debtor would be sustained for the cautioner: and if the same were found probable by writ, his incident diligence would stop the circumduction of the term, or any further procedure in the principal cause, till that incident exhibition took its ultimate effect. So in real actions for lands or annualrents, of old the defender had a term to call his warrant, his superior, or his author: but in place of that, law required that superiors and authors should be called *ab initio*, otherwise no process is to be sustained as to their rights, or as to the defender's rights founded upon their rights; so that it was a good defence, that all parties having interest are not called: but when they are called, the defender is not thereby secured; for if they do not appear, process proceeds against their rights, so far as they continue to have interest: but the defender's right will also fall in consequence, unless he force the superiors or authors to produce, which must be by incident diligences.

5. When incident diligences at the term were sustained, the user thereof was not obliged to refer the verity to the party's oath; yea, though he did, and that the haver were holden as confessed, that would not prove against the pursuer in the principal cause: yet he might have further a close of that diligence, by a decreet of exhibition, whereupon horning and caption would have followed. But defenders commonly were glad of opportunity to get long delay; and therefore, when they were not sure to recover the writs, they libelled the exhibition to be proven *prout de jure*, and seldom did the haver concern himself, but the pursuer in the principal cause turned defender in the incident: and if the user of the incident did not use diligence to proceed therein, he was allowed to crave protestation, and to do all that the other, viz. the defender in the principal cause, who is pursuer in the incident, could do to hasten it to an end, either by any defence upon informality of the incident, or by urging short terms for proving. Yet, probation by witnesses then having four terms, and after obtaining decreet of exhibition, the execution thereof was by the letters of four forms, having four several subsequent charges, the last whereof was caption, this way of incident diligence was exceedingly tedious and expensive, so that it was justly and fitly changed by the said Act of Regulation [Courts Act 1672,c.16; A.P.S. viii,80,c.40]; whereby incident diligence was not competent, unless it were sustained in the act, and then diligence was granted by horning against the havers, charging them to compear and depone, whether they have, or had the writs contained in the charge, and to produce such of them as they acknowledged by their oaths; and upon production of this charge, with the executions, a second diligence is granted against the same parties by caption, and a term assigned for executing of the caption, whereby the havers might at any time be taken, and kept in prison

till they were produced at the term, and did depone, unless they were set at liberty, upon caution to appear at the term, with consent of party, or by authority of the Lords. This method is very just; for there is the same reason to force parties, though unconcerned in the process, to prove by their writs, as by their oaths, when called as witnesses.

6. The diligences against witnesses were of old very tedious and expensive, for they were four in number, and as many terms to prove. The first was a precept to appear and bear witness, without any certification. And if this were produced at the term, a second diligence was granted, commanding the witnesses to compear, with certification that, if they compeared not, horning would be direct; and a term was assigned for their compearance. If the defender produced not that precept with the executions, the term would be circumduced; but if he did appear, horning was direct, and a third term assigned. And if that were produced, caption was granted, and a fourth term assigned. But this method was changed by an Act of Parliament, in the rescinded Parliaments, taking away letters of four forms [1647,c.43; A.P.S. VI(1), 283,c.321]; and though that Act was not restored, yet the Lords continued the custom as very convenient.

7. All these diligences are granted by the Ordinary, in the Outer House. But there are other extraordinary diligences granted by the Lords *in præsentia*, upon bill, on many divers occasions, during the dependence of the process. As, first, in competitions about lands or annualrents, if the process be dubious and intricate, the Lords, upon supplication, do sequestrate the rents, and do remit the competitors to an auditor, to determine their rights and preferences, by a decreet of ranking, when the competitors are many, that it cannot be discussed at the bar: and the Lords do name factors after hearing, if the parties offer persons, nominating the fittest, appointing them salaries, and warranting them to set lands by roup. In these processes there is dispute, decreets and acts, between every competitor and the rest, whereby some are utterly excluded, and others are preferred to have access in order, according to the validity of their rights. As also, sequestration is obtained by bill, when any piece of ground, or corns thereon, are in a dubious controversy.

Secondly, There is an incident process, for citing parties who are not present at the bar when litiscontestation is made, to appear to give their oath of calumny; which is competent at any time, before conclusion of the cause by probation, or before decreet by circumduction of the term. This incident process doth not go to a roll, but is taken summarily in, whenever it is ready, as being only incident.

Thirdly, When witnesses are old, valetudinary or sick, the Lords, even before litiscontestation, upon sufficient testificate, bearing this to be true upon the testifier's conscience, will examine witnesses to lie *in retentis*, and grant diligence for that effect.

Fourthly, If any party discover witnesses he knew not, and so declare upon oath, the Lords will grant diligence against these witnesses, and sometimes have granted the same, without such declaration. But now, when the testimonies of witnesses are patent, whereby the supplicant may see that his witnesses prove not; no other witnesses should be admitted without such an oath, seeing he hath temptation to corrupt the witnesses.

Fifthly, If parties supplicate for commission to examine parties or witnesses, who are not able to travel, through age or infirmity, the Lords will grant commission to examine them in the country; and if the supplicant have been negligent or faulty in proposing the same, the time of litiscontestation, they will nominate persons out of a list, to be named by the other party. But, if the commission be to examine witnesses in probation of tenors, or in improbations, they will name more commissioners, because two Ordinaries are requisite to examine such witnesses, when they are able to come.

Sixthly, When witnesses or parties to be examined are many, and the matter plain, the Lords will easily grant commission to be insert in the act of litiscontestation; but not if the matter be intricate, unless both persons consent, or in case of infirmity: in which case, the Lords allow the interrogators to be insert in the act or commission.

Seventhly, If any point to be proven require ocular inspection and visitation, the Lords use to give commission to some of their number to visit the ground, and examine witnesses upon the place, in the vacance, if any of them live near it; or otherwise to commissioners. But if it be near, the Lords use to execute commissions upon Mondays.

8. In all commissions for witnesses, there is a term and place of examination appointed; and letters of horning are granted against the witnesses, to appear at that time and place. But commissioners cannot examine at any other term, unless the commission bear it, and so caption cannot follow, until these commissioners' report be made. All commissions do also bear a term to report, and these who are to prove, are to produce the report, and either party should have the double of the report, which should have the subscriptions of the deponents, or of the commissioners, if they cannot subscribe: and the term is not to be circumduced, till after the day of report.

9. The hornings granted against witnesses, or against havers of writs, need not be registrate, neither do they infer the falling of escheat, but only the obtaining of caption. If witnesses in the first diligence die or go out of the country, the Lords will grant a new diligence for other witnesses in place of these, to the same term with the second diligence, against the witnesses in the first diligence, but will not give a new term for caption against these additional witnesses.

Title 42. Probation by Writ

THERE are three ordinary ways of proving points admitted to be proven in acts of litiscontestation, or acts before answer, viz. writ, witnesses, or oath of party; of which two, and sometimes all may concur for proving the same point. So writ and witnesses may concur, and when witnesses depone only that they know not or remember not, writ may be adhibited, and oath so far as is not proven by writ. And therefore the determination of the manner of probation in acts, is thus, to be proven *scripto vel juramento partis*, or *prout de jure;* that is, such points wherein witnesses are not allowed, are to be proven by the party's writ or oath: but if oath of verity be first used, there is no place for writ or witnesses: but if writ be first used, oath may be used in so far as is not proven by writ. Points to be proven *prout de jure*, comprehend all the three manners of probation, yet in the order aforesaid; which occurs especially in acts before answer, wherein particular grounds of inference are condescended on, which is not a direct, but an indirect and presumptive probation; for these circumstances are probable partly by writ, partly by witnesses and by oath of party, not only as to different circumstances, but also as to the same.

2. The proper order of these ways of probation should be first by writ, which ordinarily contains the solemn confession or acknowledgment of parties. And as verbal confession, or confession without a party's subscription in the same process, do instantly verify; so the solemn confession by writ hath a term for probation allowed: and while probation may be so had, witnesses ought not to be put to the trouble of giving unnecessary oaths. But if oath of verity be used, it is the end of all strife.

3. Probative writs are very various and of different importance in probation; and writ comprehends both *Chirographum* and *Typographum*. The most direct and plenary probation by writ is, by the written acknowledgment of the party, against whom the writ is used, whether it be declaratory or promissory, if the law allow the writ to be, or to be presumed to be, marked by the party by a mark approven in law as probative, as being written by his hand, or an ordinary sentence subjoined written with his hand, which he is known to have chosen for instructing the writ. This we see to have been the ancient custom by some of the apostle Paul's epistles. 2 Thess. iii. 17, 18. "The salutation of me Paul, with my own hand, which is the sign in every epistle: so I write. The grace of the Lord Jesus Christ be with you all. Amen." [The Authorised Version omits "me" and reads "token" for "sign".] Of a long time the attestation of writs was by the superscription or subscription of the name, designation or title of the party. Kings do superscribe, and their secretaries subscribe to their epistles, or to a breviate or docquet of larger writs; because Princes have not the time to peruse the whole body, wherein there is much of formality. Others do only subscribe.

4. In the ruder times when few could write, the subscription of the party with witnesses insert, though not subscribing, made a probative writ, which was of great inconvenience: for if the witnesses died, the direct manner of improbation was lost; and also the indirect, by comparing the subscriptions of the witnesses with their other subscriptions or hand-writ, which is competent when the witnesses subscribe: and, on the other part, if the witnesses forgot, though they were truly witnesses, the writ would be

improven, if there were not other strong adminicles. Writs were also probative, if the names of the witnesses were insert, though without a designation; and the writ was sustained, if the user thereof did condescend upon a special designation, whereby the persons understood might improve: but now, by a late statute, Parl. 1681, cap. 5. [Subscription of Deeds Act 1681, c.5; A.P.S. VIII,242,c.5] writs, after that statute, prove not, unless the witnesses subscribe and be designed.

5. The ancient form of attesting writs was by seals, being the known seal of the party, which was ordinarily his coat of arms, or if he had no arms, the initial letters of his name and surname. But, since writing became ordinary, sealing is much out of use, except where seals are solemnities, as in evidents granted by the King. Sealing was much unsurer than subscription, because coats of arms, or initial letters, were common to many persons, and were easier to be counterfeited than the hand-writ of parties, especially if they use their ordinary characters: for thereby their hand-writ is dignoscible by other holograph writs or sentences uncontroverted, and peculiar characters are easier forged, and less astructable.

6. Holograph writs subscribed are unquestionably the strongest probation by writ, and least imitable. But if they be not subscribed, they are understood to be incomplete acts, from which the party hath resiled: yet if they be written in compt-books, or upon authentic writs, they are probative, and resiling is not presumed. Writs are accounted holograph, where large sentences are written with the party's hand, although not the whole writ.

Yet bills of exchange are probative, though neither holograph, nor having witnesses insert, nor subscribing; because of the exuberant trust among merchants, and the speedy dispatch which their affairs require, whereby such bills use not to be kept for any considerable time, and if they were so kept, they would not be probative; and because it is the general custom of nations, which particular statutes cannot remedy. Also discharges by masters to their tenants are probative, being signed, though not holograph, nor having witnesses.

7. In other nations, writs are not fully probative by the subscription of parties. In England and Ireland, such writs, though subscribed by parties and witnesses, prove not, unless they be proven by the oath of the party, or by the oaths of the witnesses. But, with the subscriptions of both, they require the party's seal, and that the writ bear "signed, sealed, and delivered in presence of," &c.; and then the witnesses subscribe: but any impression upon wax makes the writ probative.

The Romans did not allow private writ, as a sufficient probation; but they trusted most to public writ, as being done in judgment, and subscribed by the clerks, who could only be churchmen, as the word clerk insinuates. But though the name continue, there is now no necessity, and seldom allowance for churchmen to be clerks or notars: yet by statute, ministers are allowed to be notars in the testaments of parties, who cannot, or are not able to write.

They did also esteem writs subscribed by Tabellions, or public notars, to be public writs, because these were authorised by sovereign authority, to redact in writ what was done or spoken amongst parties.

8. Our custom hath much more acquiesced in the subscription of parties, in the several ways and terms before expressed, and does presume the delivery of writs, if they be out of the granter's hands, being in the hands of these in whose favours they are granted, or in the hands of third parties; unless it be proven by the oath of the party, in whose favour the writs were granted, or by his writ, that they were depositated in that party's hands, either to be returned to the granter, or not to be delivered till such and such conditions were fulfilled; and by the oath of the depositar, what the conditions were, which the depositar's writ would not prove while he were alive, but might prove after his death.

9. Our custom doth not allow the instruments of notars as probative writs, except in the particular cases thereby approven. As first, When they subscribe for parties that have not skill or ability to subscribe, being at the parties' command and before witnesses. In such cases, notars used to lead the hands of the parties in subscribing their names, which now is unnecessary and out of use: but the touching of the notar's pen, after reading of the matter written, is still retained, yet it is presumed from the notar's assertion, unless the writ be improven. But if the matter exceed the value of a 100 pound Scots, obligations subscribed by notars prove not, unless there be two notars and four witnesses. 2. Instruments of seasin can only be by the instrument of a notar; for it is a solemnity which cannot be supplied otherwise. And likewise instruments of resignation and instruments of intimation of assignations, translations, or repositions, and likewise instruments of renunciation by parties renouncing the rights they had, or by tenants renouncing their possession, and so must instruments of premonition, requisition and consignation upon reversions, instruments of requisition to ward-vassals to confer with persons offered to match with them, and instruments of their keeping or not keeping of these diets, and what passed therein: and wheresoever by agreement of parties, instruments are appointed, they are understood to be by notars, though it be not expressed. Yet instruments of notars make not full probation, without some adminicle to instruct their warrant, not only in relation to the points of right, but even as to mere possession; as when tenants renounce their possession, they must deliver to their master, or (in his absence) at his dwelling-house, a renunciation subscribed by them, containing a warrant to enter summarily, without process. 3. In other cases, where parties will not do acts which they are obliged to do, or declare what they are obliged to declare, instruments taken thereupon by notars, having witnesses insert and required, are probative, which no other witnesses could prove. And whatsoever is said or done in any instrument solemn or not solemn, at the requisition of the parties, the notars are obliged to give instruments thereupon, although the points be not a part of the solemnity re-

quisite in such instruments: but these points which are no parts of the solemnity, must be astructed by the witnesses insert in the instrument, unless it be in ancient matters. The offer to pay or perform any obligation in due time, and the consignation of what is consignable, upon refusal, are probative, [11, 10,20,*supra*] although they be not necessary solemnities, because they are probable by the oath of the party, which cannot supply any solemnity, though it may hinder the party to insist upon such solemnity.

All solemn instruments of notars are, by a late statute, appointed to be subscribed by the witnesses, being done after the publication of that Act, Parl. 1681, cap. 5. [Subscription of Deeds Act, 1681,c.5; A.P.S. VIII,242, c.5]. But that reaches not to other instruments: yet it is very convenient that the witnesses should subscribe even in these, for thereby their subscription keeps them in remembrance, that they were witnesses, and were required to be witnesses.

10. All acts and deeds under the hands of the clerks of processes are probative writs, and the warrants thereof are presumed; yet so, as if they be recently quarrelled, the warrants must be produced: and in the case of reduction, upon improbation of the writs produced, as titles or probation, they must be reproduced, unless they be adminiculated, or the tenor be proven; albeit the reduction be *ex intervallo*. These public writs prove what was done by the judge, or what was said or alleged by parties, but do not prove that the things alleged were true, except in so far as the instructions thereof are expressed, generally or particularly.

11. Whatsoever writs are probative against a party, are probative against all representing that party, and in most things are probative against their singular successors. And likewise, all writs which were probative against the predecessors, or authors of parties, are probative not only against their universal, but their singular successors in personal rights; yea, in apprisings or adjudications within the legal, or in infeftments for security or payment of sums, which are satisfied by intromission, as are apprisings or adjudications.

12. There is no relevant objection in the first instance, against the extracts of clerks, or instruments of notars, where they are competent, or against summons or diligences by writers, or executions of messengers, by denying that they were clerks or notars, &c., or by denying that judges or arbiters had authority: and if the same be alleged by way of reduction, holden and reputed will be a sufficient defence. For if these objections were allowed in the first instance, they might be generally alleged in all processes, and nothing could proceed, unless all these authorities were proven, which would be a public prejudice; and therefore even improbation by way of defence, though with the oath of calumny of the proponer, is not sustained, though it be the most important defence, without consigning such an amand as may take off all suspicion of designing delay.

13. Writs not subscribed by those against whom they are adduced, nor

by their predecessors or authors, and even acts and decreets, wherein they were not parties, are *inter alios acta, quæ aliis non præjudicant*, though they may give concourse in probation. And regularly the testimonies of witnesses in one process prove not in another, unless both the parties and cause be the same, or that other witnesses cannot be found.

14. Compt-books are probative against those who made them, although they be not subscribed, nor written with their hand, if thereby there appear a long tract of their affairs; but they prove not for them.

15. Missive letters are probative, except where they relate to more solemn writs, such as bonds, bills, or accompts: for if these be not produced, letters relative thereto will not prove, because it will be presumed, that these principal writs are satisfied, when they cannot be produced. Testificates are probative in obtaining suspensions, where the reason is upon matter of fact, or even in instructing reasons of advocation.

16. Histories are probative in all cases, where fame is relevant, if they be authentic, and not contradicted by more authentic histories of the same time, as in the case of propinquity of blood, or of antiquity and priority of dignity, titles of honour, &c.

17. How far investitures and the instructions thereof are probative and effectual against others than the parties therein contained, their heirs, or successors, hath been considered in the Titles, Infeftments of Property [11,3, *supra*], or Annualrents [11,5,*supra*], Reduction [IV,20,*supra*] or Competition [IV,35,*supra*]; which need not here be repeated.

18. Probation by writ is not so firm as probation by witnesses, or by oath. For it admits contrary probation, by posterior writ or by oath, and it may be taken away by improbation: but oaths cannot be improven, albeit the writ expressing the same may be improven: neither can probation be led against the testimony of concurring witnesses, though reprobators are competent against the initials of their testimonies, for therein they are not *contestes*.

19. There are many relevant objections against the faith of writs, which appear from inspection thereof. As first, when the body of the writ, the witnesses and the parties' subscriptions do all appear to be by the same handwrit; thence it is concluded that the writ is either a copy, or is forged; and therefore it will be rejected without improbation: and if the user tenaciously adhere to it as authentic, improbation may be sustained against it by exception, without an amand.

Secondly, If the writ appear to be vitiated *in substantialibus*, by deletion, razing, or superinduction of letters and words, which may alter the same, especially if done with other ink; thence it is inferred, that it was not done at or before the subscription. What points are *de substantialibus* must be esteemed by the nature of the writ: the date not only as to the time, but as to the place, the name of the writer, or filler up of any blanks, or filler up of the date and witnesses, and the designation of witnesses, since the Act requiring their designation to be expressed [Subscription of Deeds Act, 1681,c.5; A.P.S. viii,242,c.5], are *de substantialibus* in all writs, when the question is of their being true or authentic. The worst kind of deletion is, when the words deleted cannot be read, (but if they be so scored that they can be read, it will appear whether they be *de substantialibus*,) for if they cannot be read, they will be esteemed to be such, unless the contrary appear by what precedes and follows, or that there be a marginal note bearing "the deletion from such a word, to such a word to be of consent." Razing is much more incident to writs on parchment than on paper. Superinduction is not only by adding or altering of letters, but of monosyllabs or short words, as when No or Not is interlined, not between line and line, for then it would not be respected, but between word and word. Interlining where it only makes up the sense of the sentence, gives not ground for any objection.

Thirdly, Marginal additions upon one side of a contract, and not upon the other, are probative against that party who produces that side, but are suspect if the addition be in their favour, and is not probative till it be adminiculated by posterior writs relative thereto, or by the oath of the party, or the witnesses inserted. Marginal additions are much more easily suspect, than what is in the body of the writ, where the writ is not mutual, both parties subscribing the additions: for it is not certain that the witnesses subscribed when these additions were added, and therefore though they own their subscriptions, if they do not remember the additions, albeit that will not improve the writ, yet it will make these additions improbative, if they be in favour of the receiver of the writ. Therefore, in such cases, it is very prudent to mention the number of marginal additions, with the filling up of the date and witnesses.

Fourthly, Large blanks in writs which may alter the import thereof, make writs improbative, if it appear by the hand or ink, that they differ from the body: for it will be presumed, that they are filled up after subscribing, unless the contrary be proven or adminiculated [111,1,5,*supra*]; as if the filler up of the date and witnesses do particularly mention such blanks filled up by him. But blanks for procurators in procuratories of resignation, or bailies in precepts of seasin, or blanks for filling up of particulars under a general designation expressed, or blanks for the dates of writs related, or even for the names of creditors in bonds or dispositions, or of assignees in assignations or translations, do not render the writ improbative or suspect, but have other bad consequences: for thereby arresters are in hazard to be excluded, who use only generally to interrogate the granters, whether they were debtors to the party whose goods or sums are arrested the time of the arrestment? If they depone only *negative*, as ordinarily they do, upon pretence that they knew not to whom they stood obliged by the blank-writ, they will be absolved: but if they do rightly depone, they ought to acknowledge they gave a blank writ to such a person, against whom the process may be continued, and diligence granted against him to produce the writ, and so forward till the haver be found, which ought to be upon the expenses of the granter of the blank-writ: and if the person be not found who hath the writ to his own behove, the granter of the blank-writ ought to be decerned, since through his fault the arrester is disappointed: and albeit he should depone, that he granted the writ blank, but he saw the name of such a party filled up therein, yet that quality should not be sustained, unless the same were proven by production of the writ, if it was filled up *ex intervallo* [III,1,5,*supra*].

Fifthly, Writs may be improbative by inspection of the stamp or seal of the paper, whereupon the same is written: as, if paper with such a stamp or seal was known not to be found at the time of the date the writ bears, the writ thereby is not only improbative but improven. Of this there was a memorable example, when the Earl of Haddington was President, [1616–26] at the advising of the articles of improbation of a very suspect writ, where yet there was not sufficient probation to annul or improve it; it fell instantly in the President's mind to look to the stamp of the paper, and it was found that there was none such at the time of the date the writ did bear, whereupon with common approbation, the writ was improven.

Sixthly, Writs which by their date bear to be ancient, if they be written upon paper industriously sullied to appear to be old, do thereby become suspect and improbative, unless they be adminiculated by authentic writs relative thereto.

Seventhly, Very old writs, especially charters or seasins, are suspected by the notoriety of the hand-writs of the notars that then lived, and commonly practised, which were but very few, and their hands evidently known to all who were conversant amongst ancient evidents, if the writ, or attestation, did not appear to be the hand-writing of him it bears to be writer or notary. And on the contrary, such known hand-writ will confirm an ancient writ, although it be much torn or worn, and though it have no vestige of the seal, when sealing served for subscription, or was requisite for solemnity.

20. There remains yet to be considered the interpretation of writs, for which there are many rules, both general, and as to the tenor of special clauses, such as clauses by ancient style, which is continued, although the effect be not extended to all the words expressed. So the style of inhibitions prohibits the disposal of all rights, goods, and gear, and yet reaches only to heritable rights; the like is in the style of several gifts in Exchequer and the meaning of clauses of warrandice, of clauses of conquest, clauses of substitution, clauses irritant, &c.

21. The general rules of interpretation of writs are, first, that they ought to be interpreted according to the parties that expressed the same, and the matter expressed therein. So if the person expressing be vulgar, the interpretation of their words and sentences ought to be understood according to the vulgar meaning and common sense thereof: and if the matter import that they must be legal terms, they are to be understood in the most common and vulgar sense these terms can bear. And therefore that brocard, that *verba sunt interpretanda contra proferentem, qui potuit sibi clarius legem dixisse,* or *mentem*

apertius explicasse, holds not in such vulgar persons, but in skilful persons, or where skilful persons are trusted.

Secondly, *Verba sunt interpretanda contra proferentem*, where the parties are skilful, or are known to have trusted skilful persons in forming of the writs; and therefore the same should be as much extended in favour of the other party as their sense can bear.

Thirdly, Words are more extensively to be interpreted in matters favourable, or in persons favourable, than in other cases, especially when the matter is odious, as the Roman law saith, *in dubio pro dote respondendum*. And generally *in dubio pro libertate respondendum*, and *in dubio pro innocentia respondendum*, *in dubio pro possessore respondendum*, *in dubio pro debitore respondendum*, *in dubio pro reo respondendum*.

Fourthly, *Plus valet quod agitur, quam quod simulatè concipitur:* more respect is to be had to what appears by the writ, to have been the interest and design of the parties, than to what the style appears.

Fifthly, *In claris non est locus conjecturis*. This is a correctory to the former rules, that judges may not arbitrarily interpret writs, or give them a sense inconsistent with their clear words.

Sixthly, *Nemo præsumitur donare*, under which is comprehended, *debitor non præsumitur donare:* which is more pregnant than the former general rule. Yet in other cases, when the words may bear a design to oblige, they are not to be interpreted as a deed of mere liberality; as if the words bear, that such a person delivers or obliges to deliver such and such things, they rather import loan than gift. Yet when the natural signification of the words importeth donation, or a gratuitous deed, it is to be interpreted accordingly [IV,45,15, *infra*].

Seventhly, Words in latter-wills, or donations or dispositions in contemplation of imminent death, are more favourably to be interpreted, and to be further extended than in deeds *inter vivos*. There are large treatises written *de conjecturata mente defuncti*, which are much considered in the Roman law, but are not so useful as to us; the power of testing with us being very much restricted, there being only left to the defunct a power of legating that which is called the dead's part of moveables, which is seldom the whole, sometimes the half, but most ordinarily the third of testable moveables. This our custom hath determined, that where defuncts legate, gift, oblige or dispone their whole moveables, that is understood to be with the burden of their whole moveables debts: because the gift being *per universitatem*, the burden is also meant to be *per universitatem;* whereas otherwise debts are taken off the whole head, and the wife, bairns and nearest of kin bear their shares of it: yea such donations, even *inter vivos*, are understood to be with that burden. But if the legacy, gift or disposition be special, if by evidences it appear that the defunct knew the thing legated not to be his own, the same is to be acquired, or the value thereof out of the dead's part; but if that be not known, the meaning is understood to be, that he gives it as he hath it, or pretends to it, without any warrandice, no not against his own preterite fact and deed: for defuncts are not supposed to have remembered what they have done; and what they do after the legacy, derogates therefrom: yet special legacies have this advantage, that they have no abatement by the defunct's debt, if they do not exceed dead's part.

22. As to the meaning and interpretation of special clauses, they are congested in the Indexes of the Decisions of the Lords observed by me. The particulars would be tedious and unnecessary to be here repeated, but by these indexes and decisions, they will easily be cleared; especially these clauses which are most frequently controverted, such as clauses concerning conquest, succession, and irritancies.

Title 43. Probation by Witnesses

IN all controversies witnesses are adhibited to determine, as a common rule amongst all nations; which is confirmed by the word of GOD, "In the mouth of two or three witnesses let every word be established:" [Matt.xviii,16; 11 Cor.xiii,1; cf.Deut.xvii,6; xix,15] where, by "every word," is understood every allegeance to be proven. For it is not meant that words should only be proven by witnesses, but that things should be so proven, being proponed by words written or spoken, if a just conclusion be thence inferred. But words of the mind, or thoughts, cannot be proven by witnesses, unless they be expressed by words, or other sufficient signs.

2. Thence also it followeth, that one witness cannot make sufficient probation, whatsoever be the quality or veracity of that witness, and yet the testimony of one witness may produce more faith in the judges than other two will do: this evinceth, that every thing is not a sufficient proof that makes faith to the judge. One witness may concur with other evidences to make up probation, though it be not sufficient alone.

3. Hence it is also consequent, that the probation of some points requires but two witnesses, and others require three, which must be matters of very great importance: for if the sentence had been, that every word should be proven by three witnesses, or at least by two, it had not imported so much as when it is said, that every word shall be established by two witnesses, or by three. This difference is observed in several cases in the Roman law, without any particular edict, but upon the diversity of importance of the matter, as in the making of the inventories of the estates of defuncts by their heirs, improving the hand-writ or subscription of a party *comparatione literarum*. And yet positive law may require more witnesses than three, in the most solemn and important acts, when there is no *penuria testium*: so seven witnesses were required in testaments, and five in codicils, which behoved to sign; but, in a military testament *in procinctu*, two witnesses were sufficient without signing: this doth not invalidate the natural evidence of three witnesses in itself, but only refuseth legal remedies, when the command to adhibit so many witnesses is neglected or contemned, in the same way that legal remedies are not adhibi-

ted upon naked pactions, when the authority of law requiring somewhat further, (as stipulation) which may easily be done in all cases, is neglected.

4. Upon the like grounds our law and custom hath in many things refused the testimony of witnesses, how many soever they be, where writ may, and uses to be adhibited; or where it is agreed to be adhibited. So we allow no verbal or nuncupative testaments, and no probations of legacies exceeding 100 pound Scots, and no probation by witnesses of the borrowing of money. But in matters of far greater importance, where writ uses not to be adhibited, or cannot commonly be adhibited, we allow probation by witnesses: as in all bargains, buying, selling, or bartering in markets, it were most inconvenient to require writ; and therefore in all such bargains, in or without market, witnesses are adhibited, unless it be agreed upon that writ shall be adhibited. And we refuse witnesses for proving any other promise or paction, though within the value of 100 pound Scots: neither make we any difference, whether the words be framed in the way of stipulation or not, which was a very fit difference before the skill to write became so common. We do also allow witnesses to prove the intromission or receipt of any moveable, whether fungible or not, except the borrowing of current money. Neither do we allow the probation of witnesses for payment of money, or other fungibles, where the same are established by writ, except in the case of the delivery of victual by tenants, or of the performance of a contract for a visible work, requiring a long time to work, or that which is palpably extant; so contracts for building a ship, a bridge, a house, &c. or for delivery of a ship, or for performing a voyage, though contracted in writ, may be proven to be performed by witnesses. And, though the intromission with money-rent be probable by witnesses, yet the payment of silver-rent by tenants to their masters, though within an 100 pounds, is not so probable. And generally, in all cases where writ is not only a mean of probation but a solemnity requisite, the same cannot be supplied by witnesses, or even by the oaths of parties; because without such writs, the rights whereof they are solemnities become null: yet the tenor thereof may be proven not only by oath of party, but by witnesses.

5. It is a common requisite in all witnesses, that they be solemnly sworn in presence of a Judge-Ordinary or delegate, according to the common custom of all civil nations: and therefore extrajudicial oaths, or oaths not required judicially, as aforesaid, albeit in writ, are not accounted testimonies, but testificates; which, though they may be sufficient to instruct matters of small importance, as in obtaining commissions to depone in the country, or for instructing reasons of advocation, or in concourse with other evidences, especially in matters ancient, yet they are not accounted testimonies in ordinary probation.

6. These solemn oaths of witnesses give the chief ground of the moral duty to acquiesce in the testimony of witnesses, and that it proceeds not upon statute or custom; for it is a strong ground of confidence, that *contestes* will not perjure themselves, and take GOD witness to a lie, wherein they may be

redargued by their *contestes*, and become infamous, and punishable capitally. And therefore, as parties refer to, and acquiesce in the oaths of parties swearing to their own detriment, even then when another probation is possible, much more ought they to acquiesce in the solemn oaths of more indifferent persons as witnesses. And as witnesses are habile to take away men's lives and their estates, so much more are they sufficient in lesser matters, where writ is not required.

7. Yet great caution hath been always adhibited in admitting of witnesses, because many are apt to mistake through inadvertence or precipitancy, and through the secret insinuation of favour or hatred, which even the witnesses themselves do not perceive: therefore several persons are, even by the moral law, inhabile to prove as one of two or three witnesses. As first, those who have not attained the age of discretion, whereby their senses are confirmed by exercise, to advert things as they are, and when a moral principle of justice is not considered and confirmed in them, that they can have the reverence of an oath, and the abhorrence to wrong others in their right: yet when they come to have discretion, they may bear witness in palpable things, upon their memory of what passed before they attained to discretion, wherein there can be little doubt of their mistake; as when march-stones are solemnly set, boys use sometimes to be laid down upon them and sharply whipt, whereby they will be able to remember, and be good witnesses as to these marches when they are very old, that impression on their fancy lasting long.

Secondly, Fatuous or furious persons are not capable of being witnesses, while they are in that condition, and even of things that then occurred, except they had long lucid intervals; for short intervals are hard to be known.

Thirdly, Profligate persons, who make no conscience of oaths, which may be known by their frequent lying, and swearing falsely or inconsiderately, or their being openly vitious otherwise, whereupon they are accounted as ininfamous, *infamia facti*, by such vice as relates to the matter of right, as deceivers or oppressors, or persons openly profane, being atheistical, or contemners of religion: for such are not presumed to have the reverence of an oath, and especially if they be vitious by vices relating to oaths, as if they have been corrupt witnesses by accepting of bribes, or not discovering in the preliminaries of their oath when bribes were offered, or in deponing things inconsistent, which make them inhabile in any cause. This point is sometimes too far stretched, as when persons are excluded as being heretics: for many such have reverence to an oath; and though they may be rejected as suspect, when they are to testify against these of an opposite persuasion, especially if they be zealous, yet that is not through simple inhability, but upon suspicion of inequality. Covenants have been made with these that acknowledged not the true GOD, yet having devotion to that which they adored, it gave ground of confidence in their oaths. And certainly it is much the duty of judges, in taking the oaths of parties or witnesses, to do it in these terms that would most touch the conscience of the swearers, according to their persuasion and custom. And albeit Quakers, or other fanatics, deviating from the common sentiments of mankind, do, from persuasion, refuse to give a formal oath, yet if they do that which is materially the same, as if they depone that what they are to say "is in the presence of GOD, who is their witness, and who will be their judge if they lie," it is materially an oath.

Fourthly, Husband and wife, parents and children, are commonly inhabile witnesses. And though parties would consent, yet these are not obliged to depone against one another, lest thereby disgust and prejudice should arise betwixt so near relations, or they be in too great tentation of perjury; and therefore they are exeemed from being witnesses or judges one against another, even in capital matters.

Fifthly, These who are in place of parents and children, as uncles and aunts, nephews and nieces, and also brothers and sisters, are inhabile to be witnesses for one another: but they have not the privilege to exeem themselves from being witnesses one against another. But cousin-germans, and these of greater distance, are not simply inhabile, but where more indifferent witnesses are found.

Sixthly, Enmity or malice incapacitates these to witness against these they hate. And if the enmity was upon any atrocious injury done or attempted against life or fame, an ordinary reconciliation doth not obliterate the same, unless evident friendship hath followed.

Seventhly, Interest in the cause makes witnesses inhabile as to that cause, if they can gain or lose thereby. But that *fovent consimilem causam*, is not a good objection: for that conjunction of interests relates to the relevancy, and not to the verity of the cause.

8. Positive law or custom hath been too apt to reject witnesses, who were not morally inhabile; which is very allowable where there is variety of witnesses, if the other party can give sufficient evidence thereof, as when any deed is done at a public market, burial, or marriage, or at solemn conferences before friends or arbiters, or by examination of the adducer, if he knew of any other witnesses, and who they were, or by preliminary examination of the witnesses who were the *contestes* in the point to be proven: in such cases the judge may warrantably forbear to examine that witness, till some others of the *contestes* be called: but otherwise to exclude these, who by divine law are habile, and thereby to exclude the adducer from his right, is not warrantable. And therefore, where it appears, that there could not be many witnesses, these that are present, will be admitted, though in other cases they will be rejected; as in encroachments upon men in or about their houses, if there be any vestige of the crime, witnesses are not rejected, because they are servants, or of such other relations as otherwise would exclude them. And in all clandestine acts, there is not to be expected variety of witnesses; and so suspicion should not exclude.

9. Therefore, where competent evidence is given, that other witnesses might be had, there are many grounds allowable to refuse these who are ad-

duced, with suspicion of being biassed, till others who are without suspicion be examined; as first, poverty, whereby witnesses are more capable of corruption. And therefore in our custom, it uses to be objected against witnesses, that they are not worth the King's unlaw, that is, the ordinary mulct for misdemeanors. But this ought to be considered according to the importance of the cause; which, if it be great, he who is worth the King's unlaw, is not *omni exceptione major* : for in great causes, the tentation may be great, which cannot be presumed in mean points.

Secondly, Witnesses threatened by powerful and rigorous adducers, if they did engage to depone, are corrupt, although their deposition were true. But though they did not engage, they ought in their preliminaries to declare the threats, which would purge the suspicion, showing they were not afraid thereof; otherwise they were suspect.

Thirdly, Witnesses become inhabile, by giving partial counsel; as by instigating the plea, telling the party of his interest, and offering to depone in his favour, or being present with him at consultations with lawyers, where it might be shown what was necessary to be proven. But it is no partial counsel, though persons be interrogated by parties what they know of such affairs, generally or particularly, if the motion arise not from themselves.

Fourthly, Witnesses may be rejected, if they were prompted and instructed in what terms to depone.

Fifthly, Witnesses may be rejected, if they come to the place of judicature, at the desire of the adducer, without being cited. These are called ultroneous witnesses, but should rather be called officious witnesses. But if upon other occasions they came there, and were cited, not being desired to come for that end, it is no ground of suspicion.

Sixthly, Domestic witnesses, as servants and others, though not in a servile condition, yet continued in the family of the adducer for some considerable time, are rejected as suspect, either in the case of their master or mistress, or their fellow-domestics, being in a friendship together, unless they be necessary witnesses in domestic affairs.

Seventhly, By our custom moveable tenants, who have not tacks for terms to run, are suspect witnesses.

Eighthly, Advocates, agents, factors, trustees, are suspect witnesses for these who intrust them. But they are not obliged to depone as to any secret, committed to them.

Ninthly, Good-brothers and good-sisters are suspect witnesses for one another, except it be by marrying of two sisters or two brothers, which is but *affinitas affinitatis* : and therefore they are only to be excluded, where more indifferent witnesses are found.

Tenthly, Extraordinary friendship or intimacy makes witnesses not to be *omni exceptione majores* : for such are accounted no less affectionate than brethren. Yea, unlawful amours render witnesses suspect of too much favour, or otherwise of too much hatred, if they have gone off with dissatisfaction.

Eleventhly, Women are rejected from being witnesses in causes merely civil, except they be necessary witnesses, as in the probation of a child born of that ripeness, as that it did cry or weep.

10. But, in all these objections against witnesses, where they are not simply excluded, or have interest in the cause whereby they may gain or lose, or in near collateral relation, or enmity, witnesses should not be rejected, unless other witnesses unsuspect could be found.

11. The verity of all these objections may be proven by the oath of the adducer, or by the oath of the witness, or by the oaths of other witnesses, if they be cited to a term before the witnesses be examined; but they cannot otherwise be offered to be proven, because these objections are dilators which must be instantly verified, in the first instance; but in the second instance, they may be proven, even by witnesses, if reprobatures be protested for, at the time of their examination: for otherwise parties are held as acquiescing, if they protest not; except they can give competent evidence, that the grounds of their inhability came to their knowledge after their testimony, and were of the nature of these for which witnesses might be simply rejected, as upon account of near relation, enmity, or interest in the plea: for there is no reason, that upon the other lighter grounds of suspicion (which should only take place where more indifferent witnesses are found) solemn decreets should be reduced; especially now when causes go to the roll, which makes a considerable distance of time between the examination of witnesses and the decreet, whereby parties so soon as witnesses are cited, might *incidenter* cite other witnesses to prove their inhability, which will have summary process, and might be terminated before decreet be extracted. But it hath been, and ever will be of great inconvenience, if decreets remain uncertain by reprobatures: and therefore it were most convenient, that there should be a statute for a short prescription in reprobatures.

12. So much for the hability or inhability of witnesses. The next point is, how they are adduced and examined. The ancient custom was, that, in the principal summons, there was a warrant to cite witnesses, and a blank left for their names. But seeing now causes cannot come to be disputed and determined, at the term to which persons are cited, that way of citing witnesses by the principal summons is useless, till terms be assigned for probation: and then the witnesses are cited by diligences, yet with continuation of days; so that the adducer may bring them to the bar, any day after the term to which they are cited, and then objections against them may be disputed or referred to the Ordinary on the witnesses, before they be examined; but still they must appear at the bar, and make faith: and there is put up, in the minute-book, "Avisandum and witnesses," to intimate to the other party, that the witnesses will be examined in the afternoon, unless they be adduced on Saturday, and then they are to be examined on Tuesday thereafter.

13. There are two Ordinaries for examination of the witnesses, that they be not forced to long attendance: and more are appointed, if the witnesses be

very many. If they cannot be all overtaken at one diet, the Ordinaries ought to begin with these first the next day, that the opposite party be not uncertain when to attend, and to give in interrogators, or propone and instruct objections: and if they be otherwise examined, the party will easily get a re-examination, he condescending upon the relevant particulars. The Ordinaries are judges as to the relevancy and pertinency of the interrogators, which are regulated by the tenor of the act of litiscontestation: and therefore they cannot refuse to examine upon the tenor of it: but if indirect interrogators be proponed, to expiscate the verity, parties are heard thereupon; and in case of difficulty, report is made thereanent, or upon the objections and instructions thereof.

14. Formerly the testimonies of witnesses were taken, without the hearing of any but the judge and clerk. But now, by a late statute [Evidence Act, 1686,c.18; A.P.S. VIII,599,c.30], testimonies are appointed to be published; and therefore parties and advocates are admitted to be present at the examination, but no other ought to be admitted. This was always allowed in criminals, and the reason is, because, upon the answers of witnesses, there arise emergent interrogators to expiscate the truth, which the Lords did always follow, and now they have the concourse of the parties.

15. In the testimonies of witnesses, the *ratio scientiæ* should always be expressed, that it may appear they do not depone upon fancy or conjecture, or upon deduction of consequences, but upon acts falling under sense. And therefore testimonies *ex auditu* prove not, that is, where the witness gives for the reason of his knowledge, that he heard the matter by relation of others. But, if the thing to be proven do itself fall under hearing, the testimony of the witness that heard it is valid: and therefore, if witnesses be adhibited to prove fame, the hearing of common report is sufficient, though the deponent cannot condescend upon the reporters.

16. If parties give in interrogators, for examining who were present at these acts on which the witness depones, and where and when the same were done; the same should not be refused, that thereby it may appear, whether there were witnesses not cited, which were less suspect, whom the Lords might ordain to be cited, that it might appear whether the witnesses would vary as to the circumstances of time and place, and so not be *contestes*.

17. By what hath been said, it may appear what witnesses are inhabile in any case; and what witnesses are inhabile as to some particular persons, and not to others; or as to some particular causes and not to others; and what witnesses are rejected, only where more indifferent witnesses are found, but otherwise may be received without them, or if one unsuspect be found, may be received with the same: thence also it appears, what witnesses are *omni exceptione majores*, as being neither inhabile nor suspect.

18. In examination of witnesses, each witness should be examined severally, out of the presence of the rest. And the parties and advocates ought not to be permitted to remove, till all of them be examined. Neither ought the examined witnesses to go to the same room with these not examined, to the effect the

witnesses to be examined may not be biassed, by representing to them what the former witnesses have deponed, which may very readily be unfaithfully related: for a witness that will not perjure himself in the favour or odium of a party, may yet relate his testimony otherwise than truly it was.

19. Witnesses in improbation of writs, or reprobatures, are not excluded upon exceptions, but all are taken *cum nota*, which are not parties: and if their testimonies be contrary, they may be confronted, that by minding those who differ, of circumstances, they may be convinced to join: and in advising these testimonies, respect is not had only to the number, but chiefly to these who are most free of exception.

Title 44. Probation by Oaths of Parties

PROBATION by oaths of parties, hath a moral ground and a scriptural warrant, as well as probation by witnesses. The moral ground is, that as men are obliged to perform all duties towards men, so they ought not to refuse to acknowledge the same, so that the other party be obliged to acquiesce, and not further to strive or controvert. The scriptural warrant is, "That an oath for confirmation, is the end of all strife." [Hebrews vi,16] And, therefore, as all men are obliged to remove the ground of strife, so they are obliged to give their oaths, when these are necessary, for removing it. Strife doth comprehend, not only contending by force, but contending by law. And there is convincing reason that oaths of parties should end all strife; because thereby God is called as witness of the truth, and is acknowledged as a just judge, who will punish the perjury. It is a stronger confirmation than the testimonies of witnesses; because parties' oaths are commonly against themselves, whereas witnesses swear not against themselves. Also these who assert or acknowledge by confession or writ, do not call God to be witness and judge, nor are under the atrocious crime of perjury; and confession is rather a yielding, than a positive assertion of the verity of what is confessed, as denial imports no more but not confessing, and not a positive assertion of the falsehood of the thing denied.

2. Seeing oaths of parties for confirmation must end all strife, and that the swearer runs therein the hazard of perjury and infamy, if the contrary be proven; therefore, after such oaths, there may be no other probation adduced; yea, parties ought not to be urged to swear, where the urger knows any other sufficient probation; and therefore he that is required to swear for terminating a plea, is not óbliged to swear, till the requirer not only renounce all other probation, but depone that he hath none: especially that he hath no probative writ; because the malice of some, in small matters, may be so great, as to be content to lose the point referred, so that they might make the swearer infamous, by reserving his writ to the contrary.

3. It is not every oath that can terminate pleas, and be the end of all strife, but that oath only which the Scripture calls an oath for confirmation, and which is commonly called an oath of verity, because it positively affirmeth, that what the swearer asserteth, is true. And therefore an oath of credulity is

not such an oath of verity: because the swearer doth not assert the verity of the matter, but the verity of his belief of the matter; by which, is not understood, that which is proper belief, that is, persuasion upon the testimony of faithful witnesses; but belief is the prevalent opinion or judgment of the swearer. And yet the oath of credulity ought to be true, that the swearer is so persuaded; and it is so presumed, but it terminates not the plea: for even thereafter, other probation by writ or by witnesses above exception, may be used, where, by statute or custom, they are not forbidden; much more if the party depone, that, to the best of his memory, or best of his knowledge, what he asserteth is true. Such oaths do justly exclude him who so sweareth, to insist in these points contrary to his own belief or persuasion; and therefore in that case they may terminate the plea: but an oath of verity terminates the plea *simpliciter*: yet oaths of credulity, in supplement of other evidences, may fully terminate the plea, but not alone.

4. Yea, oaths of credulity may terminate pleas in some cases, even in favour of the swearer; as the oath *in litem*, in relation to the quantity or value of goods, which positive law for conveniency allows in many cases, to prevent atrocious injuries; as in the case of spuilzie, if a spuilzie be proven, though the whole particulars libelled be not proven, the party injured is allowed to prove by his own oath what other particulars were spuilzied: or, in the case of things committed to custody, by the Edict *nautæ, caupones, stabularii*, if any thing be wanting, the party damnified may depone upon the goods contained in any coffer or cloak-bag, or other inclosure, and the law presumes, that these who receive the same in custody, do it with that hazard, and that it were uncivil to require these who trusted the same, to show not only to parties, but to witnesses what were inclosed: and as to the value, an oath of credulity, or of estimation, is in these or the like cases allowed to those damnified, yet so as if the estimation be exorbitant, the judge only can modify.

5. An oath of verity cannot be urged, in that which might infer the hazard of life or fame of the party. And this is not by positive law only, but by the common law of nations: and it is the common interest of mankind, that they should not be urged to swear against their life, limbs, or fame; and even when they are pressed to confess by torture, they are not compelled to swear, but it is sufficient to deny, that is, not to confess; because there lies upon them an obligation of self-preservation, whereby they may conceal their own crime, if it cannot otherwise be proven. Joshua did not urge Achan [Joshua vii,19–24] to confess the stealing of the Babylonish garment, nor did he say that the confession was to the glory of God, till by divine testimony the lot fell upon Achan, and then it did glorify God, to show his omniscience, veracity, and justice, by the lot, and that not only by Achan's confession, but by his digging up and showing to the people the truth thereof. Therefore it is, that in improbations in cases of forgery, or in theft and robbery, or in most cases of fraud, parties are not urged to depone, nor are they urged to depone upon the secret thoughts of their mind, either as to their judgment, or as to their pur-

pose and design: for so far has God left thoughts free, as to man's inquiry. Neither can an oath be urged to supply the want of a writ, when it is not only a mean of probation, but a solemnity requisite for completing a right, as a charter, seasin, or intimation of an assignation.

6. Oaths of verity do so far sopite pleas, that after such an oath is given, there is no more to be required than *si juratum sit;* so that there can be no remedy, though, by a criminal action, the swearer should be found perjured: and that because an oath, voluntarily referred or deferred by him who had power so to do, implies a contract to stand thereto, without any retractation, and hath the force of a transaction, and of a final and ultimate judgment; and therefore there is no appeal from sentences proceeding upon voluntary oaths, where appeals are in use.

7. An oath of verity hath the same effect, though it be extrajudical, which both affordeth action and exception. And albeit by the Roman law [D.2,14,7], naked pactions without stipulation were ineffectual, yet even an extrajudicial oath doth afford both action and exception. And though extrajudicial confessions do not always prove, but may be upon other designs than to confirm the truth; yet an extrajudicial oath doth ever prove whether it be ultroneous, or upon transaction or reference of parties.

8. An oath of verity is so effectual and extensive, and doth so fully end pleas, that it gives not only action or exception to the party who has sworn, but to his heirs and successors, yea, to his singular successors. And the oath of one *correus debendi* liberates not only him and his heirs, but all the rest and their heirs. And the oath of the principal liberates the cautioner, and his heirs, if the verity of the point be referred to his oath. Yea, though another action be intented by the same or other parties, if the plea or cause be the same, the exception of an oath of verity is sufficient to elide it, if the matter be the same: but the matter comprehends the *medium concludendi*, whereunto if the oath relate, and not simply to the verity of the conclusion, it doth not exclude the probation of the conclusion by other *media*.

9. There is another kind of oaths of verity, which is not referred nor deferred by a party, but by the judge; which therefore is not a voluntary but a necessary oath, in obedience. But it takes no place in plenary probation, in which the judge can neither command a party to swear, without consent of the other party, nor can he hinder him to refer or defer an oath, where oaths are competent: for instance, where there is *semiplena probatio*, a judge may command a party to depone, even in his own favour, when he finds that would make up a sufficient probation: such also are the oaths *ex officio*, in extraordinary cases. From these oaths there was competent an appeal, that it might be judged by the superior judge, whether the inferior did rightly urge the oath: but therein there is no contract of parties; and therefore writs after found out, may reduce sentences upon such necessary oaths, but not upon oaths voluntarily referred or deferred by parties, implying an engagement finally to stand to the oath.

10. Formerly parties were examined upon oath alone, either upon the express terms in the act whereupon they deponed, or upon interrogators given in writ by the parties, but they or their advocates were not allowed to be present: but now, since all testimonies are published, parties do not only give in written interrogators, but they and their advocates are present, and offer to the examinators verbal interrogators, from the answers made to the act or written interrogators.

11. The examinators are judges of the relevancy and pertinency of the interrogators, and in case of difficulty, they report the debates concerning them. There is great skill and prudence in ordering the interrogators, that the particular interrogators or expiscations be put first; for if the terms of the act, or more general interrogators be put first, the answers thereunto engage the deponent to answer the particulars accordingly, which they would not easily advert if the particulars were first proposed.

12. The examinator ought not to give up the interrogators to be seen by the parties that are to swear, who thereby are apt to contrive evasive answers, and are assisted therein by others: nor should he suffer them to read their answers in writ, but to answer by word. And it is his trust by new interrogators to clear all dubious answers. Yet in the case of qualified oaths, they are accustomed to relate the matter of fact in writ, and to subjoin that what they have before related is true. The main reason of allowing writ in this case is, that the other party may be ready to debate against the competency of the quality; but the examinator and the other party may propone what interrogators they see just, notwithstanding the written qualified oath. And there is a late Act of Sederunt in July 1692, prohibiting the giving in of written oaths, except in the case of qualified oaths.

13. Oaths of verity referred to parties, are sometimes by them deferred back to the referrer, wherein the question oft-times ariseth, which of the two should depone, which the judge must determine: and he that offers to defer, ought to depone that he is not clear in the matter; and therefore, if there be probability that the other party hath more occasion to be clear therein, he should not refuse to depone, but otherwise he should not be urged, because the deferrer may be clear to depone against himself, but would rather the referrer should depone, against whom he hath the ground of reproach, that he hath gained his cause by his own oath.

14. Qualified oaths are these wherein the deponent acknowledgeth that what is referred to his oath is true, but that what is referred doth not contain all the truth requisite for determining the cause, which therefore he adds as qualities of his oath. This is necessary and warrantable in many cases; especially where in any affair, a party who refers to oath, pitches upon particulars sufficient to infer the conclusion, by presumption arising therefrom, which he is not otherwise obliged to prove; as if he allege he made a bargain for ware at such a price, and delivered the same; and therefore ought to have the price. The other party may depone that the bargain was true, the ware delivered,

and that was the price; but that there were other conditions besides the price, or that the ware was not seen by the buyer, but taken on trust, and found insufficient, and upon the first discovery thereof was offered to be returned, and not being accepted, the goods being perishable, were rouped, whereby the insufficiency did appear. Or if a party should pursue another, for intromitting with goods in his possession, which presumed his right, and therefore ought to be restored, the party might depone, that he intromitted with these goods by authority of a judge, or by the consent or approbation of the party.

15. There is another oath frequently used in processes, called an oath of calumny, which may be used against pursuers as to their whole libel, or as to such parts thereof wherein they insist; or against the defender as to any defence proponed by him, or even as to his denying the verity of the pursuer's libel, and as to all replies, duplies, &c. wherein either party will be holden as confessed, if they refuse to depone; except in the cases where they are not obliged to depone or confess, which are the same as in the oath of verity.

16. There is much unclearness in the import of an oath of calumny, what the meaning of it is, and what the words ought to be; which depends mainly upon the signification of calumny, which doth always import a reflection or reproach upon the party who calumniates. And in processes, it is either a reproach against the justice or truth of the party who calumniates, that is, that he urges points unjust, or which he believes not to be true: and by the ordinary terms of oaths of calumny, wherein parties are interrogated, "whether they have just reason to affirm or deny such points," parties are in danger to swear falsely, or ignorantly; for thereby they may mean, that they have just reason to pursue or defend their own interest, or their meaning may be, that these points are not against law or reason, albeit they know nothing of the truth thereof. But the tenor and true meaning of the oath of calumny is, that parties do not affirm or deny these things that may reproach their neighbour, but when they believe that what they assert is true; which is very well determined by our ancient statute, both as to parties and their advocates, or forespeakers: Parl. 1429, cap. 125. [A.P.S. 11,19,c.16] bearing, "That advocates and forespeakers in temporal courts, shall swear, and also parties that they plead for, if they be present in the beginning, before they be heard in the cause, that the cause he trows is good and leill."

Illud juretur, quod lis sibi justa videtur.

Et si quæretur verum, non inficietur.

By this statute it appears, that the oath of calumny is an oath of credulity, that the cause is good, *i. e.* just, and leill, *i. e.* true; and that the plea appears to the deponent to be just, and that he will not deny the truth that shall be asked of him thereanent. In the plea are comprehended both the allegeances of pursuers and defenders; and therefore the terms of the oath of calumny should be by either party, that "they believe or judge that the points they insisted in are both just and true." And it is not sufficient to depone, that they think them just or equitable; or that they only believe they are true, but that they are both just and true.

17. The statute also bears, that the oath of calumny upon the libel should be before any process. And it used to be sustained, if it were deponed, that they believed some part of the libel were just and true: but now oaths of calumny are not used but in the time of dispute, and not until the points whereon they are craved are found relevant, or at least admitted to probation by an act before answer; but in formal acts of litiscontestation it is not reasonable to crave the oath of calumny, as to the justice of points, seeing the Lords have found them relevant, but only as to the verity thereof, that they believe they are true, and not calumniously proponed to procure delay.

The Lords did lately, by an Act of Sederunt [A.S. 13 Jan. 1692], alter the terms of oaths of calumny, but that Act hath not yet taken effect, and the terms of this statute are much more clear and proper, than the terms of that Act: and the oath may be fitly proposed in these terms, "whether or no the deponent doth believe, that there is more probability for the truth of the point proposed, than against the same:" for this is sufficient to clear, that the allegeance is not calumniously proponed.

18. If parties be present at the disputing of their cause, they must depone *de calumnia*, but if they be absent, the advocates who propone the points, may be put to depone *de calumnia*, whether or no they were informed by their clients, or by such as they intrusted to inform them, that the points they insisted in were true, which yet doth not hinder the parties to be cited to depone *de calumnia*, whether they did believe the truth of these points: for it is sufficient for advocates, to believe upon the information of clients, but the clients must have a better ground of belief.

19. Oaths of calumny are always competent before probation, or, even if the probation by writ or witnesses prove nothing, when they are patent, the oath of calumny may be required; but not after the conclusion of the cause, and yet even then the oath of verity may be required, if the party be present.

20. By what hath been said, the difference is evident between the oath of verity and that of calumny; that the oath of calumny doth not fully determine the plea, but only excludes the deponent from insisting in these points, which he doth not believe to be true; and doth not hinder the other party to prove these points, which the deponent did deny by his oath of calumny, but doth not prove the points to be true, and so as to require no further probation, as the oath of verity doth. The Lords, by Act of Sederunt, have declared that they will not require the oath of calumny of parties, upon their own recent fact, for they cannot believe that to be true, but when it is true, and therefore there must not first be required an oath of calumny thereupon, and when they cannot prove by witnesses or writ, they cannot then return to the oath of verity, upon the same point of proper recent fact: but in ancient facts, where the actor may have forgot, the oath of calumny may be required, and after-

wards the oath of verity, if no other probation may be had: for then the deponent must be positive of the truth of the point.

21. The moral duty to swear for ending of controversies, gives the foundation of the probation by holding parties as confessed who do not depone, when they are required or cited to depone with express certification to be holden as confessed, if they do not depone [1 v,3,30,*supra*]. This is a just and a most expedient certification: for the law presumeth they will not depone, because they are conscious they must confess what is referred to their oaths. And it takes place both in oaths of verity, and in oaths of calumny: for these who refuse to depone *de calumnia*, are held as refusing, because they are conscious their allegeance is calumnious, and that they themselves do not believe the truth of it.

22. Albeit being holden as confessed, comes in place of the oath, acknowledging the point referred thereto, yet it is not so strong a probation as the oath itself: for none can be reponed against an oath, but they may be reponed against being holden as confessed, if the execution, by which they were cited under that certification, be improven; or such impediment hindering their appearance at the term appointed, be instructed, that they neither could come, nor send to their advocates to petition for a commission to depone; as if they suddenly fell into a disease affecting the brain, or were carried away and unlawfully imprisoned; yea, if parties be holden as confessed upon exorbitant quantities, which cannot be supposed they would acknowledge, they will be reponed to their oaths; or if they defer to the party's oath who required the same.

23. The presumptive probation, by being holden as confessed, may be elided, if recently done, by other contrary probation adduced by the party holden as confessed; but not *ex intervallo*, because the other probations which might have been had on the same point, whereupon the party was holden as confessed, may be lost; for if any crave to be reponed, the other party may confirm the decreet by witnesses, which otherwise would not be receivable. And it cannot be known whether he might have found witnesses to prove, if the reposition be craved *ex intervallo*, seeing in the mean time persons might have died, or removed, who might have known the truth: and likewise a decreet upon holding parties as confessed, for whom a term hath been taken, is a decreet *in foro*, which is not quarrellable *ex intervallo*.

Title 45. Probation Extraordinary

HAVING explicated the three ordinary kinds of probation, viz. writ, witnesses and oath, there remain yet other kinds and ways of probation, which are here called extraordinary; because they are more rare and unaccustomed, and some of them are only competent to sovereign courts *ex officio nobili*, when the ordinary ways of probation occur not.

2. Probation uses to be distinguished in that which is inartificial, and that which is artificial. The former three ways of probation are called inartificial;

because they prove points expressly, directly, and *in terminis*, and so require no art or skill to make parties understand, that the point found relevant is proven: as when a libel, exception or reply, is directly and expressly proven to be true, by the oath of the parties against whom the probation is adduced, swearing that these points are true, or that they know them to be true, or that they believe them to be true, or when they say the like by an authentic writ subscribed by them, or for them, or when sufficient witnesses testify the same; for here can be no doubt or question, that the very point proposed is expressly proven. But when the probation is not direct and express, but consequential and indirect, where the point to be proven is inferred to be true by consequence, it is not equally obvious to all capacities, whether that consequence be valid or not: and therefore it is called an artificial probation, when it admits debate and reasoning whether the consequence be good or not; upon which the Lords must give interlocutor, not only when the consequence is upon matters of fact acknowledged or notour, but even when the points of fact are offered to be proven, from which being proven, that point would be inferred by consequence, which is proponed in the libel, exception, reply, or duply. And yet the interlocutor is rather concerning the verity of these points, than concerning the justice thereof; but the interlocutor may well be, that such matters of fact alleged are not relevant to infer the point proposed in the process: for the probation of the matter of fact to infer the point to be proven by consequence, cannot help or relieve the party who alleges the same, because the inference is not good.

3. But there are other extraordinary ways of probation, besides this consequential probation, inferring the truth of one point of fact, from another point of fact; such as notoriety of the verity of the point of fact, and the confession of the party, which are valid probations, and yet are neither by writ, witnesses, or oath of party. Neither do all other probations beside these three, come under the name or nature of presumptions; but all the ways of probation, besides these three, are less ordinary than they; and therefore are all joined here, under the name of extraordinary kinds and ways of probation.

4. Probation by notoriety of the verity of fact is, when the judge of proper knowledge knows, that the point to be proven is commonly known or acknowledged to be true, whether it be so known to a whole nation or to a whole vicinity. And it will not be elided, though some particular persons be ignorant of it, if the generality know it. But the particular knowledge of the judge is not probative; for the judge must proceed *secundum allegata et probata*, and cannot be both judge and witness in the same cause upon particular knowledge; and yet his knowledge of the notoriety is sufficient, but so that the notoriety may be redargued by a stronger positive probation, if it be in due time proponed and proven. But a decreet will not be found null for want of probation, when judges sustain the point to be notour, especially in a sovereign court collegiate, where the major part of the judges acknowledge the notoriety: thus all allegeances for husbands, wives, parents, children, proceed without pro-

bation of their being such, unless pregnant evidence be alleged in the contrary, which will hardly be admitted to be proven by litiscontestation, but must be instantly verified, yet may be competent by way of reduction. There are many other such cases, as when lands are libelled to lie in such a shire, such jurisdictions, or such parishes, it is taken for granted, unless the contrary be instantly proven. In the serving of brieves of heirs, or of terces of relicts, "commonly holden and reputed" is sufficient, though it be not universal, but in the vicinity, without proving the marriage of the father and mother, or of the husband and wife: yet a contrary probation, that such persons could not be lawfully married, or that they were the time of the birth married to others, if instantly verified, would stop the service, or make it null, or being proven in a reduction, would have the same effect.

Albeit judges cannot be both judges and witnesses, not only in the same point, but even in the same cause, (which is introduced that the power of judges be not too much increased) yet it reaches not to notoriety, or to what is done in presence of the judge in judgment, as what he sees and hears; for these are counted as notour. But this holds not *ex intervallo*, upon the memory of judges, even of things they have seen or heard in judgment, neither in what they have heard or seen extrajudicially, but only such as are so insert in judicial acts.

5. The next extraordinary manner of probation is, by the confession of the party, against whom any allegeance is sustained to be proven; yet it is an extraordinary probation, because there are few so ingenuous as to confess what they know to be true, neither is there a law to compel them either to confess or deny, unless the matter be referred to their oath of verity or calumny. This confession must be judicial, acknowledged by advocates at the bar, (or by their informations) being minuted by clerks, in so far as falls within the duty of advocates, who frequently acknowledge what they do not controvert, to show their ingenuity, and to give the more favour to what they do controvert.

It has been much controverted, and sometimes sustained, that when parties propone defences, without denying the libel or quantities, they should be supposed to acknowledge the same; but that hath not been universally sustained. By the Roman law in many cases, parties were put to acknowledge or deny the truth, without oath: and, in some cases, their denial doubled the value of that which they did unjustly deny, and was proven; which our custom doth not approve: and in other cases upon denial, the expense of probation lay upon the denier, which were very just and sustainable with us, having nothing penal in it; and therefore, if the alleger require the other party to confess or deny any point found relevant, if he refuse to confess the verity of that point, and if it be proven, so that it may be presumed he was not ignorant of the verity of it, he may justly be condemned in the expenses, whatever be the event of the plea.

6. But if the party be not present, when litiscontestation is made, the

question is, if his advocate may be so required? And how far the advocate's confession will be sufficient probation? As to the first, there is very good ground, that the advocate may be required to confess or deny the point to be proven: for he should insist in no point, but that which he hath asked his client whether it be true or not? At least, whether he doth believe it to be true?

And as to the last point, whatever is the proper trust and duty of advocates, obliges their clients as to the verity of allegeances; and therefore ingenuous advocates acknowledge how far they will controvert the verity of points proposed, both in matter of law, and matter of fact: but in matter of law they have less warrant, for that is the judge's part, and therefore if they yield more than the judge sees just, he ought to extend the law further than they yield; but, in matter of fact, the judge is not presumed to know, nor doth his private knowledge import, but it is proper for advocates, who are procurators by their office, to acknowledge or confess points of verity, which they will not controvert, which makes sufficient probation, being minuted by a clerk of session; or if it be contained in bills or informations given in by the advocate who returns the process for that party, which being once so done, they ought not to be permitted to retract the same, upon pretence of want of warrant, inadvertence or mistake.

7. Homologation is a kind of confession or acknowledgment of the right homologated. It hath been already considered (*Lib.* 1, *Tit.* Obligations Conventional, § 11 [1,10,11,*supra*]), what acts have been found to import homologation, and what not.

8. Extrajudicial confession is commonly held not to be probative, but to be done upon some other design, than to prove the verity of what is professed; yet when extrajudicial confession is made upon accompt of the truth of the things confessed, it may import probation; but if it be only by emission of words, it cannot be proven by witnesses, but by oath of party, who, if he acknowledge such a confession, and adject not a rational qualification, it will prove against him. But extrajudicial confession may not only be by word, but by writ, as by missive letters, wherein there are no obligements contained; so confessions before arbiters in transaction of affairs may be proven by the oath of party, or even by a decreet-arbitral, if there be no defect therein: and confessions before church-judicatures and congregations, though they be accounted extrajudicial, and in capital matters, are not sustained as probation, because to shun excommunication, men may be under temptation to acknowledge themselves guilty of that they are not; yet if any matter civil be confessed and acknowledged by writ, it is a much stronger probation than several positive presumptions; or confessions made *ad levandam conscientiam*, or for satisfying the desire of parties, being so proven, are probative, because such expressions cannot be accounted *verba jactantia*. Yea, when the Lords *ex officio* allow all evidences to be adduced, for proving any point, they will examine witnesses upon extrajudicial confession, which makes not plenary pro-

bation, but doth concur with other evidences to make up probation, if the nature of the point in question cannot be proven by an ordinary probation, and yet is not exclusive of extraordinary probation; as oft-times occurs in latent or ancient rights, or where there is suspicion of fraud.

9. Presumptions are the most important extraordinary probations. And they are of two kinds. The one is, when the points to be proven are presumed to be true, without the probation of any other point of fact. The other is, when points of fact are alleged, and thence the point to be proven is inferred, as consequent therefrom. This occurs two ways; for sometimes a point is offered to be proven simply, and when the probation is adduced, the point is not expressly proven thereby, but so much is proven, as the point to be proven is thence presumed to be true; and this occurs at the advising of probation, which formerly rested alone upon the consequences inferred by the Lords with close doors; but now parties are to be heard, whether the consequences be good, or the presumption be probative. And sometimes these consequences are demonstrative, or of necessary consequence, in which case the probation is full and sure: but these come scarce under the name of presumptions, but these consequences only that are sufficient to induce persuasion in the judge, and that have an eminent probability of the consequence. But every probability is not probative, nor deserves the name of presumption: and frequently many presumptions do concur to make up probation; and there may be many opposite probabilities, from different consequences and considerations; so that if the prevalence be not great, it will not infer against a possessor, the loss of his possession, much less against a proprietor, the loss of his property, nor will it infer an obligation against a party that is otherwise free. But if the question be about attaining the possession of that which neither party possesses, but craves to recover as their prior possession, or if the point of right be dubious, the prevalence of the presumptions, though far less than in the former cases, may infer sufficient probation: for when parties do controvert and contend, it is easy to prove the right, where there is no other contest, but if it belong to the parties contending or be *nullius;* yet the *regalia* or these things that are *inter regalia,* or belong to sovereign authority, are not accounted *nullius,* but may be declared to belong to the sovereign authority, though they do not insist: but, in other things, hardly can any thing be declared *nullius.*

10. It is a more sure way of probation, when the points of fact which are designed to prove the point in question, are expressly condescended upon in the libel or exception, &c. which uses to be done, when the alleger says, that he offers to prove such a point, in so far as he offers to prove other points of fact, from which the point to be proven is presumed, as consequent: for then before probation, there is place to debate the consequence, and so the judge must determine whether the consequence be good or not, *nam frustra probatur, quod probatum non relevat.*

11. The other kind of probation is, when the very point in question is

much more probable to be true than to be false, without adducing any other matter of fact to be proven; so that the dispute is only whether the allegeance be presumed to be true, wherein every probability infers not a probative presumption, but it must be eminent *ad convincendam conscientiam judicis*: for if it be certain by evident reason, it is not presumption but notoriety, which makes the probation.

12. This is that kind of presumption whereupon there are so large treatises of lawyers. And so presumptions are divided in three sorts, for they are either *præsumptio judicis*, *præsumptio juris*, or *præsumptio juris et de jure*.

Præsumptio judicis is when the judge finds the probability of a point (wherein the ordinary probations are not competent,) to be eminently probable to be true; unless the contrary be proven by a more positive probation.

13. *Præsumptio juris* is where law hath so presumed, but hath not statute, nor declared it for a rule: so frequently in the narrative of statutes, presumptions are expressed, as motives inducing the making of the statute, but it is the statutory words that makes it a law: yet the presumption from which the statute arises is a presumption in the law, and is stronger than the presumption of a judge alone: of these presumptions there are multitudes in the Roman law, which swell the treatises of presumptions to a great measure. There are not wanting such presumptions in our law, though we have but few statutes: yet even these presumptions admit a contrary stronger probation; and though presumptions be said *transferre onus probandi*, rather than to prove, yet they prove unless the contrary be proven. Under the presumptions of law, the presumptions of custom are to be comprehended, though they be not in written law; and so custom hath fixed many presumptions, about which there is no question, but that they are probative.

14. *Præsumptio juris et de jure* is, when the statutory or declaratory part of the written law does statute or declare such a point to be true, without further probation. This presumption is not only a presumption in the law, but a presumption which becometh a law; and therefore it admits no contrary probation. Of these, there are many examples in our law: such is the presumption of simulation from retention of possession, whereby base infeftments are postponed to posterior public infeftments; or the retention of possession of escheat-goods, which is declared to presume that the gift is to the behoof of the rebel, who was suffered long to possess; and the statute against fraudulent alienations declares, That it shall be sufficient to infer fraud in prejudice of creditors, if in the course of inchoate diligence the debtor dispone, or if he dispone without cause onerous, when he becomes insolvent.

15. Fiction of law is no presumption; for thereby the law-giver makes that which he knows not to be true, to be esteemed and held as if it were true: so the heir is *eadem persona cum defuncto*.

16. Presumptions of law with us are chiefly when, by the decisions of the Lords, such presumptions are ordinarily sustained; of which there are many more than are in our written law.

17. Presumptions are of two sorts; some are general, occurring in many causes; and others are special to particular causes. The chief general presumptions approved by our customs, are these; I. Liberty is presumed in opposition to slavery. Of this presumption we have but little use, slavery being abolished; yet there remains some vestiges of it in colliers and salters, who are astricted to these services by law, though there were no paction or engagement, which is introduced upon the common interest, these services being so necessary for this kingdom, where the feual of coal is in most parts necessary at home, and very profitable abroad; and seeing we have no salt of our own, but that which is made by the boiling of salt-water, salters are so also astricted: so that colliers and salters, while they live, must continue in these services, and the once having them in service, is a sufficient ground to detain or recover them; yet so, that if that possession hath not been lawful, another who did possess, and from whom they did unwarrantably remove, *vi, clam, aut precariò*, may recover them from the unlawful possessor.

II. Freedom from all obligations by delinquence is presumed. This presumption is to the same effect with that common brocard, *nemo præsumitur malus ;* which is to be understood of any particular delinquence or fault (albeit in general no man be free of faults, inducing obligations to reparation or punishment) even though he hath been proven to have been faulty in the same kind of fault. Yet he who is known to be habitually vitious in any particular vice, is presumed so to continue; but this alone is not a probative presumption, but an adminicle, concurring with other presumptions or probation, whereby *semi-plena probatio* may be made full; so in improbations, it may be adduced as an article of the indirect manner, that the defender hath forged other writs, albeit the party concerned do not insist, if the evidence of the forgery be clear.

III. Freedom from conventional obligations is presumed, but not from natural obligations, or these which arise from the will of God, and man's obedience thereto. Obligations also by law are presumed, and are effectual probations, and are presumed to be known, in so far as they are evident and commonly known to people of all capacities: but with exceptions in some cases, of soldiers, rusticks, women, minors and persons of weak capacity. Hence it is that in any action, wherein freedom from obligations by engagement, or obligations by the law of God, or law of man, are libelled relevantly, there needs no other probation but presumption: and if what is alleged from the law of God, be clear and relevant to infer the conclusion craved, it is presumed *præsumptione juris et de jure*, admitting no contrary probation: for it is rather a point of law, which requires no probation, than a point of fact. But the other presumptions before mentioned are but *præsumptiones juris*, which admit a contrary probation, and therefore are said *transferre onus probandi*, that is, they prove unless the contrary be proven.

IV. From the effect, the ordinary cause is presumed. From this ground many of the contracts are presumed: so he who payeth annualrent, is presumed to owe the stock; he who payeth hire, is presumed to be the conductor; he who holdeth accompt in a matter common, is presumed to be in a society, or in other cases to be a factor or trustee; he who goeth about another man's affair, is presumed to be a mandatar, or a *negotiorum gestor*, if the affair hath been begun by that other. These contracts could hardly be otherwise proven but by writ, which is seldom used, or by oath of party, wherein the hazard of the parties' faithfulness and sincerity occurreth. Yet these presumptions are but *juris*, and admit contrary probation, if the defender condescend on a more probable cause, which will prevail as a stronger probation; much more if he prove the contrary by oath of party or writ; yea, even witnesses are receivable to elide such presumptions.

V. Freedom is presumed against any servitude or *nexus realis :* as the freedom from astrictions to mills, or any other real servitude of lands, or any hypothecation of moveables, or any arrestment thereof; and therefore, if any pursue a declarator of freedom from these, he needs no further probation, but this presumption, which transfers the burden of probation upon the defender, if he allege such real burdens.

VI. All negative allegeances are presumed. And hence it is commonly said, that negatives prove themselves, and need no probation, other than this presumption. And therefore in exculpation, there is no more needful, but to libel that the party is not culpable, actor, or accessory, whereupon decreet will follow without any probation, against the parties who are cited; and they cannot insist in the contrary, while that decreet stands unreduced, though it be in absence; yet they may be reponed upon payment of expenses, if they be contumacious in not appearing; but if they appear and allege any thing contrary to the libel, they must prove the same, and the pursuer needs prove nothing, unless it be by reply to elide the defence. This presumption must be limited by what hath been said, as to the former presumptions, that it holds in negatives against obligations by engagement, but not in the negatives of natural obligations, or obligations of law; and it holds in servitudes or real burdens, except such as are introduced by law; so the negatives of hypothecation of the fruits or *invecta et illata* for rents, are not presumed when proposed by tenants.

VII. All possession is presumed to be lawful. This is *præsumptio juris*, and therefore, when possession is craved either to be retained, recovered, or quieted from molestation, there is no more to be libelled, but that the pursuer was in possession, and did not relinquish the same, which will be presumed; but that the pursuer was in possession, must be proven. But it admits the contrary probation, that the possession was *vi, clam, aut precariò*, which the defender must prove, and the pursuer is not obliged to condescend upon, or instruct any right, but only possession; unless it be by reply to elide the allegeance of violent, clandestine, or precarious possession. This presumption is introduced for the common interest of mankind, that none may disturb the possession of another, at his own hand, without order of law, and instructing a just cause for altering that possession; and that no question of right shall be meddled in, till the possession be established where it ought to be; and therefore possession makes a right several from property. This is also the rise of the distinction betwixt petitory and possessory judgments, whereby possessors defend themselves in possession, without disputing their rights summarily, but by reduction or declarator only, and enjoy the fruits and profits *medio tempore*, till they be put *in mala fide* to possess, by instructing the right of another [11,7,22,*supra*]. These actions are also elided, by obligements to quit possession, in favour of the defender, whether it be by direct obligation, or by dispositions importing the same.

VIII. Possession of moveable goods presumes the property thereof. This is the great security of commerce, which would be extremely prejudged, if men were obliged to prove the titles of their possession of moveables, and so subject themselves to the memories or faithfulness of witnesses, or to the necessity of writ in bargains which ordinarily pass currently in markets. Yet this is but *præsumptio juris*, admitting a contrary probation, even by stronger presumptions; and therefore he who insists for recovery of moveables, which he alleges to belong to himself in property, or wherein he was the lawful possessor, put out of possession, *vi, clam, aut precariò*, must condescend and prove, that he so ceased to possess, that it could not be presumed to be by commerce; as if he prove that the goods were stolen or strayed from him, or were lost by him, or that they belonged to him as succeeding to a defunct who died in possession thereof, and the like; or if he prove that he was in possession, and that the goods could not pass from him by commerce to the defender, because they were goods altogether unsuitable for him to have by commerce, as if the goods were precious moveables, which it could not be presumed that the defender could acquire by traffic for his own use, or as a merchant, or as a person intrusted for others, to whom such goods were presumable to be acquired by commerce.

IX. Long possession presumes property of real servitudes: and that, albeit there be no more title but the general title of pertinent, in any infeftment.

X. Possession of lands by him who is holden and reputed heritable possessor, wadsetter, or liferenter, presumeth sufficient title to cognosce the right, by an inquest of the most famous persons in the neighbourhood, if it be proven that the pursuer's writs and evidents were burnt, destroyed, or lost by any accident. This is a presumption of law, mentioned in our Acts of Parliament, and it differeth much from the probation of a tenor, which can be proven by two sufficient witnesses, yet requires adminicles; but here the whole writs may be lost, so that there remains no adminicle in writ: but it can no otherwise be proven, but by an inquest of the most famous persons in the neighbourhood, by a commission to the sheriff or other judge-ordinary in the place.

XI. There was a *præsumptio juris et de jure*, in favour of the king, in the case of forfeiture, whereby possession for five years, was declared sufficient to the king or his donatar, to give him right to the lands possessed by the person forfeited, being retoured by an inquest as heritable possessor thereof. Parl. 1584, cap. 2 [A.P.S. III,349,c.6]; bearing, "That all lands, baronies, lordships, annual-rents, mills, multures, fishings, tenants, tenandries and service of free tenants, and other heritages whatsomever, which have been, or hereafter shall be peaceably bruiked and possessed, by whatsomever persons forfeited, or that hereafter shall be forfeited for crimes of treason and lesemajesty, committed or that hereafter shall be committed, against his Highness and his successors, or by them to whom our Sovereign Lord and his successors should succeed by reason of the forfeiture of their nearest heirs; as their heritage by labouring the same with their own goods, setting the same to tenants, and uplifting the mails and duties thereof, as their heritage, and so reputed holden and esteemed heritable possessors thereof, by the space of five years, immediately preceding the process and sentence of forfeiture; shall belong to the king, and others deriving right from him, without showing any other right and title thereof. And also it is statute, that tacks and possessions of lands or teinds by the forfeited person, shall be put in possession of the king or his donatar, and they to remain therein for five years, that they may search the rights thereof, and shall enjoy the fruits thereof during that time." In this last point anent tacks, there is not required five years' possession by the forfeited person, but any lawful possession sufficeth. These are evidently *præsumptiones juris et de jure*, which the law not only owneth, but statutes to be a full probation. But the foresaid statute is much derogated, by cap. 33, Sess.2,Parl.1,W.&M.1690, [A.P.S. IX,225,c.104], whereby, "It is declared, that all forfeited estates shall be subject to all real actions and claims against the same, though they be not raised nor insisted in within the five years preceding the forfeiture; excepting bygone feu-duties, annualrents, and other annual prestations, for which there is no diligence within the said five years." Whereas formerly only such actions within the five years, did interrupt the presumption: yet the title of the forfeited person is still presumed, but may be excluded by a better right.

XII. It is an important general presumption, that whosoever is cited by a messenger, to compear and depone by an oath of calumny, verity or supplement, if he do not depone, he is holden as confessed. This is not by statute-law, but by custom, justly and fitly introduced by the Lords, on this presumption, that he doth not depone, because he durst not deny, which is *præsumptio juris et de jure*, which admits not a contrary probation. Yet the Lords, *ex nobili officio*, do repone parties to their oaths, when they instruct, that they were not contumacious in not compearing and deponing, or when they adduce evidences in the contrary, which is not admitted as a contrary probabtion, but is a ground to repone them to their oaths: for that for which they are holden as confessed may be true, though there were writs to prove the contrary. The probation by being holden as confessed, is a certification in summons referred to oath, and is already more fully treated with the probation by oath, *Lib.* 4, *Tit.* 44.

XIII. The certification in reductions and improbations is also by custom founded upon presumption. For, in reduction, the certification is, that the pursuer shall be preferred and put in possession, if the defender appear not and produce; which is upon this presumption, that he dare not produce, knowing that the pursuer has a better right, whereby a decreet of preference *in foro* would be recovered. And the certification in improbation is, that if the defender produce not the writs called for, they shall be holden and reputed as false and forged; and the presumption whereon this certification is grounded, is, that the defender dare not produce the writs called for, because he is conscious they would be improven: this is *præsumptio juris et de jure*, which admits of no contrary probation, but the former is only *præsumptio juris*. The like presumption in improbation is, that he who uses a writ, must abide by the truth thereof, with certification if he do not, it shall be holden as forged: the presumption is, that he is conscious of the forgery, and so accessory thereto, or otherwise he would abide by the writ.

XIV. It is a common presumption, that no man by disponing, or delivering of possession, is presumed to gift gratuitously, unless it be so expressed. And therefore he is rather presumed to give in custody, or in trust, than to gift. Yea, though it be expressed as a gift, or gratuitous disposition, it may be found a trust, not only by the oath of party, but by pregnant presumptions.

XV. It is a common presumption, that *debitor non præsumitur donare* [1,8,2; IV,42,21,*supra*]. This is a species of the former, and stronger than other presumptions of that kind: for the donor being debtor, it is strongly presumed, that he doth not dispone or deliver to gift, but to pay; yet it is not without limitation, for if the thing disponed be not liquid of the same kind with the debt, it is not presumed to be in payment; or if there be a stronger presumption that it is a gift rather than payment; so mean things given to indigent persons, are presumed rather to be for charity, than in satisfaction of a debt; or what is disponed by princes, is not presumed to be in satisfaction of a former gift or promise; or what is disponed or engaged to children, who are competently provided by former dispositions or obligements, is not presumed to be in satisfaction of the former, but as a new donation.

XVI. What is delivered by a bridegroom to a bride is presumed to be conditional, if marriage follow.

XVII. What is wittingly built or wrought on the ground of another is presumed to be a donation. This presumption is introduced by law, that such buildings be not demolished.

XVIII. Entertainment to a person that is major, without paction, is presumed to be gifted, and nothing can be demanded upon that account.

XIX. Life is presumed. This some do extend to an hundred years of age, but others only to fourscore, which is confirmed by that of the Psalmist, that the age of man is threescore ten, unless by the strength of nature he come to fourscore. Hence it is that heirs cannot be served upon presumption of the death of their predecessor, unless witnesses or fame concur in the contrary;

and hence also women may not marry in their husband's absence till that age, which yet doth not hinder them to proceed by a process of adherence, which doth not infer death, but desertion.

XX. In matters of fact ignorance is presumed, unless knowledge be proven. But this hath several limitations; as first, knowledge is presumed of these things that fall under sense, when the party was present, as to these things which moved him to be present; but not as to other things, that might have passed without his observation. Secondly, Ignorance is not presumed of the moral law, or positive law or custom, which is evident to common capacities. Neither in proper recent facts, except in these who are involved in multiplicity of affairs; but it is presumed in the acts of others, except where the party is obliged to inquire, and so to know the same. Hence comes the brocard, *Scire debes cum quo contrahis*, which doth not so much relate to the validity of rights, as to the qualification of the party with whom you contract.

XXI. In solemn acts all formalities are presumed, whereby the act might subsist, unless these formalities be specially required by law or paction.

XXII. *Probatis extremis præsumuntur media*. This presumption hath its effect in prescriptions and possessory judgments; for in the long prescription forty years' possession must be proven; and in possessory judgments seven years' possession must be proven, so that no other hath possessed seven years, since both these possessions must be continual without interruption. But it is not necessary to prove continual possession every day, every month, or even every year; but possession must be proven at least every other year, or that there hath not intermitted three years in the long prescription, or one in the short prescriptions or possessory judgment; but these are presumed *probatis extremis* [IV,40,20,*supra*].

18. The special presumptions in particular causes are mainly concerning lawful marriage, and lawful children, trust, and concerning the satisfaction of old obligations, which hath been long without payment of annualrent, and concerning the retiring of writs and evidents, and returning the same back unto the persons of the debtors. In all which the ordinary probations by writ, oath, or witnesses, do seldom occur: and therefore probation by presumption is the more necessary. But in these, presumptions are seldom direct and immediate, arising from the points of fact to be proven, as in the general presumptions, wherein the certainty or pregnant probability of the truth of the matter of fact makes it be presumed to be true, without any probation by writ, oath or witnesses: but the other kind of probation is, when some of these ordinary probations are adduced, from whence the point to be proven is deduced by consequence. No judge will sustain marriage because it is alleged, or that which is properly trust, or the satisfaction of evidents, because they are asserted. But other facts must be proven, that these may thence be inferred as necessary or very probable.

19. To return to the particulars, marriage may be proven by witnesses, which is a direct and immediate probation, but it seldom occurs except in

recent marriages which have been solemn. But in no case is it easy to be proven by writ, although the declarations or testificates of the person who officiated, of the married persons themselves, and even of the witnesses, were produced; for these are but testificates, unless the oaths of the witnesses be interposed, amongst whom he that officiated is a pregnant witness, and others that were present, though not called nor required; much less will the oaths of both the married persons prove the marriage in all cases; for that may be by collusion, to cover their fornication, or to prejudge the lawful succession by solemn marriage. And yet marriage will be more easily proven indirectly by facts whence it is presumed.

As first, marriage is proven by the *sponsalia* preceding, as by the contract of marriage, whereby the parties oblige themselves to solemnize marriage, and by copulation following, or even by antecedent promise of marriage, whatever be the way that it is obtained or granted, if copulation follow without violence; although the promise were conditional, and that the condition is no otherwise purified but by copulation, the condition is thereby presumed to be passed from, or the fraud or force in obtaining the promise. But if the copulation be not voluntary, whatever precede it does not infer the marriage.

Secondly, Contracts in impuberty are presumed not to be with the use of reason, nor are obligatory or valid, except contracts of marriage in impuberty of either or both parties, which, if copulation follow, are valid: for marriage being a divine contract, cannot receive its measures and rules from human constitution; and therefore discretion or judgment is presumed from copulation, *præsumptione juris et de jure;* and (as the canon saith) in such cases, *malitia supplet ætatem.*

Thirdly, Cohabitation, and behaving as man and wife for a considerable time, presumeth marriage, though there be neither contract, promise, nor *sponsalia* preceding, nor evidence of copulation by children. But the copulation in the former case must be proven by the tokens of virginity known to witnesses, or by present inspection of the wife's body. These are presumptions so strong, that the confession or oath of either, or both parties, will not elide the same, though they should acknowledge that they neither promised marriage *de futuro*, nor contracted the same *de præsenti*; yea, though they should acknowledge that they so cohabited to cover their fornication, that they might be free to marry others when they pleased: for all these and such things would be presumed as collusive, to dissolve the marriage upon dissonance of humours, or other designs, seeing marriage is indissolvable but by adultery or wilful desertion.

20. Filiation is presumed from marriage, whereby the children are presumed to be the lawful children of these who are proven to be married in any of the former ways, which is yet more pregnant and favourable on the part of the children, to give them the right of aliment and succession, and is the probation of the marriage betwixt these who are presumed parents, which is so strong a presumption, that the mother acknowledging another father than he

that is married to her, will not prejudge the children; much less will the assertion of the father, that the children are not his, albeit he condescend upon another to be the true father: yet if both the married persons do acknowledge that the child is not procreate betwixt them, but by another as father, who would also acknowledge the same, and own the child, it would elide the presumption. But if both married persons had first owned and treated the child as theirs, the concurring testimonies of all the three would not prejudge the child in its aliment, legitim and succession, as children of that marriage. But the impotency of the father, or his being far distant from the mother, while the child were presumable to be gotten, at least for the space of nine or ten months, is sufficient to prove the children not to be lawful children.

21. Trust may be proven by the confession, or oath of the trustee, or by his writ acknowledging the same. But it is much more frequent to prove the same indirectly, by matters of fact proven by writ, oath, or witnesses, not directly proving the trust, but indirectly, being thence inferred by the judge. The stating a right in the name of a trustee, with a backbond or declaration of the trust, is properly no trust, more than any obligation in writ, which is called *creditum*, or a trust, in so far as the debtor will voluntarily pay his creditor, and not alienate his estate to exclude him, or put him to the trouble of suits at law: so trust with a backbond is only trust in so far as the trustee, disponing for causes onerous, may betray his trust, because the backbond being personal, and not a recorded reversion, will not recover the thing intrusted. But trust properly is that which the law calleth *fidei commissum*, where there is no reversion, bond, or promise of reversion; yet the trustee knows *quid actum est*, that it was not a donation or gratuitous alienation; but that the granter did trust that the trustee would dispose of it as the truster would require: and therefore, if the trustee did not this voluntarily, it were to small purpose to refer it to his oath: for it is presumed that he who would steal, would swear; and it is the worst kind of stealth to betray trust: and therefore the law alloweth, that trust may be proven indirectly, by circumstances inferring the same.

22. There are many circumstances from which trust may be inferred; as first, if any person deliver money, and take a bond in the name of another, not being a child, or other near relation, and at the lending did not express it to be the money of that other, and did retain the bond in his own hand, thence it would be presumed that other's name were in trust to the lender's behoof, and he might be compelled to acknowledge the same, and to assign. And if any person assign or dispone a right to another, and if it be proven that he was in such circumstances, as it was not safe to keep it in his own name, and that the other, being master of the right, made no mention of it in the inventory of his estate, or did not dispose of the profits of it, it would thence be presumed, that it were in trust, to the behoof of his author, albeit it did bear a pure donation for love and favour, or to be for onerous causes and good considerations.

23. The satisfaction of an old security has been always sustained, not

only by direct probation, but by indirect, from circumstances proven: As if the creditor had long taken no profit when he had opportunity; as if he had had intromission with the debtor's estate, or was his tutor or curator, and did not retain the sum in that security, nor mention it, or did not mention it in the inventory of his estate, or if he were indigent and claimed it not, and the debtor were opulent; or if a posterior security were granted for a greater sum, without mention or accumulation of the former, and without demanding any thing upon it, it would be presumed to be comprehended in the greater security, if the profit thereof were taken and claimed, and not of the other.

24. The returning securities to the granter thereof, is much more frequently proven by presumptions from circumstances, than by direct probation; whereof this alone is *præsumptio juris, chirographum apud debitorem repertum præsumitur solutum.* Yet it may be elided by a contrary probation, that the writ came into the debtor's hand by another way than upon payment: as by finding it, or getting it up from another in whose hands it was, without the creditor's warrant, or that the security was in the author's hand with a blank assignation or disposition, albeit it was not a right to be retired upon payment, or if it was in the hands of the author who could cancel it, so that the tenor of it could hardly be proven, albeit there were no blank assignation or disposition of it: thus apprisings found in the debtor's charter–chest, after his death, the same being so proven, have been found extinct, before the law for registration of the allowance of apprising; and when the messenger was dead, and the executions not in the appriser's hands; or if therewith there was a blank assignation or disposition, which would extinguish the same; although a singular successor's name were filled up even for onerous causes, because he would be presumed to be partaker of the fraud, or to be only a trustee.

Title 46. Decreets of Session

HITHERTO have been explained the several actions and processes, competent before the Lords of Session, and the most ordinary and important defences, exceptions, replies and duplies, common, or proper to be adhibited in these processes, with the diligences for obtaining probation thereof, and the several ways of probation competent therein. There remain now to be considered, the decreets following upon the saids processes, and the executorials and executive actions for making them effectual; which actions could not fitly be explicated before decreets, they being a part of the execution thereof, and presupposing the same; as actions for making arrested goods or sums forthcoming, actions upon breach of arrestment, contraventions upon lawborrows, and adjudications of several kinds; and lastly, suspensions of decreets of Session, or other summary charges.

2. It were a superfluous and tedious repetition, to consider the matter of decreets severally, and the particular forms and tenors thereof. But it is sufficient to know the general forms of final sentences, the whole matter having

been handled before. The judicial sentences of judges are of two sorts: The one is intermediate between the dependence and termination of processes, which are therefore called interlocutors, and are done by acts of process: The other sentences are definitive, which terminate and end processes, as to the instance, action, or plea. These we call decernitures or decreets: the English call them judgments, or decrees, which do more properly signify a resolution upon choice in any free thing, than the determining the rights of parties.

3. Decreets are either absolvitor, whereby the defender is freed or assoilzied from the conclusion of the libel or process; or they are condemnator, whereby the conclusion of the process is found just and true, against the defender, in whole or in part; or they are mixed, whereby the defender is absolved from some part of the conclusion of the process, and is condemned in other parts thereof. In all the three, the decreet is either simple, when it is exactly conform to the conclusion of the process, or it is qualified by the proposal or consent of parties, or by the authority of the judge *ex proprio motu ;* which qualifications do not annul the decreet as disconform to the libel, for either party may qualify their allegeances, and though neither do it, the judge may do it.

4. Sentence definitive of the instance is, when upon any dilator, process is refused: for thereby that instance is ended, these sentences are only absolvitors *ab instantia*, the terms whereof are ordinarily, "The Lords sustain the dilator defence, and find no process upon this citation; or in this action;" which are not the same: for instance, if a spuilzie be pursued upon a citation having less time than fifteen days, there is no process on that citation; but if the dilator be, that the process is not intented within three years after committing the spuilzie, that dilator being sustained, is an absolvitor from any action of spuilzie; but it is not an absolvitor *a lite et causa*, for the pursuer may insist for wrongous intromission. But if the cause be odious, the interlocutor uses to be, "The Lords assoilzie *a libello ut libellatur*." Defenders use to neglect the extracting of such sentences, imprudently enough: for, upon supplication, the Lords may ordain the cause to be further heard, when perhaps the defender is gone, thinking himself *in tuto*; whereas, if the sentence were extracted, he were *in tuto*.

Sentences finding libels not relevant, are of this kind. For the pursuer may insist in the same cause, otherwise libelled, upon other *media*. Yea, he will seldom be hindered to alter his libel, to make it relevant, to be sustained without a new citation; but if the sentence be extracted, he cannot insist on that citation.

Protestations for not producing suspensions, or for not insisting, are absolvitors from the instance. These use to be extracted; for if they be not, the pursuer may insist at any time within the year.

Protestations containing remits in advocations, are always extracted, and are final sentences of the advocation, as to the reasons therein contained, but hinder not advocations upon new reasons, emergent after the former advocation; which should not be passed upon reasons competent and omitted the time of the former advocation: for as reasons of suspension are excluded, because competent and omitted, so ought reasons of advocation.

5. All the former absolvitors pass under their several names, and are not ordinarily called decreets, though indeed they be. But decreets, so commonly called, are also of different kinds. Some are without litiscontestation, when the points requisite for obtaining sentence are all instantly verified, by presumption, writ, oath of parties, or being holden as confessed without taking a day to depone: which sort of decreets occur, when the pursuer's libel is so instantly instructed, and there is no defence or exceptions sustained to be proven, or if exceptions be repelled in respect of replies instantly verified; or if the reply be repelled in respect of a duply instructed; or if all these be instructed, which do not import the verity of the allegeance against which they are adduced. All such decreets may be dispatched by the Ordinary, unless some point be taken to interlocutor, as to the relevancy or instruction, which makes no further stop than till the interlocutor be reported; unless the Lords appoint it to be heard in their own presence, instantly, or to go to the roll. So Ordinaries may advise all writs adduced for interest or probation, requiring no litiscontestation, and may take and advise the oaths of parties compearing, and instantly determine thereupon: albeit they are sparing to determine upon qualified oaths, or these which are not so plain and short as that they may be written and signed at the bar, in respect there is a remedy without necessity to go to the roll, because the Lords hear the oaths of parties, when the clerks offer them, if they determine the cause, and do instantly decern; but if there be any doubt of qualities adjected, the Lords either call the parties, or remit the cause to the roll. Yet if the writs produced be many, large, or intricate, the Ordinary may make a great *avisandum* to answer when the Lords call; and then the cause goes to the roll, according to the date of that *avisandum*.

6. The second kind of decreets is, when litiscontestation is made, and terms are assigned to prove. After the first term is past, the party against whom the point is to be proven, may call upon the act, and if the point to be proven be by oath, he may crave the term to be circumduced, and the party to be holden as confessed; or if the probation be by writ or witnesses, he may crave the term to be circumduced for not proving: and if that point terminate the cause, decreet passes of course. But if the party produce an executed diligence against witnesses, he will get a second term against any of the witnesses contained in the former diligence, against whom citations are produced by the charge of horning on the act, and therewith may have a caption for taking of the witnesses; which being elapsed, if the witnesses be not produced, ordinarily the term is circumduced, and decreet pronounced, if decreet follow upon that point. Yet, by supplication for more witnesses, in place of these that are dead, or out of the country, or for witnesses new come to knowledge, the party deponing that they are come to knowledge since the former diligence, will get a diligence against these other witnesses, and a term longer

than ordinary, that he may use both horning, and, in case of disobedience, caption before that term: so that there are still but two terms. Yea at the second term for witnesses, if an execution against magistrates or messengers to take the witnesses be produced, or the latency of witnesses be instructed, at least by the party's oath, a further term may be granted by the Lords on supplication. But, if no diligence be produced at the first term, or no witnesses at the last term, decreet passeth of course, the terms whereof are, "the Lords circumduce the term and decern."

7. In diligence for probation by writ, if neither writs be produced, nor horning against the havers, the term will be circumduced, and decreet pronounced. But if either writs or horning against the havers be produced, a second term will be granted, and caption against the havers. But if he who is to prove, will take a reasonable long term, by an incident diligence by way of action, for proving the having of other men's writs, if he depone *de calumnia*, that he believes that they are in the hands of such persons, against whom he hath intented the exhibition, shortly after the term was assigned, the Lords do readily allow the same; but not indefinitely without a certain term as formerly, when the user of the incident did industriously draw it in length, as far as he could, because, till the full effect thereof, the principal cause was superseded.

8. If writs be adduced *ad probandum* upon litiscontestation, the Ordinary cannot advise the same: yet if such writs be produced, as have no rational contingency with the point to be proven, he ought to reject the same, and circumduce the term. But if any writs to the purpose be produced, if no further term be craved (for the pursuer when he thinks he hath proven will readily renounce probation, yet the defender will not, till the last term be past, nor will declare the cause concluded) there the Ordinary ought to declare the cause to be concluded, and according to the act concluding the cause, it is to be inrolled in the roll of concluded causes.

9. In like manner when the probation is by witnesses, if there be any depositions, the Ordinary cannot advise the same, though they bear nothing more than that the witnesses knew nothing of the cause. And if the cause depend upon a libel or reply to be proven by the pursuer, he will readily at the first term (if he thinks he has sufficiently proven, or expects no more probation) renounce further probation, whereupon the Ordinary will hold the cause as concluded. But if the defender be to prove an exception or duply, the cause cannot be concluded without his consent, till the last term be elapsed; and then the Ordinary declares the cause to be concluded, and according to the date of these conclusions of the cause, they are inrolled amongst concluded causes.

10. If the defender compear not, or before proponing peremptors pass from his compearance, the probation is only by the pursuer, and upon the libel; which, if he instantly verify by presumption, writ, or holding the defender as confessed, he being cited by a messenger at arms with that certifica-

tion, and if the matter be competent to be proven by oath, the Ordinary will presently decern, or report in case of difficulty, and upon report will decern: yea, if he find a defect in relevancy or probation, he ought to assoilzie, which the defender though absent may extract for his security; and the Ordinary ought not to suffer the pursuer to take up his process, after absolvitor is pronounced.

11. If probation be upon litiscontestation *reo absente*, the pursuer may pass from further probation, when he pleaseth, and hold the cause as concluded: but the Ordinary cannot advise the probation, whether it be by writ or witnesses, but it must go to the roll of concluded causes. And, if the defender be cited by a messenger, personally apprehended, with certification to be holden as confessed, the Ordinary ought to hold him as confessed and decern, if he find the libel relevant, and the certification to prove the same; otherwise he ought to assoilzie.

12. These acts concluding causes are oft-times neglected to be extracted; yet the Lords use to proceed to advise upon the minute of the act concluding the cause.

13. The advising and decerning in concluded causes proceed thus: The ordinary day for advising concluded causes is Saturday; yet if the Lords find that the testimonies or writs are many, which cannot be ended in a forenoon, they appoint an afternoon for advising; and in the beginning or ending of each session, they use to proceed in concluded causes, upon other days, when that roll is far behind. For concluded causes once being inrolled, need not be wakened, though a year elapse after their inrolment: and though they be delete out of the roll for not insisting, yet they may be inrolled of new; because either party may insist in concluded causes, though the other insist not: and therefore when they are deleted because none of the parties insist, neither party can take advantage thereof, but that either party may inrol again.

14. When concluded causes are called to be advised, which is not till the process be put in the hands of the clerk of the process, that he may peruse the same, then the clerk, in presence of the advocates for one or more sides, relates the case, and reads the words of the act of litiscontestation, bearing the points that are to be proven, and then declares what is adduced for proving thereof, that either advocate may hear that he omits nothing necessary to be mentioned, which he will not fail to do, because it concerns both his trust and reputation. If the probation be by a qualified oath, or by another oath which is long and perplexed, then the user of the oath pitches upon the words which he thinks prove the point to be proven, which are accordingly read: and if the other party allege other words, to clear the meaning of these, these are also read: and if there be doubtfulness in the probation, the advocates are heard how far the oath proves, or if it be a qualified oath, they are heard whether the quality be intrinsic and competent or not. And if the probation be fully clear, the Chancellor or President, without removing of the parties,

decerns. But if there be any doubtfulness, parties and advocates remove, and the Lords advise and decern.

15. If the probation be partly by writ, and by witnesses so far as is not proven by writ, the same course is followed. And if witnesses have been used, who neither depone *affirmativè* nor *negativè*, but that they know nothing, or remember nothing of the points that are to be proven; when the party that is to prove seeth the event to be such, he may, upon supplication, obtain a citation against the defender to depone, with certification, providing it stop not the advising of the cause, and then the cause is advised upon the oath, or upon the certification to be holden as confessed, which are competent when witnesses neither affirm nor deny.

16. If the probation be only upon the testimonies of witnesses, and if the party against whom they are adduced have insisted upon reprobatures against the hability of these witnesses, if the summons of reprobature be concluded, the adducer of the witnesses may pitch upon witnesses which are not in the reprobature, and if these prove, there is no need to advise the reprobature; if not, the reprobature must be first advised. The testimonies of the reprobatures may not be *contra dicta testium*, wherein they are *contestes*, but only against their preliminary depositions, wherein they are alone, and wherein their oaths are not oaths of verity terminating the process. All these points which concern hability of witnesses are expressed, *Lib.* 4, *Tit.* 43, Probation by Witnesses. After the discussing of the reprobature (which may be either as to the preliminaries, or as to the *ratio scientiæ*) the principal cause is advised.

17. Formerly parties were not allowed to be present at the advising of the testimonies of witnesses, nor to see the testimonies: for when they were taken, none but every singular witness could be present, and when all had deponed, the Ordinary was to seal the testimonies with his own seal; and when they were opened, which was only at the time they were to be advised, so soon as decreet was pronounced, they were sealed up again, never to be opened thereafter. The reason then given for this custom was, that the witnesses might not incur malice or prejudice by their testimonies, and thereby might the more freely depone; and because all probation depends upon the faith and belief of the judges, which is their proper trust: but if the testimonies were published, debates upon their testimonies would be drawn in much more length than the debates of relevancy, whereby one court could not overtake the causes of a nation. But by a late statute, Parl. 1686, cap. 18, [A.P.S. VIII,599,c.30] the testimonies of witnesses are ordained to be published; wherein there is this advantage, that witnesses cannot be so easily suborned, or depone for favour or fead, when their particular testimonies are known; and when they are examined, parties or advocates may more effectually follow them with emergent interrogators, minding them of circumstances.

18. However, testimonies taken since that Act are published, both at the taking and advising, and so are never sealed. When they were sealed, the

Lords advised with close doors; and when they called before advising, it was only to hear if any party had any thing to say, why they should not be advised with close doors. But now parties and procurators must be called. And to prevent delay and loss of time, the advocates are appointed to prepare a condescendence upon the witnesses, whereby they think the several points are proven: and therefore the witnesses are marked by numeral figures; and if their testimonies be long, the particular words thereof pitched on are to be marked by a line on the margin, and a letter thereat: so that at every point to be proven, and at every testimony, if the probation be clear, that witness's deposition is declared to prove: if it be doubtful, parties and procurators are removed, and the Lords advise. And so soon as they find concurring witnesses to prove, they inquire no further: but if none of the marked testimonies prove, by two, or three witnesses in more arduous cases, then they assoilzie. But the Lords are not put as formerly, to read and compare all the testimonies, and to find out what is proven thereby: which of late, before the publication of testimonies, did so burden them, that they referred the same to the clerk of the process, or to some of their number, which much weakened the decreet, depending but on the trust of these; but when parties themselves are allowed to pitch on their probation, they can no more complain of it, than when they produce large writs, and are obliged to mark the clauses they insist on: and so the burden of the Lords by the publication of testimonies, is by these means somewhat eased.

19. The greatest difficulty of advising concluded causes is, by acts before answer, by which parties are not allowed to prove contrary points; but the nomination of the witnesses is not wholly in the power of either party, but a certain number is determined, which either may adduce. And if the Lords by their preliminaries find, that there were other witnesses present, called by neither party, they may, *ex proprio motu*, call these (if there be any doubtfulness) before they determine. Now, in advising these causes, oft-times the relevancy of the whole points to be proven is undetermined, and always the relevancy of some points. And though the debates upon relevancy take some time, yet not near so much as the debates on relevancy before litiscontestation: for there they do as anxiously debate upon the relevancy of these points, wherein nothing will be proven, as in others; but here the probation being first advised, what is proven, the debate will not be large whether these points be relevant or not.

20. This difficulty doth also arise in advising probation, when testimonies are inconsistent, whether they be adduced by the same party, or by opposite parties. In this these rules are to be observed: 1. An affirmative witness is much stronger probation than a negative witness; because inadvertence or forgetfulness may make the negative witness so depone, innocently, but none can innocently depone upon more than what he remembers, and did advert to: 2. There is much weight in the reason of the knowledge; so he who was near proves stronglier, either what he heard, or saw, than he that de-

pones that he heard or saw but at a distance; or he who depones that he was well acquainted with the person of whom he depones, than he who was not, but did only ask who that person was, or did express such tokens of him: 3. If the points whereon the cause depends be done at different times, the more recent will be the more pregnant proof, as that wherein circumstances will be less obliterate: 4. As to the value or quantity of things to be proven, two witnesses above exception, who prove the greatest quantity or value, are sufficient, though there be many more that prove lesser quantities or values; yet if they all concur, and be of far greater fame than the fewer witnesses that prove more, that quality may be sustained: 5. Points that fall under the proper object of one sense, are probable by less authority than other points that fall under more senses; so quantity, motion, distance, require more skilful witnesses than the existence of these objects: 6. Instrumentary witnesses being required to be witnesses, and the particulars expressed, are far more pregnant than common witnesses: 7. Witnesses of seeing of facts, by which the verity is inferred, are more pregnant than these where the same is inferred by emission of words; as in the question whether a fact be spuilzie, wrongous intromission, or warrantable intromission; a witness deponing acts of force and violence, is more pregnant than another that depones delivery by consent; because the acts of violence make a deeper impression in the memory: 8. When testimonies are contrary, *testimonia non sunt numeranda sed ponderanda :* So fewer of more reputation for faithfulness will preponderate more of less reputation.

21. If the probation be by writ, if the writs disagree, and contain both the confession or acknowledgment of the person against whom probation is led, or of his predecessors or authors, they are stronger than any other writ by clerks or notars, albeit there be less question of their subscription or attestation: and likewise the attestation of a clerk is more pregnant than the attestation of other notars. But when the acknowledgment of the original party is compared with the acknowledgment of his successors, the former is more pregnant. But if there be different acknowledgments, or declarations by the same person, *posteriora derogant prioribus*, which holds also in clauses in the same writ: for the posterior clauses, if they agree not with the former, do always qualify, correct, alter, or even take off the former, if they do fully contradict the same, or be inconsistent therewith: for parties, in forming of writs, which oft-times are very long, are unwilling to alter the whole frame, which takes long time and expenses, and therefore do rather add posterior clauses not agreeing with the former.

22. Albeit either party be absent at advising of concluded causes, yet that doth not make the decreet a decreet in absence, nor gives ground to reduce it as not *in foro contradictorio ;* because there is much more interest in judges in the matter of probation, than in the relevancy; for, albeit their believing of the truth of points proven be not absolute and arbitrary, for there must be two or three witnesses, yet there is far more latitude in their persuasion of the

point of fact, than in the point of law. And it were a great detriment to the security and quiet of the nation, if there were difference made between decreets by Ordinaries and these *in præsentia*, or by a lesser and a greater *quorum*, or by advising when either of the parties' advocates forbear to compear, having been in the cause, and attending the House, so that it is a wilful forbearance. Nor is there any reason to admit of bills, upon pretence that the witnesses have proven more or less than the Lords have found proven, to put the Lords again to go over the testimonies, when the advocates might so distinctly be heard upon all the testimonies they rested on. It is not the persuasion or trust of interested parties or their procurators, but that of the Lords, that must terminate probation.

23. By what hath been said, the difference may appear between decreets in absence, and these which are upon compearance, but passed from before proponing peremptors, and these which are upon circumduction of terms, and these which are upon advising of probation. The last two sorts are decreets *in foro contradictorio et contentioso*, wherein allowance has been given to all that could be relevantly alleged. But decreets wherein only dilators were proponed, and compearance passed from, are in the middle between decreets passed in absence, and decreets *in foro contradictorio :* for therein the defender chooseth rather to let a decreet take effect by performance, or possession, than to found upon these defences which he knew not how to prove.

24. There is a special kind of decreets called decreets of suspension, which proceed upon the suspension of former decreets or charges: and whether the decreets be absolvitor or condemnator, they are called decreets of suspension.

25. There is also a distinction between decreets of reduction and decreets reductive. The former is, when any prior decreet or charge is reduced: the latter when that decreet of reduction is reduced.

26. The tenor of decreets is much the same, as to the form thereof: for they contain, 1. The deduction of the libel, suspension or charge. 2. The compearance of parties who were either in the cause *ab initio*, or were admitted for their interest. 3. They contain a summary of all the writs produced for any of the parties. But they do not mention the witnesses adduced: yet now seeing testimonies are published, it were very fit that, in the production, mention were made of how many testimonies were adduced, without any thing of their tenor, or the names of the witnesses; for in decreets in absence, or where parties are reponed against the same, it is necessary to know how many witnesses were adduced. 4. The decernitory words are set down *verbatim* as they are in the signed sentence. And lastly, There is set down the BECAUSE of the decreet, containing the allegeances of the parties, and the interlocutors of the Lords thereupon, and even the final sentence itself is repeated.

27. It derogates much from the honour of the Session, and from the estimation and security of their decreets, and hinders the dispatch of justice, that

all things (whether in matter of law or matter of fact) are congested in their decreets, which do contain the reiterated and various disputes and interlocutors, and the frequently repeated bills and answers and interlocutors thereupon insert *verbatim:* whereby decreets arise to such a bulk, and are so nauseous to the perusers of them, that they will exceed sometimes forty sheets of paper and more; and take a long time and expensive attendance, before such decreets can be extracted. All which may be remedied by the Lords, seeing the order of the administration of justice is, by their institution, committed to them. For all these things may be allowed to be insert in the acts, whereupon decreets proceed: but there is no necessity to insert more in the decreet, than the matter of fact, whereupon the decerniture stands and is supported; whether it be in the libel, or in the exceptions, replies or duplies, containing only different matters of fact, albeit very unskilfully. Every defence is called an exception, and every answer thereto is called a reply, and the return thereto a duply. So that there needed no objections be inserted, or disputes whether these points of fact are according to law; for when the Lords find any point of fact relevant, that imports that it is according to law, and is sufficient for the effect for which it is adduced; and more is unfit, unless the particular statutes, customs, and reasons from equity and justice behoved to be insert, which is pretended by none. Neither needs this take from the clerks the benefit that custom hath allowed, according to the number of sheets in decreets; but the same might be allowed according to the number of the sheets in the acts, whereupon the decreets proceed, in which their pains do chiefly consist: for what passes at the time of decreets is seldom large.

28. To show that this proposal is practicable, some instances may clear it. 1. When there is no exception proposed, but the defences are all objections against the titles, or on the interest of parties not cited, the order of citation, or the relevancy of the libel: in all these, there is no proper exception, nor in any dilator: therefore there needs no mention of these in decreets, but of the particular defence only, whereupon no process is sustained, which is the proper BECAUSE of such decreets. Yea, though the libel insist on a particular statute, and the defender defends upon desuetude, or upon a posterior statute abrogating or derogating from the former statute; it is but an objection, and makes the libel not relevant. 2. If there be allegeances in fact proposed as exceptions, either proven by the writs produced, or offered to be proven in the proper way that such are probable, and if none of these be found relevant, then there is no necessity to mention them in the decreet, but they will still be held as proposed and repelled, or competent and omitted: and if in the second instance by suspension or reduction, the same matters of fact be repeated, not only does the said presumption make against them, but the acts of process may clear the same, as well as the decreet, if the same be recently quarrelled; and there is no reason that grounds of debate should be perpetually encouraged till prescription, but that in the most solemn acts by final sentences, *omnia præsumenda solenniter acta*, without necessity to produce

these acts, which are seldom registrate: so that the libel being found relevant, and terms assigned to prove, the decreet needs bear no more, but that the term was circumduced, for adducing no probation, or that the probation being advised, did or did not prove. 3. If exceptions in fact one or more be found relevant, and instantly verified, they must be insert in the decreet: but if they be to be proven, there needs no more be insert, but that such exceptions being found relevant, and terms assigned for proving thereof, either the terms were circumduced, for not adducing any probation in the manner found competent, and therefore decreet was given; or that the exception was found proven or not proven, and decreet accordingly pronounced. 4. Replies being properly matters of fact, instructed or offered to be proven, if they be not found relevant, they need not be expressed in the decreet; and if they be found relevant, whether they presuppose the verity of the exception or not, the tenor of the decreet will be in the same way, as hath been expressed of libels and exceptions, and so of duplies, or any further plies in fact. By this method, there will not be continued to posterity, such long relations of matter of fact, neither instructed nor offered to be proven, nor such impertinences and reflections as now are in decreets, with great ease to the Lords, who, in the second instance, may, at a short view, see the whole grounds of a decreet, and with much ease and no damage to the clerks, nor to the clients by necessitating their long attendance to extract decreets. This method is not the same with that which sometime hath been urged, viz. That decreets of Session should have no special reason or BECAUSE, but only in general, "That all the allegeances and evidences of the parties being considered *hinc inde*, the Lords decerned, &c." But here all the grounds of the decreet are to be specially expressed; so that all other grounds behoved either not to be proponed, or being proponed to have been repelled; as now allegeances, which are passed over by the Lords without interlocutors specially relating thereto, are understood to be proponed and repelled.

Title 47. Letters Executorial upon Decreets

DECREETS would be of no effect, but as bees without stings, if the law did not fix the kinds and form of the executions thereof: which do follow the decreets themselves of course, without the necessity of any special warrant in the decreet. The execution of the decreets of inferior courts are called precepts, such as precepts for paying or performing what was decerned, or for poinding; and upon decreets of removing follow precepts to remove, and precepts to eject the persons decerned to remove, and to possess the obtainer of the decreet of removing. Inferior courts have no other executions; except burghs-royal (who have a privilege to grant acts of warding) and the Admiral's privilege. See § 23, *h. t.* [IV,47,23,*infra*].

2. The decreets of the Lords of Session for attaining their effects, have letters in the King's name, commanding the parties decerned to pay and perform as is decerned. These of old, were by Letters of Four Forms, as they

were called: the first was a charge to pay or perform, without any certification; the second was a charge to the same effect, but with certification that horning would be direct; the third was horning; the fourth was caption [Contrast Craig III,2,4]. But these being tedious and expensive, every form being to be returned to Edinburgh, before the next were granted; the first two were laid aside, and only horning and caption retained. But the custom ran to the other extreme, and letters of poinding were granted without the necessity of a preceding horning.

3. But both then and now, no execution can pass within fifteen days after the dates of the decreets of inferior courts, which therefore are called the days of law; and now horning must precede poinding or possession, which are not to be granted till the days of the charge be expired, which are fifteen days in decreets upon processes, and such days as parties agree on by the clause of registration in registrable writs, and by the decreets of registration thereupon, whether summarily, both debtor and creditor, or his assignee having intimated in the creditor's life, being alive, or in case of either of their deceases, upon decreets of registration. But if the party to be charged be out of the country, the charge must be upon sixty days, at the market-cross of Edinburgh and pier of Leith. Or if he be latent, or in a place to which there is not safe access, the letters may bear warrant, to charge him at the market-cross of the head burgh of the shire, wherein he dwells, or haunts. Or if he have no certain dwelling or abode, the charge at the market-cross of Edinburgh, as *communis patria*, will be appointed by the letters. And if the party be not found personally, the charge may be at his dwelling-house, (if he have any) in the same order and with the same solemnities as is required in the execution of summons, of which formerly, *Lib*. 4, *Tit*. 38. Preliminaries of Process [IV,38,13,*supra*].

4. The same executorials are granted of course, upon any part of the King's revenue, or upon the benefices or stipends of ministers, having obtained decreets for letters conform, or having decreets of locality; and that not only in favours of the obtainers of these decreets, but also of their successors, upon production of the decreets of their predecessors, with their own act of admission: Act of Sederunt, 22d June 1687. Which letters were effectual, not only against the persons decerned in the decreets, but against their heirs or singular successors possessing the lands burdened by the said decreets. And in like manner horning is summarily granted, upon all the Acts of Parliament, bearing expressly a warrant for horning. Letters of horning were also competent for the charges of commissioners to Parliaments and Conventions of Estates; and for the contribution-money due to the Lords of Session, out of the benefices. All these hornings were called general letters, because all the particular persons were not named in them, but were contained under general heads [III,3,13,*supra*].

5. But by cap. 13, Sess. 2, Parl. 1, K. W. and Q. M. [Act 1690,c.13; A.P.S. IX,153,c.16] all general letters of horning were prohibited in the

future, and declared null, if they were used, except for the King's revenue, and minister's localities, without prejudice of the decreets for poinding of the ground, which are to have the same execution as formerly. This is, that they may proceed not only against the persons that then were heritors and possessors, but also against their successors, so long as the obtainer of the decreet and letters of poinding lives; but, after his death, the same must be transferred in the person of his heir or assignee *activè*, and in the persons of the then heritors and possessors *passivè*.

6. Yet this Act will not hinder summary charges, if the parties' names be particularly mentioned in the letters: as in the hornings for the commissioners' charges, if the names of the heritors be therein expressed, who are represented by their commissioners, albeit the *quota* be not expressed, but only the total of the charges, according to the Clerk-Register's testificate of their attendance; without necessity of a decreet calling all the saids heritors, but only containing a charge to the free-holders to meet and stent themselves, for the saids commissioners' charges, according to the valuation of their lands holden of the King. And likewise letters direct at the instance of the several Lords of Session, for their shares of the contribution-money, against those who were in use to pay the same, being expressed by name, are sufficient, without necessity of a decreet. See *Lib.* 4, *Tit.* 3, § 25.

7. Summary letters of horning are also granted on bills of exchange, by cap. 20, Parl. 1681 [Bills of Exchange Act, 1681, c.20; A.P.S. VIII,352,c.86], bearing, that "any foreign bills of exchange, from or to this realm, being duly protested for not acceptance or for not payment, and the said protest having the bill of exchange prefixed, shall be registrable within six months after the date of the said bill, in case of non-acceptance, or after falling due in case of non-payment, at the instance of the person to whom the same is made payable, or his order, that letters of horning upon a single charge of six days may pass thereon: without prejudice to pursue for exchange, re-exchange, damage or interest, by way of action or special charge." But after the six months, there is no place for summary registration or summary charge upon bills of exchange, but only by way of action. Also by this Act, they bear annualrent, in case of non-acceptance, from the date thereof, and in case of acceptance, and non-payment, from the day of falling due.

8. Letters of horning do first narrate the ground whereupon they proceed, whether it be a decreet either solemn or summary (by registrations of bonds, or other registrable writs, or bills of exchange) or a statute by which horning is appointed. Also they pass by custom in the cases aforesaid; and also upon the decreets of inferior courts, presented to the Lords: Parl. 1606, cap. 10, [A.P.S. IV,286,c.9] &c. Next follows the will or command, which contains two parts, both being directed to messengers. The one is, to command the party to pay or perform. And (in case of disobedience, the days of the charge being past) the other part is, a command to the messenger to pass to the market-cross of the head burgh of the jurisdiction, wherein the party

charged dwells, whether it be a shire, stewartry, bailiary of royalty or of regality, and there publicly to read the letters of horning, and because of disobedience of the party charged, to denounce him rebel: and to the effect the samine may be known to all concerned, the messenger must give three blasts with a horn, which is the reason why these letters are called horning: and likewise for the further publication, he must affix a copy of the letters upon the cross, immediately after the blasts of the horn. All which must be done in presence of witnesses, required to that effect, who, with the messenger, ought without delay to sign the executions of the horning, these being ordinarily taken along with the messenger, that they may be witnesses both at the charge and denunciation, since the late statute, Parl. 1681, cap. 5.[Subscription of Deeds Act, 1681,c.5; A.P.S. VIII,242,c.5]. For it is not reasonable, that the execution should depend upon the memory of the messenger and witnesses; and the letters of horning are not accounted executed, till the executions thereof be both done, written and signed as aforesaid. But as to hornings preceding that Act, the expressing of the witnesses, their names and designations, both as to the charge and denunciation, and their being required to be witnesses to these acts, with the subscription and seal, or stamp of the messenger, was sufficient: but now the subscription of the messenger and witnesses supplies the stamp, and in ancient executions any vestige of the stamp is sufficient.

9. The effects of horning so executed, whereby decreets and others above-mentioned attain their end, are different in several cases. For though the horning be not registrated, yet upon the return thereof duly executed, letters of caption sometimes pass of course, whereby the party denounced may be immediately taken and incarcerated. But if the decreet be to remove, there is, upon sight thereof, letters of possession granted for dispossessing the party decerned to remove, and for entering of the party, obtainer of the letters, to the natural possession. And if the horning and executions be registrate within the time appointed by the Act of Parliament for registration of hornings, the moveables of the party denounced, which he had the time of the denunciation, or which he shall succeed to, or acquire thereafter, become escheat and confiscated to the King, or to the Lord or bailie of regality, according to their infeftments, whereby the moveables of parties living within the regality, and denounced and registrate there, are gifted and disponed by the King to them, their heirs and successors, as pertinents of their office and jurisdiction. But hornings against witnesses, or havers of writs to be produced *ad probandum*, or any denunciation not being at the market-cross where the party denounced dwells, do not infer single or liferent escheat, but only caption. Yet denunciation against persons fugitive, or other denunciations by order of the Privy Council or Justices, being at the market-cross of the place where they sit at the time, do infer escheat single and liferent, though the party denounced dwell not there: but this is by a special statute. And likewise the party denounced and registrate at the horn is declared rebel, because

of his disobedience to the King's command; yet it is not a rebellion importing treason or any crime, because it is not presumed, that the party's not obeying was out of contempt of the King's authority and command; but because they are either not able to perform, or supinely negligent and ignorant of the denunciation and registration.

It is also a further effect of the horning duly executed and registrate, that if the party denounced be insolvent, he can thereafter do no deed (if he was not specially obliged to do it before the denunciation) that will be effectual against the creditor at whose instance the denunciation was.

10. If the party denounced be relaxed, within year and day after the denunciation, it reaches no further than his moveables that he had before the relaxation. But if he continue unrelaxed for the space of year and day, the rent and profit of all his heritable rights fall to his several superiors, not upon account of transgression against them, but because by the denunciation he is an out-law, and as *civiliter mortuus*, whereby his fees are opened to his several superiors: yea, though he be relaxed, only those moveables he acquired after his relaxation continue to him: but his liferent continues in the hands of his superiors [11,4,64; 111,3,14,*supra*].

11. Horning duly executed and registrate hath this further effect, that the party denounced as a rebel or out-law, hath no person to stand in judgment until he be relaxed. Yet when he is cited by parties, with certification, that if he compear not, he shall be holden as confessed, or that his evidents shall be reduced, or improven, as reputed false and forged, the Lords will not suffer that party to debar the party denounced with horning, by which they should both urge him to compear, and hinder him to compear. The Lords do likewise relax parties who are incarcerated, and not able to find caution, to give them *personam standi in judicio*, to the effect that their cause may be discussed while they are in prison.

12. Horning having so severe effects, the Lords do reduce the same upon the least nullity, by omission of any thing requisite in the execution and registration thereof; as is largely treated, *Lib.* 3, *Tit.* 3. Confiscation, § 1. *et seq.* But they will not sustain any nullity by way of exception; because the King's interest arising thereupon by the escheat, requires that the Officers of State should be called, especially when the horning is craved to be reduced, that the escheat may fall in consequence, unless a donatar be called or appear. But if the horning be otherwise made use of, as to debar any party from compearance, the nullities therein will be received, intimation only being made to the Officers of State: or if the horning be craved to be reduced, that the liferent-escheat may fall in consequence, the superior or his donatar must be called, whosoever the superior be; for in that the King *utitur jure communi*.

13. The second executorial on decreets is, by Letters of Caption. These letters pass of course upon production of the executions of the horning, both as to the charge and denunciation. The narrative thereof bears, that the party to be taken was orderly denounced rebel and put to the horn, for the causes

expressed in the horning; and therefore the will of the letters bears warrant to command all magistrates and messengers, to take and apprehend the person denounced, wherever he may be found within their several jurisdictions. Yet any messenger employed by the party to whom the horning belongs, may himself, without a charge to any other, apprehend the person denounced wherever he finds him; and the having of the horning is a sufficient instruction of his warrant: yea, if he think another messenger may be more able to execute the caption, or be less suspect to be intrusted with the letters, he may cause that messenger execute the same; and if he be not willing, he may charge him by the warrant of the letters to do the same.

14. All messengers should have a blazon, and a rod or wand [IV,49,7, *infra*]. The blazon is a piece of brass or silver, having the impression of the king's arms upon it, which is fixed upon the messenger's breast, so as the impression of the arms may be seen, that thereby while he charges, his authority and warrant may appear: for if any affront be done to him, when he charges without his blazon, it will not import a deforcement, unless the actor knew him to be a messenger then. From the impression of the king's arms on this blazon, messengers are called messengers at arms: for they are not military officers, but civil. The rod or wand hath a particular shape and impression, by which it may be distinguished from any other. The use thereof is to evidence his authority and warrant to execute captions or other executorials: for in the execution of captions, the messenger ought to touch the party to be taken with that rod, and then read to him the letters of caption: yet if he have witnesses and assistance sufficient to make him go to prison if he were unwilling, the not reading of the letters, or the not giving a copy thereof signed by the messenger would not annul the caption: but if the party taken should escape, the reading of the letters, or giving a copy thereof, would not have the same effect, as if the blazon were seen, or the party were touched with the rod; these being the evidences of the messenger's authority, by which the party cannot deny, but that he knew him to be a messenger at arms, and thereby might not only be liable to the penalty of deforcement, but to other penalties for his contempt and violence.

15. The caption being so far executed, the messenger or magistrate charged to execute the caption, must take the person apprehended to a lawful prison, and must deliver him to the keeper of the prison, or to some magistrate having power over him, requiring him to put him and detain him in prison: and if they refuse, or do not perform the same immediately, he may charge them by the warrant of the letters for that effect.

16. The messenger may incarcerate the party in whatever lawful prison he pleases, and is presumed to have warrant from his employers so to do: which power custom hath allowed, that debtors may the more effectually be induced to pay, but it wants not its inconvenience, putting all the burghs to the trouble of incarceration at the option, or it may be upon the pique or prejudice of the creditor or messenger. And therefore it might fitly be amended

by an Act of Parliament, or of Sederunt, requiring messengers in executing of captions, to take the party to the next lawful prison, having a secure prison-house; for, albeit every burgh-royal or burgh of regality be obliged to have a sufficient prison, yet many have not, and creditors ought not to hazard the escape of their debtors by an insufficient prison; and, albeit thereby the magistrates will be liable for the debt, yet they are not always solvent; but there is no reason they should pass by a sufficient prison.

17. Messengers ought not to detain prisoners unnecessarily in their hands, but ought to put them in prison so soon as they can; lest they prejudge their employers by heightening their expenses, upon pretences of componing with their parties, or suffer them to procure suspension before they be actually imprisoned.

18. As messengers may execute captions, by themselves immediately; so they may at discretion charge other messengers or magistrates, to execute the same; but they must attend them, and furnish them with the letters of caption, without which they can show no warrant for the incarceration: and therefore magistrates use to offer to go with the messengers foot for foot, if he can show where the person to be taken is, of which he doth show any probable evidence; but otherwise it were unreasonable that a sheriff or his depute should follow a messenger, at uncertainty, to any place of his shire. Magistrates of burghs are liable to more diligence, for executing captions, because the bounds of their town or jurisdiction is narrow; and therefore ordinarily, the messengers do of consent take their officers and other assistants, to search for and apprehend the party.

19. By magistrates, are only understood sheriffs of shires, stewarts of stewartries, bailies of regality, bailies of burghs-royal, or of burghs of regality; but, though all these be obliged to have sufficient prison-houses, and may be punished for want of them, yet they are not bound to receive prisoners whereby they would be liable for the debt in the caption, if they have no sufficient prison.

20. The executions of letters of caption ought to bear the whole diligence of the messenger user thereof, in the several cases before expressed, and especially the place where he apprehended the party, and the time thereof; that it may appear how long he was in his hands. And if he charged any magistrate or other messenger, who failed in giving due concurrence, he ought to express the same, albeit thereafter the party was taken otherwise: for these who fail in due concourse, are liable for the debt in the caption, although there were many such, as well as these who suffered the prisoner to escape; likeas all of them become *correi debendi* to the creditor; and if the party escape by violence, or otherwise, the manner of escape ought to be expressed in the execution, and the names of these who were concurring in the escape: the witnesses also in these executions ought to be required and designed, and ought to subscribe with the messenger *de recenti*.

21. There is an accessory action or diligence against these who fail in

their duty, in executing of captions, for which the Lords may grant letters of horning summarily to charge them, in the same way as they do against depositars of sums consigned, upon sight of the instrument of deposition: for there is no reason that creditors using executorials should be put to new ordinary actions; nor can such hornings be counted general letters, because the names of the parties are expressed, and their failing in their concourse appears from the executions, whether it be in the not concurring to the taking and incarcerating, or in suffering the prisoner to escape.

22. It will not be a relevant defence or reason of suspension, for magistrates suffering prisoners to escape, that they will yet take the party, albeit he be in as good condition as when he escaped; or that, upon testificates of physicians, they suffered the prisoner for his health to go out to take the air, or to go to a private house, albeit in either case there were two to guard him; for the Lords, by Act of Sederunt [A.S. 14 June 1671], prohibited the magistrates of Edinburgh to suffer prisoners to go out, without particular warrant; or the magistrates of other burghs not far distant, except in the imminency of death. And where such warrant is granted, the magistrates ought to choose the place of the prisoner's abode, that the same be secure, and the guards attending. Likeas, they do declare, that if magistrates let prisoners go out, upon any other pretence, although they restore them to prison, they shall be liable for the debt: for *squalor carceris* is an interest of the creditor, to cause the debtor to satisfy, or to discover his means, which magistrates ought not to prejudge them in. Yea, the escape of prisoners liberates not the magistrates, except in the case that provident diligence could not prevent or hinder: and therefore it is not relevant to liberate them, that the prisoner got in files, and therewith did shear off the locks or catbands of the doors of the prison; because there ought to have been more doors and catbands on either side, whereby the prisoner could not reach the outer catbands: neither yet that the prisoner cut the stanchers with files, or *aquafortis;* because the keepers of the prison ought to visit the same frequently, and to search for such instruments: for if such pretences be sustained, it will be easy for the keepers, by collusion, to suffer prisoners to escape. In like manner, the escape from messengers doth only liberate the messenger, when he useth all provident means to prevent or hinder the party to escape.

23. Captions do ordinarily proceed upon the sight of registrate hornings. But registration is not requisite against witnesses, or havers of writs, charged by diligence, to produce writs as means of probation. Captions are also granted without a preceding charge, by the Lords, upon special occasion, as if parties be suspect to leave the country, and have no visible estate in it; or when the warrant is upon contempt, or disorder in process. Any judge-ordinary, or even parties, may seize upon persons for public crimes, or for their own debts in their escape out of the kingdom, or in clear evidences of their present going about the same. There is also a special privilege of summary arresting or seizing persons by the Admiral, because his jurisdiction is

most conversant about strangers, and on that occasion, and for dispatch of strangers, he is authorized, summarily to seize persons, till they find caution *judicio sisti*, or *judicatum solvi*, or both.

24. The third executorial is by Letters of Poinding, which of old was called the brief of distress, passing out of the chancellary of course; by which the goods not only of debtors, but of their tenants and possessors of their lands, were poinded for their debts, much like the execution of the subjects of one state against another, by letters of mart. But this was justly redressed by Parl. 1469, cap. 37. [Diligence Act, 1469,c.36; A.P.S. II,96,c.12] intitled, "That the poor tenants shall pay no further than their term's mail for their Lord's debt, by the brief of distress." And custom hath further interpreted, that this distress of tenants, even for a term's mail for their Lord's debt, is not for his personal debt, but for these debts which are *debita fundi*, and that upon letters for poinding of the ground, passed upon decreets for poinding of the ground, which can extend to no further than the ground affected with the real burden contained in the letters, and the goods thereupon, in so far as they do belong to the debtor, or to the tenants, in so far as may be extended to their term's mail or rent [II,5,9,*supra*]. This kind of poinding requires no prior charge of horning, because no person is decerned to pay, and so cannot be charged, but only the ground is decerned to be distressed; and the moveables thereon to be poinded; and failing these, the ground-right and property of the lands to be apprised by the foresaid Act. Yet it cannot proceed till fifteen days after the decreet of poinding of the ground, which are the days of law, within which parties may satisfy, or procure suspension. This way of poinding is more fully explained, *Lib.* 4, *Tit.* 24, Poinding of the Ground [IV, 23,*supra*]. So that there needs no further to be here repeated.

25. Apprising is the executorial for making effectual decreets for poinding of the ground, which passeth of course as other executorials: for letters of apprising are summarily obtained thereupon by supplication; and the same order is used therein, as in apprisings upon personal debts. There is no need to say any further of apprising here, it being largely handled, *Lib.* 2, *Tit.* Infeftments, § 29. [II,1,29,*supra*] as a species thereof; and likewise *Lib.* 3, *Tit.* Dispositions [III,2,13,*supra*], as apprising is a transmission and legal vendition of lands and annualrents. See also *Lib.* 4, *Tit.* 35. § 27.

26. Hence there arises a division of poinding, in real and personal. The real poinding proceeds upon a real right affecting the ground. The personal poinding proceeds upon a personal debt, decerned to be paid by persons debtors, principals and cautioners, or other accessory debtors; whereupon letters of poinding pass of course, for poinding the readiest goods of the debtor, wherever they can be found, to the avail of the debt. And because the right of moveables is presumed by possession, all the moveables which are in the possession of the debtor, may be so poinded for his debt; and neither his assertion, nor his oath that they belong not to him, but to others, will stop the poinding: but the oath of others being offered, before the poinding be com-

plete, will stop the same, without prejudice to the creditor, to prove these stopped goods to have then belonged to his debtor; and so he may recover the same, if he be not otherwise satisfied. The messenger hath authority to take this oath, and is a kind of judge in the execution: and therefore he should not rest on the oath of parties in general, that the goods belonged to them, and not to the debtor; but he ought to cause them condescend upon their particular right, and ought to set the same down in his execution of poinding, that if there was any thing wanting to pay the debt, the creditor may return upon these goods, and that he may know that the messenger has done his duty without collusion: for the messenger may reject the oath, if he do not find a reasonable account of the title, and persons will not so particularly depone falsely, as in general, or upon their construction of the point of right, seeing they may know that such oaths in their own behalf are but as oaths of credulity, or oaths of calumny, which terminate not the point of right, so that by a future process such oaths may be easily redargued, and they appear to be perjured. These oaths to stop poindings, use to be admitted, to be given not only by the owner of the goods, but in case of his absence, without suspicion of collusion, by his wife, or children in his family. See *Lib.* 4, *Tit.* 30. Spuilzie, &c., § 6.

27. By the 35th Act, Parl. 1469 [Act 1469,c.34; A.P.S. 11,95,c.10], poinding for mails and annualrent upon holy days, is forbidden, and deferred till the third day after Whitsunday or Martinmas, which was for the rent payable at these terms, while these were accounted holy days. But these not being so accounted now, that part of the Act is in desuetude: yet still poindings on the Lord's day, or on solemn days appointed by church or state, for humiliation or thanksgiving, are void and punishable.

28. Letters of poinding are not only granted upon the Lords' decreets, solemn or summary, or upon the other summary letters of horning, but also upon the decreets of sheriffs, commissaries, or other inferior judges, the same being presented to the Lords. For though these judges may give precepts of poinding on their own decreets, yet these can have no effect without their own jurisdiction; but the letters of poinding granted by the Lords, are as extensive as if they were upon their own decreets, Parl. 1661, cap. 29. [Poinding Act, 1661,c.29; A.P.S. VII,203,c.218].

29. But no personal poinding can lawfully be put to execution until a charge of horning be given, and the days of the charge expired, by cap. 4, Parl. 1669 [A.P.S. VII,556,c.5], bearing, "That it shall not be lawful to poind moveables upon registrate bonds, or decreets for personal debts, till the parties be first charged, and the days of the charge expired; with certification, that poinding otherwise used, shall be null, and the poinders shall be punished, and proceeded against as spuilziers: but prejudice always of any decreets recovered at the instance of heritors against their tenants in their own courts; whereupon it shall be lawful to them to use poinding as formerly: and but prejudice to superiors, to use poinding against their vassals, for their feu-

duties, as they might lawfully have done of before." These exceptions leave it uncertain what was the rule for the persons excepted before, wherein the custom of the several places must be considered, at least to shun spuilzie: but, though there be no necessity for a precept to pay, as in the case of other creditors, who must use such precepts, or letters of horning, before they can lawfully poind, yet still the days of law after the decreet ought to be free, that parties decerned may satisfy or suspend.

30. The order of masters poinding their tenants is not determined by statute, but by custom, which is thus: masters do at their own gates, or other places accustomed, poind their tenants for their rents, and poinding upon any decreets of their baron-courts are so executed; because there is no warrant for letters of horning or poinding upon their decreets, neither can they exercise their jurisdiction without their own territories.

31. Poinding upon decreets of all judges ordinary must be thus: if the poinding proceed upon the precept of an inferior judge, his officers, with such assistants as they think sufficient, go to the place where the goods of the debtor are, within the jurisdiction. And if they be goods that can be driven, or brought together without hurt, they gather the same, and then they read the precept of poinding; and if there be ordinary prizers within the bounds, and the debtor offer to prize goods by them to the value of the debt, that no more need be carried to the cross than what is sufficient, the officers may not drive or carry more away, than about that quantity they estimate: or if such prizers be not offered, the officers may design prizers for that effect, and they have the choice of the goods that may be sufficient. But that apprising is not the rule of estimation, but the goods must be carried to the cross, or to the ordinary place of poinding, within the jurisdiction where they are found, and there again the letters of poinding must be read; and if there be ordinary sworn prizers, authorized by the judge-ordinary of the place, these should apprise the goods to the value of the debt, with the twentieth penny more for the sheriff-fee; but if such be not found, the officers may choose other prizers, against whom the debtor can instruct no just exception, especially indifferent persons, who are not concurring in the poinding, if they can be had.

32. The goods being so apprised, the officers must make public intimation thereof by oyesses, to convocate the people, and declare the price of the goods, they being set apart and under view; and then must require the debtor to make payment, with certification, that if he do not, he will deliver the goods apprised to the creditor, or any having his warrant, (which is sufficiently instructed by having the precept of poinding) to be used by the creditor, as his own goods, at his pleasure. If the debtor, or any to his behove, appear and offer payment, such time must be allowed before the goods be delivered, as the money may be told, and being told, the same must be delivered to the creditor, or the person intrusted for him, upon his interchanging of a discharge of the debt, and of the decreet, and letters for the same; and there must also be time to draw the discharge by sight of the officers, or judge-

ordinary of the place: and in case such discharge be not granted, the officer must not deliver the goods to the creditor, if the debtor consign the sum in the hands of the judge-ordinary of the place, or his clerk, to remain in their hands, to be given up to the creditor upon delivery of the discharge as aforesaid; which being contained in the execution of the poinding, will be a sufficient ground to charge the depositar to deliver the money upon delivery of a discharge, which the Ordinary on the Bills for the time will find sufficient, comparing it with the decreet: or if there be a notar present, it is more convenient, that the instrument of a notar be taken upon the executions than by the officers, who are oft-times ignorant. This consignation being made, the goods should be left to the debtor, owner thereof, to be disposed of as his own goods: and there may be no further execution upon that precept of poinding.

33. But if no offer and consignation of the sums as aforesaid be made, the officers, executors of the poinding, must deliver the goods apprised to the creditor, as his own goods, in satisfaction of the debt contained in the precept of poinding, in whole or in part: and he ought to offer to the debtor, a copy of the letters of poinding, and the executions signed by him and the witnesses required thereto, if he can write, or by a notar, by whose instrument the executions are formed; either of which will be a sufficient instruction of the payment of the debt. The execution upon letters of poinding by the Lords is in the same manner; but with this difference, that the execution must be done by messengers at arms.

This way of consignation is the securest and most convenient; yet if the messenger, or other executor, being a person of credit, receive the money, he may keep it as consignatar, if a discharge be not offered; and though the executor should deliver the same to the creditor, he would be in no hazard, if he offered the subscribed double of the letters of poinding and executions to the debtor, and delivered the same, if he would accept it.

34. There is an exception against poinding of moveables, by cap. 98. Parl. 1503 [Diligence Act, 1503, c.98; A.P.S. 11,254,c.45], in these terms, "It is statute and ordained, that in time to come, no manner of sheriff nor officer poind nor distrenzie the oxen, horse, nor other goods pertaining to the plough, and that labours the ground, the time of the labouring of the samine, where any other goods or land are to be apprised or poinded, according to the common law." By this statute it appeareth, that plough-goods cannot be poinded, upon decreets for poinding of the ground, albeit there be no other goods sufficient upon the ground, to satisfy the real burden contained in the decreet: because the Act bears, that plough-goods shall only be poinded, when there is neither other moveables nor lands to be poinded; so that seeing the land is always capable to be poinded, therefore the plough-goods cannot at all be so poinded: but it is not so in personal poinding; yet in either case, the exemption of plough-goods is only in plough-time, which is not to be understood of the time they are actually ploughing, but of the ordinary time that ploughs use to go, in the several places of the country: and that, whether

it be for the master's debts, or for those of the tenants or other possessors. The reason of the statute is, the public good, that the ploughing of the ground be not hindered. By "other sufficient goods on the ground," are not to be understood the household plenishing, which came not commonly under the name of goods on the ground [1,9,22,*supra*].

35. The fourth executorial is, by Letters of Possession, which take place not only upon decreets of removing, but upon all other decreets, whereby parties are decerned to be put in possession; as decreets following upon actions of ejection, intrusion, succeeding in the vice of persons removed, or decerned to remove or cede the possession, as when the servants or successors of liferenters are summarily charged to remove, or when any party is obliged by contract or obligation to enter another in possession. And, though in all other cases the days of law must first pass, and the days of the charge of horning must expire, before caption or poinding on personal debts can proceed, yet there is no reason to extend that privilege, against decreets for possession and letters of possession thereon: for if the possession be by contract, that delay is competent, according to the clause of registration, because it is so agreed, and therefore after expiring of the charge on the obligement, letters of possession are competent, to make the obligement effectual, so soon as the days of the charge are expired; and if the decreet be against unlawful possessors, they can plead no privilege: But even in ordinary removings, there should no delay be pretended upon days of law, or preceding charge; because removings being at peremptory terms, the master of the ground could not safely agree with new tenants, if he could not remove the former possessors precisely at the term. And therefore the common interest requires, that decreets of removing may be obtained before the term, to take only effect at the term; that letters of possession may immediately pass upon these decreets, to take effect at the term; albeit in other cases, parties ought not to be troubled by process, before the term.

36. The tenor of letters of possession, relate the decreet whereupon they proceed, and the will contains warrant to dispossess the parties decerned, their "wives, bairns, cottars, servants, and their goods and gear, forth and from the lands or houses in the decreet; and to enter the obtainer of the letters in the natural possession, by himself or others by his warrant, which the having of the letters does sufficiently instruct;" and the form of the execution is, if it be a house or garden that hath a door, the former possessor or any of his, being inclosed by the door, the same is opened, and they are thrust out, and the obtainer of the letters, or his order, are entered in. And if there be goods therein, the same may be all turned out of doors; and at least three particulars, or bribes (as they are called) must be turned out by the executer of the letters, and the obtainer himself may lay out the rest when he pleases. And for the possession of ground, the whole goods may be turned off the ground, or at least three bribes thereof, and the obtainer of the letters, or his order, may turn off the rest thereafter, at his pleasure: but corns or other

moveables, that cannot so be removed, do not retain any pretence of possession to the party dispossessed. All these things must be expressed in the executions of the letters of possession by messengers, who can only execute the decreets of the Lords, and by the officers of inferior courts executing decreets thereof, and signing the executions, with the witnesses required, or by notars framing the executions by way of instrument, and subscribing the same before witnesses; in all these cases, a copy of the letters of possession, and executions thereof, ought to be signed and delivered, or at least offered to the party decerned if he be unwilling to take it, that thereby he may instruct that obedience is given to the letters, lest he be distressed of new, upon pretence of being still liable as possessor, for the rents.

37. The fifth kind of executorials is by precepts out of the chancellary, upon retours; which are the decreets of the judges, to whom brieves were directed to serve heirs. Upon these retours precepts requiring superiors to infeft the apparent heirs of their vassals, being specially retoured in lands or annualrents, conform to the retour, are the executorials of the retour. The order and tenor of these retours are explained, *Lib.* 3, *Tit.* Heirs. [111,5,*supra*]. And the order and tenor of the precepts against superiors is explained, *Lib.* 2, *Tit.* Infeftments of Property [11,2,*supra*], which therefore need not to be here repeated. But it is thereby clear, that these precepts against superiors are executorials of the retours, whereby the superior is obliged to receive the vassal's heir, or otherwise to lose the benefit of the non-entry by the superiority, during that vassal's life; and the superior's superior supplies his place, and so from superior to superior, till it come to the King, who refuseth to enter no lawful heir, upon showing the refusal or non-obedience of that superior, who is the King's immediate vassal: for there can be no charge against the King, or Lords of Exchequer, for passing such infeftments; but they do immediately grant warrant, for precepts out of the chancellary, commanding the judge-ordinary of the place where the fee lies, to give seasin to the person retoured; which precepts contain a clause *capiendo securitatem*, for such things as are due to the King as superior, or his donatar: and if the judge-ordinary do not grant seasinac cordingly, the Lords on supplication, and production of the instruments of disobedience, will grant warrant to the director of the chancellary, to issue precepts to another person, as sheriff in that part, specially constitute.

38. If the fee be holden immediately of the King, precepts pass of course out of the chancellary, commanding the judge-ordinary of the place to give seasin *capiendo securitatem*, as in the former case. The tinsel of superiority upon non-obedience of these precepts is more fully handled, *Lib.* 4, *Tit.* 7.

39. The other brieves of the chancellary are explained, *Lib.* 4, *Tit.* 3. They need no executorials different from the serving of the brieves: for the serving of the brieve of idiotry is a declaratory decreet, finding the person to be incapable of managing his affairs, and therefore decerning and declaring his nearest agnate of twenty-five years complete, to be his tutor, during the

incapacity. The serving of the brieve for tutors of law, is also a declaratory decreet. The brieves of division, perambulation, or lining, being executed, do put the party in possession, and need no other execution. The brieve of terce gives also a declaratory decreet, that the pursuer was holden and reputed wife of the defunct, and therefore kenns her to a terce of lands, and others liable to a terce, by actual division of the terce from the rest of the fee, either by aiker-deal, or by allocating roums according to the rent; whereby she is put in possession, and needs no further execution.

40. The sixth kind of executorials is by Letters for making Patent Doors, when parties keep themselves or their goods within locked doors, and do not give access thereto, for executing of caption or poinding; but make such resistance as the executer cannot overcome. These pass upon execution of these executorials, when the messenger gets not access, but returns the execution thereupon; for then letters are granted for making patent doors, by force. The law of England secures every man's person and goods, to be safe and quiet, within his own doors, so that no man can enter the same, whom he doth not warrant or permit, which is a common interest of great importance; every man's house is his sanctuary; but our letters of caption passing of course, bear warrant to open doors, and to make the king's keys; so that new letters are only needful in resisting, or offering to resist; which resistance is a contempt, and a kind of deforcement, and is sufficiently instructed by the execution of the messenger, signed by him and the witnesses, required to be witnesses not only to the keeping of the doors close, and refusing entry when there is audible knocks, by the messenger, having on his blazon (which ought so to be expressed in the execution) but also bearing them to be witnesses to the resistance, or offer of resistance as aforesaid.

41. There are other extraordinary executorials, but they are not accustomed to be given by the Lords, but by the Privy Council; such as letters for charging of parties to enter their persons in prison, in such prisons as are appointed by the letters; wherein not only denunciation may pass, upon which escheat and liferent fall, but likewise in some cases, the certification of these letters is under the pain of treason, in cases where it is so appointed by statute or custom. And likewise letters of fire and sword, in case of deforcement or resistance of the ordinary executions, by continued open force in arms; especially for making letters of possession effectual. But the charges against such persons, to enter their persons in such prisons, under the pain of treason, are competent for making captions effectual, and should be first used, before letters of fire and sword, which are the last legal executions, warranting all manner of force of arms, that is competent in war; wherein, deforcement imports not only the ordinary penalty of moveables, but the pains of treason.

Title 48. Law-Burrows and the Actions on Contravention thereof

THERE is a general executorial by letters of law-burrows, which pass without citation, yet not of course, but upon the oath of the user thereof, or other sufficient proof or evidence of a custom or design of any party, to encroach upon another, by troubling them otherwise than by the course of law [1,9, 30,*supra*]. These letters must be used upon evidence of the inclination of the party complained on, to injure the other, and the will containeth a warrant, to charge the party to find caution to keep the party plaintiff secure of any illegal violence. But it reached at first only to the complainer's life, Parl. 1429, cap. 129. [Lawburrows Act, 1429,c.129; A.P.S. 11,19,c.20].

2. Formerly men were accustomed to take assurance of others, against their violence: but it was declared, Parl. 1449, cap. 12. [Act 1449,c.13; A.P.S. 11,35,c.2] "That no man needs take assurance from others, but the king's peace to be assurance to all men; that if any person dreads another, that he pass to the sheriff, or to the officers that it effeirs to, and make that knawn, or swear that he dreads him, and they shall take burrows of peace." Burrows or burgh, by our ancient style, signifies caution; so that burrows of peace signifies caution to do no act contrary to the public peace, in prejudice of the complainer swearing that he dreaded him, or giving other evidence of his ill inclination towards him, which was sufficient, although he did not swear that he was afraid of him, which might be interpreted as dishonourable. But law-burrows hath been the term continued, as more extensive, importing caution to be found against any trouble to be done to the complainer, otherwise than by the course of law. And therefore the letters did bear, "That the complainer should be harmless and skaithless, in his person and goods, otherwise than law will." And the penalty of law-burrows was at first at the discretion of the chancellor or president, Parl. 1491, cap. 27. [A.P.S. 11,225, c.8]. But thereafter the tenor thereof was further extended, and explained thus, "To find sicker surety and law-burrows, that the complainers, their wives, bairns, tenants and servants, shall be harmless and skaithless, in their bodies, lands, tacks and possessions, goods and gear, and no ways to be troubled and molested therein, by the persons complained upon, nor no others of their causing, sending, hounding out, recepting, command, assistance or ratihabition, whom they may hinder or let, directly or indirectly; otherwise than by the order of law and justice." Parl. 1581, cap. 117. [Lawburrows Act, 1581,c.117; A.P.S. 111,222,c.22]. And the penalties were to be equally divided between the king and party injured, Parl. 1579, cap. 77. [A.P.S. 111,144,c.15]. The penalty of law-burrows was thereafter determined, for every Lord 2000*l*, for every great baron 1000*l*, for every freeholder 1000 merks, for every feuar 500 merks, for every zeaman 100 merks, for every unlanded gentleman 200 merks, Parl. 1593, cap. 166. [A.P.S. IV,18,c. 13]. Yet, in extraordinary cases, the penalty is sometimes increased, when the evidences are clear, as if great violence had been already done, by men of

violent tempers: and sometimes it is abated, when the party cannot be able to find caution for such a sum.

3. Albeit law-burrows do not proceed upon decreets or dependences, as the other executorials do, yet they are truly executorials for preserving men's rights, and do proceed upon most reasonable considerations: for it were a great inconvenience, if violent men had no more to fear, than the making up the damage that a party sustains by their injuries, which many times would not be worth the pursuing for.

4. For further security, there is another statute, declaring, "That, albeit parties charged to find law-burrows, pass to the horn and find not caution, yet they shall be liable to the pains of law-burrows, contained in the letters," Parl. 1597, cap. 269. [Lawburrows Act, 1597,c.273; A.P.S. IV,140,c.40].

5. The action founded on the breach of law-burrows is called Contravention. The title in this, is, either on the charge upon the letters of law-burrows, when no caution is found; or upon the bond granted for obedience thereof, when caution is found. The former can only be against the party contravener: the latter may be against both the contravener and cautioner and may be by way of charge upon the bond of caution, the particular fact being given with the charge, as the special charge, in case the charge be suspended; especially now since the inrolments of actions takes a long time before they be discussed. But the warrant for horning should not pass of course, but upon some evidence, that the contravention is atrocious, at least upon the oath of calumny of the charger, which charge is not excluded by the Act against general letters, but it hath all the effects of other hornings: for upon the denunciation thereof, the escheat falls. Yet the special charge must be proven, and any defences against it are sustainable, though not instantly verified.

6. When caution is not found, contravention can only be by way of ordinary action. But the penalty is much more to be extended in that case, both because of the damage by the delay and expenses in discussing the ordinary action, and the want of security by caution.

7. Albeit the tenor of the letters be that the complainer shall be harmless and skaithless, yet the penalty is not incurred upon every damage, but *ex damno injuria dato*, when the damage is done wittingly and wilfully; for instance, the pasturing of cattle upon a march, when it is not wilfully done, may infer damage but not contravention, although the march be clear and uncontroverted, much less if the pasturage be upon ground controverted before the charge of law-burrows, in which case the action or charge for contravention useth to be turned into a molestation or perambulation, which is not a regular way so to alter summons, from one kind of action to another: but it is more regular and rational, when the contravener alleges, that he hath done no wrong, but did only continue his possession, as it was before the charge; in this case, if the parties' allegeances be contrary, the Lords, before answer, may allow witnesses *hinc inde*, to clear the former possession, which, if it

prove to be violent, momentary, or clandestine, it should not defend the contravener; but when the summons is turned into a molestation, the defender is
indirectly assoilzied from the contravention. Also the not payment of a debt,
though thereby skaith arise to the creditor, doth not infer contravention, because it is not properly an injury.

8. Albeit the fore-mentioned statute bearing that persons charged by
letters of lawburrows are liable for contravention, when they are denounced
for not finding caution, seems to import that the charge is not sufficient without the denunciation; yet it is the contempt of the charge, which makes it
effectual without caution: and therefore, though the charger proceed not to
denunciation, it is a favour to the contravener, who is not only liable for deeds
done after the denunciation, but after the charge: sometimes also the charge
is suspended, not upon obedience, but upon other reasons; as that the penalty
is not suitable to the quality and ability of the party charged, according to the
Act of Parliament, and then there is no caution found, for keeping the charger
skaithless; and yet it were without ground to pretend, that until that suspension were discussed, and the party denounced, there should be no contravention: but, on the contrary, if the reason of suspension be not sustained and
instructed, the charger ought not to be put to a new action of contravention,
but may insist upon the charge, and give in the deeds of contravention by
a special charge.

9. Contravention may concur with other penal actions, as spuilzie, ejection, intrusion, or succeeding in the vice. But the Lords are not accustomed
to sustain both penalties (albeit neither of the statutes bear derogation to the
other) but allow the party injured to choose which of the actions he pleases to
insist in. Yet, if the deed be atrocious against the public peace, both penalties
may be sustained; and the officers of state may insist, though the party injured do not. But where the injury is not a breach of the public peace, but
arises from the skaith done by private parties, the officers of state have not
interest in the contravention, without concourse of the private party, albeit
the penalty be divisible between the King and the party; as the concourse of
private parties is required in many other crimes.

10. Albeit the tenor of the letters of law-burrows bear, that parties shall
be harmless and skaithless not only as to injuries against themselves, but
against their wives, bairns, tenants and servants, in their bodies, lands, tacks
and possessions, goods and gear; yet these other persons have no title for
contravention, upon the law-burrows, albeit the same be indirectly in their
favour, unless the charge be also at their instance, but the penalty doth wholly
belong to the King, and to the raiser of the letters, who is injured in and by
the injury done to these other parties. And therefore the contravention will
not extend to deeds done against the lands, tacks and possessions, goods and
gear of these other persons, whence no detriment ariseth unto the charger,
but only where he is damnified in and by their damage: for if they have other
lands, tacks and possessions, not from him, encroachments thereupon will

not infer contravention by their master's charge, but only what is done in these they have from him. But injuries against their persons, whereby they are disabled or discouraged in their duty to the charger, do infer contravention. And even other atrocious injuries against wives and bairns, in their fame, as in their persons, do infer contravention, upon the charge of the husband or parent: and, albeit under the name of bairns and children, are comprehended grand-children, &c., yet if a nearer parent be alive, of the male line, and capable of managing his affairs, it were hard to extend the contravention, except upon the father's charge.

11. Contravention doth not only arise upon deeds done by the principal parties complained on, but likewise upon the deeds of others, of their causing, sending, hounding out, &c. And here the question may arise, how there points shall be proven? For, ordinarily, warrant or command is only probable *scripto* or *juramento* in civil matters, which doth not hold in criminals; and therefore, if the injury be properly criminal, witnesses are receivable, for proving the facts or deeds importing the warrant, command or ratihabition: as if the witnesses heard the principal party express words, clearly importing these accessions, and agreeing upon the words; or if they saw the party charged calling to him a tenant or a servant, who immediately did the deed of contravention, without being stopped or reproved in the doing. But if it be a lesser damage, though injurious, and not upon deeds immediately done, or upon the circumstances inferring the command, oath or writ is requisite; for what was said at one time might be countermanded at another time, and is not presumed to be a constant warrant.

12. There also arises difficulty upon the words, "whom they may stop or let," which are adjected to the warrant, command, or ratihabition, and so might be interpreted, as if contravention were not inferred, by command or ratihabition to any other than persons in the contravener's power, which were too narrow an interpretation: they might also be interpreted so as to extend to the deeds of all that the party complained on might command, and so infer contravention by the deeds of children in the family, or servants, though without warrant, command or ratihabition, which were too large an extension, unless the command or ratihabition were proven by the oath of the party charged, or by other facts inferring the same: as if a son in the family, or a domestic servant, should commit an atrocious deed against the charger, without any occasion or provocation relating to themselves, it might thence be inferred, that they did the same by warrant, or for assisting of the party charged, in avenging his quarrel.

13. The words in the tenor of law-burrows, bearing, "that the complainers, their wives, bairns, tenants and servants, shall be harmless and skaithless, in their bodies, lands, tacks, possessions, goods and gear, and no ways to be molested or troubled therein by the persons complained upon, &c." may seem to restrict the effect of law-burrows to skaith in the complainers' bodies, goods and lands; and so contravention takes no place on other injuries, such as men-

acing, reproaching, reviling, defamation; neither upon attempts against the body, as by strokes paried off, or escaped: which injuries are more atrocious than injuries in goods and gear. But the last words, "no way to molest or trouble," import, that law-burrows are even to be extended to such cases of trouble or molestation, though no other actual skaith follow.

14. The English have two sorts of law-burrows. By the one, parties are bound to the peace, not to do any deed to the party complaining against the peace. By the other, parties are bound to the good behaviour, whereby they incur the penalty in their bonds, in case they commit any thing contrary to good behaviour against the party complaining, or against any other; which is extended not only to words, but to frowns, or to any sign of contempt: but this proceeds only upon sufficient evidence that the party is habitually of ill behaviour, in which case it is both just and fit. And though we have not these terms of distinction, there is no doubt but sovereign judges, upon such evidence, may give law-burrows even to that extent, that the party complained on do no injury to the complainer any manner of way, or may take such engagements, although there be no complainer, as they may and use to do, in taking ordinary law-burrows upon evidence of inclination to violate the peace, though no party complain, as upon atrocious words, threats, or challenges to duels.

15. When law-burrows are granted, and put to execution, the same are upon the oath of the party complaining, which uses to be conceived in these terms, that he swears "he dreads the party complained on, bodily harm, &c." This hath continued since the first institution of law-burrows, which was then only extended to bodily harm: but now the oath should be sufficient, that he swears he dreads him wilful harm, in the persons or goods of himself, his wife, his bairns, tenants, or servants: for the swearing a fear of bodily harm may be looked upon as reproachful and base, as if the complainer were so afraid that he durst not defend himself. But if the complainer evidence reason to suspect such injuries, as if he produce decreets of contravention of former law-burrows, or testificates of persons above exception, of former injuries, menaces or challenges, law-burrows ought to be granted without any oath. But then they should not pass of course, but upon the judges' perusal of the evidence, and finding the same sufficient, which should be so expressed in the bill for law-burrows.

Title 49. Actions upon Deforcement

THE legal remedies for making decreets effectual, are of two sorts: The one passeth summarily of course, without citation of parties to the granting thereof, by letters executorial; of which in the former title: The other proceeds by way of action, wherein parties, if they appear, must be heard, and the procedure therein differs only from other actions, that these other do precede the decreets in the principal cause, whereas the executive actions must follow these decreets, for the execution whereof they are intented; and therefore, in the division of actions by our customs, (*Lib.* 4, *Tit.* 3.) actions were divided in discussive and executive: the one discusseth and determineth the point of right, the other puts the same so determined to execution; so that there are two kinds of executorials, to wit, letters executorial, and actions executorial.

2. The executorial actions are these; the action upon deforcement, or unwarrantably impeding letters executorial, the action upon inhibition as to landrights, and the action upon arrestment, for making arrested goods or sums forthcoming, the action for breach of arrestment, and against cautioners in loosing of arrestment, and the actions of adjudication, which are of diverse sorts. We have already spoken of magistrates and messengers being liable for the debts of rebels, when suffered to escape unwarrantably, as the same may be obtained by way of summary charge, which may, and oft-times uses to be pursued by way of action. There is also a general executorial by law-burrows and contravention thereof; of which we have also spoken.

3. The action upon deforcement is partly civil, and partly criminal, and may be pursued either way [1,9,29,*supra*]. For the deforcing of messengers, and other executors of the King's letters, albeit it be without armed force, is a crime, and may be pursued criminally for punishment; but nothing would thence arise to the party injured: and if there were not a civil remedy in favour of the party injured, to be pursued before the Lords, who are judges in the principal cause, it would be of exceeding great inconvenience, if they were necessitated to address to another judicature, to make the executorials on the Lords' sentence effectual.

4. There are three statutes in relation to deforcement. The first is, cap.84. Parl. 1587 [A.P.S. 111,460,c.57], bearing, "That all deforcers of officers, in execution of their offices, be summoned upon fifteen days' warning, civilly or criminally, at the option of the party pursuer, and their lives and goods to be in the King's will therefore." The other two statutes are as to the civil actions upon deforcement: the one is, cap. 118. Parl. 1581 [Breach of Arrestment Act, 1581,c.118; A.P.S. 111,223,c.23]; whereby, "all deforcers of the execution of sentences are to be declared to have escheated their whole moveables to the King, beside the punishment of their persons at his will; and that the party injured shall have execution, upon the first and readiest of the deforcer's goods for his debt and expenses, &c. and that the action shall be without tabling the same, or continuation thereof." This gives sufficient ground for the Lords, to take in these actions summarily, without putting them to the roll; because the roll comes in place of the table of actions which was before; yea, as the Lords do summarily charge parties (when they contemn their authority) by letters of horning, there is no less reason to charge deforcers, who show contempt against the letters in the King's name, whereas the letters upon contempt of the Lords authority, is upon contemptuous violation of acts in their own name. The other statute is, cap. 150. Parl. 1592 [Deforcement Act,1592,c. 152; A.P.S. 111,577,c.72], which extends the action upon deforcement, not only to deforcement of the execution of decreets, but statutes and ordains, "That in case any officer of arms, or sheriff in that part, or other person whatsom-

ever, the time of the execution of any summons, letters or precepts, direct by his Highness, or other judges, within this realm, or in putting of decreets to due execution, be deforced in doing of the same, the deforcers shall forfeit, amit and tyne, all and whatsoever their goods and gear moveable." This statute does also enlarge the interest of the party at whose instance the execution was: for, whereas formerly they had only preference for the sums contained in the decreet, and their expenses to be modified by the Lords, yet by this Act they have the one half of the escheat goods. And either of these may be insisted on, at the option of the party injured; so that, if the half of the escheat goods be more than their interest, they may insist for the same; but if it be less, they may insist for their interest out of the whole head. And by the last statute, it is also declared, that the execution shall be holden to be as lawful and orderly, as if there had been no hinderance by the deforcement: this can only relate to moveables, for it would make a great uncertainty in land-rights, if every deforcement should make an inchoate execution as good as a complete. The statute bears, that the deforcement is first to be verified and proven, which hath given occasion to insist upon deforcement, only by way of action, for proving the deforcement; yet the executions bearing deforcement, are sufficient proof for a summary charge, albeit further proof must be for escheating the moveables, if the charge be suspended.

5. The proper defences against this action, arise from the nullities of the executions of the several executorials, which are all competent by way of defence, because the action is penal, and the penalty very great: as if the messenger have not on his blazon, in the execution of hornings or captions; or in the execution of letters of possession; or if he do not read either of these letters, and show the signet to the party, unless he hinder him, or if the party flee away from the messenger, in the execution of caption, before he touch or attach him with his wand of peace. But it is not necessary nor convenient, that he should have on his blazon at the execution of caption, lest thereby he may scar the party to suffer him to touch him: but if he hinder him to touch him, with any weapon or staff, his offering to touch him, and showing his wand of peace is sufficient to infer deforcement: but if he be attached, he commits deforcement if he do not go along with the messenger, who is not obliged to carry him by force, though he may, but without beating or wounding him, in the execution of a civil caption; albeit more may be done in the execution of a criminal caption, as he may detain him under caption where he is.

6. It is a relevant defence, that the party attached by caption was so sick, that he was not able to go or ride.

7. In the execution of letters of poinding, it is a sufficient defence, that the messenger had not his blazon on [IV,47,14,*supra*]. And, albeit it were proven by reply, that the party knew the person executor to be a messenger, it will not be relevant, unless it be so proponed, that he knew he was in the present exercise of that office: for he might be exauctorated; neither will the duply of "holden and reputed" be sufficient in that case, because the law hath

determined the way, how the messenger should be known, viz. by his blazon, or his wand of peace. But if he make use of these when he hath not authority, the oath of the party that he knew he was not a messenger then in office, will be relevant, because persons may use these tokens of authority, who have it not; yet if the party depone he was so holden and reputed, and that he knew nothing to the contrary, the execution will be valid, and any hinderance will be reputed a deforcement.

In this execution, the messenger is judge, when parties offer to depone, that the goods offered to be poinded are not the debtor's, but their own property: wherein he may specially interrogate, to find out the truth, and if he find that the oath does not instruct, the hinderance of the execution will infer deforcement: and it will not be sufficient to prove the goods to be his own, in the action of deforcement. The reason is, because so much must be yielded to public authority, albeit when the poinding is executed, the goods may be restored by way of action.

8. In all deforcements, not only the acts of the party directly concerned infer this action, but the acts of all that he may stop or let. But he is not liable for the actions of others, who officiously, without his warrant, do stop any execution: yet so that if he be present, and do not require them to forbear, in that case he will be liable for their acts; *qui tacet consentire videtur.*

Title 50. Inhibition and Arrestment, and the Actions thereon

THE actions upon inhibition and arrestment are amongst the prime executive actions. And they may well be reckoned amongst executorials, albeit they do but hinder debtors to dispose of their estates heritable or moveable, till the creditors who take the benefit of arrestment or inhibition be satisfied. And the actions thereupon are properly executorial actions.

2. Inhibition extends only to ground-rights by infeftment, or other equivalent rights, as liferents by terce, courtesy, or reservation in the infeftments of others; but reacheth no bonds or obligements, though they bear clause of infeftment. But they reach the superior or donatar's casualties of superiority.

3. The rise of inhibitions is, from debtors dilapidating their estates in prejudice of their creditors. And they are much more ancient and extensive than the remedy by reduction *ex fraude creditorum*, which is determined by that excellent statute of Session, ratified in Parliament, *anno* 1621 [Bankruptcy Act, 1621,c.18; A.P.S. IV,615,c.18].

4. Inhibitions did proceed upon supplication to the Lords of Session, by creditors, relating and producing their decreets, or processes against the debtors, or the evidences whereupon such decreets might follow; and subsuming that their debtors were like to dilapidate their estates to their prejudice: and therefore desiring that the Lords would give order for letters in the King's name, inhibiting or prohibiting these debtors to dilapidate their estates, and the lieges to accept rights from them, till these creditors were satisfied. Which the Lords, upon probable evidence, did grant, without citation of

the debtors. The tenor of which letters were thus: "William and Mary, &c. Forasmuch as it is humbly meant and shown to us by our lovit A, that where B, by his bond, &c. (then follows a deduction of the writs whereupon inhibition is craved) And the said B, the debtor knowing that the complainer will suit execution against him, his lands and estate, for satisfying of his said obligation, action or decreet, does therefore intend, in defraud and prejudice of the complainer (as he is informed) to sell, annailzie, wadset, dispone, resign, burden or otherwise dilapidate, all and sundry his lands, heritages, teinds, tenements, annualrents, liferents, reversions, tacks, steadings, roums, possessions, corns, cattle, goods and gear, &c. Our will is herefore, &c. That ye inhibit and discharge the said B personally, or at his dwelling-place, and if he be forth of the kingdom, at the market-cross of Edinburgh, and pier and shore of Leith: that he on no ways make any private or public alienation of his lands, heritages, teinds, tenements, annualrents, liferents, reversions, tacks, steadings, roums, possessions, corns, cattle, goods and gear, or any part thereof, nor contract, or do any other deed directly or indirectly, whereby any of the saids lands, heritages, teinds, tenements, annualrents, liferents, or reversions, may be apprised, adjudged, or any ways evicted from him, in prejudice of the complainer, anent the fulfilling to him of the saids obligations, decreets, or processes. And siclike, that you, in our said name and authority foresaid, inhibit and discharge all our lieges of this realm, and all others whom it effeirs, by open proclamation at the market-cross of the shire, bailiary or regality where the said B dwells, and the lands lie, that they, nor none of them presume or take upon hand, to block, buy, take or accept any right from him, of his lands, heritages, teinds, tenements, annualrents, liferents, reversions, tacks, steadings, roums, possessions, corns, cattle, goods and year; or accept from him any bonds, obligations, or contracts, whereby any part of the same may be apprised, adjudged, or any ways evicted from the said B, &c. According to justice. Because the Lords of our Council and Session have seen the foresaid bond, obligation, decreet or process. As ye will answer, &c."

5. By this tenor, it doth appear, that inhibitions were not granted by the Lords of course, without consideration both of the debt and ground thereof, and some probability that the complainer's diligence might be prevented, before they could affect the debtor's estate: and therefore then inhibition reached the debtor's moveables. But this great inconvenience arising, that the free commerce of moveables (which ordinarily is without writ) should not pass current; therefore the Lords restricted the effect of inhibitions, that it should not extend to moveable goods, but only to the rights of lands and others above written: and yet the Lords have never changed the style of inhibition, as aforesaid; but as to moveables, they grant letters of arrestment, for arresting all sums of money not secured by infeftment, and all moveable goods and gear, to remain under sure fence and safe arrestment, until sufficient caution be found for payment of the ground of the arrestment if it shall be found due.

6. Inhibitions are only personal, and do not strike against any right made by the heirs of the person inhibited.

7. Inhibitions were long in use, before the statutes ordaining them to be registrate: and therefore the lieges could not be put *in mala fide* to buy from, or bargain with the person inhibited, unless the inhibition were published at the market-cross of the jurisdiction where he lived; and at the market-crosses of the several jurisdictions where his lands lay. But these publications easily passing observation and remembrance, great inconvenience arose to creditors and purchasers. For remedy whereof, it was statute, Parl. 1581, cap. 119. [A.P.S. 111,223,c.24]. "That all inhibitions and interdictions to be raised thereafter, for whatsomever cause, with the executions and indorsations thereof, be registrate where the person inhibited or interdicted dwells, or makes his residence: and, if the said person have his lands and heritage, or the most part thereof, lying in another sheriffdom than where he dwells, that the same be registrate in that shire. The extract of which shall be probative in all cases, except in the case of improbation. And if it shall not be so registrate, it is declared null." This nullity is only to be understood as to lands not lying in the shires where it is registrate. This Act was defective, insinuating that a registration where the most part of the lands lay, should be sufficient for the whole: for it could have effect as to no part of the lands in any other shire, the lieges whereof could not be put *in mala fide*.

8. But this statute being prejudicial to other jurisdictions than the sheriffs, the same was altered by cap. 268. Parl. 1597 [A.P.S. IV,139,c.35], "Ordaining that inhibitions, interdictions, and publications thereof, that should happen thereafter to be executed against persons dwelling within bailiaries or stewartries, as well of royalty as regality, should be executed at the market-cross of the head-burgh of the said bailiaries and stewartries, within the whilk the saids persons dwells, and registrate there. Whilk registration is declared as valid as if it had been in the sheriff's books." By this Act there was no necessity to publish or registrate in the sheriff's books, against persons within the saids stewartries or bailiaries, as is clear by its tenor; yet it appears by the registers, that messengers did frequently publish and registrate at both.

9. By cap. 265. Parl. 1597 [Act 1597,c.269; A.P.S. IV,139,c.36], "inhibitions are appointed to be registrate judicially, before a notar and four famous witnesses, by and attour the ordinary clerk. And in case the ordinary clerk refuse to registrate the same, instruments being taken thereupon, the samine may be registrate by the next sheriff, stewart, or bailie, or by the Clerk-Register and his deputes, in the Books of Council: whilk registration shall be as sufficient as if the samine letters were registrate in the sheriff, stewart, or bailie's books, where the saids persons dwell." By this Act it appears, that the inferior courts, and their clerks, had power to registrate inhibitions, without deputation from the clerk of register. And albeit they were only to be presented to the clerk of register, in case of refusal of the ordinary

clerks, yet by the ambiguity of these words, "or to the clerk-register and his deputes," there hath been always since, registers of inhibitions in every jurisdiction, and keepers thereof by deputation from the clerk-register, and likewise a General Register of Inhibitions and Interdictions at Edinburgh, that all parties might at their option registrate there (which was sufficient for inhibiting the lieges of the whole kingdom) whereby the lieges were at greater pains in searching both the General and Special Registers, and there is great advantage of registrating at the General Register: for thereby no lands of the debtor could escape; whereas, by registrating in the special registers, the inhibition extended no further than the lands in that jurisdiction where it were registrate.

But that clause of registrating judicially, &c. was thereafter rescinded as unnecessary, cap. 13. Parl. 1600 [Hornings Act, 1600,c.13; A.P.S. IV,230,c. 22], whereby the General Register at Edinburgh is established. And now of a long time the Clerk-Register has deputes not only at Edinburgh, but also at the several shires and other jurisdictions.

10. In all these statutes there is no mention of executing or publishing inhibitions at any place, but where the person inhibited dwells. Yet oft-times inhibitions are executed both in bailiaries and stewartries, where the lands lie, and at the market-cross of the shire in which the bailiaries lie: which hath arisen much from the advantage of messengers, to have the more work and the larger allowance. And sometimes they publish the same at all the crosses where the lands lie, not only when they must be registrate there, but when they are registrate in the General Register [IV,35,21,*supra*]. Hence these questions arise, 1. Whether such a custom be general, since the acts for registration of inhibitions? 2. Whether such custom doth annul the inhibitions not so published? By inspection of the General Register of Inhibitions, it appears, that inhibitions have been published, sometimes, not only in the jurisdiction where the person inhibited dwells, but also in other jurisdictions, and specially they are published and registrate both in stewartries and bailiaries, and likewise in the shires in which these jurisdictions lie, contrary to cap. 265. Parl. 1597 [A.P.S. IV,139,c.36], bearing, "That all letters of horning, relaxations, inhibitions, interdictions, and publications thereof, that should be raised at any time thereafter, and executed against whatsomever persons dwelling within bailiaries and stewartries, shall be executed at the market-cross of the head-burgh, or town of the saids bailiaries and stewartries, and registrate there: which shall be as lawful as if the same had been registrate in the sheriff-books:" whereby it appears, that inhibitions against persons dwelling within stewartries or bailiaries of royalty or regality must be executed and registrate there, and not at the head-burgh of the shire, without reservation, in case the person inhibited have lands within the shire, and without these stewartries or bailiaries. And it follows *a contrario sensu*, that if the inhibited person dwell not within stewartries and bailiaries, the inhibition needs not be published there, albeit they had lands within these stewart-

ries and bailiaries. But generally the publication of inhibitions is only at one head-burgh, albeit it cannot be doubted but many of these persons had lands in more jurisdictions than one: and specially when inhibitions are registrate in the General Register, which serves for the whole kingdom, and without inspection whereof no provident man will acquire, it were very superfluous to publish at other crosses than where the party dwells, and wherein registration is requisite in that case.

The main argument for the necessity of publication at all the market-crosses, where any of the inhibited person's lands lie, is, That the statutes for registration of inhibitions do not derogate from the former custom of publishing at all the market-crosses where the lands lie; but, on the contrary, require registration of inhibitions, and the publication thereof. But the contrary appears by the tenor of the first statute, whereby it is only requisite to publish where the person inhibited dwells, and where the most part of his lands lie; and, therefore, there is no necessity to publish at the market-crosses where his other lands lie: yet it is certain, that it will not be effectual against any lands, but where it is either registrate in the particular registers of the jurisdictions where these lands lie, or in the general register, which supplies all these registers: whence it is evident, that inhibitions may be effectual where they are registrate, though they be not there published. 2. The second act for registration of inhibitions doth yet more derogate from publishing inhibitions everywhere, where the debtor's lands lie; because it requires not publishing at the market-crosses of bailiaries or regalities, unless the person inhibited dwell there, without exception whether he have land there or not. And so an inhibition was found null, simply because it was not executed in the regality where the person inhibited dwelt, in respect of the Act of Parliament, which declares such inhibitions null, without restriction or words taxative, but indefinitely. 3. There is nothing more dubious than "where the greatest part of the inhibited person's lands lie," whether it must be greater than all the rest of his lands, or greater than any of the rest. 4. Inhibitions must be registrate within forty days after the publication thereof, which can only be reckoned after the first publication where the party inhibited dwells, otherwise it might be effectually registrate within forty days after every publication where the several lands lie.

The next reason for the publication at all the crosses where the inhibited person's lands lie, is, That it hath been a general custom so to do, and so commonly holden and believed, which is sufficient to infer a law, not only when it adds, but when it derogates from the statute law: for inhibitions are found null even in the publication, if there be not three oyesses, and yet no statute requires the same. But there is less moment in this reason: for, 1. It cannot be proven to be an universal custom. 2. Whatsoever the avarice of messengers or ignorance of parties might make them to do, *propter majorem cautelam*, is only *voluntatis*, but not *necessitatis*, unless they were by a sentence of the Lords ordained or obliged so to do. 3. Such a custom not authorized cannot derogate from the foresaid express statutes; and yet the custom is most frequent to publish both at the market-cross of the shire, and at the market-crosses of the regalities of the said shire, which is diametrically opposite to the said statute. But the common notion of a general publication hath never been adhibited to this custom, to publish both at shire and at bailiary and regality within the same, but only to the general publication at all jurisdictions where the inhibited person's lands lie. 4. The statutes require only publication where the most part of the lands lie; and yet the inhibition reaches annualrents and liferents, which will hardly be brought under the name of lands: and yet the inhibition will not affect, unless it be registrate where the lands lie, out of which the annualrents or liferents are due. And it is a dangerous thing to render inhibitions null, which the Lords cannot know how far it may go: but if they be sustained, it is easy for the Lords, by a statute of Session, to declare for the future what must be done to make inhibitions effectual. 5. As to the oyesses requisite in publication of inhibitions, this doth not infer, that these were superadded to what was before requisite for publication of inhibitions: for these oyesses were introduced as necessary to all public executions, seeing, without oyesses to call the people, or blasts of a horn to let them know a public execution affixed, no execution could be accounted public by the reading thereof, which might be done without advertence of the people of what was a-doing, and oft-times the copy affixed was pulled away, either by these unconcerned, or more frequently by these who do it upon account of the publisher, that the execution may not come to notice.

11. As to the effect of inhibitions, they extend only against voluntary facts and deeds of the party inhibited, after the first publication thereof at the market-cross where the inhibited person dwells, and not after the registration. Yet as an inchoate diligence, if it appear that the debtor did endeavour to prevent the perfecting thereof, it is a ground of reduction, (as was found in the case of Mr John Elleis against Keith) [Probably 1 Stair 327; M.5987] [1,9,15,*supra*], so that it is not restricted only to affect the lands of the regality: whereas, in other cases where it is not registrate in the general or special register, it is only invalid against the lands lying in these jurisdictions, where it is not registrate specially or generally.

12. There is this inconveniency to purchasers and creditors, that they cannot securely close bargains finally, till forty days run after the first publication. And by the late custom of the keepers of the registers, whereby they kept inhibitions uninserted very long, purchasers became altogether unsecure, even though they had an attest of the registration; which by a late decision and a subsequent law, [A.P.S. VIII,600,c.33] was declared only to affect the keeper, and these representing him; whereby these excellent statutes were in effect evacuated; which the Lords in a great part have helped by a statute of Session, [A.S. 15 July, 1692] appointing the keepers of the registers to have minute-books, wherein all things to be registrate behoved

presently to be received, and a minute made of it signed by the presenter; whereby there could be no debate concerning the time of presenting, nor durst the keeper adventure to neglect the registration within the days, having so ready a probation against him.

13. It is a nullity if the executions bear not a copy given, or offered to the party inhibited, personally, or at his dwelling-place, or at the cross of Edinburgh, and pier and shore of Leith: and the inhibiting both of the party inhibited, and the lieges at the cross, was not found sufficient, Hope, Inhibitions, Syme *contra* Coldingknows [Hope, *Maj.Pr.* 11,15,11 and 16; M.6943]; Lamb *contra* Blackburn [Hope, *Maj.Pr.* 11,15,8].

14. It is also a nullity if the executions bear not, that a copy was delivered to the party inhibited, and affixed upon the cross: for the giving or offering of that copy, or affixing thereof, is most properly the act inhibiting. It was so found, July 28, 1671, Keith *contra* Johnstoun, [1 Stair 767; M.3786] albeit the executions did bear a copy affixed upon the cross, and that the messenger mended the execution on the margin, bearing a copy given, but was not so registrate; nor was it found probable by witnesses, not being so marked.

15. Inhibition was found null, because the letters did only bear warrant to charge the person at the market-cross, &c. as out of the country, and the execution was against him personally, Jan. 24, 1627, Erskin *contra* Erskin [Durie 262; M.3682].

16. Inhibition was found null, because it bore not three oyesses, and public reading at the market-cross, which was not admitted to be supplied by witnesses, July 11, 1676, Stevinson *contra* Innes [2 Stair 443; M.3788]. Yet thereafter the Lords sustained an inhibition, where the execution did bear only, that the messenger made lawful publication and reading of the letters; because they found that style frequent in the register, and that the inhibiter offered voluntarily to prove the oyesses given. So far were they from annulling inhibitions.

17. Inhibitions do not only strike against lands acquired, where the same is registrate, but against lands thereafter acquired in the same jurisdiction, December 15, 1665, and February 27, 1667, Mr. John Elleis *contra* Keith [1 Stair 327 and 457; M.5987 and 7020]; which was not extended to lands acquired in other jurisdictions, where the inhibition was not registrate, July 18, 1672, Smeitoun *contra* [Possibly *sub anno* 1662, *Swinton* v 1 Stair 128; M.3729].

18. But inhibitions do not reduce rights which the person inhibited was obliged to grant, before the publication of the inhibition, if the obligement were special, or if there were a disposition anterior, importing that obligement. But infeftments to corroborate anterior personal obligements, not bearing an obligement to infeft, are reducible thereupon.

19. Infeftments after inhibition, by legal diligences, for a debt prior, are not reducible thereupon, but only if the debt be posterior.

20. Inhibition did not extend to wadsets or redeemable annualrents; because the creditor might always have compelled the debtor to pay, (as was found, July 16, 1667, Mr. John Elleis *contra* Reith [1 Stair 473; M.7022]) till the Lords, by Act of Sederunt, Feb. 19, 1680, did declare, "That creditors using inhibition against the debtors infeft in wadset or annualrent, if they shall make intimation, by instrument of a notar, to the persons who have right to the reversions of the said wadsets or annualrents, that the wadsetter or annualrenter stands inhibited at their instance, and shall produce, in presence of the party and notar, the inhibition duly registrate, that they will not sustain renunciations or grants of redemption, although upon true payment, not being made *bona fide*, but after intimation, as aforesaid, unless the redemption proceed by process, whereunto the user of the inhibition must be called, &c."

21. Inhibitions pass ordinarily of course without advertence; yet if any party represent, that an inhibition may not pass till it be considered, and show a reasonable cause for it, the Lords have been in use to consider, and, in several cases, to refuse inhibitions. So it was refused to a wife upon her contract of marriage with her husband, January 11, 1625, Hamilton Supplicant, [Durie 155; M.6048] where Dury doth also mention a decision, January 9, 1623, Marshal, [Durie 140; M.6036] by which inhibition was granted at the wife's instance against the husband, *stante matrimonio*, upon her contract of marriage; as to which she needed not to be authorized in that case. The diversity of the case lies in this, that, upon the contracts of merchants and trading people, whereby the husband becomes obliged to employ such sums on land or annualrent for the wife, inhibition used to be refused, unless the husband had an opulent fortune beside to trade with; otherwise the so employing of his stock would ruin his trade and family. Inhibition was also refused upon the warrandice of a discharge from the charger's fact and deed only, unless the supplicant had shown a particular hazard of distress: for warrandice is but a conditional obligation, and hath no effect till the condition exist.

22. The actions upon inhibition are only rescissory, and are spoken to *Lib.* 4, (*Tit.* Reductions) [IV,20,*supra*] and they have only effect against voluntary deeds, posterior to the executing of the inhibition. But if there was an anterior obligement, whereby the party inhibited might have been legally compelled to dispone, the disposition is not voluntary nor reducible.

23. Inhibition is a very useful remedy for securing of creditors against the dilapidation of their debtor's estate, by which their satisfaction becomes to be in hazard. But every sale by a debtor is not to be accounted dilapidation. And, if malicious or too suspicious creditors shall obtain inhibitions of course, it were worthy of an Act of Parliament, or Act of Sederunt to be ratified in Parliament, whereby the keepers of registers of inhibition should be prohibited to insert any inhibition in the register, within thirty days after the execution against the debtor, there being still ten days remaining of the forty

days required for registration of inhibitions: for the inhibition will still be received, and put in the minute-book when offered. The benefit of such an Act would be, that the debtor may shun the affront of suspicion, arising from inhibition, by offering performance; and in case of refusal, by application to the Lords, that, upon consignation of the ground of the inhibition, it may be refused; or, upon production of clear discharges of the ground of the inhibition, or in case the term of payment be not come, by giving sufficient caution for performance at the term: for, besides the prejudice to the debtor, such unwarrantable inhibition will remain in record against him and his heirs, till purged by prescription. And that register hath no allowance for inserting discharges of the inhibition, or the grounds thereof, or of any decreet of reduction thereof; so that all purchasers must keep and preserve these discharges, or sentences during the prescription. And even other creditors are not secure; for if these discharges or sentences be not found, the debts contracted after may be reduced.

24. As inhibition hath been introduced for securing creditors against dilapidation of land-rights, so arrestment hath been introduced for the benefit of creditors, that they might reach their debtor's moveable goods or sums. All sums are accounted moveable as to this effect, whereon actual infeftment has not passed, or is not standing.

25. Arrestment, and the actions arising therefrom, are more properly executorial than inhibitions: for inhibition doth only remove impediments hindering execution; but arrestment doth not only hinder the debtor, in whose hands it is made, to pay, but gives an action, whereby the right of the sums, or goods arrested, is adjudged to the creditor arresting; and thereby the former creditor is denuded, and the arrester becomes creditor.

26. There are two executive actions arising from arrestment. The one is the action for making arrested goods or sums Furthcoming, which reacheth no further than the satisfaction of the sum for which the arrestment was laid on: and the title of it were much more suitable to be Adjudication upon Arrestment: for it is as properly an adjudication of a moveable interest, as the adjudications of land-rights. And the title it has is tediously long, when it is fully expressed, and very unbecoming when it is called a furthcoming. Neither is it the making of the goods or sums furthcoming, that is the proper effect of this action; but the adjudging of them to the arrester: for if goods be arrested, the haver is liberated by producing the goods, whereby they are made furthcoming; but they become not the arrester's, until they be rouped and sold, and the price delivered to the arrester. There is no necessity here to insist further upon arrestment, and the action thereupon transmitting the right to the arrester, the same being largely treated, *Lib.* 3, (*Tit.* Assignations) [III,1,*supra*] as being a legal assignation, in the same way that adjudications of rights of the ground are legal dispositions; and both have their effects by the sentence of the judge adjudging the same to the several pursuers, in the different manners and orders prescribed by law.

27. Under arrestment is comprehended Sequestration, whereby not only the subject is arrested, to remain *in statu quo*, without the access of either party contending, till their titles be discussed; but likewise the custody of the thing controverted is intrusted, by an act and commission of the Lords, to persons nominated by them, either for the custody, or for the management thereof, and profits of the same, to be made forthcoming to the parties that shall be found to have best right. These are ordinarily called "factors constitute by the Lords," and by their commission, they have power to uplift the rents and profits, and to set and raise lands, which is ordinarily by roup, that the factors may not be in a capacity by collusion to take an under-rate. For these factors, salaries are appointed by the Lords, either before their intromission, or are reserved to be modified by the Lords, after their diligence shall appear. And when the titles of parties are determined, they have immediately access against these factors; and, albeit their decreets do not bear the same expressly, yet they do imply it.

28. Such factors are constitute upon very many occasions. As, 1. When the claims of parties reach the whole right *in solidum*, but require a long time, before, by the course of the roll, the cause can be determined, not only by discussing the relevancy, but by concluding and advising the probation, wherein different terms use to be assigned, for witnesses and diligences both ordinary and incident for production of other men's writs *ad modum probationis;* for then, seeing the subject in question would become unprofitable, or damnified *medio tempore;* therefore, upon the application of parties, the Lords appoint factors to manage in the mean time. 2. When the parties controverting do not pretend to the whole right, but a part thereof, and a preference therein, the Lords appoint factors to manage till the interests of the several pretenders be ranked and determined. 3. When apparent heirs are doubtful whether to enter heirs to their predecessors, then, upon the application of creditors or relicts having liferents, the Lords will appoint factors to manage in the mean time. 4. If any party succeed to an estate, and be out of the country to continue for a considerable time, and is perhaps ignorant of his interest; then, upon application of their relations, the Lords will appoint factors to manage, until the party concerned constitute other factors. 5. If any arrestment be made upon things on the ground of lands, such as woods, corns, peats, turfs, planting, trees, &c. if the Lords find ground of suspicion of the irregularity of either party, they will give commission to take the samine in custody: much more, if the controversy be about any moveable goods, as jewels, plate, heirship, &c. the Lords will put the samine in the custody of indifferent persons, till the rights of parties be determined.

29. The actions against these factors or keepers, are chiefly founded upon the rights of parties being determined; and is properly an action of restitution, and may be more fitly called an action for making forthcoming, than the action upon arrestment, whereby the sums or goods are adjudged to creditors arresting for their satisfaction, and thereby the right and property changed.

30. The other action upon arrestment arises properly from the breach of arrestment, whereby the arrester hath action, either for his debt, or for the half of the moveables of the breaker of arrestment, by virtue of the Acts of Parliament made thereupon. But there is no necessity to insist farther in this action here; because the breach of arrestment is a delinquence civilly cognoscible before the Lords, and therefore is explained, *Lib.* 1, *Tit.* Reparation [1, 9,29,*supra*].

Title 51. Adjudications

ADJUDICATIONS are now the great executorials by which all rights of the ground are conveyed from debtors to their creditors, by decreet of the Lords; whereby they dispone as effectually as the persons decerned themselves could do: with this difference, that, in voluntary dispositions, there are always expressed clauses of warrandice, which are not in judicial dispositions.

2. Apprisings were formerly the chief executorials, whereby all rights of the ground were conveyed, and adjudications were only extraordinary remedies, where apprising could not take place. But not only do these adjudications yet stand, as legal and ordinary by long custom, and are by several statutes authorized and extended, (as by cap. 7. Parl. 1621, [Adjudication Act, 1621,c.7; A.P.S. IV,611,c.7] cap. 18. Parl. 1669 [A.P.S. VII,576,c.39]). But further (by Act 19. Parl. 1672. [Adjudications Act, 1672,c.19; A.P.S. VIII,93,c.45]), apprisings are laid aside, and adjudications are introduced in their place, except in the case where there hath been prior apprisings of the same subject: so that now no ground-right is apprisable, except only upon the action for poinding of the ground, where the decreet decerns Letters of Apprising to be direct: whereupon apprisings must proceed with all the formalities as formerly, whereby these actions, which ought to have the most summary execution, are very tedious and expensive: and therefore there is no doubt but parties may raise adjudications upon all *debita fundi*, and if they insist only for the bygone annualrents, and not for the stock, (as frequently they do) they may insert a clause in the summons, bearing, "a power to apprise the moveables on the ground, belonging to the debtor, or to his tenants, not exceeding a term's mail; and an adjudication of the groundright and property for what remains unpaid, by the said moveables:" which no doubt the Lords would sustain. See *Lib.* 4, *Tit.* 35. § 27.

3. Adjudication doth not only convey the rights of the ground, but also the moveable sums of debtors and their moveable goods which are not in their own hands, by the actions for making forthcoming, which are adjudications upon arrestment. So that poinding is only of the goods of the debtor, which are in his own possession, which is also an adjudication of these moveables from the debtor to the creditor.

4. Beside all these adjudications, there is a new adjudication taking its rise from the 17th Act, Parl. 1681, [Judicial Sale Act, 1681,c.17; A.P.S. VIII,

351,c.83] concerning the sale of bankrupts' lands: "Whereby the Lords are authorized and impowered (upon a process at the instance of any creditor having a real right) to cognosce and try the value of estates, where the heritor is notoriously bankrupt, and the creditors are in possession thereof; and to commissionate persons to sell the lands, or any part thereof, at the rates of the country where they lie, with consent of the debtor where there is a legal reversion, or without the same where there is none: and the sale is to be by public roup, after public intimation at the head burgh of the shire, bailiary, stewartry or regality where the lands lie, and at the parish-kirk where the lands lie, and at six other adjacent parish-kirks (to be named by the Lords of Session) at the dissolution of the congregation, on a Sunday after the forenoon's sermon, by letters of intimation under the Signet, upon the Lords' deliverance: which letters are specially to express the time and place of the roup. And the creditors having real rights, and in possession, are to be specially cited upon twenty-one days, and all others concerned within or without the kingdom, at the market-crosses of these head burghs; and at the market-cross of Edinburgh, and pier and shore of Leith: and the price is to be distributed to the creditors, conform to their rights."

5. But there are some alterations made in this, by cap. 20. Parl. 1690, [Judicial Sale Act, 1690,c.20; A.P.S. IX,195,c.49] "Whereby it is statute and declared, that the buyers of bankrupts' estates, shall have right thereto by decreets of sale, to be pronounced by the Lords, adjudging the lands sold to the buyer for the price decerned, whether they be under reversion or not; and that if no buyer be found at the rate determined by the Lords, it shall be leisom for the Lords to divide the lands and other rights amongst the creditors, according to their several rights and diligences. And because the sale may be obstructed by donatars of liferent-escheat, the Lords are impowered to determine the price and value of the said liferent-escheats, and to sell land for the price thereof, according as the saids rights shall be found to have preference." By this statute the general inconvenience that did arise to debtors, by bringing in apprisings of general adjudications within the year, *pari passu* (whereby a great part of the estates of the kingdom came to be broken) is retrieved.

6. Albeit these statutes mention the "lands of bankrupts who are notoriously insolvent, and that the creditors are in possession," yet that is not to be understood as if the debtor's debts must exceed the value of his estate; but it is sufficient that his estate be so affected, as prudent persons will not buy from him, at a competent rate, with the hazard of the diligence of his creditors. And therefore it is not necessary to prove in this process, that the burden of his estate and his debts exceed the value of the estate; because the debtor hath a competent time allowed him by the saids statutes to purge the debts. For, 1. there must be proven the rental and rate of his estate and casualties thereof, according to the ordinary rate of the country. And, 2. after that probation is advised by the Lords, there must not only be an intimation at all

the parish-kirks where the lands lie, and six other kirks nearest adjacent; but the creditors in possession must be cited upon twenty-one days. And, 3. after all, the roup must proceed. So that if, in the mean time, he can sell his estate, and pay all his debt, the roup falls. Neither is it necessary, that all the estate must be possessed by creditors; but it is sufficient that a part thereof be possessed by wadsets, or annualrents, or by adjudications. And there is a great benefit not only to the creditors, but also to the debtor, that he gets a better price than he could obtain by voluntary disposition; and if there be any superplus of the price, he has it free to himself.

7. This adjudication by roup being designed as a general remedy both for debtors and creditors, the Lords do not sustain the same, unless the debtor's whole estate be contained in the process, if either the debtor or any creditor do, before the term be assigned for proving the rental, condescend and instruct, that a part of the debtor's estate is omitted in the process; as was found in the process, at the instance of Sir Francis Kinloch against Scot of Boningtoun, 1692 [1 Fountainhall 517,521; 4 B.S. 6]. In which case also, it being found that one of the kirks named by the Lords was not a parish-kirk, the intimation was ordained to be renewed, both as to the lands omitted, and as to a sixth parish-kirk of the lands libelled; because the Lords could not name *ex certa scientia*, but upon the suggestion of the pursuer.

8. These adjudications of bankrupts' estates, whether by way of sale or division, proceed summarily, as other adjudications, and are called amongst the acts, without abiding the roll: yet the allegeances and objections of debtors and co-creditors are competent to be proponed, when these adjudications are so called; and there cannot be here an adjudication repelling defences, and reserving them *contra executionem*, as in other adjudications, where one is already passed.

9. By addition of these adjudications of broken estates, there are many kinds of adjudications now in use. As, first, an adjudication for perfecting dispositions of rights of the ground which require infeftment, whether in fee or liferent, and whether in property or annualrent, when the disponer is either expressly or implicitly bound to infeft the acquirer, and oft-times to infeft himself for that effect, yet hath not performed the same; justice requiring some legal remedy to make such dispositions and obligements effectual: which would have been very tedious and expensive, if the acquirer had no other remedy, but first to use personal diligence against him to liquidate the damage, and then to apprise thereupon, whereby the acquirer having a real right if not complete, might easily be prevented by any creditor who had only a personal debt. Therefore the Lords, who, by their institution and authority, are impowered to make rules for dispatch of justice (whose power is thereby like that of the Roman Praetor, *ubi lex deest, Prætor supplet*) did sustain process at the acquirer's instance, against the disponer to fulfil, and against his superior to supply his place, and to receive the acquirer, in the same way as he might have done upon his vassal's charter of confirmation or procuratory

of resignation; and if all the superiors till the king were called, they might be so decerned in order, and at last precepts might be direct for expeding charters from the king, who is supreme superior.

But this being at first *remedium extraordinarium*, the Lords did not sustain it, so long as there was an ordinary remedy by horning and caption against the disponer, to perfect the disposition or obligement to infeft.

But now adjudications becoming so ordinary remedies, not only in this, but in many other cases, and being all executive actions, there is no ground to delay the acquirer till he obtain a decreet, and use all personal diligence, whereby he may be readily prevented by the adjudications of personal creditors: especially considering, that if the disponer be dead, there behoved to be an action against his heir, for fulfilling the disposition, and thereupon a decreet and all personal execution, before he could have a judicial disposition to supply the voluntary disposition promised: and therefore, in either case, this adjudication should proceed, unless the acquirer of his own choice should please to insist in the personal execution.

There is very convincing reason, that, upon these adjudications, if they be irredeemable, the superior should have a full year's rent; because he must accept a stranger vassal; or a modification, if the disposition be redeemable, or but a liferent-right; and if it be an annualrent, he should have a year's annualrent: for, though the Lords demurred to give a year's rent in adjudications for personal debts, because the year's rent was expressed in the Act anent apprisings, and omitted in the Act anent adjudications, yet that reason holds not in this kind of adjudications.

10. The second kind of adjudications is, when apparent heirs are pursued to fulfil their predecessors' obligements, but cannot be reached, unless they did represent the debtor; therefore, by cap. 106, Parl. 1540 [A.P.S. 11, 375,c.24], it is provided, that the apparent heirs of debtors may be charged to enter heir to any of their predecessors who were debtors, within forty days, with certification, that if they enter not, all action and execution will be competent against them, as if they were actually entered heirs. Whereupon the Lords do summarily, by supplication, without citation, grant letters to charge such apparent heirs to enter. But because the law gives the apparent heir a year to deliberate, whether he will enter heir or not; therefore the forty days within which they are charged to enter, should not terminate, till the *annus deliberandi* terminate. There is no further execution upon this charge, but it is a ground of an action whereby the apparent heir is pursued as lawfully charged to enter heir; and thereupon a decreet follows establishing the debt against him, as if he were originally debtor, whereon all personal execution, and also all real execution against any estate that the apparent heir hath, may proceed. But because he hath not that estate to which he might be heir, and hath not been entered therein; therefore such an estate could not be apprised from him, though he did not renounce to be heir, until there were a new special charge to enter heir in such particular lands, or other heritable rights,

with certification, that apprising thereof should be as effectual as if he were actually entered: and then apprising did proceed.

But if the apparent heir did renounce to be heir upon the general charge, then there was no place for a special charge, or for an apprising thereon; which the Lords supply by an action of adjudication, narrating the premises. And, albeit the foresaid Act of Parl. 1540, cap. 106. [A.P.S. 11,375,c.24] bear only, that the charge to enter heir proceed against parties being of perfect age, and for their predecessors' debts, yet by Act 27, Parl. 1621 [A.P.S. IV, 627,c.27], the same is extended to debts due by any person himself, as well as these which were addebted by his predecessors: and our custom hath promiscuously sustained charges against minors as well as against persons of perfect age. And though the foresaid Act bear, "That if the apparent heir charged, enter not, letters shall be directed to the sheriff of the shire and his deputes, to apprise the saids lands to the saids creditors, for the saids debts, if they be liquid; the which process of apprising shall have as great strength, force, and effect, as if the saids heirs were entered thereto;" yet the Lords found that method could not be effectual: and therefore supplied the same by a special charge, raised upon the decreet following on the general charge, for charging the heir to enter to such lands, and other heritable rights, specially; with certification, that if he enter not, they should be apprised from him, as if he were entered; which special charge passed upon bill, and was the immediate warrant for the apprising.

But now apprisings being laid aside, adjudication proceeds upon the general charge, whether the apparent heir renounce or not; but with this difference that if the apparent heir do not renounce, he is personally liable in all his estate, heritable and moveable: but if he renounce, his person and other estate is free, but the lands of his predecessor, who was debtor, and to whom he was apparent heir, is only adjudged. And whether the debt be liquid or not, the creditor may proceed in an action of adjudication, which hath been sustained not only for liquid but illiquid obligations, and even for obligations in fact. And by cap. 27, Parl. 1621 [A.P.S. IV,627,c.27], the apparent heir may be charged to enter, to the effect the lands to which he might have entered, might be apprised for his own debt, as well as for his predecessor's debt.

11. The third kind of adjudications is that which comes in place of apprising, upon infeftments of annualrents, or other *debita fundi*, and is in place of apprisings which proceed upon actions for poinding the ground, wherein the decreet is only for granting letters of apprising for poinding the moveables on the ground in the first place, and the ground-right and property, and all other right in the next place: for seeing now, by cap. 19, Parl. 1672 [Adjudications Act, 1672,c.19; A.P.S. VIII,93,c.45], it is statute, that in place of apprisings, the Lords of Session, upon process raised before them, at the instance of any creditor, shall adjudge the debtor's lands, &c. there is here no exception, whether the adjudication proceed upon a personal obligement, or upon a real burden upon the land: but adjudications on real burdens should

bear the same clause as in apprisings, that the moveables on the ground should be first distressed, and then the ground-right, unless the creditor proceed upon the personal obligation for the stock, or for the annualrent thereof: for then there is no warrant to poind the moveables, but the creditor has the addition of a fifth part in place of penalty or expenses; which may be always modified, whether the same be expressed or not, if the defender appear litigious. But if the adjudication be for bygone annualrents by infeftment, there uses no penalty of expenses to be granted for these; and therefore that fifth part ought not to be extended thereto: for the reason of the statute is, that the creditor is necessitate to take land for his debt. But in infeftments of annualrent the very design is to affect the land and not the debtor, and he hath access to the moveables, which personal creditors have not; neither can any land be adjudged or apprised, but that which the *debitum reale* affecteth, and whereof every part is affected: and therefore there ought to be no special adjudication of a part of the lands equivalent to the bygone annualrents, but the whole lands affected must be adjudged under reversion of ten years [IV,23, 8; IV,35,27; IV,51,2,*supra*].

12. The fourth kind of adjudication is founded upon the foresaid statute, putting adjudications in place of apprisings; whereby it is statute, "That, if the debtor appear and produce his rights, and be willing to put the creditor in possession, and to ratify the adjudication; in that case the Lords shall only adjudge so much of the debtor's lands as is sufficient to pay the debt, and a fifth part more in place of all penalty and expenses, redeemable only within five years from the date of the adjudication." And the Lords are impowered to pitch upon the lands so as may be sufficient for the creditor, and least hurtful for the debtor: the price whereof is to be rated conform to the rates of the country where the lands lie, and according to the tenor of the holding thereof, and the casualties of the same, either affecting other lands, as multures and other servitudes, or increasing the value, though giving no present rent, as wood, coal, &c. And it is declared, that the creditor shall be liable to no accompt in case of redemption; but, on the contrary, that the debtor shall be obliged to pay the annualrents of that part of the estate adjudged, to the rents whereof the creditor could not have access for payment of his annualrent.

This kind of adjudication hath been much neglected both by debtors and creditors, [IV,23,3,*supra*] whereby general adjudications have generally taken place, and, coming in *pari passu*, have rendered most debtors bankrupts, and have brought in the necessity of adjudication by sale. And albeit the Lords were impowered to decern securities for warrandice of the special adjudication, to affect the other lands, yet creditors liked better to adjudge all, and so brought themselves to a most tedious account, upon intromission, compensation, or the like exceptions competent against general adjudications, being proponed within the legal, which the least pretence of process doth prorogate. Debtors could have no advantage by general adjudications, except bankrupts whose whole estates would be exhausted by special adjudications. And others had no detriment, but only the penalty of a fifth part moie, to which the ordinary penalty and sheriff-fee was equivalent, which used not to be modified unless it were exorbitant, or that there were some defect in the formalities of the apprising.

13. The fifth kind of adjudications are the general adjudications of all the debtor's lands and heritable rights at random, without giving any evidence that the debtor had any right to them; and which is effectual though he was not actually infeft, but apparent heir; for there is no charge to enter heir required as to these adjudications. And it is a great inconvenience, that creditors may adjudge what they please to insert, and thereby lay the foundation of a plea against parties not concerned. But if parties appear and produce the evidences whereby these debtors are denuded, the Lords will not adjudge the ground-right and property, but will adjudge any other right of reversion or trust, which may be pretended competent to the debtor: or, as they did in the case of Alexander Livingstoun against the Lord Forrester, November 23, 1664 [1 Stair 232; M.10200], where they adjudged lands wherein the debtor was infeft in the property, but with the burden of a back-bond, bearing that the infeftment was only for relieving the acquirer of the disponer's debts.

This kind of adjudication is liable to all the exceptions to which apprisings were liable, which need not be further insisted in here, being so largely considered, Lib. 3. (Tit. Dispositions) [111,2,*supra*] upon apprising and adjudication, as judicial dispositions.

14. The last kind of adjudication is upon the sale or division of broken estates, wherein the estate is sold by roup, albeit the debts and burdens be not ranked before the adjudication: but the price decerned upon the roup bears annualrent from the date of the roup, and the buyer is obliged to find caution for the price, if there be any suspicion of hazard.

It was also declared, that there should be an inventory of the evidents of all the creditors, their debts and real burdens, which should be signed by the Ordinary upon the roup, and the creditors, and delivered to the buyer, and copies thereof given to the creditors, in like manner subscribed by him and the buyer, as the other was by him and the creditors, that, in case of any distress against the buyer, upon production by the buyer of that inventory, and the writs therein, each party should be liable to warrant, in so far as concerns the sum he received. As was found in the process of sale, at the instance of Dundas of Harviestoun, July 1692 [Not found].

Title 52. Suspensions, Where, of Sists of Execution, Relaxation, and Charges to set at Liberty, either upon Justice, or upon Mercy
super cessione bonorum

This title is reserved to the last place, because all executions by horning, poinding, caption, and incarceration, are stopped, till the suspensions thereof be discussed; and therefore suspensions could not be distinctly understood, until these executions, which might be suspended, were premised: and so the discussing of suspensions falls in properly here to be treated.

2. Suspension, as the name insinuates, signifieth a stopping of execution; and that either for a time, till such and such things occur and be done, as shall be decerned by decreet of suspension, or by stopping the execution for ever.

3. The last hath the like effect as a reduction; but with this difference, that decreets on suspensions cannot be again suspended or reduced upon grounds proponed and repelled, or competent and omitted, when the first decreet on the suspension was obtained, which does not so hold in reductions of other rights: for, though a reduction upon one ground be not effectual, so that the defender is assoilzied, yet a new reduction may be raised upon other grounds, on different facts, but not upon other grounds *in jure ;* which hath a great inconvenience to multiply and protract pleas: and it were worthy of a statute, that whosoever raises reduction of any right, should not be heard upon any reasons that were then competent and omitted [IV,40,16,*supra*]: For otherwise the litigious and rich might weary out the innocent, and these who are less powerful to maintain pleas.

4. Suspensions do also differ from reductions in this, that suspensions are not effectual, unless the grounds thereof be instantly verified; because there having been decreets, or that which is equivalent thereto, the effect thereof by possession or otherwise, should not be delayed upon allegeances to be proven, albeit they were not competent in the decreet or charge suspended, but should only be reserved by way of reduction; so that in the mean time, till the obtainer of the decreet or charge be put *in mala fide*, to continue his possession, he is to enjoy and spend the profits as his own. But he is not put *in mala fide* by raising a reduction, but by the production of such a right as doth evidently elide his right, and not by a dubious production, until the Lords find it to be a better right.

5. But there are some exceptions from this rule, as if a cautioner, or any interposed person do suspend, who is not supposed to have the principal debtor's writs to defend him, he will get terms both by horning and caption against the principal debtor, or others havers of these writs: or if the reason of suspension be such as the suspender is not obliged to instruct by writ, if he refer the same to the charger's oath, in that case the advocate for the charger will always take a term to produce him to depone, albeit the suspender hath not referred the reason by the suspension to his oath, and will take the shortest term, that the cause may be the sooner discussed: but if the reason of suspension be probable by witnesses, the suspender will get diligences against the witnesses.

6. Suspenders use to raise reductions with their suspensions; and, if in discussing thereof they satisfy the production, or hold it as satisfied, they will get a term to prove even by their own writs, if they depone that they are not in their power at the time, if there be any probability of verity in the reasons.

7. There is no necessity to consider here the reduction of decreets: for what is general in reductions is handled *Lib.* 4, *Tit.* 20. Reduction and Im-

probation: and what is special in the reduction of decreets of the Lords of Session, may be gathered from *Lib.* 4, *Tit.* 46. Decreets of Session. Of these specialties, this is the prime, that decreets of Session *in foro contradictorio* cannot be reduced upon what was proponed and repelled, or competent and omitted; which doth not extend to emergent reasons, or such as are known to be new come to knowledge: but, in this case, or when the decreet is either in absence simply, or by the defender's passing from his compearance before peremptors proponed, subsequent reductions will be sustained, upon distinct reasons, as in other rights: yet, more such suspensions cannot be sustained; for, after discussing of the first suspension, what was then competent, is not receivable by a posterior suspension.

8. A suspension is an action, at the instance of the suspender, against any party that hath obtained decreet, or hath obtained letters for charging the suspender to pay or perform any thing for which he is charged, and whereupon he may be denounced rebel, whereby his escheat would fall to the king, or his liferent-escheat to his superior, or whereby his person may be taken by caption and incarcerated, or his goods or sums may be poinded, or his lands may be apprised upon decreets for poinding the ground, or adjudged for these, or for personal debts. The suspension may also be against any who have obtained right to such decreets, or summary charges. But because in most cases a charge of horning must precede the other executions, therefore the defender in the suspension is always called charger.

9. Suspension cannot pass but upon a bill, which must be presented by the clerk of the bills of suspension and advocation, and not by the ordinary clerks of Session. The bill doth always mention that the supplicant is charged, or that his lands may be apprised or poinded, and then mentions the grounds of the charge, and the reasons he alleges against the same: and therefore craves warrant to summon the charger, to produce the grounds of the charge, and to hear and see the same suspended by decreet of the Lords, for the saids reasons. Likeas, the bill also contains an offer of sufficient caution, at least juratory caution, that is, that the petitioner depones that he is not able to find caution, or if he offer a cautioner whose sufficiency is doubted, he depones that he can find no better. And in case the suspender be denounced, the bill craves relaxation, and an offer of caution for escheat-goods.

10. Formerly suspensions frequently passed upon insufficient caution: but now the clerk of the bills is liable to the charger for the sufficiency of the cautioner the time he was admitted; and, on the other part, he is liable to the suspender for damage, if he refuse a sufficient cautioner; conform to an Act of Sederunt, February 18, 1686. And therefore the clerk of the bills inquires into the condition of the cautioners offered, by some persons of credit who know them; and sometimes gets persons to attest the sufficiency of the cautioner. If the clerk of the bills refuse a cautioner without reason, the Ordinary on the Bills must judge upon the grounds alleged by the clerk and the party, and in case of difficulty, adviseth with the Lords.

11. Suspensions were necessarily introduced by the Lords, especially to give hearing to those who were decerned in absence; because oft-times the executions whereupon such decreets proceeded, were not true, but only were made up indorsations by a forged executor, whereby no person was in hazard to be punished as a forger; and albeit the executer were found, it was not worth the trouble the suspender would be at, to improve the executions; but he would rather pass by the same, and dispute the reasons of suspension: yet he had this disadvantage, that where he might have had terms to prove in ordinary actions, he behoved for the most part, instantly to verify, in the suspension. Therefore the ordinary style of suspensions bears, that the decreet craved to be suspended, was for null-defence and non-compearance, the complainer never having been orderly summoned thereto.

12. There was also necessity for suspension of summary charges, which pass of course, where no hearing of the suspender could be understood; as in charges upon decreets of summary registration, without citation, or charges upon bills of exchange amongst merchants, by Act 20. Parl. 1681 [Bills of Exchange Act, 1681,c.20; A.P.S. VIII,352,c.86], see *Lib.* 4, *Tit.* 47. § 7. In like manner, summary charges are allowed by several Acts of Parliament, without citation or decreet: and they are oft-times general, neither naming the persons nor things to be performed, particularly.

13. In like manner, there was a necessity to suspend all decreets, though *in foro contradictorio*, or though they were decreets of Parliament (when no Parliament was sitting) upon obedience of the saids decreets, and upon production of the charges, discharges, or other declarations of the satisfaction thereof: for, seeing the Parliament is not a constant judicature, nor hath fixed members, nor any custom that any of the members can suspend in the intervals, the Lords of Session, who are the supreme judges-ordinary, must give remedy by suspension, upon obedience; which is understood two ways. 1. When obedience is proved by acceptation, 2. When full obedience is offered and not accepted, that being instructed by instrument, and consignation being made of what is decerned, to be given up upon demand, without discussion, it is sufficient obedience: for the party charger can possibly do no more. But if the suspender add other reasons to be discussed, the consignation is but in place of a cautioner, and imports not full obedience; nor are these other reasons competent to be discussed by the Lords.

14. The first design of suspension, was not to take from the charger the benefit of legal execution, against a suspender who had compeared in the decreet craved to be suspended, and had disputed the cause, without passing from his compearance before proponing of peremptors: and so was not to be passed upon reasons competent and omitted, or proponed and repelled, or even upon pretence of instructions alleged to be new come to knowledge, or emergent; unless the instructions be after the decreet: for the new coming of instructions to knowledge, ought to be in some way proven, and the assertion of the suspender is not sufficient probation thereof. Neither should any

decreet upon compearance be suspended, but upon reasons relevant and instantly verified at the passing of the bill.

15. Yet many abuses did creep in, in the passing of bills of suspension; so that if the reasons were relevant, the offer to instruct the same at discussion, was sustained: which ought not to have been done, except for cautioners; or probation of matters of fact, where the party charger might prove by witnesses, though he were bound by writ; which is indulged to tenants for proving delivery of victual, or performance of deeds contained in their tacks; but ought not to be sustained to others, without testificates of persons of fame, who know that the matters of fact alleged in the reasons were true. In like manner, the allegeance of being a decreet in absence for null-defence became to be sustained, without inquiry into the verity thereof, by inspection of the decreet, or testificate of the clerk of the process. As also protestations were suspended of course, upon consignation of the protestation-money. And the clerks of the bills were not held liable for the sufficiency of cautioners, or that they were at least so holden and reputed when received. By all which, the effect of decreets of Session became very uncertain.

16. And therefore the Lords have adhibited many remedies, for preventing these inconveniences. As 1. By observing an Act of Sederunt in anno 1639 [Not found], whereby it was declared, that "competent and omitted" should thenceforth be relevant, as well against reasons contrary to decreets upon suspension, as against decreets upon ordinary action: whereas formerly, suspenders might raise as many suspensions as they had several reasons; though many points are not competent in suspensions, which would have been competent in ordinary actions; for as *in judicio possessorio*, these points which require reduction or declarator, are not competent by way of exception; much less by way of suspension; and in decreets of general declarator, many things are reserved to the special declarator, which therefore are not competent in suspensions against the general declarator. Likewise points emergent after decreets on suspension, are receivable against these decreets; for they were not then competent. And seeing decreets of suspension ought only to proceed upon reasons instantly verified; therefore not only instructions new come to knowledge are receivable by suspension, if rational evidences be given that they were new come to knowledge, by testificates from those who discovered the same, but also if they were not, the time of the passing of the suspension, in the hands of the suspender, or these in his power, they should not be repelled, because not produced at the passing of the suspension, they being produced at the discussing thereof. These grounds have given rise to the custom of eiking reasons of suspension, which were not in the bill.

There are two kinds of decreets, which pass under the name of decreets of suspension. The one is condemnatory, when the letters are found orderly proceeded, either simply, or in part; or conditionally, when the letters are suspended ay and till such things be performed by the charger: in which case the charger needs not a new decreet, to instruct the performance of these, but upon performance accepted, or offered, and upon refusal, what is decerned being consigned, the charger may charge again upon his decreet, by new letters bearing the instructions of his performance, or consignation as aforesaid. The other decreet of suspension is, when the letters are suspended *simpliciter*, either for the whole articles charged for, or for a part thereof. And for distinction's sake, we shall call only these decreets *of* suspension, which are absolvitor *simpliciter*, and these decreets which are condemnator, we shall call decreets *on* suspension.

Secondly, Another remedy which the Lords adhibited against abuses by suspensions, was by ordaining the clerks of Session to give testificates from time to time, to the clerk of the bills, of decreets *in foro*; and by requiring the clerks of the bills to have an index thereof, by the names of the chargers, that the same might be shown at the passing of the bills; and if the agent for the charger desired to see the bill of suspension, the Ordinary was appointed first to consider the relevancy and competency of the reasons and the instructions, and if he found the same relevant and instructed, he was to sign the bill of that date it was read to him, or by him: and if any desired to see it, before it passed the signet, he might allow it to be seen, and give a sist of execution for a definite time, which sist (by the Act of Sederunt, Feb. 9, 1675) was not to exceed a month, from the time the bill was presented. But because several sists were granted by several Ordinaries, therefore (by Act of Sederunt, Nov. 9, 1680) fourteen days are only allowed for sists of execution, from the date the bill was signed, for the clerks inquiring into the condition of the cautioner: and all other stops (except where causes were ordained by the Lords to be discussed on the bill) are declared void. Yet upon other considerations the sist hath been continued, not exceeding a month in whole. And that it may be known, what sists are granted, the clerks of the bills are ordained to make an alphabetic inventory of bills refused or sisted, that posterior Ordinaries be not imposed on.

These sists of execution being intimated to the charger, have the same effect during their time, as a passed suspension, and any transgression thereof is receivable by complaint, as other contempts of authority.

Thirdly, Another remedy against the abuses by suspension, is, that whereas formerly, every one of the Ordinary Lords might at any time pass bills of suspension, albeit not presented by the clerk of the bills; so that parties could not know to whom to address against passing of bills; therefore the Lords (by their said Act, February 9, 1675) did ordain, that thereafter in time of session, no bill of suspension should be presented to any to be passed, but only to the Ordinary upon the Bills for the time, and only by the clerk of the bills or his servants; and in case the Ordinary refuse the bill, he should mark on the back thereof with his own hand, "Refused, in respect the reasons are not relevant or not instructed:" which bills the clerk is ordered to keep, and to mark with his hand on the back thereof, what writs are produced for instructing the bill: and if the same bill, or any new bill of suspension upon that matter be again presented, the clerk is to present the former refused bill, which the Ordinary is not to pass, till it be presented to the whole Lords in time of session, or three in time of vacance. And therefore in this case, as well as in the former of granting of sists, the clerk must keep an alphabetic index for both.

Fourthly, The next remedy against the abuses by suspension, is, that because suspension uses to be desired, upon pretence that the charge given by the messenger is general or informal, and for verifying thereof forged copies are produced, and sometimes other forged instructions, which the suspender intends to make no further use of, but to get delay and suffer protestation; therefore the Lords (by their said Act, November 9, 1680) do declare, if the charger shall produce such a suspension, or duplicate thereof under the hand of the keeper of the signet, that beside the ordinary expenses of protestation, the Ordinary will modify large expenses to the charger for the delay: and in case the suspension come to be discussed (by the suspender's insisting) the Lords declare, that they will hold these writs false and forged, and modify large expenses to the charger, but prejudice to insist against the forgers of such copies or writs.

Fifthly, Another remedy against the abuses by suspension, is, because suspenders ordinarily refer the verity of the reasons to the charger's oath, therefore the Ordinary, if he find the reason relevant, should take the oath of the charger if he be present, upon the verity of the reason, in order to the passing or refusing of the bill; and if the charger be absent, he shall take the suspender's oath of calumny thereupon: and in either of these cases, the Ordinary shall pass the bill, with this quality, that the suspender shall be liable to the charger, in the expenses he shall be at, through the purchasing of that suspension, and in discussing of the same, according as he shall depone upon these expenses, without any modification thereof, if the letters shall be found orderly proceeded.

Lastly, Because suspensions now come in by a roll, to be discussed in order as they are seen, returned and presented to the keeper of the rolls, which must require a considerable time before execution can proceed; therefore the Lords do ordinarily, upon the supplication of the charger, appoint the reasons to be discussed upon the bill, without passing the signet: in which case, the suspender is not obliged to find caution; and therefore the charger hath his option, either to discuss the cause summarily on the bill without caution, or not to demand the discussing on the bill, if he get sufficient caution. This is the most excellent remedy, for making of the decreets of Session effectual; and therefore if the chargers do only charge in time of session, they need suffer no delay in execution. And for that effect, suspensions should not pass in the vacance unless the charge had been given in vacance time, for which the copy of the charge should be produced, and the oath of the producer taken, that it is true: and even in that case, suspension cannot pass in the vacance, but by the Ordinary and two other of the Lords, viz. the nearest before him in course and the nearest after him, that are in town for the time, if the decreet be *in foro contradictorio*.

The discussing of suspensions upon the bill is ordinarily granted on the petition of the chargers, except in the case where the suspenders are incarcerated, who for the most part are not able to find sufficient caution; yet compassion and the favour of liberty may prevail with the Lords, that if the charger will not insist to discuss upon the bill, the suspender may have suspension passed upon caution, or consignation of a general disposition, if he be no further able.

And also if the suspension contain a charge to set at liberty, the said Act of Sederunt, requires, that it be not passed till intimation be instructed to have been made to the charger, of the time of presenting the bill, within the latitude of eight days, that he may answer for himself, before the liberty be granted. And in session-time, the Lords do always ordain intimation to be made to the charger's advocate, that he may be heard before the liberty be granted. For there is no reason to set debtors at liberty, after the ultimate act of personal execution, without a full consignation of the charge.

17. These remedies are so favourable for chargers, that the Lords have found it just to pass suspensions, when the suspender makes faith, that he can find either no caution, or no better caution than what he offers; he always consigning a disposition of his whole means and estate, in favour of the charger, so far as the letters shall be found orderly proceeded.

18. This also is special in suspensions of protestations, that because they do more easily pass than suspensions of decreets, upon consignation of the protestation-money; therefore it is ordained, that the clerk of the bills shall always mention in his index whether the bill for suspending a protestation be the second, third, or posterior protestation: for the third protestation cannot be suspended but *in præsentia*, or by three of the Lords met together, as aforesaid. And to that effect the Lords do declare, that if the deliverance of the bill do not bear, that the same is the second or subsequent suspension, they will recall the suspension, albeit the same be expede at the signet, conform to the Act of Sederunt, July 10, 1677.

19. And seeing chargers may so easily obtain suspensions to be discussed upon the bill, they should not urge the Ordinary to report their allegeances against passing of the bill, which takes up much time, and hath no sentence following upon it, only the bill is refused: whereupon nothing can be extracted, but only the clerk of the bills in his index of refused bills ought to express that such bills were refused *in præsentia ;* which therefore three in the vacance cannot pass upon the same reasons. Yea, if a bill be refused by three in the vacance, it cannot be passed by them, or any other three.

20. The deliverance upon a bill of suspension, ordaining it to be discussed upon the bill, hath all the effects of a suspension passed the signet, and this further, that it requires neither consignation nor caution: because the

charger may always insist to have it discussed when he pleases; and the Ordinary in that week when it passed ought to discuss it at the side-bar, whenever the charger insists. And, albeit other Ordinaries ought not to go to the side-bar, but on the proper days assigned to them, yet he who was Ordinary when such bills were appointed to be discussed, hath privilege at all times to go to the side-bar, for discussing thereof, and report, without being hindered till the ordinary diet to report in other cases.

21. If the charger do not insist to discuss upon the bill, the suspender ought not to be put to uncertain attendance: and therefore he may apply to that Ordinary who could discuss, to call the charger to insist; and if he do insist, and the suspender appear not, the Ordinary ought to grant protestation as in other suspensions: or if, upon the suspender's application, the charger compear not to insist, if he do instantly instruct his reasons, which are found relevant, he may remit the same to the Lords, and may obtain a decreet of suspension, if the Lords find the same proven by the instructions produced; or otherwise he may crave protestation against the charger for not insisting, which will have this effect, that no sentence shall pass against him till he be charged of new.

22. Suspensions do pass for diverse ends, and accordingly are of diverse tenors. They pass either for giving the party *personam standi in judicio ;* or not only for suspending further execution, but for relaxing the suspender, who was denounced by horning, or for setting the suspender at liberty; and that either upon the justice and verity of the reasons of suspension, for taking away the debt, or upon compassion and mercy to over-burdened creditors incarcerated, upon their disponing their whole estate irredeemably to their creditors, for obtaining only freedom against personal execution.

23. The first and least effect of suspension is, to give the party *personam standi in judicio ;* for when persons are charged by the King's letters, if they give not obedience, the law holds it as rebellion, and by public proclamation they are denounced rebels; after which they are debarred from compearing in judgment, either as pursuers or as defenders. Yet this being but a rebellion *fictione juris,* seeing no person will wilfully or contemptuously disobey, but are denounced either by clandestine charges which came not to their knowledge, or because they are not able to pay; therefore the Lords do not admit certification holding such persons as confessed, nor grant certifications against their writs as false and feigned: because the ground of these certifications does in these cases cease, viz. that they do wilfully forbear to appear and depone, because they are conscious they behoved to confess, or to produce their writs, because they know they would be found forged; so that the other party must either forbear to debar them, or they cannot prevail by these certifications. And when persons are incarcerated, and have reasons of suspension, relevant and competently instructed, the Lords, knowing that they behoved to be denounced before they were incarcerated, do therefore pass suspension, for giving them person to stand in judgment, that they may insist in

their reasons of suspension, wherein they are really defenders. But this kind of suspension requires no caution, and doth not contain relaxation, and is only given when the Lords refuse to suspend, and grant charge to set at liberty; which they oft-times do, though sufficient caution be offered; because incarceration is the last act of personal diligence: and therefore they only give the incarcerated person privilege to compear by his advocates, to discuss the reasons of suspension, himself remaining in prison: wherein if they prevail, the decreet of suspension will contain relaxation, and a warrant for a charge to set at liberty, the suspender finding caution in the ordinary way for escheat goods.

24. The second way of passing suspension is, when the reasons are found relevant and competently instructed, and the suspender is neither denounced nor incarcerated; for then there is no mention of giving the suspender person to stand in judgment, or a warrant to relax, or to set at liberty: yet the common rule is, that the suspension cannot pass the signet, till either consignation or sufficient caution be found, that what shall be decerned shall be paid or performed. But this cautioner cannot be charged till the suspension be first discussed. In finding this caution there is no exception, though the suspender were never so solvent, yea, though he had solvent cautioners for the same cause, bound conjunctly and severally, (whereby they are more easily reached than ordinary cautioners in suspension; for, they being bound conjunctly and severally, they have not the benefit of discussion) yet I see no reason, that if one cautioner offer another solvent cautioner, who is obliged to relieve him, that he should be refused; for the charger hath thereby immediate access against that person, which he hath not otherwise. And though the reason of suspension were never so fully instructed, as by a registrate discharge, yet caution must be found. And the clerk of the bills being liable, if the cautioner be not at least holden and reputed solvent for performance of the charge, suspenders would be very much straitened, if they had no remedy by juratory caution: for though the Lords are judges of the clerk's reasons for refusing the caution offered, yet they seldom enter in that debate, but allows him to accept of the caution as he will be answerable.

25. The clerks of the bills, for their security, do require attesters of the solvency of the cautioner offered: and if these attesters be persons of unquestionable credit, it liberates the clerks; but the attesters are *subsidiariè* liable to the charger, by way of action, only if the cautioner, when offered, was insufficient. But it hath been always sustained to liberate the attester, that the cautioner was holden and reputed solvent for the charge, the time of his attesting; which must be proven by witnesses, that it was so commonly reputed in the vicinity where he lived: yet this will be excluded, if the charger instruct by writ, that the cautioner was then under evident distresses, by registrate horning long unsuspended, or by apprisings or adjudications.

26. The remedy by juratory caution hath been allowed by the Roman law, and the custom of most civil nations: for it were hard to exclude sus-

penders from their just and competent defences, because they were not able to find caution. And therefore, if the cautioner be doubted, if the suspender depone that he can find no better, the cautioner ought to be received, unless the suspender himself be also doubted in his solvency; in which case the Lords, by Act of Sederunt, require the suspender to give a general disposition and assignation of all his estate, to stand in place of caution: and much more if the suspender can find no caution. But if the suspender have a visible estate in lands, or sufficient bonds, and offer assignation or infeftment in place of caution, if he depone he can find no better, the samine ought to be received, without putting him to a general disposition, which carries the affront of being like a *cessio bonorum*, though it be not against all the creditors.

27. The third kind of suspension is that which contains relaxation, that is, a loosing from the denunciation, whereby the moveables which the suspender acquires after relaxation fall not under his escheat, as do his other moveables; and therefore in such suspensions the suspender must not only find caution for the charger's security, but also for his escheat-goods belonging to him before the relaxation: which now is become but a mere formality: for there being no way in that state of the process to know the value of these escheat-goods, caution for any inconsiderable sum is accepted as to these escheat-goods. This way of suspension may be granted to persons incarcerated, without a charge to set them at liberty, which is seldom granted but upon consignation, or upon an unwarrantable incarceration, when either a suspension is passed the signet, and intimated by citation or other intimation; or when a warrant hath been granted to discuss the reasons on the bill, and intimated before the incarceration; or even when a sist is granted and not expired, if the same be intimated or shown before the incarceration. But after incarceration the magistrates or jailers cannot set the person incarcerated at liberty, without a warrant from the Lords, even though the charge was satisfied before the incarceration.

28. Charges to set at liberty, albeit most ordinarily granted in suspensions, yet in the former or like cases, the same may be granted without suspension; yea, upon evidence of any person's being incarcerated anywhere, without an executed caption or act of warding, the Lords will summarily, without citation, grant warrant for a charge to set at liberty.

29. The fourth kind of suspension is, of the precepts of chancellary, upon the retours of heirs, for charging their superiors to infeft them; upon which no personal execution follows, but the superior is passed by, and new precepts are granted against the superior's superior, to supply his vice. And therefore the legal remedy for such superiors is, by suspending the charges upon these precepts: but the suspension must be upon reasons instantly verified, as that the charger hath not performed that article of the retour, *faciendo domino superiori quod de jure facere tenetur*. But if it be a reason to be proven, it is only competent by way of reduction of the retour or precept.

30. The last kind of suspension is that which doth not proceed upon the

justice of any reason of suspension, but which the law hath allowed upon compassion and mercy of incarcerated debtors, who are not able to pay their debts, upon their assignation and disposition to their creditors, of their whole means and estate, heritable and moveable, real and personal. This must proceed by way of action, calling the creditors, and bearing that the pursuer is incarcerated and insolvent; and that he is willing to assign and dispone his whole means and estate to his creditors, and to deliver to them all the rights and evidents he hath, or can command thereof: and thereupon beseeching for liberty against personal execution only, and offering to depone upon what means and estate he hath, and what securities thereof he is master of.

31. This process proceeding upon compassion of human misery, and the design of the incarceration not being penal, but against defrauders or concealers of their estate, it uses to be taken in summarily without going to a roll; seeing there is no point of right to be discussed therein, especially now when it is so long ere an ordinary action can come in by the roll. It is first called for taking of the incarcerated person's oath upon his means and securities; and after the oath is returned, it is called again for obtaining a decreet of liberty, containing a warrant to charge to set at liberty. But it can only be called and discussed *in præsentia*.

32. The oath given *in cessione bonorum*, was only that the party had no other means or estate than what was contained in the inventory produced, signed by him; and that he had made no disposition nor assignation thereof, in prejudice of his creditors after his incarceration. But, by an Act of Sederunt, February 8, 1688, the formula of this oath must be in these terms, "If he hath any lands, heritages, sums of money, goods or gear belonging to him, more than is contained in the disposition and inventory produced in process; and if since his imprisonment he hath made any other disposition than that which is produced; and if he hath made any other before his imprisonment, and if he acknowledge that he hath made any other disposition before his imprisonment, that he condescend upon the same: and also that he depone, if since his imprisonment he hath put out of his hands any money, goods or gear belonging to him. And the Lords do declare that, if the pursuer shall deny, that he hath granted any other disposition, and that his oath shall be thereafter redargued, the decreet of *bonorum* obtained by him shall be void and null, and he shall never get the benefit of a *cessio bonorum* thereafter." The reason why the oath must be, "whether there be any dispositions before the incarceration," is, because the dyvour might have designedly denuded himself, and by collusion with some one creditor, got himself in prison, and so defraud all his other creditors, (as frequently they enter only into prison when their oath is to be taken) and also because the prior disposition might be fraudulent otherwise. But the words will not extend so far as to exclude the benefit of *bonorum*, except in the case of recent dispositions, and not old dispositions, which it is presumed the deponent had forgot.

33. The defences which are proper against this *cessio bonorum*, are, 1.

From the oath, if it be not conform to the formula. Yet, though he adject this quality, that he hath put nothing away during his incarceration, but what was necessary for his subsistence till sentence, it will not exclude his liberation. 2. If any thing can be instantly verified redarguing the oath; because the oath is not upon the reference of the defender, but upon the order of the judge; as if there can be any other recent disposition produced than what is acknowledged in the oath, or if the disposition anterior to the incarceration be near the time thereof, and so is presumed collusive. The reason why the defences at obtaining the decreet must be instantly verified, is, because they ought to have been proponed when the process was called for taking the defender's oath; in which case the creditors might have had a term to prove. 3. It is a relevant defence, if the party hath not been truly detained in prison, for a considerable time, that the creditors may make inquiry of any fraudulent conveyance, and that the *squalor carceris* may bring the debtor to ingenuity; for in that case only it can be thought to be an act of commiseration. 4. Thence also hath arisen this defence, viz. That the creditors offer to aliment the debtor in prison; which certainly cannot be understood, that the debtor, though alimented, can perpetually be kept in prison, but only till full search can be made, if any fraud be committed: and if offer of aliment be made, the Lords modify the quantity, and cause insert this quality, that if the aliment be not weekly paid on the day appointed, warrant is granted for a charge to set at liberty.

34. The law hath also appointed that magistrates, where dyvours are incarcerated, must not set them out, until they have the habit appointed to be worn by dyvours, as their outmost garment: and they ought to set the dyvour for some time, in the most public time of the day, upon a place appointed for that purpose, commonly called the Dyvour-stone. And these decreets bear, that the dyvour shall be no longer free from personal execution, than while that habit is upon him, when his clothes are on, and so visible that all who converse with him may see it. The reason of which severity is, to deter *Decoctores*, who lavishly spend their estates, and continue trade, when they know themselves absolutely broken: and therefore the Lords exeem some from wearing this habit, upon their proper knowledge or famous testificates, that they became poor without such faults.

35. In all suspensions, there is a day assigned for the suspender to cite the charger, and in the mean time the letters are suspended; which day ought to be according to the distance of the parties, that there may be sufficient time to use citation: but if a longer day be appointed, the charger may raise a summons for shortening that time, which therefore is called a *Prævento*, and comes in summarily as an incident process.

36. Suspension is the most general legal remedy against executorials, yet it doth not reach them all: for there is no suspending of diligence for probation before sentence, nor for suspending of inhibition or arrestment, upon account that the ground thereof is suspended. Yet the suspension has this

effect, that arrestments, though upon decreets, may be loosed upon caution; because the ground of the arrestment stands suspended. Neither doth suspension of the ground of arrestment exclude or delay the action for making forthcoming; but the party, whose goods and means are craved to be made forthcoming, may repeat the reasons of suspension, by way of defence, and may propone other defences, albeit not competent by way of suspension, but which have the ordinary course of probation. Yea a decreet ordaining moveables or sums to be made forthcoming, hath its full effect by poinding or adjudication, albeit the ground of the arrestment was suspended, whether before or after the arrestment: because the reasons of suspension might have been repeated, and if they were not repeated, they were competent and omitted, if the decreet was *in foro ;* and though it was not, yet unless it be suspended, execution may proceed thereon.

37. Suspension doth not hinder real execution by adjudication. Yet, in the same way as in arrestment and process to make forthcoming, so in the process of adjudication, the reasons of suspension may be repeated by way of defence. But, if they be not instantly verified at the discussing of that action, albeit the reasons be founded on other men's writs, or on matter of fact requiring no writ, the reasons of suspension, though relevant, will be repelled *illo loco,* but reserved *contra executionem ;* in respect that now adjudications within the year come in *pari passu ;* and in case of the division of adjudged lands, the creditors have access for choosing where they will have their shares, according to the order of the dates of adjudication, in case in a process of sale there be not found buyers. And when apprisings were in use, the charges to enter heir, nor the denunciation of lands or other heritages to be apprised, were not to be suspended: but if, at the messenger's proceeding to apprise, a suspension of the sums were produced, the messenger (unless he had assessors appointed by the Lords) did always repel the same and all other defences; unless apprising were expressly and *nominatim* suspended, which was only passed upon reasons special against the apprising, and not only against the debt apprised for; and then the messenger ought to have forborn to apprise, but might have adjourned the diet of apprising to a competent time, that the Lords might discuss the special reasons of suspension against the apprising, which they would do *incidenter ;* otherwise the messenger's proceeding were punishable as a contempt. The reason of all which was, that messengers were not skilful judges, but apprised *periculo petentis.*

38. It remains then that the proper effect of suspension is, to stop charges or denunciations of horning, or the effects of denunciation; as to give *personam standi in judicio ;* or to exclude escheat after relaxation; or to stop poinding, except on decreets of forthcoming; or to stop the entering of vassals by others than their immediate superiors, till the suspensions be discussed.

39. So much may suffice as to the passing of bills of suspension. As to the discussing of suspensions, the form thereof, wherein it differs from the dis-

cussing of ordinary actions, is thus. The charger against whom the suspension is obtained, after the day of compearance in the suspension is past, gives a short copy of the suspension to a clerk, and causeth call it in the Outer-House. If none compear for the suspender, protestation is admitted of course.

40. If an advocate compear for the suspender, then the clerk assigns a short day to him to produce the principal suspension; and at the same time the charger may give him out the charge, being the decreet, or sentence obtained. The first diet being come, the clerk calls the copy again, and assigns a second shorter time, with certification that if he produce not, protestation will be admitted: and then he calls the third time, and if the principal suspension be not produced with the charge (if it was given out in time) protestation is admitted. All which is marked by the clerk on the back of the copy, and being put in the minute-book and read, it may be extracted the next day after. But during that time, the production of the principal suspension, with the charge to the party, clerk, or keeper of the minute-book, will stop the protestation. The like order is also used for getting back of advocations, and the instructions of the principal cause, if it be given out when the copy is first called.

41. The charger's advocate, at the giving out of the charge, writeth on the back thereof, the day that it was given out, and sets his name thereto: and is not obliged to receive the suspension, unless the suspender mark on the process, that he hath seen and returned the same, expressing the date of the return, but may take out his protestation, as if the principal were not produced.

42. According to the date of the return of the charge, the suspension is inrolled; and when it comes to be discussed, the cause being called, the charger produceth the copy marked by the clerk as aforesaid, and thereupon craveth a protestation from the Ordinary, which he admits, if the suspender's advocate produce not. Yet sometimes, the charger's advocate will hold the copy for a principal, and the suspender will repeat his reasons of suspension: which though they be not admittable upon a short copy, in strict form, (because all reasons of suspension, both principal and eiked, ought to be set down in writ, and given to the charger to see) yet frequently, the charger will rather dispute the cause, than take a protestation, which is easily suspended again; and therefore will answer to the reasons as verbally repeated.

43. But if the suspender compear, and the charger do not insist, he may produce the principal suspension, and crave the letters to be suspended, "Ay and till the charge be produced;" which puts him *in tuto*, that no protestation can be taken upon the copy, till the charge be produced. Yea, if the suspender extract and produce the charge, and refer his reasons to the Lords, they will advise the same; and if they find the reasons relevant and proven, will suspend the letters *simpliciter*. In which case the decreet of suspension is as other decreets in absence, and may be reduced upon a summons of reduction: wherein the Lords will reconsider the reasons, and hear the parties de-

bate thereupon; and may recall what they formerly did, albeit *super eisdem deductis*; which they cannot do in decreets upon compearance. For when the defender is absent, the Lords do not so accurately consider the cause; seeing there is a remedy; and likewise, because, albeit they find the reasons relevant as before, yet the party may elide the same by relevant answers and duplies.

44. If both charger and suspender compear, and the principal suspension be produced; then the charger doth briefly repeat his charge or decreet suspended, and declares what he insists in. And if there be any thing general, he useth to give in a condescendence in writ, at the beginning, to be seen with the charge; which therefore is called the special charge. And if the charge have in it many members, he declares what points he insists in, *primo loco :* and if he do not, the suspender may insist upon any reason of suspension he pleaseth, against any of the points.

45. The suspender, in repeating his reason, should condescend by the number, what reason it is: and whether it be libelled or eiked: for suspenders may add or eike to their libelled reasons, if they will; so that if the reason they repeat, be neither eiked nor libelled, in strict form it may be repelled: or if the eiked reason hath not been at first produced, and seen with the suspension, it ought not to be received. Yet many times the Ordinary will indulge that favour, and cause the charger either answer it instantly, or take it up till a day, to see: which he may do, without expunging the cause out of the roll; but may call the cause again at the day appointed: and if the charger hath seen the reasons, he may proceed.

46. In like manner, reasons of suspension ought to be instantly verified by writ; unless they be referred to the charger's oath: in which case, the charger's procurators, to hasten the process, will take a day to produce the charger to give his oath. But if the reason of suspension be founded upon a writ which is not the suspender's own writ, (as when cautioners suspend upon discharges granted to the principal debtor,) the suspender will get a term to prove; as he also will, when the reasons of suspension consist *in facto*, and are to be proven by witnesses.

47. The first point of debate in suspensions is, upon the relevancy and verification of the reasons; and the next point is, upon the competency of the reasons: for many reasons are competent by way of reduction, that are not competent by way of suspension; because suspension stops the execution of a decreet already obtained, and therefore the execution should not be delayed, except upon reasons relevant, and of a short probation; but the execution ought to proceed, and if the decreet whereupon execution passed, be reduced, all that hath been taken away by the execution, will be recovered. So a reason upon minority and lesion, is not receivable by way of suspension, but by reduction; nor yet reasons upon inhibition, interdiction, iniquity, nullity, or upon any clause irritant, not being declared, (albeit it bear to take effect without declarator,) except in few cases.

48. If the reason of suspension be sustained, then the charger propones

his answer to the reason: it is termed a reason, to difference it from defences proponed in ordinary actions; because a reason of suspension is a defence in the principal cause, and the answer is a reply thereto. The answer, being proponed, is first debated, as to the relevancy and competency thereof (but it needs not be instantly verified, because the charger may delay himself); for many things are not competent by way of answer, which are relevant; as upon interdictions, inhibitions, minority, and most nullities, and clauses irritant, and failzies, which require reduction. But if the charger have a reduction, and will hold the production thereof satisfied, he may repeat the reasons of reduction by way of answer to the reason of suspension. If the answer be sustained, the suspender may propone his reply, which doth not consist in any allegeance against the relevancy or competency of the answer; but in some distinct writ, clause or fact, eliding the answer, in the same way as the answer did elide the reason: and so the charger insists in a duply, and the suspender may insist in a triply, and the charger in a quadruply, &c.

49. A beit the suspender be obliged to verify his reasons of suspension instantly, yet he needs not instruct his reply; because that riseth upon the charger's answer, and therefore he will get a term to instruct the same, or his triply.

50. Some reasons of suspension do not conclude to suspend the letters *simpliciter*, and so to take away the decreet suspended for ever, but only to suspend the same for a time: and then the decreet of suspension bears, "the Lords suspend the letters ay and while, &c." Otherwise (when the reasons conclude so, and are sustained) the decreet bears, "the Lords suspend the letters *simpliciter*."

51. If, in discussing the suspension, there be nothing admitted to be proven in the future; then decreet of suspension follows, (which is the common name both of decreets in favour of suspenders, and of decreets in favour of chargers,) whereby the Lords either find the letters orderly proceeded, simply, or ay and while such a thing be done. And sometimes the Lords suspend the letters for a part, and find the letters orderly proceeded for the rest; or otherwise the Lords suspend the letters *simpliciter*.

52. If any point be admitted to be proven, either of the reasons of suspension, or of the answer, reply, duply, &c. whether it be in favour of one of the parties only, or of both, when they have different points to be proven; then litis-contestation is made, and an act must be extracted, which is an act of litis-contestation: but ordinarily in suspensions there is a present decreet.

FINIS

APPENDIX

AFTER the second edition of the Institutions of the Law of Scotland, with the alterations from, and additions to the same, were past the press, there were several statutes enacted in the fourth session of this current Parliament of King William and Queen Mary [Parl. 1, Sess.3 (1693)], making many alterations in our former customs, partly in the matter, and partly in the manner of procedure: which occurring before this treatise went abroad, I thought it convenient to give a short account of them.

I. Whereas formerly dispositions of lands or annualrents did contain obligements upon the disponer, to grant infeftments to the acquirer, either to be holden of him, or from him of his immediate superior, by resignation or confirmation; and for that effect to grant procuratories of resignation, and precepts of seasin, aud to renew the same so oft as need were, and with all containing procuratories and precepts: yet if either the disponer or purchaser died before resignation were made, or before seasin were taken on the precept, the procuratory and precept were esteemed to become void, as being mandates failing with the mandant or mandatar; whereas indeed such mandates do only fail, which are revocable at the pleasure of the granter, and continue no longer than his pleasure, and therefore expire by his death; which ought not to be extended to procuratories of resignation and precepts of seasin, both which are irrevocable. Yet acquirers were put to great expenses, in regard that superiors were not obliged to receive upon the procuratory; and lest the purchasers might be prevented, they did ordinarily take seasin upon the disponer's precept; and if, before they agreed with the superior, either the disponer or purchaser happened to die, there was a necessity of a process against the representatives of the disponer, to enter to the fee (by being served heir therein, and infeft thereupon) and to renew procuratories or precepts to the purchasers, their heirs or assignees.

For remedy whereof, a statute was made [Act 1693,c.35; A.P.S. IX,331,c. 73], declaring, that procuratories or precepts, made, or to be made, should be effectual, though the disponer or purchaser were dead before resignation were made, or infeftment taken; and that not only in favour of the heirs, but also of the singular successors; providing their progress were insert in the instruments of seasin. But there are excepted precepts of *clare constat;* because by keeping up these, the casualties due to the superior might be shunned.

This statute will remedy a frequent inconveniency; for it was ordinary for buyers, though they might hold of the superior, to take only infeftment holden of the disponer; and then to dispone again to others, who in the same manner took infeftment holden of the first purchaser, and so forth to subsequent purchasers: whereby the proprietor might have very many superiors, all holding base. But by this statute the proprietor might take infeftment from the first superior, and thereby evacuate all the intermediate superiors; for where there is a procuratory of resignation for an infeftment from the disponer's superior, and a precept of seasin to be holden of the disponer himself, albeit the purchaser take infeftment on that precept, yet so soon as he obtains infeftment from the disponer's superior, the infeftment holden of the disponer becomes void; seeing the same fee cannot at the same time be holden of different superiors. Yet if either of the infeftments be found null, the proprietor may defend himself with the other; because in that case, there are not two infeftments. This statute was prepared, and brought into the Parliament, by the Lords of Session: and it does not only extend to procuratories of resignation, and precepts of seasin to be granted hereafter, but to resignations or seasins to be made or taken upon procuratories or precepts already granted: because it is declaratory; declaring, that procuratories of resignation, and precepts of seasin, do not fall under that general rule, *mortuo mandatore,* &c. *perimitur mandatum;* which should only be understood of ambulatory mandates, enduring no longer than the pleasure of the mandant, so that his pleasure ceaseth by his death, as well as by other ways of revocation: but procuratories of resignation and precepts of seasin are irrevocable mandates, to the behove of the mandatar; and they are no more revocable than assignations, which by their nature and style are procuratories by the cedent to the assignee *in rem suam:* for debtors are not obliged to pay to any other but the persons mentioned in the obligation, or their heirs, (which *fictione juris* are esteemed the same persons with the creditors,) and therefore unless the obligement bear expressly to assignees, the debtor is not the assignee's debtor; and so the assignee obtains payment as being the procurator or mandatar of the creditor; yet the mandate is not revocable by the death of either cedent or assignee, even by our own former custom.

II. There is another important statute passed in the same session of Parliament [Real Rights Act, 1693,c.13; A.P.S. IX,271,c.22], prepared and brought in by the Lords, taking away the difference betwixt public and private (or base) infeftments. For infeftments were esteemed private, latent, and simulate *retentâ possessione,* when the person infeft was not put in possession, the infeftment passing only between the disponer and the person infeft: but if the infeftment did proceed from the disponer's superior by resignation or confirmation; then the presumption of simulation for want of possession ceaseth; because superiors use not to grant such infeftments, but upon compositions. And therefore infeftments granted by the disponer's superior were called public infeftments, and were effectual from their dates; but the private (or base) infeftments were not effectual, till the presumption of simulation ceased, either by natural possession, or by uplifting mails and duties, or by processes for obtaining these duties: for thereby also the presumption of simulation was excluded by a stronger presumption, that the disponer would not suffer his tenants to be distressed upon a simulate infeftment. And upon the same ground, base infeftments of annualrents were not excluded by posterior public infeftments intervening between the date of the base infeftment and the first term of payment: because during that time, the annualrenter could not have payment, or action for payment of his annualrent. But this was not extended to base infeftments of property, in the same time, because those gave immediate warrant to enter in possession, though it were but by the acquirer's holding of courts as proprietor. The exclusion of simulation in base infeftments, was chiefly sustained, upon discharges granted by the persons infeft, to the tenants, upon infeftments of property, or by discharges of annualrents granted to the proprietors; which discharges might easily be made *ex post facto*: for discharges to tenants require no witnesses, albeit they be not holograph; and holograph discharges of annualrent are sufficient: and yet thereby the dates were not certain, but in either case they might have been antedated, or never delivered till competitions arose with posterior public infeftments.

By these ways of validating base infeftments, that they might not be excluded by posterior public infeftments before the base infeftments obtained possession, or action for possession, the rights of lands which are of greatest import, became very uncertain, and liable to probation by witnesses, who might instruct possession, though there were no writ to instruct the same; and thereby also many tedious and expensive actions and competitions arose about the rights of lands or annualrents. And, albeit all infeftments might have been accounted public, and neither private nor simulate after the Act of Parl. 1617 [Registration Act, 1617,c.16; A.P.S. IV,545,c.16], ordaining all seasins to be registrate, in manner expressed in that Act, and declaring all seasins not so registrate to be null, that not only purchasers, but all creditors might know the condition of their debtors, as to their rights of lands or annualrents, which are the chief grounds of credit; so that no infeftment registrate in public registers, patent to all the lieges, should after the registration have been accounted private or latent, nor was possession thereby necessary to accomplish it: yet the Act of registration of seasins, not having at first attained its full effect, the distinction of public and private infeftments was continued until this time; and accordingly purchasers and creditors acted and rested upon the difference of public and base infeftments. And therefore a statute could not justly be extended to infeftments already taken; so that this statute now passed doth only extend to infeftments and seasins to be taken hereafter. But it statutes that, in all actions and competitions of infeftments, they shall be valid and preferable according to the dates of their registration, and not according to the dates of the seasin; because it is the registration which takes away the presumption of a base infeftment's being private, latent, or simulate; whereby a base infeftment, being registrate before a public infeftment, will be preferred thereto, albeit the date of the public seasin be prior to the date of the base seasin. The reason whereof is, that the security of these who intend to purchase or lend their money, should not depend upon the dates of the seasins affecting their author's lands or annualrents; for these dates they cannot know, until they see the registers, seeing seasins are only declared null, which are not registrate within sixty days of their dates. And the time and order of their being inserted in the registers did depend upon the keepers of the several registers, who for their own profit kept the registers open, without inserting the seasins presented to them: so that it was in their power to take in seasins, even though presented after the threescore days, and might insert the same in the register, as presented within the threescore days: so that while that power continued, no purchaser or creditor could be secure, if they did not delay their bargains till the registers were filled up, which ofttimes was for the space of many months.

This statute doth not take off all difference between public and base infeftments: for infeftments are called base, not from the presumption of simulation by the latency thereof, but because infeftments holden of the disponer's superior are higher and nearer the infeftments holden of the King, than the infeftments holden of the disponer; these being lower, baser, and further from infeftments holden of the King, which are the only noble infeftments, and in respect of which, all infeftments holden of subjects are but base infeftments, not only lower but ignobler than these holden of the King, whose immediate vassals only are called *vassalli ligii*.

The distinction of public and base infeftments hath arisen of old, when most lands in Scotland were immediately holden of the King, in great baronies or tenements, and were generally ward-holdings, and are still presumed to be such, unless the contrary appear by their tenors; and therefore few of the King's vassals could give subaltern infeftments, without the King's consent or confirmation, until the Act of Parliament warranting ward-vassals to set their land in feu by infeftments: which hath received many variations, as is shown *Lib.* 2, *Tit.* Infeftments of Property [11,3,*supra*]. But then subaltern infeftments became frequent, by the King's granting blench infeftments, and by consenting to, or confirming of subaltern infeftments of ward-vassals: for by that general consent, that ward-vassals might feu their lands to sub-vassals, not only were infeftments holden of the King continued to be called public and noble, but all infeftments holden of the disponer's immediate superior, and not of himself, were preferred to infeftments holden of the disponer; and these were called base, albeit the base infeftment were prior in date, unless there had appeared some possession, or action for possession;

with this incongruity, that an infeftment holden of the disponer was a base infeftment, and yet an infeftment upon that same purchaser's resignation, holden of his author, is accounted a public infeftment, and so more noble than the infeftment of his immediate author.

Albeit the presumption of latency and simulation of infeftments holden of the disponer be taken away in time coming, by this statute; yet the exception of simulation, as being to the behove of the disponer, is not taken away, but only the presumption that it is so by want of possession. But the being to the behove of the disponer or any other person may be proven by writ, or by the oath of the person infeft, and even by pregnant presumptions arising, and inferred from matters of fact, by writ, oath, or sometimes by witnesses: amongst which, the disponer's continuing in possession, especially if he have continued long after his disposition, is amongst the most pregnant evidences of simulation or trust.

III. There was a third statute prepared by the Lords, and passed in Parliament, to prevent the inconveniency by keeping the registers open, and so being in the power of the keepers thereof, to evacuate the whole design and benefit of that excellent statute for registration of rights that might affect lands. For which effect, there is an article in the Act of Regulations, Parl. 1672 [Courts Act, 1672,c.16; A.P.S. VIII,80,c.40], appointing the keepers of registers, to have minute-books, and that the same be quarterly collationed with the registers, by the sheriffs and bailies, where the registers are kept, and two Justices of Peace, under the pain of 100*l. toties quoties* they neglect to collation, and deprivation of the keepers, and paying damage to parties, in case they fail in their duty. But though this article of the Act be not repealed, yet it hath been totally neglected: and though it had been observed, it could not have cured the inconveniency; seeing the keepers of the registers might easily transcribe these minute-books written by themselves or their servants; yea they might transcribe whole books of the register, and so take in and leave out, upon large compositions. Therefore the Lords, by an Act of Sederunt, in July, 1692 [A.S. 1 July, 1692], printed and published at the market-cross of Edinburgh, ordained that all keepers of registers, should keep minute-books of their several registers; and that, immediately upon the presenting of any writs to be registrate therein, they should set down the name and designation of the person presenting, and the day and hour when he presented the same, expressing the general designation of the lands or other rights; and that the minute of each writ presented should be signed by the presenter, and by the keeper; and that the keeper should insert the writs presented in the same order as they are in the minute-book, under the pain of deprivation and damages; conform to the said Act of Regulation. And the Lords did present the like Act to the Parliament, that it might be the more punctually observed, which accordingly is passed in an Act of Parliament [Register of Sasines Act, 1693,c.14; A.P.S. IX,271,c.23]. This Act doth fully complete the design of the acts for registration of seasins, reversions, allowances of apprisings and adjudications, hornings, inhibitions, and interdictions; all which may affect lands, not only against the granters and their heirs, but even against singular successors: and it is not possible for the keepers of the registers to alter these minute-books, in respect the minute of each right is signed by the presenter thereof, which minute is to be made patent to all the lieges gratis; which in so far may seem an alteration of the Act of Regulation, giving an allowance in money, for inspection of the register; but yet this is only making free the inspection of the minute-book.

IV. There are some other laws relating to the Session, and the manner of administrating justice therein, passed in the same session of Parliament. The first of these, was also prepared by the Lords, and is to this effect: that the Lords should name weekly an Ordinary, to prepare concluded causes, and to hear the parties condescend upon the points wherein they insist, and the particular articles in the writs, on which they insist for probation of the points admitted to probation, by the acts of litis-contestation, and of the testimonies of the particular witnesses, and of the words in these testimonies, and to make a minute thereof in writ: and that, according as the cause stands in the roll of concluded causes, and are ready to be advised. Which auditors are to put the same in a minute, to be read in presence of the parties and advocates, before the concluded cause be advised; whereby concluded causes might be the more speedily dispatched. But this Act doth not extend to acts before answer, whereby, because the allegeances of parties are contrary in matter of fact, (so that two single witnesses might carry the cause, which might be of great inconveniency.) Therefore the Lords, in these cases, allow either party to adduce such a number of witnesses, for proving such points of fact, as the Lords appoint to be insert in the act: and therefore such acts are not properly concluded causes, and so ought not to be in that roll; because not only the probation, but the relevancy is undetermined, and must be disputed before it be determined; for, though there be some arguing in the act, yet more ought not to be excluded, after the probation adduced for the matter of fact.

V. The Lords did also prepare another Act, as to the manner of signing of interlocutors by the Chancellor or President. And that in respect, that the clerks did draw interlocutors, as they conceived they were passed by the Lords, which could not be read immediately after they were written, and adjusted to what was truly done, without giving a great hinderance to the dispatch of interlocutors; therefore they were read to the Chancellor or President, daily after the Lords parted: and because the clerks sometimes mistook what passed, seeing they got no informations before, as the Lords did, there was a necessity to adjust the minutes to the interlocutors, as they verbally passed (whereby there behoved several times to be alterations of the minutes, as the clerks had first drawn them); therefore the Lords resolved to stay together, after the lawyers and others were parted, till they should jointly adjust the minutes, and put them *in mundo*. This was so far enlarged by an Act of Parliament [Interlocutors Act, 1693,c.18; A.P.S. ix,283,c.31], that all interlocutors to be signed by the Chancellor or President are ordained to pass in this manner, viz. that the question to be voted shall be drawn and read, and agreed to by the Lords before it be voted: and the interlocutor to be passed thereupon, is to be written on a paper apart, to be adjusted by the Lords, and then transcribed on the process: and that either immediately, as the interlocutors pass, or thereafter, when the Lords are sitting in judgment. By this Act, the Lords will be obliged to attend, till the interlocutors be adjusted and transcribed on the process, after the advocates and parties are dismissed; and interlocutors cannot be reported the day they are made: which hath this advantage, that if any thing be represented for altering the same, it may be more conveniently considered before pronouncing, than after; and will also have this advantage, that in reductions, there will appear no deletions, or interlining of interlocutors, and they will all remain fixed upon the process.

VI. There are two other Acts in relation to the Session, passed in the same session of Parliament, which were not prepared by the Lords, but by the Committee of Security. The one relates to reports, and the other to the hearing and advising processes in the Inner-House.

The Act concerning reports [Act 1693,c.20; A.P.S. IX,283,c.33], is to this effect, that in all disputes taken to interlocutor, to be reported in presence of the Lords, the advocates for either party must set down their allegeances, and sign the same; and likewise, the reporter must sign the whole. The certification in the Act is, that the advocate who refuses to attend, and prepare the report, shall be excluded the House for a month: for he that insists will not fail to attend: and if he do not insist, there can be no report.

This Act will put the Lords to a great deal of more pains than formerly they were at; for then the pursuer's advocate had the sight of the minutes of the dispute, and of the interlocutor of the Ordinary, if any were; (for if the Ordinary apprehend the point to be dubious, the minutes bear that he will give the Lords answer; but if he give his own interlocutor, then upon consigning of an amand, he must also give the Lords answer, unless the allegeance be evidently impertinent, and yet the party may represent the same by bill to the Lords, if he think fit); and after the pursuer's advocate had perused and adjusted the minutes, as he pretended he had, then the defender's advocates did the like; and if they differed in the points to be reported, the Ordinary behoved to adjust the same, which did much delay reports: and the minutes were frequently indistinct and large; for either party related the case, and represented the merits or favour of it, before they came to a formal and distinct point to be determined; yea, they related most of the dispute which was at the bar, whereas they ought only to have insisted in the points at interlocutor. But by this Act, the Ordinary must intimate a diet when the advocates may attend him, to adjust the minutes, either in the House in an afternoon, or at his chamber. And therefore the clerks in the Outer-House ought not to write on the process, but on a paper apart, until the points to be reported be adjusted. And the Ordinary ought to cause set down the formal points that are to be determined, in a larger character, and to cause express them in the terms of law, specially, and not in the general terms of allegeances, and set them in the due order the law requires.

These special terms of law, and the order thereof, conduce exceedingly to the dispatch of justice, and to the obtaining of distinct interlocutors. As 1. If there be any declinator proponed of any probability, the Ordinary should go no further, till that declinator be determined. 2. If other dilators be proponed, there can be no recourse to declinators: for *primus actus judicii est judicis approbatorius*. The order of proponing dilators is, first, against the form of the executions: for if these be not conform to law, it is in vain to enter upon the cause. And since executions must be signed by the executer and witnesses, which ought to be recently, that it may not depend upon their memory *ex intervallo*, there can be no altering or mending of the executions, as was ordinary before, when the advocates used to mend the executions at the bar, and offered to abide by the verity thereof, as amended; which was then received, but cannot now be admitted. And if the defender pass over any defect or informality in the executions, and proceed to any other dilator or peremptor, he cannot return to quarrel the executions, nor will it be a nullity of the decreet or act, in the second instance. 3. The next dilator in order, is upon the title of the pursuer, or of the defender. And, albeit the Ordinary allow the parties to relate the case, and the merits of it on both sides, before they come to this defence, yet in the minutes, nothing thereof should be mentioned: for the reporter hath read the process, when he reports the same, and relates summarily the contents thereof, and the points insisted on, which he must now do in presence of parties and advocates. 4. The next dilator is upon the concourse of parties necessary to be called, if any of these be not called: which uses to be expressed in these terms, "all parties having interest are not called." 5. The next dilatory defence is the competency of the process: for many cases may be relevant in one process, that will not be competent in another. And therefore it is improper to dispute the relevancy, if there be any objection against the competency: so that if any objections against the relevancy be proponed, there is no place to return to the competency. 6. The last dilatory defence is the irrelevancy, whether it be of the libel, or of the reasons of suspension, reduction, or preference.

This defence of irrelevancy is but a dilator, albeit it may assoilzie from that instance, and it hath the effect of a peremptory defence, when the other party hath no other legal mean to attain the conclusion proposed.

All these dilatory defences ought to be minuted and reported in the order and terms of law; and the reasons subjoined to each of them severally; and all the points reported ought to have their number expressed by numeral figures, whereby the clerks, in stating the question, need not resume the words, but state it thus, "whether such a point, being in the 1st, 2d, 3d, defence, &c.

should be sustained or repelled?" and then the interlocutor would follow clearly, "The Lords sustain or repel the 1st, 2d, 3d, defence, &c."

In these dilatory defences, there is nothing in fact offered to be proven: for they are all objections, and not exceptions; and therefore there ought to be no replies, albeit there may be many mutual answers, arguing the point of law. And none of these dilatory defences are to be admitted; unless they be instantly verified. And the order of discussing doth necessarily require, that after any peremptory defence proposed, there can be no recourse to dilators: neither can dilators be spun out in length to make delay; but after the first interlocutor upon dilators, none will be admitted, but those which are proponed at the next calling.

If a dilator be proponed *peremptoriè*, that is, so as if the proponer fail in the probation, he loses the cause; then it ceases to be of the nature of a dilator, and becomes a peremptor, as if he offer to improve the executions *peremptoriè*.

The next kind of defences are these which are called peremptory defences; because they elide the libel, though it be competent, relevant, and orderly proceeded. Peremptory defences do always consist in points instructed, by writs produced, or offered to be proven by such probation as the law requires in such matters of fact; and therefore in minutes and reports the peremptors ought to be distinctly expressed by larger characters.

Whence the dispute arises, first, whether those matters of fact be competent by way of exception, or only by reduction and declarator; and next, whether they be relevant to elide the libel, or the reason of suspension, or of reduction, or of preference; but the answers made to the exceptions ought not to be termed replies; for they are only objections against the exceptions; but replies are matters of fact, eliding the defence, in the same way as the defence elides the libel, &c. And the like objections are against the competency or relevancy of the replies, as were against the exceptions, and they are but objections, albeit they be answers to the replies; but the duplies are matters of fact, for eliding the replies: so that both the replies and duplies must either be instructed by the writs produced, or terms must be assigned to either or both parties, as the matter does require. And so in minutes and reports, the replies and duplies should be expressed in larger characters, and the arguments *hinc inde*, for and against them, should be subjoined to each of them severally: and if they be more in number, they should be expressed by numeral figures; whereby the clerks, in stating the questions, need not repeat the words, but only say, "whether such an exception be competent and relevant in the manner of probation offered, or not?" Whereupon the interlocutor must be, that the Lords "sustain the exception, or repel the same:" and if the exception be sustained, then the reporter proceeds to the reply; and if the reply be sustained, to the duply, &c. wherein the questions and the interlocutors are to be in the like terms.

The reporter may most conveniently, and with least ground of suspicion, cause the clerks read the exceptions in order, and so the replies and duplies, &c. But there is no necessity of reading the objections and arguments, but only to repeat the sum of them; seeing the enlargements thereof may be communicate to the Lords by their informations, put in their boxes the night before the report is made.

VII. The other Act of this last session of Parliament [Court of Session Act 1693,c.26; A.P.S. IX,305,c.42], ordains all reports, and all bills, and the written answers thereof, to be reasoned and determined with open doors, and likewise all disputes *in præsentia*, to be with open doors: so that the parties and their advocates, and all others that please, may be present, when the Lords are arguing and voting.

This is a great alteration from the 66 article of the institution of the College of Justice, institute by K. James V. anno 1537 [College of Justice Act, 1532, c.36; A.P.S. 11,335,c.2], ordaining that, advocates shall remove with the parties, after disputing their matters at the bar, and re-enter again, at the giving and pronouncing of the interlocutors. Yet the statute bears, that none may speak, whether procurators or parties, otherwise they are to be sent presently to prison.

This Act will make the Lords more liable to the irritation and malice of parties, when they hear them reason and vote against their interest; and especially in the most dubious cases, *in apicibus juris*, wherein parties can least know what is according to law; and when their advocates will extend their abilities and eloquence for their clients, which will hardly suit the *præfervida Scotorum ingenia*. For, albeit, formerly, the reasonings and votings of the Lords, in so great a judicature, and so many attendants, could be no secrets, and often were misrepresented, yet the parties were then calm, and had no certain evidence that these reports were true: but when they are at the bar, they will be in much more certainty and fervour, which may make their grudges stick the deeper, and last the longer. But there will be much less reasoning amongst the Lords than behoved to be formerly; and their prudence and generosity will oblige them to forbear all heats in reasoning.

These two Acts may foreslow the dispatch of justice; but what is thereby dispatched, will be much more distinct and clear than before.

It was the most ordinary complaint of advocates, that the Lords gave them not distinct interlocutors to all their allegeances, and thence they multiplied bills, especially upon pretence that such points as were proposed had not been noticed by the Lords, but had passed without special consideration. And next, that the influence of reporters was too great, and that though parties found themselves thereby lesed, yet the Lords were unwilling to remit the cause reported by one Lord to another. And, albeit the Lords did both by word, and by Acts of Sederunt, urge the lawyers to propone their defences, and especially their exceptions, replies, and duplies, distinctly and severally, with different characters, yet they could never obtain the same from the most part of them. But when they complained by their bills, they proposed to the

Lords a number of questions, but not in the terms and order of law, which is absolutely necessary in a formal legal debate.

But now they have no ground to suspect the influence of reporters, if they follow the terms of law and order proposed, all being read and reported in their presence; which if they do, they will certainly receive distinct interlocutors, point by point: which before could not be done, through their own fault, when their disputes were in a mass of law and fact, out of which the Lords behoved to pitch upon these points which they thought of importance, and requisite to be determined, and gave interlocutors as to these; but as to the rest, they were understood as repelled, or unnecessary to be resolved.

The difficulty is greater as to disputes *in præsentia*, and the decisions thereon: for formerly the pleaders were often so large, that they could hardly make a close, but by the hour; for if they had disputed every point apart, and had been removed, they would have so much enlarged on each point, that thereby, and by the loss of time in removing them and the crowd, there could not have been so much dispatched in a month as was ordinarily dispatched in a week, and therefore the Lords behoved to let them say all they would, before they gave their interlocutor to any point. And after all, they did ordinarily press for liberty to inform before interlocutor, when the dispute at the bar was forgot, and the Lords were necessitated to hear the same reported by the Chancellor or President, and to choose out the points that were to be determined, as was accustomed in reports from Ordinaries, which cannot quadrate with the Act for open doors: for then no time will be lost by removing, until a new cause be called; and then the parties and procurators that were in the former cause, must go out by the left hand, and pass at the great door, and so go through the waiting-room to the Outer-House; for the counter-tide of some going out the way they came in, and others coming in that same way, consumed a great deal of time.

The method then which seems will be most convenient and requisite with patent doors, in discussing causes *in præsentia*, occurs in two different cases. For first, sometimes the Lords, upon reports, appoint the whole cause to be disputed in their presence, and inrolled in the Inner-House roll, according to the date of that interlocutor. And next, sometimes they do not find it necessary to remit the whole cause to the roll of the Inner-House, but find only one single point *in jure* difficult, and not clear by law or custom, and therefore necessary to be cleared upon full debate, as a leading case, (and when that point is determined, they leave it to the Ordinary to go on in the rest,) and for that end, the Lords appoint the pleaders to be ready against the next day, or the day after it, to plead that point, and that immediately after the discussing of that cause in the ordinary roll, which was not ended when that report was made: for when the point is remitted to a longer day, several such points fall on the same day, or all the parties are not ready, which puts the point out of the pleaders' minds. There can be no more than one single dispute this way, which breeds no uncertain attendance, seeing the cause was then disputed in the Outer-House, where all parties' interests are attended.

But when a whole cause comes to be disputed *in præsentia*, the Chancellor or President must keep the pleaders to the terms of law and order before expressed; and must not let them enlarge upon dilators, but, after the first dilator proposed and argued by the pleaders, must stop them. And then, if in his opinion the dilator be not sustainable, he must ask, "if any of the Lords be for sustaining that dilator, in order as they are to be proponed?" and if none of the Lords answer, it is thence evident, that none of them are for sustaining of it: and so the clerk having written, "Repels the first dilator," the Chancellor or President pronounces, "The Lords repel the first dilator." But if the Chancellor or President's opinion be, that the dilator is to be sustained, then he asks the Lords, "if there be any for repelling this dilator?" And if none answer, all are understood to acquiesce, and he pronounces the interlocutor, "The Lords sustain the dilator," and so the cause is dismissed. And though one of the Lords be of a different judgment, yet it he be not seconded by another, the point is still sustained, or repelled as before. But if two concur in one opinion, contrary to the opinion of the Chancellor or President, presiding for the time; then the point comes to a vote. And dilators will seldom require a new reasoning among the Lords, but they will rest on the reasonings of the advocates, and so give their votes. The same was the custom when the doors were close. And it is the custom in all judicatures whatsoever, that except two at least be of a different opinion from him that presides, his opinion prevails without a vote; or otherwise no judicature were able to make any dispatch.

If the dilator be repelled, the defender's advocate is required to propone any further defence, if he have it, and in due order. And if he propone any, he cannot go back to that which in the due order was before it; as if he propone a peremptory exception, he cannot return to declinators, or other dilators. If he then propone an exception, instructed by the writs produced, he should mark the clause whereupon he insists, which must be read; otherwise he must in the terms of law say, "Absolvitor, because I offer to prove this relevant exception *prout de jure*", by writ, oath of party, notoriety or presumption: and he must not be permitted to adduce arguments to confirm his exception, till he hear the pursuer's advocate, whether he controverts the relevancy of it, or not; or if the pursuer question not the relevancy, or the manner of probation, but propones a reply in these terms, "The exception ought to be repelled, by reason of this reply, instructed by writ produced," and the clauses thereof marked, or otherwise that he offer to prove the same, and condescend on the manner of probation; in that case, the pursuer is not to give reasons to confirm his reply, till he hear whether the defender's advocate controverts the relevancy thereof, or propones a duply; in which case, if he only propone a duply, and the pursuer controvert not the relevancy thereof, the dispute is ended: and the Lords will not controvert, where the parties' advocates do not controvert. Only as to the probation, if the defence presuppose the verity of the libel, and the reply the verity of the defence, and the duply the verity of the reply; then the term is assigned, only to prove the duply: but if the exception do not presuppose the verity of the libel, either as to the matter, quantity or quality; then the term must be assigned to the pursuer, to prove that point of his libel, and to the defender, to prove that part of his exception eliding the same. But if the reply do not presuppose the verity of the defence, nor the duply the verity of the reply; then the term is to be assigned to the pursuer, to prove his libel and reply, and to the defender, to prove his defence and duply.

But if the pursuer controvert the relevancy of the defence, then either side must be allowed a competent time, to argue whether the same be relevant or not, and then must be stopped by him who presides, who, if he be of opinion that the defence is relevant, must move the question to the Lords, "if any be for repelling the defence." And if two of the Lords do not concur for repelling it, he gives the interlocutor, "that the Lords sustain the exception." But if he shall apprehend, that the dispute hath not cleared, whether the exception be relevant or not; in that case he will not propone the question to the Lords, "whether or no the same is clear?" but will desire the Lords to speak to the point; and after they have so done, if there be diversity of judgments, he will put it to the question, "Sustain the exception, or not?"

If the exception be sustained, the pursuer's advocate will be desired to propone a reply in fact, if he any have, wherein the same method will be followed as in the exception. And if the reply be sustained, the defender's advocate will proceed to the duply, if he any have, in the same manner.

But whether the exception be sustained or repelled, the defender may propone more exceptions, to be discussed in the same manner as the first. And in like manner, the pursuer in his replies, and the defender in his duplies: and if more of these be proponed, it must be with numeral figures, that the question may be summarily stated and voted.

This statute doth appoint, that not only the discussing of causes disputed *in præsentia*, and upon reports, but also that the answering of bills shall be with open doors; which doth not import the calling of parties, unless the Lords, upon reading the bills, see fit that a point be presently heard *in præsentia*: but in all other cases, the Lords, as they have already resolved and practised, will pitch upon the points in the bills, which they find deserve an answer, and will appoint the reporter to hear the parties upon these points, whether they contain any new matter, or more pregnant arguments in law. But the advocates ought to keep the terms of law, and the order before mentioned, as well in bills as in verbal disputes. And it were very convenient that no bills were read, but such as had been delivered to the clerks the night before, that they might peruse them, and have in readiness what were necessary to be considered by the Lords, when called for; showing the presenters of the bills, that they durst not read them, if they did not observe the terms and order of law, setting down the points to be resolved in larger characters, and subjoining the reasons to these points severally. The points agreed upon to be heard, must be set down on the bill as an interlocutor, and signed as other interlocutors. If the Lords find any point in the bill not to be competent and relevant, or already determined, the interlocutor will then be, "That the Lords refuse the desire of the bill, as not competent or relevant, or as already determined."

By these means, bills will not be insert in decreets, but only the dispute upon the points remitted to be heard; unless the bill be wholly refused, in which case it may be insert in the decreet; or if it be passed of course in matters notour, and require not an answer, it may also be insert; but the Lords may appoint all impertinent reflections in bills, to be delete when they are read.

If any interlocutor written on the process be recalled, the last interlocutor ought only to be insert in the decreet.

I see no ground of doubt, but this order of discussing causes upon dispute, in presence of the Lords, or by report, was always most expedient: But now, after these late statutes of Parliament, it is absolutely necessary: otherwise it were impossible for one judicature to decide and determine all civil causes which use to come before the Session. For if every allegeance in point of fact, or law, wherein pleaders differ, must come to a vote, by the concourse of two Lords desiring a vote, and the state of the question for that vote must first be written by the clerk *in mundo*, and read and acquiesced in by the Lords, (whereby the difference not only in the matter, but also in the wording, may come to a new vote,) it will then be obvious how little dispatch can be made upon the foresaid points, unless they be distinctly and orderly proponed by the pleaders. And by this the Lords can have no occasion to differ on the state of the question, unless it be as to the order of discussing: for the pleaders are to propose the points of process, which they may still reform, as they find themselves straitened by the debate, till it come to the vote, and are not obliged to stick at the more indigested points, as they were first proposed.

And therefore the pleaders ought not to insist for having a vote on every point of law or fact, wherein they differ; but only upon these points, which are the proper points of process, which being determined by a vote, will either give a decreet, or an act assigning a term for probation: as if the point to be determined be a dilator; if it be sustained, the instance is ended, unless a new dilator or peremptor be proponed: and in the same manner, if a peremptor exception be proponed; and if, in answer thereto, an objection be proponed against the competency of that exception, (which comprehends the order of proponing,) if that objection be repelled, the excipient must have absolvitor, if he instantly verify, or must have a term to prove, and so in the reply or duply: for there is always an *Ergo* expressed or implied, for obtaining a final sentence, or a term: and nothing else should be voted, except upon bills for expedients in probation.

The order by which causes are now to be discussed and determined, doth not only require that declinators should not be proponed after dilators, nor dilators after peremptors, nor either out of their just order, and that dilators should be proponed before the second vote; but likewise require that all objections against the competency or relevancy of exceptions, replies or duplies, should be proponed before the second vote as to such objections: otherwise pleaders may multiply objections, till their invention be exhausted: and if they should crave a distinct interlocutor to each of them severally, what dispatch in justice could be expected? and therefore there should be no numeral letters as to declinators, dilators, or objections; but the Lords may determine them with one or more votes as they please. None of these things clash with the late statutes, but rather are necessary consequences thence arising.

VIII. This method of discussing being very clear and plain as to ordinary actions, it remains to be considered, what difference there may be in discussing of advocations, suspensions, reductions or competitions.

1. As to advocations, the conclusion thereof is, "to remove the process from an incompetent, interested, or suspected judge, to the Lords, or to another judicature," and that upon the reasons libelled or eiked in writ. And all these reasons might have been proponed as declinators before that judge; but being proponed before the Lords, they are as nullities of what he hath done or shall do in that process, and are to be discussed as other nullities: which for the most part are objections against the jurisdiction and authority of the judge, or against the justice of his interlocutors; and therefore are discussed as objections or dilators, which must be instantly verified, in the order and manner as hath been said in declinators, dlatoris, or objections in ordinary actions.

2. What hath been said of the manner of discussing ordinary actions, will easily regulate the manner of discussing suspensions. The conclusion whereof is, "to suspend the execution and effect of decreets, either simply (which hath the effect of a reduction of the decreet) or in part, *qualificatè*, or for a time:" and that for the reasons libelled or eiked in writ, which yet the suspender may limit, qualify, or explain in the dispute. These reasons of suspension are in effect the defences in the principal cause, and the suspender is rather defender than pursuer. For he that hath right to the decreet, is in effect pursuer, and, for distinction's sake, is called charger; and therefore he must repeat and insist in his charge, before the suspender insist in any reason of suspension, so that the cause is to be treated as depending, during the suspension. And therefore the reasons of suspension are either objections against the citation, titles, interests of parties, competency, or relevancy of the action; or against the sufficiency of the probation, or the nullities in not observing necessary formalities. All these are to be discussed in the same way as dilators or objections in ordinary actions. But if the reasons of suspension would have been proper exceptions in the principal cause, they are to be discussed in the same way as in ordinary actions. First, by objection against the competency,

that, albeit the matter were entire, it would not be sustained by way of exception; or if it would then be sustained, it would not be now competent, because it was competent and omitted in the first instance; or because it is not relevant. But if they be repelled, the Lords will sustain the reason, unless a reply in fact be proposed; which reply is in a suspension called an answer to the reason, which, as a point of process, is not every answer, but an answer *in facto* proven by the production, or in some cases to be proven at a term; and therefore, when the charger answers, that *res est judicata*, (the same point being proponed in the principal cause and repelled, or in another decreet produced) against this, it may be objected, that the reason of suspension is upon matter emergent, or new come to knowledge after the decreet, which therefore cannot be excluded thereby.

3. The method of discussing reductions differeth according to the divers kinds of reductions. For if it be a reduction of a decreet, the reducer is in effect defender; and he that hath right to the decreet craved to be reduced, insists as pursuer, for removing these grounds which might annul his decreet. If he call not for the grounds and warrants of the decreet, (whether they be original writs whereupon the decreet proceeded, which parties do take up, or other warrants which remain with the clerks,) but only calls for reduction of the decreet, upon what appears from the same, without the warrants; then there is no difference between discussing a reduction and a suspension, but that a reduction doth not stop the execution and effect of the decreet: and therefore in it, terms are granted, generally, to prove the reasons of reduction; and so the manner of discussing is alike in both. But if any more than the decreet be called to be produced and reduced, then the dispute begins as to the writs which the defender is obliged to produce.

And in discussing of the production, there seldom occurreth any thing, but objections against that conclusion of the reduction, calling for production of such writs. So in reductions, all the ordinary dilators are competent against the citation, the titles, and the not calling parties necessary to be called; but nothing as to the competency, or against the relevancy, which is only to be disputed after the production is closed: but these objections are peculiar to reductions, that when the pursuer craves certification *contra non producta*, the defences are all objections against the pursuer's interest, by the titles he produces; as that he can crave certification against no writ, but that against which there is a reason of reduction libelled; or that the defender hath produced sufficiently to exclude all his titles produced, having produced a right anterior to all his titles, which is but *dilatoriè* proponed, in discussing the production; and if it be not sustained, the defender may make a further production, and allege the same upon it, but he cannot delay the certification upon any further than the second production.

When the production is closed, the pursuer then insists in his reasons of reduction; and if there be more reasons, his process is *articulatus libellus*, and every reason must be discussed accordingly. And the defender ought first to

propone his defences against the relevancy of the reasons; and then his exceptions instructed or offered to be proven, and the pursuer his objections against
the relevancy of the exceptions, and then his replies, and the defender his
objections, &c. against the pursuer's replies, and the pursuer his objections,
&c. against the defender's duplies, in the same manner as in ordinary
actions.

4. The manner of discussing competitions of right must be different, according to the divers ways the competition occurs. If it occur by a double
poinding, raised at the instance of a party, that may be distressed or troubled,
upon the different rights of several parties; he may cite them all to dispute
their rights. And in the process he is still pursuer, and may insist against any
of the parties he calleth, albeit the other party should not insist, to the effect
absolvitor may be pronounced, from any trouble upon that right he insists
against; but if another competitor produce a prior or more valid right, the
common presumption, *prior tempore potior jure*, makes the producer to be as
pursuer, both against the raiser of the double poinding, and against the competitors. And this evites the frequent altercations, what party should first insist, and so he propones his reason of preference, whereof the relevancy must
be first discussed, and the several objections against the same must either be
sustained or repelled: and if all be repelled, the competitors must propone
upon their rights by way of exception, yet the terms they use are, "that my
right produced ought to be preferred;" wherein the first right in order of
time gives the first interest to insist: so then, if the second competitor in order
of time be preferred to the first, it is his interest to insist, and so in order till
all the competitors be discussed.

If a competition of rights arise from the different parties called in the same
reduction, the pursuer, being *in libello*, may insist against any of the parties
who were cited, and have produced, as he pleaseth, to reduce that party's
right, in so far as prejudicial to the pursuer's right; and so he may proceed
against all the parties called, producing several insubordinate rights. But if
any of them exclude the pursuer's right, he is out of the field: and yet the
competition proceeds upon the several insubordinate rights, and the first
right in order of time hath interest to insist against the second right in order
of time, and if he be preferred thereto, may proceed against the rest in order
of time, while he is not excluded by any other right; but if he be excluded, he
is out of the field, and he that prevails insists against the rest, until all be discussed. This is all requisite to be known, for preventing the jangling of parties, contending who should insist and be first heard.

But if the competition arise from parties compearing for their interest, and
producing titles; then the question comes to be, whether he produces sufficient title to give him interest to defend or compete; and thence frequently
arises a competition of rights. In which case, the pursuer in the process ought
to be first heard, and may insist against any of the parties called, or compearing for his interest, till he be excluded: and then the competition proceeds

according to the anteriority of the rights produced. If the process whereon the competition ariseth be a reduction, the pursuer must proceed differently against the parties called, and the parties admitted for their interests. For the party called can make use of no right, against which certification is admitted, as to the pursuer in the reduction and obtainer of the certification; but he may propone upon any right against the parties compearing for their interest, for preferring him to them: for albeit the pursuer hath prevailed against him by the certification, yet if any compearing for their interests be preferred to the pursuer, he who is excluded by the certification, may found upon any right against him that prevails, because the certification was only in favour of the pursuer of the reduction. If the competitors be many, the competition is remitted to an auditor.

The reason why parties are admitted for their interests, though they be not called, is, to prevent pleas and the unnecessary multiplication of processes; and therefore it is not sufficient to exclude an interest, to offer to reserve it to another process; but the party must be admitted, and may insist in the process, as if it had been raised at his instance, and should get terms thereupon to prove, not only as a defender, but as a pursuer.

IX. Seeing by the above-mentioned Act, it is peremptorily statute under a high penalty, "That in all points to be voted by the Lords of Session hereafter, the question being stated, shall be first written by the clerk *in mundo*, as it shall be agreed to by the Lords, and read immediately before they go to the vote," it is evident how great weight is laid upon the stating of the vote, which if it be not clear and short, it will exceedingly retard the dispatch of causes: and therefore if the point in dispute be clear in law, whether it be dilator or peremptor, the Chancellor or President may ask the Lords, whether any of them be for sustaining it; and if none answer, may repel it. Or he may ask, if any of them be for repelling it; and if none answer, may sustain it, without necessity to write the state of the question, which is only to be done in case the matter come to a vote. But if he apprehend the point proposed to be dubious, he ought to move the Lords to speak to it, that it may appear whether they be unanimous in it, or not.

But if the dispute be upon the relevancy or competency of the libel, or upon the relevancy or competency of the exception, reply or duply, which can only consist in matters of fact, presumed, instructed, or offered to be proven; in that case, the question may most conveniently be, "Sustain the libel, or not? Sustain or repel the exception, reply, or duply", &c.?

But in all questions concerning the competency or relevancy of exceptions, replies or duplies, &c. the question proposed must bear the kind of the point proposed, whether it be exception, reply, or duply, &c. Or if the dispute be upon a reason of suspension, the terms may be, "whether the answer *in facto* to the reason," or "the reply *in facto*, are to be sustained or repelled?" But if the dispute be in a reduction or competition, the reasons are parts of the libel, and the defences *in facto* are proper exceptions, and likewise the replies and duplies, and may in the same way be put to the vote, as in ordinary actions.

In this way there can be no occasion of difference among the Lords, concerning the stating of the question; seeing it doth only relate to the points as proponed by the pleaders, expressing nothing particularly, but the special kind of the allegeance: for, seeing judges ought to proceed *secundum allegata*, the pleaders should have liberty to frame their own allegeances, expressing the several kinds of them.

This method for the Inner-House will likewise be a rule for the Outer-House, that every point to be reported be set down in the minutes, in the due order, and as the same is proponed, leaving a distance between every point, for writing therein the state of the question and the interlocutor.

X. Albeit, by the 20th Act of the same last session of Parliament [Act 1693,c.20; A.P.S. IX,283,c.33], advocates are allowed "to make their allegeances as they think fit," it imports only that it belongs to them to form the matter; but still they must keep the terms and order of law, expressing the several kinds of their allegeances. Neither should they be permitted to repeat the matter of fact, which is in the libel and charge, at the adjusting of the minutes. But they should have liberty to argue shortly what they have to say, in which they may make answers *hinc inde* several times before the clerk write any thing: and then the substance of what they have argued must be briefly dictated to the clerk; first by the defender or suspender, obviating what in the verbal reasoning the pursuer or charger's advocates said; who then may dictate their answers to the defences, and their reasons for the same severally, so as they think they may take off the pursuer's objections or replies against the same. If this order be not followed, the dictating of many mutual answers will make the minutes so large that it will take up more time in adjusting them than can be allowed to the Ordinary, by reason of his other affairs, or to the advocates, because of their consulting with their clients, drawing their informations, and reading of statutes and doctors. And much more time will be unnecessarily spent in making reports conform to the minutes.

XI. By what hath been said, it will be evident to every judicious lawyer, that the discussing and determining of process is regularly by sustaining the libel or charge as relevant or competent, or by refusing to sustain the same, which terminates the instance: for all dilators are only objections against the libel or charge, seeing the relevancy imports, that the conclusion is justly to be inferred from the premises, if they be true; and so relieves or helps the pursuer in his right: so that if the due order of citation, or the titles to be produced *in initio*, or the calling of parties necessary to be called, &c. be wanting, the libel will not relieve or help the pursuer. And in the next place, if the libel be sustained, the defender's exceptions come to be discussed, whether relevant or not, and so in the replies and duplies. But there is exception from that rule in improbations, reductions upon fraud, or declarators of trust, that parties are allowed to adduce all the adminicles and evidences they can, before answer to the relevancy, that the Lords upon the whole matter may determine according to the strongest evidences; or in other cases before answer, wherein evidences and adminicles are allowed to be adduced.

FINIS

Aufidius: Possibly Aufidius Tosca, or Aufidius Namusa, both minor Roman jurists.

Balduinus: François Baudouin (1520–73) French theologian and jurist, author of a commentary on Justinian's *Institutions*.

Baldus: Petro Baldo degli Ubaldi (c. 1325–1400) famous Italian jurist, author of many works on Roman law, *Consilia, In Codicem, In Digestum, In Institutiones, Super Feudis*, and others.

Boetius: Probably Epo Boetius (1529–99) Flemish jurist, writer on civil and canon law.

Chassanaeus; Barthelemy de Chassenez (1480–1541) French jurist and magistrate, author of *Commentaria in Consuetudines Burgundiae* (1517), *Consilia* (1530) and other works.

Connanus: François de Connan (1508–51) French jurist, author of *Commentaria juris civilis* (1538).

Cornelius: Possibly Q. Cornelius Maximus.

Corvinus: Arnold Corvinus de Belderen (c. 1620–c. 1680) author of works on civil, feudal and canon law, including a *Digesta* (1642), *Jus Canonicum de Pactis* (1648), *Jurisprudentiae Romanae Summarium* (1655), *Jus Feudale* (1660) and *Imperator Justinianus* (1668).

Covarruvias: Diego Covarruvias (or Covarrubias) y Leyva (1512–77) Spanish jurist, bishop of Segovia and then of Cuenca, author of *Variarum Resolutionum ex Pontificio Regio et Caesareo jure* (1552–70) and many other legal works.

Cowell: John Cowell (1554–1611) Regius Professor of Civil Law at Cambridge, author of *The Interpreter* (1607) a legal dictionary ordered by Parliament to be burned by the common hangman because of some of its definitions, and of *Institutiones Juris Anglicani ad methodum Institutionum Justiniani compositae et digestae* (1605).

Craig: Sir Thomas Craig of Riccartoun (1538–1608) Justice-depute of Scotland, author of *A Treatise on the Succession* (1603), *De Unione Regnorum Britanniae Tractatus* (1605) and *Jus Feudale* (1655) (translated by Lord President Clyde, 1934).

Crassus: Publius Licinius Crassus Mucianus (consul 131 B.C.), Roman jurist and Greek scholar.

Cujas: Jacques Cujas (Cujacius) (1522–90) distinguished French jurist, professor at Bourges and author of a series of works on Roman law, including *Observationum et Emendationum Libri XXVIII*. His *Opera Omnia* were published in 1658.

Donellus: Hugues Doneau (1527–91) French jurist and teacher at Leiden, author of *Commentaria ad Titulos Codicis* (1599), *Commentaria ad titulos Digestorum* (1582) and *Commentaria de jure civili* (1596).

Duarenus: François Douaren or Duaren (1509–59) professor at Bourges, reputed the most learned jurist of his time, author of *Tractatus de Feudis* (1558) and of an edition of the *Jus Civile*.

Faber: Jean Faber, Fabre or Lefevre (?–1540) French jurist, author of *Breviarium in Codicem* (1545) and *In Institutiones Commentarius* (1488).

Gallus: C. Aquilius Gallus, Roman jurist of 1st century B.C.

Gratian: Graziano (c. 1095–c. 1159) a Camaldolese monk of Bologna, compiler of the *Concordia Discordantium Canonum* or *Decretum*, a major collection of materials on canon law.

Gregorius Tholosanus: Pierre Gregoire (Petrus Gregorius Tholosanus) (1540–1597) French jurist, professor at Pont-a-mousson, author of *Syntagma juris universi* (1606), *De re publica libri XXVI* and other works.

Grotius: Hugo de Groot (1583–1645) Dutch statesman, humanist and jurist, author of *De Jure Praedae* (1604), of which one chapter, *Mare Liberum*, appeared in 1609, *De Jure Belli ac Pacis* (1625), *Inleidinge tot de Hollandsche Rechtsgeleerdheid* (Introduction to the Jurisprudence of Holland) (1631) and other works.

Gudelinus: Pierre Goudelin (1550–1619) professor at Louvain, author of *De Jure Novissimo* (1620) possibly the first systematic exposition of Netherlands law, *De Jure Feudorum* (1624) and *Syntagma Regularum Juris* (1640).

Julianus: Salvius Julianus (c. 100–169 A.D.) an outstanding Roman jurist, responsible for revision and final settlement of the praetorian edict and a member of the imperial consilium, author of *Digesta* (90 books), a treatise on civil and praetorian law, much quoted later.

Juventius: Publius Juventius Celsus (consul 129 B.C.) Roman jurist, head of the Proculian school of jurists, author of *Epistulae, Commentarii, Quaestiones* and an important *Digesta*.

Littleton: Sir Thomas Littleton (1402–81) judge of the Court of Common Pleas in England, 1466, author of *Tenures* (c. 1481) which first gave a systematic account of English land law and was the basis for Coke's First Institute, *Coke upon Littleton*.

Manlius: Possibly Manius Manilius (consul 149 B.C.) a famous Roman jurist and founder of the civil law, author of *Monumenta* and forms for contracts of sale.

Marius: John Marius (17th cent.) author of a book on *Bills of Exchange* (1651) regarded as of high authority.

Menochius: Giacomo Menochio (1532–1607) Italian jurist, teacher at Padua and Pavia, author of *De possessione* (1565) De *Praesumptionibus* (1609), *De Arbitriis* (1569), *Consilia* (1605) and other works.

Molina: Luis de Molina (1535–1600) Spanish Jesuit and theologian-jurist, teacher at Evora, author of theological works, notably *Concordia libri arbitrii cum gratiae donis* (1588), *Disputationes de Contractibus* (1601) and *De Justitia et Jure* (6 vols., 1613).

Nasica: Gaius Scipio Nasica, surnamed Optimus, of 3rd century B.C., Roman republican jurist, given a house at public expense to enable persons to consult him.

Papirius: Either Sextus Papirius, a Roman jurist, who is said to have compiled a collection of *leges regiae*, or Publius

Papirius, who made a collection of royal laws, or Gaius Papirius, who restored a collection of ordinances in the forum which had become illegible; or there may have been a collection of pontifical law made when a Papirius was *rex sacrorum*.

Paulus: Julius (c.200 A.D.) a distinguished jurist and member of the imperial consilium, author of *Institutiones, Regulae*, a commentary on the Edict, an exposition of the *jus civile*, commentaries on older jurists and monographs on many particular laws and topics.

Plinius: Gaius Plinius Secundus (23–79 A.D.) author of a *Naturalis Historia* in 36 books dealing inter alia with anthropology.

Proculus: Roman jurist of 1st century A.D. who gave his name to the Proculian school of jurists, author of *Epistulae* (a collection of opinions from his practice) and *Notae* to Labeo.

Rebuffus: Pierre Rebuffi (1487–1557) French jurist and teacher, author of works on Roman law collected in his *Opera* (1586).

Sabinus: Masurius Sabinus, Roman jurist of 1st century A.D., who gave his name to the Sabinian school of jurists, author of a standard exposition of the civil law, an *Ad Edictum praetoris urbani, De Furtis, Responsa* and other works.

Salmasius: Claude de Saumaise (1588–1653) French polymath, author of inter alia, *De Usuris* (1638), *De Modo Usurarum* (1639) and *De Foenore Trapezitico* (1640).

Scaevola: Several of this name were distinguished Roman jurists. Quintus Mucius Scaevola (consul 95 B.C.) published the first systematic treatise on civil law. Quintus Cervidius Scaevola (2nd century A.D.) gave responsa, later collected in six books and compiled a *Digesta*, the leading book of casuistic literature.

Skene: Sir John Skene of Curriehill (?1543–1617) published editions of *The Lawes and Actes of Parliament* (1597) and of *Regiam Majestatem* (1609) and a legal dictionary *De Verborum Significatione* (1597). He was Lord Clerk Register 1594–1611 and a Lord of Session (Lord Curriehill), 1594–1617.

Stephanus: Mathias Stephanus (1576–1646) German jurist, author of *Quaestiones illustres* (1608), *Notae ad Pandectarum tit. De Verborum Significatione* (1628) and other works.

Tiraquellus: André Tiraqueau (c. 1480–

1558), counsellor of the Parlement of Paris, author of *De Legibus connubialibus* (1515), *De retractu utroque municipali et conventionali* (1547), *De poenis legum, De judicis in rebus exiguis, De nobilitate et jure primogenitorum* and other works.

Ulpianus: Domitius Ulpianus (d. 228 A.D.) praefectus praetorio from 222 A.D., a voluminous writer on law and the chief source of materials for Justinian's *Digest*. He wrote *Ad Edictum Libri 81, Ad Sabinum Disputationes, Responsa, Opiniones, Institutiones, Regulae,* and *Liber Singularis Regularum.*

Vinnius: Arnold Vinnen (1588–1657) Dutch jurist, professor at Leiden, author of *Jurisprudentiae contractae sive partitionum juris civil libri IV* (1624), *In IV libros Institutionum Imperialium Commentarius* (1642), *Institutiones Justiniani cum notis* (1646) and other works on civil law.

Wesenbecius: Matthaeus Wesenbeck (1531–86) German jurist, author of *Commentarius in Institutiones* (1609), *Paratitla juris sive Commentarius in Pandectas et Codicem* (1568) *Prolegomena Jurisprudentiae* (1584).

Zasius: Ulric Zase (1461–1535) German jurist, author of *Lucubrationes* (1518), *Tractatus de Restitutione in Integrum* and other works.

Zoesius: Henri Zoes (1571–1627) Dutch jurist, author of *Commentaria de jure Feudorum* (1641), *Ad Decretales* (1647), *Ad Institutiones* (1653), *In Codicem* (1660) and *Ad Digestorum libros* (1718).

LIST OF SUBSCRIBERS

A

D. M. Abbott, Edinburgh
Aberdeen City Libraries
Norman J. Adamson, Queen's Counsel,
  Legal Secretary to the Lord Advocate
David R. Adie, Glasgow
Sir Crispin Agnew of Lochnaw, Bt,
  Slains Pursuivant at Arms
James Tait Aitken, S.S.C., Edinburgh
Douglas C. Anderson, Solicitor,
  Tillicoultry
Jack Anderson, LL.B., N.P., Aberdeen
Anderson, Banks & Co., Solicitors, Oban
Anderson, Fyfe, Stewart & Young,
  Solicitors, Glasgow
Anderson & Gardiner, Solicitors,
  Glasgow
William Angus, Solicitor, Hamilton
The Rt Hon. Lord Avonside, Senator of
  the College of Justice

B

D. K. Bain, Advocate, New St Andrews
  House, Edinburgh
J. H. Baker, St Catharine's College,
  Cambridge
Robert Lindsay Balfour
Ballantyne & Copland, Solicitors and
  Notaries, Motherwell
John G. C. Barr, Deputy Secretary, Law
  Society of Scotland, Edinburgh
T. St J. N. Bates
John Bayne, Advocate, lately Sheriff
David A. Bennett, Writer to the Signet,
  Edinburgh
Bird Semple & Crawford Herron,
  Solicitors, Glasgow
Birmingham Public Libraries
Alison A. Birrell, Solicitor, Bearsden,
  Dunbartonshire
Robert Black, Advocate, Edinburgh
John Walter Graham Blackie, Advocate,
  University Lecturer, Edinburgh
Blair & Bryden, Solicitors, Greenock
Bovey & Bovey, Solicitors, Glasgow
Edward F. Bowen, Advocate

B. Neil Bowman, Solicitor, Broughty
  Ferry, Dundee
John S. Boyle, Solicitor, Glasgow
A. W. Bradley, Professor, University of
  Edinburgh
The Hon. Lord Brand, Senator of the
  College of Justice, Gospatric House
  Dalmeny, South Queensferry
Philip H. Brodie, Advocate
William Brotherston, S.S.C., N.P.,
  Edinburgh
Alistair R. Brownlie, S.S.C., Edinburgh
M. S. R. Bruce, Queen's Counsel
Sir William Bryden, Queen's Counsel
Robert Burgess, Senior Lecturer, Uni-
  versity of East Anglia, Norwich
John Burgoyne, Solicitor, Glasgow
John H. Burnett, Principal & Vice-Chan-
  cellor, University of Edinburgh
Burnett & Reid, Solicitors, Aberdeen
Paul Burns, Solicitor, Glasgow
Burns, Veal & Gillan, Solicitors,
  Dundee
Alistair S. Burrow, Solicitor, Glasgow

C

John W. Cairns, The Queen's University
  of Belfast
The Hon. Lord Cameron, Senator of the
  College of Justice (3)
J. Alastair Cameron, Queen's Counsel,
  Edinburgh
Joseph G. S. Cameron, Writer to the
  Signet
K. J. Cameron, Advocate
C. S. Campbell, Writer to the Signet
James Campbell, Writer to the Signet
James H. Campbell, Solicitor
John D. Campbell, Edinburgh
Francis Cannon, Solicitor, Glasgow
Ronald G. Cant, St Andrews
David R. Carruthers, Solicitor, Shetland
John L. Carter, Glasgow
John B. W. Christie, Sheriff, Dundee
Michael P. Clancy, Solicitor, Cambuslang,
  Glasgow

E. M. Clive, Scottish Law Commission, Edinburgh

James J. Clyde, Queen's Counsel, 9 Heriot Row, Edinburgh

Dennis Collins, s.s.c., Dundee

Henry John Gray Connochie, B.L., Advocate in Aberdeen and Notary Public

Campbell Connon & Co., Solicitors, Aberdeen

Cornell Law Library, New York, U.S.A.

D. C. Coull, Solicitor, Aberdeen

W. M. Cowan, s.s.c., Edinburgh

Gordon S. Cowie, Professor, University of Glasgow

Elizabeth B. Crawford, Lecturer, University of Glasgow

T. J. N. Craxton, s.s.c., Edinburgh

William Scott Crosby, Advocate in Aberdeen (2)

Crown Agent, Crown Office, Edinburgh

Peter A. Cruickshank, Advocate in Aberdeen

Thomas Booth Cruickshank, 'Ellenslea', Carsphairn, by Castle Douglas

W. Douglas Cullen, Queen's Counsel, Edinburgh

Ronald C. B. Currie, Solicitor, Dunfermline

Douglas J. Cusine, Lecturer, University of Aberdeen

D

Ramsay R. Dalgety, Advocate, 196 Craigleith Road, Edinburgh

Julian S. Danskin, Solicitor, Leven

C. K. Davidson, Queen's Counsel, Dean of Faculty of Advocates

Euan F. Davidson, Glasgow

Aubrey L. Diamond, Professor, University of London

Ian S. Dickinson, Senior Lecturer, University of Strathclyde, Glasgow

John Graham Dickson, Writer to the Signet, Glencorse House, Milton Bridge, Penicuik, Midlothian

Rev. Dr Mark Dilworth, Keeper, Scottish Catholic Archives

James T. J. Dobie, Solicitor, Dumfries

Alastair G. Dobson, LL.B., F.I.C.B., A.I.B. (Scot.), Geneva, Switzerland

Robert Donald, Advocate, Aberdeen

A. G. Donaldson, Barrister-at-law, University of Edinburgh

Gordon Donaldson, H.M. Historiographer in Scotland

Arthur B. Dorman, Solicitor, Glasgow

James Hall Douglas, Procurator Fiscal, 'Tir-Nan-Og', Canmore Grove, Dunfermline

W. R. Douglas, Writer to the Signet, Edinburgh

Dundas & Wilson, C.S., Edinburgh

Dundee University Library

Rev. A. Ian Dunlop, Minister of St Stephen's, Edinburgh

The Hon. Lord Dunpark, Senator of the College of Justice

I. J. A. Dyer, Lecturer, University of Glasgow

E

East Kilbride District Council

D. A. O. Edward, Queen's Counsel, Advocate, Edinburgh

Ian Edward, Advocate in Aberdeen

The Hon. Lord Elliott, Chairman, Scottish Land Court; President, Lands Tribunal for Scotland

The Rt Hon. The Lord Emslie, Lord President of the Court of Session (2)

George M. Esson, Advocate in Aberdeen

A. J. Ewen, Aberdeen

Winifred Ewing, Solicitor, Member of European Parliament, Goodwill, Lossiemouth

F

Nicholas Fairbairn of Fordell, Queen's Counsel, M.P., H.M. Solicitor-General for Scotland, Fordell Castle, by Dunfermline

Ian C. Fairweather, s.s.c., Edinburgh

T. David Fergus, Lecturer, University of Glasgow

James R. Fiddes, Queen's Counsel, Edinburgh

Donald R. Findlay, Advocate, Edinburgh

Wilson Finnie, Lecturer, University of Edinburgh

Derick Fleming, LL.B., N.P., Rosemount, 5 Lyle Street, Greenock

John D. Ford, 83 Randolph Road, Glasgow

Ian Stewart Forrester, Advocate, Member of the New York Bar, Brussels

A. D. M. Forte, Lecturer, University of Dundee

Angus J. E. Foster, Advocate, Edinburgh

James Y. Francis, Solicitor and Notary Public, Newton Mearns

The Rt Hon. Lord Fraser of Tullybelton, Lord of Appeal in Ordinary

I. S. Fraser, Barrister-at-Law

Sir William Kerr Fraser, Permanent Under-Secretary of State, Scottish Office

James D. Friel, Senior Procurator Fiscal Depute, Glasgow

G

Galts, Solicitors, Glasgow

Wm. W. Gaunt, President, Wm. W. Gaunt & Sons, Inc., Florida, U.S.A.

Ian F. Gibb, Solicitor, Bearsden

Sir John Gibson, Queen's Counsel

Dennis C. Gilles, Professor, Department of Computing Science, University of Glasgow

William T. Gillie, Judge, Franklin County Court of Common Pleas, Hall of Justice, Columbus, Ohio, U.S.A.

M. Gordon Gillies, Queen's Counsel, Sheriff at Lanark

Glasgow University Library (2)

William M. Gordon, Professor, University of Glasgow

Douglas Grant, Sheriff

Ian D. Grant, Assistant Keeper, Scottish Record Office

Sir William Gray, Solicitor, Glasgow

Gray, Muirhead & Carmichael, Writers to the Signet, Edinburgh

George Lidderdale Gretton, Writer to the Signet, Edinburgh

Anne M. O. Griffiths

Ivor R. Guild, Writer to the Signet, Edinburgh

H

Andrew Haddon, O.B.E., Solicitor, Hawick

James Halliday, Principal Lecturer in History, College of Education, Dundee

John M. Halliday, Professor Emeritus, 129 St Vincent Street, Glasgow

A. C. Hamilton, Advocate

Alan J. Hamilton, Newton Mearns, Glasgow

David Hamilton, Glasgow

Steven F. Hamilton, Town Clerk, Glasgow

T. G. I. Hamnett, Advocate

Geoffrey J. Hand, Professor, University of Birmingham

H. J. Hanham, Cambridge, Massachusetts, U.S.A.

Anthony P. Hanlon, Student, Glasgow

Alan Harding, Professor, University of Liverpool

Michael Harkins, Student, University of Dundee

Lorna M. Harris, Solicitor

J. W. Harrison, Solicitor, Penrith, Cumberland

R. H. Helmholz, Professor

Hamish McN. Henderson, Senior Lecturer, University of Edinburgh

Lynn K. W. Herbert, Glasgow

W. John Herbert, University of Dundee

James B. Highgate, Solicitor, Glasgow

Hill & Robb, Solicitors, Stirling

Holmes, Mackillop & Co., Solicitors, Glasgow and Johnstone (2)

W. T. Hook, Advocate

J. A. D. Hope, Queen's Counsel, Edinburgh

Hughes, Dowdall & Co., Solicitors, Glasgow

The Hon. Lord Hunter, Senator of the College of Justice

R. L. C. Hunter, W.S., N.P., F.C.I. Arb., Aberdeen

David John Hustwayte, Solicitor, Doune

Gordon Milroy Hutton, Statutory (Senior) Lecturer of the National University of Ireland

I

J. Alistair M. Inglis, Professor, University of Glasgow

Godfrey W. Iredell, Braithwaite, Keswick, Cumbria

Ronald David Ireland, Sheriff of Lothian and Borders

J

R. B. Jack, Professor, University of Glasgow

James C. M. Jardine, Sheriff of Glasgow and Strathkelvin

The Hon. Lord Jauncey

William Jeffrey, Jr., Professor, University of Cincinnati, U.S.A.

Christine Johnson, M.A., Balerno

Ivor S. Johnston, Glasgow

Lt-Colonel Edmund Jones, Aboyne, Aberdeenshire

K

Amadu Mukhtar Kanu, Port Loko, Sierra Leone

David Kelbie, Sheriff of North Strathclyde at Dumbarton

Robert Reid Kerr, Sheriff, Falkirk

Maurice G. Kidd, Writer to the Signet, Barley Mill House, by West Saltoun, East Lothian

The Rt Hon. Lord Kilbrandon

The Hon. Lord Kincraig, Senator of the College of Justice

King Sons & Paterson, Solicitors, Irvine, Ayrshire

The Hon. Lord Kissen, Senator of the College of Justice

L

David K. Laing, Advocate in Aberdeen

James S. Laird, Solicitor, Glasgow

Crawford J. Langley, Solicitor, Glasgow

B. J. Lanigan, Solicitor, 7 Craigfern Drive, Blanefield

H. A. Graeme Lapsley, Solicitor, Kirkwall, Orkney

The Law Society Library, London

F. H. Lawson, Emeritus Professor, Oxford

Thomas W. Leigh, Attorney-at-Law, Monroe, Louisiana, U.S.A.

Bruce Lenman, Senior Lecturer, University of St Andrews

Robert D. Leslie, University of Edinburgh

Frederick Samuel Levine, Solicitor, Bearsden, Glasgow

Reginald N. Levitt, Sheriff of North Strathclyde at Kilmarnock

Dr John Underwood Lewis, Professor of Philosophy, The University of Windsor, Ontario, Canada

Hamish G. M. Liddell, Writer to the Signet, Pitlochry

Neil A. Lightbody, Solicitor, Edinburgh

Lindsays, Writers to the Signet

Livingstone & Company, Solicitors, Glasgow

Daniel Lockett, S.S.C., Edinburgh

J. B. T. Loudon, S.S.C., N.P.

Louisville University Law Library, Kentucky, U.S.A.

L. S. Lovat, Sheriff, Hamilton

Klaus Luig, Professor, Passau, Germany

Francis Lyall, Professor, University of Aberdeen

G. S. T. Lyon or Denholm, Solicitor, Dunino, St Andrews, Fife

George Traill Lyon, Solicitor, Kirkcaldy, Fife

James T. Lyon, Writer to the Signet (Barrister and Solicitor, Provinces of Nova Scotia and Saskatchewan) Regina, Saskatchewan, Canada

Lord Lyon King of Arms, Court of the Lord Lyon, H.M. New Register House, Edinburgh

M

Carole M. G. McAlpine, 'Windyknowe', 168 Southbrae Drive, Jordanhill, Glasgow

Colin J. MacAulay, Advocate

Walter Grieve MacAulay, M.A., LL.B., N.P., 11 Victoria Square, Stirling

William W. McBryde, Senior Lecturer, University of Aberdeen

E. B. McCabe, Solicitor, 29 Woodside Terrace Lane, Glasgow

Andrew James McCartan, Solicitor, Forres, Moray

G. D. MacCormack

D. Neil MacCormick, Professor, University of Edinburgh

Robert A. McCreadie, Lecturer, University of Edinburgh

The Hon. Lord McDonald, M.C., Senator of the College of Justice

Gregor Macdonald, Writer, Glasgow

I. H. MacDonald, Writer to the Signet

John R. Macdonald, Solicitor, Rosewell, Midlothian

Kenneth Norman MacDonald, Kildun House, Stornoway

C. N. McEachran, Advocate

His Honour, Judge Vincent K. McEwan, Queen's Counsel, Thornhill, Ontario, Canada

John A. C. McFadden, Solicitor, Dumfries

Colin H. McFadyen, Stewarton, 54 Anwoth Street, Glasgow

D. J. T. Macfadyen, Solicitor, Glenashdale, 54 Station Road, Carluke

A. Findlay McFadzean, Solicitor

David B. McGarva, Notary, North Berwick

Ian B. McGhee, M.A., LL.B., Glasgow

James M. McGhie, Advocate

John G. McGlennan, Senior Depute Procurator Fiscal, Glasgow

J. A. McGoogan, Solicitor, Coatbridge

A. E. McIlwain, Solicitor, Hamilton

John C. McInnes, Sheriff, Cupar, Fife

John Archibald McIntyre, Professor, University of Guelph, Guelph, Ontario, Canada

Malcolm McIver, Solicitor, Glasgow

Donald S. Mackay, Advocate, Edinburgh

N. A. M. Mackay, Writer to the Signet, Edinburgh

Ronald D. Mackay, Advocate

Roseanna McKenna, Lecturer, University of Stirling

Colin Scott MacKenzie, D.L., Procurator Fiscal, Stornoway

Mackenzie, Robertson & Co., Solicitors, Glasgow

Alexander J. MacLean, Solicitor and Lecturer, University of Edinburgh

Angela M. McLean, Senior Lecturer, University of Glasgow

Angus MacLeod, Solicitor, former Procurator Fiscal, 7 Oxford Terrace, Edinburgh

Calum Murray MacLeod, Solicitor, Dundee

N. W. McMillan, Solicitor, Glasgow

Hugh M. McNeill, London

Peter G. B. McNeill, Sheriff of Glasgow and Strathkelvin, at Glasgow

I.D. Macphail, Sheriff of Glasgow and Strathkelvin

A.C. Macpherson, Sheriff of South Strathclyde, Dumfries and Galloway, at Hamilton

D.F. Macquaker, Solicitor, Glasgow

Hector L. MacQueen, Lecturer, University of Edinburgh

John MacQueen, Professor, School of Scottish Studies, University of Edinburgh

Christopher MacRae, B.L., F.C.C.A., F.C.M.A., F.B.I.M., Depute Director of Building and Works

William MacRae, Solicitor, Watling Lodge, Bonnyhill Road, Falkirk, Stirlingshire

MacTruisdidh's MacFhearghuis, Fir-Lagha, Port-Righ, An T-Eilean, Sgitheanach

Roy McWhirter, Writer to the Signet, Allermuir, 15 Woodhall Road, Colinton, Edinburgh

G. Maher, University of Glasgow

J.M. & J. Mailer, Solicitors, Stirling

John Mair, 190 Bath Street, Glasgow

Enid A. Marshall, Reader, University of Stirling

L.A. Massie, Advocate, Grangewood, 9 Whitehouse Terrace, Edinburgh

Andrew F.L. Matheson, Solicitor, Newmilns, Ayrshire

Mathie, MacLuckie & Lupton, Solicitors, Stirling

David Maxwell, Queen's Counsel, Edinburgh

Joseph Mellick, O.B.E., Glasgow

D.A.Y. Menzies, Advocate, Leaston House, Humbie, East Lothian

Michael C. Meston, Professor, University of Aberdeen

Graeme I.J. Middleton, Edinburgh

William McIntosh Millar, O.B.E., Solicitor, Glasgow

D.L. Carey Miller, Senior Lecturer, University of Aberdeen

Eric James Miller, 4 Victoria Crescent Road, Glasgow

Ernest Miller, Solicitor in Hamilton and Giffnock

Norman Milne, Sheriff of North Strathclyde at Campbeltown and Oban

Milne & Mackinnon, Advocates in Aberdeen

A.G. Mitchell, Solicitor, Dundee

Iain Grant Mitchell, Advocate, Edinburgh

J. Kenneth Mitchell, Advocate, Edinburgh

Joan Monypenny of Pitmilly

George M. More, Solicitor, Edinburgh

A.C. Morrison & Richards, Advocates, Aberdeen

David Morrison, 36 Albyn Place, Aberdeen

Nigel M.P. Morrison, Advocate, Edinburgh

H.D.B. Morton, Queen's Counsel, Edinburgh

Morton, Fraser & Milligan, Writers to the Signet, Edinburgh

J. Campbell Muir, Eyemouth

Donald Muirhead, Solicitor, 'Deanston', Lefroy Street, Coatbridge

William Munro, Queen's Counsel (2)

J. Duncan Murdoch, Solicitor, Glasgow

James L. Murdoch, Lecturer, University of Glasgow

John Murray, Queen's Counsel, Edinburgh

Leonard G. Murray, Solicitor, Glasgow

Neil D. Murray, Advocate, Edinburgh

Murray, Gillies & Wilson, Solicitors, Irvine, Ayrshire

N

David N.J. Neill, Procurator Fiscal Depute, Dingwall

Douglas Chalmers Neillands, 11 Western Place, Edinburgh

J. Newall, Writer to the Signet, Edinburgh

C.G.B. Nicholson, Sheriff, Edinburgh

A.W. Noble, Advocate, Edinburgh

Sir Fraser Noble, Principal, University of Aberdeen

Iain W. Noble, Professor, University of Edinburgh

O

William Wright Orr, Senior Depute Procurator Fiscal, Glasgow

P

Alan A. Paterson, Solicitor and Lecturer, University of Edinburgh

Ann Paton, Advocate

G. Campbell H. Paton, Q.C., LL.B., LL.D., 163 Colinton Road, Edinburgh

J.B. Patrick, Sheriff, Sheriff Court, Greenock

Patrick & James, Writers to the Signet, Edinburgh

Judith J.H. Pearson, Lecturer, University of Edinburgh

George W. Penrose, Queen's Counsel, Edinburgh

James Peoples, Advocate, Edinburgh

George S. Peterson, Solicitor, Lerwick, Shetland

Hon. Mr Justice Phillips
Iain G. Pirie, Sheriff of South Strathclyde, Dumfries & Galloway, at Airdrie
Isobel Anne Poole, Sheriff
Primrose & Gordon, Solicitors
William D. Prosser, Queen's Counsel, Edinburgh

R

N. J. G. Ramsay, Sheriff, Kirkcudbright
Reading University
Colin T. Reid, Lecturer, University of Aberdeen
Ian D. Reid, Solicitor, Edinburgh
Kenneth G. C. Reid, Lecturer, University of Edinburgh
Reid, Johnston, Bell & Henderson, Solicitors and Notaries Public, Dundee
John McManus Reilly, Solicitor, Glasgow
E. Rendle, Solicitor, St Andrews
Douglas James Risk, Sheriff, Aberdeen
George Ritchie, Solicitor, Edinburgh
Brechin Robb, Solicitors, Glasgow
Gordon J. Robbie, Solicitor, Dundee
Robert Roberts, Jr., Lawyer, Shreveport, Louisiana, U.S.A.
The Hon. Lord Robertson, Senator of the College of Justice
A. O. Robertson, Solicitor, Glasgow
Donald Buchanan Robertson, Queen's Counsel, Cranshaws Castle, Cranshaws, Berwickshire
Lewis Robertson, Industrialist and Administrator, Edinburgh
Robertson, Neilson & Co., Solicitors, Glasgow
Olivia F. Robinson
Alan Rodger, Edinburgh
The Hon. Lord Ross, Senator of the College of Justice
Ian Ross, Professor of English, University of British Columbia, Canada
R. M. Ross, s.s.c., Montrose
Ross, Strachan & Scott, Solicitors, Dundee
The Royal Faculty of Procurators in Glasgow
A. M. G. Russell, Queen's Counsel, Sheriff, Grampian, Highland and Islands at Aberdeen
Florence Maxwell Russell, Dunoon, Argyll
T. F. Russell

S

St John's College Library, Oxford
D. Gerald Sadler, Writer to the Signet, Stewartry of Kirkcudbright
Alasdair Colin Sampson, Solicitor & Notary Public, Darvel, Ayrshire

T. S. Scadlock, 105 West George Street, Glasgow
The Rt Hon. The Lord Scarman, Lord of Appeal in Ordinary
R. J. D. Scott, Sheriff, Aberdeen
T. H. Scott, Solicitor of Inland Revenue for Scotland
Scottish Record Office
Brian E. Scoullar, Solicitor, Glasgow
Rev. Dr Henry R. Sefton, Lecturer, King's College, Aberdeen
W. David H. Sellar, Edinburgh
Walter G. Semple, Solicitor, Glasgow
Esmée. E. Shapiro, Lecturer, University of Glasgow
Archibald Sharp & Son, Solicitors, Glasgow
The Rev. Dr Duncan Shaw, The minister of the parish of Craigentinny, Edinburgh
Robert R. Shaw, Solicitor, Kirkwall, Orkney
H. D. Sheldon, Solicitor
H. A. Shewan, Queen's Counsel
Eric B. Simmons, Solicitor, Dunbar
William G. Simmons, Glasgow
Joyce Simpson, Solicitor, Aberdeen
David B. Smith, Sheriff of North Strathclyde at Kilmarnock
J. A. M. Smith, Solicitor, Glasgow
Sean Craufurd, Smith 11 Learmonth Terrace, Edinburgh
T. B. Smith, Professor, Queen's Counsel, Morham, Haddington
W. Leggat Smith, Solicitor, Glasgow
Ian N. Sneddon, Professor, Department of Mathematics, University of Glasgow
The Society of Procurators and Solicitors in the City and County of Perth
Society of Writers to Her Majesty's Signet, Signet Library, Parliament Square, Edinburgh
South, Forrest, MacKintosh & Merchant, Solicitors
James Spy, Advocate, Edinburgh
Steedman, Ramage & Co., Writers to the Signet, Edinburgh
David Stevenson, Department of History, University of Aberdeen
A. I. B. Stewart, Solicitor, Campbeltown
Alastair L. Stewart, Sheriff, Aberdeen
Angus Stewart, Advocate, 27 Dundas Street, Edinburgh
James Stewart, Writer to the Signet, Edinburgh
Stewart & McIsaac, Solicitors, Elgin
Stirling University Library
Hamish Stirling, Advocate
Matthew Stirling, M.A., F.C.A.

P. & J. Stormonth Darling, Writers to the Signet, Kelso

The Hon. Lord Mackenzie Stuart, Judge of the Court of Justice of the European Communities (2)

Elaine E. Sutherland, Lecturer, University of Edinburgh

John W. Sutherland, Student, University of Glasgow

R. I. Sutherland, Queen's Counsel

Robert Sutherland, Writer to the Signet

William Sutherland, Advocate in Aberdeen

T

Angus G. Taylor, Writer to the Signet, Canada (2)

William J. Taylor, Advocate, Edinburgh

Douglas Henderson Elphinstone Teesdale, Advocate, Edinburgh and Malvern

Alexander Thomson, J.P., Solicitor (Retired), Elvar, Comrie, Perthshire

Sir James Thomson, Carrbridge

James Thomson, M.A., LL.B.

Malcolm Thomson, Advocate, Edinburgh

John M. Todd, M.A., Redbourn House, St Bees, Cumbria

Turnbull, Simson & Sturrock, Writers to the Signet, Jedburgh

Colin J. Tyre, Lecturer, University of Edinburgh

U

The Library, University College, London

University of London Library

C. Ichegbo Uriri, Student, University of Glasgow

W

Alexander Walker, Messenger-at-Arms, 91 Mitchell Street, Glasgow

Adrian D. Ward, Solicitor, Barrhead

A. S. Weatherhead, Solicitor, Glasgow

David Bruce Weir, Queen's Counsel

Michael E. L. Weir, Writer to the Signet, 1 Pentland Avenue, Edinburgh

A. B. Wilkinson, Professor, University of Dundee

Ian D. Willock, Professor, University of Dundee

Roy A. Wilson, Sheriff of Grampian, Highland and Islands at Elgin

W. A. Wilson, Edinburgh

William J. Windram, LL.B., Galashiels

Stephen E. Woolman, Lecturer, University of Edinburgh

Y

David M. Young, Writer to the Signet, Edinburgh

John N. Young, Advocate

Where no department is stated, university members of staff are in the Faculty of Law.

INDEX